Matching Supply with Demand

An Introduction to Operations Management

Matching Supply with Demand

**An Introduction to
Operations Management**

Third Edition

Gérard Cachon
*The Wharton School,
University of Pennsylvania*

Christian Terwiesch
*The Wharton School,
University of Pennsylvania*

MATCHING SUPPLY WITH DEMAND: AN INTRODUCTION TO OPERATIONS MANAGEMENT, THIRD EDITION

3 4 5 6 7 8 9 0 QVS/QVS 1 0 9 8 7 6 5 4

ISBN 978-0-07-352520-4

MHID 0-07-352520-0

Vice President & Editor-in-Chief: *Brent Gordon*
Vice President of Specialized Publishing : *Janice M. Roerig-Blong*
Publisher: *Tim Vertovec*
Developmental Editor: *Gail Korosa*
Marketing Manager: *Jaime Halteman*
Editorial Coordinator: *Danielle Andries*
Project Manager: *Erin Melloy*
Design Coordinator: *Margarite Reynolds*
Cover Designer: *Studio Montage, St. Louis, Missouri*
Cover Image: *From left to right: © 2007 Getty Images, Inc.; The McGraw-Hill Companies, Inc./Christopher Kerrigan, photographer; The McGraw-Hill Companies, Inc./John Flournoy, photographer; D. Normark/ PhotoLink/Getty Images; © Lars A. Niki; Big Cheese Photo/SuperStock; Livio Sinibaldi/Getty Images; Chris Sattlberger/Getty Images; Comstock Images/Jupiterimages; Ryan McVay/Getty Images; Getty Images/OJO Images; Brand X Pictures/Getty Images.*
Buyer: *Nicole Baumgartner*
Media Project Manager: *Balaji Sundararaman*
Compositor: *Laserwords Private Limited*
Typeface: *10/12 Times New Roman*
Printer: *Quad/Graphics*

Library of Congress Cataloging-in-Publication Data

Cachon, Gérard.
  Matching supply with demand : an introduction to operations management / Gérard Cachon, Christian Terwiesch.—3rd ed.
      p. cm.
  Includes bibliographical references and index.
  ISBN-13: 978-0-07-352520-4 (alk. paper)
  ISBN-10: 0-07-352520-0 (alk. paper)
  1. Production management. I. Terwiesch, Christian. II. Title.
  TS155.C13 2013
  658.5—dc23
                                                        2011043859

www.mhhe.com

To the teachers, colleagues, and professionals who shared with us their knowledge.

About the Authors

Gérard Cachon *The Wharton School, University of Pennsylvania*

Professor Cachon is the Fred R. Sullivan Professor of Operations and Information Management at The Wharton School of the University of Pennsylvania, where he teaches a variety of undergraduate, MBA, executive, and Ph.D. courses in operations management. His research focuses on supply chain management, and operations strategy; in particular, how new technologies enhance and transform competitiveness via operations. He is a Distinguished Fellow and past president of the Manufacturing and Service Operations Society. His articles have appeared in *Harvard Business Review, Management Science, Marketing Science, Manufacturing & Service Operations Management,* and *Operations Research.* He has been on the editorial review board of five leading journals in operations management, is a former editor of *Manufacturing & Service Operations Management,* and is the current editor of *Management Science.* He has consulted with a wide range of companies, including 4R Systems, Ahold, Americold, Campbell Soup, Gulfstream Aerospace, IBM, Medtronic, and O'Neill.

Before joining The Wharton School in July 2000, Professor Cachon was on the faculty at the Fuqua School of Business, Duke University. He received a Ph.D. from The Wharton School in 1995.

He is an avid proponent of bicycle commuting (and other environmentally friendly modes of transportation). Along with his wife and four children he enjoys hiking, skiing, fishing, snorkeling, and scuba diving.

Christian Terwiesch *The Wharton School, University of Pennsylvania*

Professor Terwiesch is the Andrew M. Heller Professor at the Wharton School of the University of Pennsylvania. He also is a professor in Wharton's Operations and Information Management Department as well as a Senior Fellow at the Leonard Davis Institute for Health Economics. His research on operations management, research and development, and innovation management appears in many of the leading academic journals, including *Management Science, Operations Research, Marketing Science, and Organization Science.* He has received numerous teaching awards for his courses in Wharton's MBA and executive education programs.

Professor Terwiesch has researched with and consulted for various organizations, including a project on concurrent engineering for BMW, supply chain management for Intel and Medtronic, and product customization for Dell. Most of his current work relates to health care and innovation management. In the health care arena, some of Professor Terwiesch's recent projects include the analysis of capacity allocation for cardiac surgery procedures at the University of California–San Francisco and at Penn Medicine, the impact of emergency room crowding on hospital capacity and revenues (also at Penn Medicine), and the usage of intensive care beds in the Children's Hospital of Philadelphia. In the innovation area, recent projects include the management of the clinical development portfolio at Merck, the development of open innovation systems, and the design of patient-centered care processes in the Veterans Administration hospital system.

Professor Terwiesch's latest book, *Innovation Tournaments,* outlines a novel, process-based approach to innovation management. The book was featured by *BusinessWeek, the Financial Times,* and the *Sloan Management Review.*

Acknowledgements

We would like to acknowledge the many people who have helped us in so many different ways with this ongoing project.

We begin with the 2004 Wharton MBA class that weathered through our initial version of the text. It is not practical for us to name every student that shared comments with us, but we do wish to name the students who took the time to participate in our focus groups: Gregory Ames, Maria Herrada-Flores, Justin Knowles, Karissa Kruse, Sandeep Naik, Jeremy Stackowitz, Charlotte Walsh, and Thomas (TJ) Zerr. The 2005 MBA class enjoyed a much more polished manuscript, but nevertheless contributed numerous suggestions and identified remaining typos and errors (much to our chagrin). Since then, we have continued to receive feedback from our undergraduate, MBA, and executive MBA students at Wharton. In addition to Wharton students, we received helpful feedback from students at Texas A&M, the University of Toronto, and INSEAD.

Along with our students, we would like to thank our co-teachers in the core: Naren Agrawal, Krishnan Anand, Omar Besbes, Morris Cohen, Marshall Fisher, Richard Lai, Chris Lee, Pranab Majumder, Serguei Netessine, Kathy Pearson, Taylor Randall, Nicolas Reinecke, Daniel Snow, Stephan Spinler, Anita Tucker, Karl Ulrich, Senthil Veeraraghavan, and Yu-Sheng Zheng. In addition to useful pedagogical advice and quality testing, they shared many of their own practice problems and questions.

This book is not the first book in Operations Management, nor will it be the last. We hope we have incorporated the best practices of existing books while introducing our own innovations. The book by Anupindi et al. as well as the article by Harrison and Loch were very helpful to us, as they developed the process view of operations underlying Chapters 2 through 8. The book by Chase and Aquilano was especially useful for Chapter 10. We apply definitions and terminology from those sources whenever possible without sacrificing our guiding principles.

We also have received some indirect and direct assistance from faculty at other universities. Garrett van Ryzin's (Columbia) and Xavier de Groote's (INSEAD) inventory notes were influential in the writing of Chapters 2 and 14, and the revenue management note by Serguei Netessine (Wharton) and Rob Shumsky (Dartmouth) was the starting point for Chapter 16. The process analysis, queuing, and inventory notes and articles written by Martin Lariviere (Northwestern), Michael Harrison (Stanford), and Christoph Loch (INSEAD) were also influential in several of our chapters. Martin, being a particularly clever question designer, was kind enough to share many of his questions with us.

Matthew Drake (Duquesne University) provided us with invaluable feedback during his meticulous accuracy check of both the text and the solutions, and we thank him for his contribution.

Several brave souls actually read the entire manuscript and responded with detailed comments. These reviewers included Leslie M. Bobb (Bernard M. Baruch College), Sime Curkovic (Western Michigan University–Kalamazoo), Scott Dobos (Indiana University–Bloomington), Ricki Ann Kaplan (East Tennessee State University), and Kathy Stecke (University of Texas at Dallas).

Our Ph.D. student "volunteers," Karan Girotra, Diwas KC, Marcelo Olivares, and Fuqiang Zhang, as well as Ruchika Lal and Bernd Terwiesch, took on the tedious job of quality testing. Robert Batt, Santiago Gallino, Antonio Moreno, Greg Neubecker, Michael Van Pelt, and Bethany Schwartz helped to collect and analyze data and could frequently solve practice problems faster than we could. The text is much cleaner due to their efforts.

The many cases and practical examples that illustrate the core concepts of this book reflect our extensive collaboration with several companies, including the University of Pennsylvania Hospital System in the Philadelphia region, the Circored plant in Trinidad, the Xootr factory in New Hampshire, the An-ser call center in Wisconsin, the operations group at O'Neill in California, and the supply chain group at Medtronic in Minnesota. We have benefited from countless visits and meetings with their management teams. We thank the people of these organizations, whose role it is to match supply and demand in the "real world," for sharing their knowledge, listening to our ideas, and challenging our models. Special thanks go to Jeff Salomon and his team (Interventional Radiology), Karl Ulrich (Xootr), Allan Fromm (An-ser), Cherry Chu and John Pope (O'Neill), and Frederic Marie and John Grossman (Medtronic). Allan Fromm deserves extra credit, as he was not only willing to share with us his extensive knowledge of service operations that he gathered as a CEO of a call center company but also proofread the entire manuscript and tackled most of the practice problems. Special thanks also to the McKinsey operations practice, in particular Stephen Doig, John Drew, and Nicolas Reinecke, for sharing their practical experience on Lean Operations and the Toyota Production System.

We especially thank our friend, colleague, and cycling partner Karl Ulrich, who has been involved in various aspects of the book, starting from its initial idea to the last details of the design process, including the cover design.

Through each edition of this text we have been supported by a fantastic team at McGraw Hill: Scott Isenberg, Cynthia Douglas, Colin Kelley, Karthryn Mikulic, Dick Hercher, Danielle Andries, and Erin Melloy.

Finally, we thank our family members, some of whom were surely unwilling reviewers who nevertheless performed their family obligation with a cheerful smile.

Gérard Cachon

Christian Terwiesch

Preface

This book represents our view of the essential body of knowledge for an introductory operations management course. It has been successfully used with all types of students, from freshmen taking an introductory course in operations management, to MBAs, to executive MBAs, and even PhD students.

Our guiding principle in the development of *Matching Supply with Demand* has been "real operations, real solutions." "Real operations" means that most of the chapters in this book are written from the perspective of a specific company so that the material in this text will come to life by discussing it in a real-world context. Companies and products are simply easier to remember than numbers and equations. We have chosen a wide variety of companies, small and large, representing services, manufacturing, and retailing alike. While obviously not fully representative, we believe that—taken together—these cases provide a realistic picture of operations management problems today.

"Real solutions" means that we do not want equations and models to merely provide students with mathematical gymnastics for the sake of an intellectual exercise. We feel that professional training, even in a rigorous academic setting, requires tools and strategies that students can implement in practice. We achieve this by demonstrating how to apply our models from start to finish in a realistic operational setting. For example, we do not assume the existence of inputs such as a demand forecast or a cost parameter; we actually explain how these inputs can be obtained in practice. Furthermore, we openly address the implementation challenges of each model/strategy we discuss so that students know what to expect when the "rubber hits the pavement."

To fully deliver on "real operations, real solutions," we also must adhere to the principle of "real simple." Do not worry; "real simple" does not mean plenty of "blah-blah" without any analytical rigor. Quite the contrary. To us, "real simple" means hard analysis that is made easy to learn. This is crucial for an operations text. Our objective is to teach business leaders, not tacticians. Thus, we need students to be able to quickly develop a foundation of formal models so that they have the time to explore the big picture, that is, how operations can be transformed to provide an organization with sustainable competitive advantage and/or superior customer service. Students that get bogged down in details, equations, and analysis are not fully capturing the valuable insights they will need in their future career.

So how do we strive for "real simple"? First, we recognize that not every student comes to this material with an engineering/math background. As a result, we tried to use as little mathematical notation as possible, to provide many real-world examples, and to adhere to consistent terminology and phrasing. Second, we provide various levels of detail for each analysis. For example, every little step in an analysis is described in the text via an explicit example; then a summary of the process is provided in a "how to" exhibit, a brief listing of key notation and equations is provided at the end of each chapter, and, finally, solved practice problems are offered to reinforce learning. While we do humbly recognize, given the quantitative sophistication of this text, that "much simpler" might be more accurate than "real simple," we nevertheless hope that students will be pleasantly surprised to discover that their analytical capabilities are even stronger than they imagined.

The initial version of *Matching Supply with Demand* made its debut in portions of the operations management core course at Wharton in the 2002–2003 academic year. This edition incorporates the feedback we have received over the last 10 years from many students, executives, and colleagues, both at Wharton and abroad.

Gérard Cachon

Christian Terwiesch

Changes to This Edition

The third edition has benefited from the comments and suggestions from students, faculty, and practitioners from around the world. The book is now translated into Chinese and Korean, and what once was written as an MBA textbook has been taught to undergraduate students, MBA students, doctoral students, and executives.

The changes that we implemented were substantial, touching almost every chapter of the book. The changes can be broken up into three categories: an update of data and case examples, the addition of three chapters related to content that was not previously covered in the book, and an overall streamlining of the exposition of the existing content.

Many things have happened since we wrote the second edition three years ago. Companies have gone out of business, and new business models were invented. Toyota, the only company that has a chapter dedicated to it in this book, has gone through a major crisis with quality problems in it vehicles. Sadly enough, history also repeated itself: We used the 2007 Japanese earthquake as a motivating example on the first page of the second edition. Now, as we write the third edition, we had to witness the devastating effects of the 2011 earthquake and the effects it had on people and business. To respond to the need to stay current, we have updated data and case examples throughout the book.

We decided to add three new chapters to this book. The first new chapter is about project management—a topic that is taught in many operations courses but was previously absent from the book. The second new chapter is about sustainable operation, a topic of rapidly growing interest in academia and in practice. We also added a chapter on business model innovation. Just like the chapter on lean operations and the Toyota Production System was added as a capstone chapter for the first half of the book in the second edition, for the third edition we wanted to bring together a set of ideas that enable companies to build new business models using the lessons of matching supply with demand. The chapter was fun to write, and we hope it will also be fun to read.

We have seen many textbooks grow thick over multiple editions—nothing is more painful to an author than deleting text he or she wrote before. As much as we were committed to update the content of the book and to add fresh and relevant content, we also wanted to keep the time constraints of our readers in mind. We took some content out of the book (we will make it available on our book website, www.cachon-terwiesch.net) and streamlined the exposition of several tools. It is all about *lean* after all.

Brief Contents

Table of Contents

Chapter 1

Introduction

A central premise in economics is that prices adjust to match supply with demand: if there is excess demand, prices rise; if there is excess supply, prices fall. But while an economist may find comfort with this theory, managers in practice often do not. To them excess demand means lost revenue and excess supply means wasted resources. They fully understand that matching supply with demand is extremely difficult and requires more tools than just price adjustments.

Consider the following examples:

• In 2006, Nintendo launched the Wii game console with much success—so much success that the company could not make enough units to keep up with demand. Some entrepreneurs would wait in long lines to purchase scarce units only to turn around and sell them online for several hundred dollars over the retail price.

• In 2007, Dell lost its worldwide market share leadership to HP. Trying to regain momentum, Dell offered laptop computers to consumers in various colors. Unfortunately, problems with dust contamination in the painting process prevented Dell from ramping up production, causing long delays, which in turn caused some customers to cancel their order.

• At 4 p.m. on weekdays, it is hard to find a taxi in Manhattan because that is when taxis tend to change between shifts. Consequently, customers wait longer for a cab.

• In March 2011, a massive earthquake hit Japan, followed by devastating tsunamis. Supplies for some key automobile and electronic components were unavailable or scarce for months, disrupting production around the globe.

• In 2008, Boeing was unable to deliver on time its new 777s to Emirates Airlines because growth in demand caught its supplier of kitchen galleys off guard and short on capacity.

• In early 2002, a victim of a car crash in Germany died in a rescue helicopter after the medical team together with their dispatcher had unsuccessfully attempted to find a slot in an operating room at eight different hospitals. In the United States, every day there are thousands of patients requiring emergency care who cannot be transported to the nearest emergency room and/or have to wait considerable time before receiving care.

• The average customer to Disney World experiences only nine rides per day, in part because of long queues. To give customers a better experience (read, "more rides"), Disney developed several mechanisms to encourage customers to find rides with short or no queues.

All of these cases have in common that they suffer from a mismatch between demand and supply, with respect either to their timing or to their quantities.

This book is about how firms can design their operations to better match supply with demand. Our motivation is simply stated: By better matching supply with demand, a firm gains a significant competitive advantage over its rivals. A firm can achieve this better match through the implementation of the rigorous models and the operational strategies we outline in this book.

To somewhat soften our challenge to economic theory, we do acknowledge it is possible to mitigate demand–supply mismatches by adjusting prices. For example, the effective market price of the Wii game console did rise due to the strong demand. But this price adjustment was neither under Nintendo's control, nor did Nintendo (or its retailers) collect the extra surplus. In other words, we view that price adjustment as a symptom of a problem, rather than evidence of a healthy system. Moreover, in many other cases, price adjustments are impossible. The time period between the initiation of demand and the fulfillment through supply is too short or there are too few buyers and sellers in the market. There simply is no market for emergency care in operating rooms, waiting times in call centers, or piston rings immediately after an earthquake.

Why is matching supply with demand difficult? The short answer is that demand can vary, in either predictable or unpredictable ways, and supply is inflexible. On average, an organization might have the correct amount of resources (people, product, and/or equipment), but most organizations find themselves frequently in situations with resources in the wrong place, at the wrong time, and/or in the wrong quantity. Furthermore, shifting resources across locations or time is costly, hence the inflexibility in supply. For example, physicians are not willing to rush back and forth to the hospital as they are needed and retailers cannot afford to immediately move product from one location to another. While it is essentially impossible to always achieve a perfect match between supply and demand, successful firms continually strive for that goal.

Table 1.1 provides a sample of industries that we will discuss in this book and describes their challenge to match supply with demand. Take the airline industry (last column in Table 1.1.). For fiscal year 2007, British Airways achieved a 76.1 percent utilization; that is, a 160-seat aircraft (the average size in their fleet) had, on average, 122 seats occupied with a paying passenger and 38 seats flying empty. If British Airways could have had four more (paying) passengers on each flight, that is, increase its utilization by about 2.5 percent, its corporate profits would have increased by close to £242 million, which is about 44 percent of its operating profit for 2007. This illustrates a critical lesson: Even a seemingly small

TABLE 1.1   Examples of Supply–Demand Mismatches

	Retailing	Iron Ore Plant	Emergency Room	Pacemakers	Air Travel
Supply	Consumer electronics	Iron ore	Medical service	Medical equipment	Seats on specific flight
Demand	Consumers buying a new video system	Steel mills	Urgent need for medical service	Heart surgeon requiring pacemaker at exact time and location	Travel for specific time and destination
Supply exceeds demand	High inventory costs; few inventory turns	Prices fall	Doctors, nurses, and infrastructure are underutilized	Pacemaker sits in inventory	Empty seat
Demand exceeds supply	Forgone profit opportunity; consumer dissatisfaction	Prices rise	Crowding and delays in the ER; potential diversion of ambulances	Forgone profit (typically not associated with medical risk)	Overbooking; customer has to take different flight (profit loss)
Actions to match supply and demand	Forecasting; quick response	If prices fall too low, production facility is shut down	Staffing to predicted demand; priorities	Distribution system holding pacemakers at various locations	Dynamic pricing; booking policies

(continued)

TABLE 1.1 **Concluded**

Managerial importance	Per-unit inventory costs for consumer electronics retailing all too often exceed net profits	Prices are so competitive that the primary emphasis is on reducing the cost of supply	Delays in treatment or transfer have been linked to death	Most products (valued $20k) spend 4–5 months waiting in a trunk of a salesperson before being used	About 30% of all seats fly empty; a 1–2% increase in seat utilization makes the difference between profits and losses
Reference	Chapter 2, The Process View of the Organization; Chapter 12, Betting on Uncertain Demand: The Newsvendor Model; Chapter 13, Assemble-to-Order, Make-to-Order, and Quick Response with Reactive Capacity	Chapter 3, Understanding the Supply Process: Evaluating Process Capacity; Chapter 4, Estimating and Reducing Labor Costs	Chapter 8, Variability and Its Impact on Process Performance: Waiting Time Problems; Chapter 9, The Impact of Variability on Process Performance: Throughput Losses	Chapter 14, Service Levels and Lead Times in Supply Chains: The Order-up-to Inventory Model	Chapter 16, Revenue Management with Capacity Controls

improvement in operations, for example, a utilization increase of 2.5 percent, can have a significant effect on a firm's profitability precisely because, for most firms, their profit (if they have a profit) is a relatively small percentage of their revenue. Hence, improving the match between supply and demand is a critically important responsibility for a firm's management.

The other examples in Table 1.1 are drawn from a wide range of settings: health care delivery and devices, retailing, and heavy industry. Each suffers significant consequences due to demand–supply mismatches, and each requires specialized tools to improve and manage its operations.

To conclude our introduction, we strongly believe that effective operations management is about effectively matching supply with demand. Organizations that take the design of their operations seriously and aggressively implement the tools of operations management will enjoy a significant performance advantage over their competitors. This lesson is especially relevant for senior management given the razor-thin profit margins firms must deal with in modern competitive industries.

1.1 Learning Objectives and Framework

In this book, we look at organizations as entities that must match the supply of what they produce with the demand for their product. In this process, we will introduce a number of quantitative models and qualitative strategies, which we collectively refer to as the "tools of operations management." By "quantitative model" we mean some mathematical procedure or equation that takes inputs (such as a demand forecast, a processing rate, etc.) and outputs a number that either instructs a manager on what to do (how much inventory to buy, how many nurses to have on call, etc.) or informs a manager about a relevant performance measure (e.g., the average time a customer waits for service, the average number of patients in the emergency room, etc.). By "qualitative strategy" we mean a guiding principle: for example, increase the flexibility of your production facilities, decrease the variety of products offered, serve customers in priority order, and so forth. The next section gives a brief description of the key models and strategies we cover. Our learning objective for this book, put as succinctly as we can, is to teach students how and when to implement the tools of operations management.

Just as the tools of operations management come in different forms, they can be applied in different ways:

1. Operations management tools can be applied to ensure that resources are used as efficiently as possible; that is, the most is achieved with what we have.

2. Operations management tools can be used to make desirable trade-offs between competing objectives.

3. Operations management tools can be used to redesign or restructure our operations so that we can improve performance along multiple dimensions simultaneously.

We view our diverse set of tools as complementary to each other. In other words, our focus is neither exclusively on the quantitative models nor exclusively on the qualitative strategies. Without analytical models, it is difficult to move beyond the "blah-blah" of strategies and without strategies, it is easy to get lost in the minutia of tactical models. Put another way, we have designed this book to provide a rigorous operations management education for a strategic, high-level manager or consultant.

We will apply operations tools to firms that produce services and goods in a variety of environments—from apparel to health care, from call centers to pacemakers, and from kick scooters to iron ore fines. We present many diverse settings precisely because there does not exist a "standard" operational environment. Hence, there does not exist a single tool that applies to all firms. By presenting a variety of tools and explaining their pros and cons, students will gain the capability to apply this knowledge no matter what operational setting they encounter.

Consider how operations tools can be applied to a call center. A common problem in this industry is to find an appropriate number of customer service representatives to answer incoming calls. The more representatives we hire, the less likely incoming calls will have to wait; thus, the higher will be the level of service we provide. However, labor is the single largest driver of costs in a call center, so, obviously, having more representatives on duty also will increase the costs we incur per call.

The first use of operations management tools is to ensure that resources are used as effectively as possible. Assume we engage in a benchmarking initiative with three other call centers and find that the performance of our competitors behaves according to Figure 1.1: Competitor A is providing faster response times but also has higher costs. Competitor B has longer response times but has lower costs. Surprisingly, we find that competitor C outperforms us on both cost and service level. How can this be?

It must be that there is something that competitor C does in the operation of the call center that is smarter than what we do. Or, in other words, there is something that we do in our operations that is inefficient or wasteful. In this setting, we need to use our tools to move the firm toward the frontier illustrated in Figure 1.1. The frontier is the line that includes all benchmarks to the lower left; that is, no firm is outside the current frontier. For example, a premium service might be an important element of our business strategy, so we may choose not to compromise on service. And we could have a target that at least 90 percent of the incoming calls will be served within 10 seconds or less. But given that target, we should use our quantitative tools to ensure that our labor costs are as low as possible, that is, that we are at least on the efficiency frontier.

The second use of operations management tools is to find the right balance between our competing objectives, high service and low cost. This is similar to what is shown in Figure 1.2. In such a situation, we need to quantify the costs of waiting as well as the costs of labor and then recommend the most profitable compromise between these two objectives.

FIGURE 1.1
Local Improvement of Operations by Eliminating Inefficiencies

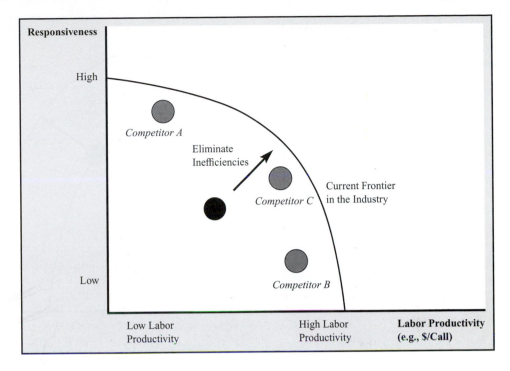

Moving to the frontier of efficiency and finding the right spot on the frontier are surely important. But outstanding companies do not stop there. The third use for our operations management tools is to fundamentally question the design of the current system itself. For example, a call center might consider merging with or acquiring another call center to gain scale economies. Alternatively, a call center might consider an investment in the development of a new technology leading to shorter call durations.

FIGURE 1.2
Trade-off between Labor Productivity and Responsiveness

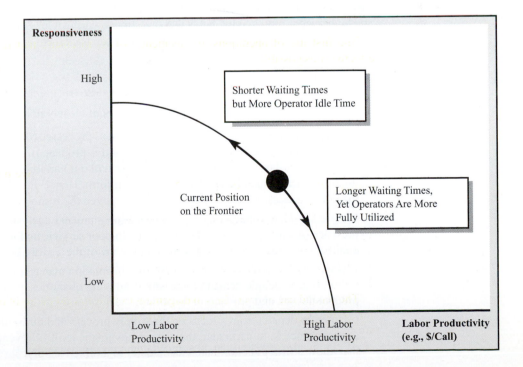

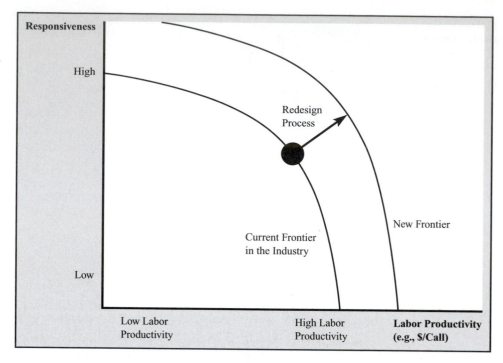

In such cases, a firm pushes the envelope, that is, moves the frontier of what previously was feasible (see Figure 1.3). Hence, a firm is able to achieve faster responsiveness and higher labor productivity. But, unfortunately, there are few free lunches: while we have improved both customer service and labor productivity, pushing out the frontier generally requires some investments in time and effort. Hence, we need to use our tools to quantify the improvements we can achieve so that we can decide whether the effort is justifiable. It is easy to tell a firm that investing in technology can lead to shorter call durations, faster service, and higher labor productivity, but is that investment worthwhile? Our objective is to educate managers so that they can provide "big ideas" and can back them up with rigorous analysis.

1.2 Road Map of the Book

This book can be roughly divided into five clusters of closely related chapters.

The first cluster, Chapters 2–7, analyzes business processes (the methods and procedures by which a service is completed or a good is produced). For the most part, the view taken in those chapters is one of process without variability in service times, production times, demand arrival, quality, and so forth. Hence, the objective is to organize the business process to maximize supply given the resources available to the firm.

Chapters 8–11 introduce variability into business process analysis. Issues include the presence of waiting times, lost demand due to poor service, and lost output due to poor quality. This cluster concludes with an overview of the Toyota Production System.

Chapters 12–15 discuss inventory control, information management, and process flexibility. Issues include demand forecasting, stocking quantities, performance measures, product design, and production flexibility.

Chapter 16 departs from a focus on the supply process and turns attention to the demand process. In particular, the chapter covers the tools of revenue management that allow a firm to better match its demand to its fixed supply.

TABLE 1.2
A High-Level Grouping of Chapters

Chapters	Theme
2–7	Process analysis without variability in service times, production rates, demand arrival, quality, etc.
8–11	Process analysis with variability in service times, production rates, demand arrival, quality, etc.
12–15	Inventory control, information management, process flexibility
16	Revenue management
17–19	Strategic operations management: supply chains, sustainability, and business models

Chapters 17–19 conclude the book with several strategic topics, including the management and control of the supply chain, sustainability, and business model innovation.

Table 1.2 summarizes these clusters.

The following provides a more detailed summary of the contents of each chapter:

• Chapter 2 defines a process, introduces the basic process performance metrics, and provides a framework for characterizing processes (the product–process matrix). Little's Law is introduced, an essential formula for understanding business processes and the link between operations management and financial accounting.

• Chapter 3 introduces process analysis tools from the perspective of a manager (as opposed to an engineer): how to determine the capacity of a process and how to compute process utilization.

• Chapter 4 looks at assembly operations with a specific focus on labor costs, an extremely important performance metric. It frequently drives location decisions (consider the current debate related to offshoring) and has—especially in service operations—a major impact on the bottom line. We define measures such as labor content, labor utilization, and idle time. We also introduce the concept of line balancing.

• Chapter 5 investigates project management, a process that is designed for a single, somewhat unique, project such as a ship, a new building, or a satellite.

• Chapter 6 connects the operational details of process analysis with key financial performance measures for a firm, such as return on invested capital. Through this chapter we discover how to make process improvement translate into enhanced financial performance for the organization.

• Chapter 7 studies production in the presence of setup times and setup costs (the EOQ model). A key issue is the impact of product variety on production performance.

• Chapter 8 explores the consequences of variability on a process. As we will discuss in the context of a call center, variability can lead to long customer waiting times and thereby is a key enemy in all service organizations. We discuss how an organization should handle the trade-off between a desire for minimizing the investment into capacity (e.g., customer service representatives) while achieving a good service experience for the customer.

• Chapter 9 continues the discussion of variability and its impact on service quality. As we will discuss in the context of emergency medicine, variability frequently can lead to situations in which demand has to be turned away because of insufficient capacity. This has substantial implications, especially in the health care environment.

• Chapter 10 details the tools of quality management, including statistical process control, six-sigma, and robust design.

• Chapter 11 describes how Toyota, via its world-famous collection of production strategies called the Toyota Production System, achieves high quality and low cost.

• Chapter 12 focuses on the management of seasonal goods with only one supply opportunity. The newsvendor model allows a manager to strike the correct balance between too much supply and too little supply.

• Chapter 13 expands upon the setting of the previous chapter by allowing additional supply to occur in the middle of the selling season. This "reactive capacity" allows a firm to better respond to early season sales information.

• Chapter 14 continues the discussion of inventory management with the introduction of lead times. The order-up-to model is used to choose replenishment quantities that achieve target availability levels (such as an in-stock probability).

• Chapter 15 highlights numerous risk-pooling strategies to improve inventory management within the supply chain: for example, location pooling, product pooling, universal design, delayed differentiation (also known as postponement), and capacity pooling.

• Chapter 16 covers revenue management. In particular, the focus is on the use of booking limits and overbooking to better match demand to supply when supply is fixed.

• Chapter 17 identifies the bullwhip effect as a key issue in the effective operation of a supply chain and offers coordination strategies for firms to improve the performance of their supply chain.

• Chapter 18 applies operations management thinking to the challenge of sustainability.

• Chapter 19 concludes the book with how operations management enables new business models. A framework is presented for understanding business model innovation that can assist in the creation of new business models.

Some of the chapters are designed to be "entry level" chapters, that is, chapters that can be read independently from the rest of the text. Other chapters are more advanced, so they at least require some working knowledge of the material in another chapter. Table 1.3 summarizes the contents of the chapters and indicates prerequisite chapters.

TABLE 1.3   Chapter Summaries and Prerequisites

Chapter	Managerial Issue	Key Qualitative Framework	Key Quantitative Tool	Prerequisite Chapters
2: The Process View of the Organization	Understanding business processes at a high level; process performance measures, inventory, flow time, and flow rate	Product–process matrix; focus on process flows	Little's Law Inventory turns and inventory costs	None
3: Understanding the Supply Process: Evaluating Process Capacity	Understanding the details of a process	Process flow diagram; finding and removing a bottleneck	Computing process capacity and utilization	Chapter 2
4: Estimating and Reducing Labor Costs	Labor costs	Line balancing; division of labor	Computing labor costs, labor utilization Minimizing idle time	Chapters 2, 3
5: Project Management	Time to project completion	Critical path	Critical path analysis	Chapters 2, 3
6: The Link between Operations and Finance	Process improvement to enhance corporate performance	Return on Invested Capital (ROIC) tree	Computing ROIC	Chapters 2, 3
7: Batching and Other Flow Interruptions: Setup Times and the Economic Order Quantity Model	Setup time and setup costs; managing product variety	Achieving a smooth process flow; deciding about setups and ordering frequency	EOQ model Determining batch sizes	Chapters 2, 3

(continued)

TABLE 1.3   **Concluded**

Chapter	Managerial Issue	Key Qualitative Framework	Key Quantitative Tool	Prerequisite Chapters
8: Variability and Its Impact on Process Performance: Waiting Time Problems	Waiting times in service processes	Understanding congestion; pooling service capacity	Waiting time formula	None
9: The Impact of Variability on Process Performance: Throughput Losses	Lost demand in service processes	Role of service buffers; pooling	Erlang loss formula Probability of diverting demand	Chapter 8
10: Quality Management, Statistical Process Control, and Six-Sigma Capability	Defining and improving quality	Statistical process control; six-sigma	Computing process capability; creating a control chart	None
11: Lean Operations and the Toyota Production System	Process improvement for competitive advantage	Lean operations; Toyota Production System	—	None
12: Betting on Uncertain Demand: The Newsvendor Model	Choosing stocking levels for seasonal-style goods	Improving the forecasting process	Forecasting demand The newsvendor model for choosing stocking quantities and evaluating performance measures	None
13: Assemble-to-Order, Make-to-Order, and Quick Response with Reactive Capacity	How to use reactive capacity to reduce demand–supply mismatch costs	Value of better demand information; assemble-to-order and make-to-order strategies	Reactive capacity models	Chapter 12
14: Service Levels and Lead Times in Supply Chains: The Order-up-to Inventory Model	Inventory management with numerous replenishments	Impact of lead times on performance; how to choose an appropriate objective function	The order-up-to model for inventory management and performance-measure evaluation	Chapter 12 is highly recommended
15: Risk Pooling Strategies to Reduce and Hedge Uncertainty	How to better design the supply chain or a product or a service to better match supply with demand	Quantifying, reducing, avoiding, and hedging uncertainty	Newsvendor and order-up-to models	Chapters 12 and 14
16: Revenue Management with Capacity Controls	How to manage demand when supply is fixed	Reserving capacity for high-paying customers; accepting more reservations than available capacity	Booking limit/protection level model; overbooking model	Chapter 12
17: Supply Chain Coordination	How to manage demand variability and inventory across the supply chain	Bullwhip effect; supply chain contracts	Supply chain contract model	Chapter 12
18: Sustainability	How to employ operations management techniques to a sustainability initiative	Measuring resource use and emissions	—	None
19: Business Model Innovation	How to create a business model innovation	Customer value curve and supply process transformation	—	None

Chapter

2

The Process View of the Organization

Matching supply and demand would be easy if business processes would be instantaneous and could immediately create any amount of supply to meet demand. Understanding the questions of "Why are business processes not instantaneous?" and "What constrains processes from creating more supply?" is thereby at the heart of operations management. To answer these questions, we need to take a detailed look at how business processes actually work. In this chapter, we introduce some concepts fundamental to process analysis. The key idea of the chapter is that it is not sufficient for a firm to create great products and services; the firm also must design and improve its business processes that supply its products and services.

To get more familiar with the process view of a firm, we now take a detailed look behind the scenes of a particular operation, namely the Department of Interventional Radiology at Presbyterian Hospital in Philadelphia.

2.1 Presbyterian Hospital in Philadelphia

Interventional radiology is a subspecialty field of radiology that uses advanced imaging techniques such as real-time X-rays, ultrasound, computed tomography, and magnetic resonance imaging to perform minimally invasive procedures.

Over the past decade, interventional radiology procedures have begun to replace an increasing number of standard "open surgical procedures" for a number of reasons. Instead of being performed in an operating room, interventional radiology procedures are performed in an angiography suite (see Figure 2.1). Although highly specialized, these rooms are less expensive to operate than conventional operating rooms. Interventional procedures are often safer and have dramatically shorter recovery times compared to traditional surgery. Also, an interventional radiologist is often able to treat diseases such as advanced liver cancer that cannot be helped by standard surgery.

Although we may not have been in the interventional radiology unit, many, if not most, of us have been in a radiology department of a hospital at some point in our life. From the perspective of the patient, the following steps need to take place before the patient can go home or return to his or her hospital unit. In process analysis, we refer to these steps as *activities*:

- Registration of the patient.
- Initial consultation with a doctor; signature of the consent form.

FIGURE 2.1
**Example of a
Procedure in an
Interventional
Radiology Unit**

Reprinted with permission of
Arrow International, Inc.

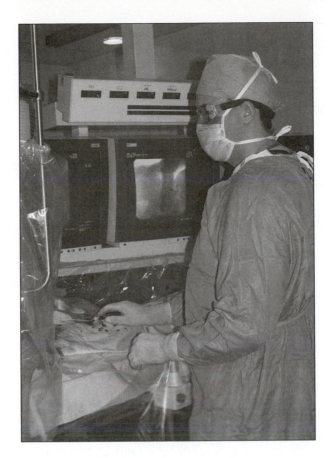

- Preparation for the procedure.
- The actual procedure.
- Removal of all equipment.
- Recovery in an area outside the angiography suite.
- Consultation with the doctor.

Figure 2.2 includes a graphical representation of these steps, called a *Gantt diagram* (named after the 19th-century industrialist Henry Gantt). It provides several useful pieces of information.

First, the Gantt chart allows us to see the process steps and their durations, which are also called *activity times* or *processing times.* The duration simply corresponds to the length of the corresponding bars. Second, the Gantt diagram also illustrates the dependence between the various process activities. For example, the consultation with the doctor can only occur once the patient has arrived and been registered. In contrast, the preparation of the angiography suite can proceed in parallel to the initial consultation.

You might have come across Gantt charts in the context of project management. Unlike process analysis, project management is typically concerned with the completion of one single project (See Chapter 5 for more details on project management.) The most well-known concept of project management is the *critical path.* The critical path is composed of all those activities that—if delayed—would lead to a delay in the overall completion time of the project, or—in this case—the time the patient has completed his or her stay in the radiology unit.

In addition to the eight steps described in the Gantt chart of Figure 2.2, most of us associate another activity with hospital care: waiting. Strictly speaking, waiting is not really

FIGURE 2.2
Gantt Chart
Summarizing the
Activities for
Interventional
Radiology

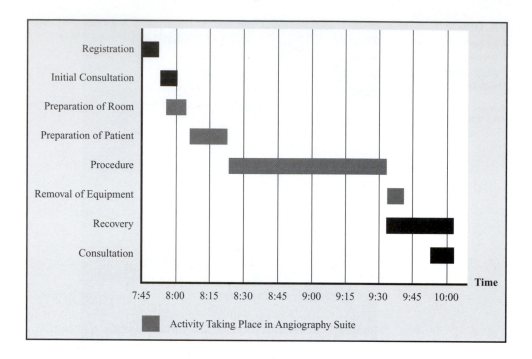

an activity, as it does not add any value to the process. However, waiting is nevertheless relevant. It is annoying for the patient and can complicate matters for the hospital unit. For this reason, waiting times take an important role in operations management. Figure 2.3 shows the actual durations of the activities for a patient arriving at 12:30, as well as the time the patient needs to wait before being moved to the angiography suite.

FIGURE 2.3
Gantt Chart
Summarizing the
Activities for a
Patient Arriving
at 12:30

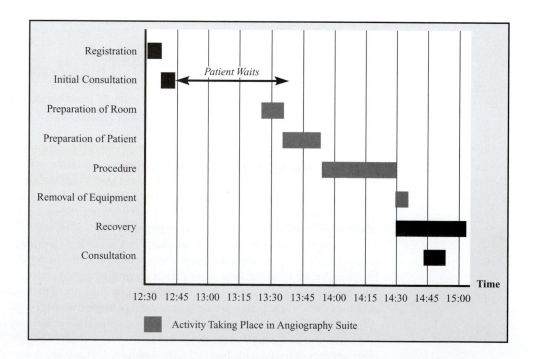

But why is there waiting time? Waiting is—to stay in the medical language for the moment—a symptom of supply–demand mismatch. If supply would be unlimited, our visit to the hospital would be reduced to the duration of the activities outlined in Figure 2.2 (the critical path). Imagine visiting a hospital in which all the nurses, technicians, doctors, and hospital administrators would just care for you!

Given that few of us are in a position to receive the undivided attention of an entire hospital unit, it is important that we not only take the egocentric perspective of the patient, but look at the hospital operations more broadly. From the perspective of the hospital, there are many patients "flowing" through the process.

The people and the equipment necessary to support the interventional radiology process deal with many patients, not just one. We refer to these elements of the process as the *process resources*. Consider, for example, the perspective of the nurse and how she/he spends her/his time in the department of interventional radiology. Obviously, radiology from the viewpoint of the nurse is not an exceptional event, but a rather repetitive endeavor. Some of the nurse's work involves direct interaction with the patient; other work—while required for the patient—is invisible to the patient. This includes the preparation of the angiography suite and various aspects of medical record keeping.

Given this repetitive nature of work, the nurse as well as the doctors, technicians, and hospital administrators think of interventional radiology as a process, not a project. Over the course of the day, they see many patients come and go. Many hospitals, including the Presbyterian Hospital in Philadelphia, have a "patient log" that summarizes at what times patients arrive at the unit. This patient log provides a picture of demand on the corresponding day. The patient log for December 2, is summarized by Table 2.1.

Many of these arrivals were probably scheduled some time in advance. Our analysis here focuses on what happens to the patient once he/she has arrived in the interventional radiology unit. A separate analysis could be performed, looking at the process starting with a request for diagnostics up to the arrival of the patient.

Given that the resources in the interventional radiology unit have to care for 11 patients on December 2, they basically need to complete the work according to 11 Gantt charts of the type outlined in Figure 2.2. This—in turn—can lead to waiting times. Waiting times arise when several patients are "competing" for the same limited resource, which is illustrated by the following two examples.

First, observe that the critical path for a typical patient takes about 2 hours. Note further that we want to care for 11 patients over a 10-hour workday. Consequently, we will have to take care of several patients at once. This would not be a problem if we had unlimited resources, nurses, doctors, space in the angiography suites, and so forth. However,

TABLE 2.1
Patient Log on December 2

Number	Patient Name	Arrival Time	Room Assignment
1		7:35	Main room
2		7:45	
3		8:10	
4		9:30	Main room
5		10:15	Main room
6		10:30	Main room
7		11:05	
8		12:35	Main room
9		14:30	Main room
10		14:35	
11		14:40	

FIGURE 2.4
**Time Patient Spent in
the Interventional
Radiology Unit (for
Patients Treated in
Main Room Only),
Including Room
Preparation Time**

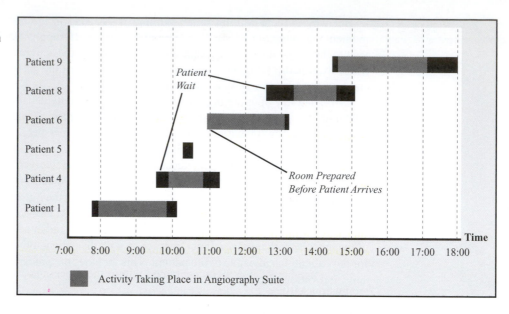

given the resources that we have, if the Gantt charts of two patients are requesting the same resource simultaneously, waiting times result. For example, the second patient might require the initial consultation with the doctor at a time when the doctor is in the middle of the procedure for patient 1. Note also that patients 1, 4, 5, 6, 8, and 9 are assigned to the same room (the unit has a main room and a second room used for simpler cases), and thus they are also potentially competing for the same resource.

A second source of waiting time lies in the unpredictable nature of many of the activities. Some patients will take much longer in the actual procedure than others. For example, patient 1 spent 1:50 hours in the procedure, while patient 9 was in the procedure for 2:30 hours (see Figure 2.4). As an extreme case, consider patient 5, who refused to sign the consent form and left the process after only 15 minutes.

Such uncertainty is undesirable for resources, as it leaves them "flooded" with work at some moments in the day and "starved" for work at other moments. Figure 2.5 summarizes at what moments in time the angiography suite was used on December 2.

By now, we have established two views to the interventional radiology:

• The view of the patient for whom the idealized stay is summarized by Figure 2.2. Mismatches between supply and demand from the patient's perspective mean having a unit of demand (i.e., the patient) wait for a unit of supply (a resource).

• The view of the resources (summarized by Figure 2.5), which experience demand–supply mismatches when they are sometimes "flooded" with work, followed by periods of no work.

As these two perspectives are ultimately two sides of the same coin, we are interested in bringing these two views together. This is the fundamental idea of process analysis.

FIGURE 2.5
**Usage of the Main
Room**

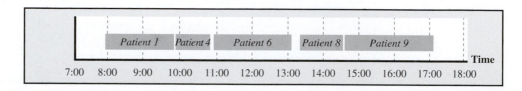

2.2   Three Measures of Process Performance

At the most aggregate level, a process can be thought of as a "black box" that uses *resources* (labor and capital) to transform *inputs* (undiagnosed patients, raw materials, unserved customers) into *outputs* (diagnosed patients, finished goods, served customers). This is shown in Figure 2.6. Chapter 3 explains the details of constructing figures like Figure 2.6, which are called *process flow diagrams.* When analyzing the processes that lead to the supply of goods and services, we first define our unit of analysis.

In the case of the interventional radiology unit, we choose patients as our *flow unit.* Choosing the flow unit is typically determined by the type of product or service the supply process is dealing with; for example, vehicles in an auto plant, travelers for an airline, or gallons of beer in a brewery.

As suggested by the term, flow units flow through the process, starting as input and later leaving the process as output. With the appropriate flow unit defined, we next can evaluate a process based on three fundamental process performance measures:

- The number of flow units contained within the process is called the *inventory* (in a production setting, it is referred to as *work-in-process, WIP*). Given that our focus is not only on production processes, inventory could take the form of the number of insurance claims or the number of tax returns at the IRS. There are various reasons why we find inventory in processes, which we discuss in greater detail below. While many of us might initially feel uncomfortable with the wording, the inventory in the case of the interventional radiology unit is a group of patients.

- The time it takes a flow unit to get through the process is called the *flow time.* The flow time takes into account that the item (flow unit) may have to wait to be processed because there are other flow units (inventory) in the process potentially competing for the same resources. Flow time is an especially important performance metric in service environments or in other business situations that are sensitive to delays, such as make-to-order production, where the production of the process only begins upon the arrival of the customer order. In a radiology unit, flow time is something that patients are likely to care about: it measures the time from their arrival at the interventional radiology unit to the time patients can go home or return to their hospital unit.

- Finally, the rate at which the process is delivering output (measured in [flow units/unit of time], e.g., units per day) is called the *flow rate* or the *throughput rate.* The maximum rate with which the process can generate supply is called the *capacity* of the process. For December 2, the throughput of the interventional radiology unit was 11 patients per day.

Table 2.2 provides several examples of processes and their corresponding flow rates, inventory levels, and flow times.

You might be somewhat irritated that we have moved away from the idea of supply and demand mismatch for a moment. Moreover, we have not talked about profits so far.

FIGURE 2.6
The Process View of an Organization

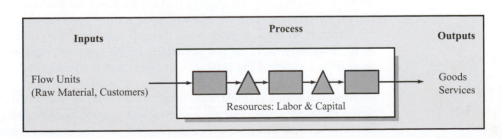

TABLE 2.2
Examples of Flow Rates, Inventories, and Flow Times

	U.S. Immigration	Champagne Industry	MBA Program	Large PC Manufacturer
Flow unit	Application for immigration benefit	Bottle of champagne	MBA student	Computer
Flow rate/ throughput	Approved or rejected visa cases: 6.3 million per year	260 million bottles per year	600 students per year	5,000 units per day
Flow time	Average processing time: 7.6 months	Average time in cellar: 3.46 years	2 years	10 days
Inventory	Pending cases: 4.0 million cases	900 million bottles	1,200 students	50,000 computers

However, note that increasing the maximum flow rate (capacity) avoids situations where we have insufficient supply to match demand. From a profit perspective, a higher flow rate translates directly into more revenues (you can produce a unit faster and thus can produce more units), assuming your process is currently *capacity constrained,* that is, there is sufficient demand that you could sell any additional output you make.

Shorter flow times reduce the time delay between the occurrence of demand and its fulfillment in the form of supply. Shorter flow times therefore also typically help to reduce demand–supply mismatches. In many industries, shorter flow times also result in additional unit sales and/or higher prices, which makes them interesting also from a broader management perspective.

Lower inventory results in lower working capital requirements as well as many quality advantages that we explore later in this book. A higher inventory also is directly related to longer flow times (explained below). Thus, a reduction in inventory also yields a reduction in flow time. As inventory is the most visible indication of a mismatch between supply and demand, we will now discuss it in greater detail.

2.3   Little's Law

Accountants view inventory as an asset, but from an operations perspective, inventory often should be viewed as a liability. This is not a snub on accountants; inventory *should* be an asset on a balance sheet, given how accountants define an asset. But in common speech, the word *asset* means "desirable thing to have" and the dictionary defines *liability* as "something that works to one's disadvantage." In this sense, inventory can clearly be a liability. This is most visible in a service process such as a hospital unit, where patients in the waiting room obviously cannot be counted toward the assets of the health care system.

Let's take another visit to the interventional radiology unit. Even without much medical expertise, we can quickly find out which of the patients are currently undergoing care from some resource and which are waiting for a resource to take care of them. Similarly, if we took a quick walk through a factory, we could identify which parts of the inventory serve as raw materials, which ones are work-in-process, and which ones have completed the production process and now take the form of finished goods inventory.

However, taking a single walk through the process—dishwasher factory or interventional radiology unit—will not leave us with a good understanding of the underlying operations. All it will give us is a snapshot of what the process looked like at one single moment in time. Unfortunately, it is this same snapshot approach that underlies most management (accounting) reports: balance sheets itemize inventory into three categories (raw materials, WIP, finished goods); hospital administrators typically distinguish between pre- and postoperative patients. But such snapshots do not tell us *why* these inventories exist in the first place! Thus, a static, snapshot approach neither helps us to analyze business processes (why is there inventory?) nor helps us to improve them (is this the right amount of inventory?).

Now, imagine that instead of our single visit to the hospital unit, we would be willing to stay for some longer period of time. We arrive early in the morning and make ourselves comfortable at the entrance of the unit. Knowing that there are no patients in the interventional radiology unit overnight, we then start recording any arrival or departure of patients. In other words, we collect data concerning the patient inflow and outflow.

At the end of our stay, we can plot a graph similar to Figure 2.7. The upper of the two curves illustrates the cumulative number of patients who have entered the unit. The curve begins at time zero (7:00) and with zero patients. If we had done the same exercise in a unit with overnight patients, we would have recorded our initial patient count there. The lower of the two curves indicates the cumulative number of patients who have left the unit. Figure 2.7 shows us that by noon, seven patients have arrived, of which five have left the unit again.

At any given moment in time, the *vertical distance* between the upper curve and the lower curve corresponds to the number of patients in the interventional radiology unit, or—abstractly speaking—the inventory level. Thus, although we have not been inside the interventional radiology unit this day, we are able to keep track of the inventory level by comparing the cumulative inflow and outflow. For example, the inventory at noon consisted of two patients.

We also can look at the *horizontal distance* between the two lines. If the patients leave the unit in the same order they entered it, the horizontal gap would measure the exact amount of time each patient spent in the interventional radiology unit. More generally, given that the length of stay might vary across patients and patients do not necessarily leave the unit in the exact same sequence in which they entered it, the average gap between the two lines provides the average length of stay.

FIGURE 2.7
Cumulative Inflow and Outflow

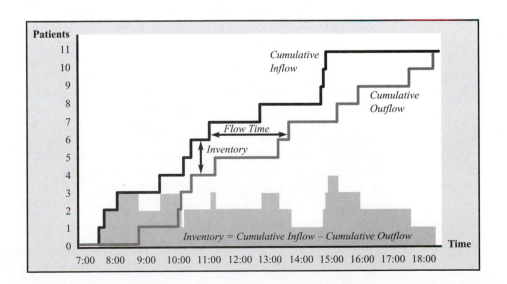

Thus, Figure 2.7 includes all three of the basic process performance measures we discussed on the previous page: flow rate (the slope of the two graphs), inventory (the vertical distance between the two graphs), and flow time (the horizontal distance between the two graphs).

Based on either the graph or the patient log, we can now compute these performance measures for December 2. We already know that the flow rate was 11 patients/day.

Next, consider inventory. Inventory changes throughout the day, reflecting the differences between inflow and outflow of patients. A "brute force" approach to compute average inventory is to count the inventory at every moment in time throughout the day, say every five minutes, and then take the average. For December 2, this computation yields an average inventory of 2.076 patients.

Next, consider the flow time, the time a patient spends in the unit. To compute that information, we need to add to the patient log, Table 2.1, the time each patient left the interventional radiology unit. The difference between arrival time and departure time would be the flow time for a given patient, which in turn would allow us to compute the average flow time across patients. This is shown in Table 2.3 and is in many ways similar to the two graphs in Figure 2.7. We can easily compute that on December 2, the average flow time was 2 hours, 4 minutes, and 33 seconds, or 2.076 hours.

At this point, you might ask: "Does the average inventory always come out the same as the average flow time?" The answer to this question is a resounding *no*. However, the fact that the average inventory was 2.076 patients and the average flow time was 2.076 hours is no coincidence either.

To see how inventory and flow time relate to each other, let us review the three performance measures, flow rate, flow time, and inventory:

- Flow rate = 11 patients per day, which is equal to one patient per hour.
- Flow time = 2.076 hours.
- Inventory = 2.076 patients.

Thus, while inventory and flow time do not have to—and, in fact, rarely are—equal, they are linked in another form. We will now introduce this relationship as Little's Law (named after John D. C. Little).

$$\text{Average inventory} = \text{Average flow rate} \times \text{Average flow time} \qquad \text{(Little's Law)}$$

Many people think of this relationship as trivial. However, it is not. Its proof is rather complex for the general case (which includes—among other nasty things—variability) and by mathematical standards is very recent.

TABLE 2.3
Calculation of Average Flow Time

Number	Patient Name	Arrival Time	Departure Time	Flow Time
1		7:35	8:50	1:15
2		7:45	10:05	2:20
3		8:10	10:10	2:00
4		9:30	11:15	1:45
5		10:15	10:30	0:15
6		10:30	13:35	3:05
7		11:05	13:15	2:10
8		12:35	15:05	2:30
9		14:30	18:10	3:40
10		14:35	15:45	1:10
11		14:40	17:20	2:40
			Average	2:04:33

Little's Law is useful in finding the third performance measure when the other two are known. For example, if you want to find out how long patients in a radiology unit spend waiting for their chest X-ray, you could do the following:

1. Observe the inventory of patients at a couple of random points during the day, giving you an average inventory. Let's say this number is seven patients: four in the waiting room, two already changed and waiting in front of the procedure room, and one in the procedure room.

2. Count the procedure slips or any other records showing how many patients were treated that day. This is the day's output. Let's say there were 60 patients over a period of 8 hours; we could say that we have a flow rate of 60/8 = 7.5 patients/hour.

3. Use Little's Law to compute Flow time = Inventory/Flow rate = 7/7.5 = 0.933 hour = 56 minutes. This tells us that, on average, it takes 56 minutes from the time a patient enters the radiology unit to the time his or her chest X-ray is completed. Note that this information would otherwise have to be computed by collecting additional data (e.g., see Table 2.3).

When does Little's Law hold? The short answer is *always.* For example, Little's Law does not depend on the sequence in which the flow units (e.g., patients) are served (remember FIFO and LIFO from your accounting class?). (However, the sequence could influence the flow time of a particular flow unit, e.g., the patient arriving first in the morning, but not the average flow time across all flow units.) Furthermore, Little's Law does not depend on randomness: it does not matter if there is variability in the number of patients or in how long treatment takes for each patient; all that matters is the average flow rate of patients and the average flow time.

In addition to the direct application of Little's Law, for example, in the computation of flow time, Little's Law is also underlying the computation of inventory costs as well as a concept known as inventory turns. This is discussed in the following section.

2.4 Inventory Turns and Inventory Costs

Using physical units as flow units (and, hence, as the inventory measure) is probably the most intuitive way to measure inventory. This could be vehicles at an auto retailer, patients in the hospital, or tons of oil in a refinery.

However, working with physical units is not necessarily the best method for obtaining an aggregate measure of inventory across different products: there is little value to saying you have 2,000 units of inventory if 1,000 of them are paper clips and the remaining 1,000 are computers. In such applications, inventory is often measured in some monetary unit, for example, $5 million worth of inventory.

Measuring inventory in a common monetary unit facilitates the aggregation of inventory across different products. This is why total U.S. inventory is reported in dollars. To illustrate the notion of monetary flow units, consider Kohl's Corp, a large U.S. retailer. Instead of thinking of Kohl's stores as sodas, toys, clothes, and bathroom tissues (physical units), we can think of its stores as processes transforming goods valued in monetary units into sales, which also can be evaluated in the form of monetary units.

As can easily be seen from Kohl's balance sheet, on January 31, 2011, the company held an inventory valued at $3.036 billion (see Table 2.4). Given that our flow unit now is the "individual dollar bill," we want to measure the flow rate through Kohl's operation.

The direct approach would be to take "sales" as the resulting flow. Yet, this measure is inflated by Kohl's gross profit margin; that is, a dollar of sales is measured in sales dol-

TABLE 2.4   **Excerpts from Financial Statements of Kohl's and Walmart (All Numbers in Millions)**

Source: Taken from 10-K filings.

	2011	2010	2009	2008	2007
Kohl's					
Revenue	$ 18,391	$ 17,178	$ 16,389	$ 16,474	$ 15,544
Cost of Goods Sold	$ 11,359	$ 10,679	$ 10,332	$ 10,459	$ 9,890
Inventory	$ 3,036	$ 2,923	$ 2,799	$ 2,856	$ 2,588
Net Income	$ 1,114	$ 991	$ 885	$ 1,084	$ 1,109
Walmart					
Revenue	$418,952	$ 405,046	$ 401,244	$374,526	$344,992
Cost of Goods Sold	$307,646	$2,97,500	$2,99,419	$280,198	$258,693
Inventory	$ 36,318	$ 33,160	$ 34,511	$ 35,180	$ 33,685
Net Income	$ 16,389	$ 14,335	$ 13,188	$ 12,884	$ 12,036

lars, while a dollar of inventory is measured, given the present accounting practice, in a cost dollar. Thus, the appropriate measure for flow rate is the cost of goods sold, or COGS for short.

With these two measures—flow rate and inventory—we can apply Little's Law to compute what initially might seem a rather artificial measure: how long does the average flow unit (dollar bill) spend within the Kohl's system before being turned into sales, at which point the flow units will trigger a profit intake. This corresponds to the definition of flow time.

$$\text{Flow rate} = \text{Cost of goods sold} = \$11{,}359 \text{ million/year}$$
$$\text{Inventory} = \$3{,}036 \text{ million}$$

Hence, we can compute flow time via Little's Law as

$$\text{Flow time} = \frac{\text{Inventory}}{\text{Flow rate}}$$

$$= \$3{,}036 \text{ million}/\$11{,}359 \text{ million/year} = 0.267 \text{ year} = 97 \text{ days}$$

Thus, we find that it takes Kohl's—on average—97 days to translate a dollar investment into a dollar of—hopefully profitable—revenues.

This calculation underlies the definition of another way of measuring inventory, namely in terms of *days of supply.* We could say that Kohl's has 97 days of inventory in their process. In other words, the average item we find at Kohl's spends 97 days in Kohl's supply chain.

Alternatively, we could say that Kohl's turns over its inventory 365 days/year/97 days = 3.74 times per year. This measure is called *inventory turns.* Inventory turns is a common benchmark in the retailing environment and other supply chain operations:

$$\text{Inventory turns} = \frac{1}{\text{Flow time}}$$

TABLE 2.5
Inventory Turns and Margins for Selected Retail Segments

Source: Based on Gaur, Fisher, and Raman 2005.

Retail Segment	Examples	Annual Inventory Turns	Gross Margin
Apparel and accessory	Ann Taylor, GAP	4.57	37%
Catalog, mail-order	Spiegel, Lands End	8.60	39%
Department stores	Sears, JCPenney	3.87	34%
Drug and proprietary stores	Rite Aid, CVS	5.26	28%
Food stores	Albertson's, Safeway, Walmart	10.78	26%
Hobby, toy/game stores	Toys R Us	2.99	35%
Home furniture/equipment	Bed Bath & Beyond	5.44	40%
Jewelry	Tiffany	1.68	42%
Radio, TV, consumer electronics	Best Buy, CompUSA	4.10	31%
Variety stores	Kohl's, Walmart, Target	4.45	29%

To illustrate this application of Little's Law further, consider Walmart, one of Kohl's competitors. Repeating the same calculations as outlined on the previous page, we find the following data about Walmart:

$$\text{Cost of goods sold} = \$307,646 \text{ million/year}$$
$$\text{Inventory} = \$36,318 \text{ million}$$
$$\text{Flow time} = \$36,318 \text{ million}/\$307,646 \text{ million/year}$$
$$= 0.118 \text{ year} = 43.1 \text{ days}$$
$$\text{Inventory turns} = 1/43.1 \text{ turns/day}$$
$$= 365 \text{ days/year} \times 1/43.1 \text{ turns/day} = 8.47 \text{ turns per year}$$

Thus, we find that Walmart is able to achieve substantially higher inventory turns than Kohl's. Table 2.5 summarizes inventory turn data for various segments of the retailing industry. Table 2.5 also provides information about gross margins in various retail settings (keep them in mind the next time you haggle for a new sofa or watch!).

Inventory requires substantial financial investments. Moreover, the inventory holding cost is substantially higher than the mere financial holding cost for a number of reasons:

- Inventory might become obsolete (think of the annual holding cost of a microprocessor).
- Inventory might physically perish (you don't want to think of the cost of holding fresh roses for a year).
- Inventory might disappear (also known as theft or shrink).
- Inventory requires storage space and other overhead cost (insurance, security, real estate, etc.).
- There are other less tangible costs of inventory that result from increased wait times (because of Little's Law, to be discussed in Chapter 8) and lower quality (to be discussed in Chapter 11).

Given an annual cost of inventory (e.g., 20 percent per year) and the inventory turn information as computed above, we can compute the per-unit inventory cost that a process (or a supply chain) incurs. To do this, we take the annual holding cost and divide it by the number of times the inventory turns in a year:

$$\text{Per-unit inventory costs} = \frac{\text{Annual inventory costs}}{\text{Annual inventory turns}}$$

Exhibit 2.1

CALCULATING INVENTORY TURNS AND PER-UNIT INVENTORY COSTS

1. Look up the value of inventory from the balance sheet.
2. Look up the cost of goods sold (COGS) from the earnings statement; do *not* use sales!
3. Compute inventory turns as

$$\text{Inventory turns} = \frac{\text{COGS}}{\text{Inventory}}$$

4. Compute per-unit inventory costs as

$$\text{Per-unit inventory costs} \quad \frac{\text{Annual inventory costs}}{\text{Inventory turns}}$$

Note: The annual inventory cost needs to account for the cost of financing the inventory, the cost of depreciation, and other inventory-related costs the firm considers relevant (e.g., storage, theft).

For example, a company that works based on a 20 percent annual inventory cost and that turns its inventory six times per year incurs per-unit inventory costs of

$$\frac{20\% \text{ per year}}{6 \text{ turns per year}} = 3.33\%$$

In the case of Kohl's (we earlier computed that the inventory turns 3.74 times per year), and assuming annual holding costs of 20 percent per year, this translates to inventory costs of about 5.35 percent of the cost of goods sold (20%/3.74 = 5.35). The calculations to obtain per unit inventory costs are summarized in Exhibit 2.1.

To stay in the retailing context a little longer, consider a retailer of consumer electronics who has annual inventory costs of 30 percent (driven by financial costs and obsolescence). Assuming the retailer turns its inventory about four times per year (see Table 2.5.), we obtain a per-unit inventory cost of 30%/4 = 7.5%. Consider a TV in the retailer's assortment that is on the shelf with a price tag of $300 and is procured by the retailer for $200. Based on our calculation, we know that the retailer incurs a $200 × 7.5% = $15 inventory cost for each such TV that is sold. To put this number into perspective, consider Figure 2.8.

Figure 2.8 plots the relationship between gross margin and inventory turns for consumer electronics retailers (based on Gaur, Fisher, and Raman 2005). Note that this graph does not imply causality in this relationship. That is, the model does not imply that if a firm increases its gross margin, its inventory turns will decline automatically. Instead, the way to look at Figure 2.8 is to think of gross margin for a given set of products as being fixed by the competitive environment. We can then make two interesting observations:

- A retailer can decide to specialize in products that turn very slowly to increase its margins. For example, Radio Shack is known for its high margins, as they carry many products in their assortment that turn only once or twice a year. In contrast, Best Buy is carrying largely very popular items, which exposes the company to stiffer competition and lower gross margins.
- For a given gross margin, we observe dramatic differences concerning inventory turns. For example, inventory turns vary between four and nine times for a 15 percent gross margin. Consider retailer A and assume that all retailers work with a 30 percent annual holding cost. Based on the annual inventory turns of 4.5, retailer A faces a 6.66 percent per-unit inventory cost. Now, compare this to competing retailer B, who turns its inventory eight times per year. Thus, retailer B operates with 3.75 percent per-unit inventory

FIGURE 2.8
**Relationship between
Inventory Turns and
Gross Margin**

Source: Based on Gaur, Fisher,
and Raman 2005.

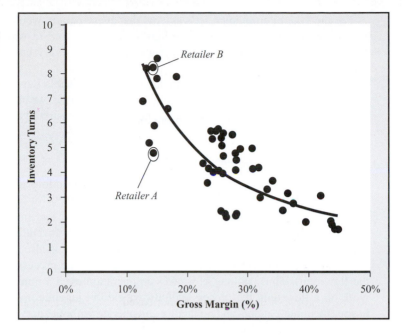

costs, almost a 3 percent cost advantage over retailer A. Given that net profits in this industry segment are around 2 percent of sales, such a cost advantage can make the difference between profits and bankruptcy.

2.5 Five Reasons to Hold Inventory

While Little's Law allows us to compute the average inventory in the process (as long as we know flow time and flow rate), it offers no help in answering the question we raised previously: Why is there inventory in the process in the first place? To understand the need for inventory, we can no longer afford to take the black-box perspective and look at processes from the outside. Instead, we have to look at the process in much more detail.

As we saw from Figure 2.7, inventory reflected a deviation between the inflow into a process and its outflow. Ideally, from an operations perspective, we would like Figure 2.7 to take the shape of two identical, straight lines, representing process inflow and outflow. Unfortunately, such straight lines with zero distance between them rarely exist in the real world. De Groote (1994) discusses five reasons for holding inventory, that is, for having the inflow line differ from the outflow line: (1) the time a flow unit spends in the process, (2) seasonal demand, (3) economies of scale, (4) separation of steps in a process, and (5) stochastic demand. Depending on the reason for holding inventory, inventories are given different names: pipeline inventory, seasonal inventory, cycle inventory, decoupling inventory/ buffers, and safety inventory. It should be noted that these five reasons are not necessarily mutually exclusive and that, in practice, there typically exist more than one reason for holding inventory.

Pipeline Inventory

This first reason for inventory reflects the time a flow unit has to spend in the process in order to be transformed from input to output. Even with unlimited resources, patients still need to spend time in the interventional radiology unit; their flow time would be the length of the critical path. We refer to this basic inventory on which the process operates as *pipeline inventory*.

For the sake of simplicity, let's assume that every patient would have to spend exactly 1.5 hours in the interventional radiology unit, as opposed to waiting for a resource to become available, and that we have one patient arrive every hour. How do we find the pipeline inventory in this case?

The answer is obtained through an application of Little's Law. Because we know two of the three performance measures, flow time and flow rate, we can figure out the third, in this case inventory: with a flow rate of one patient per hour and a flow time of 1.5 hours, the average inventory is

$$\text{Inventory} = 1[\text{patient/hour}] \times 1.5[\text{hours}] = 1.5 \text{ patients}$$

which is the number of patients undergoing some value-adding activity. This is illustrated by Figure 2.9.

In certain environments, you might hear managers make statements of the type "we need to achieve zero inventory in our process." If we substitute Inventory = 0 into Little's Law, the immediate result is that a process with zero inventory is also a process with zero flow rate (unless we have zero flow time, which means that the process does not do anything to the flow unit). Thus, as long as it takes an operation even a minimum amount of time to work on a flow unit, the process will always exhibit pipeline inventory. There can be no hospital without patients and no factory can operate without some work in process!

Little's Law also points us toward the best way to reduce pipeline inventory. As reducing flow rate (and with it demand and profit) is typically not a desirable option, the *only* other way to reduce pipeline inventory is by reducing flow time.

Seasonal Inventory

Seasonal inventory occurs when capacity is rigid and demand is variable. Two examples illustrate this second reason for inventory. Campbell's Soup sells more chicken noodle soup in January than in any other month of the year (see Chapter 17)—not primarily because of cold weather, but because Campbell's discounts chicken noodle soup in January. June is the next biggest sales month, because Campbell's increases its price in July.

So much soup is sold in January that Campbell's starts production several months in advance and builds inventory in anticipation of January sales. Campbell's could wait longer to start production and thereby not build as much inventory, but it would be too costly to assemble the needed capacity (equipment and labor) in the winter only to dismantle that capacity at the end of January when it is no longer needed.

In other words, as long as it is costly to add and subtract capacity, firms will desire to smooth production relative to sales, thereby creating the need for seasonal inventory.

FIGURE 2.9
Pipeline Inventory

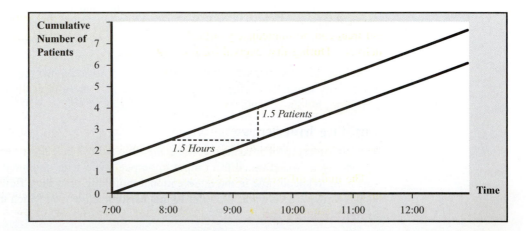

FIGURE 2.10
Seasonal Inventory—
Sugar

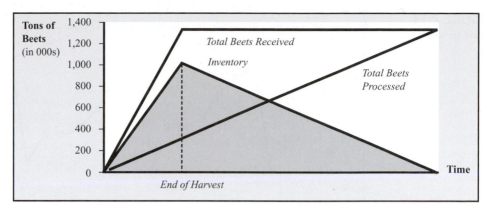

An extreme case of seasonal inventory can be found in the agricultural and food processing sector. Due to the nature of the harvesting season, Monitor Sugar, a large sugar cooperative in the U.S. Midwest, collects all raw material for their sugar production over a period of six weeks. At the end of the harvesting season, they have accumulated—in the very meaning of the word—a pile of sugar beets, about 1 million tons, taking the form of a 67-acre sugar beets pile.

Given that food processing is a very capital-intense operation, the process is sized such that the 1.325 million tons of beets received and the almost 1 million tons of inventory that is built allow for a nonstop operation of the production plant until the beginning of the next harvesting season. Thus, as illustrated by Figure 2.10, the production, and hence the product outflow, is close to constant, while the product inflow is zero except for the harvesting season.

Cycle Inventory

Throughout this book, we will encounter many situations in which it is economical to process several flow units collectively at a given moment in time to take advantage of scale economies in operations.

The scale economics in transportation processes provide a good example for the third reason for inventory. Whether a truck is dispatched empty or full, the driver is paid a fixed amount and a sizeable portion of the wear and tear on the truck depends on the mileage driven, not on the load carried. In other words, each truck shipment incurs a fixed cost that is independent of the amount shipped. To mitigate the sting of that fixed cost, it is tempting to load the truck completely, thereby dividing the fixed cost across the largest number of units.

In many cases, this indeed may be a wise decision. But a truck often carries more product than can be immediately sold. Hence, it takes some time to sell off the entire truck delivery. During that interval of time, there will be inventory. This inventory is labeled *cycle inventory* as it reflects that the transportation process follows a certain shipment cycle (e.g., a shipment every week).

Figure 2.11 plots the inventory level of a simple tray that is required during the operation in the interventional radiology unit. As we can see, there exists a "lumpy" inflow of units, while the outflow is relatively smooth. The reason for this is that—due to the administrative efforts related to placing orders for the trays—the hospital only places one order per week.

The major difference between cycle inventory and seasonal inventory is that seasonal inventory is due to temporary imbalances in supply and demand due to variable demand (soup) or variable supply (beets) while cycle inventory is created due to a cost motivation.

FIGURE 2.11
Cycle Inventory

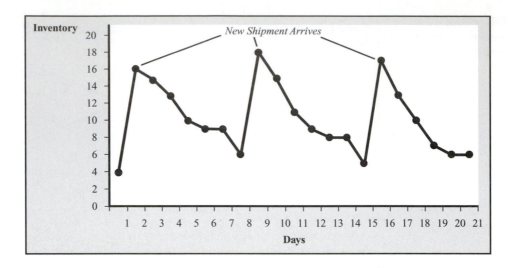

Decoupling Inventory/Buffers

Inventory between process steps can serve as buffers. An inventory buffer allows management to operate steps independently from each other. For example, consider two workers in a garment factory. Suppose the first worker sews the collar onto a shirt and the second sews the buttons. A buffer between them is a pile of shirts with collars but no buttons. Because of that buffer, the first worker can stop working (e.g., to take a break, repair the sewing machine, or change thread color) while the second worker keeps working. In other words, buffers can absorb variations in flow rates by acting as a source of supply for a downstream process step, even if the previous operation itself might not be able to create this supply at the given moment in time.

An automotive assembly line is another example of a production process that uses buffers to decouple the various stations involved with producing the vehicle. In the absence of such buffers, a disruption at any one station would lead to a disruption of all the other stations, upstream and downstream. Think of a bucket brigade to fight a fire: There are no buffers between firefighters in a bucket brigade, so nobody can take a break without stopping the entire process.

Safety Inventory

The final reason for inventory is probably the most obvious, but also the most challenging: stochastic demand. Stochastic demand refers to the fact that we need to distinguish between the predicted demand and the actually realized demand. In other words, we typically face variation in demand relative to our demand prediction. Note that this is different from variations in predictable demand, which is called *seasonality,* like a sales spike of Campbell's chicken noodle soup in January. Furthermore, stochastic demand can be present along with seasonal demand: January sales can be known to be higher than those for other months (seasonal demand) and there can be variation around that known forecast (stochastic demand).

Stochastic demand is an especially significant problem in retailing environments or at the finished goods level of manufacturers. Take a book retailer that must decide how many books to order of a given title. The book retailer has a forecast for demand, but forecasts are (at best) correct on average. Order too many books and the retailer is faced with leftover inventory. Order too few and valuable sales are lost. This trade-off can be managed, as we will discover in Chapter 12, but not eliminated (unless there are zero forecast errors).

FIGURE 2.12
Safety Inventory at a Blood Bank

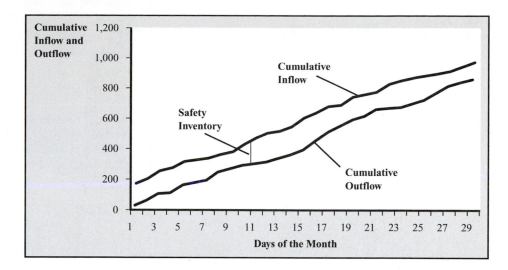

The resulting inventory thereby can be seen as a way to hedge against the underlying demand uncertainty. It might reflect a one-shot decision, for example, in the case of a book retailer selling short-life-cycle products such as newspapers or magazines. If we consider a title with a longer product life cycle (e.g., children's books), the book retailer will be able to replenish books more or less continuously over time.

Figure 2.12 shows the example of the blood bank in the Presbyterian Hospital in Philadelphia. While the detailed inflow and consumption of blood units vary over the course of the month, the hospital always has a couple of days of blood in inventory. Given that blood perishes quickly, the hospital wants to keep only a small inventory at its facility, which it replenishes from the regional blood bank operated by the Red Cross.

2.6 The Product–Process Matrix

Processes leading to the supply of goods or services can take many different forms. Some processes are highly automated, while others are largely manual. Some processes resemble the legendary Ford assembly line, while others resemble more the workshop in your local bike store. Empirical research in operations management, which has looked at thousands of processes, has identified five "clusters" or types of processes. Within each of the five clusters, processes are very similar concerning variables such as the number of different product variants they offer or the production volume they provide. Table 2.6 describes these different types of processes.

By looking at the evolution of a number of industries, Hayes and Wheelwright (1979) observed an interesting pattern, which they referred to as the product–process matrix (see Figure 2.13). The product–process matrix stipulates that over its life cycle, a product typically is initially produced in a job shop process. As the production volume of the product increases, the production process for the product moves from the upper left of the matrix to the lower right.

For example, the first automobiles were produced using job shops, typically creating one product at a time. Most automobiles were unique; not only did they have different colors or add-ons, but they differed in size, geometry of the body, and many other aspects. Henry Ford's introduction of the assembly line corresponded to a major shift along the diagonal of the product–process matrix. Rather than producing a couple of products in a job shop, Ford produced thousands of vehicles on an assembly line.

TABLE 2.6
Process Types and Their Characteristics

	Examples	Number of Different Product Variants	Product Volume (Units/Year)
Job shop	• Design company • Commercial printer • Formula 1 race car	High (100+)	Low (1–100)
Batch process	• Apparel sewing • Bakery • Semiconductor wafers	Medium (10–100)	Medium (100–100k)
Worker-paced line flow	• Auto assembly • Computer assembly	Medium (1–50)	High (10k–1M)
Machine-paced line flow	• Large auto assembly	Low (1–10)	High (10k–1M)
Continuous process	• Paper mill • Oil refinery • Food processing	Low (1–10)	Very high

Note that the "off-diagonals" in the product–process matrix (the lower left and the upper right) are empty. This reflects that it is neither economical to produce very high volumes in a job shop (imagine if all of the millions of new vehicles sold in the United States every year were handcrafted in the same manner as Gottlieb Daimler created the first automobile) nor does it make sense to use an assembly line in order to produce only a handful of products a year.

We have to admit that few companies—if any—would be foolish enough to produce a high-volume product in a job shop. However, identifying a process type and looking at the product–process matrix is more than an academic exercise in industrial history. The usefulness of the product–process matrix lies in two different points:

1. Similar process types tend to have similar problems. For example, as we will discuss in Chapter 4, assembly lines tend to have the problem of line balancing (some workers working harder than others). Batch-flow processes tend to be slow in responding to

FIGURE 2.13
Product–Process Matrix

Source: Hayes and Wheelwright (1979).

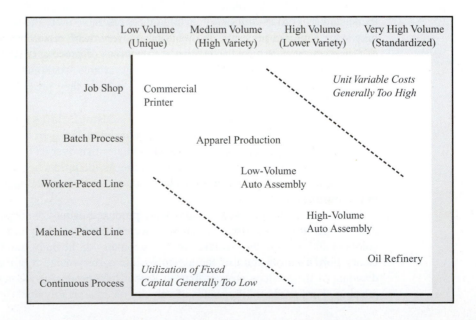

customer demand (see Chapter 7). Thus, once you know a process type, you can quickly determine what type of problems the process is likely to face and what solution methods are most appropriate.

2. The "natural drift" of industries toward the lower right of Figure 2.13 enables you to predict how processes are likely to evolve in a particular industry. Consider, for example, the case of eye surgery. Up until the 1980s, corrective eye surgery was done in large hospitals. There, doctors would perform a large variety of very different eye-related cases. Fifteen years later, this situation had changed dramatically. Many highly specialized eye clinics have opened, most of them focusing on a limited set of procedures. These clinics achieve high volume and, because of the high volume and the lower variety of cases, can operate at much higher levels of efficiency. Similarly, semiconductor production equipment used to be assembled on a one-by-one basis, while now companies such as Applied Materials and Kulicke & Soffa operate worker-paced lines.

2.7 Summary

In this chapter, we emphasized the importance of looking at the operations of a firm not just in terms of the products that the firm supplies, but also at the processes that generate the supply. Looking at processes is especially important with respect to demand–supply mismatches. From the perspective of the product, such mismatches take the form of waiting times; from the perspective of the process, they take the form of inventory.

For any process, we can define three fundamental performance measures: inventory, flow time, and flow rate. The three measures are related by Little's Law, which states that the average inventory is equal to the average flow time multiplied by the average flow rate.

Little's Law can be used to find any of the three performance measures, as long as the other two measures are known. This is specifically important with respect to flow time, which is in practice frequently difficult to observe directly.

A measure related to flow time is inventory turns. Inventory turns, measured by 1/(flow time), captures how fast the flow units are transformed from input to output. It is an important benchmark in many industries, especially retailing. Inventory turns are also the basis of computing the inventory costs associated with one unit of supply.

2.8 Further Reading

De Groote (1994) is a very elegant note describing the basic roles of inventory. This note, as well as many other notes and articles by de Groote, takes a very "lean" perspective to operations management, resembling much more the tradition of economics as opposed to engineering.

Gaur, Fisher, and Raman (2005) provide an extensive study of retailing performance. They present various operational measures, including inventory turns, and show how they relate to financial performance measures.

The Hayes and Wheelwright (1979) reference is widely recognized as a pioneering article linking operations aspects to business strategy. Subsequent work by Hayes, Wheelwright, and Clark (1988) established operations as a key source for a firm's competitive advantage.

2.9 Practice Problems

Q2.1*   **(Dell)** What percentage of cost of a Dell computer reflects inventory costs? Assume Dell's yearly inventory cost is 40 percent to account for the cost of capital for financing the inventory, the warehouse space, and the cost of obsolescence. In other words, Dell incurs a cost of $40 for a $100 component that is in the company's inventory for one entire year. In 2001, Dell's 10-k reports showed that the company had $400 million in inventory and COGS of $26,442 million.

Q2.2   **(Airline)** Consider the baggage check-in of a small airline. Check-in data indicate that from 9 a.m. to 10 a.m., 255 passengers checked in. Moreover, based on counting the number of

(* indicates that the solution is at the end of the book)

passengers waiting in line, airport management found that the average number of passengers waiting for check-in was 35. How long did the average passenger have to wait in line?

Q2.3   **(Inventory Cost)** A manufacturing company producing medical devices reported $60,000,000 in sales over the last year. At the end of the same year, the company had $20,000,000 worth of inventory of ready-to-ship devices.

a. Assuming that units in inventory are valued (based on COGS) at $1,000 per unit and are sold for $2,000 per unit, how fast does the company turn its inventory? The company uses a 25 percent per year cost of inventory. That is, for the hypothetical case that one unit of $1,000 would sit exactly one year in inventory, the company charges its operations division a $250 inventory cost.

b. What—in absolute terms—is the per unit inventory cost for a product that costs $1,000?

Q2.4**   **(Apparel Retailing)** A large catalog retailer of fashion apparel reported $100,000,000 in revenues over the last year. On average, over the same year, the company had $5,000,000 worth of inventory in their warehouses. Assume that units in inventory are valued based on cost of goods sold (COGS) and that the retailer has a 100 percent markup on all products.

a. How many times each year does the retailer turn its inventory?

b. The company uses a 40 percent per year cost of inventory. That is, for the hypothetical case that one item of $100 COGS would sit exactly one year in inventory, the company charges itself a $40 inventory cost. What is the inventory cost for a $30 (COGS) item? You may assume that inventory turns are independent of the price.

Q2.5   **(LaVilla)** LaVilla is a village in the Italian Alps. Given its enormous popularity among Swiss, German, Austrian, and Italian skiers, all of its beds are always booked in the winter season and there are, on average, 1,200 skiers in the village. On average, skiers stay in LaVilla for 10 days.

a. How many new skiers are arriving—on average—in LaVilla every day?

b. A study done by the largest hotel in the village has shown that skiers spend on average $50 per person on the first day and $30 per person on each additional day in local restaurants. The study also forecasts that—due to increased hotel prices—the average length of stay for the 2003/2004 season will be reduced to five days. What will be the percentage change in revenues of local restaurants compared to last year (when skiers still stayed for 10 days)? Assume that hotels continue to be fully booked!

Q2.6   **(Highway)** While driving home for the holidays, you can't seem to get Little's Law out of your mind. You note that your average speed of travel is about 60 miles per hour. Moreover, the traffic report from the WXPN traffic chopper states that there is an average of 24 cars going in your direction on a one-quarter mile part of the highway. What is the flow rate of the highway (going in your direction) in cars per hour?

Q2.7   **(Industrial Baking Process)** Strohrmann, a large-scale bakery in Pennsylvania, is laying out a new production process for their packaged bread, which they sell to several grocery chains. It takes 12 minutes to bake the bread. How large an oven is required so that the company is able to produce 4,000 units of bread per hour (measured in the number of units that can be baked simultaneously)?

Q2.8**   **(Mt. Kinley Consulting)** Mt. Kinley is a strategy consulting firm that divides its consultants into three classes: associates, managers, and partners. The firm has been stable in size for the last 20 years, ignoring growth opportunities in the 90s, but also not suffering from a need to downsize in the recession at the beginning of the 21st century. Specifically, there have been—and are expected to be—200 associates, 60 managers, and 20 partners.

The work environment at Mt. Kinley is rather competitive. After four years of working as an associate, a consultant goes "either up or out"; that is, becomes a manager or is dismissed from the company. Similarly, after six years, a manager either becomes a partner or is dismissed. The company recruits MBAs as associate consultants; no hires are made at the manager or partner level. A partner stays with the company for another 10 years (a total of 20 years with the company).

a. How many new MBA graduates does Mt. Kinley have to hire every year?

b. What are the odds that a new hire at Mt. Kinley will become partner (as opposed to being dismissed after 4 years or 10 years)?

Q2.9 **(Major U.S. Retailers)** The following table shows financial data (year 2004) for Costco Wholesale and Walmart, two major U.S. retailers.

	Costco	Walmart
	($ Millions)	($ Millions)
Inventories	$ 3,643	$ 29,447
Sales (net)	$48,106 13.4%	$286,103 24.6%
COGS	$41,651	$215,493

Source: Compustat, WRDS.

Assume that both companies have an average annual holding cost rate of 30 percent (i.e., it costs both retailers $3 to hold an item that they procured for $10 for one entire year).

a. How many days, on average, does a product stay in Costco's inventory before it is sold? Assume that stores are operated 365 days a year.

b. How much lower is, on average, the inventory cost for Costco compared to Walmart of a household cleaner valued at $5 COGS? Assume that the unit cost of the household cleaner is the same for both companies and that the price and the inventory turns of an item are independent.

Q2.10 **(McDonald's)** The following figures are taken from the 2003 financial statements of McDonald's and Wendy's.[1] Figures are in million dollars.

	McDonald's	Wendy's
Inventory	$ 129.4	$ 54.4
Revenue	17,140.5	3,148.9
Cost of goods sold	11,943.7	1,634.6
Gross profit	5,196.8	1,514.4

a. In 2003, what were McDonald's inventory turns? What were Wendy's inventory turns?

b. Suppose it costs both McDonald's and Wendy's $3 (COGS) per their value meal offerings, each sold at the same price of $4. Assume that the cost of inventory for both companies is 30 percent a year. Approximately how much does McDonald's save in inventory cost *per value meal* compared to that of Wendy's? You may assume the inventory turns are independent of the price.

[1] Example adopted from an About.com article (http://beginnersinvest.about.com/cs/investinglessons/1/blles3mcwen.htm). Financial figures taken from Morningstar.com.

You can view a video of how problems marked with a ** are solved by going on www.cachon-terwiesch.net and follow the links under 'Solved Practice Problems'

Chapter 3

Understanding the Supply Process: Evaluating Process Capacity

In the attempt to match supply with demand, an important measure is the maximum amount that a process can produce in a given unit of time, a measure referred to as the *process capacity*. To determine the process capacity of an operation, we need to analyze the operation in much greater detail compared to the previous chapter. Specifically, we need to understand the various activities involved in the operation and how these activities contribute toward fulfilling the overall demand.

In this chapter, you will learn how to perform a process analysis. Unlike Chapter 2, where we felt it was sufficient to treat the details of the operation as a black box and merely focus on the performance measures inventory, flow time, and flow rate, we now will focus on the underlying process in great detail.

Despite this increase in detail, this chapter (and this book) is not taking the perspective of an engineer. In fact, in this chapter, you will learn how to take a fairly technical and complex operation and simplify it to a level suitable for managerial analysis. This includes preparing a process flow diagram, finding the capacity and the bottleneck of the process, computing the utilization of various process steps, and computing a couple of other performance measures.

We will illustrate this new material with the Circored plant, a joint venture between the German engineering company Lurgi AG and the U.S. iron ore producer Cleveland Cliffs. The Circored plant converts iron ore (in the form of iron ore fines) into direct reduced iron (DRI) briquettes. Iron ore fines are shipped to the plant from mines in South America; the briquettes the process produces are shipped to various steel mills in the United States.

The example of the Circored process is particularly useful for our purposes in this chapter. The underlying process is complex and in many ways a masterpiece of process engineering (see Terwiesch and Loch [2002] for further details). At first sight, the process is so complex that it seems impossible to understand the underlying process behavior without a detailed background in engineering and metallurgy. This challenging setting allows us to demonstrate how process analysis can be used to "tame the beast" and create a managerially useful view of the process, avoiding any unnecessary technical details.

3.1 How to Draw a Process Flow Diagram

The best way to begin any analysis of an operation is by drawing a *process flow diagram.* A process flow diagram is a graphical way to describe the process and it will help us to structure the information that we collect during the case analysis or process improvement project. Before we turn to the question of how to draw a process flow diagram, first consider alternative approaches to how we could capture the relevant information about a process.

Looking at the plant from above (literally), we get a picture as is depicted in Figure 3.1. At the aggregate level, the plant consists of a large inventory of iron ore (input), the plant itself (the resource), and a large inventory of finished briquettes (output). In many ways, this corresponds to the black box approach to operations taken by economists and many other managerial disciplines.

In an attempt to understand the details of the underlying process, we could turn to the engineering specifications of the plant. Engineers are interested in a detailed description of the various steps involved in the overall process and how these steps are functioning. Such descriptions, typically referred to as specifications, were used in the actual construction of the plant. Figure 3.2 provides one of the numerous specification drawings for the Circored process.

Unfortunately, this attempt to increase our understanding of the Circored process is also only marginally successful. Like the photograph, this view of the process is also a rather static one: It emphasizes the equipment, yet provides us with little understanding of how the iron ore moves through the process. In many ways, this view of a process is similar to taking the architectural drawings of a hospital and hoping that this would lead to insights about what happens to the patients in this hospital.

In a third—and final—attempt to get our hands around this complex process, we change our perspective from the one of the visitor to the plant (photo in Figure 3.1) or the engineers who built the plant (drawing in Figure 3.2) to the perspective of the iron ore itself

FIGURE 3.1
Photo of the Circored Plant

Source: Terwiesch and Loch 2002.

FIGURE 3.2   Engineering Drawing

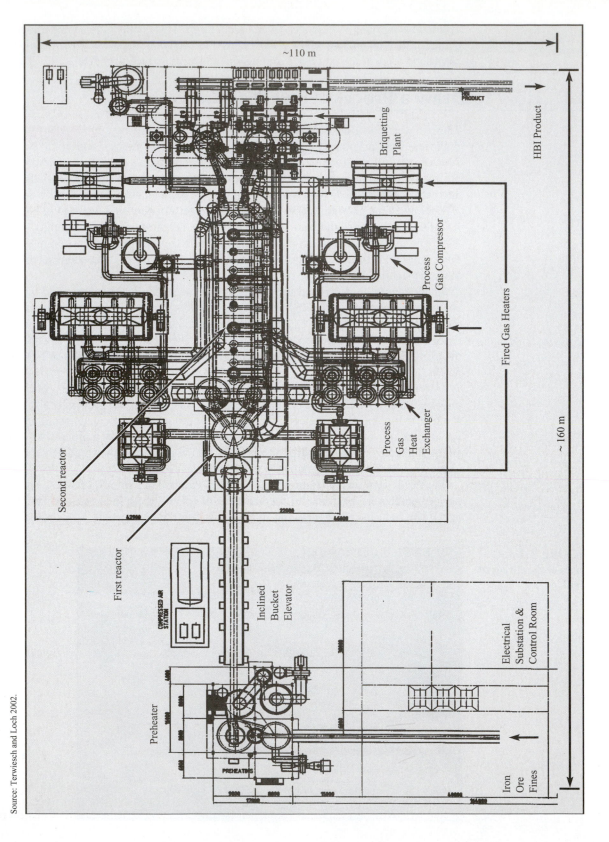

Source: Terwiesch and Loch 2002.

and how it flows through the process. Thus, we define a unit of iron ore—a ton, a pound, or a molecule—as our flow unit and "attach" ourselves to this flow unit as it makes its journey through the process. This is similar to taking the perspective of the patient in a hospital, as opposed to taking the perspective of the hospital resources. For concreteness, we will define our flow unit to be a ton of iron ore.

To draw a process flow diagram, we first need to focus on a part of the process that we want to analyze in greater detail; that is, we need to define the *process boundaries* and an appropriate level of detail. The placement of the process boundaries will depend on the project we are working on. For example, in the operation of a hospital, one project concerned with patient waiting time might look at what happens to the patient waiting for a lab test (e.g., check-in, waiting time, encounter with the nurse). In this project, the encounter with the doctor who requested the lab test would be outside the boundaries of the analysis. Another project related to the quality of surgery, however, might look at the encounter with the doctor in great detail, while either ignoring the lab or treating it with less detail.

A process operates on flow units, which are the entities flowing through the process (e.g., patients in a hospital, cars in an auto plant, insurance claims at an insurance company). A process flow diagram is a collection of boxes, triangles, and arrows (see Figure 3.3). Boxes stand for process activities, where the operation adds value to the flow unit. Depending on the level of detail we choose, a process step (a box) can itself be a process.

Triangles represent waiting areas or *buffers* holding inventory. In contrast to a process step, inventories do not add value; thus, a flow unit does not have to spend time in them. However, as discussed in the previous chapter, there are numerous reasons why the flow unit might spend time in inventory even if it will not be augmented to a higher value there.

FIGURE 3.3
Elements of a Process

Source: Terwiesch and Loch 2002.

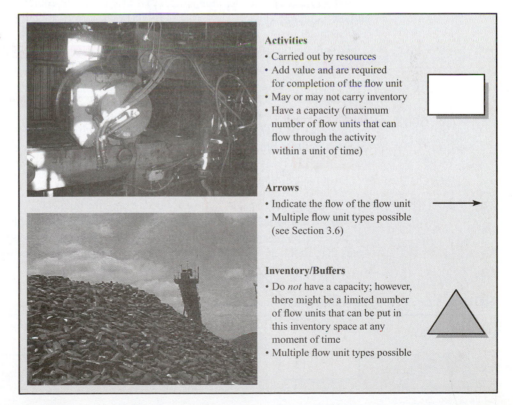

Activities
- Carried out by resources
- Add value and are required for completion of the flow unit
- May or may not carry inventory
- Have a capacity (maximum number of flow units that can flow through the activity within a unit of time)

Arrows
- Indicate the flow of the flow unit
- Multiple flow unit types possible (see Section 3.6)

Inventory/Buffers
- Do *not* have a capacity; however, there might be a limited number of flow units that can be put in this inventory space at any moment of time
- Multiple flow unit types possible

FIGURE 3.4
Process Flow
Diagram, First Step

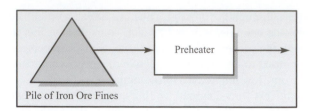

The arrows between boxes and triangles represent the route the flow unit takes through the process. If there are different flow units that take different routes through the process, it can be helpful to use different colors for the different routes. An example of this is given at the end of this chapter.

In the Circored plant, the first step the flow unit encounters in the process is the *preheater*, where the iron ore fines (which have a texture like large-grained sand) are dried and heated. The heating is achieved through an inflow of high-pressured air, which is blown into the preheater from the bottom. The high-speed air flow "fluidizes" the ore, meaning that the mixed air–ore mass (a "sandstorm") circulates through the system as if it was a fluid, while being heated to a temperature of approximately 850–900°C.

However, from a managerial perspective, we are not really concerned with the temperature in the preheater or the chemical reactions happening therein. For us, the preheater is a resource that receives iron ore from the initial inventory and processes it. In an attempt to take record of what the flow unit has experienced up to this point, we create a diagram similar to Figure 3.4.

From the preheater, a large bucket elevator transports the ore to the second process step, the *lock hoppers.* The lock hoppers consist of three large containers, separated by sets of double isolation valves. Their role is to allow the ore to transition from an oxygen-rich environment to a hydrogen atmosphere.

Following the lock hoppers, the ore enters the *circulating fluid bed reactor*, or *first reactor*, where the actual reduction process begins. The reduction process requires the ore to be in the reactor for 15 minutes, and the reactor can hold up to 28 tons of ore.

After this first reduction, the material flows into the *stationary fluid bed reactor*, or *second reactor.* This second reaction takes about four hours. The reactor is the size of a medium two-family home and contains 400 tons of the hot iron ore at any given moment in time. In the meantime, our diagram from Figure 3.4 has extended to something similar to Figure 3.5.

A couple of things are worth noting at this point:

• When creating Figure 3.5, we decided to omit the bucket elevator. There is no clear rule on when it is appropriate to omit a small step and when a step would have to be included in the process flow diagram. A reasonably good rule of thumb is to only include those process steps that are likely to affect the process flow or the economics of the process. The bucket

FIGURE 3.5   Process Flow Diagram (to Be Continued)

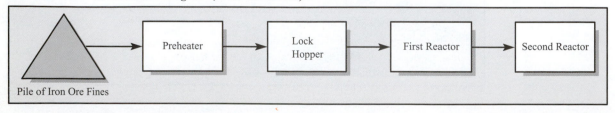

FIGURE 3.6 **Completed Process Flow Diagram for the Circored Process**

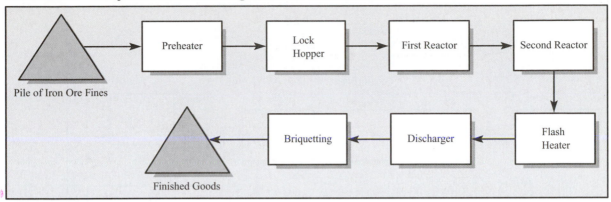

elevator is cheap, the flow units spend little time on it, and this transportation step never becomes a constraint for the process. So it is not included in our process flow diagram.

• The reaction steps are boxes, not triangles, although there is a substantial amount of ore in them, that is, they do hold inventory. The reduction steps are necessary, value-adding steps. No flow unit could ever leave the system without spending time in the reactors. This is why we have chosen boxes over triangles here.

Following the second reactor, the reduced iron enters the *flash heater*, in which a stream of high-velocity hydrogen carries the DRI to the top of the plant while simultaneously reheating it to a temperature of 685°C.

After the flash heater, the DRI enters the *pressure let-down system (discharger)*. As the material passes through the discharger, the hydrogen atmosphere is gradually replaced by inert nitrogen gas. Pressure and hydrogen are removed in a reversal of the lock hoppers at the beginning. Hydrogen gas sensors assure that material leaving this step is free of hydrogen gas and, hence, safe for briquetting.

Each of the three *briquetting* machines contains two wheels that turn against each other, each wheel having the negative of one-half of a briquette on its face. The DRI is poured onto the wheels from the top and is pressed into briquettes, or iron bars, which are then moved to a large pile of finished goods inventory.

This completes our journey of the flow unit through the plant. The resulting process flow diagram that captures what the flow unit has experienced in the process is summarized in Figure 3.6.

When drawing a process flow diagram, the sizes and the exact locations of the arrows, boxes, and triangles do not carry any special meaning. For example, in the context of Figure 3.6, we chose a "U-shaped" layout of the process flow diagram, as otherwise we would have had to publish this book in a larger format.

In the absence of any space constraints, the simplest way to draw a process flow diagram for a process such as Circored's is just as one long line. However, we should keep in mind that there are more complex processes; for example, a process with multiple flow units or a flow unit that visits one and the same resource multiple times. This will be discussed further at the end of the chapter.

Another alternative in drawing the process flow diagram is to stay much closer to the physical layout of the process. This way, the process flow diagram will look familiar for engineers and operators who typically work off the specification drawings (Figure 3.2) and it might help you to find your way around when you are visiting the "real" process. Such an approach is illustrated by Figure 3.7.

FIGURE 3.7 Completed Process Flow Diagram for the Circored Process

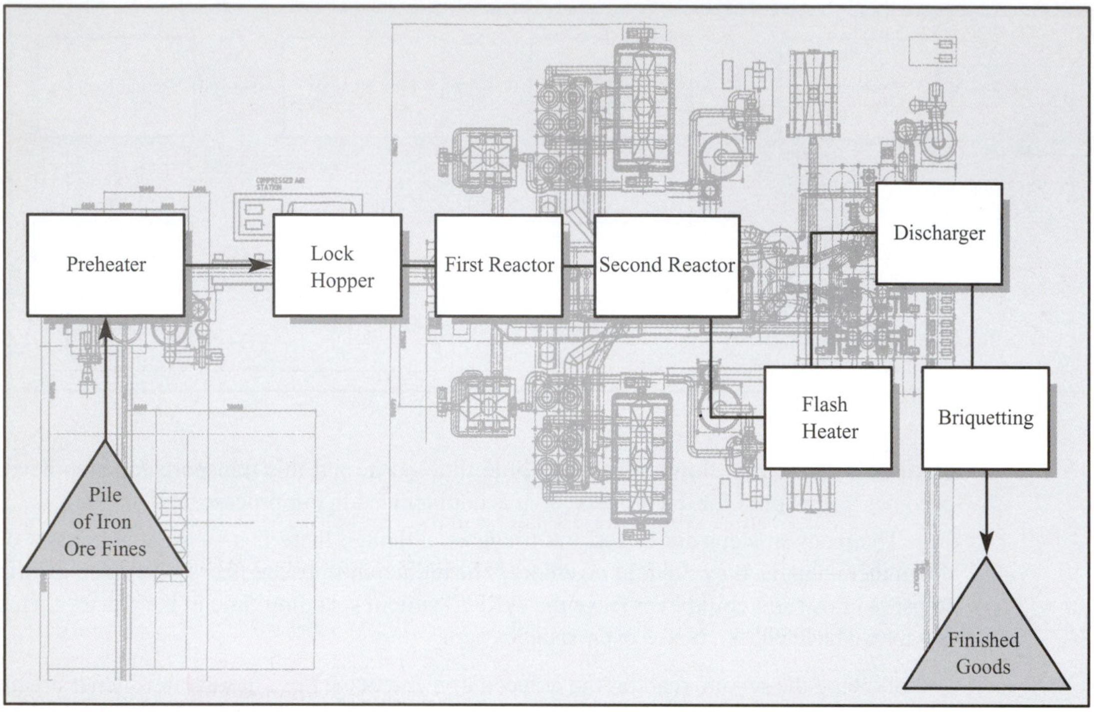

3.2 Bottleneck, Process Capacity, and Flow Rate (Throughput)

From a supply perspective, the most important question that arises is how much direct reduced iron the Circored process can supply in a given unit of time, say one day. This measure is the *capacity* of the process, which we also call the *process capacity*. Not only can capacity be measured at the level of the overall process, it also can be measured at the level of the individual resources that constitute the process. Just as we defined the process capacity, we define the capacity of a resource as the maximum amount the resource can produce in a given time unit.

Note that the process capacity measures how much the process *can* produce, opposed to how much the process actually *does* produce. For example, consider a day where—due to a breakdown or another external event—the process does not operate at all. Its capacity would be unaffected by this, yet the flow rate would reduce to zero. This is similar to your car, which might be able to drive at 130 miles per hour (capacity), but typically—or better, hopefully—only drives at 65 miles per hour (flow rate).

As the completion of a flow unit requires the flow unit to visit every one of the resources in the process, the overall process capacity is determined by the resource with the smallest capacity. We refer to that resource as the *bottleneck*. It provides the weakest link in the overall process chain, and, as we know, a chain is only as strong as its weakest link. More formally, we can write the process capacity as

Process capacity = Minimum{Capacity of resource 1, . . . , Capacity of resource n}

where there are a total of n resources. How much the process actually does produce will depend not only on its capability to create supply (process capacity), but also on the demand for its output as well as the availability of its input. As with capacity, demand and the available input should be measured as rates, that is, as flow units per unit of time. For this process, our flow unit is one ton of ore, so we could define the available input and the demand in terms of tons of ore per hour.

FIGURE 3.8   **Supply-Constrained (left) and Demand-Constrained (right) Processes**

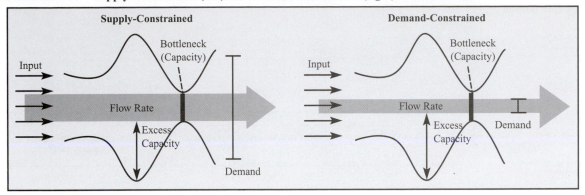

The combination of available input, demand, and process capacity yields the rate at which our flow unit actually flows through the process, called the *flow rate:*

Flow rate = Minimum{Available input, Demand, Process capacity}

If demand is lower than supply (i.e., there is sufficient input available and the process has enough capacity), the process would produce at the rate of demand, independent of the process capacity. We refer to this case as *demand-constrained.* Note that in this definition demand also includes any potential requests for the accumulation of inventory. For example, while the demand for Campbell's chicken noodle soup might be lower than process capacity for the month of November, the process would not be demand-constrained if management decided to accumulate finished goods inventory in preparation for the high sales in the month of January. Thus, demand in our analysis refers to everything that is demanded from the process at a given time.

If demand exceeds supply, the process is *supply-constrained.* Depending on what limits product supply, the process is either input-constrained or capacity-constrained.

Figure 3.8 summarizes the concepts of process capacity and flow rate, together with the notion of demand- versus supply-constrained processes. In the case of the supply-constrained operation, there is sufficient input; thus, the supply constraint reflects a capacity constraint.

To understand how to find the bottleneck in a process and thereby determine the process capacity, consider each of the Circored resources. Note that all numbers are referring to tons of process output. The actual, physical weight of the flow unit might change over the course of the process.

Finding the bottleneck in many ways resembles the job of a detective in a crime story; each activity is a "suspect," in the sense that it could potentially constrain the overall supply of the process:

- The preheater can process 120 tons per hour.
- The lock hoppers can process 110 tons per hour.
- The analysis of the reaction steps is somewhat more complicated. We first observe that at any given moment of time, there can be, at maximum, 28 tons in the first reactor. Given that the iron ore needs to spend 15 minutes in the reactor, we can use Little's Law (see Chapter 2) to see that the maximum amount of ore that can flow through the reactor— and spend 15 minutes in the reactor—is

$$28 \text{ tons} = \text{Flow rate} \times 0.25 \text{ hour} \implies \text{Flow rate} = 112 \text{ tons/hour}$$

Thus, the capacity of the first reactor is 112 tons per hour. Note that a shorter reaction time in this case would translate to a higher capacity.

TABLE 3.1
Capacity Calculation

Process Step	Calculations	Capacity
Preheater		120 tons per hour
Lock hoppers		110 tons per hour
first reactor	Little's Law: Flow rate = 28 tons/0.25 hour	112 tons per hour
Second reactor	Little's Law: Flow rate = 400 tons/4 hours	100 tons per hour
Flash heater		135 tons per hour
Discharger		118 tons per hour
Briquetting machine	Consists of three machines: 3 × 55 tons per hour	165 tons per hour
Total process	Based on bottleneck, which is the stationary reactor	**100 tons per hour**

- We can apply a similar logic for the second reactor, which can hold up to 400 tons:

$$400 \text{ tons} = \text{Flow rate} \times 4 \text{ hours} => \text{Flow rate} = 100 \text{ tons/hour}$$

Thus, the capacity (the maximum possible flow rate through the resource) of the second reactor is 100 tons per hour.

- The flash heater can process 135 tons per hour.
- The discharger has a capacity of 118 tons per hour.
- Each of the three briquetting machines has a capacity of 55 tons per hour. As the briquetting machines collectively form one resource, the capacity at the briquetting machines is simply 3 × 55 tons per hour = 165 tons per hour.

The capacity of each process step is summarized in Table 3.1.

Following the logic outlined above, we can now identify the first reactor as the bottleneck of the Circored process. The overall process capacity is computed as the minimum of the capacities of each resource (all units are in tons per hour):

$$\text{Process capacity} = \text{Minimum } \{120, 110, 112, 100, 135, 118, 165\} = 100$$

3.3 How Long Does It Take to Produce a Certain Amount of Supply?

There are many situations where we need to compute the amount of time required to create a certain amount of supply. For example, in the Circored case, we might ask, "How long does it take for the plant to produce 10,000 tons?" Once we have determined the flow rate of the process, this calculation is fairly straightforward. Let X be the amount of supply we want to fulfill. Then,

$$\text{Time to fullfill } X \text{ units} = \frac{X}{\text{Flow rate}}$$

To answer our question,

$$\text{Time to produce } 10,000 \text{ tons} = \frac{10,000 \text{ tons}}{100 \text{ tons/hour}} = 100 \text{ hours}$$

Note that this calculation assumes the process is already producing output, that is, the first unit in our 10,000 tons flows out of the process immediately. If the process started empty, it would take the first flow unit time to flow through the process. Chapter 4 provides the calculations for that case.

Note that in the previous equation we use flow rate, which in our case is capacity because the system is supply-constrained. However, if our system were demand-constrained, then the flow rate would equal the demand rate.

3.4 Process Utilization and Capacity Utilization

Given the first-of-its-kind nature of the Circored process, the first year of its operation proved to be extremely difficult. In addition to various technical difficulties, demand for the product (reduced iron) was not as high as it could be, as the plant's customers (steel mills) had to be convinced that the output created by the Circored process would be of the high quality required by the steel mills.

While abstracting from details such as scheduled maintenance and inspection times, the plant was designed to achieve a process capacity of 876,000 tons per year (100 tons per hour × 24 hours/day × 365 days/year, see above), the demand for iron ore briquettes was only 657,000 tons per year. Thus, there existed a mismatch between demand and potential supply (process capacity).

A common measure of performance that quantifies this mismatch is utilization. We define the *utilization* of a process as

$$\text{Utilization} = \frac{\text{Flow rate}}{\text{Capacity}}$$

Utilization is a measure of how much the process *actually produces* relative to how much it *could produce* if it were running at full speed (i.e., its capacity). This is in line with the example of a car driving at 65 miles per hour (flow rate), despite being able to drive at 130 miles per hour (capacity): the car utilizes 65/130 = 50 percent of its potential.

Utilization, just like capacity, can be defined at the process level or the resource level. For example, the utilization of the process is the flow rate divided by the capacity of the process. The utilization of a particular resource is the flow rate divided by that resource's capacity.

For the Circored case, the resulting utilization is

$$\text{Utilization} = \frac{657,000 \text{ tons per year}}{876,000 \text{ tons per year}} = 0.75 = 75\%$$

In general, there are several reasons why a process might not produce at 100 percent utilization:

- If demand is less than supply, the process typically will not run at full capacity, but only produce at the rate of demand.
- If there is insufficient supply of the input of a process, the process will not be able to operate at capacity.
- If one or several process steps only have a limited availability (e.g., maintenance and breakdowns), the process might operate at full capacity while it is running, but then go into periods of not producing any output while it is not running.

Given that the bottleneck is the resource with the lowest capacity and that the flow rate through all resources is identical, the bottleneck is the resource with the highest utilization.

In the case of the Circored plant, the corresponding utilizations are provided by Table 3.2. Note that all resources in a process with only one flow unit have the same flow

TABLE 3.2
Utilization of the Circored Process Steps Including Downtime

Process Step	Calculations	Utilization
Preheater	657,000 tons/year/[120 tons/hour × 8,760 hours/year]	62.5%
Lock hoppers	657,000 tons/year/[110 tons/hour × 8,760 hours/year]	68.2%
First reactor	657,000 tons/year/[112 tons/hour × 8,760 hours/year]	66.9%
Second reactor	657,000 tons/year/[100 tons/hour × 8,760 hours/year]	75.0%
Flash heater	657,000 tons/year/[135 tons/hour × 8,760 hours/year]	55.6%
Discharger	657,000 tons/year/[118 tons/hour × 8,760 hours/year]	63.6%
Briquetting	657,000 tons/year/[165 tons/hour × 8,760 hours/year]	45.5%
Total process	657,000 tons/year/[100 tons/hour × 8,760 hours/year]	**75%**

rate, which is equal to the overall process flow rate. In this case, this is a flow rate of 657,000 tons per year.

Measuring the utilization of equipment is particularly common in capital-intensive industries. Given limited demand and availability problems, the bottleneck in the Circored process did not operate at 100 percent utilization. We can summarize our computations graphically, by drawing a utilization profile. This is illustrated by Figure 3.9.

Although utilization is commonly tracked, it is a performance measure that should be handled with some care. Specifically, it should be emphasized that the objective of most businesses is to maximize profit, not to maximize utilization. As can be seen in Figure 3.9, there are two reasons in the Circored case for why an individual resource might not achieve 100 percent utilization, thus exhibiting excess capacity.

- First, given that no resource can achieve a higher utilization than the bottleneck, every process step other than the bottleneck will have a utilization gap relative to the bottleneck.

FIGURE 3.9 **Utilization Profile**

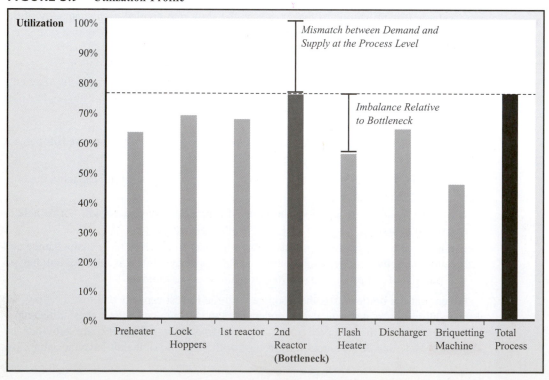

TABLE 3.3
Utilization of the Circored Process Steps Assuming Unlimited Demand and No Downtime

Process Step	Calculations	Utilization
Preheater	100/120	83.3%
Lock hoppers	100/110	90.9%
First reactor	100/112	89.3%
Second reactor	100/100	100.0%
Flash heater	100/135	74.1%
Discharger	100/118	84.7%
Briquetting machine	100/165	60.6%
Total process	**100/100**	**100%**

- Second, given that the process might not always be capacity-constrained, but rather be input- or demand-constrained, even the bottleneck might not be 100 percent utilized. In this case, every resource in the process has a "base level" of excess capacity, corresponding to the difference between the flow rate and the bottleneck capacity.

Note that the second reason disappears if there is sufficient market demand and full resource availability. In this case, only the bottleneck achieves a 100 percent utilization level. If the bottleneck in the Circored plant were utilized 100 percent, we would obtain an overall flow rate of 876,000 tons per year, or, equivalently 100 tons per hour. The resulting utilization levels in that case are summarized in Table 3.3.

3.5 Workload and Implied Utilization

Given the way we defined utilization (the ratio between flow rate and capacity), utilization can never exceed 100 percent. Thus, utilization only carries information about excess capacity, in which case utilization is strictly less than 100 percent. In contrast, we cannot infer from utilization by how much demand exceeds the capacity of the process. This is why we need to introduce an additional measure.

We define the *implied utilization* of a resource as

$$\text{Implied utilization} = \frac{\text{Demand}}{\text{Capacity}}$$

The implied utilization captures the mismatch between what could flow through the resource (demand) and what the resource can provide (capacity). Sometimes the "demand that could flow through a resource" is called the *workload.* So you can also say that the implied utilization of a resource equals its workload divided by its capacity.

Assume that demand for the Circored ore would increase to 1,095,000 tons per year (125 tons per hour). Table 3.4 calculates the resulting levels of implied utilization for the Circored resources.

TABLE 3.4
Implied Utilization of the Circored Process Steps Assuming a Demand of 125 Tons per Hour and No Downtime

Process Step	Calculations	Implied Utilization	Utilization
Preheater	125/120	104.2%	83.3%
Lock hoppers	125/110	113.6%	90.9%
First reactor	125/112	111.6%	89.3%
Second reactor	125/100	125%	100.0%
Flash heater	125/135	92.6%	74.1%
Discharger	125/118	105.9%	84.7%
Briquetting machine	125/165	75.8%	60.6%
Total process	**125/100**	**125%**	**100%**

Several points in the table deserve further discussion:

- Unlike utilization, implied utilization can exceed 100 percent. Any excess over 100 percent reflects that a resource does not have the capacity available to meet demand.

- The fact that a resource has an implied utilization above 100 percent does not make it the bottleneck. As we see in Table 3.4, it is possible to have several resources with an implied utilization above 100 percent. However, there is only one bottleneck in the process! This is the resource where the implied utilization is the highest. In the Circored case, this is—not surprisingly—the first reactor. Would it make sense to say that the process has several bottlenecks? No! Given that we can only operate the Circored process at a rate of 100 tons per hour (the capacity of the first reactor), we have ore flow through every resource of the process at a rate of 100 tons per hour. Thus, while several resources have an implied utilization above 100 percent, all resources other than the first reactor have excess capacity (their utilizations in Table 3.4 are below 100 percent). That is why we should not refer to them as bottlenecks.

- Having said this, it is important to keep in mind that in the case of a capacity expansion of the process, it might be worthwhile to add capacity to these other resources as well, not just to the bottleneck. In fact, depending on the margins we make and the cost of installing capacity, we could make a case to install additional capacity for all resources with an implied utilization above 100 percent. In other words, once we add capacity to the current bottleneck, our new process (with a new bottleneck) could still be capacity-constrained, justifying additional capacity to other resources.

3.6   Multiple Types of Flow Units

Choosing an appropriate flow unit is an essential step when preparing a process flow diagram. While, for the examples we have discussed so far, this looked relatively straightforward, there are many situations that you will encounter where this choice requires more care. The two most common complications are

- The flow of the unit moving through the process breaks up into multiple flows. For example, in an assembly environment, following an inspection step, good units continue to the next processing step, while bad units require rework.

- There are multiple types of flow units, representing, for example, different customer types. In an emergency room, life-threatening cases follow a different flow than less complicated cases.

The critical issue in choosing the flow unit is that you must be able to express all demands and capacities in terms of the chosen flow unit. For example, in the Circored process, we chose one ton of ore to be the flow unit. Thus, we had to express each resource's capacity and the demand in terms of tons of ore. Given that the process only makes ore, the choice of the flow unit was straightforward. However, consider the following example involving multiple product or customer types. An employment verification agency receives resumés from consulting firms and law firms with the request to validate information provided by their job candidates.

Figure 3.10 shows the process flow diagram for this agency. Note that while the three customer types share the first step and the last step in the process (filing and sending confirmation letter), they differ with respect to other steps:

- For internship positions, the agency provides information about the law school/business school the candidate is currently enrolled in as well as previous institutions of higher education and, to the extent possible, provides information about the applicant's course choices and honors.

FIGURE 3.10 Process Flow Diagram with Multiple Product Types

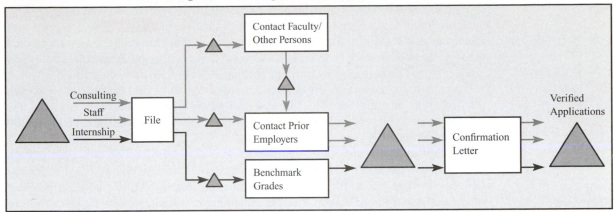

- For staff positions, the agency contacts previous employers and analyzes the letters of recommendation from those employers.
- For consulting/lawyer positions, the agency attempts to call former supervisors and/or colleagues in addition to contacting the previous employers and analyzes the letters of recommendation from those employers.

As far as demand, this process receives 3 consulting, 11 staff, and 4 internship applications per hour. Table 3.5 also provides the capacities of each activity, in applications per hour. Given that the workload on each activity as well as all of the capacities can be expressed in terms of "applications per hour," we can choose "one application" as our flow unit, despite the fact that there are multiple types of applications.

The next step in our process analysis is to find the bottleneck. In this setting this is complicated by the *product mix* (different types of customers flowing through one process). For example, the process step "contact persons" might have a very long processing time, resulting in a low capacity for this activity. However, if the workload on this activity (applications per hour) is also very low, then maybe this low capacity is not an issue.

TABLE 3.5 Finding the Bottleneck in the Multiproduct Case

| | Processing Time | Number of Workers | Capacity | Workload [Applications/Hour] | | | | Implied Utilization |
				Consulting	Staff	Interns	Total	
File	3 [min./appl.]	1	1/3 [appl./min.] = 20 [appl./hour]	3	11	4	18	18/20 = 90%
Contact persons	20 [min./appl.]	2	2/20 [appl./min.] = 6 [appl./hour]	3	0	0	3	3/6 = 50%
Contact employers	15 [min./appl.]	3	3/15 [appl./min.] = 12 [appl./hour]	3	11	0	14	14/12 = 117%
Grade/school analysis	8 [min./appl.]	2	2/8 [appl./min.] = 15 [appl./hour]	0	0	4	4	4/15 = 27%
Confirmation letter	2 [min./appl.]	1	1/2 [appl./min.] = 30 [appl./hour]	3	11	4	18	18/30 = 60%

To find the bottleneck and to determine capacity in a multiproduct situation, we need to compare each activity's capacity with its demand. The analysis is given in Table 3.5.

To compute the demand on a given activity as shown in Table 3.5, it is important to remember that some activities (e.g., filing the applications) are requested by all product types, whereas others (e.g., contacting faculty and former colleagues) are requested by one product type. This is (hopefully) clear by looking at the process flow diagram.

To complete our analysis, divide each activity's demand by its capacity to yield each activity's implied utilization. This allows us to find the busiest resource. In this case, it is "contact prior employers", so this is our bottleneck. As the implied utilization is above 100 percent, the process is capacity-constrained.

The flow unit "one application" allowed us to evaluate the implied utilization of each activity in this process, but it is not the only approach. Alternatively, we could define the flow unit as "one minute of work." This might seem like an odd flow unit, but it has an advantage over "one application." Before explaining its advantage, let's figure out how to replicate our analysis of implied utilization with this new flow unit.

As before, we need to define our demands and our capacities in terms of our flow unit. In the case of capacity, each worker has "60 minutes of work" available per hour. (By definition, we all do!) So the capacity of an activity is (Number of workers) × 60 [minutes/hour]. For example "contact persons" has two workers. So its capacity is $2 \times 60 = 120$ minutes of work per hour. Each worker has 60 "minutes of work" available per hour, so two of them can deliver 120 minutes of work.

Now turn to the demands. There are 11 staff applications to be processed each hour and each takes 3 minutes. So the demand for staff applications is $11 \times 3 = 33$ minutes per hour. Now that we know how to express the demands and the capacities in terms of the "minutes of work," the implied utilization of each activity is again the ratio of the amount demanded from the activity to the activity's capacity. Table 3.6 summarizes these calculations. As we would expect, this method yields the same implied utilizations as the "one application" flow unit approach.

So if "one application" and "one minute of work" give us the same answer, how should we choose between these approaches? In this situation, you would work with the approach that you find most intuitive (which is probably "one application," at least initially) because they both allow us to evaluate the implied utilizations. However, the "one minute of work" approach is more robust. To explain why, suppose it took 3 minutes to file a staff application, 5 minutes to file a consulting application, and 2 minutes to file an internship application. In this case, we get into trouble if we define the flow unit to be "one application"—with that flow unit, we cannot express the capacity of the file activity! If we receive only internship applications, then filing could process $60/2 = 30$ applications per hour. However, if we receive only consulting applications, then filing can only process $60/5 = 12$ applications per hour. The number of applications per hour that filing can process depends on the mix of applications! The "minute of work" flow unit completely solves that problem—no matter what mix of applications is sent to filing, with one worker, filing has 60 minutes of work available per hour. Similarly, for a given mix of applications, we can also evaluate the workload on filing in terms of minutes of work (just as is done in Table 3.6.

To summarize, choose a flow unit that allows you to express all demands and capacities in terms of that flow unit. An advantage of the "minute of work" (or "hour of work," "day of work," etc.) approach is that it is possible to do this even if there are multiple types of products or customers flowing through the process.

So what is the next step in our process analysis? We have concluded that it is capacity-constrained because the implied utilization of "contact employers" is greater

TABLE 3.6 Using "One Minute of Work" as the Flow Unit to Find the Bottleneck in the Multiproduct Case

| | Processing Time | Number of Workers | Capacity | Workload [Minutes/Hour] | | | | Implied Utilization |
				Consulting	Staff	Interns	Total	
File	3 [min./appl.]	1	60 [min./hour]	3×3	11×3	4×3	54	54/60 = 90%
Contact persons	20 [min./appl.]	2	120 [min./hour]	3×20	0	0	60	60/120 = 50%
Contact employers	15 [min./appl.]	3	180 [min./hour]	3×15	11×15	0	210	210/180 = 117%
Grade/school analysis	8 [min./appl.]	2	120 [min./hour]	0	0	4×8	32	32/120 = 27%
Confirmation letter	2 [min./appl.]	1	60 [min./hour]	3×2	11×2	4×2	36	36/60 = 60%

than 100 percent—it is the bottleneck. Given that it is the only activity with an implied utilization greater than 100 percent, if we are going to add capacity to this process, "contact employers" should be the first candidate—in the current situation, they simply do not have enough capacity to handle the current mix of customers. Notice, if the mix of customers changes, this situation might change. For example, if we started to receive fewer staff applications (which have to flow through "contact employers") and more internship applications (which do not flow through "contact employers") then the workload on "contact employers" would decline, causing its implied utilization to fall as well. Naturally, shifts in the demands requested from a process can alter which resource in the process is the bottleneck.

Although we have been able to conclude something useful with our analysis, one should be cautious to not conclude too much when dealing with multiple types of products or customers. To illustrate some potential complications, consider the following example. At the international arrival area of a major U.S. airport, 15 passengers arrive per minute, 10 of whom are U.S. citizens or permanent residents and 5 are visitors.

The immigration process is organized as follows. Passengers disembark their aircraft and use escalators to arrive in the main immigration hall. The escalators can transport up to 100 passengers per minute. Following the escalators, passengers have to go through immigration. There exist separate immigration resources for U.S. citizens and permanent residents (they can handle 10 passengers per minute) and visitors (which can handle 3 visitors per minute). After immigration, all passengers pick up their luggage. Luggage handling (starting with getting the luggage off the plane and ending with moving the luggage onto the conveyor belts) has a capacity of 10 passengers per minute. Finally, all passengers go through customs, which has a capacity of 20 passengers per minute.

We calculate the implied utilization levels in Table 3.7. Notice when evaluating implied utilization we assume the demand on luggage handling is 10 U.S. citizens and 5 visitors even though we know (or discover via our calculations) that it is not possible for 15 passengers to arrive to luggage handling per minute (there is not enough capacity in immigration). We do this because we want to compare the potential demand on each resource with its capacity to assess its implied utilization. Consequently, we can evaluate each resource's implied utilization in isolation from the other resources.

Based on the values in Table 3.7, the bottleneck is immigration for visitors because it has the highest implied utilization. Furthermore, because its implied utilization is

TABLE 3.7
Calculating Implied Utilization in Airport Example

Resource	Demand for U.S. Citizens and Permanent Residents [Pass./Min.]	Demand for Visitors [Pass./Min.]	Capacity [Pass./Min.]	Implied Utilization
Escalator	10	5	100	15/100 = 15%
Immigration—U.S. residents	10	0	10	10/10 = 100%
Immigration—visitors	0	5	3	5/3 = 167%
Luggage handling	10	5	10	15/10 = 150%
Customs	10	5	20	15/20 = 75%

greater than 100 percent, the process is supply-constrained. Given that there is too little supply, we can expect queues to form. Eventually, those queues will clear because the demand rate of arriving passengers will at some point fall below capacity (otherwise, the queues will just continue to grow, which we know will not happen indefinitely at an airport). But during the times in which the arrival rates of passengers is higher than our capacity, where will the queues form? The answer to this question depends on how we prioritize work.

The escalator has plenty of capacity, so no priority decision needs to be made there. At immigration, there is enough capacity for 10 U.S. citizens and 3 visitors. So 13 passengers may be passed on to luggage handling, but luggage handling can accommodate only 10 passengers. Suppose we give priority to U.S. citizens. In that case, all of the U.S. citizens proceed through luggage handling without interruption, and a queue of visitors will form at the rate of 3 per minute. Of course, there will also be a queue of visitors in front of immigration, as it can handle only 3 per minute while 5 arrive per minute. With this priority scheme, the outflow from this process will be 10 US citizens per minute. However, if we give visitors full priority at luggage handling, then a similar analysis reveals that a queue of U.S. citizens forms in front of luggage handling, and a queue of visitors forms in front of immigration. The outflow is 7 U.S. citizens and 3 visitors.

The operator of the process may complain that the ratio of U.S. citizens to visitors in the outflow (7 to 3) does not match the inflow ratio (2 to 1), even though visitors are given full priority. If we were to insist that those ratios match, then the best we could do is have an outflow of 6 U.S. citizens and 3 visitors—we cannot produce more than 3 visitors per minute given the capacity of immigration, so the 2 to 1 constraint implies that we can "produce" no more than 6 U.S. citizens per minute. Equity surely has a price in this case—we could have an output of 10 passengers per minute, but the equity constraint would limit us to 9 passengers per minute. To improve upon this output while maintaining the equity constraint, we should add more capacity at the bottleneck—immigration for visitors.

3.7 Summary

Figure 3.11 is a summary of the major steps graphically. Exhibits 3.1 and 3.2 summarize the steps required to do the corresponding calculations for a single flow unit and multiple flow units, respectively.

Exhibit 3.1

STEPS FOR BASIC PROCESS ANALYSIS WITH ONE TYPE OF FLOW UNIT

1. Find the capacity of every resource; if there are multiple resources performing the same activity, add their capacities together.
2. The resource with the lowest capacity is called the *bottleneck*. Its capacity determines the capacity of the entire process (*process capacity*).
3. The flow rate is found based on

$$\text{Flow rate} = \text{Minimum \{Available input, Demand, Process capacity\}}$$

4. We find the utilization of the process as

$$\text{Utilization} = \frac{\text{Flow rate}}{\text{Capacity}}$$

The utilization of each resource can be found similarly.

Any process analysis should begin with the creation of a process flow diagram. This is especially important for the case of multiple flow units, as their flows are typically more complex.

Next, we need to identify the bottleneck of the process. As long as there exists only one type of flow unit, this is simply the resource with the lowest capacity. However, for more general cases, we need to perform some extra analysis. Specifically, if there is a product mix, we have to compute the requested capacity (workload) at each resource and then compare it to the available capacity. This corresponds to computing the implied utilization, and we identify the bottleneck as the resource with the highest implied utilization.

Finally, once we have found the bottleneck, we can compute a variety of performance measures. As in the previous chapter, we are interested in finding the flow rate. The flow rate also allows us to compute the process utilization as well as the utilization profile across resources. Utilizations, while not necessarily a business goal by themselves, are important measures in many industries, especially capital-intensive industries.

FIGURE 3.11   **Summary of Process Analysis**

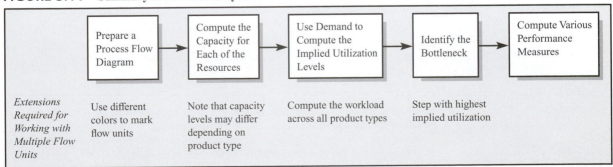

Exhibit 3.2

STEPS FOR BASIC PROCESS ANALYSIS WITH MULTIPLE TYPES OF FLOW UNITS

1. For each resource, compute the number of minutes that the resource can produce; this is 60 [min./hour] × Number of resources within the resource pool.
2. Create a process flow diagram, indicating how the flow units go through the process; use multiple colors to indicate the flow of the different flow units.
3. Create a table indicating how much workload each flow unit is consuming at each resource:

   - The rows of the table correspond to the resources in the process.
   - The columns of the table correspond to the different types of flow units.
   - Each cell of the table should contain one of the following:

   If flow unit does not visit the corresponding resource, 0;
   Otherwise, demand per hour of the corresponding flow unit × processing time.
4. Add up the workload of each resource across all flow units.
5. Compute the implied utilization of each resource as

$$\text{Implied utilization} = \frac{\text{Result of step 4}}{\text{Result of step 1}}$$

The resource with the highest implied utilization is the bottleneck.

The preceding approach is based on Table 3.6; that is, the flow unit is "one minute of work."

3.8 Practice Problems

Q3.1* **(Process Analysis with One Flow Unit)** Consider a process consisting of three resources:

Resource	Processing Time [Min./Unit]	Number of Workers
1	10	2
2	6	1
3	16	3

What is the bottleneck? What is the process capacity? What is the flow rate if demand is eight units per hour? What is the utilization of each resource if demand is eight units per hour?

Q3.2* **(Process Analysis with Multiple Flow Units)** Consider a process consisting of five resources that are operated eight hours per day. The process works on three different products, A, B, and C:

Resource	Number of Workers	Processing Time for A [Min./Unit]	Processing Time for B [Min./Unit]	Processing Time for C [Min./Unit]
1	2	5	5	5
2	2	3	4	5
3	1	15	0	0
4	1	0	3	3
5	2	6	6	6

Demand for the three different products is as follows: product A, 40 units per day; product B, 50 units per day; and product C, 60 units per day.

What is the bottleneck? What is the flow rate for each flow unit assuming that demand must be served in the mix described above (i.e., for every four units of A, there are five units of B and six units of C)?

(* indicates that the solution is at the end of the book)

Q3.3   **(Cranberries)** International Cranberry Uncooperative (ICU) is a competitor to the National Cranberry Cooperative (NCC). At ICU, barrels of cranberries arrive on trucks at a rate of 150 barrels per hour and are processed continuously at a rate of 100 barrels per hour. Trucks arrive at a uniform rate over eight hours, from 6:00 a.m. until 2:00 p.m. Assume the trucks are sufficiently small so that the delivery of cranberries can be treated as a continuous inflow. The first truck arrives at 6:00 a.m. and unloads immediately, so processing begins at 6:00 a.m. The bins at ICU can hold up to 200 barrels of cranberries before overflowing. If a truck arrives and the bins are full, the truck must wait until there is room in the bins.

   a. What is the maximum number of barrels of cranberries that are waiting on the trucks at any given time?

   b. At what time do the trucks stop waiting?

   c. At what time do the bins become empty?

   d. ICU is considering using seasonal workers in addition to their regular workforce to help with the processing of cranberries. When the seasonal workers are working, the processing rate increases to 125 barrels per hour. The seasonal workers would start working at 10:00 a.m. and finish working when the trucks stop waiting. At what time would ICU finish processing the cranberries using these seasonal workers?

Q3.4   **(Western Pennsylvania Milk Company)** The Western Pennsylvania Milk Company is producing milk at a fixed rate of 5,000 gallons/hour. The company's clients request 100,000 gallons of milk over the course of one day. This demand is spread out uniformly from 8 a.m. to 6 p.m. If there is no milk available, clients will wait until enough is produced to satisfy their requests.

    The company starts producing at 8 a.m. with 25,000 gallons in finished goods inventory. At the end of the day, after all demand has been fulfilled, the plant keeps on producing until the finished goods inventory has been restored to 25,000 gallons.

    When answering the following questions, treat trucks/milk as a continuous flow process. Begin by drawing a graph indicating how much milk is in inventory and how much milk is "back-ordered" over the course of the day.

   a. At what time during the day will the clients have to start waiting for their requests to be filled?

   b. At what time will clients stop waiting?

   c. Assume that the milk is picked up in trucks that hold 1,250 gallons each. What is the maximum number of trucks that are waiting?

   d. Assume the plant is charged $50 per hour per waiting truck. What are the total waiting time charges on a day?

Q3.5**   **(Bagel Store)** Consider a bagel store selling three types of bagels that are produced according to the process flow diagram outlined below. We assume the demand is 180 bagels a day, of which there are 30 grilled veggie, 110 veggie only, and 40 cream cheese. Assume that the workday is 10 hours long and each resource is staffed with one worker.

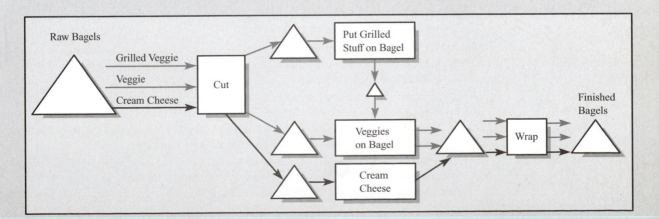

Moreover, we assume the following Processing times:

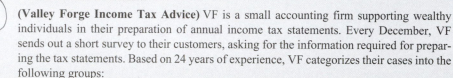

	Cut	Grilled Stuff	Veggies	Cream Cheese	Wrap
Processing time	3 [min./bagel]	10 [min./bagel]	5 [min./bagel]	4 [min./bagel]	2 [min./bagel]

Processing times are independent of which bagel type is processed at a resource (for example, cutting a bagel takes the same time for a cream cheese bagel as for a veggie bagel).

a. Where in the process is the bottleneck?

b. How many units can the process produce within one hour, assuming the product mix has to remain constant?

Q3.6 **(Valley Forge Income Tax Advice)** VF is a small accounting firm supporting wealthy individuals in their preparation of annual income tax statements. Every December, VF sends out a short survey to their customers, asking for the information required for preparing the tax statements. Based on 24 years of experience, VF categorizes their cases into the following groups:

- Group 1 (new customers, easy): 15 percent of cases
- Group 2 (new customers, complex): 5 percent of cases
- Group 3 (repeat customers, easy): 50 percent of cases
- Group 4 (repeat customers, complex): 30 percent of cases

Here, "easy" versus "complex" refers to the complexity of the customer's earning situation.

In order to prepare the income tax statement, VF needs to complete the following set of activities. Processing times (and even which activities need to be carried out) depend on which group a tax statement falls into. All of the following processing times are expressed in minutes per income tax statement.

Group	Filing	Initial Meeting	Preparation	Review by Senior Accountant	Writing
1	20	30	120	20	50
2	40	90	300	60	80
3	20	No meeting	80	5	30
4	40	No meeting	200	30	60

The activities are carried out by the following three persons:

- Administrative support person: filing and writing.
- Senior accountant (who is also the owner): initial meeting, review by senior accountant.
- Junior accountant: preparation.

Assume that all three persons work eight hours per day and 20 days a month. For the following questions, assume the product mix as described above. Assume that there are 50 income tax statements arriving each month.

a. Which of the three persons is the bottleneck?

b. What is the (implied) utilization of the senior accountant? The junior accountant? The administrative support person?

c. You have been asked to analyze which of the four product groups is the most profitable. Which factors would influence the answer to this?

d. How would the process capacity of VF change if a new word processing system would reduce the time to write the income tax statements by 50 percent?

Q3.7 **(Car Wash Supply Process)** CC Car Wash specializes in car cleaning services. The services offered by the company, the exact service time, and the resources needed for each of them are described in the table following:

Service	Description	Processing Time	Resource Used
A. Wash	Exterior car washing and drying	10 min.	1 automated washing machine
B. Wax	Exterior car waxing	10 min.	1 automated waxing machine
C. Wheel cleaning	Detailed cleaning of all wheels	7 min.	1 employee
D. Interior cleaning	Detailed cleaning inside the car	20 min.	1 employee

The company offers the following packages to their customers:

- Package 1: Includes only car wash (service A).
- Package 2: Includes car wash and waxing (services A and B).
- Package 3: Car wash, waxing, and wheel cleaning (services A, B, and C).
- Package 4: All four services (A, B, C, and D).

Customers of CC Car Wash visit the station at a constant rate (you can ignore any effects of variability) of 40 customers per day. Of these customers, 40 percent buy Package 1, 15 percent buy Package 2, 15 percent buy Package 3, and 30 percent buy Package 4. The mix does not change over the course of the day. The store operates 12 hours a day.

a. What is the implied utilization of the employee doing the wheel cleaning service?

b. Which resource has the highest implied utilization?

For the next summer, CC Car Wash anticipates an increase in the demand to 80 customers per day. Together with this demand increase, there is expected to be a change in the mix of packages demanded: 30 percent of the customers ask for Package 1, 10 percent for Package 2, 10 percent for Package 3, and 50 percent for Package 4. The company will install an additional washing machine to do service A.

c. What will be the new bottleneck in the process?

d. How many customers a day will not be served? Which customers are going to wait? Explain your reasoning!

Q3.8 **(Starbucks)** After an "all night" study session the day before their last final exam, four students decide to stop for some much-needed coffee at the campus Starbucks. They arrive at 8:30 a.m. and are dismayed to find a rather long line.

Fortunately for the students, a Starbucks executive happens to be in line directly in front of them. From her, they learn the following facts about this Starbucks location:

I. There are three employee types:

- There is a single cashier who takes all orders, prepares nonbeverage food items, grinds coffee, and pours drip coffee.
- There is a single frozen drink maker who prepares blended and iced drinks.
- There is a single espresso drink maker who prepares espressos, lattes, and steamed drinks.

II. There are typically four types of customers:

- Drip coffee customers order only drip coffee. This requires 20 seconds of the cashier's time to pour the coffee.
- Blended and iced drink customers order a drink that requires the use of the blender. These drinks take on average 2 minutes of work of the frozen drink maker.
- Espresso drink customers order a beverage that uses espresso and/or steamed milk. On average, these drinks require 1 minute of work of the espresso drink maker.
- Ground coffee customers buy one of Starbucks' many varieties of whole bean coffee and have it ground to their specification at the store. This requires a total of 1 minute of the cashier's time (20 seconds to pour the coffee and 40 seconds to grind the whole bean coffee).

III. The customers arrive uniformly at the following rates from 7 a.m. (when the store opens) until 10 a.m. (when the morning rush is over), with no customers arriving after 10 a.m.:

- Drip coffee customers: 25 per hour.
- Blended and iced drink customers: 20 per hour.
- Espresso drink customers: 70 per hour.
- Ground coffee customers: 5 per hour.

IV. Each customer spends, on average, 20 seconds with the cashier to order and pay.

V. Approximately 25 percent of all customers order food, which requires an additional 20 seconds of the cashier's time per transaction.

While waiting in line, the students reflect on these facts and they answer the following questions:

a. What is the implied utilization of the frozen drink maker?

b. Which resource has the highest implied utilization?

From their conversation with the executive, the students learn that Starbucks is considering a promotion on all scones (half price!), which marketing surveys predict will increase the percentage of customers ordering food to 30 percent (the overall arrival rates of customers will *not* change). However, the executive is worried about how this will affect the waiting times for customers.

c. How do the levels of implied utilization change as a response to this promotion?

Q3.9 **(Paris Airport)** Kim Opim, an enthusiastic student, is on her flight over from Philadelphia (PHL) to Paris. Kim reflects upon how her educational experiences from her operations courses could help explain the long wait time that she experienced before she could enter the departure area of Terminal A at PHL. As an airline representative explained to Kim, there are four types of travelers in Terminal A:

- Experienced short-distance (short-distance international travel destinations are Mexico and various islands in the Atlantic) travelers: These passengers check in online and do not speak with any agent nor do they take any time at the kiosks.
- Experienced long-distance travelers: These passengers spend 3 minutes with an agent.
- Inexperienced short-distance travelers: These passengers spend 2 minutes at a kiosk; however, they do not require the attention of an agent.
- Inexperienced long-distance travelers: These passengers need to talk 5 minutes with an agent.

After a passenger checks in online, or talks with an agent, or uses a kiosk, the passenger must pass through security, where they need 0.5 minutes independent of their type. From historical data, the airport is able to estimate the arrival rates of the different customer types at Terminal A of Philadelphia International:

- Experienced short-distance travelers: 100 per hour
- Experienced long-distance travelers: 80 per hour
- Inexperienced short-distance travelers: 80 per hour
- Inexperienced long-distance travelers: 40 per hour

At this terminal, there are four security check stations, six agents, and three electronic kiosks. Passengers arrive uniformly from 4 p.m. to 8 p.m., with the entire system empty prior to 4 p.m. (the "midafternoon lull") and no customers arrive after 8 p.m. All workers must stay on duty until the last passenger is entirely through the system (e.g., has passed through security).

a. What are the levels of implied utilization at each resource?

b. At what time has the last passenger gone through the system? Note: If passengers of one type have to wait for a resource, passengers that do not require service at the resource can pass by the waiting passengers!

c. Kim, an experienced long-distance traveler, arrived at 6 p.m. at the airport and attempted to move through the check-in process as quickly as she could. How long did she have to wait before she was checked at security?

d. The airline considers showing an educational program that would provide information about the airport's check-in procedures. Passenger surveys indicate that 80 percent of the inexperienced passengers (short or long distance) would subsequently act as experienced passengers (i.e., the new arrival rates would be 164 experienced short-distance, 112 experienced long-distance, 16 inexperienced short-distance, and 8 inexperienced long-distance [passengers/hour]). At what time has the last passenger gone through the system?

You can view a video of how problems marked with a ** are solved by going on www. cachon-terwiesch.net and follow the links under 'Solved Practice Problems'

Chapter 4

Estimating and Reducing Labor Costs

The objective of any process should be to create value (make profits), not to maximize the utilization of every resource involved in the process. In other words, we should not attempt to produce more than what is demanded from the market, or from the resource downstream in the process, just to increase the utilization measure. Yet, the underutilization of a resource, human labor or capital equipment alike, provides opportunities to improve the process. This improvement can take several forms, including:

- If we can reduce the excess capacity at some process step, the overall process becomes more efficient (lower cost for the same output).
- If we can use capacity from underutilized process steps to increase the capacity at the bottleneck step, the overall process capacity increases. If the process is capacity-constrained, this leads to a higher flow rate.

In this chapter, we discuss how to achieve such process improvements. Specifically, we discuss the concept of line balancing, which strives to avoid mismatches between what is supplied by one process step and what is demanded from the following process step (referred to as the process step downstream). In this sense, line balancing attempts to match supply and demand within the process itself.

We use Novacruz Inc. to illustrate the concept of line balancing and to introduce a number of more general terms of process analysis. Novacruz is the producer of a high-end kick scooter, known as the Xootr (pronounced "zooter"), displayed in Figure 4.1.

4.1 Analyzing an Assembly Operation

With the increasing popularity of kick scooters in general, and the high-end market segment for kick scooters in particular, Novacruz faced a challenging situation in terms of organizing their production process. While the demand for their product was not much higher than 100 scooters per week in early March 2000, it grew dramatically, soon reaching 1,200 units per week in the fall of 2000. This demand trajectory is illustrated in Figure 4.2.

First consider March 2000, during which Novacruz faced a demand of 125 units per week. At this time, the assembly process was divided between three workers (resources) as illustrated by Figure 4.3.

The three workers performed the following activities. In the first activity, the first 30 of the overall 80 parts are assembled, including the fork, the steer support, and the t-handle.

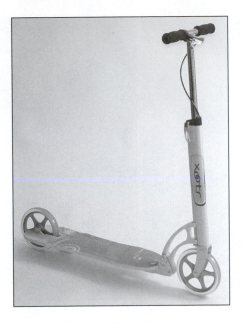

Given the complexity of this assembly operation, it takes about 13 minutes per scooter to complete this activity. We refer to the 13 minutes/unit as the *processing time.* Depending on the context, we will also refer to the processing time as the *activity time* or the *service time* Note that in the current process, each activity is staffed with exactly one worker.

In the second activity, a worker assembles the wheel, the brake, and some other parts related to the steering mechanism. The second worker also assembles the deck. This step is somewhat faster and its processing time is 11 minutes per unit. The scooter is completed by the third worker, who wipes off the product, applies the decals and grip tape, and conducts the final functional test. The processing time is about 8 minutes per unit.

FIGURE 4.2
Lifecycle Demand
Trajectory for Xootrs

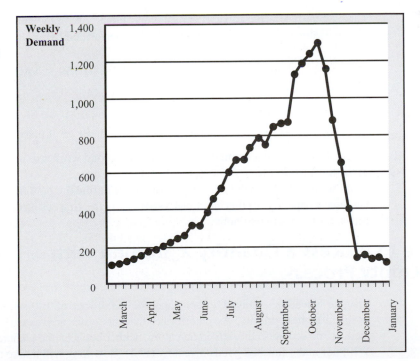

FIGURE 4.3
Current process layout

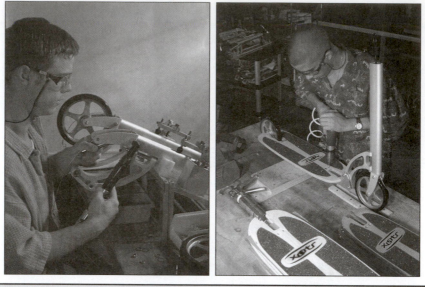

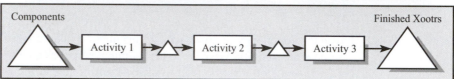

To determine the capacity of an individual resource or a group of resources performing the same activity, we write:

$$\text{Capacity} = \frac{\text{Number of resources}}{\text{Processing time}}$$

This is intuitive, as the capacity grows proportionally with the number of workers.

For example, for the first activity, which is performed by one worker, we write:

$$\text{Capacity} = \frac{1}{13 \text{ minutes/scooter}} = 0.0769 \text{ scooter/minute}$$

which we can rewrite as

$$0.0769 \text{ scooter/minute} \times 60 \text{ minutes/hour} = 4.6 \text{ scooters/hour}$$

Similarly, we can compute capacities of the second worker to be 5.45 scooters/hour and of the third worker to be 7.5 scooters/hour.

As we have done in the preceding chapter, we define the bottleneck as the resource with the lowest capacity. In this case, the bottleneck is the first resource, resulting in a process capacity of 4.6 scooters/hour.

4.2   Time to Process a Quantity *X* Starting with an Empty Process

Imagine Novacruz received a very important rush order of 100 scooters, which would be assigned highest priority. Assume further that this order arrives early in the morning and there are no scooters currently in inventory, neither between the resources (work-in-process, WIP) nor in the finished goods inventory (FGI). How long will it take to fulfill this order?

As we are facing a large order of scooters, we will attempt to move as many scooters through the system as possible. Therefore, we are capacity-constrained and the flow rate of the process is determined by the capacity of the bottleneck (one scooter every 13 minutes). The time between the completions of two subsequent flow units is called the *cycle time* of a process and will be defined more formally in the next section.

We cannot simply compute the time to produce 100 units as 100 units/0.0769 unit/ minute = 1,300 minutes because that calculation assumes the system is producing at the bottleneck rate, one unit every 13 minutes. However, that is only the case once the system is "up and running." In other words, the first scooter of the day, assuming the system starts the day empty (with no work in process inventory), takes even longer than 13 minutes to complete. How much longer depends on how the line is paced.

The current system is called a *worker-paced* line because each worker is free to work at his or her own pace: if the first worker finishes before the next worker is ready to accept the parts, then the first worker puts the completed work in the inventory between them. Eventually the workers need to conform to the bottleneck rate; otherwise, the inventory before the bottleneck would grow too big for the available space. But that concern is not relevant for the first unit moving through the system, so the time to get the first scooter through the system is 13 + 11 + 8 = 32 minutes. More generally:

$$\text{Time through an empty worker-paced process} = \text{Sum of the processing times}$$

An alternative to the worker-paced process is a machine-paced process as depicted in Figure 4.4. In a machine-paced process, all of the steps must work at the same rate even with the first unit through the system. Hence, if a machine-paced process were used, then the first Xootr would be produced after 3 × 13 minutes, as the conveyor belt has the same speed at all three process steps (there is just one conveyor belt, which has to be paced to the slowest step). More generally,

$$\text{Time through an empty machine-paced process}$$
$$= \text{Number of resources in sequence} \times \text{Processing time of the bottleneck step}$$

Now return to our worker-paced process. After waiting 32 minutes for the first scooter, it only takes an additional 13 minutes until the second scooter is produced and from then onwards, we obtain an additional scooter every 13 minutes. Thus, scooter 1 is produced after 32 minutes, scooter 2 after 32 + 13 = 45 minutes, scooter 3 after 32 + (2 × 13) = 58 minutes, scooter 4 after 32 + (3 × 13) = 71 minutes, and so on.

More formally, we can write the following formula. The time it takes to finish X units starting with an empty system is

$$\text{Time to finish } X \text{ units starting with an empty system}$$
$$= \text{Time through an empty process} + \frac{X - 1 \text{ unit}}{\text{Flow rate}}$$

You may wonder whether it is always necessary to be so careful about the difference between the time to complete the first unit and all of the rest of the units. In this case, it is because the number of scooters is relatively small, so each one matters. But

FIGURE 4.4
A Machine-Paced Process Layout
(Note: conveyor belt is only shown for illustration)

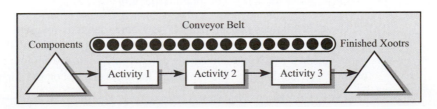

Exhibit 4.1

TIME TO PROCESS A QUANTITY _X_ STARTING WITH AN EMPTY PROCESS

1. Find the time it takes the flow unit to go through the empty system:
   - In a worker-paced line, this is the sum of the processing times.
   - In a machine-paced line, this is the cycle time × the number of stations.

2. Compute the capacity of the process (see previous methods). Since we are producing _X_ units as fast as we can, we are capacity-constrained; thus,

$$\text{Flow rate} = \text{Process capacity}$$

3. Time to finish _X_ units

$$= \text{Time through empty process} + \frac{X - 1 \text{ unit}}{\text{Flow rate}}$$

Note: If the process is a continuous process, we can use _X_ instead.

---

imagine a continuous-flow process such as a cranberry processing line. Suppose you want to know how long it takes to produce five tons of cranberries. Let's say a cranberry weighs one gram, so five tons equals five million cranberries. Now how long does it take to produce five million cranberries? Strictly speaking, we would look at the time it takes the first berry to flow through the system and then add the time for the residual 4,999,999 berries. However, for all computational purposes, five million minus one is still five million, so we can make our life a little easier by just ignoring this first berry:

Time to finish X units with a continuous-flow process

$$= \text{Time through an empty process} + \frac{X \text{ units}}{\text{Flow rate}}$$

Exhibit 4.1 summarizes the calculations leading to the time it takes the process to produce X units starting with an empty system.

4.3 Labor Content and Idle Time

What is the role of labor cost in the production of the Xootr? Let's look first at how much actual labor is involved in the assembly of the Xootr. Towards this end, we define the _labor content_ as the sum of the processing times of the three workers. In this case, we compute a labor content of

Labor content = Sum of processing times with labor

$$= 13 \text{ minutes/unit} + 11 \text{ minutes/unit} + 8 \text{ minutes/unit}$$

$$= 32 \text{ minutes per unit}$$

These 32 minutes per unit reflect how much labor is invested into the production of one scooter. We could visualize this measure as follows. Let's say there would be a slip of paper attached to a Xootr and each worker would write the amount of time spent working on the Xootr on this slip. The sum of all numbers entered on the slip is the labor content.

Assume that the average hourly rate of the assembly employees is $12 per hour (and thus $0.20 per minute). Would the resulting cost of labor then be 32 minutes/unit $\times$ $0.20/minute = $6.40/unit? The answer is a clear *no*! The reason for this is that the labor content is a measure that takes the perspective of the flow unit but does not reflect any information about how the process is actually operated.

Assume—for illustrative purposes—that we would hire an additional worker for the second activity. As worker 2 is not a constraint on the overall output of the process, this would probably not be a wise thing to do (and that is why we call it an illustrative example). How would the labor content change? Not at all! It would still require the same 32 minutes of labor to produce a scooter. However, we have just increased our daily wages by 33 percent, which should obviously be reflected in our cost of direct labor.

To correctly compute the cost of direct labor, we need to look at two measures:

- The number of scooters produced per unit of time (the flow rate).
- The amount of wages we pay for the same time period.

Above, we found that the process has a capacity of 4.6 scooters an hour, or 161 scooters per week (we assume the process operates 35 hours per week). Given that demand is currently 125 scooters per week (we are demand-constrained), our flow rate is at 125 scooters per week.

Now, we can compute the cost of direct labor as

$$\text{Cost of direct labor} = \frac{\text{Total wages per unit of time}}{\text{Flow rate per unit of time}}$$

$$= \frac{\text{Wages per week}}{\text{Scooters produced per week}}$$

$$= \frac{3 \times \$12/h \times 35\,h/week}{125 \text{ scooters/week}}$$

$$= \frac{\$1,260/week}{125 \text{ scooters/week}} = \$10.08/scooter$$

Why is this number so much higher than the number we computed based on the direct labor content? The difference between the two numbers reflects underutilization, or what we will refer to as *idle time*. In this case, there are two sources of idle time:

- The process is never able to produce more than its bottleneck. In this case, this means one scooter every 13 minutes. However, if we consider worker 3, who only takes eight minutes on a scooter, this translates into a 5-minute idle time for every scooter built.
- If the process is demand-constrained, even the bottleneck is not operating at its full capacity and, consequently also exhibits idle time. Given a demand rate of 125 scooters/week, that is, 3.57 scooters/hour or one scooter every 16.8 minutes, all three workers get an extra 3.8 minutes of idle time for every scooter they make.

This reflects the utilization profile and the sources of underutilization that we discussed in Chapter 3 with the Circored process.

Note that this calculation assumes the labor cost is fixed. If it were possible to shorten the workday from the current 7 hours of operations to 5 hours and 25 minutes (25 scooters a day $\times$ 1 scooter every 13 minutes), we would eliminate the second type of idle time.

More formally, define the following:

$$\text{Cycle time} = \frac{1}{\text{Flow rate}}$$

Cycle time provides an alternative measure of how fast the process is creating output. As we are producing one scooter every 16.8 minutes, the cycle time is 16.8 minutes. Similar to what we did intuitively above, we can now define the idle time for worker i as the following:

Idle time for a single worker $=$ Cycle time $-$ Processing time of the single worker

Note that this formula assumes that every activity is staffed with exactly one worker. The idle time measures how much unproductive time a worker has for every unit of output produced. These calculations are summarized by Table 4.1.

If we add up the idle time across all workers, we obtain the total idle time that is incurred for every scooter produced:

$$3.8 + 5.8 + 8.8 = 18.4 \text{ minutes/unit}$$

Now, apply the wage rate of $12 per hour ($0.20/minute $\times$ 18.4 minutes/unit) and, voilà, we obtain exactly the difference between the labor cost we initially expected based on the direct labor content alone ($6.40 per unit) and the actual cost of direct labor computed above.

As a final measure of process efficiency, we can look at the average labor utilization of the workers involved in the process. We can obtain this number by comparing the labor content with the amount of labor we have to pay for (the labor content and the idle time):

$$\text{Average labor utilization} = \frac{\text{Labor content}}{\text{Labor content} + \text{Sum of idle times across workers}}$$

$$= \frac{32[\text{minutes per unit}]}{32[\text{minutes per unit}] + 18.4[\text{minutes per unit}]} = 63.5\%$$

TABLE 4.1
Basic Calculations Related to Idle Time

	Worker 1	Worker 2	Worker 3
Processing time	13 minutes/unit	11 minutes/unit	8 minutes/unit
Capacity	$\frac{1}{13}$ unit/minute	$\frac{1}{11}$ unit/minute	$\frac{1}{8}$ unit/minute
	= 4.61 units/hour	= 5.45 units/hour	= 7.5 units/hour
Process capacity	Minimum {4.61 units/h, 5.45 units/h, 7.5 units/h} = 4.61 units/hour		
Flow rate	Demand = 125 units/week = 3.57 units/hour Flow rate = Minimum {demand, process capacity} = 3.57 units/hour		
Cycle time	1/3.57 hours/unit = 16.8 minutes/unit		
Idle time	16.8 minutes/unit − 13 minutes/unit = 3.8 minutes/unit	16.8 minutes/unit − 11 minutes/unit = 5.8 minutes/unit	16.8 minutes/unit − 8 minutes/unit = 8.8 minutes/unit
Utilization	3.57/4.61 = 77%	3.57/5.45 = 65.5%	3.57/7.5 = 47.6%

Exhibit 4.2

SUMMARY OF LABOR COST CALCULATIONS

1. Compute the capacity of all resources; the resource with the lowest capacity is the bottleneck (see previous methods) and determines the process capacity.
2. Compute Flow rate = Min{Available input, Demand, Process capacity}; then compute

$$\text{Cycle time} = \frac{1}{\text{Flow rate}}$$

3. Compute the total wages (across all workers) that are paid per unit of time:

$$\text{Cost of direct labor} = \frac{\text{Total wages}}{\text{Flow rate}}$$

4. Compute the idle time across all workers at resource i

Idle time across all workers at resource i = Cycle time × (Number of workers at resource i) − Processing time at resource i

5. Compute the labor content of the flow unit: this is the sum of all processing times involving direct labor.
6. Add up the idle times across all resources (total idle time); then compute

$$\text{Average labor utilization} = \frac{\text{Labor content}}{\text{Labor content} + \text{Total idle time}}$$

An alternative way to compute the same number is by averaging the utilization level across the three workers:

$$\text{Average labor utilization} = \tfrac{1}{3} \times (\text{Utilization}_1 + \text{Utilization}_2 + \text{Utilization}_3) = 63.4\%$$

where Utilization$_i$ denotes the utilization of the ith worker. Exhibit 4.2 summarizes the calculations related to our analysis of labor costs. It includes the possibility that there are multiple workers performing the same activity.

4.4 Increasing Capacity by Line Balancing

Comparing the utilization levels in Table 4.1 reveals a strong imbalance between workers: while worker 1 is working 77 percent of the time, worker 3 is only active about half of the time (47.6 percent to be exact). Imbalances within a process provide micro-level mismatches between what could be supplied by one step and what is demanded by the following steps. _Line balancing_ is the act of reducing such imbalances. It thereby provides the opportunity to

- Increase the efficiency of the process by better utilizing the various resources, in this case labor.
- Increase the capacity of the process (without adding more resources to it) by reallocating either workers from underutilized resources to the bottleneck or work from the bottleneck to underutilized resources.

While based on the present demand rate of 125 units per week and the assumption that all three workers are a fixed cost for 35 hours per week, line balancing would change neither the flow rate (process is demand-constrained) nor the cost of direct labor (assuming the 35 hours per week are fixed); this situation changes with the rapid demand growth experienced by Novacruz.

Consider now a week in May, by which, as indicated by Figure 4.1, the demand for the Xootr had reached a level of 200 units per week. Thus, instead of being demand-constrained, the process now is capacity-constrained, specifically, the process now is constrained by worker 1, who can produce one scooter every 13 minutes, while the market demands scooters at a rate of one scooter every 10.5 minutes (200 units/week/35 hours/week = 5.714 units/hour).

Given that worker 1 is the constraint on the system, all her idle time is now eliminated and her utilization has increased to 100 percent. Yet, workers 2 and 3 still have idle time:

- The flow rate by now has increased to one scooter every 13 minutes or $\frac{1}{13}$ unit per minute (equals $\frac{1}{13} \times 60 \times 35 = 161.5$ scooters per week) based on worker 1.

- Worker 2 has a capacity of one scooter every 11 minutes, that is, $\frac{1}{11}$ unit per minute. Her utilization is thus Flow rate/Capacity$_2 = \frac{1}{13}/\frac{1}{11} = \frac{11}{13} = 84.6\%$.

- Worker 3 has a capacity of one scooter every 8 minutes. Her utilization is thus $\frac{1}{13}/\frac{1}{8} = \frac{8}{13} = 61.5\%$.

Note that the increase in demand not only has increased the utilization levels across workers (the average utilization is now $\frac{1}{3} \times (100\% + 84.6\% + 61.5\%) = 82\%$), but also has reduced the cost of direct labor to

$$
\begin{aligned}
\text{Cost of direct labor} &= \frac{\text{Total wages per unit of time}}{\text{Flow rate per unit of time}} \\
&= \frac{\text{Wages per week}}{\text{Scooters produced per week}} \\
&= \frac{3 \times \$12/\text{hour} \times 35 \text{ hours/week}}{161.5 \text{ scooters/week}} \\
&= \frac{\$1,260/\text{week}}{161.5 \text{ scooters/week}} = \$7.80/\text{scooter}
\end{aligned}
$$

Now, back to the idea of line balancing. Line balancing attempts to evenly (fairly!) allocate the amount of work that is required to build a scooter across the three process steps.

In an ideal scenario, we could just take the amount of work that goes into building a scooter, which we referred to as the labor content (32 minutes/unit), and split it up evenly between the three workers. Thus, we would achieve a perfect line balance if each worker could take 32/3 minutes/unit; that is, each would have an identical processing time of 10.66 minutes/unit.

Unfortunately, in most processes, it is not possible to divide up the work that evenly. Specifically, the activities underlying a process typically consist of a collection of *tasks* that cannot easily be broken up. A closer analysis of the three activities in our case reveals the task structure shown in Table 4.2.

For example, consider the last task of worker 1 (assemble handle cap), which takes 118 seconds per unit. These 118 seconds per unit of work can only be moved to another worker in their entirety. Moreover, we cannot move this task around freely, as it obviously would not be feasible to move the "assemble handle cap" task to after the "seal carton" task.

TABLE 4.2
Task Durations

Worker	Tasks	Task Duration [seconds/unit]
Worker 1	Prepare cable	30
	Move cable	25
	Assemble washer	100
	Apply fork, threading cable end	66
	Assemble socket head screws	114
	Steer pin nut	49
	Brake shoe, spring, pivot bolt	66
	Insert front wheel	100
	Insert axle bolt	30
	Tighten axle bolt	43
	Tighten brake pivot bolt	51
	Assemble handle cap	118
		Total: 792
Worker 2	Assemble brake lever and cable	110
	Trim and cap cable	59
	Place first rib	33
	Insert axles and cleats	96
	Insert rear wheel	135
	Place second rib and deck	84
	Apply grip tape	56
	Insert deck fasteners	75
		Total: 648
Worker 3	Inspect and wipe off	95
	Apply decal and sticker	20
	Insert in bag	43
	Assemble carton	114
	Insert Xootr and manual	94
	Seal carton	84
		Total: 450

However, we could move the 118 seconds per unit from worker 1 to worker 2. In this case, worker 1 would now have an processing time of 674 seconds per unit and worker 2 (who would become the new bottleneck) would have an processing time of 766 seconds per unit. The overall process capacity is increased, we would produce more scooters, and the average labor utilization would move closer to 100 percent.

But can we do better? Within the scope of this book, we only consider cases where the sequence of tasks is given. Line balancing becomes more complicated if we can resequence some of the tasks. For example, there exists no technical reason why the second to last task of worker 2 (apply grip tape) could not be switched with the subsequent task (insert deck fasteners). There exist simple algorithms and heuristics that support line balancing in such more complex settings. Yet, their discussion would derail us from our focus on managerial issues.

But even if we restrict ourselves to line balancing solutions that keep the sequence of tasks unchanged, we can further improve upon the 766-second cycle time we outlined above. Remember that the "gold standard" of line balancing, the even distribution of the labor content across all resources, suggested an processing time of 10.66 minutes per unit, or 640 seconds per unit.

Moving the "assemble handle cap" task from worker 1 to worker 2 was clearly a substantial step in that direction. However, worker 2 has now 126 seconds per unit (766 seconds/ unit − 640 seconds/unit) more than what would be a balanced workload. This situation can be improved if we take the worker's last two tasks (apply grip tape, insert deck fasteners) and move the corresponding 56 + 75 seconds/unit = 131 seconds/unit to worker 3.

The new processing times would be as follows:

- Worker 1: 674 seconds per unit (792 − 118 seconds/unit).
- Worker 2: 635 seconds per unit (648 + 118 − 56 − 75 seconds/unit).
- Worker 3: 581 seconds per unit (450 + 56 + 75 seconds/unit).

Are they optimal? No! We can repeat similar calculations and further move work from worker 1 to worker 2 (tighten brake pivot bolt, 51 seconds per unit) and from worker 2 to worker 3 (place second rib and deck, 84 seconds per unit). The resulting (final) processing times are now

- Worker 1: 623 seconds per unit (674 − 51 seconds/unit).
- Worker 2: 602 seconds per unit (635 + 51 − 84 seconds/unit).
- Worker 3: 665 seconds per unit (581 + 84 seconds/unit).

To make sure we have not "lost" any work on the way, we can add up the three new processing times and obtain the same labor content (1,890 seconds per unit) as before. The resulting labor utilization would be improved to

$$\text{Average labor utilization} = \text{Labor content} / (\text{Labor content} + \text{Total idle time})$$
$$= 1,890 / (1,890 + 42 + 63 + 0) = 94.7\%$$

The process improvement we have implemented based on line balancing is sizeable in its economic impact. Based on the new bottleneck (worker 3), we see that we can produce one Xootr every 665 seconds, thereby having a process capacity of $\frac{1}{665}$ units/second × 3,600 seconds/hour × 35 hours/week = 189.5 units per week. Thus, compared to the unbalanced line (161.5 units per week), we have increased process capacity (and flow rate) by 17 percent (28 units) without having increased our weekly spending rate on labor. Moreover, we have reduced the cost of direct labor to $6.65/unit.

Figure 4.5 summarizes the idea of line balancing by contrasting cycle time and task allocation of the unbalanced line (before) and the balanced line (after).

4.5 Scale Up to Higher Volume

As indicated by Figure 4.2, demand for the Xootr increased dramatically within the next six months and, by July, had reached a level of 700 units per week. Thus, in order to maintain a reasonable match between supply and demand, Novacruz had to increase its process capacity (supply) further.

To increase process capacity for a worker-paced line, in this case from 189.5 units per week (see balanced line with three workers above) to 700 units per week, additional workers are needed. While the fundamental steps involved in building a Xootr remain unchanged, we have several options to lay out the new, high-volume process:

- Using the exact same layout and staffing plan, we could replicate the—now balanced—process and add another (and another, . . .) worker-paced line with three workers each.
- We could assign additional workers to the three process steps, which would increase the capacity of the steps and hence lead to a higher overall process capacity.
- We could divide up the work currently performed by three workers, thereby increasing the specialization of each step (and thus reducing processing times and hence increasing capacity).

FIGURE 4.5
Graphical Illustration of Line Balance

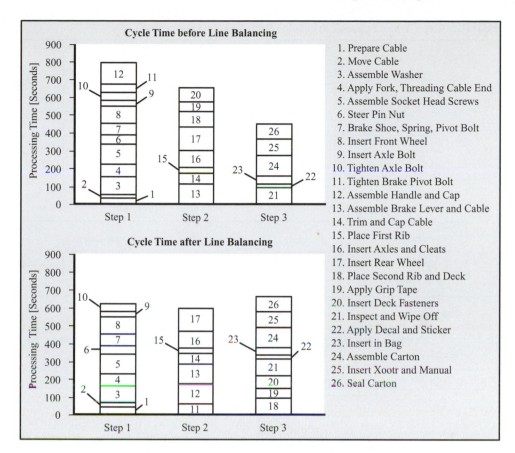

We will quickly go through the computations for all three approaches. The corresponding process flow diagrams are summarized in Figure 4.6.

Increasing Capacity by Replicating the Line

As the capacity of the entire operation grows linearly with the number of replications, we could simply add three replications of the process to obtain a new total capacity of 4×189.5 units/week = 758 units per week.

The advantage of this approach is that it would allow the organization to benefit from the knowledge it has gathered from their initial process layout. The downside of this approach is that it keeps the ratio of workers across the three process steps constant (in total, four people do step 1, four at step 2, and four at step 3), while this might not necessarily be the most efficient way of allocating workers to assembly tasks (it keeps the ratio between workers at each step fixed).

Alternatively, we could just add two replications and obtain a process capacity of 568.5 units per week and make up for the remaining 131.5 units (700 − 568.5 units/week) by adding overtime. Given that the 131.5 units to be produced in overtime would be spread over three lines, each line would have to produce 131.53/3 = 43.84 units per week corresponding to 8.1 hours of overtime per week (43.83 units/week/5.41 units/hour).

Under the assumption that we could use overtime, the average labor utilization would remain unchanged at 94.7 percent.

Increasing Capacity by Selectively Adding Workers

While the first approach assumed the number of workers at each process step to be the same, such a staffing might not necessarily be optimal. Specifically, we observe that (after the

FIGURE 4.6 **Three Process Layouts for High-Volume Production**

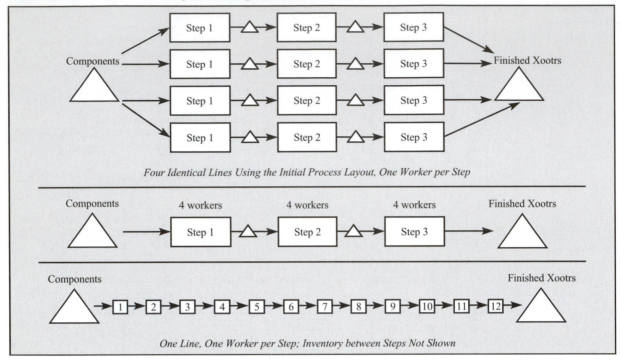

Four Identical Lines Using the Initial Process Layout, One Worker per Step

One Line, One Worker per Step; Inventory between Steps Not Shown

rebalancing) the third step is the bottleneck (processing time of 665 seconds per unit). Thus, we feel tempted to add over-proportionally more workers to this step than to the first two.

Given that we defined the capacity at each resource as the number of workers divided by the corresponding processing time, we can write the following:

$$\text{Requested capacity} = \frac{\text{Number of workers}}{\text{Activity time}}$$

For step 1, this calculation yields (700 units per week at 35 hours per week is 0.00555 unit per second):

$$0.00555 \text{ unit/second} = \frac{\text{Number of workers}}{623 \text{ seconds per unit}}$$

Thus, the number of workers required to meet the current demand is $0.00555 \times 623 = 3.46$ workers. Given that we cannot hire half a worker (and ignoring overtime for the moment), this means we have to hire four workers at step 1. In the same way, we find that we need to hire 3.34 workers at step 2 and 3.69 workers at step 3.

The fact that we need to hire a total of four workers for each of the three steps reflects the good balance that we have achieved above. If we would do a similar computation based on the initial numbers (792,648,450 seconds/unit for workers 1, 2, and 3 respectively; see Table 3.2), we would obtain the following:

- At step 1, we would hire 0.00555 unit/second = Number of workers/792 seconds/unit; therefore, Number of workers = 4.4.
- At step 2, we would hire 0.00555 unit/second = Number of workers/648 seconds/unit; therefore, Number of workers = 3.6.
- At step 3, we would hire 0.00555 unit/second = Number of workers/450 seconds/unit; therefore, Number of workers = 2.5.

Thus, we observe that a staffing that allocates extra resources to activities with longer processing times (5 workers for step 1 versus 4 for step 2 and 3 for step 3) provides an alternative way of line balancing.

Note also that if we had just replicated the unbalanced line, we would have had to add four replications as opposed to the three replications of the balanced line (we need five times step 1). Thus, line balancing, which at the level of the individual worker might look like "hair-splitting," debating about every second of worker time, at the aggregate level can achieve very substantial savings in direct labor cost.

At several places throughout the book, we will discuss the fundamental ideas of the Toyota Production System, of which line balancing is an important element. In the spirit of the Toyota Production System, idle time is considered as waste (*muda*) and therefore should be eliminated from the process to the extent possible.

Increasing Capacity by Further Specializing Tasks

Unlike the previous two approaches to increase capacity, the third approach fundamentally alters the way the individual tasks are assigned to workers. As we noted in our discussion of line balancing, we can think of each activity as a set of individual tasks. Thus, if we increase the level of specialization of workers and now have each worker only be responsible for one or two tasks (as opposed to previously an activity consisting of 5 to 10 tasks), we would be able to reduce processing time and thereby increase the capacity of the line.

Specifically, we begin our analysis by determining a targeted cycle time based on demand: in this case, we want to produce 700 units per week, which means 20 scooters per hour or one scooter every three minutes. How many workers does it take to produce one Xootr every three minutes?

The answer to this question is actually rather complicated. The reason for this complication is as follows. We cannot compute the capacity of an individual worker without knowing which tasks this worker will be in charge of. At the same time, we cannot assign tasks to workers, as we do not know how many workers we have.

To break this circularity, we start our analysis with the staffing we have obtained under the previous approaches, that is, 12 workers for the entire line. Table 4.3 shows how we can assign the tasks required to build a Xootr across these 12 workers.

Following this approach, the amount of work an individual worker needs to master is reduced to a maximum of 180 seconds. We refer to this number as the *span of control.* Given that this span of control is much smaller than under the previous approaches (665 seconds), workers will be able to perform their tasks with significantly less training. Workers are also likely to improve upon their processing times more quickly as specialization can increase the rate of learning.

The downside of this approach is its negative effect on labor utilization. Consider what has happened to labor utilization:

$$\text{Average labor utilization} = \frac{\text{Labor content}}{\text{Labor content} + \text{Sum of idle time}}$$

$$= \frac{1890}{1{,}890 + 25 + 0 + 65 + 7 + 11 + 11 + 51 + 45 + 40 + 10 + 3 + 2} = 87.5\%$$

Note that average labor utilization was 94.7 percent (after balancing) with three workers. Thus, specialization (smaller spans of control) makes line balancing substantially more complicated. This is illustrated by Figure 4.7.

The reason for this decrease in labor utilization, and thus the poorer line balance, can be found in the granularity of the tasks. Since it is not possible to break up the individual tasks further, moving a task from one worker to the next becomes relatively more significant. For example, when we balanced the three-worker process, moving a 51-second-per-unit

TABLE 4.3
**Processing times
and Task Allocation
under Increased
Specialization**

Worker	Tasks	Task Duration [seconds/unit]
Worker 1	Prepare cable	30
	Move cable	25
	Assemble washer	100
		Total: 155
Worker 2	Apply fork, threading cable end	66
	Assemble socket head screws	114
		Total: 180
Worker 3	Steer pin nut	49
	Brake shoe, spring, pivot bolt	66
		Total: 115
Worker 4	Insert front wheel	100
	Insert axle bolt	30
	Tighten axle bolt	43
		Total: 173
Worker 5	Tighten brake pivot bolt	51
	Assemble handle cap	118
		Total: 169
Worker 6	Assemble brake lever and cable	110
	Trim and cap cable	59
		Total: 169
Worker 7	Place first rib	33
	Insert axles and cleats	96
		Total: 129
Worker 8	Insert rear wheel	135
		Total: 135
Worker 9	Place second rib and deck	84
	Apply grip tape	56
		Total: 140
Worker 10	Insert deck fasteners	75
	Inspect and wipe off	95
		Total: 170
Worker 11	Apply decal and sticker	20
	Insert in bag	43
	Assemble carton	114
		Total: 177
Worker 12	Insert Xootr and manual	94
	Seal carton	84
		Total: 178
	Total labor content	1,890

task to another step accounted for just 8 percent of the step's work (674 seconds per unit). In a 12-step process, however, moving the same 51-second-per-unit task is now relative to a 169-second-per-unit workload for the step, thereby accounting for 30 percent of work. For this reason, it is difficult to further improve the allocation of tasks to workers relative to what is shown in Figure 4.7.

The observation that line balancing becomes harder with an increase in specialization can best be understood if we "turn this reasoning on its head": line balancing becomes

FIGURE 4.7
Line Balance in a Highly Specialized Line
(Different shades represent different tasks)

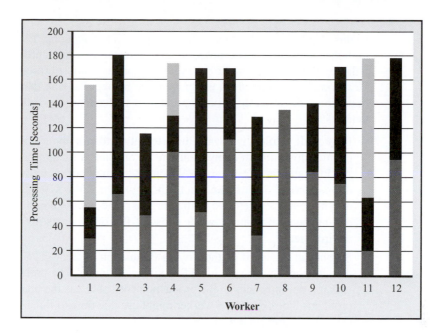

easier with a decrease in specialization. To see this, consider the case of having one single worker do all the tasks in the process. The corresponding labor utilization would be 100 percent (assuming there is enough demand to keep at least one worker busy), as, by definition, this one person also would be the bottleneck.

The idea of having one resource perform all activities of the process is referred to as a work cell. The process flow diagram of a work cell is illustrated by Figure 4.8. Since the processing time at a work cell with one worker is the same as the labor content, we would have a capacity per work cell of $\frac{1}{1,890}$ unit per second = 1.9048 units per hour, or 66.67 units per week. Already 11 work cells would be able to fulfill the demand of 700 Xootrs per week. In other words, the improved balance that comes with a work cell would allow us to further improve efficiency.

Again, the downside of this approach is that it requires one worker to master a span of control of over 30 minutes, which requires a highly trained operator. Moreover, Novacruz found that working with the 12-person line and the corresponding increase in specialization led to a substantial reduction in processing times.

FIGURE 4.8
Parallel Work Cells
(Only three work cells are shown)

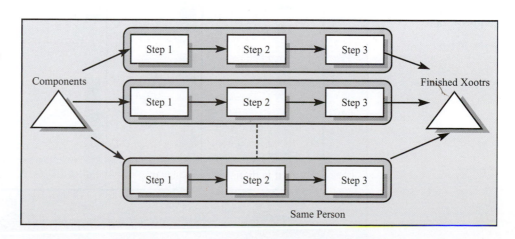

4.6 Summary

In this chapter, we introduced the concept of line balancing. Line balancing attempts to eliminate idle time from the process and thereby increase labor utilization. At first sight, line balancing seems to belong in the same category as "hair-splitting" and "penny-counting." However, it is important to understand the managerial role that line balancing plays in operations. Specifically, it is important to understand the following three managerial benefits:

- First of all, while it is always more tempting to talk about dollars rather than pennies, pennies do matter in many industries. Consider, for example, the computer industry. All PC manufacturers purchase from the same pool of suppliers of processors, disk drives, optical devices, and so forth. Thus, while the $10 of labor cost in a computer might seem small relative to the purchase price of the computer, those $10 are under our managerial control, while most of the other costs are dictated by the market environment.

- Second, in the spirit of the Toyota Production System (TPS), idle time is waste and thereby constitutes what in TPS is known as *muda*. The problem with *muda*/idle time is that it not only adds to the production costs, but has the potential to hide many other problems. For example, a worker might use idle time to finish or rework a task that she could not complete during the allocated processing time. While this does not lead to a direct, out-of-pocket cost, it avoids the root cause of the problem, which, when it surfaces, can be fixed.

- Third, while the $10 labor cost in the assembly operation of a PC manufacturer discussed above might seem like a low number, there is much more labor cost involved in the PC than $10. What appears as procurement cost for the PC maker is to some extent labor cost for the suppliers of the PC maker. If we "roll up" all operations throughout the value chain leading to a PC, we find that the cost of labor is rather substantial. This idea is illustrated in Figure 4.9 for the case of the automotive industry: while for a company like an automotive company assembly labor costs seem to be only a small element of costs, the 70 percent of costs that are procurement costs themselves include assembly labor costs from suppliers, subsuppliers, and so forth. If we look at all costs in the value chain (from an automotive company to their fifth-tier supplier), we see that about a quarter of costs in the automotive supply chain are a result of labor costs. A consequence of this observation is that it is not enough to improve our own operations

FIGURE 4.9
Sources of Cost in the Supply Chain

Source: Whitney 2004.

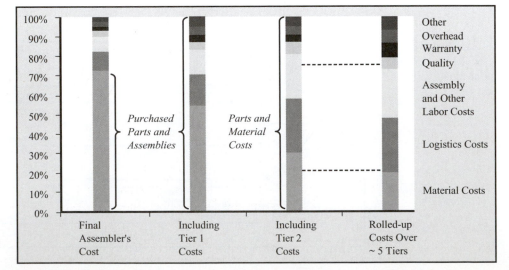

internally, but to spread such improvements throughout the supplier network, as this is where the biggest improvement opportunities are hidden. This concept of supplier development is another fundamental concept of the Toyota Production System.

In addition to these three factors, line balancing also illustrates an important—and from a managerial perspective very attractive—property of operations management. Line balancing improves per-unit labor cost (productivity) and does not require any financial investments in assets! To improve labor productivity, we would typically attempt to automate parts of the assembly, which would lower the per-unit labor cost, but at the same time require a higher investment of capital. Such an approach would be most likely if we operated in a high-wage location such as Germany or France. In contrast, we could try to operate the process with little or no automation but have a lot of labor time invested in the process. Such an approach would be more likely if we moved the process to a low-wage location such as China or Taiwan.

This tension is illustrated by Figure 4.10. The horizontal axis of Figure 4.10. shows the return on the assets tied up in the manufacturing process. High returns are desirable, which could be achieved by using little automation and a lot of labor. The vertical axis shows the productivity of labor, which would be maximized if the process were highly automated. As can be seen in Figure 4.10, there exists a tension (trade-off) between the dimensions, visible in the form of an efficient frontier. Thus, changes with respect to the level of automation would move the process up or down the frontier. One dimension is traded against the other.

In contrast, the effect of line balancing in the context of Figure 4.10 is very different. Line balancing improves labor productivity without any additional investment. To the extent that line balancing allows the firm to eliminate some currently underutilized resources using production equipment, line balancing also reduces the required assets. Thus, what from a strategic perspective seems like a simple, one-dimensional positioning problem along the technology frontier now has an additional dimension. Rather than simply taking the current process as given and finding a good strategic position, the firm should attempt to improve its process capability and improve along both performance dimensions simultaneously.

FIGURE 4.10
Trade-off between Labor Productivity and Capital Investment

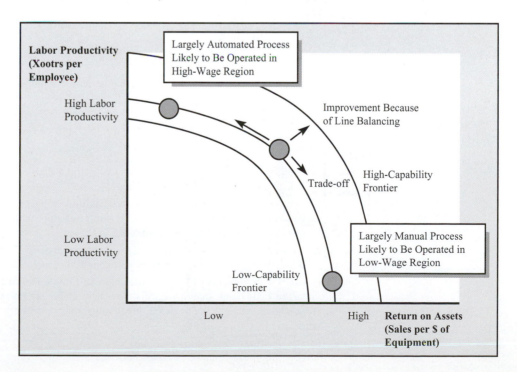

4.7 Further Reading

Bartholdi and Eisenstein (1996) develop the concept of a bucket brigade, which corresponds to a line operation that is self-balancing. In this concept, workers move between stations and follow relatively simple decision rules that determine which task should be performed next.

Whitney (2004) presents a systematic approach to design and production of mechanical assemblies. This book introduces mechanical and economic models of assemblies and assembly automation. The book takes a system view of assembly, including the notion of product architecture, feature-based design, computer models of assemblies, analysis of mechanical constraint, assembly sequence analysis, tolerances, system-level design for assembly and JIT methods, and economics of assembly automation.

4.8 Practice Problems

Q4.1* **(Empty System, Labor Utilization)** Consider a process consisting of three resources in a worker-paced line and a wage rate of $10 per hour. Assume there is unlimited demand for the product.

Resource	Processing time (minutes)	Number of Workers
1	10	2
2	6	1
3	16	3

a. How long does it take the process to produce 100 units starting with an empty system?

b. What is the average labor content?

c. What is the average labor utilization?

d. What is the cost of direct labor?

Q4.2** **(Assign Tasks to Workers)** Consider the following six tasks that must be assigned to four workers on a conveyor-paced assembly line (i.e., a machine-paced line flow). Each worker must perform at least one task.

	Time to Complete Task (seconds)
Task 1	30
Task 2	25
Task 3	35
Task 4	40
Task 5	15
Task 6	30

The current conveyor-paced assembly line configuration assigns the workers in the following way:

- Worker 1: Task 1
- Worker 2: Task 2
- Worker 3: Tasks 3, 4
- Worker 4: Tasks 5, 6

a. What is the capacity of the current line?

b. Now assume that tasks are allocated to maximize capacity of the line, subject to the conditions that (1) a worker can only perform two adjacent operations and (2) all tasks need to be done in their numerical order. What is the capacity of this line now?

c. Now assume that tasks are allocated to maximize capacity of the line and that tasks can be performed in any order. What is the maximum capacity that can be achieved?

Q4.3 **(PowerToys)** PowerToys Inc. produces a small remote-controlled toy truck on a conveyor belt with nine stations. Each station has, under the current process layout, one worker assigned to it. Stations and processing times are summarized in the following table:

(* indicates that the solution is at the end of the book)

Station	Task	Processing Times (seconds)
1	Mount battery units	75
2	Insert remote control receiver	85
3	Insert chip	90
4	Mount front axle	65
5	Mount back axle	70
6	Install electric motor	55
7	Connect motor to battery unit	80
8	Connect motor to rear axle	65
9	Mount plastic body	80

a. What is the bottleneck in this process?

b. What is the capacity, in toy trucks per hour, of the assembly line?

c. What is the direct labor cost for the toy truck with the current process if each worker receives $15/hour, expressed in dollars per toy truck?

d. What would be the direct labor cost for the toy truck if work would be organized in a work cell, that is, one worker performs all tasks? Assume that the processing times would remain unchanged (i.e., there are no specialization gains).

e. What is the utilization of the worker in station 2?

Because of a drastically reduced forecast, the plant management has decided to cut staffing from nine to six workers per shift. Assume that (i) the nine tasks in the preceding table cannot be divided; (ii) the nine tasks are assigned to the six workers in the most efficient way possible; and (iii) if one worker is in charge of two tasks, the tasks have to be adjacent (i.e., one worker cannot work on tasks 1 and 3).

f. How would you assign the nine tasks to the six workers?

g. What is the new capacity of the line (in toy trucks per hour)?

Q4.4   **(12 Tasks to 4 Workers)** Consider the following tasks that must be assigned to four workers on a conveyor-paced assembly line (i.e., a machine-paced line flow). Each worker must perform at least one task. There is unlimited demand.

	Time to Complete Task (seconds)
Task 1	30
Task 2	25
Task 3	15
Task 4	20
Task 5	15
Task 6	20
Task 7	50
Task 8	15
Task 9	20
Task 10	25
Task 11	15
Task 12	20

The current conveyor-paced assembly-line configuration assigns the workers in the following way:

- Worker 1: Tasks 1, 2, 3
- Worker 2: Tasks 4, 5, 6
- Worker 3: Tasks 7, 8, 9
- Worker 4: Tasks 10, 11, 12

a. What is the capacity of the current line?

b. What is the direct labor content?

c. What is the average labor utilization (do not consider any transient effects such as the line being emptied before breaks or shift changes)?

d. How long would it take to produce 100 units, starting with an empty system?

The firm is hiring a fifth worker. Assume that tasks are allocated to the five workers to maximize capacity of the line, subject to the conditions that (i) a worker can only perform adjacent operations and (ii) all tasks need to be done in their numerical order.

e. What is the capacity of this line now?

Again, assume the firm has hired a fifth worker. Assume further that tasks are allocated to maximize capacity of the line and that tasks can be performed in any order.

f. What is the maximum capacity that can be achieved?

g. What is the minimum number of workers that could produce at an hourly rate of 72 units? Assume the tasks can be allocated to workers as described in the beginning (i.e., tasks cannot be done in any order).

Q4.5** **(Geneva Watch)** The Geneva Watch Corporation manufactures watches on a conveyor belt with six stations. One worker stands at each station and performs the following tasks:

Station	Tasks	Processing Time (seconds)
A: Preparation 1	Heat-stake lens to bezel	14
	Inspect bezel	26
	Clean switch holes	10
	Install set switch in bezel	<u>18</u>
	Total time for A	68
B: Preparation 2	Check switch travel	23
	Clean inside bezel	12
	Install module in bezel	<u>25</u>
	Total time for B	60
C: Battery installation	Install battery clip on module	20
	Heat-stake battery clip on module	15
	Install 2 batteries in module	22
	Check switch	<u>13</u>
	Total time for C	70
D: Band installation	Install band	45
	Inspect band	<u>13</u>
	Total time for D	58
E: Packaging preparation	Cosmetic inspection	20
	Final test	<u>55</u>
	Total time for E	75
F: Watch packaging	Place watch and cuff in display box	20
	Place cover in display box base	14
	Place owner's manual, box into tub	<u>30</u>
	Total time for F	64

These six workers begin their workday at 8:00 a.m. and work steadily until 4:00 p.m. At 4:00, no new watch parts are introduced into station A and the conveyor belt continues until all of the work-in-process inventory has been processed and leaves station F. Thus, each morning the workers begin with an empty system.

a. What is the bottleneck in this process?

b. What is the capacity, in watches per hour, of the assembly line (ignore the time it takes for the first watch to come off the line)?

c. What is the direct labor content for the processes on this conveyor belt?

d. What is the utilization of the worker in station B (ignore the time it takes for the first watch to come off the line)?

e. How many minutes of idle time will the worker in station C have in one hour (ignore the time it takes for the first watch to come off the line)?

f. What time will it be (within one minute) when the assembly line has processed 193 watches on any given day?

Q4.6   **(Yoggo Soft Drink)** A small, privately owned Asian company is producing a private-label soft drink, Yoggo. A machine-paced line puts the soft drinks into plastic bottles and then packages the bottles into boxes holding 10 bottles each. The machine-paced line is comprised of the following four steps: (1) the bottling machine takes 1 second to fill a bottle, (2) the lid machine takes 3 seconds to cover the bottle with a lid, (3) a labeling machine takes 5 seconds to apply a label to a bottle, and (4) the packaging machine takes 4 seconds to place a bottle into a box. When a box has been filled with 10 bottles, a worker tending the packaging machine removes the filled box and replaces it with an empty box. Assume that the time for the worker to remove a filled box and replace it with an empty box is negligible and hence does not affect the capacity of the line. At step 3 there are two labeling machines that each process alternating bottles, that is, the first machine processes bottles 1, 3, 5, . . . and the second machine processes bottles 2, 4, 6, . . . Problem data are summarized in the table following.

Process Step	Number of Machines	Seconds per Bottle
Bottling	1	1
Applying a lid	1	3
Labeling	2	5
Packaging	1	4

a. What is the process capacity (bottles/hour) for the machine-paced line?

b. What is the bottleneck in the process?

c. If one more identical labeling machine is added to the process, how much is the increase in the process capacity going to be (in terms of bottles/hour)?

d. What is the implied utilization of the packaging machine if the demand rate is 60 boxes/hour? Recall that a box consists of 10 bottles.

Q4.7   **(Atlas Inc.)** Atlas Inc. is a toy bicycle manufacturing company producing a five-inch small version of the bike that Lance Armstrong rode to win his first Tour de France. The assembly line at Atlas Inc. consists of seven work stations, each performing a single step. Stations and processing times are summarized here:

*   Step 1 (30 sec.): The plastic tube for the frame is cut to size.
*   Step 2 (20 sec.): The tube is put together.
*   Step 3 (35 sec.): The frame is glued together.
*   Step 4 (25 sec.): The frame is cleaned.
*   Step 5 (30 sec.): Paint is sprayed onto the frame.
*   Step 6 (45 sec.): Wheels are assembled.
*   Step 7 (40 sec.): All other parts are assembled to the frame.

Under the current process layout, workers are allocated to the stations as shown here:

*   Worker 1: Steps 1, 2
*   Worker 2: Steps 3, 4
*   Worker 3: Step 5
*   Worker 4: Step 6
*   Worker 5: Step 7

a. What is the bottleneck in this process?

b. What is the capacity of this assembly line, in finished units/hour?

c. What is the utilization of Worker 4, ignoring the production of the first and last units?

d. How long does it take to finish production of 100 units, starting with an empty process?

e. What is the average labor utilization of the workers, ignoring the production of the first and last units?

f. Assume the workers are paid $15 per hour. What is the cost of direct labor for the bicycle?

g. Based on recommendations of a consultant, Atlas Inc. decides to reallocate the tasks among the workers to achieve maximum process capacity. Assume that if a worker is in charge of two tasks, then the tasks have to be adjacent to each other. Also, assume that the sequence of steps cannot be changed. What is the maximum possible capacity, in units per hour, that can be achieved by this reallocation?

h. Again, assume a wage rate of $15 per hour. What would be the cost of direct labor if one single worker would perform all seven steps? You can ignore benefits of specialization, set-up times, or quality problems.

i. On account of a reduced demand forecast, management has decided to let go of one worker. If work is to be allocated among the four workers such that (i) the tasks can't be divided, (ii) if one worker is in charge of two tasks, the tasks have to be adjacent, (iii) the tasks are assigned in the most efficient way and (iv) each step can only be carried out by one worker, what is the new capacity of the line (in finished units/hour)?

Q4.8   **(Glove Design Challenge)** A manufacturer of women's designer gloves has employed a team of students to redesign her manufacturing unit. They gathered the following information. The manufacturing process consists of four activities: (1) fabric cutting; (2) dyeing; (3) stitching, done by specially designed machines; and (4) packaging. Processing times are shown below. Gloves are moved between activities by a conveyor belt that paces the flow of work (machine-paced line).

Process Step	Number of Machines	Minutes per Glove
Cutting	1	2
Dyeing	1	4
Stitching	1	3
Packaging	1	5

a. What is the process capacity in gloves/hour?

b. Which one of the following statements is true?

   i.   The capacity of the process increases by reducing the dyeing time.

   ii. If stitching time increases to 5 min./glove, the capacity of the process remains unchanged, but "time through an empty machine-paced process" increases.

   iii. By reducing packaging time, the process capacity increases.

   iv. By reducing cutting time, the capacity of the process increases.

c. What is the implied utilization of the packaging machine if the demand rate is 10 gloves/hour?

d. What is the flow time for a glove?

Q4.9   **(Worker-Paced Line)**

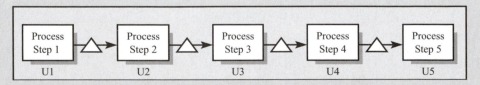

The accompanying diagram depicts a five-step, worker-paced headphone manufacturing plant. The headphones are meant to be used with iPods and DVD players. Step 1 involves a worker bending a metal strip into an arc shape. In step 2, the metal arc is fitted with a plastic sleeve. In step 3, the headphones are fitted at the end of the metal and plastic strips. In step 4, the wires are soldered into the headphones. Step 5 involves a specially designed packaging unit. After the plant has been operational for a couple of hours, the manager inspects the plant. He is particularly interested in cutting labor costs. He observes the following. The process is capacity constrained and the entire process produces 36 units in one hour. U1 through U5 denote the utilization at steps 1 through 5 respectively. Currently, there is a single worker at each step and the utilizations are as follows: U1 = 4/30, U2 = 4/15, U3 = 4/5, U4 = 1, U5 = 2/5.

Answer the following questions based on the given data and information.

a. What is the capacity of step 5?

b. Which step is the bottleneck?

c. Which process step has the highest capacity?

d. If the wage rate is $36 per hour per person, what is the direct labor cost per unit?

You can view a video of how problems marked with a ** are solved by going on www. cachon-terwiesch.net and follow the links under 'Solved Practice Problems'

Chapter 5

Project Management

In the previous chapters, we established the process view of the organization.[1] Processes are all about repetition—we don't perform an operation once, we perform it over and over again. This process management view fits many, if not most, operations problems well. Mining and production plants, back offices of insurances or banks, hospitals, and call centers are all about repetition, and many flow units journey through the corresponding processes on a daily basis.

There are, however, a number of operations for which the repetition-based approach of process management is less appropriate. Consider, for example, a major construction project, the development of a new product, or the planning of a wedding party. In these situations, your primary concern is about planning the completion of one flow unit, and typically, you would like to see this completion to happen sooner rather than later.

Whether you care about the completion of one or many flow units often depends on which role you play in an operation. While most of us think about one wedding (at a time) and thus should think of a wedding event as a project, a wedding planner organizes numerous weddings and thus should think of weddings as flow units in a process. Similarly, a developer working on the launch of a new product or the construction worker building a new office complex are likely to think about their work as a project, while many echelons up in the organization, the vice president of product development or the owner of a real estate development company think about these projects as flow units in a big process.

We define a *project* as a temporary (and thus nonrepetitive) operation. Projects have a limited time frame, have one or more specific objectives, a temporary organizational structure, and thus often are operated in a more ad-hoc, improvised management style. In this chapter, you will learn the basics of project management, including:

- Mapping out the various activities that need to be completed as part of the project.
- Computing the completion time of the project based on the critical path.
- Accelerating a project to achieve an earlier completion time.
- Understanding the types of uncertainty a project faces and how to deal with them.

5.1 Motivating Example

Unmanned aerial vehicles (UAVs) are aircrafts that are flown without a human being on board. They are either controlled remotely or have built-in navigation intelligence to

[1] The authors gratefully acknowledge the help of Christoph Loch and Stylios Kavadias, whose case study on the Dragonfly UAV is the basis for the motivating example in this chapter.

FIGURE 5.1
UAV Offered
by Boeing

Unmanned aerial vehicles
(UAVs)

determine their direction. Most of their applications lie in the military arena, but UAVs can also be used for scientific exploration or search-and-rescue operations (see Figure 5.1).

We use the example of the development of a UAV to illustrate several tools and techniques of project management. In particular, we look at the decision situation of a developer who has just completed a prototype UAV and now is putting together a more detailed proposal for commercial development (see Kavadias, Loch, and De Meyer for further details. The authors gratefully acknowledge the help of Christoph Loch and Stylios Kavadias, whose case study on the Dragonfly UAV is the basis for the chapter). Table 5.1 lists the activities that need to be done to complete the proposal. Note that this entirely captures the work required for the proposal, not the actual development itself.

A quick (and rather naïve) view of Table 5.1 is that the total time to complete the proposal will be $9 + 3 + 11 + 7 + 8 + 6 + 21 + 10 + 15 + 5 = 95$ days. Alternatively, one might (equally naively) claim, the proposal development should take 21 days, the duration of the longest activity.

Both of these views omit an important aspect of the nature of project management. Some, but not all, of the activities are dependent on each other. For example, activity A_3 (aerodynamics analysis) requires the completion of activity A_2 (prepare and discuss surface models). Such dependencies are also referred to as *precedence relationships*. They can be summarized in a *dependency matrix* as shown in Table 5.2. In the dependency matrix, each

TABLE 5.1
Activities for the
UAV Proposal
Development

Activity	Description	Expected Duration (days)
A_1	Prepare preliminary functional and operability requirements, and create preliminary design configuration	9
A_2	Prepare and discuss surface models	3
A_3	Perform aerodynamics analysis and evaluation	11
A_4	Create initial structural geometry, and prepare notes for finite element structural simulation	7
A_5	Develop structural design conditions	8
A_6	Perform weights and inertia analyses	6
A_7	Perform structure and compatibility analyses and evaluation	21
A_8	Develop balanced free-body diagrams and external applied loads	10
A_9	Establish internal load distributions, evaluate structural strength stiffness; preliminary manufacturing planning and analysis	15
A_{10}	Prepare proposal	5

TABLE 5.2 Dependency Matrix for the UAV

		Information-Providing Activity (Upstream)									
		A_1	A_2	A_3	A_4	A_5	A_6	A_7	A_8	A_9	A_{10}
Information-Receiving Activity (Downstream)	A_1										
	A_2	X									
	A_3		X								
	A_4		X								
	A_5				X						
	A_6				X						
	A_7			X			X				
	A_8			X		X	X				
	A_9								X		
	A_{10}							X		X	

column represents an activity that provides information, and each row indicates an activity that receives information. An entry in column *i* and row *j* suggests that the activity in the i-th column (A_i) provides information to the activity in the j-th row (A_j). We also say that A_i precedes A_j or that A_j is dependent of A_i. Dependent activities require information or physical outputs from the input providing activities. The dependency matrix implicitly suggests a sequencing of the activities and thus dictates the flow of the project. The project will start with activity A_1, because it does not have any input providing activities. It will end with activity A_{10}. Similar to process flow terminology, people often refer to a preceding activity as "upstream" and the dependent activity as "downstream."

5.2 Critical Path Method

There exist multiple approaches to represent project information as displayed in Tables 5.1 and 5.2. In the *activity-on-node (AON) representation,* nodes correspond to project activities and arrows correspond to precedence relationships (with an arrow going from the input providing activity to the corresponding dependent activity). In this chapter, we focus on the AON representation because it is similar to the process flow diagrams that we discuss in the other chapters of this book.

To create an AON representation of a project, we start with the activity that requires no input, in our case that is activity A_1. We then work our way through the dependency matrix, mimicking the evolution of the project:

1. We create a node in the form of a box for the activity, including its name as well as its expected duration.
2. After creating the node for the activity, we consider the activity as done. Thus, all information provided by the activity to its dependent activities is now available. We can draw a line through the corresponding column, and draw an arrow out of the activity for each dependency (for each "X").
3. Next, we look for any other activity in the dependency matrix that has all its information providing activities completed and go back to step 1 until we have worked ourselves to the last activity.

FIGURE 5.2 **Activity on node (AON) representation of the UAV project. Left part of the box is the activity name; right part is the activity duration**

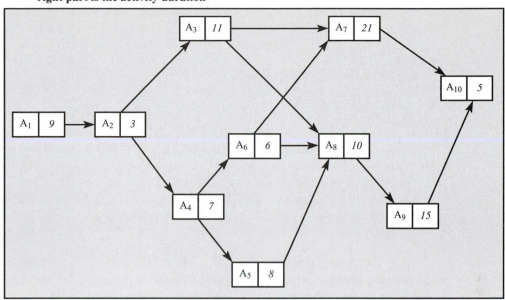

If we repeatedly execute these three steps, we obtain a graph as shown in Figure 5.2. This graph provides a practical and visual way to illustrate the evolution of the project. It resembles the process flow diagram introduced in Chapter 3.

5.3 Computing Project Completion Time

Despite the similarity between process flow diagram and the AON representation, we should remember the fundamental difference between process management and project management. In process management, we directed our attention to the resource that had the lowest capacity, the bottleneck. If each activity in the process flow diagram was staffed by one worker (or machine), the bottleneck was the activity with the longest activity time.

What matters for the completion time of the project, however, is not the individual activity times, but the completion time of the entire project. This completion time requires ALL activities to be completed. In fact, we will see that in the UAV project, the activity with the longest duration (A_7) will not constrain the duration of the overall project.

So, how long then will the project in Figure 5.2 take? This turns out to be a tricky question. It is intuitive that the project can be carried out in less than $9 + 3 + 11 + 7 + 8 + 6 + 21 + 10 + 15 + 5 = 95$ days (the sum of the activity times). Some activities can be carried out in parallel and so the 10 activities do not create a 10-person relay race. On the other hand, the degree to which we can execute the activities in parallel is limited by the dependency matrix. For example, activity A_3 requires the completion of activity A_2, which, in turn, requires the completion of activity A_1. Things get even more convoluted as we consider activity A_7. For it to be complete, A_3 and A_6 have to be complete. A_3, in turn, requires completion of A_2 and A_1, while A_6 requires completion of A_4, which, once again, requires completion of A_2 and A_1. What a mess!

To correctly compute the completion time of the project, a more structured approach is needed. This approach is based on considering all possible paths through the network in Figure 5.2. A path is a sequence of nodes (activities) and (directional) arrows. For example, the sequence $A_1, A_2, A_3, A_7, A_{10}$ is a path. Every path can be assigned a duration by simply adding up the durations of the activities that constitute the path. The duration of the path $A_1, A_2, A_3, A_7, A_{10}$ is $9 + 3 + 11 + 21 + 5 = 49$ days.

The number of paths through the AON representation depends on the shape of the dependency matrix. In the easiest case, every activity would just have one information-providing activity and one dependent activity. In such a (relay race) project, the dependency matrix had just one entry per row and one entry per column. The duration of the project would be the sum of the activity times. Every time one activity provides information to multiple activities, the number of paths is increased.

In the UAV project and its project graph shown in Figure 5.2, we can identify the following paths connecting the first activity (A_1) with the last activity (A_{10}):

$$A_1 - A_2 - A_3 - A_7 - A_{10} \text{ with a duration of } 9 + 3 + 11 + 21 + 5 = 49 \text{ days}$$

$$A_1 - A_2 - A_3 - A_8 - A_9 - A_{10} \text{ with a duration of } 9 + 3 + 11 + 10 + 15 + 5 = 53 \text{ days}$$

$$A_1 - A_2 - A_4 - A_6 - A_7 - A_{10} \text{ with a duration of } 9 + 3 + 7 + 6 + 21 + 5 = 51 \text{ days}$$

$$A_1 - A_2 - A_4 - A_6 - A_8 - A_9 - A_{10} \text{ with a duration of } 9 + 3 + 7 + 6 + 10 + 15 + 5 = 55 \text{ days}$$

$$A_1 - A_2 - A_4 - A_5 - A_8 - A_9 - A_{10} \text{ with a duration of } 9 + 3 + 7 + 8 + 10 + 15 + 5 = 57 \text{ days}$$

The path with the longest duration is called the critical path. Its duration determines the duration of the overall project. In our case, the critical path is $A_1 - A_2 - A_4 - A_5 - A_8 - A_9 - A_{10}$ and the resulting project duration is 57 days. Note that A_7, the activity with the longest duration, is not on the *critical path*.

5.4   Finding the Critical Path and Creating a Gantt Chart

The exercise of identifying every possible path through the project graph along with its duration is a rather tedious exercise. The more activities and the more dependency relationships we have, the greater the number of paths we have to evaluate before we find the one we truly care about, the *critical path*.

Fortunately, there is a simpler way to compute the project duration. The idea behind this easier way is to compute the earliest possible start time for each activity. For each activity, we can find the *earliest start time (EST)* by looking at the earliest time all information providing activities have been completed. The earliest start time of the first activity is time zero. The *earliest completion time (ECT)* of an activity is the earliest start time plus the activity duration. We then work our way through the project graph, activity by activity, starting from the first activity and going all the way to the last.

More formally, we can define the following algorithm to compute the earliest completion time of the project. The approach is similar to our method of coming up with the graphical representation of the project graph:

1. Start with the activity that has no information-providing activity and label that activity as the start. The earliest start time of that activity is defined as 0. The earliest completion time is the duration of this activity.
2. Identify all activities that can be initiated at this point (i.e., have all information-providing activities complete). For a given such activity i, compute the earliest start time as:

$$EST(A_i) = \text{Max}\{ECT(A_j)\}, \text{ where } A_j \text{ are all activities providing input to } A_i$$

3. Compute the earliest completion time of A_i as

$$ECT(A_i) = EST(A_i) + \text{Duration}(A_i)$$

4. Consider activity i as completed, and identify any further activities that now can be initiated. Go back to step 2.

TABLE 5.3
Computing the Completion Time of a Project (table is created row by row, starting with the first activity)

Activity	Earliest Start Time (EST)	Expected Duration (days)	Earliest Completion Time (ECT)
A_1	0	9	9
A_2	$ECT(A_1) = 9$	3	12
A_3	$ECT(A_2) = 12$	11	23
A_4	$ECT(A_2) = 12$	7	19
A_5	$ECT(A_4) = 19$	8	27
A_6	$ECT(A_4) = 19$	6	25
A_7	$Max\{ECT(A_3),ECT(A_6)\}$ $= Max\{23,25\} = 25$	21	46
A_8	$Max\{ECT(A_3), ECT(A_5),ECT(A_6)\}$ $= Max\{23, 27, 25\} = 27$	10	37
A_9	$ECT(A_8) = 37$	15	52
A_{10}	$ECT(A_9) = 52$	5	57

This algorithm is illustrated in Table 5.3. The table is created from the top to the bottom, one activity at a time. As you construct a given row i, you have to ask yourself, "What activities provide information to i? What activities does i depend on?" You can see this by reading row i in the dependency matrix, or you can see this in the project graph.

Based on the earliest start and earliest completion time, we can create a Gantt chart for the project. The *Gantt chart* is basically a timeline with the activities included as bars. Gantt charts are probably the most commonly used visualization for project time lines. Note that unlike the AON representation, the Gantt chart itself does not capture the dependencies of the activities. Based on the previously explained computations of the earliest start and completion times, we have already ensured that activities only get initiated when all required information is available.

The Gantt chart for the UAV project is shown in Figure 5.3.

5.5   Computing Slack Time

It lies in the nature of the critical path that any delay in activities on the critical path will immediately cause a delay in the overall project. For example, a one-day delay in activity A_9 will automatically delay the overall project by one day. However, this is not true for

FIGURE 5.3
Gantt Chart for the UAV Project

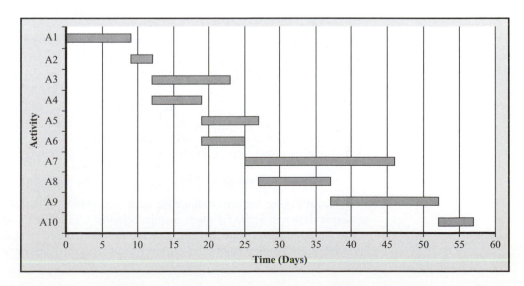

activities that are not part of the critical path. We can delay activity A_7 even by several days (six to be exact) without affecting the overall completion of the project. In other words, activity A_7 has some built in "wiggle room." The technical term for this wiggle room is *slack time*. It is the amount of time an activity can be delayed without affecting the overall completion time of the project.

The slack time of an activity is determined based on an additional set of calculations known as the late start schedule. So far, we have computed the earliest start time (EST) and earliest completion time (ECT) of each activity by going through the project from beginning to end. We now compute the *latest start time (LST)* and *latest completion time (LCT)* for each activity such that the project still completes on time. We do this by beginning with the last activity and working our way backward through the project until we reach the beginning. Thus, we start with the last activity (A_{10}) and end with the first activity (A_1).

So, let's start with the last activity. Assuming we want to complete the project as early as possible, we define the LCT of the last activity as being the same as its ECT:

$$\text{LCT(Last activity)} = \text{ECT(Last activity)}$$
$$\text{LCT}(A_{10}) = \text{ECT}(A_{10}) = 57$$

There exist some cases in which an early completion is not desired—instead, there exists a target time at which the project should be complete. In this case, we can define the LCT of the last activity as the target date.

The latest start time of the last activity is simply the latest completion time minus the duration of the last activity:

$$\text{LST(Last activity)} = \text{LCT(Last activity)} - \text{Duration(Last activity)}$$
$$\text{LST}(A_{10}) = \text{LCT}(A_{10}) - 5 = 57 - 5 = 52$$

More generally, we define the LCT for an activity as the smallest (earliest) LST value of all activities that are depending on it and the LST as the LCT minus the duration. Consider activity A_9, which only has A_{10} as a dependent activity. Thus, we can define:

$$\text{LCT}(A_9) = \text{LST}(A_{10}) = 52$$
$$\text{LST}(A_9) = \text{LCT}(A_9) - \text{Duration}(A_9) = 52 - 15 = 37$$

In the same manner, we compute:

$$\text{LCT}(A_8) = \text{LST}(A_9) = 37$$
$$\text{LST}(A_8) = \text{LCT}(A_8) - \text{Duration}(A_8) = 37 - 10 = 27$$

Next, consider activity A_7, the activity we previously observed to have some slack time.

$$\text{LCT}(A_7) = \text{LST}(A_{10}) = 52$$
$$\text{LST}(A_7) = \text{LCT}(A_7) - \text{Duration}(A_7) = 52 - 21 = 31$$

Note the difference between the earliest start time of A_7, which was 25, and the latest start time of A7, which we just found to be 31. In other words, we can delay the start of A_7 by six days without affecting the overall completion time of the project.

Based on this observation, we define the slack of an activity as:

$$\text{Slack time} = \text{Latest start time} - \text{Earliest start time}$$

In the same way, we can compute the other information of the late schedule. This information is shown in Table 5.4. Note that the columns LST and LCT are computed by going backward through the project graph; thus, we start with the rows at the bottom of the table and work our way up. As expected, the slack time of all activities on the critical path is zero.

TABLE 5.4
Computation of Slack Time

Activity	EST	Duration	ECT	LCT	LST = LCT − Duration	Slack = LST − EST
A_1	0	9	9	$LST(A_2) = 9$	$9 − 9 = 0$	0
A_2	9	3	12	$Min\{LST(A_3),LST(A_4)\}$ $= Min\{16,12\} = 12$	$12 − 3 = 9$	0
A_3	12	11	23	$Min\{LST(A_7),LST(A_8)\}$ $= Min\{31,27\} = 27$	$27 − 11 = 16$	$27 − 23 = 4$
A_4	12	7	19	$Min\{LST(A_5),LST(A_6)\}$ $= Min\{19,21\} = 19$	$19 − 7 = 12$	0
A_5	19	8	27	$LST(A_8) = 27$	$27 − 8 = 19$	0
A_6	19	6	25	$Min\{LST(A_7),LST(A_8)\}$ $= Min\{31,27\} = 27$	$27 − 6 = 21$	$27 − 25 = 2$
A_7	25	21	46	$LST(A_{10}) = 52$	$52 − 21 = 31$	$52 − 46 = 6$
A_8	27	10	37	$LST(A_9) = 37$	$37 − 10 = 27$	0
A_9	37	15	52	$LST(A_{10}) = 52$	$52 − 15 = 37$	0
A_{10}	52	5	57	57	$57 − 5 = 52$	0

What is the benefit of knowing how much slack time there is associated with an activity? The main benefit from knowing the slack time information is as follows:

- *Potentially delay the start of the activity:* To the extent that we can delay the start of an activity without delaying the overall project, we might prefer a later start over an earlier start. Because activities are often associated with direct expenses, simple discounted cash flow calculations suggest that the start times be delayed wherever possible.

- *Accommodate the availability of resources:* Internal or external resources might not always be available when we need them. Slack time provides us with a way to adjust our schedule (as shown in the Gantt chart) without compromising the completion time of the overall project.

Exhibit 5.1 summarizes the steps to plan the time line of a project and to identify the critical path as well as the slack times of the activities. Based on this information, we can

FIGURE 5.4
Augmented Project Graph. The top row includes the earliest start time, the duration, and the earliest completion time. The middle row is the activity name. The bottom row is the latest start time, the slack, and the latest completion time.

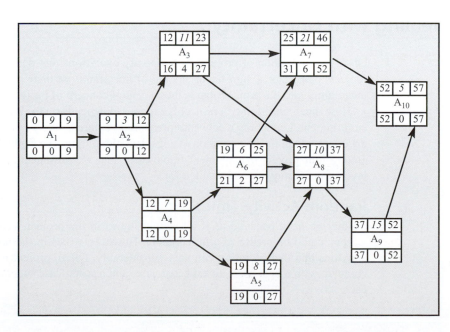

Exhibit 5.1

SUMMARY OF CALCULATIONS FOR A CRITICAL PATH ANALYSIS

1. Identify all activities that constitute the project.
2. Determine the dependencies among the activities by either creating a dependency matrix or by creating the project graph. Make sure there exists no circularity in the dependencies (i.e., the dependency matrix only has entries to the lower left of the diagonal and the project graph does not contain any loops).
3. Compute the earliest start time (EST) and the earliest completion time (ECT) by working forward through the project graph (from start to end).

$$\text{EST}(A_i) = \text{Max}\{\text{ECT}(A_j)\}, \text{ where } A_j \text{ are all activities providing input to } A_i$$

$$\text{ECT}(A_i) = \text{EST}(A_i) + \text{Duration}(A_i)$$

4. Compute the latest start time (LST) and the latest completion time (LCT) by working backward through the project graph (from end to start)

$$\text{LCT}(A_i) = \text{Min}\{\text{LST}(A_j)\}, \text{ where } A_j \text{ are all activities receiving input from } A_i$$

$$\text{LST}(A_i) = \text{LCT}(A_i) - \text{Duration}(A_i)$$

5. Compute the slack of an activity as

$$\text{Slack}(A_i) = \text{LST}(A_i) - \text{EST}(A_i)$$

6. Create the critical path by highlighting all activities with zero slack.

augment the initial project graph and present all information we computed for each activity in a graphical format, similar to what is similar to what is shown in Figure 5.2. This representation, as shown in Figure 5.4., is the output of many commercial software packages dealing with project management as well as a set of consulting tools.

Note that all of these computations assume that there exists no uncertainty in the activity durations (and dependencies). Uncertainty is the subject of the next section.

5.6 Dealing with Uncertainty

Given our definition of projects as temporary operations that deal with nonroutine work, projects often face a significant amount of uncertainty at their outset. Incorporating this uncertainty into the project plan is thus a central concern of project management.

How much uncertainty a project is exposed to depends on the nature of a project and its environment. Launching a new entrepreneurial venture is likely to be associated with more uncertainty than the construction of a residential building. We find it helpful to distinguish among four project management frameworks that we present in increasing order of the level of uncertainty they are suited for.

Random Activity Times

So far, we have behaved as if all activity times in the project were deterministic—that is, they could be predicted with certainty. However, it lies in the nature of many project activities that their duration can vary considerably. Often, project managers are asked to come up with a best-case, an expected-case, and a worst-case scenario for the duration of each activity.

FIGURE 5.5
Procedure Durations in the operating room for Open Heart Surgery

(Data taken from Olivares et al.)

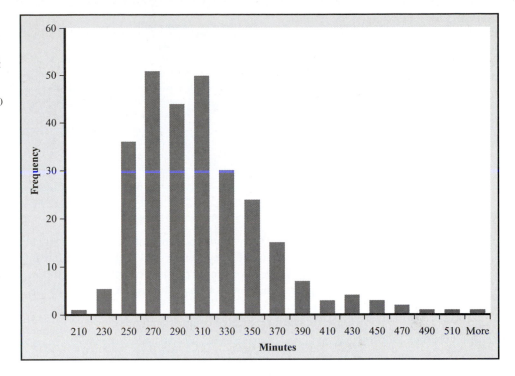

With that information in mind, it is possible to compute the variance of an activity time as well as the probability of meeting a certain due date. This is similar to the logic of uncertain activity times in waiting models that we explore in Chapter 8. Figure 5.5 shows the activity durations for a sample of cardiac surgeries in the operating room of a large hospital. We observe that there exists a considerable amount of procedure variation. Moreover, we observe that the distribution is not symmetric: activity durations that are more than double the mean duration can happen—the distribution has a "long tail."

When facing uncertainty in the activity time durations, it is important to understand that uncertainty in activity duration is a bad thing because it, on average, will lead to a later completion time of the project. It is a misconception that uncertainties in activity times will cancel each other out, just as the statement, "Put your head in the freezer and your feet in the oven and the average temperature you are exposed to is just about right," makes little sense. In a similar manner, variation in activity duration will not cancel out. When some activities are completed early and others are completed late, the overall impact on the project duration is almost always undesirable.

To see this, consider the simple project graph displayed in Figure 5.6. On the left side of the figure, we have a project with deterministic activity times. Given the activity durations of 5 days for A_1, 4 days for A_2, and 6 days for A_3, as well as the dependency structure shown by the project graph, the critical path of this project is $A_1 - A_3$ and the completion time is 11. Now, consider the activity times on the ride side of the figure. A_1 now has a

FIGURE 5.6
Simple Example of a Project with Uncertainty in the Activity Duration

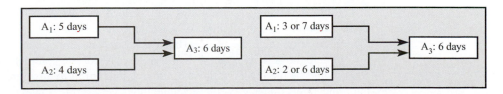

TABLE 5.5
Example Calculations for a Small Project with Three Activities (based on Figure 5.6)

Scenario	Probability	Explanation	Start of A_3	Completion
A_1 late and A_2 late	0.25	A_1 would take 7 days (during which time, the 6 days of A_2 will also be completed)	7	13
A_1 early, A_2 late	0.25	A_2 would take 6 days (during which time, the 3 days of A_1 would also be completed)	6	12
A_1 late, A_2 early	0.25	A_1 would take 7 days (during which time, the 2 days of A_2 would also be completed)	7	13
A_1 early and A_2 early	0.25	A_1 would take 3 days (during which time, the 2 days of A_2 would also be completed)	3	9

completion time of 3 days with a 50% probability and 7 days with a 50% probability and A_2 has a completion time of 2 days with a 50% probability and 6 days with a 50% probability.

Note that in expectation (on average) the completion times of A_1 and A_2 have not changed. But the expected completion time of the project has. To see this, consider the calculations displayed in Table 5.5.

Observe that the expected completion time is:

$$0.25 \times 13 \text{ days} + 0.25 \times 12 \text{ days} + 0.25 \times 13 \text{ days} + 0.25 \times 9 \text{ days} = 11.75 \text{ days}$$

almost one day (0.75 day, to be exact) longer than in the deterministic base case. Note that this relies on a rather optimistic assumption in the case that both activities are completed early: we implicitly assume that A_3 has the flexibility of starting earlier than planned, when both A_1 and A_2 are completed early. If we cannot benefit from the early completion of activities, the overall penalty we incur from uncertainty would be even higher.

In the first three scenarios, we are slower than the deterministic completion time of 11 days. Only in the last case are we faster. Thus, we are not just exposed to the risk of the project running later than in the deterministic case, but we will be running later on average.

The reason for this effect is that the critical path of the project can potentially shift. In other words, an activity not on the critical path might delay the overall project because of a longer than expected duration. While A_2 was not on the critical path in the deterministic base case, we saw that it was holding up the project (and thus was on the critical path) in the second scenario analyzed earlier. Unfortunately, many books and software packages ignore this effect and pretend that the variance of the overall project duration can be directly computed from the variances of the activity times on the critical path. This is simply incorrect—a rigorous evaluation of the overall project duration almost always requires some Monte Carlo simulation.

Beyond avoiding this simple, yet very common mistake, correctly estimating the duration of the activity is a challenge. Estimates of activity durations are often inflated, especially when working with internal resources: because nobody on the team wants to be blamed for potential schedule overruns, it is common to quote excessively long estimates of activity durations (the estimates are "padded"). This is especially common if there exists no threat of substitution for a resource, as is common with resources internal to the organization (e.g., the IT department). Resources simply declare that it takes 10 days to complete the activity, even if their true forecast for the completion is 5 days. After all, what would be the incentive for the resource to commit to an aggressive schedule? Once the project gets under way, the schedule looks very tight. However, if one truly observes the execution of the project, most activities make little progress, and the corresponding resources are either idle or working on other projects, even if they are associated with the critical path. Obtaining honest (unbiased) activity durations is thus essential. One technique is to compare actual activity durations with their forecasts, similar to what we discuss in Chapter 12.

However, estimates of activity durations can also be underestimated, especially when working with external resources: if contractors for a project are asked to submit a time estimate, they have a substantial incentive to underestimate the project completion time because this increases their likelihood of being selected for the project. Once on the job, however, they know that they cannot be easily kicked out of the project should their activity run late. For example, consider the OR data from Figure 5.5 discussed earlier. If we compare the actual time taken in the OR with the time estimates made initially when the OR was booked, it turns out that, on average, procedures take 10 percent longer than initially forecasted. The reason for this is that doctors often want to get a particular slot on the OR schedule—and they know that they are more likely to get a slot in the near future if their procedure time is short. However, they also know that once they have started the procedure, there exists no way to penalize them for a schedule overrun. With this in mind, they simply promise overly optimistic activity durations. Again, obtaining unbiased activity durations is important. Project contracts, and especially late completion penalties, are also an instrument to consider when working with external parties.

Potential Iteration/Rework Loops

The previously introduced dependency matrix (see Table 5.2) had an important property—all dependencies were on the lower left of the diagonal. In other words, there existed a one-way path from the beginning of the project to the end.

In practice, however, projects often require iteration. In fact, the previously discussed UAV project commonly (in about 3 out of 10 cases) iterates between activities A_4 and A_9. Such iterations are typical for product development and innovation projects where problem solving can be a more organic, iterative process. It is often referred to as rework.

In general, such *rework loops* are more likely to happen in high-uncertainty environments. For example, a development team for an Internet platform might want to adjust its business plan after having launched a beta prototype, creating a rework loop. In contrast, we hope that the architect in charge of a major construction project does not want to revisit her drawings after the first tenants moved into the building. Consequently, project planning tools such as Gantt charts and the critical path method are more valuable for low-uncertainty projects, and they can provide a false sense of planning accuracy when applied in high-uncertainty environments.

Several tools exist for modeling and analyzing projects with iteration. We restrict ourselves to the main insight from this line of research. The presence of iteration loops typically dominates the effect of uncertain activity duration. In other words, when faced with the potential of some activities taking longer than expected and an unexpected iteration requiring reworking one or multiple previously completed activities, a project manager should focus on the threat of the iteration because it has a stronger effect on the overall completion time.

Decision Tree/Milestones/Exit Option

The previous two types of uncertainty reflected the question, "When will the project be completed?" Activities might take a little longer (uncertain activity times) or sometimes might even have to be repeated (rework loops), but in the end, we always complete the project.

Often, however, a more fundamental question is of essence to the project manager: "Will we complete this project at all, or should we terminate the project?" Such uncertainty is common in many innovation settings, include venture capital–funded projects or pharmaceutical research and development (R&D). For example, only a small fraction of R&D projects that enter phase 1 clinical trials will be launched in the market. More than 80 percent of the projects will be canceled along the way.

Project management techniques as reviewed earlier are inappropriate for handling this type of uncertainty. The threat of terminating the project because of new market data (market uncertainty) or new technical data (technological uncertainty) looms so large that it trumps the previously discussed types of uncertainty.

Decision trees map out the potential scenarios that can occur once the uncertainty is resolved and the potential set of actions that can be taken in each scenario. A key insight that can be derived from such models is the observation that it is often substantially cheaper to exit a project early, instead of letting costs escalate and then exiting the project later on at higher costs. The project management implication of this is that it is very desirable to move activities that resolve this type of uncertainty (feasibility studies, market research) to the early part of the project.

Unknown Unknowns

When Christopher Columbus set out to find a new way to sail to India, he (most likely) did not set up a project plan. Even for modern time explorers, be it in sailing or in business, there exist situations where the amount of uncertainty we face is simply too large to make any careful planning process meaningful. In such settings, we face so much uncertainty that we don't even know what we don't know. We face *unknown unknowns*, also referred to as *unk-unks*.

It lies in the nature of many high-uncertainty projects that they will not be completed. In that sense, a timely abandonment often is the goal as it avoids an escalation in costs. Often, a useful exercise is to simply list all variables in the project that are currently not known and to look for activities that would help resolve these unknowns. At any moment in time, the project manager should then attempt to spend as little as possible to learn enough to decide whether or not to move forward with the project. This technique, also referred to as *discovery-driven planning,* will help resolve some uncertainties and potentially identify new ones.

Exhibit 5.2 summarizes these levels of project uncertainty. The main point is that different project management tools apply to different projects, depending on the amount of uncertainty they face. It is neither advisable to use a high-uncertainty tool (such as decision trees) for a low-uncertainty project (why would you want to evaluate an exit option every day in an ongoing construction project?) nor vice versa (why try to find and optimize the critical path if you do not even know if you are in business next quarter?).

5.7   How to Accelerate Projects

Project managers typically pursue a combination of three objectives: project completion time, project cost (budget), and the quality of the accomplished work. Sometimes, these objectives are in conflict with another. This then creates a trade-off among the three dimensions, similar to what we have seen in other chapters of this book (e.g., the trade-off between call center responsiveness and efficiency in Chapter 1).

Consider the development of the UAV discussed earlier. Most likely, more time would allow the developers to put together an even more convincing proposal. Similarly, if budget would not be a constraint, it might be possible to outsource at least some work, which, if it shortens the duration of a critical path activity, would lead to an earlier project completion time.

Beyond trading off one goal against another goal, we can also try to "break the trade-off" and just be smarter about how we manage the project. The following provides a set of inexpensive

Exhibit 5.2

SUMMARY OF DIFFERENT UNCERTAINTY LEVELS IN A PROJECT

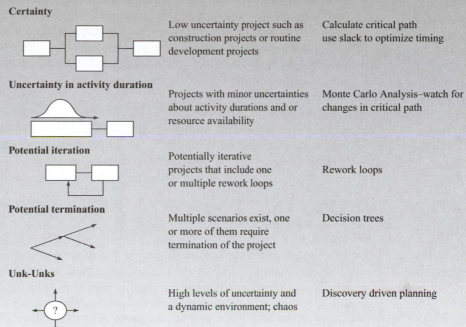

Certainty	Low uncertainty project such as construction projects or routine development projects	Calculate critical path use slack to optimize timing
Uncertainty in activity duration	Projects with minor uncertainties about activity durations and or resource availability	Monte Carlo Analysis–watch for changes in critical path
Potential iteration	Potentially iterative projects that include one or multiple rework loops	Rework loops
Potential termination	Multiple scenarios exist, one or more of them require termination of the project	Decision trees
Unk-Unks	High levels of uncertainty and a dynamic environment; chaos	Discovery driven planning

actions a project manager can take to accelerate the completion time of the project without necessarily sacrificing the quality of the accomplished work or the project budget:

- *Start the project early:* The last day before the project's due date is typically a day of stress and busyness. In contrast, the first day of the project is typically characterized by little action. This effect is similar to the "term paper syndrome" well familiar to most students. It reflects human optimism and overconfidence in the ability to complete work in the future. At the risk of stating the obvious—a day at the beginning of the project is equally long as a day at the end of the project—why do little or no work on the former and jam all the work into the latter?

- *Manage the project scope:* One of the most common causes of delay in projects is that the amount of work that is part of the project changes over the course of the project. Features are added and engineering change orders requested. If such changes occur late in the project, they often cause significant project delays and budget overruns for relatively little increased quality. For this reason, it is advisable to finalize the scope of the project early on.

- *Crash activities:* Often, an increase in spending allows for a faster completion time of a project. Contractors are willing to work overtime for a premium, and expensive equipment might help further shorten activity duration. However, the reverse is not always true. Projects that take excessively long are not necessarily cheaper. Because typically there are some fixed costs associated with a project, a project that drags on forever might actually be also very expensive.

- *Overlap critical path activities:* A central assumption underlying the dependency matrix shown in Table 5.2 has been that an activity that is dependent on an information-providing activity needs to wait until that activity is completed. However, it is often possible to allow the dependent activity to start early, relying on preliminary information from the information-providing activity. For example, it seems plausible that the activity "Building design" should be completed before starting the activity "Building construction." However, does this imply that all of the design has to be completed? Or, maybe, would it be possible to begin digging the foundation of the building while the designers are still finalizing the shape of the windows? By identifying the exact dependencies among activities, it is often possible to provide the dependent activity with a head start.

5.8 Literature/ Further Reading

Loch et al. (2006) provide a comprehensive framework of managing projects with uncertainty. The authors use many illustrative examples and target experienced project managers as their audience.

Terwiesch and Ulrich (2009) deal with far-horizon innovation projects as well as multiple challenges associated with financial evaluations of innovation projects.

Ulrich and Eppinger (2011) is the classic textbook for product development and includes an easy-to-follow introductory chapter on project management and project organization.

5.9 Practice Problems

Q5.1*   **(Venture Fair)** In order to participate at a venture fair, Team TerraZ is preparing a project plan for their new-product offering. The team plans to spend 3 days on ideation. Once ideation is complete, the team aims to interview 20 potential customers (6 days) and to engage in a careful analysis of competing products (12 days). Following the customer interviews, the team expects to spend 10 days on careful user observation and 4 days on sending out e-mail surveys. These two activities are independent from each other, but both require that the interviews be completed. With the input from the customer observation and the e-mail surveys, the team then plans to spend 5 days on putting together the target specifications for the product. This activity also requires the analysis of competing products to be complete.

After the target specifications, the team aims to create a product design, which will take 10 days. With the product design complete, they plan to get price quotes (6 days) and build a prototype (4 days) that they then want to test out with some customers (5 days). Once the prototype has been tested and the price quotes are in, they can put together their information material for the venture fair (3 days).

a.   Create a dependency matrix for the activities described, and build a project graph.

b.   Find the critical path. What is the latest time the team can start working, assuming the venture fair is scheduled for April 18?

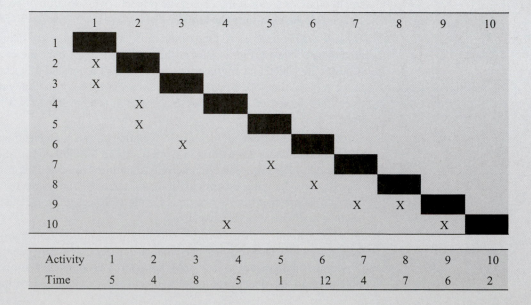

	1	2	3	4	5	6	7	8	9	10
1	■									
2	X	■								
3	X		■							
4		X		■						
5		X			■					
6			X			■				
7					X		■			
8						X		■		
9							X	X	■	
10				X					X	■

Activity	1	2	3	4	5	6	7	8	9	10
Time	5	4	8	5	1	12	4	7	6	2

Q5.2   **(10 Activities)** Consider the dependency matrix and the activity durations provided above.

    a. Build a project graph, visually depicting the evolution of this project.

    b. Find the critical path. What is the earliest time that the project can be completed?

    c. For each activity, compute the late start, the late completion, and the slack time.

Q5.3**   **(Graduation Party)** Thierry, Ute, and Vishal are getting ready for their last period in the MBA program. Following the final exams, they intend to throw a big party with many of their friends from back home. Presently, they have identified the following set of activities that need to be completed. They decide to not spend any work on preparing the party until all final exams are over. Moreover, they aim to spend a 3-day beach vacation as early as possible, but not before all party planning activities are completed.

On June 10, they will enter the final exam week, which will take 5 days. They then want to arrange for live music (which will take 5 days), evaluate a number of potential party sites (6 days), and prepare a guest list, which includes inviting their friends and receiving the RSVPs (7 days). They want to visit their two most promising party sites, which they expect to take 4 days. However, this can only be done once they have completed the list of party sites. Once they have finished the guest list and received the RSVPs, they want to book hotel rooms for their friends and create a customized T-shirt with their names on it as well as the name of the guest. Hotel room reservation (3 days) and T-shirt creation (6 days) are independent from each other, but both of them require the guest list to be complete. Once they have picked the party site, they want to have a meeting on site with an event planner, which they expect to take 4 days. And then, once all work is completed, they plan to take off to the beach.

    a. Create a dependency matrix for the activities described.

    b. Build a project graph, visually depicting the evolution of this project.

    c. Find the critical path. What is the earliest time that the three can go to the beach?

    d. For each activity, compute the late start, the late completion, and the slack time.

Q5.4   **(Three Activities with Uncertainty)** A small project consists of three activities: A, B, and C. To start activity C, both activities A and B need to be complete. Activity A takes 3 days with a probability of 50 percent and 5 days with a probability of 50 percent, and so does Activity B. Activity C takes 1 day. What is the expected completion time of the project?

You can view a video of how problems marked with a ** are solved by going on www. cachon-terwiesch.net and follow the links under 'Solved Practice Problems'

Chapter

6

The Link between Operations and Finance

To the reader new to the area of operations management, the previous chapters might have appeared more technical than expected.[1] After all, most of the performance measures we used were concepts such as balancing the line to increase labor utilization, reducing inventories, improving flow time, and so on. But WHY do we have to worry about these measures? Do they really matter to our job? Or, asked differently, what is the objective of all this?

The objective of most incorporated organizations is to create economic value. Those who have money invested in the enterprise want to see a return on their money—a return that exceeds the return that they would get if they invested their money differently, for example, in a bond, a savings account, or a competing organization. Economic value is created whenever the return on invested capital (ROIC) in a corporation exceeds the cost of capital (the weighted average cost of capital, WACC, is an important concept from the field of corporate finance). This is visible in the basic value equation:

$$\text{Economic value created } = \text{ Invested capital} \times (\text{ROIC} - \text{WACC})$$

Since the cost of capital cannot be changed easily in the short term, our focus here is on the return on invested capital. More details about corporate valuation can be found in Koller, Goedhart, and Wessels (2005).

In this chapter, we show the link between the operational variables we have discussed previously (and that are discussed throughout this book) and ROIC. This is an ambitious task. In many organizations, not to mention business school courses, the topics of operations management and corporate finance are rather remote from each other.

Given this fundamental disconnect, managers and consultants often struggle with questions such as "What performance measures should we track?"; "How do operational performance measures impact the bottom line performance?"; or "How do we go about improving processes to achieve various operational performance improvements, including cost savings, lead-time reduction, or increases in product variety?"

[1] The authors thank Stephen Doig and Taylor Randall for their input to this chapter. They are especially grateful to Paul Downs for providing them with detailed data about his company.

The objective of this chapter is to provide readers with a set of tools that support them in analyzing the operational performance of a company and to guide them in increasing the overall value of the firm by improving its operations. We will do this in three steps. First, we introduce the ROIC tree, also known as the KPI tree (KPI stands for key performance indicators). Second, we show how to value operational improvement opportunities, that is, predicting by how much the ROIC improves if we improve our process along some of the operational measures defined elsewhere in the book. Third, we provide examples of KPI trees and look at how we can read financial statements to get a sense of the operational performance of a firm. The first two steps will be illustrated using the case of a small Pennsylvania furniture company, Paul Downs Cabinetmakers.

6.1 Paul Downs Cabinetmakers

Paul Downs started making furniture in 1986 in a small shop in Manayunk, Pennsylvania. (Manayunk, pronounced "Man-ee-yunk," is a hip neighborhood in Philadelphia.) Over the years, his business outgrew four shops and is now operating in a 33,000-square-foot facility in Bridgeport, Pennsylvania. The company focuses on high-end, residential furniture. Figure 6.1(a) shows one of their most popular dining table models.

Paul Downs' production facility includes machines and other wood-processing equipment valued at about $450,000. There is an annual depreciation associated with the machines (reflecting the duration of their useful life) of $80,000. Rents for the showroom and the factory amount to roughly $150,000 per year. Other indirect costs for the company are about $100,000 per year for marketing related expenses, $180,000 for management and administration, and $60,000 for a highly skilled worker in charge of finishing furniture and conducting a quality inspection.

The company has two major types of inventory. There is about $20,000 tied up in raw materials. This is wood that is purchased from suppliers in large order quantities (see Chapter 7 for further details on order quantities). When purchasing wood, Paul Downs needs to pay his suppliers roughly one month in advance of receiving the shipment. There is also about $50,000 of work-in-process inventory. This corresponds to furniture that is in the process of being completed.

Furniture production, especially in the high-end segment, is a very manual process and requires a highly skilled workforce. Paul employs 12 cabinetmakers (see Figure 6.1(b)), many of whom have been with his company for more than a decade. The cabinetmakers

FIGURE 6.1 **Finished Product and Work in Progress from Paul Downs' Production Facility**

Source: Paul Downs

(a)   (b)

work about 220 days in a year (on average about 8 hours per day). The typical wage rate for a cabinetmaker is $20 per hour.

To finish a typical piece of furniture, a worker needs about 40 hours. This corresponds to our previous concept of an processing time. The work is organized in work cells. Instead of having the cabinetmakers specialize in one aspect of furniture making (e.g., cutting, sanding, or polishing), a cabinetmaker handles a job from beginning to end. Of their overall number of hours worked, cabinetmakers spend about 15 percent of their time building fixtures and setting up machines (more on setup times in the Chapter 7). Given the modern production equipment, a good part of this includes programming computer-controlled machines. Since the cabinetmakers are organized in work cells, it would be too expensive to equip each cell with all wood-working equipment; instead, the cabinetmakers share the most expensive tools. This leads to an occasional delay if multiple cabinetmakers need access to the same unit of equipment at the same time. Consequently, cabinetmakers spend about 10 percent of their time waiting for a particular resource to become available.

From a design perspective, a typical piece of furniture requires about 30 kg of wood. In addition to this wood, about 25 percent additional wood is needed to account for scrap losses, primarily in the cutting steps of a job. Wood costs about $10 per kg.

Purchasing high-end furniture is not cheap—customers pay about $3,000 for a dining table like the one shown in Figure 6.1(a). Typically, customers are expected to pay 50 percent of the price as a down payment. They then receive their furniture about three months later. This delay reflects the custom nature of the end product as well as the fact that Paul Downs's facility at the moment is fully utilized, that is, there is more demand than what can be processed by the factory.

6.2   Building an ROIC Tree

As the owner of the firm, Paul Downs is primarily interested in creating economic value and thus in increasing the ROIC of his firm. The problem with respect to increasing ROIC is that ROIC, in and of itself, is not a lever that is under direct managerial control. It can be computed at the end of a quarter or a year, but while a manager might go to work in the morning thinking, "Today, I will increase my ROIC by 5 percent," it is not at all clear how to achieve that objective. The idea behind building an ROIC tree is to cascade the high-level financial metric into its key operational ingredients, thereby revealing the levers a manager can use to improve ROIC. To use a metaphor from the sciences, to understand how a biological cell works, we need to explain the behavior of its component molecules.

Let's begin by writing down our overall goal, the ROIC:

$$\text{ROIC} = \frac{\text{Return}}{\text{Invested capital}}$$

Now, let's do a simple algebraic manipulation and write

$$\text{ROIC} = \frac{\text{Return}}{\text{Invested capital}} = \frac{\text{Return}}{\text{Revenue}} \times \frac{\text{Revenue}}{\text{Invested capital}}$$

The first ratio, Return/Revenue, is the company's margin. The second ratio, Revenue/Invested capital, is called the company's capital turns. Note that it resembles the measure of inventory turns that we introduced in Chapter 2. This simple, though elegant, way of decomposing the ROIC into margin and asset turns is often referred to as the DuPont model. DuPont was among the pioneers introducing financial performance measures to its business units.

Companies and industries differ widely with respect to how they achieve a specific ROIC. Some industries are asset-intensive: the capital turns are low, but their margins are significant. Others require little capital. Such industries are typically easier to enter for new competitors, leading to relatively thin margins.

Now, back to Paul Downs. As advisors to Paul, we can now help him improve his business by saying: "Paul, to improve your ROIC, you need to either increase your margin or turn your assets faster . . ." It is unlikely that this advice would ensure our future career as management consultants.

Nevertheless, let's keep pushing the same logic further and now decompose margin and asset turns into their drivers. Consider margin first. Based on standard accounting logic, we can write the Return (profits) of the firm as

$$\text{Return} = \text{Revenue} - \text{Fixed costs} - \text{Production volume} \times \text{Variable costs}$$

Because this is not an accounting book, and to be consistent with our definitions throughout the book, let us use "Flow rate" instead of "Production volume." Given the above equation, and keeping in mind that Revenue = Flow rate × Price, we can rewrite the previous equation by dividing both sides by Revenue, which yields

$$\frac{\text{Return}}{\text{Revenue}} = \frac{\text{Revenue}}{\text{Revenue}} - \frac{\text{Fixed costs}}{\text{Revenue}} - \frac{\text{Flow rate} \times \text{Variable costs}}{\text{Revenue}}$$

$$= 1 - \frac{\text{Fixed costs}}{\text{Flow rate} \times \text{Price}} - \frac{\text{Flow rate} \times \text{Variable costs}}{\text{Flow rate} \times \text{Price}}$$

$$= 1 - \frac{\text{Fixed costs}}{\text{Flow rate} \times \text{Price}} - \frac{\text{Variable costs}}{\text{Price}}$$

Using a similar logic as we used for margin, we can write asset turns as

$$\frac{\text{Revenue}}{\text{Invested capital}} = \frac{\text{Flow rate} \times \text{Price}}{\text{Invested capital}}$$

Our overall ROIC equation can now be written as

$$\text{ROIC} = \left[1 - \frac{\text{Fixed costs}}{\text{Flow rate} \times \text{Price}} - \frac{\text{Variable costs}}{\text{Price}} \right] \times \frac{\text{Flow rate} \times \text{Price}}{\text{Invested capital}}$$

Because ultimately, we want to be able to express the ROIC as a function of its atomic ingredients such as wage rates, processing times, idle times, and so forth, we need to continue this process further. To avoid an explosion of mathematical equations, we prefer to write them in tree forms (see Figure 6.2).

Now, consider the four variables that we discovered as drivers of margins in greater detail: Flow rate, Fixed costs, Variable costs, and Price.

To focus our analysis on the operations aspects of this case, we assume Price has already been established—in other words, we do not consider Price to be one of our potential levers. Of course, we could take our operations-focused analysis and modify it appropriately to conduct a similar marketing-focused analysis that concentrates on the pricing decision. In general though, we caution the reader not to "build a machine with too many moving parts"—especially at the start of a project, looking at an operation in detail, one simply needs to make some assumptions. Otherwise, one runs the risk of getting lost in the complexity.

Next, consider the variable costs. In our example, the variable costs are driven primarily by the consumption of wood. In some cases, one also could consider the cost of labor as a variable cost (especially if workers get paid part of their salary on a piece-rate basis).

FIGURE 6.2
ROIC Tree

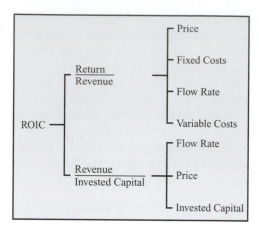

Yet, in our case, the number of cabinetmakers, as well as their hourly wages, is given and thus constitutes a fixed cost. Focusing on wood expenses, we can write the variable costs of a piece of furniture as

$$\text{Variable cost} = \text{Price of wood} \times \text{Wood per table}$$
$$= \text{Price of wood} \times (\text{Wood in final table} + \text{Cutting loss})$$

Now, let us turn our attention to Flow rate. Recall from our earlier definition that

$$\text{Flow rate} = \text{Min}\{\text{Demand, Process capacity}\}$$

Because we assume that there is enough demand at the moment, Flow rate is determined by Process capacity. But what determines capacity in this case? The main constraint on this operation is the work of the cabinetmakers. The number of units of furniture that we can produce per year depends on

- The number of available worker hours, which is determined by the number of cabinetmakers multiplied by the hours each cabinetmaker works per year.
- The time a worker needs for a piece of furniture, which is determined by the amount of time it takes a cabinetmaker to wait for a machine to become available, the time to set up the machine, and the actual time to do the work.

Figure 6.3 summarizes these calculations in tree format. The figure also shows how we can make the tree more informative by adding the corresponding mathematical symbols into it.

FIGURE 6.3
The Drivers of Process Capacity

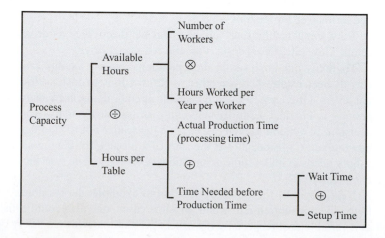

FIGURE 6.4
ROIC Tree for
Fixed Costs

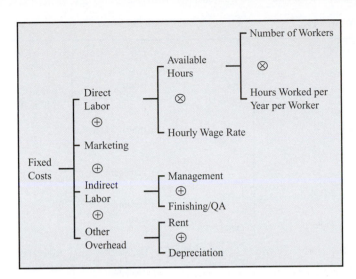

Finally, let us consider the Fixed costs. They include expenses for marketing, the labor expenses for overhead (inspection, administration), rent, depreciation, and the cost of the workforce. Figure 6.4 summarizes the main components.

It should be noted that one should be very careful how to measure depreciation. It is important to distinguish between the loss of value of a machine (e.g., a reduction in its useful life) and the depreciation as it is calculated for tax purposes. Following the standard practice of valuation and corporate finance, our emphasis is on the former view of depreciation. Note further that we do not include taxes in our analysis here (i.e., we compute the pre-tax ROIC).

Combining our previous work, we now can extend Figure 6.2 to a more complete picture of ROIC drivers as shown in Figure 6.5. Note that, based on this extended tree, we now have achieved an important part of our objective for this chapter—we have created a direct linkage between the ROIC and "down-to-earth" operational variables such as idle time, setup time, processing time, and flow rate.

To complete our ROIC tree, we now need to turn to the asset-turn branch of the tree and explore it to the same level of detail as we have explored the margin branch. Because we can take the Flow rate (and the Price) from our previous analysis, what is left to be done is a refined analysis of the invested capital. Capital is invested in plant, property, and equipment (PP&E) as well as in three forms of working capital:

- Inventory includes the inventory of raw materials (wood) as well as all work-in-process inventory (WIP), that is, a pile of semi-finished pieces of furniture.

- Prepayments to suppliers include money that we have sent to our suppliers but for which we have not received the associated shipment of raw materials.

- Any money we are waiting to receive from our customers for products that we have already shipped to them. While in most businesses this part of the balance sheet requires an investment in capital, the situation, in our case, is much more favorable. As customers pay us a down payment well in advance of receiving their furniture, this line item actually corresponds to an inexpensive form of cash. For this reason, we should label this item "unearned revenues" so as not to upset any of the accountants in our readership.

Figure 6.6 summarizes the components in invested capital in tree format. When we compute the amount of money that we need to invest in accounts payable, we first need to find out how much money we spend on wood purchasing every year. Because we have to pay our supplier one month in advance, at any given point, we have one-twelfth of the yearly payment tied up as capital. A similar logic applies to the unearned revenues.

FIGURE 6.5 **Expanded ROIC Tree**

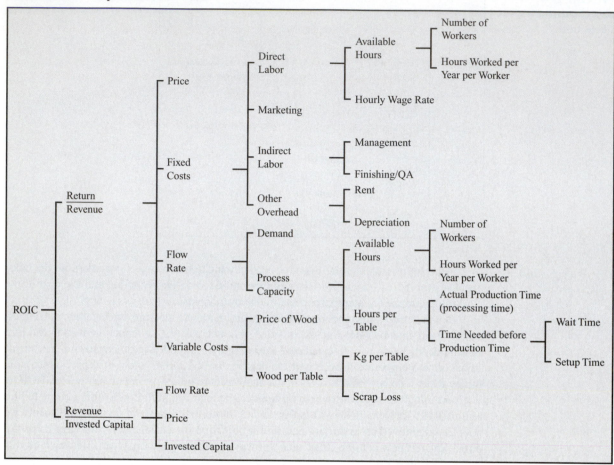

This completes the development of the ROIC tree. We now have expressed our key financial performance measure, ROIC, as a function of detailed operational variables. We have explained the behavior of the cell by looking at its molecules and ultimately at its atoms.

FIGURE 6.6
ROIC Tree for
Invested Capital

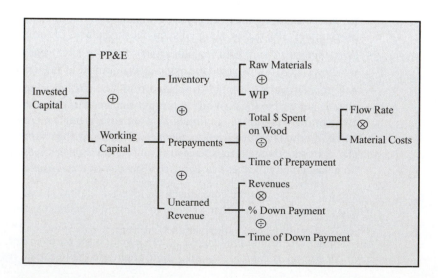

6.3　Valuing Operational Improvements

Understanding the link between processing times, wage rates, and other operational variables, and ROIC is certainly a useful motivation to illustrate that these variables are worthwhile studying—they are a nice teaser in a book chapter. But are they also useful in practice? What is the benefit of all this work?

The key benefit of the calculations defined above is that we can now assign a value tag to each of the operational levers that we potentially might pull to improve our operations. As the owner, manager, or consultant of the company, one can do many things to improve the ROIC such as

- Cut wages.
- Change the design so that the work required to make a piece of furniture is reduced.
- Reduce the time workers spend waiting for a machine.
- Reduce the setup times.
- Change the payment terms with the supplier, and so on.

But which of these actions are worth pursuing? All of them are likely to come along with some cost, and at the very minimum they will require management time and attention. So, which ones pay back these costs? Or, put differently, where is the juice worth the squeeze?

We thus want to find out how a change in one of the operational variables leads to a change in ROIC. This can require a lot of tedious calculations, so it is best to conduct this analysis using Excel. Figure 6.7 shows our full tree in spreadsheet format. It also populates the tree with numbers, creating a complete picture of the operations of the furniture we make.

Note that one variable might occur at multiple locations in such a spreadsheet model. Consider, for example, the variable Flow Rate in our furniture example. Flow rate shows up in the revenue part of the tree. It also shows up as part of the material costs. And, finally, it also shows up in the working capital calculation as downpayments depend on revenue (and thus flow rate) as well as material costs depend on flow rate. Thus, when building the spread sheet, it is important to keep all these usages of one variables connected, i.e., driven by the same cell. Put differently, an increase in flow rate is not just giving us more revenues. It also creates more material costs, it adds working capital by increasing the downpayments, and it reduces our working capital by adding to the prepaid expenses

Once we are equipped with such a spreadsheet model, we can easily find the impact of an operational variable by changing the corresponding cell and observing the change in the cell corresponding to the ROIC.

Before we do this, let's develop some intuition. What will happen if we reduce the setup times by five percentage points (from 15 percent to 10 percent)? Of course, shorter setup times are a good thing and we expect the ROIC to improve. Put differently, if somebody offered us to reduce setup times for free, we would happily take him or her up on the offer.

The crucial question is thus: by how much will the ROIC improve? What will happen to the root of our tree (ROIC) if we wiggle it at one of its leaves (setup time)? Will the ROIC change by 1 percent? More? Or less?

It is hard to answer such a question based on intuition. When asked to make a guess without out a formal analytical model, most people we know argue along the following line: "There are many variables that influence ROIC. So, changing one of them by five percentage points will have an effect substantially smaller than a five-percentage-point ROIC improvement." This logic is in line with the tree metaphor: if you wiggle a tree at any one of its leaves, you do not expect big movements at its roots.

Table 6.1 shows that this argument does not hold. In fact, this guess is well off the mark. A five-percentage-point change in setup times leads in our example to an 18.8-percentage-point improvement in ROIC (i.e., it raises ROIC from the base case of 12.3 percent to 31.1 percent).

FIGURE 6.7 **ROIC Tree in Excel**

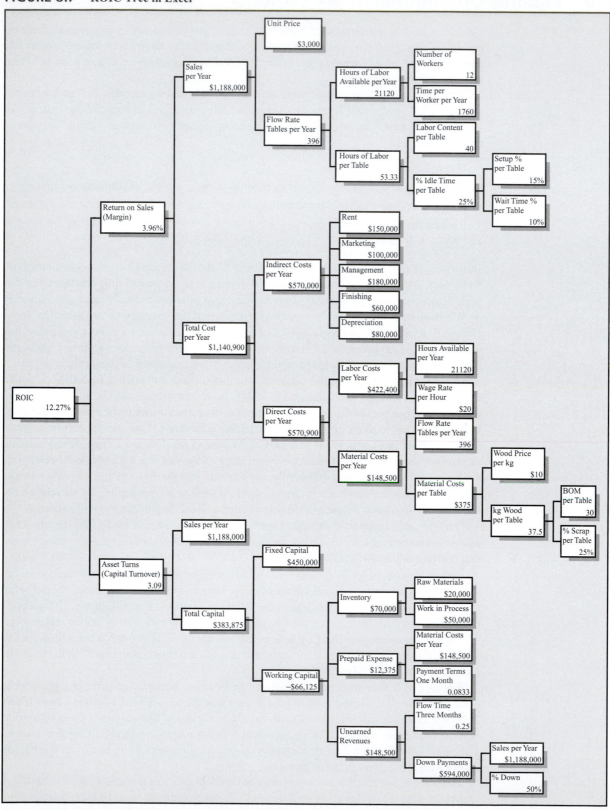

TABLE 6.1 ROIC after the Improvement

Scenario	Base Case	$1/hr Lower Wages	5 Percent Shorter Setups	$10k per Year Lower Rent	2 hr/Table Lower Labor Content	5 Percent Lower Scrap Rate
ROIC [%]	12.3	17.7	31.1	14.8	27.0	13.8

What looked like a small and, at least from a financial perspective, unimportant variable turns out to be a key driver of financial performance. When an operational variable behaves this way, we refer to it as an operational value driver.

A couple of observations are helpful to better understand the role of setup times as an operational value driver.

- If we take a second look at our ROIC tree (see Figure 6.7), we see that setup times drive ROIC in multiple ways. Setup time is a driver of margins, the upper branch of the tree, as shorter setups allow us to produce more and hence to spread out the fixed costs over more units. Moreover, setup times also impact asset turns—we get more revenues out of the same capital investment because setup times influence sales-per-year, which is a component of asset turns.

- This analysis is based on the assumption that there exists enough demand to support a 26-unit increase in sales (the new flow rate would be 422). If the company had been constrained by demand, it is easy to see that shorter setup times would have (marginally) improved ROIC only if we could have used our productivity improvement to reduce the number of cabinetmakers.

- We have considered a one-third reduction in setup times (from 15 percent to 10 percent). As we will discuss in Chapter 7, such a reduction in setup times is indeed feasible and plausible.

A second look at Table 6.1 reveals that process improvements that yield a higher flow rate (lower setup times and lower labor content) are having the biggest impact on ROIC. Figure 6.8 illustrates this logic.

Independent of flow rate, we have to pay $992,400 per year for fixed costs, including the salaries for the cabinetmakers as well as the other items discussed in Figure 6.4. Once these fixed costs are covered (i.e., we exceed the break-even volume), every additional unit of flow rate leads to a $2,625 ($3,000 price minus $375 for wood consumption) increase in profit. As can be seen by the shaded area in Figure 6.8, the small increase in flow rate

FIGURE 6.8
Fixed Costs versus Variable Costs

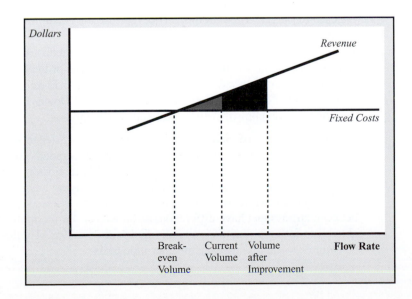

Exhibit 6.1

HOW TO CREATE AN ROIC TREE

1. Start with the objective (ROIC) on one side of the tree.
2. Decompose a variable into its components.

   - Example: ROIC = Income/Invested Capital
   - Relationships of variables can be a + b, a − b, a/b, or a × b.

3. Decide which branches of the tree have an impact and are important.

   - What are the main cost drivers (80/20 rule)?
   - What are the strategic levers of the company?
   - Which inputs are most likely to change?

4. Expand important branches (return to step 2).
5. End with measures that can be tied to operational strategy.
6. Populate the tree with actual numbers.
7. Reflect on the tree to see if it makes sense.

   - Benchmark performance.
   - Perform sensitivity analysis.

leads to a big increase in profits. This logic is true for all high fixed-cost operations such as hotels, airlines, and many other services. Chapter 16 will discuss this effect further.

Exhibit 6.1 summarizes the key steps of building an ROIC tree and evaluating potential operational improvements. Such a tree is a powerful starting point for consultants entering a new engagement looking at their client's operations, for a general manager who wants to have a comprehensive understanding of what drives value in his/her business, and for private equity investors that intend to quickly increase the value of a firm by fixing parts of its operation.

6.4 Analyzing Operations Based on Financial Data

In the previous section, we have looked at a relatively small business and built an ROIC tree that was grounded in a detailed understanding of the company's operations. Alternatively, we can start the analysis based on publicly available data (most often, this would be the case for larger firms). In this section, we use the example of the airline industry to illustrate the usefulness of the ROIC tree method.

The first step in our analysis is to identify firms in an industry that have demonstrated and sustained superior financial performance. In the case of the U.S. airline industry, the prime candidate for a success story is clearly Southwest Airlines.

Second, we build an ROIC tree as we did in the Paul Downs case. When analyzing an airline, the following bits of airline vocabulary are helpful:

- Instead of thinking of an airline selling tickets, it is easier to think of an airline selling *revenue passenger miles* (RPMs). An RPM corresponds to transporting a paying customer for one mile. A flight from Philadelphia to Boston, for example, with 200 passengers would correspond to 447 miles × 200 paying passengers = 89,400 RPMs. By focusing on RPM, we avoid some of the problems associated with comparisons between airlines that have different route structures. Furthermore, as we will see, variable costs for an airline are generally tied to the number of miles flown, so it is also convenient to express revenue on a per-mile basis.

- The capacity of an airline is determined by the number and the sizes of its aircrafts. This leads to a measure known as the *available seat miles* (ASMs). One ASM corresponds to one airline seat (with or without a passenger in it) flying for one mile.
- Airlines only make money if they can turn their ASMs into RPMs: a seat with a paying customer is good; an empty seat is not. The ratio RPM/ASM is called the *load factor*—it strongly resembles our definition of utilization as it looks at how many revenue passenger miles the airline creates relative to how much it could create if every seat were filled. Clearly, the load factor must always be less than one—other than small infants sitting on a parent's lap, airlines do not allow two paying customers to occupy the same seat.

Figure 6.9 summarizes a simplified version of an ROIC tree for an airline. There exist, of course, many more levels of details that could be analyzed, including aspects of fleet age and composition, size of flight crews, the percentage of flying time of an aircraft, and so on. But since we are growing this tree from the left to the right, any additional level of detail could be simply tagged on to our analysis in Figure 6.9.

FIGURE 6.9
ROIC Tree for a Generic Airline
(Profit corresponds to pretax income)

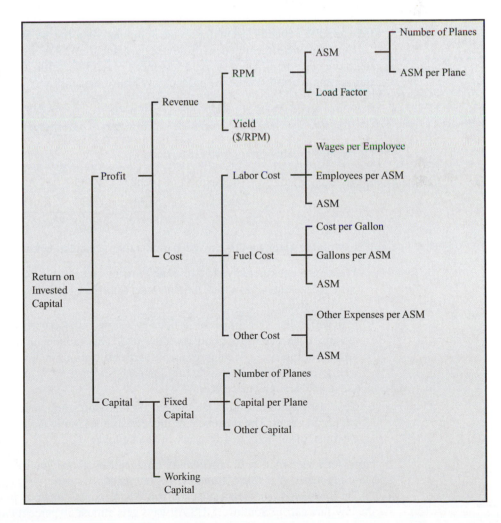

As a third step, we want to explore why the financially high-performing firm is doing better than its peers. A good diagnostic tool toward this end is the following method we call productivity ratios. We can write productivity as

$$\text{Productivity} = \frac{\text{Revenue}}{\text{Cost}}$$

and we can write labor productivity as

$$\text{Labor productivity} = \frac{\text{Revenue}}{\text{Labor cost}}$$

and see that Southwest's labor is substantially more productive than US Airways' labor. The Southwest labor productivity ratio is 3.31, which is almost 40 percent higher than the one for US Airways. The following calculations are illustrated with data from the year 2000. We use this old data for two reasons. First, from 1998 to 2000, Southwest managed to double its market capitalization—a financial performance that none of its competitors even came close to. So, clearly, in the eyes of Wall Street, Southwest did something right. Second, following the terrorist attacks of September 2001, the airline industry entered a long period of bankruptcies and restructuring processes, which makes reading the financial statements during these periods somewhat more complicated. At the end of the chapter, we will provide additional data for the more recent years.

But where does the productivity advantage come from? Are Southwest employees serving more customers? Do they make less money? From the ratio alone, we cannot tell. For this reason, we will rewrite the productivity measure as follows:

$$\text{Productivity} = \frac{\text{Revenue}}{\text{Cost}} = \frac{\text{Revenue}}{\text{Flow rate}} \times \frac{\text{Flow rate}}{\text{Resource}} \times \frac{\text{Resource}}{\text{Cost}}$$

Or, applied to labor productivity in airlines:

$$\text{Labor productivity} = \frac{\text{Revenue}}{\text{Labor cost}} = \underbrace{\frac{\text{Revenue}}{\text{RPM}}}_{\text{Yield}} \times \underbrace{\frac{\text{RPM}}{\text{ASM}} \times \frac{\text{ASM}}{\text{Employees}}}_{\text{Efficiency}} \times \underbrace{\frac{\text{Employees}}{\text{Labor costs}}}_{\text{Cost}}$$

It is helpful to break up this expanded productivity calculation into three pieces:

- Yields: the operational yield (Revenue/Flow rate) measures how much money the firm can squeeze out of its output, the flow rate. This measure is largely driven by the firm's pricing power.
- Efficiency: the transformation efficiency (Flow rate/Resource) measures how many resources we need to support the flow rate. This number is determined by how we utilize our resources. It captures the resource utilization (in our case, the load factor) as well as the inherent processing times at each resource (how many available seat miles can a single employee serve?).
- Cost: the cost of resources (Resource/Cost) measures how much of a resource we can get per $1 spent. The reciprocal of this measure is simply the cost of that resource, for example, the average yearly salary of an employee.

Now, let's see what these productivity ratios tell us about Southwest's source of higher labor productivity. Table 6.2 summarizes our results.

The results of our diagnostics confirm US Airways' superior pricing power. Unlike the low-fare carrier Southwest, US Airways gets almost 50 percent more money for every

TABLE 6.2 **Comparison between US Airways and Southwest**

Airline	Operational Yield [$/RPM]	Load Factor [%]	ASM per Employee	Number of Employees/Million US$ of Labor Costs	Overall Labor Productivity
US Airways	0.197	0.70	0.37	47.35	2.43
Southwest	0.135	0.69	0.53	67.01	3.31

Note: The 47.35 in the second column from the right can also be expressed as US Airways' average wage: $1,000,000/47.35 = $21,119 is the quarterly wage rate for an employee.

passenger mile. Interestingly, both firms operate at roughly the same load factor. However, Southwest (more than!) offsets its pricing disadvantage with the last two ratios:

- A Southwest employee is able to support 50 percent more ASMs compared to a US Airways employee (0.53 as opposed to 0.37)
- While being paid about a 50 percent lower salary (for the same money you pay 47 US Airways employees, you can hire 67 Southwest employees). Note that this number has changed substantially since 2001. In fact, now, Southwest employees earn substantially higher wages than their counterparts at US Airways—wages have moved in the direction of productivity differences.

As a fourth and final step of our analysis, we can now look at how much money US Airways would save if it could imitate one or several of the productivity ratios from Southwest. For example, we can ask the following two questions:

- How much money would US Airways save if it could support as many ASMs with an employee as Southwest does?
- How much money would US Airways save if it paid Southwest wages?

Figure 6.10 summarizes the cost-saving opportunities. Consider the potential savings that US Airways would obtain from paying its employees Southwest wages first. US

FIGURE 6.10
Potential US Airways Cost Savings

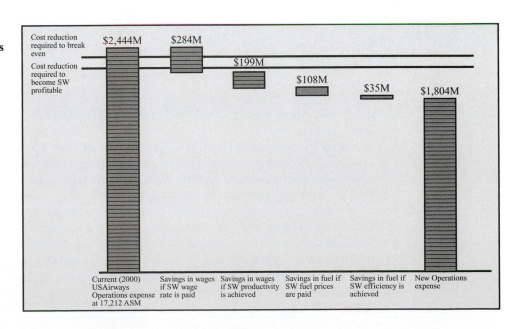

Airways has 45,833 employees on its payroll. The average salary was $21,120 per quarter (see also Table 6.2) compared to $14,922 for the average Southwest employee. If we paid US Airways employees Southwest wages, we would hence save

$$45,833 \times (\$21,120 - \$14,922) = \$284,072,934$$

Next, consider the savings potential if we could have a US Airways employee achieve the same level of productivity as a Southwest employee. It takes US Airways 45,833 employees to service 17,212 ASM, translating to 17,212/45,833 = 0.37 ASM per employee. As we saw in Table 6.2, Southwest is able to service 0.53 ASM per employee. So,

$$17,212 \text{ ASM}/(0.53 \text{ ASM/employee}) = 32,475 \text{ employees}$$

is the number of workers that US Airways would need if it achieved Southwest's labor productivity. This leads to a possible head-count reduction of 13,358 employees (45,833 − 32,475). Given the average US Airways salary of $21,120 per quarter, this corresponds to a quarterly savings opportunity of

$$\$21,120 \text{ per employee} \times 13,358 \text{ employees} = \$282,120,960$$

Note that the savings we would obtain from such an increase in productivity are not savings "on top of" the savings potential reflecting an adjustment of US Airways wages to the Southwest level. In other words, the total (combined) savings from the adjustment in labor cost and the increase in productivity would not be $284,072,934 + $282,120,960. The reason for this is simply that once we have cut salaries, the savings that we get from reducing the number of workers to reflect productivity gains are smaller (they would be the new, lower salary of $14,922 per employee per quarter instead of the higher salary of $21,120).

So, if we want to compute the additional savings we obtain from a productivity increase assuming that the US Airways wages already have been adjusted to the Southwest level, we compute

$$\$14,922 \text{ per employee} \times 13,358 \text{ employees} = \$199,328,076$$

Figure 6.10 also shows and analyzes another productivity advantage of Southwest—the company's ability to procure cheap jet fuel (which is a result of clever—or lucky—investments in fuel hedges).

US Airways would save $108M if it could purchase jet fuel at Southwest's purchasing conditions. And if, on top of it, it could match Southwest's fuel efficiency, it would save another $35M.

Unlike the analysis that we did in the Paul Downs case, the approach summarized in Figure 6.10 is much more of a top-down analysis. Before entering the details of the operations (what does Southwest do differently that their labor can support more ASMs), we start out our analysis by broadly exploring the size of various opportunities.

In general, the top-down approach is most useful when analyzing competing organizations or when there simply are limited data available about operational details, thus, when the analysis happens from "the outside in." In contrast, it should be emphasized that for the management within an operation, the level of granularity that we have outlined in Figure 6.10 is vastly insufficient. Sizing the opportunity is only the first step; the real challenge then is to cascade the labor productivity disadvantage further, all the way into the

FIGURE 6.11
The Airline Industry in 2010

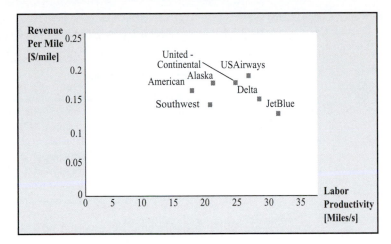

minutes it takes to board an airplane, the durations of the worker breaks, the number of employees at a gate, and so on.

As far as the airline industry is concerned, it has been interesting to notice what has happened between 2000 and 2006. In 2000, the average US Airways salary was 41 percent higher than that of the average Southwest employee. By 2006, Southwest salaries had caught up and even exceeded the 2000 salaries of US Airways. US Airways salaries, on the other hand, had decreased to the 2000 level of Southwest! While salaries changed dramatically, the productivity advantage of Southwest did not. In fact, in 2006, Southwest continued to have a 50 percent higher labor productivity than US Airways.

By 2010, the industry had changed even further, as is illustrated in Figure 6.11. On the vertical dimension, the graph shows the amount of money the average passenger was paying for one mile of air travel on the various carriers. This amount is expressed relative to the industry average. On the horizontal dimension, we show how many passenger miles an airline can generate with one dollar of labor cost, again, relative to the industry average. All data is based on FY2010. Note that the Southwest advantage from 10 years prior has disappeared. While each employee, on average, served more passengers compared to other airlines, Southwest employees were paid substantially above industry average (see preceding discussion), leading to an overall labor productivity that is below industry average. However, because of lower fuel costs/higher fuel efficiency as well as lower other expenses (such as landing fees, commissions, sales and marketing expenses), Southwest still turned substantial profits, despite paying its employees well. As we discuss in Chapter 19, a new player managed to disrupt the industry, JetBlue became the "new Southwest."

6.5 Summary

In this chapter, we have provided a link between the operations of a company and its financial performance. This link can be studied at the micro level, as we have done in the Paul Downs case, or it can be done starting with the financial statements, as we have done in the airline case. Either way, operational variables are key drivers of a company's financial performance. Value creation takes place in the operations of a company and so, to increase the economic value of a company, a detailed analysis of operations is a must.

6.6 Further Reading

Koller, Goedhart, and Wessels (2005) is an excellent book on topics related to valuation and corporate finance. Compared to most other finance books, it is very hands-on and does not shy away from the operational details of business.

Cannon, Randall, and Terwiesch (2007) study the empirical relationship between operational variables and future financial performance in the airline industry.

6.7 Practice Problems

Q6.1*   **(Crazy Cab)** Crazy Cab is a small taxi cab company operating in a large metropolitan area. The company operates 20 cabs. Each cab is worth about $20k. The metropolitan area also requires that each cab carry a medallion (a type of license). Medallions are currently traded at $50k. Cab drivers make $8 per hour and are available for every time of the day. The average cab is used for 40 trips per day. The average trip is three miles in length. Passengers have to pay $2 as a fixed fee and $2 per mile they are transported. Fuel and other costs, such as maintenance, are $0.20 per mile. The cab drives about 40 percent of the distance without a paying passenger in it (e.g. returning from a drop-off location, picking up a passenger, etc.)

a.   Draw an ROIC tree for the cab company.

b.   Populate the tree with numbers. Make assumptions to explore operational variables in as much detail as possible (e.g., assumptions about gas prices, gas consumption, etc.).

c.   Which of the variables would you classify as operational value drivers?

d.   Analyze the labor efficiency and the efficiency of using the fleet of cabs using productivity ratios.

Q6.2**   **(Penne Pesto)** Penne Pesto is a small restaurant in the financial district of San Francisco. Customers order from a variety of pasta dishes. The restaurant has 50 seats and is always full during the four hours in the evening. It is not possible to make reservations at Penne; most guests show up spontaneously on their way home from work. If there is no available seat, guests simply move on to another place.

On average, a guest spends 50 minutes in the restaurant, which includes 5 minutes until the guest is seated and the waiter has taken the order, an additional 10 minutes until the food is served, 30 minutes to eat, and 5 minutes to handle the check-out (including waiting for the check, paying, and leaving). It takes the restaurant another 10 minutes to clean the table and have it be ready for the next guests (of which there are always plenty). The average guest leaves $20 at Penne, including food, drink, and tip (all tips are collected by the restaurant, employees get a fixed salary).

The restaurant has 10 waiters and 10 kitchen employees, each earning $90 per evening (including any preparation, the 4 hours the restaurant is open, and clean-up). The average order costs $5.50 in materials, including $4.50 for the food and $1 for the average drink. In addition to labor costs, fixed costs for the restaurant include $500 per day of rent and $500 per day for other overhead costs.

The restaurant is open 365 days in the year and is full to the last seat even on weekends and holidays. There is about $200,000 of capital tied up in the restaurant, largely consisting of furniture, decoration, and equipment.

a.   How many guests will the restaurant serve in one evening?

b.   What is the Return on Invested Capital for the owner of the restaurant?

c.   Assume that you could improve the productivity of the kitchen employees and free up one person who would be helping to clean up the table. This would reduce the clean-up to 5 minutes instead of 10 minutes. What would be the new ROIC?

d.   What would be the new ROIC if overhead charges could be reduced by $100 per day?

Q6.3   **(Philly Air)** PhillyAir Inc. offers low cost air travel between Philadelphia and Atlantic City. Philly Air's invested capital is $5,000,000, corresponding to the investment in the two planes the company owns. Each of the two planes can carry 50 passengers. Each plane does 12 daily trips from Philadelphia to Atlantic City and 12 from Atlantic City to Philadelphia. The price is $100 for each one-way ticket. The current load factor is 70 percent (ie., 35 seats are sold on the average flight). The annual cost of operating the service and running the business is $60,000,000 (including all costs, such as labor, fuel, marketing, gate fees, landing fees, maintenance, etc). The company operates 365 days a year.

a. Draw an ROIC (return on invested capital) tree for the company that incorporates all of the above information.

b. What is the current ROIC?

c. What is the minimum load factor at which the company breaks even?

d. What load factor would the company have to achieve so that it obtained a 10 percentage-point increase in the ROIC (e.g. an ROIC increasing from 5 percent to 15 percent)?

Q6.4   **(Oscar's Office Building)** Oscar is considering getting into the real estate business. He's looking at buying an existing office building for $1.8 million in cash. He wants to estimate what his return on invested capital (ROIC) will be on an annual basis. The building has 14,000 square feet of rentable space. He'd like to set the rent at $4.00 per square foot per month. However, he knows that demand depends on price. He estimates that the percentage of the building he can fill roughly follows the equation:

$$\% \text{ Occupied} = 2 - 0.3 \times \text{Rent}$$

(rent is in dollars per square foot per month)

So, at $4.00, Oscar thinks he can fill about 80 percent of the office space.

Oscar considers two categories of costs: variable costs, which are a function of the square feet occupied, and fixed costs. Fixed costs will be $8,000 per month and include such items as insurance, maintenance, and security. Variable costs cover such things as electricity and heat and run $1.25 per month for each square foot occupied.

a. Draw an ROIC (return on invested capital) tree for the company.

b. What is the ROIC?

c. What would be the new ROIC be if Oscar decides to charge rent of $5.00 per square foot per month?

Q6.5   **(OPIM Bus Inc.)** OPIM Bus Inc. offers low-cost bus transportation between Philadelphia and Bryn Mawr. The invested capital is $500,000, corresponding to the investment in the two vehicles it owns. Each of the two buses can carry 50 passengers. Each bus does 12 daily trips from Philadelphia to Bryn Mawr and 12 from Bryn Mawr to Philadelphia. The price is $10 for each one-way ticket. The current load factor is 70 percent (i.e., 35 seats are sold on average). The annual cost of operating the service and running the business is $6 million. The company operates 365 days a year.

a. Draw an ROIC (return on invested capital) tree for the company.

b. What is the current ROIC?

c. What is the minimum load factor at which the company breaks even?

d. What load factor would the company have to achieve so that it obtained a 10 percentage-point increase in the ROIC (e.g. an ROIC increasing from 5 percent to 15 percent)?

You can view a video of how problems marked with a ** are solved by going on www. cachon-terwiesch.net and follow the links under 'Solved Practice Problems'

7

Batching and Other Flow Interruptions: Setup Times and the Economic Order Quantity Model

Up to this point, we were working under the assumption that during every X units of time, one flow unit would enter the process and one flow unit would leave the process. We defined X as the process cycle time. In the scooter example of Chapter 4, we established a cycle time of three minutes in conjunction with Table 4.3, allowing us to fulfill demand of 700 scooters per week.

In an ideal process, a cycle time of three minutes would imply that every resource receives one flow unit as an input each three-minute interval and creates one flow unit of output each three-minute interval. Such a smooth and constant flow of units is the dream of any operations manager, yet it is rarely feasible in practice. There are several reasons for why the smooth process flow is interrupted, the most important ones being setups and variability in processing times or quality levels. The focus of this chapter is on set-ups, which are an important characteristic of batch-flow operations. Problems related to variability are discussed in Chapters 8 and 9. And quality problems are discussed in Chapter 10.

To discuss setups, we return to the Xootr production process. In particular, we consider the computer numerically controlled (CNC) milling machine which is responsible for making two types of parts on each Xootr—the steer support and two ribs (see Figure 7.1). The steer support attaches the Xootr's deck to the steering column, and the ribs help the deck support the weight of the rider. Once the milling machine starts producing one of these parts, it can produce them reasonably quickly. However, a considerable setup time, or changeover time, is needed before the production of each part type can begin. Our primary objective is to understand how setups like these influence the three basic performance measures of a process: inventory, flow rate, and flow time.

FIGURE 7.1 **Milling Machine (left) and Steer Support Parts (right)**

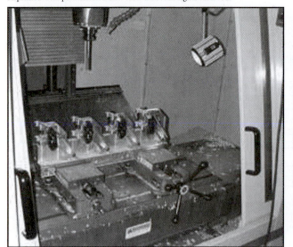 

7.1 The Impact of Setups on Capacity

To evaluate the capacity of the milling machine, we need some more information. Specifically, once set up to produce a part, the milling machine can produce steer supports at the rate of one per minute and can produce ribs at the rate of two per minute. Recall, each Xootr needs one steer support and two ribs. Furthermore, one hour is needed to set up the milling machine to start producing steer supports and one hour is also needed to begin producing ribs. Although no parts are produced during those setup times, it is not quite correct to say that nothing is happening during those times either. The milling machine operator is busy calibrating the milling machine so that it can produce the desired part.

It makes intuitive sense that the following production process should be used with these two parts: set up the machine to make steer supports, make some steer supports, set up the machine to make ribs, make some ribs, and finally, repeat this sequence of setups and production runs. We call this repeating sequence a *production cycle*: one production cycle occurs immediately after another, and all productions cycles "look the same" in the sense that they have the same setups and production runs.

We call this a batch production process because parts are made in batches. Although it may be apparent by what is meant by a "batch", it is useful to provide a precise definition:

A *batch* is a collection of flow units.

Throughout our analysis, we assume that batches are produced in succession. That is, once the production of one batch is completed, the production of the next batch begins and all batches contain the same number and type of flow unit.

Given that a batch is a collection of flow units, we need to define our flow unit in the case of the Xootr. Each Xootr needs one steer support and two ribs, so let's say the flow unit is a "component set" and each component set is composed of those three parts. Hence, each production cycle produces a batch of component sets.

One might ask why we did not define the flow unit to be one of the two types of parts. For example, we could call the steering supports made in a production run a batch of steering supports. However, our interest is not specifically on the capacity to make steering supports or ribs in isolation. We care about the capacity for component sets because one component

FIGURE 7.2   **The Impact of Setup Times on Capacity**

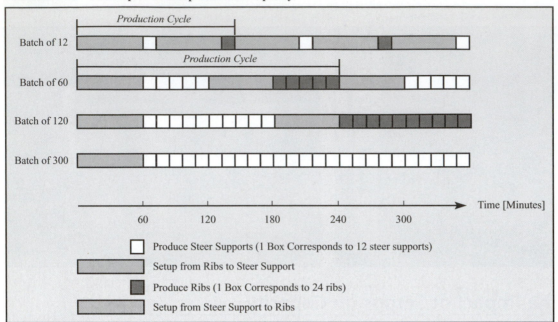

set is needed for each Xootr. Thus, for the purpose of this analysis, it makes more sense to define the flow unit as a component set and to think in terms of a batch of component sets.

Because no output is produced while the resource is in setup mode, it is fairly intuitive that frequent setups lead to lower capacity. To understand how setups reduce the capacity of a process, consider Figure 7.2. The impact of setups on capacity is fairly intuitive. As nothing is produced at a resource during setup, the more frequently a resource is set up, the lower its capacity. As discussed above, the milling machine underlying the example of Figure 7.2 has the following processing times/setup times:

- It takes one minute to produce one steer support unit (of which there is one per Xootr).
- It takes 60 minutes to change over the milling machine from producing steer supports to producing ribs (setup time).
- It takes 0.5 minute to produce one rib; because there are two ribs in a Xootr, this translates to one minute/per component set.
- Finally, it takes another 60 minutes to change over the milling machine back to producing steer supports.

Now consider the impact that varying the batch size has on capacity. Recall that we defined capacity as the maximum flow rate at which a process can operate. If we produce in small batches of 12 component sets per batch, we spend a total of two hours of setup time (one hour to set up the production for steer supports and one hour to set up the production of ribs) for every 12 component sets we produce. These two hours of setup time are lost from regular production.

The capacity of the resource can be increased by increasing the batch size. If the machine is set up every 60 units, the capacity-reducing impact of setup can be spread out over 60 units. This results in a higher capacity for the milling machine. Specifically, for a batch size of 60, the milling machine could produce at 0.25 component set per minute. Table 7.1 summarizes the capacity calculations for batch sizes of 12, 60, 120, and 300.

TABLE 7.1
The Impact of Setups on Capacity

Batch Size	Time to Complete One Batch [minutes]	Capacity [units/minute]
12	60 minutes (set up steering support) + 12 minutes (produce steering supports) + 60 minutes (set up ribs) + 12 minutes (produce ribs) _____ 144 minutes	12/144 = 0.0833
60	60 minutes (set up steering support) + 60 minutes (produce steering supports) + 60 minutes (set up ribs) + 60 minutes (produce ribs) _____ 240 minutes	60/240 = 0.25
120	60 minutes (set up steering support) + 120 minutes (produce steering supports) + 60 minutes (set up ribs) + 120 minutes (produce ribs) _____ 360 minutes	120/360 = 0.333
300	60 minutes (set up steering support) + 300 minutes (produce steering supports) + 60 minutes (set up ribs) + 300 minutes (produce ribs) _____ 720 minutes	300/720 = 0.4166

Generalizing the computations in Table 7.1, we can compute the capacity of a resource with setups as a function of the batch size:

$$\text{Capacity given batch size} = \frac{\text{Batch size}}{\text{Setup time} + \text{Batch size} \times \text{Processing time}}$$

Basically, the above equation is spreading the "unproductive" setup time over the members of a batch. To use the equation, we need to be precise about what we mean by batch size, the setup time, and processing time:

• The batch size is the number of flow units that are produced in one "cycle" (i.e., before the process repeats itself, see Figure 7.2).

• The setup time includes all setups in the production of the batch. In this case, this includes $S = 60$ minutes + 60 minutes = 120 minutes. It can also include any other nonproducing time associated with the production of the batch. For example, if the production of each batch requires a 10-minute worker break, then that would be included. Other "setup times" can include scheduled maintenance or forced idled time (time in which literally nothing is happening with the machine—it is neither producing nor being prepped to produce).

• The processing time includes all production time that is needed to produce one complete flow unit of output at the milling machine. In this case, this includes 1 minute/unit for the steer support as well as two times 0.5 minute/unit for the two ribs. The processing time is thus $p = 1$ minute/unit + 2×0.5 minute/unit = 2 minutes/unit. Notice that the processing time is 2 minutes even though no single component set is actually produced over a single period of 2 minutes of length. Due to setups, the processing time for a component set is divided over two periods of one minute each, and those two periods can be separated by a considerable amount of time. Nevertheless, from

FIGURE 7.3
Capacity as a
Function of the
Batch Size

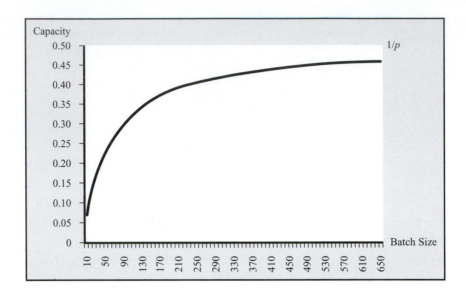

the perspective of calculating the capacity of the milling machine when operated with a given batch size, it does not matter whether each component set is produced over a continuous period of time or disjointed periods of time. All that matters is that a total of 2 minutes is needed for each component set.

Given these definitions, say we operate with a batch size of 100 units. Our capacity in this case would be

$$\text{Capacity (for } B = 100) = \frac{\text{Batch size}}{\text{Setup time} + \text{Batch size} \times \text{Processing time}}$$

$$= \frac{100 \text{ units}}{120 \text{ minutes} + 100 \text{ units} \times 2 \text{ minutes/unit}}$$

$$= 0.3125 \text{ unit/minute}$$

No matter how large a batch size we choose, we will never be able to produce faster than one unit every p units of time. Thus, $1/p$ can be thought of as the maximum capacity the process can achieve. This is illustrated in Figure 7.3.

7.2 Interaction between Batching and Inventory

Given the desirable effect that large batch sizes increase capacity, why not choose the largest possible batch size to maximize capacity? While large batch sizes are desirable from a capacity perspective, they typically require a higher level of inventory, either within the process or at the finished goods level. Holding the flow rate constant, we can infer from Little's Law that such a higher inventory level also will lead to longer flow times. This is why batch-flow operations generally are not very fast in responding to customer orders (remember the last time you bought custom furniture?).

The interaction between batching and inventory is illustrated by the following two examples. First, consider an auto manufacturer producing a sedan and a station wagon on the same assembly line. For simplicity, assume both models have the same demand rate, 400 cars per day each. The metal stamping steps in the process preceding final assembly

FIGURE 7.4   **The Impact of Batch Sizes on Inventory**

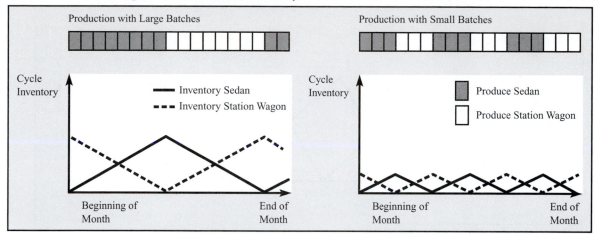

are characterized by especially long setup times. Thus, to achieve a high level of capacity, the plant runs large production batches and produces sedans from the first of a month to the 15th and station wagons from the 16th to the end of the month.

However, it seems fairly unrealistic to assume that customers only demand sedans at the beginning of the month and station wagons at the end of the month. In other words, producing in large batches leads to a mismatch between the rate of supply and the rate of demand.

Thus, in addition to producing enough to cover demand in the first half of the month, to satisfy demand for sedans the company needs to produce 15 days of demand to inventory, which then fulfills demand while the line produces station wagons. This is illustrated by the left side of Figure 7.4. Observe that the average level of inventory is 3,000 cars for each of the two models. Now, ignoring setup times for a moment, consider the case in which the firm produces 400 station wagons and 400 sedans a day. In this setting, one would only need to carry 0.5 day of cycle inventory, a dramatic reduction in inventory. This is illustrated by the right side of Figure 7.4. Thus, smaller batches translate to lower inventory levels!

In the ideal case, which has been propagated by Toyota Production Systems under the word *heijunka* or *mixed-model* production, the company would alternate between producing one sedan and producing one station wagon, thereby producing in batch sizes of one. This way, a much better synchronization of the demand flow and the production flow is achieved and cycle inventory is eliminated entirely.

Second, consider a furniture maker producing chairs in batch sizes of 100. Starting with the wood-cutting step and all the way through the finishing process, the batch of 100 chairs would stay together as one entity.

Now, take the position of one chair in the batch. What is the most dominant activity throughout the process? Waiting! The larger the batch size, the longer the time the flow unit waits for the other "members" of the same batch—a situation comparable with going to the barber with an entire class of children. Given Little's Law, this increase in wait time (and thereby flow time) leads to a proportional increase in inventory.

With these observations, we can turn our attention back to the milling machine at Nova Cruz. Similar to Figure 7.4, we can draw the inventory of components (ribs and steer supports) over the course of a production cycle. Remember that the assembly process following the milling machine requires a supply of one unit every three minutes. This one

FIGURE 7.5 **The Impact of Setup Times on Capacity**

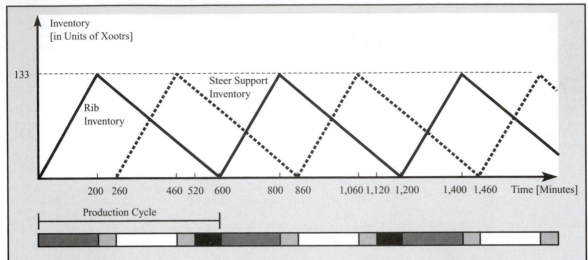

unit consists, from the view of the milling machine, of two ribs and a steer support unit. If we want to ensure a sufficient supply to keep the assembly process operating, we have to produce a sufficient number of ribs such that during the time we do not produce ribs (e.g., setup time and production of steer support) we do not run out of ribs. Say the milling machine operates with a batch size of 200 units, $B = 200$. In that case, the inventory of ribs changes as follows:

• During the production of ribs, inventory accumulates. As we produce ribs for one scooter per minute, but only supply ribs to the assembly line at a rate of one scooter every three minutes, rib inventory accumulates at the rate of two scooters per three minutes, or 2/3 scooters per minute.

• Because we produce for 200 minutes, the inventory of ribs at the end of the production run is 200 minutes × 2/3 scooters per minute = 133 scooters (i.e., 266 ribs).

• How long does the rib inventory for 133 scooters last? The inventory ensures supply to the assembly for 400 minutes (cycle time of assembly operations was three minutes). After these 400 minutes, we need to start producing ribs again. During these 400 minutes, we have to accommodate two setups (together 120 minutes) and 200 minutes for producing the steer supports.

The resulting production plan as well as the corresponding inventory levels are summarized by Figure 7.5. Notice that each production cycle takes 600 minutes, and this includes 80 minutes of idle time. Why do we insert additional idle time into the milling machine's production schedule? The answer is that without the idle time, the milling machine would produce too quickly given our batch size of 200 units. To explain, assembly takes 200 units × 3 minute/unit = 600 minutes to produce a batch of 200 scooters. The milling machine only needs 520 minutes to produce that batch of 600 scooters (120 minutes of setup and 400 minutes of production). Hence, if the milling machine produced one batch after another (without any idle time between them), it would produce 200 components sets every 520 minutes (or 200/520 = 0.3846 components sets per minute), which is faster than assembly can use them (which is 1/3 component sets per minute). This analysis suggests that maybe we want to choose a different batch size, as we see in the next section.

7.3   Choosing a Batch Size in the Presence of Setup Times

When choosing an appropriate batch size for a process flow, it is important to balance the conflicting objectives: capacity and inventory. Large batches lead to large inventory; small batches lead to losses in capacity.

In balancing these two conflicting objectives, we benefit from the following two observations:

- Capacity at the bottleneck step is extremely valuable (as long as the process is capacity-constrained, i.e., there is more demand than capacity) as it constrains the flow rate of the entire process.

- Capacity at a nonbottleneck step is free, as it does not provide a constraint on the current flow rate.

This has direct implications for choosing an appropriate batch size at a process step with setups.

- If the setup occurs at the bottleneck step (and the process is capacity-constrained), it is desirable to increase the batch size, as this results in a larger process capacity and, therefore, a higher flow rate.

- If the setup occurs at a nonbottleneck step (or the process is demand-constrained), it is desirable to decrease the batch size, as this decreases inventory as well as flow time.

The scooter example summarized by Figure 7.6 illustrates these two observations and how they help us in choosing a good batch size. Remember that B denotes the batch size, S the setup time, and p the per unit processing time.

The process flow diagram in Figure 7.6 consists of only two activities: the milling machine and the assembly operations. We can combine the assembly operations into one activity, as we know that its slowest step (bottleneck of assembly) can create one Xootr every three minutes.

To determine the capacity of the milling machine for a batch size of 12, we apply the formula

$$\text{Capacity }(B) = \frac{\text{Batch size}}{\text{Setup time} + \text{Batch size} \times \text{Processing time}}$$

$$= \frac{B}{S + B \times p} = \frac{12}{120 + 12 \times 2} = 0.0833 \text{ unit/minute}$$

The capacity of the assembly operation is easily computed based on its bottleneck capacity of $\frac{1}{3}$ unit per minute. Note that for $B = 12$, the milling machine is the bottleneck.

FIGURE 7.6

Data from the Scooter Case about Setup Times and Batching

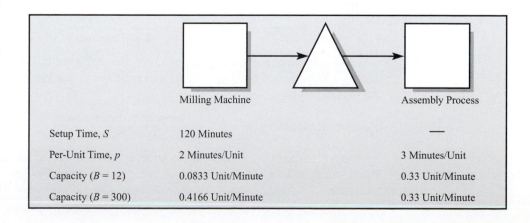

	Milling Machine	Assembly Process
Setup Time, S	120 Minutes	—
Per-Unit Time, p	2 Minutes/Unit	3 Minutes/Unit
Capacity ($B = 12$)	0.0833 Unit/Minute	0.33 Unit/Minute
Capacity ($B = 300$)	0.4166 Unit/Minute	0.33 Unit/Minute

Next consider, what happens to the same calculations if we increase the batch size from 12 to 300. While this does not affect the capacity of the assembly operations, the capacity of the milling machine now becomes

$$\text{Capacity } (B) = \frac{B}{S + B \times p} = \frac{300}{120 + 300 \times 2} = 0.4166 \text{ unit/minute}$$

Thus, we observe that the location of the bottleneck has shifted from the milling machine to the assembly operation, just by modifying the batch size. Now which of the two batch sizes is the "better" one, 12 or 300?

• The batch size of 300 is clearly too large. The milling machine incurs idle time as the overall process is constrained by the (substantially) smaller capacity of the assembly operations (note, based on Figure 7.5, we know that even for the smaller batch size of $B = 200$, there exists idle time at the milling machine). This large batch size is likely to create unnecessary inventory problems as described above.

• The batch size of 12 is likely to be more attractive in terms of inventory. Yet, the process capacity has been reduced to 0.0833 unit per minute, leaving the assembly operation starved for work.

As a batch size of 12 is too small and a batch size of 300 is too large, a good batch size is "somewhere in between." Specifically, we are interested in the smallest batch size that does not adversely affect process capacity.

To find this number, we equate the capacity of the step with setup (in this case, the milling machine) with the capacity of the step from the remaining process that has the smallest capacity (in this case, the assembly operations):

$$\frac{B}{120 + B \times 2} = \frac{1}{3}$$

and solve this equation for B:

$$\frac{B}{120 + B \times 2} = \frac{1}{3}$$

$$3 \times B = 120 + 2 \times B$$

$$B = 120$$

which gives us, in this case, $B = 120$. This algebraic approach is illustrated by Figure 7.7. If you feel uncomfortable with the calculus outlined above (i.e., solving the equation for the batch size B), or you want to program the method directly into Excel or another software package, you can use the following equation:

$$\text{Recommended batch size} = \frac{\text{Flow rate} \times \text{Setup time}}{1 - \text{Flow rate} \times \text{Processing time}}$$

which is equivalent to the analysis performed above. To see this, simply substitute Setup time = 120 minutes, Flow rate = 0.333 unit per minute, and Processing time = 2 minutes per unit and obtain

$$\text{Recommended batch size} = \frac{\text{Flow rate} \times \text{Setup time}}{1 - \text{Flow rate} \times \text{Processing time}} = \frac{0.333 \times 120}{1 - 0.333 \times 2} = 120$$

Figure 7.7 shows the capacity of the process step with setup, which increases with the batch size B, and for very high values of batch size B approaches $1/p$ (similar to the graph in Figure 7.3). As the capacity of the assembly operation does not depend on the batch size, it corresponds to a constant (flat line).

Exhibit 7.1

FINDING A GOOD BATCH SIZE IN THE PRESENCE OF SETUP TIMES

1. Compute Flow rate = Minimum {Available input, Demand, Process capacity}.
2. Define the production cycle, which includes the processing and setups of all flow units in a batch.
3. Compute the time in a production cycle that the resource is in setup; setup times are those times that are independent of the batch size.
4. Compute the time in a production cycle that the resource is processing; this includes all the processing times that are incurred per unit (i.e., are repeated for every member of the batch).
5. Compute the capacity of the resource with setup for a given batch size:

$$\text{Capacity } (B) = \frac{B}{\text{Setup time} + B \times \text{Processing time}}$$

6. We are looking for the batch size that leads to the lowest level of inventory without affecting flow rate; we find this by solving the equation

$$\text{Capacity } (B) = \text{Flow rate}$$

for the batch size *B*. This also can be done directly using the following formula:

$$\text{Recommended batch size} = \frac{\text{Flow rate} \times \text{Setup time}}{1 - \text{Flow rate} \times \text{Processing time}}$$

The overall process capacity is—in the spirit of the bottleneck idea—the minimum of the two graphs. Thus, before the graphs intersect, the capacity is too low and flow rate is potentially given up. After the intersection point, the assembly operation is the bottleneck and any further increases in batch size yield no return. Exhibit 7.1 provides a summary of the computations leading to the recommended batch size in the presence of setup times.

FIGURE 7.7

Choosing a "Good" Batch Size

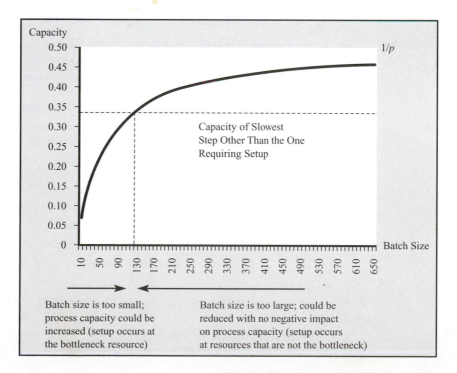

123

7.4   Setup Times and Product Variety

As we have seen in the case of the Xootr production process, setup times often occur due to the need to change over production from one product to another. This raises the following question: What is the impact of product variety on a process with setup times? To explore this question, let's consider a simple process that makes two kinds of soup: chicken noodle and tomato.

Demand for chicken soup is 100 gallons per hour, while demand for tomato soup is 75 gallons per hour. Switching from one type of soup to another requires 30 minutes to clean the production equipment so that one flavor does not disrupt the flavor of the next soup. Once production begins, the process can make 300 gallons per hour of either type of soup. Given these parameters, let's evaluate a production cycle that minimizes inventory while satisfying demand.

We first need to define our flow unit. In this case, it is natural to let our flow unit be one gallon of soup. Hence, a production cycle of soup contains a certain number of gallons, some chicken and some tomato. In this case, a "batch" is the set of gallons produced in a production cycle. While the plant manager is likely to refer to batches of tomato soup and batches of chicken soup individually, and unlikely to refer to the batch that combines both flavors, we cannot analyze the production process of tomato soup in isolation from the production process of chicken soup. (For example, if we dedicate more time to tomato production, then we will have less time for chicken noodle production.) Because we are ultimately interested in our capacity to make soup, we focus our analysis at the level of the production cycle and refer to the entire production within that cycle as a "batch."

Our desired flow rate is 175 gallons per hour (the sum of demand for chicken and tomato), the setup time is 1 hour (30 minutes per soup and two types of soup) and the processing time is 1/300 hour per gallon. The batch size that minimizes inventory while still meeting our demand is then

$$\text{Recommended batch size} = \frac{\text{Flow rate} \times \text{Setup time}}{1 - \text{Flow rate} \times \text{Processing time}} = \frac{175 \times (2 \times 1/2)}{1 - 175 \times (1/300)} = 420 \text{ gallons}$$

We should produce in proportion to demand (otherwise at least one of the flavors will have too much production and at least one will have too little), so of the 420 gallons, $420 \times 100/(100 + 75) = 240$ gallons should be chicken soup and the remainder, $420 - 240 = 180$ gallons, should be tomato.

To understand the impact of variety on this process, suppose we were to add a third kind of soup to our product offering, onion soup. Furthermore, with onion soup added to the mix, demand for chicken remains 100 gallons per hour, and demand for tomato continues to be 75 gallons per hour, while onion now generates 30 gallons of demand on its own. In some sense, this is an ideal case for adding variety—the new variant adds incrementally to demand without stealing any demand from the existing varieties.

The desired flow rate is now $100 + 75 + 30 = 205$, the setup time is 1.5 hours (three setups per batch), and the inventory minimizing quantity for the production cycle is

$$\text{Recommended batch size} = \frac{\text{Flow rate} \times \text{Setup time}}{1 - \text{Flow rate} \times \text{Processing time}} = \frac{205 \times (3 \times 1/2)}{1 - 205 \times (1/300)} = 971 \text{ gallons}$$

Again, we should produce in proportion to demand: $971 \times (100/205) = 474$ gallons of chicken, $971 \times (75/205) = 355$ gallons of tomato, and $971 \times (30/205) = 142$ gallons of onion.

So what happened when we added to variety? In short, we need more inventory. Our first hint of this is the size of the batch (the amount of soup across all flavors that is produced in a production cycle)—420 gallons without onion, while 971 gallons with onion. We can explore this further by evaluating the maximum inventory of chicken soup in either case. (Average inventory of chicken soup is half of its peak inventory.) In our original case, during production, inventory of chicken soup increases at the rate of $300 - 100 = 200$ gallons per hour. Production of 240 gallons of chicken soup requires 240/300 hours. So, peak inventory of chicken soup is $200 \times (240/300) = 160$ gallons. The analogous calculation with onion included yields a peak inventory of $200 \times (474/300) = 316$ gallons, a 98 percent increase in the amount of inventory needed!

Why did inventory of chicken soup increase when onion soup was added to the mix? Setup times are to blame. With more varieties in the production mix, the production process has to set up more often per production cycle. This reduces the capacity of the production cycle (no soup is made during a setup). To increase the capacity back to the desired flow rate (which is even higher now), we need to operate with larger batches (longer production cycles), and they lead to more inventory.

One may argue that the previous analysis is too optimistic—adding onion soup to the mix should steal some demand away from the other flavors. It turns out that our result is not sensitive to this assumption. To demonstrate, let's consider the opposite extreme—adding onion soup does not expand overall demand, it only steals demand from the other flavors. Specifically, the overall flow rate remains 175 gallons per hour, with or without onion soup. Furthermore, with onion soup, the demand rate for chicken, tomato, and onion are 80, 65, and 30 gallons per hour, respectively. The processing time is still 1/300 gallons per hour, and the setup time per batch is now 1.5 hours (three changeovers due to three types of soup). The batch size that minimizes our inventory while meeting our demand is

$$\text{Recommended batch size} = \frac{\text{Flow rate} \times \text{Setup time}}{1 - \text{Flow rate} \times \text{Processing time}} = \frac{175 \times (3 \times 1/2)}{1 - 175 \times (1/300)} = 630 \text{ gallons}$$

Inventory does not increase as much in this case, but it still increases.

The conclusion from this investigation is that setup times and product variety do not mix very well. Consequently, there are two possible solutions to this challenge. The first is to offer only a limited amount of variety. That was Henry Ford's approach when he famously declared that "You can have any color Model-T you want, as long as it is black." While a convenient solution for a production manager, it is not necessarily the best strategy for satisfying demand in a competitive environment.

The other approach to the incompatibility of setups and variety is to work to eliminate setup times. This is the approach advocated by Shigeo Shingo, one of the most influential thought leader in manufacturing. When he witnessed changeover times of more than an hour in an automobile plant, he responded with the quote, "The flow must go on," meaning that every effort must be made to ensure a smooth flow of production. One way to ensure a smooth flow is to eliminate or reduce setup times. Shigeo Shingo developed a powerful technique for doing exactly that, which we will revisit later in the chapter.

7.5 Setup Time Reduction

Despite improvement potential from the use of "good" batch sizes and smaller transfer batches, setups remain a source of disruption of a smooth process flow. For this reason, rather than taking setups as "God-given" constraints and finding ways to accommodate them, we should find ways that directly address the root cause of the disruption.

This is the basic idea underlying the single minute exchange of die (SMED) method. The creators of the SMED method referred to any setup exceeding 10 minutes as an unacceptable source of process flow disruption. The 10-minute rule is not necessarily meant to be taken literally: the method was developed in the automotive industry, where setup times used to take as much as four hours. The SMED method helps to define an aggressive, yet realistic setup time goal and to identify potential opportunities of setup time reduction.

The basic underlying idea of SMED is to carefully analyze all tasks that are part of the setup time and then divide those tasks into two groups, *internal* setup tasks and *external* setup tasks.

- Internal setup tasks are those tasks that can only be executed while the machine is stopped.
- External setup tasks are those tasks that can be done while the machine is still operating, meaning they can be done *before* the actual changeover occurs.

Experience shows that companies are biased toward using internal setups and that, even without making large investments, internal setups can be translated into external setups.

Similar to our discussion about choosing a good batch size, the biggest obstacles to overcome are ineffective cost accounting procedures. Consider, for example, the case of a simple heat treatment procedure in which flow units are moved on a tray and put into an oven. Loading and unloading of the tray is part of the setup time. The acquisition of an additional tray that can be loaded (or unloaded) while the other tray is still in process (before the setup) allows the company to convert internal setup tasks to external ones. Is this a worthwhile investment?

The answer is, as usual, it depends. SMED applied to nonbottleneck steps is not creating any process improvement at all. As discussed previously, nonbottleneck steps have excessive capacity and therefore setups are entirely free (except for the resulting increase in inventory). Thus, investing in any resource, technical or human, is not only wasteful, but it also takes scarce improvement capacity/funds away from more urgent projects. However, if the oven in the previous example were the bottleneck step, almost any investment in the acquisition of additional trays suddenly becomes a highly profitable investment.

The idea of internal and external setups as well as potential conversion from internal to external setups is best visible in car racing. Any pit stop is a significant disruption of the race car's flow toward the finish line. At any point and any moment in the race, an entire crew is prepared to take in the car, having prepared for any technical problem from tire changes to refueling. While the technical crew might appear idle and underutilized throughout most of the race, it is clear that any second they can reduce from the time the car is in the pit (internal setups) to a moment when the car is on the race track is a major gain (e.g., no race team would consider mounting tires on wheels during the race; they just put on entire wheels).

7.6 Balancing Setup Costs with Inventory Costs: The EOQ Model

Up to now, our focus has been on the role of setup times, as opposed to setup costs. Specifically, we have seen that setup time at the bottleneck leads to an overall reduction in process capacity. Assuming that the process is currently capacity-constrained, setup times thereby carry an opportunity cost reflecting the overall lower flow rate (sales).

Independent of such opportunity costs, setups frequently are associated with direct (out-of-pocket) costs. In these cases, we speak of setup costs (as opposed to setup times). Consider, for example, the following settings:

- The setup of a machine to process a certain part might require scrapping the first 10 parts that are produced after the setup. Thus, the material costs of these 10 parts constitute a setup cost.

• Assume that we are charged a per-time-unit usage fee for a particular resource (e.g., for the milling machine discussed above). Thus, every minute we use the resource, independent of whether we use it for setup or for real production, we have to pay for the resource. In this case, "time is money" and the setup time thereby translates directly into setup costs. However, as we will discuss below, one needs to be very careful when making the conversion from setup times to setup costs.

• When receiving shipments from a supplier, there frequently exists a fixed shipment cost as part of the procurement cost, which is independent of the purchased quantity. This is similar to the shipping charges that a consumer pays at a catalog or online retailer. Shipping costs are a form of setup costs.

All three settings reflect *economies of scale:* the more we order or produce as part of a batch, the more units there are in a batch over which we can spread out the setup costs.

If we can reduce per-unit costs by increasing the batch size, what keeps us from using infinitely (or at least very large) batches? Similar to the case of setup times, we again need to balance our desire for large batches (fewer setups) with the cost of carrying a large amount of inventory.

In the following analysis, we need to distinguish between two cases:

• If the quantity we order is produced or delivered by an outside supplier, all units of a batch are likely to arrive at the same time.

• In other settings, the units of a batch might not all arrive at the same time. This is especially the case when we produce the batch internally.

Figure 7.8 illustrates the inventory levels for the two cases described above. The lower part of Figure 7.8 shows the case of the outside supplier and all units of a batch arriving at the same moment in time. The moment a shipment is received, the inventory level jumps up by the size of the shipment. It then falls up to the time of the next shipment.

The upper part of Figure 7.8 shows the case of units created by a resource with (finite) capacity. Thus, while we are producing, the inventory level increases. Once we stop production, the inventory level falls. Let us consider the case of an outside supplier first (lower part of Figure 7.8). Specifically, consider the case of the Xootr handle caps that Nova Cruz sources from a supplier in Taiwan for $0.85 per unit. Note that the maximum inventory of handle caps occurs at the time we receive a shipment from Taiwan. The inventory is then depleted at the rate of the assembly operations, that is, at a flow rate, *R,* of 700 units (pairs of handle caps) per week, which is equal to one unit every three minutes.

For the following computations, we make a set of assumptions. We later show that these assumptions do not substantially alter the optimal decisions.

• We assume that production of Xootrs occurs at a constant rate of one unit every three minutes. We also assume our orders arrive on time from Taiwan. Under these two assumptions, we can deplete our inventory all the way to zero before receiving the next shipment.

• There is a fixed setup cost per order that is independent of the amount ordered. In the Xootr case, this largely consists of a $300 customs fee.

• The purchase price is independent of the number of units we order, that is, there are no quantity discounts. We talk about quantity discounts in the next section.

The objective of our calculations is to minimize the cost of inventory and ordering with the constraint that we must never run out of inventory (i.e., we can keep the assembly operation running).

FIGURE 7.8
Different Patterns of Inventory Levels

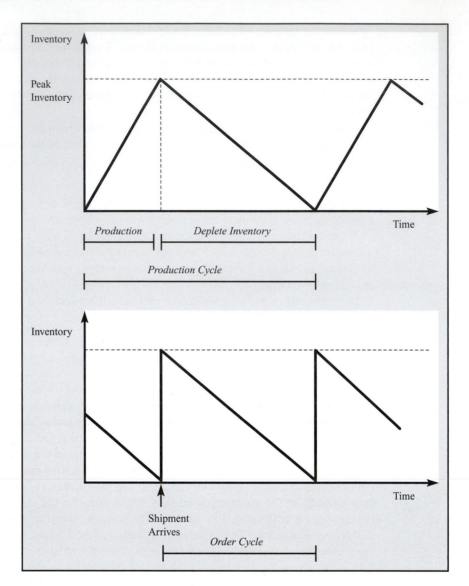

We have three costs to consider: purchase costs, delivery fees, and holding costs. We use 700 units of handle caps each week no matter how much or how frequently we order. Thus, we have no excuse for running out of inventory and there is nothing we can do about our purchase costs of

$$\$0.85/\text{unit} \times 700 \text{ units/week} = \$595 \text{ per week}$$

So when choosing our ordering policy (when and how much to order), we focus on minimizing the sum of the other two costs, delivery fees and inventory costs.

The cost of inventory depends on how much it costs us to hold one unit in inventory for a given period of time, say one week. We can obtain the number by looking at the annual inventory costs and dividing that amount by 52. The annual inventory costs need to account for financing the inventory (cost of capital, especially high for a start-up like Nova Cruz), costs of storage, and costs of obsolescence. Nova Cruz uses an annual inventory cost of 40 percent. Thus, it costs Nova Cruz 0.7692 percent to hold a piece of inventory for one week. Given that a handle cap costs $0.85 per unit, this translates to an inventory cost of $h = 0.007692 \times \$0.85/\text{unit} = \$0.006538$ per unit per week. Note that the annual holding cost needs to include the cost of capital as well as any other cost of inventory (e.g., storage, theft, etc).

How many handle caps will there be, on average, in Nova Cruz's inventory? As we can see in Figure 7.8, the average inventory level is simply

$$\text{Average inventory} = \frac{\text{Order quantity}}{2}$$

If you are not convinced, refer in Figure 7.8 to the "triangle" formed by one order cycle. The average inventory during the cycle is half of the height of the triangle, which is half the order quantity, $Q/2$. Thus, for a given inventory cost, h, we can compute the inventory cost per unit of time (e.g., inventory costs per week):

$$\text{Inventory costs [per unit of time]} = \frac{1}{2}\text{ Order quantity} \times h = \frac{1}{2}Q \times h$$

Before we turn to the question of how many handle caps to order at once, let's first ask ourselves how frequently we have to place an order. Say at time 0 we have I units in inventory and say we plan our next order to be Q units. The I units of inventory will satisfy demand until time I/R (in other words, we have I/R weeks of supply in inventory). At this time, our inventory will be zero if we don't order before then. We would then again receive an order of Q units (if there is a lead time in receiving this order, we simply would have to place this order earlier).

Do we gain anything by receiving the Q handle caps earlier than at the time when we have zero units in inventory? Not in this model: demand is satisfied whether we order earlier or not and the delivery fee is the same too. But we do lose something by ordering earlier: we incur holding costs per unit of time the Q units are held.

Given that we cannot save costs by choosing the order time intelligently, we must now work on the question of how much to order (the order quantity). Let's again assume that we order Q units with every order and let's consider just one order cycle. The order cycle begins when we order Q units and ends when the last unit is sold, Q/R time units later. For example, with $Q = 1,000$, an order cycle lasts 1,000 units/700 units per week = 1.43 weeks. We incur one ordering fee (setup costs), K, in that order cycle, so our setup costs per week are

$$\text{Setup costs [per unit of time]} = \frac{\text{Setup cost}}{\text{Length of order cycle}}$$

$$= \frac{K}{Q/R} = \frac{K \times R}{Q}$$

Let $C(Q)$ be the sum of our average delivery cost per unit time and our average holding cost per unit time (per week):

$$\text{Per unit of time cost } C(Q) = \text{Setup costs} + \text{Inventory costs}$$

$$= \frac{K \times R}{Q} + \frac{1}{2} \times h \times Q$$

Note that purchase costs are not included in $C(Q)$ for the reasons discussed earlier. From the above we see that the delivery fee per unit time decreases as Q increases: we amortize the delivery fee over more units. But as Q increases, we increase our holding costs.

Figure 7.9 graphs the weekly costs of delivery, the average weekly holding cost, and the total weekly cost, $C(Q)$. As we can see, there is a single order quantity Q that minimizes the total cost $C(Q)$. We call this quantity Q^*, the economic order quantity, or *EOQ* for short. Hence the name of the model.

FIGURE 7.9 **Inventory and Ordering Costs for Different Order Sizes**

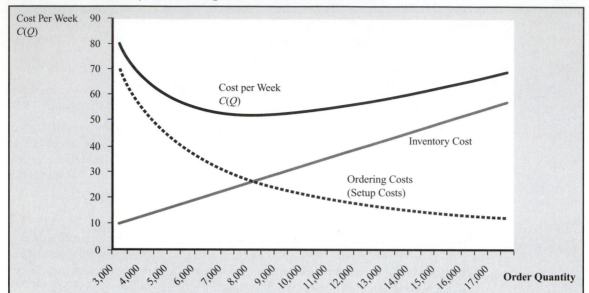

From Figure 7.9 it appears that Q^* is the quantity at which the weekly delivery fee equals the weekly holding cost. In fact, that is true, as can be shown algebraically. Further, using calculus it is possible to show that

$$\text{Economic order quantity} = \sqrt{\frac{2 \times \text{Setup cost} \times \text{Flow rate}}{\text{Holding cost}}}$$

$$Q^* = \sqrt{\frac{2 \times K \times R}{h}}$$

As our intuition suggests, as the setup costs K increase, we should make larger orders, but as holding costs h increase, we should make smaller orders.

We can use the above formula to establish the economic order quantity for handle caps:

$$Q^* = \sqrt{\frac{2 \times \text{Setup cost} \times \text{Flow rate}}{\text{Holding cost}}}$$

$$= \sqrt{\frac{2 \times 300 \times 700}{0.006538}} = 8,014.69$$

The steps required to find the economic order quantity are summarized by Exhibit 7.2.

7.7 Observations Related to the Economic Order Quantity

If we always order the economic order quantity, our cost per unit of time, $C(Q^*)$, can be computed as

$$C(Q^*) = \frac{K \times R}{Q^*} + \frac{1}{2} \times h \times Q^* = \sqrt{2 \times K \times R \times h}$$

Exhibit 7.2

FINDING THE ECONOMIC ORDER QUANTITY

1. Verify the basic assumptions of the EOQ model:

   - Replenishment occurs instantaneously.
   - Demand is constant and not stochastic.
   - There is a fixed setup cost K independent of the order quantity.

2. Collect information on

   - Setup cost, K (only include out-of-pocket cost, not opportunity cost).
   - Flow rate, R.
   - Holding cost, h (not necessarily the yearly holding cost; needs to have the same time unit as the flow rate).

3. For a given order quantity Q, compute

$$\text{Inventory costs [per unit of time]} = \frac{1}{2} Q \times h$$

$$\text{Setup costs [per unit of time]} = \frac{K \times R}{Q}$$

4. The economic order quantity minimizes the sum of the inventory and the setup costs and is

$$Q^{*} = \sqrt{\frac{2 \times K \times R}{h}}$$

The resulting costs are

$$C(Q^{*}) = \sqrt{2 \times K \times R \times h}$$

While we have done this analysis to minimize our average cost per unit of time, it should be clear that Q^* would minimize our average cost per unit (given that the rate of purchasing handle caps is fixed). The cost per unit can be computed as

$$\text{Cost per unit} = \frac{C(Q^{*})}{R} = \sqrt{\frac{2 \times K \times h}{R}}$$

As we would expect, the per-unit cost is increasing with the ordering fee K as well as with our inventory costs. Interestingly, the per-unit cost is decreasing with the flow rate R. Thus, if we doubled our flow rate, our ordering costs increase by less than a factor of 2. In other words, there are economies of scale in the ordering process: the per-unit ordering cost is decreasing with the flow rate R. Put yet another way, an operation with setup and inventory holding costs becomes more efficient as the demand rate increases.

While we have focused our analysis on the time period when Nova Cruz experienced a demand of 700 units per week, the demand pattern changed drastically over the product life cycle of the Xootr. As discussed in Chapter 4, Nova Cruz experienced a substantial demand growth from 200 units per week to over 1,000 units per week. Table 7.2 shows how increases in demand rate impact the order quantity as well as the per-unit cost of the handle caps. We observe that, due to scale economies, ordering and inventory costs are decreasing with the flow rate R.

TABLE 7.2

Scale Economies in
the EOQ Formula

Flow Rate, R	Economic Order Quantity, Q*	Per-Unit Ordering and Inventory Cost, C(Q*)/ R	Ordering and Inventory Costs as a Percentage of Total Procurement Costs
200	4,284	0.14 [$/unit]	14.1%
400	6,058	0.10	10.4%
600	7,420	0.08	8.7%
800	8,568	0.07	7.6%
1,000	9,579	0.06	6.8%

A nice property of the economic order quantity is that the cost function, $C(Q)$, is relatively flat around its minimum Q^* (see graph in Figure 7.9). This suggests that if we were to order Q units instead of Q^*, the resulting cost penalty would not be substantial as long as Q is reasonably close to Q^*. Suppose we order only half of the optimal order quantity, that is, we order $Q^*/2$. In that case, we have

$$C(Q^*/2) = \frac{K \times R}{Q^*/2} + \frac{1}{2} \times h \times Q^*/2 = \frac{5}{4} \times \sqrt{2 \times K \times R \times h} = \frac{5}{4} \times C(Q^*)$$

Thus, if we order only half as much as optimal (i.e., we order twice as frequently as optimal), then our costs increase only by 25 percent. The same holds if we order double the economic order quantity (i.e., we order half as frequently as optimal).

This property has several important implications:

• Consider the optimal order quantity $Q^* = 8,014$ established above. However, now also assume that our supplier is only willing to deliver in predefined quantities (e.g., in multiples of 5,000). The robustness established above suggests that an order of 10,000 will only lead to a slight cost increase (increased costs can be computed as $C(Q = 10,000) = \$53.69$, which is only 2.5 percent higher than the optimal costs).

• Sometimes, it can be difficult to obtain exact numbers for the various ingredients in the EOQ formula. Consider, for example, the ordering fee in the Nova Cruz case. While this fee of \$300 was primarily driven by the \$300 for customs, it also did include a shipping fee. The exact shipping fee in turn depends on the quantity shipped and we would need a more refined model to find the order quantity that accounts for this effect. Given the robustness of the EOQ model, however, we know that the model is "forgiving" with respect to small misspecifications of parameters.

A particularly useful application of the EOQ model relates to *quantity discounts*. When procuring inventory in a logistics or retailing setting, we frequently are given the opportunity to benefit from quantity discounts. For example:

• We might be offered a discount for ordering a full truckload of supply.
• We might receive a free unit for every five units we order (just as in consumer retailing settings of "buy one, get one free").
• We might receive a discount for all units ordered over 100 units.
• We might receive a discount for the entire order if the order volume exceeds 50 units (or say \$2,000).

We can think of the extra procurement costs that we would incur from not taking advantage of the quantity discount—that is, that would result from ordering in smaller quantities—as a setup cost. Evaluating an order discount therefore boils down to a comparison between inventory costs and setup costs (savings in procurement costs), which we can do using the EOQ model.

If the order quantity we obtain from the EOQ model is sufficiently large to obtain the largest discount (the lowest per-unit procurement cost), then the discount has no impact on our order size. We go ahead and order the economic order quantity. The more interesting case occurs when the EOQ is less than the discount threshold. Then we must decide if we wish to order more than the economic order quantity to take advantage of the discount offered to us.

Let's consider one example to illustrate how to think about this issue. Suppose our supplier of handle caps gives us a discount of 5 percent off the entire order if the order exceeds 10,000 units. Recall that our economic order quantity was only 8,014. Thus, the question is "should we increase the order size to 10,000 units in order to get the 5 percent discount, yet incur higher inventory costs, or should we simply order 8,014 units?"

We surely will not order more than 10,000; any larger order does not generate additional purchase cost savings but does increase inventory costs. So we have two choices: either stick with the EOQ or increase our order to 10,000. If we order $Q^* = 8,014$ units, our total cost per unit time is

$$700 \text{ units/week} \times \$0.85/\text{unit} + C(Q^*)$$
$$= \$595/\text{week} + \$52.40/\text{week}$$
$$= \$647.40/\text{week}$$

Notice that we now include our purchase cost per unit time of 700 units/week × $0.85/ unit. The reason for this is that with the possibility of a quantity discount, our purchase cost now depends on the order quantity.

If we increase our order quantity to 10,000 units, our total cost per unit time would be

$$700 \text{ units/week} \times \$0.85/\text{unit} \times 0.95 + C(10,000)$$
$$= \$565.25/\text{week} + \$52.06/\text{week}$$
$$= \$617.31/\text{week}$$

where we have reduced the procurement cost by 5 percent (multiplied by 0.95) to reflect the quantity discount. (*Note:* The 5 percent discount also reduces the holding cost h in $C(.)$) Given that the cost per week is lower in the case of the increased order quantity, we want to take advantage of the quantity discount.

After analyzing the case of all flow units of one order (batch) arriving simultaneously, we now turn to the case of producing the corresponding units internally (upper part of Figure 7.8).

All computations we performed above can be easily transformed to this more general case (see, e.g., Nahmias 2005). Moreover, given the robustness of the economic order quantity, the EOQ model leads to reasonably good recommendations even if applied to production settings with setup costs. Hence, we will not discuss the analytical aspects of this. Instead, we want to step back for a moment and reflect on how the EOQ model relates to our discussion of setup times at the beginning of the chapter.

A common mistake is to rely too much on setup *costs* as opposed to setup *times*. For example, consider the case of Figure 7.6 and assume that the monthly capital cost for the milling machine is $9,000, which corresponds to $64 per hour (assuming four weeks of 35 hours each). Thus, when choosing the batch size, and focusing primarily on costs, Nova Cruz might shy away from frequent setups. Management might even consider using the economic order quantity established above and thereby quantify the impact of larger batches on inventory holding costs.

There are two major mistakes in this approach:

• This approach to choosing batch sizes ignores the fact that the investment in the machine is already sunk.

• Choosing the batch size based on cost ignores the effect setups have on process capacity. As long as setup costs are a reflection of the cost of capacity—as opposed to direct financial setup costs—they should be ignored when choosing the batch size. It is the overall process flow that matters, not an artificial local performance measure! From a capacity perspective, setups at nonbottleneck resources are free. And if the setups do occur at the bottleneck, the corresponding setup costs not only reflect the capacity costs of the local resource, but of the entire process!

Thus, when choosing batch sizes, it is important to distinguish between setup costs and setup times. If the motivation behind batching results from setup times (or opportunity costs of capacity), we should focus on optimizing the process flow. Section 7.3 provides the appropriate way to find a good batch size. If we face "true" setup costs (in the sense of out-of-pocket costs) and we only look at a single resource (as opposed to an entire process flow), the EOQ model can be used to find the optimal order quantity.

Finally, if we encounter a combination of setup times and (out-of-pocket) setup costs, we should use both approaches and compare the recommended batch sizes. If the batch size from the EOQ is sufficiently large so that the resource with the setup is not the bottleneck, minimizing costs is appropriate. If the batch size from the EOQ, however, makes the resource with the setups the bottleneck, we need to consider increasing the batch size beyond the EOQ recommendation.

7.8   Other Flow Interruptions: Buffer or Suffer

In addition to illustrating the SMED method, the race car example also helps to illustrate how the concept of batching can be applied to *continuous process flows,* as opposed to discrete manufacturing environments. First of all, we observe that the calculation of the average speed of the race car is nothing but a direct application of the batching formula introduced at the beginning of this chapter:

$$\text{Average speed (number of miles between stops)} =$$

$$\frac{\text{Number of miles between stops}}{\text{Duration of the stop} + \text{Time to cover one mile} \times \text{Number of miles between stops}}$$

In continuous flow processes, the quantity between two flow interruptions is frequently referred to as a production run.

Consider the production of orange juice, which is produced in a continuous flow process. At an abstract level, orange juice is produced in a three-step process: extraction, filtering, and bottling. Given that the filter at the second process step has to be changed regularly, the process needs to be stopped for 30 minutes following every four hours of production. While operating, the step can produce up to 100 barrels per hour.

To determine the capacity of the filtering step, we use

$$\text{Capacity } (B) = \frac{B}{S + B \times p}$$

$$= \frac{\text{Amount processed between two stops}}{\text{Duration of stop} + \text{Time to produce one barrel} \times \text{Amount processed between two stops}}$$

$$= \frac{400 \text{ barrels}}{30 \text{ minutes} + 60/100 \text{ minutes per barrel} \times 400 \text{ barrels}}$$

$$= \frac{400 \text{ barrels}}{270 \text{ minutes}}$$

$$= 1.48 \ barrels/minute = 88.88 \ barrels/hour$$

FIGURE 7.10

Data for the Production of Orange Juice

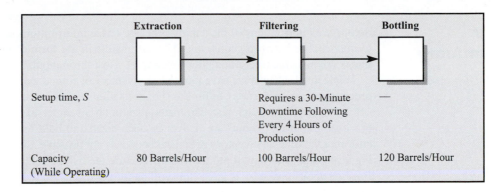

	Extraction	Filtering	Bottling
Setup time, S	—	Requires a 30-Minute Downtime Following Every 4 Hours of Production	—
Capacity (While Operating)	80 Barrels/Hour	100 Barrels/Hour	120 Barrels/Hour

While in the case of batch flow operations we have allowed for substantial buffer sizes between process steps, the process as described in Figure 7.10 is currently operating without buffers. This has substantial implications for the overall flow rate.

Analyzing each step in isolation would suggest that the extraction step is the bottleneck, which would give us a process capacity of 80 barrels per hour. However, in the absence of buffers, the extraction step needs to stop producing the moment the filtering step is shut down. Thus, while running, the process is constrained by the extraction step, producing an output of 80 barrels per hour, and while being shut down, the process step is constrained by the filtering step (at 0 barrel per hour).

Previously, we considered the setup step in isolation from the rest of the process. That is a valid analysis if the setup step indeed works in isolation from the rest of the process, that is, if there is sufficient inventory (buffers) between steps. That assumption is violated here: The filtering step cannot operate at 88 barrels per hour because it is constrained by the extraction step of 80 barrels per hour.

For this reason, when we use our equation

$$\text{Capacity} = \frac{\text{Amount processed between two stops}}{\text{Duration of stop} + \text{Time to produce one barrel} \times \text{Amount processed between two stops}}$$

it is important that we acknowledge that we are producing at a rate of 80 barrels per hour (i.e., $\frac{1}{80}$ hour per barrel) while we are at the filtering step. This leads to the following computation of process capacity:

$$\text{Capacity} = \frac{320 \text{ barrels}}{0.5 \text{ hour} + \dfrac{1}{80} \text{ hour per barrel} \times 320 \text{ barrels}}$$

$$= 320 \text{ barrels}/4.5 \text{ hours}$$

$$= 71.11 \text{ barrels/hour}$$

This prompts the following interesting observation: In the presence of flow interruptions, buffers can increase process capacity. Practitioners refer to this phenomenon as "buffer or suffer," indicating that flow interruptions can be smoothed out by introducing buffer inventories. In the case of Figure 7.10, the buffer would need to absorb the outflow of the extraction step during the downtime of the reduction step. Thus, adding a buffer between these two steps would indeed increase process capacity up to the level where, with 80 barrels per hour, the extraction step becomes the bottleneck.

7.9 Summary

Setups are interruptions of the supply process. These interruptions on the supply side lead to mismatches between supply and demand, visible in the form of inventory and—where this is not possible (see orange juice example)—lost throughput.

While in this chapter we have focused on inventory of components (handle caps), work-in-process (steer support parts), or finished goods (station wagons versus sedans, Figure 7.4), the supply–demand mismatch also can materialize in an inventory of waiting customer orders. For example, if the product we deliver is customized and built to the specifications of the customer, holding an inventory of finished goods is not possible. Similarly, if we are providing a substantial variety of products to the market, the risk of holding completed variants in finished goods inventory is large (this will be further discussed in Chapter 15). Independent of the form of inventory, a large inventory corresponds to long flow times (Little's Law). For this reason, batch processes are typically associated with very long customer lead times.

In this chapter, we discussed tools to choose a batch size. We distinguished between setup times and setup costs. To the extent that a process faces setup times, we need to extend our process analysis to capture the negative impact that setups have on capacity. We then want to look for a batch size that is large enough to not make the process step with the setup the bottleneck, while being small enough to avoid excessive inventory.

To the extent that a process faces (out-of-pocket) setup costs, we need to balance these costs against the cost of inventory. We discussed the EOQ model for the case of supply arriving in one single quantity (sourcing from a supplier), as well as the case of internal production. Figure 7.11 provides a summary of the major steps you should take when analyzing processes with flow interruptions, including setup times, setup costs, or machine downtimes. There are countless extensions to the EOQ model to capture, among other things, quantity discounts, perishability, learning effects, inflation, and quality problems.

Our ability to choose a "good" batch size provides another example of process improvement. Consider a process with significant setup times at one resource. As a manager of this process, we need to balance the conflicting objectives of

- Fast response to customers (short flow times, which correspond, because of Little's Law, to low inventory levels), which results from using small batch sizes.
- Cost benefits that result from using large batch sizes. The reason for this is that large batch sizes enable a high throughput, which in turn allows the firm to spread out its fixed costs over a maximum number of flow units.

FIGURE 7.11 **Summary of Batching**

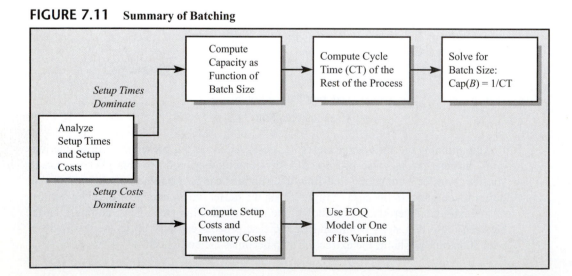

FIGURE 7.12
Choosing a Batch Size

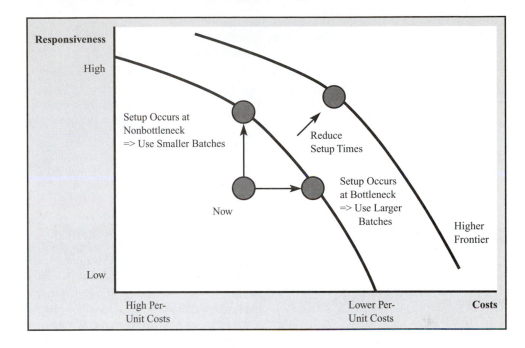

This tension is illustrated by Figure 7.12. Similar to the case of line balancing, we observe that adjustments in the batch size are not trading in one performance measure against the other, but allow us to improve by reducing current inefficiencies in the process.

Despite our ability to choose batch sizes that mitigate the tension between inventory (responsiveness) and costs, there ultimately is only one way to handle setups: eliminate them wherever possible or at least shorten them. Setups do not add value and are therefore wasteful.

Methods such as SMED are powerful tools that can reduce setup times substantially. Similarly, the need for transfer batches can be reduced by locating the process resources according to the flow of the process.

7.10 Further Reading

Nahmias (2005) is a widely used textbook in operations management that discusses, among other things, many variants of the EOQ model.

7.11 Practice Problems

Q7.1*   **(Window Boxes)** Metal window boxes are manufactured in two process steps: stamping and assembly. Each window box is made up of three pieces: a base (one part A) and two sides (two part Bs).

The parts are fabricated by a single stamping machine that requires a setup time of 120 minutes whenever switching between the two part types. Once the machine is set up, the processing time for each part A is one minute while the processing time for each part B is only 30 seconds.

Currently, the stamping machine rotates its production between one batch of 360 for part A and one batch of 720 for part B. Completed parts move from the stamping machine to the assembly only after the entire batch is complete.

At assembly, parts are assembled manually to form the finished product. One base (part A) and two sides (two part Bs), as well as a number of small purchased components, are required for each unit of final product. Each product requires 27 minutes of labor time

(* indicates that the solution is at the end of the book)

to assemble. There are currently 12 workers in assembly. There is sufficient demand to sell every box the system can make.

　　a. What is the capacity of the stamping machine?

　　b. What batch size would you recommend for the process?

Q7.2** **(PTests)** Precision Testing (PTests) does fluid testing for several local hospitals. Consider their urine testing process. Each sample requires 12 seconds to test, but after 300 samples, the equipment must be recalibrated. No samples can be tested during the recalibration process and that process takes 30 minutes.

　　a. What is PTest's maximum capacity to test urine samples (in samples per hour)?

　　b. Suppose 2.5 urine samples need to be tested per minute. What is the smallest batch size (in samples) that ensures that the process is not supply constrained? (Note; A batch is the number of tests between calibrations.)

　　c. PTest also needs to test blood samples. There are two kinds of tests that can be done— a "basic" test and a "complete" test. Basic tests require 15 seconds per sample, whereas "complete" tests require 1.5 minutes per sample. After 100 tests, the equipment needs to be cleaned and recalibrated, which takes 20 minutes. Suppose PTest runs the following cyclic schedule: 70 basic tests, 30 complete tests, recalibrate, and then repeat. With this schedule, how many *basic* tests can they complete per minute on average?

Q7.3 **(Gelato)** Bruno Fruscalzo decided to set up a small production facility in Sydney to sell to local restaurants that want to offer gelato on their dessert menu. To start simple, he would offer only three flavors of gelato: fragola (strawberry), chocolato (chocolate), and bacio (chocolate with hazelnut). After a short time he found his demand and setup times to be

	Fragola	Chocolato	Bacio
Demand (kg/hour)	10	15	5
Setup time (hours)	3/4	1/2	1/6

Bruno first produces a batch of fragola, then a batch of chocolato, then a batch of bacio and then he repeats that sequence. For example, after producing bacio and before producing fragola, he needs 45 minutes to set up the ice cream machine, but he needs only 10 minutes to switch from chocolato to bacio. When running, his ice cream machine produces at the rate of 50 kg per hour no matter which flavor it is producing (and, of course, it can produce only one flavor at a time).

　　a. Suppose Bruno wants to minimize the amount of each flavor produced at one time while still satisfying the demand for each of the flavors. (He can choose a different quantity for each flavor.) If we define a batch to be the quantity produced in a single run of each flavor, how many kilograms should he produce in each batch?

　　b. Given your answer in part (a), how many kilograms of fragola should he make with each batch?

　　c. Given your answer in part (a), what is the maximum inventory of chocolato? (Assume production and demand occur at constant rates.)

Q7.4 **(Two-step)** Consider the following two step process:

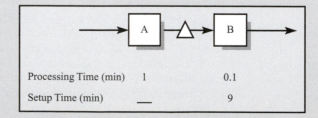

Processing Time (min)	1	0.1
Setup Time (min)	—	9

Step A has a processing time of 1 minute per unit, but no setup is required. Step B has an processing time of 0.1 minute per unit, but a setup time of 9 minutes is require per batch. A buffer with ample inventory is allowed between the two steps.

a. Suppose units are produced in batches of 5 (i.e., after each set of 5 units are produced, step B must incur a setup of 9 minutes). What is the capacity of the process (in units per minute)?

b. What is the batch size that maximizes the flow rate of this process with minimal inventory? Assume there is ample demand.

c. Now suppose the inventory buffer is removed between steps A and B:

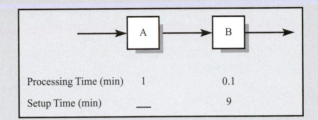

| Processing Time (min) | 1 | 0.1 |
| Setup Time (min) | — | 9 |

Thus, when B is being set up, A cannot work because there is no place to put its completed units. Once B has finished its setup and is ready to work on units, A can resume its work because B is now ready to accept A's output. What batch size achieves a flow rate of 0.82 unit per minute?

Q7.5 **(Simple Setup)** Consider the following batch flow process consisting of three process steps performed by three machines:

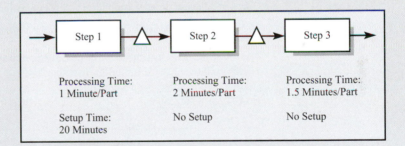

Step 1	Step 2	Step 3
Processing Time: 1 Minute/Part	Processing Time: 2 Minutes/Part	Processing Time: 1.5 Minutes/Part
Setup Time: 20 Minutes	No Setup	No Setup

Work is processed in batches at each step. Before a batch is processed at step 1, the machine has to be set up. During a setup, the machine is unable to process any product.

a. Assume that the batch size is 50 parts. What is the capacity of the process?

b. For a batch size of 10 parts, which step is the bottleneck for the process?

c. Using the current production batch size of 50 parts, how long would it take to produce 20 parts starting with an empty system? Assume that the units in the batch have to stay together (no smaller transfer batches allowed) when transferred to step 2 and to step 3. A unit can leave the system the moment it is completed at step 3. Assume step 1 needs to be set up before the beginning of production.

d. Using the current production batch size of 50 parts, how long would it take to produce 20 parts starting with an empty system? Assume that the units in the batch do *not* have to stay together; specifically, units are transferred to the next step the moment they are completed at any step. Assume step 1 needs to be set up before the beginning of production.

e. What batch size would you choose, assuming that all units of a batch stay together for the entire process?

Q7.6   **(Setup Everywhere)** Consider the following batch-flow process consisting of three process steps performed by three machines:

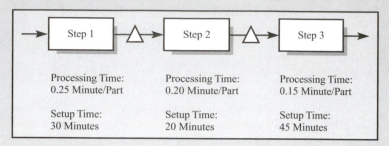

Work is processed in batches at each step. Before a batch is processed at a step, the machine at that step must be set up. (During a setup, the machine is unable to process any product.) Assume that there is a dedicated setup operator for each machine (i.e., there is always someone available to perform a setup at each machine.)

a. What is the capacity of step 1 if the batch size is 35 parts?

b. For what batch sizes is step 1 (2, 3) the bottleneck?

Q7.7   **(JCL Inc.)** JCL Inc. is a major chip manufacturing firm that sells its products to computer manufacturers like Dell, HP, and others. In simplified terms, chip making at JCL Inc. involves three basic operations: depositing, patterning, and etching.

- **Depositing:** Using chemical vapor deposition (CVD) technology, an insulating material is deposited on the wafer surface, forming a thin layer of solid material on the chip.

- **Patterning:** Photolithography projects a microscopic circuit pattern on the wafer surface, which has a light-sensitive chemical like the emulsion on photographic film. It is repeated many times as each layer of the chip is built.

- **Etching:** Etching removes selected material from the chip surface to create the device structures.

The following table lists the required processing times and setup times at each of the steps. There is unlimited space for buffer inventory between these steps. Assume that the unit of production is a wafer, from which individual chips are cut at a later stage.

Note: A Setup can only begin once the batch has arrived at the machine.

Process Step	1 Depositing	2 Patterning	3 Etching
Setup time	45 min.	30 min.	20 min.
Processing time	0.15 min./unit	0.25 min./unit	0.20 min./unit

a. What is the process capacity in units per hour with a batch size of 100 wafers?

b. For the current batch size of 100 wafers, how long would it take to produce 50 wafers? Assume that the batch needs to stay together during deposition and patterning (i.e., the firm does not work with transfer batches that are less than the production batch). However, the 50 wafers can leave the process the moment all 50 wafers have passed through the etching stage. Recall that a setup can only be started upon the arrival of the batch at the machine.

c. For what batch size is step 3 (etching) the bottleneck?

d. Suppose JCL Inc. came up with a new technology that eliminated the setup time for step 1 (deposition), but increased the processing time to 0.45 min./unit. What would be the batch size you would choose so as to maximize the overall capacity of the process, assuming all units of a batch stay together for the entire process?

Q7.8   **(Kinga Doll Company)** Kinga Doll Company manufactures eight versions of its popular girl doll, Shari. The company operates on a 40-hour work week. The eight versions differ in doll skin, hair, and eye color, enabling most children to have a doll with a similar appearance to them. It currently sells an average of 4,000 dolls (spread equally among its eight versions) per week to boutique toy retailers. In simplified terms, doll making at Kinga involves three basic operations: molding the body and hair, painting the face, and dressing the doll. Changing over between versions requires setup time at the molding and painting stations due to the different colors of plastic pellets, hair, and eye color paint required. The table below lists the setup times for a batch and the processing times for each unit at each step. Unlimited space for buffer inventory exists between these steps.

Assume that (i) setups need to be completed first, (ii) a setup can only start once the batch has arrived at the resource, and (iii) all flow units of a batch need to be processed at a resource before any of the units of the batch can be moved to the next resource.

Process Step	1 Molding	2 Painting	3 Dressing
Setup time	15 min.	30 min.	No setup
Processing time	0.25 min./unit	0.15 min./unit	0.30 min./unit

a. What is the process capacity in units per hour with a batch size of 500 dolls?

b. What is the time it takes for the first batch of 500 dolls to go through an empty process?

c. Which batch size would minimize inventory without decreasing the process capacity?

d. Which batch size would minimize inventory without decreasing the current flow rate?

Q7.9 **(Bubba Chump Shrimp)** The Bubba Chump Shrimp Company processes and packages shrimp for sale to wholesale seafood distributors. The shrimp are transported to the main plant by trucks that carry 1,000 pounds (lb) of shrimp. Once the continuous flow processing of the shrimp begins, *no* inventory is allowed in buffers due to spoilage and all of the shrimp must be processed within 12 hours to prevent spoilage. The processing begins at the sorter, where the trucks dump the shrimp onto a conveyor belt that feeds into the sorter, which can sort up to 500 lb per hour. The shrimp then proceed to the desheller, which can process shrimp at the rate of 400 lb per hour. However, after 3 hours and 45 minutes of processing, the desheller must be stopped for 15 minutes to clean out empty shrimp shells that have accumulated. The veins of the shrimp are then removed in the deveining area at a maximum rate of 360 lb per hour. The shrimp proceed to the washing area, where they are processed at 750 lb per hour. Finally, the shrimp are packaged and frozen.

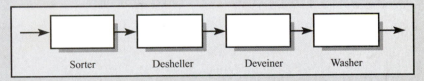

Sorter   Desheller   Deveiner   Washer

Note: All unit weights given are in "final processed shrimp." You do *not* need to account for the weight of the waste in the deshelling area. The plant operates continuously for 12 hours per day beginning at 8:00 a.m. Finally, there is negligible time to fill the system in the morning.

a. What is the daily process capacity of the desheller (in isolation from the other processes)?

b. What is the daily process capacity of the deveiner (in isolation from the other processes)?

c. What is the daily process capacity of the processing plant (excluding the packaging and freezing)?

d. If five trucks arrive one morning at 8:00 a.m., what is the total number of pounds of shrimp that must be wasted?

Q7.10* **(Cat Food)** Cat Lovers Inc. (CLI) is the distributor of a very popular blend of cat food that sells for $1.25 per can. CLI experiences demand of 500 cans per week on average. They order the cans of cat food from the Nutritious & Delicious Co. (N&D). N&D sells cans to CLI at $0.50 per can and charges a flat fee of $7 per order for shipping and handling.

　　CLI uses the economic order quantity as their fixed order size. Assume that the opportunity cost of capital and all other inventory cost is 15 percent annually and that there are 50 weeks in a year.

　　a. How many cans of cat food should CLI order at a time?

　　b. What is CLI's total order cost for one year?

　　c. What is CLI's total holding cost for one year?

　　d. What is CLI's weekly inventory turns?

Q7.11* **(Beer Distributor)** A beer distributor finds that it sells on average 100 cases a week of regular 12-oz. Budweiser. For this problem assume that demand occurs at a constant rate over a 50-week year. The distributor currently purchases beer every two weeks at a cost of $8 per case. The inventory-related holding cost (capital, insurance, etc.) for the distributor equals 25 percent of the dollar value of inventory per year. Each order placed with the supplier costs the distributor $10. This cost includes labor, forms, postage, and so forth.

　　a. Assume the distributor can choose any order quantity it wishes. What order quantity minimizes the distributor's total inventory-related costs (holding and ordering)?

　　　For the next three parts, assume the distributor selects the order quantity specified in part (a).

　　b. What are the distributor's inventory turns per year?

　　c. What is the inventory-related cost per case of beer sold?

　　d. Assume the brewer is willing to give a 5 percent quantity discount if the distributor orders 600 cases or more at a time. If the distributor is interested in minimizing its total cost (i.e., purchase and inventory-related costs), should the distributor begin ordering 600 or more cases at a time?

Q7.12** **(Millennium Liquors)** Millennium Liquors is a wholesaler of sparkling wines. Their most popular product is the French Bete Noire. Weekly demand is for 45 cases. Assume demand occurs over 50 weeks per year. The wine is shipped directly from France. Millennium's annual cost of capital is 15 percent, which also includes all other inventory-related costs. Below are relevant data on the costs of shipping, placing orders, and refrigeration.

　　• Cost per case: $120

　　• Shipping cost (for any size shipment): $290

　　• Cost of labor to place and process an order: $10

　　• Fixed cost for refrigeration: $75/week

　　a. Calculate the weekly holding cost for one case of wine.

　　b. Use the EOQ model to find the number of cases per order and the average number of orders per year.

　　c. Currently orders are placed by calling France and then following up with a letter. Millennium and its supplier may switch to a simple ordering system using the Internet. The new system will require much less labor. What would be the impact of this system on the ordering pattern?

Q7.13 **(Powered by Koffee)** Powered by Koffee (PBK) is a new campus coffee store. PBK uses 50 bags of whole bean coffee every month, and you may assume that demand is perfectly steady throughout the year.

　　PBK has signed a year-long contract to purchase its coffee from a local supplier, Phish Roasters, for a price of $25 per bag and an $85 fixed cost for every delivery independent

(* indicates that the solution is at the end of the book)

of the order size. The holding cost due to storage is $1 per bag per month. PBK managers figure their cost of capital is approximately 2 percent per month.

a. What is the optimal order size, in bags?

b. Given your answer in (a), how many times a year does PBK place orders?

c. Given your answer in (a), how many months of supply of coffee does PBK have on average?

d. On average, how many dollars per month does PBK spend to hold coffee (including cost of capital)?

Suppose that a South American import/export company has offered PBK a deal for the next year. PBK can buy a years' worth of coffee directly from South America for $20 per bag and a fixed cost for delivery of $500. Assume the estimated cost for inspection and storage is $1 per bag per month and the cost of capital is approximately 2 percent per month.

e. Should PBK order from Phish Roasters or the South American import/export company? Quantitatively justify your answer.

Chapter

8

Variability and Its Impact on Process Performance: Waiting Time Problems

For consumers, one of the most visible—and probably annoying—forms of supply–demand mismatches is waiting time. As consumers, we seem to spend a significant portion of our life waiting in line, be it in physical lines (supermarkets, check-in at airports) or in "virtual" lines (listening to music in a call center, waiting for a response e-mail).

It is important to distinguish between different types of waiting time:

• Waiting time predictably occurs when the expected demand rate exceeds the expected supply rate for some limited period of time. This happens especially in cases of constant capacity levels and demand that exhibits seasonality. This leads to implied utilization levels of over 100 percent for some time period. Queues forming at the gate of an airport after the flight is announced are an example of such queues.

• As we will see in the next section, in the presence of variability, queues also can arise if the implied utilization is below 100 percent. Such queues can thereby be fully attributed to the presence of variability, as there exists, on average, enough capacity to meet demand.

While the difference between these two types of waiting time probably does not matter much to the customer, it is of great importance from the perspective of operations management. The root cause for the first type of waiting time is a capacity problem; variability is only a secondary effect. Thus, when analyzing this type of a problem, we first should use the tools outlined in Chapters 3, 4, and 7 instead of focusing on variability.

The root cause of the second type of waiting time is variability. This makes waiting time unpredictable, both from the perspective of the customer as well as from the perspective of the operation. Sometimes, it is the customer (demand) waiting for service (supply) and, sometimes, it is the other way around. Demand just never seems to match supply in these settings.

Analyzing waiting times and linking these waiting times to variability require the introduction of new analytical tools, which we present in this chapter. We will discuss the tools for analyzing waiting times based on the example of An-ser Services, a call-center operation in

Wisconsin that specializes in providing answering services for financial services, insurance companies, and medical practices. Specifically, the objective of this chapter is to

- Predict waiting times and derive some performance metrics capturing the service quality provided to the customer.
- Recommend ways of reducing waiting time by choosing appropriate capacity levels, redesigning the service system, and outlining opportunities to reduce variability.

8.1   Motivating Example: A Somewhat Unrealistic Call Center

For illustrative purposes, consider a call center with just one employee from 7 A.M. to 8 A.M. Based on prior observations, the call-center management estimates that, on average, a call takes 4 minutes to complete (e.g., giving someone driving directions) and there are, on average, 12 calls arriving in a 60-minute period, that is, on average, one call every 5 minutes.

What will be the average waiting time for a customer before talking to a customer service representative? From a somewhat naïve perspective, there should be no waiting time at all. Since the call center has a capacity of serving 60/4 = 15 calls per hour and calls arrive at a rate of 12 calls per hour, supply of capacity clearly exceeds demand. If anything, there seems to be excess service capacity in the call center since its utilization, which we defined previously (Chapter 3) as the ratio between flow rate and capacity, can be computed as

$$\text{Utilization} = \frac{\text{Flow rate}}{\text{Capacity}} = \frac{12 \text{ calls per hour}}{15 \text{ calls per hour}} = 80\%$$

First, consider the arrivals and processing times as depicted in Figure 8.1. A call arrives exactly every 5 minutes and then takes exactly 4 minutes to be served. This is probably the weirdest call center that you have ever seen! No need to worry, we will return to "real operations" momentarily, but the following thought experiment will help you grasp how variability can lead to waiting time.

Despite its almost robotlike processing times and the apparently very disciplined customer service representative ("sorry, 4 minutes are over; thanks for your call"), this call center has one major advantage: no incoming call ever has to wait.

FIGURE 8.1
A Somewhat Odd Service Process

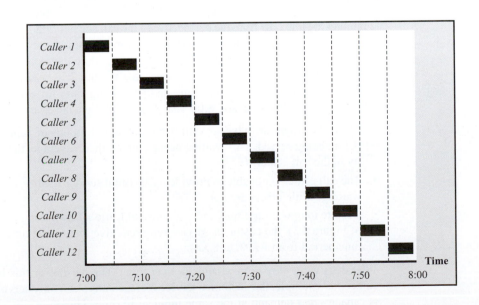

FIGURE 8.2
Data Gathered at a Call Center

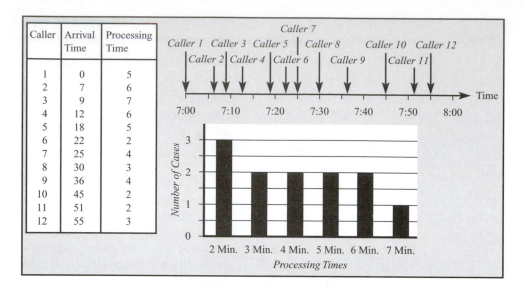

Caller	Arrival Time	Processing Time
1	0	5
2	7	6
3	9	7
4	12	6
5	18	5
6	22	2
7	25	4
8	30	3
9	36	4
10	45	2
11	51	2
12	55	3

Assuming that calls arrive like kick scooters at an assembly line and are then treated by customer service representatives that act like robots reflects a common mistake managers make when calculating process performance. These calculations look at the process at an aggregate level and consider how much capacity is available over the entire hour (day, month, quarter), yet ignore how the requests for service are spaced out within the hour.

If we look at the call center on a minute-by-minute basis, a different picture emerges. Specifically, we observe that calls do not arrive like kick scooters appear at the end of the assembly line, but instead follow a much less systematic pattern, which is illustrated by Figure 8.2.

Moreover, a minute-by-minute analysis also reveals that the actual service durations also vary across calls. As Figure 8.2 shows, while the average processing time is 4 minutes, there exist large variations across calls, and the actual processing times range from 2 minutes to 7 minutes.

Now, consider how the hour from 7:00 A.M. to 8:00 A.M. unfolds. As can be seen in Figure 8.2, the first call comes in at 7:00 A.M. This call will be served without waiting time, and it takes the customer service representative 5 minutes to complete the call. The following 2 minutes are idle time from the perspective of the call center (7:05–7:07). At 7:07, the second call comes in, requiring a 6-minute processing time. Again, the second caller does not have to wait and will leave the system at 7:13. However, while the second caller is being served, at 7:09 the third caller arrives and now needs to wait until 7:13 before beginning the service.

Figure 8.3 shows the waiting time and processing time for each of the 12 customers calling between 7:00 A.M. and 8:00 A.M. Specifically, we observe that

- Most customers do have to wait a considerable amount of time (up to 10 minutes) before being served. This waiting occurs, although, on average, there is plenty of capacity in the call center.

- The call center is not able to provide a consistent service quality, as some customers are waiting, while others are not.

- Despite long waiting times and—because of Little's Law—long queues (see lower part of Figure 8.3), the customer service representative incurs idle time repeatedly over the time period from 7 A.M. to 8 A.M.

Why does variability not average out over time? The reason for this is as follows. In the call center example, the customer service representative can only serve a customer if there is capacity *and* demand at the same moment in time. Therefore, capacity can never "run

FIGURE 8.3
Detailed Analysis of Call Center

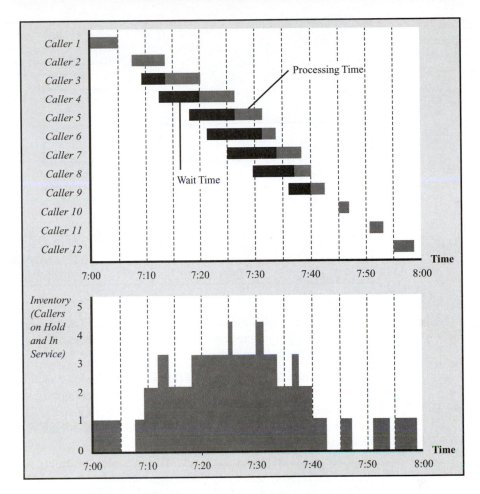

ahead" of demand. However, demand can "run ahead" of capacity, in which case the queue builds up. The idea that inventory can be used to decouple the supply process from demand, thereby restoring the flow rate to the level achievable in the absence of variability, is another version of the "buffer or suffer" principle that we already encountered in Chapter 7. Thus, if a service organization attempts to achieve the flow-rate levels feasible based on averages, long waiting times will result (unfortunately, in those cases, it is the customer who gets "buffered" and "suffers").

Taking the perspective of a manager attempting to match supply and demand, our objectives have not changed. We are still interested in calculating the three fundamental performance measures of an operation: inventory, flow rate, and flow time. Yet, as the above example illustrated, we realize that the process analysis tools we have discussed up to this point in the book need to be extended to appropriately deal with variability.

8.2 Variability: Where It Comes From and How It Can Be Measured

As a first step toward restoring our ability to understand a process's basic performance measures in the presence of variability, we take a more detailed look at the concept of variability itself. Specifically, we are interested in the sources of variability and how to measure variability.

FIGURE 8.4
Variability and Where It Comes From

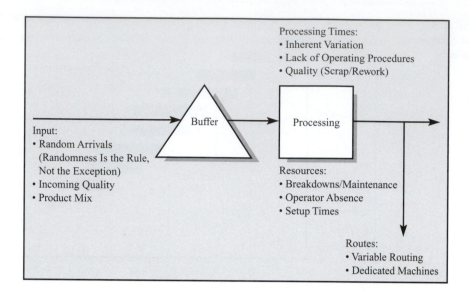

Why is there variability in a process to begin with? Drawing a simple (the most simple) process flow diagram suggests the following four sources of variability (these four sources are summarized in Figure 8.4):

• Variability from the inflow of flow units. The biggest source of variability in service organizations comes from the market itself. While some patterns of the customer-arrival process are predictable (e.g., in a hotel there are more guests checking out between 8 A.M. and 9 A.M. than between 2 P.M. and 3 P.M.), there always remains uncertainty about when the next customer will arrive.

• Variability in processing times. Whenever we are dealing with human operators at a resource, it is likely that there will be some variability in their behavior. Thus, if we would ask a worker at an assembly line to repeat a certain activity 100 times, we would probably find that some of these activities were carried out faster than others. Another source of variability in processing times that is specific to a service environment is that in most service operations, the customer him/herself is involved in many of the tasks constituting the processing time. At a hotel front desk, some guests might require extra time (e.g., the guest requires an explanation for items appearing on his or her bill), while others check out faster (e.g., simply use the credit card that they used for the reservation and only return their room key).

• Random availability of resources. If resources are subject to random breakdowns, for example, machine failures in manufacturing environments or operator absenteeism in service operations, variability is created.

• Random routing in case of multiple flow units in the process. If the path a flow unit takes through the process is itself random, the arrival process at each individual resource is subject to variability. Consider, for example, an emergency room in a hospital. Following the initial screening at the admissions step, incoming patients are routed to different resources. A nurse might handle easy cases, more complex cases might be handled by a general doctor, and severe cases are brought to specific units in the hospital (e.g., trauma center). Even if arrival times and processing times are deterministic, this random routing alone is sufficient to introduce variability.

In general, any form of variability is measured based on the standard deviation. In our case of the call center, we could measure the variability of call durations based on collecting some data and then computing the corresponding standard deviation. The problem with this approach is that the standard deviation provides an *absolute* measure of variability. Does a standard deviation of 5 minutes indicate a high variability? A 5-minute standard deviation for call durations (processing times) in the context of a call center seems like a large number. In the context of a 2-hour surgery in a trauma center, a 5-minute standard deviation seems small.

For this reason, it is more appropriate to measure variability in *relative* terms. Specifically, we define the *coefficient of variation* of a random variable as

$$\text{Coefficient of variation} = \text{CV} = \frac{\text{Standard deviation}}{\text{Mean}}$$

As both the standard deviation and the mean have the same measurement units, the coefficient of variation is a unitless measure.

8.3 Analyzing an Arrival Process

Any process analysis we perform is only as good as the information we feed into our analysis. For this reason, Sections 8.3 and 8.4 focus on data collection and data analysis for the upcoming mathematical models. As a manager intending to apply some of the following tools, this data analysis is essential. However, as a student with only a couple of hours left to the final exam, you might be better off jumping straight to Section 8.5.

Of particular importance when dealing with variability problems is an accurate representation of the demand, which determines the timing of customer arrivals.

Assume we got up early and visited the call center of An-ser; say we arrived at their offices at 6:00 A.M. and we took detailed notes of what takes place over the coming hour. We would hardly have had the time to settle down when the first call comes in. One of the An-ser staff takes the call immediately. Twenty-three seconds later, the second call comes in; another 1:24 minutes later, the third call; and so on.

We define the time at which An-ser receives a call as the *arrival time*. Let AT_i denote the arrival time of the ith call. Moreover, we define the time between two consecutive arrivals as the *interarrival time*, IA. Thus, $IA_i = AT_{i+1} - AT_i$. Figure 8.5 illustrates these two definitions.

If we continue this data collection, we accumulate a fair number of arrival times. Such data are automatically recorded in call centers, so we could simply download a file that looks like Table 8.1.

Before we can move forward and introduce a mathematical model that predicts the effects of variability, we have to invest in some simple, yet important, data analysis. A major risk related to any mathematical model or computer simulation is that these tools always provide

FIGURE 8.5 **The Concept of Interarrival Times**

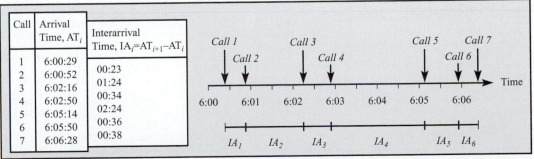

Call	Arrival Time, AT_i	Interarrival Time, $IA_i = AT_{i+1} - AT_i$
1	6:00:29	
2	6:00:52	00:23
3	6:02:16	01:24
4	6:02:50	00:34
5	6:05:14	02:24
6	6:05:50	00:36
7	6:06:28	00:38

TABLE 8.1   Call Arrivals at An-ser on April 2, from 6:00 A.M. to 10:00 A.M.

6:00:29	6:52:39	7:17:57	7:33:51	7:56:16	8:17:33	8:28:11	8:39:25	8:55:56	9:21:58
6:00:52	6:53:06	7:18:10	7:34:05	7:56:24	8:17:42	8:28:12	8:39:47	8:56:17	9:22:02
6:02:16	6:53:07	7:18:17	7:34:19	7:56:24	8:17:50	8:28:13	8:39:51	8:57:42	9:22:02
6:02:50	6:53:24	7:18:38	7:34:51	7:57:39	8:17:52	8:28:17	8:40:02	8:58:45	9:22:30
6:05:14	6:53:25	7:18:54	7:35:10	7:57:51	8:17:54	8:28:43	8:40:09	8:58:49	9:23:13
6:05:50	6:54:18	7:19:04	7:35:13	7:57:55	8:18:03	8:28:59	8:40:23	8:58:49	9:23:29
6:06:28	6:54:24	7:19:40	7:35:21	7:58:26	8:18:12	8:29:06	8:40:34	8:59:32	9:23:45
6:07:37	6:54:36	7:19:41	7:35:44	7:58:41	8:18:21	8:29:34	8:40:35	8:59:38	9:24:10
6:08:05	6:55:06	7:20:10	7:35:59	7:59:12	8:18:23	8:29:38	8:40:46	8:59:45	9:24:30
6:10:16	6:55:19	7:20:11	7:36:37	7:59:20	8:18:34	8:29:40	8:40:51	9:00:14	9:24:42
6:12:13	6:55:31	7:20:26	7:36:45	7:59:22	8:18:46	8:29:45	8:40:58	9:00:52	9:25:07
6:12:48	6:57:25	7:20:27	7:37:07	7:59:22	8:18:53	8:29:46	8:41:12	9:00:53	9:25:15
6:14:04	6:57:38	7:20:38	7:37:14	7:59:36	8:18:54	8:29:47	8:41:26	9:01:09	9:26:03
6:14:16	6:57:44	7:20:52	7:38:01	7:59:50	8:18:58	8:29:47	8:41:32	9:01:31	9:26:04
6:14:28	6:58:16	7:20:59	7:38:03	7:59:54	8:19:20	8:29:54	8:41:49	9:01:55	9:26:23
6:17:51	6:58:34	7:21:11	7:38:05	8:01:22	8:19:25	8:30:00	8:42:23	9:02:25	9:26:34
6:18:19	6:59:41	7:21:14	7:38:18	8:01:42	8:19:28	8:30:01	8:42:51	9:02:30	9:27:02
6:19:11	7:00:50	7:21:46	7:39:00	8:01:56	8:20:09	8:30:08	8:42:53	9:02:38	9:27:04
6:20:48	7:00:54	7:21:56	7:39:17	8:02:08	8:20:23	8:30:23	8:43:24	9:02:51	9:27:27
6:23:33	7:01:08	7:21:58	7:39:35	8:02:26	8:20:27	8:30:23	8:43:28	9:03:29	9:28:25
6:24:25	7:01:31	7:23:03	7:40:06	8:02:29	8:20:44	8:30:31	8:43:47	9:03:33	9:28:37
6:25:08	7:01:39	7:23:16	7:40:23	8:02:39	8:20:54	8:31:02	8:44:23	9:03:38	9:29:09
6:25:19	7:01:56	7:23:19	7:41:34	8:02:47	8:21:12	8:31:11	8:44:49	9:03:51	9:29:15
6:25:27	7:04:52	7:23:48	7:42:20	8:02:52	8:21:12	8:31:19	8:45:05	9:04:11	9:29:52
6:25:38	7:04:54	7:24:01	7:42:33	8:03:06	8:21:25	8:31:20	8:45:10	9:04:33	9:30:47
6:25:48	7:05:37	7:24:09	7:42:51	8:03:58	8:21:28	8:31:22	8:45:28	9:04:42	9:30:58
6:26:05	7:05:39	7:24:45	7:42:57	8:04:07	8:21:43	8:31:23	8:45:31	9:04:44	9:30:59
6:26:59	7:05:42	7:24:56	7:43:23	8:04:27	8:21:44	8:31:27	8:45:32	9:04:44	9:31:03
6:27:37	7:06:37	7:25:01	7:43:34	8:05:53	8:21:53	8:31:45	8:45:39	9:05:22	9:31:55
6:27:46	7:06:46	7:25:03	7:43:43	8:05:54	8:22:19	8:32:05	8:46:24	9:06:01	9:33:08
6:29:32	7:07:11	7:25:18	7:43:44	8:06:43	8:22:44	8:32:13	8:46:27	9:06:12	9:33:45
6:29:52	7:07:24	7:25:39	7:43:57	8:06:47	8:23:00	8:32:19	8:46:40	9:06:14	9:34:07
6:30:26	7:07:46	7:25:40	7:43:57	8:07:07	8:23:02	8:32:59	8:46:41	9:06:41	9:35:15
6:30:32	7:09:17	7:25:46	7:45:07	8:07:43	8:23:12	8:33:02	8:47:00	9:06:44	9:35:40
6:30:41	7:09:34	7:25:48	7:45:32	8:08:28	8:23:30	8:33:27	8:47:04	9:06:48	9:36:17
6:30:53	7:09:38	7:26:30	7:46:22	8:08:31	8:24:04	8:33:30	8:47:06	9:06:55	9:36:37
6:30:56	7:09:53	7:26:38	7:46:38	8:09:05	8:24:17	8:33:40	8:47:15	9:06:59	9:37:23
6:31:04	7:09:59	7:26:49	7:46:48	8:09:15	8:24:19	8:33:47	8:47:27	9:08:03	9:37:37
6:31:45	7:10:29	7:27:30	7:47:00	8:09:48	8:24:26	8:34:19	8:47:40	9:08:33	9:37:38
6:33:49	7:10:37	7:27:36	7:47:15	8:09:57	8:24:39	8:34:20	8:47:46	9:09:32	9:37:42
6:34:03	7:10:54	7:27:50	7:47:53	8:10:39	8:24:48	8:35:01	8:47:53	9:10:32	9:39:03
6:34:15	7:11:07	7:27:50	7:48:01	8:11:16	8:25:03	8:35:07	8:48:27	9:10:46	9:39:10
6:36:07	7:11:30	7:27:56	7:48:14	8:11:30	8:25:04	8:35:25	8:48:48	9:10:53	9:41:37
6:36:12	7:12:02	7:28:01	7:48:14	8:11:38	8:25:07	8:35:29	8:49:14	9:11:32	9:42:58
6:37:21	7:12:08	7:28:17	7:48:50	8:11:49	8:25:16	8:36:13	8:49:19	9:11:37	9:43:27
6:37:23	7:12:18	7:28:25	7:49:00	8:12:00	8:25:22	8:36:14	8:49:20	9:11:50	9:43:37
6:37:57	7:12:18	7:28:26	7:49:04	8:12:07	8:25:31	8:36:23	8:49:40	9:12:02	9:44:09
6:38:20	7:12:26	7:28:47	7:49:48	8:12:17	8:25:32	8:36:23	8:50:19	9:13:19	9:44:21
6:40:06	7:13:16	7:28:54	7:49:50	8:12:40	8:25:32	8:36:29	8:50:38	9:14:00	9:44:32
6:40:11	7:13:21	7:29:09	7:49:59	8:12:41	8:25:45	8:36:35	8:52:11	9:14:04	9:44:37
6:40:59	7:13:22	7:29:27	7:50:13	8:12:42	8:25:48	8:36:37	8:52:29	9:14:07	9:44:44
6:42:17	7:14:04	7:30:02	7:50:27	8:12:47	8:25:49	8:37:05	8:52:40	9:15:15	9:45:10
6:43:01	7:14:07	7:30:07	7:51:07	8:13:40	8:26:01	8:37:11	8:52:41	9:15:26	9:46:15
6:43:05	7:14:49	7:30:13	7:51:31	8:13:41	8:26:04	8:37:12	8:52:43	9:15:27	9:46:44
6:43:57	7:15:19	7:30:50	7:51:40	8:13:52	8:26:11	8:37:35	8:53:03	9:15:36	9:49:48
6:44:02	7:15:38	7:30:55	7:52:05	8:14:04	8:26:15	8:37:44	8:53:08	9:15:40	9:50:19
6:45:04	7:15:41	7:31:24	7:52:25	8:14:41	8:26:28	8:38:01	8:53:19	9:15:40	9:52:53
6:46:13	7:15:57	7:31:35	7:52:32	8:15:15	8:26:28	8:38:02	8:53:30	9:15:40	9:53:13
6:47:01	7:16:28	7:31:41	7:53:10	8:15:25	8:26:37	8:38:10	8:53:32	9:15:41	9:53:15
6:47:10	7:16:36	7:31:45	7:53:18	8:15:39	8:26:58	8:38:15	8:53:44	9:15:46	9:53:50
6:47:35	7:16:40	7:31:46	7:53:19	8:15:48	8:27:07	8:38:39	8:54:25	9:16:12	9:54:24
6:49:23	7:16:45	7:32:13	7:53:51	8:16:09	8:27:09	8:38:40	8:54:28	9:16:34	9:54:48
6:50:54	7:16:50	7:32:16	7:53:52	8:16:10	8:27:17	8:38:44	8:54:49	9:18:02	9:54:51
6:51:04	7:17:08	7:32:16	7:54:04	8:16:18	8:27:26	8:38:49	8:55:05	9:18:06	9:56:40
6:51:17	7:17:09	7:32:34	7:54:16	8:16:26	8:27:29	8:38:57	8:55:05	9:20:19	9:58:25
6:51:48	7:17:09	7:32:34	7:54:26	8:16:39	8:27:35	8:39:07	8:55:14	9:20:42	9:59:19
6:52:17	7:17:19	7:32:57	7:54:51	8:17:16	8:27:54	8:39:20	8:55:22	9:20:44	
6:52:17	7:17:22	7:33:13	7:55:13	8:17:24	8:27:57	8:39:20	8:55:25	9:20:54	
6:52:31	7:17:22	7:33:36	7:55:35	8:17:28	8:27:59	8:39:21	8:55:50	9:21:55	

us with a number (or a set of numbers), independent of the accuracy with which the inputs we enter into the equation reflect the real world.

Answering the following two questions before proceeding to any other computations improves the predictions of our models substantially.

- Is the arrival process *stationary;* that is, is the expected number of customers arriving in a certain time interval constant over the period we are interested in?
- Are the interarrival times *exponentially distributed,* and therefore form a so-called *Poisson* arrival process?

We now define the concepts of stationary arrivals and exponentially distributed interarrival times. We also describe how these two questions can be answered, both in general as well as in the specific setting of the call center described previously. We also discuss the importance of these two questions and their impact on the calculations in this and the next chapter.

Stationary Arrivals

Consider the call arrival pattern displayed in Table 8.1. How tempting it is to put these data into a spreadsheet, compute the mean and the standard deviation of the interarrival times over that time period, and end the analysis of the arrival pattern at this point, assuming that the mean and the standard deviation capture the entire behavior of the arrival process. Five minutes with Excel, and we could be done!

However, a simple graphical analysis (Figure 8.6) of the data reveals that there is more going on in the arrival process than two numbers can capture. As we can see graphically in Figure 8.6, the average number of customers calling within a certain time interval (e.g., 15 minutes) is not constant over the day.

To capture such changes in arrival processes, we introduce the following definitions:

- An arrival process is said to be *stationary* if, for any time interval (e.g., an hour), the expected number of arrivals in this time interval only depends on the length of the time interval, not on the starting time of the interval (i.e., we can move a time interval of a fixed length back and forth on a time line without changing the expected number of arrivals). In the context of Figure 8.6, we see that the arrival process is not stationary. For example, if we take a 3-hour interval, we see that there are many more customers arriving from 6 A.M. to 9 A.M. than there are from 1 A.M. to 4 A.M.
- An arrival process exhibits *seasonality* if it is not stationary.

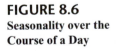

FIGURE 8.6
Seasonality over the Course of a Day

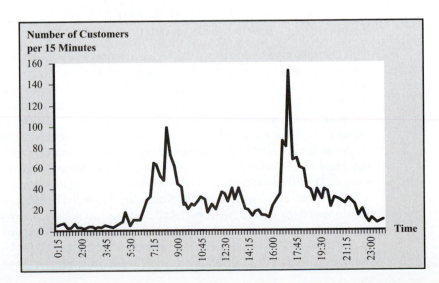

FIGURE 8.7   **Test for Stationary Arrivals**

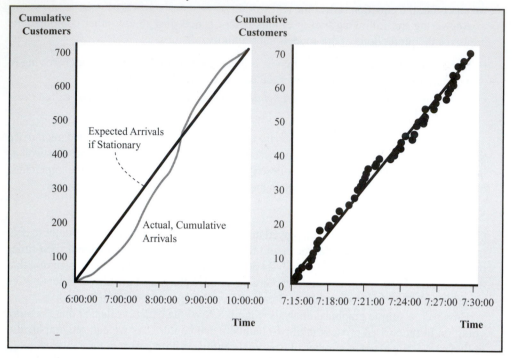

When analyzing an arrival process, it is important that we distinguish between changes in demand (e.g., the number of calls in 15 minutes) that are a result of variability and changes in demand that are a result of seasonality. Both variability and seasonality are unpleasant from an operations perspective. However, the effect of seasonality alone can be perfectly predicted ex ante, while this is not possible for the case of variability (we might know the expected number of callers for a day, but the actual number is a realization of a random variable).

Based on the data at hand, we observe that the arrival process is not stationary over a period of several hours. In general, a simple analysis determines whether a process is stationary.

1. Sort all arrival times so that they are increasing in time (label them as $AT_1 \ldots AT_n$).
2. Plot a graph with (x AT_i; $y = i$) as illustrated by Figure 8.7.
3. Add a straight line from the lower left (first arrival) to the upper right (last arrival).

If the underlying arrival process is stationary, there will be no significant deviation between the graph you plotted and the straight line. In this case, however, in Figure 8.7 (left) we observe several deviations between the straight line and the arrival data. Specifically, we observe that for the first hour, fewer calls come in compared to the average arrival rate from 6 A.M. to 10 A.M. In contrast, around 8:30 A.M., the arrival rate becomes much higher than the average. Thus, our analysis indicates that the arrival process we face is not stationary.

When facing nonstationary arrival processes, the best way to proceed is to divide up the day (the week, the month) into smaller time intervals and have a separate arrival rate for each interval. If we then look at the arrival process within the smaller intervals—in our case, we use 15-minute intervals—we find that the seasonality within the interval is relatively low. In other words, within the interval, we come relatively close to a stationary arrival stream. The stationary behavior of the interarrivals within a 15-minute interval is illustrated by Figure 8.7 (right).

Figure 8.7 (left) is interesting to compare with Figure 8.7 (right): the arrival process behaves as stationary "at the micro-level" of a 15-minute interval, yet exhibits strong seasonality over the course of the entire day, as we observed in Figure 8.6. Note that the peaks in Figure 8.6 correspond to those time slots where the line of "actual, cumulative arrivals" in Figure 8.7 grows faster than the straight line "predicted arrivals."

In most cases in practice, the context explains this type of seasonality. For example, in the case of An-ser, the spike in arrivals corresponds to people beginning their day, expecting that the company they want to call (e.g., a doctor's office) is already "up and running." However, since many of these firms are not handling calls before 9 A.M., the resulting call stream is channeled to the answering service.

Exponential Interarrival Times

Interarrival times commonly are distributed following an *exponential distribution*. If IA is a random interarrival time and the interarrival process follows an exponential distribution, we have

$$\text{Probability } \{IA \leq t\} = 1 - e^{-\frac{t}{a}}$$

where a is the average interarrival time as defined above. Exponential functions are frequently used to model interarrival time in theory as well as practice, both because of their good fit with empirical data as well as their analytical convenience. If an arrival process has indeed exponential interarrival times, we refer to it as a *Poisson arrival process*.

It can be shown analytically that customers arriving independently from each other at the process (e.g., customers calling into a call center) form a demand pattern with exponential interarrival times. The shape of the cumulative distribution function for the exponential distribution is given in Figure 8.8. The average interarrival time is in minutes. An important property of the exponential distribution is that the standard deviation is also equal to the average, a.

Another important property of the exponential distribution is known as the *memoryless property*. The memoryless property simply states that the number of arrivals in the next time slot (e.g., 1 minute) is independent of when the last arrival has occurred.

To illustrate this property, consider the situation of an emergency room. Assume that, on average, a patient arrives every 10 minutes and no patients have arrived for the last

FIGURE 8.8   **Distribution Function of the Exponential Distribution (left) and an Example of a Histogram (right)**

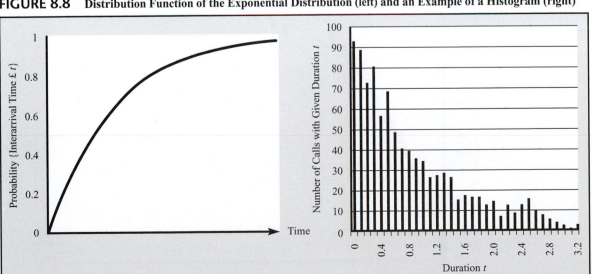

20 minutes. Does the fact that no patients have arrived in the last 20 minutes increase or decrease the probability that a patient arrives in the next 10 minutes? For an arrival process with exponential interarrival times, the answer is *no*.

Intuitively, we feel that this is a reasonable assumption in many settings. Consider, again, an emergency room. Given that the population of potential patients for the ER is extremely large (including all healthy people outside the hospital), we can treat new patients as arriving independently from each other (the fact that Joan Wiley fell off her mountain bike has nothing to do with the fact that Joe Hoop broke his ankle when playing basketball).

Because it is very important to determine if our interarrival times are exponentially distributed, we now introduce the following four-step diagnostic procedure:

1. Compute the interarrival times $IA_1 \ldots IA_n$.
2. Sort the interarrival times in increasing order; let a_i denote the ith smallest interarrival time (a_1 is the smallest interarrival time; a_n is the largest).
3. Plot pairs ($x = a_i, y = i/n$). The resulting graph is called an empirical distribution function.
4. Compare the graph with an exponential distribution with "appropriately chosen parameter." To find the best value for the parameter, we set the parameter of the exponential distribution equal to the average interarrival time we obtain from our data. If a few observations from the sample are substantially remote from the resulting curve, we might adjust the parameter for the exponential distribution "manually" to improve fit.

Figure 8.9 illustrates the outcome of this process. If the underlying distribution is indeed exponential, the resulting graph will resemble the analytical distribution as in the case of Figure 8.9. Note that this procedure of assessing the goodness of fit works also for any other distribution function.

Nonexponential Interarrival Times

In some cases, we might find that the interarrival times are not exponentially distributed. For example, we might encounter a situation where arrivals are scheduled (e.g., every hour), which typically leads to a lower amount of variability in the arrival process.

FIGURE 8.9
Empirical versus Exponential Distribution for Interarrival Times

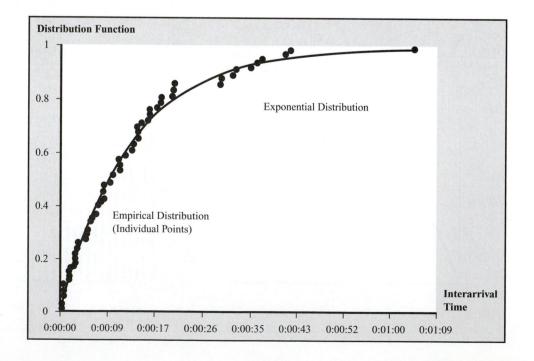

FIGURE 8.10

How to Analyze a Demand/Arrival Process

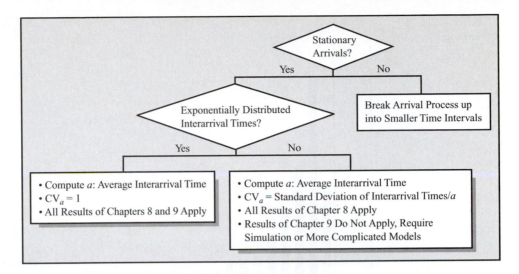

While in the case of the exponential distribution the mean interarrival time is equal to the standard deviation of interarrival times and, thus, one parameter is sufficient to characterize the entire arrival process, we need more parameters to describe the arrival process if interarrival times are not exponentially distributed.

Following our earlier definition of the coefficient of variation, we can measure the variability of an arrival (demand) process as

$$CV_a = \frac{\text{Standard deviation of interarrival time}}{\text{Average interarrival time}}$$

Given that for the exponential distribution the mean is equal to the standard deviation, its coefficient of variation is equal to 1.

Summary: Analyzing an Arrival Process

Figure 8.10 provides a summary of the steps required to analyze an arrival process. It also shows what to do if any of the assumptions required for the following models (Chapters 8 and 9) are violated.

8.4   Processing Time Variability

Just as exact arrival time of an individual call is difficult to predict, so is the actual duration of the call. Thus, service processes also have a considerable amount of variability from the supply side. Figure 8.11 provides a summary of call durations for the case of the An-ser call center. From the perspective of the customer service representative, these call durations are the processing times. As mentioned previously, we will use the words *processing time, processing time,* and *processing time* interchangeably.

We observe that the variability in processing times is substantial. While some calls were completed in less than a minute, others took more than 10 minutes! Thus, in addition to the variability of demand, variability also is created within the process.

There have been reports of numerous different shapes of processing time distributions. For the purposes of this book, we focus entirely on their mean and standard deviation. In other words, when we collect data, we do not explicitly model the distribution of the processing times, but assume that the mean and standard deviation capture all the relevant information. This information is sufficient for all computations in Chapters 8 and 9.

FIGURE 8.11
Processing Times in Call Center

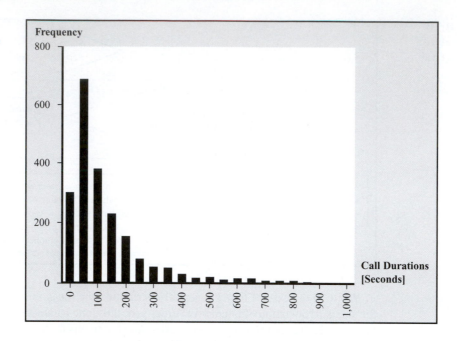

Based on the data summarized in Figure 8.11, we compute the mean processing time as 120 seconds and the corresponding standard deviation as 150 seconds. As we have done with the interarrival times, we can now define the coefficient of variation, which we obtain by

$$CV_p = \frac{\text{Standard deviation of processing time}}{\text{Average processing time}}$$

Here, the subscript p indicates that the CV measures the variability in the processing times. As with the arrival process, we need to be careful not to confuse variability with seasonality. Seasonality in processing times refers to known patterns of call durations as a function of the day of the week or the time of the day (as Figure 8.12 shows, calls take significantly longer on weekends than during the week). Call durations also differ depending on the time of the day.

FIGURE 8.12
Average Call Durations: Weekday versus Weekend

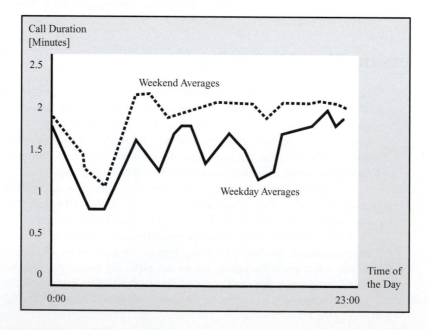

The models we introduce in Chapters 8 and 9 require a stationary service process (in the case of seasonality in the service process, just divide up the time line into smaller intervals, similar to what we did with the arrival process) but do not require any other properties (e.g., exponential distribution of processing time). Thus, the standard deviation and mean of the processing time are all we need to know.

8.5 Predicting the Average Waiting Time for the Case of One Resource

Based on our measures of variability, we now introduce a simple formula that restores our ability to predict the basic process performance measures: inventory, flow rate, and flow time.

In this chapter, we restrict ourselves to the most basic process diagram, consisting of one buffer with unlimited space and one single resource. This process layout corresponds to the call center example discussed above. Figure 8.13 shows the process flow diagram for this simple system.

Flow units arrive to the system following a demand pattern that exhibits variability. On average, a flow unit arrives every a time units. We labeled a as the average interarrival time. This average reflects the mean of interarrival times IA_1 to IA_n. After computing the standard deviation of the IA_1 to IA_n interarrival times, we can compute the coefficient of variation CV_a of the arrival process as discussed previously.

Assume that it takes on average p units of time to serve a flow unit. Similar to the arrival process, we can define p_1 to p_n as the empirically observed processing times and compute the coefficient of variation for the processing times, CV_p, accordingly. Given that there is only one single resource serving the arriving flow units, the capacity of the server can be written as $1/p$.

As discussed in the introduction to this chapter, we are considering cases in which the capacity exceeds the demand rate; thus, the resulting utilization is strictly less than 100 percent. If the utilization were above 100 percent, inventory would predictably build up and we would not need any sophisticated tools accounting for variability to predict that flow units will incur waiting times. However, the most important insight of this chapter is that flow units incur waiting time even if the server utilization is below 100 percent.

Given that capacity exceeds demand and assuming we never lose a customer (i.e., once a customer calls, he or she never hangs up), we are demand-constrained and, thus, the flow rate R is the demand rate. (Chapter 9 deals with the possibility of lost customers.) Specifically, since a customer arrives, on average, every a units of time, the flow rate $R = 1/a$. Recall that we can compute utilization as

$$\text{Utilization} = \frac{\text{Flow rate}}{\text{Capacity}} = \frac{1/a}{1/p} = p/a < 100\%$$

Note that, so far, we have not applied any concept that went beyond the deterministic process analysis we discussed in Chapters 3 to 7.

FIGURE 8.13

A Simple Process with One Queue and One Server

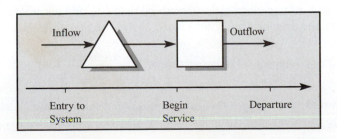

FIGURE 8.14
A Simple Process with One Queue and One Server

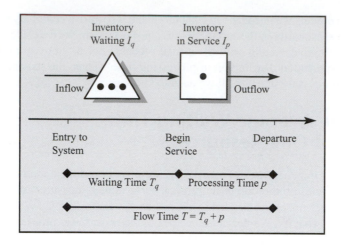

Now, take the perspective of a flow unit moving through the system (see Figure 8.14). A flow unit can spend time waiting in the queue (in a call center, this is the time when you listen to Music of the '70s). Let T_q denote the time the flow unit has to spend in the queue waiting for the service to begin. The subscript q denotes that this is only the time the flow unit waits in the queue. Thus, T_q does *not* include the actual processing time, which we defined as p. Based on the waiting time in the queue T_q and the average processing time p, we can compute the flow time (the time the flow unit will spend in the system) as

$$\text{Flow time} = \text{Time in queue} + \text{Processing time}$$
$$T = T_q + p$$

Instead of taking the perspective of the flow unit, we also can look at the system as a whole, wondering how many flow units will be in the queue and how many will be in service. Let I_q be defined as the inventory (number of flow units) that are in the queue and I_p be the number of flow units in process. Since the inventory in the queue I_q and the inventory in process I_p are the only places we can find inventory, we can compute the overall inventory in the system as $I = I_q + I_p$.

As long as there exists only one resource, I_p is a number between zero and one: sometimes there is a flow unit in service ($I_p = 1$); sometimes there is not ($I_p = 0$). The probability that at a random moment in time the server is actually busy, working on a flow unit, corresponds to the utilization. For example, if the utilization of the process is 30 percent, there exists a .3 probability that at a random moment in time the server is busy. Alternatively, we can say that over the 60 minutes in an hour, the server is busy for

$$.3 \times 60 \, [\text{minutes/hour}] = 18 \text{ minutes}$$

While the inventory in service I_p and the processing time p are relatively easy to compute, this is unfortunately not the case for the inventory in the queue I_q or the waiting time in the queue T_q.

Based on the processing time p, the utilization, and the variability as measured by the coefficients of variation for the interarrival time CV_a and the processing time CV_p, we can compute the average waiting time in the queue using the following formula:

$$\text{Time in queue} = \text{Processing time} \times \left(\frac{\text{Utilization}}{1 - \text{Utilization}} \right) \times \left(\frac{\text{CV}_a^2 + \text{CV}_p^2}{2} \right)$$

The formula does not require that the processing times or the interarrival times follow a specific distribution. Yet, for the case of nonexponential interarrival times, the formula only approximates the expected time in the queue, as opposed to being 100 percent exact. The formula should be used only for the case of a stationary process (see Section 8.3 for the definition of a stationary process as well as for what to do if the process is not stationary).

The above equation states that the waiting time in the queue is the product of three factors:

- The waiting time is expressed as multiples of the processing time. However, it is important to keep in mind that the processing time also directly influences the utilization (as Utilization = Processing time/Interarrival time). Thus, one should not think of the waiting time as increasing linearly with the processing time.

- The second factor captures the utilization effect. Note that the utilization has to be less than 100 percent. If the utilization is equal to or greater than 100 percent, the queue continues to grow. This is not driven by variability, but simply by not having the requested capacity. We observe that the utilization factor is nonlinear and becomes larger and larger as the utilization level is increased closer to 100 percent. For example, for Utilization = 0.8, the utilization factor is $0.8/(1 - 0.8) = 4$; for Utilization = 0.9, it is $0.9/(1 - 0.9) = 9$; and for Utilization = 0.95, it grows to $0.95/(1 - 0.95) = 19$.

- The third factor captures the amount of variability in the system, measured by the average of the squared coefficient of variation of interarrival times CV_a and processing times CV_p. Since CV_a and CV_p affect neither the average processing time p nor the utilization u, we observe that the waiting time grows with the variability in the system.

The best way to familiarize ourselves with this newly introduced formula is to apply it and "see it in action." Toward that end, consider the case of the An-ser call center at 2:00 A.M. in the morning. An-ser is a relatively small call center and they receive very few calls at this time of the day (see Section 8.3 for detailed arrival information), so at 2:00 A.M., there is only one person handling incoming calls.

From the data we collected in the call center, we can quickly compute that the average processing time at An-ser at this time of the day is around 90 seconds. Given that we found in the previous section that the processing time does depend on the time of the day, it is important that we use the processing time data representative for these early morning hours: Processing time $p = 90$ seconds.

Based on the empirical processing times we collected in Section 8.4, we now compute the standard deviation of the processing time to be 120 seconds. Hence, the coefficient of variation for the processing time is

$$CV_p = 120 \text{ seconds}/90 \text{ seconds} = 1.3333$$

From the arrival data we collected (see Figure 8.6), we know that at 2:00 A.M. there are 3 calls arriving in a 15-minute interval. Thus, the interarrival time is $a = 5$ minutes $= 300$ seconds. Given the processing time and the interarrival time, we can now compute the utilization as

$$\text{Utilization} = \text{Processing time/Interarrival time } (= p/a)$$
$$= 90 \text{ seconds}/300 \text{ seconds} = 0.3$$

Concerning the coefficient of variation of the interarrival time, we can take one of two approaches. First, we could take the observed interarrival times and compute the standard deviation empirically. Alternatively, we could view the arrival process during the time period as random. Given the good fit between the data we collected and the exponential distribution (see Figure 8.9), we assume that arrivals follow a Poisson process (interarrival times are exponentially distributed). This implies a coefficient of variation of

$$CV_a = 1$$

Substituting these values into the waiting time formula yields

$$\text{Time in queue} = \text{Processing time} \times \left(\frac{\text{Utilization}}{1 - \text{Utilization}} \right) \times \left(\frac{CV_a^2 + CV_p^2}{2} \right)$$

$$= 90 \times \frac{0.3}{1 - 0.3} \times \frac{1^2 + 1.3333^2}{2}$$

$$= 53.57 \text{ seconds}$$

Note that this result captures the average waiting time of a customer before getting served. To obtain the customer's total time spent for the call, including waiting time and processing time, we need to add the processing time p for the actual service. Thus, the flow time can be computed as

$$T = T_q + p = 53.57 \text{ seconds} + 90 \text{ seconds} = 143.57 \text{ seconds}$$

It is important to point out that the value 53.57 seconds provides the average waiting time. The actual waiting times experienced by individual customers vary. Some customers get lucky and receive service immediately; others have to wait much longer than 53.57 seconds. This is discussed further below.

Waiting times computed based on the methodology outlined above need to be seen as long-run averages. This has the following two practical implications:

- If the system would start empty (e.g., in a hospital lab, where there are no patients before the opening of the waiting room), the first couple of patients are less likely to experience significant waiting time. This effect is transient: Once a sufficient number of patients have arrived, the system reaches a "steady-state." Note that given the 24-hour operation of An-ser, this is not an issue in this specific case.

- If we observe the system for a given time interval, it is unlikely that the average waiting time we observe within this interval is exactly the average we computed. However, the longer we observe the system, the more likely the expected waiting time T_q will indeed coincide with the empirical average. This resembles a casino, which cannot predict how much money a specific guest will win (or typically lose) in an evening, yet can well predict the economics of the entire guest population over the course of a year.

Now that we have accounted for the waiting time T_q (or the flow time T), we are able to compute the resulting inventory. With $1/a$ being our flow rate, we can use Little's Law to compute the average inventory I as

$$I = R \times T = \frac{1}{a} \times (T_q + p)$$

$$= 1/300 \times (53.57 + 90) = 0.479$$

Thus, there is, on average, about half a customer in the system (it is 2:00 A.M. after all . . .). This inventory includes the two subsets we defined as inventory in the queue (I_q) and inventory in process (I_p):

- I_q can be obtained by applying Little's Law, but this time, rather than applying Little's Law to the entire system (the waiting line and the server), we apply it only to the waiting line in isolation. If we think of the waiting line as a mini process in itself (the corresponding process flow diagram consists only of one triangle), we obtain a flow time of T_q. Hence,

$$I_q = 1/a \times T_q = 1/300 \times 53.57 = 0.179$$

- At any given moment in time, we also can look at the number of customers that are currently talking to the customer service representative. Since we assumed there would only be one representative at this time of the day, there will never be more than one caller at this stage. However, there are moments in time when no caller is served, as the utilization of the employee is well below 100 percent. The average number of callers in service can thus be computed as

$$I_p = \text{Probability\{0 callers talking to representative\}} \times 0$$
$$+ \text{Probability\{1 caller talking to representative\}} \times 1$$
$$I_p = (1 - u) \times 0 + u \times 1 = u$$

In this case, we obtain $I_p = 0.3$.

8.6 Predicting the Average Waiting Time for the Case of Multiple Resources

After analyzing waiting time in the presence of variability for an extremely simple process, consisting of just one buffer and one resource, we now turn to more complicated operations. Specifically, we analyze a waiting time model of a process consisting of one waiting area (queue) and a process step performed by multiple, identical resources.

We continue our example of the call center. However, now we consider time slots at more busy times over the course of the day, when there are many more customer representatives on duty in the An-ser call center. The basic process layout is illustrated in Figure 8.15.

Let m be the number of parallel servers we have available. Given that we have m servers working in parallel, we now face a situation where the average processing time is likely to be much longer than the average interarrival time. Taken together, the m resources have a capacity of m/p, while the demand rate continues to be given by $1/a$. We can compute the utilization u of the service process as

$$\text{Utilization} = \frac{\text{Flow rate}}{\text{Capacity}} = \frac{1/\text{Interarrival time}}{(\text{Number of resources}/\text{Processing time})}$$
$$= \frac{1/a}{m/p} = \frac{p}{a \times m}$$

Similar to the case with one single resource, we are only interested in the cases of utilization levels below 100 percent.

FIGURE 8.15
A Process with One Queue and Multiple, Parallel Servers ($m = 5$)

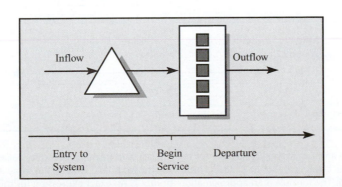

Inflow — Outflow

Entry to System — Begin Service — Departure

The flow unit will initially spend T_q units of time waiting for service. It then moves to the next available resource, where it spends p units of time for service. As before, the total flow time is the sum of waiting time and processing time:

$$\text{Flow time} = \text{Waiting time in queue} + \text{Processing time}$$
$$T = T_q + p$$

Based on the processing time p, the utilization u, the coefficients of variation for both service (CV_p) and arrival process (CV_a) as well as the number of resources in the system (m), we can compute the average waiting time T_q using the following formula:[1]

$$\text{Time in queue} = \left(\frac{\text{Processing time}}{m}\right) \times \left(\frac{\text{Utilization}^{\sqrt{2(m+1)}-1}}{1 - \text{Utilization}}\right) \times \left(\frac{CV_a^2 + CV_p^2}{2}\right)$$

As in the case of one single resource, the waiting time is expressed as the product of the processing time, a utilization factor, and a variability factor. We also observe that for the special case of $m = 1$, the above formula is exactly the same as the waiting time formula for a single resource. Note that all other performance measures, including the flow time (T), the inventory in the system (I), and the inventory in the queue (I_q), can be computed as discussed before.

While the above expression does not necessarily seem an inviting equation to use, it can be programmed without much effort into a spreadsheet. Furthermore, it provides the average waiting time for a system that otherwise could only be analyzed with much more sophisticated software packages.

Unlike the waiting time formula for the single resource case, which provides an exact quantification of waiting times as long as the interarrival times follow an exponential distribution, the waiting time formula for multiple resources is an approximation. The formula works well for most settings we encounter, specifically if the ratio of utilization u to the number of servers m is large (u/m is high).

Now that we have computed waiting time, we can again use Little's Law to compute the average number of flow units in the waiting area I_q, the average number of flow units in service I_p, and the average number of flow units in the entire system $I = I_p + I_q$. Figure 8.16 summarizes the key performance measures.

FIGURE 8.16
Summary of Key Performance Measures

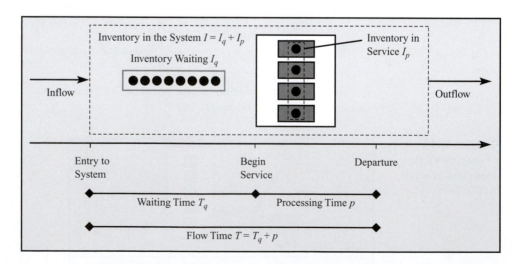

[1] Hopp and Spearman (1996); the formula initially had been proposed by Sakasegawa (1977) and used successfully by Whitt (1983). For $m = 1$, the formula is exactly the same as in the previous section. The formula is an approximation for $m > 1$. An exact expression for this case does not exist.

Exhibit 8.1

SUMMARY OF WAITING TIME CALCULATIONS

1. Collect the following data:

   - Number of servers, m
   - Processing time, p
   - Interarrival time, a
   - Coefficient of variation for interarrival (CV_a) and processing time (CV_p)

2. Compute utilization: $u = \dfrac{p}{a \times m}$

3. Compute expected waiting time:

$$T_q = \left(\frac{\text{Processing time}}{m}\right) \times \left(\frac{\text{Utilization}^{\sqrt{2(m+1)}-1}}{1 - \text{Utilization}}\right) \times \left(\frac{CV_a^2 + CV_p^2}{2}\right)$$

4. Based on T_q, we can compute the remaining performance measures as

$$\text{Flow time } T = T_q + p$$
$$\text{Inventory in service } I_p = m \times u$$
$$\text{Inventory in the queue } I_q = T_q/a$$
$$\text{Inventory in the system } I = I_p + I_q$$

Note that in the presence of multiple resources serving flow units, there can be more than one flow unit in service simultaneously. If u is the utilization of the process, it is also the utilization of each of the m resources, as they process demand at the same rate. We can compute the expected number of flow units at any of the m resources *in isolation* as

$$u \times 1 + (1 - u) \times 0 = u$$

Adding up across the m resources then yields

$$\text{Inventory in process} = \text{Number of resources} \times \text{Utilization}$$
$$I_p = m \times u$$

We illustrate the methodology using the case of An-ser services. Assuming we would work with a staff of 10 customer service representatives (CSRs) for the 8:00 A.M. to 8:15 A.M. time slot, we can compute the utilization as follows:

$$\text{Utilization } u = \frac{p}{a \times m} = \frac{90 \text{ [seconds/call]}}{11.39 \times 10 \text{ [seconds/call]}} = 0.79$$

where we obtained the interarrival time of 11.39 seconds between calls by dividing the length of the time interval (15 minutes = 900 seconds) by the number of calls received over the interval (79 calls). This now allows us to compute the average waiting time as

$$T_q = \left(\frac{p}{m}\right) \times \left(\frac{u^{\sqrt{2(m+1)}-1}}{1 - u}\right) \times \left(\frac{CV_a^2 + CV_p^2}{2}\right)$$

$$= \left(\frac{90}{10}\right) \times \left(\frac{0.79^{\sqrt{2(10+1)}-1}}{1 - 0.79}\right) \times \left(\frac{1 + 1.3333^2}{2}\right) = 24.98 \text{ seconds}$$

The most important calculations related to waiting times caused by variability are summarized in Exhibit 8.1.

8.7 Service Levels in Waiting Time Problems

So far, we have focused our attention on the average waiting time in the process. However, a customer requesting service from our process is not interested in the average time he or she waits in queue or the average total time to complete his or her request (waiting time T_q and flow time T respectively), but in the wait times that he or she experiences personally.

Consider, for example, a caller who has just waited for 15 minutes listening to music while on hold. This caller is likely to be unsatisfied about the long wait time. Moreover, the response from the customer service representative of the type "we are sorry for your delay, but our average waiting time is only 4 minutes" is unlikely to reduce this dissatisfaction.

Thus, from a managerial perspective, we not only need to analyze the average wait time, but also the likelihood that the wait time exceeds a certain *target wait time* (*TWT*). More formally, we can define the *service level* for a given target wait time as the percentage of customers that will begin service in TWT or less units of waiting time:

$$\text{Service level} = \text{Probability}\{\text{Waiting time} \leq \text{TWT}\}$$

This service level provides us with a way to measure to what extent the service is able to respond to demand within a consistent waiting time. A service level of 95 percent for a target waiting time of TWT = 2 minutes means that 95 percent of the customers are served in less than 2 minutes of waiting time.

Figure 8.17 shows the empirical distribution function (see Section 8.3 on how to create this graph) for waiting times at the An-ser call center for a selected time slot. Based on the graph, we can distinguish between two groups of customers. About 65 percent of the customers did not have to wait at all and received immediate service. The remaining 35 percent of the customers experienced a waiting time that strongly resembles an exponential distribution.

We observe that the average waiting time for the entire calling population (not just the ones who had to wait) was, for this specific sample, about 10 seconds. For a target wait time TWT = 30 seconds, we find a service level of 90 percent; that is, 90 percent of the callers had to wait 30 seconds or less.

FIGURE 8.17
Empirical Distribution of Waiting Times at An-ser

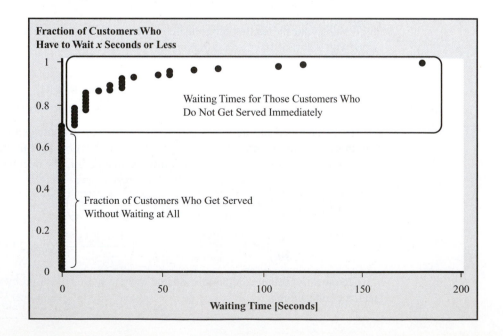

Service levels as defined above are a common performance measure for service operations in practice. They are used internally by the firm in charge of delivering a certain service. They also are used frequently by firms that want to outsource a service, such as a call center, as a way to contract (and track) the responsiveness of their service provider.

There is no universal rule of what service level is right for a given service operation. For example, responding to large public pressure, the German railway system (Deutsche Bundesbahn) has recently introduced a policy that 80 percent of the calls to their customer complaint number should be handled within 20 seconds. Previously, only 30 percent of the calls were handled within 20 seconds. How fast you respond to calls depends on your market position and the importance of the incoming calls for your business. A service level that worked for the German railway system (30 percent within 20 seconds) is likely to be unacceptable in other, more competitive environments.

8.8 Economic Implications: Generating a Staffing Plan

So far, we have focused purely on analyzing the call center for a given number of customer service representatives (CSRs) on duty and predicted the resulting waiting times. This raises the managerial question of how many CSRs An-ser should have at work at any given moment in time over the day. The more CSRs we schedule, the shorter the waiting time, but the more we need to pay in terms of wages.

When making this trade-off, we need to balance the following two costs:

- Cost of waiting, reflecting increased line charges for 1-800 numbers and customer dissatisfaction (line charges are incurred for the actual talk time as well as for the time the customer is on hold).
- Cost of service, resulting from the number of CSRs available.

Additional costs that could be factored into the analysis are

- Costs related to customers calling into the call center but who are not able to gain access even to the waiting line, that is, they receive a busy signal (blocked customers; this will be discussed further in Chapter 9).
- Costs related to customers who hang up while waiting for service.

In the case of An-ser, the average salary of a CSR is $10 per hour. Note that CSRs are paid independent of being idle or busy. Variable costs for a 1-800 number are about $0.05 per minute. A summary of various costs involved in managing a call center—or service operations in general—is given by Figure 8.18.

FIGURE 8.18
Economic Consequences of Waiting

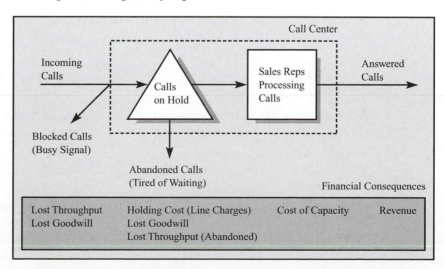

TABLE 8.2
Determining the Number of CSRs to Support Target Wait Time

Number of CSRs, m	Utilization $u = p/(a \times m)$	Expected Wait Time T_q [seconds] Based on Waiting Time Formula
8	0.99	1221.23
9	0.88	72.43
10	0.79	24.98
11	0.72	11.11
12	0.66	5.50
13	0.61	2.89
14	0.56	1.58

When deciding how many CSRs to schedule for a given time slot, we first need to decide on how responsive we want to be to our customers. For the purpose of our analysis, we assume that the management of An-ser wants to achieve an average wait time of 10 seconds. Alternatively, we also could set a service level and then staff according to a TWT constraint, for example, 95 percent of customers to be served in 20 seconds or less.

Now, for a given arrival rate, we need to determine the number of CSRs that will correspond to an average wait time of 10 seconds. Again, consider the time interval from 8:00 A.M. to 8:15 A.M. Table 8.2 shows the utilization level as well as the expected wait time for different numbers of customer service representatives. Note that using fewer than 8 servers would lead to a utilization above one, which would mean that queues would build up independent of variability, which is surely not acceptable.

Table 8.2 indicates that adding CSRs leads to a reduction in waiting time. For example, while a staff of 8 CSRs would correspond to an average waiting time of about 20 minutes, the average waiting time falls below 10 seconds once a twelfth CSR has been added. Thus, working with 12 CSRs allows An-ser to meet its target of an average wait time of 10 seconds. In this case, the actual service would be even better and we expect the average wait time for this specific time slot to be 5.50 seconds.

Providing a good service level does come at the cost of increased labor. The more CSRs are scheduled to serve, the lower is their utilization. In Chapter 4 we defined the cost of direct labor as

$$\text{Cost of direct labor} = \frac{\text{Total wages per unit of time}}{\text{Flow rate per unit of time}}$$

where the total wages per unit of time are determined by the number of CSRs m times their wage rate (in our case, \$10 per hour or 16.66 cents per minute) and the flow rate is determined by the arrival rate. Therefore,

$$\text{Cost of direct labor} = \frac{m \times 16.66 \text{ cents/minute}}{1/a} = a \times m \times 16.66 \text{ cents/minute}$$

An alternative way of writing the cost of labor uses the definition of utilization ($u = p/(a \times m)$). Thus, in the above equation, we can substitute p/u for $a \times m$ and obtain

$$\text{Cost of direct labor} = \frac{p \times 16.66 \text{ cents/minute}}{u}$$

This way of writing the cost of direct labor has a very intuitive interpretation: The actual processing time p is inflated by a factor of 1/Utilization to appropriately account for idle time. For example, if utilization were 50 percent, we are charged a \$1 of idle time penalty

TABLE 8.3
Economic
Implications of
Various Staffing
Levels

Number of Servers	Utilization	Cost of Labor per Call	Cost of Line Charges per Call	Total Cost per Call
8	0.988	0.2531	1.0927	1.3458
9	0.878	0.2848	0.1354	0.4201
10	0.790	0.3164	0.0958	0.4122
11	0.718	0.3480	0.0843	0.4323
12	0.658	0.3797	0.0796	0.4593
13	0.608	0.4113	0.0774	0.4887
14	0.564	0.4429	0.0763	0.5193
15	0.527	0.4746	0.0757	0.5503

for every \$1 we spend on labor productively. In our case, the utilization is 66 percent; thus, the cost of direct labor is

$$\text{Cost of direct labor} = \frac{1.5 \ \text{minutes/call} \times 16.66 \ \text{cents/minute}}{0.66} = 38 \ \text{cents/call}$$

This computation allows us to extend Table 8.2 to include the cost implications of the various staffing scenarios (our calculations do not consider any cost of lost goodwill). Specifically, we are interested in the impact of staffing on the cost of direct labor per call as well as in the cost of line charges.

Not surprisingly, we can see in Table 8.3 that moving from a very high level of utilization of close to 99 percent (using 8 CSRs) to a more responsive service level, for example, as provided by 12 CSRs, leads to a significant increase in labor cost.

At the same time, though, line charges drop from over \$1 per call to almost \$0.075 per call. Note that \$0.075 per call is the minimum charge that can be achieved based on staffing changes, as it corresponds to the pure talk time.

Adding line charges and the cost of direct labor allows us to obtain total costs. In Table 8.3, we observe that total costs are minimized when we have 10 CSRs in service.

However, we need to be careful in labeling this point as the optimal staffing level, as the total cost number is a purely internal measure and does not take into account any information about the customer's cost of waiting. For this reason, when deciding on an appropriate staffing level, it is important to set acceptable service levels for waiting times as done in Table 8.2 and then staffing up to meet these service levels (opposed to minimizing internal costs).

If we repeat the analysis that we have conducted for the 8:00 A.M. to 8:15 A.M. time slot over the 24 hours of the day, we obtain a staffing plan. The staffing plan accounts for both the seasonality observed throughout the day as well as the variability and the resulting need for extra capacity. This is illustrated by Figure 8.19.

When we face a nonstationary arrival process as in this case, a common problem is to decide into how many intervals one should break up the time line to have close to a stationary arrival process within a time interval (in this case, 15 minutes). While we cannot go into the theory behind this topic, the basic intuition is this: It is important that the time intervals are large enough so that

- We have enough data to come up with reliable estimates for the arrival rate of the interval (e.g., if we had worked with 30-second intervals, our estimates for the number of calls arriving within a 30-second time interval would have been less reliable).
- Over the course of an interval, the queue needs sufficient time to reach a "steady state"; this is achieved if we have a relatively large number of arrivals and service completions within the duration of a time interval (more than 10).

FIGURE 8.19
**Staffing and
Incoming Calls over
the Course of a Day**

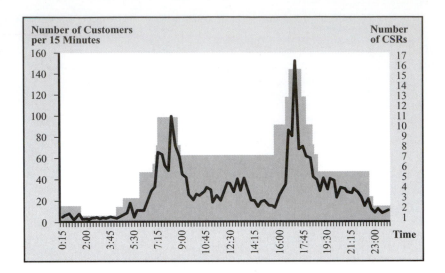

In practice, finding a staffing plan can be somewhat more complicated, as it needs to account for

- Breaks for the operators.
- Length of work period. It is typically not possible to request an operator to show up for work for only a one-hour time slot. Either one has to provide longer periods of time or one would have to temporarily route calls to other members of the organization (supervisor, back-office employees).

Despite these additional complications, the analysis outlined above captures the most important elements typical for making supply-related decisions in service environments.

8.9   Impact of Pooling: Economies of Scale

Consider a process that currently corresponds to two (m) demand arrival processes that are processed by two (m) identical servers. If demand cannot be processed immediately, the flow unit waits in front of the server where it initially arrived. An example of such a system is provided in Figure 8.20 (left).

Here is an interesting question: Does combining the two systems into a single system with one waiting area and two (m) identical servers lead to lower average waiting times? We refer to such a combination of multiple resources into one "mega-resource" as *pooling*.

FIGURE 8.20
**The Concept of
Pooling**

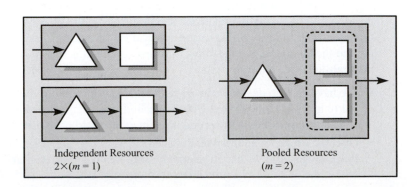

Consider, for example, two small food services at an airport. For simplicity, assume that both of them have a customer arrival stream with an average interarrival time a of 4 minutes and a coefficient of variation equal to one. The processing time p is three minutes per customer and the coefficient of variation for the service process also is equal to one. Consequently, both food services face a utilization of $p/a = 0.75$.

Using our waiting time formula, we compute the average waiting time as

$$T_q = \text{Processing time} \times \left(\frac{\text{Utilization}}{1 - \text{Utilization}} \right) \times \left(\frac{\text{CV}_a^2 + \text{CV}_p^2}{2} \right)$$

$$= 3 \times \left(\frac{0.75}{1 - 0.75} \right) \times \left(\frac{1 + 1}{2} \right)$$

$$= 3 \times (0.75/0.25) = 9 \text{ minutes}$$

Now compare this with the case in which we combine the capacity of both food services to serve the demand of both services. The capacity of the pooled process has increased by a factor of two and now is $\frac{2}{3}$ unit per minute. However, the demand rate also has doubled: If there was one customer every four minutes arriving for service 1 and one customer every four minutes arriving for service 2, the pooled service experiences an arrival rate of one customer every $a = 2$ minutes (i.e., two customers every four minutes is the same as one customer every two minutes).

We can compute the utilization of the pooled process as

$$u = \frac{p}{a \times m}$$

$$= 3/(2 \times 2) = 0.75$$

Observe that the utilization has not changed compared to having two independent services. Combining two processes with a utilization of 75 percent leads to a pooled system with a 75 percent utilization. However, a different picture emerges when we look at the waiting time of the pooled system. Using the waiting time formula for multiple resources, we can write

$$T_q = \left(\frac{\text{Processing time}}{m} \right) \times \left(\frac{\text{Utilization}^{\sqrt{2(m+1)}-1}}{1 - \text{Utilization}} \right) \times \left(\frac{\text{CV}_a^2 + \text{CV}_p^2}{2} \right)$$

$$= \left(\frac{3}{2} \right) \times \left(\frac{0.75^{\sqrt{2(2+1)}-1}}{1 - 0.75} \right) \times \left(\frac{1 + 1}{2} \right) = 3.95 \text{ minutes}$$

In other words, the pooled process on the right of Figure 8.20 can serve the same number of customers using the same processing time (and thereby having the same utilization), but in only *half* the waiting time!

While short of being a formal proof, the intuition for this result is as follows. The pooled process uses the available capacity more effectively, as it prevents the case that one resource is idle while the other faces a backlog of work (waiting flow units). Thus, pooling identical resources balances the load for the servers, leading to shorter waiting times. This behavior is illustrated in Figure 8.21.

Figure 8.21 illustrates that for a given level of utilization, the waiting time decreases with the number of servers in the resource pool. This is especially important for higher levels of utilization. While for a system with one single server waiting times tend to "go

FIGURE 8.21
How Pooling Can
Reduce Waiting Time

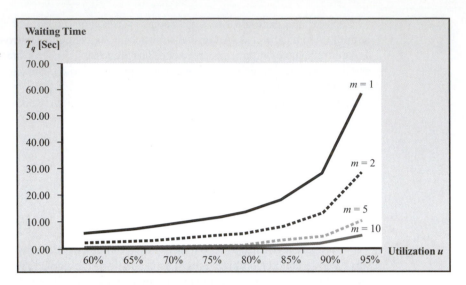

through the roof" once the utilization exceeds 85 percent, a process consisting of 10 identical servers can still provide reasonable service even at utilizations approaching 95 percent.

Given that a pooled system provides better service than individual processes, a service organization can benefit from pooling identical branches or work groups in one of two forms:

- The operation can use pooling to reduce customer waiting time without having to staff extra workers.

- The operation can reduce the number of workers while maintaining the same responsiveness.

These economic benefits of pooling can be illustrated nicely within the context of the An-ser case discussed above. In our analysis leading to Table 8.2, we assumed that there would be 79 calls arriving per 15-minute time interval and found that we would need 12 CSRs to serve customers with an average wait time of 10 seconds or less.

Assume we could pool An-ser's call center with a call center of comparable size; that is, we would move all CSRs to one location and merge both call centers' customer populations. Note that this would not necessarily require the two call centers to "move in" with each other; they could be physically separate as long as the calls are routed through one joint network.

Without any consolidation, merging the two call centers would lead to double the number of CSRs and double the demand, meaning 158 calls per 15-minute interval. What would be the average waiting time in the pooled call center? Or, alternatively, if we maintained an average waiting time of 10 seconds or less, how much could we reduce our staffing level? Table 8.4 provides the answers to these questions.

First, consider the row of 24 CSRs, corresponding to pooling the entire staff of the two call centers. Note specifically that the utilization of the pooled call center is not any different from what it was in Table 8.2. We have doubled the number of CSRs, but we also have doubled the number of calls (and thus cut the interarrival time by half). With 24 CSRs, we expect an average waiting time of 1.2 seconds (compared to almost 6 seconds before).

Alternatively, we could take the increased efficiency benefits resulting from pooling by reducing our labor cost. We also observe from Table 8.4 that a staff of 20 CSRs would be able to answer calls with an average wait time of 10 seconds. Thus, we could increase

TABLE 8.4
Pooling Two Call Centers

Number of CSRs	Utilization	Expected Wait Time [seconds]	Labor Cost per Call	Line Cost per Call	Total Cost
16	0.988	588.15	0.2532	0.5651	0.8183
17	0.929	72.24	0.2690	0.1352	0.4042
18	0.878	28.98	0.2848	0.0992	0.3840
19	0.832	14.63	0.3006	0.0872	0.3878
20	0.790	8.18	0.3165	0.0818	0.3983
21	0.752	4.84	0.3323	0.0790	0.4113
22	0.718	2.97	0.3481	0.0775	0.4256
23	0.687	1.87	0.3639	0.0766	0.4405
24	0.658	1.20	0.3797	0.0760	0.4558
25	0.632	0.79	0.3956	0.0757	0.4712
26	0.608	0.52	0.4114	0.0754	0.4868
27	0.585	0.35	0.4272	0.0753	0.5025
28	0.564	0.23	0.4430	0.0752	0.5182
29	0.545	0.16	0.4589	0.0751	0.5340
30	0.527	0.11	0.4747	0.0751	0.5498

utilization to almost 80 percent, which would lower our cost of direct labor from $0.3797 to $0.3165. Given an annual call volume of about 700,000 calls, such a saving would be of significant impact for the bottom line.

Despite the nice property of pooled systems outlined above, pooling should not be seen as a silver bullet. Specifically, pooling benefits are much lower than expected (and potentially negative) in the following situations:

• Pooling benefits are significantly lower when the systems that are pooled are not truly independent. Consider, for example, the idea of pooling waiting lines before cash registers in supermarkets, similar to what is done at airport check-ins. In this case, the individual queues are unlikely to be independent, as customers in the current, nonpooled layout will intelligently route themselves to the queue with the shortest waiting line. Pooling in this case will have little, if any, effect on waiting times.

• Similar to the concept of line balancing we introduced earlier in this book, pooling typically requires the service workforce to have a broader range of skills (potentially leading to higher wage rates). For example, an operator sufficiently skilled that she can take orders for hiking and running shoes, as well as provide answering services for a local hospital, will likely demand a higher wage rate than someone who is just trained to do one of these tasks.

• In many service environments, customers value being treated consistently by the same person. Pooling several lawyers in a law firm might be desirable from a waiting-time perspective but ignores the customer desire to deal with one point of contact in the law firm.

• Similarly, pooling can introduce additional setups. In the law-firm example, a lawyer unfamiliar with the situation of a certain client might need a longer time to provide some quick advice on the case and this extra setup time mitigates the operational benefits from pooling.

• Pooling can backfire if pooling combines different customer classes because this might actually increase the variability of the service process. Consider two clerks working in a retail bank, one of them currently in charge of simple transactions (e.g., processing time of 2 minutes per customer), while the other one is in charge of more complex cases (e.g., processing time of 10 minutes). Pooling these two clerks makes the service process more variable and might actually increase waiting time.

8.10 Priority Rules in Waiting Lines

Choosing an appropriate level of capacity helps to prevent waiting lines from building up in a process. However, in a process with variability, it is impossible to eliminate waiting lines entirely. Given, therefore, that at some point in time some customers will have to wait before receiving service, we need to decide on the order in which we permit them access to the server. This order is determined by a *priority rule,* sometimes also referred to as a queuing discipline.

Customers are assigned priorities by adding a (small) step at the point in the process where customers arrive. This process step is called the *triage step.* At triage, we collect information about some of the characteristics of the arriving customer, which we use as input for the priority rule. Below we discuss priority rules based on the following characteristics:

- The processing time or the expected processing time of the customer (processing-time-dependent priority rules).
- Processing-time-independent priority rules, including priority rules based on customer arrival time and priority rules based on customer importance or urgency.

Processing-Time-Dependent Priority Rules

If it is possible to observe the customer's processing time or his or her expected processing time prior to initiating the service process, this information should be incorporated when assigning a priority to the customer. The most commonly used service-time-dependent priority rule is the shortest processing time (SPT) rule.

Under the SPT rule, the next available server is allocated to the customer with the shortest (expected) processing time of all customers currently in the waiting line. The SPT rule is extremely effective and performs well, with respect to the expected waiting time as well as to the variance of the waiting time. If the processing times are not dependent on the sequence with which customers are processed, the SPT rule can be shown to lead to the shortest average flow time. Its basic intuition is summarized by Figure 8.22.

Processing-Time-Independent Priority Rules

In many cases, it is difficult or impossible to assess the processing time or even the expected processing time prior to initiating the service process. Moreover, if customers are able to misrepresent their processing time, then they have an incentive to suggest that their processing time is less than it really is when the SPT rule is applied (e.g., "Can I just ask a quick question? . . ."). In contrast, the customer arrival time is easy to observe and difficult for the customer to manipulate.

For example, a call center receiving calls for airline reservations knows the sequence with which callers arrive but does not know which customer has already gathered all relevant information and is ready to order and which customer still requires explanation and discussion.

FIGURE 8.22 **The Shortest Processing time (SPT) Rule (used in the right case)**

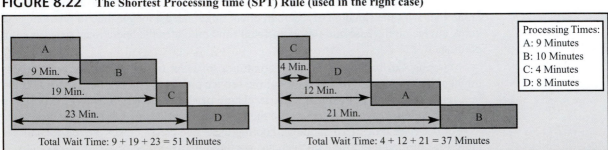

The most commonly used priority rule based on arrival times is the first-come, first-served (FCFS) rule. With the FCFS rule, the next available server is allocated to the customer in the waiting line with the earliest arrival time.

In addition to using arrival time information, many situations in practice require that characteristics such as the urgency or the importance of the case are considered in the priority rule. Consider the following two examples:

- In an emergency room, a triage nurse assesses the urgency of each case and then assigns a priority to the patient. Severely injured patients are given priority, independent of their arrival times.

- Customers calling in for investor services are likely to experience different priorities, depending on the value of their invested assets. Customers with an investment of greater than $5 million are unlikely to wait, while customers investing only several thousand dollars might wait for 20 minutes or more.

Such urgency-based priority rules are also independent of the processing time. In general, when choosing a service-time-independent priority rule, the following property should be kept in mind: Whether we serve customers in the order of their arrival, in the reverse order of their arrival (last-come, first-served), or even in alphabetical order, the expected waiting time does not change. Thus, higher priority service (shorter waiting time) for one customer always requires lower priority (longer waiting time) for other customers.

From an implementation perspective, one last point is worth noting. Using priority rules other than FCFS might be perceived as unfair by the customers who arrived early and are already waiting the longest. Thus, while the average waiting time does not change, serving latecomers first increases the variance of the waiting time. Since variability in waiting time is not desirable from a service-quality perspective, the following property of the FCFS rule is worth remembering: Among service-time-independent priority rules, the FCFS rule minimizes the variance of waiting time and flow time.

8.11   Reducing Variability

In this chapter, we have provided some new methods to evaluate the key performance measures of flow rate, flow time, and inventory in the presence of variability. We also have seen that variability is the enemy of all operations (none of the performance measures improves as variability increases). Thus, in addition to just taking variability as given and adjusting our models to deal with variability, we should always think about ways to reduce variability.

Ways to Reduce Arrival Variability

One—somewhat obvious—way of achieving a match between supply and demand is by "massaging" demand such that it corresponds exactly to the supply process. This is basically the idea of *appointment systems* (also referred to as reservation systems in some industries).

Appointment systems have the potential to reduce the variability in the arrival process as they encourage customers to arrive at the rate of service. However, one should not overlook the problems associated with appointment systems, which include

- Appointment systems do not eliminate arrival variability. Customers do not perfectly arrive at the scheduled time (and some might not arrive at all, "no-shows"). Consequently, any good appointment system needs ways to handle these cases (e.g., extra charge or extra waiting time for customers arriving late). However, such actions are typically very difficult to implement, due to what is perceived to be "fair" and/or "acceptable," or because variability in processing times prevents service providers from always keeping on schedule (and if the doctor has the right to be late, why not the patient?).

- What portion of the available capacity should be reserved in advance. Unfortunately, the customers arriving at the last minute are frequently the most important ones: emergency operations in a hospital do not come through an appointment system and business travelers paying 5 to 10 times the fare of low-price tickets are not willing to book in advance (this topic is further explored in the revenue management chapter, Chapter 16).

The most important limitation, however, is that appointment systems might reduce the variability of the arrival process as seen by the operation, but they do not reduce the variability of the true underlying demand. Consider, for example, the appointment system of a dental office. While the system (hopefully) reduces the time the patient has to wait before seeing the dentist on the day of the appointment, this wait time is not the only performance measure that counts, as the patient might already have waited for three months between requesting to see the dentist and the day of the appointment. Thus, appointment systems potentially hide a much larger supply–demand mismatch and, consequently, any good implementation of an appointment system includes a continuous measurement of both of the following:

- The inventory of customers who have an appointment and are now waiting for the day they are scheduled to go to the dentist.
- The inventory of customers who wait for an appointment in the waiting room of the dentist.

In addition to the concept of appointment systems, we can attempt to influence the customer arrival process (though, for reasons similar to the ones discussed, not the true underlying demand pattern) by providing incentives for customers to avoid peak hours. Frequently observed methods to achieve this include

- Early-bird specials at restaurants or bars.
- Price discounts for hotels during off-peak days (or seasons).
- Price discounts in transportation (air travel, highway tolls) depending on the time of service.
- Pricing of air travel depending on the capacity that is already reserved.

It is important to point out that, strictly speaking, the first three items do not reduce variability; they level expected demand and thereby reduce seasonality (remember that the difference between the two is that seasonality is a pattern known already ex ante). The fourth item refers to the concept of revenue management, which is discussed in Chapter 16.

Ways to Reduce Processing Time Variability

In addition to reducing variability by changing the behavior of our customers, we also should consider how to reduce internal variability. However, when attempting to standardize activities (reducing the coefficient of variation of the processing times) or shorten processing times, we need to find a balance between operational efficiency (call durations) and the quality of service experienced by the customer (perceived courtesy).

Figure 8.23 compares five of An-ser's operators for a specific call service along these two dimensions. We observe that operators NN, BK, and BJ are achieving relatively short call durations while being perceived as friendly by the customers (based on recorded calls). Operator KB has shorter call durations, yet also scores lower on courtesy. Finally, operator NJ has the longest call durations and is rated medium concerning courtesy.

Based on Figure 8.23, we can make several interesting observations. First, observe that there seems to exist a frontier capturing the inherent trade-off between call duration and courtesy. Once call durations for this service go below 2.5 minutes, courtesy seems hard to maintain. Second, observe that operator NJ is away from this frontier, as he is neither

FIGURE 8.23
**Operator
Performance
Concerning Call
Duration and
Courtesy**

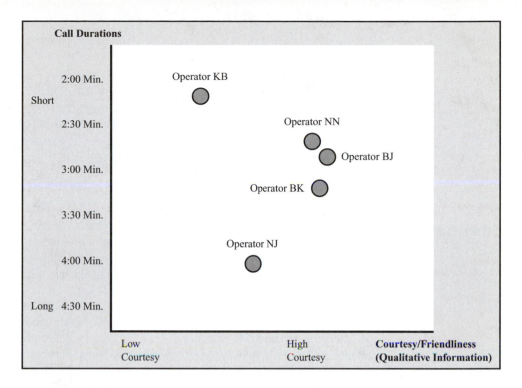

overly friendly nor fast. Remarkably, this operator also has the highest variability in call durations, which suggests that he is not properly following the operating procedures in place (this is not visible in the graph).

To reduce the inefficiencies of operators away from the frontier (such as NJ), call centers invest heavily in training and technology. For example, technology allows operators to receive real-time instruction of certain text blocks that they can use in their interaction with the customer (scripting). Similarly, some call centers have instituted training programs in which operators listen to audio recordings of other operators or have operators call other operators with specific service requests. Such steps reduce both the variability of processing times as well as their means and, therefore, represent substantial improvements in operational performance.

There are other improvement opportunities geared primarily toward reducing the variability of the processing times:

• Although in a service environment (or in a make-to-order production setting) the operator needs to acknowledge the idiosyncrasy of each customer, the operator still can follow a consistent process. For example, a travel agent in a call center might use predefined text blocks (scripts) for his or her interaction with the customer (welcome statement, first question, potential up-sell at the end of the conversation). This approach allowed operators NN, BK, and BJ in Figure 8.23 to be fast and friendly. Thus, being knowledgeable about the process (when to say what) is equally important as being knowledgeable about the product (what to say).

• Processing times in a service environment—unlike processing times in a manufacturing context—are not under the complete control of the resource. The customer him/herself plays a crucial part in the activity at the resource, which automatically introduces a certain amount of variability (e.g., having the customer provide his or her credit card number, having the customer bag the groceries, etc.) What is the consequence of this? At least from a variability perspective, the answer is clear: Reduce the involvement of the customer during the service at a scarce resource wherever possible (note that if the customer involvement does not occur at a scarce resource, having the customer be involved and thereby do part of the work might be very desirable, e.g., in a self-service setting).

- Variability in processing times frequently reflects quality problems. In manufacturing environments, this could include reworking a unit that initially did not meet specifications. However, rework also occurs in service organizations (e.g., a patient who is released from the intensive care unit but later on readmitted to intensive care can be thought of as rework).

Many of these concepts are discussed further in Chapter 10.

8.12 Summary

In this chapter, we have analyzed the impact of variability on waiting times. As we expected from our more qualitative discussion of variability in the beginning of this chapter, variability causes waiting times, even if the underlying process operates at a utilization level of less than 100 percent. In this chapter, we have outlined a set of tools that allows us to quantify this waiting time, with respect to both the average waiting time (and flow time) as well as the service level experienced by the customer.

There exists an inherent tension between resource utilization (and thereby cost of labor) and responsiveness: Adding service capacity leads to shorter waiting times but higher costs of labor (see Figure 8.24). Waiting times grow steeply with utilization levels. Thus, any responsive process requires excess capacity. Given that capacity is costly, it is important that only as much capacity is installed as is needed to meet the service objective in place for the process. In this chapter, we have outlined a method that allows a service operation to find the point on the frontier that best supports their business objectives (service levels).

However, our results should be seen not only as a way to predict/quantify the waiting time problem. They also outline opportunities for improving the process. Improvement opportunities can be broken up into capacity-related opportunities and system-design-related opportunities, as summarized below.

FIGURE 8.24
Balancing Efficiency with Responsiveness

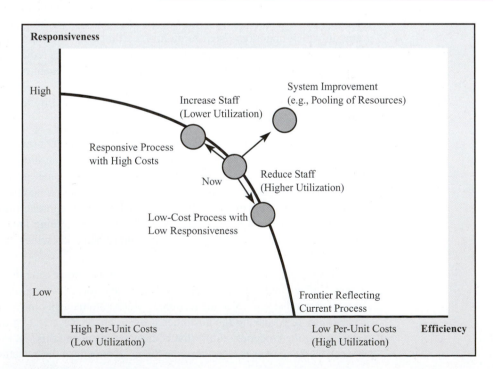

Capacity-Related Improvements

Operations benefit from flexibility in capacity, as this allows management to adjust staffing levels to predicted demand. For example, the extent to which a hospital is able to have more doctors on duty at peak flu season is crucial in conducting the staffing calculations outlined in this chapter. A different form of flexibility is given by the operation's ability to increase capacity in the case of unpredicted demand. For example, the extent to which a bank can use supervisors and front-desk personnel to help with unexpected spikes in inbound calls can make a big difference in call center waiting times. This leads to the following two improvement opportunities:

- Demand (and sometimes supply) can exhibit seasonality over the course of the day. In such cases, the waiting time analysis should be done for individual time intervals over which the process behaves relatively stationary. System performance can be increased to the extent the organization is able to provide time-varying capacity levels that mirror the seasonality of demand (e.g., Figure 8.19).

- In the presence of variability, a responsive process cannot avoid excess capacity, and thereby will automatically face a significant amount of idle time. In many operations, this idle time can be used productively for tasks that are not (or at least are less) time critical. Such work is referred to as background work. For example, operators in a call center can engage in outbound calls during times of underutilization.

System-Design-Related Improvements

Whenever we face a trade-off between two conflicting performance measures, in this case between responsiveness and efficiency, finding the right balance between the measures is important. However, at least equally important is the attempt to improve the underlying process, shifting the frontier and allowing for higher responsiveness and lower cost (see Figure 8.24). In the context of services suffering from variability-induced waiting times, the following improvement opportunities should be considered:

- By combining similar resources into one joint resource pool (pooling resources), we are able to either reduce wait times for the same amount of capacity or reduce capacity for the same service level. Processes that face variability thereby exhibit very strong scale economies.

- Variability is not exogenous and we should remember to reduce variability wherever possible.

- By introducing a triage step before the actual service process that sequences incoming flow units according to a priority rule (service-time-dependent or service-time-independent), we can reduce the average wait time, assign priority to the most important flow units, or create a waiting system that is perceived as fair by customers waiting in line.

8.13 Further Reading

Gans, Koole, and Mandelbaum (2003) is a recent overview on call-center management from a queuing theory perspective. Further quantitative tools on queueing can be found in Hillier and Lieberman (2002).

Hall (1997) is a very comprehensive and real-world-focused book that provides numerous tools related to variability and its consequences in services and manufacturing.

8.14 Practice Problems

Q8.1* **(Online Retailer)** Customers send e-mails to a help desk of an online retailer every 2 minutes, on average, and the standard deviation of the interarrival time is also 2 minutes. The online retailer has three employees answering e-mails. It takes on average 4 minutes to write a response e-mail. The standard deviation of the processing times is 2 minutes.

(* indicates that the solution is at the end of the book)

a. Estimate the average customer wait before being served.

b. How many e-mails would there be, on average, that have been submitted to the online retailer but not yet answered?

Q8.2**   **(My-law.com)** My-law.com is a recent start-up trying to cater to customers in search of legal services who are intimidated by the idea of talking to a lawyer or simply too lazy to enter a law office. Unlike traditional law firms, My-law.com allows for extensive interaction between lawyers and their customers via telephone and the Internet. This process is used in the upfront part of the customer interaction, largely consisting of answering some basic customer questions prior to entering a formal relationship.

In order to allow customers to interact with the firm's lawyers, customers are encouraged to send e-mails to my-lawyer@My-law.com. From there, the incoming e-mails are distributed to the lawyer who is currently "on call." Given the broad skills of the lawyers, each lawyer can respond to each incoming request.

E-mails arrive from 8 A.M. to 6 P.M. at a rate of 10 e-mails per hour (coefficient of variation for the arrivals is 1). At each moment in time, there is exactly one lawyer "on call," that is, sitting at his or her desk waiting for incoming e-mails. It takes the lawyer, on average, 5 minutes to write the response e-mail. The standard deviation of this is 4 minutes.

a. What is the average time a customer has to wait for the response to his/her e-mail, ignoring any transmission times? *Note:* This includes the time it takes the lawyer to start writing the e-mail *and* the actual writing time.

b. How many e-mails will a lawyer have received at the end of a 10-hour day?

c. When not responding to e-mails, the lawyer on call is encouraged to actively pursue cases that potentially could lead to large settlements. How much time on a 10-hour day can a My-law.com lawyer dedicate to this activity (assume the lawyer can instantly switch between e-mails and work on a settlement)?

To increase the responsiveness of the firm, the board of My-law.com proposes a new operating policy. Under the new policy, the response would be highly standardized, reducing the standard deviation for writing the response e-mail to 0.5 minute. The average writing time would remain unchanged.

d. How would the amount of time a lawyer can dedicate to the search for large settlement cases change with this new operating policy?

e. How would the average time a customer has to wait for the response to his/her e-mail change? *Note:* This includes the time until the lawyer starts writing the e-mail *and* the actual writing time.

Q8.3**   **(Car Rental Company)** The airport branch of a car rental company maintains a fleet of 50 SUVs. The interarrival time between requests for an SUV is 2.4 hours, on average, with a standard deviation of 2.4 hours. There is no indication of a systematic arrival pattern over the course of a day. Assume that, if all SUVs are rented, customers are willing to wait until there is an SUV available. An SUV is rented, on average, for 3 days, with a standard deviation of 1 day.

a. What is the average number of SUVs parked in the company's lot?

b. Through a marketing survey, the company has discovered that if it reduces its daily rental price of $80 by $25, the average demand would increase to 12 rental requests per day and the average rental duration will become 4 days. Is this price decrease warranted? Provide an analysis!

c. What is the average time a customer has to wait to rent an SUV? Please use the initial parameters rather than the information in part (b).

d. How would the waiting time change if the company decides to limit all SUV rentals to *exactly* 4 days? Assume that if such a restriction is imposed, the average interarrival time will increase to 3 hours, with the standard deviation changing to 3 hours.

Q8.4   **(Tom Opim)** The following situation refers to Tom Opim, a first-year MBA student. In order to pay the rent, Tom decides to take a job in the computer department of a local department store. His only responsibility is to answer telephone calls to the department, most of which are inquiries about store hours and product availability. As Tom is the only person answering calls, the manager of the store is concerned about queuing problems.

Currently, the computer department receives an average of one call every 3 minutes, with a standard deviation in this interarrival time of 3 minutes.

Tom requires an average of 2 minutes to handle a call. The standard deviation in this processing time is 1 minute.

The telephone company charges $5.00 per hour for the telephone lines whenever they are in use (either while a customer is in conversation with Tom or while waiting to be helped).

Assume that there are no limits on the number of customers that can be on hold and that customers do not hang up even if forced to wait a long time.

a. For one of his courses, Tom has to read a book (*The Pole,* by E. Silvermouse). He can read 1 page per minute. Tom's boss has agreed that Tom could use his idle time for studying, as long as he drops the book as soon as a call comes in. How many pages can Tom read during an 8-hour shift?

b. How long does a customer have to wait, on average, before talking to Tom?

c. What is the average total cost of telephone lines over an 8-hour shift? Note that the department store is billed whenever a line is in use, including when a line is used to put customers on hold.

Q8.5   **(Atlantic Video)** Atlantic Video, a small video rental store in Philadelphia, is open 24 hours a day, and—due to its proximity to a major business school—experiences customers arriving around the clock. A recent analysis done by the store manager indicates that there are 30 customers arriving every hour, with a standard deviation of interarrival times of 2 minutes. This arrival pattern is consistent and is independent of the time of day. The checkout is currently operated by one employee, who needs on average 1.7 minutes to check out a customer. The standard deviation of this check-out time is 3 minutes, primarily as a result of customers taking home different numbers of videos.

a. If you assume that every customer rents at least one video (i.e., has to go to the check-out), what is the average time a customer has to wait in line before getting served by the checkout employee, not including the actual checkout time (within 1 minute)?

b. If there are no customers requiring checkout, the employee is sorting returned videos, of which there are always plenty waiting to be sorted. How many videos can the employee sort over an 8-hour shift (assume no breaks) if it takes exactly 1.5 minutes to sort a single video?

c. What is the average number of customers who are at the checkout desk, either waiting or currently being served (within 1 customer)?

d. Now assume *for this question only* that 10 percent of the customers do not rent a video at all and therefore do not have to go through checkout. What is the average time a customer has to wait in line before getting served by the checkout employee, not including the actual checkout time (within 1 minute)? Assume that the coefficient of variation for the arrival process remains the same as before.

e. As a special service, the store offers free popcorn and sodas for customers waiting in line at the checkout desk. (*Note:* The person who is currently being served is too busy with paying to eat or drink.) The store owner estimates that every minute of customer waiting time costs the store 75 cents because of the consumed food. What is the optimal number of employees at checkout? Assume an hourly wage rate of $10 per hour.

Q8.6   **(RentAPhone)** RentAPhone is a new service company that provides European mobile phones to American visitors to Europe. The company currently has 80 phones available at Charles de Gaulle Airport in Paris. There are, on average, 25 customers per day requesting a phone. These requests arrive uniformly throughout the 24 hours the store is open. (*Note:* This means customers arrive at a faster rate than 1 customer per hour.) The corresponding coefficient of variation is 1.

Customers keep their phones on average 72 hours. The standard deviation of this time is 100 hours.

Given that RentAPhone currently does not have a competitor in France providing equally good service, customers are willing to wait for the telephones. Yet, during the waiting period, customers are provided a free calling card. Based on prior experience, RentAPhone found that the company incurred a cost of $1 per hour per waiting customer, independent of day or night.

a. What is the average number of telephones the company has in its store?

b. How long does a customer, on average, have to wait for the phone?

c. What are the total monthly (30 days) expenses for telephone cards?

d. Assume RentAPhone could buy additional phones at $1,000 per unit. Is it worth it to buy one additional phone? Why?

e. How would waiting time change if the company decides to limit all rentals to *exactly* 72 hours? Assume that if such a restriction is imposed, the number of customers requesting a phone would be reduced to 20 customers per day.

Q8.7   **(Webflux Inc.)** Webflux is an Internet-based DVD rental business specializing in hard-to-find, obscure films. Its operating model is as follows. When a customer finds a film on the Webflux Web site and decides to watch it, she puts it in the virtual shopping cart. If a DVD is available, it is shipped immediately (assume it can be shipped during weekends and holidays, too). If not available, the film remains in the customer's shopping cart until a rented DVD is returned to Webflux, at which point it is shipped to the customer if she is next in line to receive it. Webflux maintains an internal queue for each film and a returned DVD is shipped to the first customer in the queue (first-in, first-out).

Webflux has one copy of the 1990 film *Sundown, the Vampire in Retreat,* starring David Carradine and Bruce Campbell. The average time between requests for the DVD is 10 days, with a coefficient of variation of 1. On average, a customer keeps the DVD for 5 days before returning it. It also takes 1 day to ship the DVD to the customer and 1 day to ship it from the customer back to Webflux. The standard deviation of the time between shipping the DVD out from Webflux and receiving it back is 7 days (i.e., it takes on average 7 days to (a) ship it, (b) have it with the customer, and (c) ship it back); hence, the coefficient of variation of this time is 1.

a. What is the average time that a customer has to wait to receive *Sundown, the Vampire in Retreat* DVD after the request? Recall it takes 1 day for a shipped DVD to arrive at a customer address (i.e., in your answer, you have to include the 1-day shipping time).

b. On average, how many customers are in Webflux's internal queue for *Sundown?* Assume customers do not cancel their items in their shopping carts.

Thanks to David Carradine's renewed fame after the recent success of *Kill Bill Vol. I* and *II* which he starred in, the demand for *Sundown* has spiked. Now the average interarrival time for the DVD requests at Webflux is 3 days. Other numbers (coefficient of variation, time in a customer's possession, shipping time) remain unchanged. *For the following question only,* assume sales are lost for customers who encounter stockouts; that is those who cannot find a DVD on the Webflux Web site simply navigate away without putting it in the shopping cart.

c. To satisfy the increased demand, Webflux is considering acquiring a second copy of the *Sundown* DVD. If Webflux owns a total of two copies of *Sundown* DVDs (whether in Webflux's internal stock, in customer's possession, or in transit), what percentage of the customers are turned away because of a stockout? (*Note:* To answer this question, you will need material from Chapter 9.)

Q8.8   **(Security Walking Escorts)** A university offers a walking escort service to increase security around campus. The system consists of specially trained uniformed professional security officers that accompany students from one campus location to another. The service is operated 24 hours a day, seven days a week. Students request a walking escort by phone. Requests for escorts are received, on average, every 5 minutes with a coefficient of variation of 1. After receiving a request, the dispatcher contacts an available escort (via a mobile phone), who immediately proceeds to pick up the student and walk her/him to her/his destination. If there are no escorts available (that is, they are all either walking a student to her/his destination or walking to pick up a student), the dispatcher puts the request in a queue until an escort becomes available. An escort takes, on average, 25 minutes for picking up a student and taking her/him to her/his desired location (the coefficient of variation of this time is also 1). Currently, the university has 8 security officers who work as walking escorts.

a. How many security officers are, on average, available to satisfy a new request?

b. How much time does it take—on average—from the moment a student calls for an escort to the moment the student arrives at her/his destination?

For the next two questions, consider the following scenario. During the period of final exams, the number of requests for escort services increases to 19.2 per hour (one request every 3.125 minutes). The coefficient of variation of the time between successive requests equals 1. However, if a student requesting an escort finds out from the dispatcher that her/his request would have to be put in the queue (i.e., all security officers are busy walking other students), the student cancels the request and proceeds to walk on her/his own.

c. How many students per hour who called to request an escort end up canceling their request and go walking on their own? (*Note:* To answer this question, you will need material from Chapter 9.)

d. University security regulations require that at least 80 percent of the students' calls to request walking escorts have to be satisfied. What is the minimum number of security officers that are needed in order to comply with this regulation?

Q8.9 **(Mango Electronics Inc.)** Mango Electronics Inc. is a *Fortune* 500 company that develops and markets innovative consumer electronics products. The development process proceeds as follows.

Mango researches new technologies to address unmet market needs. Patents are filed for products that have the requisite market potential. Patents are granted for a period of 20 years starting from the date of issue. After receiving a patent, the patented technologies are then developed into marketable products at five independent development centers. Each product is only developed at one center. Each center has all the requisite skills to bring any of the products to market (a center works on one product at a time). On average, Mango files a patent every 7 months (with standard deviation of 7 months). The average development process lasts 28 months (with standard deviation of 56 months).

a. What is the utilization of Mango's development facilities?

b. How long does it take an average technology to go from filing a patent to being launched in the market as a commercial product?

c. How many years of patent life are left for an average product launched by Mango Electronics?

Q8.10 **(UPS Shipping)** A UPS employee, Davis, packs and labels three types of packages: basic packages, business packages, and oversized packages. Business packages take priority over basic packages and oversized packages because those customers paid a premium to have guaranteed two-day delivery. During his nine-hour shift, he has, on average, one container of packages containing a variety of basic, business, and oversized packages to process every 3 hours. As soon as Davis processes a package, he passes it to the next employee, who loads it onto a truck. The times it takes him to process the three different types of packages and the average number of packages per container are shown in the table below.

	Basic	Business	Oversized
Average number of minutes to label and package each unit	5 minutes	4 minutes	6 minutes
Average number of units per container	10	10	5

Davis currently processes packages from each container as follows. First, he processes all business packages in the container. Then he randomly selects either basic packages or oversized packages for processing until the container is empty. However, his manager suggested to Davis that, for each container, he should process all the business packages first, second the basic packages, and last the oversized packages.

a. If Davis follows his supervisor's advice, what will happen to Davis's utilization?

b. What will happen to the average time that a package spends in the container?

You can view a video of how problems marked with a ** are solved by going on www. cachon-terwiesch.net and follow the links under 'Solved Practice Problems'

The Impact of Variability on Process Performance: Throughput Losses

After having analyzed waiting times caused by variability, we now turn to a second undesirable impact variability has on process performance: *throughput loss.* Throughput losses occur in the following cases, both of which differ from the case of flow units patiently waiting for service discussed in Chapter 8:

- There is a limited buffer size and demand arriving when this buffer is full is lost.
- Flow units are impatient and unwilling or unable to spend too much time waiting for service, which leads to flow units leaving the buffer before being served.

Analyzing processes with throughput losses is significantly more complicated compared to the case of patient customers discussed in Chapter 8. For this reason, we focus our analysis on the simplest case of throughput loss, which assumes that the buffer size is zero, that is, there is no buffer. We will introduce a set of analytical tools and discuss their application to time-critical emergency care provided by hospitals, especially trauma centers. In these settings, waiting times are not permissible and, when a trauma center is fully utilized, incoming ambulances are diverted to other hospitals.

There exist more general models of variability that allow for buffer sizes larger than zero, yet due to their complexity, we only discuss those models conceptually. Again, we start the chapter with a small motivating example.

9.1 Motivating Examples: Why Averages Do Not Work

Consider a street vendor who sells custom-made sandwiches from his truck parked along the sidewalk. Demand for these sandwiches is, on average, one sandwich in a five-minute time slot. However, the actual demand varies, and thus sometimes no customer places an order, while at other times the owner of the truck faces one or two orders. Customers are not willing to wait for sandwiches and leave to go to other street vendors if they cannot be served immediately.

TABLE 9.1
Street Vendor
Example of
Variability

Scenario	Demand	Capacity	Flow Rate
A	0	0	0
B	0	1	0
C	0	2	0
D	1	0	0
E	1	1	1
F	1	2	1
G	2	0	0
H	2	1	1
I	2	2	2
Average	1	1	$\frac{5}{9}$

The capacity leading to the supply of sandwiches over a five-minute time slot also varies and can take the values 0, 1, or 2 with equal probabilities (the variability of capacity might reflect different order sizes or operator absenteeism). The average capacity therefore is one, just as is the average demand.

From an aggregate planning perspective, demand and supply seem to match, and on average, the truck should be selling at a flow rate of one sandwich every five minutes:

$$\text{Flow rate} = \text{Minimum}\{\text{Demand, Capacity}\} = \text{Minimum}\{1, 1\} = 1$$

Now, consider an analysis that is conducted at the more detailed level. If we consider the potential outcomes of both the demand and the supply processes, we face nine possible scenarios, which are summarized in Table 9.1.

Consider each of the nine scenarios. But instead of averaging demand and capacity and then computing the resulting flow rate (as done above, leading to a predicted flow rate of one), we compute the flow rate for each of the nine scenarios and then take the average across scenarios. The last column in Table 9.1 provides the corresponding calculations.

Note that for the first three scenarios (Demand = 0), we are not selling a single sandwich. However, if we look at the last three scenarios (Demand = 2), we cannot make up for this loss, as we are constrained by capacity. Thus, even while demand is booming (Demand = 2), we are selling on average one sandwich every five minutes.

If we look at the average flow rate that is obtained this way, we observe that close to half of the sales we expected to make based on our aggregate analysis do not materialize! The explanation for this is as follows: In order to sell a sandwich, the street vendor needed demand (a customer) and supply (the capacity to make a sandwich) at the same moment in time. Flow rate could have been improved if the street vendor could have moved some supply to inventory and thereby stored it for periods of time in which demand exceeded supply, or, vice versa, if the street vendor could have moved some demand to a backlog of waiting customers and thereby stored demand for periods of time in which supply exceeded demand: another example of the "buffer or suffer" principle.

9.2 Ambulance Diversion

Now, let's move from analyzing a "cooked-up" food-truck to a problem of much larger importance, with respect to both its realism as well as its relevance. Over the last couple of years, reports have shown a substantial increase in visits to emergency departments. At the same time many hospitals, in response to increasing cost pressure, have downsized important resources that are part of the emergency care process. This has led to a decrease in the number of hours hospitals are "open" for emergency patients arriving by helicopter or ambulance.

Under U.S. federal law, all hospitals that participate in Medicare are required to screen—and, if an emergency condition is present, stabilize—any patient who comes to the emergency department, regardless of the individual's ability to pay.[1] Under certain circumstances where a hospital lacks staffing or facilities to accept additional emergency patients, the hospital may place itself on "diversion status" and direct en route ambulances to other hospitals.

In total, the General Accounting Office estimates that about two of every three hospitals went on diversion at least once during the fiscal year 2001. Moreover, the study estimates that about 2 in every 10 of these hospitals were on diversion for more than 10 percent of the time, and about 1 in every 10 was on diversion for more than 20 percent of the time—or about five hours per day.

We focus our analysis on trauma cases, that is, the most severe and also the most urgent type of emergency care. A triage system evaluates the patients while they are in the ambulance/helicopter and directs the arrival to the emergency department (less severe cases) or the trauma center (severe cases). Thus, the trauma center only receives patients who have had a severe trauma.

9.3 Throughput Loss for a Simple Process

Consider the following situation of a trauma center in a hospital in the Northeastern United States. Incoming patients are moved into one of three trauma bays. On average, patients spend two hours in the trauma bay. During that time, the patients are diagnosed and, if possible, stabilized. The most severe cases, which are difficult or impossible to stabilize, spend very little time in a trauma bay and are moved directly to the operating room.

Given the severe conditions of patients coming into the trauma center, any delay of care can have fatal consequences for the patient. Thus, having patients wait for service is not an option in this setting. If, as a result of either frequent arrivals or long service times, all three trauma bays are utilized, the trauma center has to move to the ambulance diversion status defined above.

We model the trauma center as a process flow diagram consisting of no buffer and multiple parallel resources (see Figure 9.1). Given that we have three trauma bays (and corresponding staff) available, there can be a maximum of three patients in the process. Once

FIGURE 9.1
Process Flow Diagram for Trauma Center

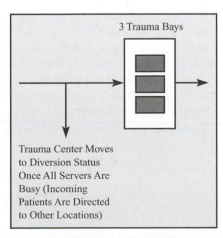

---

[1] The following definitions and statistics are taken from the report "Hospital Emergency Departments," GAO-03-460, given by the General Accounting Office to the U.S. Senate.

all three bays are in use, the trauma center informs the regional emergency system that it has to go on diversion status; that is, any patients needing trauma services at that time are transported to other hospitals in the region.

The trauma center we analyze handles about 2,000 cases per year. For our analysis, we focus on the late evening hours, during which, on average, a new patient arrives every three hours. In addition to traffic rush hour, the late evening hours are among the busiest for the trauma center, as many of the incoming cases are results of vehicle accidents (alcohol-induced car accidents tend to happen in the evening) and victims of violence (especially in the summer months, many violent crimes occur in the evening hours).

Thus, we have a new patient every $a = 3$ hours and it takes, on average, $p = 2$ hours of time to get the patient out of the trauma center. In our analysis, we assume that the trauma bays are the resources and that there is sufficient staff to operate all three bays simultaneously, if the need arises.

Given that there are three trauma bays available, the capacity of the trauma center is

$$\text{Capacity} = \frac{\text{Number of resources}}{\text{Processing time}} = \frac{3}{2 \text{ hours}/\text{patient}}$$
$$= 1.5 \text{ patients per hour}$$

Since incoming patients arrive randomly, we use exponential interarrival times and consequently face a coefficient of variation of CV_a equal to one. The coefficient of variation of the service time in this case turns out to be above one (many medical settings are known to have extremely high variability). However, as we will see below, the following computations do not depend on the service time variability and apply to any service time distribution.

We are interested in analyzing the following performance measures:

- What percent of the time will the trauma center have to go on diversion status? Similarly, how many patients are diverted because all three trauma bays are utilized?

- What is the flow rate through the trauma center, that is, how many patients are treated every unit of time (e.g., every day)?

The most difficult, yet also most important step in our analysis is computing the probability with which the process contains m patients, P_m. This probability is of special importance, as once m patients are in the trauma center, the trauma center needs to divert any incoming requests until it has discharged a patient. The probability of having all m servers busy, P_m, depends on two variables:

- The *implied utilization.* Given that some patients are not admitted to the process (and thereby do not contribute to throughput), we no longer need to impose the condition that the capacity exceeds the demand rate ($1/a$). This assumption was necessary in the previous chapter, as otherwise the waiting line would have "exploded." In a system that automatically "shuts down" the process in case of high demand, this does not happen. Hence, u now includes the case of a utilization above 100 percent, which is why we speak of the implied utilization (Demand rate/Capacity) as opposed to utilization (Flow rate/Capacity).

- The number of resources (trauma bays) m.

We begin our analysis by computing the implied utilization:

$$u = \frac{\text{Demand rate}}{\text{Capacity}} = \frac{0.3333 \text{ patient per hour}}{1.5 \text{ patients per hour}} = 0.2222$$

Based on the implied utilization u and the number of resources m, we can use the following method to compute the probability that all m servers are busy, P_m. Define $r = u \times m = p/a$. Thus, $r = 0.67$.

TABLE 9.2
Finding the
Probability $P_m(r)$
Using the Erlang
Loss Table from
Appendix B

				Erlang Loss Table			
				m			
		1	2	3	4	5	6 ...
	0.10	0.0909	0.0045	0.0002	0.0000	0.0000	0.0000
	0.20	0.1667	0.0164	0.0011	0.0001	0.0000	0.0000
	0.25	0.2000	0.0244	0.0020	0.0001	0.0000	0.0000
	0.30	0.2308	0.0335	0.0033	0.0003	0.0000	0.0000
r	0.33	0.2500	0.0400	0.0044	0.0004	0.0000	0.0000
	0.40	0.2857	0.0541	0.0072	0.0007	0.0001	0.0000
	0.50	0.3333	0.0769	0.0127	0.0016	0.0002	0.0000
	0.60	0.3750	0.1011	0.0198	0.0030	0.0004	0.0000
	0.67	0.4000	0.1176	0.0255	0.0042	0.0006	0.0001
	0.70	0.4118	0.1260	0.0286	0.0050	0.0007	0.0001
	0.75	0.4286	0.1385	0.0335	0.0062	0.0009	0.0001
	...						

We can then use the *Erlang loss formula* table (Appendix B) to look up the probability that all *m* resources are utilized and hence a newly arriving flow unit has to be rejected. First, we find the corresponding row heading in the table ($r = 0.67$) indicating the ratio of processing time to interarrival time (see Table 9.2). Second, we find the column heading ($m = 3$) indicating the number of resources. The intersection of that row with that column is

$$\text{Probability\{all } m \text{ servers busy\}} = P_m(r) = 0.0255 \quad \text{(Erlang loss formula)}$$

Thus, we find that our trauma center, on average, will be on diversion for 2.5 percent of the time, which corresponds to about 0.6 hour per day and about 18 hours per month.

A couple of remarks are in order to explain the impact of the processing time-to-interarrival-time ratio *r* and the number of resources *m* on the probability that all servers are utilized:

• The probability $P_m(r)$ and hence the analysis do not require the coefficient of variation for the service process. The analysis only applies to the (realistic) case of exponentially distributed interarrival times; therefore, we implicitly assume that the coefficient of variation for the arrival process is equal to one.

• The formula underlying the table in Appendix B is attributed to the work of Agner Krarup Erlang, a Danish engineer who invented many (if not most) of the models that we use in Chapters 8 and 9 for his employer, the Copenhagen Telephone Exchange. In this context, the arrivals were incoming calls for which there was either a telephone line available or not (in which case the calls were lost, which is why the formula is also known as the *Erlang loss formula*).

• At the beginning of Appendix B, we provide the formula that underlies the Erlang loss formula table. We can use the formula directly to compute the probability $P_m(r)$ for a given processing-time-to-interarrival-time ratio *r* and the number of resources *m*.

In addition to the probability that all resources are utilized, we also can compute the number of patients that will have to be diverted. Since demand for trauma care continues at a rate of $1/a$ independent of the diversion status of the trauma center, we obtain our flow rate as

$$\text{Flow rate} = \text{Demand rate} \times \text{Probability that not all servers are busy}$$
$$= 1/a \times (1 - P_m) = \tfrac{1}{3} \times 0.975 = 0.325 \text{ patient per hour}$$

Similarly, we find that we divert ⅓ × 0.025 = 0.0083 patient per hour = 0.2 patient per day.

The case of the trauma center provides another example of how variability needs to be accommodated in a process by putting excess capacity in place. A utilization level of 22 percent in an environment of high fixed costs seems like the nightmare of any administrator. Yet, from the perspective of a person in charge of creating a responsive process, absolute utilization numbers should always be treated with care: The role of the trauma center is not to maximize utilization; it is to help people in need and ultimately save lives.

One main advantage of the formula outlined above is that we can quickly evaluate how changes in the process affect ambulance diversion. For example, we can compute the probability of diversion that would result from an increased utilization. Such a calculation would be important, both to predict diversion frequencies, as well as to predict flow rate (e.g., number of patients served per month).

Consider, for example, a utilization of 50 percent. Such a case could result from a substantial increase in arrival rate (e.g., consider the case that a major trauma center in the area closes because of the financial problems of its hospital).

Based on the increased implied utilization, $u = 0.5$, and the same number of trauma bays, $m = 3$, we compute $r = u \times m = 1.5$. We then use the Erlang loss formula table to look up the probability $P_m(r)$ that all m servers are utilized:

$$P_3(1.5) = 0.1343$$

Thus, this scenario of increased utilization would lead to ambulance diversion more than 13 percent of the time, corresponding to close to 100 hours of diversion every month.

Figure 9.2 shows the relationship between the level of implied utilization and the probability that the process cannot accept any further incoming arrivals. As we can see, similar to waiting time problems, there exist significant scale economies in loss systems: While a 50 percent utilization would lead to a diversion probability of 30 percent with one server ($m = 1$), it only leads to a 13 percent diversion probability with three servers and less than 2 percent for 10 servers.

Exhibit 9.1 summarizes the computations required for the Erlang loss formula.

FIGURE 9.2

Implied Utilization versus Probability of Having All Servers Utilized

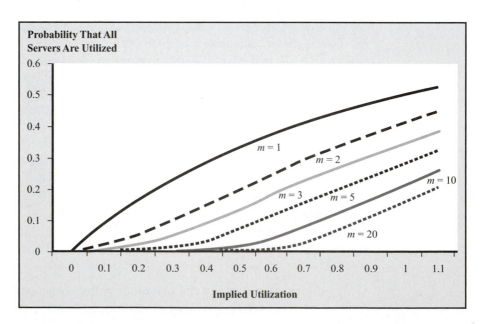

Exhibit 9.1

USING THE ERLANG LOSS FORMULA

1. Define $r = \dfrac{p}{a}$ where p is the processing time and a is the interarrival time

2. Use the Erlang loss formula table in Appendix B to look up the probability that all servers are busy:

$$\text{Probability \{all } m \text{ servers are busy\}} = P_m(r)$$

3. Compute flow rate based on

$$\text{Flow rate} = \text{Demand rate} \times \text{Probability that not all servers are busy}$$
$$R = 1/a \times (1 - P_m)$$

4. Compute lost customers as

$$\text{Customers lost} = \text{Demand rate} \times \text{Probability that all servers are busy}$$
$$= 1/a \times P_m$$

9.4 Customer Impatience and Throughput Loss

In Chapter 8 we analyzed a process in which flow units patiently waited in a queue until it was their turn to be served. In contrast, in the case of the trauma center, we have analyzed a process in which flow units never waited but, when all servers were busy, were turned immediately into lost flow units (were routed to other hospitals).

These two cases, a waiting problem on one side and a loss problem on the other side, are important, yet they also are extreme cases concerning the impact of variability on process performance. Many interesting applications that you might encounter are somewhere in between these two extremes. Without going into a detailed analysis, it is important that we at least discuss these intermediate cases at the conceptual level.

The first important intermediate case is a waiting problem in which there is a buffer that allows a limited number of flow units to wait for service. The limit of the buffer size might represent one of these situations:

- In a call center, there exist a maximum number of calls that can be on hold simultaneously; customers calling in when all these lines are in use receive a busy signal (i.e., they don't even get to listen to the 70s music!). Similarly, if one thinks of a queue in front of a drive-through restaurant, there exist a maximum number of cars that can fit in the queue; once this maximum is reached, cars can no longer line up.

- Given that, as a result of Little's Law, the number of customers in the queue can be translated into an expected wait time, a limit on the queue size might simply represent a maximum amount of time customers would be willing to wait. For example, customers looking at a queue in front of a movie theater might simply decide that the expected wait time is not justified by the movie they expect to see.

Although we will not discuss them in this book, there exist mathematical models to analyze this type of problem and for a given maximum size of the buffer, we can compute the usual performance measures, inventory, flow rate, and wait time (see, e.g., Hillier and Liebermann (2002)).

For the case of a single server, Figure 9.3 shows the relationship between the number of available buffers and the probability that all buffers are full; that is, the probability that the process can no longer accept incoming customers. As we can see, this probability

FIGURE 9.3

Impact of Buffer Size on the Probability P_m for Various Levels of Implied Utilization as well as on the Throughput of the Process in the Case of One Single Server

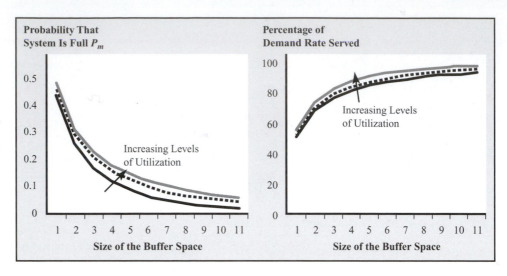

is quickly decreasing as we add more and more buffer space. Note that the graph shifts up as we increase the level of utilization, which corresponds to the intuition from earlier chapters.

Since we can compute the throughput of the system as

$$(1 - \text{Probability that all buffers are full}) \times \text{Demand rate}$$

we also can interpret Figure 9.3 as the throughput loss. The right part of Figure 9.3 shows the impact of buffer size on throughput. Even for a single server and a utilization of 90 percent, we need more than 10 buffers to come close to restoring the throughput we would expect in the absence of variability.

The second intermediate case between a waiting problem and a loss problem resembles the first case but is different in the sense that customers always enter the system (As opposed to not even joining the queue), but then leave the queue unserved as they become tired of waiting. The technical term for this is "customers *abandon* the queue" or the customers *balk*. This case is very common in call centers that have very long wait times. However, for call centers with high service levels for short target wait times, such as in the case of the An-ser call center discussed in Chapter 8, there are very few abandonment cases (this is why we could safely ignore customers abandoning the queue for our analysis in Chapter 8).

Figure 9.4 shows an example of call center data (collected by Gans, Koole, and Mandelbaum (2003)) in a setting with long waiting times. The horizontal axis shows how long customers had to wait before talking to an agent. The vertical axis represents the percentage of customers hanging up without being served. We observe that the longer customers have to wait, the larger the proportion of customers lost due to customer impatience.

There are three types of improvement opportunities for the two intermediate cases, limited buffer space and abandoning customers:

- Reduce wait times. Similar to our prior analysis, anything we can do to reduce wait times (intelligently choose capacity, reduce variability, etc.) helps reduce throughput losses resulting from customer impatience.

- Increase the maximum number of flow units that can be in the buffer. This can be achieved by either altering the actual buffer (adding more space, buying more telephone lines) or increasing the customers' willingness to tolerate waiting.

- Avoid customers leaving that have already waited. Having customers wait and then leave is even worse than having customers leave immediately, so it is important to

FIGURE 9.4
Impact of Waiting Time on Customer Loss

Source: Gans, Koole, and Mandelbaum, 2003.

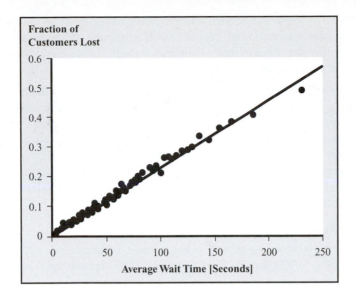

avoid this case as much as possible. One way of achieving this is to reduce the perceived waiting duration by giving customers meaningful tasks to do (e.g., key in some information, help reduce the actual service time) or by creating an environment where waiting is not too painful (two generations of operations managers were told to install mirrors in front of elevators, so we are not going to repeat this suggestion). Obviously, mirrors at elevators and playing music in call centers alone do not solve the problem entirely; however, these are changes that are typically relatively inexpensive to implement. A more meaningful (and also low-cost) measure would be to communicate the expected waiting time upfront to the customer (e.g., as done in some call centers or in Disney's theme parks). This way, customers have expectations concerning the wait time and can make a decision whether or not to line up for this service (Disney case) or can even attempt to run other errands while waiting for service (call center case).

9.5 Several Resources with Variability in Sequence

After having analyzed variability and its impact on process performance for the case of very simple processes consisting of just one resource, we now extend our analysis to more complicated process flow diagrams.

Specifically, we analyze a sequence of resources as described in the process flow diagram in Figure 9.5. Such processes are very common, both in manufacturing and service environments:

- The kick-scooter assembly process that we analyzed in Chapter 4 consists (ignoring variability) of multiple resources in sequence.

FIGURE 9.5
A Serial Queuing System with Three Resources

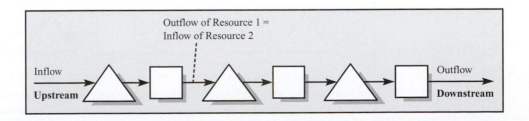

- As an example of a service process consisting of multiple resources in sequence, consider the immigration process at most U.S. airports. When arriving in the United States, travelers first have to make their way through the immigration authority and then line up at customs (see chapter 4).

A complicating factor in the analysis of such processes is that the subsequent resources do not operate independently from each other: The departure process of the first resource is the arrival process of the second resource, and so forth. Thus, the variability of the arrival process of the second resource depends on the variability of the arrival process of the first resource and on the variability of the service process of the first resource. What a mess!

Independent of our ability to handle the analytical challenges related to such processes, which also are referred to as tandem queues, we want to introduce some basic intuition of how such processes behave.

The Role of Buffers

Similar to what we have seen in the example of impatient customers and limited buffer space (Figure 9.3), buffers have the potential to improve the flow rate through a process. While, in the case of a single resource, buffers increase flow rate as they reduce the probability that incoming units are denied access to the system, the impact of buffers in *tandem queues* is somewhat more complicated. When looking at a tandem queue, we can identify two events that lead to reductions in flow rate (see Figure 9.6):

- A resource is *blocked* if it is unable to release the flow unit it has just completed as there is no buffer space available at the next resource downstream.
- A resource is *starved* if it is idle and the buffer feeding the resource is empty.

In the trauma center example discussed at the beginning of the chapter, blocking is the most important root cause of ambulance diversion. The actual time the trauma surgeon needs to care for a patient in the trauma bay is only, on average, one hour. However, on average, patients spend one additional hour in the trauma bay waiting for a bed in the intensive care unit (ICU) to become available. Since, during this time, the trauma bay cannot be used for newly arriving patients, a full ICU "backs up" and blocks the trauma center. The study of the General Accounting Office on emergency department crowding and ambulance diversion, mentioned above, pointed to the availability of ICU beds as the single largest source leading to ambulance diversion.

FIGURE 9.6
The Concepts of Blocking and Starving

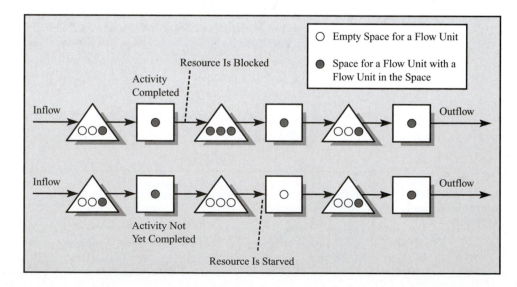

It is important to understand that the effects of blocking can snowball from one resource to additional resources upstream. This can be illustrated in the hospital setting outlined above. Consider a patient who is ready to be discharged from a general care unit at 11 A.M. However, as the patient wants to be picked up by a family member, the patient can only leave at 5 P.M. Consequently, the unit cannot make the bed available to newly arriving patients, including those who come from the ICU. This, in turn, can lead to a patient in the ICU who is ready to be discharged but now needs to wait in the ICU bed. And, yes, you guessed right, this in turn can lead to a patient in the trauma center, who could be moved to the ICU, but now has to stay in the trauma bay. Thus, in a process with limited buffer space, all resources are dependent on another. This is why we defined buffers that help management to relax these dependencies as *decoupling inventory* (Chapter 2).

Blocking and starving can be easily avoided by adding buffers. The buffers would have to contain a sufficient number of flow units so as to avoid starvation of the downstream resource. At the same time, the buffer should have enough space to prevent the resource upstream from ever being blocked. Several hospitals have recently experimented with introducing discharge rooms for patients who are ready to go home from a general care unit: Even a buffer at the end of the process (healthy patient) will reduce the probability that an incoming trauma patient has to be diverted because of a fully utilized trauma center.

In addition to the probability of not being able to admit newly arriving flow units, an important performance measure for our process continues to be the flow rate. Figure 9.7 uses simulation to compare four process layouts of three resources with variability. This situation corresponds to a worker-paced line, with one worker at every resource. The processing times are exponentially distributed with means of 6.5 minutes/unit, 7 minutes/unit, and 6 minutes/unit respectively.

Based on averages, we would expect the process to produce one unit of output every seven minutes. However, in the absence of any buffer space, the process only produces at a rate of one unit every 11.5 minutes (upper left). The process does not realize its full capacity, as the bottleneck is frequently blocked (station 2 has completed a flow unit but cannot forward it to station 3) or starved (station 2 wants to initiate production of the next flow unit but does not receive any input from upstream).

FIGURE 9.7   **Flow Rate Compared at Four Configurations of a Queuing System (Cycle times computed using simulation)**

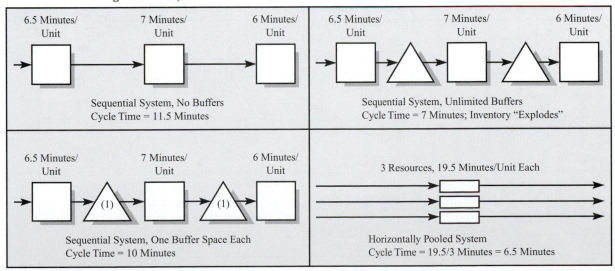

If we introduce buffers to this process, the flow rate improves. Even just allowing for one unit in buffer before and after the bottleneck increases the output to one unit every 10 minutes (lower left). If we put no limits on buffers, the process is able to produce the expected flow rate of one unit every seven minutes (upper right). Yet, we also observe that the buffer between the first and the second steps will grow very rapidly.

Finally, the lower-right part of Figure 9.7 outlines an alternative way to restore the flow rate, different from the concept of "buffer or suffer" (in fact, the flow rate is even a little larger than in the case of the upper right). By combining the three activities into one activity, we eliminate starving and blocking entirely. This concept is called *horizontal pooling,* as it resembles the concept of pooling identical activities and their previously separate arrival streams that we discussed in Chapter 8. Observe further the similarities between horizontal pooling and the concept of a work cell discussed in Chapter 4.

Given the cost of inventory as well as its detrimental impact on quality discussed in Chapter 10, we need to be careful in choosing where and how much inventory (buffer space) we allow in the process. Since the bottleneck is the constraint limiting the flow rate through the process (assuming sufficient demand), we want to avoid the bottleneck being either starved or blocked. Consequently, buffers are especially helpful right before and right after the bottleneck.

9.6 Summary

Variability not only impacts inventory and wait time but potentially also leads to losses in throughput. In this chapter, we have presented and analyzed the simplest case of such loss systems, consisting of multiple parallel resources with no buffer. The key computations for this case can be done based on the Erlang loss formula.

We then extended our discussion to the case in which customers potentially wait for service but are sufficiently impatient that a loss in throughput can still occur.

Figure 9.8 shows an overview of the various types of scenarios we discussed and, at least partially, analyzed. On the very left of the figure is the waiting problem of Chapter 8; on the very right is the no-buffer loss system (Erlang loss system) presented at the beginning of this chapter. In between are the intermediate cases of impatient customers. Observe that the four process types share a lot of similarities. For example, a wait system with limited, but large, buffer size is likely to behave very similarly to a pure waiting problem.

FIGURE 9.8   Different Types of Variability Problems

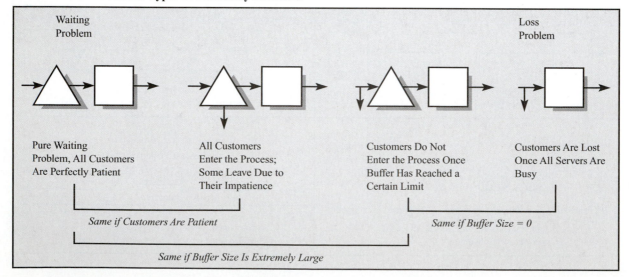

Similarly, as the buffer size approaches zero, the system behavior approaches the one of the pure loss system. Finally, we also looked at the case of several resources in series, forming a sequence of queues.

From a managerial perspective, the primary objective continues to be to reduce variability wherever possible. All concepts we discussed in Chapter 8 still apply, including the ideas to reduce the variability of service times through standardization and training.

However, since we cannot reduce variability entirely, it is important that we create processes that are robust enough so that they can accommodate as much of the remaining variability as possible. The following should be kept in mind to address throughput loss problems resulting from variability:

- *Use Buffers.* Nowhere else in this book is the concept of "buffer or suffer" so visible as in this chapter. To protect process resources, most importantly the bottleneck, from variability, we need to add buffers to avoid throughput losses of the magnitude in the example of Figure 9.7. In a sequence of resources, buffers are needed right before and right after the bottleneck to avoid the bottleneck either starving or becoming blocked.

- *Keep track of demand.* A major challenge in managing capacity-related decisions in a process with customer loss is to collect *real* demand information, which is required to compute the implied utilization level. Why is this difficult? The moment our process becomes sufficiently full that we cannot admit any new flow units (all trauma bays are utilized, all lines are busy in the call center), we lose demand, and, even worse, we do not even know how much demand we lose (i.e., we also lose the demand information). A common mistake that can be observed in practice is that managers use flow rate (sales) and utilization (Flow rate/Capacity) when determining if they need additional capacity. As we have discussed previously, utilization is by definition less than 100 percent. Consequently, the utilization measure always gives the impression that there is sufficient capacity in place. The metric that really matters is demand divided by capacity (implied utilization), as this reveals what sales could be if there were sufficient capacity.

- *Use background work.* Similar to what we discussed in Chapter 8 with respect to waiting time problems, we typically cannot afford to run a process at the low levels of utilization discussed in the trauma care setting. Instead, we can use less time-critical work to use potential idle time in a productive manner. However, a word of caution is in order. To qualify as background work, this work should not interfere with the time-critical work. Thus, it must be possible to interrupt or delay the processing of a unit of background work. Moreover, we have to ensure that background work does not compete for the same resource as time-critical work further downstream. For example, it has been reported that elective surgery (at first sight a great case of background work for a hospital) can lead to ambulance diversion, as it competes with trauma care patients for ICU capacity.

9.7 Further Reading

Gans, Koole, and Mandelbaum (2003), referenced in Chapter 8, is also a great reading with respect to customer loss patterns. Again, we refer the interested readers to Hillier and Lieberman (2002) and Hall (1997) for additional quantitative methods.

9.8 Practice Problems

Q9.1* **(Loss System)** Flow units arrive at a demand rate of 55 units per hour. It takes, on average, six minutes to serve a flow unit. Service is provided by seven servers.

    a. What is the probability that all seven servers are utilized?

    b. How many units are served every hour?

    c. How many units are lost every hour?

(* indicates that the solution is at the end of the book)

Q9.2** **(Home Security)** A friend of yours approaches you with the business idea of a private home security service. This private home security service guarantees to either dispatch one of their own five guards immediately if one of their customers sends in an alarm or, in the case that all five guards are responding to other calls, direct the alarm to the local police. The company receives 12 calls per hour, evenly distributed over the course of the day.

The local police charges the home security company $500 for every call that the police responds to. It takes a guard, on average, 90 minutes to respond to an alarm.

a. What fraction of the time are incoming alarms directed to the police?

b. How much does the home security company have to pay the local police every month?

Q9.3** **(Video Store)** A small video store has nine copies of the DVD *Captain Underpants, The Movie* in its store. There are 15 customers every day who request this movie for their children. If the movie is not on the shelf, they leave and go to a competing store. Customers arrive evenly distributed over 24 hours.

The average rental duration is 36 hours.

a. What is the likelihood that a customer going to the video store will find the movie available?

b. Assume each rental is $5. How much revenue does the store make per day from the movie?

c. Assume each child that is not able to obtain the movie will receive a $1 bill. How much money would the store have to give out to children requesting *Captain Underpants* every day?

d. Assume the demand for the movie will stay the same for another six months. What would be the payback time (not considering interest rates) for purchasing an additional copy of the movie at $50? Consider the extra revenues related to question b and the potential cost savings (part (c)).

Q9.4 **(Gas Station)** Consider the situation of Mr. R. B. Cheney, who owns a large gas station on a highway in Vermont. In the afternoon hours, there are, on average, 1,000 cars per hour passing by the gas station, of which 2 percent would be willing to stop for refueling. However, since there are several other gas stations with similar prices on the highway, potential customers are not willing to wait and bypass Cheney's gas station.

The gas station has six spots that can be used for filling up vehicles and it takes a car, on average, five minutes to free up the spot again (includes filling up and any potential delay caused by the customer going inside the gas station).

a. What is the probability that all six spots are taken?

b. How many customers are served every hour?

Q9.5 **(Two Workstations)** Suppose a process contains two workstations that operate with no buffer between them.

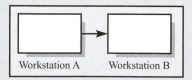

Workstation A   Workstation B

Now consider the three possible scenarios below:

Scenario	Processing Time of Workstation A	Processing Time of Workstation B
Scenario 1	5 minutes	5 minutes
Scenario 2	5 minutes	4 minutes or 6 minutes equally likely
Scenario 3	5 minutes	3 minutes or 5 minutes equally likely

a. Which of the three scenarios will have, on average, the highest flow rate?

b. Which of the three scenarios will have, on average, the lowest flow time?

Q9.6   **(XTremely Fast Service Inc.)** XTremely Fast Service Inc. is a call center with several business units. One of its business units, Fabulous 4, currently staffs four operators who work eight hours per day Monday through Friday. They provide customer support for a mail-order catalog company. Assume customers call Fabulous 4 during business hours and that—on average—a call arrives every 3 minutes (standard deviation of the interarrival time is equal to 3 minutes). You do NOT have to consider any seasonality in this call arrival pattern. If all four staff members are busy, the customer is rerouted to another business unit instead of being put on hold. Suppose the processing time for each call is 5 minutes on average.

a. What is the probability that an incoming call is *not* processed by Fabulous 4?

b. Suppose that Fabulous 4 receives $1 for each customer that it processes. What is Fabulous 4's daily revenue?

c. Suppose Fabulous 4 pays $5 for every call that gets routed to another business unit. What is its daily transfer payment to the other business unit?

Q9.7   **(Gotham City Ambulance Services)** Gotham City Ambulance Services (GCAS) owns eight ambulances. On average, emergencies are reported to GCAS every 15 minutes (with a coefficient of variation of 1, no seasonality exists). If GCAS has available ambulances, it immediately dispatches one. If there are no ambulances available, the incident is served by the emergency services at a neighboring community. You can assume that in the neighboring community, there is always an ambulance available. On average, an ambulance and its crew are engaged for 1.5 hours (with a coefficient of variation of 1.5) on every call. GCAS operates 24 hours a day.

a. What fraction of the emergencies reported to GCAS are handled by the emergency services at the neighboring community?

b. How many emergencies are served by GCAS during an average 24-hour day?

c. GCAS updated the operating procedures for its staff. This led to a reduction in the coefficient of variation of the time spent on each trip by its staff from 1.5 to 1.25. How will this training program affect the number of emergencies attended to by the GCAS?

d. New regulations require that every emergency service respond to at least 95 percent of all incidents reported in its area of service. Does GCAS need to buy more ambulances to meet this requirement? If yes, how many ambulances will be required? (Assume that the mean time spent on each trip cannot be changed.)

You can view a video of how problems marked with a ** are solved by going on www. cachon-terwiesch.net and follow the links under 'Solved Practice Problems'

10

Quality Management, Statistical Process Control, and Six-Sigma Capability

Many production and service processes suffer from quality problems. Airlines lose baggage, computer manufacturers ship laptops with defective disk drives, pharmacies distribute wrong medications to patients, and postal services lose or misdeliver articles by mail. In addition to these quality problems directly visible to consumers, many quality problems remain hidden from the perspective of the consumer, as they are detected and corrected within the boundaries of the process. For example, products arriving at the end of an assembly process might not pass final inspection, requiring that components be disassembled, reworked, and put together again. Although hidden to the consumer, such quality problems have a profound impact on the economics of business processes.

The main purpose of this chapter is to understand quality problems and to improve business processes with respect to quality. We will do this in five steps:

1. We first introduce the methodology of statistical process control, a powerful method that allows an organization to detect quality problems and to measure the effectiveness of process improvement efforts.

2. We introduce various ways to measure the capability of a process, including the concept of six sigma.

3. One way to achieve a high process capability is to build a process that is sufficiently robust so that deviations from the desired process behavior do not automatically lead to defects.

4. We then discuss how quality problems impact the process flow, thereby extending the process analysis discussion we started in Chapters 3 and 4. Specifically, we analyze how quality problems affect flow rate as well as the location of the bottleneck.

5. We conclude this chapter with a brief description of how to organize and implement quality improvement projects using structured problem-solving techniques.

10.1 Controlling Variation: Practical Motivation

Variation is the root cause of all quality problems. To see this, imagine a process without any variation. In this case, the process would either always function as desired, in which case we would not need a chapter on quality, or it would never function as desired, in which case it would be unlikely that our organization would be in business to begin with. We might face variation with respect to durations, as we have discussed in Chapters 8 and 9, but also could encounter variation with respect to other measures, such as the courtesy of a customer service representative in a call center or the physical dimensions of a manufactured component. Thus, (once again) understanding variation, including its sources and its measurement, is essential to improve our operation.

As an example, consider the production of the steer support for the Xootr kick scooter discussed in Chapter 4.[1] The component is obtained via extrusion from aluminum and subsequent refinement at a computer-controlled machine tool (CNC machine). Figures 10.1 and 10.2 show the engineering drawing and the component in the assembly. Despite the fact that every steer support component is refined by the CNC machine, there still exists some variation with respect to the exact geometry of the output. This variation is the result of many causes, including differences in raw materials, the way the component is placed

---

[1] The authors thank Karl Ulrich of Xootr LLC for his invaluable input.

FIGURE 10.1   **Engineering Drawing of the Steer Support, a Critical Component of the Xootr Scooter**
The height of the steer support is specified by the dimensions (shown in the lower center portion of the drawing) as falling between 79.900 and 80.000 mm.

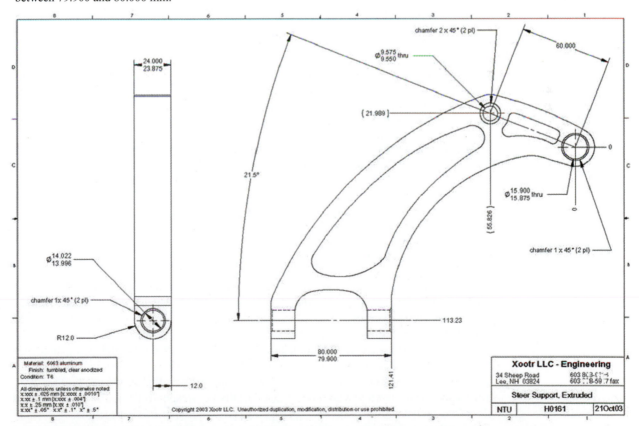

FIGURE 10.2
Steer Support within Xootr Scooter Assembly
The height of the steer support must closely match the opening in the lower handle.

in the machine, the temperature of the room at the time of the processing, an occasional mistake in programming the CNC machine, or some of the many other factors that we discuss further below.

According to the design of the product, the ideal steer support would measure 79.950 mm; the drawing specifies that the height must fall between 79.900 mm and 80.000 mm. If the height is less than 79.900 mm, the part may rattle excessively because it fits loosely. If the height is greater than 80.000 mm, then the part may not fit in the available gap in the handle assembly.

Given that variation of the steer support's height can cause quality problems, the engineers of the company (Xootr LLC) monitor the height very carefully. Every day, a sample of components is taken and measured accurately. Xootr engineers use *statistical process control (SPC)* to achieve the following:

- The company wants to achieve a consistent process that meets the specification as often as possible. SPC allows Xootr LLC to define performance measures that objectively describe the company's ability to produce according to their specifications.

- While a certain amount of variation seems natural, SPC allows Xootr LLC to quickly identify any "abnormally" large variation or changes in the underlying geometry.

10.2 The Two Types of Variation

Before we introduce the method of SPC, it is helpful to reflect a little more about the potential sources of variation. Following the work by W. A. Shewhart and W. E. Deming, we distinguish between two types of variation. *Common causes* of variation refer to constant variation reflecting pure randomness in the process. At the risk of being overly poetic for an operations management textbook, let us note that no two snowflakes are alike and no two flowers are exactly identical. In the same way, there is inherent variation in any business process and consequently no two steer support parts that Xootr can build will be exactly identical. Given that common-cause variation corresponds to "pure" randomness, a plot of the heights for a sample of steer support parts would have a shape similar to the normal distribution. Thus, for the case of common-cause variation, we cannot predict the exact outcome for the randomness in every single flow unit, yet we can describe the underlying randomness in the form of a statistical distribution that applies to the larger population.

Assignable causes of variation are those effects that result in changes of the parameters of the underlying statistical distribution of the process. For example, a mistake in programming the CNC machine, an operator error, or wear and tear of the extrusion machine would be assignable causes. Such causes are not common for all steer support parts; they only affect a subset. For those parts affected by the assignable cause, the distribution of heights looks statistically different and might have a higher variance or a different mean. The objective of many process improvement projects is to "assign" changes in process behavior to such causes and then to prevent them from recurring in the future.

To understand the notion of common causes of variation and how they differ from assignable causes, consider the following illustrative example. Take a piece of paper and write three rows, each containing the capital letter R eight times. Use your "normal" writing hand for the first row. Then, switch hands and write the eight Rs in the second row with the hand that you typically do not write with. Finally, for the last row, use your "normal" writing hand for the first four Rs and then switch hands for the last four. The outcome is likely to resemble what is shown in Figure 10.3.

The first row of Rs looks relatively consistent. While not every letter is exactly the same, there exists some (common-cause) variation from one letter to the next. In the second row, we observe a much larger (common-cause) variation with respect to the shape of the eight Rs. However, just as in the first row, there exists no obvious pattern that would allow us to predict the shape of the next letter (e.g., it is not possible to predict the shape of the sixth letter based on the first five letters in the same row). The pattern of letters in the last row is different. Following the fourth R, the process changes substantially. This variation can be clearly assigned to the cause of switching hands.

The distinction between common causes of variation and assignable causes is not a universal truth; it depends on the degree of knowledge of the observer. For example, to a layman, the movement of the Dow Jones Industrial Index might appear totally random, while an experienced trader can easily point to specific causes (earnings announcements, information releases by the government or rating agencies) that explain certain patterns of the market. Thus, just as the layman might learn and understand patterns that currently appear random to her, a process observer will discover new assignable causes in variation that she previously fully attributed to common causes.

FIGURE 10.3
Examples for Variation Types

The objective of statistical process control is to

- Alert management to assignable causes (i.e., in the case of the third row, we want to set off an alarm as soon after the fifth letter as possible). However, we do not want to alert management to the small variation from one letter to the next in the first two rows.
- Measure the amount of variation in the process, creating an objective measure of consistency (i.e., we want some way to measure that the first row is "better" than the second row).
- Assign causes to variation that currently is perceived as pure randomness and subsequently control these causes, leading to reduced variation and a higher consistency in outcomes.

10.3   Constructing Control Charts

Control charts are graphical tools to statistically distinguish between assignable and common causes of variation. Control charts visualize variation, thereby enabling the user to judge whether the observed variation is due to common causes or assignable causes, such as the breakdown of a machine or an operator mistake.

Control charts are part of a larger set of tools known as statistical process control, a quality movement that goes back to the 1930s, and over the decades included the "quality gurus" W. A. Shewhart, W. E. Deming, and J. M. Juran. Control charts have recently become fashionable again as they are an integral part of the six-sigma movement, introduced by Motorola and publicized widely by General Electric. Although their origin lies in the manufacturing domain, control charts are applicable to service processes equally well. At the end of this section, we discuss an application of control charts in a call center setting.

In order to distinguish between assignable and common causes of variation concerning a specific process outcome, control charts track the process outcome over time. Such process outcomes could be the physical size of a component that is assembled into a scooter or the time it takes a customer service representative to answer a call.

Given that data collection in many environments is costly, control charts are frequently based on samples taken from the process, as opposed to assessing every individual flow unit. Common sample sizes for control charts range between 2 and 10. When constructing a control chart, a sample is drawn in each of several time periods for typically 20 to 50 time periods. In the Xootr case, we will create a control chart based on one month of data and five units sampled every day.

Control charts plot data over time in a graph similar to what is shown in Figure 10.4. The x-axis of the control chart captures the various time periods at which samples from the

FIGURE 10.4
A Generic Control Chart

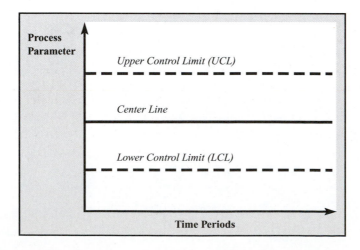

process are taken. For the two types of control charts that we discuss in this section, the y-axis plots one of the following two metrics:

- In the $\overline{X}$ chart (pronounced "X-bar chart"), the y-axis corresponds to the mean of each sample. $\overline{X}$ charts can be used to document trends over time and to identify unexpected drifts (e.g., resulting from the wear of a tool) or jumps (e.g., resulting from a new person operating a process step), corresponding to assignable causes of variation.

$$\overline{X} = \frac{x_1 + x_2 + \cdots + x_n}{n}$$

where n is the sample size in each period.

- In the R (range) chart, the y-axis corresponds to the range of each sample. The range is the difference between the highest value in the sample and the lowest value in the sample. Thus,

$$R = \max\{x_1, x_2, \ldots x_n\} - \min\{x_1, x_2, \ldots x_n\}$$

Instead of using the range of the sample, an alternative measure of variability is the standard deviation. The main reason why control charts have historically focused on the range instead of the standard deviation lies in its simplicity with respect to computation and explanation to a broad set of people in an organization.

To familiarize ourselves with the control chart methodology introduced up to this point, consider the data, displayed in Table 10.1, the Xootr engineers collected related to the

TABLE 10.1

Measurements of Steer Support Dimension in Groups of Five Observations

Period	X_1	X_2	X_3	X_4	X_5	Mean	Range
1	79.941	79.961	79.987	79.940	79.956	79.957	0.047
2	79.953	79.942	79.962	79.956	79.944	79.951	0.020
3	79.926	79.986	79.958	79.964	79.950	79.957	0.059
4	79.960	79.970	79.945	79.967	79.967	79.962	0.025
5	79.947	79.933	79.932	79.963	79.954	79.946	0.031
6	79.950	79.955	79.967	79.928	79.963	79.953	0.039
7	79.971	79.960	79.941	79.962	79.918	79.950	0.053
8	79.970	79.952	79.946	79.928	79.970	79.953	0.043
9	79.960	79.957	79.944	79.945	79.948	79.951	0.016
10	79.936	79.945	79.961	79.958	79.947	79.949	0.025
11	79.911	79.954	79.968	79.947	79.918	79.940	0.057
12	79.950	79.955	79.992	79.964	79.940	79.960	0.051
13	79.952	79.945	79.955	79.945	79.952	79.950	0.010
14	79.973	79.986	79.942	79.978	79.979	79.972	0.044
15	79.931	79.962	79.935	79.953	79.937	79.944	0.031
16	79.966	79.943	79.919	79.958	79.923	79.942	0.047
17	79.960	79.941	80.003	79.951	79.956	79.962	0.061
18	79.954	79.958	79.992	79.935	79.953	79.959	0.057
19	79.910	79.950	79.947	79.915	79.994	79.943	0.083
20	79.948	79.946	79.943	79.935	79.920	79.939	0.028
21	79.917	79.949	79.957	79.971	79.968	79.952	0.054
22	79.973	79.959	79.971	79.947	79.949	79.960	0.026
23	79.920	79.961	79.937	79.935	79.934	79.937	0.041
24	79.937	79.934	79.931	79.934	79.964	79.940	0.032
25	79.945	79.954	79.957	79.935	79.961	79.950	0.026
					Average	79.951	0.0402

height of the steer support component. The data show five observations for each day over a 25-day period. Based on the above definitions of $\overline{X}$ and R, we can compute the last two columns of the table.

For example, for day 14, $\overline{X}$ is computed as

$$\overline{X} = (79.973 + 79.986 + 79.942 + 79.978 + 79.979)/5 = 79.972$$

Similarly, for day 14, R is computed as

$$R = \max\{79.973, \ 79.986, \ 79.942, \ 79.978, \ 79.979\}$$
$$- \min\{79.973, \ 79.986, \ 79.942, \ 79.978, \ 79.979\} = 0.044$$

After computing the mean and the range for every period, we proceed to compute the average range and the average $\overline{X}$ across all days. The average across all $\overline{X}$s is frequently called $\overline{\overline{X}}$ (pronounced "X-double bar"), reflecting that it is an average across averages, and the average range is called $\overline{R}$ (pronounced "R-bar"). As we can see at the bottom of Table 10.1, we have

$$\overline{\overline{X}} = 79.951 \quad \text{and} \quad \overline{R} = 0.0402$$

In creating the $\overline{X}$ chart, we use the computed value of $\overline{\overline{X}}$ as a center line and plot the values of $\overline{X}$ for each day. For the R-chart, we plot the value of R in a chart that uses the average range, $\overline{R}$, as the center line.

Finally, we have to include the control limits in the charts. We set the control limits such that when we observe an entry for $\overline{X}$ or R outside the control limits (i.e., above the upper control or below the lower control), we can say with 99.7 percent confidence that the process has gone "out of control." Fortunately, we do not have to statistically derive the control limits. Instead, we can use a set of precomputed parameters (summarized in Table 10.2) to compute the control limits based on the following equations:

$$\text{Upper control limit for } \overline{X} = \overline{\overline{X}} + A_2 \times \overline{R} = 79.951 + 0.58 \times 0.0402 = 79.974$$

$$\text{Lower control limit for } \overline{X} = \overline{\overline{X}} - A_2 \times \overline{R} = 79.951 - 0.58 \times 0.0402 = 79.928$$

$$\text{Upper control limit for } R = D_4 \times \overline{R} = 2.11 \times 0.0402 = 0.0848$$

$$\text{Lower control limit for } R = D_3 \times \overline{R} = 0 \times 0.0402 = 0$$

TABLE 10.2
Control Chart Parameters for 99.7 Percent Confidence

Number of Observations in Subgroup (n)	Factor for X-Bar Chart (A_2)	Factor for Lower Control Limit in R Chart (D_3)	Factor for Upper Control Limit in R chart (D_4)	Factor to Estimate Standard Deviation (d_2)
2	1.88	0	3.27	1.128
3	1.02	0	2.57	1.693
4	0.73	0	2.28	2.059
5	0.58	0	2.11	2.326
6	0.48	0	2.00	2.534
7	0.42	0.08	1.92	2.704
8	0.37	0.14	1.86	2.847
9	0.34	0.18	1.82	2.970
10	0.31	0.22	1.78	3.078

FIGURE 10.5
X-bar Chart
and *R* Chart

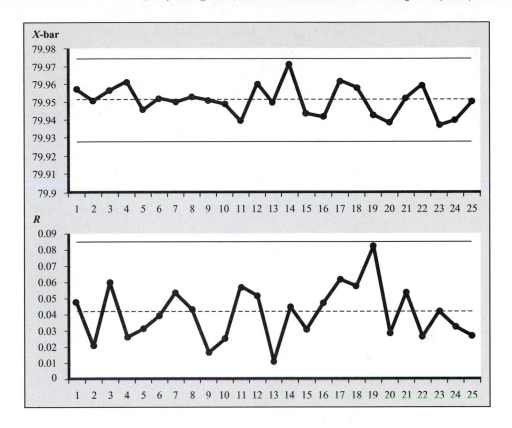

The control charts obtained this way allow for a visual assessment of the variation of the process. The definition of control limits implies that 99.7 percent of the sample points are expected to fall between the upper and lower control limits. Thus, if any point falls outside the control limits, we can claim with a 99.7 percent confidence level that the process has gone "out of control," that is, that an assignable cause has occurred.

In addition to an observation $\overline{X}$ falling above the upper control limit or below the lower control limit, a sequence of eight subsequent points above (or below) the center line also should be seen as a warning sign justifying further investigation (in the presence of only common causes of variation, the probability of this happening is simply $(0.5)^8 = 0.004$, which corresponds to a very unlikely event).

Figure 10.5 shows the control charts for the Xootr. We observe that the production process for the steer support is well in control. There seems to be an inherent randomness in the exact size of the component. Yet, there is no systematic pattern such as a drift or a sudden jump outside the control limits.

10.4 Control Chart Example from a Service Setting

To illustrate an application of control charts in a service setting, we turn back to the case of the An-ser call center, the answering service in Wisconsin that we discussed in conjunction with the waiting time formula in Chapter 8. An-ser is interested in an analysis of call durations for a particular type of incoming call, as both mean and variance of call durations impact the customer waiting time (see Chapter 8).

To analyze call durations for this particular type of incoming call, An-ser collected the data displayed in Table 10.3 over a period of 27 days. Similar to the Xootr case, we

TABLE 10.3
Data for a Control Chart at An-ser

Period	X_1	X_2	X_3	X_4	X_5	Mean	Range
1	1.7	1.7	3.7	3.6	2.8	2.7	2
2	2.7	2.3	1.8	3.0	2.1	2.38	1.2
3	2.1	2.7	4.5	3.5	2.9	3.14	2.4
4	1.2	3.1	7.5	6.1	3.0	4.18	6.3
5	4.4	2.0	3.3	4.5	1.4	3.12	3.1
6	2.8	3.6	4.5	5.2	2.1	3.64	3.1
7	3.9	2.8	3.5	3.5	3.1	3.36	1.1
8	16.5	3.6	2.1	4.2	3.3	5.94	14.4
9	2.6	2.1	3.0	3.5	2.1	2.66	1.4
10	1.9	4.3	1.8	2.9	2.1	2.6	2.5
11	3.9	3.0	1.7	2.1	5.1	3.16	3.4
12	3.5	8.4	4.3	1.8	5.4	4.68	6.6
13	29.9	1.9	7.0	6.5	2.8	9.62	28.0
14	1.9	2.7	9.0	3.7	7.9	5.04	7.1
15	1.5	2.4	5.1	2.5	10.9	4.48	9.4
16	3.6	4.3	2.1	5.2	1.3	3.3	3.9
17	3.5	1.7	5.1	1.8	3.2	3.06	3.4
18	2.8	5.8	3.1	8.0	4.3	4.8	5.2
19	2.1	3.2	2.2	2.0	1.0	2.1	2.2
20	3.7	1.7	3.8	1.2	3.6	2.8	2.6
21	2.1	2.0	17.1	3.0	3.3	5.5	15.1
22	3.0	2.6	1.4	1.7	1.8	2.1	1.6
23	12.8	2.4	2.4	3.0	3.3	4.78	10.4
24	2.3	1.6	1.8	5.0	1.5	2.44	3.5
25	3.8	1.1	2.5	4.5	3.6	3.1	3.4
26	2.3	1.8	1.7	11.2	4.9	4.38	9.5
27	2.0	6.7	1.8	6.3	1.6	3.68	5.1
					Average	**3.81**	**5.85**

can compute the mean and the range for each of the 27 days. From this, we can then compute the overall mean:

$$\overline{\overline{X}} = 3.81 \text{ minutes}$$

and the average range

$$\overline{R} = 5.85 \text{ minutes}$$

We then compute the control limits using the constants from Table 10.2:

Upper control limit for $\overline{X} = \overline{\overline{X}} + A_2 \times \overline{R} = 3.81 + 0.58 \times 5.85 = 7.20$

Lower control limit for $\overline{X} = \overline{\overline{X}} - A_2 \times \overline{R} = 3.81 - 0.58 \times 5.85 = 0.42$

Upper control limit for $R = D_4 \times \overline{R} = 2.11 \times 5.85 = 12.34$

Lower control limit for $R = D_3 \times \overline{R} = 0 \times 5.85 = 0$

Combining the control limits with the values of the mean, $\overline{X}$, and the range, R, we obtain the control charts shown in Figure 10.6.

As we can see in Figure 10.6, the call durations exhibit a fair amount of variation. This leads to a large average range, R-bar (lower part of Figure 10.6), and explains the

FIGURE 10.6
Control Charts for the An-ser Case

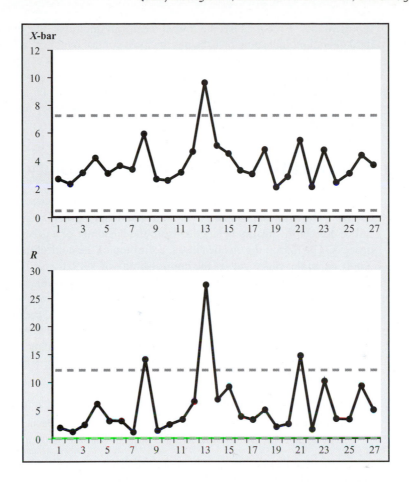

large interval between the upper and lower control limits. Despite these relatively "forgiving" control limits, we observe that the process moves out of control on day 13, when the mean, $\overline{X}$, jumps up to 9.62 (upper part of Figure 10.6). There are also two additional days when the R chart indicates an abnormally large variation in the process.

Going back to the data we collected (Table 10.3), we see that this exceptionally large mean is driven by one long call duration of almost half an hour. Despite having one observation drive the result, we know with 99.7 percent confidence that this long duration was not just "bad luck" but indeed reflects an assignable cause. Thus, further investigation is warranted.

In this particular case, An-ser management discovered that several calls on the days in question were handled by an operator that typically handled different types of calls. Further data analysis revealed large operator-to-operator variation for the exact same type of call. This is visible in Table 10.4. Note that all calls are of the same type, so that the duration difference can fully be attributed to the operator. Table 10.4 indicates that customer service

TABLE 10.4
Comparison of Operators

	CSR 1	CSR 2	CSR 3	CSR 4	CSR 5
Mean	2.95	3.23	7.63	3.08	4.26
Standard deviation	0.96	2.36	7.33	1.87	4.41

representative 1 (CSR 1) has the lowest mean call durations. She also has the lowest standard deviation, indicating that she has the most control over her calls. In fact, listening to a sample of randomly recorded calls indicated that CSR 1 fully complied with the script for the call type. In contrast, CSR 3 took more than twice as long when answering the same calls. Moreover, her standard deviation was seven times as large. Listening to a sample of recorded calls from CSR 3 confirmed a lack of consistency and large deviations with respect to the established script.

10.5　Design Specifications and Process Capability

So far, we have focused our discussion on the question to what extent the process is "in control." However, it is important to understand that a process that is in control might still fail to deliver the quality demanded from the customer or a downstream operation in the process. The reason for this lies in the definition of the control limits. Consider again the Xootr example. Since we set the control limits of 79.928 and 79.974 according to how the process performed in the past (25 days in the case above), we only measure to what extent the process is operating in line with its historical behavior (in the spirit of the letter R in Figure 10.3, the first two rows were "in control," despite the poor handwriting in the second row). This, however, contains little information about the degree to which the process is meeting the *design specifications* of 79.900 mm to 80.000 mm.

The consistency requirement from the customer typically takes the form of a design specification. A design specification includes

- A *target value* (79.950 mm in the case of the steer support component).
- A *tolerance level,* describing the range of values that are acceptable from the customer's perspective, [79.900 mm, 80.000 mm] for the steer support.

Again, note that design specifications are driven by the needs of the downstream process or by the end customer, while control limits are driven by how the process step has been operating in the past. Thus, it is very well possible that a process is "in control" yet incapable of providing sufficiently tight tolerances demanded by the customer. Vice versa, we say that a process, while being "in control," is capable if it can produce output according to the design specifications.

So, how do we know if a given process is capable of meeting the tolerance level established by the design specifications? This depends on

- The tightness of the design specification, which we can quantify as the difference between the upper specification level (USL) and the lower specification level (LSL).
- The amount of variation in the current process, which we can estimate based on the range R. For small sample sizes, we can translate the range R into an estimator of the standard deviation using the following equation:

$$\hat{\sigma} = \overline{R}/d_2$$

where $\hat{\sigma}$ stands for the estimated standard deviations and the values of d_2 are summarized in Table 10.2. For the steer support point, we have:

$$\hat{\sigma} = \overline{R}/d_2$$
$$= \frac{0.0402}{2.326} = 0.017283$$

Note that one also can estimate the standard deviation using a traditional statistical approach.

Thus, to increase the capability of the process in meeting a given set of design specifications, we either have to increase the tolerance level or decrease the variability in the process. We can combine these two measures into a single score, which is frequently referred to as the *process capability* index:

$$C_p = \frac{\text{USL} - \text{LSL}}{6\hat{\sigma}}$$

Thus, the process capability index C_p measures the allowable tolerance relative to the actual variation of the process. Figure 10.7 compares different values of C_p for a given set of design specifications. As we can see, the much lower variation (σ_B) of the process in the lower part of the figure will make it less likely that a defect will occur; that is, that the process creates a flow unit that falls above the upper specification limit or below the lower specification limit.

For the steer support component, we compute the process capability measure as follows:

$$C_p = \frac{\text{USL} - \text{LSL}}{6\hat{\sigma}} = \frac{80.000 - 79.900}{6 \times 0.017283} = 0.964345$$

A capability index of $C_p = 1$ would correspond to a process that meets the quality requirements 99.7 percent of the time. In other words, the process would have 28 defects per 10,000 units.

Traditionally, quality experts have recommended a minimum process capability index of 1.33. However, Motorola, as part of its six-sigma program, now postulates that all efforts should be made to obtain a process capability C_p of 2.0 at every individual step.

FIGURE 10.7

Comparison of Three-Sigma and Six-Sigma Process Capability

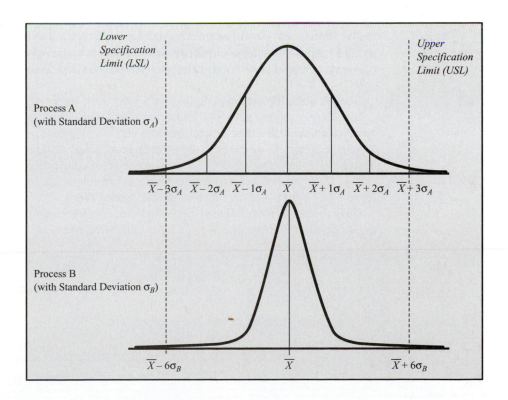

This is statistically equivalent to requiring that the USL is six standard deviations above the mean and the LSL is six standard deviations below the mean. This explains the name "six-sigma" (see Figure 10.7).

Xootr LLC uses process capability scores to compare different production technologies. For example, recently, the company considered streamlining its production process for the steer support component. Instead of extruding the part and then machining it, management suggested eliminating the machining step and using the extruded part directly for production.

Xootr LLC conducted a formal analysis of this proposal based on the process capability index C_p. Collecting data similar to Table 10.1, the company found that eliminating the machining step would lead to a dramatic increase in defects, reflecting a much lower process capability index (the design specifications have not changed and there is a much higher variation in height in absence of the machining step), and hence decided not to pursue this potentially cheaper production process.

10.6   Attribute Control Charts

Rather than collecting data concerning a specific variable and then comparing this variable with specification limits to determine if the associated flow unit is defective or not, it is frequently desirable to track the percentage of defective items in a given sample. This is especially the case if it is difficult to come up with a single variable, such as length or duration, that captures the degree of specification conformance. This is the idea behind *attribute control charts*.

To construct an attribute control chart, we need to be able to distinguish defective from nondefective flow units. In contrast to variable control charts, this distinction does not have to be made based on a single dimension. It could be the result of many variables with specification limits and even qualitative factors, as long as they can be measured consistently. For example, an airline tracking defects corresponding to lost luggage, a pharmacy trying to reduce the number of patients that were provided the wrong drugs, or a data entry operation struggling with handwriting recognition all would likely use an attribute control chart.

Sample sizes for attribute control charts tend to be larger, typically ranging from 50 to 200. Larger sample sizes are needed in particular if defects are relatively rare events. Samples are collected over several periods, just as in the case of variable control charts. Within each sample we evaluate the percentage of defective items. Let p denote this percentage. We then compute the average percentage of defects over all samples, which we call $\bar{p}$. This "average across averages" is the center line in our attribute control chart, just as we used $\bar{X}$ as the center line for variable control charts.

To compute the control limits, we first need to obtain an estimate of the standard deviation of defects. This estimate is given by the following equation:

$$\text{Estimated standard deviation} = \sqrt{\frac{\bar{p}(1 - \bar{p})}{\text{Sample size}}}$$

We then compute the upper and lower control limits:

$$\text{UCL} = \bar{p} + 3 \times \text{Estimated standard deviation}$$
$$\text{LCL} = \bar{p} - 3 \times \text{Estimated standard deviation}$$

Thus, we again set control limits such that the process is allowed to vary three standard deviations in each direction from the mean.

Whether one should use a variable control chart or an attribute control chart depends on the type of problem at hand.

- If there exists a single, measurable variable that determines if a unit is defective or not, one should always use variable control charts. The advantage of the variable control chart is that it makes use of valuable information that is discarded in attribute control charts. For example, if three sampled units were all very close to (yet still below) the upper specification limit, they would be classified as "nondefective" in the spirit of attribute control charts. In contrast, the variable control chart would use this information as leading to an increased estimated probability that a future unit might be above the upper specification limit.

- If there are many potential causes of defects, variable-based control charts are difficult to implement. Thus, when measuring defects in activities such as order entry in a call center, baggage handling for an airline, or drug handling in a pharmacy, attribute-based control charts should be used.

Given the multiple potential root causes of a defect, it is frequently desirable to find which of these root causes accounts for the majority of the problems. The Pareto diagram is a graphical way to identify the most important causes of process defects. To create a Pareto diagram, we need to collect data on the number of defect occurrences as well as the associated defect types. We can then plot simple bars with heights indicating the relative occurrences of the defect types. It is also common to plot the cumulative contribution of the defect types. An example of a Pareto diagram is shown in Figure 10.8. The figure categorizes defects related to customer orders at Xootr LLC.

Pareto charts were introduced to quality management by J. M. Juran, who observed that managers spent too much time trying to fix "small" problems while not paying enough attention to "big" problems. The Pareto principle, also referred to as the 80-20 rule, postulates that 20 percent of causes account for 80 percent of the problems. In the context of quality, the Pareto principle implies that a few defect types account for the majority of defects.

10.7 Robust Process Design

As discussed above, variation in a process parameter such as the geometry of a part or the duration of a service activity is at the root of all quality problems. So identifying the sources of variation and eliminating them should always be the first priority when aiming for a quality improvement.

However, eliminating variation is not always possible. Especially when dealing with human resources (e.g., assembly-line workers) or human flow units (patients, calls in a call center), we are always exposed to variation that is beyond our control. Moreover, often the sources of variation might be under our control, yet their elimination might be prohibitively expensive.

For these reasons, instead of just fighting variation, we also need to be able to accommodate it. We need to design processes that are robust, that is, that do not fall apart and produce defects the moment they are exposed to variation. A good tennis player should always aim to hit the ball with the sweet spot of her racket, yet a good tennis racket also should be "forgiving" in that it does not lead to a poor shot the moment the hit is less than perfect.

To understand the concept of robust process design, consider the following illustrative example. Many universities and business schools are blessed (or cursed) with on-site restaurants, coffee shops, or cafeterias. As part of their baking operations, a large coffee shop needs to define an operating procedure to bake chocolate chip cookies.

FIGURE 10.8
Sources of Problems with Customer Orders at Xootr

Cause of Defect	Absolute Number	Percentage	Cumulative Percentage
Browser error	43	39%	39%
Order number out of sequence	29	26%	65%
Product shipped, but credit card not billed	16	15%	80%
Order entry mistake	11	10%	90%
Product shipped to billing address	8	7%	97%
Wrong model shipped	3	3%	100%
Total	**110**		

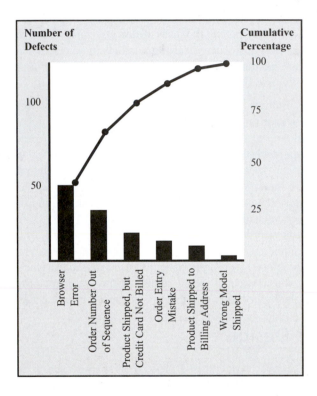

There are many important product attributes customers care about when it comes to the chocolate chip cookies that they purchase for $1.19 a piece. Yet, probably the most important one is the cookie's chewiness—is it too soft and still tastes like it is "half-baked" or is it too hard and crunches like a brick. The two key parameters that determine the chewiness are the bake time (the duration that the cookies are in the oven) and the oven temperature.

To state it formally:

$$\text{Chewiness of cookie} = F_1(\text{Bake time}) + F_2(\text{Oven temperature})$$

where F_1 and F_2 are two functions illustrated in Figure 10.9.

Note that there exists more than one way to obtain any given chewiness value. We can bake the cookie for 24 minutes at 240 degrees (process design A) or we can bake them for 21 minutes at 280 degrees (process design B). For the sake of argument, say that, from the customer's perspective, these two are identical.

A reality of baking cookies and selling them fresh is that this type of process is often exposed to a fair bit of variation. The typical operator involved in this process has received

FIGURE 10.9
Two Different Process Recipes for Making Chocolate Chip Cookies

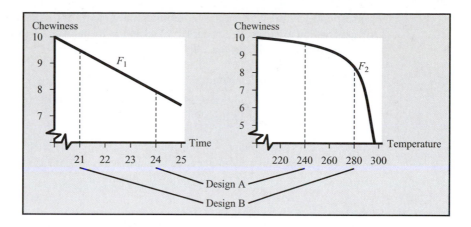

little training and is paid a relatively low wage rate. Often, the baking is carried out by operators who also have other responsibilities (i.e., they don't sit next to the oven during the baking time), making it likely that the baking time can vary ± 1 minute from the recipe and/or the actual oven temperature can vary ± 10 degrees.

So, which process recipe should we use? Process design A or process design B? From the customer's perspective and ignoring the effect of variation, it seems as if this choice does not matter. However, keeping the effect of variation in the actual baking time in mind, a second look at Figure 10.9 reveals that going for the 21-minute baking time can be a risky endeavor. The shorter baking time requires us to use a higher oven temperature. And, at this high oven temperature, even small variations in baking time and oven temperature (especially too high temperatures) can lead to bad outcomes.

For this reason, we say that process design A is more robust—it is more tolerant of variation in the process parameters. We can formalize the concept of robustness by looking at a two-dimensional plot such as shown in Figure 10.10. The figure shows a set of lines that

FIGURE 10.10
Cookie Example (continued)

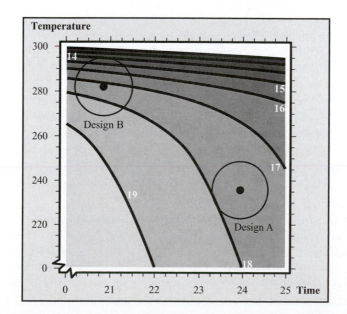

correspond to time–temperature combinations yielding the same chewiness. Each shade of grey in the figure hence roughly corresponds to the same expected chewiness. Now, compare design A with design B in the figure by including

- A dot for the time–temperature combination.
- A circle around the dot that corresponds to all possible time–temperature combinations that might be chosen as a result of variation.

What makes process recipe A more robust is that the circle capturing all likely variations of the recipe stays entirely in one area of chewiness: we can afford a variation in the input parameters without suffering a variation in the output.

10.8 Impact of Yields and Defects on Process Flow

Defects, as described in previous sections, have a profound impact on the process flow. In this section, we discuss processes consisting of a sequence of process steps, of which at least one step suffers from detectable quality problems. In other words, there exists at least one step at which units are separated into "good units" and "defective units." Whereas good items can continue processing at the next operation, defective units either have to be *reworked* or are *eliminated from the process* (known as scrapped in the manufacturing context).

- In the case of the Xootr, the company scraps all steer support parts that do not meet the specifications as discussed previously.
- In contrast, Xootr LLC reworks Xootrs that require adjustments in the brake assembly. These Xootrs are rerouted to a separate operator in charge of rework. This (highly skilled) operator disassembles the brake (typically scrapping the brake cable) and adjusts the brake as needed, thereby creating a sellable Xootr.

The following examples help illustrate that the ideas of rework and flow unit elimination are by no means restricted to manufacturing:

- Following heart surgery, patients typically spend time recovering in the intensive care unit. While most patients can then be moved to a regular unit (and ultimately be sent home), some patients are readmitted to the intensive care unit in case of complications. From the perspective of the ICU, patients who have been discharged to regular units but then are readmitted to the ICU constitute rework.
- The recruitment process of large firms, most prominently the one of consulting companies, also exhibits a large percentage of flow units that are eliminated before the end of the process. For every offer made, consulting firms process hundreds of résumés and interview dozens of job candidates (possibly staged in several rounds). Typically, job candidates are eliminated from the applicant pool—rework (a job candidate asked to repeat her first-round interviews) is very rare.
- Pharmaceutical development analyzes thousands of chemical compounds for every new drug that enters the market. The initial set of compounds is reduced through a series of tests, many of which are very costly. After a test, some units are allowed to proceed to the next phase, while others are eliminated from the set of potential compounds for the clinical indication the company is looking for.

We define the *yield* of a resource as:

$$\text{Yield of resource} = \frac{\text{Flow rate of units processed successfully at the resource}}{\text{Flow rate}}$$

$$= 1 - \frac{\text{Flow rate of defects at the resource}}{\text{Flow rate}}$$

Thus, the yield of a resource measures the percentage of good units that are processed at this resource. Similarly, we can define yields at the level of the overall process:

$$\text{Process yield} = \frac{\text{Flow rate of units processed successfully}}{\text{Flow rate}} = 1 - \frac{\text{Flow rate of defects}}{\text{Flow rate}}$$

Obviously, the words *defects* and *rework* sound harsh in some of the examples described above, especially if we are dealing with human flow units. However, the following concepts and calculations apply equally well for disk drives that have to be reworked because they did not meet the specifications of final tests and patients that have to be readmitted to intensive care because they did not recover as quickly as required to safely stay in a regular hospital unit.

It also should be pointed out that a defect does not always reflect the failure of a process step, but can reflect inherent randomness (common cause variation) in the process or differences with respect to the flow units at the beginning of the process. For example, dismissing a chemical compound as a potential cure for a given disease, does not imply that previous development steps did not do their job correctly. Instead, the development steps have simply revealed a (previously unknown) undesirable property of the chemical compound. Similarly, it lies in the nature of a recruiting process that its yield (percentage of applications resulting in a job) is well below 100 percent.

Rework

Rework means that some steps prior to the detection of the problem must be redone, or some additional process steps are required to transform a defective unit into a good unit. Two examples of rework are shown in Figure 10.11 (inventory locations are left out for simplicity).

In the upper part of the figure, defective units are taken out of the regular process and moved to a separate rework operation. This is common in many production processes

FIGURE 10.11
Two Processes with Rework

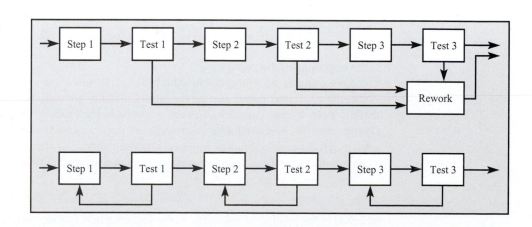

such as in the Xootr example discussed above. If the rework step is always able to turn a defective unit into a good unit, the process yield would return to 100 percent. In the lower part of the figure, defective units are reworked by the same resource that previously processed the unit. The readmission of a patient to the intensive care unit corresponds to such a case.

Rework changes the utilization profile of the process. Compared to the case of no defects, rework means that a resource has additional work flowing to it, which in turn increases utilization. As a consequence, rework can potentially change the location of the bottleneck.

Thus, when analyzing the influence of yields (and rework) on process capacity, we need to distinguish between bottleneck and nonbottleneck resources. If rework involves only nonbottleneck machines with a large amount of idle time, it has a negligible effect on the overall process capacity (note that it will still have cost implications, reflecting costs of material and extra labor at the rework step).

In many cases, however, rework is severe enough to make a resource a bottleneck (or, even worse, rework needs to be carried out on the bottleneck). As the capacity of the bottleneck equals the capacity of the overall process, all capacity invested in rework at the bottleneck is lost from the perspective of the overall process.

Eliminating Flow Units from the Process

In many cases, it is not possible or not economical to rework a flow unit and thereby transform a defective unit into a good unit. Once the Xootr machine has produced a defective steer support unit, it is almost impossible to rework this unit into a nondefective unit. Instead, despite an approximate material cost of $12 for the unit, the company scraps the unit and produces a replacement for it.

Similarly, a consulting firm searching for a new hire will prefer to simply reject the application, instead of investing in training to improve the job candidate's skills. If defective units are eliminated from the process, final output of good units is correspondingly reduced.

Strictly speaking, eliminating flow units from the process is a special form of rework, where all operations between the step where the defective unit leaves the process and the beginning of the process have to be reworked. Given that all operations up to the point of defect detection have to be reworked, the earlier we can detect and eliminate the corresponding flow unit, the less we waste capacity. This wasted capacity reflects that more units need to be started in the process than are finished. For example, to get 100 good units at the end of the process, we have to start with

$$\text{Number of units started to get 100 good units} = 100/\text{Process yield}$$

at the beginning of the process.

Two examples of processes in which defective units are eliminated are shown in Figure 10.12. In the upper part of the figure, defects are only detected at the end, and thereby have wasted capacity of every resource in the process. In the lower part of the figure, a test is conducted after every process step, which allows for the early elimination of defective parts, leading to less wasted capacity.

In a process in which defective units are eliminated, we can write the process yield as

$$\text{Process yield} = y_1 \times y_2 \times \cdots \times y_m$$

where m is the number of resources in the sequence and y_i is the yield of the ith resource.

FIGURE 10.12
Process with Scrap

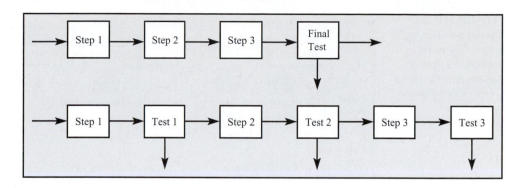

Cost Economics and Location of Test Points

In addition to their effect on capacity, yields determine the value that a good unit has at various stages in the process. What is the value of a good unit in the process? The answer to this question will differ depending on whether we are capacity constrained or whether we are constrained by demand.

Consider the demand-constrained case first. At the beginning of the process, the value of a good item equals its input cost (the cost of raw material in the case of production). The value of a good unit increases as it moves through the process, even if no additional material is being added. Again, let y_n be the yield at the nth stage. The value leaving resource n is approximately $1/y_n$ times the sum of the value entering stage n plus any variable costs we incur at stage n.

The capacity-constrained case is fundamentally different. At the end of the process, the marginal extra revenue of the unit determines the value of a good unit. Yet, at the beginning of the process, the value of a good unit still equals its input costs. So should the valuation of a good unit be cost-based working forward or price-based working backwards? The discontinuity between these two approaches comes at the bottleneck operation. After the bottleneck, value is based on selling price; before the bottleneck, it is based on cost.

For example, assume that Xootr LLC is currently demand-constrained and we want to value a flow unit as it moves through the process. We should do this using a cost-based calculation, as—independent of a defect in this flow unit—we will achieve the same sales rate (i.e., we fulfill demand). In contrast, if Xootr LLC is capacity-constrained, we have to factor in the marginal extra revenue for those flow units that have already passed the bottleneck.

As a consequence of this, the costs that arise with detecting a defect dramatically increase as a flow unit moves through the process to market. Consider the case of a nonreworkable defect occurring at a prebottleneck resource, as depicted in Figure 10.13. If the defect is detected before the bottleneck, the costs of this defect are simply the costs of the materials that went into the unit up to the detection of the defect. However, if the defect is detected after the bottleneck and the process is currently capacity-constrained, the unit is almost as valuable as a complete unit. In the extreme case, if the defect is detected on the market, we are likely to incur major costs related to warranty, field repair, liability, and so forth. For this reason, in a capacity-constrained process, it is essential to have an inspection step prior to the bottleneck.

At a more conceptual level, Figure 10.13 relates to an idea referred to as *quality at the source,* an element of the Toyota Production System emphasizing that defects should be

FIGURE 10.13
**Cost of a Defect as
a Function of Its
Detection Location,
Assuming a Capacity-
Constrained Process**

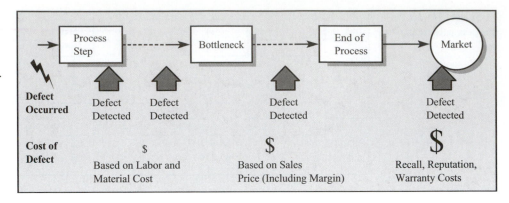

detected right when and where they occur, as opposed to being detected in a remote final inspection step. In addition to the cost benefits discussed above, another advantage of quality at the source is that the correction of the root cause that led to the defect is typically much easier to identify at the place and time when the defect is made. While a worker in charge of a process step that leads to a defect is likely to remember the context of the defect, figuring out what went wrong with a unit at a final inspection step is typically much harder.

Defects and Variability

Quality losses and yield-related problems not only change the capacity profile of a process, but they also cause variability. A yield of 90 percent means not that every tenth flow unit is defective, but that there is a 10 percent probability of a defect occurring. Thus, yield losses increase variability, which—as we have seen in Chapters 8 and 9—is the enemy of capacity.

Consider again the process flow diagram in the lower part of Figure 10.11, that is, a process where defective units are immediately reworked by repeating the operation. Even if the actual activity time is deterministic, yield losses force items into multiple visits at the same resource, and thus make the effective activity time for a *good* item a random variable.

Capacity losses due to variability can be partially compensated by allowing inventory after each operation with yields below 100 percent. The larger these buffers, the more the capacity-reducing impact of variability is reduced. However, additional inventory increases costs and flow times; it also can hurt the detection and solution of quality problems, as we discussed in Chapter 9.

10.9 A Process for Improvement

The strength of the statistical process control techniques discussed in this chapter results from their combination of collecting actual data with using professional analysis techniques.

The importance of data collection cannot be overemphasized. In many industries, collecting data about process performance is the exception rather than the norm. Once you have collected data, process improvement meetings turn fact-based and objective as opposed to being largely subjective. While most manufacturing facilities by now routinely collect data about their processes, most service processes are lagging behind. Only in the last couple of years have service providers in banking or health care started to systemically track process data. This is somewhat surprising given that services are often blessed with loads of data because of their electronic workflow management systems.

But a successful process improvement project needs more than data. It is important to statistically analyze data. Otherwise, every small, random change in the process (including common cause variation) is interpreted as meaningful and acted upon. The tools outlined above help to separate the important from the unimportant.

In addition to statistical tools, it is also essential to have a clear action plan on how to organize a project aiming at process improvement. A well executed process improvement project tends to go through the following steps:

- You sense a problem and explore it broadly.
- You formulate a specific problem to work on/state a specific improvement theme.
- You collect data and analyze the situation.
- You find the root causes.
- You plan a solution and implement it.
- You evaluate the effects of the solution.
- You standardize the process to include the new solution if it is good.
- Then you take on the next problem.

Figure 10.14 summarizes the tools introduced in this chapter by outlining a systematic process to achieve quality improvement.

The focus of the improvement project is guided by where defects are most costly and hence improvements have the biggest economic impact. Typically, this involves the bottleneck resource. We then collect data and analyze it, determining process capabilities and exact yields. This helps us understand the impact of defects on the process flow and ultimately on the economics of the process.

We have a choice between thinking of defects in a binary way (defect versus no defect) or based on a specific set of customer specifications (upper and lower specification limits). In the former case, we use attribute control charts; otherwise we use regular control charts as introduced previously in this chapter. This analysis lets us determine our current process capability. By classifying the defects and assigning them to causes (Pareto analysis), we also can find out the most significant root causes.

We then either eliminate these root causes or, using the robust process design logic, attempt to minimize their sensitivity to variation in process parameters. The resulting improved process is monitored and analyzed in the same way as previously, which either confirms or disconfirms the usefulness of our action. This is an iterative process, reflecting that there are multiple (potentially interacting) causes and a potentially limited understanding of the process.

FIGURE 10.14

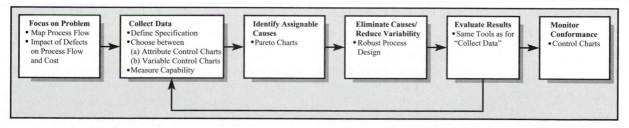

Finally, control charts help with respect to standardizing a solution and in determining the degree of conformance with the new process design. They will also alert us of an emergence of any new assignable causes.

10.10 Further Reading

Wadsworth, Stephens, and Godfrey (1986) provide an excellent overview of various control charting methods. Their book also includes several examples of implementation. Breyfogle (1999) provides a detailed overview of many tools and definitions underlying six sigma. Interested readers also should look at the initial Motorola document about six sigma, which is summarized in Motorola (1987).

Six-sigma training is often done using a catapult to help illustrate that it often is better to consistently hit a spot that is slightly off target as opposed to occasionally hitting the target, yet hit a wide range of different points as well. See www.xpult.com for more details on six sigma and catapults.

More details on quality can be found in the earlier work by Juran (1951) or the more recent work Juran (1989).

Bohn and Terwiesch (1999) provide a framework for analyzing the economics of yield-driven processes, which we used as the foundation for the discussion of rework and scrap.

Ulrich and Eppinger (2011) is an excellent source for more details about robust process design and the design of experiments to improve products and processes.

Finally, the small booklet "Memory Jogger" is a highly effective manual for the quality improvement tools discussed in this chapter and beyond.

10.11 Practice Problems

Q10.1   **(Quality)** Consider the following potential quality problems:

- Wine that is served in a restaurant sometimes is served too warm, while at other times it is served too cold.
- A surgeon in a hospital follows the hygiene procedures in place on most days, but not all days.
- A passenger traveling with an airline might be seated at a seat with a defective audio system.
- An underwriter in a bank might sometimes accidentally approve loans to consumers that are not creditworthy.

For each of these potential problems:

a. What type of data would you collect?

b. What type of control charts would you use?

Q10.2   **(Process with Rework)** Consider the following three-stage production process of glass ceramics, which is operated as a worker-paced line.

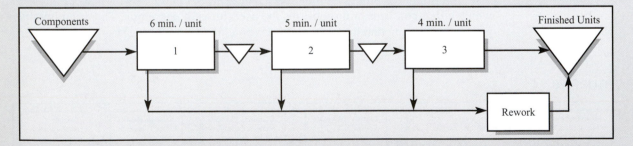

The process is experiencing severe quality problems related to insufficiently trained workers. Specifically, 20 percent of the parts going through operation 1 are badly processed by the operator. Rather than scrapping the unit, it is moved to a highly skilled rework operator, who can correct the mistake and finish up the unit completely within 15 minutes.

The same problem occurs at station 2, where 10 percent of the parts are badly processed, requiring 10 minutes of rework. Station 3 also has a 10 percent ratio of badly processed parts, each of them requiring 5 minutes by the rework operator.

a. What is the utilization of station 2 if work is released into the process at a rate of 5 units per hour?

b. Where in the process is the bottleneck? Why? (Remember, the bottleneck is the resource with the lowest capacity, independent of demand.)

c. What is the process capacity?

Chapter 11

Lean Operations and the Toyota Production System

Toyota is frequently associated with high quality as well as overall operational excellence, and, as we will discuss in this chapter, there are good reasons for this association—Toyota has enjoyed decades of economic success while changing the history of operations management.

- Various elements of the company's famous Toyota Production System (TPS) are covered throughout this book, but in this chapter we will review and summarize the components of TPS, as well as a few that have not been discussed in earlier chapters.
- We also will illustrate how the various elements of TPS are intertwined, thereby making it difficult to adapt some elements while not adapting others.

As we will discuss, one of the key objectives of TPS is the elimination of "waste" from processes such as idle time, unnecessary inventory, defects, and so forth. As a result, people often refer to (parts of) TPS as "lean operations." The expression "lean operations" has been especially popular in service industries.

11.1 The History of Toyota

To appreciate the elegance and success of the Toyota Production System, it is helpful to go back in time and compare the history of the Toyota Motor Company with the history of the Ford Motor Corporation.

Inspired by moving conveyor belts at slaughterhouses, Henry Ford pioneered the use of the assembly line in automobile production. The well-known Model T was the first mass-produced vehicle that was put together on an assembly line using interchangeable parts. Working with interchangeable parts allowed Ford to standardize assembly tasks, which had two important benefits. First, it dramatically reduced variability, and thereby increased quality. Second, it streamlined the production process, thereby making both manual and automated assembly tasks faster.

With the luxury of hindsight, it is fair to say that Ford's focus was on running his automotive production process with the goal of utilizing his expensive production equipment as much as possible, thereby allowing him to crunch out the maximum number of vehicles. Ford soon reached an unmatched production scale—in the early days of the Model T, 9 out of 10 automotive vehicles in the world were produced by Ford! Benefiting from his scale economies, Ford drove the price of a Model T down, which made it afford- able to the American middle class, an enormous market that was well suited to be served by mass production.

The Toyota Motor Corporation grew out of Toyota Industries, a manufacturer of automated looms, just prior to World War II. Toyota supported the Japanese army by supplying it with military trucks. Given the shortages of most supplies in Japan at that time, Toyota trucks were equipped with only one headlight and had an extremely simplistic design. As we will see, both the heritage as a loom maker as well as the simplicity of its first vehicle product had consequences for the future development of Toyota.

Following the war, shortages in Japan were even more severe. There existed virtually no domestic market for vehicles and little cash for the acquisition of expensive production equipment. The United States had an active role in the recovery process of Japan and so it is not surprising that the American production system had a strong influence on the young automaker. Toyota's early vehicles were in part produced using secondhand U.S. equip- ment and also otherwise had significant resemblances with the U.S. brands of Dodge and Chevrolet.

As inspiring as the Western industrial engineering must have been to Toyota, replicat- ing it was out of the question. Mass production, with its emphasis on scale economies and large investments in machinery, did not fit Toyota's environment of a small domestic market and little cash.

Out of this challenging environment of scarcity, Toyota's management created the various elements of a system that we now refer to as the Toyota Production System (TPS). TPS was not invented overnight—it is the outcome of a long evolution that made Toyota the most successful automaker in the world and the gold standard for operations management.

Following a long period of growth, Toyota became the world's top automaker in the year 2008. Since then, Toyota experienced two crises. First, in the fourth quarter of 2009 and first quarter of 2010, Toyota recalled several million vehicles in response to reports of unintended vehicle acceleration. Toyota executives were questioned by the U.S. Congress, and the numerous reasons for a set of fatal accidents were widely discussed in the U.S. media. Early in 2011, the National Highway Traffic Safety Administration, in collaboration with NASA, released a report that identified driver error, as the main root cause behind the accidents (in most instances, drivers confused the gas pedal with the brake pedal). Despite the negative publicity associated with the recalls, Toyota was able to keep its position as the world's top automaker.

Second, following the Japanese earthquake of March 2011, Toyota was forced to shut down several of its assembly plants. Moreover, the company (and others) faced supply shortages of important automotive parts. The full impact of the earthquake on Toyota's 2011 production and its relative impact compared to other automakers is still unclear as we write this third edition.

But enough about Toyota—this chapter is not about Toyota, but it is about TPS. Many other industries are implementing TPS, with examples ranging from health care to banking. You can use TPS in your organization, whether you work for Toyota or for the German government. And, even Toyota does not always follow TPS. Thus, the power of TPS does not depend on Toyota's position in the ranking of the world's top automakers.

11.2   TPS Framework

While TPS is frequently associated with certain buzzwords such as JIT, kanban, and kaizen, one should not assume that simply implementing any of these concepts would lead to the level of operational excellence at Toyota. TPS is not a set of off-the-shelf solutions for various operational problems, but instead a complex configuration of various routines ranging from human resource management to the management of production processes.

Figure 11.1 summarizes the architecture of TPS. At the top, we have the principle of waste reduction. Below, we have a set of methods that help support the goal of waste reduction. These methods can be grouped into JIT methods (JIT stands for just-in-time) and quality improvement methods. There exist strong interdependencies among the various methods. We will discuss some of these interdependencies throughout this chapter, especially the interaction between JIT and quality.

Collectively, these methods help the organization to attack the various sources of waste that we will define in the next section. Among them are overproduction, waiting, transport, overprocessing, and inventory, all of which reflect a mismatch between supply and demand. So the first set of methods that we will discuss (Section 11.4) relate to synchronizing the

FIGURE 11.1   The Basic Architecture of TPS
(The numbers in the black circles correspond to the related section numbers of this chapter.)

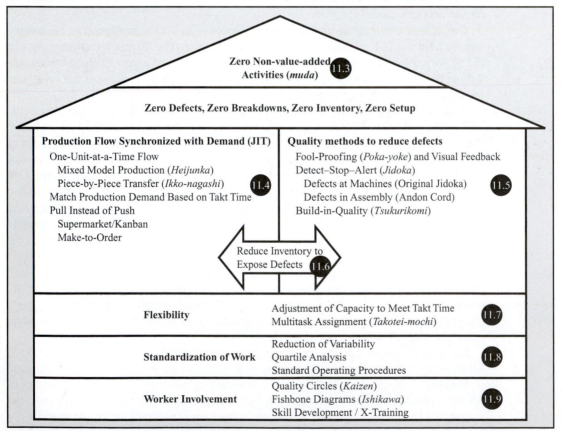

production flow with demand. Output should be produced exactly when the customer wants it and in the quantity demanded. In other words, it should be produced just in time.

If we want to obtain a flow rate of the process that reliably matches demand while also following the just-in-time idea, we have to operate a process with no defects and no breakdowns. This is a direct consequence of our discussion in Chapters 8 and 9 (buffer or suffer): defects create variability and the only way we can obtain our target flow rate in a process with variability is to use buffers.

Toyota's strong emphasis on quality lets the company overcome the buffer-or-suffer tension: by producing with zero defects and zero breakdowns, the company neither has to suffer (sacrifice flow rate) nor to buffer (hold inventory). For this reason, and the fact that defects are associated with the waste of rework, quality management is the second pillar around which TPS is built.

Both JIT and quality management require some foundational methods such as the standardization of work (which eliminates variability), the flexibility to scale up and down process capacity in response to fluctuations in demand, and a set of human resource management practices.

11.3   The Seven Sources of Waste

In the late 1980s, a research consortium known as the International Motor Vehicle Program (IMVP) conducted a global benchmarking of automotive plants. The study compared quality and productivity data from plants in Asia, Europe, and North America. The results were a clear indication of how far Toyota already had journeyed in redesigning the historical concept of mass production.

Consider the data displayed in Table 11.1, which compares the General Motors Framingham assembly plant with the Toyota Takaoka assembly plant. The Toyota plant was about twice as productive and had three times fewer defects compared to the GM plant making a comparable vehicle. Moreover, it used its manufacturing space more efficiently and turned its components and parts inventory dramatically faster.

While the data underlying this exhibit are already 25 years old, they are still of high relevance today. First, the IMVP study in many ways was the first true proof of the superiority of TPS. For that reason, it constituted a milestone in the history of industrialization. Second, while all large automotive manufacturers have made substantial improvements since the initial data collection, two more recent rounds of benchmarking (see Holweg and Pil 2004) documented that the productivity of Japanese manufacturers has been a moving target. While U.S. and European manufacturers could improve their productivity, the Japanese producers have continued to improve theirs so that Toyota still enjoys a substantial competitive advantage today.

TABLE 11.1
General Motors Framingham Assembly Plant versus Toyota Takaoka Assembly Plant (Based on 1986 benchmarking data from the IMVP Assembly Plant Survey.)

Source: Womack, Jones, and Roos (1991).

	GM Framingham	Toyota Takaoka
Gross Assembly Hours per Car	40.7	18
Assembly Defects per 100 Cars	130	45
Assembly Space per Car	8.1	4.8
Inventories of Parts (average)	2 weeks	2 hours

Notes: Gross assembly hours per car are calculated by dividing total hours of effort in the plant by the total number of cars produced.
Defects per car were estimated from the JD Power Initial Quality Survey for 1987.
Assembly Space per Car is square feet per vehicle per year, corrected for vehicle size.
Inventories of Parts are a rough average for major parts.

What accounts for the difference in productivity between the GM and the Toyota plant? Both processes end up with a very comparable car after all. The difference in productivity is accounted for by all the things that GM did that did not contribute to the production of the vehicle: non-value-added activities. TPS postulates the elimination of such non-value-added activities, which are also referred to as *muda*.

There are different types of muda. According to T. Ohno, one of the thought leaders with respect to TPS, there are seven sources of waste:

1. Overproduction. Producing too much, too soon, leads to additional waste in the forms of material handling, storage, and transportation. The Toyota Production System seeks to produce only what the customer wants and when the customer wants it.

2. Waiting. In the spirit of "matching supply with demand," there exist two types of waiting. In some cases, a resource waits for flow units, leading to idle time at the resource. Utilization measures the amount of waiting of this type—a low utilization indicates the resource is waiting for flow units to work on. In other cases, flow units wait for resources to become available. As a consequence, the flow time is longer than the value-added time. A good measure for this second type of waiting is the percentage of flow time that is value-added time (in the language of Chapter 8, this is the processing time, p, relative to the flow time, $T = T_q + p$). Both types of waiting reflect a poorly balanced process and can be reduced by using the tools outlined in Chapter 4.

3. Transport. Internal transport, be it carrying around half-finished computers, wheeling patients through the hospital, or carrying around folders with insurance claims, corresponds to the third source of waste. Processes should be laid out such that the physical layout reflects the process flow to minimize the distances flow units must travel through a process.

4. Overprocessing. A close analysis of activity times reveals that workers often spend more time on a flow unit than necessary. A worker might excessively polish the surface of a piece of metal he just processed or a doctor might ask a patient the same questions that a nurse has asked five minutes earlier.

5. Inventory. In the spirit of matching supply with demand, any accumulation of inventory has the potential to be wasteful. Inventory is closely related to overproduction and often indicates that the JIT methods have not (yet) been implemented correctly. Not only is inventory often non-value-adding, it often hides other problems in the process as it leads to long information turnaround times and eases the pressure to find and eliminate underlying root causes (see Section 11.6 for more details).

6. Rework. A famous saying in the Toyota Production System and the associated quality movement has been "Do it right the first time." As we have discussed in the previous chapter, rework increases variability and consumes capacity from resources. Not only does rework exist in manufacturing plants, it is also (unfortunately) common in service operations. For example, hospitals all too frequently repeat X-rays because of poor image quality or readmit patients to the intensive care unit.

7. Motion. There are many ways to perform a particular task such as the tightening of a screw on the assembly line or the movement of a patient from a wheelchair into a hospital bed. But, according to the early pioneers of the industrial revolution, including Frederick Taylor and Frank and Lillian Gilbreth, there is only one "right way." Every task should be carefully analyzed and should be optimized using a set of tools that today is known as ergonomics. To do otherwise is wasteful.

Just as we have seen in the context of line balancing, the objective of waste reduction is to maximize the percentage of time a resource is engaged in value-adding activity by reducing the non-value-added (wasteful) activities as much as possible.

At this point, a clarification of wording is in order. TPS's objective is to achieve zero waste, including zero inventory and zero defects. However, this objective is more an aspirational one than it is a numerical one. Consider the objective of zero inventory and recall from Little's Law: Inventory = Flow rate × Flow time. Thus, unless we are able to produce at the speed of light (flow time equal to zero), the only way to achieve zero inventory is by operating at zero flow rate—arguably, not a desirable outcome. So, of course, Toyota's factories don't operate at zero inventory, but they operate at a low level of inventory and keep on decreasing this low level. The same holds for zero defects. Defects happen in each of Toyota's assembly plants many, many times a shift. But they happen less often than elsewhere and are always thought of as a potential for process improvement.

It is important to emphasize that the concept of waste is not unique to manufacturing. Consider, for example, the day of a nurse in a large hospital. In an ideal world, a nurse is there to care for patients. Independent of managed care, this is both the ambition of the nurse and the desire of the patient. However, if one carefully analyzes the workday of most nurses, a rather different picture emerges. Most nurses spend less than half of their time helping patients and waste the other time running around in the hospital, doing paperwork, searching for medical supplies, coordinating with doctors and the hospital administration, and so on. (See Tucker [2004] for an excellent description of nursing work from an operations management perspective.) This waste is frustrating for the nurse, leads to poor care for the patient, and is expensive for the health care provider.

Once we have reduced waste, we can perform the same work, yet at lower costs. In a process that is currently capacity constrained, waste reduction is also a way to increase output (flow rate) and hence revenues. As we have discussed in Chapter 6, the economic impact of these improvements can be dramatic.

A useful way to analyze and describe the effects of waste is the Overall Equipment Effectiveness (OEE) framework, used by McKinsey and other consulting firms. The objective of the framework is to identify what percentage of a resource's time is true, value-added time and what percentage is wasted. This provides a good estimate for the potential for process improvement before engaging in waste reduction.

As is illustrated by Figure 11.2, we start the OEE analysis by documenting the total available time of the resource. From this total time (100 percent), some time is wasted on machine breakdowns (or, in the case of human resources, absenteeism) and setup times, leading to an available time that is substantially less than the total planned time (in this

FIGURE 11.2
The Overall Equipment Effectiveness Framework

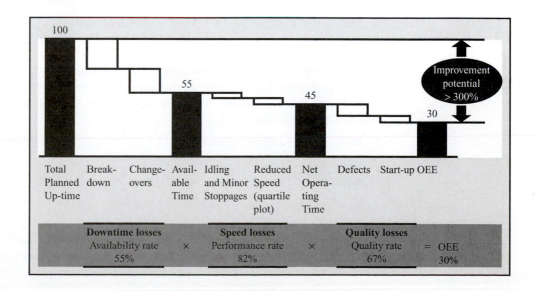

	Downtime losses		Speed losses		Quality losses	
	Availability rate	×	Performance rate	×	Quality rate	= OEE
	55%		82%		67%	30%

case, only 55 percent of the total planned time is available for production). However, not all of the remaining 55 percent is value-added time. Because of poor process balance, the resource is likely to be occasionally idle. Also, the resource might not operate at an optimum speed, as the activity time includes some waste and some incidental work that does not add direct customer value. In the case of Figure 11.2, 82 percent of the available time is used for operation, which leaves a total of 45 percent (= 55% × 82%). If one then factors in a further waste of capacity resulting from defects, rework, and start-ups (67 percent), we see that only 30 percent (55% × 82% × 67%) of the available capacity is used to really add value!

The following two examples illustrate the usefulness of the OEE framework in non-manufacturing settings. They also illustrate that wasting as much as half of the capacity of an expensive resource is much more common than one might expect:

- In the loan underwriting process of a major consumer bank, a recent case study documented that a large fraction of the underwriting capacity is not used productively. Unproductive time included (a) working on loans that are unlikely to be accepted by customers because the bank has already taken too long to get a response back to the customer, (b) idle time, (c) processing loans that resources preceding underwriting already could have rejected because of an obviously low creditworthiness of the application, (d) incidental activities of paper handling, and (e) attempting to reach customers on the phone but failing to do so. The study estimates that only 40 percent of the underwriting capacity is used in a value-adding way.

- In the operating rooms of a major hospital, the capacity is left unused because of (a) gaps in the schedule, (b) procedure cancellation, (c) room cleaning time, (d) patient preparation time, and (e) procedure delays because of the doctor or the anesthesiologist arriving late. After completing waste identification, the hospital concluded that only 60 percent of its operating room time was used productively. One might argue that patient preparation is a rather necessary and hence value-adding step prior to surgery. Yet, it is not clear that this step has to happen in the operating room. In fact, some hospitals are now using the tools of setup time reduction discussed in Chapter 7 and preparing the patient for surgery outside of the operating room so that the changeover from one surgical procedure to another is reduced.

11.4   JIT: Matching Supply with Demand

Just-in-time (JIT) is about matching supply with demand. The goal is to create a supply process that forms a smooth flow with its demand, thereby giving customers exactly what they need, when they need it.

In this section, we discuss three steps toward achieving a JIT process. The three steps build on each other and hence should be taken in the order they are presented. They presume that the process is already in-control (see Chapter 10) using standardized tasks and is able to achieve reliable quality:

1. Achieve a *one-unit-at-a-time* flow.
2. Produce at the rate of customer demand.
3. Implement a *pull system* using *kanban* or *make-to-order production*.

Achieve One-Unit-at-a-Time Flow

Compare the following two technologies that move people from one level of a building to another: an escalator and an elevator. Most of us associate plenty of waiting with elevators—we wait for the elevator to arrive and we wait stuck between dozens of people as the elevator stops at seemingly every floor. Escalators, in contrast, keep people moving toward their destination, no waiting and no jamming of people.

People waiting for and standing in elevators are like batches in a production setting. Chapter 7 already has discussed the concepts of SMED, the reduction of setup times that makes small production batches economically possible. In TPS, production plans are designed to avoid large batches of the same variant. Instead, product variants are mixed together on the assembly line (mixed-model production, which is also known as *heijunka*), as discussed in Chapter 7.

In addition to reducing setup times, we also should attempt to create a physical layout for our resources that closely mirrors the process flow. In other words, two resources that are close to each other in the process flow diagram also should be co-located in physical space. This avoids unnecessary transports and reduces the need to form transport batches. This way flow units can flow one unit at a time from one resource to the next (*ikko-nagashi*).

Produce at the Rate of Customer Demand

Once we have created a one-unit-at-a-time flow, we should make sure that our flow rate is in line with demand. Historically, most large-scale operations have operated their processes based on forecasts. Using planning software (often referred to as MRP, for materials requirement planning, and ERP, for enterprise resource planning), work schedules were created for the various subprocesses required to create the final product.

Forecasting is a topic for itself (see Chapter 12), but most forecasts have the negative property of not being right. So at the end of a planning period (e.g., one month), the ERP system would update its next production plan, taking the amount of inventory in the process into account. This way, in the long run, production more or less matches demand. Yet, in the day-to-day operations, extensive periods of substantial inventories or customer backorders exist.

TPS aims at reducing finished goods inventory by operating its production process in synchronization with customer orders. This is true for both the overall number of vehicles produced as well as with respect to the mix of vehicles across various models.

We translate customer demand into production rate (flow rate) using the concept of takt time. Takt time is derived from the German word *takt,* which stands for "tact" or "clock." Just like an orchestra needs to follow a common tact imposed by the conductor, a JIT process should follow the tact imposed by demand. Takt time calculations are identical to what we have seen with demand rate and flow rate calculations in earlier chapters.

Implement Pull Systems

The synchronization with the aggregate level of demand through takt time is an important step toward the implementation of JIT. However, inventory not only exists at the finished-goods level, but also throughout the process (work-in-process inventory). Some parts of the process are likely to be worker paced with some (hopefully modest) amount of inventory between resources. We now have to design a coordination system that coordinates these resources by controlling the amount of inventory in the process. We do this by implementing a pull system.

In a pull system, the resource furthest downstream (i.e., closest to the market) is paced by market demand. In addition to its own production, it also relays the demand information to the next station upstream, thus ensuring that the upstream resource also is paced by demand. If the last resource assembles two electronics components into a computer, it relays the demand for two such components to the next resource upstream. This way, the external demand is transferred step by step through the process, leading to an information flow moving in the opposite direction relative to the physical flow of the flow units.

Such a demand-driven pull system is in contrast to a *push system* where flow units are allowed to enter the process independent of the current amount of inventory in process. Especially if the first resources in the process have low levels of utilization—and are thereby likely to flood the downstream with inventory—push systems can lead to substantial inventory in the process.

To implement a pull system, TPS advocates two forms of process control:

- In kanban-based pull (also known as fill-up or supermarket pull), the upstream replenishes what demand has withdrawn from the downstream.
- Make-to-order refers to the release of work into a system only when a customer order has been received for that unit.

Consider the kanban system first. *Kanban* refers to a production and inventory control system in which production instructions and parts delivery instructions are triggered by the consumption of parts at the downstream step (Fujimoto 1999).

In a kanban system, standardized returnable parts containers circulate between the upstream and the downstream resources. The upstream resource is authorized to produce a unit when it receives an empty container. In other words, the arrival of an empty container triggers a production order. The term *kanban* refers to the card that is attached to each container. Consequently, kanban cards are frequently called work authorization forms.

A simplified description of a kanban system is provided by Figure 11.3. A downstream resource (right) consumes some input component that it receives from its upstream resource (left). The downstream resource empties containers of these input components—the downstream resource literally takes the part out of the container for its own use, thereby creating an empty container, which in turn, as already mentioned, triggers a production order for the upstream resource. Thus, the use of kanban cards between all resources in the process provides an effective and easy-to-implement mechanism for tying the demand of the process (downstream) with the production of the resources (upstream). They therefore enforce a match between supply and demand.

The main advantage of a kanban system is that there can never be more inventory between two resources than what has been authorized by the kanban cards—the upstream resource can only produce when it has an empty container, so production stops when all of the containers are full, thereby limiting the inventory to the number of containers. In contrast, with a push system, the upstream resource continues to produce as long as it has work. For example, suppose the upstream resource is a lathe that produces the legs for a wood chair. With a push system, the lathe keeps producing legs as long as it has blocks of wood to work on. With a kanban system, the lathe produces a set of chair legs only if it has an empty kanban. Hence, with a kanban system, the lathe stops working only when it runs out of kanbans, whereas with a push system the lathe only stops working when it runs out of raw materials. The distinction can lead to very different behavior. In a push system, inventory can simply "happen" to management because there is theoretically no limit to the amount of inventory that can pile up after a resource (e.g., think of the plant manager walking through

FIGURE 11.3
The Operation of a Kanban System

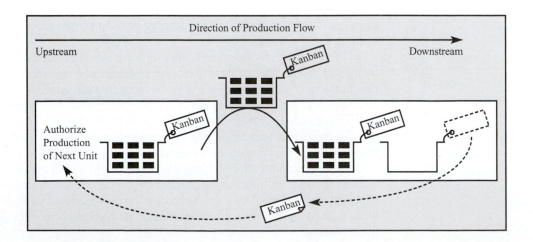

the process and saying, "Wow, we have a lot of inventory at this step today"). In contrast, in a kanban system the amount of inventory becomes a managerial decision variable—the maximum inventory is controlled via the number of kanban cards in the process.

As an alternative to a kanban system, we also can implement a pull system using a make-to-order process. As is suggested by the term "make-to-order," resources in such a process only operate after having received an explicit customer order. Typically, the products corresponding to these orders then flow through the process on a first-in, first-out (FIFO) basis. Each flow unit in the make-to-order process is thereby explicitly assigned to one specific customer order. Consider the example of a rear-view mirror production in an auto plant to see the difference between kanban and make-to-order. When the operator in charge of producing the interior rear-view mirror at the plant receives the work authorization through the kanban card, it has not yet been determined which customer order will be filled with this mirror. All that is known is that there are—at the aggregate—a sufficient number of customer orders such that production of this mirror is warranted. Most likely, the final assembly line of the same auto plant (including the mounting of the rear-view mirror) will be operated in a make-to-order manner, that is, the operator putting in the mirror can see that it will end up in the car of Mr. Smith.

Many organizations use both forms of pull systems. Consider computer maker Dell. Dell's computers are configured in work cells. Processes supplying components are often operated using kanban. Thus, rear-view mirrors at Toyota and power supplies at Dell flow through the process in sufficient volume to meet customer demand, yet are produced in response to a kanban card and have not yet been assigned to a specific order.

When considering which form of a pull system one wants to implement, the following should be kept in mind:

- Kanban should be used for products or parts (a) that are processed in high volume and limited variety, (b) that are required with a short lead time so that it makes economic sense to have a limited number of them (as many as we have kanban cards) preproduced, and (c) for which the costs and efforts related to storing the components are low.

- Make-to-order should be used when (a) products or parts are processed in low volume and high variety, (b) customers are willing to wait for their order, and (c) it is expensive or difficult to store the flow units. Chapter 13 will explain the costs and benefits of a make-to-order production system.

11.5   Quality Management

If we operate with no buffers and want to avoid the waste of rework, operating at zero defects is a must. To achieve zero defects, TPS relies on defect prevention, rapid defect detection, and a strong worker responsibility with respect to quality.

Defects can be prevented by "fool-proofing" many assembly operations, that is, by making mistakes in assembly operations physically impossible (*poka-yoke*). Components are designed in a way that there exists one single way of assembling them.

If, despite defect prevention, a problem occurs, TPS attempts to discover and isolate this problem as quickly as possible. This is achieved through the *jidoka* concept. The idea of jidoka is to stop the process immediately whenever a defect is detected and to alert the line supervisor. This idea goes back to the roots of Toyota as a maker of automated looms. Just like an automated loom should stop operating in the case of a broken thread, a defective machine should shut itself off automatically in the presence of a defect.

Shutting down the machine forces a human intervention in the process, which in turn triggers process improvement (Fujimoto 1999). The jidoka concept has been generalized to include any mechanism that stops production in response to quality problems, not just for automated machines. The most well-known form of jidoka is the *Andon cord,* a cord running adjacent to assembly lines that enables workers to stop production if they detect a defect. Just like the jidoka automatic shut-down of machines, this procedure dramatizes manufacturing problems and acts as a pressure for process improvements.

A worker pulling the Andon cord upon detecting a quality problem is in sharp contrast to Henry Ford's historical assembly line that would leave the detection of defects to a final inspection step. In TPS, "the next step is the customer" and every resource should only let those flow units move downstream that have been inspected and evaluated as good parts. Hence, quality inspection is "built in" (*tsukurikomi*) and happens at every step in the line, as opposed to relying on a final inspection step alone.

The idea of detect–stop–alert that underlies the jidoka principle is not just a necessity to make progress towards implementing the zero inventory principle. Jidoka also benefits from the zero inventory principle, as large amounts of work-in-process inventory achieve the opposite of jidoka: they delay the detection of a problem, thereby keeping a defective process running and hiding the defect from the eyes of management. This shows how the various TPS principles and methods are interrelated, mutually strengthening each other.

To see how work-in-process inventory is at odds with the idea of jidoka, consider a sequence of two resources in a process, as outlined in Figure 11.4. Assume the activity times at both resources are equal to one minute per unit. Assume further that the upstream resource (on the left) suffers quality problems and—at some random point in time—starts producing bad output. In Figure 11.4, this is illustrated by the resource producing squares instead of circles. How long will it take until a quality problem is discovered? If there is a large buffer between the two resources (upper part of Figure 11.4), the downstream resource will continue to receive good units from the buffer. In this example, it will take seven minutes before the downstream resource detects the defective flow unit. This gives the upstream resource seven minutes to continue producing defective parts that need to be either scrapped or reworked.

Thus, the time between when the problem occurred at the upstream resource and the time it is detected at the downstream resource depends on the size of the buffer between the two resources. This is a direct consequence of Little's Law. We refer to the time between creating a defect and receiving the feedback about the defect as the *information turn-around time* (*ITAT*). Note that we assume in this example that the defect is detected in the next resource downstream. The impact of inventory on quality is much worse if defects only get detected at the end of the process (e.g., at a final inspection step). In this case, the

FIGURE 11.4
Information Turnaround Time and Its Relationship with Buffer Size

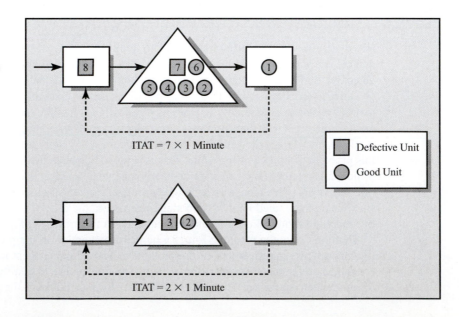

ITAT is driven by all inventory downstream from the resource producing the defect. This motivates the built-in inspection we mentioned above.

11.6   Exposing Problems through Inventory Reduction

Our discussion on quality reveals that inventory covers up problems. So to improve a process, we need to turn the "inventory hiding quality problems" effect on its head: we want to reduce inventory to expose defects and then fix the underlying root cause of the defect.

Recall that in a kanban system, the number of kanban cards—and hence the amount of inventory in the process—is under managerial control. So we can use the kanban system to gradually reduce inventory and thereby expose quality problems. The kanban system and its approach to buffers can be illustrated with the following metaphor. Consider a boat sailing on a canal that has numerous rocks in it. The freight of the boat is very valuable, so the company operating the canal wants to make sure that the boat never hits a rock. Figure 11.5 illustrates this metaphor.

One approach to this situation is to increase the water level in the canal. This way, there is plenty of water over the rocks and the likelihood of an accident is low. In a production setting, the rocks correspond to quality problems (defects), setup times, blocking or starving, breakdowns, or other problems in the process and the ship hitting a rock corresponds to lost throughput. The amount of water corresponds to the amount of inventory in the process (i.e., the number of kanban cards), which brings us back to our previous "buffer-or-suffer" discussion.

An alternative way of approaching the problem is this: instead of covering the rocks with water, we also could consider reducing the water level in the canal (reduce the number of kanban cards). This way, the highest rocks are exposed (i.e., we observe a process problem), which provides us with the opportunity of removing them from the canal. Once this has been accomplished, the water level is lowered again, until—step by step—all rocks are removed from the canal. Despite potential short-term losses in throughput, the advantage of this approach is that it moves the process to a better frontier (i.e., it is better along multiple dimensions).

This approach to inventory reduction is outlined in Figure 11.6. We observe that we first need to accept a short-term loss in throughput reflecting the reduction of inventory (we stay on the efficient frontier, as we now have less inventory). Once the inventory level is lowered, we are able to identify the most prominent problems in the process (rocks in the water). Once identified, these problems are solved and thereby the process moves to a more desirable frontier.

Both in the metaphor and in our ITAT discussion above, inventory is the key impediment to learning and process improvement. Since with kanban cards, management is in

FIGURE 11.5   **More or Less Inventory? A Simple Metaphor**

Source: Stevenson 2006.

FIGURE 11.6
Tension between Flow Rate and Inventory Levels/ITAT

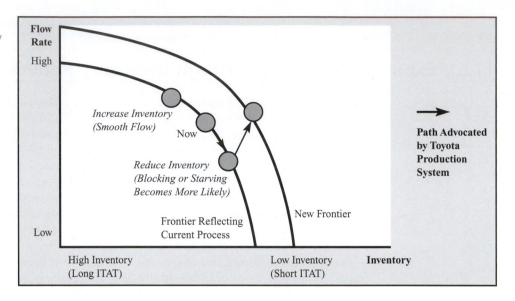

control of the inventory level, it can proactively manage the tension between the short-term need of a high throughput and the long-term objective of improving the process.

11.7   Flexibility

Given that there typically exist fluctuations in demand from the end market, TPS attempts to create processes with sufficient flexibility to meet such fluctuations. Since forecasts are more reliable at the aggregate level (across models or components, see discussion of pooling in Chapter 8 and again in Chapter 15), TPS requests workers to be skilled in handling multiple machines.

- When production volume has to be decreased for a product because of low demand, TPS attempts to assign some workers to processes creating other products and to have the remaining workers handle multiple machines simultaneously for the process with the low-demand product.

- When production volume has to be increased for a product because of high demand, TPS often uses a second pool of workers (temporary workers) to help out with production. Unlike the first pool of full-time employees (typically with lifetime employment guarantee and a broad skill set), these workers are less skilled and can only handle very specific tasks.

Consider the six-step operation shown in Figure 11.7. Assume all activities have an activity time of one minute per unit. If demand is low (right), we avoid idle time (low average labor utilization) by running the process with only three operators (typically, full-time employees). In this case, each operator is in charge of two minutes of work, so we would achieve a flow rate of 0.5 unit per minute. If demand is high (left in the Figure 11.7), we assign one worker to each step, that is, we bring in additional (most likely temporary) workers. Now, the flow rate can be increased to one unit per minute.

This requires that the operators are skilled in multiple assembly tasks. Good training, job rotation, skill-based payment, and well-documented standard operating procedures are essential requirements for this. This flexibility also requires that we have a multitiered workforce consisting of highly skilled full-time employees and a pool of temporary workers (who do not need such a broad skill base) that can be called upon when demand is high.

Such multitask flexibility of workers also can help decrease idle time in cases of activities that require some worker involvement but are otherwise largely automated. In these

FIGURE 11.7 **Multi-task Flexibility**

(Note: The figure assumes a 1 minute/unit activity time at each station.)

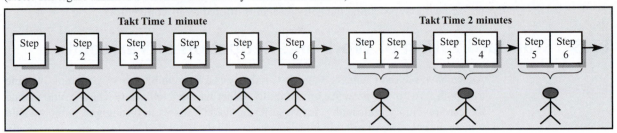

cases, a worker can load one machine and while this machine operates, the worker—instead of being idle—operates another machine along the process flow (*takotei-mochi*). This is facilitated if the process flow is arranged in a U-shaped manner, in which case a worker can share tasks not only with the upstream and the downstream resource, but also with another set of tasks in the process. Another important form of flexibility relates to the ability of one plant to produce more than one vehicle model. Consider the data displayed in Figure 11.8. The left part of the figure shows how Ford's vehicles are allocated to Ford's production plants. As we can see, many vehicles are dedicated to one plant and many of the plants can only produce a small set of vehicles. Consequently, if demand increases relative to the plant's capacity, that plant is unlikely to have sufficient capacity to fulfill it. If demand decreases, the plant is likely to have excess capacity.

In an ideal world, the company would be able to make every model in every plant. This way, high demand from one model would cancel out with low demand from another one, leading to better plant utilization and more sales. However, such capacity pooling would require the plants to be perfectly flexible—requiring substantial investments in production tools and worker skills. An interesting alternative to such perfect flexibility is the concept of partial flexibility, also referred to as *chaining*. The idea of chaining is that every car can be made in two plants and that the vehicle-to-plant assignment creates a chain that connects as many vehicles and plants as possible. As we will see in Chapter 15, such partial flexibility results in almost the same benefits of full flexibility, yet at dramatically lower costs. The right side of Figure 11.8 shows the vehicle-to-plant assignment of

FIGURE 11.8 **Vehicle-to-Plant Assignments at Ford (Left) and at Nissan (right).**

Source: Moreno and Terwiesch (2011).

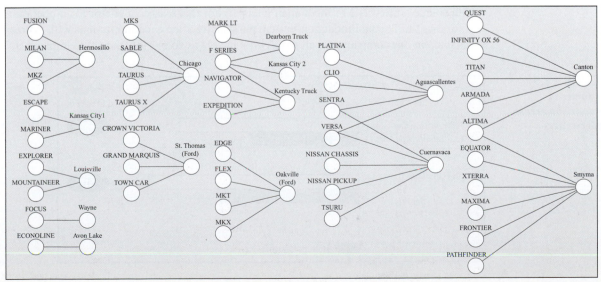

Nissan (North America) and provides an illustrative example of partial flexibility. In an environment of volatile demand, this partial flexibility has allowed Nissan to keep its plants utilized without providing the hefty discounts offered by its competitors.

11.8   Standardization of Work and Reduction of Variability

As we have seen in Chapters 8 and 9, variability is a key inhibitor in our attempt to create a smooth flow. In the presence of variability, either we need to buffer (which would violate the zero inventory philosophy) or we suffer occasional losses in throughput (which would violate the principle of providing the customer with the requested product when demanded). For this reason, the Toyota Production System explicitly embraces the concepts of variability measurement, control, and reduction discussed in Chapter 10.

The need for stability in a JIT process and the vulnerability of an unbuffered process were visible in the computer industry following the 1999 Taiwanese earthquake. Several of the Taiwanese factories that were producing key components for computer manufacturers around the world were forced to shut down their production due to the earthquake. Such an unpredicted shutdown was more disruptive for computer manufacturers with JIT supply chains than those with substantial buffers (e.g., in the form of warehouses) in their supply chains (Papadakis 2002).

Besides earthquakes, variability occurs because of quality defects (see above) or because of differences in activity times for the same or for different operators. Figure 11.9 shows performance data from a large consumer loan processing organization. The figure compares the performance of the top-quartile operator (i.e., the operator who has 25 percent of the other operators achieving a higher performance and 75 percent of the operators achieving a lower performance) with the bottom quartile operator (the one who has 75 percent of the operators achieving a higher performance). As we can see, there can exist dramatic differences in the productivity across employees.

A quartile analysis is a good way to identify the presence of large differences across operators and to estimate the improvement potential. For example, we could estimate what would happen to process capacity if all operators would be trained so that they achieve a performance in line with the current top-quartile performance.

11.9   Human Resource Practices

We have seen seven sources of waste, but the Toyota Production System also refers to an eighth source—the waste of the human intellect. For this reason, a visitor to an operation that follows the Toyota Production System philosophy often encounters signs with expressions like "In our company, we all have two jobs: (1) to do our job and (2) to improve it."

FIGURE 11.9
Productivity Comparison across Underwriters

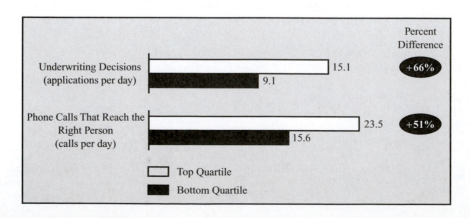

To illustrate different philosophies toward workers, consider the following two quotes. The first one comes from the legendary book *Principles of Scientific Management* written by Frederick Taylor, which still makes an interesting read almost a century after its first appearance (once you have read the quote below, you will at least enjoy Taylor's candid writing style). The second quote comes from Konosuka Matsushita, the former chairman of Panasonic.

Let us look at Taylor's opinion first and consider his description of pig iron shoveling, an activity that Taylor studied extensively in his research. Taylor writes: "This work is so crude and elementary that the writer firmly believes that it would be possible to train an intelligent gorilla so as to become a more efficient pig-iron handler than any man can be."

Now, consider Matsushita, whose quote almost reads like a response to Taylor:

> We are going to win and you are going to lose. There is nothing you can do about it, because the reasons for failure are within yourself. With you, the bosses do the thinking while the workers wield the screw drivers. You are convinced that this is the way to run a business. For you, the essence of management is getting the ideas out of the heads of the bosses and in to the hands of the labour. [. . .] Only by drawing on the combined brainpower of all its employees can a firm face up to the turbulence and constraints of today's environment.

TPS, not surprisingly, embraces Matsushita's perspective of the "combined brainpower." We have already seen the importance of training workers as a source of flexibility.

Another important aspect of the human resource practices of Toyota relates to process improvement. Quality circles bring workers together to jointly solve production problems and to continuously improve the process (*kaizen*). Problem solving is very data driven and follows a standardized process, including control charts, fishbone (Ishikawa) diagrams, the "Five Whys," and other problem-solving tools. Thus, not only do we standardize the production process, we also standardize the process of improvement.

Ishikawa diagrams (also known as *fishbone diagrams* or cause–effect diagrams) graphically represent variables that are causally related to a specific outcome, such as an increase in variation or a shift in the mean. When drawing a fishbone diagram, we typically start with a horizontal arrow that points at the name of the outcome variable we want to analyze. Diagonal lines then lead to this arrow representing main causes. Smaller arrows then lead to these causality lines, creating a fishbonelike shape. An example of this is given by Figure 11.10. Ishikawa diagrams are simple yet powerful problem-solving tools that can be used to structure brainstorming sessions and to visualize the causal structure of a complex system.

A related tool that also helps in developing causal models is known as the "Five Whys." The tool is prominently used in Toyota's organization when workers search for the root cause of a quality problem. The basic idea of the "Five Whys" is to continually question ("Why did this happen?") whether a potential cause is truly the root cause or is merely a symptom of a deeper problem.

In addition to these operational principles, TPS includes a range of human resource management practices, including stable employment ("lifetime employment") for the core workers combined with the recruitment of temporary workers; a strong emphasis on skill development, which is rewarded financially through skill-based salaries; and various other aspects relating to leadership and people management.

11.10   Lean Transformation

How do you turn around an existing operation to achieve operational excellence as we have discussed it above? Clearly, even an operations management textbook has to acknowledge that there is more to a successful operational turnaround than the application of a set of tools.

McKinsey, as a consulting firm with a substantial part of its revenues resulting from operations work, refers to the set of activities required to improve the operations of a client

FIGURE 11.10   Example of an Ishikawa Diagram

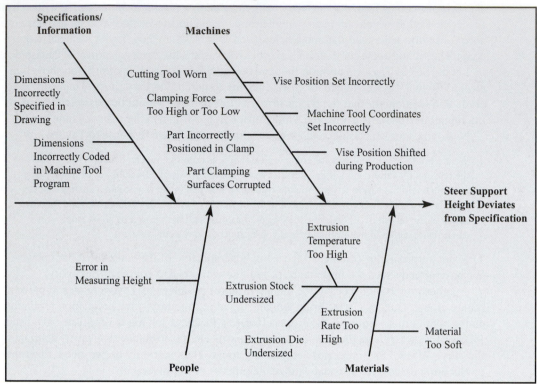

as a *lean transformation.* There exist three aspects to such a lean transformation: the operating system, a management infrastructure, and the mindsets and behaviors of the employees involved.

With the operating system, the firm refers to various aspects of process management as we have discussed in this chapter and throughout this book: an emphasis on flow, matching supply with demand, and a close eye on the variability of the process.

But technical solutions alone are not enough. So the operating system needs to be complemented by a management infrastructure. A central piece of this infrastructure is performance measurement. Just as we discussed in Chapter 6, defining finance-level performance measures and then cascading them into the operations is a key struggle for many companies. Moreover, the performance measures should be tracked over time and be made transparent throughout the organization. The operator needs to understand which performance measures he or she is supposed to achieve and how these measures contribute to the bigger picture. Management infrastructure also includes the development of operator skills and the establishment of formal problem-solving processes.

Finally, the mindset of those involved in working in the process is central to the success of a lean transformation. A nurse might get frustrated from operating in an environment of waste that is keeping him or her from spending time with patients. Yet, the nurse, in all likelihood, also will be frustrated by the implementation of a new care process that an outsider imposes on his or her ward. Change management is a topic well beyond the scope of this book: open communication with everyone involved in the process, collecting and discussing process data, and using some of the tools discussed in Chapter 10 as well as with respect to kaizen can help make the transformation a success.

11.11 Further Reading

Readers who want to learn more about TPS are referred to excellent reading, such as Fujimoto (1999) or Ohno (1988), from which many of the following definitions are taken.

Fujimoto (1999) describes the evolution of the Toyota Production System. While not a primary focus of the book, it also provides excellent descriptions of the main elements of the Toyota Production System. The results of the benchmarking studies are reported in Womack, Jones, and Roos (1991) and Holweg and Pil (2004).

Bohn and Jaikumar (1992) is a classic reading that challenges the traditional, optimization-focused paradigm of operations management. Their work stipulates that companies should not focus on optimizing decisions for their existing business processes, but rather should create new processes that can operate at higher levels of performance.

Drew, McCallum, and Roggenhofer (2004) describe the "Journey to Lean," a description of the steps constituting a lean transformation as described by a group of McKinsey consultants.

Tucker (2004) provides a study of TPS-like activities from the perspective of nurses who encounter quality problems in their daily work. Moreno and Terwiesch discuss flexibility strategies in the U.S. automotive industry and analyze if and to what extent firms with flexible production systems are able to achieve higher plant utilization and lower price discounts.

The Wikipedia entries for Toyota, Ford, Industrial Revolution, Gilbreth, and Taylor are also interesting summaries and were helpful in compiling the historical reviews presented in this chapter.

11.12 Practice Problems

Q11.1 **(Three Step)** Consider a worker-paced line with three process steps, each of which is staffed with one worker. The sequence of the three steps does not matter for the completion of the product. Currently, the three steps are operated in the following sequence.

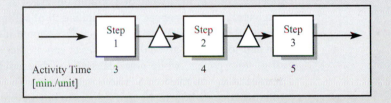

a. What would happen to the inventory in the process if the process were operated as a push system?

b. Assuming you would have to operate as a push system, how would you resequence the three activities?

c. How would you implement a pull system?

Q11.2 **(Six Step)** Consider the following six-step worker-paced process. Each resource is currently staffed by one operator. Demand is 20 units per hour. Over the past years, management has attempted to rebalance the process, but given that workers can only complete tasks that are adjacent to each other, no further improvement has been found.

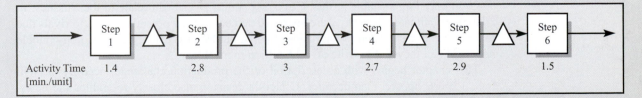

a. What would you suggest to improve this process? (*Hint:* Think "out of the box.")

12

Betting on Uncertain Demand: The Newsvendor Model[1]

Matching supply and demand is particularly challenging when supply must be chosen before observing demand and demand is stochastic (uncertain). To illustrate this point, suppose you are the owner of a simple business: selling newspapers. Each morning you purchase a stack of papers with the intention of selling them at your newsstand at the corner of a busy street. Even though you have some idea regarding how many newspapers you can sell on any given day, you never can predict demand for sure. Some days you sell all of your papers, while other days end with unsold newspapers to be recycled. As the newsvendor, you must decide how many papers to buy at the start of each day. Because you must decide how many newspapers to buy before demand occurs, unless you are very lucky, you will not be able to match supply to demand. A decision tool is needed to make the best out of this difficult situation. The *newsvendor model* is such a tool.

You will be happy to learn that the newsvendor model applies in many more settings than just the newsstand business. The essential issue is that you must take a firm bet (how much inventory to order) before some random event occurs (demand) and then you learn that you either bet too much (demand was less than your order) or you bet too little (demand exceeded your order). This trade-off between "doing too much" and "doing too little" occurs in other settings. Consider a technology product with a long lead time to source components and only a short life before better technology becomes available. Purchase too many components and you risk having to sell off obsolete technology. Purchase too few and you may forgo sizable profits. Cisco is a company that can relate to these issues: In 2000 they estimated that they were losing 10 percent of their potential orders to rivals due to long lead times created by shortages of parts; but by early 2001, the technology bubble had burst and they had to write off $2.5 billion in inventory.

This chapter begins with a description of the production challenge faced by O'Neill Inc., a sports apparel manufacturer. O'Neill's decision also closely resembles the newsvendor's task. We then describe the newsvendor model in detail and apply it to O'Neill's problem. We also show how to use the newsvendor model to forecast a number of performance measures relevant to O'Neill.

[1] Data in this chapter have been disguised to protect confidential information.

12.1 O'Neill Inc.

O'Neill Inc. is a designer and manufacturer of apparel, wetsuits, and accessories for water sports: surf, dive, waterski, wake-board, triathlon, and wind surf. Their product line ranges from entry-level products for recreational users, to wetsuits for competitive surfers, to sophisticated dry suits for professional cold-water divers (e.g., divers that work on oil platforms in the North Sea). O'Neill divides the year into two selling seasons: Spring (February through July) and Fall (August through January). Some products are sold in both seasons, but the majority of their products sell primarily in a single season. For example, waterski is active in the Spring season whereas recreational surf products sell well in the Fall season. Some products are not considered fashionable (i.e., they have little cosmetic variety and they sell from year to year), for example, standard neoprene black booties. With product names like "Animal," "Epic," "Hammer," "Inferno," and "Zen," O'Neill clearly also has products that are subject to the whims of fashion. For example, color patterns on surf suits often change from season to season to adjust to the tastes of the primary user (15–30-year-old males from California).

O'Neill operates its own manufacturing facility in Mexico, but it does not produce all of its products there. Some items are produced by the TEC Group, O'Neill's contract manufacturer in Asia. While TEC provides many benefits to O'Neill (low cost, sourcing expertise, flexible capacity, etc.), they do require a three-month lead time on all orders. For example, if O'Neill orders an item on November 1, then O'Neill can expect to have that item at its distribution center in San Diego, California, ready for shipment to customers, only on January 31.

To better understand O'Neill's production challenge, let's consider a particular wetsuit used by surfers and newly redesigned for the upcoming spring season, the Hammer 3/2. (The "3/2" signifies the thickness of the neoprene on the suit: 3 mm thick on the chest and 2 mm everywhere else.) Figure 12.1 displays the Hammer 3/2 and O'Neill's logo. O'Neill has decided to let TEC manufacture the Hammer 3/2. Due to TEC's three-month lead time, O'Neill needs to submit an order to TEC in November before the start of the spring season. Using past sales data for similar products and the judgment of its designers and sales representatives, O'Neill developed a forecast of 3,200 units for total demand during the spring season for the Hammer 3/2. Unfortunately, there is considerable uncertainty in that forecast despite the care and attention placed on the formation of the forecast. For example, it is O'Neill's experience that 50 percent of the time the actual demand deviates from their initial forecast by more than 25 percent of the forecast. In other words, only 50 percent of the time is the actual demand between 75 percent and 125 percent of their forecast.

Although O'Neill's forecast in November is unreliable, O'Neill will have a much better forecast for total season demand after observing the first month or two of sales. At that time, O'Neill can predict whether the Hammer 3/2 is selling slower than forecast, in which case O'Neill is likely to have excess inventory at the end of the season, or whether the Hammer 3/2 is more popular than predicted, in which case O'Neill is likely to stock out. In the latter case, O'Neill would love to order more Hammers, but the long lead time from Asia prevents O'Neill from receiving those additional Hammers in time to be useful. Therefore, O'Neill essentially must "live or dive" with its single order placed in November.

Fortunately for O'Neill, the economics on the Hammer are pretty good. O'Neill sells the Hammer to retailers for $190 while it pays TEC $110 per suit. If O'Neill has leftover inventory at the end of the season, it is O'Neill's experience that they are able to sell that inventory for $90 per suit. Figure 12.2 summarizes the time line of events and the economics for the Hammer 3/2.

So how many units should O'Neill order from TEC? You might argue that O'Neill should order the forecast for total demand, 3,200, because 3,200 is the most likely outcome.

FIGURE 12.1
O'Neill's Hammer
3/2 Wetsuit and Logo
for the Surf Market

The forecast is also the value that minimizes the expected absolute difference between the actual demand and the production quantity; that is, it is likely to be close to the actual demand. Alternatively, you may be concerned that forecasts are always biased and therefore suggest an order quantity less than 3,200 would be more prudent. Finally, you might argue that because

FIGURE 12.2
Time Line of Events
and Economics for
O'Neill's Hammer
3/2 Wetsuit

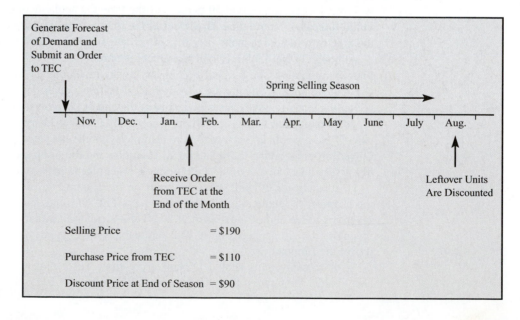

the gross margin on the Hammer is more than 40 percent ((190 − 110)/190 = 0.42), O'Neill should order more than 3,200 in case the Hammer is a hit. We next define the newsvendor model and then discuss what the newsvendor model recommends for an order quantity.

12.2   An Introduction to the Newsvendor Model

The newsvendor model considers a setting in which you have only one production or procurement opportunity. Because that opportunity occurs well in advance of a single selling season, you receive your entire order just before the selling season starts. Stochastic demand occurs during the selling season. If demand exceeds your order quantity, then you sell your entire order. But if demand is less than your order quantity, then you have leftover inventory at the end of the season.

There is a fixed cost per unit ordered: for the Hammer 3/2, Cost = 110. It is important that Cost includes only costs that depend on the number of units ordered; amortized fixed costs should not be included, because they are unaffected by our order quantity decision. In other words, this cost figure should include all costs that vary with the order quantity and no costs that do not vary with the order quantity. There is a fixed price for each unit you sell; in this case, Price = 190.

If there is leftover inventory at the end of the season, then there is some value associated with that inventory. To be specific, there is a fixed *Salvage value* that you earn on each unit of leftover inventory: with the Hammer, the Salvage value = 90. It is possible that leftover inventory has no salvage value whatsoever, that is, Salvage value = 0. It is also possible leftover inventory is costly to dispose, in which case the salvage value may actually be a salvage cost. For example, if the product is a hazardous chemical, then there is a cost for disposing of leftover inventory; that is, Salvage value < 0 is possible.

To guide your production decision, you need a forecast for demand. O'Neill's initial forecast for the Hammer is 3,200 units for the season. But it turns out (for reasons that are explained later) you need much more than just a number for a forecast. You need to have a sense of how accurate your forecast is; you need a forecast on your forecast error! For example, in an ideal world, there would be absolutely no error in your forecast: if the forecast is 3,200 units, then 3,200 units is surely the demand for the season. In reality, there will be error in the forecast, but forecast error can vary in size. For example, it is better to be 90 percent sure demand will be between 3,100 and 3,300 units than it is to be 90 percent sure demand will be between 2,400 and 4,000 units. Intuition should suggest that you might want to order a different amount in those two situations.

To summarize, the newsvendor model represents a situation in which a decision maker must make a single bet (e.g., the order quantity) before some random event occurs (e.g., demand). There are costs if the bet turns out to be too high (e.g., leftover inventory that is salvaged for a loss on each unit). There are costs if the bet turns out to be too low (the opportunity cost of lost sales). The newsvendor model's objective is to bet an amount that correctly balances those opposing forces. To implement the model, we need to identify our costs and how much demand uncertainty we face. We have already identified our costs, so the next section focuses on the task of identifying the uncertainty in Hammer 3/2 demand.

12.3   Constructing a Demand Forecast

The newsvendor model balances the cost of ordering too much against the cost of ordering too little. To do this, we need to understand how much demand uncertainty there is for the Hammer 3/2, which essentially means we need to be able to answer the following question:

What is the probability demand will be less than or equal to Q units?

for whatever Q value we desire. In short, we need a *distribution function*. Recall from statistics, every random variable is defined by its distribution function, $F(Q)$, which is the probability the outcome of the random variable is Q or lower. In this case the random variable is demand for the Hammer 3/2 and the distribution function is

$$F(Q) = \text{Prob}\{\text{Demand is less than or equal to } Q\}$$

For convenience, we refer to the distribution function, $F(Q)$, as our demand forecast because it gives us a complete picture of the demand uncertainty we face. The objective of this section is to explain how we can use a combination of intuition and data analysis to construct our demand forecast.

Distribution functions come in two forms. *Discrete distribution functions* can be defined in the form of a table: There is a set of possible outcomes and each possible outcome has a probability associated with it. The following is an example of a simple discrete distribution function with three possible outcomes:

Q	F(Q)
2,200	0.25
3,200	0.75
4,200	1.00

The Poisson distribution is an example of a discrete distribution function that we will use extensively. With *continuous distribution functions* there are an unlimited number of possible outcomes. Both the exponential and the normal are continuous distribution functions. They are defined with one or two parameters. For example, the normal distribution is defined by two parameters: its mean and its standard deviation. We use μ to represent the mean of the distribution and σ to represent the standard deviation. (μ is the Greek letter mu and σ is the Greek letter sigma.) This notation for the mean and the standard deviation is quite common, so we adopt it here.

In some situations, a discrete distribution function provides the best representation of demand, whereas in other situations a continuous distribution function works best. Hence, we work with both types of distribution functions.

Now let's turn to the complex task of actually creating the forecast. As mentioned in Section 12.1, the Hammer 3/2 has been redesigned for the upcoming spring season. As a result, actual sales in the previous season might not be a good guide for expected demand in the upcoming season. In addition to the product redesign, factors that could influence expected demand include the pricing and marketing strategy for the upcoming season, changes in fashion, changes in the economy (e.g., is demand moving toward higher or lower price points), changes in technology, and overall trends for the sport. To account for all of these factors, O'Neill surveyed the opinion of a number of individuals in the organization on their personal demand forecast for the Hammer 3/2. The survey's results were averaged to obtain the initial 3,200-unit forecast. This represents the "intuition" portion of our demand forecast. Now we need to analyze O'Neill's available data to further develop the demand forecast.

Table 12.1 presents data from O'Neill's previous spring season with wetsuits in the surf category. Notice that the data include both the original forecasts for each product as well as its actual demand. The original forecast was developed in a process that was comparable to the one that led to the 3,200-unit forecast for the Hammer 3/2 for this season. For example, the forecast for the Hammer 3/2 in the previous season was 1,300 units, but actual demand was 1,696 units.

TABLE 12.1
Forecasts and Actual Demand Data for Surf Wetsuits from the Previous Spring Season

Product Description	Forecast	Actual Demand	Error*	A/F Ratio**
JR ZEN FL 3/2	90	140	−50	1.56
EPIC 5/3 W/HD	120	83	37	0.69
JR ZEN 3/2	140	143	−3	1.02
WMS ZEN-ZIP 4/3	170	163	7	0.96
HEATWAVE 3/2	170	212	−42	1.25
JR EPIC 3/2	180	175	5	0.97
WMS ZEN 3/2	180	195	−15	1.08
ZEN-ZIP 5/4/3 W/HOOD	270	317	−47	1.17
WMS EPIC 5/3 W/HD	320	369	−49	1.15
EVO 3/2	380	587	−207	1.54
JR EPIC 4/3	380	571	−191	1.50
WMS EPIC 2MM FULL	390	311	79	0.80
HEATWAVE 4/3	430	274	156	0.64
ZEN 4/3	430	239	191	0.56
EVO 4/3	440	623	−183	1.42
ZEN FL 3/2	450	365	85	0.81
HEAT 4/3	460	450	10	0.98
ZEN-ZIP 2MM FULL	470	116	354	0.25
HEAT 3/2	500	635	−135	1.27
WMS EPIC 3/2	610	830	−220	1.36
WMS ELITE 3/2	650	364	286	0.56
ZEN-ZIP 3/2	660	788	−128	1.19
ZEN 2MM S/S FULL	680	453	227	0.67
EPIC 2MM S/S FULL	740	607	133	0.82
EPIC 4/3	1,020	732	288	0.72
WMS EPIC 4/3	1,060	1,552	−492	1.46
JR HAMMER 3/2	1,220	721	499	0.59
HAMMER 3/2	1,300	1,696	−396	1.30
HAMMER S/S FULL	1,490	1,832	−342	1.23
EPIC 3/2	2,190	3,504	−1,314	1.60
ZEN 3/2	3,190	1,195	1,995	0.37
ZEN-ZIP 4/3	3,810	3,289	521	0.86
WMS HAMMER 3/2 FULL	6,490	3,673	2,817	0.57

*Error = Forecast − Actual demand
**A/F ratio = Actual demand divided by Forecast

So how does O'Neill know actual demand for a product that stocks out? For example, how does O'Neill know that actual demand was 1,696 for last year's Hammer 3/2 if they only ordered 1,500 units? Because retailers order via phone or fax, O'Neill can keep track of each retailer's initial order, that is, the retailer's demand before the retailer knows a product is unavailable. (However, life is not perfect: O'Neill's phone representatives do not always record a customer's initial order into the computer system, so there is even some uncertainty with that figure. We'll assume this is a minor issue and not address it in our analysis.) In other settings, a firm may not be able to know actual demand with that level of precision. For example, a retailer of O'Neill's products probably does not get to observe what demand could be for the Hammer 3/2 once the Hammer is out of stock at the retailer. However, that retailer would know when during the season the Hammer stocked out and, hence, could use that information to forecast how many additional units could have been sold during the remainder of the season. Therefore, even if a firm cannot directly observe lost sales, a firm should be able to obtain a reasonable estimate for what demand could have been.

FIGURE 12.3
Forecasts and Actual Demand for Surf Wetsuits from the Previous Season

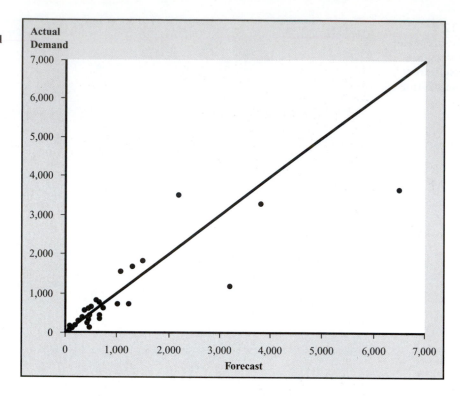

As can be seen from the data, the forecasts ranged from a low of 90 units to a high of 6,490 units. There was also considerable forecast error: O'Neill goofed with the Women's Hammer 3/2 Full suit with a forecast nearly 3,000 units above actual demand, while the forecast for the Epic 3/2 suit was about 1,300 units too low. Figure 12.3 gives a scatter plot of forecasts and actual demand. If forecasts were perfect, then all of the observations would lie along the diagonal line.

While the absolute errors for some of the bigger products are dramatic, the forecast errors for some of the smaller products are also significant. For example, the actual demand for the Juniors Zen Flat Lock 3/2 suit was more than 150 percent greater than forecast. This suggests that we should concentrate on the relative forecast errors instead of the absolute forecast errors.

Relative forecast errors can be measured with the *A/F ratio:*

$$A/F \text{ ratio} = \frac{\text{Actual demand}}{\text{Forecast}}$$

An accurate forecast has an A/F ratio = 1, while an A/F ratio above 1 indicates the forecast was too low and an A/F ratio below 1 indicates the forecast was too high. Table 12.1 displays the A/F ratios for our data in the last column.

Those A/F ratios provide a measure of the forecast accuracy from the previous season. To illustrate this point, Table 12.2 sorts the data in ascending A/F order. Also included in the table is each product's A/F rank in the order and each product's percentile, the fraction of products that have that A/F rank or lower. (For example, the product with the fifth A/F ratio has a percentile of 5/33 = 15.2 percent because it is the fifth product out of 33 products in the data.) We see from the data that actual demand is less than 80 percent of the forecast for one-third of the products (the A/F ratio 0.8 has a percentile of 33.3) and

TABLE 12.2
Sorted A/F Ratios for Surf Wetsuits from the Previous Spring Season

Product Description	Forecast	Actual Demand	A/F Ratio*	Rank	Percentile**
ZEN-ZIP 2MM FULL	470	116	0.25	1	3.0
ZEN 3/2	3,190	1,195	0.37	2	6.1
ZEN 4/3	430	239	0.56	3	9.1
WMS ELITE 3/2	650	364	0.56	4	12.1
WMS HAMMER 3/2 FULL	6,490	3,673	0.57	5	15.2
JR HAMMER 3/2	1,220	721	0.59	6	18.2
HEATWAVE 4/3	430	274	0.64	7	21.2
ZEN 2MM S/S FULL	680	453	0.67	8	24.2
EPIC 5/3 W/HD	120	83	0.69	9	27.3
EPIC 4/3	1,020	732	0.72	10	30.3
WMS EPIC 2MM FULL	390	311	0.80	11	33.3
ZEN FL 3/2	450	365	0.81	12	36.4
EPIC 2MM S/S FULL	740	607	0.82	13	39.4
ZEN-ZIP 4/3	3,810	3,289	0.86	14	42.4
WMS ZEN-ZIP 4/3	170	163	0.96	15	45.5
JR EPIC 3/2	180	175	0.97	16	48.5
HEAT 4/3	460	450	0.98	17	51.5
JR ZEN 3/2	140	143	1.02	18	54.5
WMS ZEN 3/2	180	195	1.08	19	57.6
WMS EPIC 5/3 W/HD	320	369	1.15	20	60.6
ZEN-ZIP 5/4/3 W/HOOD	270	317	1.17	21	63.6
ZEN-ZIP 3/2	660	788	1.19	22	66.7
HAMMER S/S FULL	1,490	1,832	1.23	23	69.7
HEATWAVE 3/2	170	212	1.25	24	72.7
HEAT 3/2	500	635	1.27	25	75.8
HAMMER 3/2	1,300	1,696	1.30	26	78.8
WMS EPIC 3/2	610	830	1.36	27	81.8
EVO 4/3	440	623	1.42	28	84.8
WMS EPIC 4/3	1,060	1,552	1.46	29	87.9
JR EPIC 4/3	380	571	1.50	30	90.9
EVO 3/2	380	587	1.54	31	93.9
JR ZEN FL 3/2	90	140	1.56	32	97.0
EPIC 3/2	2,190	3,504	1.60	33	100.0

*A/F ratio = Actual demand divided by Forecast
**Percentile = Rank divided by total number of wetsuits (33)

actual demand is greater than 125 percent of the forecast for 27.3 percent of the products (the A/F ratio 1.25 has a percentile of 72.7).

Given that the A/F ratios from the previous season reflect forecast accuracy in the previous season, maybe the current season's forecast accuracy will be comparable. Hence, we want to find a distribution function that will match the accuracy we observe in Table 12.2. We will use the normal distribution function to do this. Before getting there, we need a couple of additional results.

Take the definition of the A/F ratio and rearrange terms to get

$$\text{Actual demand} = \text{A/F ratio} \times \text{Forecast}$$

For the Hammer 3/2, the forecast is 3,200 units. Note that the forecast is not random, but the A/F ratio is random. Hence, the randomness in actual demand is directly related to the randomness in the A/F ratio. Using standard results from statistics and the above equation, we get the following results:

$$\text{Expected actual demand} = \text{Expected A/F ratio} \times \text{Forecast}$$

and

$$\text{Standard deviation of demand} = \text{Standard deviattion of A/F ratios} \times \text{Forecast}$$

Expected actual demand, or *expected demand* for short, is what we should choose for the mean for our normal distribution, μ. The average A/F ratio in Table 12.2 is 0.9976. Therefore, expected demand for the Hammer 3/2 in the upcoming season is $0.9976 \times 3{,}200 = 3{,}192$ units. In other words, if the initial forecast is 3,200 units and the future A/F ratios are comparable to the past A/F ratios, then the mean of actual demand is 3,192 units. So let's choose 3,192 units as our mean of the normal distribution.

This decision may raise some eyebrows: If our initial forecast is 3,200 units, why do we not instead choose 3,200 as the mean of the normal distribution? Because 3,192 is so close to 3,200, assigning 3,200 as the mean probably would lead to a good order quantity as well. However, suppose the average A/F ratio were 0.90, that is, on average, actual demand is 90 percent of the forecast. It is quite common for people to have overly optimistic forecasts, so an average A/F ratio of 0.90 is possible. In that case, expected actual demand would only be $0.90 \times 3{,}200 = 2{,}880$. Because we want to choose a normal distribution that represents actual demand, in that situation it would be better to choose a mean of 2,880 even though our initial forecast is 3,200. (Novice golfers sometimes adopt an analogous strategy. If a golfer consistently hooks the ball to the right on her drives, then she should aim to the left of the flag. In an ideal world, there would be no hook to her shot nor a bias in the forecast. But if the data say there is a hook, then it should not be ignored. Of course, the golfer and the forecaster also should work on eliminating the bias.)

Now that we have a mean for our normal distribution, we need a standard deviation. The second equation above tells us that the standard deviation of actual demand equals the standard deviation of the A/F ratios times the forecast. The standard deviation of the A/F ratios in Table 12.2 is 0.369. (Use the "stdev()" function in Excel.) So the standard deviation of actual demand is the standard deviation of the A/F ratios times the initial forecast: $0.369 \times 3{,}200 = 1{,}181$. Hence, to express our demand forecast for the Hammer 3/2, we can use a normal distribution with a mean of 3,192 and a standard deviation of 1,181. See Exhibit 12.1 for a summary of the process of choosing a mean and a standard deviation for a normal distribution forecast.

Now that we have the parameters of a normal distribution that will express our demand forecast, we need to be able to find $F(Q)$. There are two ways this can be done. The first way is to use spreadsheet software. For example, in Excel use the function Normdist(Q, 3192, 1181, 1). The second way, which does not require a computer, is to use the Standard Normal Distribution Function Table in Appendix B.

The *standard normal* is a particular normal distribution: its mean is 0 and its standard deviation is 1. To introduce another piece of common Greek notation, let $\Phi(z)$ be the distribution function of the standard normal. Even though the standard normal is a continuous distribution, it can be "chopped up" into pieces to make it into a discrete distribution. The Standard Normal Distribution Function Table is exactly that; that is, it is the discrete version of the standard normal distribution. The full table is in Appendix B, but Table 12.3 reproduces a portion of the table.

The format of the Standard Normal Distribution Function Table makes it somewhat tricky to read. For example, suppose you wanted to know the probability that the outcome of a standard normal is 0.51 or lower. We are looking for the value of $\Phi(z)$ with $z = 0.51$. To find that value, pick the row and column in the table such that the first number in the row and the first number in the column add up to the z value you seek. With $z = 0.51$, we are looking for the row that begins with 0.50 and the column that begins with 0.01, because the sum of those two

Exhibit 12.1

A PROCESS FOR USING HISTORICAL A/F RATIOS TO CHOOSE A MEAN AND STANDARD DEVIATION FOR A NORMAL DISTRIBUTION FORECAST

Step 1. Assemble a data set of products for which the forecasting task is comparable to the product of interest. In other words, the data set should include products that you expect would have similar forecast error to the product of interest. (They may or may not be similar products.) The data should include an initial forecast of demand and the actual demand. We also need forecast for the item for the upcoming season.

Step 2. Evaluate the A/F ratio for each product in the data set. Evaluate the average of the A/F ratios (that is, the expected A/F ratio) and the standard deviation of the A/F ratios. (In Excel use the average() and stdev() functions.)

Step 3. The mean and standard deviation of the normal distribution that we will use as the forecast can now be evaluated with the following two equations:

$$\text{Expected demand} = \text{Expected A/F ratio} \times \text{Forecast}$$

$$\text{Standard deviation of demand} = \text{Standard deviation of A/F ratios} \times \text{Forecast}$$

where the forecast in the above equations is the forecast for the item for the upcoming season.

values equals 0.51. The intersection of that row with that column gives $\Phi(z)$; from Table 12.3 we see that $\Phi(0.51) = 0.6950$. Therefore, there is a 69.5 percent probability the outcome of a standard normal is 0.51 or lower.

But it is unlikely that our demand forecast will be a standard normal distribution. So how can we use the standard normal to find $F(Q)$; that is, the probability demand will be Q or lower given that our demand forecast is some other normal distribution? The answer is that we convert the quantity we are interested in, Q, into an equivalent quantity for the standard normal. In other words, we find a z such that $F(Q) = \Phi(z)$; that is, the probability demand is less than or equal to Q is the same as the probability the outcome of a standard normal is z or lower. That z is called the *z-statistic.* Once we have the appropriate z-statistics, we then just look up $\Phi(z)$ in the Standard Normal Distribution Function Table to get our answer.

To convert Q into the equivalent z-statistic, use the following equation:

$$z = \frac{Q - \mu}{\sigma}$$

For example, suppose we are interested in the probability that demand for the Hammer 3/2 will be 4,000 units or lower, that is, $Q = 4,000$. With a normal distribution that has mean 3,192 and standard deviation 1,181, the quantity $Q = 4,000$ has a z-statistic of

$$z = \frac{4,000 - 3,192}{1,181} = 0.68$$

TABLE 12.3
A Portion of the Standard Normal Distribution Function Table, $\Phi(z)$

z	0.00	0.01	0.02	0.03	0.04	0.05	0.06	0.07	0.08	0.09
0.3	0.6179	0.6217	0.6255	0.6293	0.6331	0.6368	0.6406	0.6443	0.6480	0.6517
0.4	0.6554	0.6591	0.6628	0.6664	0.6700	0.6736	0.6772	0.6808	0.6844	0.6879
0.5	0.6915	0.6950	0.6985	0.7019	0.7054	0.7088	0.7123	0.7157	0.7190	0.7224
0.6	0.7257	0.7291	0.7324	0.7357	0.7389	0.7422	0.7454	0.7486	0.7517.	0.7549
0.7	0.7580	0.7611	0.7642	0.7673	0.7704	0.7734	0.7764	0.7794	0.7823	0.7852
0.8	0.7881	0.7910	0.7939	0.7967	0.7995	0.8023	0.8051	0.8078	0.8106	0.8133
0.9	0.8159	0.8186	0.8212	0.8238	0.8264	0.8269	0.8315	0.8340	0.8365	0.8389
1.0	0.8413	0.8438	0.8461	0.8485	0.8508	0.8531	0.8554	0.8577	0.8599	0.8621

Exhibit 12.2

A PROCESS FOR EVALUATING THE PROBABILITY DEMAND IS EITHER LESS THAN OR EQUAL TO Q (WHICH IS $F(Q)$) OR MORE THAN Q (WHICH IS $1 - F(Q)$)

If the demand forecast is a normal distribution with mean μ and standard deviation σ, then follow steps A and B:

A. Evaluate the z-statistic that corresponds to Q:

$$z = \frac{Q - \mu}{\sigma}$$

B. The probability demand is less than or equal to Q is $\Phi(z)$. With Excel $\Phi(z)$ can be evaluated with the function Normsdist(z); otherwise, look up $\Phi(z)$ in the Standard Normal Distribution Function Table in Appendix B. If you want the probability demand is greater than Q, then your answer is $1 - \Phi(z)$.

If the demand forecast is a discrete distribution function table, then look up $F(Q)$, which is the probability demand is less than or equal to Q. If you want the probability demand is greater than Q, then the answer is $1 - F(Q)$.

Therefore, the probability demand for the Hammer 3/2 is 4,000 units or lower is $\Phi(0.68)$; that is, it is the same as the probability the outcome of a standard normal is 0.68 or lower. According to the Standard Normal Distribution Function Table (see Table 12.3 for convenience), $\Phi(0.68) = 0.7517$. In other words, there is just over a 75 percent probability that demand for the Hammer 3/2 will be 4,000 or fewer units. Exhibit 12.2 summarizes the process of finding the probability demand will be less than or equal to some Q (or more than Q).

You may recall that it has been O'Neill's experience that demand deviated by more than 25 percent from their initial forecast for 50 percent of their products. We can now check whether that experience is consistent with our normal distribution forecast for the Hammer 3/2. Our initial forecast is 3,200 units. So a deviation of 25 percent or more implies demand is either less than 2,400 units or more than 4,000 units. The z-statistic for $Q = 2,400$ is $z = (2400 - 3192)/1181 = -0.67$, and from the Standard Normal Distribution Function Table, $\Phi(-0.67) = 0.2514$. (Find the row with -0.60 and the column with -0.07.) If there is a 25.14 percent probability demand is less than 2,400 units and a 75.17 percent probability that demand is less than 4,000 units, then there is a $75.17 - 25.14 = 50.03$ percent probability that demand is between 2,400 and 4,000 units. Hence, O'Neill's initial assertion regarding forecast accuracy is consistent with our normal distribution forecast of demand.

To summarize, the objective in this section is to develop a detailed demand forecast. A single "point forecast" (e.g., 3,200 units) is not sufficient. We need to quantify the amount of variability that may occur about our forecast; that is, we need a distribution function. We obtained this distribution function by fitting a normal distribution to our historical forecast accuracy data, Table 12.2.

12.4 The Expected Profit-Maximizing Order Quantity

The next step after assembling all of our inputs (selling price, cost, salvage value, and demand forecast) is to choose an order quantity. The first part in that process is to decide what is our objective. A natural objective is to choose our production/procurement quantity to maximize our expected profit. This section explains how to do this. Section 12.6 considers other possible objectives.

Before revealing the actual procedure for choosing an order quantity to maximize expected profit, it is helpful to explore the intuition behind the solution. Consider again O'Neill's Hammer 3/2 ordering decision. Should we order one unit? If we do, then there is a very good chance we will sell the unit: With a forecast of 3,192 units, it is likely we sell at least one unit. If we sell the unit, then the gain from that unit equals $190 − $110 = $80 (the selling price minus the purchase cost). The *expected* gain from the first unit, which equals the probability of selling the first unit times the gain from the first unit, is then very close to $80. However, there is also a slight chance that we do not sell the first unit, in which case we incur a loss of $110 − $90 = $20. (The loss equals the difference between the purchase cost and the discount price.) But since the probability we do not sell that unit is quite small, the *expected* loss on the first unit is nearly $0. Given that the expected gain from the first unit clearly exceeds the expected loss, the profit from ordering that unit is positive. In this case it is a good bet to order at least one unit.

After deciding whether to order one unit, we can now consider whether we should order two units, and then three units, and so forth. Two things happen as we continue this process. First, the probability that we sell the unit we are considering decreases, thereby reducing the expected gain from that unit. Second, the probability we do not sell that unit increases, thereby increasing the expected loss from that unit. Now imagine we order the 6,400th unit. The probability of selling that unit is quite low, so the expected gain from that unit is nearly zero. In contrast, the probability of *not* selling that unit is quite high, so the expected loss is nearly $20 on that unit. Clearly it makes no sense to order the 6,400th unit. This pattern is illustrated in Figure 12.4. We see that from some unit just above 4,000 the expected gain on that unit equals its expected loss.

Let's formalize this intuition some more. In the newsvendor model, there is a trade-off between ordering too much (which could lead to costly leftover inventory) and ordering too little (which could lead to the opportunity cost of lost sales). To balance these forces, it is useful to think in terms of a cost for ordering too much and a cost for ordering too little. Maximizing expected profit is equivalent to minimizing those costs. To be specific, let C_o be the *overage cost,* the loss incurred when a unit is ordered but not sold. In other words, the overage cost is the per-unit cost of overordering. For the Hammer 3/2, we have $C_o = 20$.

FIGURE 12.4
The Expected Gain and Expected Loss from the *Q*th Hammer 3/2 Ordered by O'Neill

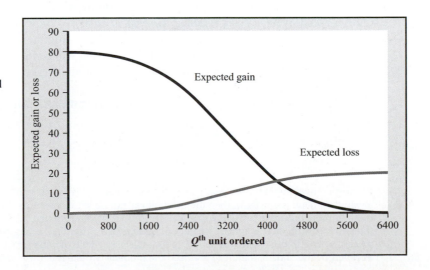

In contrast to C_o, let C_u be the *underage cost,* the opportunity cost of not ordering a unit that could have been sold. The following is an equivalent definition for C_u: C_u is the gain from selling a unit. In other words, the underage cost is the per-unit opportunity cost of underordering. For the Hammer 3/2, $C_u = 80$. Note that the overage and underage costs are defined for a *single unit.* In other words, C_o is not the total cost of all leftover inventory; instead, C_o is the cost *per unit* of leftover inventory. The reason for defining C_o and C_u for a single unit is simple: We don't know how many units will be left over in inventory, or how many units of demand will be lost, but we do know the cost of each unit left in inventory and the opportunity cost of each lost sale.

Now that we have defined the overage and underage costs, we need to choose Q to strike the balance between them that results in the maximum expected profit. Based on our previous reasoning, we should keep ordering additional units until the expected loss equals the expected gain.

The expected loss on a unit is the cost of having the unit in inventory (the overage cost) times the probability it is left in inventory. For the Qth unit, that probability is $F(Q)$: It is left in inventory if demand is less than Q.[2] Therefore, the expected loss is $C_o \times F(Q)$. The expected gain on a unit is the benefit of selling a unit (the underage cost) times the probability the unit is sold, which in this case occurs if demand is greater than Q. The probability demand is greater than Q is $(1 - F(Q))$. Therefore, the expected gain is $C_u \times (1 - F(Q))$.

It remains to find the order quantity Q that sets the expected loss on the Qth unit equal to the expected gain on the Qth unit:

$$C_o \times F(Q) = C_u \times (1 - F(Q))$$

If we rearrange terms in the above equation, we get

$$F(Q) = \frac{C_u}{C_o + C_u} \qquad\qquad \textbf{(12.1)}$$

The profit-maximizing order quantity is the order quantity that satisfies the above equation. If you are familiar with calculus and would like to see a more mathematically rigorous derivation of the optimal order quantity, see Appendix D.

So how can we use equation (12.1) to actually find Q? Let's begin by just reading it. It says that the order quantity that maximizes expected profit is the order quantity Q such that demand is less than or equal to Q with probability $C_u/(C_o + C_u)$. That ratio with the underage and overage costs is called the *critical ratio.* We now have an explanation for why our forecast must be a distribution function. To choose the profit-maximizing order quantity, we need to find the quantity such that demand will be less than that quantity with a particular probability (the critical ratio). The mean alone (i.e., just a sales forecast) is insufficient to do that task.

Let's begin with the easy part. We know for the Hammer 3/2 that $C_u = 80$ and $C_o = 20$, so the critical ratio is

$$\frac{C_u}{C_o + C_u} = \frac{80}{20 + 80} = 0.8$$

---

[2] That statement might bother you. You might recall that $F(Q)$ is the probability demand is Q or lower. If demand is exactly Q, then the Qth unit will not be left in inventory. Hence, you might argue that it is more precise to say that $F(Q - 1)$ is the probability the Qth unit is left in inventory. However, the normal distribution assumes demand can be any value, including values that are not integers. If you are willing to divide each demand into essentially an infinite number of fractional pieces, as is assumed by the normal, then $F(Q)$ is indeed the probability there is leftover inventory. If you are curious about the details, see Appendix D.

We are making progress, but now comes the tricky part: We need to find the order quantity Q such that there is a 80 percent probability that demand is Q or lower.

There are two ways to find a Q such that there is an 80 percent probability that demand will be Q or smaller. The first is to use the Excel function, Normsinv(), and the second is to use the Standard Normal Distribution Function Table. If you have Excel available, the first method is the easiest, but they both follow essentially the same process, as we will see.

If we have Excel, to find the optimal Q, we begin by finding the z statistic such that there is an 80 percent probability the outcome of a standard normal is z or lower. Then we convert that z into the Q we seek. To find our desired z, use the following Excel function:

$$z = \text{Normsinv(Critical ratio)}$$

In our case, the critical ratio is 0.80 and Normsinv(0.80) returns 0.84. That means that there is an 80 percent chance the outcome of a standard normal will be 0.84 or lower. That would be our optimal order quantity if demand followed a standard normal distribution. But our demand is not standard normal. It is normal with mean 3192 and standard deviation 1181. To convert our z into an order quantity that makes sense for our actual demand forecast, we use the following equation:

$$Q = \mu + z \times \sigma$$

where
$$\mu = \text{Mean of the normal distribution}$$
$$\sigma = \text{Standard deviation of the normal distribution}$$

Hence, using our Excel method, the expected profit maximizing order quantity for the Hammer 3/2 is $Q = 3{,}192 + 0.84 \times 1{,}181 = 4{,}184$.

The second method to find Q is to use the Standard Normal Distribution Function Table. Again, we want to find the z such that the probability the standard normal is z or less is equal to the critical ratio, which in this case is 0.80. Looking at Table 12.3, we see that $\Phi(0.84) = 0.7995$ and $\Phi(0.85) = 0.8023$, neither of which is exactly the 0.80 probability we are looking for: $z = 0.84$ yields a slightly lower probability (79.95 percent) and $z = 0.85$ yields a slightly higher probability (80.23 percent). What should we do? The rule is simple, which we will call the *round-up rule:*

Round-up rule. Whenever you are looking up a target value in a table and the target value falls between two entries, choose the entry that leads to the larger order quantity.

In this case the larger quantity is $z = 0.85$, so we will go with 0.85. Now, like with our Excel process, we convert that z into a $Q = 3{,}192 + 0.85 \times 1{,}181 = 4{,}196$.

Why do our two methods lead to different answers? In short, Excel does not implement the round-up rule. But that raises the next question. Is it OK to use Excel to get our answer? The answer is "yes." To explain, when demand is normally distributed, there will be a small difference between the Excel answer, using the Normsinv() function, and the Standard Normal Distribution Function Table answer. In this case, the difference between the two is only 12 units, which is less than 0.3 percent away from 4,196.

Therefore, the expected profit with either of these order quantities will be essentially the same. Furthermore, Excel provides a convenient means to perform this calculation quickly.

So, if Excel is the quick and easy method, why should we bother with the Standard Normal Distribution Function Table and the round-up rule? Because when our demand forecast is a discrete distribution function, the round-up rule provides the more accurate answer. (Recall, a discrete distribution function assumes that the only possible outcomes

Exhibit 12.3

A PROCEDURE TO FIND THE ORDER QUANTITY THAT MAXIMIZES EXPECTED PROFIT IN THE NEWSVENDOR MODEL

Step 1: Evaluate the critical ratio: $\dfrac{C_u}{C_o + C_u}$. In the case of the Hammer 3/2, the underage cost is $C_u =$ Price $-$ Cost and the overage cost is $C_o =$ Cost $-$ Salvage value.

Step 2: If the demand forecast is a normal distribution with mean μ and standard deviation σ, then follow steps A and B:

    A. Find the optimal order quantity if demand had a standard normal distribution. One method to achieve this is to find the z value in the Standard Normal Distribution Function Table such that

$$\Phi(z) = \frac{C_u}{C_o + C_u}$$

    (If the critical ratio value does not exist in the table, then find the two z values that it falls between. For example, the critical ratio 0.80 falls between $z = 0.84$ and $z = 0.85$. Then choose the larger of those two z values.) A second method is to use the Excel function Normsinv: $z =$ Normsinv(Critical ratio).

    B. Convert z into the order quantity that maximizes expected profit, Q:
    $Q = \mu + z \times \sigma$

---

are integers.) This is particularly valuable when expected demand is small, say, 10 units, or 1 unit, or even 0.25 unit. In those cases, the normal distribution function does not model demand well (in part, because it is a continuous distribution function). Furthermore, it can make a big difference (in terms of expected profit) whether one or two units are ordered. Hence, the value of understanding the round-up rule.

This discussion probably has left you with one final question—Why is the round-up rule the right rule? The critical ratio is actually closer to 0.7995 (which corresponds to $z = 0.84$) than it is to 0.8023 (which corresponds to $z = 0.85$). That is why Excel chooses $z = 0.84$. Shouldn't we choose the z value that leads to the probability that is closest to the critical ratio? In fact, that is not the best approach. The critical ratio equation works with the following logic—keep ordering until you get to the first order quantity such that the critical ratio is less than the probability demand is that order quantity or lower. That logic leads the rule to "step over" the critical ratio and then stop, that is, the round-up rule. Excel, in contrast, use the "get as close to the critical ratio as possible" rule. If you are hungry for a more in-depth explanation and justification, see Appendix D. Otherwise, stick with the round-up rule, and you will be fine. Exhibit 12.3 summarizes these steps.

12.5 Performance Measures

The previous section showed us how to find the order quantity that maximizes our expected profit. This section shows us how to evaluate a number of relevant performance measures. As Figure 12.5 indicates, these performance measures are closely related. For example, to evaluate expected leftover inventory, you first evaluate expected lost sales (which has up to three inputs: the order quantity, the loss function table, and the standard deviation of demand), then expected sales (which has two inputs: expected lost sales and expected demand), and then expected leftover inventory (which has two inputs: expected sales and the order quantity).

FIGURE 12.5

The Relationships between Initial Input Parameters (boxes) and Performance Measures (ovals)

Note: Some performance measures require other performance measures as inputs; for example, expected sales requires expected demand and expected lost sales as inputs.

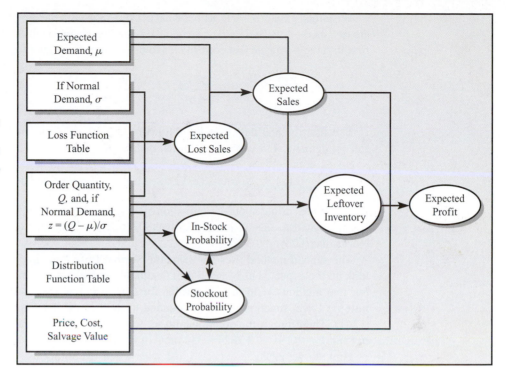

These performance measures can be evaluated for any order quantity, not just the expected profit-maximizing order quantity. To emphasize this point, this section evaluates these performance measures assuming 3,500 Hammer 3/2s are ordered. See Table 13.1 for the evaluation of these measures with the optimal order quantity, 4,196 units.

Expected Lost Sales

Let's begin with *expected lost sales,* which is the expected number of units by which demand (a random variable) exceeds the order quantity (a fixed threshold). (Because order quantities are measured in physical units, sales and lost sales are measured in physical units as well, not in monetary units.) For example, if we order 3,500 units of the Hammer but demand could have been high enough to sell 3,821 units, then we would lose $3,821 - 3,500 = 321$ units of demand. Expected lost sales is the amount of demand that is not satisfied, which should be of interest to a manager even though the opportunity cost of lost sales does not show up explicitly on any standard accounting document.

Note that we are interested in the *expected* lost sales. Demand can be less than our order quantity, in which case lost sales is zero, or demand can exceed our order quantity, in which case lost sales is positive. Expected lost sales is the average of all of those events (the cases with no lost sales and all cases with positive lost sales).

How do we find expected lost sales for any given order quantity? When demand is normally distributed, use the following equation:

$$\text{Expected lost sales} = \sigma \times L(z)$$

where
$$\sigma = \text{Standard deviation of the normal distribution representing demand}$$
$$L(z) = \text{Loss function with the standard normal distribution}$$

We already know $\sigma = 1,181$ but what is $L(z)$? Like with the optimal order quantity, there are two methods to find $L(z)$, one using Excel and one using a table. With either method, we first find the z-statistic that corresponds to our chosen order quantity, $Q = 3,500$:

$$z = \frac{Q - \mu}{\sigma} = \frac{3,500 - 3,192}{1,181} = 0.26$$

The first method then uses the following Excel formula to evaluate the expected lost sales if demand were a standard normal distribution, $L(z)$:

$$L(z) = \text{Normdist}(z,0,1,0) - z*(1 - \text{Normsdist}(z))$$

(If you are curious about the derivation of the above function, see Appendix D.) In this case, Excel provides the following answer: $L(0.26) = \text{Normdist}(0.26,0,1,0) - 0.26*(1 - \text{Normsdist}(0.26)) = 0.2824$.

The second method uses the Standard Normal Loss Function Table in Appendix B to look up the expected lost sales. From that table we see that $L(0.26) = 0.2824$. In this case, our two methods yield the same value for $L(z)$, which always is the case when we input into the Excel function a z value rounded to the nearest hundredth (e.g., 0.26 instead of 0.261). Therefore, if the order quantity is 3,500 Hammer 3/2s, then we can expect to lose $\sigma \times L(z) = 1,181 \times 0.2824 = 334$ units of demand.

How do we evaluate expected lost sales when we do not use a normal distribution to model demand? In that situation we need a table to tell us what expected lost sales is for our chosen order quantity. For example, Appendix B provides the loss function for the Poisson distribution with different means. Appendix C provides a procedure to evaluate the loss function for any discrete distribution function. We relegate this procedure to the appendix because it is computationally burdensome; that is, it is the kind of calculation you want to do on a spreadsheet rather than by hand.

Exhibit 12.4 summarizes the procedures for evaluating expected lost sales.

Expected Sales

Each unit of demand results in either a sale or a lost sale, so

$$\text{Expected sales} + \text{Expected lost sales} = \text{Expected demand}$$

We already know expected demand: It is the mean of the demand distribution, μ. Rearrange terms in the above equation and we get

$$\text{Expected sales} = \mu - \text{Expected lost sales}$$

Therefore, the procedure to evaluate expected sales begins by evaluating expected lost sales. See Exhibit 12.5 for a summary of this procedure.

Let's evaluate expected sales if 3,500 Hammers are ordered and the normal distribution is our demand forecast. We already evaluated expected lost sales to be 334 units. Therefore, Expected sales $= 3,192 - 334 = 2,858$ units.

Notice that expected sales is always less than expected demand (because expected lost sales is never negative). While you might get lucky and sell more than the mean demand, on average you cannot sell more than the mean demand.

Exhibit 12.4

EXPECTED LOST SALES EVALUATION PROCEDURE

If the demand forecast is a normal distribution with mean μ and standard deviation σ, then follow steps A through D:

A. Evaluate the z-statistic for the order quantity Q: $z = \dfrac{Q - \mu}{\sigma}$.

B. Use the z-statistic to look up in the Standard Normal Loss Function Table the expected lost sales, $L(z)$, with the standard normal distribution.

C. Expected lost sales $= \sigma \times L(z)$.

D. With Excel, expected lost sales can be evaluated with the following equation:

$$\text{Expected lost sales} = \sigma * (\text{Normdist}(z,0,1,0) - z*(1 - \text{Normsdist}(z)))$$

If the demand forecast is a discrete distribution function table, then expected lost sales equals the loss function for the chosen order quantity, $L(Q)$. If the table does not include the loss function, then see Appendix C for how to evaluate it.

Expected Leftover Inventory

Expected leftover inventory is the average amount that demand (a random variable) is less than the order quantity (a fixed threshold). (In contrast, expected lost sales is the average amount by which demand exceeds the order quantity.)

The following equation is true because every unit purchased is either sold or left over in inventory at the end of the season:

$$\text{Expected sales} + \text{Expected leftover inventory} = Q$$

Rearrange the above equation to obtain

$$\text{Expected leftover inventory} = Q - \text{Expected sales}$$

We know the quantity purchased, Q. Therefore, we can easily evaluate expected leftover inventory once we have evaluated expected sales. See Exhibit 12.5 for a summary of this procedure.

If the demand forecast is a normal distribution and 3,500 Hammers are ordered, then expected leftover inventory is $3,500 - 2,858 = 642$ units because we evaluated expected sales to be 2,858 units.

It may seem surprising that expected leftover inventory and expected lost sales can both be positive. While in any particular season there is either leftover inventory or lost sales, but not both, we are interested in the expectation of those measures over all possible outcomes. Therefore, each *expectation* can be positive.

Expected Profit

We earn Price − Cost on each unit sold and we lose Cost − Salvage value on each unit we do not sell, so our expected profit is

$$\text{Expected profit} = [(\text{Price} - \text{Cost}) \times \text{Expected sales}]$$
$$- [(\text{Cost} - \text{Salvage value}) \times \text{Expected leftover inventory}]$$

Therefore, we can evaluate expected profit after we have evaluated expected sales and leftover inventory. See Exhibit 12.5 for a summary of this procedure.

Exhibit 12.5

EXPECTED SALES, EXPECTED LEFTOVER INVENTORY, AND EXPECTED PROFIT EVALUATION PROCEDURES

Step 1.   Evaluate expected lost sales (see Exhibit 12.4). All of these performance measures can be evaluated directly in terms of expected lost sales and several known parameters: μ = Expected demand; Q = Order quantity; Price; Cost; and Salvage value.

Step 2.   Use the following equations to evaluate the performance measure of interest.

$$\text{Expected sales} = \mu - \text{Expected lost sales}$$
$$\text{Expected leftover inventory} = Q - \text{Expected sales}$$
$$= Q - \mu + \text{Expected lost sales}$$
$$\text{Expected profit} = [(\text{Price} - \text{Cost}) \times \text{Expected sales}]$$
$$- [(\text{Cost} - \text{Salvage value}) \times \text{Expected leftover inventory}]$$

With an order quantity of 3,500 units and a normal distribution demand forecast, the expected profit for the Hammer 3/2 is

$$\text{Expected profit} = (\$80 \times 2{,}858) - (\$20 \times 642) = \$215{,}800$$

In-Stock Probability and Stockout Probability

A common measure of customer service is the in-stock probability. The in-stock probability is the probability the firm ends the season having satisfied all demand. (Equivalently, the in-stock probability is the probability the firm has stock available for every customer.) That occurs if demand is less than or equal to the order quantity,

$$\text{In-stock probability} = F(Q)$$

The stockout probability is the probability the firm stocks out for some customer during the selling season (i.e., a lost sale occurs). Because the firm stocks out if demand exceeds the order quantity,

$$\text{Stockout probability} = 1 - F(Q)$$

(The firm either stocks out or it does not, so the stockout probability equals 1 minus the probability demand is Q or lower.) We also can see that the stockout probability and the in-stock probability are closely related:

$$\text{Stockout probability} = 1 - \text{In-stock probability}$$

See Exhibit 12.6 for a summary of the procedure to evaluate these probabilities. With an order quantity of 3,500 Hammers, the z-statistic is $z = (3{,}500 - 3{,}192)/1{,}181 = 0.26$. From the Standard Normal Distribution Function Table, we find $\Phi(0.26) = 0.6026$, so the in-stock probability is 60.26 percent. The stockout probability is $1 - 0.6026 = 39.74$ percent.

The in-stock probaility is not the only measure of customer service. Another popular measure is the *fill rate*. The fill rate is the probability a customer is able to purchase a unit (i.e., does not experience a stockout). Interestingly, this is not the same as the in-stock probability, which is the probability that all demand is satisfied. For example, if $Q = 100$ and demand turns out to be 101, then most customers were able to purchase a unit but the firm did not satisfy all demand. See Appendix D for more information regarding how to evaluate the fill rate.

Exhibit 12.6

12.6 Choosing an Order Quantity to Meet a Service Objective

Maximizing expected profit is surely a reasonable objective for choosing an order quantity, but it is not the only objective. As we saw in the previous section, the expected profit-maximizing order quantity may generate an unacceptable in-stock probability from the firm's customer service perspective. This section explains how to determine an order quantity that satisfies a customer service objective, in particular, a minimum in-stock probability.

Suppose O'Neill wants to find the order quantity that generates a 99 percent in-stock probability with the Hammer 3/2. The in-stock probability is $F(Q)$. So we need to find an order quantity such that there is a 99 percent probability that demand is that order quantity or lower. Given that our demand forecast is normally distributed, we first find the z-statistic that achieves our objective with the standard normal distribution. In the Standard Normal Distribution Function Table, we see that $\Phi(2.32) = 0.9898$ and $\Phi(2.33) = 0.9901$. Again, we choose the higher z-statistic, so our desired order quantity is now $Q = \mu + z \times \sigma = 3{,}192 + 2.33 \times 1{,}181 = 5{,}944$. You can use Excel to avoid looking up a probability in the Standard Normal Distribution Function Table to find z:

$$z = \text{Normsinv(In-stock probability)}$$

Notice that a substantially higher order quantity is needed to generate a 99 percent in-stock probability than the one that maximizes expected profit (4,196). Exhibit 12.7 summarizes the process for finding an order quantity to satisfy a target in-stock probability.

12.7 Managerial Lessons

Now that we have detailed the process of implementing the newsvendor model, it is worthwhile to step back and consider the managerial lessons it implies.

With respect to the forecasting process, there are three key lessons.

• For each product, it is insufficient to have just a forecast of expected demand. We also need a forecast for how variable demand will be about the forecast. That uncertainty in the forecast is captured by the standard deviation of demand.

Exhibit 12.7

A PROCEDURE TO DETERMINE AN ORDER QUANTITY THAT SATISFIES A TARGET IN-STOCK PROBABILITY

If the demand forecast is a normal distribution with mean μ and standard deviation σ, then follow steps A and B:

A. Find the *z*-statistic in the Standard Normal Distribution Function Table that satisfies the in-stock probability, that is,

$$\Phi(z) = \text{In-stock probability}$$

If the in-stock probability falls between two *z* values in the table, choose the higher *z*. In Excel, *z* can be found with the following formula:

$$z = \text{Normsinv(In-stock probability)}.$$

B. Convert the chosen *z*-statistic into the order quantity that satisfies our target in-stock probability,

$$Q = \mu + z \times \sigma$$

If the demand forecast is a discrete distribution function table, then find the order quantity in the table such that $F(Q)$ = In-stock probability. If the in-stock probability falls between two entries in the table, choose the entry with the larger order quantity.

• It is important to track actual demand. Two common mistakes are made with respect to this issue. First, do not forget that actual demand may be greater than actual sales due to an inventory shortage. If it is not possible to track actual demand after a stockout occurs, then you should attempt a reasonable estimate of actual demand. Second, actual demand includes potential sales only at the regular price. If you sold 1,000 units in the previous season, but 600 of them were at the discounted price at the end of the season, then actual demand is closer to 400 than 1,000.

• You need to keep track of past forecasts and forecast errors in order to assess the standard deviation of demand. Without past data on forecasts and forecast errors, it is very difficult to choose reasonable standard deviations; it is hard enough to forecast the mean of a distribution, but forecasting the standard deviation of a distribution is nearly impossible with just a "gut feel." Unfortunately, many firms fail to maintain the data they need to implement the newsvendor model correctly. They might not record the data because it is an inherently undesirable task to keep track of past errors: Who wants to have a permanent record of the big forecasting goofs? Alternatively, firms may not realize the importance of such data and therefore do not go through the effort to record and maintain it.

There are also a number of important lessons from the order quantity choice process.

• The profit-maximizing order quantity generally does not equal expected demand. If the underage cost is greater than the overage cost (i.e., it is more expensive to lose a sale than it is to have leftover inventory), then the profit-maximizing order quantity is larger than expected demand. (Because then the critical ratio is greater than 0.50.) On the other hand, some products may have an overage cost that is larger than the underage cost. For such products, it is actually best to order less than the expected demand.

- The order quantity decision should be separated from the forecasting process. The goal of the forecasting process is to develop the best forecast for a product's demand and therefore should proceed without regard to the order quantity decision. This can be frustrating for some firms. Imagine the marketing department dedicates considerable effort to develop a forecast and then the operations department decides to produce a quantity above the forecast. The marketing department may feel that their efforts are being ignored or their expertise is being second-guessed. In addition, they may be concerned that they would be responsible for ensuring that all of the production is sold even though their forecast was more conservative. The separation between the forecasting and the order quantity decision also implies that two products with the same mean forecast may have different expected profit-maximizing order quantities, either because they have different critical ratios or because they have different standard deviations.

- Explicit costs should not be overemphasized relative to opportunity costs. Inventory at the end of the season is the explicit cost of a demand–supply mismatch, while lost sales are the opportunity cost. Overemphasizing the former relative to the latter will cause you to order less than the profit-maximizing order quantity.

- It is important to recognize that choosing an order quantity to maximize expected profit is only one possible objective. It is also a very reasonable objective, but there can be situations in which a manager may wish to consider an alternative objective. For example, maximizing expected profit is wise if you are not particularly concerned with the variability of profit. If you are managing many different products so that the realized profit from any one product cannot cause undue hardship on the firm, then maximizing expected profit is a good objective to adopt. But if you are a startup firm with a single product and limited capital, then you might not be able to absorb a significant profit loss. In situations in which the variability of profit matters, it is prudent to order less than the profit-maximizing order quantity. The expected profit objective also does not consider customer service explicitly in its objective. With the expected profit-maximizing order quantity for the Hammer 3/2, the in-stock probability is about 80 percent. Some managers may feel this is an unacceptable level of customer service, fearing that unsatisfied customers will switch to a competitor. Figure 12.6 displays the trade-off between

FIGURE 12.6

The Trade-off between Profit and Service with the Hammer 3/2

The circle indicates the in-stock probability and the expected profit of the optimal order quantity, 4,196 units.

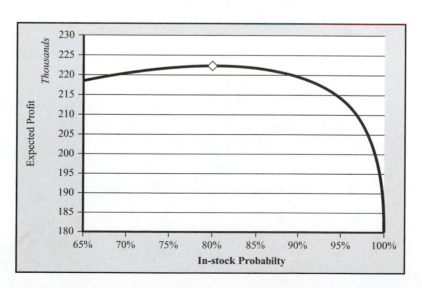

service and expected profit. As we can see, the expected profit curve is reasonably flat around the maximum, which occurs with an in-stock probability that equals 80 percent. Raising the in-stock probability to 90 percent may be considered worthwhile because it reduces profits by slightly less than 1 percent. However, raising the in-stock dramatically, say, to 99 percent, may cause expected profits to fall too much—in that case by nearly 10 percent.

- Finally, while it is impossible to perfectly match supply and demand when supply must be chosen before random demand, it is possible to make a smart choice that balances the cost of ordering too much with the cost of ordering too little. In other words, uncertainty should not invite ad hoc decision making.

12.8 Summary

The newsvendor model is a tool for making a decision when there is a "too much–too little" challenge: Bet too much and there is a cost (e.g., leftover inventory), but bet too little and there is a different cost (e.g., the opportunity cost of lost sales). (See Table 12.4 for a summary of the key notation and equations.) To make this trade-off effectively, it is necessary to have a complete forecast of demand. It is not enough to just have a single sales forecast; we need to know the potential variation about that sales forecast. With a forecast model of demand (e.g., normal distribution with mean 3,192 and standard deviation 1,181), we can choose a quantity to maximize expected profit or to achieve a desired in-stock probability. For any chosen quantity, we can evaluate several performance measures, such as expected sales and expected profit.

TABLE 12.4
Summary of Key Notation and Equations in Chapter 12

Q = Order quantity　　C_u = Underage cost　　C_o = Overage cost　　Critical ratio $= \dfrac{C_u}{C_o + C_u}$

μ = Expected demand　　　σ = Standard deviation of demand

$F(Q)$: Distribution function　　　　　$\Phi(Q)$: Distribution function of the standard normal

Expected actual demand = Expected A/F ratio $\times$ Forecast

Standard deviation of actual demand = Standard deviation of A/F ratios $\times$ Forecast

Expected profit-maximizing order quantity: $F(Q) = \dfrac{C_u}{C_o + C_u}$

z-statistic or normalized order quantity: $z = \dfrac{Q - \mu}{\sigma}.$

$Q = \mu + z \times \sigma$

$L(z)$ = Expected lost sales with the standard normal distribution

Expected lost sales $= \sigma \times L(z)$　　Expected sales $= \mu -$ Expected lost sales

Excel: Expected lost sales $= \sigma * ($Normdist$(z,0,1,0) - z * (1 - $Normsdist$(z)))$

Expected leftover inventory $= Q -$ Expected sales

Expected profit $= [($Price $-$ Cost$) \times$ Expected sales]
$\quad - [($Cost $-$ Salvage value$) \times$ Expected leftover inventory]

In-stock probability $= F(Q)$　　　　Stockout probability $= 1 -$ In-stock probability

Excel: $z = $ Normsinv(Target in-stock probability)

Excel: In-stock probability $=$ Normsdist(z)

12.9 Further Reading

The newsvendor model is one of the most extensively studied models in operations management. It has been extended theoretically along numerous dimensions (e.g., multiple periods have been studied, the pricing decision has been included, the salvage values could depend on the quantity salvaged, the decision maker's tolerance for risk can be incorporated into the objective function, etc.)

Several textbooks provide more technical treatments of the newsvendor model than this chapter. See Nahmias (2005), Porteus (2002), or Silver, Pyke, and Peterson (1998).

For a review of the theoretical literature on the newsvendor model, with an emphasis on the pricing decision in a newsvendor setting, see Petruzzi and Dada (1999).

12.10 Practice Problems

Q12.1* **(McClure Books)** Dan McClure owns a thriving independent bookstore in artsy New Hope, Pennsylvania. He must decide how many copies to order of a new book, *Power and Self-Destruction,* an exposé on a famous politician's lurid affairs. Interest in the book will be intense at first and then fizzle quickly as attention turns to other celebrities. The book's retail price is $20 and the wholesale price is $12. The publisher will buy back the retailer's leftover copies at a full refund, but McClure Books incurs $4 in shipping and handling costs for each book returned to the publisher. Dan believes his demand forecast can be represented by a normal distribution with mean 200 and standard deviation 80.

   a. Dan will consider this book to be a blockbuster for him if it sells more than 400 units. What is the probability *Power and Self-Destruction* will be a blockbuster?

   b. Dan considers a book a "dog" if it sells less than 50 percent of his mean forecast. What is the probability this exposé is a "dog"?

   c. What is the probability demand for this book will be within 20 percent of the mean forecast?

   d. What order quantity maximizes Dan's expected profit?

   e. Dan prides himself on good customer service. In fact, his motto is "McClure's got what you want to read." How many books should Dan order if he wants to achieve a 95 percent in-stock probability?

   f. If Dan orders the quantity chosen in part e to achieve a 95 percent in-stock probability, then what is the probability that "Dan won't have what some customer wants to read" (i.e., what is the probability some customer won't be able to purchase a copy of the book)?

   g. Suppose Dan orders 300 copies of the book. What would Dan's expected profit be in this case?

Q12.2* **(EcoTable Tea)** EcoTable is a retailer of specialty organic and ecologically friendly foods. In one of their Cambridge, Massachusetts, stores, they plan to offer a gift basket of Tanzanian teas for the holiday season. They plan on placing one order and any leftover inventory will be discounted at the end of the season. Expected demand for this store is 4.5 units and demand should be Poisson distributed. The gift basket sells for $55, the purchase cost to EcoTable is $32, and leftover baskets will be sold for $20.

   a. If they purchase only 3 baskets, what is the probability that some demand will not be satisfied?

   b. If they purchase 10 baskets, what is the probability that they will have to mark down at least 3 baskets?

   c. How many baskets should EcoTable purchase to maximize its expected profit?

   d. Suppose they purchase 4 baskets. How many baskets can they expect to sell?

   e. Suppose they purchase 6 baskets. How many baskets should they expect to have to mark down at the end of the season?

(* indicates that the solution is in Appendix E)

f. Suppose EcoTable wants to minimize its inventory while satisfying all demand with at least a 90 percent probability. How many baskets should they order?

g. Suppose EcoTable orders 8 baskets. What is its expected profit?

Q12.3* **(Pony Express Creations)** Pony Express Creations Inc. (www.pony-ex.com) is a manufacturer of party hats, primarily for the Halloween season. (80 percent of their yearly sales occur over a six-week period.) One of their popular products is the Elvis wig, complete with sideburns and metallic glasses. The Elvis wig is produced in China, so Pony Express must make a single order well in advance of the upcoming season. Ryan, the owner of Pony Express, expects demand to be 25,000 and the following is his entire demand forecast:

Q	Prob($D = Q$)	F(Q)	L(Q)
5,000	0.0181	0.0181	20,000
10,000	0.0733	0.0914	15,091
15,000	0.1467	0.2381	10,548
20,000	0.1954	0.4335	6,738
25,000	0.1954	0.6289	3,906
30,000	0.1563	0.7852	2,050
35,000	0.1042	0.8894	976
40,000	0.0595	0.9489	423
45,000	0.0298	0.9787	168
50,000	0.0132	0.9919	61
55,000	0.0053	0.9972	21
60,000	0.0019	0.9991	7
65,000	0.0006	0.9997	2
70,000	0.0002	0.9999	0
75,000	0.0001	1.0000	0

Prob($D = Q$) = Probability demand D equals Q
$F(Q)$ = Probability demand is Q or lower
$L(Q)$ = Expected lost sales if Q units are ordered

The Elvis wig retails for $25, but Pony Express's wholesale price is $12. Their production cost is $6. Leftover inventory can be sold to discounters for $2.50.

a. Suppose Pony Express orders 40,000 Elvis wigs. What is the chance they have to liquidate 10,000 or more wigs with a discounter?

b. What order quantity maximizes Pony Express's expected profit?

c. If Pony Express wants to have a 90 percent in-stock probability, then how many Elvis wigs should be ordered?

d. If Pony Express orders 50,000 units, then how many wigs can they expect to have to liquidate with discounters?

e. If Pony Express insists on a 100 percent in-stock probability for its customers, then what is its expected profit?

Q12.4* **(Flextrola)** Flextrola, Inc., an electronics systems integrator, is planning to design a key component for their next-generation product with Solectrics. Flextrola will integrate the component with some software and then sell it to consumers. Given the short life cycles of such products and the long lead times quoted by Solectrics, Flextrola only has one opportunity to place an order with Solectrics prior to the beginning of its selling season. Flextrola's demand during the season is normally distributed with a mean of 1,000 and a standard deviation of 600.

(* indicates that the solution is in Appendix E)

Solectrics' production cost for the component is $52 per unit and it plans to sell the component for $72 per unit to Flextrola. Flextrola incurs essentially no cost associated with the software integration and handling of each unit. Flextrola sells these units to consumers for $121 each. Flextrola can sell unsold inventory at the end of the season in a secondary electronics market for $50 each. The existing contract specifies that once Flextrola places the order, no changes are allowed to it. Also, Solectrics does not accept any returns of unsold inventory, so Flextrola must dispose of excess inventory in the secondary market.

a. What is the probability that Flextrola's demand will be within 25 percent of its forecast?

b. What is the probability that Flextrola's demand will be more than 40 percent greater than its forecast?

c. Under this contract, how many units should Flextrola order to maximize its expected profit?

For parts d through i, assume Flextrola orders 1,200 units.

d. What are Flextrola's expected sales?

e. How many units of inventory can Flextrola expect to sell in the secondary electronics market?

f. What is Flextrola's expected gross margin percentage, which is (Revenue − Cost)/Revenue?

g. What is Flextrola's expected profit?

h. What is Solectrics' expected profit?

i. What is the probability that Flextrola has lost sales of 400 units or more?

j. A sharp manager at Flextrola noticed the demand forecast and became wary of assuming that demand is normally distributed. She plotted a histogram of demands from previous seasons for similar products and concluded that demand is better represented by the log normal distribution. Figure 12.7 plots the density function for both the log normal

FIGURE 12.7
Density Function

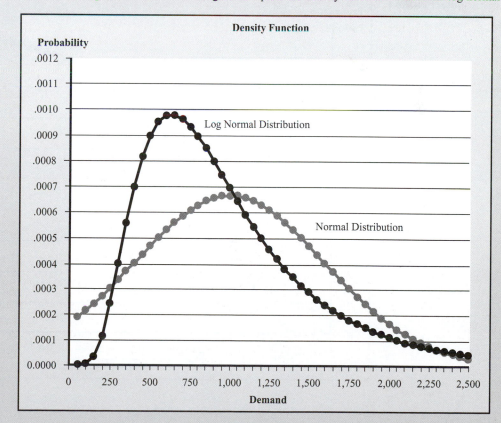

and the normal distribution, each with mean of 1,000 and standard deviation of 600. Figure 12.8 plots the distribution function for both the log normal and the normal. Using the more accurate forecast (i.e., the log normal distribution), approximately how many units should Flextrola order to maximize its expected profit?

Q12.5*   **(Fashionables)** Fashionables is a franchisee of The Limited, the well-known retailer of fashionable clothing. Prior to the winter season, The Limited offers Fashionables the choice of five different colors of a particular sweater design. The sweaters are knit overseas by hand, and because of the lead times involved, Fashionables will need to order its assortment in advance of the selling season. As per the contracting terms offered by The Limited, Fashionables also will not be able to cancel, modify, or reorder sweaters during the selling season. Demand for each color during the season is normally distributed with a mean of 500 and a standard deviation of 200. Further, you may assume that the demands for each sweater are independent of those for a different color.

The Limited offers the sweaters to Fashionables at the wholesale price of $40 per sweater and Fashionables plans to sell each sweater at the retail price of $70 per unit. The Limited delivers orders placed by Fashionables in truckloads at a cost of $2,000 per truckload. The transportation cost of $2,000 is borne by Fashionables. Assume unless otherwise specified that all the sweaters ordered by Fashionables will fit into one truckload. Also assume that all other associated costs, such as unpacking and handling, are negligible.

The Limited does not accept any returns of unsold inventory. However, Fashionables can sell all of the unsold sweaters at the end of the season at the fire-sale price of $20 each.

FIGURE 12.8
Distribution Function

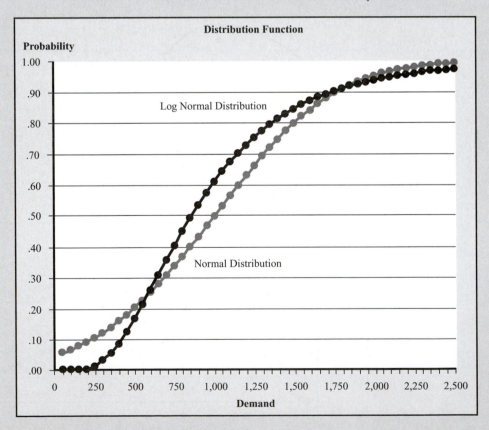

(* indicates that the solution is in Appendix E)

a. How many units of each sweater type should Fashionables order to maximize its expected profit?

b. If Fashionables wishes to ensure a 97.5 percent in-stock probability, what should its order quantity be for each type of sweater?

For parts c and d, assume Fashionables orders 725 of each sweater.

c. What is Fashionables' expected profit?

d. What is the stockout probability for each sweater?

e. Now suppose that The Limited announces that the unit of truckload capacity is 2,500 total units of sweaters. If Fashionables orders more than 2,500 units in total (actually, from 2,501 to 5,000 units in total), it will have to pay for two truckloads. What now is Fashionables' optimal order quantity for each sweater?

Q12.6** **(Teddy Bower Parkas)** Teddy Bower is an outdoor clothing and accessories chain that purchases a line of parkas at $10 each from its Asian supplier, TeddySports. Unfortunately, at the time of order placement, demand is still uncertain. Teddy Bower forecasts that its demand is normally distributed with mean of 2,100 and standard deviation of 1,200. Teddy Bower sells these parkas at $22 each. Unsold parkas have little salvage value; Teddy Bower simply gives them away to a charity.

a. What is the probability this parka turns out to be a "dog," defined as a product that sells less than half of the forecast?

b. How many parkas should Teddy Bower buy from TeddySports to maximize expected profit?

c. If Teddy Bower wishes to ensure a 98.5 percent in-stock probability, how many parkas should it order?

For parts d and e, assume Teddy Bower orders 3,000 parkas.

d. Evaluate Teddy Bower's expected profit.

e. Evaluate Teddy Bower's stockout probability

Q12.7 **(Teddy Bower Boots)** To ensure a full line of outdoor clothing and accessories, the marketing department at Teddy Bower insists that they also sell waterproof hunting boots. Unfortunately, neither Teddy Bower nor TeddySports has expertise in manufacturing those kinds of boots. Therefore, Teddy Bower contacted several Taiwanese suppliers to request quotes. Due to competition, Teddy Bower knows that it cannot sell these boots for more than $54. However, $40 per boot was the best quote from the suppliers. In addition, Teddy Bower anticipates excess inventory will need to be sold off at a 50 percent discount at the end of the season. Given the $54 price, Teddy Bower's demand forecast is for 400 boots, with a standard deviation of 300.

a. If Teddy Bower decides to include these boots in its assortment, how many boots should it order from its supplier?

b. Suppose Teddy Bower orders 380 boots. What would its expected profit be?

c. John Briggs, a buyer in the procurement department, overheard at lunch a discussion of the "boot problem." He suggested that Teddy Bower ask for a quantity discount from the supplier. After following up on his suggestion, the supplier responded that Teddy Bower could get a 10 percent discount if they were willing to order at least 800 boots. If the objective is to maximize expected profit, how many boots should it order given this new offer?

Q12.8 **(Land's End)** Geoff Gullo owns a small firm that manufactures "Gullo Sunglasses." He has the opportunity to sell a particular seasonal model to Land's End. Geoff offers Land's End two purchasing options:

• Option 1. Geoff offers to set his price at $65 and agrees to credit Land's End $53 for each unit Land's End returns to Geoff at the end of the season (because those units did not sell). Since styles change each year, there is essentially no value in the returned merchandise.

- Option 2.   Geoff offers a price of $55 for each unit, but returns are no longer accepted. In this case, Land's End throws out unsold units at the end of the season.

This season's demand for this model will be normally distributed with mean of 200 and standard deviation of 125. Land's End will sell those sunglasses for $100 each. Geoff 's production cost is $25.

a. How much would Land's End buy if they chose option 1?

b. How much would Land's End buy if they chose option 2?

c. Which option will Land's End choose?

d. Suppose Land's End chooses option 1 and orders 275 units. What is Geoff Gullo's expected profit?

Q12.9   **(CPG Bagels)** CPG Bagels starts the day with a large production run of bagels. Throughout the morning, additional bagels are produced as needed. The last bake is completed at 3 P.M. and the store closes at 8 P.M. It costs approximately $0.20 in materials and labor to make a bagel. The price of a fresh bagel is $0.60. Bagels not sold by the end of the day are sold the next day as "day old" bagels in bags of six, for $0.99 a bag. About two-thirds of the day-old bagels are sold; the remainder are just thrown away. There are many bagel flavors, but for simplicity, concentrate just on the plain bagels. The store manager predicts that demand for plain bagels from 3 P.M. until closing is normally distributed with mean of 54 and standard deviation of 21.

a. How many bagels should the store have at 3 P.M. to maximize the store's expected profit (from sales between 3 P.M. until closing)? (*Hint:* Assume day-old bagels are sold for $0.99/6 = $0.165 each; i.e., don't worry about the fact that day-old bagels are sold in bags of six.)

b. Suppose that the store manager is concerned that stockouts might cause a loss of future business. To explore this idea, the store manager feels that it is appropriate to assign a stockout cost of $5 per bagel that is demanded but not filled. (Customers frequently purchase more than one bagel at a time. This cost is per bagel demanded that is not satisfied rather than per customer that does not receive a complete order.) Given the additional stockout cost, how many bagels should the store have at 3 P.M. to maximize the store's expected profit?

c. Suppose the store manager has 101 bagels at 3 P.M. How many bagels should the store manager expect to have at the end of the day?

Q12.10** **(The Kiosk)** Weekday lunch demand for spicy black bean burritos at the Kiosk, a local snack bar, is approximately Poisson with a mean of 22. The Kiosk charges $4.00 for each burrito, which are all made before the lunch crowd arrives. Virtually all burrito customers also buy a soda that is sold for 60¢. The burritos cost the Kiosk $2.00, while sodas cost the Kiosk 5¢. Kiosk management is very sensitive about the quality of food they serve. Thus, they maintain a strict "No Old Burrito" policy, so any burrito left at the end of the day is disposed of. The distribution function of a Poisson with mean 22 is as follows:

Q	F(Q)	Q	F(Q)	Q	F(Q)	Q	F(Q)
1	0.0000	11	0.0076	21	0.4716	31	0.9735
2	0.0000	12	0.0151	22	0.5564	32	0.9831
3	0.0000	13	0.0278	23	0.6374	33	0.9895
4	0.0000	14	0.0477	24	0.7117	34	0.9936
5	0.0000	15	0.0769	25	0.7771	35	0.9962
6	0.0001	16	0.1170	26	0.8324	36	0.9978
7	0.0002	17	0.1690	27	0.8775	37	0.9988
8	0.0006	18	0.2325	28	0.9129	38	0.9993
9	0.0015	19	0.3060	29	0.9398	39	0.9996
10	0.0035	20	0.3869	30	0.9595	40	0.9998

a. Suppose burrito customers buy their snack somewhere else if the Kiosk is out of stock. How many burritos should the Kiosk make for the lunch crowd?

b. Suppose that any customer unable to purchase a burrito settles for a lunch of Pop-Tarts and a soda. Pop-Tarts sell for 75¢ and cost the Kiosk 25¢. (As Pop-Tarts and soda are easily stored, the Kiosk never runs out of these essentials.) Assuming that the Kiosk management is interested in maximizing profits, how many burritos should they prepare?

You can view a video of how problems marked with a ** are solved by going on www. cachon-terwiesch.net and follow the links under 'Solved Practice Problems'

13

Assemble-to-Order, Make-to-Order, and Quick Response with Reactive Capacity[1]

A firm facing the newsvendor problem can manage, but not avoid, the possibility of a demand–supply mismatch: order too much and inventory is left over at the end of the season, but order too little and incur the opportunity cost of lost sales. The firm finds itself in this situation because it commits to its entire supply before demand occurs. This mode of operation is often called *make-to-stock* because all items enter finished goods inventory (stock) before they are demanded. In other words, with make-to-stock, the identity of an item's eventual owner is not known when production of the item is initiated.

To reduce the demand–supply mismatches associated with make-to-stock, a firm could attempt to delay at least some production until better demand information is learned. For example, a firm could choose to begin producing an item only when it receives a firm order from a customer. This mode of operation is often called *make-to-order* or *assemble-to-order.* Dell Computer is probably the most well-known and most successful company to have implemented the assemble-to-order model.

Make-to-stock and make-to-order are two extremes in the sense that with one all production begins well before demand is received, whereas with the other production begins only after demand is known. Between any two extremes there also must be an intermediate option. Suppose the lead time to receive an order is short relative to the length of the selling season. A firm then orders some inventory before the selling season starts so that some product is on hand at the beginning of the season. After observing early season sales, the firm then submits a second order that is received well before the end of the season (due to the short lead time). In this situation, the firm should make a conservative initial order and use the second order to strategically respond to initial season sales: Slow-selling products are not replenished midseason, thereby reducing leftover inventory, while fast-selling products are replenished, thereby reducing lost sales.

The capability to place multiple orders during a selling season is an integral part of *Quick Response.* Quick Response is a set of practices designed to reduce the cost of mismatches

---

[1] The data in this chapter have been modified to protect confidentiality.

between supply and demand. It began in the apparel industry as a response to just-in-time practices in the automobile industry and has since migrated to the grocery industry under the label *Efficient Consumer Response.*

The aspect of Quick Response discussed in this chapter is the use of *reactive capacity,* that is, capacity that allows a firm to place one additional order during the season, which retailers often refer to as a "second buy." As in Chapter 12, we use O'Neill Inc. for our case analysis. Furthermore, we assume throughout this chapter that the normal distribution with mean 3,192 and standard deviation 1,181 is our demand forecast for the Hammer 3/2.

The first part of this chapter evaluates and minimizes the demand–supply mismatch cost to a make-to-stock firm, that is, a firm that has only a single ordering opportunity, as in the newsvendor model. Furthermore, we identify situations in which the cost of demand–supply mismatches is large. Those are the situations in which there is the greatest potential to benefit from Quick Response with reactive capacity or make-to-order production. The second part of this chapter discusses make-to-order relative to make-to-stock. The third part studies reactive capacity: How should we choose an initial order quantity when some reactive capacity is available? And, as with the newsvendor model, how do we evaluate several performance measures? The chapter concludes with a summary and managerial implications.

13.1 Evaluating and Minimizing the Newsvendor's Demand–Supply Mismatch Cost

In this section, the costs associated in the newsvendor model with demand–supply mismatches are identified, then two approaches are outlined for evaluating the expected demand–supply mismatch cost, and finally we show how to minimize those costs. For ease of exposition, we use the shorthand term *mismatch cost* to refer to the "expected demand–supply mismatch cost."

In the newsvendor model, the mismatch cost is divided into two components: the cost of ordering too much and the cost of ordering too little. Ordering too much means there is leftover inventory at the end of the season. Ordering too little means there are lost sales. The cost for each unit of leftover inventory is the overage cost, which we label C_o. The cost for each lost sale is the underage cost, which we label C_u. (See Chapter 12 for the original discussion of these costs.) Therefore, the mismatch cost in the newsvendor model is the sum of the expected overage cost and the expected underage cost:

$$\text{Mismatch cost} = (C_o \times \text{Expected leftover inventory}) + (C_u \times \text{Expected lost sales}) \tag{13.1}$$

Notice that the mismatch cost includes both a tangible cost (leftover inventory) and an intangible opportunity cost (lost sales). The former has a direct impact on the profit and loss statement, but the latter does not. Nevertheless, the opportunity cost of lost sales should not be ignored.

Not only does equation (13.1) provide us with the definition of the mismatch cost, it also provides us with our first method for evaluating the mismatch cost because we already know how to evaluate the expected leftover inventory and the expected lost sales (from Chapter 12). Let's illustrate this method with O'Neill's Hammer 3/2 wetsuit. The Hammer has a selling price of $190 and a purchase cost from the TEC Group of $110. Therefore, the underage cost is $190 − $110 = $80 per lost sale. Leftover inventory is sold at $90, so the overage cost is $110 − $90 = $20 per wetsuit left at the end of the season. The expected profit-maximizing order quantity is 4,196 units. Using the techniques

TABLE 13.1
Summary of Performance Measures for O'Neill's Hammer 3/2 Wetsuit When the Expected Profit-Maximizing Quantity Is Ordered and the Demand Forecast Is Normally Distributed with Mean 3,192 and Standard Deviation 1,181

Order quantity, Q	= 4,196 units
Expected demand, μ	= 3,192 units
Standard deviation of demand, σ	= 1,181
Expected lost sales	= 130 units
Expected sales	= 3,062 units
Expected leftover inventory	= 1,134 units
Expected revenue	= $683,840
Expected profit	= $222,280

Expected lost sales = $1,181 \times L(0.85) = 1,181 \times 0.11 = 130$
Expected sales = $3,192 - 130 = 3,062$
Expected leftover inventory = $4,196 - 3,062 = 1,134$
Expected revenue = Price $\times$ Expected sales + Salvage value $\times$ Expected leftover inventory
$= \$190 \times 3,062 + \$90 \times 1,134 = \$683,840$
Expected profit = $(\$190 - \$110) \times 3,062 - (\$110 - \$90) \times 1,134 = \$222,280$

described in Chapter 12, for that order quantity we can evaluate several performance measures, summarized in Table 13.1. Therefore, the mismatch cost for the Hammer 3/2, despite ordering the expected profit-maximizing quantity, is

$$(\$20 \times 1,134) + (\$80 \times 130) = \$33,080$$

Now let's consider a second approach for evaluating the mismatch cost. Imagine O'Neill had the opportunity to purchase a magic crystal ball. Even before O'Neill needs to submit its order to TEC, this crystal ball reveals to O'Neill the exact demand for the entire season. O'Neill would obviously order from TEC the demand quantity observed with this crystal ball. As a result, O'Neill would be in the pleasant situation of avoiding all mismatch costs (there would be no excess inventory and no lost sales) while still providing immediate product availability to its customers. In fact, the only function of the crystal ball is to eliminate all mismatch costs: for example, the crystal ball does not change demand, increase the selling price, or decrease the production cost. Thus, the difference in O'Neill's expected profit with the crystal ball and without it must equal the mismatch cost: The crystal ball increases profit by eliminating mismatch costs, so the profit increase must equal the mismatch cost. Therefore, we can evaluate the mismatch cost by first evaluating the newsvendor's expected profit, then evaluating the expected profit with the crystal ball, and finally taking the difference between those two figures.

We already know how to evaluate the newsvendor's expected profit (again, see Chapter 12). So let's illustrate how to evaluate the expected profit with the crystal ball. If O'Neill gets to observe demand before deciding how much to order from TEC, then there will not be any leftover inventory at the end of the season. Even better, O'Neill will not stock out, so every unit of demand turns into an actual sale. Hence, O'Neill's expected sales with the crystal ball equal expected demand, which is μ. We already know that O'Neill's profit per sale is the gross margin, the retail price minus the production cost, Price − Cost. Therefore O'Neill's expected profit with this crystal ball is expected demand times the profit per unit of demand, which is (Price − Cost) $\times \mu$. In fact, O'Neill can never earn a higher expected profit than it does with the crystal ball: There is nothing better than having no leftover inventory and earning the full margin on every unit of potential demand. Hence, let's call that profit the *maximum profit:*

$$\text{Maximum profit} = (\text{Price} - \text{Cost}) \times \mu$$

O'Neill's maximum profit with the Hammer 3/2 is $80 \times 3,192 = $255,360. We already know that the newsvendor expected profit is $222,280. So the difference between the maximum profit (i.e., crystal ball profit) and the newsvendor expected profit is O'Neill's mismatch costs. That figure is $255,360 − $222,280 = $33,080, which matches our calculation with our first method (as it should). To summarize, our second method for evaluating the mismatch cost uses the following equation:

$$\text{Mismatch cost} = \text{Maximum profit} - \text{Expected profit}$$

Incidentally, you can also think of the mismatch cost as the most O'Neill should be willing to pay to purchase the crystal ball; that is, it is the value of perfect demand information.

The second method for calculating the mismatch cost emphasizes that there exists an easily evaluated maximum profit. We might not be able to evaluate expected profit precisely if there is some reactive capacity available to the firm. Nevertheless, we do know that no matter what type of reactive capacity the firm has, that reactive capacity cannot be as good as the crystal ball we just described. Therefore, the expected profit with any form of reactive capacity must be more than the newsvendor's expected profit but less than the maximum profit.

You now may be wondering about how to minimize the mismatch cost and whether that is any different than maximizing the newsvendor's expected profit. The short answer is that these are effectively the same objective, that is, the quantity that maximizes profit also minimizes mismatch costs. One way to see this is to look at the equation above: If expected profit is maximized and the maximum profit does not depend on the order quantity, then the difference between them, which is the mismatch cost, must be minimized.

Now that we know how to evaluate and minimize the mismatch cost, we need to get a sense of its significance. In other words, is $33,080 a big problem or a little problem? To answer that question, we need to compare it with something else. The maximum profit is one reference point: the demand–supply mismatch cost as a percentage of the maximum profit is $33,080/$255,360 = 13 percent. You may prefer expected sales as a point of comparison: the demand–supply mismatch cost per unit of expected sales is $33,080/3,062 = $10.8. Alternatively, we can make the comparison with expected revenue, $683,840, or expected profit, $222,280: the demand–supply mismatch cost is approximately 4.8 percent of total revenue ($33,080/$683,840) and 14.9 percent of expected profit ($33,080/$222,280). Companies in the sports apparel industry generally have net profit in the range of 2 to 5 percent of revenue. Therefore, eliminating the mismatch cost from the Hammer 3/2 could potentially double O'Neill's net profit! That is an intriguing possibility.

13.2 When Is the Mismatch Cost High?

No matter which comparison you prefer, the mismatch cost for O'Neill is significant, even if the expected profit-maximizing quantity is ordered. But it is even better to know what causes a large demand–supply mismatch. To answer that question, let's first choose our point of comparison for the mismatch cost. Of the ones discussed at the end of the previous section, only the maximum profit does not depend on the order quantity chosen: unit sales, revenue, and profit all clearly depend on Q. In addition, the maximum profit is representative of the potential for the product: we cannot do better than earn the maximum profit. Therefore, let's evaluate the mismatch cost as a percentage of the maximum profit.

We next need to make an assumption about how much is ordered before the selling season, that is, clearly the mismatch cost depends on the order quantity Q. Let's adopt the natural assumption that the expected profit-maximizing quantity is ordered, which, as we discussed in the previous section, also happens to minimize the newsvendor's mismatch cost.

If we take the equations for expected lost sales and expected leftover inventory from Chapter 12, plug them into our first mismatch cost equation (13.1), and then do several algebraic manipulations, we arrive at the following observations:

- The expected demand–supply mismatch cost becomes larger as demand variability increases, where demand variability is measured with the coefficient of variation, σ/μ.

- The expected demand–supply mismatch cost becomes larger as the critical ratio, $C_u/(C_o + C_u)$, becomes smaller.

(If you want to see the actual equations and how they are derived, see Appendix D.)

It is intuitive that the mismatch cost should increase as demand variability increases—it is simply harder to get demand to match supply when demand is less predicable. The key insight is how to measure demand variability. The *coefficient of variation* is the correct measure. You may recall in Chapter 8 we discussed the coefficient of variation with respect to the variability of the processing time (CV_p) or the interarrival time to a queue (CV_a). This coefficient of variation, σ/μ, is conceptually identical to those coefficients of variation: it is the ratio of the standard deviation of a random variable (in this case demand) to its mean.

It is worthwhile to illustrate why the coefficient of variation is the appropriate measure of variability in this setting. Suppose you are informed that the standard deviation of demand for an item is 800. Does that tell you enough information to assess the variability of demand? For example, does it allow you to evaluate the probability actual demand will be less than 75 percent of your forecast? In fact, it does not. Consider two cases, in the first the forecast is for 1,000 units and in the second the forecast is for 10,000 units. Demand is less than 75 percent of the 1,000-unit forecast if demand is less than 750 units. What is the probability that occurs? First, normalize the value 750:

$$Z = \frac{Q - \mu}{\sigma} = \frac{750 - 1,000}{800} = -0.31$$

Now use the Standard Normal Distribution Function Table to find the probability demand is less than 750: $\Phi(-0.31) = 0.3783$. With the forecast of 10,000, the comparable event has demand that is less than 7,500 units. Repeating the same process yields $z = (7,500 - 10,000)/800 = -3.1$ and $\Phi(-3.1) = 0.0009$. Therefore, with a standard deviation of 800, there is about a 38 percent chance demand is less than 75 percent of the first forecast but much less than a 1 percent chance demand is less than 75 percent of the second forecast. In other words, the standard deviation alone does not capture how much variability there is in demand. Notice that the coefficient of variation with the first product is 0.8 (800/1,000), whereas it is much lower with the second product, 0.08 (800/10,000).

For the Hammer 3/2, the coefficient of variation is 1,181/3,192 = 0.37. While there is no generally accepted standard for what is a "low," "medium," or "high" coefficient of variation, we offer the following guideline: Demand variability is rather low if the coefficient of variation is less than 0.25, medium if it is in the range 0.25 to 0.75, and high with anything above 0.75. A coefficient of variation above 1.5 is extremely high, and anything above 3 would imply that the demand forecast is essentially meaningless.

Table 13.2 provides data to allow you to judge for yourself what is a "low," "medium," and "high" coefficient of variation.

TABLE 13.2
Forecast Accuracy Relative to the Coefficient of Variation When Demand Is Normally Distributed

Coefficient of Variation	Probability Demand Is Less Than 75% of the Forecast	Probability Demand Is within 25% of the Forecast
0.10	0.6%	98.8%
0.25	15.9	68.3
0.50	30.9	38.3
0.75	36.9	26.1
1.00	40.1	19.7
1.50	43.4	13.2
2.00	45.0	9.9
3.00	46.7	6.6

Recall from Chapters 8 and 9 that the coefficient of variation with an exponential distribution is always one. Therefore, if two processes have exponential distributions, they always have the same amount of variability. The same is not true with the normal distribution because with the normal distribution the standard deviation is adjustable relative to the mean.

Our second observation above relates mismatch costs to the critical ratio. In particular, products with low critical ratios and high demand variability have high mismatch costs and products with high critical ratios and low demand variability have low mismatch costs. Table 13.3 displays data on the mismatch cost for various coefficients of variation and critical ratios.

As we have already mentioned, it is intuitive that the mismatch cost should increase as demand variability increases. The intuition with respect to the critical ratio takes some more thought. A very high critical ratio means there is a large profit margin relative to the loss on each unit of excess inventory. Greeting cards are good examples of products that might have very large critical ratios: the gross margin on each greeting card is large while the production cost is low. With a very large critical ratio, the optimal order quantity is quite large, so there are very few lost sales. There is also a substantial amount of leftover inventory, but the cost of each unit left over in inventory is not large at all, so the total cost of leftover inventory is relatively small. Therefore, the total mismatch cost is small. Now consider a product with a low critical ratio, that is, the per-unit cost of excess inventory is much higher than the cost of each lost sale. Perishable items often fall into this category as well as items that face obsolescence. Given that excess inventory is expensive, the optimal order quantity is quite low, possibly lower than expected demand. As a result, excess inventory is not a problem, but lost sales are a big problem, resulting in a high mismatch cost.

TABLE 13.3
The Mismatch Cost (as a Percentage of the Maximum Profit) When Demand Is Normally Distributed and the Newsvendor Expected Profit-Maximizing Quantity Is Ordered

Coefficient of Variation	Critical Ratio					
	0.4	0.5	0.6	0.7	0.8	0.9
0.10	10%	8%	6%	5%	3%	2%
0.25	24%	20%	16%	12%	9%	5%
0.40	39%	32%	26%	20%	14%	8%
0.55	53%	44%	35%	27%	19%	11%
0.70	68%	56%	45%	35%	24%	14%
0.85	82%	68%	55%	42%	30%	17%
1.00	97%	80%	64%	50%	35%	19%

13.3   Reducing Mismatch Costs with Make-to-Order

When supply is chosen before demand is observed (make-to-stock), there invariably is either too much or too little supply. A purely hypothetical solution to the problem is to find a crystal ball that reveals demand before it occurs. A more realistic solution is to initiate production of each unit only after demand is observed for that unit, which is often called make-to-order or assemble-to-order. This section discusses the pros and cons of make-to-order with respect to its ability to reduce mismatch costs.

In theory, make-to-order can eliminate the entire mismatch cost associated with make-to-stock (i.e., newsvendor). With make-to-order, there is no leftover inventory because production only begins after a firm order is received from a customer. Thus, make-to-order saves on expensive markdown and disposal expenses. Furthermore, there are no lost sales with make-to-order because each customer order is eventually produced. Therefore, products with a high mismatch cost (low critical ratios, high demand variability) would benefit considerably from a switch to make-to-order from make-to-stock.

But there are several reasons to be wary of make-to-order. For one, even with make-to-order, there generally is a need to carry component inventory. Although components may be less risky than finished goods, there still is a chance of having too many or too few of them. Next, make-to-order is never able to satisfy customer demands immediately; that is, customers must wait to have their order filled. If the wait is short, then demand with make-to-order can be nearly as high as with make-to-stock. But there is also some threshold beyond which customers do not wait. That threshold level depends on the product: customers are generally less willing to wait for diapers than they are for custom sofas.

It is helpful to think of queuing theory (Chapters 8 and 9) to understand what determines the waiting time with make-to-order. No matter the number of servers, a key characteristic of a queuing system is that customer service begins only after a customer arrives to the system, just as production does not begin with make-to-order until a customer commits to an order. Another important feature of a queuing system is that customers must wait to be processed if all servers are busy, just as a customer must wait with make-to-order if the production process is working on the backlog of orders from previous customers.

To provide a reference point for this discussion, suppose O'Neill establishes a make-to-order assembly line for wetsuits. O'Neill could keep in inventory the necessary raw materials to fabricate wetsuits in a wide array of colors, styles, and quality levels. Wetsuits would then be produced as orders are received from customers. The assembly line has a maximum production rate, which would correspond to the service rate in a queue. Given that demand is random, the interarrival times between customer orders also would be random, just as in a queuing system.

A key insight from queuing is that a customer's expected waiting time depends nonlinearly (a curve, not a straight line) on the system's utilization (the ratio of the flow rate to capacity): As the utilization approaches 100 percent, the waiting time approaches infinity. (See Figure 8.21.) As a result, if O'Neill wishes to have a reasonably short waiting time for customers, then O'Neill must be willing to operate with less than 100 percent utilization, maybe even considerably less than 100 percent. Less than 100 percent utilization implies idle capacity; for example, if the utilization is 90 percent, then 10 percent of the time the assembly line is idle. Therefore, even with make-to-order production, O'Neill experiences demand–supply mismatch costs. Those costs are divided into two types: idle capacity and lost sales from customers who are unwilling to wait to receive their product. When comparing make-to-stock with make-to-order, you could say that make-to-order replaces the cost of leftover inventory with the cost of idle capacity. Whether or not make-to-order is preferable depends on the relative importance of those two costs.

While a customer's expected waiting time may be significant, customers are ultimately concerned with their total waiting time, which includes the processing time. With make-to-order, the processing time has two components: the time in production and the time from production to actual delivery. Hence, successful implementation of make-to-order generally requires fast and easy assembly of the final product. Next, keeping the delivery time to an acceptable level either requires paying for fast shipping (e.g., air shipments) or moving production close to customers (to reduce the distance the product needs to travel). Fast shipping increases the cost of *every* unit produced, and local production (e.g., North America instead of Asia) may increase labor costs. See Chapter 19 for more discussion.

Although make-to-order is not ideal for all products, Dell discovered that make-to-order is particularly well suited for personal computers for several reasons: Inventory is very expensive to hold because of obsolescence and falling component prices; labor is a small portion of the cost of a PC, in part because the modular design of PCs allows for fast and easy assembly; customers are primarily concerned with price and customization and less concerned with how long they must wait for delivery (i.e., they are patient) and unique design features (i.e., it is hard to differentiate one PC from another with respect to design); there is a large pool of educated customers who are willing to purchase without physically seeing the product (i.e., the phone/Internet channels work); and the cost to transport a PC is reasonable (relative to its total value). The same logic suggests that make-to-order is more challenging in the automobile industry. For example, assembling a vehicle is challenging, customization is less important to consumers, consumers do not like to wait to receive their new vehicle (at least in the United States), and moving vehicles around is costly (relative to their value). Indeed, Toyota once announced that it planned to produce a custom-ordered vehicle in only five days (Simison 1999). However, the company quietly backed away from the project.

As already mentioned, make-to-order is not ideal for all products. Koss Corp., a headphone maker, is an example of a company that discovered that make-to-order is not always a magic bullet (Ramstad 1999). The company experimented with make-to-order and discovered it was unable to provide timely deliveries to its customers (retailers) during its peak season. In other words, demand was variable, but Koss's capacity was not sufficiently flexible. Because it began to lose business due to its slow response time, Koss switched back to make-to-stock so that it would build up inventory before its peak demand period. For Koss, holding inventory was cheaper than losing sales to impatient customers. To summarize, make-to-order eliminates some of the demand–supply mismatches associated with make-to-stock, but make-to-order has its own demand–supply mismatch issues. For example, make-to-order eliminates leftover inventory but it still carries component inventory. More importantly, to ensure acceptable customer waiting times, make-to-order requires some idle capacity, thereby potentially increasing labor and delivery costs.

13.4 Quick Response with Reactive Capacity

O'Neill may very well conclude that make-to-order production is not viable either in Asia (due to added shipping expenses) or in North America (due to added labor costs). If pure make-to-order is out of the question, then O'Neill should consider some intermediate solution between make-to-stock (the newsvendor) and make-to-order (a queue). With the newsvendor model, O'Neill commits to its entire supply before *any* demand occurs; whereas with make-to-order, O'Neill commits to supply only after *all* demand occurs. The intermediate solution is to commit to some supply before demand but then maintain the option to produce additional supply after some demand is observed. The capacity associated with that later supply is called *reactive capacity* because it allows O'Neill to react to the demand information it learns before committing to the second order. The ability to make multiple replenishments (even if just one replenishment) is a central goal in Quick Response.

Suppose O'Neill approaches TEC with the request that TEC reduce its lead time. O'Neill's motivation behind this request is to try to create the opportunity for a replenishment during the selling season. Recall that the Spring season spans six months, starting in February and ending in July. (See Figure 12.2.) It has been O'Neill's experience that a hot product in the first two months of the season (i.e., a product selling above forecast) almost always turns out to be a hot product in the rest of the season. As a result, O'Neill could surely benefit from the opportunity to replenish the hot products midseason. For example, suppose TEC offered a one-month lead time for a midseason order. Then O'Neill could submit to TEC a second order at the end of the second month (March) and receive that replenishment before the end of the third month, thereby allowing that inventory to serve demand in the second half of the season. Figure 13.1 provides a time line in this new situation.

While it is clear that O'Neill could benefit from the second order, offering a second order with a one-month lead time can be costly to TEC. For example, TEC might need to reserve some capacity to respond to O'Neill's order. If O'Neill's second order is not as large as TEC anticipated, then some of that reserved capacity might be lost. Or O'Neill's order might be larger than anticipated, forcing TEC to scramble for extra capacity, at TEC's expense. In addition, the one-month lead time may force the use of faster shipping, which again could increase costs. The issue is whether the cost increases associated with the second order justify the mismatch cost savings for O'Neill. To address this issue, let's suppose that TEC agrees to satisfy O'Neill's second order but insists on a 20 percent premium for those units to cover TEC's anticipated additional expenses. Given this new opportunity, how should O'Neill adjust its initial order quantity and how much are mismatch costs reduced?

Choosing order quantities with two ordering opportunities is significantly more complex than choosing a single order quantity (i.e., the newsvendor problem). For instance, in addition to our forecast for the entire season's demand, now we need to worry about developing a forecast for demand in the second half of the season given what we observe in the first two months of the season. Furthermore, we do not know what will be our initial sales when we submit our first order, so that order must anticipate all possible outcomes for initial sales and then the appropriate response in the second order for all of those outcomes. In addition, we may stock out within the first half of the season if our first order is not large enough.

FIGURE 13.1
Time Line of Events for O'Neill's Hammer 3/2 Wetsuit with Unlimited, but Expensive, Reactive Capacity

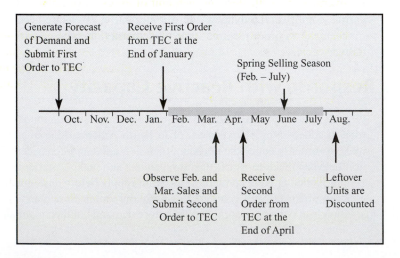

Finally, even after observing initial sales, some uncertainty remains regarding demand in the second half of the season.

Even though we now face a complex problem, we should not let the complexity overwhelm us. A good strategy when faced with a complex problem is to make it less complex, that is, make some simplifying assumptions that allow for analytical tractability while retaining the key qualitative features of the complex problem. With that strategy in mind, let's assume (1) we do not run out of inventory before the second order arrives and (2) after we observe initial sales we are able to perfectly predict sales in the remaining portion of the season. Assumption 1 is not bad as long as the first order is reasonably large, that is, large enough to cover demand in the first half of the season with a high probability. Assumption 2 is not bad if initial sales are a very good predictor of subsequent sales, which has been empirically observed in many industries.

Our simplifying assumptions are enough to allow us to evaluate the optimal initial order quantity and then to evaluate expected profit. Let's again consider O'Neill's initial order for the Hammer 3/2. It turns out that O'Neill still faces the "too much–too little" problem associated with the newsvendor problem even though O'Neill has the opportunity to make a second order. To explain, note that if the initial order quantity is too large, then there will be leftover inventory at the end of the season. The second order does not help at all with the risk of excess inventory, so the "too much" problem remains.

We also still face the "too little" issue with our initial order, but it takes a different form than in our original newsvendor problem. Recall, with the original newsvendor problem, ordering too little leads to lost sales. But the second order prevents lost sales: After we observe initial sales, we are able to predict total demand for the remainder of the season. If that total demand exceeds our initial order, we merely choose a second order quantity to ensure that all demand is satisfied. This works because of our simplifying assumptions: Lost sales do not occur before the second order arrives, there is no quantity limit on the second order, and initial sales allow us to predict total demand for the season.

Although the second order opportunity eliminates lost sales, it does not mean we should not bother with an initial order. Remember that units ordered during the season are more expensive than units ordered before the season. Therefore, the penalty for ordering too little in the first order is that we may be required to purchase additional units in the second order at a higher cost.

Given that the initial order still faces the "too little–too much" problem, we can actually use the newsvendor model to find the order quantity that maximizes expected profit. The overage cost, C_o, per unit of excess inventory is the same as in the original model; that is, the overage cost is the loss on each unit of excess inventory. Recall that for the Hammer 3/2 Cost = 110 and Salvage value = 90. So $C_o = 20$.

The underage cost, C_u, per unit of demand that exceeds our initial order quantity is the additional premium we must pay to TEC for units in the second order. That premium is 20 percent, which is 20% × 110 = 22. In other words, if demand exceeds our initial order quantity, then the penalty for ordering too little is the extra amount we must pay TEC for each of those units (i.e., we could have avoided that premium by increasing the initial order). Even though we must pay this premium to TEC, we are still better off having the second ordering opportunity: Paying TEC an extra $22 for each unit of demand that exceeds our initial order quantity is better than losing the $80 margin on each of those units if we did not have the second order. So $C_u = 22$.

We are now ready to calculate our optimal initial order quantity. (See Exhibit 12.3 for an outline of this process.) First, evaluate the critical ratio:

$$\frac{C_u}{C_o + C_u} = \frac{22}{20 + 22} = 0.5238$$

Next find the z value in the Standard Normal Distribution Function Table that corresponds to the critical ratio 0.5238: $\Phi(0.05) = 0.5199$ and $\Phi(0.06) = 0.5239$, so let's choose the higher z value, $z = 0.06$. Now convert the z value into an order quantity for the actual demand distribution with $\mu = 3,192$ and $\sigma = 1,181$:

$$Q = \mu + z \times \sigma = 3,192 + 0.06 \times 1,181 = 3,263$$

Therefore, O'Neill should order 3,263 Hammer 3/2s in the first order to maximize expected profit when a second order is possible. Notice that O'Neill should still order a considerable amount in its initial order so as to avoid paying TEC the 20 percent premium on too many units. However, O'Neill's initial order of 3,263 units is considerably less than its optimal order of 4,196 units when the second order is not possible.

Even though O'Neill must pay a premium with the second order, O'Neill's expected profit should increase by this opportunity. (The second order does not prevent O'Neill from ordering 4,196 units in the initial order, so O'Neill cannot be worse off.) Let's evaluate what that expected profit is for any initial order quantity Q. Our maximum profit has not changed. The best we can do is earn the maximum gross margin on every unit of demand,

$$\text{Maximum profit} = (\text{Price} - \text{Cost}) \times \mu = (190 - 110) \times 3,192 = 255,360$$

The expected profit is the maximum profit minus the mismatch costs:

$$\text{Expected profit} = \text{Maximum profit} - (C_o \times \text{Expected leftover inventory})$$
$$- (C_u \times \text{Expected second order quantity})$$

The first mismatch cost is the cost of leftover inventory and the second is the additional premium that O'Neill must pay TEC for all of the units ordered in the second order. We already know how to evaluate expected leftover inventory for any initial order quantity. (See Exhibit 12.5 for a summary.) We now need to figure out the expected second order quantity.

If we order Q units in the first order, then we make a second order only if demand exceeds Q. In fact, our second order equals the difference between demand and Q, which would have been our lost sales if we did not have a second order. This is also known as the loss function. Therefore,

$$\text{Expected second order quantity} = \text{Newsvendor's expected lost sales}$$

We already know how to evaluate the newsvendor's expected lost sales. (See Exhibit 12.4 for a summary.) First look up $L(z)$ in the Standard Normal Loss Function Table for the z value that corresponds to our order quantity, $z = 0.06$. We find in that table $L(0.06) = 0.3697$. Next, finish the calculation:

$$\text{Expected lost sales} = \sigma \times L(z) = 1,181 \times 0.3697 = 437$$

Recall that

$$\text{Expected sales} = \mu - \text{Expected lost sales} = 3,192 - 437 = 2,755$$

where expected sales is the quantity the newsvendor would sell with an order quantity of 3,263. We want to evaluate expected sales for the newsvendor so that we can evaluate the last piece we need:

$$\text{Expected leftover inventory} = Q - \text{Expected sales} = 3,263 - 2,755 = 508$$

We are now ready to evaluate expected profit for the Hammer 3/2 if there is a second order:

$$\text{Expected profit} = \text{Maximum profit} - (C_o \times \text{Expected leftover inventory})$$
$$- (C_u \times \text{Expected second order quantity})$$
$$= \$255,360 - (\$20 \times 508) - (\$22 \times 437)$$
$$= \$235,586$$

Recall that O'Neill's expected profit with just one ordering opportunity is $222,280. Therefore, the second order increases profit by ($235,586 − $222,280)/$222,280 = 6.0 percent even though TEC charges a 20 percent premium for units in the second order. We also can think in terms of how much the second order reduces the mismatch cost. Recall that the mismatch cost with only one order is $33,080. Now the mismatch cost is $255,360 − $235,586 = $19,744, which is a 40 percent reduction in the mismatch cost (1 − $19,774/$33,080). In addition, O'Neill's in-stock probability increases from about 80 percent to essentially 100 percent and the number of leftover units at the end of the season that require markdowns to sell is cut in half (from 1,134 to 508). Therefore, even though reactive capacity in the form of a midseason replenishment does not eliminate all mismatch costs, it provides a feasible strategy for significantly reducing mismatch costs.

13.5 Summary

With the newsvendor's make-to-stock system, the firm commits to its entire supply before any updated demand information is learned. As a result, there are demand–supply mismatch costs that manifest themselves in the form of leftover inventory or lost sales. This chapter identifies situations in which the mismatch cost is high and considers several improvements to the newsvendor situation to reduce those mismatch costs.

Mismatch costs are high (as a percentage of a product's maximum profit) when a product has a low critical ratio and/or a high coefficient of variation. A low critical ratio implies that the cost of leftover inventory is high relative to the cost of a lost sale. Perishable products or products that face obsolescence generally have low critical ratios. The coefficient of variation is the ratio of the standard deviation of demand to expected demand. It is high for products that are hard to forecast. Examples include new products, fashionable products, and specialty products with small markets. The important lesson here is that actions that lower the critical ratio or increase the coefficient of variation also increase demand–supply mismatch costs.

Make-to-order is an extreme solution to the newsvendor situation. With make-to-order, the firm begins producing an item only after the firm has an order from a customer. In other words, production begins only when the ultimate owner of an item becomes known. A key advantage with make-to-order is that leftover inventory is eliminated. However, a make-to-order system is not immune to the problems of demand–supply mismatches because it behaves like a queuing system. As a result, customers must wait to be satisfied and the length of their waiting time is sensitive to the amount of idle capacity.

The intermediate solution between make-to-order and make-to-stock has the firm commit to some production before any demand information is learned, but the firm also has the capability to react to early demand information via a second order, which is called reactive capacity. Reactive capacity can substantially reduce (but not eliminate) the newsvendor's mismatch cost. Still, this approach may be attractive because it does not suffer from all of the challenges faced by make-to-order.

Table 13.4 provides a summary of the key notation and equations presented in this chapter.

TABLE 13.4
A Summary of the Key Notation and Equations in Chapter 13

Q = Order quantity
C_u = Underage cost C_o = Overage cost
μ = Expected demand σ = Standard deviation of demand

Mismatch cost = (C_o × Expected leftover inventory) + (C_u × Expected lost sales)
          = Maximum profit − Expected profit

Maximum profit = (Price − Cost) × μ

Coefficient of variation = Standard deviation/Expected demand

13.6 Further Reading

More responsive, more flexible, more reactive operations have been the goal over the last 20 years in most industries, in large part due to the success of Dell Inc. in the personal computer business. For an insightful review of Dell's strategy, see Magretta (1998). See McWilliams and White (1999) for an interview with Michael Dell on his views on how the auto industry should change with respect to its sales and production strategy.

For a comprehensive treatment of Quick Response in the apparel industry, see Abernathy, Dunlop, Hammond, and Weil (1999), Vitzthum (1998) describes how Zara, a Spanish fashion retailer, is able to produce "fashion on demand."

Fisher (1997) discusses the pros and cons of flexible supply chains and Zipkin (2001) does the same for mass customization. Karmarkar (1989) discusses the pros and cons of push versus pull production systems.

See Fisher and Raman (1996) or Fisher, Rajaram, and Raman (2001) for technical algorithms to optimize order quantities when early sales information and reactive capacity are available.

13.7 Practice Problems

Q13.1* **(Teddy Bower)** Teddy Bower sources a parka from an Asian supplier for $10 each and sells them to customers for $22 each. Leftover parkas at the end of the season have no salvage value. (Recall Q12.6.) The demand forecast is normally distributed with mean 2,100 and standard deviation 1,200. Now suppose Teddy Bower found a reliable vendor in the United States that can produce parkas very quickly but at a higher price than Teddy Bower's Asian supplier. Hence, in addition to parkas from Asia, Teddy Bower can buy an unlimited quantity of additional parkas from this American vendor at $15 each after demand is known.

   a. Suppose Teddy Bower orders 1,500 parkas from the Asian supplier. What is the probability that Teddy Bower will order from the American supplier once demand is known?

   b. Again assume that Teddy Bower orders 1,500 parkas from the Asian supplier. What is the American supplier's expected demand; that is, how many parkas should the American supplier expect that Teddy Bower will order?

   c. Given the opportunity to order from the American supplier at $15 per parka, what order quantity from its Asian supplier now maximizes Teddy Bower's expected profit?

   d. Given the order quantity evaluated in part c, what is Teddy Bower's expected profit?

   e. If Teddy Bower didn't order any parkas from the Asian supplier, then what would Teddy Bower's expected profit be?

Q13.2* **(Flextrola)** Flextrola, Inc., an electronics system integrator, is developing a new product. As mentioned in Q11.4, Solectrics can produce a key component for this product. Solectrics sells this component to Flextrola for $72 per unit and Flextrola must submit its order well in advance of the selling season. Flextrola's demand forecast is a normal distribution with mean of 1,000 and standard deviation of 600. Flextrola sells each unit, after integrating some software, for $131. Leftover units at the end of the season are sold for $50.

(* indicates that the solution is at the end of the book)

Xandova Electronics (XE for short) approached Flextrola with the possibility of also supplying Flextrola with this component. XE's main value proposition is that they offer 100 percent in-stock and one-day delivery on all of Flextrola's orders, no matter when the orders are submitted. Flextrola promises its customers a one-week lead time, so the one-day lead time from XE would allow Flextrola to operate with make-to-order production. (The software integration that Flextrola performs can be done within one day.) XE's price is $83.50 per unit.

a. Suppose Flextrola were to procure exclusively from XE. What would be Flextrola's expected profit?

b. Suppose Flextrola plans to procure from both Solectrics and XE; that is, Flextrola will order some amount from Solectrics before the season and then use XE during the selling season to fill demands that exceed that order quantity. How many units should Flextrola order from Solectrics to maximize expected profit?

c. Concerned about the potential loss of business, Solectrics is willing to renegotiate their offer. Solectrics now offers Flextrola an "options contract": Before the season starts, Flextrola purchases Q options and pays Solectrics $25 per option. During the selling season, Flextrola can exercise up to the Q purchased options with a one-day lead time—that is, Solectrics delivers on each exercised option within one day—and the exercise price is $50 per unit. If Flextrola wishes additional units beyond the options purchased, Solectrics will deliver units at XE's price, $83.50. For example, suppose Flextrola purchases 1,500 options but then needs 1,600 units. Flextrola exercises the 1,500 options at $50 each and then orders an additional 100 units at $83.50 each. How many options should Flextrola purchase from Solectrics?

d. Continuing with part c, given the number of options purchased, what is Flextrola's expected profit?

Q13.3* **(Wildcat Cellular)** Marisol is new to town and is in the market for cellular phone service. She has settled on Wildcat Cellular, which will give her a free phone if she signs a one-year contract. Wildcat offers several calling plans. One plan that she is considering is called "Pick Your Minutes." Under this plan, she would specify a quantity of minutes, say x, per month that she would buy at 5¢ per minute. Thus, her upfront cost would be $0.05x$. If her usage is less than this quantity x in a given month, she loses the minutes. If her usage in a month exceeds this quantity x, she would have to pay 40¢ for each extra minute (that is, each minute used beyond x). For example, if she contracts for $x = 120$ minutes per month and her actual usage is 40 minutes, her total bill is $120 \times 0.05 = \$6.00$. However, if actual usage is 130 minutes, her total bill would be $\$120 \times 0.05 + (130 - 120) \times 0.40 = \$10.00$. The same rates apply whether the call is local or long distance. Once she signs the contract, she cannot change the number of minutes specified for a year. Marisol estimates that her monthly needs are best approximated by the normal distribution, with a mean of 250 minutes and a standard deviation of 24 minutes.

a. If Marisol chooses the "Pick Your Minutes" plan described above, how many minutes should she contract for?

b. Instead, Marisol chooses to contract for 240 minutes. Under this contract, how much (in dollars) would she expect to pay at 40 cents per minute?

c. A friend advises Marisol to contract for 280 minutes to ensure limited surcharge payments (i.e., the 40-cents-per-minute payments). Under this contract, how many minutes would she expect to waste (i.e., unused minutes per month)?

d. If Marisol contracts for 260 minutes, what would be her approximate expected monthly cell phone bill?

e. Marisol has decided that she indeed does not like surcharge fees (the 40-cents-per-minute fee for her usage in excess of her monthly contracted minutes). How many minutes should she contract for if she wants only a 5 percent chance of incurring any surcharge fee?

(* indicates that the solution is at the end of the book)

f. Wildcat Cellular offers another plan called "No Minimum" that also has a $5.00 fixed fee per month but requires no commitment in terms of the number of minutes per month. Instead, the user is billed 7¢ per minute for her actual usage. Thus, if her actual usage is 40 minutes in a month, her bill would be $5.00 + 40 × 0.07 = $7.80. Marisol is trying to decide between the "Pick Your Minutes" plan described above and the "No Minimum" plan. Which should she choose?

Q13.4** **(Sarah's Wedding)** Sarah is planning her wedding. She and her fiancé have signed a contract with a caterer that calls for them to tell the caterer the number of guests that will attend the reception a week before the actual event. This "final number" will determine how much they have to pay the caterer; they must pay $60 per guest that they commit to. If, for example, they tell the caterer that they expect 90 guests, they must pay $5,400 (= 90 × $60) even if only, say, 84 guests show up. The contract calls for a higher rate of $85 per extra guest for the number of guests beyond what the couple commits to. Thus, if Sarah and her fiancé commit to 90 guests but 92 show up, they must pay $5,570 (the original $5,400 plus 2 × $85).

The problem Sarah faces is that she still does not know the exact number of guests to expect. Despite asking that friends and family members reply to their invitations a month ago, some uncertainty remains: her brother may—or may not—bring his new girlfriend; her fiancé's college roommate may—or may not—be able to take a vacation from work; and so forth. Sarah has determined that the expected number of guests (i.e., the mean number) is 100, but the actual number could be anywhere from 84 to 116:

Q	f(Q)	F(Q)	L(Q)		Q	f(Q)	F(Q)	L(Q)
84	0.0303	0.0303	16.00		101	0.0303	0.5455	3.64
85	0.0303	0.0606	15.03		102	0.0303	0.5758	3.18
86	0.0303	0.0909	14.09		103	0.0303	0.6061	2.76
87	0.0303	0.1212	13.18		104	0.0303	0.6364	2.36
88	0.0303	0.1515	12.30		105	0.0303	0.6667	2.00
89	0.0303	0.1818	11.45		106	0.0303	0.6970	1.67
90	0.0303	0.2121	10.64		107	0.0303	0.7273	1.36
91	0.0303	0.2424	9.85		108	0.0303	0.7576	1.09
92	0.0303	0.2727	9.09		109	0.0303	0.7879	0.85
93	0.0303	0.3030	8.36		110	0.0303	0.8182	0.64
94	0.0303	0.3333	7.67		111	0.0303	0.8485	0.45
95	0.0303	0.3636	7.00		112	0.0303	0.8788	0.30
96	0.0303	0.3939	6.36		113	0.0303	0.9091	0.18
97	0.0303	0.4242	5.76		114	0.0303	0.9394	0.09
98	0.0303	0.4545	5.18		115	0.0303	0.9697	0.03
99	0.0303	0.4848	4.64		116	0.0303	1.0000	0.00
100	0.0303	0.5152	4.12					

Q = Number of guests that show up to the wedding
$f(Q)$ = Density function = Prob{Q guests show up}
$F(Q)$ = Distribution function = Prob{Q or fewer guests show up}
$L(Q)$ = Loss function = Expected number of guests above Q

a. How many guests should Sarah commit to with the caterer?

b. Suppose Sarah commits to 105 guests. What is Sarah's expected bill?

c. Suppose that the caterer is willing to alter the contract so that if fewer than the number of guests they commit to show up, they will get a partial refund. In particular, they only have to pay $45 for each "no-show." For example, if they commit to 90 but only 84 show, they will have to pay 84 × $60 + 6 × $45 = $5,310. Now how many guests should she commit to?

d. The caterer offers Sarah another option. She could pay $70 per guest, no matter how many guests show up; that is, she wouldn't have to commit to any number before the wedding. Should Sarah prefer this option or the original option ($60 per committed guest and $85 each guest beyond the commitment)?

Q13.5 **(Lucky Smokes)** Lucky Smokes currently operates a warehouse that serves the Virginia market. Some trucks arrive at the warehouse filled with goods to be stored in the warehouse. Other trucks arrive at the warehouse empty to be loaded with goods. Based on the number of trucks that arrive at the warehouse in a week, the firm is able to accurately estimate the total number of labor hours that are required to finish all of the loading and unloading. The following histogram plots these estimates for each week over the past two

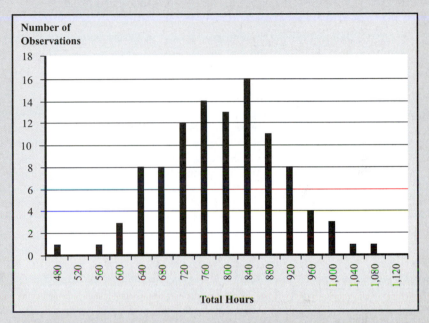

years. (There are a total of 104 weeks recorded in the graph.) For example, there were three weeks in this period that required 600 total labor hours and only one week that recorded 1,080 hours of required labor.

The mean of the data is 793 and the standard deviation is 111. Labor is the primary variable cost in the operation of a warehouse. The Virginia warehouse employed 20 workers, who were guaranteed at least 40 hours of pay per week. Thus, in weeks with less than 800 hours of required labor, the workers either went home early on some days or were idle. On weeks with more than 800 hours of required labor, the extra hours were obtained with overtime. Workers were paid time and a half for each hour of overtime.

You have been placed in charge of a new warehouse scheduled to serve the North Carolina market. Marketing suggests that the volume for this warehouse should be comparable to the Virginia warehouse. Assume that you must pay each worker for at least 40 hours of work per week and time and a half for each hour of overtime. Assume there is no limit on overtime for a given week. Further, assume you approximate your workload requirement with a normal distribution.

a. If you hire 22 workers, how many weeks a year should you expect to use overtime?

b. If you hire 18 workers, how many weeks a year will your workers be underutilized?

c. If you are interested in minimizing your labor cost, how many workers should you hire (again, assuming your workload forecast is normally distributed)?

d. You are now concerned the normal distribution might not be appropriate. For example, you can't hire 20.5 workers. What is the optimal number of workers to hire if you use the empirical distribution function constructed with the data in the above histogram?

Q13.6   **(Shillings)** You are traveling abroad and have only American dollars with you. You are currently in the capital but you will soon be heading out to a small town for an extended stay. In the town, no one takes credit cards and they only accept the domestic currency (shillings). In the capital, you can convert dollars to shillings at a rate of two shillings per dollar. In the town, you learn that one dollar only buys 1.6 shillings. Upon your return to the capital at the end of your trip, you can convert shillings back to dollars at a rate of 2.5 shillings per dollar. You estimate that your expenditures in the town will be normally distributed with mean of 400 shillings and standard deviation of 100 shillings.

a.   How many dollars should you convert to shillings before leaving the capital?

b.   After some thought, you feel that it might be embarrassing if you run out of shillings and need to ask to convert additional dollars, so you really do not want to run out of shillings. How many dollars should you convert to shillings if you want to ensure there is no more than a 1 in 200 chance you will run out of shillings?

Q13.7   **(TEC)** Consider the relationship between TEC and O'Neill with unlimited, but expensive, reactive capacity. Recall that TEC is willing to give O'Neill a midseason replenishment (see Figure 13.1) but charges O'Neill a 20 percent premium above the regular wholesale price of $110 for those units. Suppose TEC's gross margin is 25 percent of its selling price for units produced in the first production run. However, TEC estimates that its production cost per unit for the second production run (any units produced during the season after receiving O'Neill's second order) is twice as large as units produced for the initial order. Wetsuits produced that O'Neill does not order need to be salvaged at the end of the season. With O'Neill's permission, TEC estimates it can earn $30 per suit by selling the extra suits in Asian markets.

a.   What is TEC's expected profit with the traditional arrangement (i.e., a single order by O'Neill well in advance of the selling season)? Recall that O'Neill's optimal newsvendor quantity is 4,101 units.

b.   What is TEC's expected profit if it offers the reactive capacity to O'Neill and TEC's first production run equals O'Neill's first production order? Assume the demand forecast is normally distributed with mean 3,192 and standard deviation 1,181. Recall, O'Neill's optimal first order is 3,263 and O'Neill's expected second order is 437 units.

c.   What is TEC's optimal first production quantity if its CEO authorizes its production manager to choose a quantity that is greater than O'Neill's first order?

d.   Given the order chosen in part c, what is TEC's expected profit? (*Warning:* This is a hard question.)

Q13.8   **(Office Supply Company)** Office Supply Company (OSC) has a spare parts warehouse in Alaska to support its office equipment maintenance needs. Once every six months, a major replenishment shipment is received. If the inventory of any given part runs out before the next replenishment, then emergency air shipments are used to resupply the part as needed. Orders are placed on January 15 and June 15, and orders are received on February 15 and July 15, respectively.

OSC must determine replenishment quantities for its spare parts. As an example, historical data show that total demand for part 1AA-66 over a six-month interval is Poisson with mean 6.5. The cost of inventorying the unneeded part for six months is $5 (which includes both physical and financial holding costs and is charged based on inventory at the end of the six-month period). The variable production cost for 1AA-66 is $37 per part. The cost of a regular, semiannual shipment is $32 per part, and the cost of an emergency shipment is $50 per part.

It is January 15 and there are currently three 1AA-66 parts in inventory. How many parts should arrive on February 15?

Q13.9*   **(Steve Smith)** Steve Smith is a car sales agent at a Ford dealership. He earns a salary and benefits, but a large portion of his income comes from commissions: $350 per vehicle sold for the first five vehicles in a month and $400 per vehicle after that. Steve's historical sales can be well described with a Poisson distribution with mean 5.5; that is, on average, Steve sells 5.5 vehicles per month. On average, how much does Steve earn in commissions per month?

(* indicates that the solution is at the end of the book)

You can view a video of how problems marked with a ** are solved by going on www. cachon-terwiesch.net and follow the links under 'Solved Practice Problems'

Chapter

14

Service Levels and Lead Times in Supply Chains: The Order-up-to Inventory Model[1]

Many products are sold over a long time horizon with numerous replenishment opportunities. To draw upon a well-known example, consider the Campbell Soup Company's flagship product, chicken noodle soup. It has a long shelf life and future demand is assured. Hence, if in a particular month Campbell Soup has more chicken noodle soup than it needs, it does not have to dispose of its excess inventory. Instead, Campbell needs only wait for its pile of inventory to draw down to a reasonable level. And if Campbell finds itself with less inventory than it desires, its soup factory cooks up another batch. Because obsolescence is not a major concern and Campbell is not limited to a single production run, the newsvendor model (Chapters 12 and 13) is not the right inventory tool for this setting. The right tool for this job is the *order-up-to model*.

Although multiple replenishments are feasible, the order-up-to model still faces the "too little–too much" challenge associated with matching supply and demand. Because soup production takes time (i.e., there is a lead time to complete production), Campbell cannot wait until its inventory draws down to zero to begin production. (You would never let your vehicle's fuel tank go empty before you begin driving to a refueling station!) Hence, production of a batch should begin while there is a sufficient amount of inventory to buffer against uncertain demand while we wait for the batch to finish. Since buffer inventory is not free, the objective with the order-up-to model is to strike a balance between running too lean (which leads to undesirable stockouts, i.e., poor service) and running too fat (which leads to inventory holding costs).

Instead of soup, this chapter applies the order-up-to model to the inventory management of a technologically more sophisticated product: a pacemaker manufactured by Medtronic Inc. We begin with a description of Medtronic's supply chain for pacemakers and then detail the order-up-to model. Next, we consider how to use the model to hit target service

[1] Data in this chapter have been modified to protect confidentiality.

levels, discuss what service targets are appropriate, and explore techniques for controlling how frequently we order. We conclude with general managerial insights.

14.1 Medtronic's Supply Chain

Medtronic is a designer and manufacturer of medical technology. They are well known for their line of cardiac rhythm products, and, in particular, pacemakers, but their product line extends into numerous other areas: products for the treatment of cardiovascular diseases and surgery, diabetes, neurological diseases, spinal surgery, and eye/nose/throat diseases.

Inventory in Medtronic's supply chain is held at three levels: manufacturing facilities, distribution centers (DCs), and field locations. The manufacturing facilities are located throughout the world, and they do not hold much finished goods inventory. In the United States there is a single distribution center, located in Mounds View, Minnesota, responsible for the distribution of cardiac rhythm products. That DC ships to approximately 500 sales representatives, each with his or her own defined territory. All of the Medtronic DCs are responsible for providing very high availability of inventory to the sales representatives they serve in the field, where availability is measured with the in-stock probability.

The majority of finished goods inventory is held in the field by the sales representatives. In fact, field inventory is divided into two categories: consignment inventory and trunk inventory. Consignment inventory is inventory owned by Medtronic at a customer's location, usually a closet in a hospital. Trunk inventory is literally inventory in the trunk of a sales representative's vehicle. A sales representative has easy access to both of these kinds of field inventory, so they can essentially be considered a single pool of inventory.

Let's now focus on a particular DC, a particular sales representative, and a particular product. The DC is the one located in Mounds View, Minnesota. The sales representative is Susan Magnotto and her territory includes the major medical facilities in Madison, Wisconsin. Finally, the product is the InSync ICD Model 7272 pacemaker, which is displayed in Figure 14.1.

A pacemaker is demanded when it is implanted in a patient via surgery. Even though a surgeon can anticipate the need for a pacemaker for a particular patient, a surgeon may not know the appropriate model for a patient until the actual surgery. For this reason, and for the need to maintain a good relationship with each physician, Susan attends each surgery and always carries the various models that might be needed. Susan can replenish her inventory after an implant by calling an order in to Medtronic's Customer Service, which then sends the request to the Mounds View DC. If the model she requests is available in inventory at the DC, then it is sent to her via an overnight carrier. The time between when Susan orders a unit and when she receives the unit is generally one day, and rarely more than two days.

The Mounds View DC requests replenishments from the production facilities on a weekly basis. With the InSync pacemaker, there is currently a three-week lead time to receive each order.

For the InSync pacemaker, Figure 14.2 provides one year's data on monthly shipments and end-of-month inventory at the Mounds View DC. Figure 14.3 provides data on monthly implants (i.e., demand) and inventory for the InSync pacemaker in Susan's territory over the same year. As can be seen from the figures, there is a considerable amount

FIGURE 14.1
Medtronic's InSync ICD Pacemaker

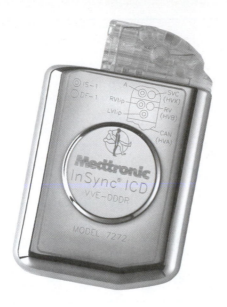

of variation in the number of units demanded at the DC and in particular in Susan's territory. Interestingly, it appears that there is more demand in the summer months in Susan's territory, but the aggregate shipments through the DC do not indicate the same pattern. Therefore, it is reasonable to conclude that the "pattern" observed in Susan's demand data is not real: Just like a splotch of ink might look like something on a piece of paper, random events sometimes appear to form a pattern.

FIGURE 14.2
Monthly Shipments (bar) and End-of-Month Inventory (line) for the InSync Pacemaker at the Mounds View Distribution Center

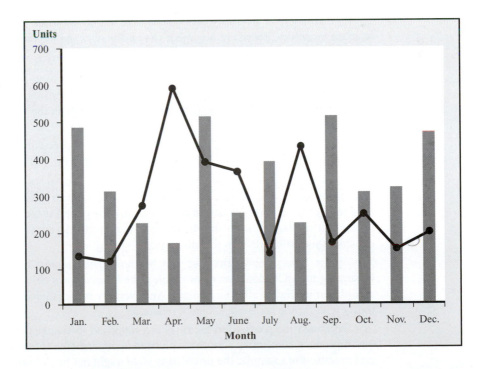

FIGURE 14.3
Monthly Implants (bar) and End-of-Month Inventory (line) for the InSync Pacemaker in Susan's Territory

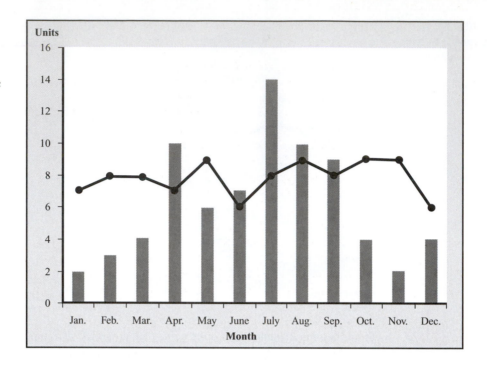

As a sales representative, Susan's primary responsibility is to ensure that Medtronic's products are the choice products of physicians in her territory. To encourage active sales effort, a considerable portion of her yearly income is derived from bonuses to achieve aggressive sales thresholds.

If the decision on inventory investment were left up to Susan, she would err on the side of extra inventory. There are a number of reasons why she would like to hold a considerable amount of inventory:

• Due to the sales incentive system, Susan never wants to miss a sale due to a lack of inventory. Because patients and surgeons do not tolerate waiting for back-ordered inventory, if Susan does not have the right product available, then the sale is almost surely lost to a competitor.

• Medtronic's products are generally quite small, so it is possible to hold a considerable amount of inventory in a relatively small space (e.g., the trunk of a vehicle).

• Medtronic's products have a relatively long shelf life, so spoilage is not a major concern. (However, spoilage can be a concern if a rep fails to stick to a "first-in-first-out" regime, thereby allowing a unit to remain in inventory for a disproportionately long time. Given that spoilage is not a significant issue if first-in-first-out is implemented, we'll not consider this issue further in this discussion.)

• While Susan knows that she can be replenished relatively quickly from the DC (assuming the DC has inventory available), she is not always able to find the time to place an order immediately after an implant. An inventory buffer thereby allows her some flexibility with timing her replenishment requests.

• Although the production facilities are supposed to ensure that the DCs never stock out of product, sometimes a product can become unavailable for several weeks, if not several months. For example, the *production yield* might not be as high as initially planned or a supplier of a key component might be capacity-constrained. Whatever the cause, having a few extra units of inventory helps protect Susan against these shortages.

To ensure that each sales representative holds a reasonable amount of inventory, each sales representative is given a *par level* for each product. The par level specifies the maximum number of units the sales representative can have on-order plus on-hand at any given time. Therefore, once a sales representative's inventory equals her par level, she cannot order an additional unit until one is implanted. The par levels are set quarterly based on previous sales and anticipated demand. If a sales representative feels a higher par level is warranted, he or she can request an adjustment. Even though Medtronic does not wish to give the sales representative full reign over inventory, due to Medtronic's large gross margins, neither does Medtronic want to operate too lean.

An issue for Medtronic is whether its supply chain is supporting its aggressive growth objectives. This chapter first considers the management of field inventory. As of now, the sales representatives are responsible for managing their own inventory (within the limits of set par levels), but maybe a computer-based system should be considered that would choose stocking levels and automatically replenish inventory. This system would relieve Susan Magnotto and other representatives from the task of managing inventory so that they can concentrate on selling product. While that is attractive to Susan, a reduction in product availability is nonnegotiable. After exploring the management of field inventory, attention is turned to the management of the Mounds View distribution center inventory. It is essential that the DC provide excellent availability to the field representatives without holding excessive inventory.

14.2 The Order-up-to Model Design and Implementation

The order-up-to model is designed to manage inventory for a product that has the opportunity for many replenishments over a long time horizon. This section describes the assumptions of the model and how it is implemented in practice. The subsequent sections consider the evaluation of numerous performance measures, how historical data can be used to choose a distribution to represent demand, and how to calibrate the model to achieve one of several possible objectives.

We are working with a single product that is sold over a long period of time. Opportunities to order replenishment inventory occur at regular intervals. The time between two ordering opportunities is called a *period,* and all of the periods are of the same duration. While one day seems like a natural period length for the InSync pacemaker in the field (e.g., in Susan's territory), one week is a more natural period length for the Mounds View DC. In other settings, the appropriate period length could be an hour, a month, or any other interval. See Section 14.8 for additional discussion on the appropriate period length. For the sake of consistency, let's also assume that orders are submitted at the same point in time within the period, say, at the beginning of the period.

Random demand occurs during each period. As with the newsvendor model, among the most critical inputs to the order-up-to model are the parameters of the demand distribution, which is the focus of Section 14.4. However, it is worth mentioning that the model assumes the same demand distribution represents demand in every period. This does not mean that actual demand is the same in every period; it just means that each period's demand is the outcome of a single distribution. The model can be extended to accommodate more complex demand structures, but, as we will see, our simpler structure is adequate for our task.

Receiving a replenishment is the third event within each period. We assume that replenishments are only received at the beginning of a period, before any demand occurs in the period. Hence, if a shipment arrives during a period, then it is available to satisfy demand during that period.

Replenishment orders are received after a fixed amount of time called the *lead time,* which is represented with the variable l. The lead time is measured in periods; if one day is a period, then the lead time to receive an order should be measured in days. Hence, not only should the period length be chosen so that it matches the frequency at which orders can be made and replenishments can be received, it also should be chosen so that the replenishment lead time can be measured in an integer (0, 1, 2, . . .) number of periods.

There is no limit to the quantity that can be ordered within a period, and no matter the order quantity, the order is always received in the lead time number of periods. Therefore, supply in this model is not capacity-constrained, but delivery of an order does take some time.

Inventory left over at the end of a period is carried over to the next period; there is no obsolescence, theft, or spoilage of inventory.

To summarize, at the start of each period, a replenishment order can be submitted and a replenishment can be received, then random demand occurs. There is no limit imposed on the quantity of any order, but an order is received only after l periods. For example, if the period length is one day and $l = 1$, then a Monday morning order is received Tuesday morning. Each period has the same duration and the same sequence of events occurs in each period (order, receive, demand). Figure 14.4 displays the sequence of events over a sample of three periods when the lead time to receive orders is one period, $l = 1$.

Now let's define several terms we use to describe our inventory system and then we show how the order-up-to level is used to choose an order quantity.

On-order inventory is relatively intuitive: The on-order inventory is the number of units that we ordered in previous periods that we have not yet received. Our on-order inventory should never be negative, but it can be zero.

On-hand inventory is also straightforward: It is the number of units of inventory we have on-hand, immediately available to serve demand.

Back-order is the number of units on back order, that is, the total amount of demand that has occurred but has not been satisfied. To get the mathematics of the order-up-to model to work precisely, it is necessary to assume that *all* demand is eventually filled, that is, if demand occurs and no units are available in current inventory, then that demand is back-ordered and filled as soon as inventory becomes available. In other words, the order-up-to model assumes there are no lost sales. In some settings, this is not a problem: complete back-ordering is commonplace in the management of inventory between two firms within a supply chain. However, as with the InSync pacemaker in the field, when end consumers generate demand (instead of a firm), the back-order assumption is probably

FIGURE 14.4
Sample Sequence of Events in the Order-up-to Model with a One-Period Lead Time, $l = 1$, to Receive Orders

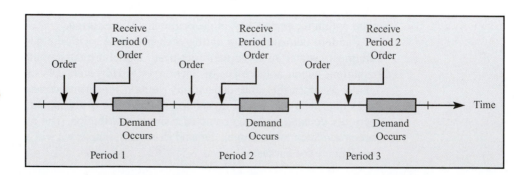

violated (at least to some extent). Nevertheless, if the order-up-to level is chosen so that back orders are rare, then the order-up-to model is a reasonable approximation. Hence, we use it for the InSync pacemaker to manage both the DC inventory as well as Susan's field inventory.

The next measure combines on-hand inventory with the back order:

$$\text{Inventory level} = \text{On-hand inventory} - \text{Back order}$$

Unlike the on-hand inventory and the back order, which are never negative, the inventory level can be negative. It is negative when we have units back-ordered. For example, if the inventory level is -3, then there are three units of demand waiting to be filled.

The following measure combines all of the previous measures:

$$\text{Inventory position} = \text{On-order inventory} + \text{On-hand inventory} - \text{Back order}$$
$$= \text{On-order inventory} + \text{Inventory level}$$

The *order-up-to level* is the maximum inventory position we are willing to have. Let's denote the order-up-to level with the variable S. For example, if $S = 2$, then we are allowed an inventory position up to two units, but no more. Our order-up-to level is essentially equivalent to the par level Medtronic currently uses. It has also been referred to as the *base stock level*. (The order-up-to model is sometimes called the *base stock model*.)

The implementation of our order-up-to policy is relatively straightforward: If we observe at the beginning of any period that our inventory position is less than the order-up-to level S, then we order enough inventory to raise our inventory position to S; that is, in each period, we order the difference between S and the inventory position:

$$\text{Each period's order quantity} = S - \text{Inventory position}$$

Because the inventory position includes our on-order inventory, after we submit the order, our inventory position immediately increases to S.

To illustrate an ordering decision, suppose we observe at the beginning of a period that our inventory level is -4 (four units are back-ordered), our on-order inventory is one, and our chosen order-up-to level is $S = 3$. In this situation, we need to order six units: our inventory position is $1 - 4 = -3$ and our order quantity should be S minus the inventory position, $3 - (-3) = 6$.

If we find ourselves in a period with an inventory position that is greater than S, then we should not order anything. Eventually our inventory position will drop below S. After that time, we will begin ordering and our inventory position will never again be greater than S as long as we do not change S (because we only order to raise our inventory position to S, never more).

Notice that our inventory position drops below S only when demand occurs. Suppose $S = 3$ and we observe that our inventory position is one at the beginning of the period. If we followed our order-up-to policy in the previous period, then we must have had an inventory position of three after our order in the previous period. The only way that we could then observe an inventory position of one in this period is if two units of demand occurred in the previous period. Thus, we will order two units in this period (to raise our inventory position back to $S = 3$). Hence,

The order quantity in each period exactly equals the demand in the previous period in the order-up-to inventory model.

Due to this observation, an order-up-to policy is sometimes called a *one-for-one ordering policy:* each unit of demand triggers an order for one replenishment unit.

The order-up-to model is an example of a system that operates on the pull principle of production/inventory control. The key feature of a *pull system* is that production-replenishment of a unit is only initiated when a demand of another unit occurs. Therefore, in a pull system, inventory is pulled through the system only by the occurrence of demand. In contrast, with a *push system,* production-replenishment occurs in anticipation of demand. The newsvendor model is a push system. A kanban system, which is a critical component of any just-in-time system, operates with pull. (See Chapter 11.) Pull systems impose the discipline to prevent the excessive buildup of inventory, but they do not anticipate shifts in future demand. Thus, pull systems are most effective when average demand remains steady, as we have assumed in our order-up-to model.

14.3   The End-of-Period Inventory Level

The inventory level (on-hand inventory minus the back order) is an important metric in the order-up-to model: If the inventory level is high, then we incur holding costs on on-hand inventory, but if the inventory level is low, then we may not be providing adequate availability to our customers. Hence, we need to know how to control the inventory level via our decision variable, the order-up-to level. The following result suggests there actually is a relatively simple relationship between them:

The inventory level measured at the end of a period equals the order-up-to level S *minus demand over* l + 1 *periods.*

If that result is (magically) intuitive to you, or if you are willing to believe it on faith, then you can now skip ahead to the next section. For the rest of us, the remainder of this section explains and derives that result.

We'll derive our result with the help of a seemingly unrelated example. Suppose at a neighborhood picnic you have a large pot with 30 cups of soup in it. Over the course of the picnic, you add 20 additional cups of soup to the pot and a total of 40 cups are served. How many cups of soup are in the pot at the end of the picnic? Not too hard: start with 30, add 20, and then subtract 40, so you are left with 10 cups of soup in the pot. Does the answer change if you first subtract 40 cups and then add 20 cups? The answer is no as long as people are patient. To explain, if we subtract 40 cups from the original 30 cups, then we will have -10 cups, that is, there will be people waiting in line to receive soup. Once the 20 cups are added, those people in line are served and 10 cups remain. The sequence of adding and subtracting does not matter precisely because everyone is willing to wait in line, that is, there are no lost sales of soup. In other words, the sequence of adding and subtracting does not matter, only the total amount added and the total amount subtracted matter.

Does the answer change in our soup example if the 20 cups are added one cup at a time or in random quantities (e.g., sometimes half a cup, sometime a whole cup, sometimes more than a cup)? Again, the answer is no: the increments by which the soup is added or subtracted do not matter, only the total amount added or subtracted.

Keep the soup example in mind, but let's switch to another example. Suppose a firm uses the order-up-to model, its order-up-to level is $S = 3$, and the lead time is two days, $l = 2$. What is the inventory level at the end of any given day? This seems like a rather hard question to answer, but let's tackle it anyway. To provide a concrete reference, randomly choose a period, say period 10. Let *IL* be the inventory level at the start of period 10. We use a variable for the inventory level because we really do not know the exact inventory level. It turns out, as we will see, that we do not need to know the exact inventory level.

After we submit our order in period 10, we will have a total of $3 - IL$ units on order. When we implement the order-up-to model, we must order so that our inventory level

(*IL*) plus our on-order inventory (3 − *IL*) equals our order-up-to level (3 = *IL* + 3 − *IL*). Some of the on-order inventory may have been ordered in period 10, some of it in period 9. No matter when the on-order inventory was ordered, it will *all* be received by the end of period 12 because the lead time is two periods. For example, the period 10 order is received in period 12, so all of the previously ordered inventory should have been received by period 12 as well.

Now recall the soup example. Think of *IL* as the amount of soup you start with. How much is added to the "pot of inventory" over periods 10 to 12? That is the amount that was on order in period 10, that is, 3 − *IL*. So the pot starts with *IL* and then 3 − *IL* is added over periods 10 to 12. How much is subtracted from the pot of inventory over periods 10 to 12? Demand is what causes subtraction from the pot of inventory. So it is demand over periods 10 to 12 that is subtracted from inventory; that is, demand over the *l* + 1 periods (10 to 12 are three periods). So how much is in the pot of inventory at the end of period 12? The answer is simple: just as in the soup example, it is how much we start with (*IL*), plus the amount we add (3 − *IL*), minus the amount we subtract (demand over periods 10 to 12):

$$\text{Inventory level at the end of period 12} = IL + 3 - IL - \text{Demand in periods 10 to 12}$$
$$= 3 - \text{Demand in periods 10 to 12}$$

In other words, our inventory level at the end of a period is the order-up-to level (in this case 3) minus demand over *l* + 1 periods (in this case, periods 10 to 12). Hence, we have derived our result.

Just as in the soup example, it does not matter the sequence by which inventory is added or subtracted; all that matters is the total amount that is added (3 − *IL*) and the total amount that is subtracted (total demand over periods 10 to 12). (This is why the back-order assumption is needed.) Nor do the increments by which inventory is added or subtracted matter. In other words, we can add and subtract at constant rates, or we could add and subtract at random rates; either way, it is only the totals that matter.

You still may be a bit confused about why it is demand over *l* + 1 periods that is relevant rather than demand over just *l* periods. Recall that we are interested in the inventory level at the *end* of the period, but we make our ordering decision at the *start* of a period. The time from when an order is placed at the start of a period to the end of the period in which the order arrives is actually *l* + 1 periods' worth of demand.

Now you might wonder why we initiated our analysis at the start of a period, in this case period 10. Why not begin by measuring the inventory position at some other time during a period? The reason is that the inventory position measured at the start of a period is always equal to the order-up-to level, but we cannot be sure about what the inventory position will be at any other point within a period (because of random demand). Hence, we anchor our analysis on something we know for sure, which is that the inventory position equals *S* at the start of every period when an order-up-to policy is implemented.

To summarize, in the order-up-to model, the inventory level at the end of a period equals the order-up-to level *S* minus demand over *l* + 1 periods. Therefore, while we need to know the distribution of demand for a single period, we also need to know the distribution of demand over *l* + 1 periods.

14.4 Choosing Demand Distributions

Every inventory management system must choose a demand distribution to represent demand. In our case, we need a demand distribution for the Mounds View DC and Susan Magnotto's territory. Furthermore, as discussed in the previous section, we need a demand distribution for one period of demand and a demand distribution for $l + 1$ periods of demand. As we will see, the normal distribution works for DC demand, but the Poisson distribution is better for demand in Susan's territory.

The graph in Figure 14.2 indicates that Mounds View's demand is variable, but it appears to have a stable mean throughout the year. This is a good sign: as we already mentioned, the order-up-to model assumes average demand is the same across periods. Average demand across the sample is 349 and the standard deviation is 122.38. Seven months of the year have demand less than the mean, so the demand realizations appear to be relatively symmetric about the mean. Finally, there do not appear to be any extreme outliers in the data: the maximum is 1.35 standard deviations from the mean and the minimum is 1.46 standard deviations from the mean. Overall, the normal distribution with a mean of 349 and a standard deviation of 122.38 is a reasonable choice to represent the DC's monthly demand.

However, because the DC orders on a weekly basis and measures its lead time in terms of weeks, the period length for our order-up-to model applied to the DC should be one week. Therefore, we need to pick a distribution to represent weekly demand; that is, we have to chop our monthly demand distribution into a weekly demand distribution. If we are willing to make the assumption that one week's demand is independent of another week's demand, and if we assume that there are 4.33 weeks per month (52 weeks per year/12 months), then we can convert the mean and standard deviation for our monthly demand distribution into a mean and standard deviation for weekly demand:

$$\text{Expected weekly demand} = \frac{\text{Expected monthly demand}}{4.33}$$

$$\text{Standard deviation of weekly demand} = \frac{\text{Standard deviation of monthly demand}}{\sqrt{4.33}}$$

Exhibit 14.1 summarizes the process of converting demand distributions from one period length to another.

In the case of the Mounds View DC, expected weekly demand is $349/4.33 = 80.6$ and the standard deviation of weekly demand is $122.38/\sqrt{4.33} = 58.81$. So we will use a normal distribution with mean 80.6 and standard deviation 58.81 to represent weekly demand at the Mounds View DC.

We also need demand for the InSync pacemaker over $l + 1$ periods, which in this case is demand over $3 + 1 = 4$ weeks. Again using Exhibit 14.1, demand over four weeks has mean $4 \times 80.6 = 322.4$ and standard deviation $\sqrt{4} \times 58.81 = 117.6$.

Now consider demand for the InSync pacemaker in Susan's territory. From the data in Figure 14.3, total demand over the year is 75 units, which translates into average demand of 6.25 (75/12) units per month, 1.44 units per week (75/52), and 0.29 (1.44/5) unit per day, assuming a five-day week.

Our estimate of 0.29 unit per day for expected demand implicitly assumes expected demand on any given day of the year is the same as for any other day of the year. In other words, there is no seasonality in demand across the year, within a month, or within a week. There probably is not too much promotion-related volatility in demand (buy one pacemaker, get one free), nor is there much volatility due to gift giving (what more could a dad want than a new pacemaker under the Christmas tree). There probably is not much variation within the week (the same number of implants on average on Friday as on Monday) or within the month. However, those conjectures could be tested with more refined data. Furthermore, from the data in Figure 14.2, it appears demand is stable throughout the year and

Exhibit 14.1

HOW TO CONVERT A DEMAND DISTRIBUTION FROM ONE PERIOD LENGTH TO ANOTHER

If you wish to divide a demand distribution from a long period length (e.g., a month) into n short periods (e.g., a week), then

$$\text{Expected demand in the short period} = \frac{\text{Expected demand in the long period}}{n}$$

$$\text{Standard deviation of demand in the short period} =$$
$$\frac{\text{Standard deviation of demand in the long period}}{\sqrt{n}}$$

If you wish to combine demand distributions from n short periods (e.g., a week) into one long period (e.g, a three-week period, $n = 3$), then

$$\text{Expected demand in the long period} = n \times \text{Expected demand in the short period}$$

$$\text{Standard deviation of demand in the long period} =$$
$$\sqrt{n} \times \text{Standard deviation of demand in the short period}$$

The above equations assume the same demand distribution represents demand in each period and demands across periods are independent of each other.

there are no upward or downward trends in the data. Hence, our assumption of a constant expected daily demand is reasonable.

Using Exhibit 14.1, if average demand over one day is 0.29 unit, then expected demand over $l + 1$ days must be $2 \times 0.29 = 0.58$.

Unlike the normal distribution, which is defined by two parameters (its mean and its standard deviation), the Poisson distribution is defined by only a single parameter, its mean. For the InSync pacemaker, it is natural to choose the mean equal to the observed mean demand rate: 0.29 for demand over one period and 0.58 for demand over two periods. Even though the Poisson distribution does not allow you to choose any standard deviation while holding the mean fixed, the Poisson distribution does have a standard deviation:

$$\text{Standard deviation of a Poisson distribution} = \sqrt{\text{Mean of the distribution}}$$

For example, with a mean of 0.29, the standard deviation is $\sqrt{0.29} = 0.539$. Table 14.1 provides the distribution and density functions for the chosen Poisson distributions.

TABLE 14.1

The Distribution and Density Functions for Two Poisson Distributions. In Excel, $F(S)$ is evaluated with the function POISSON(S, *Expected demand*, 1) and $f(S)$ is evaluated with the function POISSON(S, *Expected demand*, 0).

	Mean Demand = 0.29			Mean Demand = 0.58	
S	$F(S)$	$f(S)$	S	$F(S)$	$f(S)$
0	0.74826	0.74826	0	0.55990	0.55990
1	0.96526	0.21700	1	0.88464	0.32474
2	0.99672	0.03146	2	0.97881	0.09417
3	0.99977	0.00304	3	0.99702	0.01821
4	0.99999	0.00022	4	0.99966	0.00264
5	1.00000	0.00001	5	0.99997	0.00031

$F(S) = \text{Prob}\{\text{Demand is less than or equal to } S\}$
$f(S) = \text{Prob}\{\text{Demand is exactly equal to } S\}$

FIGURE 14.5

The Distribution (left graph) and Density Functions (right graph) of a Poisson Distribution with a Mean of 0.29 (bullets and dashed lines) and a Normal Distribution with a Mean of 0.29 and a Standard Deviation of 0.539 (solid line)

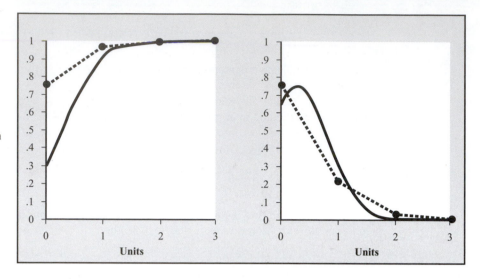

Because it can be hard to visualize a distribution from a table, Figure 14.5 displays the graphs of the distribution and density functions of the Poisson distribution with mean 0.29. For comparison, the comparable functions for the normal distribution are also included. (The dashed lines with the Poisson distribution are only for visual effect; that is, those functions exist only for integer values.)

The graphs in Figure 14.5 highlight that the Poisson and normal distributions are different in two key respects: (1) the Poisson distribution is discrete (it has integer outcomes), whereas the normal distribution is continuous, and (2) the distribution and density functions for those two distributions have different shapes. The fractional quantity issue is not a major concern if demand is 500 units (or probably even 80 units), but it is a concern when average demand is only 0.29 unit. Ideally, we want a discrete demand distribution like the Poisson.

Yet another argument can be made in support of the Poisson distribution as our model for demand in Susan's territory. Recall that with the queuing models (Chapters 8 and 9) we use the exponential distribution to describe the time between customer arrivals, which is appropriate if customers arrive independently of each other; that is, the arrival time of one customer does not provide information concerning the arrival time of another customer. This is particularly likely if the arrival rate of customers is quite slow, as it is with the InSync pacemaker. So it is likely that the interarrival time of InSync pacemaker demand has an exponential distribution. And here is the connection to the Poisson distribution: If the interarrival times are exponentially distributed, then the number of arrivals in any fixed interval of time has a Poisson distribution. For example, if the interarrival times between InSync pacemaker demand in Susan's territory are exponentially distributed with a mean of 3.45 days, then the average number of arrivals (demand) per day has a Poisson distribution with a mean of $1/3.45 = 0.29$ unit.

If we had daily demand data, we would be able to confirm whether or not our chosen Poisson distribution is a good fit to the data. Nevertheless, absent those data, we have probably made the best educated guess.

To summarize, we shall use a normal demand distribution with mean 80.6 and standard deviation 58.81 to represent weekly demand for the InSync pacemaker at the Mounds View DC and a normal demand distribution with mean 322.4 and standard deviation 117.6 to represent demand over $l + 1 = 4$ weeks. We will use a Poisson distribution with mean 0.29 to represent daily demand in Susan Magnotto's territory and a Poisson distribution with mean 0.58 to represent demand over $l + 1 = 2$ days.

14.5   Performance Measures

This section considers the evaluation of several performance measures with the order-up-to method. We consider these measures at two locations in the supply chain: Susan Magnotto's territory and the Mounds View distribution center.

Recall we use a Poisson distribution with mean 0.29 to represent daily demand in Susan's territory and a Poisson distribution with mean 0.58 to represent demand over $l + 1 = 2$ days. We shall evaluate the performance measures assuming Susan uses $S = 3$ as her order-up-to level. The Mounds View weekly demand is normally distributed with mean 80.6 and standard deviation 58.81 and over $l + 1 = 4$ weeks it is normally distributed with mean $\mu = 322.4$ and standard deviation $\sigma = 117.6$. We evaluate the performance measures assuming the order-up-to level $S = 625$ is implemented at Mounds View.

Figure 14.6 summarizes the necessary inputs to evaluate each performance measure.

In-Stock and Stockout Probability

A *stockout* occurs when demand arrives and there is no inventory available to satisfy that demand immediately. A stockout is not the same as being *out of stock,* which is the condition of having no inventory on hand. With our definition of a stockout, we must be out of stock *and* a demand must occur. Thus, if we are out of stock and no demand occurs, then a stockout never happened. We are *in stock* in a period if all demand was satisfied in that period. With this definition, if we start a period with five units and demand is five units, then we are in stock in that period even though we end the period without inventory.

The *in-stock probability* is the probability we are in stock in a period, and the *stockout probability* is the probability a stockout occurs. We used these same definitions in the newsvendor model, Chapter 12. As in the newsvendor model, an alternative measure is the fill rate, which is the probability a customer will be able to purchase an item. See Appendix D for the procedure to evaluate the fill rate in the order-up-to model.

FIGURE 14.6

The Relationship between Inputs (boxes) and Performance Measures (ovals) in the Order-up-to Model

μ = Expected demand over $l + 1$ periods and σ = Standard deviation of demand over $l + 1$ periods.

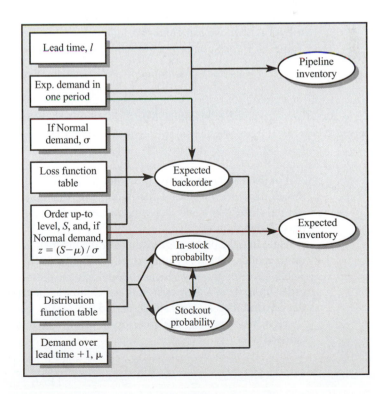

A stockout causes a back order. Hence, a stockout occurs in a period if one or more units are back-ordered at the end of the period. If there are back orders at the end of the period, then the inventory level at the end of the period is negative. The main result from Section 14.3 is that the inventory level is related to the order-up-to level and demand over $l + 1$ periods in the following way:

Inventory level at the end of the period $= S -$ Demand over $l + 1$ periods

Therefore, the inventory level at the end of the period is negative if demand over $l + 1$ periods exceeds the order-up-to level. Therefore,

Stockout probability $=$ Prob{Demand over $l + 1$ periods $> S$}

$= 1 -$ Prob{Demand over $l + 1$ periods $\leq S$}   **(14.1)**

Equation (14.1) is actually an approximation of the stockout probability, but it happens to be an excellent approximation if the chosen service level is high (i.e., if stockouts are rare). See Appendix D for why equation (14.1) is an approximation and for the exact, but more complicated, stockout probability equation.

Because either all demand is satisfied immediately from inventory or not, we know that the

In-stock probability $= 1 -$ Stockout probability

Combining the above equation with equation (14.1), we get

In-stock probability $= 1 -$ Stockout probability

$=$ Prob{Demand over $l + 1$ periods $\leq S$}

The above probability equations do not depend on which distribution has been chosen to represent demand, but the process for evaluating those probabilities does depend on the particular demand distribution.

When the demand distribution is given in the form of a table, as with the Poisson distribution, then we can obtain the in-stock probability directly from the table. Looking at Table 14.1, for Susan's territory with an order-up-to level $S = 3$,

In-stock probability $=$ Prob{Demand over $l + 1$ periods ≤ 3}

$= 99.702\%$

Stockout probability $= 1 -$ Prob{Demand over $l + 1$ periods ≤ 3}

$= 1 - 0.99702$

$= 0.298\%$

For the Mounds View distribution center, we need to work with the normal distribution. Recall that with the normal distribution you first do the analysis as if demand is a standard normal distribution and then you convert those outcomes into the answers for the actual normal distribution.

Note that the process for evaluating the in-stock and stockout probabilities in the order-up-to model, which is summarized in Exhibit 14.2, is identical to the one described in Table 12.4 for the newsvendor model except the order quantity Q is replaced with the order-up-to level S. However, it is critical to use the demand forecast for $l + 1$ periods, not the demand forecast for a single period (unless the lead time happens to be 0).

First, we normalize the order-up-to level, which is $S = 625$, using the parameters for demand over $l + 1$ periods:

$$z = \frac{S - \mu}{\sigma} = \frac{625 - 322.4}{117.6} = 2.57$$

Exhibit 14.2

Next, we look up $\Phi(z)$ (the probability the outcome of a standard normal is less than or equal to z) in the Standard Normal Distribution Function Table in Appendix B: $\Phi(2.57) = 0.9949$. Therefore, with $S = 625$, the in-stock probability for the DC is 99.49 percent. The stockout probability is $1 - \Phi(z) = 0.0051$, or 0.51 percent.

Expected Back Order

The *expected back order* is the expected number of back orders at the end of any period. We need the expected back order to evaluate the expected on-hand inventory, which is of direct interest to any manager.

Recall from Section 14.3 that the inventory level at the end of the period is S minus demand over $l + 1$ periods. Hence, if demand over $l + 1$ periods is greater than S, then there will be back orders. The number of back orders equals the difference between demand over $l + 1$ periods and S. Therefore, in the order-up-to model, the expected back order equals the loss function of demand over $l + 1$ periods evaluated at the threshold S. *Note:* This is analogous to the expected lost sales in the newsvendor model. In the order-up-to model, the number of units back-ordered equals the difference between random demand over $l + 1$ periods and S; in the newsvendor model, the expected lost sales are the difference between random demand and Q. So all we need to evaluate the expected back order is the loss function of demand over $l + 1$ periods.

Let's begin with the expected back order in Susan's territory. Recall that with a discrete distribution function table, we need to have a column that has the loss function $L(S)$. Table 14.2 displays the loss function we need. (Appendix C describes how to use the data

TABLE 14.2
Distribution and Loss Function for Two Poisson Distributions

	Mean Demand = 0.29			Mean Demand = 0.58	
S	F(S)	L(S)	S	F(S)	L(S)
0	0.74826	0.29000	0	0.55990	0.58000
1	0.96526	0.03826	1	0.88464	0.13990
2	0.99672	0.00352	2	0.97881	0.02454
3	0.99977	0.00025	3	0.99702	0.00335
4	0.99999	0.00001	4	0.99966	0.00037
5	1.00000	0.00000	5	0.99997	0.00004

$F(S) = \text{Prob}\{\text{Demand is less than or equal to } S\}$
$L(S) = \text{Loss function} = \text{Expected back order} = \text{Expected amount demand exceeds } S$

Exhibit 14.3

EXPECTED BACK ORDER EVALUATION FOR THE ORDER-UP-TO MODEL

If the demand over $l + 1$ periods is a normal distribution with mean μ and standard deviation σ, then follow steps A through D (see Exhibit 14.1 for the process of evaluating μ and σ if you have demand over a single period):

A. Evaluate the z-statistic for the order-up-to level S: $z = \dfrac{S - \mu}{\sigma}$.

B. Use the z-statistic to look up in the Standard Normal Loss Function Table the expected loss with the standard normal distribution, $L(z)$.

C. Expected back order $= \sigma \times L(z)$.

D. With Excel, expected back order can be evaluated with the following equation:

$$\text{Expected back order} = \sigma * (\text{Normdist } (z, 0, 1, 0) - z*(1 - \text{Normsdist } (z)))$$

If the demand forecast for $l + 1$ periods is a discrete distribution function table, then expected back order equals $L(S)$, where $L(S)$ is the loss function. If the table does not include the loss function, then see Appendix C for a procedure to evaluate it.

in Table 14.1 to evaluate $L(S)$.) Appendix B has the loss function table for other Poisson distributions. With $S = 3$ and mean demand over $l + 1$ periods equal to 0.58, we see that $L(3) = 0.00335$. Therefore, the expected back order in Susan's territory is 0.00335 unit if she operates with $S = 3$.

With the Mounds View DC, we follow the process of evaluating expected lost sales with a normal distribution. (See Exhibit 12.4.) First, find the z-statistic that corresponds to the order-up-to level:

$$z = \frac{S - \mu}{\sigma} = \frac{625 - 322.4}{117.6} = 2.57$$

Note again that we are using the mean and standard deviation of the normal distribution that represents demand over $l + 1$ periods. Now look up in the Standard Normal Distribution Loss Function Table the loss function with the standard normal distribution and a z-statistic of 2.57: $L(2.57) = 0.0016$. Next, convert that expected loss with the standard normal distribution into the expected back order:

$$\text{Expected back order} = \sigma \times L(z) = 117.6 \times 0.0016 = 0.19$$

Exhibit 14.3 summarizes the process.

Expected On-Hand Inventory

Expected on-hand inventory, or just *expected inventory* for short, is the expected number of units of inventory at the end of a period. We choose to measure inventory at the end of the period because that is when inventory is at its lowest point in the period.

Recall that the inventory level at the end of a period is equal to the order-up-to level S minus demand over $l + 1$ periods. Hence, inventory at the end of a period is the difference between S and demand over $l + 1$ periods: if $S = 5$ and demand over $l + 1$ periods is three, then there are two units left in inventory. In other words, expected inventory is the expected amount by which S exceeds demand over $l + 1$ periods. Referring to the insights

Exhibit 14.4

EVALUATION OF EXPECTED ON-HAND INVENTORY, AND PIPELINE/EXPECTED ON-ORDER INVENTORY IN THE ORDER-UP-TO MODEL

For the expected on-hand inventory:

A. Evaluate the expected back order (see Exhibit 14.3).

B. Expected on-hand inventory = S − Expected demand over l + 1 periods + Expected back order.

See Exhibit 14.1 for how to evaluate *expected demand over l* + 1 periods.

For the pipeline inventory (which is also known as expected on-order inventory):

$$\text{Expected on-order inventory} = \text{Expected demand in one period} \times \text{Lead time}$$

from the newsvendor model, if we think of S in terms of the order quantity and demand over $l + 1$ periods in terms of "sales," then inventory is analogous to "leftover inventory." Recall that in the newsvendor model

$$\begin{aligned}\text{Expected leftover inventory} &= Q - \text{Expected sales}\\ &= Q - \mu + \text{Expected lost sales}\end{aligned}$$

As a result, in the order-up-to model

$$\text{Expected inventory} = S - \text{Expected demand over } l + 1 \text{ periods} + \text{Expected back order}$$

In Susan's territory with $S = 3$, the expected inventory is $3 - 0.58 + 0.00335 = 2.42$. At the Mounds View DC with $S = 625$, the expected inventory is $625 - 322.4 + 0.19 = 302.8$. Exhibit 14.4 summarizes the process.

Pipeline Inventory/Expected On-Order Inventory

Pipeline inventory, which also will be called *expected on-order inventory,* is the average amount of inventory on order at any given time. It is relevant because Medtronic owns the inventory between the Mounds View distribution center and Susan Magnotto's territory. To evaluate pipeline inventory, we refer to Little's Law, described in Chapter 2,

$$\text{Inventory} = \text{Flow rate} \times \text{Flow time}$$

Now let's translate the terms in the Little's Law equation into the comparable terms in this setting: inventory is the number of units on order; flow rate is the expected demand in one period (the expected order in a period equals expected demand in one period, so on-order inventory is being created at a rate equal to expected demand in one period); and flow time is the lead time, since every unit spends l periods on order. Therefore,

$$\text{Expected on-order inventory} = \text{Expected demand in one period} \times \text{Lead time}$$

In the case of the InSync pacemaker, Susan's territory has $0.29 \times 1 = 0.29$ unit on order on average and the Mounds View DC has $80.6 \times 3 = 241.8$ units on order. Exhibit 14.4 summarizes the process.

The expected on-order inventory is based on demand over l periods of time, and not $l + 1$ periods of time. Furthermore, the above equation for the expected on-order inventory holds for any demand distribution because Little's Law depends only on average rates, and not on the variability of those rates.

14.6   Choosing an Order-up-to Level to Meet a Service Target

This section discusses the actual choice of InSync order-up-to levels for Susan Magnotto's territory and the Mounds View DC. To refer to a previously mentioned analogy, the order-up-to level is somewhat like the point in the fuel gauge of your car at which you decide to head to a refueling station. The more you are willing to let the dial fall below the "E," the higher the chance you will run out of fuel. However, while increasing that trigger point in the fuel gauge makes you feel safer, it also increases the average amount of fuel you drive around with. With that trade-off in mind, this section considers choosing an order-up-to level to minimize inventory while achieving an in-stock probability no lower than an in-stock target level. This objective is equivalent to minimizing inventory while yielding a stockout probability no greater than one minus the in-stock target level.

Given Medtronic's large gross margin, let's say we want the in-stock probability to be at least 99.9 percent for the InSync pacemaker in Susan's territory as well as at the Mounds View DC. With a 99.9 percent in-stock probability, a stockout should occur no more than 1 in 1,000 days on average. Section 14.7 discusses whether we have chosen a reasonable target.

From Section 14.5 we know that the in-stock probability is the probability demand over $l + 1$ periods is S or lower. Hence, when demand is modeled with a discrete distribution function, we find the appropriate order-up-to level by looking directly into that table. From Table 14.2, we see that in Susan's territory, $S = 0$ clearly does not meet our objective with an in-stock probability of about 56 percent, that is, $F(0) = 0.5599$. Neither is $S = 3$ sufficient because it has an in-stock probability of about 99.7 percent. However, with $S = 4$ our target is met: the in-stock probability is 99.97 percent. In fact, $S = 4$ exceeds our target by a considerable amount: that translates into one stockout every $1/0.00034 = 2,941$ days, or one stockout every 11.31 years, if we assume 260 days per year.

With the Mounds View DC, we must work with the normal distribution. We first find the order-up-to level that meets our in-stock probability service requirement with the standard normal distribution and then convert that standard normal order-up-to level to the order-up-to level that corresponds to the actual demand distribution. In the Standard Normal Distribution Function Table, we see that $\Phi(3.08) = 0.9990$, so an order-up-to level of 3.08 would generate our desired in-stock probability if demand over $l + 1$ periods followed a standard normal. It remains to convert that z-statistic into an order-up-to level: $S = \mu + z \times \sigma$. Remember that the mean and standard deviation should be from the normal distribution of demand over $l + 1$ periods. Therefore,

$$S = 322.4 + 3.08 \times 117.62 = 685$$

See Exhibit 14.5 for a summary of the process to choose an order-up-to level to achieve a target in-stock probability.

14.7   Choosing an Appropriate Service Level

So far in our discussion, we have chosen high service levels because we suspect that a high service level is appropriate. This section puts more rigor behind our hunch. For the sake of brevity, we'll explicitly consider only the management of field inventory. At the end of the section, we briefly discuss the management of distribution center inventory.

The appropriate service level minimizes the cost of holding inventory plus the cost of poor service. The holding cost of inventory is usually expressed as a *holding cost rate,* which is the cost of holding one unit in inventory for one year, expressed as a percentage of the item's cost. For example, if a firm assigns its holding cost rate to be 20 percent, then it

Exhibit 14.5

HOW TO CHOOSE AN ORDER-UP-TO LEVEL *S* TO ACHIEVE AN IN-STOCK PROBABILITY TARGET IN THE ORDER-UP-TO MODEL

If the demand over $l + 1$ periods is a normal distribution with mean μ and standard deviation σ, then follow steps A and B (see Exhibit 14.1 for the process of evaluating μ and σ if you have demand over a single period):

A. In the Standard Normal Distribution Function Table, find the probability that corresponds to the target in-stock probability. Then find the *z*-statistic that corresponds to that probability. If the target in-stock probability falls between two entries in the table, choose the entry with the larger *z*-statistic.

In Excel the appropriate *z*-statistic can be found with the following equation:

$$z = \text{Normsinv}(\text{Target in-stock probability})$$

B. Convert the *z*-statistic chosen in part A to an order-up-to level: $S = \mu + z \times \sigma$. Recall that you are using the mean and standard deviation of demand over $l + 1$ periods.

If the demand forecast for $l + 1$ periods is a discrete distribution function table, then find the *S* in the table such that $F(S)$ equals the target in-stock probability, where $F(S)$ is the probability demand is less than or equal to *S* over $l + 1$ periods. If the target in-stock probability falls between two entries in the table, choose the larger *S*.

---

believes the cost of holding a unit in inventory for one year equals 20 percent of the item's cost. The holding cost includes the opportunity cost of capital, the cost of spoilage, obsolescence, insurance, storage, and so forth, all variable costs associated with holding inventory. Because Medtronic is a growing company, with a high internal opportunity cost of capital, let's say their holding cost rate is 35 percent for field inventory. We'll use the variable h to represent the holding cost. See Chapter 2 for additional discussion on the holding cost rate.

If we assume the InSync pacemaker has a 75 percent gross margin, then the cost of an InSync pacemaker is $(1 - 0.75) \times \text{Price} = 0.25 \times \text{Price}$, where Price is the selling price.[2] Therefore, the annual holding cost is $0.35 \times 0.25 \times \text{Price} = 0.0875 \times \text{Price}$ and the daily holding cost, assuming 260 days per year, is $0.875 \times \text{Price}/260 = 0.000337 \times \text{Price}$.

The cost of poor service requires some thought. We first need to decide how we will measure poor service and then decide on a cost for poor service. In the order-up-to model, a natural measure of poor service is the occurrence of a back order. Therefore, we say that we incur a cost for each unit back-ordered and we'll let the variable b represent that cost. We'll also refer to the variable b as the *back-order penalty cost*. Now we must decide on an appropriate value for b. A natural focal point with field inventory (i.e., inventory for serving final customers) is to assume each back order causes a lost sale and the cost of a lost sale equals the product's gross margin. However, if you believe there are substantial long-run implications of a lost sale (e.g., the customer will switch his or her future business to a competitor), then maybe the cost of a lost sale is even higher than the gross margin. On the other hand, if customers are somewhat patient, that is, a back order does not automatically lead to a lost sale, then maybe the cost of a back order is lower than the gross margin. In the case of Medtronic, the former story is more likely. Let's suppose each back order leads to a lost sale and, to be conservative, the cost of a back order is just the gross margin; that is, $b = 0.75 \times \text{Price}$.

Now let's minimize Medtronic's holding and back-order costs. The holding cost in a period is h times the number of units in inventory (which we measure at the end of the

---

[2] Medtronic's gross margin across all products, as reported on their income statement, is approximately 80 percent. Because there are competing products, we assume the actual gross margin of the InSync is slightly lower than this average.

period). The back-order cost in a period is b times the number of units back-ordered.[3] As a result, we face the "too little–too much" challenge: Choose S too high and incur excessive inventory holding costs; but if S is too low, then we incur excessive back-order costs. We can actually use the newsvendor logic to strike the correct balance.

Our overage cost is $C_o = h$: the consequence of setting S too high is inventory and the cost per unit of inventory per period is h. Our underage cost is $C_u = b$: back orders are the consequence of setting S too low and the cost per back order is b. In the newsvendor model, we chose an order quantity Q such that the critical ratio equals the probability demand is Q or lower, which is the same as the probability that a stockout does not occur. In the order-up-to model, the probability a stockout does not occur in a period is

$$\text{Prob\{Demand over } l + 1 \text{ periods} \leq S\}$$

Hence, the order-up-to level that minimizes costs in a period satisfies the following newsvendor equation:

$$\text{Prob\{Demand over } l + 1 \text{ periods} \leq S\} = \frac{C_u}{C_o + C_u} = \frac{b}{h + b} \qquad \textbf{(14.2)}$$

For Medtronic, the critical ratio is

$$\frac{b}{h + b} = \frac{(0.75 \times \text{Price})}{(0.00037 \times \text{Price}) + (0.75 \times \text{Price})} = 0.9996$$

Notice the following with respect to equation (14.2):

- We do not need to know the product's actual price, Price, because it cancels out of both the numerator and the denominator of the critical ratio.
- It is important that we use the holding cost per unit per period to evaluate the critical ratio because the order-up-to level determines the expected inventory in a period. In other words, h should be the holding cost for a single unit for a single period.

Now we are ready to justify our service level based on costs. Recall that

$$\text{In-stock probability} = \text{Prob\{Demand over } l + 1 \text{ periods} \leq S\}$$

If we combine the above equation with equation (14.2), then the in-stock probability that is consistent with cost minimization is

$$\text{In-stock probability} = \text{Critical ratio} = \frac{b}{h + b} \qquad \textbf{(14.3)}$$

In other words, the appropriate in-stock probability equals the critical ratio. Recall that we chose 99.9 percent as our target in-stock probability. Even though that might seem high, our calculations above suggest that an in-stock probability of up to 99.96 percent is consistent with cost minimization.

---

[3] If you have been reading carefully, you might realize that this is not entirely correct. The back-order cost in a period is b times the number of demands *in that period* that are back-ordered, that is, we do not incur the cost b per unit that became back-ordered in a previous period and still is on back order. However, with a high in-stock probability, it should be the case that units are rarely back-ordered, and if they are back-ordered, then they are back-ordered for no more than one period. Hence, with a high in-stock probability, assuming the back-order cost is b times the number of units back-ordered is an excellent approximation.

TABLE 14.3
The Optimal Target In-Stock Probability for Various Gross Margins
The annual holding cost rate is 35 percent, the back order penalty cost equals the gross margin, and inventory is reviewed daily.

Gross Margin	Optimal Target In-Stock Probability	Gross Margin	Optimal Target In-Stock Probability
1%	88.24%	35%	99.75%
2	93.81	57	99.90
3	95.83	73	99.95
4	96.87	77	99.96
6	97.93	82	99.97
12	99.02	87	99.98
21	99.50	93	99.99

Holding inventory is not cheap for Medtronic (35 percent holding cost rate), but due to Medtronic's large gross margins, the underage cost ($0.75 \times$ Price) is still about 2,200 times greater than the overage cost ($0.000337 \times$ Price)! With such a lopsided allocation of costs, it is no surprise that the appropriate in-stock probability is so high.

Table 14.3 indicates for various gross margins the optimal target in-stock probability. We can see that an obscene gross margin is needed (93 percent) to justify a 99.99 percent in-stock probability, but a modest gross margin (12 percent) is needed to justify a 99 percent in-stock probability.

Now consider the appropriate service level at the distribution center. While the opportunity cost of capital remains the same whether it is tied up in inventory in the field or at the distribution center, all other inventory holding costs are likely to be lower at the distribution center (e.g., physical space, theft, spoilage, insurance, etc.). But even with a lower holding cost, the appropriate service level at the distribution center is unlikely to be as high as it is in the field because the distribution center's back-order cost should be lower. Why? A back order in the field is likely to lead to a lost sale, but a back order at the distribution center does not necessarily lead to a lost sale. Each field representative has a buffer of inventory and that buffer might prevent a lost sale as long as the back order at the distribution center does not persist for too long. This is not to suggest that the appropriate in-stock probability at the distribution center is low. Rather, it suggests that the appropriate in-stock probability might not be 99.9 percent.[4]

The main insight from this section is that the optimal target in-stock probability in the order-up-to model is likely to be quite high (99 percent and above), even with a relatively modest gross margin and high annual holding cost rate. However, that result depends on two key assumptions: back orders lead to lost sales and inventory does not become obsolete. The latter assumption highlights a connection and a useful contrast between the order-up-to model and the newsvendor model. In the newsvendor model, obsolescence is the primary concern; that is, demand is not expected to continue into the future, so leftover inventory is expensive. As a result, optimal service levels in the newsvendor model are rarely as high as in the order-up-to model. Furthermore, the appropriate model to employ depends on where a *product* is in its *life cycle*. Up to and including the mature stage of a product's life cycle, the order-up-to model is more appropriate. As a product's end of life approaches, the newsvendor model is needed. Some products have very long life cycles—for example, chicken noodle soup—so the newsvendor model is never needed. Others have very short life cycles—for example, O'Neill's Hammer 3/2—so a firm is relegated to the newsvendor model almost immediately. It is the products with an intermediate life

---

[4] Evaluation of the appropriate in-stock probability for the distribution center is beyond the scope of this discussion. However, simulation can be a useful tool to begin to understand the true back-order cost at the distribution center. Via simulation it is possible to estimate the likelihood that a back order at the distribution center causes a lost sale in the field.

cycle (one to two years)—for example, the InSync pacemaker—that can be very tricky to manage. A firm should start thinking in terms of the order-up-to model and then switch to the newsvendor model shortly before the product dies. Many firms botch this "end-of-life" transition: by holding on to high service levels too long, they find themselves with far too much inventory when the product becomes obsolete.

14.8 Controlling Ordering Costs

In our analysis of Medtronic's supply chain, the focus has been on the service level (the in-stock probability) and the expected amount of inventory on hand at the end of each period. Although we have not addressed the issue of *order frequency* (i.e., how many shipments are made each year to the DC or to each sales territory), there are other settings for which it is important to control the order frequency. For example, most online book shoppers realize, due to how online retailers charge for shipping, that five separate orders with one book in each order is generally more expensive than one book order containing the same five books. In other words, when there is a significant cost incurred with each order that is independent of the amount ordered (i.e., a fixed cost), it is necessary to be smart about how often orders are made. The focus of this section is on how we can account for fixed ordering costs in the order-up-to model.

As we have already seen, in the order-up-to model, the order quantity in a period equals the demand in the previous period. Hence, an order is submitted in a period whenever demand in the previous period is not zero. Therefore, the probability we submit an order in a period is $1 - \text{Prob\{Demand in one period} = 0\}$ and the frequency at which we submit orders is

$$\frac{1 - \text{Prob\{Demand in one period} = 0\}}{\text{Length of period}}$$

For example, if there is a 90 percent probability we order in a period and a period is two weeks, then our order frequency is 0.9/2 weeks = 0.45 order per week. If demand occurs frequently, so the probability of zero demand is very small no matter the length of the period, then it follows that we can reduce our ordering frequency by increasing the length of our period; that is, we are likely to submit nearly twice as many orders with a one-week period than with a two-week period. But increasing the length of the period is costly from the perspective of inventory holding costs. We illustrate that point via an example.

Suppose all orders are received precisely eight weeks after they are submitted to a supplier, weekly demand is normally distributed with mean 100 and standard deviation 75, the target in-stock probability is 99.25 percent, and demands across weeks are independent. We can choose a period length of one, two, four, or eight weeks. If the period is one week, then the lead time is eight periods, whereas if the period length is four weeks, then the lead time is two periods. Using the methods developed in the previous sections, we can determine the end-of-period average inventory for each period length. Those results are summarized in Table 14.4. The table reveals that our end-of-period inventory is indeed higher as we lengthen the period. But that is not really a fair comparison across our different options.

As we have already stated, the average order quantity equals average demand in the previous period. Thus, our average order quantity with a period length of one week is 100 units, whereas our average order quantity with an eight-week period is 800 units. Figure 14.7 plots the average inventory level over time for our four options; on average, inventory increases at the start of the period by the average order quantity and then decreases at the rate of 100 units per week, that is, average inventory follows a "saw-toothed" pattern. (Due to randomness in demand, the actual inventory pattern varies around those patterns, but those saw-toothed

TABLE 14.4
Analysis of Ending Inventory for Different Period Lengths
In each case, the delivery time is eight weeks and demand is normally distributed and independent across weeks.

	Period Length (in weeks)			
	1	**2**	**4**	**8**
One period expected demand	100	200	400	800
One period standard deviation	75.0	106.1	150.0	212.1
Lead time (in periods)	8	4	2	1
Target in-stock probability	99.25%	99.25%	99.25%	99.25%
z	2.43	2.43	2.43	2.43
S	1,447	1,576	1,831	2,329
Average back order	0.56	0.59	0.65	0.75
Average ending inventory	548	577	632	730

patterns capture the average behavior of inventory.) The average inventory over time is the average end-of-period inventory plus half of the average order quantity, which for our four options is 598, 677, 832, and 1,130 respectively. Hence, longer periods mean less-frequent ordering but more inventory.

Incidentally, you may recall that the graphs in Figure 14.7 resemble Figure 2.11 in Chapter 2. Back in Chapter 2 we used the term *cycle inventory* to refer to the inventory held due to lumpy ordering. In this case, the average cycle inventory would be half of the average order quantity: with four-week periods, the average cycle inventory is $400/2 = 200$ units. The average end-of-period inventory is often referred to as *safety inventory* because that is the inventory that is needed to buffer demand variability. The average inventory over time is then safety inventory plus cycle inventory.

To balance the cost of more inventory with the benefit of fewer orders, we need information about holding and ordering costs. Let's say this item costs $50, annual holding costs are

FIGURE 14.7
Average Inventory Pattern over Time for Four Different Period Lengths
Upper left, one week; upper right, two weeks; lower left, four weeks; and lower right, eight weeks.

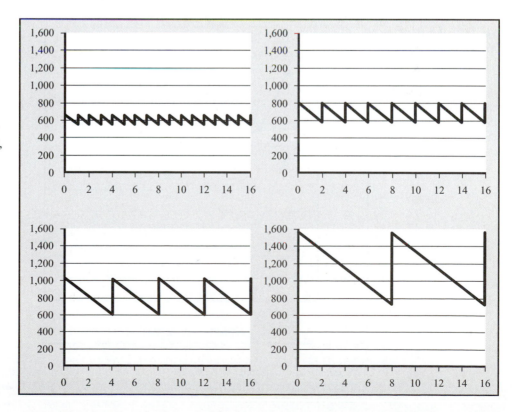

25 percent, and we incur a fixed cost of $275 per shipment (e.g., we could be talking about a truck delivery). If the period length is one week, then the average inventory is 598 units, which has value 598 × $50 = $29,900 and costs us 25% × $29,900 = $7,475 per year. With mean demand of 100 and a standard deviation of 75, the z-statistic for 0 is (0 − 100)/75 = −1.33. Hence, the probability we order in any given week is 1 − Φ(−1.33) = 0.91.[5] With 52 weeks per year, we can expect to make 0.91 × 52 = 47.32 orders per year for a total ordering cost of 47.32 × $275 = $13,013. Total cost is then $7,475 + $13,013 = $20,488. Repeating those calculations for the remaining three period-length options reveals their annual costs to be $15,398, $13,975, and $15,913. Figure 14.8 plots those costs as well as the inventory holding and ordering costs of the four options.

Figure 14.8 reveals that our best option is to set the period length to four weeks (which implies the lead time is then two periods). A shorter period length results in too many orders so the extra ordering costs dominate the reduced holding costs. A longer period suffers from too much inventory.

Although this analysis has been done in the context of the order-up-to model, it may very well remind you of another model, the *Economic Order Quantity (EOQ)* model discussed in Chapter 7. Recall that in the EOQ model there is a fixed cost per order/batch K and a holding cost per unit per unit of time h and demand occurs at a constant flow rate R; in this case, $R = 100$ per week or $R = 5,200$ per year. The key difference between our model and the EOQ model is that here we have random demand whereas the EOQ model assumes demand occurs at a constant rate. Nevertheless, it is interesting to evaluate the EOQ model in this setting. We already know that the fixed ordering cost is K $275. The holding cost per unit per year is 25% × $50 = $12.5. So the EOQ quantity (see Chapter 7) is

$$Q = \sqrt{\frac{2 \times K \times R}{h}} = \sqrt{\frac{2 \times 275 \times 5200}{12.5}} = 478$$

FIGURE 14.8
Annual Ordering Costs (squares), Inventory Costs (diamonds), and Total Costs (circles) for Periods of Length One, Two, Four, and Eight Weeks

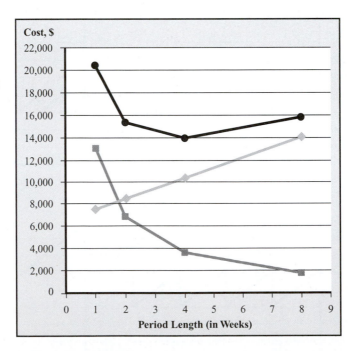

(Note that we need to use the yearly flow rate because the holding cost is per unit per year.) Hence, the EOQ model suggests that each order should be for 478 units, which implies submitting an order every $478/100 = 4.78$ weeks. (This follows from Little's Law.) Hence, even though the order-up-to and the EOQ models are different, the EOQ model's recommendation is quite similar (order every 4.78 weeks versus order every 4 weeks). Although we have only demonstrated this for one example, it can be shown that the EOQ model generally gives a very good recommendation for the period length (note that the EOQ actually recommends an order quantity that can then be converted to a period length).

One limitation of our order-up-to model is that the lead time must equal an integer number of periods. In our example, because the delivery time is eight weeks, this allows us to choose period lengths of one, two, four, or eight, but we cannot choose a period length of 3 or 5 or 4.78 weeks (because with a period length of 3 weeks the lead time is 2.67 periods, i.e., deliveries would be received two-thirds of the way into a period instead of at the beginning of the period). If the delivery time were three weeks, then we would be even more restricted in our period length options. Fortunately, the order-up-to model can be extended to handle situations in which the lead time is a fraction of the period length. But that extension is beyond the scope of this text, and, rest assured, the qualitative insights from our model carry over to that more complex setting.

So we have shown that we can adjust our period length in the order-up-to model to control our ordering costs. Furthermore, the average order quantity with the optimal period length will approximately equal the EOQ quantity. (Hence, the EOQ formula gives us an easy way to check if our period length is reasonable.) One advantage of this approach is that we submit orders on a regular schedule. This is a useful feature if we need to coordinate the orders across multiple items. For example, since we incur a fixed cost per truck shipment, we generally deliver many different products on each truck because no single product's demand is large enough to fill a truck (imagine sending a tractor trailer load of spices to a grocery store). In that situation, it is quite useful to order items at the same time so that the truck can be loaded quickly and we can ensure a reasonably full shipment (given that there is a fixed cost per shipment, it makes sense to utilize the cargo capacity as much as possible). Therefore, we need only ensure that the order times of different products align.

Instead of using fixed order intervals, as in the order-up-to model, we could control ordering costs by imposing a minimum order quantity. For example, we could wait for Q units of demand to occur and then order exactly Q units. With such a policy, we would order on average every Q/R units of time, but due to the randomness in demand, the time between orders would vary. Not surprisingly, the EOQ quantity provides an excellent recommendation for that minimum order quantity, but we omit the analytical details as they are beyond the scope of this text. The important insight from this discussion is that it is possible to control ordering costs by restricting ourselves to a periodic schedule of orders (as in the order-up-to model) or we could restrict ourselves to a minimum order quantity. With the first option, there is little variability in the timing of orders, which facilitates the coordination of orders across multiple items, but the order quantities are variable (which may increase handling costs). With the second option, the order quantities are not variable (we always order Q), but the timing of those orders varies.

14.9 Managerial Insights

This section discusses general managerial insights from the order-up-to model.

One of the key lessons from the queuing and newsvendor chapters is that variability in demand is costly. (Recall that the mismatch cost in the newsvendor model is increasing with the coefficient of variation, which is the ratio of the standard deviation of demand to expected

FIGURE 14.9
The Trade-off between Inventory and In-Stock with Normally Distributed Demand and Mean 100 over *l* **+ 1 Periods**
The curves differ in the standard deviation of demand over *l* + 1 periods: 60, 50, 40, 30, 20,10 from top to bottom.

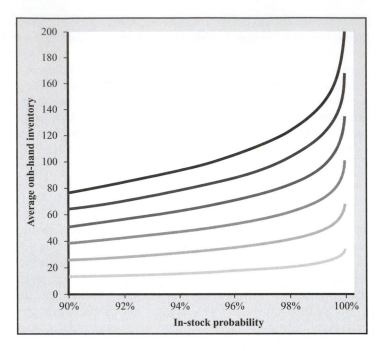

demand.) That result continues to hold in the order-up-to model. Figure 14.9 illustrates the result graphically. The figure presents the trade-off curve between the in-stock probability and expected inventory: as the desired in-stock probability increases, so does the required amount of inventory. Furthermore, we see that for any given in-stock probability, the expected inventory increases in the standard deviation of demand over *l* + 1 periods: increased variability means more inventory is needed on average to achieve a fixed service level.

In addition to the variability in demand, the expected inventory in the order-up-to model is sensitive to the lead time, as illustrated by Figure 14.10: as the lead time is reduced, so is the required inventory for any service target.

While expected inventory depends on the variability of demand and the lead time, the expected on-order inventory, or pipeline inventory, depends only on the lead time. Therefore, while reducing the uncertainty in demand reduces expected inventory, pipeline

FIGURE 14.10
The Impact of Lead Time on Expected Inventory for Four In-Stock Targets
In-Stock targets are 99.9, 99.5, 99.0, and 98 percent, top curve to bottom curve, respectively. Demand in one period is normally distributed with mean 100 and standard deviation 60.

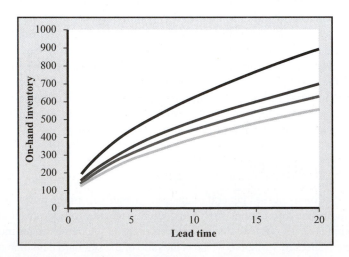

FIGURE 14.11
Expected Inventory (circles) and Total Inventory (squares), Which Is Expected Inventory Plus Pipeline Inventory, with a 99.9 Percent In-Stock Requirement
Demand in one period is normally distributed with mean 100 and standard deviation 60.

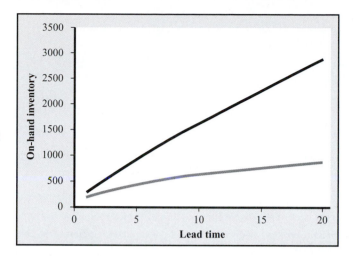

inventory can only be reduced with a faster lead time. (Actually, reducing demand also reduces pipeline inventory, but that is rarely an attractive option, and reducing demand does not even reduce pipeline inventory when it is measured relative to the demand rate, e.g., with inventory turns or days of demand.) Furthermore, the amount of pipeline inventory can be considerable, especially for long lead times, as demonstrated in Figure 14.11, where the distance between the two curves is the pipeline inventory, which is clearly growing as the lead time increases.

14.10 Summary

This chapter illustrates the application of the order-up-to model to one product, the InSync pacemaker, at two different levels in Medtronic's supply chain: the Mounds View distribution center and Susan Magnotto's Madison, Wisconsin, territory. The order-up-to model periodically reviews (weekly at Mounds View, daily for Susan) the inventory position at a location and submits an order, which is received after a fixed lead time, to raise the inventory position to an order-up-to level. The order-up-to level is chosen, based on the demand distribution, to minimize inventory while maintaining a service standard such as an in-stock probability.

The analysis of the order-up-to model reveals that raising the desired service level increases the required inventory investment and the amount of inventory needed increases nonlinearly as the target service level increases. In other words, as high service levels are desired, proportionally more inventory is needed.

There are two other key factors that determine the amount of inventory that is needed: the variability of demand, measured by the coefficient of variation, and the length of the lead time. Just as we saw in the newsvendor model, an increase in the coefficient of variation leads to an increase in the amount of inventory needed for any fixed service level.

The length of the lead time is critical for two reasons. First, a reduction in the lead time reduces the amount of inventory needed at any location. Second, and maybe even more importantly, a reduction in the lead time reduces the amount of inventory in transit between locations, that is, the pipeline inventory. In fact, reducing the lead time is the only way to reduce the pipeline inventory: While reducing the variability of demand reduces the expected inventory at a location, it has no effect on pipeline inventory because of Little's Law.

Table 14.5 provides a summary of the key notation and equations presented in this chapter.

TABLE 14.5
Summary of Key Notation and Equations in Chapter 14

l = Lead time

S = Order-up-to level

Inventory level = On-hand inventory − Back order

Inventory position = On-order inventory + Inventory level

In-stock probability = 1 − Stockout probability

= Prob{Demand over l + 1 periods ≤ S}

Expected back order:

If demand over l + 1 periods is normally distributed with mean μ and standard deviation σ:

Expected back order = $\sigma \times L(z)$, where $z = (S - \mu)/\sigma$

In Excel:

Expected back order = $\sigma*(\text{Normdist}(z,0,1,0) - z*(1 - \text{Normsdist}(z)))$

If demand over l + 1 periods is a discrete distribution function table, then
Expected back order = $L(S)$

Expected inventory = S − Expected demand over l + 1 periods + Expected back order

Expected on-order inventory = Expected demand in one period × Lead time

14.11 Further Reading

The order-up-to model is just one of many possible inventory policies that could be implemented in practice. For example, there are policies that account for stochastic lead times, lost sales, and/or batch ordering (ordering in integer multiples of a fixed batch quantity). However, no matter what extensions are included, the key insights remain: Inventory increases as demand variability increases or as the lead time increases.

See Zipkin (2000) for an extensive treatment of the theory of inventory management. For less technical, but still sophisticated, treatments, see Nahmias (2005) or Silver, Pyke, and Peterson (1998). Those texts cover the additional polices we discussed in the chapter (for example, a minimum order quantity with a fixed lead time and stochastic demand). In addition, they discuss the issue of the appropriate service level for upstream stages in a supply chain.

See Simchi-Levi, Kaminsky, and Simchi-Levi (2003) and Chopra and Meindl (2004) for managerial discussions of supply-chain management.

14.12 Practice Problems

Q14.1*   **(Furniture Store)** You are the store manager at a large furniture store. One of your products is a study desk. Weekly demand for the desk is normally distributed with mean 40 and standard deviation 20. The lead time from the assembly plant to your store is two weeks and you order inventory replenishments weekly. You use the order-up-to model to control inventory.

a. Suppose your order-up-to level is $S = 220$. You are about to place an order and note that your inventory level is 100 and you have 85 desks on order. How many desks will you order?

b. Suppose your order-up-to level is $S = 220$. You are about to place an order and note that your inventory level is 160 and you have 65 desks on order. How many desks will you order?

c. What is the optimal order-up-to level if you want to target a 98 percent in-stock probability?

d. Suppose your order-up-to level is $S = 120$. What is your expected on-hand inventory?

e. Suppose your order-up-to level is $S = 120$. Your internal cost of capital is 15 percent and each desk costs $200. What is your total cost of capital for the year for inventory in the store?

(* indicates that the solution is at the end of the book)

Q14.2* **(Campus Bookstore)** A campus bookstore sells the Palm m505 handheld for $399. The wholesale price is $250 per unit. The store estimates that weekly demand averages 0.5 unit and has a Poisson distribution. The bookstore's annual inventory holding cost is 20 percent of the cost of inventory. Assume orders are made weekly and the lead time to receive an order from the distributor is four weeks.

    a. What base stock level minimizes inventory while achieving a 99 percent in-stock probability?

    b. Suppose the base stock level is $S = 4$. What is the average pipeline inventory?

    c. Suppose the base stock level is $S = 5$. What is the average inventory held at the end of the week in the store?

    d. Suppose the base stock level is $S = 6$. What is the probability a stockout occurs during a week (i.e., some customer is back-ordered)?

    e. Suppose the base stock level is $S = 6$. What is the probability the store is out of stock (i.e., has no inventory) at the end of a week?

    f. Suppose the base stock level is $S = 6$. What is the probability the store has one or more units of inventory at the end of a week?

The bookstore is concerned that it is incurring excessive ordering costs by ordering weekly. For parts g and h, suppose the bookstore now submits orders every two weeks. The demand forecast remains the same and the lead time is still four weeks.

    g. What base stock level yields at least a 99 percent in-stock probability while minimizing inventory?

    h. What is the average pipeline stock?

Q14.3* **(Quick Print)** Quick Print Inc. uses plain and three-hole-punched paper for copying needs. Demand for each paper type is highly variable. Weekly demand for the plain paper is estimated to be normally distributed with mean 100 and standard deviation 65 (measured in boxes). Each week, a replenishment order is placed to the paper factory and the order arrives five weeks later. All copying orders that cannot be satisfied immediately due to the lack of paper are back-ordered. The inventory holding cost is about $1 per box per year.

    a. Suppose that Quick Print decides to establish an order-up-to level of 700 for plain paper. At the start of this week, there are 523 boxes in inventory and 180 boxes on order. How much will Quick Print order this week?

    b. What is Quick Print's optimal order-up-to level for plain paper if Quick Print operates with a 99 percent in-stock probability?

Q14.4* **(Main Line Auto Distributor)** Main Line Auto Distributor is an auto parts supplier to local garage shops. None of its customers have the space or capital to store all of the possible parts they might need so they order parts from Main Line several times a day. To provide fast service, Main Line uses three pickup trucks to make its own deliveries. Each Friday evening, Main Line orders additional inventory from its supplier. The supplier delivers early Monday morning. Delivery costs are significant, so Main Line only orders on Fridays. Consider part A153QR, or part A for short. Part A costs Main Line $175 and Main Line sells it to garages for $200. If a garage orders part A and Main Line is out of stock, then the garage finds the part from some other distributor. Main Line has its own capital and space constraints and estimates that each unit of part A costs $0.50 to hold in inventory per week. (Assume you incur the $0.50 cost for units left in inventory at the end of the week, not $0.50 for your average inventory during the week or $0.50 for your inventory at the start of the week.) Average weekly demand for this part follows a Poisson distribution with mean 1.5 units. Suppose it is Friday evening and Main Line currently doesn't have any part A's in stock. The distribution and loss functions for a Poisson distribution with mean 1.5 can be found in Appendix B.

    a. How many part A's should Main Line order from the supplier?

(* indicates that the solution is at the end of the book)

b. Suppose Main Line orders three units. What is the probability Main Line is able to satisfy all demand during the week?

c. Suppose Main Line orders four units. What is the probability Main Line is *not* able to satisfy all demand during the week?

d. If Main Line seeks to hit a target in-stock probability of 99.5 percent, then how many units should Main Line order?

e. Suppose Main Line orders five units. What is Main Line's expected holding cost for the upcoming week?

Q14.5* **(Hotspices.com)** You are the owner of Hotspices.com, an online retailer of hip, exotic, and hard-to-find spices. Consider your inventory of saffron, a spice (generally) worth more by weight than gold. You order saffron from an overseas supplier with a shipping lead time of four weeks and you order weekly. Average quarterly demand is normally distributed with a mean of 415 ounces and a standard deviation of 154 ounces. The holding cost per ounce per week is $0.75. You estimate that your back-order penalty cost is $50 per ounce. Assume there are 4.33 weeks per month.

a. If you wish to minimize inventory holding costs while maintaining a 99.25 percent in-stock probability, then what should your order-up-to level be?

b. If you wish to minimize holding and back-order penalty costs, then what should your order-up-to level be?

c. Now consider your inventory of pepperoncini (Italian hot red peppers). You can order this item daily and your local supplier delivers with a two-day lead time. While not your most popular item, you do have enough demand to sell the five-kilogram bag. Average demand per day has a Poisson distribution with mean 1.0. The holding cost per bag per day is $0.05 and the back-order penalty cost is about $5 per bag. What is your optimal order-up-to level?

Q14.6** **(Blood Bank)** Dr. Jack is in charge of the Springfield Hospital's Blood Center. Blood is collected in the regional Blood Center 200 miles away and delivered to Springfield by airplane. Dr. Jack reviews blood reserves and places orders every Monday morning for delivery the following Monday morning. If demand begins to exceed supply, surgeons postpone nonurgent procedures, in which case blood is back-ordered.

Demand for blood on every given week is normal with mean 100 pints and standard deviation 34 pints. Demand is independent across weeks.

a. On Monday morning, Dr. Jack reviews his reserves and observes 200 pints in on-hand inventory, no back orders, and 73 pints in pipeline inventory. Suppose his order-up-to level is 285. How many pints will he order? Choose the closest answer.

b. Dr. Jack targets a 99 percent in-stock probability. What order-up-to level should he choose? Choose the closest answer.

c. Dr. Jack is planning to implement a computer system that will allow daily ordering (seven days per week) and the lead time to receive orders will be one day. What will be the average order quantity?

Q14.7** **(Schmears Shirts)** Schmears Inc. is a catalog retailer of men's shirts. Daily demand for a particular SKU (style and size) is Poisson with mean 1.5. It takes three days for a replenishment order to arrive from Schmears' supplier and orders are placed daily. Schmears uses the order-up-to model to manage its inventory of this shirt.

a. Suppose Schmears uses an order-up-to level of 9. What is the average number of shirts on order?

b. Now suppose Schmears uses an order-up-to level of 8. What is the probability during any given day that Schmears does not have sufficient inventory to meet the demand from all customers?

c. Suppose Schmears wants to ensure that 90 percent of customer demand is satisfied immediately from stock. What order-up-to level should they use?

(* indicates that the solution is at the end of the book)

d. Schmears is considering a switch from a "service-based" stocking policy to a "cost-minimization" stocking policy. They estimate their holding cost per shirt per day is $0.01. Forty-five percent of customers order more than one item at a time, so they estimate their stockout cost on this shirt is $6 per shirt. What order-up-to level minimizes the sum of their holding and back-order costs?

Q14.8 **(ACold)** ACold Inc. is a frozen food distributor with 10 warehouses across the country. Iven Tory, one of the warehouse managers, wants to make sure that the inventory policies used by the warehouse are minimizing inventory while still maintaining quick delivery to ACold's customers. Since the warehouse carries hundreds of different products, Iven decided to study one. He picked Caruso's Frozen Pizza. Demand for CFPs averages 400 per day with a standard deviation of 200. Weekly demand (five days) averages 2,000 units with a standard deviation of 555. Since ACold orders at least one truck from General Foods each day (General Foods owns Caruso's Pizza), ACold can essentially order any quantity of CFP it wants each day. In fact, ACold's computer system is designed to implement a base stock policy for each product. Iven notes that any order for CFPs arrives four days after the order. Further, it costs ACold $0.01 per day to keep a CFP in inventory, while a back order is estimated to cost ACold $0.45.

a. What base stock level should Iven choose for CFPs if his goal is to minimize holding and back-order costs?

b. Suppose the base stock level 2,800 is chosen. What is the average amount of inventory on order?

c. Suppose the base stock level 2,800 is chosen. What is the annual holding cost? (Assume 260 days per year.)

d. What base stock level minimizes inventory while maintaining a 97 percent in-stock probability?

Q14.9 **(Cyber Chemicals)** Cyber Chemicals uses liquid nitrogen on a regular basis. Average daily demand is 178 gallons with a standard deviation of 45. Due to a substantial ordering cost, which is estimated to be $58 per order (no matter the quantity in the order), Cyber currently orders from its supplier on a weekly basis. Cyber also incurs holding costs on its inventory. Cyber recognizes that its inventory is lowest at the end of the week but prefers a more realistic estimate of its average inventory. In particular, Cyber estimates its average inventory to be its average end-of-week inventory plus half of its average order quantity. The holding cost Cyber incurs on that average inventory is $0.08 per gallon per week. Cyber's supplier delivers in less than a day. Assume 52 weeks per year, five days per week.

a. Cyber wishes to maintain a 99.9 percent in-stock probability. If it does so, what is Cyber's annual inventory holding cost?

b. What is Cyber's annual ordering cost?

c. Should Cyber consider ordering every two weeks?

Q14.10 **(Southern Fresh)** Shelf space in the grocery business is a valuable asset. Every good supermarket spends a significant amount of effort attempting to determine the optimal shelf space allocation across products. Many factors are relevant to this decision: the profitability of each product, the size of each product, the demand characteristics of each product, and so forth. Consider Hot Bull corn chips, a local favorite. Average daily demand for this product is 55, with a standard deviation of 30. Bags of Hot Bull can be stacked 20 deep per facing. (A facing is the width on a shelf required to display one item of a product.) Deliveries from Southern Fresh's central warehouse occur two days after a store manager submits an order. (Actually, in most stores, orders are generated by a centralized computer system that is linked to its point-of-sales data. But even these orders are received two days after they are transmitted.)

a. How many facings are needed to achieve a 98.75 percent in-stock probability?

b. Suppose Southern Fresh allocates 11 facings to Hot Bull corn chips. On average, how many bags of Hot Bull are on the shelf at the end of the day?

c. Although Southern Fresh does not want to incur the cost of holding inventory, it does want to leave customers with the impression that it is well stocked. Hence, Southern Fresh employees continually roam the aisles of the store to adjust the presentation of the product. In particular, they shift product around so that there is an item in each facing whenever possible. Suppose Southern Fresh allocates 11 facings to Hot Bull corn chips. What is the probability that at the end of the day there will be an empty facing, that is, a facing without any product?

You can view a video of how problems marked with a ** are solved by going on www. cachon-terwiesch.net and follow the links under 'Solved Practice Problems'

Chapter 15

Risk-Pooling Strategies to Reduce and Hedge Uncertainty[1]

Uncertainty is the bane of operations. No matter in what form—for example, uncertain demand, uncertain supply, or uncertain quality—operational performance never benefits from the presence of uncertainty. Previous chapters have discussed models for coping with uncertainty (e.g., queuing, newsvendor, and order-up-to) and have emphasized the need to quantify uncertainty. Some strategies for reducing and hedging uncertainty have already been suggested: combine servers in a queuing system (Chapter 9); reduce uncertainty by collecting data to ensure that the best demand forecast is always implemented (Chapter 12); establish make-to-order production and invest in reactive capacity to better respond to demand (Chapter 13).

This chapter explores several additional strategies based on the concept of risk pooling. The idea behind risk pooling is to redesign the supply chain, the production process, or the product to either reduce the uncertainty the firm faces or hedge uncertainty so that the firm is in a better position to mitigate the consequence of uncertainty. Several types of risk pooling are presented (location pooling, virtual pooling, product pooling, lead time pooling, and capacity pooling), but these are just different names to describe the same basic phenomenon. With each strategy, we work through a practical example to illustrate its effectiveness and to highlight the situations in which the strategy is most appropriate.

15.1 Location Pooling

The newsvendor and the order-up-to inventory models are tools for deciding how much inventory to put at a single location to serve demand. An equally important decision, and one that we have ignored so far, is in how many different locations should the firm store inventory to serve demand. To explain, consider the Medtronic supply chain discussed in Chapter 14. In that supply chain, each sales representative in the field manages a cache of inventory to serve the rep's territory and there is a single distribution center to serve the entire U.S. market. Should there be one stockpile of inventory per sales representative or should the demands from multiple territories be served from a single location? Should

[1] Data in this chapter have been disguised to protect confidentiality.

there be a single distribution center or should the U.S. market demand be divided among multiple distribution centers? We explore those questions in this section.

Pooling Medtronic's Field Inventory

Let's begin with where to locate Medtronic's field inventory. Instead of the current system in which each sales representative manages his or her own inventory, maybe the representatives in adjacent territories could share inventory. For example, Medtronic could rent a small space in a centrally located and easily accessible location (e.g., a back room in a strip mall off the interchange of two major highways) and two to five representatives could pool their inventory at that location. Sharing inventory means that each representative would only carry inventory needed for immediate use; that is, each representative's trunk and consignment inventory would be moved to this shared location. Control of the pooled inventory would be guided by an automatic replenishment system based on the order-up-to model. What impact would this new strategy have on inventory performance?

Recall that average daily demand for Medtronic's InSync pacemaker in Susan Magnotto's Madison, Wisconsin, territory is represented with a Poisson distribution with mean 0.29 unit per day. For the sake of argument, let's suppose there are several other territories adjacent to Susan's, each with a single sales representative and each with average daily demand of 0.29 unit for the InSync pacemaker. Instead of each representative carrying his or her own inventory, now they share a common pool of inventory. We refer to the combined territories in this new system as the *pooled territory* and the inventory there as the *pooled inventory*. In contrast, we refer to the territories in the current system as the *individual territories* and the inventory in one of those territories as the *individual inventory*. We refer to the strategy of combining the inventory from multiple territories/locations into a single location as *location pooling*. We have already evaluated the expected inventory with the current individual territory system, so now we need to evaluate the performance of the system with pooled territories, that is, the impact of location pooling.

The order-up-to model is used to manage the inventory at the pooled territory. The same aggressive target in-stock probability is used for the pooled territory as is used at the individual territories, 99.9 percent. Furthermore, the lead time to replenish the pooled territory is also one day. (There is no reason to believe the lead time to the pooled territory should be different than to the individual territories.)

As discussed in Chapter 14, if the Poisson distribution represents demand at two different territories, then their combined demand has a Poisson distribution with a mean that equals the sum of their means. (See Exhibit 14.1.) For example, suppose Susan shares inventory with two nearby sales representatives and they all have mean demand for the InSync pacemaker of 0.29 unit per day. Then total demand across the three territories is Poisson with mean $3 \times 0.29 = 0.87$ unit per day. We then can apply the order-up-to model to that pooled territory assuming a lead time of one day and a mean demand of 0.87 unit.

Table 15.1 presents data on the impact of pooling the sales representatives' territories. To achieve the 99.9 percent in-stock probability for three sales representatives requires $S = 7$, where S is the order-up-to level. If Susan's inventory is not combined with another representative's, then (as we evaluated in Chapter 14) $S = 4$ is needed to hit the target in-stock probability. The expected inventory at the pooled location is 5.3 units, in contrast to 3.4 units for each individual location. However, the total inventory for three individual locations is $3 \times 3.4 = 10.2$ units. Hence, pooling three locations reduces expected inventory by about 48 percent $[(10.2 - 5.3)/10.2]$, without any degradation in service!

TABLE 15.1
The Impact on InSync Pacemaker Inventory from Pooling Sales Representatives' Territories
Demand at each territory is Poisson with average daily demand of 0.29 unit, the target in-stock probability is 99.9 percent, and the lead time is one day.

Number of Territories Pooled	Pooled Territory's Expected Demand per Day (a)	S	Expected Inventory		Pipeline Inventory	
			Units (b)	Days-of-Demand (b/a)	Units (c)	Days-of-Demand (c/a)
1	0.29	4	3.4	11.7	0.29	1.0
2	0.58	6	4.8	8.3	0.58	1.0
3	0.87	7	5.3	6.1	0.87	1.0
4	1.16	8	5.7	4.9	1.16	1.0
5	1.45	9	6.1	4.2	1.45	1.0
6	1.74	10	6.5	3.7	1.74	1.0
7	2.03	12	7.9	3.9	2.03	1.0
8	2.32	13	8.4	3.6	2.32	1.0

There is another approach to make the comparison between pooled territories and individual territories: Evaluate each inventory quantity relative to the demand it serves, that is, calculate expected inventory measured in days-of-demand rather than units:

$$\text{Expected inventory in days-of-demand} = \frac{\text{Expected inventory in units}}{\text{Expected daily demand}}$$

Table 15.1 also provides that measure of expected inventory. We see that inventory at each individual territory equals 3.4/0.29 = 11.7 days-of-demand whereas inventory at three pooled territories equals only 5.3/0.87 = 6.1 days-of-demand. Using our days-of-demand measure, we see that pooling three territories results in a 48 percent [(11.7 − 6.1)/11.7] reduction in inventory investment. We obtain the same inventory reduction (48 percent) because the two measures of inventory, units and days-of-demand, only differ by a constant factor (the expected daily demand). Hence, we can work with either measure.

While pooling two or three territories has a dramatic impact on inventory, Table 15.1 indicates that there are decreasing marginal returns to pooling territories; that is, each new territory added to the pool brings a smaller reduction in inventory than the previous territory added to the pool. For example, adding two more territories to a pool of six (to make a total of eight combined territories) has very little impact on the inventory investment (3.6 days-of-demand versus 3.7 days-of-demand), whereas adding two more territories to a pool of one (to make a total of three combined territories) has a dramatic impact in inventory (6.1 days-of-demand versus 11.7 days-of-demand). This is good news: the majority of the benefit of pooling territories comes from the first couple of territories combined, so there is little value in trying to combine many territories together.

Although location pooling generally reduces inventory, a careful observer of the data in Table 15.1 would discover that this is not always so: adding the seventh location to the pool slightly increases inventory (3.9 days-of-demand versus 3.7 days-of-demand). This is due to the restriction that the order-up-to level must be an integer (0, 1, 2, . . .) quantity. As a result, the in-stock probability might be even higher than the target: the in-stock probability with six pooled territories is 99.90 percent, whereas it is 99.97 percent with seven pooled territories. Overall, this issue does not invalidate the general trend that location pooling reduces inventory.

This discussion obviously leads to the question of why does location pooling reduce the required inventory investment? We'll find a good answer by looking at how demand variability changes as locations are added to the pooled location. And, as we have already discussed, the coefficient of variation (the ratio of the standard deviation to the mean) is our choice for measuring demand variability.

Recall that the standard deviation of a Poisson distribution equals the square root of its mean. Therefore,

$$\text{Coefficient of variation of a Poisson distribution} =$$
$$\frac{\text{Standard deviation}}{\text{Mean}} = \frac{\sqrt{\text{Mean}}}{\text{Mean}} = \frac{1}{\sqrt{\text{Mean}}} \quad \textbf{(15.1)}$$

As the mean of a Poisson distribution increases, its coefficient of variation decreases, that is, the Poisson distribution becomes less variable. Less variable demand leads to less inventory for any given service level. Hence, combining locations with Poisson demand reduces the required inventory investment because a higher demand rate implies less variable demand. However, because the coefficient of variation decreases with the square root of the mean, it decreases at a decreasing rate. In other words, each incremental increase in the mean has a proportionally smaller impact on the coefficient of variation, and, hence, on the expected inventory investment.

Figure 15.1 displays the relationship between inventory and the coefficient of variation for the data in Table 15.1. Notice that the decreasing pattern in inventory closely mimics the decreasing pattern in the coefficient of variation.

In addition to the total expected inventory in the field, we also are interested in the total pipeline inventory (inventory on order between the distribution center and the field). Table 15.1 provides the pipeline inventory in terms of units and in terms of days-of-demand. While location pooling decreases the expected inventory in days-of-demand, it has absolutely no impact on the pipeline inventory in terms of days-of-demand! Why? Little's

FIGURE 15.1
The Relationship between Expected Inventory (circles) and the Coefficient of Variation (squares) as Territories Are Pooled
Demand in each territory is Poisson with mean 0.29 unit per day, the target in-stock probability is 99.9 percent, and the lead time is one day.

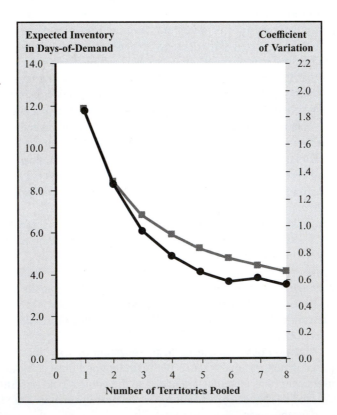

TABLE 15.2

Using Location Pooling to Raise the In-Stock Probability While Maintaining the Same Inventory Investment

Demand at each territory is Poisson with average daily demand of 0.29 unit, and the lead time is one day.

Number of Territories Pooled	Pooled Territory's Expected Demand per Day	S	Expected Inventory		
			Units	Days-of-Demand	In-Stock Probability
1	0.29	4	3.4	11.7	99.96615%
2	0.58	8	6.8	11.7	99.99963
3	0.87	12	10.3	11.8	100.00000

Law governs pipeline inventory, and Little's Law depends on averages, not variability. Hence, because pooling territories reduces the variability of demand, it reduces expected inventory in the field, but it has no impact on the pipeline inventory. As we mentioned before, the only way to reduce pipeline inventory is to get a faster lead time.

While we can exploit location pooling to reduce inventory while maintaining a service level, we also can use location pooling to increase our service level. For example, we could choose an order-up-to level in the pooled territory that generates the same inventory investment as the individual territories (measured in days-of-demand) and see how much higher our in-stock could be. Table 15.2 presents those data for pooling up to three territories; beyond three territories we can raise the in-stock to essentially 100 percent with the same inventory investment as the individual territories.

Because the in-stock probability target with individual territories is so high (99.9 percent), it probably makes better sense to use location pooling to reduce the inventory investment rather than to increase the service level. However, in other settings it may be more desirable to increase the service level, especially if the target service level is deemed to be too low.

Figure 15.2 provides another perspective on this issue. It displays the inventory–service trade-off curves with four different degrees of location pooling: individual territories, two territories pooled, four territories pooled, and eight territories pooled. As displayed in the figure, pooling territories shifts the inventory–service trade-off curve down and to the right. Hence, location pooling gives us many options: we can choose to (1) maintain the same service with less inventory, (2) maintain the same inventory with a higher service, or (3) reduce inventory and increase service simultaneously (i.e., "we can have our cake and eat it too"). We saw a similar effect when pooling servers in a queuing environment. There you can use pooling to reduce waiting time without having to staff extra workers, or you can reduce workers while maintaining the same responsiveness, or a combination of both. Furthermore, we should note that these results are not specific to the order-up-to model or Poisson demand; they are quite general and we use this model and demand only to illustrate our point.

Although our analysis highlights the potential dramatic benefit of location pooling, this does not imply that Medtronic should pool territories without further thought. There will be an explicit storage cost for the space to house the pooled inventory, whereas the current system does not have a storage cost for trunk and consignment inventory. However, location pooling might reduce theft and spoilage costs because inventory is stored in fewer locations. Furthermore, location pooling probably would reduce shipping costs because the number of items per delivery is likely to increase.

The greatest concern with location pooling is the impact on the efficiency of the sales representatives. Even if only a few territories are pooled, it is likely that the pooled location would not be as convenient to each sales representative as their own individual inventory.

The physical separation between user and inventory can be mitigated via *virtual pooling:* Representatives maintain control of their inventory, but inventory information is

FIGURE 15.2

The Inventory–
Service Trade-off
Curve for Different
Levels of Location
Pooling

The curves represent,
from highest to
lowest, individual
territories, two pooled
territories, four
pooled territories,
and eight pooled
territories. Demand
in each territory is
Poisson with mean
0.29 unit per day and
the lead time is
one day.

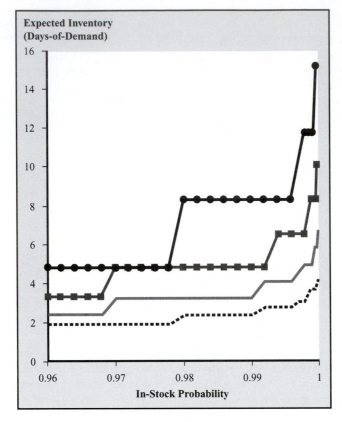

shared among all representatives so that each rep can obtain inventory from the central distribution center and any other rep that has excess inventory. Although virtual pooling has its own challenges (e.g., the additional cost of maintaining the necessary information systems, the added expense of transshipping inventory among territories, and the sticky design issue of how to decide when inventory can be taken from one rep to be given to another rep), it can still be better than the current system that has isolated pockets of inventory.

Medtronic's Distribution Center(s)

Now let's turn our attention to the distribution center. For the U.S. market, Medtronic currently operates a single distribution center in Mounds View, Minnesota. Suppose Medtronic were to subdivide the United States into two or more regions, with each region assigned a single distribution center. This idea is location pooling in reverse. Hence, the total inventory investment is likely to increase. Let's see by how much.

Recall that weekly demand of the InSync Pacemaker at the Mounds View DC is normally distributed with mean 80.6 and standard deviation 58.81. There is a three-week lead time and the target in-stock probability is 99.9 percent. Table 15.3 provides data on the expected inventory required given the number of DCs Medtronic operates.

Table 15.3 reveals that it is indeed costly to subdivide the U.S. market among multiple distribution centers: eight DCs require nearly three times more inventory to achieve the same service level as a single DC! (To be precise, it requires 12.8/4.5 = 2.84 times more inventory.)

TABLE 15.3
The Increase in Inventory Investment as More Distribution Centers Are Operated
Assume demand is equally divided among the DCs, demands across DCs are independent, total demand is normally distributed with mean 80.6 and standard deviation 58.8, and the lead time is three weeks in all situations.

Number of DCs	Weekly Demand Parameters at Each DC			Expected Inventory at Each DC	
	Mean	Standard Deviation	Coefficient of Variation	Units	Weeks-of-Demand
1	80.6	58.8	0.73	364	4.5
2	40.3	41.6	1.03	257	6.4
3	26.9	34.0	1.26	210	7.8
4	20.2	29.4	1.46	182	9.0
5	16.1	26.3	1.63	163	10.1
6	13.4	24.0	1.79	148	11.0
7	11.5	22.2	1.93	137	11.9
8	10.1	20.8	2.06	127	12.8

In this situation, the connection between the coefficient of variation and the expected inventory savings from location pooling (or "dissavings" from location disintegration, as in this case) is even stronger than we saw with field inventory, as displayed in Figure 15.3. In fact, expected inventory and the coefficient of variation in this setting are proportional to one another (i.e., their ratio is a constant no matter the number of distribution centers).

Electronic Commerce

No discussion on location pooling is complete without discussing electronic commerce. One of the well-known advantages to the e-commerce model, especially with respect to e-tailers, is the ability to operate with substantially lower inventory. As our analysis suggests, keeping inventory in fewer locations should allow an e-tailer to turn inventory much faster than a comparable brick-and-mortar retailer. However, there are extra costs to position inventory in a warehouse rather than in a neighborhood store: shipping individual

FIGURE 15.3
The Expected Inventory in Units (circles) and the Coefficient of Variation (squares) Depending on the Number of Distribution Centers Medtronic Operates
Demand is assumed to be equally divided and independent across distribution centers. The target in-stock probability is 99.9 percent and the lead time is three weeks in all cases.

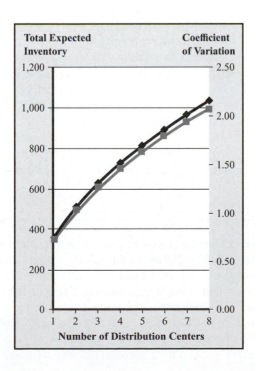

items to consumers is far more expensive than shipping in bulk to retail stores and, while physical stores need not be constructed, an e-tailer needs to invest in the technology to create an electronic store (i.e., user interface, logistics management, etc.).

We also saw that there are declining returns to location pooling. Not surprisingly, while many e-tailers, such as Amazon.com, started with a single distribution center, they now operate several distribution centers in the United States. This requires that some products are stored in multiple locations, but it also means that the average customer is located closer to a distribution center, which accelerates the average delivery time and reduces shipping costs.

The ability to offer customers a huge product selection is another advantage of the e-commerce model, possibly the most important advantage. While we have focused on using location pooling to reduce inventory, location pooling also can enable a broad product assortment. Consider an item that sells but is a rather slow seller. Unfortunately for most businesses, the majority of products fall into that category. To include this item in the product assortment requires at least one unit. Placing one unit in hundreds of locations may not be economical, but it may be economical to place a few units in a single location.

To illustrate this point, consider a slow-moving product that could be sold by a retailer with 200 stores. The product would sell at each store at the average rate of 0.01 unit per week. Consequently, the retailer's total demand across all stores is $0.01 \times 200 = 2$ per week. You may think this is ridiculously slow, but in fact there are many products that sell at this pace. For example, Brynjolfsson, Hu, and Smith (2003) estimated that 40 percent of Amazon's sales came from items that sold no more than 1.5 units per week. Returning to our example, suppose this retailer must stock at least one unit in each store (the product must be available at the store). Given each store's sales rate, the retailer will stock only one unit and each item will spend nearly two years ($1/0.01 = 100$ weeks) on the shelf. That sales rate implies a measly 0.5 inventory turn (inventory is turned over once every two years). To finalize this analysis, if inventory cost 20 percent per year to hold (capital cost and, more importantly, the cost of shelf space), then this item will incur $2 \times 20\% = 40$ percent in holding costs. Most retailers do not have anywhere near a 40 percent gross margin, so it is unlikely that this product is profitable—the retailer cannot carry this item profitably because it just doesn't turn fast enough. Now contrast those economics with an e-tailer with one warehouse. If the e-tailer's demand is Poisson with mean two per week, replenishment lead time is two weeks, and the target in-stock is 99 percent, we can use the order-up-to model to determine that the retailer will have on average about six units of inventory. If total yearly demand is about 104 units (52 weeks at 2 per week), then our e-tailer turns inventory $104/6 = 17.3$ times per year. The e-tailer stands a chance to make money stocking this item, whereas the brick-and-mortar retailer does not. To summarize, there are many slow selling products in this world (which can sum up to a lot of sales, as evidenced by Amazon.com), but location pooling may be necessary for a retailer to profitably include them in the assortment.

15.2   Product Pooling

The previous section considered serving demand with fewer inventory locations. A closely related idea is to serve demand with fewer products. To explain, consider O'Neill's Hammer 3/2 wetsuit discussed in Chapters 12 and 13. The Hammer 3/2 we studied is targeted to the market for surfers, but O'Neill sells another Hammer 3/2 that serves the market for recreational divers. The two wetsuits are identical with the exception that the surf Hammer has the "wave" logo (see Figure 12.1) silk screened on the chest, while the dive Hammer has O'Neill's dive logo, displayed in Figure 15.4. O'Neill's current product line has two products to serve demand for a Hammer 3/2 wetsuit, some of it from surfers, the

FIGURE 15.4
O'Neill's Logo for
Dive Wetsuits

other portion from divers. An alternative is to combine these products into a single product to serve all Hammer 3/2 wetsuit demand, that is, a *universal design*. The strategy of using a universal design is called *product pooling*. This section focuses on the merits of the product-pooling strategy with a universal design.

Recall that demand for the surf Hammer is normally distributed with mean 3,192 and standard deviation 1,181. For the sake of simplicity, let's assume demand for the dive Hammer is also normally distributed with the same mean and standard deviation. Both wetsuits sell for $190, are purchased from O'Neill's supplier for $110, and are liquidated at the end of the season for $90.

We have already evaluated the optimal order quantity and expected profit for the surf Hammer: ordering 4,196 units earns an expected profit of $222,280 (see Table 13.1). Because the dive Hammer is identical to the surf Hammer, it has the same optimal order quantity and expected profit. Therefore, the total profit from both Hammer wetsuits is 2 × $222,280 = $444,560.

Now let's consider what O'Neill should do if it sold a single Hammer wetsuit, which we call the universal Hammer. We need a distribution to represent demand for the universal Hammer and then we need an order quantity. Expected demand for the universal Hammer is 3,192 × 2 = 6,384 units. If demand in the dive market is independent of demand in the surf market, then the standard deviation for the universal Hammer is $1,181 \times \sqrt{2} = 1,670$ (see Exhibit 14.1). The underage cost for the universal Hammer is still $C_u = 190 - 110 = 80$ and the overage cost is still $C_o = 110 - 90 = 20$. Hence, the critical ratio has not changed:

$$\frac{C_u}{C_o + C_u} = \frac{80}{20 + 80} = 0.8$$

The corresponding *z*-statistic is still 0.85, and so the optimal order quantity is

$$Q = \mu + \sigma \times z = 6,384 + 1,670 \times 0.85 = 7,804$$

The expected profit with the universal Hammer is

$$\begin{aligned}
\text{Expected profit} &= (C_u \times \text{Expected sales}) - (C_o \times \text{Expected leftover inventory}) \\
&= (80 \times 6,200) - (20 \times 1,604) \\
&= \$463,920
\end{aligned}$$

Therefore, pooling the surf and dive Hammers together can potentially increase profit by 4.4 percent [(463,920 − 444,560)/444,560]. This profit increase is 1.4 percent of the expected revenue when O'Neill sells two wetsuits. Given that net profit in this industry ranges from 2 percent to 5 percent of revenue, this potential improvement is not trivial.

As with the location pooling examples at Medtronic, the potential benefit O'Neill receives from product pooling occurs because of a reduction in the variability of demand. With two Hammer wetsuits, O'Neill faces a coefficient of variation of about 0.37 with each suit. With a universal Hammer, the coefficient of variation is about $1{,}670/6{,}384 = 0.26$. Recall from Chapter 13 that the mismatch cost in the newsvendor model is directly proportional to the coefficient of variation, hence the connection between a lower coefficient of variation and higher expected profit.

Given this link between the coefficient of variation and the benefit of product pooling, it is important for us to understand how product pooling influences the coefficient of variation. In this example, as well as the Medtronic examples in the previous two sections, we make a key assumption that the demands we are combining are independent. Recall that independence means that the outcome of one demand provides no information about the outcome of the other demand. There are many settings in which demands are indeed independent. But there are also situations in which demands are not independent.

The link between two random events can be measured by their correlation, which ranges from -1 to 1. Independent random events have zero correlation. Positive correlation means two random events tend to move in lock step; that is, when one is high, the other tends to be high as well, and when one is low, the other tends to be low as well. In contrast, negative correlation means two random events tend to move in opposite directions; that is, when one is high, the other tends to be low, and when one is low, the other tends to be high.

We can illustrate the effect of correlation graphically with two products. Figure 15.5 displays the outcome of 100 random demand realizations for two products in three scenarios. (For example, if the random demands of the two products are five and seven respectively, then a point is plotted at {5,7}.) In the first scenario, the products' demands are negatively correlated, in the second they are independent, and in the third they are positively correlated. In the independent scenario (scenario two), we see that the outcomes form a "cloud" that roughly fits into a circle; that is, the outcome of one demand says nothing about the outcome of the other demand. In the negative correlation scenario (scenario one), the outcome cloud is a downward-sloping ellipse: high demand with one product suggests low demand with the other product. The positive correlation scenario (scenario three) also has an outcome cloud shaped like an ellipse, but now it is upward sloping: high demand with one product suggests high demand with the other product.

Many different demand outcomes lead to the same total demand. For example, in the graphs in Figure 15.5, the total demand is 20 units if the products' demands are {0,20}, {1,19}, . . . , {19,1}, {20,0}. In other words, all of the points along the dashed line in each graph have total demand of 20 units. In general, all points along the same downward-sloping 45° line have the same total demand. Because the outcome ellipse in the negative correlation scenario is downward sloping along a 45° line, the total demands of those outcomes are nearly the same. In contrast, because the outcome ellipse in the positive correlation scenario is *upward* sloping, those outcomes generally sum to different total demands. In other words, we expect to see more variability in the total demand with positive correlation than with negative correlation.

We can now be more precise about the impact of correlation. If we combine two demands with the same mean μ and standard deviation σ, then the pooled demand has the following parameters:

$$\text{Expected pooled demand} = 2 \times \mu$$

$$\text{Standard deviation of pooled demand} = \sqrt{2 \times (1 + \text{Correlation})} \times \sigma$$

FIGURE 15.5
Random Demand for Two Products
In the graphs, x-axis is product 1 and y-axis is product 2. In scenario 1 (upper-left graph), the correlation is −0.90; in scenario 2 (upper-right graph), the correlation is 0; and in scenario 3 (the lower graph), the correlation is 0.90. In all scenarios, demand is normally distributed for each product with mean 10 and standard deviation 3.

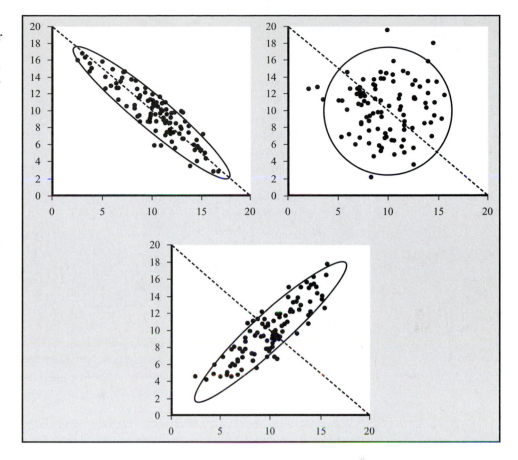

Notice that the correlation has no impact on the expected demand, but it does influence the standard deviation. Furthermore, the above equations are equivalent to the ones we have been using (e.g., Exhibit 14.1) when the correlation is zero, that is, when the two demands are independent.

The coefficient of variation for the pooled demand is then

$$\text{Coefficient of variation of pooled demand} = \sqrt{\frac{1}{2}(1 + \text{Correlation})} \times \left(\frac{\sigma}{\mu}\right)$$

As the correlation increases, the coefficient of variation of pooled demand increases as well, just as the graphs in Figure 15.5 suggest.

Now let's visualize what happens when we choose quantities for both the dive and the surf suits. Figure 15.6 displays the result of our quantity choices for different demand outcomes. For example, if the demand outcome is in the lower-left-hand "square" of the graph, then we have leftover surf and dive suits. The ideal outcome is if demand for each suit happens to equal its order quantity, an outcome labeled with a circle in the graph. The demand–supply mismatch penalty increases as the demand outcome moves further away from that ideal point in any direction.

The comparable graph for the universal Hammer is different, as is shown in Figure 15.7. Now any demand outcome along the downward-sloping 45° line (circles) is an ideal outcome because total demand equals the quantity of universal suits. In other words, the number of ideal demand outcomes with the universal suit has expanded considerably relative

FIGURE 15.6
**The Inventory/
Stockout Outcome
Given the Order
Quantities for Surf
and Dive Suits,
Q_{surf} and Q_{dive}**

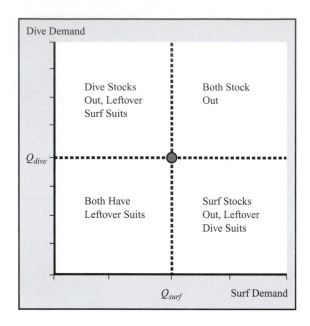

to the single ideal demand outcome with two suits. How likely are we to be close to one of those ideal points? Figure 15.7 also superimposes the three "outcome clouds" from Figure 15.5. Clearly, with negative correlation we are more likely to be close to an ideal point (the downward-sloping ellipse) and with positive correlation we are least likely to be near an ideal point.

We can confirm the intuition developed with the graph in Figure 15.7 by actually evaluating O'Neill's optimal order quantity for the universal Hammer 3/2 and its expected profit for the entire range of correlations. We first notice that the optimal order quantity for the Hammer 3/2 is generally *not* the sum of the optimal order quantities of the two suits. For example, O'Neill's total order with two wetsuits is $4,196 \times 2 = 8,392$ units, but with correlation 0.2 the optimal order for the universal Hammer is 7,929 units and with correlation -0.7 the optimal order is 7,162.

FIGURE 15.7
**Outcomes for the
Universal Hammer
Given Q Units
Purchased**
Outcomes on the
diagonal line with
circles are ideal; there
is no leftover inventory
and no stockouts.
Outcomes below and
to the left of that line
have leftover suits;
outcomes to the right
and above that line
result in stockouts.
Ellipses identify
likely outcomes under
different correlations.

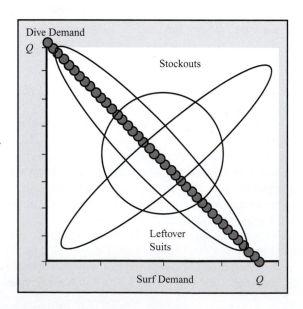

The results with respect to expected profit are displayed in Figure 15.8: We indeed see that the expected profit of the universal Hammer declines as surf and dive demand become more positively correlated.

The extreme ends in Figure 15.8 are interesting. With perfectly positive correlation (i.e., correlation = 1), there is absolutely no benefit from inventory pooling: The expected profit with the universal Hammer is $444,560, and that is also the profit with two Hammer wetsuits! At the other end of the spectrum, correlation = −1, the coefficient of variation of total Hammer demand is 0, and so the maximum profit is achieved, $510,720! In fact, in that situation, the optimal order quantity for universal suits is just 6,384 units, which also happens to be the expected demand for universal suits. (This makes sense; we only earn the maximum profit if we sell on average the expected demand and we never have leftover inventory.)

While we have been discussing the impact of demand correlation on the efficacy of product pooling, this issue applies even with location pooling. If the demands at two locations are negatively correlated, then location pooling is even more effective than if the demands were merely independent. And if demands are positively correlated across locations, then location pooling is less effective than we evaluated, given our assumption of independence.

We also should discuss the conditions that we can expect when demand has a particular type of correlation. Positive correlation can occur if the products are linked to some common source of uncertainty, for example, general economic conditions. For example, positive correlation is likely to be present if all of a firm's products tend to perform poorly in a depressed economy and perform well in a robust economy. Negative correlation is present when there is relatively little uncertainty with respect to total category sales but substantial uncertainty with respect to the allocation of those sales across the product line. For example,

FIGURE 15.8

The Correlation between Surf and Dive Demand for the Hammer 3/2 and the Expected Profit of the Universal Hammer Wetsuit (decreasing curve) and the Coefficient of Variation of Total Demand (increasing curve)

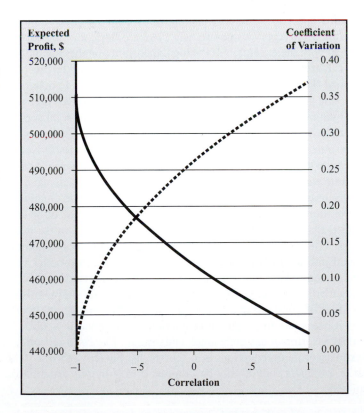

a firm selling fashionable jackets may know pretty well how many jackets will sell in total but have considerable uncertainty over which colors will be hot this season.

To summarize, a key benefit of a universal design is the reduction in demand variability, which leads to better performance in terms of matching supply and demand (e.g., higher profit or lower inventory for a targeted service level). But there are drawbacks to a universal design strategy as well:

• A universal design may not provide the needed functionality to consumers with special needs. For example, most bicycle manufacturers produce road bikes designed for fast touring on well-paved roads and mountain bikes for tearing through rugged trails. They even sell hybrid bikes that have some of the features of a road bike as well as some of the features of a mountain bike. But it is not sufficient to just sell a hybrid bike because it would not satisfy the high-performance portions of the road and mountain bike segments. The lower functionality of a universal design for some segments implies that it might not capture the same total demand as a set of focused designs.

• A universal design may be more expensive or it may be cheaper to produce than focused products. Because a universal design is targeted to many different uses, either it has components that are not necessary to some consumers or it has components that are of better quality than needed by certain consumers. These extra components or the extra quality increases a universal design's cost relative to focused designs. However, it is often cheaper to manufacture or procure a large quantity of a single component than small quantities of a bunch of components; that is, there are economies of scale in production and procurement. In that sense, a universal design may be cheaper.

• A universal design may eliminate some brand/price segmentation opportunities. By definition, a universal design has a single brand/price, but a firm may wish to maintain distinct brands/prices. As with the concern regarding functionality, a single brand/price may not be able to capture the same demand as multiple brands/prices.

With respect to O'Neill's Hammer 3/2 wetsuit, it appears that the first two concerns regarding a universal design are not relevant: Given that the surf and dive Hammers are identical with the exception of the logo, their functionality should be identical as well, and there is no reason to believe their production costs should be much different. However, the universal Hammer wetsuit does eliminate the opportunity to maintain two different O'Neill logos, one geared for the surf market and one geared for the dive market. If it is important to maintain these separate identities (e.g., you might not want serious surfers to think they are purchasing the same product as recreational divers), then maybe two suits are needed. On the other hand, if you wish to portray a single image for O'Neill, then maybe it is even better to have a single logo, in which case two different wetsuits make absolutely no sense.

While we have concentrated on the benefits of serving demand with a universal design, this discussion provides a warning for firms that may be engaging in excessive product proliferation. Every firm wishes to be "customer focused" or "customer oriented," which suggests that a firm should develop products to meet all of the needs of its potential customers. Truly innovative new products that add to a firm's customer base should be incorporated into a firm's product assortment. But if extra product variety merely divides a fixed customer base into smaller pieces, then the demand–supply mismatch cost for each product will increase. Given that some of the demand–supply mismatch costs are indirect (e.g., loss of goodwill due to poor service), a firm might not even realize the additional costs it bears due to product proliferation. Every once in a while a firm realizes that its product assortment has gone amok and *product line rationalization* is sorely needed. The trick to assortment reductions is to "cut the fat, but leave the meat (and surely the bones)"; that is, products should only be dropped if they merely cannibalize demand from other products.

15.3 Lead Time Pooling: Consolidated Distribution and Delayed Differentiation

Location and product pooling, discussed in the previous two sections, have limitations: location pooling creates distance between inventory and customers and product pooling potentially degrades product functionality. This section studies two strategies that address those limitations: consolidated distribution and delayed differentiation. Both of those strategies use a form of risk pooling that we call lead time pooling.

Consolidated Distribution

The key weakness of location pooling is that inventory is moved away from customers, thereby preventing customers from physically seeing a product before purchase, thus increasing the time a customer must wait to receive a product and generally increasing the delivery cost. However, as we have learned, it also can be costly to position inventory near every customer. A major reason for this cost is the problem of having product in the wrong place. For example, with Medtronic's approximately 500 sales territories, it is highly unlikely that all 500 territories will stock out at the same time. If a stockout occurs in one territory, it is quite likely that there is some other territory that has inventory to spare, even maybe a nearby territory. This imbalance of inventory occurs because a firm faces two different kinds of uncertainty, even with a single product: uncertainty with respect to total demand (e.g., how many InSync pacemakers are demanded in the United States on a particular day) and uncertainty with respect to the allocation of that demand (e.g., how many InSync pacemakers are demanded in each territory in the United States on a particular day). The consolidated-distribution strategy attempts to keep inventory close to customers while hedging against the second form of uncertainty.

We'll demonstrate the consolidated-distribution strategy via a retail example. Imagine demand for a single product occurs in 100 stores and average weekly demand per store follows a Poisson distribution with a mean of 0.5 unit per week. Each store is replenished directly from a supplier with an eight-week lead time. To provide good customer service, the retailer uses the order-up-to model and targets a 99.5 percent in-stock probability. The top panel of Figure 15.9 displays a schematic of this supply chain. Let's evaluate the amount of inventory the retailer needs.

With an eight-week lead time and a mean demand of 0.5 unit per week, the expected demand over $l + 1$ periods is $(8 + 1) \times 0.5 = 4.5$. From the Poisson Distribution Function Table in Appendix B we see that with a mean of 4.5, the order-up-to level $S = 10$ yields an in-stock probability of 99.33 percent and $S = 11$ yields an in-stock probability of 99.76 percent, so we need to choose $S = 11$ for each store. According to the Poisson Loss Function Table in Appendix B, with mean demand of 4.5 units over $l + 1$ periods and an order-up-to level $S = 11$, the expected back order is 0.00356 unit per week. Hence, each of the 100 stores will have the following expected inventory:

$$\text{Expected inventory} = S - \text{Expected demand over } l + 1 \text{ periods}$$
$$+ \text{ Expected back order}$$
$$= 11 - 4.5 + 0.00356$$
$$= 6.50356$$

The total inventory among the 100 stores is then $6.504 \times 100 = 650.4$ units.

Now suppose the retailer builds a distribution center to provide consolidated distribution. The distribution center receives all shipments from the supplier and then replenishes each of the retail stores; it allows for consolidated distribution. The lead time for the distribution

FIGURE 15.9

Two Retail Supply Chains, One with Direct Shipments from the Supplier, the Other with Consolidated Distribution in a Distribution Center

Expected weekly demand at each store is 0.5 unit and the target in-stock probability is 99.5 percent.

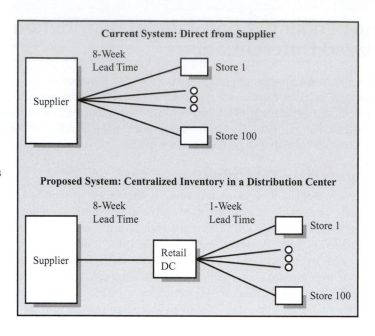

center remains eight weeks from the supplier. The lead time to replenish each of the retail stores is one week. To ensure a reliable delivery to the retail stores, the distribution center operates with a high in-stock probability, 99.5 percent. The bottom panel in Figure 15.9 displays the proposed supply chain with a distribution center.

The distribution center provides the retailer with a centralized location for inventory while still allowing the retailer to position inventory close to the customer. In contrast, the location pooling strategy would just create the centralized inventory location, eliminating the 100 stores close to customers. Therefore, this centralized-inventory strategy resembles location pooling without the major drawback of location pooling. But what does it do for the total inventory investment?

We can repeat the evaluation of the inventory investment for each store, assuming a 99.5 percent in-stock probability target and now a one-week lead time. From the Poisson Distribution Function Table, given expected demand over $l + 1$ periods is 1.0 unit, the order-up-to level $S = 4$ generates an in-stock probability of 99.63 percent. The resulting expected inventory per store is 3.00 units, nearly a 54 percent reduction in inventory from the direct-supply model (3.00 versus 6.5 units)! Because each store now receives a one-week lead time instead of an eight-week lead time, the inventory at the retail stores is dramatically reduced.

Now we need to evaluate the inventory at the distribution center. The demand at the distribution center equals the orders from the retail stores. On average, the retail stores order 0.5 unit per week; that is, the average inflow (i.e., order) into a store must equal the average outflow (i.e., demand), otherwise inventory either builds up continuously (if the inflow exceeds the outflow) or dwindles down to zero (if the outflow exceeds the inflow). Because the retail stores' total demand is $100 \times 0.5 = 50$ units per week, the average demand at the distribution center also must be 50 units per week.

While we can be very sure of our estimate of the distribution center's expected demand, the distribution center's standard deviation of demand is not immediately apparent. The standard deviation of demand at each retailer is $\sqrt{0.50} = 0.707$. (Recall that with Poisson demand, the standard deviation equals the square root of the mean.) Hence, if demand were independent across all stores, then the standard deviation of total demand would be

$0.707 \times \sqrt{100} = 7.07$. However, if there is positive correlation across stores, then the standard deviation would be higher, and with negative correlation the standard deviation would be lower. The only way to resolve this issue is to actually evaluate the standard deviation of total demand from historical sales data (the same data we used to estimate the demand rate of 0.5 unit per week at each store). Suppose we observe that the standard deviation of total weekly demand is 15. Hence, there is evidence of positive correlation in demand across the retail stores.

We now need to choose a distribution to represent demand at the distribution center. In this case, the Poisson is not the best choice. The standard deviation of a Poisson distribution is the square root of its mean, which in this case would be $\sqrt{50} = 7.07$. Because we have observed the standard deviation to be significantly higher, the Poisson distribution would not provide a good fit with the data. Our alternative, and a reasonable choice, is the normal distribution with mean 50 and standard deviation 15. Using the techniques from Chapter 14, we can determine that the distribution center's expected inventory is about 116 units if its target in-stock is 99.5 percent, the lead time is eight weeks, and weekly demand is normally distributed with mean 50 and standard deviation 15.

The only inventory that we have not counted so far is the pipeline inventory. In the direct-delivery model, there is pipeline inventory between the supplier and the retail stores. Using Little's Law, that pipeline inventory equals $0.5 \times 100 \times 8 = 400$ units. The consolidated-distribution model has the same amount of inventory between the supplier and the distribution center. However, with both models let's assume that pipeline inventory is actually owned by the supplier (e.g., the retailer does not start to pay for inventory until it is received). Hence, from the retailer's perspective, that inventory is not a concern. On the other hand, the retailer does own the inventory between the distribution center and the retail stores in the consolidated-distribution model. Again using Little's Law, there are $0.5 \times 100 \times 1 = 50$ units in that pipeline.

Table 15.4 summarizes the retailer's inventory in both supply chain structures. For comparison, the location pooling strategy is also included. With location pooling, all of the stores are eliminated and the retailer ships to customers from a central distribution center. Because that distribution center has an eight-week lead time and faces the same demand distribution as the DC in the consolidated-distribution strategy, its expected inventory is also 116 units.

We see from Table 15.4 that the consolidated-distribution strategy is able to reduce the expected inventory investment 28 percent $[(650 - 466)/650]$ relative to the original direct-delivery structure. In fact, the advantage of the consolidated-distribution strategy is even better than this analysis suggests. The cost of holding one unit of inventory at a retail store is surely substantially higher than the cost of holding one unit in a distribution center: retail shelf space is more expensive than DC space, shrinkage is a greater concern, and so forth. Because the consolidated-distribution model reduces retail inventory by more than 50 percent, merely adding up the total inventory in the system underestimates the value of the consolidated-distribution model.

TABLE 15.4
Retail Inventory with Three Supply Chain Structures

	Direct Delivery Supply Chain	Consolidated-Distribution Supply Chain	Location Pooling
Expected total inventory at the stores	650	300	0
Expected inventory at the DC	0	116	116
Pipeline inventory between the DC and the stores	0	50	0
Total	650	466	116

Interestingly, the consolidated-distribution model outperforms direct delivery even though the total lead time from the supplier to the retail stores is increased by one week due to the routing of all inventory through the DC. Why is inventory reduced despite the longer total lead time? As mentioned earlier, in this system there are two types of uncertainty: uncertainty with total demand in a given week and uncertainty with the allocation of that demand over the retail stores. When inventory leaves the supplier, the retailer is essentially betting on how much inventory will be needed eight weeks later. However, in the direct-delivery model, the retailer also must predict *where* that inventory is needed; that is, the retailer must gamble on a total quantity and an allocation of that quantity across the retail stores. There is uncertainty with the total inventory needed, but even more uncertainty with where that inventory is needed. The consolidated-distribution model allows the retailer to avoid that second gamble: The retailer only needs to bet on the amount of inventory needed for the central distribution center. In other words, while the retailer must commit to a unit's final destination in the direct-delivery model, in the consolidated-distribution model the retailer delays that commitment until the unit arrives at the distribution center. It is precisely because the DC allows the retailer to avoid that second source of uncertainty that the consolidated-distribution model can outperform the direct-delivery model.

The consolidated-distribution model exploits what is often called *lead time pooling*. Lead time pooling can be thought of as combining the lead times for multiple inventory locations. Actually, it is easier to explain graphically: in Figure 15.9 we see that the 100 connections between the supplier and the retail stores in the direct-delivery model (four of which are actually drawn) are pooled into a single connection between the supplier and the DC in the consolidated-distribution model.

We saw that demand correlation influenced the effectiveness of product pooling and location pooling. Not surprisingly, demand correlation has the same effect here. The greater the correlation, the higher the standard deviation of demand at the distribution center. Figure 15.10 displays supply chain inventory with the consolidated-distribution model over a range of demand variability for the distribution center. As retail demand becomes

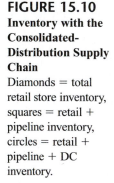

FIGURE 15.10
Inventory with the Consolidated-Distribution Supply Chain
Diamonds = total retail store inventory, squares = retail + pipeline inventory, circles = retail + pipeline + DC inventory.

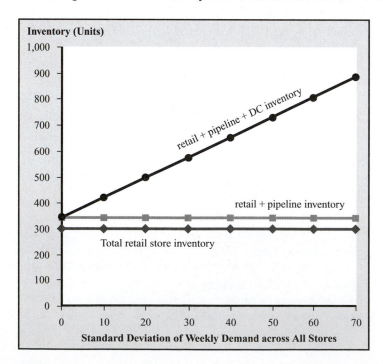

FIGURE 15.11

Inventory with the Consolidated-Distribution Supply Chain (squares) and the Direct-Delivery Supply Chain (circles) with Different Supplier Lead Times

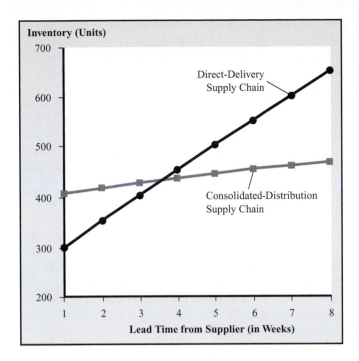

more negatively correlated, the inventory in the consolidated-distribution model declines. However, we have seen that inventory can be reduced even with some positive correlation: The consolidated-distribution model outperforms direct delivery if the DC's standard deviation is about 40 or lower.

Another factor that determines the attractiveness of the consolidated-distribution model relative to the direct-delivery model is the lead time from the supplier. Figure 15.11 displays total supply chain inventory with both models for various supplier lead times. The direct-delivery model performs better than the consolidated-distribution model if the supplier's lead time is three weeks or fewer; otherwise, the consolidated-distribution model does better. This occurs because lead time pooling is most effective as the lead time increases. In particular, the lead time before the distribution center (i.e., from the supplier) should be longer than the lead time after the distribution center (i.e., to the stores).

To summarize, a central inventory location (i.e., a distribution center) within a supply chain can exploit lead time pooling to reduce the supply chain's inventory investment while still keeping inventory close to customers. This strategy is most effective if total demand is less variable than demand at the individual stores and if the lead time before the distribution center is much longer than the lead time after the distribution center.

While we have concentrated on the inventory impact of the consolidated distribution strategy, that strategy has other effects on the supply chain. We have not included the extra cost of operating the distribution center, even though we did mention that the holding cost for each unit of inventory at the distribution center is likely to be lower than at the retail stores. Furthermore, we have not included the extra transportation cost from the DC to the retailer. A common critique of this kind of supply chain is that it clearly increases the distance a unit must travel from the supplier to the retailer. However, there are some additional benefits of a distribution center that we also have not included.

A DC enables a retailer to take better advantage of temporary price discounts from the supplier; that is, it is easier to store a large buy at the DC than at the retail stores. (See the Trade Promotions and Forward Buying part of Section 17.1 for an analytical model of this issue.) The DC also will facilitate more frequent deliveries to the retail stores. With the direct-delivery model, each store receives a shipment from each supplier. It is generally not economical to make partial truckload shipments, what is referred to as a "less-than-load" or LTL shipment. Therefore, in our example, the retailer receives weekly shipments from the supplier because the retailer would not be able to order a full truckload for each store on a more frequent basis.

But with a DC, more frequent shipments are economical. The DC allows the retailer to put products from multiple suppliers into a truck bound for a store. Because now a truck is filled with products from multiple suppliers, it can be filled more frequently. As a result, with the DC in the supply chain, each store might be able to receive a full truckload per day, whereas without the DC each store can only receive a shipment every week. (This argument also is used to justify the airlines' "hub-and-spoke" systems: It may be difficult to consistently fill a plane from Gainesville to Los Angeles on a daily basis, but Delta Airlines offers service between those two cities via its Atlanta hub because the Atlanta–Los Angeles leg can be filled with passengers flying from other southeast cities.) More frequent deliveries reduce inventory even further than our analysis suggests. (See Section 14.8 for more discussion.) Even the DC may be able to order more frequently from the supplier than weekly because the DC consolidates the orders from all of the retailers. In fact, while the lead time pooling benefit of a DC in this example is significant, it is quite possible that some of these other reasons for operating a DC are even more important.

Delayed Differentiation

Consolidated distribution is a strategy that uses lead time pooling to provide some of the benefits of location pooling without moving inventory far away from customers. Delayed differentiation is the analogous strategy with respect to product pooling; that is, delayed differentiation hedges the uncertainty associated with product variety without taking the variety away from customers. We'll illustrate delayed differentiation with our Hammer 3/2 example from O'Neill.

Recall that the Hammer 3/2 is sold by O'Neill in two versions: a surf wetsuit with the traditional wave logo silk-screened on the chest and a dive wetsuit with O'Neill's dive logo put in the same place. The product-pooling approach to this variety is to eliminate it: sell only one Hammer 3/2 suit with a single logo. However, that is an extreme solution and there may be reasons to maintain two different products.

The problem with two different products is that we might run out of surf Hammers while we have extra dive Hammers. In that situation, it would be great if we could just erase the dive logo and put on the surf logo, since the rest of the wetsuit is identical. Better yet, if we just stocked "logo-less" or generic wetsuits, then we could add the appropriate logo as demand arrives. That strategy is called *delayed differentiation* because we are delaying the differentiation of the wetsuit into its final form until after we observe demand.

Several things are necessary to make this delayed-differentiation strategy work. First, we need to be able to silk-screen the logo onto the generic wetsuit. This is a nontrivial issue. Currently the logo is silk-screened onto the chest piece before it is sewn into the suit. Silk-screening the logo onto a complete suit is substantially harder and may require some redesigning of the silk-screening process. Assuming we can overcome that technical difficulty, we still need to be able to add the silk screen quickly so that there is not much delay between the time a wetsuit is requested and when it is shipped. Hence, we'll need a sufficient amount of idle capacity in that process to ensure fast delivery even though demand may fluctuate throughout the season.

If these challenges are resolved, then we are left with deciding how many of the generic wetsuits to order and evaluating the resulting profit savings. In fact, we have already completed those steps. If we assume that we only silk-screen the logo onto wetsuits when we receive a firm demand for a surf or dive wetsuit, then we never keep finished goods inventory; that is, we only have to worry about our generic wetsuit inventory. The demand for the generic wetsuit is identical to the demand for the universal wetsuit; that is, it is the sum of surf Hammer demand and dive Hammer demand. The economics of the generic suit are the same as well: They sell for the same price, they have the same production cost, and we'll assume they have the same salvage value. (In some cases, the salvage value of the generic suit might be higher or lower than the salvage value of the finished product, but in this case it is plausibly about the same.) Therefore, as with the universal design analysis, we need to decide how many generic wetsuits to order given they are sold for $190 each, they cost $110 each, they will be salvaged for $90 each, and demand is normally distributed with mean 6,384 and standard deviation 1,670.

Using our analysis from the section on product pooling, the optimal order quantity is 7,840 units with the delayed differentiation strategy and expected profit increases to $463,920. Although product pooling and delayed differentiation result in the same numerical analysis, the two strategies are different. Delayed differentiation still offers multiple wetsuits to consumers, so their demands are not pooled together as with a universal design. Instead, delayed differentiation works like lead time pooling with consolidated distribution: a key differentiating feature of the product is delayed until after better demand information is observed; with location pooling that feature is the product's final destination (i.e., store) and with delayed differentiation that feature is the product's logo. Furthermore, product pooling does not require a significant modification to the production process, whereas delayed differentiation does require a change to the silk-screening process. In other applications, delayed differentiation may require a more dramatic change to the process and/or the product design.

In general, delayed differentiation is an ideal strategy when

1. Customers demand many versions, that is, variety is important.
2. There is less uncertainty with respect to total demand than there is for individual versions.
3. Variety is created late in the production process.
4. Variety can be added quickly and cheaply.
5. The components needed to create variety are inexpensive relative to the generic component (i.e., the main body of the product).

Let's explain further each of the five points just mentioned. (1) If variety isn't important, then the firm should offer fewer variants or just a universal design. (2) There should be less uncertainty with total demand so there will be few demand–supply mismatches with the generic component. In general, the more negative correlation across product variants the better, since negative correlation reduces uncertainty in the total demand. (3) Just as we saw that consolidated distribution works best if the supplier lead time to the distribution center is long relative to the lead time from the distribution center to the retail stores, delayed differentiation is most valuable if there is a long lead time to produce the generic component and a short lead time to convert the generic component into a finished product. (4) If adding variety to the generic component is too slow, then the waiting time for customers may be unacceptable, thereby rendering delayed differentiation unacceptable. In addition, if adding variety at the end of the process is costly, then the inventory savings from delayed differentiation may not be worth the extra production cost. (5) Finally, delayed differentiation saves inventory of the generic component (e.g., the generic wetsuit) but does not save inventory of the differentiating components. Hence, delayed differentiation is most useful if the majority of the product's value is in the generic component.

Delayed differentiation is particularly appropriate when variety is associated with the cosmetic features of a product, for example, color, labels, and packaging. For example, suppose a company such as Black and Decker sells power drills to both Home Depot and Walmart. Those are two influential retailers; as a result, they may wish to have slightly different packaging, and, in particular, they might wish to have different product codes on their packages so that consumers cannot make direct price comparisons. The power drill company could store drills in the two different packages, but that creates the possibility of having Home Depot drills available while Walmart drills are stocked out. Because it is relatively easy to complete the final packaging, the delayed-differentiation strategy only completes the packaging of drills after it receives firm orders from the retailers. Furthermore, packaging material is cheap compared to the drill, so while the firm doesn't want to have excessive inventory of drills, it isn't too costly to have plenty of packages available.

Retail paints provide another good example for the application of delayed differentiation. Consumers surely do not want a universal design when it comes to paint color, despite Henry Ford's famous theory of product assortment.[2] But at the same time, a store cannot afford to keep paint available in every possible shade, hue, tone, sheen, and color. One alternative is for paint to be held in a central warehouse and then shipped to customers as needed, that is, a location pooling strategy. Given the vast variety of colors, it is not clear that even a location pooling strategy can be economical. Furthermore, paint is very costly to ship directly to consumers, so that pretty much kills that idea. Instead, the paint industry has developed equipment so that a retailer can use generic materials to mix any color in their vast catalog. The final production process takes some time, but an acceptable amount of time for consumers (5 to 15 minutes). The in-store production equipment is probably more expensive than mixing paints at a factory, but again, the extra cost here is worth it. Hence, by redesigning the product to add variety at the very end of the production process (i.e., even after delivery to the retail store), paint companies are able to economically provide consumers with extensive variety.

Delayed differentiation can even be used if the "generic component" can be sold to some customers without additional processing. To explain, suppose a company sells two different quality levels of a product, for example, a fast and a slow printer or a fast and a slow microprocessor. These quality differences might allow a firm to price discriminate and thereby increase its overall margins. However, the quality difference might not imply radically different costs or designs. For example, it might be possible to design the fast and the slow printers such that a fast printer could be converted into a slow printer merely by adding a single chip or by flipping a single switch. Hence, the firm might hold only fast printers so they can serve demand for fast printers immediately. When demand for a slow printer occurs, then a fast printer is taken from inventory, the switch is flipped to make it a slow printer, and then it is shipped as a slow printer.

Delayed differentiation is indeed a powerful strategy. In fact, it bears a remarkable resemblance to another powerful strategy, make-to-order production (Chapter 13). With make-to-order production, a firm only begins making a product after it receives a firm order from a customer. Dell Inc. has used the make-to-order strategy with remarkable effectiveness in the personal computer industry. With delayed differentiation, a generic component is differentiated into a final product only after demand is received for that final product. So what is the difference between these two ideas? In fact, they are conceptually quite similar. Their difference is one of degree. Delayed differentiation is thought of as a strategy that stores nearly finished product and completes the remaining few production steps with essentially no delay. Make-to-order is generally thought to apply to a situation in which the remaining production steps from components to a finished unit are more substantial, therefore involving more than a trivial delay. Hence, delayed differentiation and make-to-order occupy two ends of the same spectrum with no clear boundary between them.

[2] Consumers can have any Model T they want, as long as it is black.

15.4   Capacity Pooling with Flexible Manufacturing[3]

Delayed differentiation takes advantage of completely flexible capacity at the end of the manufacturing process; that is, the final production step is capable of taking a generic component and converting it into any final product. Unfortunately, the luxury of complete flexibility is not always available or affordable to a firm, especially if one considers a larger portion of the manufacturing process. This section studies how a firm can use risk pooling with flexible capacity, but not necessarily completely flexible capacity. See also Section 11.7 for additional discussion on capacity flexibility.

To provide a context, consider the manufacturing challenge of an auto manufacturer such as General Motors. GM operates many different assembly plants and produces many different vehicles. Assembly capacity is essentially fixed in this industry over a substantial time horizon due to rigid labor contracts and the extensive capital requirements of an assembly plant. However, demand for individual vehicles can be quite variable: some products are perennially short on capacity, while others seem to always have too much capacity. To alleviate the resulting demand–supply mismatches, auto manufacturers continually strive for more manufacturing flexibility, that is, the ability to produce more than one vehicle type with the same capacity. GM could use flexible manufacturing to move capacity from slow-selling products to fast-selling products, thereby achieving higher sales and higher capacity utilization. But flexibility is not free: Tooling and assembly equipment capable of making more than one vehicle is more expensive than dedicated equipment and equipment capable of making any vehicle (complete flexibility) is extremely expensive. So how much flexibility does GM need and where should that flexibility be installed?

Let's define a specific problem that is representative of the challenge GM faces. There are 10 manufacturing plants and 10 vehicles (e.g., Chevy Malibu, GMC Yukon XL, etc). For now each plant is assigned to produce just one vehicle, that is, there is no flexibility in the network. Capacity for each vehicle is installed before GM observes the vehicle's demand in the market. Demand is uncertain: a normal distribution represents each vehicle's demand with mean 100 and standard deviation 40. For a slight twist on the distribution, let's assume the minimum demand is 20 and the maximum demand is 180; that is, the normal distribution is truncated so that excessively extreme outcomes are not possible.[4] Even though we impose upper and lower bounds on demand, demand is still quite uncertain, a level of uncertainty that is typical in the auto industry. One last point with respect to demand: We assume the demands for each vehicle are independent; therefore, the correlation between the demands for any two vehicles is zero.

Each plant has a capacity to produce 100 units. If demand exceeds capacity for a vehicle, then the excess is lost. If demand is less than capacity, then demand is satisfied but capacity is idle. Figure 15.12 displays this situation graphically: The left-hand side of the figure represents the 10 production plants; the right-hand side represents the 10 vehicle types; and the lines are "links" that indicate which plant is capable of producing which vehicles. In the "no flexibility" situation, each plant is capable of producing only one vehicle, so there is a total of 10 links. The configuration with the smallest amount of flexibility has 11 links, an example of which is displayed on the right-hand side of Figure 15.12. With 11 links, one plant is capable of producing two different vehicles. As we add more links, we add more flexibility. Total flexibility is achieved when we have 100 links, that is, every

---

[3] This section is based on the research reported in Jordon and Graves (1995).

[4] In other words, any outcome of the normal distribution that is either lower than 20 or higher than 180 is ignored and additional random draws are made until an outcome is received between 20 and 180. There is only a 4.6 percent chance that an outcome of a normal distribution is greater than two standard deviations from the mean (as in this case).

FIGURE 15.12
Two Configurations, One with No Flexibility (10 links) and One with Limited Flexibility (11 links)

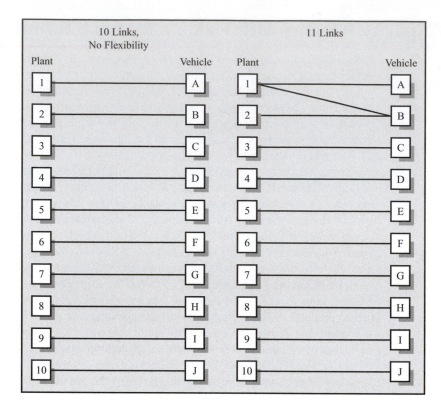

plant is able to produce every product. Figure 15.13 displays the full flexibility configuration as well as one of the possible configurations with 20 links.

With each configuration, we are interested in evaluating the expected unit sales and expected capacity utilization. Unfortunately, for most configurations, it is quite challenging to evaluate those performance measures analytically. However, we can obtain accurate estimates of those performance measures via simulation. Each iteration of the simulation draws random demand for each product and then allocates the capacity to maximize unit sales within the constraints of the feasible links. For example, in the configuration with 11 links displayed in Figure 15.12, suppose in one of the iterations that demand for vehicle A is 85 units and vehicle B is 125 units. In that case, plant 2 uses its entire 100 units of capacity to produce vehicle B and plant 1 uses its entire 100 units of capacity to produce 85 units of vehicle A and 15 units of vehicle B, thereby only losing 10 units of potential vehicle B sales. Our estimate of each performance measure is just its average across the iterations. After many iterations, our estimates will be quite accurate.

Via simulation we find that with no flexibility, expected unit sales are 853 units and expected capacity utilization is 85.3 percent. With 11 links, the expected unit sales increase to 858 units and capacity utilization increases to 85.8 percent. We do slightly better with this additional flexibility when demand for vehicle B exceeds plant 2's capacity and demand for vehicle A is below plant 1's capacity, because then plant 1 can use its capacity to produce both vehicles A and B (as in our previous example). Figure 15.14 provides data on the performance of configurations with 10 to 20 links and the full flexibility configuration.

Figure 15.14 reveals that total flexibility is able to increase our performance measures considerably: Capacity utilization jumps to 95.4 percent and expected sales increase to 954 units. But what is more remarkable is that adding only 10 additional links produces nearly the same outcome as full flexibility, which has an additional 90 links: capacity utilization is 94.9 percent with 20 links and expected sales are 949 units. Apparently, there is very little incremental value to the additional flexibility achieved by adding the 11th

FIGURE 15.13
Flexibility Configurations with Approximately Equal Capability to Respond to Demand Uncertainty

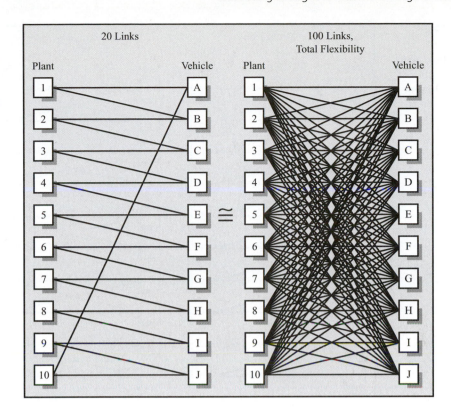

through the 90th additional links to the no-flexibility configuration. In other words, given that installing flexibility is costly, it is unlikely that total flexibility will be economically rational. This result has a similar feel to our finding that with location pooling, the majority of the benefit is captured by pooling only a few locations.

FIGURE 15.14
Impact of Incrementally Adding Flexibility on Expected Sales and Capacity Utilization

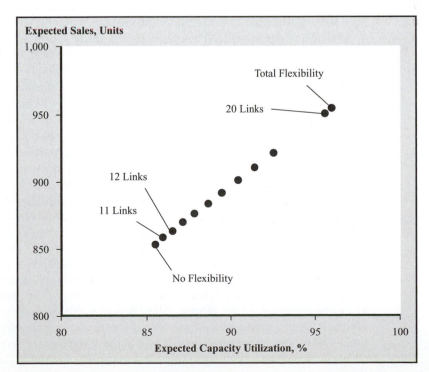

FIGURE 15.15
Flexibility Configurations with the Same Number of Links but Different Number of Chains

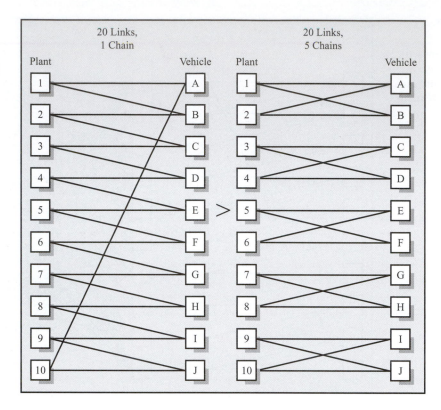

It may seem surprising that capacity pooling increases utilization, given that pooling server capacity in a queuing system has no impact on utilization, as discussed in Chapter 9. The key difference is that in a queuing system, demand is never lost; it just has to wait longer than it might want to be served. Hence, the amount of demand served is independent of how the capacity is structured. Here, demand is lost if there isn't a sufficient amount of capacity. Therefore, more flexibility increases the demand served, which increases the utilization of the capacity.

Although flexibility with 20 links can perform nearly as well as total flexibility with 100 links, not every configuration with 20 links performs that well. Figure 15.13 displays the particular 20-link configuration that nearly equals total flexibility. The effectiveness of that configuration can be explained by the concept of *chaining.* A chain is a group of plants and vehicles that are connected via links. For example, in the 11-link configuration displayed in Figure 15.12, the first two plants and vehicles form a single chain and the remaining plant–vehicle pairs form eight additional chains. With the 20-link configuration displayed in Figure 15.13, there is a single chain, as there is with the total flexibility configuration.

In general, flexibility configurations with the longest and fewest chains for a given number of links perform the best. Figure 15.15 displays two 20-link configurations, one with a single chain (the same one as displayed in Figure 15.13) and the other with five chains. We already know that the single chain configuration has expected sales of 949 units. Again via simulation, we discover that the 20-link configuration with five chains generates expected sales of only 896 units, which compares to the 853 expected unit sales with no-flexibility.

Long chains are beneficial because they facilitate the reallocation of capacity to respond to demand. For example, suppose demand for vehicle A is less than expected, but demand for vehicle G is very strong. If both vehicles are in the same chain, then plant 1's idle capacity can be shifted along the chain to help fill vehicle G's demand: plant 1 produces some vehicle B, plant 2 produces some of both vehicles B and C, and so forth so that both plants 6 and 7 can produce some vehicle G. If both of those vehicles are not part of the same chain (as in our five-chain configuration), then this swapping of capacity is not possible.

In addition to how flexibility is configured, there are two additional issues worth mentioning that influence the value of flexibility: correlation and total capacity. So far we have assumed that demands across vehicles are independent. We learned with the other risk-pooling strategies that risk pooling becomes more effective as demand becomes more negatively correlated. The same holds here: With pooled capacity, the uncertainty in total demand is more important than the uncertainty with individual products; hence, negative correlation is preferred. However, this does not mean that two negatively correlated products must be produced in the same plant. Instead, it is sufficient that two negatively correlated products are produced in the same chain. This is a valuable insight if the negatively correlated products are physically quite different (e.g., a full-size truck and a compact sedan) because producing them in the same chain might be far cheaper than producing them in the same plant.

The total available capacity also influences the effectiveness of flexibility. Suppose capacity for each plant were only 20 units. In that case, each plant would always operate at 100 percent utilization, so flexibility has no value. The end result is the same with the other extreme situation. If each plant could produce 180 units, then flexibility is again not needed because every plant is sure to have idle capacity. In other words, flexibility is more valuable when capacity and demand are approximately equal, as in our numerical examples.

Figure 15.16 further emphasizes that flexibility is most valuable with intermediate amounts of capacity: The biggest gap between the no-flexibility trade-off curve and the 20-link trade-off curve occurs when total capacity equals expected total demand, 1,000 units.

Figure 15.16 illustrates another observation: flexibility and capacity are substitutes. For example, to achieve expected sales of 950 units, GM can either install total capacity of 1,250 units with no flexibility or 1,000 units of capacity with 20-link flexibility. If capacity is cheap relative to flexibility, then the high-capacity–no-flexibility option may

FIGURE 15.16

Expected Sales and Capacity Utilization
Shown are seven different capacities (*C*) and two configurations, one with no flexibility (10 links) and one with 20 links and one chain (displayed in Figure 15.15). In each case, the total capacity is equally divided among the 10 products and expected total demand is 1,000 units.

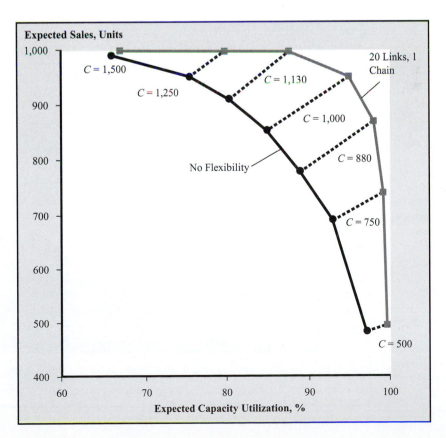

TABLE 15.5
Fiscal Year 2005 Results for Several Contract Manufacturers

Company	Revenue*	Cost of Goods*	Gross Margin
Hon-Hai Precision Industries	101,946	92,236	9.5%
Flextronics	28,680	27,166	5.3%
Jabil Circuits	13,409	12,148	9.4%
Celestica	6,526	6,012	7.9%
Sanmina-SCI	6,319	5,750	9.0%
Benchmark Electronics	2,402	2,174	9.5%
Plexus	2,013	1,770	12.1%

* In millions of dollars

be preferable. But if capacity is expensive relative to flexibility (especially given that we only need 10 additional links of flexibility), then the low-capacity–some-flexibility option may be better.

So far, our discussion has focused on a single firm and its flexibility within its own network of resources. However, if a firm cannot implement flexible capacity on its own, another option is to hire a firm that essentially provides this service for them. In fact, there is an entire industry doing just this—the contract manufacturing industry. These are companies that generally do not have their own products or brands. What they sell is capacity—flexible capacity that is used for all of their clients. For example, Flextronics could be assembling circuit boards for IBM, Hewlett-Packard, and Cisco Systems. The same equipment and often the same components are used by these multiple manufacturers, so, instead of each one investing in its own capacity and component inventory, Flextronics pools their needs. In other words, while any of these companies could produce its own circuit boards, because of capacity pooling. Flextronics is able to produce them with higher utilization and therefore lower cost. This added efficiency allows Flextronics to charge a margin, albeit a rather thin margin, as indicated in Table 15.5.

Figure 15.17 displays the revenue growth from seven leading electronics contract manufacturers. (There are contract manufacturers in other industries as well, such as pharmaceuticals.) It shows that the industry barely existed before 1992, and then there was a huge increase in sales leading up to 2000. The bursting of the telecom bubble gave the industry

FIGURE 15.17
Total Revenue of Seven Leading Contract Manufacturers by Fiscal Year: Hon-Hai Precision Industries, Flextronics, Jabil Circuits, Celestica, Sanmina-SCI, Benchmark Electronics and Plexus.
Note: The fiscal years of these firms vary somewhat, so total revenue in a calendar year will be slightly different.

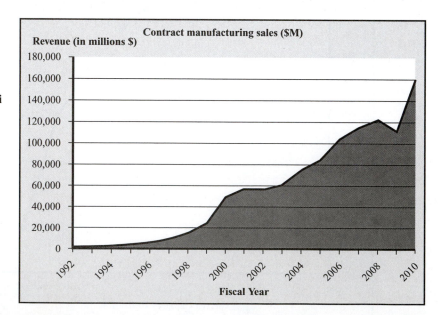

a pause in the early 2000s, and then it proceeded to gain momentum again, with the 2008–2009 dip caused by the worldwide recession. Hon-Hai Precision Industries is the clear leader in this group, as shown in Table 15.5. Apple is one of its more visible customers, and Apple's success has been a substantial contributor to Hon-Hai's revenue growth.

To summarize, this section considers the pooling of capacity via manufacturing flexibility. The main insights are

- A limited amount of flexibility can accommodate demand uncertainty nearly as well as total flexibility as long as the flexibility is configured to generate long chains.
- Flexibility should be configured so that negatively correlated products are part of the same chain but need not be produced in the same plant.
- Flexibility is most valuable when total capacity roughly equals expected demand.
- It may be possible to purchase flexibility by working with a contract manufacturer.

Therefore, it is generally neither necessary nor economically rational for a firm to sink the huge investment needed to achieve total flexibility. Flexibility is surely valuable, but it should not be installed haphazardly. Finally, while we have used the context of automobile manufacturing to illustrate these insights, they nevertheless apply to workers in service environments. For example, it is not necessary to cross-train workers so that they can handle every task (full flexibility). Instead, it is sufficient to train workers so that long chains of skills are present in the organization.

15.5 Summary

This chapter describes and explores several different strategies that exploit risk pooling to better match supply and demand. Each has its strengths and limitations. For example, location pooling is very effective at reducing inventory but moves inventory away from customers. Consolidated distribution is not as good as location pooling at reducing inventory, but it keeps inventory near customers. Product pooling with a universal design is also quite useful but might limit the functionality of the products offered. Delayed differentiation addresses that limitation but probably requires redesigning the product/process and may introduce a slight delay to fulfill demand. Capacity pooling can increase sales and capacity utilization but requires flexible capacity, which is probably not free and may be quite expensive. Hence, these are effective strategies as long as they are applied in the appropriate settings.

Even though we considered a variety of situations and models (e.g., order-up-to and newsvendor), we have developed some consistent observations:

- A little bit of risk pooling goes a long way. With location pooling, it is usually necessary to pool only a few locations, not all of them. With capacity pooling, a little bit of flexibility, as long as it is properly designed (i.e., long chains), yields nearly the same outcome as full flexibility.
- Risk-pooling strategies are most effective when demands are negatively correlated because then the uncertainty with total demand is much less than the uncertainty with any individual item/location. It follows that these strategies become less effective as demands become more positively correlated.
- Risk-pooling strategies do not help reduce pipeline inventory. That inventory can only be reduced by moving inventory through the system more quickly.
- Risk-pooling strategies can be used to reduce inventory while maintaining the same service (in-stock probability) or they can be used to increase service while holding the same inventory, or a combination of those improvements.

Table 15.6 provides a summary of the key notation and equations presented in this chapter.

TABLE 15.6
Summary of Notation and Key Equations in Chapter 15

The combination of two demands with the same mean and standard deviation yields

$$\text{Expected pooled demand} = 2 \times \mu$$

$$\text{Standard deviation of pooled demand} = \sqrt{2 \times (1 + \text{Correlation})} \times \sigma$$

$$\text{Coefficient of variation of pooled demand} = \sqrt{\frac{1}{2}(1 + \text{Correlation})} \times \left(\frac{\sigma}{\mu}\right)$$

15.6 Further Reading

In recent years, risk-pooling strategies have received considerable attention in the academic community as well as in practice.

Lee (1996) provides a technical treatment of the delayed-differentiation strategy. A more managerial description of delayed differentiation can be found in Feitzinger and Lee (1997). Brown, Lee, and Petrakian (2000) describe the application of delayed differentiation at a semiconductor firm. Simchi-Levi, Kaminsky, and Simchi-Levi (2003) and Chopra and Meindl (2004) cover risk-pooling strategies in the context of supply chain management.

Ulrich and Eppinger (2011) discuss the issues of delayed differentiation and product architecture from the perspective of a product development team.

Upton (1994, 1995) provides broad discussions on the issue of manufacturing flexibility.

15.7 Practice Problems

Q15.1* **(Egghead)** In 1997 Egghead Computers ran a chain of 50 retail stores all over the United States. Consider one type of computer sold by Egghead. Demand for this computer at each store on any given week was independently and normally distributed with a mean demand of 200 units and a standard deviation of 30 units. Inventory at each store is replenished directly from a vendor with a 10-week lead time. At the end of 1997, Egghead decided it was time to close their retail stores, put up an Internet site, and begin filling customer orders from a single warehouse.

    a. By consolidating the demand into a single warehouse, what will be the resulting standard deviation of weekly demand for this computer faced by Egghead? Assume Egghead's demand characteristics before and after the consolidation are identical.

    b. Egghead takes physical possession of inventory when it leaves the supplier and grants possession of inventory to customers when it leaves Egghead's shipping dock. In the consolidated distribution scenario, what is the pipeline inventory?

Q15.2* **(Two Products)** Consider two products, A and B. Demands for both products are normally distributed and have the same mean and standard deviation. The coefficient of variation of demand for each product is 0.6. The estimated correlation in demand between the two products is −0.7. What is the coefficient of variation of the total demand of the two products?

Q15.3* **(Fancy Paints)** Fancy Paints is a small paint store. Fancy Paints stocks 200 different SKUs (stock-keeping units) and places replenishment orders weekly. The order arrives one month (let's say four weeks) later. For the sake of simplicity, let's assume weekly demand for each SKU is Poisson distributed with mean 1.25. Fancy Paints maintains a 95 percent in-stock probability.

    a. What is the average inventory at the store at the end of the week?

    b. Now suppose Fancy Paints purchases a color-mixing machine. This machine is expensive, but instead of stocking 200 different SKU colors, it allows Fancy Paints to stock only five basic SKUs and to obtain all the other SKUs by mixing. Weekly demand for each SKU is normally distributed with mean 50 and standard deviation 8. Suppose Fancy Paints maintains a 95 percent in-stock probability for each of the five colors. How much inventory on average is at the store at the end of the week?

    c. After testing the color-mixing machine for a while, the manager realizes that a 95 percent in-stock probability for each of the basic colors is not sufficient: Since mixing requires the presence of multiple mixing components, a higher in-stock probability for components is needed to maintain a 95 percent in-stock probability for the individual SKUs. The manager decides that a 98 percent in-stock probability for each of the five basic SKUs should be

(* indicates that the solution is at the end of the book)

adequate. Suppose that each can costs $14 and 20 percent per year is charged for holding inventory (assume 50 weeks per year). What is the change in the store's holding cost relative to the original situation in which all paints are stocked individually?

Q15.4*   **(Burger King)** Consider the following excerpts from a *Wall Street Journal* article on Burger King (Beatty, 1996):

> Burger King intends to bring smiles to the faces of millions of parents and children this holiday season with its "Toy Story" promotion. But it has some of them up in arms because local restaurants are running out of the popular toys . . . Every Kids Meal sold every day of the year comes with a giveaway, a program that has been in place for about six years and has helped Grand Metropolitan PLC's Burger King increase its market share. Nearly all of Burger King's 7,000 U.S. stores are participating in the "Toy Story" promotion . . . Nevertheless, meeting consumer demand still remains a conundrum for the giants. That is partly because individual Burger King restaurant owners make their tricky forecasts six months before such promotions begin. "It's asking you to pull out a crystal ball and predict exactly what consumer demand is going to be," says Richard Taylor, Burger King's director of youth and family marketing. "This is simply a case of consumer demand outstripping supply." The long lead times are necessary because the toys are produced overseas to take advantage of lower costs . . . Burger King managers in Houston and Atlanta say the freebies are running out there, too . . . But Burger King, which ordered nearly 50 million of the small plastic dolls, is "nowhere near running out of toys on a national level."

Let's consider a simplified analysis of Burger King's situation. Consider a region with 200 restaurants served by a single distribution center. At the time the order must be placed with the factories in Asia, demand (units of toys) for the promotion at each restaurant is forecasted to be gamma distributed with mean 2,251 and standard deviation 1,600. A discrete version of that gamma distribution is provided in the following table, along with a graph of the density function:

Q	F(Q)	L(Q)		Q	F(Q)	L(Q)
0	0.0000	2,251.3		6,500	0.9807	31.4
500	0.1312	1,751.3		7,000	0.9865	21.7
1,000	0.3101	1,316.9		7,500	0.9906	15.0
1,500	0.4728	972.0		8,000	0.9934	10.2
2,000	0.6062	708.4		8,500	0.9954	6.9
2,500	0.7104	511.5		9,000	0.9968	4.6
3,000	0.7893	366.6		9,500	0.9978	3.0
3,500	0.8480	261.3		10,000	0.9985	1.9
4,000	0.8911	185.3		10,500	0.9989	1.2
4,500	0.9224	130.9		11,000	0.9993	0.6
5,000	0.9449	92.1		11,500	0.9995	0.3
5,500	0.9611	64.5		12,000	1.0000	0.0
6,000	0.9726	45.1				

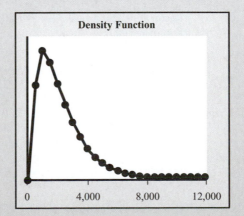

Density Function

(* indicates that the solution is at the end of the book)

Suppose, six months in advance of the promotion, Burger King must make a single order for each restaurant. Furthermore, Burger King wants to have an in-stock probability of at least 85 percent.

a. Given those requirements, how many toys must each restaurant order?

b. How many toys should Burger King expect to have at the end of the promotion?

Now suppose Burger King makes a single order for all 200 restaurants. The order will be delivered to the distribution center and each restaurant will receive deliveries from that stockpile as needed. If demands were independent across all restaurants, total demand would be $200 \times 2,251 = 450,200$ with a standard deviation of $\sqrt{200} \times 1,600 = 22,627$. But it is unlikely that demands will be independent across restaurants. In other words, it is likely that there is positive correlation. Nevertheless, based on historical data, Burger King estimates the coefficient of variation for the total will be half of what it is for individual stores. As a result, a normal distribution will work for the total demand forecast.

c. How many toys must Burger King order for the distribution center to have an 85 percent in-stock probability?

d. If the quantity in part c is ordered, then how many units should Burger King expect to have at the end of the promotion?

e. If Burger King ordered the quantity evaluated in part a (i.e., the amount such that each restaurant would have its own inventory and generate an 85 percent in-stock probability) but kept that entire quantity at the distribution center and delivered to each restaurant only as needed, then what would the DC's in-stock probability be?

Q15.5* **(Livingston Tools)** Livingston Tools, a manufacturer of battery-operated, hand-held power tools for the consumer market (such as screwdrivers and drills), has a problem. Its two biggest customers are "big box" discounters. Because these customers are fiercely price competitive, each wants exclusive products, thereby preventing consumers from making price comparisons. For example, Livingston will sell the exact same power screwdriver to each retailer, but Livingston will use packing customized to each retailer (including two different product identification numbers). Suppose weekly demand of each product to each retailer is normally distributed with mean 5,200 and standard deviation 3,800. Livingston makes production decisions on a weekly basis and has a three-week replenishment lead time. Because these two retailers are quite important to Livingston, Livingston sets a target in-stock probability of 99.9 percent.

a. Based on the order-up-to model, what is Livingston's average inventory of each of the two versions of this power screwdriver?

b. Someone at Livingston suggests that Livingston stock power screwdrivers without putting them into their specialized packaging. As orders are received from the two retailers, Livingston would fulfill those orders from the same stockpile of inventory, since it doesn't take much time to actually package each tool. Interestingly, demands at the two retailers have a slight negative correlation, -0.20. By approximately how much would this new system reduce Livingston's inventory investment?

Q15.6 **(Restoration Hardware)** Consider the following excerpts from a *New York Times* article (Kaufman, 2000):

> Despite its early promise . . . Restoration has had trouble becoming a mass-market player. . . . What went wrong? High on its own buzz, the company expanded at breakneck speed, more than doubling the number of stores, to 94, in the year and a half after the stock offering . . . Company managers agree, for example, that Restoration's original inventory system, which called for all furniture to be kept at stores instead of at a central warehouse, was a disaster.

Let's look at one Restoration Hardware product, a leather chair. Average weekly sales of this chair in each store is Poisson with mean 1.25 units. The replenishment lead time is 12 weeks. (This question requires using Excel to create Poisson distribution and loss function tables that are not included in the appendix. See Appendix C for the procedure to evaluate a loss function table.)

(* indicates that the solution is at the end of the book)

    a. If each store holds its own inventory, then what is the company's annual inventory turns if the company policy is to target a 99.25 percent in-stock probability?

    b. Suppose Restoration Hardware builds a central warehouse to serve the 94 stores. The lead time from the supplier to the central warehouse is 12 weeks. The lead time from the central warehouse to each store is one week. Suppose the warehouse operates with a 99 percent in-stock probability, but the stores maintain a 99.25 percent in-stock probability. If only inventory at the retail stores is considered, what are Restoration's annual inventory turns?

Q15.7** **(Study Desk)** You are in charge of designing a supply chain for furniture distribution. One of your products is a study desk. This desk comes in two colors: black and cherry. Weekly demand for each desk type is normal with mean 100 and standard deviation 65 (demands for the two colors are independent). The lead time from the assembly plant to the retail store is two weeks and you order inventory replenishments weekly. There is no finished goods inventory at the plant (desks are assembled to order for delivery to the store).

    a. What is the expected on-hand inventory of desks at the store (black and cherry together) if you maintain a 97 percent in-stock probability for each desk color?

You notice that only the top part of the desk is black or cherry; the remainder (base) is made of the standard gray metal. Hence, you suggest that the store stock black and cherry tops separately from gray bases and assemble them when demand occurs. The replenishment lead time for components is still two weeks. Furthermore, you still choose an order-up-to level for each top to generate a 97 percent in-stock probability.

    b. What is the expected on-hand inventory of black tops?

    c. How much less inventory of gray bases do you have on average at the store with the new in-store assembly scheme relative to the original system in which desks are delivered fully assembled? (*Hint:* Remember that each assembled desk requires one top and one base.)

Q15.8 **(O'Neill)** One of O'Neill's high-end wetsuits is called the Animal. Total demand for this wetsuit is normally distributed with a mean of 200 and a standard deviation of 130. In order to ensure an excellent fit, the Animal comes in 16 sizes. Furthermore, it comes in four colors, so there are actually 64 different Animal SKUs (stock-keeping units). O'Neill sells the Animal for $350 and its production cost is $269. The Animal will be redesigned this season, so at the end of the season leftover inventory will be sold off at a steep mark-down. Because this is such a niche product, O'Neill expects to receive only $100 for each leftover wetsuit. Finally, to control manufacturing costs, O'Neill has a policy that at least five wetsuits of any size/color combo must be produced at a time. Total demand for the smallest size (extra small-tall) is forecasted to be Poisson with mean 2.00. Mean demand for the four colors are black = 0.90, blue = 0.50, green = 0.40, and yellow = 0.20.

    a. Suppose O'Neill already has no extra small-tall Animals in stock. What is O'Neill's expected profit if it produces one batch (five units) of extra small-tall black Animals?

    b. Suppose O'Neill announces that it will only sell the Animal in one color, black. If O'Neill suspects this move will reduce total demand by 12.5 percent, then what now is its expected profit from the black Animal?

Q15.9* **(Consulting Services)** A small economic consulting firm has four employees, Alice, Bob, Cathy, and Doug. The firm offers services in four distinct areas, Quotas, Regulation, Strategy, and Taxes. At the current time Alice is qualified for Quotas, Bob does Regulation, and so on. But this isn't working too well: the firm often finds it cannot compete for business in one area because it has already committed to work in that area while in another area it is idle. Therefore, the firm would like to train the consultants to be qualified in more than one area. Which of the following assignments is likely to be most beneficial to the firm?

a.

	Alice	Bob	Cathy	Doug
Qualified areas:	Quotas	Regulation	Strategy	Taxes
	Regulation	Taxes	Quotas	Strategy

b.

	Alice	Bob	Cathy	Doug
Qualified areas:	Quotas Regulation	Regulation Quotas	Strategy Taxes	Taxes Strategy

c.

	Alice	Bob	Cathy	Doug
Qualified areas:	Quotas Regulation	Regulation Quotas	Strategy Regulation	Taxes Quotas

d.

	Alice	Bob	Cathy	Doug
Qualified areas:	Quotas Strategy	Regulation Taxes	Strategy Quotas	Taxes Regulation

e.

	Alice	Bob	Cathy	Doug
Qualified areas:	Quotas Strategy	Regulation Taxes	Strategy Quotas	Taxes Regulation

You can view a video of how problems marked with a ** are solved by going on www. cachon-terwiesch.net and follow the links under 'Solved Practice Problems'

Chapter 16

Revenue Management with Capacity Controls

The operations manager constantly struggles with a firm's supply process to better match it to demand. In fact, most of our discussion in this text has concentrated on how the supply process can be better organized, structured, and managed to make it more productive and responsive. But if supply is so inflexible that it cannot be adjusted to meet demand, then another approach is needed. In particular, this chapter takes the opposite approach: Instead of matching supply to demand, we explore how demand can be adjusted to match supply. The various techniques for achieving this objective are collected under the umbrella term *revenue management,* which is also referred to as *yield management.* Broadly speaking, revenue management is the science of maximizing the revenue earned from a fixed supply.

This chapter discusses two specific techniques within revenue management: *protection levels/booking limits* and *overbooking.* (We will see that protection levels and booking limits are really two different concepts that implement the same technique.) Those techniques perform revenue management via capacity controls; that is, they adjust over time the availability of capacity. Prices are taken as fixed, so protection levels and overbooking attempt to maximize revenue without changing prices.

We begin the chapter with a brief introduction to revenue management: its history, its success stories, and some "margin arithmetic" to explain why it can be so powerful. We next illustrate the application of protection levels and overbooking to an example from the hotel industry. The final sections discuss the implementation of these techniques in practice and summarize insights.

16.1 Revenue Management and Margin Arithmetic

Revenue management techniques were first developed in the airline industry in the early 1980s. Because each flown segment is a perishable asset (once a plane leaves the gate, there are no additional opportunities to earn additional revenue on that particular flight), the airlines wanted to maximize the revenue they earned on each flight, which is all the more important given the razor-thin profit margins in the industry. For example, a typical airline operates with about 73 percent of its seats filled but needs to fill about 70 percent of its seats to breakeven: on a 100-seat aircraft, the difference between making and losing money is measured by a handful of passengers.

Firms that implement revenue management techniques generally report revenue increases in the range of 3 to 7 percent with relatively little additional capital investment. The importance of that incremental revenue can be understood with the use of "margin arithmetic." A firm's net profit equation is straightforward:

$$\text{Profit} = R \times M - F = \text{Net profit \%} \times R$$

where

$$R = \text{Revenue}$$
$$M = \text{Gross margin as a percentage of revenue}$$
$$F = \text{Fixed costs}$$
$$\text{Net profit \%} = \text{Net profit as a percentage of revenue}$$

A firm's net profit as a percentage of its revenue (Net profit %) is generally in the range of 1 to 10 percent.

Now let's suppose we implement revenue management and increase revenue. Let Revenue increase be the percentage increase in revenue we experience, which, as has already been mentioned, is typically in the 3 to 7 percent range. Our percentage change in profit is then

$$\begin{aligned}
\text{\% change in profit} &= \frac{[(100\% + \text{Revenue increase}) \times R \times M - F] - [R \times M - F]}{R \times M - F} \\
&= \frac{\text{Revenue increase} \times R \times M}{R \times M - F} \\
&= \frac{\text{Revenue increase} \times M}{\text{Net profit \%}}
\end{aligned}$$

(The second line above cancels out terms in the numerator such as the fixed costs. The third line replaces the denominator with Net profit % $\times$ R and then cancels R from both the numerator and denominator.) Table 16.1 presents data evaluated with the above equation for various gross margins, revenue increases, and net profits as a percentage of revenues. The table illustrates that a seemingly small increase in revenue can have a significant impact on profit, especially when the gross margin is large. Thus, a 3 to 7 percent increase in revenue can easily generate a 50 to 100 percent increase in profit, especially in a high-gross-margin setting; revenue management indeed can be an important set of tools. We next illustrate in detail two of the tools in that set with an example from the hotel industry.

TABLE 16.1
Percentage Change in Profit for Different Gross Margins, Revenue Increases, and Net Profits as a Percentage of Revenue

	Net Profit % = 2%					Net Profit % = 6%			
		Revenue increase					Revenue increase		
Gross Margin	1%	2%	5%	8%	Gross Margin	1%	2%	5%	8%
100%	50%	100%	250%	400%	100%	17%	33%	83%	133%
90	45	90	225	360	90	15	30	75	120
75	38	75	188	300	75	13	25	63	100
50	25	50	125	200	50	8	17	42	67
25	13	25	63	100	25	4	8	21	33
15	8	15	38	60	15	3	5	13	20

16.2   Protection Levels and Booking Limits

The Park Hyatt Philadelphia at the Bellevue, located at Walnut and Broad in downtown Philadelphia, has 118 king/queen rooms that it offers to both leisure and business travelers.[1] Leisure travelers are more price sensitive and tend to reserve rooms well in advance of their stay. Business travelers are generally willing to pay more for a room, in part because they tend to book much closer to the time of their trip and in part because they wish to avoid the additional restrictions associated with the discount fare (e.g., advance purchase requirements and more restrictive cancellation policies). With leisure travelers in mind, the Hyatt offers a $159 discount fare for a midweek stay, which contrasts with the regular fare of $225. We'll refer to these as the low and high fares and use the notation $r_l = 159$ and $r_h = 225$ (r stands for revenue and the subscript indicates l for low fare or h for high fare).

Suppose today is April 1, but we are interested in the Hyatt's bookings on May 29th, which is a midweek night. The Hyatt knows that there will be plenty of travelers willing to pay the low fare, so selling all 118 rooms by May 29th is not a problem. However, all else being equal, the Hyatt would like those rooms to be filled with high-fare travelers rather than low-fare travelers. Unfortunately, there is little chance that there will be enough demand at the high fare to fill the hotel and the lost revenue from an empty room is significant: Once May 29th passes, the Hyatt can never again earn revenue from that capacity. So the Hyatt's challenge is to extract as much revenue as possible from these two customer segments for its May 29th rooms; that is, we wish to maximize revenue.

The objective to maximize revenue implicitly assumes that the variable cost of an occupied room is inconsequential. The zero-variable cost assumption is reasonable for an airline. It is probably less appropriate for a hotel, given that an occupied room requires additional utilities and cleaning staff labor. Nevertheless, we stick with the traditional maximize-revenue objective in this chapter. If the variable cost of a customer is significant, then the techniques we present can be easily modified to implement a maximize-profit objective. (For example, see Practice Problems Q16.8 and Q16.10.)

Returning to our example, the Hyatt could just accept bookings in both fare classes as they occur until either it has 118 reservations or May 29th arrives; the first-come, first-served regime is surely equitable. With that process, it is possible the Hyatt has all 118 rooms reserved one week before May 29th. Unfortunately, because business travelers tend to book late, in that situation it is likely some high-fare travelers will be turned away in that last week; the Hyatt is not allowed to cancel a low-fare reservation to make room for a high-fare traveler. Turning away a high-fare reservation is surely a lost revenue opportunity.

There is a better way than just accepting reservations on a first-come, first-served basis. Instead, the Hyatt could reserve a certain number of rooms just for the high-fare travelers, that is, to protect some rooms for last-minute bookings. This is formalized with the concept of protection levels and booking limits.

The *protection level* for a fare is the number of rooms that are reserved for that fare or higher. We let Q represent our protection level for the high fare. If $Q = 35$, then we protect 35 rooms for the high fare. What does it mean to "protect" 35 rooms? It means that at all

---

[1] The Park Hyatt in Philadelphia does have 118 king/queen rooms, but the demand and fare data in this case are disguised. Furthermore, the revenue management techniques described in the chapter are meant to be representative of how the Park Hyatt could do revenue management, but should not be taken to represent the Park Hyatt's actual operating procedures.

times there must always be *at least* 35 rooms that could be reserved with the high fare. For example, suppose there were 83 rooms reserved at the low fare, 30 rooms reserved at the high fare, and 5 unreserved rooms. Because there are enough unreserved rooms to allow us to possibly have 35 high-fare rooms, we have not violated our protection level.

But now suppose the next traveler requests a low-fare reservation. If we were to allow that reservation, then we would no longer have enough unreserved rooms to allow at least 35 high-fare rooms. Therefore, according to our protection level rule, we would not allow that low-fare reservation. In fact, the limit of 83 has a name; it is called a booking limit: The *booking limit* for a fare is the maximum number of reservations allowed at that fare or lower. There is a relationship between the high-fare protection level and the low-fare booking limit:

$$\text{High-fare protection level } = \text{ Capacity } - \text{ Low-fare booking limit} \qquad \textbf{(16.1)}$$

In order to have at least 35 rooms available for the high fare (its protection level), the Hyatt cannot allow any more than 83 reservations at the low fare (its booking limit) as long as the total number of allowed reservations (capacity) is 118.

You might now wonder about the protection level for the low fare and the booking limit for the high fare. There is no need to protect any rooms at the low fare because the next best alternative is for the room to go empty. So the protection level for the low fare is 0. Analogously, we are willing to book as many rooms as possible at the high fare because there is no better alternative, so the booking limit on the high fare should be set to at least 118. (As we will see in the next section, we may even wish to allow more than 118 bookings.)

Given that we have defined a booking limit to be the maximum number of reservations allowed for a fare class *or lower,* we have implicitly assumed that our booking limits are *nested.* With *nested booking limits,* it is always true that if a particular fare class is open (i.e., we are willing to accept reservations at that fare class), then we are willing to accept all higher fare classes as well. It is also true that if a particular fare class is closed, then all lower fare classes are closed as well. For reasons beyond the scope of this discussion, nested booking limits may not be optimal. Nevertheless, because nested booking limits make intuitive sense, most revenue management systems operate with nested booking limits. So, throughout our discussion, we shall assume nested booking limits.

So now let's turn to the issue of choosing a booking limit for the low fare or, equivalently, a protection level for the high fare. As in many operational decisions, we again face the "too much–too little" problem. If we protect too many rooms for the high-fare class, then some rooms might remain empty on May 29th. To explain, suppose one week before May 29th we have 83 low-fare bookings but only 10 high-fare bookings. Because we have reached the low-fare booking limit, we "close down" that fare and only accept high-fare bookings in the last week. If only 20 additional high-fare bookings arrive, then on May 29th we have five unreserved rooms, which we might have been able to sell at the low fare. Nevertheless, those five rooms go empty. So protecting too many rooms for a fare class can lead to empty rooms.

But the Hyatt can also protect too few rooms. Suppose one week before May 29th we have 80 low-fare bookings and 35 high-fare bookings. Because only 35 rooms are protected for the high fare, the remaining three unreserved rooms could be taken at the low fare. If they are reserved at the low fare, then some high-fare travelers might be turned away; that is, the Hyatt might end up selling a room at the low fare that could have been sold at a high fare. If the protection level were three rooms higher, then those three unreserved rooms could only go at the high fare. Therefore, because the low-fare bookings tend to come before the high-fare bookings, it is possible to protect too few rooms for the high fare.

Our discussion so far suggests the Hyatt could use the newsvendor model logic to choose a protection level. (Peter Belobaba of MIT first developed this approach and labeled it the "Expected Marginal Seat Revenue" analysis. See Belobaba, 1989) To implement the model, we need a forecast of high-fare demand and an assessment of the underage and overage costs. Let's say the Hyatt believes a Poisson distribution with mean 27.3 represents the number of high-fare travelers on May 29th. (This forecast could be constructed using booking data from similar nights, similar times of the year, and managerial intuition.) Table 16.2 provides a portion of the distribution function for that Poisson distribution.

Now we need an overage cost C_o and an underage cost C_u. The underage cost is the cost per unit of setting the protection level too low (i.e., "under" protecting). If we do not protect enough rooms for the high fare, then we sell a room at the low fare that could have been sold at the high fare. The lost revenue is the difference between the two fares, that is, $C_u = r_h - r_l$.

The overage cost is the cost per unit of setting the protection level too high (i.e., "over" protecting). If we set the protection level too high, it means that we did not need to protect so many rooms for the high-fare customers. In other words, demand at the high fare is less than Q, our protection level. If Q were lower, then we could have sold another room at the low fare. Hence, the overage cost is the incremental revenue of selling a room at the low fare: $C_o = r_l$. According to the newsvendor model, the optimal protection level (i.e., the one that maximizes revenue, which is also the one that minimizes the overage and underage costs) is the Q such that the probability the high-fare demand is less than or equal to Q equals the critical ratio, which is

$$\frac{C_u}{C_o + C_u} = \frac{r_h - r_l}{r_l + (r_h - r_l)} = \frac{r_h - r_l}{r_h} = \frac{225 - 159}{225} = 0.2933$$

In words, we want to find the Q such that there is a 29.33 percent probability high-fare demand is Q or lower. From Table 16.2, we see that $F(23) = 0.2381$ and $F(24) = 0.3040$, so the optimal protection level is $Q = 24$ rooms. (Recall the round-up rule: When the critical ratio falls between two values in the distribution function table, choose the entry that leads to the higher decision variable.) The corresponding booking limit for the low fare is $118 - 24 = 94$ rooms.

TABLE 16.2
The Distribution and Loss Function for a Poisson with Mean 27.3

Q	F(Q)	L(Q)	Q	F(Q)	L(Q)	Q	F(Q)	L(Q)
10	0.0001	17.30	20	0.0920	7.45	30	0.7365	1.03
11	0.0004	16.30	21	0.1314	6.55	31	0.7927	0.77
12	0.0009	15.30	22	0.1802	5.68	32	0.8406	0.56
13	0.0019	14.30	23	0.2381	4.86	33	0.8803	0.40
14	0.0039	13.30	24	0.3040	4.10	34	0.9121	0.28
15	0.0077	12.31	25	0.3760	3.40	35	0.9370	0.19
16	0.0140	11.31	26	0.4516	2.78	36	0.9558	0.13
17	0.0242	10.33	27	0.5280	2.23	37	0.9697	0.09
18	0.0396	9.35	28	0.6025	1.76	38	0.9797	0.06
19	0.0618	8.39	29	0.6726	1.36	39	0.9867	0.04

In some situations, it is more convenient to express a booking limit as an *authorization level:* The authorization level for a fare class is the percentage of available capacity that can be reserved at that fare or lower. For example, a booking limit of 94 rooms corresponds to an authorization level of 80 percent (94/118) because 80 percent of the Hyatt's rooms can be reserved at the low fare. The process of evaluating protection levels and booking limits is summarized in Exhibit 16.1.

If the Hyatt uses a protection level of 24 rooms, then the Hyatt's expected revenue is higher than if no protection level is used. How much higher? To provide some answer to that question, we need to make a few more assumptions. First, let's assume that there is ample low-fare demand. In other words, we could easily book all 118 rooms at the low fare. Second, let's assume the low-fare demand arrives before any high-fare bookings. Hence, if we do not protect any rooms for the high fare, then the low-fare customers will reserve all 118 rooms before any high-fare customer requests a reservation.

Given our assumptions, the Hyatt's revenue without any protection level would be $118 \times \$159 = \$18,762$: all 118 rooms are filled at the low fare. If we protect 24 rooms, then we surely fill 94 rooms at the low fare, for an expected revenue of $94 \times \$159 = \$14,946$. What is the expected revenue from the 24 protected rooms? Given that high-fare demand is Poisson with mean 27.3, from Table 16.2 we see that we can expect to turn away 4.1 high-fare bookings, that is, the loss function is $L(24) = 4.1$. In other words, we can expect to lose 4.1 high-fare bookings. Our expected high-fare bookings is analogous to expected sales in the newsvendor model, so

$$\begin{aligned} \text{Expected high-fare bookings} &= \text{Expected high-fare demand} - \text{Expected lost sales} \\ &= 27.3 - 4.1 \\ &= 23.2 \end{aligned}$$

In other words, we expect to have 23.2 high-fare reservations if we protect 24 rooms and high-fare demand is Poisson with mean 27.3. Therefore, because the Hyatt protects fewer rooms than expected demand, the Hyatt can expect to sell most of the rooms it protects with very few empty rooms. To be precise, of the 24 protected rooms, only 0.8 of them is expected to be empty:

$$\begin{aligned} \text{Expected number of empty rooms} &= Q - \text{Expected high-fare bookings} \\ &= 24 - 23.2 \\ &= 0.8 \end{aligned}$$

This makes sense. The incremental revenue of selling a high fare is only $66, but the cost of an empty room is $159, so a conservative protection level is prudent.

If the Hyatt expects to sell 23.2 rooms at the high fare, then the revenue from those rooms is $23.2 \times \$225 = \$5,220$. Total revenue when protecting 24 rooms is then $\$14,946 + \$5,220 = \$20,166$. Hence, our expected revenue increases by $(20,166 - 18,762) / 18,762 = 7.5$ percent. As a point of reference, we can evaluate the *maximum expected revenue,* which is achieved if we sell to every high-fare customer and sell all remaining rooms at the low fare:

$$\begin{aligned} \text{Maximum expected revenue} &= 27.3 \times \$225 + (118 - 27.3) \times \$159 \\ &= \$20,564 \end{aligned}$$

Thus, the difference between the maximum expected revenue and the revenue earned by just selling at the low fare is $\$20,564 - \$18,762 = \$1,802$. The Hyatt's revenue with a

Exhibit 16.1

EVALUATING THE OPTIMAL PROTECTION LEVEL FOR THE HIGH FARE OR THE OPTIMAL BOOKING LIMIT FOR THE LOW FARE WHEN THERE ARE TWO FARES AND REVENUE MAXIMIZATION IS THE OBJECTIVE

Step 1. Evaluate the critical ratio:

$$\text{Critical ratio} = \frac{C_u}{C_o + C_u} = \frac{r_h - r_l}{r_h}$$

Step 2. Find the Q such that $F(Q)$ = Critical ratio, where $F(Q)$ is the distribution function of high-fare demand:

a. If $F(Q)$ is given in table form, then find the Q in the table such that $F(Q)$ equals the critical ratio. If the critical ratio falls between two entries in the table, choose the entry with the higher Q.

b. If high-fare demand is normally distributed with mean μ and standard deviation σ, then find the z-statistic in the Standard Normal Distribution Function Table such that $\Phi(z)$ = Critical ratio. If the critical ratio falls between two entries in the table, choose the entry with the higher z. Finally, convert the chosen z into Q: $Q = \mu + z \times \sigma$.

Step 3. The optimal high-fare protection level is Q evaluated in Step 2. The optimal low-fare booking limit is Capacity − Q, where Capacity is the number of allowed reservations.

protection level falls short of the maximum expected revenue by only \$20,564 − \$20,166 = \$398. Hence, a protection level for the high fare allows the Hyatt to capture about 78 percent (1 − \$398/\$1,802) of its potential revenue improvement.

A revenue increase of 7.5 percent is surely substantial given that it is achieved without the addition of capacity. Nevertheless, we must be reminded of the assumptions that were made. We assumed there is ample demand for the low fare. If low-fare demand is limited, then a protection level for the high fare is less valuable and the incremental revenue gain is smaller. For example, if the sum of low- and high-fare demand is essentially always lower than 118 rooms, then there is no need to protect the high fare. More broadly, revenue management with protection levels is most valuable when operating in a capacity-constrained situation.

The second key assumption is that low-fare demand arrives before high-fare demand. If some high-fare demand "slips in" before the low-fare demand snatches up all 118 rooms, then the revenue estimate without a protection level, \$18,762, is too low. In other words, even if we do not protect any rooms for the high fare, it is possible that we would still obtain some high-fare bookings.

Although we would need to look at actual data to get a more accurate sense of the potential revenue improvement by using protection levels, our estimate is in line with the typical revenue increases reported in practice due to revenue management, 3 to 7 percent.

Now that we have considered a specific example of booking limits at a hotel, it is worth enumerating the characteristics of a business that are conducive to the application of booking limits.

- *The same unit of capacity can be used to sell to different customer segments.* It is easy for an airline to price discriminate between leisure and business travelers when the capacity that is being sold is different, for example, a coach cabin seat and a first-class seat. Those are clearly distinguishable products/services. Booking limits are applied when the capacity sold to different segments is identical; for example, a coach seat on an aircraft or a king/queen room in the Hyatt sold at two different fares.

• *There are distinguishable customer segments and the segments have different price sensitivity.* There is no need for protection levels when the revenue earned from all customers is the same, for example, if there is a single fare. Booking limits are worthwhile if the firm can earn different revenue from different customer segments with the same type of capacity. Because the same unit of capacity is being sold, it is necessary to discriminate between the customer segments. This is achieved with *fences:* additional restrictions that are imposed on the low fare that prevent high-fare customers from purchasing with the low fare. Typical fences include advanced purchase requirements, Saturday night stay requirements, cancellation fees, change fees, and so forth. Of course, one could argue that these fences make the low and high fares different products; for example, a full-fare coach ticket is not the same product as a supersaver coach ticket even if they both offer a seat in the coach cabin. True, these are different products in the broad sense, but they are identical products with respect to the capacity they utilize.

• *Capacity is perishable.* An unused room on May 29th is lost forever, just as an unused seat on a flight cannot be stored until the next flight. In contrast, capacity in a production facility can be used to make inventory, which can be sold later whenever capacity exceeds current demand.

• *Capacity is restrictive.* If the total demand at the leisure and business fares is rarely greater than 118 rooms, then the Hyatt has no need to establish protection levels or booking limits. Because capacity is expensive to install and expensive to change over time, it is impossible for a service provider to always have plenty of capacity. (Utilization would be so low that the firm would surely not be competitive and probably not viable.) But due to seasonality effects, it is possible that the Hyatt has plenty of capacity at some times of the year and not enough capacity at other times. Booking limits are not needed during those lull times but are quite useful during the peak demand periods.

• *Capacity is sold in advance.* If we were allowed to cancel a low-fare reservation whenever someone requested a high-fare reservation (i.e., bump a low-fare passenger off the plane without penalty), then we would not need to protect seats for the high fare: We would accept low-fare bookings as they arrive and then cancel as many as needed to accommodate the high-fare travelers. Similarly, we do not need protection levels if we were to conduct an auction just before the flight departs. For example, imagine a situation in which all potential demand would arrive at the airport an hour or so before the flight departs and then an auction is conducted to determine who would earn a seat on that flight. This is a rather silly way to sell airline seats, but in other contexts there is clearly a movement toward more auctionlike selling mechanisms. Because the auction ensures that capacity is sold to the highest bidders, there is no need for protection levels.

• *A firm wishes to maximize revenue, has the flexibility to charge different prices, and may withhold capacity from certain segments.* A hotel is able to offer multiple fares and withhold fares. In other words, even though the practice of closing a discount fare means the principle of first-come, first-served is violated, this practice is generally not viewed as unethical or unscrupulous. However, there are settings in which the violation of first-come, first-served, or the charging of different prices, or the use of certain fences is not acceptable to consumers, for example, access to health care.

• *A firm faces competition from a "discount competitor."* The low fares charged by People Express, a low-frills airline started after deregulation, were a major motivation for the development of revenue management at American Airlines. In order to compete in the low-fare segment, American was forced to match People Express's fares. But American did not want to have its high-fare customers paying the low fare. Booking limits and low-fare fences were the solution to the problem: American could compete at the low-fare segment without destroying the revenue from its profitable high-fare customers. People Express did not install a revenue management system and quickly went bankrupt after American's response.

16.3   Overbooking

In many service settings, customers are allowed to make reservations and then either are allowed to cancel their reservations with relatively short notice, or just fail to show up to receive their service. For example, on May 28th, the Hyatt might have all of its 118 rooms reserved for May 29th but then only 110 customers might actually show up, leaving eight rooms empty and not generating any revenue. Overbooking, described in this section, is one solution to the no-show problem. If the Hyatt chooses to overbook, then that means the Hyatt accepts more than 118 reservations even though a maximum of 118 guests can be accommodated. Overbooking is also common in the airline industry: In the United States, airlines deny boarding to about one million passengers annually (Stringer, 2002). Furthermore, it has been estimated that prohibiting overbooking would cost the world's airlines $3 billion annually due to no-shows (Cross, 1995).

Let the variable Y represent the number of additional reservations beyond capacity that the Hyatt is willing to accept, that is, up to $118 + Y$ reservations are accepted. Overbooking can lead to two kinds of outcomes. On a positive note, the number of no-shows can be greater than the number of overbooked reservations, so all the actual customers can be accommodated and more customers are accommodated than would have been without overbooking. For example, suppose the Hyatt accepts 122 reservations and there are six no-shows. As a result, 116 rooms are occupied, leaving only two empty rooms, which is almost surely fewer empty rooms than if the Hyatt had only accepted 118 reservations.

On the negative side, the Hyatt can get caught overbooking. For example, if 122 reservations are accepted, but there are only two no-shows, then 120 guests hold reservations for 118 rooms. In that situation, two guests need to be accommodated at some other hotel and the Hyatt probably must give some additional compensation (e.g., cash or free future stay) to mitigate the loss of goodwill with those customers.

In deciding the proper amount of overbooking, there is a "too much–too little" trade-off: Overbook too much and the hotel angers some customers, but overbook too little and the hotel has the lost revenue associated with empty rooms. Hence, we can apply the newsvendor model to choose the appropriate Y. We first need a forecast of the number of customers that will not show up based on historical data. Let's say the Hyatt believes for the May 29th night that the no-show distribution is Poisson with mean 8.5. Table 16.3 provides the distribution function.[2]

---

[2] A careful reader will notice that our distribution function for no-shows is independent of the number of reservations made. In other words, we have assumed the average number of no-shows is 8.5 whether we make 118 reservations or 150 reservations. Hence, a more sophisticated method for choosing the overbooking quantity would account for the relationship between the number of reservations allowed and the distribution function of no-shows. While that more sophisticated method is conceptually similar to our procedure, it is also computationally cumbersome. Therefore, we shall stick with our heuristic method. Fortunately, our heuristic method performs well when compared against the more sophisticated algorithm.

TABLE 16.3
Poisson Distribution Function with Mean 8.5

Q	F(Q)	Q	F(Q)
0	0.0002	10	0.7634
1	0.0019	11	0.8487
2	0.0093	12	0.9091
3	0.0301	13	0.9486
4	0.0744	14	0.9726
5	0.1496	15	0.9862
6	0.2562	16	0.9934
7	0.3856	17	0.9970
8	0.5231	18	0.9987
9	0.6530	19	0.9995

Next, we need underage and overage costs. If the Hyatt chooses Y to be too low, then there will be empty rooms on May 29th (i.e., the Hyatt "under" overbooked). If the Hyatt indeed has plenty of low-fare demand, then those empty rooms could have at least been sold for $r_l = \$159$, so the underage cost is $C_u = r_l = 159$. Surprisingly, the underage cost does not depend on whether customers are allowed to cancel without penalty or not. To explain, suppose we accepted 120 reservations, but there are three no-shows. If reservations are refundable, we collected revenue from 117 customers (because the three no-shows are given a refund) but could have collected revenue from the one empty room. If reservations are not refundable, we collect revenue from 120 customers, but, again, we could have collected revenue from the one empty room. In each case our incremental revenue is $159 from the one additional room we could have sold had we accepted one more reservation.

If the Hyatt chooses Y to be too high, then there will be more guests than rooms. The guests denied a room need to be accommodated at some other hotel and Hyatt offers other compensation. The total cost to Hyatt for each of those guests is estimated to be about $350, so the overage cost is $C_o = 350$. *Note:* This cost is net of any revenue collected from the customer. For example, if the reservation is not refundable, then the Hyatt incurs $509 in total costs due to the denial of service, for a net cost of $350 ($509−$159), whereas if the reservation is refundable, then the Hyatt incurs $350 in total costs due to the denial of service. Either way, the Hyatt is $350 worse off for each customer denied a room.

The critical ratio is

$$\frac{C_u}{C_o + C_u} = \frac{159}{350 + 159} = 0.3124$$

Looking in Table 16.3, we see that $F(6) = 0.2562$ and $F(7) = 0.3856$, so the optimal quantity to overbook is $Y = 7$. In other words, the Hyatt should allow up to $118 + 7 = 125$ reservations for May 29th. Exhibit 16.2 summarizes the process of evaluating the optimal quantity to overbook.

If the Hyatt chooses to overbook by seven reservations and if the Hyatt indeed receives 125 reservations, then there is about a 26 percent chance $(F(6) = 0.2562)$ that the Hyatt will find itself overbooked on May 29th. Because it is not assured that the Hyatt will receive that many reservations, the actual frequency of being overbooked would be lower.

A natural question is how should the Hyatt integrate its protection-level/booking-limit decision with its overbooking decision. The following describes a reasonable heuristic.

Exhibit 16.2

THE PROCESS TO EVALUATE THE OPTIMAL QUANTITY TO OVERBOOK

Step 1. Evaluate the critical ratio:

$$\text{Critical ratio} = \frac{C_u}{C_o + C_u} = \frac{r_l}{\text{Cost per bumped customer} + r_l}$$

Step 2. Find the Y such that $F(Y)$ = Critical ratio, where $F(Y)$ is the distribution function of no-shows:

    a. If $F(Y)$ is given in table form, then find the Y in the table such that $F(Y)$ equals the critical ratio. If the critical ratio falls between two entries in the table, choose the entry with the higher Y.

    b. If no-shows are normally distributed with mean μ and standard deviation σ, then find the z-statistic in the Standard Normal Distribution Function Table such that $\Phi(z)$ = Critical ratio. If the critical ratio falls between two entries in the table, choose the entry with the higher z. Finally, convert the chosen z into Y: $Y = \mu + z \times \sigma$.

Step 3. Y is the optimal amount to overbook; that is, the number of allowed reservations is Y + Capacity, where Capacity is the maximum number of customers that can actually be served.

If the Hyatt is willing to overbook by seven rooms, that is, $Y = 7$, then its effective capacity is $118 + 7 = 125$ rooms. Based on the forecast of high-fare demand and the underage and overage costs associated with protecting rooms for the high-fare travelers, we determined that the Hyatt should protect 24 rooms for the high fare. Using equation (16.1), that suggests the booking limit for the low fare should be

$$\text{Low-fare booking limit} = \text{Capacity} - \text{High-fare protection level}$$
$$= 125 - 24$$
$$= 101$$

The high-fare booking limit would then be 125, that is, the Hyatt accepts up to 101 low-fare reservations and up to 125 reservations in total.

16.4   Implementation of Revenue Management

Although the applications of revenue management described in this chapter present a reasonably straightforward analysis, in practice there are many additional complications encountered in the implementation of revenue management. A few of the more significant complications are discussed below.

Demand Forecasting

We saw that forecasts are a necessary input to the choice of both protection levels and overbooking quantities. As a result, the choices made are only as good as the inputted forecasts; as the old adage says, "garbage in, garbage out." Fortunately, reservation systems generally provide a wealth of information to formulate these forecasts. Nevertheless, the forecasting task is complicated by the presence of seasonality, special events (e.g., a convention in town), changing fares (both the firm's own fares as well as the competitors' fares), and truncation (once a booking limit is reached, most systems do not capture the lost demand at that fare level), among others. Furthermore, it is possible that the revenue management decisions themselves might influence demand and, hence, the forecasts used to make those decisions. As a result, with any successful revenue management system, a considerable amount of care and effort is put into the demand forecasting task.

Dynamic Decisions

Our analysis provided a decision for a single moment in time. However, fares and forecasts change with time and, as a result, booking limits need to be reviewed frequently (generally daily). In fact, sophisticated systems take future adjustments into consideration when setting current booking limits.

Variability in Available Capacity

A hotel is a good example of a service firm that generally does not have much variation in its capacity: it is surely difficult to add a room to a hotel and the number of rooms that cannot be occupied is generally small. The capacity of an airline's flight is also rigid but maybe less so than a hotel's capacity because the airline can choose to switch the type of aircraft used on a route. However, a car rental company's capacity at any given location is surely variable and not even fully controllable by the firm. Hence, those firms also must forecast the amount of capacity they think will be available at any given time.

Reservations Coming in Groups

If there is a convention in town for May 29th, then the Hyatt may receive a single request for 110 rooms at the low fare. Although this request violates the booking limit, the booking limit was established assuming reservations come one at a time. It is clearly more costly to turn away a single block of 110 reservations than it is to turn away one leisure traveler.

Effective Segmenting of Customers

We assumed there are two types of customers: a low-fare customer and a high-fare customer. In reality, this is too simplistic. There surely exist customers that are willing to pay the high fare, but they are also more than willing to book at the low fare if given the opportunity. Hence, fences are used to separate out customers by their willingness to pay. Well-known fences include advance purchase requirements, cancellation fees, change fees, Saturday night stay requirements, and so on. But these fences are not perfect; that is, they do not perfectly segment out customers. As a result, there is often spillover demand from one fare class to another. It is possible that more effective fences exist, but some fences might generate stiff resistance from customers. For example, a firm could regulate a customer's access to various fare classes based on his or her annual income, or the average price the customer paid in past service encounters, but those schemes will surely not receive a warm reception.

Multiple Fare Classes

In our application of revenue management, we have two fare classes: a low fare and a high fare. In reality there can be many more fare classes. With multiple fare classes, it becomes necessary to forecast demand for each fare class and to establish multiple booking limits.

Software Implementation

While the investment in revenue management software is often reasonable relative to the potential revenue gain, it is nevertheless not zero. Furthermore, revenue management systems often have been constrained by the capabilities of the reservation systems they must work with. In other words, while the revenue management software might be able to make a decision as to whether a fare class should be open or closed (i.e., whether to accept a request for a reservation at a particular fare), it also must be able to communicate that decision to the travel agent or customer via the reservation system. Finally, there can even be glitches in the revenue management software, as was painfully discovered by American Airlines. Their initial software had an error that prematurely closed down the low-fare class on flights with many empty seats (i.e., it set the low-fare class booking limit too low). American Airlines discovered the error only when they realized that the load on those flights was too low (the load is the percent of seats occupied; it is the utilization of the aircraft). By that time it was estimated $50 million in revenue had been lost. Hence, properly chosen booking limits can increase revenue, but poorly chosen booking limits can decrease revenue. As a result, careful observation of a revenue management system is always necessary.

Variation in Capacity Purchase: Not All Customers Purchase One Unit of Capacity

Even if two customers pay the same fare, they might be different from the firm's perspective. For example, suppose one leisure traveler requests one night at the low fare whereas another requests five nights at the low fare. While these customers pay the same amount for a given night, it is intuitive that turning away the second customer is more costly. In fact, it may even be costlier than turning away a single high-fare reservation.

Airlines experience a challenge similar to a hotel's multinight customer. Consider two passengers traveling from Chicago (O'Hare) to New York (JFK) paying the discount fare. For one passenger JFK is the final destination, whereas the other passenger will fly from JFK to London (Heathrow) on another flight with the same airline. The revenue management system should recognize that a multileg passenger is more valuable than a single-leg customer. But booking limits just defined for each fare class on the O'Hare–JFK segment do not differentiate between these two customers. In other words, the simplest version of revenue management does *single-leg* or *single-segment control* because the decision rules are focused on the fares of a particular segment in the airline's network. Our example from the Hyatt could be described as *single-night control* because the focus is on a room for one evening.

One solution to the multileg issue is to create a booking limit for each fare class–itinerary combination, not just a booking limit for each fare class on each segment. This is called *origin-destination control,* or *O-D control* for short. For example, suppose there are three fare classes, Y, M, Q (from highest to lowest), on two itineraries, O'Hare–JFK and O'Hare–Heathrow (via JFK):

Fare Class	O'Hare to JFK	O'Hare to Heathrow
Y	$724	$1,610
M	475	829
Q	275	525

Six booking limits could be constructed to manage the inventory on the O'Hare–JFK leg. For example:

Fare Class	O'Hare to JFK	O'Hare to Heathrow
Y		100
M		68
Y	60	
Q		40
M	35	
Q	20	

Hence, it would be possible to deny a Q fare request to an O'Hare–JFK passenger while accepting a Q fare request to an O'Hare–Heathrow passenger: There could be 20 Q fare reservations on the O'Hare–JFK itinerary but fewer than 40 reservations between the M and Q fares on the O'Hare–JFK itinerary and the Q fare on the O'Hare–Heathrow itinerary. If there were only three booking limits on that leg, then all Q fare requests are either accepted or rejected, but it is not possible to accept some Q fare requests while denying others.

While creating a booking limit for each fare class–itinerary combination sounds like a good idea, unfortunately, it is not a practical idea for most revenue management applications. For example, there could be thousands of possible itineraries that use the O'Hare–JFK leg. It would be a computational nightmare to derive booking limits for such a number of itineraries on each possible flight leg, not to mention an implementation challenge. One solution to this problem is *virtual nesting*. With virtual nesting, a limited number of *buckets* are created, each with its own booking limit, each with its own set of fare class–itinerary combinations. Fare class–itinerary combinations are assigned to buckets in such a way that the fare class–itinerary combinations within the same bucket have similar value to the firm, while fare class–itinerary combinations in different buckets have significantly different values.

For example, four buckets could be created for our example, labeled 0 to 3:

Bucket	Itinerary	Fare class
0	O'Hare to Heathrow	Y
1	O'Hare to Heathrow	M
	O'Hare to JFK	Y
2	O'Hare to Heathrow	Q
	O'Hare to JFK	M
3	O'Hare to JFK	Q

The O'Hare–JFK Y fare is combined into one bucket with the O'Hare–Heathrow M fare because they generate similar revenue ($724 and $829), whereas the O'Hare–Heathrow Y fare is given its own bucket due to its much higher revenue ($1,610). Thus, with virtual nesting, it is possible to differentiate among the customers on the same leg willing to pay the same fare. Furthermore, virtual nesting provides a manageable solution if there are many different fare classes and many different types of customers (e.g., customers flying different itineraries or customers staying a different number of nights in a hotel).

While virtual nesting was the first solution implemented for this issue, it is not the only solution. A more recent, and more sophisticated, solution is called *bid-price control*. Let's explain bid-price controls in the context of our airline example. The many different itineraries that use the O'Hare–JFK segment generate different revenue to the airline, but they all use the same unit of capacity, a coach seat on the O'Hare to JFK flight. With bid-price control, each type of capacity on each flight segment is assigned a *bid price*. Then, a fare class–itinerary combination is accepted as long as its fare exceeds the sum of the bid prices of the flight legs in its itinerary. For example, the bid prices could be

	O'Hare to JFK	JFK to Heathrow
Bid price	$290	$170

Hence, an O'Hare–JFK itinerary is available as long as its fare exceeds $290 and an O'Hare–Heathrow itinerary (via JFK) is available as long as its fare exceeds $290 + $170 = $460. Therefore, on the O'Hare–JFK itinerary, the Y and M fare classes would be open (fares $724 and $475 respectively); while on the O'Hare–Heathrow itinerary, all fares would be available (because the lowest Q fare, $525, exceeds the total bid price of $460).

With bid-price control, there is a single bid price on each flight segment, so it is a relatively intuitive and straightforward technique to implement. The challenge with bid-price control is to find the correct bid prices. That challenge requires the use of sophisticated optimization techniques.

16.5 Summary

Revenue management is the science of using pricing and capacity controls to maximize revenue given a relatively fixed supply/capacity. This chapter focuses on the capacity control tools of revenue management: protection levels/booking limits and overbooking. Protection levels/booking limits take advantage of the price differences between fares and the generally staggered nature of demand arrivals; that is, low-fare reservations made by leisure travelers usually occur before high fare reservations made by business travelers. By establishing a booking limit for low fares, it is possible to protect enough capacity for the later-arriving high fares. Overbooking is useful when customer reservations are not firm; if a portion of the customers can be expected to not use the capacity they reserved, then it is wise to accept more reservations than available capacity.

The science of revenue management is indeed quite complex and continues to be an extremely active area of research. Despite these challenges, revenue management has been proven to be a robust and profitable tool, as reflected in the following quote by Robert Crandall, former CEO of AMR and American Airlines (Smith, Leimkuhler, and Darrow, 1992):

> I believe that revenue management is the single most important technical development in transportation management since we entered the era of airline deregulation in 1979 . . . The development of revenue management models was a key to American Airlines' survival in the post-deregulation environment. Without revenue management we were often faced with two unsatisfactory responses in a price competitive marketplace. We could match deeply discounted fares and risk diluting our entire inventory, or we could not match and certainly lose market share. Revenue management gave us a third alternative—match deeply discounted fares on a portion of our inventory and close deeply discounted inventory when it is profitable to save space for later-booking higher value customers. By adjusting the number of reservations which are available at these discounts, we can adjust our minimum available fare to account for differences in demand. This creates a pricing structure which responds to demand on a flight-by-flight basis. As a result, we can more effectively match our demand to supply.

Table 16.4 provides a summary of the key notation and equations presented in this chapter.

TABLE 16.4
Summary of Key Notation and Equations in Chapter 16

Choosing protection levels and booking limits:

With two fares, r_h = high fare and r_l = low fare, the high-fare protection level Q has the following critical ratio:

$$\text{Critical ratio} = \frac{C_u}{C_o + C_u} = \frac{r_h - r_l}{r_h}$$

(Find the Q such that the critical ratio is the probability high-fare demand is less than or equal to Q.)

Low-fare booking limit = Capacity − Q

Choosing an overbooking quantity Y:

Let r_l be the low fare. The optimal overbooking quantity Y has the following critical ratio:

$$\text{Critical ratio} = \frac{C_u}{C_o + C_u} = \frac{r_l}{\text{Cost per bumped customer} + r_l}$$

16.6 Further Reading

For a brief history of the development of revenue management, see Cross (1995). For a more extensive history, see Cross (1997). Cross (1997) also provides a detailed overview of revenue management techniques.

See Talluri and van Ryzin (2004) for an extensive treatment of the state of the art in revenue management for both theory and practice. Two already-published reviews on the theory of revenue management are McGill and van Ryzin (1999) and Weatherford and Bodily (1992).

Applications of revenue management to car rentals, golf courses, and restaurants can be found in Geraghty and Johnson (1997), Kimes (2000) and Kimes, Chase, Choi, Lee, and Ngonzi (1998).

16.7 Practice Problems

Q16.1* **(The Inn at Penn)** The Inn at Penn hotel has 150 rooms with standard queen-size beds and two rates: a full price of $200 and a discount price of $120. To receive the discount price, a customer must purchase the room at least two weeks in advance (this helps to distinguish between leisure travelers, who tend to book early, and business travelers, who value the flexibility of booking late). For a particular Tuesday night, the hotel estimates that the demand from leisure travelers could fill the whole hotel while the demand from business travelers is distributed normally with a mean of 70 rooms and a standard deviation of 29.

a. Suppose 50 rooms are protected for full-price rooms. What is the booking limit for the discount rooms?

b. Find the optimal protection level for full-price rooms (the number of rooms to be protected from sale at a discount price).

c. The Sheraton declared a fare war by slashing business travelers' prices down to $150. The Inn at Penn had to match that fare to keep demand at the same level. Does the optimal protection level increase, decrease, or remain the same? Explain your answer.

d. What number of rooms (on average) remain unfilled if we establish a protection level of 61 for the full-priced rooms?

e. If The Inn were able to ensure that every full-price customer would receive a room, what would The Inn's expected revenue be?

f. If The Inn did not choose to protect any rooms for the full price and leisure travelers book before business travelers, then what would The Inn's expected revenue be?

g. Taking the assumptions in part f and assuming now that The Inn protects 50 rooms for the full price, what is The Inn's expected revenue?

Q16.2* **(Overbooking The Inn at Penn)** Due to customer no-shows, The Inn at Penn hotel is considering implementing overbooking. Recall from Q16.1 that The Inn at Penn has 150 rooms, the full fare is $200, and the discount fare is $120. The forecast of no-shows

(* indicates that the solution is at the end of the book)

is Poisson with a mean of 15.5. The distribution and loss functions of that distribution are as follows:

Y	F(Y)	L(Y)	Y	F(Y)	L(Y)	Y	F(Y)	L(Y)
8	0.0288	7.52	14	0.4154	2.40	20	0.8944	0.28
9	0.0552	6.55	15	0.5170	1.82	21	0.9304	0.18
10	0.0961	5.61	16	0.6154	1.33	22	0.9558	0.11
11	0.1538	4.70	17	0.7052	0.95	23	0.9730	0.06
12	0.2283	3.86	18	0.7825	0.65	24	0.9840	0.04
13	0.3171	3.08	19	0.8455	0.44	25	0.9909	0.02

The Inn is sensitive about the quality of service it provides alumni, so it estimates the cost of failing to honor a reservation is $325 in lost goodwill and explicit expenses.

a. What is the optimal overbooking limit, that is, the maximum reservations above the available 150 rooms that The Inn should accept?

b. If The Inn accepts 160 reservations, what is the probability The Inn will not be able to honor a reservation?

c. If The Inn accepts 165 reservations, what is the probability The Inn will be fully occupied?

d. If The Inn accepts 170 reservations, what is the expected total cost incurred due to bumped customers?

Q16.3* **(WAMB)** WAMB is a television station that has 25 thirty-second advertising slots during each evening. It is early January and the station is selling advertising for Sunday, March 24. They could sell all of the slots right now for $4,000 each, but, because on this particular Sunday the station is televising the Oscar ceremonies, there will be an opportunity to sell slots during the week right before March 24 for a price of $10,000. For now, assume that a slot not sold in advance *and* not sold during the last week is worthless to WAMB. To help make this decision, the salesforce has created the following probability distribution for last-minute sales:

Number of Slots, x	Probability Exactly x Slots Are Sold
8	0.00
9	0.05
10	0.10
11	0.15
12	0.20
13	0.10
14	0.10
15	0.10
16	0.10
17	0.05
18	0.05
19	0.00

a. How many slots should WAMB sell in advance?

b. In practice, there are companies willing to place standby advertising messages: if there is an empty slot available (i.e., this slot was not sold either in advance or during the last week), the standby message is placed into this slot. Since there is no guarantee that such a slot will be available, standby messages can be placed at a much lower cost. Now suppose that if a slot is not sold in advance *and* not sold during the last week, it will be used for a standby promotional message that costs advertisers $2,500. Now how many slots should WAMB sell in advance?

(* indicates that the solution is at the end of the book)

    c. Suppose WAMB chooses a booking limit of 10 slots on advanced sales. In this case, what is the probability there will be slots left over for stand-by messages?

    d. One problem with booking for March 24 in early January is that advertisers often withdraw their commitment to place the ad (typically this is a result of changes in promotional strategies; for example, a product may be found to be inferior or an ad may turn out to be ineffective). Because of such opportunistic behavior by advertisers, media companies often overbook advertising slots. WAMB estimates that in the past the number of withdrawn ads has a Poisson distribution with mean 9. Assume each withdrawn ad slot can still be sold at a standby price of $2,500 although the company misses an opportunity to sell these slots at $4,000 a piece. Any ad that was accepted by WAMB but cannot be accommodated (because there isn't a free slot) costs the company $10,000 in penalties. How many slots (at most) should be sold?

    e. Over time, WAMB saw a steady increase in the number of withdrawn ads and decided to institute a penalty of $1,000 for withdrawals. (Actually, the company now requires a $1,000 deposit on any slot. It is refunded only if WAMB is unable to provide a slot due to overbooking.) The expected number of withdrawn ads is expected to be cut in half (to only 4.5 slots). Now how many slots (at most) should be sold?

Q16.4* **(Designer Dress)** A fashion retailer in Santa Barbara, California, presents a new designer dress at one of the "by invitation only" fashion shows. After the show, the dress will be sold at the company's boutique store for $10,000 apiece. Demand at the boutique is limited due to the short time the dress remains fashionable and is estimated to be normal with mean 70 and standard deviation 40. There were only 100 dresses produced to maintain exclusivity and high price. It is the company's policy that all unsold merchandise is destroyed.

    a. How many dresses remain unsold on average at the end of the season?

    b. What is the retailer's expected revenue?

    c. Fashion companies often sell a portion of new merchandise at exhibitions for a discount while the product is still "fresh" in the minds of the viewers. The company decides to increase revenues by selling a certain number of dresses at a greatly discounted price of $6,000 during the show. Later, remaining dresses will be available at the boutique store for a normal price of $10,000. Typically, all dresses offered at the show get sold, which, of course, decreases demand at the store: it is now normal with mean 40 and standard deviation 25. How many dresses should be sold at the show?

    d. Given your decision in part c, what is expected revenue?

    e. Given your decision in part c, how many dresses are expected to remain unsold?

Q16.5* **(Overbooking PHL-LAX)** On a given Philadelphia–Los Angeles flight, there are 200 seats. Suppose the ticket price is $475 on average and the number of passengers who reserve a seat but do not show up for departure is normally distributed with mean 30 and standard deviation 15. You decide to overbook the flight and estimate that the average loss from a passenger who will have to be bumped (if the number of passengers exceeds the number of seats) is $800.

    a. What is the maximum number of reservations that should be accepted?

    b. Suppose you allow 220 reservations. How much money do you expect to pay out in compensation to bumped passengers?

    c. Suppose you allow 220 reservations. What is the probability that you will have to deal with bumped passengers?

Q16.6 **(PHL-LAX)** Consider the Philadelphia–Los Angeles flight discussed in Q16.5. Assume the available capacity is 200 seats and there is no overbooking. The high fare is $675 and the low fare is $375. Demand for the low fare is abundant while demand for the high fare is normally distributed with a mean of 80 and standard deviation 35.

    a. What is the probability of selling 200 reservations if you set an optimal protection level for the full fare?

(* indicates that the solution is at the end of the book)

b. Suppose a protection level of 85 is established. What is the average number of lost high-fare passengers?

c. Continue to assume a protection level of 85 is established. What is the expected number of unoccupied seats?

d. Again assume a protection level of 85 is established. What is the expected revenue from the flight?

Q16.7** **(Annenberg)** Ron, the director at the Annenberg Center, is planning his pricing strategy for a musical to be held in a 100-seat theater. He sets the full price at $80 and estimates demand at this price to be normally distributed with mean 40 and standard deviation 30. Ron also decides to offer student-only advance sale tickets discounted 50 percent off the full price. Demand for the discounted student-only tickets is usually abundant and occurs well before full price ticket sales.

a. Suppose Ron sets a 50-seat booking limit for the student-only tickets. What is the number of full-price tickets that Ron expects to sell?

b. Based on a review of the show in another city, Ron updates his demand forecast for full-price tickets to be normal with mean 60 and standard deviation 40, but he does not change the prices. What is the optimal protection level for full-price seats?

c. Ron realizes that having many empty seats negatively affects the attendees' value from the show. Hence, he decides to change the discount given on student-only tickets from 50 percent off the full price to 55 percent off the full price and he continues to set his protection level optimally. (The demand forecast for full-price tickets remains as in b, normal with mean 60 and standard deviation 40.) How will this change in the student-only discount price affect the expected number of empty seats? (Will they increase, decrease, or remain the same or it is not possible to determine what will happen?)

d. Ron knows that on average eight seats (Poisson distributed) remain empty due to no-shows. Ron also estimates that it is 10 times more costly for him to have one more attendee than seats relative to having one empty seat in the theater. What is the maximum number of seats to sell in excess of capacity?

Q16.8 **(Park Hyatt)** Consider the example of the Park Hyatt Philadelphia discussed in the text. Recall that the full fare is $225, the expected full-fare demand is Poisson with mean 27.3, the discount fare is $159, and there are 118 king/queen rooms. Now suppose the cost of an occupied room is $45 per night. That cost includes the labor associated with prepping and cleaning a room, the additional utilities used, and the wear and tear on the furniture and fixtures. Suppose the Park Hyatt wishes to maximize expected profit rather than expected revenue. What is the optimal protection level for the full fare?

Q16.9 **(MBA Admissions)** Each year the admissions committee at a top business school receives a large number of applications for admission to the MBA program and they have to decide on the number of offers to make. Since some of the admitted students may decide to pursue other opportunities, the committee typically admits more students than the ideal class size of 720 students. You were asked to help the admissions committee estimate the appropriate number of people who should be offered admission. It is estimated that in the coming year the number of people who will not accept the admission offer is normally distributed with mean 50 and standard deviation 21. Suppose for now that the school does not maintain a waiting list, that is, all students are accepted or rejected.

a. Suppose 750 students are admitted. What is the probability that the class size will be at least 720 students?

b. It is hard to associate a monetary value with admitting too many students or admitting too few. However, there is a mutual agreement that it is about two times more expensive to have a student in excess of the ideal 720 than to have fewer students in the class. What is the appropriate number of students to admit?

c. A waiting list mitigates the problem of having too few students since at the very last moment there is an opportunity to admit some students from the waiting list. Hence, the admissions committee revises its estimate: It claims that it is five times more expensive to have a student in excess of 720 than to have fewer students accept among the initial group of admitted students. What is your revised suggestion?

Q16.10** (Air Cargo) An air cargo company must decide how to sell its capacity. It could sell a portion of its capacity with long-term contracts. A long-term contract specifies that the buyer (the air cargo company's customer) will purchase a certain amount of cargo space at a certain price. The long-term contract rate is currently $1,875 per standard unit of space. If long-term contracts are not signed, then the company can sell its space on the spot market. The spot market price is volatile, but the expected future spot price is around $2,100. In addition, spot market demand is volatile: sometimes the company can find customers; other times it cannot on a short-term basis. Let's consider a specific flight on a specific date. The company's capacity is 58 units. Furthermore, the company expects that spot market demand is normally distributed with mean 65 and standard deviation 45. On average, it costs the company $330 in fuel, handling, and maintenance to fly a unit of cargo.

a. Suppose the company relied exclusively on the spot market, that is, it signed no long-term contracts. What would be the company's expected profit?

b. Suppose the company relied exclusively on long-term contracts. What would be the company's expected profit?

c. Suppose the company is willing to use both the long-term and the spot markets. How many units of capacity should the company sell with long-term contracts to maximize *revenue?*

d. Suppose the company is willing to use both the long-term and the spot markets. How many units of capacity should the company sell with long-term contracts to maximize *profit?*

You can view a video of how problems marked with a ** are solved by going on www. cachon-terwiesch.net and follow the links under 'Solved Practice Problems'

Chapter 17

Supply Chain Coordination

Supply chain performance depends on the actions taken by all of the organizations in the supply chain; one weak link can negatively affect every other location in the chain. While everyone supports in principle the objective of optimizing the supply chain's performance, each firm's primary objective is the optimization of its own performance. And unfortunately, as shown in this chapter, self-serving behavior by each member of the supply chain can lead to less than optimal supply chain performance. In those situations, the firms in the supply chain can benefit from better operational coordination.

In this chapter we explore several challenges to supply chain coordination. The first challenge is the *bullwhip effect:* the tendency for demand variability to increase, often considerably, as you move up the supply chain (from retailer, to distributor, to factory, to raw material suppliers, etc.). Given that variability in any form is problematic for effective operations, it is clear the bullwhip effect is not a desirable phenomenon. We identify the causes of the bullwhip effect and propose several techniques to combat it.

A second challenge to supply chain coordination comes from the *incentive conflicts* among the supply chain's independent firms: An action that maximizes one firm's profit might not maximize another firm's profit. For example, one firm's incentive to stock more inventory, or to install more capacity, or to provide faster customer service, might not be the same as another firm's incentive, thereby creating some conflict between them. We use a stylized example of a supply chain selling sunglasses to illustrate the presence and consequences of incentive conflicts. Furthermore, we offer several remedies to this problem.

17.1 The Bullwhip Effect: Causes and Consequences

Barilla is a leading Italian manufacturer of pasta. Figure 17.1 plots outbound shipments of pasta from one of its Cortese distribution center over a one-year period along with the orders Cortese placed on Barilla's upstream factories. Think of the outbound shipments as what was demanded of Cortese by its downstream customers and the orders as what Cortese demanded from its upstream suppliers. Clearly, Cortese's demand on its upstream suppliers is more volatile than the demand Cortese faces from its customers.

This pattern, in which a stage in the supply chain amplifies the volatility of its orders relative to its demand, is called the *bullwhip effect*. If there are several stages (or levels) in the supply chain (e.g., retailer, wholesaler, distributor, factory), then this amplification can feed

FIGURE 17.1
Barilla's Cortese Distribution Center Orders and Shipments

Source: Harvard Business School, Barilla Spa case.

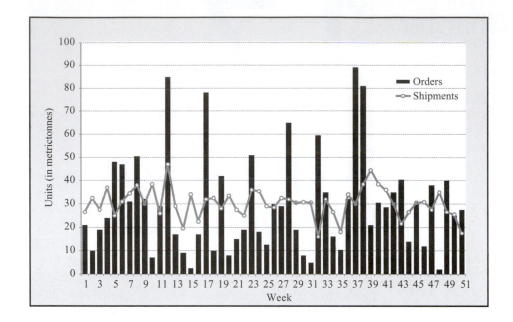

on itself—one level further amplifies the amplified volatility of its downstream customer. This accentuation of volatility resembles the increased amplitude one observes as a whip is cracked—hence the name, the bullwhip effect. In fact, Procter & Gamble coined the term to describe what they observed in their diaper supply chain: They knew that final demand for diapers was reasonably stable (consumption by babies), but the demands requested on their diaper factories were extremely variable. Somehow variability was propagating up their supply chain.

The bullwhip effect does not enhance the performance of a supply chain: Increased volatility at any point in the supply chain can lead to product shortages, excess inventory, low utilization of capacity, and/or poor quality. It impacts upstream stages in the supply chain, which must directly face the impact of variable demand, but it also indirectly affects downstream stages in the supply chain, which must cope with less reliable replenishments from upstream stages. Hence, it is extremely important that its causes be identified so that cures, or at least mitigating strategies, can be developed.

Figure 17.1 provides a real-world example of the bullwhip effect, but to understand the causes of the bullwhip effect, it is helpful to bring it into the laboratory, that is, to study it in a controlled environment. Our controlled environment is a simple supply chain with two levels. The top level has a single supplier and the next level has 20 retailers, each with one store. Let's focus on a single product, a product in which daily demand has a Poisson distribution with mean 1.0 unit at each retailer. Hence, total consumer demand follows a Poisson distribution with mean 20.0 units. (Recall that the sum of Poisson distributions is also a Poisson distribution.) Figure 17.2 displays this supply chain.

Before we can identify the causes of the bullwhip effect, we must agree on how we will measure and identify it. We use the following definition:

The bullwhip effect is present in a supply chain if the variability of demand at one level of the supply chain is greater than the variability of demand at the next downstream level in the supply chain, where variability is measured with the coefficient of variation.

For example, if the coefficient of variation in the supplier's demand (which is the sum of the retailers' orders) is greater than the coefficient of variation of the retailers' total demand, then the bullwhip effect is present in our supply chain.

FIGURE 17.2
A Supply Chain with One Supplier and 20 Retailers
Daily demand at each retailer follows a Poisson distribution with mean 1.0 unit.

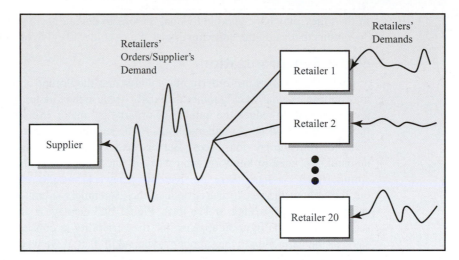

We already know how to evaluate the coefficient of variation in the retailers' total demand: Total demand is Poisson with mean 20, so the standard deviation of demand is $\sqrt{20} = 4.47$ and the coefficient of variation is $4.47/20 = 0.22$. The coefficient of variation of the supplier's demand (i.e., the coefficient of variation of the retailers' orders) depends on how the retailers place orders with the supplier.

Interestingly, while the way in which the retailers submit orders to the supplier can influence the standard deviation of the retailers' orders, it cannot influence the mean of the retailers' orders. To explain, due to the law of the conservation of matter, what goes into a retailer must equal what goes out of the retailer on average; otherwise, the amount inside the retailer will not be stable: If more goes in than goes out, then the inventory at the retailer continues to grow, whereas if less goes in than goes out, then inventory at the retailer continues to fall. Hence, no matter how the retailers choose to order inventory from the supplier, the mean of the supplier's demand (i.e., the retailers' total order) equals the mean of the retailers' total demand. In this case, the supplier's mean demand is 20 units per day, just as the mean of consumer demand is 20 units per day. We can observe this in Figure 17.1 as well: Cortese's average shipment is about 30 tonnes and their average order is also about 30 tonnes.

To evaluate the coefficient of variation in the supplier's demand, we still need to evaluate the standard deviation of the supplier's demand, which does depend on how the retailers submit orders. Let's first suppose that the retailers use an order-up-to policy to order replenishments from the supplier.

A key characteristic of an order-up-to policy is that the amount ordered in any period equals the amount demanded in the previous period (see Chapter 14). As a result, if all of the retailers use order-up-to policies with daily review, then their daily orders will match their daily demands. In other words, there is no bullwhip effect!

If all retailers use an order-up-to policy (with a constant order-up-to level S), then the standard deviation of the retailers' orders in one period equals the standard deviation of consumer demand in one period; that is, there is no bullwhip effect.

So we started our experiment with the intention of finding a cause of the bullwhip effect and discovered that the bullwhip effect need not occur in practice. It does not occur when every member at the same level of the supply chain implements a *"demand-pull"* inventory policy each period, that is, their orders each period exactly match their demands. Unfortunately, firms do not always adopt such "distortion-free" inventory management.

In fact, they may have good individual reasons to deviate from such behavior. It is those deviations that cause the bullwhip effect. We next identify five of them.

Order Synchronization

Suppose the retailers use order-up-to policies, but they order only once per week. They may choose to order weekly rather than daily because they incur a fixed cost per order and therefore wish to reduce the number of orders they make. (See Section 14.8.) Hence, at the start of each week, a retailer submits to the supplier an order that equals the retailer's demand from the previous week. But because we are interested in the supplier's *daily* demand, we need to know on which day of the week each retailer's week begins. For simplicity let's assume there are five days per week and the retailers are evenly spaced out throughout the week; that is, four of the 20 retailers submit orders on Monday, four submit orders on Tuesday, and so forth. Figure 17.3 displays a simulation outcome of this scenario. From the figure it appears that the variability in consumer demand is about the same as the variability in the supplier's demand. In fact, if we were to simulate many more periods and evaluate the standard deviations of those two data series, we would, in fact, discover that the standard deviation of consumer demand *exactly* equals the standard deviation of the supplier's demand. In other words, we still have not found the bullwhip effect.

But we made a critical assumption in our simulation. We assumed the retailers' order cycles were evenly spaced throughout the week: the same number of retailers order on Monday as on Wednesday as on Friday. But that is unlikely to be the case in practice: firms tend to prefer to submit their orders on a particular day of the week or a particular day of the month. To illustrate the consequence of this preference, let's suppose the retailers tend to favor the beginning and the end of the week: nine retailers order on Monday, five on Tuesday, one on Wednesday, two on Thursday, and three on Friday. Figure 17.4 displays the simulation outcome with that scenario.

We have discovered the bullwhip effect! The supplier's daily demand is clearly much more variable than consumer demand. For this particular sample, the coefficient of variation of the supplier's demand is 0.78 even though the coefficient of variation of consumer demand is only 0.19: the supplier's demand is about four times more variable than consumer demand! And this is not the result of a particularly strange demand pattern; that is,

FIGURE 17.3
Simulated Daily Consumer Demand (solid line) and Daily Supplier Demand (circles)
Supplier demand equals the sum of the retailers' orders.

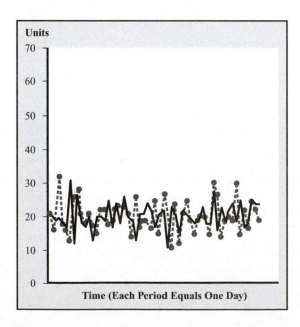

FIGURE 17.4
Simulated Daily Consumer Demand (solid line) and Supplier Demand (circles) When Retailers Order Weekly
Nine retailers order on Monday, five on Tuesday, one on Wednesday, two on Thursday, and three on Friday.

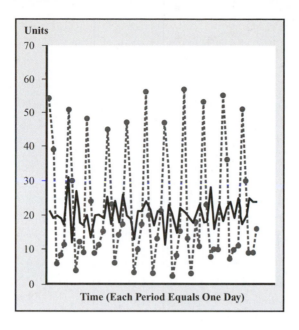

the same qualitative result is obtained if a very long interval of time is simulated. In fact, for comparison, you can note that the consumer demand in Figure 17.4 is identical to consumer demand in Figure 17.3.

Not only do we now observe the bullwhip effect, we have just identified one of its causes, *order synchronization:* If the retailers' order cycles become even a little bit synchronized, that is, they tend to cluster around the same time period, then the bullwhip effect emerges. While the retailers order on average to match average consumer demand, due to their order synchronization there will be periods in which they order considerably more than the average and periods in which they order considerably less than the average, thereby imposing additional demand volatility on the supplier.

Order synchronization also can be observed higher up in the supply chain. For example, suppose the supplier implements a materials requirement planning (MRP) system to manage the replenishment of component inventory. (This is a computer system that determines the quantity and timing of component inventory replenishments based on future demand forecasts and production schedules.) Many firms implement their MRP systems on a monthly basis. Furthermore, many implement their systems to generate replenishment orders in the first week of the month. So a supplier's supplier may receive a flood of orders for its product during the first week of the month and relatively little demand later in the month. This has been called *MRP jitters* or the *hockey stick phenomenon* (the graph of demand over the month looks like a series of hockey sticks, a flat portion and then a spike up).

Order Batching

We argued that the retailers might wish to order weekly rather than daily to avoid incurring excessive ordering costs. This economizing on ordering costs also can be achieved by *order batching:* each retailer orders so that each order is an integer multiple of some batch size. For example, now let's consider a scenario in which each retailer uses a batch size of 15 units. This batch size could represent a case or a pallet or a full truckload. Let's call it a pallet. By ordering only in increments of 15 units, that is, in pallet quantities, the retailer can facilitate the movement of product around the warehouse and the loading of product onto trucks. How does the retailer decide when to order a pallet? A natural rule is to order a batch whenever the accumulated demand since the last order exceeds the batch size.

FIGURE 17.5
Simulated Daily Consumer Demand (solid line) and Supplier Demand (circles) When Retailers Order in Batches of 15 Units
Every 15th demand, a retailer orders one batch from the supplier that contains 15 units.

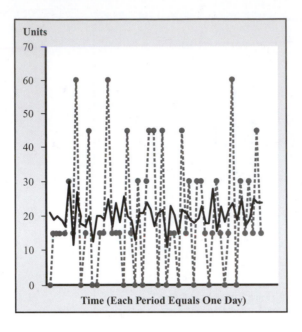

Therefore, in this example, every 15th demand triggers an order for a pallet. Naturally, ordering in batches economizes on the number of orders the retailer must make:

$$\text{Average number of periods between orders} = \frac{\text{Batch size}}{\text{Mean demand per period}}$$

In this situation, the retailer orders on average every 15/1 = 15 periods.

Figure 17.5 displays a simulation outcome with batch ordering. Because the retailers only order in pallet quantities, the supplier's demand equals a multiple of 15: on some days there are no orders, on most days one pallet is ordered by some retailer, on a few days there are up to four pallets ordered.

We again observe the bullwhip effect: The variability of the supplier's demand is considerably greater than the variability of consumer demand. To be specific, the supplier's demand has a coefficient of variation equal to 0.87 in this example, which contrasts with the 0.19 coefficient of variation for consumer demand. Thus, we have identified a second cause of the bullwhip effect, *order batching:* The bullwhip effect emerges when retailers order in batches that contain more than one unit (e.g., pallet quantities or full truckload quantities). Again, the retailers' total order on average equals average consumer demand, but not the variability of their orders. This occurs because, due to the batch quantity requirement, the retailer's order quantity in a period generally does not match the retailer's demand in that period: it tends to be either greater than or less than consumer demand. In other words, the batch quantity requirement forces the retailer to order in a way that is more variable than consumer demand even though, on average, it equals consumer demand.

Trade Promotions and Forward Buying

Suppliers in some industries offer their retailers *trade promotions:* a discount off the wholesale price that is available only for a short period of time. Trade promotions cause retailers to buy on-deal, also referred to as a *forward buy,* which means they purchase much more than they need to meet short-term needs. Trade promotions are a key tool for a supplier when the supplier wants to engage in the practice of *channel stuffing:* providing incentives to induce retailers (the channel) to hold more inventory than needed for the

FIGURE 17.6

On-Hand Inventory of Chicken Noodle Soup at a Retailer under Two Procurement Strategies

The first strategy, called demand-pull (lower sawtooth), has the retailer ordering 100 cases each week. The second strategy, called forward buying (upper sawtooth), has the retailer ordering 2,600 cases twice per year.

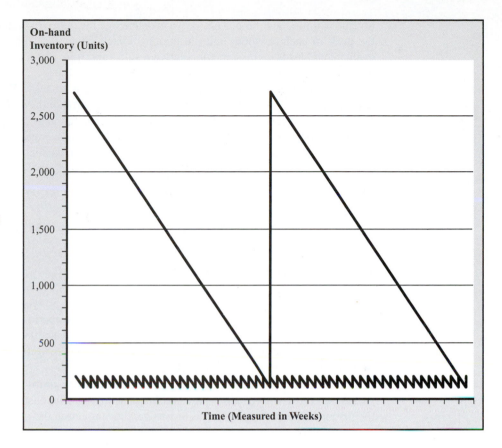

short term. Because with trade promotions many retailers purchase at the same time (order synchronization) and because they order in large quantities (order batching), trade promotions are capable of creating an enormous bullwhip. Let's illustrate this with another simple scenario.

Suppose a supplier sells chicken noodle soup; let's consider one of the supplier's retailers. The supplier's regular price of chicken noodle soup is $20 per case, but twice a year the supplier offers an 8 percent discount for cases purchased during a one-week period, for example, the first week in January and the first week in July. The retailer sells on average 100 cases of soup per week and likes to carry a one-week safety stock, that is, the retailer does not let its inventory fall below 100 cases. To avoid unnecessary complications, let's further assume that the retailer's order at the beginning of a week is delivered immediately and demand essentially occurs at a constant rate. The retailer's annual holding cost rate is 24 percent of the dollar value of its inventory.

We now compare the retailer's profit with two different ordering strategies. With the first strategy, the retailer orders every week throughout the year; with the second strategy, the retailer orders only twice per year—during the trade promotion. We call the first strategy *demand-pull* because the retailer matches orders to current demand. The second strategy is called *forward buying* because each order covers a substantial portion of future demand. Figure 17.6 displays the retailer's on-hand inventory over the period of one year with both ordering strategies.

With demand-pull, the retailer's inventory "saw-tooths" between 200 and 100 units, with an average of 150 units. With forward buying, the retailer's inventory also "saw-tooths" but now between 2,700 and 100, with an average of 1,400 units. Note, although throughout the text we measure inventory at the end of each period, here, we are measuring average inventory throughout time. That is, we take average inventory to be the midpoint between the peak of each sawtooth and the trough of each sawtooth. This approach is easier to evaluate and leads to the same qualitative results (and from a practical perspective, nearly the same quantitative result as well).

Let's now evaluate the retailer's total cost with each strategy. With demand-pull, the retailer's average inventory is 150 units. During the two promotion weeks, the average inventory in dollars is $150 \times \$18.4 = \$2,760$ because the promotion price is $\$20 \times (1 - 0.08) = \$18.40$. During the remaining 50 weeks of the year, the average inventory in dollars is $150 \times \$20 = \$3,000$. The weighted average inventory in dollars is

$$\frac{(\$2,760 \times 2) + (\$3,000 \times 50)}{52} = \$2,991$$

The annual holding cost on that inventory is $\$2,991 \times 24\% = \$718$.

The purchased cost during the year is

$$(\$20 \times 100 \times 50) + (\$18.40 \times 100 \times 2) = \$103,680$$

because 100 units are purchased at the regular price over 50 weeks of the year and 100 units are purchased at the discount price during the two promotion weeks of the year. The demand-pull strategy's total cost is $\$718 + \$103,680 = \$104,398$.

The analysis of the forward buying strategy is analogous to the demand-pull strategy. A summary is provided in Table 17.1.

From Table 17.1 we see that forward buying is more profitable to the retailer than weekly ordering with demand-pull: the forward buying total cost is 2.4 percent less than the demand-pull strategy, which is a considerable amount in the grocery industry. We can conclude that a relatively small trade promotion can rationally cause a retailer to purchase a significant volume of product. In fact, the retailer may wish to purchase enough product to cover its demand until the supplier's next promotion. In contrast, it is highly unlikely that an 8 percent discount would induce consumers to purchase a six-month supply of chicken noodle soup; rational retailers are more price sensitive than consumers.

The impact of the trade promotion on the supplier is not good. Imagine the supplier sells to many retailers, all taking advantage of the supplier's trade promotion. Hence, the retailers' orders become synchronized (they order during the same trade promotion weeks of the year) and they order in very large batch quantities (much more than is needed to cover their immediate needs). In other words, trade promotions combine order synchronization and order batching to generate a significant bullwhip effect.

Interestingly, with the forward buying strategy, the retailer does not ever purchase at the regular price. Hence, if the supplier were to offer the retailer the $18.40 price

TABLE 17.1

Analysis of Total Holding and Procurement Costs for Two Ordering Strategies

In demand-pull, the retailer orders every week; in forward buying, the retailer orders twice per year during the supplier's trade promotions.

	Demand-Pull	Forward Buying
Annual purchase (units)	5,200	5,200
Average inventory (units)	150	1,400
Average inventory	$2,991	$25,760
Holding cost (24% of average inventory cost)	$718	$6,182
Units purchased at regular price	5,000	0
Units purchased at discount price	200	5,200
Total purchase cost	$103,680	$95,680
Total holding plus procurement cost	$104,398	$101,862

FIGURE 17.7
One Retailer's Purchases of Campbell's Chicken Noodle Soup over One Year

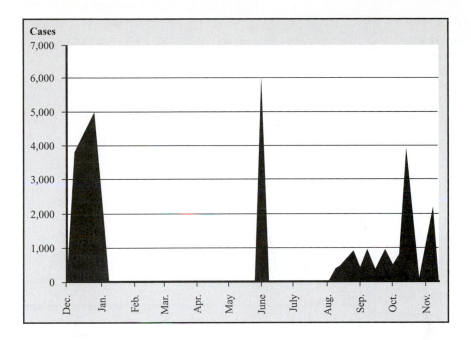

throughout the year (instead of just during the two trade promotion weeks), then the supplier's revenue would be the same. However, the retailer could then order on a weekly basis, thereby reducing the retailer's holding cost. It is not too difficult to calculate that the retailer's total cost in this constant-price scenario is $96,342, which is 5.4 percent less than the forward buying cost and 7.7 percent less than the original demand-pull strategy. Thus, due to forward buying, the supply chain's costs are about 5 percent higher than they need be without providing any benefit to the firms in the supply chain (the retailer surely does not benefit from holding extra inventory and the supplier does not benefit from higher revenue).

While our analysis has been with a theoretical supply chain of chicken noodle soup, Campbell Soup would concur that this analysis is consistent with their experience. For example, Figure 17.7 presents data on one retailer's purchases of Campbell's Chicken Noodle Soup over the course of the year. This product is traditionally promoted in January and June even though consumers primarily eat soup during the winter months.[1] As a result, this retailer requires substantial storage space to hold its forward buys. Other retailers may lack the financial and physical capabilities to be so aggressive with forward buying, but they nevertheless will take advantage of trade promotions to some extent. This is confirmed by Figure 17.8, which shows total consumption and shipments of Campbell's Chicken Noodle Soup over a one-year period: Shipments are clearly more volatile than consumption, thereby indicating the presence of the bullwhip effect.

Due to the trade promotion spike in demand in January of every year, Campbell Soup must put its chicken deboning plants on overtime from September through October, its canning plant works overtime November through December, and its shipping facility works overtime throughout January. All of these activities add to production costs, and all because of a spike in demand caused by the company's own pricing.

The negative effects of forward buying also are not limited to the supplier's operational efficiency. Some retailers purchase on-deal with no intention of selling those units

---

[1] Campbell's traditionally raises the price of its Chicken Noodle Soup during the summer, so the June buy avoids the imminent price increase. While this is technically not a promotion, the analysis is quite similar and the effect is essentially the same as a trade promotion.

FIGURE 17.8
Total Shipments
to Retailers and
Consumption by
Consumers of
Campbell's Chicken
Noodle Soup over
a One-Year Period
(roughly July to July)

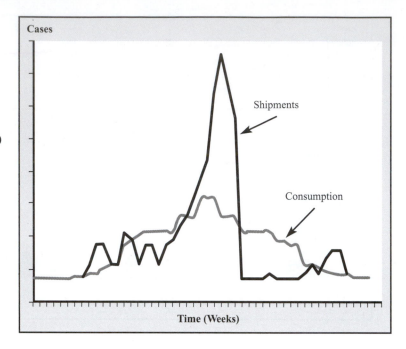

to consumers. Instead, they intend on selling to other retailers that cannot take advantage of the deal due to either physical or capital constraints. Those retailers that sell to other retailers are called *diverters* and that practice is called *diversion*. In addition to extra handling (which reduces quality and leads to spoilage), diversion needlessly adds to transportation costs. It also should be mentioned that diversion occurs when a supplier attempts to lower its price in one region of the country while maintaining a higher price in another region, possibly because the supplier faces a regional competitor in the former region. That form of diversion was greatly reduced in the grocery industry when several national grocery chains emerged (Kroger, Safeway, etc.) in the late 1980s and early 1990s. Those national chains insisted that they would receive a single low price from their suppliers, thereby preventing regional price discrimination.

Reactive and Overreactive Ordering

So far in our experimental supply chains, we have assumed the retailer knows what expected demand is in each period even though demand could be stochastic. This is a reasonable assumption for well-established products such as chicken noodle soup. But for many other products, a retailer might not know expected demand with certainty. And this uncertainty creates a complication for the retailer's inventory management.

Suppose the retailer observes higher-than-usual demand in one period. How should the retailer react to this observation? One explanation for this outlier is that it occurred merely due to random fluctuation. In that case, the retailer probably should not change her expectation of future demand and so not change how she manages inventory. But there is another explanation for the outlier: It could signal that demand has shifted, suggesting the product's actual expected demand is higher than previously thought. If that explanation is believed, then the retailer should increase her order quantity to cover the additional future demand; otherwise she will quickly stock out. In other words, it is rational for a retailer to increase her order quantity when faced with an unusually high demand observation. Analogously, the retailer should decrease her order quantity when faced with an unusually low demand observation because future demand may be weaker than previously thought.

Hence, when a retailer cannot be sure that demand is stable over time, a retailer should rationally react aggressively to possible shifts in demand.

These reactions by the retailer contribute to the bullwhip effect. Suppose the retailer's high-demand observation is really due to random fluctuation. As a result, future demand will not be higher than expected even though the retailer reacted to this information by ordering more inventory. Hence, the retailer will need to reduce future orders so that the excess inventory just purchased can be drawn down. Ordering more than needed now and less than needed later implies the retailer's orders are more volatile than the retailer's demand, which is the bullwhip effect.

While it can be rational to react to extreme demand observations, it is also human nature to *over*react to such information, that is, to act too aggressively. For example, a high-demand signal may rationally warrant a 125 percent increase in a retailer's order quantity, but a retailer may "play it safe" and order 150 percent more just in case. Unfortunately, the retailer might not realize the consequence of this action. Suppose the retailer is replenished by a wholesaler, who is replenished by a distributor, who is replenished by a supplier. The retailer sees a blip in demand and so reacts with a larger order. The retailer's order is the wholesaler's demand, and so the wholesaler sees an even larger blip in demand. The wholesaler reacts and increases his order, which surprises the distributor. So the distributor reacts with an increased order, so large that the supplier only concludes that demand has accelerated substantially. In other words, overreactions can propagate up the supply chain, thereby generating a bullwhip effect.

Shortage Gaming

Under normal circumstances, a retailer will only order as much inventory as needed to cover short-term needs, in particular, the inventory needed to cover demand until the next possible replenishment. But it is not always known when the next possible replenishment will occur. If demand is increasing and capacity is constrained, then a retailer may anticipate a long wait for the next possible replenishment. A rational response is to order plenty of inventory, while inventory is potentially available, in case future replenishment opportunities do not materialize.

Imagine a supply chain with one supplier, a hot-selling product, limited capacity, and multiple retailers. Each retailer knows capacity is tight: While it is possible the supplier will have enough capacity to fill all of the retailers' orders, it is quite likely the supplier will not have enough capacity. The retailers also know that if the supplier runs out of capacity, then the supplier will allocate that scarce capacity to the retailers. The supplier may very well use a proportional allocation scheme: a retailer's share of the capacity is proportional to the retailer's order quantity relative to the total order quantity. For example, if a retailer orders 10 units and the other retailers order a total of 40 units, then the retailer will get a one-fifth share of the capacity (10 / (10 + 40)). When this situation occurs with a product, it is often said that the product is *on allocation;* that is, the supplier must allocate capacity because the total amount demanded by retailers exceeds available capacity.

Knowing that a product may be put on allocation, what should a retailer's ordering strategy be? Returning to our example, the retailer wants 10 units but anticipates only one-fifth of that order will be delivered. Hence, if 10 units are ordered, only 2 units will be received, far less than the retailer wants. An obvious solution is to instead order 50 units: if the retailer receives one-fifth of the order, and 50 units are ordered, then the retailer will receive the desired quantity, 10 units. But the other retailers are probably thinking the same thing. So they too may order much more than needed in anticipation of receiving only a fraction of their order. This behavior of ordering more than needed due to the anticipation of a possible capacity shortage is called *shortage gaming* or *order inflation.*

Shortage gaming can result in quite a mess for the supply chain. Some retailers may receive far less than they could sell (because they did not inflate their order enough) while others might actually receive much more than they can sell (because they inflated their order too much). For instance, the retailer in our example can order 50 units and actually receive 12 units, still only a fraction of the retailer's order, but 2 units more than wanted. Furthermore, order inflation contributes to the bullwhip effect: Once a supplier's customers believe that capacity may be constrained, the supplier's customers may inflate their orders substantially, thereby creating excessive volatility in the supplier's demand. Interestingly, this may occur even if there is enough capacity to satisfy the retailers' desired quantity; all that is needed to create order inflation is the belief among the retailers that they may not get their full order.

A supplier also can exacerbate the bullwhip effect with her own actions via shortage gaming. For example, suppose a supplier allows retailers to return unsold inventory. This was a common practice in the PC industry: Suppliers such as IBM would allow distributors to return any PC at any time for a full refund and IBM would even pay for shipping costs. With little risk associated with having too much inventory, distributors focused on the risk of having too little inventory, especially if they had less inventory than they wanted due to a capacity shortage (which was common). Hence, distributors actively participated in shortage gaming.

In the PC industry, it was also common to allow distributors to submit orders that could be canceled without penalty before the order was delivered. In effect, the distributor would be allowed to return an order even before receiving the order. Again, this practice mitigated the distributors' risk of excess ordering, so the focus turned to the risk of not receiving enough product. Distributors would submit excessively large orders knowing full well that they would later cancel a portion of their order. The amount that they would later cancel would depend on how well the product was selling and the available capacity. Not surprisingly, these *phantom orders,* as they are called in the industry (orders that are submitted even though a larger portion of them will disappear, like a phantom), create a bullwhip effect and substantial headaches for the supplier: the supplier receives plenty of orders but does not know what fraction of them will materialize into actual accepted deliveries.

17.2 Bullwhip Effect: Mitigating Strategies

This section discusses how firms have changed their business practices to combat the bullwhip effect. In the grocery industry, many of these changes came with the *Efficient Consumer Response* initiative that was initiated in the early 1990s. The claim was that this set of business practices, if fully implemented, could reduce U.S. grocery industry costs by $30 billion.

Not surprisingly, effective change begins with an understanding of root causes. In the case of the bullwhip effect, we identified five causes in the previous section: order synchronization, order batching, trade promotions, overreactive ordering, and shortage gaming.

Sharing Information

Greater information sharing about actual demand between the stages of the supply chain is an intuitive step toward reducing the bullwhip effect. As we saw in the simulations reported in the previous section, the pattern of retail orders may have very little resemblance to the pattern of retail demand. As a result, when retail orders are fluctuating wildly, it can be extremely difficult for a supplier to correctly forecast demand trends and it is not surprising at all if the supplier overreacts to those data. By giving the supplier frequent access to actual consumer demand data, the supplier can better assess trends in demand and plan accordingly.

But sharing current demand data is often not enough to mitigate the bullwhip effect. Demand also can be influenced by retailer actions on pricing, merchandizing, promotion, advertising, and assortment planning. As a result, a supplier cannot accurately forecast sales for a product unless the supplier knows what kind of treatment that product will receive from its retailers. Without that information, the supplier may not build sufficient capacity for a product that the retailers want to support, or the supplier may build too much capacity of a product that generates little interest among the retailers. Both errors may be prevented if the supplier and retailers share with each other their intentions. This sharing process is often labeled *collaborative planning, forecasting, and replenishment,* or CPFR for short.

While it is quite useful for a retailer to share information with its upstream suppliers, it also can be useful for a supplier to share information on availability with its downstream retailers. For example, a supplier may be aware of a component shortage that will lead to a shortage in a product that a retailer intends to promote. By sharing that information, the retailer could better allocate its promotional effort. It also can be useful to share information when the supplier knows that a capacity shortage will not occur, thereby preventing some shortage gaming.

Smoothing the Flow of Product

It is important to recognize that information sharing is quite helpful for reducing the bullwhip effect, but it is unlikely to eliminate it. The bullwhip effect is also a result of physical limitations in the supply chain like order synchronization and order batching.

Order synchronization can be reduced by eliminating reasons why retailers may wish to order at the same time (such as trade promotions). Coordinating with retailers to schedule them on different order cycles also helps.

Reducing order batching means smaller and more frequent replenishments. Unfortunately, this objective conflicts with the desire to control ordering, transportation, and handling costs. The fixed cost associated with each order submitted to the supplier can be reduced with the use of computerized automatic replenishment systems for deciding when and how much to order. In addition, some kind of technology standard, like *electronic data interchange* (EDI), is needed so that orders can be transmitted in an electronic format that can be received by the supplier.

Transportation costs can conflict with small batches because the cost of a truck shipment depends little on the amount that is shipped. Hence, there are strong incentives to ship in full truckloads. There are also economies of scale in handling inventory, which is why it is cheaper to ship in cases than in individual units and cheaper to move pallets rather than individual cases. So the trick is to find a way to have more frequent replenishments while still controlling handling and transportation costs.

One solution is for multiple retailers to consolidate their orders with a supplier through a distributor. By ordering from a distributor rather than directly from a supplier, a retailer can receive the supplier's products on a more frequent basis and still order in full truckloads. The difference is that with direct ordering, the retailer is required to fill a truck with the supplier's products whereas by going through a distributor, the retailer can fill a truck with product from multiple suppliers that sell through that distributor.

Eliminating Pathological Incentives

As we saw in the previous section, trade promotions provide an extremely strong incentive for a retailer to forward buy and forward buying creates a substantial bullwhip effect. A constant wholesale price completely eliminates this incentive. Furthermore, a constant wholesale price might not even cost the supplier too much in revenue, especially if the majority of the retailers never purchased at the regular price.

However, there are perceived negatives associated with eliminating trade promotions. Suppliers began using trade promotions to induce retailers to offer consumer promotions with the objective of using these consumer promotions to increase final consumer demand. And, in fact, trade promotion did succeed somewhat along these lines: Most retailers would cut the retail price during a trade promotion, thereby passing on at least a portion of the deal to consumers. Hence, if trade promotions can no longer be used to induce retailers to conduct consumer promotions, and if consumer promotions are deemed to be necessary, then suppliers must develop some other tool to generate the desired consumer promotions.

Generous returns and order cancellation policies are the other self-inflicted pathological incentives because they lead to shortage gaming and phantom ordering. One solution is to either eliminate these policies or at least make them less generous. For example, the supplier could agree to only partially refund returned units or the supplier could limit the number of units that can be returned or the supplier could limit the time in which they can be returned. The supplier also could impose an order cancellation penalty or require a non-refundable deposit when orders are submitted.

Shortage gaming also can be eliminated by forgoing retailer orders altogether. To explain how this could work, suppose a supplier knows that a product will be on allocation, which means that each retailer will want more than it can receive. So the supplier does not even bother collecting retailer orders. Instead, the supplier could announce an allocation to each retailer proportional to the retailer's past sales. In the auto industry, this scheme is often called *turn-and-earn:* if a dealer turns a vehicle (i.e., sells a vehicle), then the dealer earns the right to another vehicle. Turn-and-earn allocation achieves several objectives: it ensures the supplier's entire capacity is allocated; it allocates more capacity to the higher-selling retailers, which makes intuitive sense; and it motivates retailers to sell more of the supplier's product. For example, in the auto industry, a supplier can use the allocation of a hot-selling vehicle to encourage a dealer to increase its sales effort for all vehicles so that the dealer can defend its allocation. While this extra motivation imposed on dealers is probably beneficial to the auto manufacturers, it is debatable whether it benefits dealers.

Using Vendor-Managed Inventory

Procter & Gamble and Walmart were among the first companies to identify the bullwhip effect and to take multiple significant steps to mitigate it. (Campbell's Soup was another early innovator in North America.) The set of changes they initiated are often collected under the label *Vendor-Managed Inventory,* or VMI for short. While many firms have now implemented their own version of VMI, VMI generally includes the following features:

- The retailer no longer decides when and how much inventory to order. Instead, the supplier decides the timing and quantity of shipments to the retailer. The firms mutually agree on an objective that the supplier will use to guide replenishment decisions (e.g., a target in-stock probability). The supplier's "reach" into the retailer can vary: In some applications, the supplier merely manages product in the retailer's distribution center and the retailer retains responsibility of replenishments from the distribution center to the stores. In other applications, the supplier manages inventory all the way down to the retailer's shelves. The scope of the supplier's reach also can vary by application: Generally, the supplier only controls decisions for its own products, but in some cases the supplier assumes responsibility for an entire category, which generally includes making replenishment decisions for the supplier's competitor's products on behalf of the retailer.

- If the supplier is going to be responsible for replenishment decisions, the supplier also needs information. Hence, with VMI the retailer shares with the supplier demand data (e.g., distribution center withdrawals and/or retail store point-of-sale data, POS data for short). The supplier uses those data as input to an automatic replenishment system; that is, a computer program that decides the timing and quantity of replenishments for each product and at each location managed. In addition to normal demand movements, the supplier must be made aware of potential demand shifts that can be anticipated. For example, if the retailer is about to conduct a consumer promotion that will raise the base level of demand by a factor of 20, then the supplier needs to be aware of when that promotion will occur. These computer-guided replenishment systems are often referred to as *continuous replenishment* or *continuous product replenishment*. However, these are somewhat misnomers since product tends to be replenished more frequently but not continuously.

- The supplier and the retailer eliminate trade promotions. This is surely necessary if the retailer is going to give the supplier control over replenishment decisions because a retailer will not wish to forgo potential forward-buying profits. Hence, the adoption of VMI usually includes some agreement that the supplier will maintain a stable price and that price will be lower than the regular price to compensate the retailer for not purchasing on a deal.

The innovations included in VMI are complementary and are effective at reducing the bullwhip effect. For example, transferring replenishment control from the retailer to the supplier allows the supplier to control the timing of deliveries, thereby reducing, if not eliminating, any order synchronization effects. VMI also allows a supplier to ship in smaller lots than the retailer would order, thereby combating the order-batching cause of the bullwhip. For example, prior to the adoption of VMI, many of Campbell Soup's customers would order three to five pallets of each soup type at a time, where a pallet typically contains about 200 cases. They would order in multiple pallets to avoid the cost of frequent ordering. With VMI Campbell Soup decided to ship fast-moving soups in pallet quantities and slower-moving varieties in mixed pallet quantities (e.g., in one-half- or one-quarter-pallet quantities). Frequent ordering was not an issue for Campbell Soup because they implemented an automatic replenishment system. But Campbell Soup was still concerned about handling and transportation costs. As a result, with VMI Campbell Soup continued to ship in full truckloads, which are about 20 pallets each. However, with VMI each of the 20 pallets could be a different product, whereas before VMI there would be fewer than 20 products loaded onto each truck (because more than one pallet would be ordered for each product). Hence, with VMI it was possible to maintain full truckloads while ordering each product more frequently because each product was ordered in smaller quantities.

In some cases VMI also assists with order batching because it allows the supplier to combine shipments to multiple retailers. Before VMI it would be essentially impossible for two retailers to combine their order to construct a full truckload. But if the supplier has a VMI relationship with both retailers, then the supplier can combine their orders onto a truck as long as the retailers are located close to each other. By replenishing each retailer in smaller than full truckload batches, the supplier reduces the bullwhip effect while still maintaining transportation efficiency.

VMI also can combat the overreaction cause of the bullwhip effect. Because demand information is shared, the supplier is less likely to overreact to changes in the demand. In addition, because VMI is implemented with computer algorithms that codify replenishment strategies, a VMI system is not as emotionally fickle as a human buyer.

While VMI changes many aspects of the supply chain relationship between a supplier and retailer, some aspects of that relationship are generally not disturbed. For example, VMI eliminates trade promotions, but it does not necessarily seek to eliminate consumer promotions. Consumer promotions also can contribute to the bullwhip effect, but there are several reasons why they do not tend to increase volatility as much as trade promotions: Not every retailer runs a consumer promotion at the same time, so order synchronization is not as bad as with a trade promotion, and consumers do not forward buy as much as retailers. In addition, while some companies are willing to forgo trade promotions, only a few are willing to forgo consumer promotions as well: Consumer promotions are viewed as a competitive necessity.

The Countereffect to the Bullwhip Effect: Production Smoothing

Due to the numerous causes of the bullwhip effect, one might expect that the bullwhip effect is a potential problem in nearly any supply chain. But this leads to the following questions: Does the bullwhip effect indeed exist in every supply chain? Is there any natural force that counteracts the bullwhip effect? The short answers are no, the bullwhip effect need not exist everywhere, because there is indeed a force that works to reduce it.

Figure 17.9 shows the monthly inflow and outflow of goods for general merchandisers (such as Walmart, Target, and Kohl's) in the United States over a 10-year period. Outflow of goods is analogous to demand—it is the dollar volume of goods that leaves general merchandisers, presumably into the hands of final customers. The inflow of goods is the dollar volume of goods purchased by general merchandisers. The figure reveals that the inflow of goods is actually less variable than the outflow of goods. Put another way, the demand seen by the suppliers of the general merchandisers (the inflow series) is less variable than the demand seen by the general merchandisers themselves (the outflow series)—we do not observe the bullwhip effect (at least at the aggregate level of an entire industry and at the monthly time interval). Why?

Looking at these retailers' demand, we see a noticeable fourth-quarter spike each year, which is particularly strong in November and especially in December. Intuitively, this is the annual holiday season sales surge. This annual spike presents retailers with a significant operational challenge—not only do customers need to be helped, shelves need to be replenished. Replenishing on a just-in-time basis requires a substantial amount of labor, but hiring that many seasonal workers for such a short time would be very expensive (just November and December). Instead, retailers start the process of moving product into their warehouses and stores at the start of the quarter, September and October. Each year, as Figure 17.9 reveals, retailers have a net inflow of goods during those months—inflows are greater than outflows (i.e., they build up their inventory). This prepositioning of inventory allows them to smooth out the inflow of product, thereby reducing the amount of work that needs to be done at the very busiest time of the year. In effect, retailers engage in production smoothing–build inventory during slow times and draw down inventory during hectic times so that the burden on your workforce is not too great. Apparently, it is cheaper to preposition inventory than it is to have large fluctuations in the number of employees.

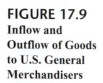

FIGURE 17.9
Inflow and Outflow of Goods to U.S. General Merchandisers

Source: U.S. Census Bureau, Monthly retail trade data.

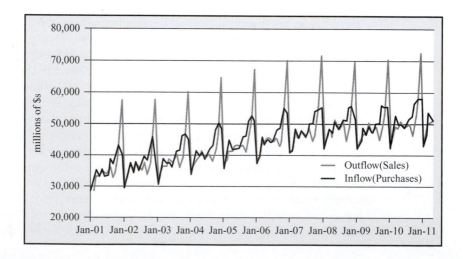

Due to this production-smoothing strategy, the suppliers to these retailers actually experience less volatility in their demand than the retailers do.

In general, when a retailer (or any other firm) faces highly seasonal demand (i.e., predictably variable demand), that retailer will have an incentive to engage in production smoothing. This, as we have seen, will act as a force to counteract the bullwhip effect. Whether this force is strong enough to eliminate the bullwhip effect or not depends on how seasonal demand is and how strong the bullwhip forces are. For general merchandisers, the holiday sales spike is sufficiently large and predictable that it overwhelms the bullwhip forces, at least when measured at the industry level and with monthly data. For individual retailers, individual products, and shorter time intervals (weekly or daily), the bullwhip effect may reemerge.

Although seasonality tends to dampen (or eliminate) the bullwhip effect, seasonality is still (almost by definition) a source of variability in the supply chain. But while it creates variability, it does not contribute to amplification—even the suppliers to general merchandisers experience considerable variability and seasonality in their demand, but it is less than the variability faced by their downstream customers.

17.3   Incentive Conflicts in a Sunglasses Supply Chain

The bullwhip effect deteriorates supply chain performance by propagating demand variability up the supply chain. But optimal supply chain performance is also not guaranteed in the absence of the bullwhip effect. This section considers the incentive conflicts that can occur between two firms in a supply chain even without the presence of the bullwhip effect. We illustrate these conflicts with a detailed example based on a supply chain for sunglasses.

Zamatia Ltd. (pronounced zah-MAH-tee-ah, to the cognoscenti) is an Italian upscale maker of eyewear. UV Inc., short for Umbra Visage, is one of their retailers in the United States. To match UV's stylish assortment, UV only operates small boutique stores located in trendy locations. We focus on one of their stores located in Miami Beach, Florida. Zamatia manufactures its sunglasses in Europe and Asia, so the replenishment lead time to the United States is long. Furthermore, the selling season for sunglasses is short and styles change significantly from year to year. As a result, UV receives only one delivery of Zamatia glasses before each season. As with any fashion product, some styles sell out quickly while others are left over at the end of the season.

Consider Zamatia's entry-level sunglasses for the coming season, the Bassano. UV purchases each one of those pairs of sunglasses from Zamatia for $75 and retails them for $115. Zamatia's production and shipping costs per pair are $35. At the end of the season, UV generally needs to offer deep discounts to sell remaining inventory; UV estimates that it will only be able to fetch $25 per leftover Bassano at the Miami Beach store. UV's Miami Beach store believes this season's demand for the Bassano can be represented by a normal distribution with a mean of 250 and a standard deviation of 125.

UV's procurement quantity decision can be made with the use of the newsvendor model (Chapter 12). Let Q be UV's order quantity. UV's underage cost per unit is $C_u = \$115 - \$75 = \$40$, that is, each lost sale due to underordering costs UV the opportunity cost of $40. UV's overage cost per unit is $C_o = \$75 - \$25 = \$50$; the consequence of leftover inventory is substantial. UV's critical ratio is

$$\frac{C_u}{C_o + C_u} = \frac{40}{50 + 40} = \frac{4}{9} = 0.4444$$

Hence, to maximize expected profit, UV should choose an order quantity such that 44.4 percent is the probability there is some leftover inventory and 55.6 percent is the probability there is a stockout.

From the Standard Normal Distribution Function Table, we find $\Phi(-0.14) = 0.4443$ and $\Phi(-0.13) = 0.4483$, so the optimal z-statistic is -0.13 and the optimal order quantity is

$$Q = \mu + z \times \sigma = 250 - 0.13 \times 125 = 234$$

Using the equations and procedures described in Chapter 12, we also are able to evaluate several performance measures for UV's store:

$$\text{Expected sales (units)} = 192$$
$$\text{Expected leftover inventory} = 42$$
$$\text{Expected profit} = \$5,580$$

Zamatia's profit from selling the Bassano at UV's Miami Beach store is $234 \times \$40 = \$9,360$, where 234 is the number of Bassano sunglasses that UV purchases and \$40 is Zamatia's gross margin (\$75 − \$35 = \$40).

While Zamatia might be quite pleased with this situation (it does earn \$9,360 relative to UV's \$5,580), it should not be. The total supply chain's profit is \$14,940, but it could be higher. To explain, suppose we choose an order quantity to maximize the supply chain's profit, that is, the combined expected profits of Zamatia and UV. In other words, what order quantity would a firm choose if the firm owned both Zamatia and UV? We call this the *supply chain optimal quantity* because it is the quantity that maximizes the *integrated supply chain.*

We can still use the newsvendor model to evaluate the supply chain's order quantity decision and performance measures. Each lost sale costs the supply chain the difference between the retail price and the production cost, \$115 − \$35 = \$80; that is, the supply chain's underage cost is $C_u = 80$. Each leftover Bassano costs the supply chain the difference between the production cost and the salvage value, \$35 − \$25 = \$10; that is, the supply chain's overage cost is $C_o = 10$. The supply chain's critical ratio is

$$\frac{C_u}{C_o + C_u} = \frac{80}{10 + 80} = 0.8889$$

The appropriate z-statistic for that critical ratio is 1.23 because $\Phi(1.22) = 0.8888$ and $\Phi(1.23) = 0.8907$. The supply chain's expected profit-maximizing order quantity is then

$$Q = \mu + z \times \sigma = 250 + 1.23 \times 125 = 404$$

which is considerably higher than UV's order of 234 units. The supply chain's performance measures can then be evaluated assuming the supply chain optimal order quantity, 404 units:

$$\text{Expected sales (units)} = 243$$
$$\text{Expected leftover inventory} = 161$$
$$\text{Expected profit} = \$17,830$$

Thus, while Zamatia and UV currently earn an expected profit of \$14,940, their supply chain could enjoy an expected profit that is about 19 percent higher, \$17,830.

Why does the current supply chain perform significantly worse than it could? The obvious answer is that UV does not order enough Bassanos: UV orders 234 of them, but the supply chain's optimal order quantity is 404 units. But why doesn't UV order enough? Because UV is acting in its own self-interest to maximize its own profit. To explain further, UV must pay Zamatia \$75 per pair of sunglasses and so UV acts as if the cost to

TABLE 17.2
UV's Order Quantity Q and Performance Measures for Several Possible Wholesale Price Contracts

	Wholesale Price			
	$35	$65	$75	$85
C_u	$80	$50	$40	$30
C_o	$10	$40	$50	$60
Critical ratio	0.8889	0.5556	0.4444	0.3333
z	1.23	0.14	−0.13	−0.43
Q	404	268	234	196
Expected sales	243	209	192	169
Expected leftover inventory	161	59	42	27
Umbra's expected profit	$17,830	$8,090	$5,580	$3,450
Zamatia's expected profit	$0	$8,040	$9,360	$9,800
Supply chain's profit	$17,830	$16,130	$14,940	$13,250

produce each Bassano is $75, not the actual $35. From UV's perspective, it does not matter if the actual production cost is $35, $55, or even $0; its "production cost" is $75. UV correctly recognizes that it only makes $40 on each sale but loses $50 on each leftover pair. Hence, UV is prudent to order cautiously.

UV's trepidation with respect to ordering is due to a phenomenon called *double marginalization.* Because UV's profit margin ($40) is one of two profit margins in the supply chain, and necessarily less than the supply chain's total profit margin ($80), UV orders less than the supply chain optimal quantity. In other words, because UV only earns a portion ($40) of the total benefit of each sale ($80), UV is not willing to purchase as much inventory as would be optimal for the supply chain.

This example illustrates an important finding:

> *Even if every firm in a supply chain chooses actions to maximize its own expected profit, the total profit earned in the supply chain may be less than the entire supply chain's maximum profit.*

In other words, rational and self-optimizing behavior by each member of the supply chain does not necessarily lead to optimal supply chain performance. So what can be done about this? That is the question we explore next.

There is an obvious solution to get UV to order more Bassanos: Zamatia could reduce the wholesale price. A lower wholesale price increases UV's underage cost (gross margin) and decreases the overage cost (loss on leftover inventory), thereby making stockouts costlier and leftover inventory less consequential. More technically, reducing the wholesale price increases UV's critical ratio, which leads UV to order more. Table 17.2 provides some data on supply chain performance with various wholesale prices.

We indeed see that if Zamatia were to reduce its wholesale price from $75 to $65, then UV would increase its Bassano order from 234 to 268 units. UV is quite happy: Its profit increases from $5,580 to $8,090. Furthermore, the supply chain's profit increases from $14,905 to $16,130. In fact, why stop with a $10 wholesale price reduction? If Zamatia were to reduce the wholesale price down to the production cost, $35, then (1) UV orders the supply chain optimal quantity, 404 units, and (2) the supply chain's profit is optimal, $17,830! That strategy is called *marginal cost pricing* because the supplier only charges the retailer the marginal cost of production.

But while marginal cost pricing is terrific for UV and the supply chain, it is disastrous for Zamatia: by definition, Zamatia's profit plunges to zero with marginal cost pricing.

We now see a classic tension within a supply chain: An increase in one firm's profit might come at the expense of a decrease in the other firm's profit. Some might refer to this distributive situation as a *zero-sum game,* but in fact it is even worse! In a zero-sum game, two parties negotiate over how to split a fixed reward (in this case, the total profit), but in this situation the total amount to be allocated between Zamatia and UV is not even fixed: Increasing Zamatia's profit may result in a smaller total profit to be shared.

With respect to the allocation of supply chain profit, firms should care about two things:

1. The size of a firm's piece of the "pie," where the pie refers to the supply chain's total profit.
2. The size of the total "pie," that is, the supply chain's total profit.

Number 1 is obvious: every firm always wants a larger piece of the pie. Number 2 is less obvious. For a fixed piece of the pie, why should a firm care about the size of the pie, that is, the size of the other firm's piece? "Petty jealousy" is not the answer. The answer is that it is always easier to divide a bigger pie: If a pie gets bigger, then it is possible to give everyone a bigger piece, that is, everyone can be better off if the pie is made bigger. In practice this is often referred to as a *win-win* deal, that is, both parties are better off.

Turning back to our discussion of the wholesale price for Zamatia and UV, we see that arguing over the wholesale price is akin to arguing over each firm's piece of the pie. And in the process of arguing over how to divide the pie, the firms may very well end up destroying part of the pie, thereby serving no one. What these firms need is a tool that first maximizes the size of the pie ($17,830) and then allows them to decide how to divide it between them without damaging any part of it. Such a tool is discussed in the next section.

17.4 Buy-Back Contracts

Without changing the wholesale price, Zamatia would get UV to order more Bassano sunglasses if Zamatia could mitigate UV's downside risk of leftover inventory: UV loses a considerable amount ($50) on each unit it is stuck with at the end of the season. One solution is for Zamatia to buy back from UV all leftover sunglasses for a full refund of $75 per pair; that is, Zamatia could offer UV a *buy-back contract,* also called a *returns policy.*

Unfortunately, buy-back contracts introduce new costs to the supply chain. In particular, UV must ship leftover inventory back to Zamatia, which it estimates costs about $1.50 per pair. And then there is the issue of what Zamatia will do with these leftover Bassano sunglasses when it receives them. One possibility is that Zamatia just throws them out, thereby "earning" a zero salvage value on each leftover Bassano. However, Zamatia may be able to sell a portion of its leftover inventory to a European retailer that may be experiencing higher sales or Zamatia may be able to collect some revenue via an outlet store. It is even possible that Zamatia has higher salvage revenue from each Bassano at the end of the season than UV. But let's suppose Zamatia is able to earn $26.50 per Bassano at the end of the season. Hence, from the perspective of the supply chain, it does not matter whether UV salvages these sunglasses at the end of the season (which earns $25) or if Zamatia salvages these sunglasses at the end of the season (which also earns $25, net of the shipping cost). In contrast, Zamatia and UV might care which firm does the salvaging of leftover inventory. We later expand upon this issue.

Let's begin the analysis of UV's optimal order quantity given the buy-back contract. UV's underage cost with this buy-back contract is still the opportunity cost of a lost sale, which is $C_u = \$115 - \$75 = \$40$. However, UV's overage cost has changed. Now UV only loses $1.50 per leftover pair due to Zamatia's generous full refund returns policy, $C_o = \$1.50$. UV's critical ratio is

$$\frac{C_u}{C_o + C_u} = \frac{40}{1.5 + 40} = 0.9639$$

With a critical ratio of 0.9639, the optimal z-statistic is 1.8 (i.e., $\Phi(1.79) = 0.9633$ and $\Phi(1.8) = 0.9641$), so UV's optimal order quantity is now

$$Q = \mu + z \times \sigma = 250 + 1.8 \times 125 = 475$$

We can evaluate UV's expected profit and discover that it has increased from \$5,580 (with no refund on returns) to \$9,580 with the returns policy. Furthermore, with an order quantity of 475 units, UV's expected leftover inventory is 227 units.

Zamatia has surely provided an incentive to UV to increase its order quantity, but is this offer also good for Zamatia? Zamatia's expected profit has several components: It sells 475 units to UV at the beginning of the season, which generates $475 \times \$75 = \$35,625$ in revenue; its production cost is $475 \times \$35 = \$16,625$; it expects to pay UV $227 \times \$75 = \$17,025$ to buy back the expected 227 units of leftover inventory; and it collects $227 \times \$26.5 = \$6,016$ in salvage revenue. Combining those components together yields an expected profit of \$7,991 for Zamatia, which is *lower* than Zamatia's profit without the returns policy, \$9,350.

How did Zamatia go wrong with this buy-back contract? Zamatia did encourage UV to order more Bassano sunglasses by reducing UV's exposure to leftover inventory risk. But Zamatia reduced that risk so much that UV actually ordered more than the supply chain optimal quantity, thereby setting Zamatia up for a large bill when leftover inventory gets shipped back. Is there a compromise between the wholesale price contract with too little inventory and the full refund buy-back contract with too much inventory? (Of course there is.)

Instead of giving a full refund on returned inventory, Zamatia could give a partial refund. For example, suppose Zamatia offers to buy back inventory from UV for \$65 per pair. This is still not a bad deal for UV. Its underage cost remains $C_u = 40$, but now its overage cost is $C_o = \$1.50 + \$75 - \$65 = \$11.50$: each unit left over costs UV the \$1.50 to ship back and due to the partial credit, it loses an additional \$10 per unit. Table 17.3 provides data on UV's optimal order quantity, expected sales, expected leftover inventory, and expected profit. The table also indicates Zamatia's profit with this partial refund is \$9,528, which is slightly better than its profit without a buy-back at all. Furthermore, the supply chain's total profit has jumped to \$17,600, which is reasonably close to the maximum profit, \$17,830. One way to evaluate the quality of a contract is by its *supply chain efficiency,* which is the fraction of the optimal profit the supply chain achieves. In this case, efficiency is 17,600 / 17,830 = 99 percent; that is, the supply chain earns 99 percent of its potential profit.

Instead of holding the wholesale price fixed and reducing the buy-back price, Zamatia could hold the buy-back price fixed and increase the wholesale price. For example, it could

TABLE 17.3
UV's Order Quantity Q and Performance Measures for Several Possible Wholesale Price Contracts

Wholesale price	\$75	\$75	\$75	\$85
Buy-back price	\$55	\$65	\$75	\$75
C_u	\$40	\$40	\$40	\$30
C_o	\$21.50	\$11.50	\$1.50	\$11.50
Critical ratio	0.6504	0.7767	0.9639	0.7229
z	0.39	0.77	1.80	0.60
Q	299	346	475	325
Expected sales	221	234	248	229
Expected leftover inventory	78	112	227	96
Expected profits:				
Umbra	\$7,163	\$8,072	\$9,580	\$5,766
Zamatia	\$9,737	\$9,528	\$7,990	\$11,594
Supply chain	\$16,900	\$17,600	\$17,570	\$17,360

increase the wholesale price to $85 and still agree to buy back inventory for $75. That contract indeed works well for Zamatia: it earns a whopping $11,594. It even is not a bad deal for UV: its profit is $5,766, which is still better than the original situation without any refund on returned inventory. But overall supply chain performance has slipped a bit: efficiency is now only 17,360 / 17,830 = 97 percent.

While we seem to be making some progress, we also seem to be fishing around without much guidance. There are many possible combinations of wholesale prices and buy-back prices, so what combinations should we be considering? Recall from the previous section that our objective should be to maximize the size of the pie and then worry about how to divide it. Every firm can be given a bigger piece if the pie is made bigger. So let's first look for wholesale/buy-back price combinations that maximize supply chain profit. In other words, we are looking for a wholesale price and a buy-back price such that UV's expected profit-maximizing order quantity given those terms is the supply chain optimal order quantity, 404 Bassanos. If we find such a contract, then we say that contract "coordinates the supply chain" because the supply chain achieves 100 percent efficiency, that is, it earns the maximum supply chain profit.

We could hunt for our desired wholesale/buy-back price combinations in Excel (for every wholesale price, slowly adjust the buy-back price until we find the one that makes UV order 404 Bassanos), or we could take a more direct route by using the following equation:

$$\text{Buy-back price} = \text{Shipping cost} + \text{Price} - (\text{Price} - \text{Wholesale price})$$
$$\times \left(\frac{\text{Price} - \text{Salvage value}}{\text{Price} - \text{Cost}} \right) \qquad \textbf{(17.1)}$$

In other words, if we have chosen a wholesale price, then equation (17.1) gives us the buy-back price that would cause UV to choose the supply chain optimal order quantity. In that case, the pie would be maximized; that is, we coordinate the supply chain and supply chain efficiency is 100 percent! (If you are curious about how to derive equation (17.1), see Appendix D.)

Let's evaluate equation (17.1) with the wholesale price of $75:

$$\text{Buy-back price} = \$1.50 + \$115 - (\$115 - \$75) \times \left(\frac{\$115 - \$25}{\$115 - \$35} \right) = \$71.50$$

Hence, if the wholesale price is $75 and Zamatia agrees to buy back leftover inventory for $71.50 per pair, then UV orders 404 Bassano sunglasses and the supply chain earns the maximum profit, $17,830.

Table 17.4 provides performance data for several different wholesale prices assuming equation (17.1) is used to choose the buy-back price.

Interestingly, with a wholesale price of $75, the firms split the supply chain's profit, that is, each earns $8,915. In that case, UV does much better than just a wholesale price contract, but Zamatia does worse. However, both firms do significantly better with the wholesale price of $85 and the buy-back price of $82.75 than they do with the original contract we considered (just a $75 wholesale price and no buy-back).

Table 17.4 reveals some remarkable observations:

• There are many different wholesale price/buy-back price pairs that maximize the supply chain's profit. In other words, there are many different contracts that achieve 100 percent supply chain efficiency.

TABLE 17.4
Performance Measures When the Buy-Back Price Is Chosen to Coordinate the Supply Chain—to Ensure 100 percent Supply Chain Efficiency

Wholesale price	$35	$45	$55	$65	$75	$85	$95	$105
Buy-back price	$26.50	$37.75	$49.00	$60.25	$71.50	$82.75	$94.00	$105.25
C_u	$80	$70	$60	$50	$40	$30	$20	$10
C_o	$10.00	$8.75	$7.50	$6.25	$5.00	$3.75	$2.50	$1.25
Critical ratio	0.8889	0.8889	0.8889	0.8889	0.8889	0.8889	0.8889	0.8889
z	1.23	1.23	1.23	1.23	1.23	1.23	1.23	1.23
Q	404	404	404	404	404	404	404	404
Expected sales	243	243	243	243	243	243	243	243
Expected leftover inventory	161	161	161	161	161	161	161	161
Expected profits:								
Umbra	$17,830	$15,601	$13,373	$11,144	$8,915	$6,686	$4,458	$2,229
Zamatia	$0	$2,229	$4,458	$6,686	$8,915	$11,144	$13,373	$15,601
Supply chain	$17,830	$17,830	$17,830	$17,830	$17,830	$17,830	$17,830	$17,830

• Virtually any allocation of the supply chain's profit between the two firms is feasible; that is, there exist contracts that give the lion's share of the profit to the supplier, contracts that equally divide the profit, and contracts that give the lion's share to the retailer.

• The firms now truly do face a zero-sum game; that is, increasing one firm's profit means the other firm's profit decreases. However, at least now the sum that they can fight over is the maximum possible.

Which contracts will the firms ultimately agree upon? We cannot really say. If Zamatia is the better negotiator or if it is perceived to have more bargaining power than UV, then we would expect Zamatia might get UV to agree to a buy-back contract with a high wholesale price. Even though Zamatia's profit can increase substantially, it is important to note that UV's profit also may increase relative to the status quo because buy-back contracts increase the size of the pie. However, if UV has the stronger negotiating skills, then it is possible UV will secure a contract that it favors (a buy-back contract with a low wholesale price).

17.5 More Supply Chain Contracts

The previous section focused on buy-back contracts, but those are not the only type of contracts that are implemented in supply chains. This section briefly describes several other types of contracts and how they may alleviate supply chain incentive conflicts. This is by no means an exhaustive list of the types of contracts that are observed in practice.

Quantity Discounts

Quantity discounts are quite common, but they come in many different forms. For example, with an all-unit quantity discount, a buyer receives a discount on all units if the quantity ordered exceeds a threshold; whereas with an incremental quantity discount, a buyer receives a discount on all units purchased above a threshold. No matter the form, quantity discounts encourage buyers to order additional inventory because the purchase price of the last unit purchased is decreasing with the amount purchased (See Section 7.6.) In the context of the newsvendor model, a quantity discount increases the underage cost, thereby increasing the critical ratio. In contrast, recall that the buy-back contract increases the critical ratio by decreasing the overage cost.

Options Contracts

With an options contract, a buyer pays one price to purchase options, say w_o, and another price to exercise the purchased options, w_e. These contracts are often used when a buyer wants a supplier to build capacity well in advance of the selling season. At that time, the buyer has only an uncertain forecast of demand. As the selling season approaches, the buyer anticipates that she will have a much better demand forecast, but by then it is too late to build additional capacity if demand is quite high. Without the options contract, the supplier bears all of the supply chain's risk, so the supplier is likely to build too little capacity. The options contract allows the firms to share the risk of demand–supply mismatches: The supplier earns at least something upfront (the option's price) while the buyer doesn't have to pay for all of the unused capacity (the exercise price is paid only on capacity actually exercised). Hence, just as with buy-back contracts, options contracts are able in some settings to achieve 100 percent supply chain efficiency (i.e., the supplier builds the right amount of capacity) and arbitrarily divide the supply chain's profit between the two firms (i.e., there is more than one options contract that achieves supply chain coordination).

Revenue Sharing

With revenue sharing, a retailer pays a wholesale price per unit purchased to a supplier but then also pays a portion of the revenue earned on that unit to the supplier. As with buy-back contracts, revenue sharing allows the firms in the supply chain to share the risk of demand–supply mismatches: The retailer pays something to the supplier upfront (the wholesale price) but only pays an additional amount if the unit actually generates revenue (the revenue share).

The most notable application of revenue sharing occurred in the video-rental industry. Back around 1998, the standard wholesale price contract was predominant in the industry: studios would sell videocassettes to video rental retailers for about $60 to $75 per tape and retailers would keep all rental revenue. At a rental price of about $3, retailers could only break even on a tape if it rented more than 20 times. But because demand for tapes generally starts high upon its release and fades quickly, retailers could not afford to purchase too many tapes. As a result, availability of newly released movies was quite low, driving many consumers to consider other entertainment forms (cable TV, pay-per-view, etc.). Considering that the manufacturing cost of a tape is quite low, it is clear that maximizing supply chain profit requires additional tapes at the retailer.

Around 1998 the industry's biggest player, Blockbuster, negotiated revenue sharing deals with the major studios. With revenue sharing, the retailer pays a far lower wholesale price (about $8) but shares a portion of the rental revenue (about 50 percent). With those terms, the breakeven on a tape reduces to fewer than six rentals, thereby allowing Blockbuster to justify purchasing many more tapes. They used their additional availability to launch their "Guaranteed to be there" and "Go home happy" marketing campaigns.

Quantity Flexibility Contracts

Consider an ongoing relationship between a buyer and a supplier. For example, the buyer is Sun Microsystems, the supplier is Sony, and the product is a monitor. Sun's demand fluctuates over time, but Sun nevertheless wants Sony to build enough capacity to satisfy all of Sun's needs, which could be either higher or lower than forecasted. But since Sun probably doesn't incur the cost of idle capacity, Sun is biased toward giving Sony overly rosy forecasts in the hope that Sony will respond to the forecast by building extra capacity. But Sony is no fool; that is, Sony knows that Sun is biased toward optimistic forecasts and so Sony may view Sun's forecasts with a skeptical eye. Unfortunately, Sun may actually have an optimistic forecast, but due to its lack of credibility with Sony, Sony may not respond with additional capacity.

The problem in this relationship is that Sony bears the entire risk of excess capacity; hence, Sun is biased toward rosy forecasts. One solution is to implement *quantity flexibility (QF) contracts:* with a QF contract, Sun provides an initial forecast but then must purchase some quantity within a certain percentage of that forecast. For example, suppose the firms agree to a 25 percent QF contract. Furthermore, it is the first quarter of the year and Sun forecasts its demand for the fourth quarter will be 2,000 units. By the time the fourth quarter rolls around, Sun is committed to purchasing from Sony at least 1,500 units (75 percent of the forecast) and Sony is committed to delivering up to 2,500 units (125 percent of the forecast) should Sun need more than the forecast. If demand turns out to be low, Sony is somewhat protected by the lower collar, whereas if demand turns out to be high, Sun can take advantage of that upside by knowing that Sony has some additional capacity (up to the upper collar). Hence, via quantity flexibility contracts, it can be shown that both firms are better off; that is, the supply chain pie gets bigger and each firm gets a bigger share.

Price Protection

In the PC industry, distributors are concerned with holding too much inventory because that inventory could become obsolete; that is, they must sell that inventory at deeply discounted prices. But there is another concern with holding too much inventory. Suppose a distributor purchases 1,000 computers today at $2,000 each, but one week later the supplier cuts the price to $1,800. Unless the distributor sells the entire batch of 1,000 computers in the next week, the distributor would be better off to purchase fewer computers at $2,000 and to purchase the remainder one week later at $1,800. In other words, the tendency of suppliers to cut their wholesale prices frequently and without notice creates an incentive among distributors to be cautious in the purchase quantities. If distributors then curtail their purchases below the supply chain optimal amount, it can be beneficial to provide them with an incentive to increase their order quantities.

Allowing distributors to return inventory helps to encourage distributors to order more inventory, but it is not the only way. *Price protection* is another way: with price protection, a supplier compensates the distributor for any price reductions on remaining inventory. For example, suppose at the end of the week the distributor sold 700 computers purchased at $2,000, but has 300 computers remaining. With price protection, the supplier would then send the distributor a check for $300 \times ($2,000 - $1,800) = $60,000$. In other words, the distributor becomes indifferent between purchasing 1,000 computers for $2,000 now and purchasing 700 computers for $2,000 now and 300 computers for $1,800 in one week.

17.6 Summary

Optimal supply chain performance is not guaranteed even if every firm in the supply chain optimizes its own performance. Self-interest and decentralized decision making do not naturally lead to 100 percent supply chain efficiency. As a result, firms in a supply chain can benefit from better coordination of their actions.

The bullwhip effect (the propagation of demand variability up the supply chain) provides a serious challenge to supply chain operations. There are many causes of the bullwhip effect (order synchronization, order batching, trade promotions, overreactive ordering, and shortage gaming) and more than one of them can be present at the same time. Solutions to the bullwhip effect such as sharing demand information, removing pathological incentives, and Vendor-Managed Inventory are designed to combat those root causes.

The bullwhip effect is not the only challenge posed upon supply chains. Given the terms of trade between supply chain members, it is quite possible that supply chain actions will not be taken because of conflicting incentives. For example, with a simple wholesale price contract, it is generally found that the retailer's incentive to order inventory leads it to order less than the supply chain optimal amount of inventory, a phenomenon called double marginalization. Fortunately, incentive conflicts can be alleviated or even eliminated with the use of carefully designed contractual terms such as buy-back contracts.

17.7 Further Reading

For a description of the causes, consequences, and solutions to the bullwhip effect, see Lee, Padmanabhan, and Whang (1997).

Buzzell, Quelch, and Salmon (1990) provide a history of trade promotions and discuss their pros and cons.

For the original research on buy-back contracts, see Pasternack (1985). For a more managerial description of the application of buy-back contracts, see Padmanabhan and Png (1995). For a review of the theoretical literature on supply chain contracting, see Cachon (2004).

17.8 Practice Problems

Q17.1* **(Buying Tissues)** P&G, the maker of Puffs tissues, traditionally sells these tissues for $9.40 per case, where a case contains eight boxes. A retailer's average weekly demand is 25 cases of a particular Puffs SKU (color, scent, etc.). P&G has decided to change its pricing strategy by offering two different plans. With one plan, the retailer can purchase that SKU for the everyday-low-wholesale price of $9.25 per case. With the other plan, P&G charges the regular price of $9.40 per case throughout most of the year, but purchases made for a single delivery at the start of each quarter are given a 5 percent discount. The retailer receives weekly shipments with a one-week lead time between ordering and delivery. Suppose with either plan the retailer manages inventory so that at the end of each week there is on average a one-week supply of inventory. Holding costs are incurred at the rate of 0.4 percent of the value of inventory at the end of each week. Assume 52 weeks per year.

a. Suppose the retailer chose the first plan ($9.25 per case throughout the year). What is the retailer's expected annual purchasing and inventory holding cost?

b. Suppose the retailer chooses the second plan and only buys at the discount price ($9.40 is the regular price and a 5 percent discount for delivery at the start of each quarter). What is the retailer's expected annual purchasing and inventory holding cost?

c. Consider the first plan and propose a new everyday-low wholesale price. Call this the third plan. Design your plan so that both P&G and the retailer prefer it relative to the second plan.

Q17.2* **(Returning books)** Dan McClure is trying to decide on how many copies of a book to purchase at the start of the upcoming selling season for his bookstore. The book retails at $28.00. The publisher sells the book to Dan for $20.00. Dan will dispose of all of the unsold copies of the book at 75 percent off the retail price, at the end of the season. Dan estimates that demand for this book during the season is normal with a mean of 100 and a standard deviation of 42.

a. How many books should Dan order to maximize his expected profit?

b. Given the order quantity in part a what is Dan's expected profit?

c. The publisher's variable cost per book is $7.50. Given the order quantity in part a, what is the publisher's expected profit?

The publisher is thinking of offering the following deal to Dan. At the end of the season, the publisher will buy back unsold copies at a predetermined price of $15.00. However, Dan would have to bear the costs of shipping unsold copies back to the publisher at $1.00 per copy.

(* indicates that the solution is at the end of the book)

d. How many books should Dan order to maximize his expected profits given the buy-back offer?

e. Given the order quantity in part d, what is Dan's expected profit?

f. Assume the publisher is able on average to earn $6 on each returned book net the publisher's handling costs (some books are destroyed while others are sold at a discount and others are sold at full price). Given the order quantity in part d what is the publisher's expected profit?

g. Suppose the publisher continues to charge $20 per book and Dan still incurs a $1 cost to ship each book back to the publisher. What price should the publisher pay Dan for returned books to maximize the supply chain's profit (the sum of the publisher's profit and Dan's profit)?

Q17.3** **(Component options)** Handi Inc., a cell phone manufacturer, procures a standard display from LCD Inc. via an options contract. At the start of quarter 1 (Q1), Handi pays LCD $4.50 per option. At that time, Handi's forecast of demand in Q2 is normally distributed with mean 24,000 and standard deviation 8,000. At the start of Q2, Handi learns exact demand for Q2 and then exercises options at the fee of $3.50 per option, (for every exercised option, LCD delivers one display to Handi). Assume Handi starts Q2 with no display inventory and displays owned at the end of Q2 are worthless. Should Handi's demand in Q2 be larger than the number of options held, Handi purchases additional displays on the spot market for $9 per unit.

For example, suppose Handi purchases 30,000 options at the start of Q1, but at the start of Q2 Handi realizes that demand will be 35,000 units. Then Handi exercises all of its options and purchases 5,000 additional units on the spot market. If, on the other hand, Handi realizes demand is only 27,000 units, then Handi merely exercises 27,000 options.

a. Suppose Handi purchases 30,000 options. What is the expected number of options that Handi will exercise?

b. Suppose Handi purchases 30,000 options. What is the expected number of displays Handi will buy on the spot market?

c. Suppose Handi purchases 30,000 options. What is Handi's expected total procurement cost?

d. How many options should Handi purchase from LCD?

e. What is Handi's expected total procurement cost given the number of purchased options from part d?

Q17.4 **(Selling Grills)** Smith and Jackson Inc. (SJ) sells an outdoor grill to Cusano's Hardware Store. SJ's wholesale price for the grill is $185. (The wholesale price includes the cost of shipping the grill to Cusano). Cusano sells the grill for $250 and SJ's variable cost per grill is $100. Suppose Cusano's forecast for season sales can be described with a Poisson distribution with mean 8.75. Furthermore, Cusano plans to make only one grill buy for the season. Grills left over at the end of the season are sold at a 75 percent discount.

a. How many grills should Cusano order?

b. What is Cusano's expected profit given Cusano's order in part a?

c. What is SJ's expected profit given Cusano's order in part a?

d. To maximize the supply chain's total profit (SJ's profit plus Cusano's profit), how many grills should be shipped to Cusano's Hardware?

Suppose SJ were to accept unsold grills at the end of the season. Cusano would incur a $15 shipping cost per grill returned to SJ. Among the returned grills, 45 percent of them are damaged and SJ cannot resell them the following season, but the remaining 55 percent can be resold to some retailer for the full wholesale price of $185.

e. Given the possibility of returning grills to SJ, how many grills should be sent to Cusano's to maximize the supply chain's total profit?

Suppose SJ gives Cusano a 90 percent credit for each returned grill, that is, SJ pays Cusano $166.50 for each returned grill. Cusano still incurs a $15 cost to ship each grill back to SJ.

f. How many grills should Cusano order to maximize his profit?

g. What is Cusano's expected profit given Cusano's order in part f?

h. What is SJ's expected profit given Cusano's order in part f?

i. To maximize the supply chain's total profit, what should SJ's credit percentage be? (The current credit is 90 percent.)

Dave Luna, the director of marketing and sales at SJ, suggests yet another arrangement. He suggests that SJ offer an advanced purchase discount. His plan works as follows: there is a 10 percent discount on any grill purchased before the season starts (the prebook order), but then retailers are able to purchase additional grills as needed during the season at the regular wholesale price (at-once orders). With this plan, retailers are responsible for selling any excess grills at the end of the season, that is, SJ will not accept returns. Assume SJ makes enough grills to satisfy Cusano's demand during the season and any leftover grills can be sold the next season at full price.

j. Given this advanced purchase discount plan, how many grills should Cusano prebook to maximize his profit?

k. What is Cusano's expected profit given Cusano's prebook order quantity in part j?

l. What is SJ's expected profit from sales to Cusano this season given Cusano's prebook order quantity in part j?

m. As a thought experiment, which one of these contractual arrangements would you recommend to SJ?

You can view a video of how problems marked with a ** are solved by going on www. cachon-terwiesch.net and follow the links under 'Solved Practice Problems'

Chapter

18

Sustainable Operations

Seven billion. That is the estimate of the world's population in October 2011, projected to rise to 9 billion by 2050. It is a lot of people, and it is just one reason that sustainability has become an important topic of discussion. This chapter explores how operations influences sustainability and how sustainable thinking can influence operations management. We start with some background to motivate the topic of sustainability, and then we outline the business case for focusing attention on sustainability. Finally we conclude with a discussion of how the tools of good operations management can be applied to a sustainability initiative.

18.1 Sustainability: Background

Sustainable business practices are said to be those that sustain people and the planet. That is, by implementing these practices we will be as well off in the future as we are now. This is a broad definition, and so sustainable business practices can be divided into many domains. We highlight five of them:

- Energy
- Water
- Materials
- Agriculture, fishing, and forestry
- People

We primarily focus on energy, but the others are discussed briefly as well.

Energy

Sustainability is often associated with "global warming" or, the more preferred term, "climate change." The evidence for climate change comes from many sources. Figure 18.1 displays the steady increase in our atmospheric carbon dioxide. (This is also referred to as the Keeling curve, in recognition of the scientist Charles Keeling, who began collecting these data more than 50 years ago.) Interestingly, we can see the Earth "breathing" in these data—because there is more land in the Northern Hemisphere than the Southern Hemisphere, carbon dioxide levels drop as vegetation grows in the northern summer and then increases again as the vegetation dies off in the winter.

Carbon dioxide is not harmful to humans or plants, but it does cause the Earth to retain heat, as if adding a blanket to our atmosphere: We are already about 1°C warmer than we were at the start of the Industrial Revolution. This temperature change may not seem large, but it has already contributed to melting glaciers and rising sea levels. In fact, it has been estimated that if all of the ice sitting on Greenland were to melt, sea level would rise more

FIGURE 18.1

Atmospheric Carbon Dioxide Measured At Mauna Loa, Hawaii

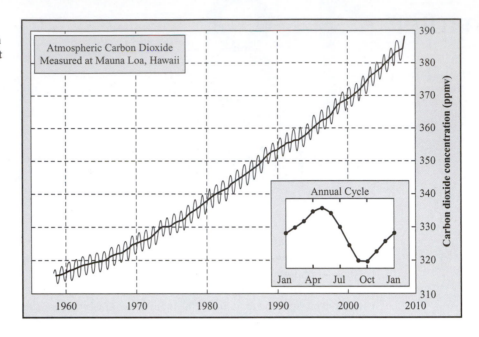

than 20 feet. Higher average temperatures may also change the severity or frequency of adverse weather and influence rainfall patterns. Finally, a significant amount of the carbon dioxide we emit is absorbed by the oceans, which increases the acidity of the ocean, thus contributing to coral degradation, among other consequences.

Data from ice core samples indicates that our current levels of carbon dioxide are not unprecedented. However, the data also show that the Earth has experienced a rapid increase in carbon dioxide levels as over the last 100 years.

Carbon dioxide is not the only *greenhouse gas (GHG),* nor is it the most prevalent. The most common greenhouse gas is actually water vapor. But human activity is not directly contributing additional water vapor to the atmosphere. Two of the other major GHGs are methane and nitrous oxide. Methane comes from landfills (decomposition of organic matter), natural gas production, and digestion/manure from animals (such as cattle, milking cows, and pigs). Fertilizers are the main source of nitrous oxide. A set of chlorofluorocarbons provide the other greenhouse gases.

Given equal weights, greenhouse gases have different warming potentials. Just like it is useful to express the output of different countries in a common currency (say, the U.S. dollar), it is useful to express total emissions in terms of a common unit. That unit is called a *carbon dioxide equivalent (CO$_2$e)*. The CO$_2$e of carbon dioxide is 1, whereas it is 21 for methane and 310 for nitrous oxide. That means that 1 kilogram of methane is equivalent (in warming potential) to 21 kilograms of carbon dioxide, and 1 kilogram of nitrous oxide is equivalent to 310 kilograms of carbon dioxide.

In 2009, U.S. emissions of carbon dioxide were 5.2 billion metric tons of CO$_2$e. Generation of electricity is the largest contributor to emissions (41 percent of the total) followed by transportation (33 percent). With electricity, coal is the major fuel responsible for emissions in the United States, followed by natural gas. For transportation, emissions primarily come from the combustion of gasoline, diesel, and jet fuel.

With transportation it is relatively straightforward to tally up total emissions—just count the amount of fuel burned. For example, the combustion of 1 gallon of gasoline emits 8.8 kilograms of carbon dioxide into the atmosphere.

FIGURE 18.2
Emissions from Electricity from Different Countries and Regions

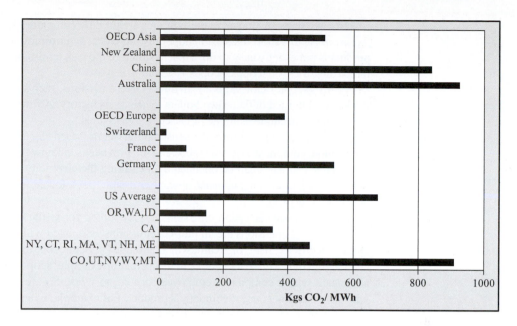

Counting emissions with electricity is more difficult. A company is likely to know how many kilowatt-hours they consumed, but what fuel was used to produce that power? The electricity on a grid comes from many different sources. Therefore, the emissions associated with electricity vary considerably across different countries and regions within countries, as indicated in Figure 18.2. For example, France relies heavily on nuclear power (relatively low CO_2 emissions), whereas Australia and China rely on coal. Within the United States, the Pacific Northwest produces much of its electricity with hydro (low emissions), whereas the mountain states again rely on coal.

Although the energy source is relevant, the efficiency of that energy also matters. For example, in transportation we are interested not only in total emissions but emissions per kilogram per kilometer of product transported. Figure 18.3 shows that there is considerable variation in this measure across different modes.

FIGURE 18.3
Emissions per Tonne Hauled per Kilometer Traveled for Various Modes of Transportation

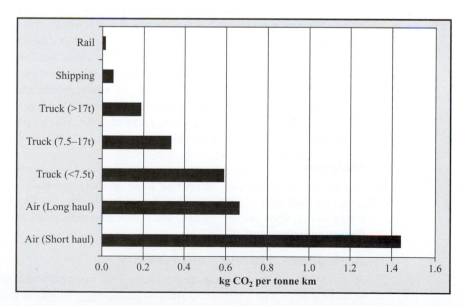

Data like those displayed in these figures are used by companies to evaluate their *carbon footprint.* As this short discussion hopefully indicates, determining the carbon footprint of a product is not exactly easy to do. To help structure the task, emissions are often divided into three categories, or scopes: scopes 1, 2, and 3.

A firm's *scope 1* emissions are all direct GHG emissions, such as fuel burned in their own trucks or oil burned in their own boilers to heat their factory. A firm can usually obtain good data to get an accurate estimate of its scope 1 emissions.

Scope 2 emissions are from the consumption of purchased electricity, heat, or steam. This can be more complicated to assess because the firm needs to know the source of its electricity. Reasonable estimates can be obtained by measuring the electricity at each of the company's locations and then using published average emissions per kilowatt for those locations (like the data in Figure 18.3).

Scope 3 emissions are all emissions not accounted for in the other two scopes. In particular, scope 3 emissions are all indirect emissions associated with the firm (other than purchased electricity, heat, or steam, which is scope 2). Scope 3 emissions are by far the most challenging of the three categories to measure. For example, scope 3 includes the emissions associated with a company's employees driving to work. So are the emissions associated with how customers use a company's product. For example, when Philips sells a lightbulb to a customer, the emissions associated with the use of that lightbulb are part of Philips' scope 3 emissions. Scope 3 also includes all upstream emissions associated with a product. For example, if Apple assembles an iPod in China through a subcontractor, then that subcontractor's electricity usage is part of Apple's scope 3 emissions. So are the emissions of that contractor's suppliers. And so on.

As you can imagine, scope 3 emissions may be substantially larger than the other two scope emissions. Scope 3 is also probably the most difficult to assess. Estimates must be made regarding customer usage of products, employee travel, and supplier emissions. The data collection challenge is substantial. To assist firms with their carbon footprinting, two nonprofit organizations, the Carbon Disclosure Project and the World Resource Initiative, have put together extensive guidelines.

Water

There is plenty of water on the planet, but fresh water is only 2.5 percent of it, and more than two-thirds of that is locked up in glaciers and ice sheets. In addition, the fresh water we do have is not evenly distributed; more importantly, it is not always found in the same places we choose to live. Consequently, water conservation is a critical issue in much of the world.

Consider a pair of jeans. Water is needed to grow the cotton for the jeans (an astonishing 1,800 gallons per pair). Water is needed in the manufacturing process (to wash the fabric, create the stonewash look, and so on), and, of course, water is used by the customer to wash his or her jeans. As this example illustrates, the water usage associated with a product can be substantial and associated with many different phases of the product's life cycle (e.g. production, usage, and disposal).

Material

In addition to water, many companies focus on their materials usage, in both raw materials and packaging. Considerations include switching to more sustainable materials (more abundant or easily recycled) and lighter materials (to reduce the energy needed in transportation).

Agriculture, Fishing, and Forestry

Sustainable agriculture includes issues like soil management and crop selection (in addition to water usage). The objective of sustainable fishing practices is to ensure that fish stocks remain robust and healthy. Forestry has similar concerns—can timber be harvested in a way that maintains the productivity of the land and the biodiversity of its environment?

People

Although sustainability is often associated with natural resources, many companies now include people in their sustainability objectives—the people involved in the delivery of a company's products and services should be treated with respect and given the opportunity to live a good life. For example, children should not be forced to work, but rather be given access to education and workers should be provided with a safe working environment.

18.2 Sustainability: The Business Case

While the adoption of sustainability goals and practices may be considered the "right thing to do," it is not immediately clear that it is the reason firms should adopt sustainability. Firms also have a responsibility to their investors, so management should have an interest in long-run value. There are at least three arguments for why sustainability can be compatible with maximizing profit:

- Build a brand
- Protect a brand
- Lower costs

Some customers value sustainability and are willing to pay a premium to know that they are purchasing a product or service that they view as good for the environment and good for the people involved in the production process. Hence, sustainability can be used to build a brand. Patagonia, the outdoor apparel company, has taken this approach. It provides high-quality clothing but also emphasizes the sustainability of its clothing. Patagonia customers may be willing to pay a premium for its products because they value Patagonia's commitment to sustainability.

Some customers are not willing to pay a premium, but at the same time they are not willing to participate in practices that they view as inappropriate, distasteful, or downright wrong. Take Nike. It has established a formidable brand based, in part, on well-placed associations with outstanding athletes. It has a strong interest to maintain that brand by ensuring that the company does not become associated with practices that could be viewed as inappropriate by its customers.

Finally, although there is no doubt that some sustainable practices increase costs, there are also many opportunities to reduce costs and simultaneously make your company's offerings more sustainable. As already discussed, carbon emissions are closely linked to energy usage. Reduce energy usage and you naturally become more sustainable. And because energy costs money, reducing energy usage also leads to cost savings. Similarly, if you reduce the amount of material used in your packaging, you need to purchase less of it and need to spend less to move it. Consistent with this view, Figure 18.4 displays a list of projects that McKinsey argues yield net savings from the perspective of sustainability.

To understand how to read Figure 18.4, consider the third project from the left, "Residential buildings—lighting." It has a negative "cost" of about $90 per CO_2e, which means that while there are out-of-pocket costs associated with making lighting in residential buildings more sustainable (e.g., purchasing compact florescents or LEDs), the net savings (e.g., in terms of reduced electricity usage) is actually positive. In other words, a project like this is a "free lunch"—society saves money and reduces emissions at the same time.

FIGURE 18.4   **Costs and Benefits of Carbon-Reducing Projects**

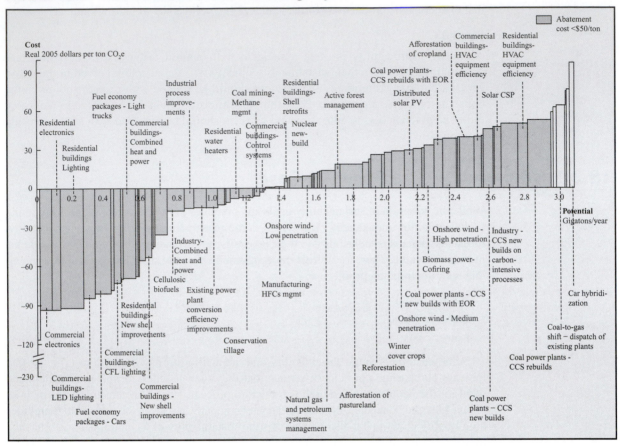

Figure 18.4 also includes projects that reduce emissions with a net cost. For example, "Coal power plants—CCS rebuild" costs about $50 per metric ton of CO_2e. ("CCS" stands for "carbon capture and sequestration," a process that captures the CO_2 from electricity production before it is emitted to the atmosphere).

Data like those in Figure 18.3 can be used to estimate the total cost of achieving CO_2 emission reduction targets; companies should prioritize their projects so that they start with the "free lunch" ones. They are the ones with the highest return on investment.

18.3 Sustainability and Operations Management

Throughout this text, we have articulated many principles to help managers improve their operations. Fortunately, those principles can be applied to sustainability initiatives as well. To begin, recall from Chapter 1 the notion of trade-offs and a production frontier. Figure 18.5 draws a simple frontier curve in which, at some point, it becomes necessary to sacrifice either sustainability or profits. However, as suggested earlier (see Figure 18.4), it is entirely possible, and probably likely, that a firm will not find itself on the frontier when it begins its sustainability initiative. Given that it has not focused on sustainability before, the firm may be able to identify projects in which it can improve sustainability and simultaneously increase profits; that is, it can move from the interior toward the frontier.

FIGURE 18.5
The Sustainability and Profit Frontier Curve

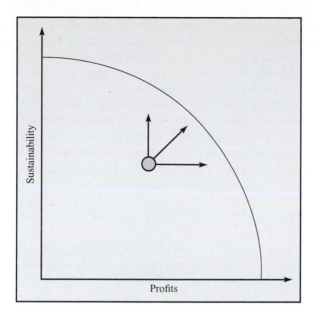

So how should a firm begin the process of identifying promising projects? Like all strategies to improve operations, begin with collecting data (Chapters 3 and 12). This is absolutely critical in the context of sustainability. You cannot improve something that you do not measure. But it is also a challenging task for several reasons. First, many companies will not have systems in place to easily gather data on electricity consumption, fuel purchases, and water usage, in part because these commodities may not be purchased centrally.

Next, even when you find your electricity usage, as already mentioned, it is not immediately obvious how to translate that number into a carbon emission—you need to know how that electricity was produced.

Third, it is not always easy to know how to allocate usage numbers to various product lines. In some sense, this is a classic accounting problem (How do you allocate fixed overhead to various items?), but the problem is no easier to solve in the context of sustainability. For example, suppose you want to determine the carbon footprint of a gallon of milk. Cows belch (among other types of "emissions"), giving off methane. It is possible to estimate the amount of methane emitted per cow, but how should that methane be allocated across the various products produced with that cow (e.g., milk and leather)?

Finally, once you have completed your task for scope 1 and 2 emissions, you need to look both up and down your supply chain, i.e., you need to consider scope 3 activities. If the data challenges are tough within the firm, they only get compounded when you must consider the boundaries outside of the firm. Despite these challenges, it is worthwhile to collect data even when the data are less than perfect.

With data in hand, one of the first tasks could be to use the Pareto diagram tool from quality management (Chapter 10): rank-order different sources of emissions, water usage, or chemical use to prioritize opportunities for improvement. In doing this prioritization, it is also important to collect data on traditional quality defects (like warranty claims). If a defective product is made in China and shipped to the United States, then not only are the materials in the product potentially wasted, the firm incurs wasted emission costs associated with transporting the item.

Just like good quality management is consistent with sustainability, the ideas of process and lean management are consistent with sustainability (Chapter 11). For example, a major goal of process management is to increase utilization and capacity with the same set of resources (Chapters 4 and 6). Many of these resources have fixed emissions or water usage. For example, the cost of lighting a facility may act like a fixed cost; the building is lit during the eight hours of a shift whether the shift produces at 75 percent capacity or 90 percent capacity. Consequently, any reduction in wasted resources is likely to reduce the carbon or water footprint of an item because more units are produced with the same overhead (such as lighting). The same is true of lean management—by identifying root causes of waste, such as with a Ishikawa diagram (see Chapter 11), more output can be produced with no more or maybe even less energy and water.

It is also important to note that collecting sustainability data can change how a firm focuses on its process design. Consider Levi Strauss, a leading maker of denim jeans. Normally, Levi's might focus on reducing labor content or the amount of fabric for each pair of jeans. Those are surely valuable activities, but when you discover the amount of water used in the production process (as mentioned earlier), the focus may turn to developing new processes that do not require as much water.

Not only can sustainability influence a firm's thinking within its own processes, sustainability can strongly influence its supply chain strategy. Take the issue of location. In the environmental movement, location is often a lightning rod for activists. For example, "localvores" advocate eating food that is grown locally to avoid emissions associated with transportation. Another popular expression is the notion of "food miles"—the distance food has to travel to reach your plate. However, it is important to note that transportation is only one part of the total impact of a product, albeit an important part. The production process also matters, such as the amount of electricity (and the source of the electricity) along with other inputs (such as the amount of fertilizer used). For example, bauxite is mined in Australia, but it is smelted into aluminum in New Zealand. While moving the bauxite to New Zealand is costly (including the emissions aspect), the electricity on the south island of New Zealand is made with hydro power. Given that a significant amount of electricity is needed to make aluminum, doing it in New Zealand is better than doing it in Australia with its coal-powered plants (see Figure 18.2).

In addition to location, the mode of transportation is important for supply chain management. A key lesson over the past 20 to 30 years has been that many good things can come with speed: With faster lead times, you generally need less inventory to hit target service levels, or you can increase service levels with the same amount of inventory (Chapter 14). However, sustainability provides a new perspective on this approach. As we see in Figure 18.3, faster usually means dirtier, at least in terms of transportation emissions. However, if faster means less inventory and less inventory can lead to smaller buildings, then it is possible that total emissions could decrease—smaller buildings require less heating, cooling, and lighting.

While a firm should be careful about evaluating its transportation mode, it appears that delayed differentiation is likely to be a sustainability friendly strategy (Chapter 15). By adding components late in the supply chain, the firm's inventory investment can be reduced. What was not mentioned in Chapter 15 is that this also tends to lighten the product in the transportation stage. A lighter product requires less energy to move around. For example, instead of bottling wine in Argentina and sending the bottles to the United States, some wineries transport their wine from South America in large steel containers. The steel vessel weighs proportionally less than the glass bottles (note, the ratio of surface area to volume decreases as volume increases), so even if there are no risk pooling benefits from this strategy, there is an environmental benefit.

In general, packaging provides significant opportunities for sustainability improvements. Sticking with the spirits industry, French champagne manufacturers have recently focused on the size and shape of their bottles: Can they reduce the amount of glass in the bottle (and therefore its weight), while still maintaining the strength needed to store the champagne inside at high pressure? Like the glass in champagne, nearly all products require some form of packaging. And unlike most products, which you hope will last for at least a couple of uses, if not several years' worth of use, packaging is almost always immediately discarded after its first "use." Hence, changing to more environmentally friendly materials, reducing the weight of the materials, and redesigning the packaging to allow for recycling for reuse are all worthwhile strategies.

18.4 Summary

Sustainability and the environment are important topics that have grabbed the attention of many CEOs. At its heart, sustainability is about the efficient use of resources, which is precisely the aim of operations management. Hence, the tools of operations management apply naturally to any sustainability initiative.

18.5 Further Reading

For an introduction to the science related to climate change, visit http://www.epa.gov/climatechange/. For more details on climate change, consider the latest report from the The Intergovernmental Panel on Climate Change (http://www.ipcc.ch/). For a discussion on sustainability and corporate strategy, see Porter and Kramer (2011). For guides on how to assess the carbon footprint of a product, visit the Carbon Disclosure project (https://www.cdproject.net) or the World Resource Initiative (www.wri.org).

18.6 Practice Problems

Q18.1*   **(Bauxite to New Zealand)** Australian bauxite ore is shipped 3,000 kilometers to New Zealand in a bulk cargo ship. The ship carries 300,000 metric tonnes of ore and consumers 1,400,000 liters of fuel oil on the journey. Fuel oil emits 38.2 kgs CO_2 per liter. For bauxite ore shipped from Australia to New Zealand, what is the emission of CO_2 (in kgs) per tonne kilometer traveled?

Q18.2   A consumer who lives in New York switches from a 60 watt incandescent light bulb to an 8 watt LED. Assume usage remains the same, which is 4 hours per day on average. Electricity costs the consumer $0.12 per kWh. (A kWh is the amount of electricity need to produce 1000 watts of energy for 1 hour.) The incandescent light bulb costs $0.40. The LED costs $12.00. The LED lasts 27,000 hours whereas the incandescent light bulb lasts 1000 hours.

   a. Including the cost of replacement bulbs and the cost of electricity, how long does it take for the LED to breakeven? (That is, after how much time will the consumer have spent as much with the LED as with the incandescent light bulb.)

   b. The consumer's electricity emits 450 kgs CO_2/MWh. (1 MWh = 1000 kWh.) How many kgs of CO_2 would the consumer emit to operate the 60 watt light bulb for one year?

19

Business Model Innovation

Netflix changed the video industry and drove Blockbuster into bankruptcy. Zipcar is emerging as a credible substitute for owning a vehicle. Both of these companies started by offering a service that differed substantially from what was the norm, not only in terms of what service customers were offered, but also in how each company delivered its service. Both are innovators and, in particular, both are examples of *business model innovation*—a term that has become a recent buzzword, used to explain the success of a number of rapidly growing businesses.

To be complete, one should acknowledge that such radical innovations are by no means a recent phenomenon. Dell revolutionized the computer industry over the course of the 1990s, a time period in which Southwest Airlines redefined air travel. One might even argue that Gottlieb Daimler and Henry Ford redefined transportation and forced many producers of horse carts out of business. Nevertheless, modern technology has surely enabled a steady stream of business model innovations in recent times.

The purpose of this chapter is to understand the forces behind such new business models. Instead of compiling a set of buzzwords and anecdotes, we want to present a solid framework that helps you understand and create new business models. Not surprisingly, given the title of our book, our framework is based on the idea that a firm can increase its profitability by identifying new and better ways in which it can match supply with demand. More specifically, in this chapter, we aim to explain:

• The economic forces behind the new business models of Netflix and Zipcar.

• The different ways in which a firm can innovate and which of these innovations classify as business model innovations.

• How a new business model can increase customer utility and often draw a new set of customers into the market.

• The ways in which a firm can leverage its operations to deliver on this utility while maximizing its profitability.

19.1 Zipcar and Netflix

In case you are not familiar with Zipcar and Netflix, this section describes what they offer and how they offer it.

Zipcar is a car-sharing company that was founded in 2000. Within 10 years, the company grew to an 8,000-vehicle fleet that serves a customer base of some 560,000 members. Members

FIGURE 19.1
Zipcar Locations in Philadelphia

Source: Google Maps.

can reserve vehicles online or by phone—they can do so minutes prior to their vehicle usage or several months in advance. There are generally many locations to choose from within a neighborhood (see Figure 19.1). At the time of use, a customer unlocks the vehicle using his or her access card (which is provided when signing up as a customer), or, more recently, an iPhone app. An annual membership costs about $60, and vehicles can be used for hourly rates that are as low as $7.50 (actual rates vary depending on make and model, as well as the time of the day and the day of the week). The hourly rate includes gas, maintenance, and insurance—members refuel the vehicle when needed and get reimbursed for the fuel expenses (many gas stations also accept the access card as a form of payment). After use, members return the vehicle by parking it in a designated space. Members are responsible for leaving the vehicle in a clean condition, ready to be used by the next member. All of this happens without the presence of a Zipcar employee.

Now let's switch to our second business model innovation, Netflix. Given the speed with which the video market has evolved from video rental companies, such as Block-buster, to today's streaming video solutions of Netflix, Apple, or Amazon, it is easy to forget how Netflix started its success. The company began in 1997 in California. By 2010, it had a collection of more than 100,000 titles, which were available to its more than 10 million subscribers for a monthly flat fee. In 2011, there were 58 shipping locations in the United States, handling an estimated volume of about 2.5 million DVDs per day.

A member manages an ordered list (the Netflix queue) of movies she or he is interested in watching. Movies are sent to the member by U.S. Postal delivery in DVD format. They can be kept by the member as long as desired (no late fees), with the constraint that at any given time the member can only have three DVDs at home (that number varies depending on the subscription plan). To get a new DVD, the subscriber needs to return one of the DVDs through the U.S. Postal Service. Once a movie is returned, another movie from the customer's queue is mailed to the customer. Netflix tries to send the movie at the top of a customer's queue, but if it is not available, possibly because it is a newly released popular title, Netflix may instead send another movie from the customer's queue.

The fact that Netflix now is largely used as a video on-demand service provides an interesting case study on how quickly new business models come and go. With Apple and Amazon streaming video in return for either rental fees or subscription plans, Netflix's amazing physical supply chain is transitioning to the virtual world. And, once again, a new business model has to be invented.

19.2 Innovation and Value Creation

The Netflix and Zipcar examples illustrate two ways in which firms innovated to supply solutions to the needs of their customers. We define an *innovation* as a novel match between a solution and a need so that value is created (see Terwiesch and Ulrich 2009). Our definition is best explained in a profit maximization paradigm.

Customers have a utility function and purchase a product or service if their utility of consumption exceeds the price. Mind you, a consumer's utility includes many components and certainly can include nonmonetary rewards, such as a preference for environmental conservation or the well-being of a group of workers. Independent of the particular components, consumers care about their net utility:

$$\text{Net utility} = \text{Utility} - \text{Price}$$

where Price is meant to include the total cost of owning the product or receiving the service. Firms, on the other side, have a profit goal. They obtain profits that can be summarized in a simple equation:

$$\text{Profits} = \text{Flow rate} \times (\text{Price} - \text{Average cost})$$

Because price reduces the net utility of the (potential) customer and increases profits, there exists an inherent tension between the interests of the customer and that of the firm. Some may argue that it is possible to produce a substantial innovation in terms of price (e.g., charging a subscription fee for music or bundling the cost of a cell phone into monthly service fees). However, we focus on two other means to generate an innovation:

- Change the way a product or service meets customer needs, thereby generating more utility. For example, we could change the performance of our service along one or more attributes, or create new attributes. It is even possible that an attribute is eliminated all together. In the end, if we create more utility for customers, we can command higher prices and draw more customers to our offerings.
- Change the way we supply the product or service. In other words, deliver the same level of customer utility, but develop a more efficient solution for doing so, thereby lowering our average cost.

As an illustration how these forces play out, consider the airline industry and the data that we discussed in Chapter 6. What matters to airlines is how much they can charge per revenue passenger mile (the yield) and how much it costs them to supply that mile. Because labor is the biggest cost driver in the industry, labor cost relative to revenue passenger miles provides a useful measure of efficiency. Over the course of the 1990s and early 2000s, Southwest was able to grow quickly and gain a significant market share. Relative to legacy carriers, customers paid only 80 percent of what the other carriers were charging, but Southwest was profitable because it produced the same service with double the efficiency.

How was that possible? Some of this is achieved through more efficient operations (see Chapter 6). However, Southwest also offered a different service. Many customers flying Southwest would not previously have been in the market for air travel at all. They might have taken a Greyhound bus or simply stayed at home. Southwest identified that unmet need: no frills air travel for an aggressive price. And, over that time period, Southwest was by far the most profitable—despite being the low-end player in the market.

Interestingly, just a couple of years later, history repeated itself. By 2005, Southwest's labor costs increased substantially, similar to the level of the legacy carriers. This time, JetBlue took the position of the low-cost airline, obtaining a labor productivity that was almost double what Southwest was able to provide (and thus, almost four times of what the legacy carriers offered). This allowed JetBlue to even further expand the market for air travel.

The success of JetBlue is visible in Figure 19.2. On the vertical dimension, the graph shows the amount of money the average passenger was paying for one mile of air travel on the various carriers. This amount is expressed relative to the industry average. On the horizontal dimension, we show how many passenger miles an airline can generate with $1.00 of labor cost, again, relative to the industry average. We observe that JetBlue was able to provide a service that was 60 percent more efficient in labor usage relative to the industry average. That allowed them to charge prices that were 40 percent lower compared to their competitors. Southwest in this time period had fallen behind in labor productivity. While each employee, on average, served more passengers compared to other airlines, Southwest employees were paid substantially above industry average. However, because of lower fuel costs/higher fuel efficiency as well as lower other expenses (such as landing fees, commissions, sales and marketing expenses), Southwest still turned substantial profits.

Note that a low-cost, efficiency-driven strategy might not be the only way to succeed. Imagine a hypothetical airline Golden Air, which caters to the very high end of the market: Limo service, business lounges, and new planes. The decisive question is this: "Are customers willing to pay premium prices for the premium services Golden Air could offer?" For the major carriers, the answer we get out of Figure 19.2 is clear: No airline is able to obtain prices that are substantially above industry average. Some companies, like NetJet, are active in this space, but for the most part, air travel seems to be a commoditized market.

So a firm can create a business model innovation either by improving customer utility or by improving operating efficiency. But firms are constantly coming up with new ways to meet customer needs and new business processes. Should we label all of these innovations as business model innovations? Clearly not. For example, it may be valuable for an airline to develop a baggage handling system that allows its baggage handlers to increase their output by 5 percent per shift, but this is not an innovation that customers would notice. Similarly, a pharmaceutical company may develop a new and useful compound, but this is what pharmaceutical companies do.

We suggest that a business model innovation is something that has the potential to fundamentally shift an industry. Usually, a business model innovation involves a simultaneous

FIGURE 19.2
Benchmarking of the Major U.S. Airlines

Source: Data based on 2005 reports.

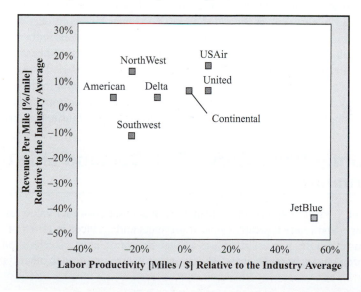

FIGURE 19.3
**Different Levels
of Innovation**

Source: Adapted from
Terwiesch and Ulrich 2009.

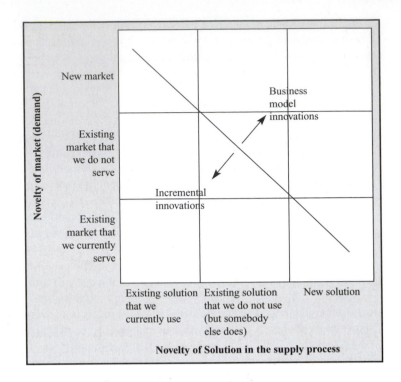

and significant shift in what customer needs are fulfilled and how the firm goes about filling them. Both Netflix and Zipcar meet these criteria—at the risk of not being particularly precise, both Netflix and Zipcar feel like very different ways of doing things. Netflix provides movie watching, just like Blockbuster, but doing it via a queue maintained on the Internet, and shipping DVDs by mail is not even close to how Blockbuster offered its service. At a high level, Zipcar is another car rental service, but its dense network of locations and extensive customer involvement makes it substantially different than the traditional car rental companies like Hertz, Avis, or National.

A useful way to measure the degree to which an innovation is substantial and deserves being labeled a new business model is explained in Figure 19.3. The lower left in the figure corresponds to refinements of existing technologies and solutions, but the company continues to serve its existing customers. The upper left represents an attempt to use existing solutions to reach new customers by entering new markets, either in the form of new geographic markets or in the form of new market segments. Either way, these innovations are rather incremental in nature and do not deserve to be labeled a new business model.

We want to reserve the term *business model innovation* for innovations that are characterized by substantial novelty in needs (and thus new customers) as well as solutions (and thus new operations). Business model innovations are thus in the upper right of Figure 19.3.

19.3 The Customer Value Curve: The Demand Side of Business Model Innovation

Let's start to explore how a firm generates more customer value (or net *utility,* if you prefer). Marketers typically think of products and services in terms of their attributes—cars, for example, possess attributes of fuel economy, style, acceleration, and ride quality. To keep our focus on business model innovation (as opposed to other types of innovation such as new pricing schemes or new product designs), we look at the following four categories of customer attributes:

- Price
- Preference fit
- Transactional efficiency
- Quality

Price includes not only the total payment to the firm (and possibly other entities, such as sales taxes), but potentially other price-related attributes such as the timing of the payments. For example, Zipcar charges an annual fee and a per-usage fee, as we discussed above. Together, these payments create a total cost for the service of transportation.

Preference fit refers to the firm's ability to provide the consumer with the product or service they want or need. In other words, how well does the firm satisfy the customer's need. Customers are often very heterogeneous in their preferences. They wear different size jeans, like different songs or movies, and enjoy eating different types of food. Often, this category of attributes is labeled "product variety." We prefer the term "preference fit" because customers do not care about "variety" per se. For example, as a customer of a video rental service, the number of titles the service makes available is, by itself, not the attribute you care about. Instead, you want to find a movie that you want to watch. Thus, variety is simply a means to an end. Preference fit is clearly a key strength of the Netflix business model—it offers a tremendous variety of movies.

Transactional efficiency has two major components that influence how easy it is to do business with a firm:

- How much effort does the customer need to exert in the process of communicating and fulfilling her or his needs. For example, one important strength of Netflix is that customers can browse through a huge video selection online, from the comfort of their home. Similarly, the advantage of Zipcar over other car rental services is that (urban) customers only have to walk a couple of blocks before getting to a vehicle.
- How much time elapses between when the customer identifies the need and when the need is fulfilled. This subdimension of transactional efficiency was initially seen as the Achilles heel in the Netflix model. After all, it can take two or three days between making a change in the Netflix queue (and returning a DVD) to receive the next DVD. Interestingly, the assumption that there should be only a few customers who would want to wait that long was proven wrong. Given the other subdimension of transactional efficiency and the strong preference fit, customers apparently are willing to ignore (or at least overlook) this attribute.

One may argue that transactional efficiency is really a part of preference fit. But transactional efficiency is rarely the need that a customer has. For example, with Zipcar, the need is transportation. Customer may like that they have nearby access to a Zipcar, but that just means that they recognize a low transactional cost of satisfying their true need (to be able to use a car). Thus, while transactional efficiency is surely important to customers, it deserves to be considered separately from preference fit.

Quality includes the subdimensions of conformance quality and performance quality. Conformance quality measures consistency and thus captures how closely the firm's offering matches what it claims it offers. This dimension is closely related to our discussion of six sigma in Chapter 6. Performance quality captures the utility that a typical customer derives from the product or service. In the case of Zipcar, conformance quality relates to the cleanliness and functioning of the vehicle. Performance quality relates to the vehicle types that are available.

TABLE 19.1   **The Four Categories of Attributes Mapped out for Zipcar and Netflix**

	Zipcar	Netflix
Reference services	Traditional car rental (Hertz) and car ownership.	Traditional movie rental service (Blockbuster) and DVD ownership.
Price	Cheaper than Hertz, especially when rented by the hour. Cheaper than owning for occasional drivers.	Cheaper than Blockbuster for frequent viewers. Cheaper than buying the DVD (unless a movie is watched many times).
Preference fit	Some selection of vehicles but not as wide a variety of vehicles as Hertz. Relative to owning a vehicle, it is possible to have access to multiple vehicles.	More variety to choose from than Blockbuster or DVD ownership.
Transactional efficiency: effort by the customer	Short walk to the car makes Zipcar easier on the customer compared to Hertz. However, relative to parking a vehicle in your driveway, the effort is greater.	As easy as purchasing a DVD on Amazon; less effort compared to going to a rental store.
Transactional efficiency: time elapsed between demand and fulfillment	Short relative to Hertz (because of the proximity to the vehicles). Long relative to owning a car.	Much longer time to fulfillment relative to rental outlet.
Quality: conformance	Potential concern about cleanliness of a vehicle, fuel level, and availability (does the previous customer return the car on time?).	Potential loss of DVD in the mail.
Quality: performance	Acceptable (unless you are used to a Porsche).	Not relevant.

A firm's offering can be mapped onto these four categories of attributes (See Table 19.1.) The customer *value curve* is a graphic depiction of a company's relative performance across these attributes. Figure 19.4 (upper part) shows the value curves for Zipcar relative to owning a vehicle as well as relative to renting a vehicle. There are a limited number of vehicles at each location, so preference fit scores low with respect to vehicle type. Conformance quality is not as good as the traditional rental car service because there is no Zipcar employee available to clean cars as they arrive or to ensure that the gas tank is full and the previous customer may not return the vehicle on time. However, relative to a traditional rental car company, Zipcar scores high in terms of transactional efficiency—after a few clicks and a short walk, you can be driving a Zipcar where you need to go. The lower part of Figure 19.4 shows the value curves for Netflix relative to going to a Blockbuster store as well as relative to purchasing a DVD. Netflix's approach was different than the one chosen by Zipcar. Netflix decided to sacrifice on the dimension of transactional efficiency (time elapsed). In return, it was able to offer an amazing number of movie titles, moving the industry to a new level of preference fit.

A key observation is that business model innovation often involves a smart sacrifice—dramatically improve one attribute of the value curve at the expense of another, possibly even an attribute that is viewed as a "sacred cow" in the industry. This suggests a strategy for developing a new business model innovation: (1) map out existing attributes, and then (2) consider which ones can be dramatically improved and which ones can be sacrificed. In thinking through how to shift the value curve, it is essential to not be biased by what currently

FIGURE 19.4
Value Curves for
Zipcar and Netflix

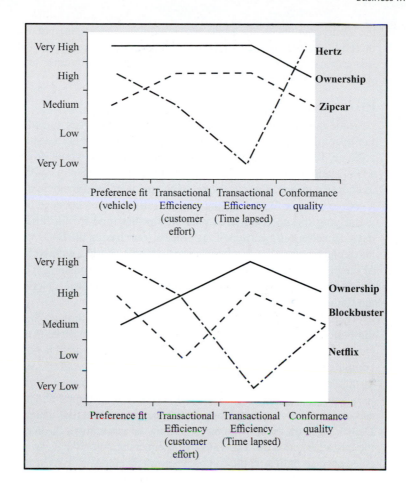

exists. It is also useful to ignore how those attributes could be delivered (the solution). Once a set of attributes is developed, the next section provides possible solutions for delivering them profitably.

19.4 Solutions: The Supply Side of Business Model Innovation

It is important to know that business model innovation often dramatically shifts the customer value curve. But we also need a solution that will do this profitably. That is the topic of this section.

Among the business model innovations we have observed, we have noticed that they generally involve changes to one or more of the following components of the firm's operations:

- Process timing
- Process location
- Process standardization

In all cases, shifts in these three dimensions can lead to substantial reductions in the cost to deliver the service and/or substantial changes in the customer value curve. They do this basically through one of three mechanisms. For one, they allow a firm to take advantage of specialized high-volume assets (e.g., large, automated sorting equipment). Alternatively, they allow the firm to use the same assets as competitors (e.g., the same type of employees, the same equipment, the same size buildings, and so on) but with a higher utilization, thereby, in effect, reducing the cost of those assets. Finally, they allow a firm to purchase less expensive assets (e.g., cheaper labor, inexpensive tooling, small buildings, and so on) while achieving the same level and quality of output.

Process Timing

At some moment in time, a customer realizes that she has a need for a product or service. For example, she might decide at 7 p.m. on a Friday night that she wants to watch a movie at home. What are her options? With Blockbuster, she would drive to a local store, choose a DVD, and return home. She might start the movie by 8 p.m. With Netflix, she would have to choose a movie, place it on her queue, and wait for the movie to arrive, hopefully within a couple of days. With Blockbuster, the fulfillment of the need can occur within hours of identifying the need, whereas with Netflix the time to fulfillment is better measured in days. Blockbuster's portion of the process (purchasing the DVD, placing it on a store shelf) takes place before the customer's need occurs, whereas with Netflix, a substantial portion of the process (packing the DVD and mailing it to the customer) occurs only after the customer's need is identified. In short, relative to Blockbuster, Netflix substantially changed the timing of its process.

There are several advantages to changing a process's timing. To start, delaying the process until after a customer reveals her need allows the firm to make better supply choices, which can lead to higher utilization of critical assets. To illustrate this point, consider the personal computer industry over the 20-year period from 1985 to 2005. With the traditional model a supplier, say, Hewlett-Packard (HP), assembles a personal computer (PC), ships the PC to a distributor or retailer, and then it is sold to a customer, about two months *after* it was assembled. That is, most of the process occurred before the customer's need was identified. Dell changed the process timing by starting the assembly of the personal computer only after the customer's need was revealed. Consequently, components are not assembled into a finished product until after the company knows that there is demand for the finished product. In contrast, with the traditional model, HP must guess at how many of each type of PC will be wanted in two months. Of course, Dell has to guess at how many components it needs, but this is a much simpler task than guessing the number of each PC type.

If delaying process timing is so wonderful, why don't all firms do it? Well, there are some disadvantages to the delay as well. For one, if you delay work until after a customer announces his or her desire, then it will generally take longer to fulfill that desire. Like with Netflix, Dell customers cannot just drive home with their new toy. More subtlety, while delaying a process can help manage one asset, it can make it more difficult to manage a different asset. In Dell's case, beyond components, another crucial asset is assembly labor. Dell will naturally have variations in the total number of PCs demanded each day. If it hires enough assembly capacity to cover every peak day, on most days that labor will be partially idle. If it hires only enough labor to cover average demand, then its backlog of PCs could grow substantially. In effect, for Dell, the assembly process acts like a queuing process. And as we saw in Chapter 8, as the utilization in a queuing process approaches 100 percent, waiting times tend to get very long. So Dell faces a trade-off. Hire many workers and have low labor utilization but small delays between customer orders and shipping, or hire only a little bit more than what is needed to cover average demand and have high labor utilization and long delays between customer orders and shipping. HP, on the other hand, does not face nearly the same challenge. Because there is a two-month period between assembly and customer demand, HP can operate with very high labor utilization—some PCs are made three months before they sell, others one month before they sell, but either way they are made well in advance of sales. What Dell demonstrated is that, when component prices were dropping, it was more important to manage the component asset than the assembly labor asset.

While Dell changed the timing of its processes to make better supply choices, process timing can also be used to lower the direct cost of a process. IKEA, the Swedish furniture company, provides an example of this approach. IKEA's innovation is to sell (reasonably) stylish and functional furniture that needs to be assembled by the customer—the company sacrifices performance quality (there is no comparison between IKEA's furniture and Ethan Allen) and transactional efficiency (few people actually enjoy the time needed to assemble furniture), but it significantly improves on the price dimension of the value curve. It did this by changing process timing. With traditional furniture, final assembly occurs before the customer announces his intention to purchase, whereas with IKEA final assembly occurs after the purchase. Consequently, final assembly is done by the consumer. This allows IKEA to reduce transportation costs (shipping knocked down furniture is less expensive than fully assembled furniture) and labor costs (employees are paid explicitly, whereas customers provide only implicit labor).

Returning to the Netflix example, one may ask how process timing works to Netflix's advantage. It is not that Netflix manufactures DVDs after customers place them in their viewing queue or that it allows them to use cheaper materials. Instead, delaying the fulfillment of the service enables Netflix to change another dimension of their process, their process location, as we discuss next.

Process Location

Changing where a process takes place can lead to a significant business model innovation. For example, Blockbuster, at its peak, operated more than 5,000 stores in the United States, each probably drawing customers from a limited geographic area that did not extend much more than 5 to 10 miles beyond each store. In contrast, Netflix operates about 60 fulfillment centers, two orders of magnitude fewer than Blockbuster. Clearly, via the U.S. mail, these centers could serve customers from much further away than a Blockbuster store.

In general, if you operate with fewer locations, then each location potentially has access to a greater pool of demand, but, at the same time, this expands the distance between customers and products. Demand aggregation works to the favor of the company, whereas moving away from customers works against the firm.

Consider the benefits of *demand aggregation,* which are analogous to the benefits of economies of scale. Scale economies arise for many reasons, but the most relevant ones for our context are:

- Trade-off between fixed and variable cost: If you engage in an activity many, many times, you might consider automating the activity or otherwise investing in some resource that can complete the activity at very low variable cost. However, if you only operate the activity occasionally, such an investment would not pay off. For example, an expensive, high-performance lawn mower that reduces the time to cut the lawn by 20 percent is likely to be a worthy investment for a professional gardener, yet most homeowners would hesitate to make this investment and rather spend a little more time for each cut.

- Learning: The more often you perform an activity, the better you will get at it, and the more effort you are likely to spend at analyzing and improving the activity. When employees more quickly learn how to do their job, they become productive more quickly, effectively lowering the firm's labor costs.

- Opportunities for dedicated resources: A Swiss Army knife does many tasks, but none as well as could be done by a dedicated tool. Similarly, while a person can do many tasks, he or she will naturally be better at some tasks than others. Consequently, with high demand it becomes feasible to utilize assets that are particularly good at narrow tasks (i.e., faster or cheaper at those tasks). For example, doctors in a small emergency department have to be prepared for all types of cases, making their work highly unpredictable and full of variability. In large emergency departments, in contrast, the volume of patients is sufficiently large to put the patients on different tracks. In so-called fast tracks, nurse practitioners take care of runny noses, trauma experts deal with trauma cases, and emergency physicians deal with other medical conditions. In this way, each track experiences less variability in the tasks it faces, thereby improving the efficiency of their work.

- Statistical economies of scale: As demand gets aggregated, it is generally observed that it also becomes less variable (in the sense of its coefficient of variation). Lower variability means that for any given level of service, the firm can utilize its assets more efficiently—the asset (e.g., inventory, people or equipment) spends less time waiting for customers, and there are fewer cases in which customers wait around for the asset to become available. This is essentially the idea of *demand pooling.* See Chapter 15.

Netflix took advantage of economies of scale in several ways. Its fulfillment centers implemented specialized sorting equipment to ensure a fast and efficient turnaround of DVDs from one customer to the next (high fixed cost, low variable cost equipment). But Netflix really exploited statistical economies of scale to dramatically increase the number of movie titles in its selection. For example, a Blockbuster store may offer 5,000 movie titles at any one time. If it were to offer more obscure titles, most of those titles would sit on the shelf for a long time before a customer request comes along, all the while incurring capital costs for the DVD and space costs for the shelf it sits on. It should be clear that Blockbuster may not be able to make money stocking obscure titles. Netflix, on the other hand, can carry those titles because each of its fulfillment centers serves much greater demand. Consequently, even a couple of copies may turn over fast enough to justify buying the DVD and the space it occupies (which would be cheaper on a per-square-foot basis that prime store-front real estate that Blockbuster would use). So, by operating with far fewer locations, Netflix is able to dramatically expand the variety it offers customers—and make a profit doing so.

Of course, there are two downsides to Netflix's model. First, customers must wait to receive their selection, lowering transactional efficiency. Second, Netflix has to explicitly pay the U.S. Postal Service to deliver the product. As always, the business model only works if the extra utility customers obtain makes them pay prices that are high enough to cover the firm's costs and to create a profit.

Zipcar also takes advantage of a process location change, but in a different direction than Netflix—instead of moving away from the customer, Zipcar moves closer to customers. Demand variability increases as we reduce the amount of demand aggregation; hence, variety will have to be compromised. Each location will not have the same selection of vehicles as a Hertz operation located at an airport. But, here, customers are willing to give up variety for the convenience of a car that is potentially within walking distance from their home. By moving closer to customers relative to Hertz, we expect that the utilization of Zipcar's cars is lower than Hertz's utilization. While this may increase Zipcar's cost, it is important to keep in mind that Zipcar also provides improved transactional efficiency—the convenience of a nearby car—which generates additional customer value.

Although Hertz provides one reference point for Zipcar, the other reference point is car ownership. And because Zipcar's cars are further from customers than their own vehicle, one would expect that Zipcar's utilization is higher than individual ownership. Consider the following, back-of-the-envelope calculations. Net of its subscription fee, Zipcar obtained annual revenues of about $200 million from its 8,000 vehicles (see Zipcar annual report in 2010). This translates to a $200 million/8,000 vehicles = $25,000 per year per vehicle. If we assume an average hourly rental fee of some $10 per hour, we see that the average Zipcar vehicle is likely to be rented out for 2,500 hours per year (more than 6 hours per day). Given that there are 365 days/year $\times$ 24 hours/day = 8,760 hours per year, we obtain a vehicle utilization of 2,500 hours used/8,760 hours available = 28.53 percent. Most consumers, especially those who either own multiple vehicles or use their vehicle only lightly, have a vehicle utilization that is substantially below this (if you use your vehicle 2 hours per day, your utilization is 2 hours/24 hours = 8.33 percent). Thus, by aggregating the demand across multiple consumers, Zipcar enables a threefold increase in asset utilization. This is a source of value.

While one might assume there is a single sweet spot in the process location spectrum, it seems that there can be multiple approaches that work. For example, take Redbox, which operates vending machines that act as a DVD rental store and are found in convenient locations such as supermarkets. In contrast to Netflix, Redbox moved closer to customers than even a Blockbuster store. As expected, variety is sacrificed—each Redbox can only stock a hundred or so titles. But there is a gain in convenience to the customers and cost—a Redbox is much cheaper than a Blockbuster store (less square footage, no employees needed on a constant basis). Both Netflix and Redbox work. The fact that each occupies a position on either end of Blockbuster (one with more variety, further away from customers, and the other with less variety, closer to customers) has certainly contributed to Blockbuster's struggles.

Of course, moving a process away from customers can also allow the firm to move the process to a location with cheaper labor or land or equipment. Outsourcing and offshoring are two strategies closely linked to this idea. For example, Nike was one of the first companies in the athletic shoe industry to move its production from the United States to Asia. Now this is viewed as the "traditional business model," but at the time it was indeed a significant departure from standard practice. It worked—in large part due to process standardization, as we discuss next.

Process Standardization

Higher education is a relatively unstandardized process. Two professors teaching the same topic, even if they plan to give the same exam, generally do not teach in exactly the same way. Even the same professor is unlikely to deliver the exact same lecture twice. Contrast this with how a McDonald's hamburger is made—although by the laws of statistics, no two hamburgers are exactly identical (see Chapter 10), nor is the process of making them, that process is surely more standardized relative to higher education.

A standardized process is one that has been defined so that it can be easily repeated; consequently, its output is relatively consistent. For example, before McDonald's, hamburgers were served at diners that made their hamburgers their own way. Each employee probably used a different amount of meat to construct the patty, and there was no standard process for cooking them (e.g., flip the burger once on the grill or several times). The owner of the diner probably gave the cook no more instruction than "cook hamburgers when customers order them." In contrast, McDonald's created uniform hamburger patties (size and shape), cooked them in a consistent manner, and even applied the toppings in a particular way. McDonald's standardized the process of making hamburgers.

There are some significant implications of process standardization, some of which can lead to business model innovations or be key enablers of business model innovation. For one, standardizing a process generally means that less skill is needed to complete the process, which means that less expensive labor or capital can be used in the process. Returning to our restaurant example, the cook in a diner probably demands hire wages than the employees in a McDonald's because that person is responsible for making more decisions that influence the quality of the output. In a more standardized process, employees do not need to make as many decisions, and they command lower wages.

For a more modern example, consider the role of process standardization in the case of Zipcar's business model. Access to vehicles is standardized by eliminating the traditional (nonstandardized) keys. Instead, a universal access card lets customers use any Zipcar vehicle—there is no need to exchange physical keys that are specific to individual vehicles. Consequently, there is no need to have a physical person present at each location to maintain proper control of these keys.

Process standardization is also a key enabler of the contract manufacturing industry discussed in Chapter 15. A contract manufacturer can use its manufacturing facilities to build products for multiple clients precisely because the process of making these components has been standardized (e.g., stuffing electronic circuit boards with integrated circuits). As hinted earlier, Nike was able to successfully send production of its shoes overseas because it was able to standardize the process of describing how to build the shoe and the actual manufacturing process. As a result, two different factories could make the same shoe, and they could be indistinguishable to a customer.

Of course, there are negative implications to process standardization. The most common one is a loss of variety (a potential reduction in preference fit). A customer does not tell McDonald's how they want their hamburger cooked. Nor does the selection of hamburgers change from month to month. In contrast, the menu at Le Bec Fin (a high-end restaurant in Philadelphia serving French cuisine) rarely stays constant from month to month; the chefs at Le Bec Fin are highly paid, are well trained, and certainly insist on changing the menu (so that their customers are unlikely to see the same menu on subsequent visits, each of which costs $150 or more per person). But as with all business model innovation, process standardization may lead to a smart sacrifice. For example, is it possible to standardize higher education so that you can deliver a valuable product to customers at much lower cost? This is an open question.

19.5 Unsuccessful Business Model Innovation

As with most innovation, business model innovation is not always successful. It is possible that a firm tries to exploit a change in process location but ends up with a product that just does not deliver enough incremental value to be profitable. In fact, there are surely more unsuccessful business model innovations than successful ones—we just do not hear about the unsuccessful ones as often.

Webvan provides a nice example of a reasonably well-known and surely unsuccessful business model innovation. Webvan tried to be an Internet grocer: Customers would order their groceries on the Web and then Webvan would deliver them to their homes.

Webvan provides a clear example of a process location change. With a traditional grocer, customers drive to a store to select among items that the company has stocked there. Webvan eliminated the store, following a demand aggregation strategy. Customers no longer drove to their groceries. Instead, Webvan drove groceries to customers. At first sight, this looks like a brilliant business model innovation—very much like a Netflix for groceries.

Unfortunately for Webvan, this did not lead to a higher utilization of its assets. Most of its warehouses were poorly utilized, and many of its vans were driven around partially full. Furthermore, instead of using "cheap" self-serve labor from customers (customers provide the service of picking their groceries and bringing them to the checkout counter), they utilized "expensive" employees paid explicitly by the company.

The Webvan example does not prove that that there will be no successful business model innovation in groceries. It merely illustrates that it can be a challenge to develop a successful business model, including a supply process that profitably matches supply with demand.

**19.6
Summary**

Innovation is a novel match between a solution and a need. We identified four key needs as they relate to business model innovation, which together make the customer value curve: price, preference fit, transactional efficiency and quality. A successful business model innovation generally involves some smart sacrifice—dramatically improving along one dimension while sacrificing some other dimension. For example, preference fit may be enhanced by increasing the variety offered while reducing some dimension of transactional efficiency (such as the time to fulfill the need). To achieve a substantial shift in the customer value curve, a firm can change the timing of a process, the location process, and/or the level of standardization of a process. These approaches are illustrated for Netflix and Zipcar, along with several other examples.

**19.7
Further
Reading**

For a strategic discussion of how a firm can radically change its positioning in the market to make "the competition irrelevant", see Chan Kim and Mauborgne (2005). See Terwiesch and Ulrich (2009) for more on the innovation process.

Appendix A

Statistics Tutorial

This appendix provides a brief tutorial to the statistics needed for the material in this book.

Statistics is about understanding and quantifying uncertainty (or, if you prefer, variability). So suppose we are interested in an event that is stochastic, that is, it has an uncertain outcome. For example, it could be the demand for a product, the number of people that call us between 10:00 a.m. and 10:15 a.m., the amount of time until the arrival of the next patient to the emergency room, and so forth. In each case, the outcome of this stochastic event is some number (units of demand, minutes between arrival, etc.). This stochastic event can also be called a *random variable*. Because our random variable could represent a wide variety of situations, for the purpose of this tutorial, let's give our random variable a generic name, *X*.

All random variables have an *expected value,* which is also called the *mean.* Depending on the context, we use different symbols to represent the mean. For example, we generally use the Greek symbol μ to represent the mean of our stochastic demand whereas we use a to represent the mean of the interarrival time of customers to a queuing system. A random variable is also characterized by its *standard deviation,* which roughly describes the amount of uncertainty in the distribution, or how "spread out" the distribution is. The Greek symbol σ is often used to describe the standard deviation of a random variable. Uncertainty also can be measured with the *variance* of a random variable. The variance of a random variable is closely related to its standard deviation: it is the square of the standard deviation:

$$\text{Variance} = (\text{Standard deviation})^2 = \sigma^2$$

Hence, it is sufficient to just work with the standard deviation because the variance can always be evaluated quickly once you know the standard deviation.

The standard deviation measures the absolute amount of uncertainty in a distribution, but it is often useful to think about the relative amount of uncertainty. For example, suppose we have two random variables, one with mean 20 and the other with mean 200. Suppose further they both have standard deviations equal to 10, that is, they have the same absolute amount of uncertainty. A standard deviation of 10 means there is about a two-thirds chance the outcome of the random variable will be within 10 units of the mean. Being within 10 units of a mean of 20 is much more variable in a relative sense than being within 10 units of a mean of 200: in the first case we have a two-thirds chance of being within 50 percent of the mean, whereas in the second case we have a two-thirds chance of being within 5 percent of the mean. Hence, we need a relative measure of uncertainty. We'll use the *coefficient of variation,* which is the standard deviation of a distribution divided by its mean, for example, σ/μ. In some cases we will use explicit variables to represent the coefficient of variation. For example, in our work with queuing systems, we will let CV_a be the coefficient of variation of the arrival times to the queue and CV_p be the coefficient of variation of the service times in the queue.

Every random variable is defined by its *distribution function* and its *density function*. (Actually, only one of those functions is sufficient to define the random variable, but that is a picky point.) Let's say $F(Q)$ is the distribution function of X and $f(Q)$ is the density function. The density function returns the probability our stochastic event will be exactly Q, while the distribution function returns the probability our stochastic event will be Q or lower:

$$F(Q) = \text{Prob}\{X \text{ will be less than or equal to } Q\}$$

$$f(q) = \text{Prob}\{X \text{ will be exactly } Q\}$$

There are an infinite number of possible distribution and density functions, but a few of the more useful ones have been given names. The *normal distribution* is probably the most well-known distribution: the density function of the normal distribution is shaped like a bell. The normal distribution is defined with two parameters, its mean and its standard deviation, that is, a μ and a σ. The distribution and density functions of a normal distribution with mean 1,000 and standard deviation 300 are displayed in Figure A.1.

Distribution functions are always increasing from 0 to 1 and often have an S shape. Density functions do not have a typical pattern: some have the bell shape like the normal; others are downward curving.

While there are an infinite number of normal distributions (essentially any mean and standard deviation combination), there is one normal distribution that is particularly useful, the *standard normal*. The standard normal distribution has mean 0 and standard deviation 1. Because the standard normal is a special distribution, its distribution function is given special notation: the distribution function of the standard normal is $\Phi(z)$; that is, $\Phi(z)$ is the

FIGURE A.1

Distribution (solid line) and Density (circles) Functions of a Normal Distribution with Mean 1,000 and Standard Deviation 300

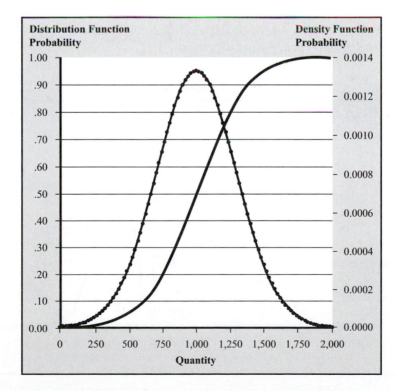

TABLE A.1
The Density Function
$f(Q)$ and Distribution
Function $F(Q)$ of a
Poisson Distribution
with Mean 1.25

Q	f(Q)	F(Q)
0	0.28650	0.28650
1	0.35813	0.64464
2	0.22383	0.86847
3	0.09326	0.96173
4	0.02914	0.99088
5	0.00729	0.99816
6	0.00152	0.99968
7	0.00027	0.99995
8	0.00004	0.99999
9	0.00001	1.00000

probability the outcome of a standard normal distribution is z or lower. The density function of the standard normal is $\phi(z)$. (Φ and ϕ are the upper- and lowercase, respectively, of the Greek letter phi.)

The normal distribution is a *continuous distribution* because all outcomes are possible, even fractional quantities such as 989.56. The *Poisson distribution* is also common, but it is a *discrete distribution* because the outcome of a Poisson random variable is always an integer value (i.e., 0, 1, 2, . . .). The Poisson distribution is characterized by a single parameter, its mean. The standard deviation of a Poisson distribution equals the square root of its mean:

$$\text{Standard deviation of a Poisson distribution} = \sqrt{\text{Mean of the Poisson distribution}}$$

While the outcome of a Poisson distribution is always an integer, the mean of the Poisson does not need to be an integer. The distribution and density functions of a Poisson distribution with mean 1.25 are displayed in Table A.1. Figure A.2 displays the density function of six different Poisson distributions. Unlike the familiar bell shape of the normal distribution, we can see that there is no standard shape for the Poisson: with a very low mean, the Poisson is a downward-sloping curve, but then as the mean increases, the Poisson begins to adopt a bell-like shape.

FIGURE A.2   **The Density Function of Six Different Poisson Distributions with Means 0.625, 1.25, 2.5, 5, 10, and 20**

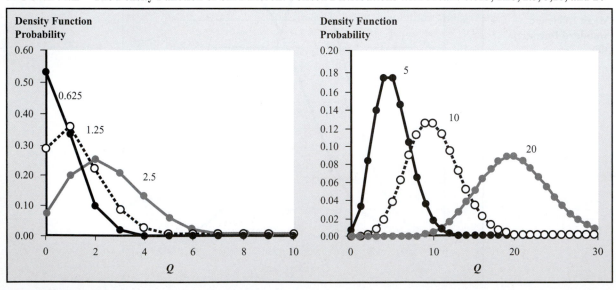

Because the outcome of a Poisson distribution is never negative and always integer, the Poisson generally better fits data with a low mean, say less than 20. For large means (say more than 20), the Poisson generally does not fit data as well as the normal for two reasons: (1) the Poisson adopts a bell-like shape, so it does not provide a shape advantage, and (2) the Poisson's standard deviation *must* equal the square root of the mean, so it does not allow the flexibility to expand or contract the width of the bell like the normal does (i.e., the normal allows for different bell shapes with the same mean but the Poisson only allows one bell shape for a given mean).

We also make extensive use of the exponential distribution in this text because it provides a good representation of the interarrival time of customers (i.e., the time between customer arrivals). The exponential distribution is characterized by a single parameter, its mean. We'll use a as the mean of the interarrival time. So if X is the interarrival time of customers and it is exponentially distributed with mean a, then the distribution function of X is

$$\text{Prob}\{X \text{ is less than or equal to } t\} = F(X) = 1 - e^{-t/a}$$

where e in the above equation is the natural constant that approximately equals 2.718282. In Excel you would write the exponential distribution function with the Exp function: $1 - \text{Exp}(-t/a)$. Notice that the exponential distribution function is a continuous distribution, which makes sense given that we are talking about time. Figure A.3 displays the distribution and density functions of an exponential distribution with mean 0.8.

The exponential distribution and the Poisson distribution are actually closely related. If the interarrival time of customers is exponentially distributed with mean a, then the

FIGURE A.3

Distribution (solid line) and Density (circles) Functions of an Exponential Distribution with Mean 0.8

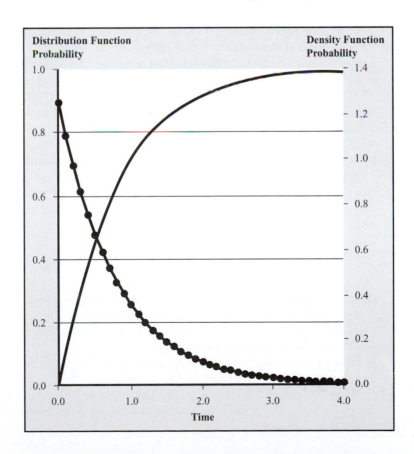

number of customers that arrive over an interval of a unit of time is Poisson distributed with mean $1/a$. For example, if the interarrival time of customers is exponentially distributed with a mean of 0.8 (as in Figure A.3), then the number of customers that arrive in one unit of time has a Poisson distribution with mean $1/0.8 = 1.25$ (as in Table A.1).

Other commonly used distributions include the negative binomial and the gamma, but we will not make much use of them in this text.

Finding the Probability *X* Will Be Less Than *Q* or Greater Than *Q*

When working with a random variable, we often need to find the probability the outcome of the random variable will be less than a particular quantity or more than the particular quantity. For example, suppose X has a Poisson distribution with mean 1.25. What is the probability X will be four units or fewer? That can be answered with the distribution function: from Table A.1, $F(4) = 99.088$ percent. What is the probability X will be greater than four units, that is, that it is five or more units? X is either Q or fewer units or it is more than Q units, so

$$\text{Prob}\{X \text{ is } Q \text{ or fewer units}\} + \text{Prob}\{X \text{ is more than } Q \text{ units}\} = 1$$

If we rearrange terms in the above equation, we get

$$\text{Prob}\{X \text{ is more than } Q \text{ units}\} = 1 - \text{Prob}\{X \text{ is } Q \text{ or fewer units}\} = 1 - F(Q)$$

Hence, X will be greater than four units with probability $1 - F(4) = 0.00912$.

A tricky issue in these evaluations is the difference between the "probability X is fewer than Q" and the "probability X is Q or fewer." The first case does not include the outcome that X exactly equals Q, whereas the second case does. For example, when we evaluate the "probability X is more than Q units," we are not including the outcome that X equals Q units. Therefore, be aware of this issue and remember that $F(Q)$ is the probability X is Q or fewer; that is, it includes the probability that X exactly equals Q units.

We also need to find the probability X is more or less than Q when X is normally distributed. Working with the normal distribution is not too hard because all normal distributions, no matter their mean or standard deviation, are related to the standard normal distribution, which is why the standard normal is special and important. Hence, we can find out the probability X will be more or less than Q by working with the standard normal distribution.

Suppose X is normally distributed with mean 1,000 and standard deviation 300 ($\mu = 1,000$, $\sigma = 300$) and we want to find the probability X will be less than $Q = 1,600$ units. First convert Q into the equivalent order quantity if X followed the standard normal distribution. That equivalent order quantity is z, which is called the *z-statistic*:

$$z = \frac{Q - \mu}{\sigma} = \frac{1,600 - 1,000}{300} = 2.0$$

Hence, the quantity 1,600 relative to a normal distribution with mean 1,000 and standard deviation 300 is equivalent to the quantity 2.0 relative to a standard normal distribution. The probability we are looking for is then $\Phi(2.0)$, which we can find in the Standard Normal Distribution Function Table in Appendix B: $\Phi(2.0) = 0.9772$. In other words, there is a 97.72 percent chance X is less than 1,600 units if X follows a normal distribution with mean 1,000 and standard deviation 300.

What is the probability X will be greater than 1,600 units? That is just $1 - \Phi(2.0) = 0.0228$; that is, the probability X will be greater than 1,600 units is just 1 minus the probability X will be less than 1,600 units.

With the normal distribution, unlike the Poisson distribution, we do not need to worry too much about the distinction between the "probability X is fewer than Q" and the "probability X is Q or fewer." With the Poisson distribution, there can be a significant probability that the outcome is exactly Q units because the Poisson distribution is a discrete distribution and usually has a low mean, which implies that there are relatively few possible outcomes. The normal distribution is continuous, so there essentially is no distinction between "X being exactly Q units" and "X being just a tiny fraction below Q units."

Expected Value

We often need to know the expected value of something happening. For example, suppose we make a decision and there are two possible outcomes, G for good and B for bad; that is, $X =$ G or $X =$ B. If the outcome is G, then we earn $100, but if the outcome is B, we lose $40. Furthermore, we know the following probabilities: Prob$\{X =$ G$\} = 0.25$ and Prob$\{X =$ B$\} = 0.75$. (Note, these probabilities must sum to 1 because they are the only two possible outcomes.) The expected value of this decision is

$$\$100 \times \text{Prob}\{X = \text{G}\} + (-\$40 \times \text{Prob}\{X = \text{B}\})$$
$$= \$100 \times 0.25 + (-\$40 \times 0.75)$$
$$= -\$5$$

In words, to evaluate the expected value, we multiply the probability of each outcome with the value of each outcome and then sum up all of those calculations.

The Loss Function

In statistics the distribution and density functions are well known and used often. Less well known in statistics is the *loss function,* but we make extensive use of it in this text. The loss function $L(Q)$ is the expected amount X is greater than Q. In other words, the expected loss is the expected amount a random variable X exceeds a chosen threshold Q.

To explain further, let X be a Poisson distribution with mean 1.25 and say our chosen threshold is $Q = 2$. (Table A.1 has the distribution function.) If $X = 3$, then X exceeds Q by one unit. If $X = 4$, then X exceeds Q by two units and if $X = 5$, then X exceeds Q by three units, and so on. Furthermore, if X is 2 or fewer, then X exceeds Q by 0 units. The loss function is the expected value of all of those events; that is, $L(2)$ is the expected amount by which X exceeds Q. Table A.2 provides those calculations for $L(2)$.

TABLE A.2
Calculation of the Loss Function for $Q = 2$ and a Poisson Distribution with Mean 1.25

Q	$f(Q)$ (a)	Amount X Exceeds 2 (b)	(a $\times$ b)
0	0.286505	0	0.00000
1	0.358131	0	0.00000
2	0.223832	0	0.00000
3	0.093263	1	0.09326
4	0.029145	2	0.05829
5	0.007286	3	0.02186
6	0.001518	4	0.00607
7	0.000271	5	0.00136
8	0.000042	6	0.00025
9	0.000006	7	0.00004
10	0.000001	8	0.00001
$L(2) =$ Total of last column =			0.18114

FIGURE A.4   **Calculation of the Loss Function for a Bell-like Distribution Function That Has Discrete Outcomes 0, 10, . . . , 200.**

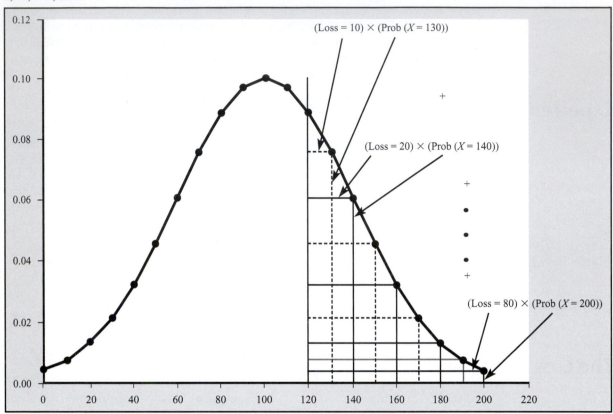

Figure A.4 gives a graphical perspective on the loss function. Depicted is a density function of a random variable X that has a bell shape like a normal distribution, but the only possible outcomes are 0, 10, 20, . . . , 190, and 200. Suppose we are interested in $L(120)$, the expected loss function evaluated at the threshold of $Q = 120$. If $X <= 120$, there is no loss; that is, the random variable does not exceed the threshold Q. If $X = 130$, then the loss is $130 - 120 = 10$, so we take that loss and multiply it by the probability it occurs. We repeat that procedure for the remaining possible outcomes that generate a loss (140 through 200) and sum those values to yield $L(120) = 7.486$. In other words, the random variable X exceeds the fixed threshold $Q = 120$ on average by 7.486. This might strike you as too low given that the losses ranged in our calculations from 10 to 80, but remember that for most outcomes there is actually no loss, that is, X is less than or equal to Q.

We displayed the calculation of the loss function with a discrete random variable in Figure A.4, but conceptually we can do the same calculation with a continuous random variable such as the normal. The only difference is that there is a lot more work to do with a continuous random variable because we need to multiply every possible loss by its probability and sum all of those calculations.

At this point you (hopefully) understand that the loss function is not conceptually difficult, but it is a "pain in the neck" to evaluate. Fortunately, Appendix C provides an easier way to evaluate the loss function of a discrete random variable. But even that easier way requires a decent amount of work, more work than should be done by hand. In other words, either you have a spreadsheet to help you evaluate the loss function or you should have a table that has already been evaluated for you, as in the following for the Poisson with mean 1.25:

Q	f(Q)	F(Q)	L(Q)
0	0.286505	0.286505	1.25000
1	0.358131	0.644636	0.53650
2	0.223832	0.868468	0.18114
3	0.093263	0.961731	0.04961
4	0.029145	0.990876	0.01134
5	0.007286	0.998162	0.00221
6	0.001518	0.999680	0.00038
7	0.000271	0.999951	0.00006
8	0.000042	0.999993	0.00001
9	0.000006	0.999999	0.00000
10	0.000001	1.000000	0.00000

If X is normally distributed, then our loss function is already provided to us in Appendix B. Actually, the loss function of the standard normal distribution is provided, that is, the Standard Normal Loss Function Table gives us $L(z)$, the expected loss function if X is a standard normal distribution. Because we often work with a different normal distribution, we need to learn how to convert the answer we get from that table into the answer that is appropriate for the normal distribution we are working with.

Suppose X is normally distributed with mean 1,000 and standard deviation 300. We are interested in the loss function with $Q = 1,600$. Just as we did when we were looking for the probability X will be greater than Q, first convert Q into the corresponding z value for the standard normal distribution:

$$z = \frac{Q - \mu}{\sigma} = \frac{1,600 - 1,000}{300} = 2.0$$

In other words, $Q = 1,600$ and a normal distribution with mean 1,000 and standard deviation 300 is equivalent to $z = 2.0$ and a standard normal distribution. Next, look up $L(z)$ in the Standard Normal Loss Function Table: $L(z) = 0.0085$. In other words, 0.0085 unit is the expected amount a standard normal will exceed the threshold of $z = 2.0$. Finally, we need to convert that value in the loss function to the value for the actual normal distribution. We use the following equation to do that:

$$L(Q) = \sigma \times L(z)$$

which in this case means

$$L(1,600) = 300 \times 0.0085 = 2.55$$

Hence, if $Q = 1,600$ and X is normally distributed with mean 1,000 and standard deviation 300, then the expected amount X will exceed Q is only 2.55 units. Why is the loss function so small? We evaluated the probability X exceeds Q to be only 2.28 percent, so most of the time X exceeds Q by 0 units.

Independence, Correlation, and Combining (or Dividing) Random Variables

We often need to combine several random variables or to divide a random variable. For example, if we have five random variables, each one representing demand on a particular day of the week, we might want to combine them into a single random variable that represents weekly demand. Or we might have a random variable that represents monthly demand and we might want to divide it into random variables that represent weekly demand. In addition to combining and dividing random variables across time, we may wish to combine or divide random variables across products or categories.

Suppose you wish to combine n random variables, labeled $X_1, X_2, \ldots, X_n$, into a single random variable X; that is, you want $X = X_1 + X_2 + \cdots + X_n$. Furthermore, we assume each of the n original random variables comes from the same "family," for example, they are all normal or all Poisson. Hence, the combined random variable X is also part of the same family: the sum of two normally random variables is normally distributed; the sum of two Poisson random variables is Poisson; and so forth. So we need a mean to describe X and maybe a standard deviation. The mean of X is easy to evaluate:

$$\mu = \mu_1 + \mu_2 + \cdots + \mu_n$$

In other words, the mean of X is just the sum of the means of the n individual random variables.

If we need a standard deviation for X and the n random variables are independent, then the standard deviation of X is

$$\sigma = \sqrt{\sigma_1^2 + \sigma_2^2 + \cdots + \sigma_n^2}$$

In words, the standard deviation of X is the square root of the sum of the variances of the n random variables. If the n random variables have the same standard deviation (i.e., $\sigma_1 = \sigma_2 = \ldots = \sigma_n$), then the above simplifies to $\sigma = \sqrt{n} \times \sigma_1$.

The key condition in our evaluation of the standard deviation of X is that the n individual random variables are independent. Roughly speaking, two random variables are *independent* if the outcome of one random variable has no influence on the outcome of the other random variable. For example, if one has a rather high demand outcome, then that provides no information as to whether the other random variable will have a high or low outcome.

Two random variables are *correlated* if the outcome of one random variable provides information about the outcome of the other random variable. Two random variables are *positively correlated* if their outcomes tend to move in lock step: if one is high, then the other tends to be high, and if one is low, the other tends to be low. Two random variables are *negatively correlated* if their outcomes tend to move in opposite step: if one is high, then the other tends to be low, and if one is low, the other tends to be high.

The correlation between two random variables can range from -1 to 1. A correlation of -1 means the two are perfectly negatively correlated: as one random variable's outcome increases, the other one's outcome surely decreases. The other extreme is perfectly positively correlated, which means a correlation of 1: as one random variable's outcome increases, the other one's outcome surely increases as well. In the middle is independence: if two random variables are independent, then their correlation is 0.

So how do we evaluate the standard deviation of X when X is the sum of two random variables that may not be independent? Use the following equation:

$$\text{Standard deviation of } X = \sigma = \sqrt{\sigma_1^2 + \sigma_2^2 + 2 \times \sigma_1 \times \sigma_2 \times \text{Correlation}}$$

where *Correlation* in the above equation is the correlation between X_1 and X_2.

Appendix B

Tables

This appendix contains the Erlang Loss Function Table and the distribution and loss function tables for the standard normal distribution and several Poisson distributions.

Erlang Loss Function Table

The Erlang Loss Function Table contains the probability that a process step consisting of m parallel resources contains m flow units, that is, all m resources are utilized. Interarrival times of flow units (e.g., customers or data packets, etc.) are exponentially distributed with mean a and service times have a mean p (service times do not have to follow an exponential distribution).

Because there is no buffer space, if a flow unit arrives and all m servers are busy, then that arriving flow unit leaves the system unserved (i.e., the flow unit is lost). The columns in the table correspond to the number of resources m and the rows in the table correspond to $r = p/a$; that is, the ratio between the service time and the interarrival time. The following two pages include two tables, one for small values of r and one for larger values of r.

Example: Find the probability $P_m(r)$ that a process step consisting of three parallel resources must deny access to newly arriving units. Flow units arrive one every $a = 3$ minutes with exponential interarrival times and take $p = 2$ minutes to serve. First, define $r = p/a = 2/3 = 0.67$ and find the corresponding row heading. Second, find the column heading for $m = 3$. The intersection of that row with that column is $P_m(r) = 0.0255$.

Note that $P_m(r)$ can be computed directly based on the following formula

$$\text{Probability\{all } m \text{ servers busy\}} = P_m(r)$$

$$= \frac{\dfrac{r^m}{m!}}{1 + \dfrac{r^1}{1!} + \dfrac{r^2}{2!} + \cdots + \dfrac{r^m}{m!}} \quad \text{(Erlang loss formula)}$$

The exclamation mark (!) in the equation refers to the factorial of an integer number. To compute the factorial of an integer number x, write down all numbers from 1 to x and then multiply them with each other. For example, $4! = 1 \times 2 \times 3 \times 4 = 24$. This calculation can be done with the Excel function FACT(x).

Erlang Loss Table

$r = p/a$	1	2	3	4	5	6	7	8	9	10
0.10	0.0909	0.0045	0.0002	0.0000	0.0000	0.0000	0.0000	0.0000	0.0000	0.0000
0.20	0.1667	0.0164	0.0011	0.0001	0.0000	0.0000	0.0000	0.0000	0.0000	0.0000
0.25	0.2000	0.0244	0.0020	0.0001	0.0000	0.0000	0.0000	0.0000	0.0000	0.0000
0.30	0.2308	0.0335	0.0033	0.0003	0.0000	0.0000	0.0000	0.0000	0.0000	0.0000
0.33	0.2500	0.0400	0.0044	0.0004	0.0000	0.0000	0.0000	0.0000	0.0000	0.0000
0.40	0.2857	0.0541	0.0072	0.0007	0.0001	0.0000	0.0000	0.0000	0.0000	0.0000
0.50	0.3333	0.0769	0.0127	0.0016	0.0002	0.0000	0.0000	0.0000	0.0000	0.0000
0.60	0.3750	0.1011	0.0198	0.0030	0.0004	0.0000	0.0000	0.0000	0.0000	0.0000
0.67	0.4000	0.1176	0.0255	0.0042	0.0006	0.0001	0.0000	0.0000	0.0000	0.0000
0.70	0.4118	0.1260	0.0286	0.0050	0.0007	0.0001	0.0000	0.0000	0.0000	0.0000
0.75	0.4286	0.1385	0.0335	0.0062	0.0009	0.0001	0.0000	0.0000	0.0000	0.0000
0.80	0.4444	0.1509	0.0387	0.0077	0.0012	0.0002	0.0000	0.0000	0.0000	0.0000
0.90	0.4737	0.1757	0.0501	0.0111	0.0020	0.0003	0.0000	0.0000	0.0000	0.0000
1.00	0.5000	0.2000	0.0625	0.0154	0.0031	0.0005	0.0001	0.0000	0.0000	0.0000
1.10	0.5238	0.2237	0.0758	0.0204	0.0045	0.0008	0.0001	0.0000	0.0000	0.0000
1.20	0.5455	0.2466	0.0898	0.0262	0.0063	0.0012	0.0002	0.0000	0.0000	0.0000
1.25	0.5556	0.2577	0.0970	0.0294	0.0073	0.0015	0.0003	0.0000	0.0000	0.0000
1.30	0.5652	0.2687	0.1043	0.0328	0.0085	0.0018	0.0003	0.0001	0.0000	0.0000
1.33	0.5714	0.2759	0.1092	0.0351	0.0093	0.0021	0.0004	0.0001	0.0000	0.0000
1.40	0.5833	0.2899	0.1192	0.0400	0.0111	0.0026	0.0005	0.0001	0.0000	0.0000
1.50	0.6000	0.3103	0.1343	0.0480	0.0142	0.0035	0.0008	0.0001	0.0000	0.0000
1.60	0.6154	0.3299	0.1496	0.0565	0.0177	0.0047	0.0011	0.0002	0.0000	0.0000
1.67	0.6250	0.3425	0.1598	0.0624	0.0204	0.0056	0.0013	0.0003	0.0001	0.0000
1.70	0.6296	0.3486	0.1650	0.0655	0.0218	0.0061	0.0015	0.0003	0.0001	0.0000
1.75	0.6364	0.3577	0.1726	0.0702	0.0240	0.0069	0.0017	0.0004	0.0001	0.0000
1.80	0.6429	0.3665	0.1803	0.0750	0.0263	0.0078	0.0020	0.0005	0.0001	0.0000
1.90	0.6552	0.3836	0.1955	0.0850	0.0313	0.0098	0.0027	0.0006	0.0001	0.0000
2.00	0.6667	0.4000	0.2105	0.0952	0.0367	0.0121	0.0034	0.0009	0.0002	0.0000
2.10	0.6774	0.4156	0.2254	0.1058	0.0425	0.0147	0.0044	0.0011	0.0003	0.0001
2.20	0.6875	0.4306	0.2400	0.1166	0.0488	0.0176	0.0055	0.0015	0.0004	0.0001
2.25	0.6923	0.4378	0.2472	0.1221	0.0521	0.0192	0.0061	0.0017	0.0004	0.0001
2.30	0.6970	0.4449	0.2543	0.1276	0.0554	0.0208	0.0068	0.0019	0.0005	0.0001
2.33	0.7000	0.4495	0.2591	0.1313	0.0577	0.0220	0.0073	0.0021	0.0005	0.0001
2.40	0.7059	0.4586	0.2684	0.1387	0.0624	0.0244	0.0083	0.0025	0.0007	0.0002
2.50	0.7143	0.4717	0.2822	0.1499	0.0697	0.0282	0.0100	0.0031	0.0009	0.0002
2.60	0.7222	0.4842	0.2956	0.1612	0.0773	0.0324	0.0119	0.0039	0.0011	0.0003
2.67	0.7273	0.4923	0.3044	0.1687	0.0825	0.0354	0.0133	0.0044	0.0013	0.0003
2.70	0.7297	0.4963	0.3087	0.1725	0.0852	0.0369	0.0140	0.0047	0.0014	0.0004
2.75	0.7333	0.5021	0.3152	0.1781	0.0892	0.0393	0.0152	0.0052	0.0016	0.0004
2.80	0.7368	0.5078	0.3215	0.1837	0.0933	0.0417	0.0164	0.0057	0.0018	0.0005
2.90	0.7436	0.5188	0.3340	0.1949	0.1016	0.0468	0.0190	0.0068	0.0022	0.0006
3.00	0.7500	0.5294	0.3462	0.2061	0.1101	0.0522	0.0219	0.0081	0.0027	0.0008
3.10	0.7561	0.5396	0.3580	0.2172	0.1187	0.0578	0.0249	0.0096	0.0033	0.0010
3.20	0.7619	0.5494	0.3695	0.2281	0.1274	0.0636	0.0283	0.0112	0.0040	0.0013
3.25	0.7647	0.5541	0.3751	0.2336	0.1318	0.0666	0.0300	0.0120	0.0043	0.0014
3.30	0.7674	0.5587	0.3807	0.2390	0.1362	0.0697	0.0318	0.0130	0.0047	0.0016
3.33	0.7692	0.5618	0.3843	0.2426	0.1392	0.0718	0.0331	0.0136	0.0050	0.0017
3.40	0.7727	0.5678	0.3915	0.2497	0.1452	0.0760	0.0356	0.0149	0.0056	0.0019
3.50	0.7778	0.5765	0.4021	0.2603	0.1541	0.0825	0.0396	0.0170	0.0066	0.0023
3.60	0.7826	0.5848	0.4124	0.2707	0.1631	0.0891	0.0438	0.0193	0.0077	0.0028
3.67	0.7857	0.5902	0.4191	0.2775	0.1691	0.0937	0.0468	0.0210	0.0085	0.0031
3.70	0.7872	0.5929	0.4224	0.2809	0.1721	0.0960	0.0483	0.0218	0.0089	0.0033
3.75	0.7895	0.5968	0.4273	0.2860	0.1766	0.0994	0.0506	0.0232	0.0096	0.0036
3.80	0.7917	0.6007	0.4321	0.2910	0.1811	0.1029	0.0529	0.0245	0.0102	0.0039
3.90	0.7959	0.6082	0.4415	0.3009	0.1901	0.1100	0.0577	0.0274	0.0117	0.0046
4.00	0.8000	0.6154	0.4507	0.3107	0.1991	0.1172	0.0627	0.0304	0.0133	0.0053

Erlang Loss Table

					m					
$r = p / a$	1	2	3	4	5	6	7	8	9	10
1.0	0.5000	0.2000	0.0625	0.0154	0.0031	0.0005	0.0001	0.0000	0.0000	0.0000
1.5	0.6000	0.3103	0.1343	0.0480	0.0142	0.0035	0.0008	0.0001	0.0000	0.0000
2.0	0.6667	0.4000	0.2105	0.0952	0.0367	0.0121	0.0034	0.0009	0.0002	0.0000
2.5	0.7143	0.4717	0.2822	0.1499	0.0697	0.0282	0.0100	0.0031	0.0009	0.0002
3.0	0.7500	0.5294	0.3462	0.2061	0.1101	0.0522	0.0219	0.0081	0.0027	0.0008
3.5	0.7778	0.5765	0.4021	0.2603	0.1541	0.0825	0.0396	0.0170	0.0066	0.0023
4.0	0.8000	0.6154	0.4507	0.3107	0.1991	0.1172	0.0627	0.0304	0.0133	0.0053
4.5	0.8182	0.6480	0.4929	0.3567	0.2430	0.1542	0.0902	0.0483	0.0236	0.0105
5.0	0.8333	0.6757	0.5297	0.3983	0.2849	0.1918	0.1205	0.0700	0.0375	0.0184
5.5	0.8462	0.6994	0.5618	0.4358	0.3241	0.2290	0.1525	0.0949	0.0548	0.0293
6.0	0.8571	0.7200	0.5902	0.4696	0.3604	0.2649	0.1851	0.1219	0.0751	0.0431
6.5	0.8667	0.7380	0.6152	0.4999	0.3939	0.2991	0.2174	0.1501	0.0978	0.0598
7.0	0.8750	0.7538	0.6375	0.5273	0.4247	0.3313	0.2489	0.1788	0.1221	0.0787
7.5	0.8824	0.7679	0.6575	0.5521	0.4530	0.3615	0.2792	0.2075	0.1474	0.0995
8.0	0.8889	0.7805	0.6755	0.5746	0.4790	0.3898	0.3082	0.2356	0.1731	0.1217
8.5	0.8947	0.7918	0.6917	0.5951	0.5029	0.4160	0.3356	0.2629	0.1989	0.1446
9.0	0.9000	0.8020	0.7064	0.6138	0.5249	0.4405	0.3616	0.2892	0.2243	0.1680
9.5	0.9048	0.8112	0.7198	0.6309	0.5452	0.4633	0.3860	0.3143	0.2491	0.1914
10.0	0.9091	0.8197	0.7321	0.6467	0.5640	0.4845	0.4090	0.3383	0.2732	0.2146
10.5	0.9130	0.8274	0.7433	0.6612	0.5813	0.5043	0.4307	0.3611	0.2964	0.2374
11.0	0.9167	0.8345	0.7537	0.6745	0.5974	0.5227	0.4510	0.3828	0.3187	0.2596
11.5	0.9200	0.8410	0.7633	0.6869	0.6124	0.5400	0.4701	0.4033	0.3400	0.2811
12.0	0.9231	0.8471	0.7721	0.6985	0.6264	0.5561	0.4880	0.4227	0.3604	0.3019
12.5	0.9259	0.8527	0.7804	0.7092	0.6394	0.5712	0.5049	0.4410	0.3799	0.3220
13.0	0.9286	0.8579	0.7880	0.7192	0.6516	0.5854	0.5209	0.4584	0.3984	0.3412
13.5	0.9310	0.8627	0.7952	0.7285	0.6630	0.5987	0.5359	0.4749	0.4160	0.3596
14.0	0.9333	0.8673	0.8019	0.7373	0.6737	0.6112	0.5500	0.4905	0.4328	0.3773
14.5	0.9355	0.8715	0.8081	0.7455	0.6837	0.6230	0.5634	0.5052	0.4487	0.3942
15.0	0.9375	0.8755	0.8140	0.7532	0.6932	0.6341	0.5761	0.5193	0.4639	0.4103
15.5	0.9394	0.8792	0.8196	0.7605	0.7022	0.6446	0.5880	0.5326	0.4784	0.4258
16.0	0.9412	0.8828	0.8248	0.7674	0.7106	0.6546	0.5994	0.5452	0.4922	0.4406
16.5	0.9429	0.8861	0.8297	0.7739	0.7186	0.6640	0.6102	0.5572	0.5053	0.4547
17.0	0.9444	0.8892	0.8344	0.7800	0.7262	0.6729	0.6204	0.5687	0.5179	0.4682
17.5	0.9459	0.8922	0.8388	0.7859	0.7334	0.6814	0.6301	0.5795	0.5298	0.4811
18.0	0.9474	0.8950	0.8430	0.7914	0.7402	0.6895	0.6394	0.5899	0.5413	0.4935
18.5	0.9487	0.8977	0.8470	0.7966	0.7467	0.6972	0.6482	0.5998	0.5522	0.5053
19.0	0.9500	0.9002	0.8508	0.8016	0.7529	0.7045	0.6566	0.6093	0.5626	0.5167
19.5	0.9512	0.9027	0.8544	0.8064	0.7587	0.7115	0.6647	0.6183	0.5726	0.5275
20.0	0.9524	0.9050	0.8578	0.8109	0.7644	0.7181	0.6723	0.6270	0.5822	0.5380
20.5	0.9535	0.9072	0.8611	0.8153	0.7697	0.7245	0.6797	0.6353	0.5913	0.5480
21.0	0.9545	0.9093	0.8642	0.8194	0.7749	0.7306	0.6867	0.6432	0.6001	0.5576
21.5	0.9556	0.9113	0.8672	0.8234	0.7798	0.7364	0.6934	0.6508	0.6086	0.5668
22.0	0.9565	0.9132	0.8701	0.8272	0.7845	0.7420	0.6999	0.6581	0.6167	0.5757
22.5	0.9574	0.9150	0.8728	0.8308	0.7890	0.7474	0.7061	0.6651	0.6244	0.5842
23.0	0.9583	0.9168	0.8754	0.8343	0.7933	0.7525	0.7120	0.6718	0.6319	0.5924
23.5	0.9592	0.9185	0.8780	0.8376	0.7974	0.7575	0.7177	0.6783	0.6391	0.6003
24.0	0.9600	0.9201	0.8804	0.8408	0.8014	0.7622	0.7232	0.6845	0.6461	0.6079
24.5	0.9608	0.9217	0.8827	0.8439	0.8053	0.7668	0.7285	0.6905	0.6527	0.6153
25.0	0.9615	0.9232	0.8850	0.8469	0.8090	0.7712	0.7336	0.6963	0.6592	0.6224
25.5	0.9623	0.9246	0.8871	0.8497	0.8125	0.7754	0.7385	0.7019	0.6654	0.6292
26.0	0.9630	0.9260	0.8892	0.8525	0.8159	0.7795	0.7433	0.7072	0.6714	0.6358
26.5	0.9636	0.9274	0.8912	0.8552	0.8192	0.7835	0.7479	0.7124	0.6772	0.6422
27.0	0.9643	0.9287	0.8931	0.8577	0.8224	0.7873	0.7523	0.7174	0.6828	0.6483
27.5	0.9649	0.9299	0.8950	0.8602	0.8255	0.7910	0.7565	0.7223	0.6882	0.6543
28.0	0.9655	0.9311	0.8968	0.8626	0.8285	0.7945	0.7607	0.7269	0.6934	0.6600
28.5	0.9661	0.9323	0.8985	0.8649	0.8314	0.7979	0.7646	0.7315	0.6985	0.6656
29.0	0.9667	0.9334	0.9002	0.8671	0.8341	0.8013	0.7685	0.7359	0.7034	0.6710
29.5	0.9672	0.9345	0.9019	0.8693	0.8368	0.8045	0.7722	0.7401	0.7081	0.6763
30.0	0.9677	0.9356	0.9034	0.8714	0.8394	0.8076	0.7758	0.7442	0.7127	0.6813
30.5	0.9683	0.9366	0.9050	0.8734	0.8420	0.8106	0.7793	0.7482	0.7172	0.6863
31.0	0.9688	0.9376	0.9064	0.8754	0.8444	0.8135	0.7827	0.7521	0.7215	0.6910
31.5	0.9692	0.9385	0.9079	0.8773	0.8468	0.8164	0.7860	0.7558	0.7257	0.6957
32.0	0.9697	0.9394	0.9093	0.8791	0.8491	0.8191	0.7892	0.7594	0.7297	0.7002

Distribution and Loss Function Tables

The Standard Normal Distribution Function Table contains the probability that the outcome of a standard normal random variable is z or smaller. The table provides z values up to two significant digits. Find the row and column headings that add up to the z value you are looking for. The intersection of that row and column contains the probability you seek, $\Phi(z)$.

Example (1): Find the probability that a standard normal random variable generates an outcome that is $z = -1.54$ or lower. First, find the row heading -1.5. Second, find the column heading -0.04 because $(-1.5) + (-0.04) = -1.54$. The intersection of that row with that column is $\Phi(-1.54) = 0.0618$.

Example (2): Find the probability that a standard normal random variable generates an outcome that is $z = 0.52$ or lower. First, find the row heading 0.5. Second, find the column heading 0.02 because $(0.5) + (0.02) = 0.52$. The intersection of that row with that column is $\Phi(0.52) = 0.6985$.

The Standard Normal Loss Function Table is organized in the same way as the Standard Normal Distribution Function Table.

The Poisson Distribution Function Table provides the probability a Poisson distribution with a given mean (column heading) is S or fewer.

The Poisson Loss Function Table provides the expected amount the outcome of a Poisson distribution with a given mean (column heading) exceeds S.

Example (3): With mean 2.25 and $S = 2$, the loss function of a Poisson distribution is 0.69795: look in the column heading for the mean 2.25 and the row with $S = 2$.

Standard Normal Distribution Function Table, $\Phi(z)$

z	−0.09	−0.08	−0.07	−0.06	−0.05	−0.04	−0.03	−0.02	−0.01	0.00
−4.0	0.0000	0.0000	0.0000	0.0000	0.0000	0.0000	0.0000	0.0000	0.0000	0.0000
−3.9	0.0000	0.0000	0.0000	0.0000	0.0000	0.0000	0.0000	0.0000	0.0000	0.0000
−3.8	0.0001	0.0001	0.0001	0.0001	0.0001	0.0001	0.0001	0.0001	0.0001	0.0001
−3.7	0.0001	0.0001	0.0001	0.0001	0.0001	0.0001	0.0001	0.0001	0.0002	0.0002
−3.6	0.0001	0.0001	0.0001	0.0001	0.0001	0.0001	0.0001	0.0002	0.0002	0.0002
−3.5	0.0002	0.0002	0.0002	0.0002	0.0002	0.0002	0.0002	0.0002	0.0002	0.0002
−3.4	0.0002	0.0003	0.0003	0.0003	0.0003	0.0003	0.0003	0.0003	0.0003	0.0003
−3.3	0.0003	0.0004	0.0004	0.0004	0.0004	0.0004	0.0004	0.0005	0.0005	0.0005
−3.2	0.0005	0.0005	0.0005	0.0006	0.0006	0.0006	0.0006	0.0006	0.0007	0.0007
−3.1	0.0007	0.0007	0.0008	0.0008	0.0008	0.0008	0.0009	0.0009	0.0009	0.0010
−3.0	0.0010	0.0010	0.0011	0.0011	0.0011	0.0012	0.0012	0.0013	0.0013	0.0013
−2.9	0.0014	0.0014	0.0015	0.0015	0.0016	0.0016	0.0017	0.0018	0.0018	0.0019
−2.8	0.0019	0.0020	0.0021	0.0021	0.0022	0.0023	0.0023	0.0024	0.0025	0.0026
−2.7	0.0026	0.0027	0.0028	0.0029	0.0030	0.0031	0.0032	0.0033	0.0034	0.0035
−2.6	0.0036	0.0037	0.0038	0.0039	0.0040	0.0041	0.0043	0.0044	0.0045	0.0047
−2.5	0.0048	0.0049	0.0051	0.0052	0.0054	0.0055	0.0057	0.0059	0.0060	0.0062
−2.4	0.0064	0.0066	0.0068	0.0069	0.0071	0.0073	0.0075	0.0078	0.0080	0.0082
−2.3	0.0084	0.0087	0.0089	0.0091	0.0094	0.0096	0.0099	0.0102	0.0104	0.0107
−2.2	0.0110	0.0113	0.0116	0.0119	0.0122	0.0125	0.0129	0.0132	0.0136	0.0139
−2.1	0.0143	0.0146	0.0150	0.0154	0.0158	0.0162	0.0166	0.0170	0.0174	0.0179
−2.0	0.0183	0.0188	0.0192	0.0197	0.0202	0.0207	0.0212	0.0217	0.0222	0.0228
−1.9	0.0233	0.0239	0.0244	0.0250	0.0256	0.0262	0.0268	0.0274	0.0281	0.0287
−1.8	0.0294	0.0301	0.0307	0.0314	0.0322	0.0329	0.0336	0.0344	0.0351	0.0359
−1.7	0.0367	0.0375	0.0384	0.0392	0.0401	0.0409	0.0418	0.0427	0.0436	0.0446
−1.6	0.0455	0.0465	0.0475	0.0485	0.0495	0.0505	0.0516	0.0526	0.0537	0.0548
−1.5	0.0559	0.0571	0.0582	0.0594	0.0606	0.0618	0.0630	0.0643	0.0655	0.0668
−1.4	0.0681	0.0694	0.0708	0.0721	0.0735	0.0749	0.0764	0.0778	0.0793	0.0808
−1.3	0.0823	0.0838	0.0853	0.0869	0.0885	0.0901	0.0918	0.0934	0.0951	0.0968
−1.2	0.0985	0.1003	0.1020	0.1038	0.1056	0.1075	0.1093	0.1112	0.1131	0.1151
−1.1	0.1170	0.1190	0.1210	0.1230	0.1251	0.1271	0.1292	0.1314	0.1335	0.1357
−1.0	0.1379	0.1401	0.1423	0.1446	0.1469	0.1492	0.1515	0.1539	0.1562	0.1587
−0.9	0.1611	0.1635	0.1660	0.1685	0.1711	0.1736	0.1762	0.1788	0.1814	0.1841
−0.8	0.1867	0.1894	0.1922	0.1949	0.1977	0.2005	0.2033	0.2061	0.2090	0.2119
−0.7	0.2148	0.2177	0.2206	0.2236	0.2266	0.2296	0.2327	0.2358	0.2389	0.2420
−0.6	0.2451	0.2483	0.2514	0.2546	0.2578	0.2611	0.2643	0.2676	0.2709	0.2743
−0.5	0.2776	0.2810	0.2843	0.2877	0.2912	0.2946	0.2981	0.3015	0.3050	0.3085
−0.4	0.3121	0.3156	0.3192	0.3228	0.3264	0.3300	0.3336	0.3372	0.3409	0.3446
−0.3	0.3483	0.3520	0.3557	0.3594	0.3632	0.3669	0.3707	0.3745	0.3783	0.3821
−0.2	0.3859	0.3897	0.3936	0.3974	0.4013	0.4052	0.4090	0.4129	0.4168	0.4207
−0.1	0.4247	0.4286	0.4325	0.4364	0.4404	0.4443	0.4483	0.4522	0.4562	0.4602
0.0	0.4641	0.4681	0.4721	0.4761	0.4801	0.4840	0.4880	0.4920	0.4960	0.5000

(continued)

Standard Normal Distribution Function Table, $\Phi(z)$ (Concluded)

z	0.00	0.01	0.02	0.03	0.04	0.05	0.06	0.07	0.08	0.09
0.0	0.5000	0.5040	0.5080	0.5120	0.5160	0.5199	0.5239	0.5279	0.5319	0.5359
0.1	0.5398	0.5438	0.5478	0.5517	0.5557	0.5596	0.5636	0.5675	0.5714	0.5753
0.2	0.5793	0.5832	0.5871	0.5910	0.5948	0.5987	0.6026	0.6064	0.6103	0.6141
0.3	0.6179	0.6217	0.6255	0.6293	0.6331	0.6368	0.6406	0.6443	0.6480	0.6517
0.4	0.6554	0.6591	0.6628	0.6664	0.6700	0.6736	0.6772	0.6808	0.6844	0.6879
0.5	0.6915	0.6950	0.6985	0.7019	0.7054	0.7088	0.7123	0.7157	0.7190	0.7224
0.6	0.7257	0.7291	0.7324	0.7357	0.7389	0.7422	0.7454	0.7486	0.7517	0.7549
0.7	0.7580	0.7611	0.7642	0.7673	0.7704	0.7734	0.7764	0.7794	0.7823	0.7852
0.8	0.7881	0.7910	0.7939	0.7967	0.7995	0.8023	0.8051	0.8078	0.8106	0.8133
0.9	0.8159	0.8186	0.8212	0.8238	0.8264	0.8289	0.8315	0.8340	0.8365	0.8389
1.0	0.8413	0.8438	0.8461	0.8485	0.8508	0.8531	0.8554	0.8577	0.8599	0.8621
1.1	0.8643	0.8665	0.8686	0.8708	0.8729	0.8749	0.8770	0.8790	0.8810	0.8830
1.2	0.8849	0.8869	0.8888	0.8907	0.8925	0.8944	0.8962	0.8980	0.8997	0.9015
1.3	0.9032	0.9049	0.9066	0.9082	0.9099	0.9115	0.9131	0.9147	0.9162	0.9177
1.4	0.9192	0.9207	0.9222	0.9236	0.9251	0.9265	0.9279	0.9292	0.9306	0.9319
1.5	0.9332	0.9345	0.9357	0.9370	0.9382	0.9394	0.9406	0.9418	0.9429	0.9441
1.6	0.9452	0.9463	0.9474	0.9484	0.9495	0.9505	0.9515	0.9525	0.9535	0.9545
1.7	0.9554	0.9564	0.9573	0.9582	0.9591	0.9599	0.9608	0.9616	0.9625	0.9633
1.8	0.9641	0.9649	0.9656	0.9664	0.9671	0.9678	0.9686	0.9693	0.9699	0.9706
1.9	0.9713	0.9719	0.9726	0.9732	0.9738	0.9744	0.9750	0.9756	0.9761	0.9767
2.0	0.9772	0.9778	0.9783	0.9788	0.9793	0.9798	0.9803	0.9808	0.9812	0.9817
2.1	0.9821	0.9826	0.9830	0.9834	0.9838	0.9842	0.9846	0.9850	0.9854	0.9857
2.2	0.9861	0.9864	0.9868	0.9871	0.9875	0.9878	0.9881	0.9884	0.9887	0.9890
2.3	0.9893	0.9896	0.9898	0.9901	0.9904	0.9906	0.9909	0.9911	0.9913	0.9916
2.4	0.9918	0.9920	0.9922	0.9925	0.9927	0.9929	0.9931	0.9932	0.9934	0.9936
2.5	0.9938	0.9940	0.9941	0.9943	0.9945	0.9946	0.9948	0.9949	0.9951	0.9952
2.6	0.9953	0.9955	0.9956	0.9957	0.9959	0.9960	0.9961	0.9962	0.9963	0.9964
2.7	0.9965	0.9966	0.9967	0.9968	0.9969	0.9970	0.9971	0.9972	0.9973	0.9974
2.8	0.9974	0.9975	0.9976	0.9977	0.9977	0.9978	0.9979	0.9979	0.9980	0.9981
2.9	0.9981	0.9982	0.9982	0.9983	0.9984	0.9984	0.9985	0.9985	0.9986	0.9986
3.0	0.9987	0.9987	0.9987	0.9988	0.9988	0.9989	0.9989	0.9989	0.9990	0.9990
3.1	0.9990	0.9991	0.9991	0.9991	0.9992	0.9992	0.9992	0.9992	0.9993	0.9993
3.2	0.9993	0.9993	0.9994	0.9994	0.9994	0.9994	0.9994	0.9995	0.9995	0.9995
3.3	0.9995	0.9995	0.9995	0.9996	0.9996	0.9996	0.9996	0.9996	0.9996	0.9997
3.4	0.9997	0.9997	0.9997	0.9997	0.9997	0.9997	0.9997	0.9997	0.9997	0.9998
3.5	0.9998	0.9998	0.9998	0.9998	0.9998	0.9998	0.9998	0.9998	0.9998	0.9998
3.6	0.9998	0.9998	0.9999	0.9999	0.9999	0.9999	0.9999	0.9999	0.9999	0.9999
3.7	0.9999	0.9999	0.9999	0.9999	0.9999	0.9999	0.9999	0.9999	0.9999	0.9999
3.8	0.9999	0.9999	0.9999	0.9999	0.9999	0.9999	0.9999	0.9999	0.9999	0.9999
3.9	1.0000	1.0000	1.0000	1.0000	1.0000	1.0000	1.0000	1.0000	1.0000	1.0000
4.0	1.0000	1.0000	1.0000	1.0000	1.0000	1.0000	1.0000	1.0000	1.0000	1.0000

Standard Normal Loss Function Table, $L(z)$

z	−0.09	−0.08	−0.07	−0.06	−0.05	−0.04	−0.03	−0.02	−0.01	0.00
−4.0	4.0900	4.0800	4.0700	4.0600	4.0500	4.0400	4.0300	4.0200	4.0100	4.0000
−3.9	3.9900	3.9800	3.9700	3.9600	3.9500	3.9400	3.9300	3.9200	3.9100	3.9000
−3.8	3.8900	3.8800	3.8700	3.8600	3.8500	3.8400	3.8300	3.8200	3.8100	3.8000
−3.7	3.7900	3.7800	3.7700	3.7600	3.7500	3.7400	3.7300	3.7200	3.7100	3.7000
−3.6	3.6900	3.6800	3.6700	3.6600	3.6500	3.6400	3.6300	3.6200	3.6100	3.6000
−3.5	3.5900	3.5800	3.5700	3.5600	3.5500	3.5400	3.5301	3.5201	3.5101	3.5001
−3.4	3.4901	3.4801	3.4701	3.4601	3.4501	3.4401	3.4301	3.4201	3.4101	3.4001
−3.3	3.3901	3.3801	3.3701	3.3601	3.3501	3.3401	3.3301	3.3201	3.3101	3.3001
−3.2	3.2901	3.2801	3.2701	3.2601	3.2502	3.2402	3.2302	3.2202	3.2102	3.2002
−3.1	3.1902	3.1802	3.1702	3.1602	3.1502	3.1402	3.1302	3.1202	3.1103	3.1003
−3.0	3.0903	3.0803	3.0703	3.0603	3.0503	3.0403	3.0303	3.0204	3.0104	3.0004
−2.9	2.9904	2.9804	2.9704	2.9604	2.9505	2.9405	2.9305	2.9205	2.9105	2.9005
−2.8	2.8906	2.8806	2.8706	2.8606	2.8506	2.8407	2.8307	2.8207	2.8107	2.8008
−2.7	2.7908	2.7808	2.7708	2.7609	2.7509	2.7409	2.7310	2.7210	2.7110	2.7011
−2.6	2.6911	2.6811	2.6712	2.6612	2.6512	2.6413	2.6313	2.6214	2.6114	2.6015
−2.5	2.5915	2.5816	2.5716	2.5617	2.5517	2.5418	2.5318	2.5219	2.5119	2.5020
−2.4	2.4921	2.4821	2.4722	2.4623	2.4523	2.4424	2.4325	2.4226	2.4126	2.4027
−2.3	2.3928	2.3829	2.3730	2.3631	2.3532	2.3433	2.3334	2.3235	2.3136	2.3037
−2.2	2.2938	2.2839	2.2740	2.2641	2.2542	2.2444	2.2345	2.2246	2.2147	2.2049
−2.1	2.1950	2.1852	2.1753	2.1655	2.1556	2.1458	2.1360	2.1261	2.1163	2.1065
−2.0	2.0966	2.0868	2.0770	2.0672	2.0574	2.0476	2.0378	2.0280	2.0183	2.0085
−1.9	1.9987	1.9890	1.9792	1.9694	1.9597	1.9500	1.9402	1.9305	1.9208	1.9111
−1.8	1.9013	1.8916	1.8819	1.8723	1.8626	1.8529	1.8432	1.8336	1.8239	1.8143
−1.7	1.8046	1.7950	1.7854	1.7758	1.7662	1.7566	1.7470	1.7374	1.7278	1.7183
−1.6	1.7087	1.6992	1.6897	1.6801	1.6706	1.6611	1.6516	1.6422	1.6327	1.6232
−1.5	1.6138	1.6044	1.5949	1.5855	1.5761	1.5667	1.5574	1.5480	1.5386	1.5293
−1.4	1.5200	1.5107	1.5014	1.4921	1.4828	1.4736	1.4643	1.4551	1.4459	1.4367
−1.3	1.4275	1.4183	1.4092	1.4000	1.3909	1.3818	1.3727	1.3636	1.3546	1.3455
−1.2	1.3365	1.3275	1.3185	1.3095	1.3006	1.2917	1.2827	1.2738	1.2650	1.2561
−1.1	1.2473	1.2384	1.2296	1.2209	1.2121	1.2034	1.1946	1.1859	1.1773	1.1686
−1.0	1.1600	1.1514	1.1428	1.1342	1.1257	1.1172	1.1087	1.1002	1.0917	1.0833
−0.9	1.0749	1.0665	1.0582	1.0499	1.0416	1.0333	1.0250	1.0168	1.0086	1.0004
−0.8	0.9923	0.9842	0.9761	0.9680	0.9600	0.9520	0.9440	0.9360	0.9281	0.9202
−0.7	0.9123	0.9045	0.8967	0.8889	0.8812	0.8734	0.8658	0.8581	0.8505	0.8429
−0.6	0.8353	0.8278	0.8203	0.8128	0.8054	0.7980	0.7906	0.7833	0.7759	0.7687
−0.5	0.7614	0.7542	0.7471	0.7399	0.7328	0.7257	0.7187	0.7117	0.7047	0.6978
−0.4	0.6909	0.6840	0.6772	0.6704	0.6637	0.6569	0.6503	0.6436	0.6370	0.6304
−0.3	0.6239	0.6174	0.6109	0.6045	0.5981	0.5918	0.5855	0.5792	0.5730	0.5668
−0.2	0.5606	0.5545	0.5484	0.5424	0.5363	0.5304	0.5244	0.5186	0.5127	0.5069
−0.1	0.5011	0.4954	0.4897	0.4840	0.4784	0.4728	0.4673	0.4618	0.4564	0.4509
0.0	0.4456	0.4402	0.4349	0.4297	0.4244	0.4193	0.4141	0.4090	0.4040	0.3989

(*continued*)

Standard Normal Loss Function Table, $L(z)$ (Concluded)

z	0.00	0.01	0.02	0.03	0.04	0.05	0.06	0.07	0.08	0.09
0.0	0.3989	0.3940	0.3890	0.3841	0.3793	0.3744	0.3697	0.3649	0.3602	0.3556
0.1	0.3509	0.3464	0.3418	0.3373	0.3328	0.3284	0.3240	0.3197	0.3154	0.3111
0.2	0.3069	0.3027	0.2986	0.2944	0.2904	0.2863	0.2824	0.2784	0.2745	0.2706
0.3	0.2668	0.2630	0.2592	0.2555	0.2518	0.2481	0.2445	0.2409	0.2374	0.2339
0.4	0.2304	0.2270	0.2236	0.2203	0.2169	0.2137	0.2104	0.2072	0.2040	0.2009
0.5	0.1978	0.1947	0.1917	0.1887	0.1857	0.1828	0.1799	0.1771	0.1742	0.1714
0.6	0.1687	0.1659	0.1633	0.1606	0.1580	0.1554	0.1528	0.1503	0.1478	0.1453
0.7	0.1429	0.1405	0.1381	0.1358	0.1334	0.1312	0.1289	0.1267	0.1245	0.1223
0.8	0.1202	0.1181	0.1160	0.1140	0.1120	0.1100	0.1080	0.1061	0.1042	0.1023
0.9	0.1004	0.0986	0.0968	0.0950	0.0933	0.0916	0.0899	0.0882	0.0865	0.0849
1.0	0.0833	0.0817	0.0802	0.0787	0.0772	0.0757	0.0742	0.0728	0.0714	0.0700
1.1	0.0686	0.0673	0.0659	0.0646	0.0634	0.0621	0.0609	0.0596	0.0584	0.0573
1.2	0.0561	0.0550	0.0538	0.0527	0.0517	0.0506	0.0495	0.0485	0.0475	0.0465
1.3	0.0455	0.0446	0.0436	0.0427	0.0418	0.0409	0.0400	0.0392	0.0383	0.0375
1.4	0.0367	0.0359	0.0351	0.0343	0.0336	0.0328	0.0321	0.0314	0.0307	0.0300
1.5	0.0293	0.0286	0.0280	0.0274	0.0267	0.0261	0.0255	0.0249	0.0244	0.0238
1.6	0.0232	0.0227	0.0222	0.0216	0.0211	0.0206	0.0201	0.0197	0.0192	0.0187
1.7	0.0183	0.0178	0.0174	0.0170	0.0166	0.0162	0.0158	0.0154	0.0150	0.0146
1.8	0.0143	0.0139	0.0136	0.0132	0.0129	0.0126	0.0123	0.0119	0.0116	0.0113
1.9	0.0111	0.0108	0.0105	0.0102	0.0100	0.0097	0.0094	0.0092	0.0090	0.0087
2.0	0.0085	0.0083	0.0080	0.0078	0.0076	0.0074	0.0072	0.0070	0.0068	0.0066
2.1	0.0065	0.0063	0.0061	0.0060	0.0058	0.0056	0.0055	0.0053	0.0052	0.0050
2.2	0.0049	0.0047	0.0046	0.0045	0.0044	0.0042	0.0041	0.0040	0.0039	0.0038
2.3	0.0037	0.0036	0.0035	0.0034	0.0033	0.0032	0.0031	0.0030	0.0029	0.0028
2.4	0.0027	0.0026	0.0026	0.0025	0.0024	0.0023	0.0023	0.0022	0.0021	0.0021
2.5	0.0020	0.0019	0.0019	0.0018	0.0018	0.0017	0.0017	0.0016	0.0016	0.0015
2.6	0.0015	0.0014	0.0014	0.0013	0.0013	0.0012	0.0012	0.0012	0.0011	0.0011
2.7	0.0011	0.0010	0.0010	0.0010	0.0009	0.0009	0.0009	0.0008	0.0008	0.0008
2.8	0.0008	0.0007	0.0007	0.0007	0.0007	0.0006	0.0006	0.0006	0.0006	0.0006
2.9	0.0005	0.0005	0.0005	0.0005	0.0005	0.0005	0.0004	0.0004	0.0004	0.0004
3.0	0.0004	0.0004	0.0004	0.0003	0.0003	0.0003	0.0003	0.0003	0.0003	0.0003
3.1	0.0003	0.0003	0.0002	0.0002	0.0002	0.0002	0.0002	0.0002	0.0002	0.0002
3.2	0.0002	0.0002	0.0002	0.0002	0.0002	0.0002	0.0001	0.0001	0.0001	0.0001
3.3	0.0001	0.0001	0.0001	0.0001	0.0001	0.0001	0.0001	0.0001	0.0001	0.0001
3.4	0.0001	0.0001	0.0001	0.0001	0.0001	0.0001	0.0001	0.0001	0.0001	0.0001
3.5	0.0001	0.0001	0.0001	0.0001	0.0000	0.0000	0.0000	0.0000	0.0000	0.0000
3.6	0.0000	0.0000	0.0000	0.0000	0.0000	0.0000	0.0000	0.0000	0.0000	0.0000
3.7	0.0000	0.0000	0.0000	0.0000	0.0000	0.0000	0.0000	0.0000	0.0000	0.0000
3.8	0.0000	0.0000	0.0000	0.0000	0.0000	0.0000	0.0000	0.0000	0.0000	0.0000
3.9	0.0000	0.0000	0.0000	0.0000	0.0000	0.0000	0.0000	0.0000	0.0000	0.0000
4.0	0.0000	0.0000	0.0000	0.0000	0.0000	0.0000	0.0000	0.0000	0.0000	0.0000

Poisson Distribution Function Table

					Mean					
S	0.05	0.10	0.15	0.20	0.25	0.30	0.35	0.40	0.45	0.50
0	0.95123	0.90484	0.86071	0.81873	0.77880	0.74082	0.70469	0.67032	0.63763	0.60653
1	0.99879	0.99532	0.98981	0.98248	0.97350	0.96306	0.95133	0.93845	0.92456	0.90980
2	0.99998	0.99985	0.99950	0.99885	0.99784	0.99640	0.99449	0.99207	0.98912	0.98561
3	1.00000	1.00000	0.99998	0.99994	0.99987	0.99973	0.99953	0.99922	0.99880	0.99825
4	1.00000	1.00000	1.00000	1.00000	0.99999	0.99998	0.99997	0.99994	0.99989	0.99983
5	1.00000	1.00000	1.00000	1.00000	1.00000	1.00000	1.00000	1.00000	0.99999	0.99999
6	1.00000	1.00000	1.00000	1.00000	1.00000	1.00000	1.00000	1.00000	1.00000	1.00000

					Mean					
S	0.55	0.60	0.65	0.70	0.75	0.80	0.85	0.90	0.95	1.00
0	0.57695	0.54881	0.52205	0.49659	0.47237	0.44933	0.42741	0.40657	0.38674	0.36788
1	0.89427	0.87810	0.86138	0.84420	0.82664	0.80879	0.79072	0.77248	0.75414	0.73576
2	0.98154	0.97688	0.97166	0.96586	0.95949	0.95258	0.94512	0.93714	0.92866	0.91970
3	0.99753	0.99664	0.99555	0.99425	0.99271	0.99092	0.98887	0.98654	0.98393	0.98101
4	0.99973	0.99961	0.99944	0.99921	0.99894	0.99859	0.99817	0.99766	0.99705	0.99634
5	0.99998	0.99996	0.99994	0.99991	0.99987	0.99982	0.99975	0.99966	0.99954	0.99941
6	1.00000	1.00000	0.99999	0.99999	0.99999	0.99998	0.99997	0.99996	0.99994	0.99992
7	1.00000	1.00000	1.00000	1.00000	1.00000	1.00000	1.00000	1.00000	0.99999	0.99999
8	1.00000	1.00000	1.00000	1.00000	1.00000	1.00000	1.00000	1.00000	1.00000	1.00000

					Mean					
S	1.25	1.50	1.75	2.00	2.25	2.50	2.75	3.00	3.25	3.50
0	0.28650	0.22313	0.17377	0.13534	0.10540	0.08208	0.06393	0.04979	0.03877	0.03020
1	0.64464	0.55783	0.47788	0.40601	0.34255	0.28730	0.23973	0.19915	0.16479	0.13589
2	0.86847	0.80885	0.74397	0.67668	0.60934	0.54381	0.48146	0.42319	0.36957	0.32085
3	0.96173	0.93436	0.89919	0.85712	0.80943	0.75758	0.70304	0.64723	0.59141	0.53663
4	0.99088	0.98142	0.96710	0.94735	0.92199	0.89118	0.85538	0.81526	0.77165	0.72544
5	0.99816	0.99554	0.99087	0.98344	0.97263	0.95798	0.93916	0.91608	0.88881	0.85761
6	0.99968	0.99907	0.99780	0.99547	0.99163	0.98581	0.97757	0.96649	0.95227	0.93471
7	0.99995	0.99983	0.99953	0.99890	0.99773	0.99575	0.99265	0.98810	0.98174	0.97326
8	0.99999	0.99997	0.99991	0.99976	0.99945	0.99886	0.99784	0.99620	0.99371	0.99013
9	1.00000	1.00000	0.99998	0.99995	0.99988	0.99972	0.99942	0.99890	0.99803	0.99669
10	1.00000	1.00000	1.00000	0.99999	0.99998	0.99994	0.99986	0.99971	0.99944	0.99898
11	1.00000	1.00000	1.00000	1.00000	1.00000	0.99999	0.99997	0.99993	0.99985	0.99971
12	1.00000	1.00000	1.00000	1.00000	1.00000	1.00000	0.99999	0.99998	0.99996	0.99992
13	1.00000	1.00000	1.00000	1.00000	1.00000	1.00000	1.00000	1.00000	0.99999	0.99998
14	1.00000	1.00000	1.00000	1.00000	1.00000	1.00000	1.00000	1.00000	1.00000	1.00000
15	1.00000	1.00000	1.00000	1.00000	1.00000	1.00000	1.00000	1.00000	1.00000	1.00000

(*continued*)

Poisson Distribution Function Table   (Concluded)

						Mean						
S	3.75	4.00	4.25	4.50	4.75	5.00	5.25	5.50	5.75	6.00	6.25	6.50
0	0.02352	0.01832	0.01426	0.01111	0.00865	0.00674	0.00525	0.00409	0.00318	0.00248	0.00193	0.00150
1	0.11171	0.09158	0.07489	0.06110	0.04975	0.04043	0.03280	0.02656	0.02148	0.01735	0.01400	0.01128
2	0.27707	0.23810	0.20371	0.17358	0.14735	0.12465	0.10511	0.08838	0.07410	0.06197	0.05170	0.04304
3	0.48377	0.43347	0.38621	0.34230	0.30189	0.26503	0.23167	0.20170	0.17495	0.15120	0.13025	0.11185
4	0.67755	0.62884	0.58012	0.53210	0.48540	0.44049	0.39777	0.35752	0.31991	0.28506	0.25299	0.22367
5	0.82288	0.78513	0.74494	0.70293	0.65973	0.61596	0.57218	0.52892	0.48662	0.44568	0.40640	0.36904
6	0.91372	0.88933	0.86169	0.83105	0.79775	0.76218	0.72479	0.68604	0.64639	0.60630	0.56622	0.52652
7	0.96238	0.94887	0.93257	0.91341	0.89140	0.86663	0.83925	0.80949	0.77762	0.74398	0.70890	0.67276
8	0.98519	0.97864	0.97023	0.95974	0.94701	0.93191	0.91436	0.89436	0.87195	0.84724	0.82038	0.79157
9	0.99469	0.99187	0.98801	0.98291	0.97636	0.96817	0.95817	0.94622	0.93221	0.91608	0.89779	0.87738
10	0.99826	0.99716	0.99557	0.99333	0.99030	0.98630	0.98118	0.97475	0.96686	0.95738	0.94618	0.93316
11	0.99947	0.99908	0.99849	0.99760	0.99632	0.99455	0.99216	0.98901	0.98498	0.97991	0.97367	0.96612
12	0.99985	0.99973	0.99952	0.99919	0.99870	0.99798	0.99696	0.99555	0.99366	0.99117	0.98798	0.98397
13	0.99996	0.99992	0.99986	0.99975	0.99957	0.99930	0.99890	0.99831	0.99749	0.99637	0.99487	0.99290
14	0.99999	0.99998	0.99996	0.99993	0.99987	0.99977	0.99963	0.99940	0.99907	0.99860	0.99794	0.99704
15	1.00000	1.00000	0.99999	0.99998	0.99996	0.99993	0.99988	0.99980	0.99968	0.99949	0.99922	0.99884
16	1.00000	1.00000	1.00000	0.99999	0.99999	0.99998	0.99996	0.99994	0.99989	0.99983	0.99972	0.99957
17	1.00000	1.00000	1.00000	1.00000	1.00000	0.99999	0.99999	0.99998	0.99997	0.99994	0.99991	0.99985
18	1.00000	1.00000	1.00000	1.00000	1.00000	1.00000	1.00000	0.99999	0.99999	0.99998	0.99997	0.99995
19	1.00000	1.00000	1.00000	1.00000	1.00000	1.00000	1.00000	1.00000	1.00000	0.99999	0.99999	0.99998

						Mean						
S	6.75	7.00	7.25	7.50	7.75	8.00	8.25	8.50	8.75	9.00	9.25	9.50
0	0.00117	0.00091	0.00071	0.00055	0.00043	0.00034	0.00026	0.00020	0.00016	0.00012	0.00010	0.00007
1	0.00907	0.00730	0.00586	0.00470	0.00377	0.00302	0.00242	0.00193	0.00154	0.00123	0.00099	0.00079
2	0.03575	0.02964	0.02452	0.02026	0.01670	0.01375	0.01131	0.00928	0.00761	0.00623	0.00510	0.00416
3	0.09577	0.08177	0.06963	0.05915	0.05012	0.04238	0.03576	0.03011	0.02530	0.02123	0.01777	0.01486
4	0.19704	0.17299	0.15138	0.13206	0.11487	0.09963	0.08619	0.07436	0.06401	0.05496	0.04709	0.04026
5	0.33377	0.30071	0.26992	0.24144	0.21522	0.19124	0.16939	0.14960	0.13174	0.11569	0.10133	0.08853
6	0.48759	0.44971	0.41316	0.37815	0.34485	0.31337	0.28380	0.25618	0.23051	0.20678	0.18495	0.16495
7	0.63591	0.59871	0.56152	0.52464	0.48837	0.45296	0.41864	0.38560	0.35398	0.32390	0.29544	0.26866
8	0.76106	0.72909	0.69596	0.66197	0.62740	0.59255	0.55770	0.52311	0.48902	0.45565	0.42320	0.39182
9	0.85492	0.83050	0.80427	0.77641	0.74712	0.71662	0.68516	0.65297	0.62031	0.58741	0.55451	0.52183
10	0.91827	0.90148	0.88279	0.86224	0.83990	0.81589	0.79032	0.76336	0.73519	0.70599	0.67597	0.64533
11	0.95715	0.94665	0.93454	0.92076	0.90527	0.88808	0.86919	0.84866	0.82657	0.80301	0.77810	0.75199
12	0.97902	0.97300	0.96581	0.95733	0.94749	0.93620	0.92341	0.90908	0.89320	0.87577	0.85683	0.83643
13	0.99037	0.98719	0.98324	0.97844	0.97266	0.96582	0.95782	0.94859	0.93805	0.92615	0.91285	0.89814
14	0.99585	0.99428	0.99227	0.98974	0.98659	0.98274	0.97810	0.97257	0.96608	0.95853	0.94986	0.94001
15	0.99831	0.99759	0.99664	0.99539	0.99379	0.99177	0.98925	0.98617	0.98243	0.97796	0.97269	0.96653
16	0.99935	0.99904	0.99862	0.99804	0.99728	0.99628	0.99500	0.99339	0.99137	0.98889	0.98588	0.98227
17	0.99976	0.99964	0.99946	0.99921	0.99887	0.99841	0.99779	0.99700	0.99597	0.99468	0.99306	0.99107
18	0.99992	0.99987	0.99980	0.99970	0.99955	0.99935	0.99907	0.99870	0.99821	0.99757	0.99675	0.99572
19	0.99997	0.99996	0.99993	0.99989	0.99983	0.99975	0.99963	0.99947	0.99924	0.99894	0.99855	0.99804
20	0.99999	0.99999	0.99998	0.99996	0.99994	0.99991	0.99986	0.99979	0.99969	0.99956	0.99938	0.99914
21	1.00000	1.00000	0.99999	0.99999	0.99998	0.99997	0.99995	0.99992	0.99988	0.99983	0.99975	0.99964
22	1.00000	1.00000	1.00000	1.00000	0.99999	0.99999	0.99998	0.99997	0.99996	0.99993	0.99990	0.99985
23	1.00000	1.00000	1.00000	1.00000	1.00000	1.00000	0.99999	0.99999	0.99998	0.99998	0.99996	0.99994
24	1.00000	1.00000	1.00000	1.00000	1.00000	1.00000	1.00000	1.00000	0.99999	0.99999	0.99999	0.99998

Poisson Loss Function Table

					Mean					
S	0.05	0.10	0.15	0.20	0.25	0.30	0.35	0.40	0.45	0.50
0	0.05000	0.10000	0.15000	0.20000	0.25000	0.30000	0.35000	0.40000	0.45000	0.50000
1	0.00123	0.00484	0.01071	0.01873	0.02880	0.04082	0.05469	0.07032	0.08763	0.10653
2	0.00002	0.00016	0.00052	0.00121	0.00230	0.00388	0.00602	0.00877	0.01219	0.01633
3	0.00000	0.00000	0.00002	0.00006	0.00014	0.00028	0.00051	0.00084	0.00131	0.00194
4	0.00000	0.00000	0.00000	0.00000	0.00001	0.00002	0.00003	0.00007	0.00011	0.00019
5	0.00000	0.00000	0.00000	0.00000	0.00000	0.00000	0.00000	0.00000	0.00001	0.00002
6	0.00000	0.00000	0.00000	0.00000	0.00000	0.00000	0.00000	0.00000	0.00000	0.00000

					Mean					
S	0.55	0.60	0.65	0.70	0.75	0.80	0.85	0.90	0.95	1.00
0	0.55000	0.60000	0.65000	0.70000	0.75000	0.80000	0.85000	0.90000	0.95000	1.00000
1	0.12695	0.14881	0.17205	0.19659	0.22237	0.24933	0.27741	0.30657	0.33674	0.36788
2	0.02122	0.02691	0.03342	0.04078	0.04901	0.05812	0.06813	0.07905	0.09089	0.10364
3	0.00276	0.00379	0.00508	0.00664	0.00850	0.01070	0.01325	0.01620	0.01955	0.02334
4	0.00029	0.00044	0.00063	0.00089	0.00121	0.00162	0.00212	0.00274	0.00347	0.00435
5	0.00003	0.00004	0.00007	0.00010	0.00015	0.00021	0.00029	0.00039	0.00052	0.00069
6	0.00000	0.00000	0.00001	0.00001	0.00002	0.00002	0.00003	0.00005	0.00007	0.00009
7	0.00000	0.00000	0.00001	0.00001	0.00002	0.00002	0.00003	0.00005	0.00007	0.00009
8	0.00000	0.00000	0.00001	0.00001	0.00001	0.00002	0.00003	0.00004	0.00006	0.00008

					Mean					
S	1.25	1.50	1.75	2.00	2.25	2.50	2.75	3.00	3.25	3.50
0	1.25000	1.50000	1.75000	2.00000	2.25000	2.50000	2.75000	3.00000	3.25000	3.50000
1	0.53650	0.72313	0.92377	1.13534	1.35540	1.58208	1.81393	2.04979	2.28877	2.53020
2	0.18114	0.28096	0.40165	0.54134	0.69795	0.86938	1.05366	1.24894	1.45356	1.66609
3	0.04961	0.08980	0.14562	0.21802	0.30729	0.41320	0.53511	0.67213	0.82313	0.98693
4	0.01134	0.02416	0.04481	0.07514	0.11672	0.17077	0.23815	0.31936	0.41454	0.52357
5	0.00221	0.00558	0.01191	0.02249	0.03870	0.06195	0.09353	0.13462	0.18619	0.24901
6	0.00038	0.00113	0.00278	0.00592	0.01134	0.01993	0.03270	0.05070	0.07501	0.10662
7	0.00006	0.00020	0.00058	0.00139	0.00297	0.00574	0.01026	0.01719	0.02728	0.04134
8	0.00001	0.00003	0.00011	0.00029	0.00070	0.00149	0.00292	0.00529	0.00902	0.01460
9	0.00000	0.00000	0.00002	0.00006	0.00015	0.00035	0.00076	0.00149	0.00273	0.00472
10	0.00000	0.00000	0.00000	0.00001	0.00003	0.00008	0.00018	0.00038	0.00076	0.00141
11	0.00000	0.00000	0.00000	0.00000	0.00001	0.00002	0.00004	0.00009	0.00020	0.00039
12	0.00000	0.00000	0.00000	0.00000	0.00000	0.00000	0.00001	0.00002	0.00005	0.00010
13	0.00000	0.00000	0.00000	0.00000	0.00000	0.00000	0.00000	0.00000	0.00001	0.00002
14	0.00000	0.00000	0.00000	0.00000	0.00000	0.00000	0.00000	0.00000	0.00000	0.00001
15	0.00000	0.00000	0.00000	0.00000	0.00000	0.00000	0.00000	0.00000	0.00000	0.00000

(continued)

Poisson Loss Function Table (Concluded)

					Mean							
S	3.75	4.00	4.25	4.50	4.75	5.00	5.25	5.50	5.75	6.00	6.25	6.50
0	3.75000	4.00000	4.25000	4.50000	4.75000	5.00000	5.25000	5.50000	5.75000	6.00000	6.25000	6.50000
1	2.77352	3.01832	3.26426	3.51111	3.75865	4.00674	4.25525	4.50409	4.75318	5.00248	5.25193	5.50150
2	1.88523	2.10989	2.33915	2.57221	2.80840	3.04717	3.28804	3.53065	3.77467	4.01983	4.26593	4.51278
3	1.16230	1.34800	1.54286	1.74579	1.95575	2.17182	2.39316	2.61903	2.84877	3.08180	3.31763	3.55582
4	0.64606	0.78147	0.92907	1.08808	1.25763	1.43684	1.62483	1.82073	2.02371	2.23300	2.44788	2.66766
5	0.32361	0.41030	0.50919	0.62019	0.74303	0.87734	1.02260	1.17824	1.34362	1.51806	1.70086	1.89134
6	0.14649	0.19543	0.25413	0.32312	0.40277	0.49330	0.59479	0.70716	0.83024	0.96374	1.10727	1.26038
7	0.06021	0.08476	0.11582	0.15417	0.20052	0.25548	0.31958	0.39320	0.47663	0.57004	0.67348	0.78690
8	0.02259	0.03363	0.04839	0.06758	0.09192	0.12211	0.15882	0.20268	0.25426	0.31402	0.38238	0.45966
9	0.00778	0.01226	0.01861	0.02732	0.03893	0.05402	0.07318	0.09704	0.12620	0.16126	0.20276	0.25123
10	0.00247	0.00413	0.00662	0.01023	0.01529	0.02219	0.03136	0.04326	0.05842	0.07733	0.10056	0.12862
11	0.00073	0.00129	0.00219	0.00356	0.00559	0.00849	0.01253	0.01801	0.02528	0.03471	0.04673	0.06178
12	0.00020	0.00038	0.00067	0.00116	0.00191	0.00304	0.00469	0.00702	0.01026	0.01462	0.02040	0.02790
13	0.00005	0.00010	0.00019	0.00035	0.00061	0.00102	0.00165	0.00257	0.00391	0.00579	0.00838	0.01187
14	0.00001	0.00003	0.00005	0.00010	0.00018	0.00032	0.00054	0.00089	0.00141	0.00217	0.00325	0.00477
15	0.00000	0.00001	0.00001	0.00003	0.00005	0.00010	0.00017	0.00029	0.00048	0.00077	0.00119	0.00181
16	0.00000	0.00000	0.00000	0.00001	0.00001	0.00003	0.00005	0.00009	0.00015	0.00026	0.00042	0.00066
17	0.00000	0.00000	0.00000	0.00000	0.00000	0.00001	0.00001	0.00003	0.00005	0.00008	0.00014	0.00022
18	0.00000	0.00000	0.00000	0.00000	0.00000	0.00000	0.00000	0.00001	0.00001	0.00002	0.00004	0.00007
19	0.00000	0.00000	0.00000	0.00000	0.00000	0.00000	0.00000	0.00000	0.00000	0.00001	0.00001	0.00002

					Mean							
S	6.75	7.00	7.25	7.50	7.75	8.00	8.25	8.50	8.75	9.00	9.25	9.50
0	6.75000	7.00000	7.25000	7.50000	7.75000	8.00000	8.25000	8.50000	8.75000	9.00000	9.25000	9.50000
1	5.75117	6.00091	6.25071	6.50055	6.75043	7.00034	7.25026	7.50020	7.75016	8.00012	8.25010	8.50007
2	4.76025	5.00821	5.25657	5.50525	5.75420	6.00335	6.25268	6.50214	6.75170	7.00136	7.25108	7.50086
3	3.79599	4.03784	4.28109	4.52551	4.77090	5.01711	5.26399	5.51142	5.75931	6.00759	6.25618	6.50502
4	2.89176	3.11961	3.35072	3.58466	3.82103	4.05949	4.29974	4.54153	4.78462	5.02882	5.27395	5.51988
5	2.08880	2.29260	2.50210	2.71672	2.93589	3.15912	3.38593	3.61589	3.84863	4.08378	4.32105	4.56015
6	1.42257	1.59331	1.77203	1.95815	2.15112	2.35036	2.55532	2.76549	2.98036	3.19947	3.42238	3.64868
7	0.91016	1.04302	1.18519	1.33631	1.49597	1.66373	1.83912	2.02167	2.21087	2.40625	2.60732	2.81362
8	0.54606	0.64173	0.74671	0.86095	0.98434	1.11669	1.25777	1.40726	1.56485	1.73015	1.90277	2.08229
9	0.30712	0.37082	0.44267	0.52292	0.61174	0.70924	0.81546	0.93037	1.05387	1.18580	1.32597	1.47411
10	0.16204	0.20132	0.24694	0.29932	0.35885	0.42586	0.50062	0.58334	0.67418	0.77321	0.88047	0.99594
11	0.08031	0.10280	0.12973	0.16156	0.19876	0.24175	0.29094	0.34671	0.40936	0.47920	0.55644	0.64127
12	0.03746	0.04945	0.06427	0.08232	0.10403	0.12983	0.16013	0.19537	0.23593	0.28221	0.33454	0.39326
13	0.01648	0.02245	0.03007	0.03965	0.05152	0.06603	0.08354	0.10445	0.12913	0.15798	0.19137	0.22968
14	0.00685	0.00964	0.01332	0.01809	0.02418	0.03185	0.04137	0.05304	0.06718	0.08413	0.10422	0.12782
15	0.00270	0.00392	0.00559	0.00783	0.01077	0.01459	0.01947	0.02561	0.03326	0.04266	0.05409	0.06783
16	0.00101	0.00152	0.00223	0.00322	0.00456	0.00636	0.00872	0.01178	0.01569	0.02063	0.02678	0.03436
17	0.00036	0.00056	0.00085	0.00126	0.00184	0.00264	0.00372	0.00517	0.00706	0.00952	0.01266	0.01663
18	0.00012	0.00020	0.00031	0.00047	0.00071	0.00105	0.00152	0.00217	0.00304	0.00420	0.00573	0.00770
19	0.00004	0.00007	0.00011	0.00017	0.00026	0.00040	0.00059	0.00087	0.00125	0.00177	0.00248	0.00342
20	0.00001	0.00002	0.00004	0.00006	0.00009	0.00014	0.00022	0.00033	0.00049	0.00072	0.00103	0.00145
21	0.00000	0.00001	0.00001	0.00002	0.00003	0.00005	0.00008	0.00012	0.00019	0.00028	0.00041	0.00059
22	0.00000	0.00000	0.00000	0.00001	0.00001	0.00002	0.00003	0.00004	0.00007	0.00010	0.00016	0.00023
23	0.00000	0.00000	0.00000	0.00000	0.00000	0.00001	0.00001	0.00001	0.00002	0.00004	0.00006	0.00009
24	0.00000	0.00000	0.00000	0.00000	0.00000	0.00000	0.00000	0.00000	0.00001	0.00001	0.00002	0.00003

Evaluation of the Loss Function

The loss function $L(Q)$ is the expected amount a random variable exceeds a fixed value. For example, if the random variable is demand, then $L(Q)$ is the expected amount demand is greater than Q. See Appendix A, Statistics Tutorial, for a more extensive description of the loss function.

This appendix describes how the loss function of a discrete distribution function can be efficiently evaluated. (Appendix A gives one solution method, but it is inefficient.) If you need to evaluate the loss function of a continuous distribution, then convert the continuous distribution into a discrete distribution by "chopping it up" into many pieces. For example, the standard normal table is the discrete (i.e., "chopped up") version of the continuous standard normal distribution function.

Let N be the number of quantities in the distribution function and let $Q_1, Q_2, Q_3, \ldots, Q_N$ be those quantities. For example, take the empirical distribution function in Chapter 12, repeated here for convenience:

Q	F (Q)	Q	F(Q)	Q	F(Q)
800	0.0303	2,592	0.3636	3,936	0.6970
1,184	0.0606	2,624	0.3939	4,000	0.7273
1,792	0.0909	2,752	0.4242	4,064	0.7576
1,792	0.1212	3,040	0.4545	4,160	0.7879
1,824	0.1515	3,104	0.4848	4,352	0.8182
1,888	0.1818	3,136	0.5152	4,544	0.8485
2,048	0.2121	3,264	0.5455	4,672	0.8788
2,144	0.2424	3,456	0.5758	4,800	0.9091
2,208	0.2727	3,680	0.6061	4,928	0.9394
2,304	0.3030	3,744	0.6364	4,992	0.9697
2,560	0.3333	3,808	0.6667	5,120	1.0000

$F(Q)$ = Probability demand is less than or equal to the quantity Q

With this distribution function, there are 33 quantities, so $N = 33$ and $Q_1 = 800$, $Q_2 = 1,184, \ldots,$ and $Q_{33} = 5,120$. Furthermore, recall that we use μ to represent expected demand, which in this case is $\mu = 3,192$.

We can recursively evaluate the loss function, which means we start with $L(Q_1)$ and then use $L(Q_1)$ to evaluate $L(Q_2)$, and then use $L(Q_2)$ to evaluate $L(Q_3)$, and so forth.

The expected lost sales if we order Q_1 (which in this case is 800 units) are

$$L(Q_1) = \mu - Q_1 = 3{,}192 - 800 = 2{,}392$$

Expected lost sales if we order Q_2 are

$$
\begin{aligned}
L(Q_2) &= L(Q_1) - (Q_2 - Q_1) \times (1 - F(Q_1)) \\
&= 2{,}392 - (1{,}184 - 800) \times (1 - 0.0303) \\
&= 2{,}020
\end{aligned}
$$

Expected lost sales if we order Q_3 are

$$
\begin{aligned}
L(Q_3) &= L(Q_2) - (Q_3 - Q_2) \times (1 - F(Q_2)) \\
&= 2{,}020 - (1{,}792 - 1{,}184) \times (1 - 0.0606) \\
&= 1{,}448
\end{aligned}
$$

In general, the ith expected lost sales are

$$L(Q_i) = L(Q_{i-1}) - (Q_i - Q_{i-1}) \times (1 - F(Q_{i-1}))$$

So you start with $L(Q_1) = \mu - Q_1$ and then you evaluate $L(Q_2)$, and then $L(Q_3)$, up to $L(Q_N)$. The resulting table is

Q	F(Q)	L(Q)	Q	F(Q)	L(Q)	Q	F(Q)	L(Q)
800	0.0303	2,392	2,592	0.3636	841	3,936	0.6970	191
1,184	0.0606	2,020	2,624	0.3939	821	4,000	0.7273	171
1,792	0.0909	1,448	2,752	0.4242	744	4,064	0.7576	154
1,792	0.1212	1,448	3,040	0.4545	578	4,160	0.7879	131
1,824	0.1515	1,420	3,104	0.4848	543	4,352	0.8182	90
1,888	0.1818	1,366	3,136	0.5152	526	4,544	0.8485	55
2,048	0.2121	1,235	3,264	0.5455	464	4,672	0.8788	36
2,144	0.2424	1,160	3,456	0.5758	377	4,800	0.9091	20
2,208	0.2727	1,111	3,680	0.6061	282	4,928	0.9394	8
2,304	0.3030	1,041	3,744	0.6364	257	4,992	0.9697	5
2,560	0.3333	863	3,808	0.6667	233	5,120	1.0000	1

Q = Order quantity
$F(Q)$ = Probability demand is less than or equal to the order quantity
$L(Q)$ = Loss function (the expected amount demand exceeds Q)

With this empirical distribution example, the quantities differ by more than one unit, for example, $Q_2 - Q_1 = 384$. Now suppose the demand forecast is the Poisson distribution with mean 1.25. The distribution function is given in Table A.1 but is repeated here for convenience:

Q	f(Q)	F(Q)
0	0.28650	0.28650
1	0.35813	0.64464
2	0.22383	0.86847
3	0.09326	0.96173
4	0.02914	0.99088
5	0.00729	0.99816
6	0.00152	0.99968
7	0.00027	0.99995
8	0.00004	0.99999
9	0.00001	1.00000

Now we have $Q_1 = 0$, $Q_2 = 1$, and so forth. We find the expected lost sales with the same process: $L(Q_1) = 1.25 - 0 = 1.25$ and

$$
\begin{aligned}
L(Q_2) &= L(Q_1) - (Q_2 - Q_1) \times (1 - F(Q_1)) \\
&= 0.53650 - (2 - 1) \times (1 - 0.64469) \\
&= 0.18114
\end{aligned}
$$

Completing the table yields

Q	f(Q)	F(Q)	L(Q)
0	0.28650	0.28650	1.25000
1	0.35813	0.64464	0.53650
2	0.22383	0.86847	0.18114
3	0.09326	0.96173	0.04961
4	0.02914	0.99088	0.01134
5	0.00729	0.99816	0.00221
6	0.00152	0.99968	0.00038
7	0.00027	0.99995	0.00006
8	0.00004	0.99999	0.00001
9	0.00001	1.00000	0.00000

Appendix D

Equations and Approximations

This appendix derives in detail some equations and explains several approximations.

Derivation, via Calculus, of the Order Quantity That Maximizes Expected Profit for the Newsvendor (Chapter 12)

Let the selling price be p, the purchase cost per unit be c, and the salvage revenue from leftover inventory be v. The expected profit function is

$$\pi(Q) = -cQ + p\left(\int_0^Q xf(x)dx + (1 - F(Q))Q\right) + v\int_0^Q (Q - x)f(x)dx$$

$$= (p - c)Q + \int_0^Q (p - v)xf(x)dx - (p - v)F(Q)Q$$

where $f(x)$ is the density function and $F(x)$ is the distribution function ($Prob(D = x)$ and $Prob(D \le x)$, respectively, where D is the random variable representing demand).

Via integration by parts, the profit function can be written as

$$\pi(Q) = (p - c)Q + (p - v)\left(QF(Q) - \int_0^Q F(x)dx\right) - (p - v)F(Q)Q$$

Differentiate the profit function and remember that the derivative of the distribution function equals the density function, that is, $dF(x)/dx = f(x)$

$$\frac{d\pi(Q)}{dQ} = (p - c) + (p - v)(F(Q) + Qf(Q) - F(Q)) - (p - v)(F(Q) + f(Q)Q)$$

$$= (p - c) - (p - v)F(Q)$$

and

$$\frac{d^2\pi(Q)}{dQ^2} = -(p - v)f(Q)$$

Because the second derivative is negative, the profit function is concave, so the solution to the first-order condition provides the optimal order quantity:

$$\frac{d\pi(Q)}{dQ} = (p - c) - (p - v)F(Q) = 0$$

Rearrange terms in the above equation and you get

$$F(Q) = \frac{p - c}{p - v}$$

Note that $C_o = c - v$ and $C_u = p - c$, so the above can be written as

$$F(Q) = \frac{C_u}{C_u + C_o}$$

The Round-up Rule (Chapter 12)

To understand why the round-up rule is correct, we need to derive the optimal order quantity with a discrete distribution function. Suppose demand will be one of a finite set of outcomes, $D \in \{d_1, d_2, \ldots, d_n\}$. For example, with the empirical distribution function for the Hammer 3/2, the possible demand outcomes included $\{800, 1{,}184, \ldots, 5{,}120\}$. Clearly, the optimal order quantity will equal one of these possible demand outcomes. Suppose we have decided to order d_i units and we are deciding whether to order d_{i+1} units. This is prudent if the expected gain from this larger order quantity is at least as large as the expected cost. The expected gain is

$$C_u(d_{i+1} - d_i)(1 - F(d_i))$$

because we sell an additional $(d_{i+1} - d_i)$ units if demand is greater than d_i, which occurs with probability $1 - F(d_i)$. The expected loss is

$$C_o(d_{i+1} - d_i)F(d_i)$$

because we need to salvage an additional $(d_{i+1} - d_i)$ units if demand is d_i or fewer, which occurs with probability $F(d_i)$. So we should increase our order from d_i to d_{i+1} when

$$C_u(d_{i+1} - d_i)(1 - F(d_i)) \geq C_o(d_{i+1} - d_i)F(d_i)$$

which simplifies to

$$\frac{C_u}{C_o + C_u} \geq F(d_i)$$

Thus, if the critical ratio is greater than $F(d_i)$, then we should increase our order from d_i to d_{i+1}. When the critical ratio is greater than $F(d_i)$ but less than $F(d_{i+1})$, in other words, between the two entries in the table, we should order d_{i+1} units and not increase our order quantity further. Put another way, we choose the larger order quantity when the critical ratio falls between two entries in the table. That is the round-up rule.

The common error is to want to choose the order quantity that yields $F()$ closest to the critical ratio. But that can lead to a suboptimal action. To illustrate, suppose demand was Poisson with mean 1.0, $C_u = 1$, and $C_o = 0.21$. The critical ratio is 0.83, which is about in the middle between $F(1) = 0.74$ and $F(2) = 0.92$. However, expected profit with an order quantity of two units is about 20 percent higher than the profit with an order quantity of one unit. That said, if $F(d_i)$ and $F(d_{i+1})$ are reasonably close together, then choosing the lower order quantity is not going to cause a significant profit loss.

Derivation of the Standard Normal Loss Function (Chapter 12)

We wish to derive the following equation for the standard normal loss function:

$$L(z) = \phi(z) - z(1 - \Phi(z))$$

Begin with the density function of the standard normal distribution,

$$\phi(z) = \frac{1}{\sqrt{2\pi}} e^{-z^2/2}$$

and differentiate

$$\frac{d\phi(z)}{dz} = -z \frac{1}{\sqrt{2\pi}} e^{-z^2/2} = -z\phi(z)$$

Let $L(z)$ be the expected loss function:v

$$L(z) = \int_z^\infty (x - z)\phi(x)dx$$

$$= \int_z^\infty x\phi(x)dx - \int_z^\infty z\phi(x)dx$$

The first integral is

$$\int_z^\infty x\phi(x)dx = -\phi(x) \big|_z^\infty = \phi(z)$$

because $d\phi(x)/dx = -x\phi(x)$ and the second integral is

$$\int_z^\infty z\phi(x)dx = z(1 - \Phi(z))$$

Thus, $L(z) = \phi(z) - z(1 - \Phi(z))$.

Evaluation of the Fill Rate (Chapter 12)

The fill rate is the probability a customer finds an item available for purchase. This is not the same as the in-stock probability, which is the probability that all demand is satisfied. (To see why, suppose 9 units are available, but 10 customers arrive to make a purchase. The firm is not in-stock, because there will be one person who is unable to purchase a unit. However, each customer has a 9 out of 10 chance to be one of the lucky customers that can purchase an item.)

The fill rate can be evaluated with the following formula:

$$\text{Fill rate} = \frac{\text{Expected sales}}{\text{Expected demand}} = \frac{\text{Expected sales}}{\mu}$$

For example, if O'Neill orders 3,500 Hammer 3/2 wetsuits, then we evaluated in the Chapter 12 that their Expected sales = 2,858. Expected demand is 3,192, so the fill rate would be

$$\text{Fill rate} = \frac{2,858}{3,192} = 89.5\%$$

Mismatch Cost as a Percentage of the Maximum Profit (Chapter 13)

We will use the following notation:

μ	= Expected demand
σ	= Standard deviation of demand
Q	= Expected profit-maximizing order quantity
$z = (Q-\mu)/\sigma$	= Normalized order quantity
$\phi(z)$	= Density function of the standard normal distribution
$\Phi(z)$	= Distribution function of the standard normal

The easiest way to evaluate $\phi(z)$ is to use the Excel function Normdist(z,0,1,0), but it also can be evaluated by hand with the following function:

$$\phi(z) = e^{-(1/2)\times z^2}/\sqrt{2 \times \pi}$$

Begin with the mismatch cost as a percentage of the maximum profit

$$\begin{aligned}\text{Mismatch cost as a \% of the} &= (C_o \times \text{Expected leftover inventory})/(\mu \times C_u) \\ \text{maximum profit} &\quad + (C_u \times \text{Expected lost sales}) / (\mu \times C_u)\end{aligned} \quad \textbf{(D.1)}$$

We also know the following:

$$\begin{aligned}\text{Expected leftover inventory} &= (Q - \text{Expected sales}) \\ &= (Q - \mu + \text{Expected lost sales})\end{aligned} \quad \textbf{(D.2)}$$

and we can rearrange $Q = \mu + z \times \sigma$ into

$$z \times \sigma = (Q - \mu) \quad \textbf{(D.3)}$$

Substitute equation (D.3) into equation (D.2), then substitute that equation into equation (D.1) and simplify:

$$\text{Mismatch cost as a \% of the maximum profit} = ((C_o \times z \times \sigma) + (C_o + C_u) \times \text{Expected lost sales})/(\mu \times C_u) \qquad \textbf{(D.4)}$$

Recall that

$$\text{Expected lost sales} = \sigma \times (\phi(z) - z \times (1 - \Phi(z)))$$

$$= \sigma \times \left(\phi(z) - z \times \frac{C_o}{C_o + C_u} \right) \qquad \textbf{(D.5)}$$

where the second line in that equation follows from the critical ratio, $\Phi(z) = C_u/(C_o + C_u)$. Substitute equation (D.5) into equation (D.4) and simplify to obtain equation (13.2):

$$\text{Mismatch cost as a \% of the maximum profit} = \left(\frac{\phi(z)}{\Phi(z)} \right) \times \left(\frac{\sigma}{\mu} \right)$$

The above equation is composed of two terms, $\phi(z)/\Phi(z)$ and σ/μ, so the mismatch cost is high when the product of those two terms is high. The second term is the coefficient of variation, which we discussed in the text. The first term is the ratio of the standard normal density function to the standard normal distribution function evaluated at the normalized order quantity. It depends on z and z depends on the critical ratio (the higher the critical ratio, the higher the optimal z-statistic). In fact, a simple plot reveals that as the critical ratio increases, $\phi(z)/\Phi(z)$ decreases. Thus, the mismatch cost becomes smaller as the critical ratio increases. In other words, all else being equal, between two products, the product with the lower critical ratio has the higher mismatch cost.

Exact Stockout Probability for the Order-up-to Model (Chapter 14)

Recall our main result from Section 14.3 that the inventory level at the end of the period equals S minus demand over $l + 1$ periods. If the inventory level is negative at the end of that interval, then one or more units are back-ordered. A stockout occurs in the last period of that interval if there is at least one unit back-ordered and the most recent back order occurred in that last period. Equation (14.1) in Chapter 14 acknowledges the first part of that statement (at least one unit is back-ordered), but it ignores that second part (the most recent back order must occur in the last period).

For example, suppose $l = 1$ and $S = 2$. If demand over two periods is three units, then there is one unit back-ordered at the end of the second period. As long as one of those three units of demand occurred in the second period, then a stockout occurred in the second period. A stockout does not occur in the second period only if all three units of demand occurred in the first period. Hence, the exact equation for the stockout probability is

$$\text{Stockout probability} = \text{Prob\{Demand over } l + 1 \text{ periods} > S\}$$
$$- \text{Prob\{Demand over } l \text{ periods} > S\}$$
$$\times \text{Prob\{Demand in one period} = 0\}$$

Equation (14.1) is an approximation because it ignores the second term in the exact equation above. The second term is the probability that the demand over $l + 1$ periods occurs only in the first l periods; that is, there is no demand in the $(l + 1)$th period. If the service level is high, then the second term should be small. Notice that the approximation overestimates the true stockout probability because it does not subtract the second term. Hence, the approximation is conservative.

If each period's demand is a Poisson distribution with mean 0.29 and there is a two-period lead time, then the approximate and exact stockout probabilities are

	Stockout Probability	
S	**Approximation**	**Exact**
0	44.010%	25.174%
1	11.536	8.937
2	2.119	1.873
3	0.298	0.280
4	0.034	0.033
5	0.003	0.003
6	0.000	0.000

Fill Rate for the Order-up-to Model (Chapter 14)

The fill rate is the probability that a customer is able to purchase a unit immediately (i.e., the customer is not backordered). The fill rate can be evaluated with the following equation:

$$\text{Fill rate} = 1 - \frac{\text{Expected back order}}{\text{Expected demand in one period}}$$

The logic behind the above equation is as follows: The number of customers in a period is the expected demand in one period, and the number of customers who are not served in a period is the expected back order, so the ratio of the expected back order to the expected demand is the fraction of customers who are not served. One minus the fraction of customers who are not served is the fraction of customers who are served, which is the fill rate. Note that this logic does not depend on the particular demand distribution (but the evaluation of the expected back order does depend on the demand distribution).

You also might wonder why the denominator of the fraction in the fill rate equation is the expected demand over a single period and not the expected demand over $l + 1$ periods. We are interested in the fraction of customers who are not served immediately from stock (one minus that fraction is the expected fill rate). The lead time influences the fraction of customers in a period who are not served (the expected back order), but it does not influence the number of customers we have. Therefore, the lead time influences the numerator of that ratio (the number of customers who are not served) but not the denominator (the number of customers who arrive).

The above equation for the fill rate is actually an approximation of the fill rate. It happens to be an excellent approximation if the fill rate is reasonably high (say, 90 percent or higher). The advantage of that formula is that it is reasonably easy to work with. However, the remainder of this section derives the exact formula.

The fill rate is one minus the probability of not being served in a period, which is the following:

$$\text{Probability of not being served} = \frac{\text{Expected back orders that occur in a period}}{\text{Expected demand in one period}}$$

We know the denominator of that fraction, the expected demand in one period. We need to determine the numerator. The expected back orders that occur in a period are not quite the same as the expected back order in a period. The difference is that some of the back order might not have occurred in the period. (This is the same issue with the evaluation of the stockout probability.) For example, if the back order in a period is four units and demand in the period was three units, then only three of the four back orders actually occurred in that period; the remaining back-ordered unit was a carryover from a previous period.

Let's define some new notation. Let

$$B(l) = \text{Expected back orders if the lead time is } l$$

Hence, $B(l)$ is what we have been calling the *expected back order*.

The expected back order at the end of the $(l + 1)$th period of an interval of $l + 1$ periods is $B(l)$. If we subtract from those back orders the ones that were back-ordered at the end of the lth period in that interval, then we have the number of back orders that occurred in that last period of the interval. Hence,

$$\text{Probability of not being served} = \frac{B(l) - B(l - 1)}{\text{Expected demand in one period}}$$

The numerator of the above fraction, in words, is the expected back order minus what the expected back order would be if the lead time were one period faster. Our exact fill rate equation is thus

$$\text{Expected fill rate} = 1 - \frac{\text{Expected back order} - B(l - 1)}{\text{Expected demand in one period}}$$

The first fill rate equation presented in this section is an approximation because it does not subtract $B(l - 1)$ from the expected back order in the numerator. If the service level is very high, then $B(l - 1)$ will be very small, which is why the equation in the chapter is a good approximation.

If demand is Poisson with mean 0.29 per period and the lead time is one period, then

	Expected Fill Rate	
S	Approximation	Exact
0	−100.000%	0.000%
1	51.759	64.954
2	91.539	92.754
3	98.844	98.930
4	99.871	99.876
5	99.988	99.988
6	99.999	99.999

The approximation underestimates the fill rate, especially when the fill rate is low. However, the approximation is accurate for high fill rates.

Coordinating Buy-Back Price (Chapter 17)

If the wholesale price has been chosen, then we want to find the buy-back price that will lead the retailer to order the supply chain profit-maximizing quantity. This can be achieved if the retailer's critical ratio equals the supply chain's critical ratio because it is the critical ratio that determines the optimal order quantity.

Let's define some notation:

p = Retail price

c = Production cost

v = Retailer's salvage value

t = Shipping cost

w = wholesale price

b = buy-back price

The supply chain's critical ratio is $(p - c)/(p - v)$ because $C_u = p - c$ and $C_o = c - v$. The retailer's underage cost with the buy-back contract is $C_u = p - w$ and its overage cost is $C_o = t + w - b$ (i.e., the shipping cost plus the amount not credited by the supplier on returned inventory, $w - b$). Hence, the retailer's critical ratio equals the supply chain's critical ratio when

$$\frac{p - c}{p - v} = \frac{p - w}{(t + w - b) + p - w}$$

If we take the above equation and rearrange terms, we get equation (17.1).

Appendix E

Solutions to Selected Practice Problems

This appendix provides solutions to marked (*) practice problems.

Chapter 2

Q2.1 (Dell)

The following steps refer directly to Exhibit 2.1.

Step 1. For 2001, we find in Dell's 10-k: Inventory = $400 (in millions)

Step 2. For 2001, we find in Dell's 10-k: COGS = $26,442 (in millions)

Step 3. Inventory turns $= \dfrac{\$26,442/\text{Year}}{\$400} = 66.105$ turns per year

Step 4. Per-unit inventory cost $= \dfrac{40\% \text{ per year}}{66.105 \text{ per year}} = 0.605$ percent per unit

Chapter 3

Q3.1 (Single Flow Unit)

The following steps refer directly to Exhibit 3.1.

Step 1. We first compute the capacity of the three resources:

$$\text{Resource 1} : \frac{2}{10} \text{ unit per minute} = 0.2 \text{ unit per minute}$$

$$\text{Resource 2} : \frac{1}{6} \text{ unit per minute} = 0.1666 \text{ unit per minute}$$

$$\text{Resource 3} : \frac{3}{16} \text{ unit per minute} = 0.1875 \text{ unit per minute}$$

Step 2. Resource 2 has the lowest capacity; process capacity therefore is 0.1666 unit per minute, which is equal to 10 units per hour.

Step 3. Flow rate $=$ Min{Process capacity, Demand}

$$= \text{Min\{8 units per hour, 10 units per hour\}} = 8 \text{ units per hour}$$

This is equal to 0.1333 unit per minute.

Step 4. We find the utilizations of the three resources as

Resource 1: 0.1333 unit per minute/0.2 unit per minute = 66.66 percent
Resource 2: 0.1333 unit per minute/0.1666 unit per minute = 80 percent
Resource 3: 0.1333 unit per minute/0.1875 unit per minute = 71.11 percent

Q3.2 (Multiple Flow Units)

The following steps refer directly to Exhibit 3.2.

Step 1. Each resource can contribute the following capacity (in minutes of work per day):

Resource	Number of Workers	Minutes per Day
1	2	$2 \times 8 \times 60 = 960$
2	2	$2 \times 8 \times 60 = 960$
3	1	$1 \times 8 \times 60 = 480$
4	1	$1 \times 8 \times 60 = 480$
5	2	$2 \times 8 \times 60 = 960$

Step 2. Process flow diagram:

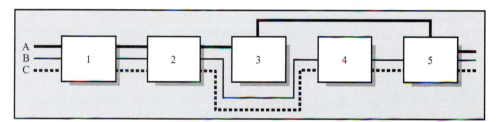

Step 3. We create a table indicating how much capacity will be consumed by the three products at the resources.

Resource	Capacity Requirement from A	Capacity Requirement from B	Capacity Requirement from C
1	$5 \times 40 = 200$	$5 \times 50 = 250$	$5 \times 60 = 300$
2	$3 \times 40 = 120$	$4 \times 50 = 200$	$5 \times 60 = 300$
3	$15 \times 40 = 600$	$0 \times 50 = 0$	$0 \times 60 = 0$
4	$0 \times 40 = 0$	$3 \times 50 = 150$	$3 \times 60 = 180$
5	$6 \times 40 = 240$	$6 \times 50 = 300$	$6 \times 60 = 360$

Step 4. Add up the rows to get the workload for each resource:

Workload for resource 1: $200 + 250 + 300 = 750$
Workload for resource 2: $120 + 200 + 300 = 620$
Workload for resource 3: $600 + 0 + 0 = 600$
Workload for resource 4: $0 + 150 + 180 = 330$
Workload for resource 5: $240 + 300 + 360 = 900$

Resource	Minutes per Day (see Step 1)	Workload per Day (see Step 4)	Implied Utilization (Step 4/Step 1)
1	960	750	0.78
2	960	620	0.65
3	480	600	1.25
4	480	330	0.69
5	960	900	0.94

Step 5. Compute implied utilization levels. Hence, resource 3 is the bottleneck. Thus, we cannot produce units A at a rate of 40 units per day. Since we are overutilized by 25 percent, we can produce units A at a rate of 32 units per day (four units per hour). Assuming the ratio between A, B, and C is constant (40:50:60), we will produce B at five units per hour and C at six units per hour. If the ratio between A, B, and C is *not* constant, this answer changes. In this case, we would produce 32 units of A and produce products B and C at the rate of demand (50 and 60 units per day respectively).

Chapter 4

Q4.1 (Empty System, Labor Utilization)

Part a

The following computations are based on Exhibit 4.1 in the book. Time to complete 100 units:

Step 1. The process will take $10 + 6 + 16$ minutes $= 32$ minutes to produce the first unit.

Step 2. Resource 2 is the bottleneck and the process capacity is 0.1666 unit per minute.

Step 3. Time to finish 100 units $= 32$ minutes $+ \dfrac{99 \text{ units}}{0.166 \text{ unit/minute}} = 626$ minutes

Parts b, c, and d

We answer these three questions together by using Exhibit 4.2 in the book.

Step 1. Capacities are

$$\text{Resource 1} : \frac{2}{10} \text{ unit/minute} = 0.2 \text{ unit/minute}$$

$$\text{Resource 2} : \frac{1}{6} \text{ unit/minute} = 0.1666 \text{ unit/minute}$$

$$\text{Resource 3} : \frac{3}{16} \text{ unit/minute} = 0.1875 \text{ unit/minute}$$

Resource 2 is the bottleneck and the process capacity is 0.1666 unit/minute.

Step 2. Since there is unlimited demand, the flow rate is determined by the capacity and therefore is 0.1666 unit/minute; this corresponds to a cycle time of 6 minutes/unit.

Step 3. Cost of direct labor $= \dfrac{6 \times \$10/\text{hour}}{60 \text{ minutes/hour} \times 0.1666 \text{ unit/minute}} = \$6/\text{unit}$

Step 4. Compute the idle time of each worker for each unit:

$$\text{Idle time for workers at resource 1} = 6 \text{ minutes/unit} \times 2 - 10 \text{ minutes/unit}$$
$$= 2 \text{ minutes/unit}$$

$$\text{Idle time for worker at resource 2} = 6 \text{ minutes/unit} \times 1 - 6 \text{ minutes/unit}$$
$$= 0 \text{ minute/unit}$$

$$\text{Idle time for workers at resource 3} = 6 \text{ minutes/unit} \times 3 - 16 \text{ minutes/unit}$$
$$= 2 \text{ minutes/unit}$$

Step 5. Labor content $= 10 + 6 + 16$ minutes/unit $= 32$ minutes/unit

Step 6. Average labor utilization $= \dfrac{32}{32 + 4} = 0.8888$

Chapter 5

Q5.1 (Venture Fair)

Part a
Dependency Matrix:

			Information-Providing Activity (Upstream)										
			1	2	3	4	5	6	7	8	9	10	11
	1	Ideation											
	2	Interview Customers	X										
	3	Analyze Competing Products	X										
Information-Receiving Activity (Downstream)	4	User/Customer Observation		X									
	5	Send E-Mail Surveys		X									
	6	Target Specifications			X	X	X						
	7	Product Design						X					
	8	Get Price Quotes							X				
	9	Build Prototype							X				
	10	Test Prototype with Customers									X		
	11	Prepare Info for Venture Fair								X		X	
Activity			1	2	3	4	5	6	7	8	9	10	11
Days			3	6	12	10	4	5	10	6	4	5	3

Part b
The critical path is A1→A2→A4→A6→A7→A9→A10→A11, which has a total duration of $3 + 6 + 10 + 5 + 10 + 4 + 5 + 3 = 46$. If the project team must have the materials finished by the day before the project fair (April 17th), then they must begin no later than March 3rd (29 days of work in March and 17 days in April).

Chapter 6

Q6.1 (Crazy Cab)

Part a/b

ROIC Tree:

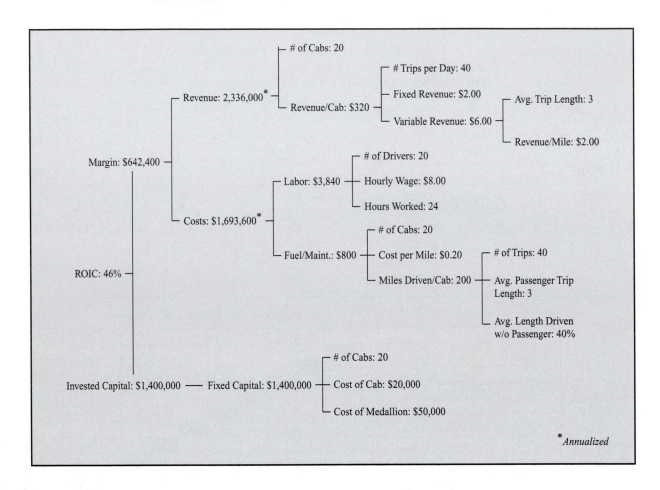

Part c

There are several variables that could be classified as operational value drivers including the number of trips per day, the average trip length, the drivers' hourly wage, and the average distance driven without passengers. Other variables such as the revenue per passenger mile, the fixed fees and the maintenance/fuel cost per mile driven are harder for management to influence because they are either regulated through the cab medallions or are strongly influenced by fuel prices (management could, however, invest in more fuel-efficient cars to reduce this cost).

Given the high capital investments associated with purchasing a cab and medallion, as well as the fixed labor requirements it is important that each cab maximizes its revenue. An additional trip is almost pure profit, particularly if it replaces idle driving time between passengers.

Part d

$$\text{Labor Efficiency} = \text{Revenue/Labor Costs}$$
$$= \text{Revenue/Mile} \times \text{Mile/Trip} \times \text{Trips/Day} \times \text{Day/Labor Costs}$$

In this equation, the first ratio measures the company's operational yield, which is largely a reflection of the company's pricing power. The next two ratios are measures of efficiency: the length of each trip and the number of daily trips, respectively. The final ratio is a measure of the cost of a resource, in this instance the company's labor costs.

A similar equation can be evaluated to determine the efficiency of each cab within the fleet:

$$\text{Cab Efficiency} = \text{Revenue/Cab}$$
$$= \text{Revenue/Mile} \times \text{Mile/Trip} \times \text{Trips/Cab}$$

Chapter 7

Q7.1 (Window Boxes)

The following computations are based on Exhibit 7.1.

Part a

Step 1. Since there is sufficient demand, the step (other than the stamping machine) that determines flow rate is assembly. Capacity at assembly is $\frac{12}{27}$ unit/minute.

Step 2. The production cycle consists of the following parts:
- Setup for A (120 minutes).
- Produce parts A (360×1 minute).
- Setup for B (120 minutes).
- Produce parts B (720×0.5 minute).

Step 3. There are two setups in the production cycle, so the setup time is 240 minutes.

Step 4. Every completed window box requires one part A (one minute per unit) and two parts B (2×0.5 minute per unit). Thus, the per-unit activity time is two minutes per unit.

Step 5. Use formula

$$\text{Capacity given batch size} = \frac{360 \text{ units}}{240 \text{ minutes} + 360 \text{ units} \times 2 \text{ minutes/unit}}$$
$$= 0.375 \text{ unit/minute}$$

Step 6. Capacity at stamping for a general batch size is

$$\frac{\text{Batch size}}{240 \text{ minutes} + \text{Batch size} \times 2 \text{ minutes/unit}}$$

We need to solve the equation

$$\frac{\text{Batch size}}{240 \text{ minutes} + \text{Batch size} \times 2 \text{ minutes/unit}} = \frac{12}{27}$$

for the batch size. The batch size solving this equation is Batch size = 960. We can obtain the same number directly by using

$$\text{Recommended batch size} = \frac{\text{Flow rate} \times \text{Setup time}}{1 - \text{Flow rate} \times \text{Time per unit}} = \frac{\frac{12}{27} \times 240}{1 - \frac{12}{27} \times 2} = 960$$

Q7.10 (Cat Food)

$$\frac{7 \times 500}{EOQ} = 1.62$$

Part a

Holding costs are $0.50 \times 15\%/50 = 0.0015$ per can per week. Note, each can is purchased for $0.50, so that is the value tied up in inventory and therefore determines the holding cost. The EOQ is then

Part b

The ordering cost is $7 per order. The number of orders per year is 500/EOQ. Thus, order cost = $/week = 81$/year

Part c

The average inventory level is EOQ/2. Inventory costs per week are thus $0.5 \times EOQ \times 0.0015 = \$1.62$. Given 50 weeks per year, the inventory cost per year is $81

Part d

Inventory turns 5 Flow rate/Inventory
    Flow Rate 5 500 cans per week
    Inventory 5 0.5 3 EOQ
    Thus, Inventory Turns = R/(0.5×EOQ) = 0.462 turns per week = 23.14 turns per year

Q7.11 (Beer Distributor)

The holding costs are 25% per year = 0.5% per week = 8*0.005 = $0.04 per week

$$\frac{7 \times 500}{EOQ} = 1.62$$

Part a

EOQ=

Part b

Inventory turns = Flow Rate/Inventory = $100 \times 50/(0.5 \times EOQ) = 5000/EOQ = 44.7$ turns per year

Part c

Per unit inventory cost =

Part d

You would never order more than Q = 600
    For Q = 600, we would get the following costs: $0.5 \times 600 \times 0.04 \times 0.95 + 10 \times 100/600 = 13.1$
    The cost per unit would be 13.1/100 = $0.131
    The quantity discount would save us 5%, which is $0.40 per case. However, our operating costs increase by $0.131 - 0.089 = \$0.042$. Hence, the savings outweigh the cost increase and it is better to order 600 units at a time.

Chapter 8

Q8.1 (Online Retailer)

Part a

We use Exhibit 8.1 for our computations.

Step 1. We collect the basic ingredients for the waiting time formula:

Activity time = 4 minutes

$$CV_p = \frac{2}{4}$$

Interarrival time = 2 minutes

$CV_a = 1$

Number of resources = 3

Step 2. This allows us to compute utilization as

$$p/am = 4/(2 \times 3) = 0.6666$$

Step 3. We then use the waiting time formula

$$T_q \approx \left(\frac{4}{3}\right) \times \left(\frac{0.666^{\sqrt{2(3+1)}-1}}{1 - 0.6666}\right) \times \left(\frac{1^2 + 0.5^2}{2}\right) = 1.19 \text{ minutes}$$

Step 4. We find the

Inventory in service: $I_p = m \times u = 3 \times 0.666 = 2$

Inventory in the queue: $I_q = T_q/a = 1.19/2 = 0.596$

Inventory in the system: $I = I_p + I_q = 2.596$

Part b

The number of e-mails that have been received but not yet answered corresponds to the total inventory of e-mails. We find this to be 2.596 e-mails (see Step 4 above).

Chapter 9

Q9.1 (Loss System)

We use Exhibit 9.1 to answer parts a through c.

Step 1. The interarrival time is 60 minutes per hour divided by 55 units arriving per hour, which is an interarrival time of $a = 1.0909$ minutes/unit. The processing time is $p = 6$ minutes/unit; this allows us to compute $r = p/a = 6/1.0909 = 5.5$.

Step 2. With $r = 5.5$ and $m = 7$, we can use the Erlang Loss Formula Table to look up $P_7(5.5)$ as 0.1525. Alternatively, we can use the actual loss formula (see Appendix C) to compute the probability that all seven servers are utilized:

$$\text{Prob \{all 7 servers are busy\}} = P_7(5.5) = \frac{\dfrac{5.5^7}{7!}}{1 + \dfrac{5.5^1}{1!} + \dfrac{5.5^2}{2!} + \cdots + \dfrac{5.5^7}{7!}} = 0.1525$$

Step 3. Compute the flow rate: $R = 1/a \times (1 - P_m) = 1/1.0909 \times (1 - 0.153) = 0.77$ unit per minute or 46.585 units per hour.

Step 4. Compute lost customers:

$$\text{Customers lost} = 1/a \times P_m = 1/1.0909 \times 0.153 = 0.14 \text{ unit per minute}$$

which corresponds to 8.415 units per hour.

Thus, from the 55 units that arrive every hour, 46.585 will be served and 8.415 will be lost.

Chapter 12

Q12.1 (McClure Books)

Part a

We first find the z-statistic for 400 (Dan's blockbuster threshold): $z = (400 - 200)/80 = 2.50$. From the Standard Normal Distribution Function Table, we see that $\Phi(2.50) = 0.9938$. So there is a 99.38 percent chance demand is 400 or fewer. Demand is greater than 400 with probability $1 - \Phi(2.50) = 0.0062$; that is, there is only a 0.62 percent chance this is a blockbuster.

Part b

We first find the z-statistic for 100 units (Dan's dog threshold): $z = (100 - 200)/80 = -1.25$. From the Standard Normal Distribution Function Table, we see that $\Phi(-1.25) = 0.1056$. So there is a 10.56 percent chance demand is 100 or fewer; that is, there is a 10.56 percent chance this book is a dog.

Part c

Demand is within 20 percent of the mean if it is between $1.2 \times 200 = 240$ and $0.8 \times 200 = 160$. Using Exhibit 12.2, we first find the z-statistic for 240 units (the upper limit on that range): $z = (240 - 200)/80 = 0.5$. From the Standard Normal Distribution Function Table, we see that $\Phi(0.5) = 0.6915$. Repeat the process for the lower limit on the range: $z = (160 - 200)/80 = -0.5$ and $\Phi(-0.5) = 0.3085$. The probability demand is between 160 and 240 is $\Phi(0.5) - \Phi(-0.50) = 0.6915 - 0.3085 = 0.3830$; that is, 38.3 percent.

Part d

The underage cost is $C_u = 20 - 12 = 8$. The salvage value is $12 - 4 = 8$ because Dan can return leftover books for a full refund ($12) but incurs a $4 cost of shipping and handling. Thus, the overage cost is cost minus salvage value: $C_o = 12 - 8 = 4$. The critical ratio is $C_u/(C_o + C_u) = 8/12 = 0.6667$. In the Standard Normal Distribution Function Table, we see that $\Phi(0.43) = 0.6664$ and $\Phi(0.44) = 0.6700$, so use the round-up rule and choose $z = 0.44$. Now convert z into the order quantity for the actual demand distribution: $Q = \mu + z \times \sigma = 200 + 0.44 \times 80 = 235.2$.

Part e

We want to find a z such that $\Phi(z) = 0.95$. In the Standard Normal Distribution Function Table, we see that $\Phi(1.64) = 0.9495$ and $\Phi(1.65) = 0.9505$, so use actual $200 + 1.65 \times 80 = 332$.

Part f

If the in-stock probability is 95 percent, then the stockout probability (which is what we are looking for) is 1 minus the in-stock, that is, $1 - 95\% = 5$ percent.

Part g

The z-statistic for 300 units is $z = (300 - 200)/80 = 1.25$. From the Standard Normal Loss Function Table, we see that $L(1.25) = 0.0506$. Expected lost sales are $\sigma \times L(1.25) = 4.05$. Expected sales are $200 - 4.05 = 195.95$, expected leftover inventory is $300 - 195.95 = 104.05$, and

$$
\begin{aligned}
\text{Expected profit} &= (\text{Price} - \text{Cost}) \times \text{Expected sales} \\
&\quad - (\text{Cost} - \text{Salvage value}) \times \text{Expected leftover inventory} \\
&= (20 - 12) \times 195.95 - (12 - 8) \times 104.05 \\
&= 1151.4
\end{aligned}
$$

Q12.2 (EcoTable Tea)

Part a

We need to evaluate the stockout probability with $Q = 3$. From the Poisson Distribution Function Table, $F(3) = 0.34230$. The stockout probability is $1 - F(3) = 65.8$ percent.

Part b

They will need to mark down three or more baskets if demand is seven or fewer. From the Poisson Distribution Function Table, $F(7) = 0.91341$, so there is a 91.3 percent probability this will occur.

Part c

First evaluate their critical ratio. The underage cost (or cost of a lost sale) is $\$55 - \$32 = \$23$. The overage cost (or the cost of having a unit left in inventory) is $\$32 - \$20 = \$12$. The critical ratio is $C_u/(C_o + C_u) = 0.6571$. From the Poisson Distribution Function Table, with a mean of 4.5, we see that $F(4) = 0.53210$ and $F(5) = 0.70293$, so we apply the round-up rule and order five baskets.

Part d

With four baskets, expected lost sales is 1.08808, according to the Poisson Loss Function Table. Expected sales is then $4.5 - 1.08808 = 3.4$.

Part e

With six baskets, expected lost sales is 0.32312, according to the Poisson Loss Function Table. Expected sales is then $4.5 - 0.32312 = 4.17688$. Expected leftover inventory is then $6 - 4.17688 = 1.72312 \approx 1.8$.

Part f

From the Poisson Distribution Function Table, $F(6) = 0.83105$ and $F(7) = 0.91314$. Hence, order seven baskets to achieve at least a 90 percent in-stock probability (in fact, the in-stock probability will be 91.3 percent).

Part g

If they order eight baskets, then expected lost sales is 0.06758. Expected sales is $4.5 - 0.06758 = 4.43242$. Expected leftover inventory is $8 - 4.43242 = 3.56758$. Profit is then $\$23 \times 4.43242 - \$12 \times 3.56758 = \$59.13$.

Q12.3 (Pony Express Creations)

Part a

If they purchase 40,000 units, then they need to liquidate 10,000 or more units if demand is 30,000 units or lower. From the table provided, $F(30,000) = 0.7852$, so there is a 78.52 percent chance they need to liquidate 10,000 or more units.

Part b

The underage cost is $C_u = 12 - 6 = 6$, the overage cost is $C_o = 6 - 2.5 = 3.5$, and the critical ratio is $6/(3.5 + 6) = 0.6316$. Looking in the demand forecast table, we see that $F(25,000) = 0.6289$ and $F(30,000) = 0.7852$, so use the round-up rule and order 30,000 Elvis wigs.

Part c

We want to find a Q such that $F(Q) = 0.90$. From the demand forecast table, we see that $F(35,000) = 0.8894$ and $F(40,000) = 0.9489$, so use the round-up rule and order 40,000 Elvis wigs. The actual in-stock probability is then 94.89 percent.

Part d

If $Q = 50,000$, then expected lost sales from the table are only 61 units. Expected leftover inventory $= Q - \mu +$ Expected lost sales $= 50,000 - 25,000 + 61 = 25,061$.

Part e

A 100 percent in-stock probability requires an order quantity of 75,000 units. With $Q = 75,000$, then expected lost sales from the table are only two units. Use Exhibit 12.5 to evaluate expected sales, expected leftover inventory, and expected profit. Expected sales are expected demand minus expected lost sales $= 25,000 - 2 = 24,998$. Expected leftover inventory is $75,000 - 24,998 = 50,002$.

$$
\begin{aligned}
\text{Expected profit} &= (\text{Price} - \text{Cost}) \times \text{Expected sales} \\
&\quad - (\text{Cost} - \text{Salvage value}) \times \text{Expected leftover inventory} \\
&= (12 - 6) \times 24,998 - (6 - 2.5) \times 50,002 \\
&= -25,019
\end{aligned}
$$

So a 100 percent in-stock probability is a money-losing proposition.

Q12.4 (Flextrola)

Part a

It is within 25 percent of the forecast if it is greater than 750 and less than 1,250. Use Exhibit 12.2. The z-statistic for 750 is $z = (750 - 1,000)/600 = -0.42$ and the z-statistic for 1,250 is $z = (1,250 - 1,000)/600 = 0.42$. From the Standard Normal Distribution Function Table, we see that $\Phi(-0.42) = 0.3372$ and $\Phi(0.42) = 0.6628$. So there is a 33.72 percent chance demand is less than 750 and a 66.28 percent chance it is less than 1,250. The chance it is between 750 and 1,250 is the difference in those probabilities: $0.6628 - 0.3372 = 0.3256$.

Part b

The forecast is for 1,000 units. Demand is greater than 40 percent of the forecast if demand exceeds 1,400 units. Use Exhibit 12.2. Find the z-statistic that corresponds to 1,400 units:

$$z = \frac{Q - \mu}{\sigma} = \frac{1,400 - 1,000}{600} = 0.67$$

From the Standard Normal Distribution Function Table, $\Phi(0.67) = 0.7486$. Therefore, there is almost a 75 percent probability that demand is less than 1,400 units. The probability that demand is greater than 1,400 units is $1 - \Phi(0.67) = 0.2514$, or about 25 percent.

Part c

To find the expected profit-maximizing order quantity, first identify the underage and overage costs. The underage cost is $C_u = 121 - 72 = 49$ because each lost sale costs Flextrola its gross margin. The overage cost is $C_o = 72 - 50 = 22$ because each unit of leftover inventory can only be sold for $50. Now evaluate the critical ratio:

$$\frac{C_u}{C_o + C_u} = \frac{49}{22 + 49} = 0.6901$$

Look up the critical ratio in the Standard Normal Distribution Function Table: $\Phi(0.49) = 0.6879$ and $\Phi(0.50) = 0.6915$, so choose $z = 0.50$. Now convert the z-statistic into an order quantity: $Q = \mu + z \times \sigma = 1,000 + 0.5 \times 600 = 1,300$.

Part d

Use Exhibit 12.4 to evaluate expected lost sales and then Exhibit 12.5 to evaluate expected sales. If $Q = 1,200$, then the corresponding z-statistic is $z = (Q - \mu)/\sigma = (1,200 - 1,000)/600 = 0.33$. From the Standard Normal Distribution Loss Table, we see that $L(0.33) = 0.2555$. Expected lost sales are then $\sigma \times L(z) = 600 \times 0.2555 = 153.3$. Finally, recall that expected sales equal expected demand minus expected lost sales: Expected sales $= 1,000 - 153.3 = 846.7$.

Part e

Flextrola sells its leftover inventory in the secondary market, which equals Q minus expected sales $1,200 - 846.7 = 353.3$.

Part f

To evaluate the expected gross margin percentage, we begin with

$$\begin{aligned}
\text{Expected revenue} &= (\text{Price} \times \text{Expected sales}) \\
&\quad + (\text{Salvage value} \times \text{Expected leftover inventory}) \\
&= (121 \times 846.7) + (50 \times 353.3) \\
&= 120,116
\end{aligned}$$

Then we evaluate expected cost $= Q \times c = 1,200 \times 72 = 86,400$. Finally, expected gross margin percentage $= 1 - 86,400/120,116 = 28.1$ percent.

Part g

Use Exhibit 12.5 and the results from parts d and e to evaluate expected profit:

$$\text{Expected profit} = (\text{Price} - \text{Cost}) \times \text{Expected sales}$$
$$- (\text{Cost} - \text{Salvage value}) \times \text{Expected leftover inventory}$$
$$= (121 - 72) \times 846.7 - (72 - 50) \times 353.3$$
$$= 33,716$$

Part h

Solectric's expected profit is $1,200 \times (72 - 52) = 24,000$ because units are sold to Flextrola for \$72 and each unit has a production cost of \$52.

Part i

Flextrola incurs 400 or more units of lost sales if demand exceeds the order quantity by 400 or more units; that is, if demand is 1,600 units or greater. The z-statistic that corresponds to 1,600 is $z = (Q - \mu)/\sigma = (1,600 - 1,000)/600 = 1$. In the Standard Normal Distribution Function Table, $\Phi(1) = 0.8413$. Demand exceeds 1,600 with the probability $1 - \Phi(1) = 15.9$ percent.

Part j

The critical ratio is 0.6901. From the graph of the distribution function, we see that the probability demand is less than 1,150 with the log normal distribution about 0.70. Hence, the optimal order quantity with the log normal distribution is about 1,150 units.

Q12.5 (Fashionables)

Part a

The underage cost is $C_u = 70 - 40 = 30$ and the overage cost is $C_o = 40 - 20 = 20$. The critical ratio is $C_u/(C_o + C_u) = 30/50 = 0.6$. From the Standard Normal Distribution Function Table, $\Phi(0.25) = 0.5987$ and $\Phi(0.26) = 0.6026$, so we choose $z = 0.26$. Convert that z-statistic into an order quantity $Q = \mu + z \times \sigma = 500 + 0.26 \times 200 = 552$. Note that the cost of a truckload has no impact on the profit-maximizing order quantity.

Part b

We need to find the z in the Standard Normal Distribution Function Table such that $\Phi(z) = 0.9750$ because $\Phi(z)$ is the in-stock probability. We see that $\Phi(1.96) = 0.9750$, so we choose $z = 1.96$. Convert to $Q = \mu + z \times \sigma = 500 + 1.96 \times 200 = 892$.

Part c

If 725 units are ordered, then the corresponding z-statistic is $z = (Q - \mu)/\sigma = (725 - 500)/200 = 1.13$. We need to evaluate lost sales, expected sales, and expected leftover inventory before we can evaluate the expected profit. Expected lost sales with the standard normal is obtained from the Standard Normal Loss Function Table, $L(1.13) = 0.0646$. Expected lost sales are $\sigma \times L(z) = 200 \times 0.0646 = 12.9$. Expected sales are $500 - 12.9 = 487.1$. Expected leftover inventory is $725 - 487.1 = 237.9$. Expected profit is

$$\text{Expected profit} = (70 - 40) \times 487.1 - (40 - 20) \times 237.9$$
$$= 9,855$$

So the expected profit per sweater type is 9,855. The total expected profit is five times that amount, minus 2,000 times the number of truckloads required.

Part d

The stockout probability is the probability demand exceeds the order quantity 725, which is $1 - \Phi(1.13) = 12.9$ percent.

Part e

If we order the expected profit-maximizing order quantity for each sweater, then that equals $5 \times 552 = 2,760$ sweaters. With an order quantity of 552 sweaters, expected lost sales are $56.5 = 200 \times L(0.26) = 200 \times 0.2824$, expected sales are $500 - 56.5 = 443.5$, and expected leftover inventory is $552 - 443.5 = 108.5$. Expected profit per sweater type is

$$\text{Expected profit} = (70 - 40) \times 443.5 - (40 - 20) \times 108.5$$
$$= 11,135$$

Because two truckloads are required, the total profit is then $5 \times 11,136 - 2 \times 2,000 = 51,675$. If we order only 500 units per sweater type, then we can evaluate the expected profit per sweater to be 11,010. Total profit is then $5 \times 11,010 - 2,000 = 53,050$. Therefore, we are better off just ordering one truckload with 500 sweaters of each type.

Chapter 13

Q13.1 (Teddy Bower)

Part a

Teddy will order from the American supplier if demand exceeds 1,500 units. With $Q = 1,500$, the z-statistic is $z = (1,500 - 2,100)/1,200 = -0.5$. From the Standard Normal Distribution Function Table, we see that $\Phi(-0.50) = 0.3085$, which is the probability that demand is 1,500 or fewer. The probability that demand exceeds 1,500 is $1 - \Phi(-0.50) = 0.6915$, or about 69 percent.

Part b

The supplier's expected demand equals Teddy's expected lost sales with an order quantity of 1,500 parkas. From the Standard Normal Loss Function Table, $L(-0.50) = 0.6978$. Expected lost sales are $\sigma \times L(z) = 1,200 \times 0.6978 = 837.4$.

Part c

The overage cost is $C_o = 10 - 0 = 10$ because leftover parkas must have been purchased in the first order at a cost of $10 and they have no value at the end of the season. The underage cost is $C_u = 15 - 10 = 5$ because there is a $5 premium on units ordered from the American vendor. The critical ratio is $5/(10 + 5) = 0.3333$. From the Standard Normal Distribution Function Table, we see that $\Phi(-0.44) = 0.3300$ and $\Phi(-0.43) = 0.3336$, so choose $z = -0.43$. Convert to Q: $Q = 2,100 - 0.43 \times 1,200 = 1,584$.

Part d

First evaluate some performance measures. We already know that with $Q = 1,584$ the corresponding z is -0.43. From the Standard Normal Loss Function Table, $L(-0.43) = 0.6503$. Expected lost sales are then $1,200 \times 0.6503 = 780.4$; that is the expected order quantity to the American vendor. If the American vendor were not available, then expected sales would be $2,100 - 780.4 = 1,319.6$. Expected leftover inventory is then $1,584 - 1,319.6 = 264.4$. Now evaluate expected profit with the American vendor option available. Expected revenue is $2,100 \times 22 = \$46,200$. The cost of the first order is $1,584 \times 10 = \$15,840$. Salvage revenue from leftover inventory is $264.4 \times 0 = 0$. Finally, the cost of the second order is $780.4 \times 15 = \$11,706$. Thus, profit is $46,200 - 15,840 - 11,706 = \$18,654$.

Part e

If Teddy only sources from the American supplier, then expected profit would be $(\$22 - \$15) \times 2,100 = \$14,700$ because expected sales would be 2,100 units and the gross margin on each unit is $\$22 - \$15 = \$7$.

Q13.2 (Flextrola)

Part a

Expected sales $= 1,000$ and the gross margin per sale is $121 - 83.5 = \$37.5$. Expected profit is then $1,000 \times \$37.5 = \$37,500$.

Part b

$C_o = 72 - 50 = 22$; $C_u = 83.5 - 72 = 11.5$; therefore, the premium on orders from XE is $\$11.5$. The critical ratio is $11.5/(22 + 11.5) = 0.3433$. From the Standard Normal Distribution Function Table, $\Phi(-0.41) = 0.3409$ and $\Phi(-0.40) = 0.3446$, so $z = -0.40$. Convert to Q: $Q = 1,000 - 0.4 \times 600 = 760$.

Part c

The underage cost on an option is the change in profit if one additional option had been purchased that could be exercised. For example, if 700 options are purchased, but demand is 701, then 1 additional option could have been purchased. The cost of the option plus exercising it is $\$25 + \$50 = \$75$. The cost of obtaining the unit without the option is $\$83.5$, so purchasing the option would have saved $C_u = \$83.5 - \$75 = \$8.5$. The overage cost on an option is the extra profit that could have been earned if the option were not purchased assuming it isn't needed. For example, if demand were 699, then the last option would not be necessary. The cost of that unnecessary option is $C_o = \$25$. The critical ratio is $8.5/(25 + 8.5) = 0.2537$. From the Standard Normal Distribution Function Table, $\Phi(-0.67) = 0.2514$ and $\Phi(-0.66) = 0.2546$, so $z = -0.66$. Convert to Q: $Q = 1,000 - 0.66 \times 600 = 604$.

Part d

Evaluate some performance measures. Expected number of units ordered beyond the purchased options (expected lost sales) is $\sigma \times L(-0.66) = 600 \times 0.8128 = 487.7$. Expected number of options exercised (expected sales) is $1,000 - 487.7 = 512.3$. Expected revenue is $1,000 \times \$121 = \$121,000$. So profit is revenue minus the cost of purchasing options $(604 \times \$25 = \$15,100)$, minus the cost of exercising options $(512.3 \times \$50 = \$25,615)$, minus the cost of units purchased without options $(487.7 \times \$83.5 = \$40,723)$: Profit $= 121,000 - 15,100 - 25,615 - 40,723 = \$39,562$.

Q13.3 (Wildcat Cellular)

Part a

The underage cost is $C_u = 0.4 - 0.05 = \$0.35$: if her usage exceeds the minutes she purchases then she could have lowered her cost by $\$0.35$ per minute if she had purchased more minutes. The overage cost is $0.05 = C_o$ because each minute purchased but not used provides no value. The critical ratio is $0.35/(0.05 + 0.35) = 0.8749$. From the Standard Normal

Distribution Funtion Table Func Table $\Phi(1.15) = 0.8749$ and $\Phi(1.16) = 0.8770$, so $z = 1.16$. Convert to Q: $Q = 250 + 1.16 \times 24 = 278$.

Part b

We need to evaluate the number of minutes used beyond the quantity purchased (Expected lost sales). $z = (240 - 250)/24 = -0.42$, $L(-0.42) = 0.6436$, and expected lost sales = $24 \times 0.6436 = 15.4$ minutes. Each minute costs $0.4, so the total surcharge is $15.4 \times \$0.4 = \$6.16$.

Part c

Find the corresponding z-statistic: $z = (280 - 250)/24 = 1.25$. Now evaluate performance measures. $L(1.25) = 0.0506$, and Expected lost sales = $24 \times 0.0506 = 1.2$ minutes, that is, only 1.2 minutes are needed on average beyond the 280 purchased. The minutes used out of the 280 (Expected sales) is $250 - 1.2 = 248.8$. The unused minutes (Expected left over inventory) is $280 - 248.8 = 31.2$.

Part d

Find the corresponding z-statistic: $z = (260 - 250)/24 = 0.42$. The number of minutes needed beyond the 260 is Expected lost sales: $L(0.42) = 0.2236$, and Expected lost sales = $24 \times 0.2236 = 5.4$ minutes. Total bill is $260 \times 0.05 + 5.4 \times 0.4 = \$15.16$.

Part e

From the Standard Normal Distribution Function Table $\Phi(1.64) = 0.9495$ and $\Phi(1.65) = 0.9505$, so with $z = 1.65$ there is a 95.05 percent chance the outcome of a Standard Normal is less than z. Convert to Q: $Q = 250 + 1.65 \times 24 = 290$.

Part f

With "Pick Your Minutes," the optimal number of minutes is 278. The expected bill is then $14.46: $z = (278 - 250)/24 = 1.17$; $L(1.17) = 0.0596$; Expected surcharge minutes = $24 \times 0.0596 = 1.4$; Expected surcharge = $\$0.4 \times 1.4 = \$0.56$; Purchase cost is $278 \times 0.05 = \$13.9$; so the total is $\$13.9 + 0.56$. With "No Minimum," the total bill is $22.5: minutes cost $\$0.07 \times 250 = \$17.5$; plus the fixed fee, $5. So she should stick with the original plan.

Q13.9 (Steve Smith)

For every car Smith sells, he gets $350 and an additional $50 for every car sold over five cars. Look in the Poisson Loss Function Table for mean 5.5: the expected amount by which the outcome exceeds zero is $L(0) = 5.5$ (same as the mean) and the expected amount by which the outcome exceeds five is $L(5) = 1.178$. Therefore, the expected commission is $(350 \times 5.5) + (50 \times 1.178) = 1,984$.

Chapter 14

Q14.1 (Furniture Store)

Part a

Inventory position = Inventory level + On-order = $100 + 85 = 185$. Order enough to raise the inventory position to the order-up-to level, in this case, $220 - 185 = 35$ desks.

Part b

As in part a, Inventory position = $160 + 65 = 225$. Because the inventory position is above the order-up-to level, 220, you do not order additional inventory.

Part c

Use Exhibit 14.5. From the Standard Normal Distribution Function Table: $\Phi(2.05) = 0.9798$ and $\Phi(2.06) = 0.9803$, so choose $z = 2.06$. The lead time l is 2, so $\mu = (2 + 1) \times 40 = 120$ and $\sigma = \sqrt{2 + 1} \times 20 = 34.64$.

$$S = \mu + z \times \sigma = 120 + 2.06 \times 34.64 = 191.36$$

Part d

Use Exhibit 14.4. The z-statistic that corresponds to $S = 120$ is $S = (120 - 120)/34.64 = 0$. Expected back order is $\sigma \times L(0) = 34.64 \times 0.3989 = 13.82$. Expected on-hand inventory is $S - \mu +$ Expected back order $= 120 - 120 + 13.82 = 13.82$.

Part e

From part d, on-hand inventory is 13.82 units, which equals $13.82 \times \$200 = \$2,764$. Cost of capital is 15 percent, so the cost of holding inventory is $0.15 \times \$2,764 = \$414.60$.

Q14.2 (Campus Bookstore)

Part a

Use Exhibit 14.5. Mean demand over $l + 1$ periods is $0.5 \times (4 + 1) = 2.5$ units. From the Poisson Distribution Function Table, with mean 2.5 we have $F(6) = 0.9858$ and $F(7) = 0.9958$, so choose $S = 7$ to achieve a 99 percent in-stock.

Part b

Use Exhibit 14.4. Pipeline inventory is $l \times$ Expected demand in one period $= 4 \times 0.5 = 2$ units. The order-up-to level has no influence on the pipeline inventory.

Part c

Use Exhibit 14.4. From the Poisson Loss Function Table with mean 2.5, Expected back order $= L(5) = 0.06195$. Expected on-hand inventory $= 5 - 2.5 + 0.06195 = 2.56$ units.

Part d

A stockout occurs if demand is seven or more units over $l + 1$ periods, which is one minus the probability demand is six or fewer in that interval. From the Poisson Distribution Function Table with mean 2.5, we see that $F(6) = 0.9858$ and $1 - F(6) = 0.0142$; that is, there is about a 1.4 percent chance of a stockout occurring.

Part e

The store is out of stock if demand is six or more units over $l + 1$ periods, which is one minus the probability demand is five or fewer in that interval. From the Poisson Distribution Function Table with mean 2.5, we see that $F(5) = 0.9580$ and $1 - F(5) = 0.0420$; that is, there is about a 4.2 percent chance of being out of inventory at the end of any given week.

Part f

The store has one or more units of inventory if demand is five or fewer over $l + 1$ periods. From part e, $F(5) = 0.9580$; that is, there is about a 96 percent chance of having one or more units at the end of any given week.

Part g

Use Exhibit 14.5. Now the lead time is two periods (each period is two weeks and the total lead time is four weeks, or two periods). Demand over one period is 1.0 unit. Demand over $l + 1$ periods is $(2 + 1) \times 1 = 3.0$ units. From the Poisson Distribution Function Table with mean 3.0, we have $F(7) = 0.9881$ and $F(8) = 0.9962$, so choose $S = 8$ to achieve a 99 percent in-stock.

Part h

Use Exhibit 14.4. Pipeline inventory is average demand over l periods $= 2 \times 1 = 2.0$ units.

Q14.3 (Quick Print)

Part a

If $S = 700$ and the inventory position is $523 + 180 = 703$, then 0 units should be ordered because the inventory position exceeds the order-up-to level.

Part b

Use Exhibit 14.5. From the Standard Normal Distribution Function Table, $\Phi(2.32) = 0.9898$ and $\Phi(2.33) = 0.9901$, so choose $z = 2.33$. Convert to $S = \mu + z \times \sigma = 600 + 2.33 \times 159.22 = 971$.

Q14.4 (Main Line Auto Distributor)

Part a

Use equation (14.2). The critical ratio is $\$25/(\$0.5 + \$25) = 0.98039$. The lead time is $l = 0$, so demand over $(l + 1)$ periods is Poisson with mean 1.5. From the Poisson Distribution Function Table with mean 1.5, we see $F(3) = 0.9344$ and $F(4) = 0.9814$, so choose $S = 4$. There is currently no unit on order or on hand, so order to raise the inventory position to four: order four units.

Part b

The in-stock probability is the probability demand is satisfied during the week. With $S = 3$ the in-stock is $F(3) = 0.9344$, that is, a 93 percent probability.

Part c

Demand is not satisfied if demand is five or more units, which is $1 - [F(4) = 0.9814] = 1 - 0.9814 = 0.0186$, or about 1.9 percent.

Part d

Use Exhibit 14.5. From the Poisson Distribution Function Table with mean 1.5, $F(4) = 0.9814$ and $F(5) = 0.9955$, so choose $S = 5$ to achieve a 99.5 percent in-stock probability.

Part e

Use Exhibit 14.4. If $S = 5$, then from the Poisson Loss Function Table with mean 1.5, we see expected back order $= L(5) = 0.0056$. Expected on-hand inventory is $S -$ Demand over $(l + 1)$ periods $+$ Expected back order $= 5 - 1.5 + 0.0056 = 3.51$ units. The holding cost is $3.51 \times \$0.5 = \$1.76$.

Q14.5 (Hotspices.com)

Part a

From the Standard Normal Distribution Function Table, $\Phi(2.43) = 0.9925$; so choose $z = 2.43$. Convert to S: $S = \mu + z \times \sigma = 159.62 + 2.43 \times 95.51 = 392$.

Part b

Use equation (14.3). The holding cost is $h = 0.75$ and the back-order penalty cost is 50. The critical ratio is $50/(0.75 + 50) = 0.9852$. From the Standard Normal Distribution Function Table, $\Phi(2.17) = 0.9850$ and $\Phi(2.18) = 0.9854$, so choose $z = 2.18$. Convert to $S = \mu + z \times \sigma = 159.62 + 2.18 \times 95.51 = 368$.

Part c

Use equation (14.3). The holding cost is $h = 0.05$ and the back-order penalty cost is 5. The critical ratio is $5/(0.05 + 5) = 0.9901$. Lead time plus one demand is Poisson with mean $1 \times 3 = 3$. From the Poisson Distribution Function Table, with $\mu = 3$, $F(7) = 0.9881$ and $F(8) = 0.9962$, so $S = 8$ is optimal.

Chapter 15

Q15.1 (Egghead)

Part a

New standard deviation is $30 \times \sqrt{50} = 212$.

Part b

Pipeline inventory = Expected demand per week $\times$ Lead time = $200 \times 50 \times 10 = 100{,}000$.

Q15.2 (Two Products)

The coefficient of total demand (pooled demand) is the coefficient of the product's demand times the square root of (1 + Correlation)/2. Therefore, $\sqrt{(1 - 0.7)/2} \times 0.6 = 0.23$.

Q15.3 (Fancy Paints)

Part a

Assume Fancy Paints implements the order-up-to inventory model. Find the appropriate order-up-to level. With a lead time of 4 weeks, the relevant demand is demand over $4 + 1 = 5$ weeks, which is $5 \times 1.25 = 6.25$. From the Poisson Distribution Function Table, $F(10) = 0.946$ and $F(11) = 0.974$, a base stock level $S = 11$ is needed to achieve at least a 95 percent in-stock probability. On-hand inventory at the end of the week is $S - 6.25 -$ Expected back order. From the Poisson Distribution Function Loss Function Table, the Expected back order is $L(11) = 0.04673$. Thus, on-hand inventory for one SKU is $11 - 6.25 + 0.04673 = 4.8$ units. There are 200 SKUs, so total inventory is $200 \times 4.8 = 960$.

Part b

The standard deviation over (4 + 1) weeks is $\sigma = \sqrt{5} \times 8 = 17.89$ and $\mu = 5 \times 50 = 250$. From the Standard Normal Distribution Function Table, we see that $\Phi(1.64) = 0.9495$ and $\Phi(1.65) = 0.9505$, so we choose $z = 1.65$ to achieve the 95 percent in-stock probability. The base stock level is then $S = \mu + z \times \sigma = 250 + 1.65 \times 17.89 = 279.5$. From the Standard Normal Loss Function Table, $L(1.65) = 0.0206$. So, on-hand inventory for one product is $S - 250$ + Expected back order = $279.5 - 250 + 17.89 \times 0.0206 =$ 29.9. There are five basic SKUs, so total inventory in the store is $29.9 \times 5 = 149.5$.

Part c

The original inventory investment is $960 \times \$14 = \$13,440$, which incurs holding costs of $\$13,440 \times 0.20 = \$2,688$. Repeat part b, but now the target in-stock probability is 98 percent. From the Standard Normal Distribution Function Table, we see that $F(2.05) = 0.9798$ and $F(2.06) = 0.9803$, so we choose $z = 2.06$ to achieve the 98 percent in-stock probability. The base stock level is then $S = \mu + z \times \sigma = 250 + 2.06 \times 17.89 = 286.9$. From the Standard Normal Loss Function Table, $L(2.06) = 0.0072$. So, on-hand inventory for one product is $S - 250$ + Expected back order = $286.9 - 250 + 17.89 \times 0.0072 = 37.0$. There are five basic SKUs, so total inventory in the store is $37.0 \times 5 = 185$. With the mixing machine, the total inventory investment is $185 \times \$14 = \$2,590$. Holding cost is $\$2,590 \times 0.2 = \$518$, which is only 19 percent (518/2688) of the original inventory holding cost.

Q15.4 (Burger King)

Part a

Use the newsvendor model to determine an order quantity. Use Exhibit 12.7. From the table we see that $F(3,500) = 0.8480$ and $F(4,000) = 0.8911$, so order 4,000 for each store.

Part b

Use Exhibit 12.4 to evaluate expected lost sales and Exhibit 12.5 to evaluate the expected leftover inventory. Expected lost sales come from the table, $L(4,000) = 185.3$. Expected sales are $\mu - 185.3 = 2,251 - 185.3 = 2,065.7$. Expected leftover inventory is Q minus expected sales, $4,000 - 2,065.7 = 1,934.3$. Across 200 stores there will be $200 \times 1,934.3 = 386,860$ units left over.

Part c

The mean is 450,200. The coefficient of variation of individual stores is $1,600/2,251 = 0.7108$. The coefficient of variation of total demand, we are told, is one-half of that, $0.7108/2 = 0.3554$. Hence, the standard deviation of total demand is $450,200 \times 0.3554 = 160,001$. To find the optimal order quantity to hit an 85 percent in-stock probability, use Exhibit 12.7. From the Standard Normal Distribution Function Table, we see $\Phi(1.03) = 0.8485$ and $\Phi(1.04) = 0.8508$, so choose $z = 1.04$. Convert to $Q = 450,200 + 1.04 \times 160,001 = 616,601$.

Part d

Expected lost sales $= 160,001 \times L(z) = 160,001 \times 0.0772 = 12,352$. Expected sales $= 450,200 - 12,352 = 437,848$. Expected leftover inventory $= 616,601 - 437,848 = 178,753$, which is only 46 percent of what would be left over if individual stores held their own inventory.

Part e

The total order quantity is $4,000 \times 200 = 800,000$. With a mean of 450,200 and standard deviation of 160,001 (from part c), the corresponding z is $(800,000 - 450,200)/160,001 = 2.19$. From the Standard Normal Distribution Function Table, we see $\Phi(2.19) = 0.9857$, so the in-stock probability would be 98.57 percent instead of 89.11 percent if the inventory were held at each store.

Q15.5 (Livingstion Tools)

Part a

With a lead time of 3 weeks, μ (3 + 1) × 5,200 = 20,800 and $\sigma = \sqrt{3+1} \times 3,800 = 7,600$. The target expected back orders is (5,200/7,600) × (1 − 0.999) = 0.0007. From the Standard Normal Distribution Function Table, we see that Φ (3.10) = 0.9990, so we choose z = 3.10 to achieve the 99.9 percent in-stock probability. Convert to S = 20,800 + 3.10 × 7,600 = 44,360. Expected back order is 7,600 × 0.0003 = 2.28. Expected on-hand inventory for each product is 44,360 − 20,800 + 2.28 = 23,562. The total inventory for the two is 2 × 23,562 = 47,124.

Part b

Weekly demand for the two products is 5,200 × 2 = 10,400. The standard deviation of the two products is $\sqrt{2 \times (1 - \text{Correlation})}$ × Standard deviation of one product = $\sqrt{2 \times (1 - 0.20)} \times 3,800 = 4,806.66$. Lead time plus one expected demand is 10,400 × 4 = 41,600. Standard deviation over $(I + 1)$ periods is $\sqrt{(3+1)} \times 4,806.66 = 9,613$. Now repeat the process in part a with the new demand parameters. Convert to S = 41,600 + 3.10 × 9,613 = 71,401. Expected back order is 9,613 × 0.0003 = 2.88. Expected on-hand inventory is 71,401 − 41,600 + 2.88 = 29,804. The inventory investment is reduced by (47,124 − 29,804)/47,124 = 37 percent.

Q15.9 (Consulting Services)

Option a provides the longest chain, covering all four areas. This gives the maximum flexibility value to the firm, so that should be the chosen configuration. To see that it forms a long chain, Alice can do Regulations, as well as Bob. Bob can do Taxes, as well as Doug. Doug can do Strategy, as well as Cathy. Cathy can do Quota, as well as Alice. Hence, there is a single chain among all four consultants. The other options do not form a single chain.

Chapter 16

Q16.1 (The Inn at Penn)

Part a

The booking limit is capacity minus the protection level, which is 150 − 50 = 100; that is, allow up to 100 bookings at the low fare.

Part b

Use Exhibit 16.1. The underage cost is C_u = 200 − 120 = 80 and the overage cost is C_o = 120. The critical ratio is 80/(120 + 80) = 0.4. From the Standard Normal Distribution Function Table, we see $\Phi(-0.26)$ = 0.3974 and $\Phi(-0.25)$ = 0.4013, so choose z = −0.25. Evaluate Q: Q = 70 − 0.25 × 29 = 63.

Part c

Decreases. The lower price for business travelers leads to a lower critical ratio and hence to a lower protection level; that is, it is less valuable to protect rooms for the full fare.

Part d

The number of unfilled rooms with a protection level of 61 is the same as expected leftover inventory. Evaluate the critical ratio, z = (61 − 70)/29 = −0.31. From the Standard Normal Loss Function Table, $L(z)$ = 0.5730. Expected lost sales are 29 × 0.5730 = 16.62 and expected leftover inventory is 61 − 70 + 16.62 = 7.62. So we can expect 7.62 rooms to remain empty.

Part e

$70 \times \$200 + (150 - 70) \times \$120 = \$23,600$ because, on average, 70 rooms are sold at the high fare and $150 - 70 = 80$ are sold at the low fare.

Part f

$150 \times \$120 = \$18,000$.

Part g

If 50 are protected, we need to determine the number of rooms that are sold at the high fare. The z statistic is $(50 - 70)/29 = -0.69$. Expected lost sales are $29 \times L(-0.69) = 24.22$. Expected sales are $70 - 24.22 = 45.78$. Revenue is then $(150 - 50) \times \$120 + 45.78 \times \$200 = \$21,155$.

Q16.2 (Overbooking The Inn at Penn)

Part a

Use Exhibit 16.2. The underage cost is $120, the discount fare. The overage cost is $325. The critical ratio is $120/(325 + 120) = 0.2697$. From the table, $F(12) = 0.2283$ and $F(13) = 0.3171$, so the optimal overbook quantity is 13.

Part b

A reservation cannot be honored if there are nine or fewer no-shows. $F(9) = 0.0552$, so there is a 5.5 percent chance the hotel will be overbooked.

Part c

It is fully occupied if there are 15 or fewer no-shows, which has probability $F(15) = 0.5170$.

Part d

Bumped customers equal 20 minus the number of no-shows, so it is equivalent to left-over inventory. Lost sales are $L(20) = 0.28$, expected sales are $15.5 - 0.28 = 15.22$, and expected leftover inventory/bumped customers $= 20 - 15.22 = 4.78$. Each one costs $325, so the total cost is $\$325 \times 4.78 = \$1,554$.

Q16.3 (WAMB)

Part a

First evaluate the distribution function from the density function provided in the table: $F(8) = 0$, $F(9) = F(8) + 0.05 = 0.05$, $F(10) = F(9) + 0.10 = 0.15$, and so on. Let Q denote the number of slots to be protected for sale later and let D be the demand for slots at $10,000 each. If $D > Q$, we reserved too few slots and the underage penalty is $C_u = \$10,000 - \$4,000 = \$6,000$. If $D < Q$, we reserved too many slots and the overage penalty is $C_o = \$4,000$. The critical ratio is $6,000/(4,000 + 6,000) = 0.6$. From the table, we find $F(13) = 0.6$, so the optimal protection quantity is 13. Therefore, WAMB should sell $25 - 13 = 12$ slots in advance.

Part b

The underage penalty remains the same. The overage penalty is now $C_o = \$4,000 - \$2,500 = \$1,500$. Setting the protection level too high before meant lost revenue on the slot, but now at least $2,500 can be gained from the slot, so the loss is only $1,500. The critical ratio is $6,000/(1,500 + 6,000) = 0.8$. From the table, $F(15) = 0.8$, so protect 15 slots and sell $25 - 15 = 10$ in advance.

Part c

If the booking limit is 10, there are 15 slots for last-minute sales. There will be standby messages if there are 14 or fewer last-minute sales, which has probability $F(14) = 0.70$.

Part d

Over-overbooking means the company is hit with a $10,000 penalty, so $C_o = 10,000$. Under-overbooking means slots that could have sold for $4,000 are actually sold at the standby price of $2,500, so $C_u = 4,000 - 2,500 = 1,500$. The critical ratio is $1,500/(10,000 + 1,500) = 0.1304$. From the Poisson Distribution Function Table with mean 9.0, $F(5) = 0.1157$ and $F(6) = 0.2068$, so the optimal overbooking quantity is six, that is, sell up to 31 slots.

Part e

The overage cost remains the same: we incur a penalty of $10,000 for each bumped customer (and we refund the $1,000 deposit of that customer, too). The underage cost also remains the same. To explain, suppose they overbooked by two slots but there are three withdrawals. Because they have one empty slot, they sell it for $2,500. Had they overbooked by one more (three slots), then they would have collected $4,000 on that last slot instead of the $2,500, so the difference is $C_u = \$4,000-\$2,500 = \$1,500$. Note, the nonrefundable amount of $1,000 is collected from the three withdrawals in either scenario, so it doesn't figure into the change in profit by overbooking one more unit. The critical ratio is $1,500/(10,000 + 1,500) = 0.1304$. From the Poisson Distribution Function Table with mean 4.5, $F(1) = 0.0611$ and $F(2) = 0.17358$, so the optimal overbooking quantity is two, that is, sell up to 27 slots.

Q16.4 (Designer Dress)

Part a

The z-statistic is $(100 - 70)/40 = 0.75$. Expected lost sales are $40 \times L(z) = 40 \times 0.1312 = 5.248$. Expected sales are $70 - 5.248 = 64.752$. Expected leftover inventory is $100 - 64.752 = 35.248$.

Part b

Expected revenue is $10,000 \times 64.752 = \$647,520$.

Part c

Use Exhibit 16.1. The underage cost is $10,000 - \$6,000 = \$4,000$ because under-protecting boutique sales means a loss of $4,000 in revenue. Overprotecting means a loss of $6,000 in revenue. The critical ratio is $4,000/(6,000 + 4,000) = 0.4$. From the Standard Normal Distribution Function Table, we see $\Phi(-0.26) = 0.3974$ and $\Phi(-0.25) = 0.4013$, so choose $z = -0.25$. Evaluate Q: $Q = 40 - 0.25 \times 25 = 33.75$. So protect 34 dresses for sales at the boutique, which means sell $100 - 34 = 66$ dresses at the show.

Part d

If 34 dresses are sent to the boutique, then expected lost sales are $\sigma \times L(z) = 25 \times L(-0.25) = 25 \times 0.5363 = 13.41$. Expected sales are $40 - 13.41 = 26.59$. So revenue is $26.59 \times \$10,000 + (100 - 34) \times 6,000 = \$661,900$.

Part e

From part d, expected sales are 26.59, so expected leftover inventory is $34 - 26.59 = 7.41$ dresses.

Q16.5 (Overbooking, PHL-LAX)

Part a

Use Exhibit 16.2. The overage cost is $800 (over-overbooking means a bumped passenger, which costs $800). The underage cost is $475 (an empty seat). The critical ratio is $475/(800 + 475) = 0.3725$. From the Standard Normal Distribution Function Table, we see $\Phi(-0.33) = 0.3707$ and $\Phi(-0.32) = 0.3745$, so choose $z = -0.32$. Evaluate Y: $Y = 30 - 0.32 \times 15 = 25.2$. So the maximum number of reservations to accept is $200 + 25 = 225$.

Part b

$220 - 200 = 20$ seats are overbooked. The number of bumped passengers equals 20 minus the number of no-shows, which is equivalent to leftover inventory with an order quantity of 20. The z-statistic is $(20-30)/15 = -0.67$. $L(-0.67) = 0.8203$, so lost sales are $15 \times 0.8203 = 12.3$. Sales are $30 - 12.3 = 17.7$ and expected leftover inventory is $20 - 17.7 = 2.3$. If 2.3 customers are bumped, then the payout is $800 \times 2.3 = \$1,840$.

Part c

You will have bumped passengers if there are 19 or fewer no-shows. The z-statistic is $(19 - 30)/15 = -0.73$. $\Phi(-0.73) = 0.2317$, so there is about a 23 percent chance there will be bumped passengers.

Chapter 17

Q17.1 (Buying Tissues)

Part a

If orders are made every week, then the average order quantity equals one week's worth of demand, which is 25 cases. If at the end of the week there is one week's worth of inventory, then the average inventory is $25/2 + 25 = 37.5$. (In this case, inventory "saw-tooths" from a high of two weeks' worth of inventory down to one week, with an average of 1.5 weeks.) On average the inventory value is $37.5 \times 9.25 = \$346.9$. The holding cost per year is $52 \times 0.4\% = 20.8$ percent. Hence, the inventory holding cost with the first plan is $20.8\% \times \$346.9 = \$72$. Purchase cost is $52 \times 25 \times \$9.25 = \$12,025$. Total cost is $\$12,025 + \$72 = \$12,097$.

Part b

Four orders are made each year; each order on average is for $(52/4) \times 25 = 325$ units. Average inventory is then $325/2 + 25 = 187.5$. The price paid per unit is $\$9.40 \times 0.95 = \$8.93$. The value of that inventory is $187.5 \times \$8.93 = \$1,674$. Annual holding costs are $\$1,674 \times 20.8\% = \$348$. Purchase cost is $52 \times 25 \times \$8.93 = \$11,609$. Total cost is $\$348 + \$11,609 = \$11,957$.

Part c

P&G prefers our third plan as long as the price is higher than in the second plan, $8.93. But the retailer needs a low enough price so that its total cost with the third plan is not greater than in the second plan, $11,957 (from part b). In part a, we determined that the annual holding cost with a weekly ordering plan is approximately $72. If we lower the price, the annual holding cost will be a bit lower, but $72 is a conservative approximation of the holding cost. So the retailer's purchase cost should not exceed $11,957 − $72 = $11,885. Total purchase quantity is 25 × 52 = 1,300 units. So if the price is $11,885/1,300 = $9.14, then the retailer will be slightly better off (relative to the second plan) and P&G is much better off (revenue of $12,012 instead of $11,885).

Q17.2 (Returning Books)

Part a

Use the newsvendor model. The overage cost is C_o = Cost − Salvage value = $20 − $28/4 = $13. The underage cost is C_u = Price − Cost = $28 − $20 = $8. The critical ratio is 8/(13 + 8) = 0.3810. Look up the critical ratio in the Standard Normal Distribution Function Table to find the appropriate z statistic = −0.30. The optimal order quantity is $Q = \mu + z \times \sigma = 100 - 0.30 \times 42 = 87$.

Part b

Expected lost sales = $L(z) \times \sigma = 0.5668 \times 42 = 23.81$, where we find $L(z)$ from the Standard Normal Loss Function Table and $z = -0.30$ (from part a). Expected sales = μ − Expected lost sales = 100 − 23.81 = 76.2. Expected leftover inventory = Q − Expected sales = 87 − 76.2 = 10.8. Profit = Price × Expected sales + Salvage value × Expected leftover inventory − Q × Cost = $28 × 76.2 + $7 × 10.8 − 87 × $20 = $469.

Part c

The publisher's profit = Q × (Wholesale price − Cost) = 87 × ($20 − $7.5) = $1,087.5.

Part d

The underage cost remains the same because a lost sale still costs Dan the gross margin, C_u = $8. However, the overage cost has changed because Dan can now return books to the publisher. He buys each book for $20 and then returns leftover books for a net salvage value of $15 − $1 (due to the shipping cost) = $14. So his overage cost is now C_o = Cost − Salvage value = $20 − $14 = $6. The critical ratio is 8/(6 + 8) = 0.5714. Look up the critical ratio in the Standard Normal Distribution Function Table to find the appropriate z statistic = 0.18. The optimal order quantity is $Q = \mu + z \times \sigma = 100 + 0.18 \times 42 = 108$.

Part e

Expected lost sales = $L(z) \times \sigma = 0.3154 \times 42 = 13.2$, where we find $L(z)$ from the Standard Normal Loss Function Table and $z = 0.18$ (from part d). Expected sales = μ − Expected lost sales = 100 − 13.2 = 86.8. Expected leftover inventory = Q − Expected sales = 108 − 86.8 = 21.2. Profit = Price × Expected sales + Salvage value × Expected leftover inventory − Q × Cost = $28 × 86.8 + $14 × 21.2 − 108 × $20 = $567.

Part f

The publisher's sales revenue is $20 × 108 = $2,160. Production cost is $7.5 × 108 = $810. The publisher pays Dan $15 × 21.2 = $318. The publisher's total salvage revenue on returned books is $6 × 21.2 = $127.2. Profit is then $2,160 − $810 − $318 + $127.2 = $1,159. Note that both the publisher and Dan are better off with this buy-back arrangement.

Part g

Equation (17.1) in the text gives the buy-back price that coordinates the supply chain (that is, maximizes the supply chain's profit). That buy-back price is $1 + $28 − ($28 − $20) × ($28 − $6)/($28 − $7.5) = $20.41. Note, the publisher's buy-back price is actually higher than the wholesale price because the publisher needs to subsidize Dan's shipping cost to return books: Dan's net loss on each book returned is $20 − (20.41 − 1) = $0.59.

Chapter 18

Q18.1 (Bauxite to New Zealand)

Total emissions on the journey is $1,400,000 \times 38.2 = 53,480,000$ kgs CO_2. The journey transports $300,000 \times 3,000 = 900,000,000$ tonne kms. So emissions are $53,480,000$ kgs $CO_2/900,000,000$ tonne kms = 0.059 kgs CO_2 per tonne km.

Glossary

A

abandoning   Refers to flow units leaving the process because of lengthy waiting times.

activity   Value-adding steps in a process where resources process flow units.

activity on node (AON) representation   A way to graphically illustrate the project dependencies in which activities correspond to nodes in a graph.

activity time   The duration that a flow unit has to spend at a resource, not including any waiting time; also referred to as service time or processing time.

A/F ratio   The ratio of actual demand (A) to forecasted demand (F). Used to measure forecast accuracy.

Andon cord   A cord running adjacent to assembly lines that enables workers to stop production if they detect a defect. Just like the jidoka automatic shut-down of machines, this procedure dramatizes manufacturing problems and acts as a pressure for process improvements.

appointment   Predefined times at which the flow unit supposedly enters the process; used to reduce variability (and seasonality) in the arrival process.

assemble-to-order   Also known as make-to-order. A manufacturing system in which final assembly of a product only begins once a firm order has been received. Dell Inc. uses assemble-to-order with personal computers.

asset turns   See capital turns.

assignable causes of variation   Those effects that result in changes of the parameters of the underlying statistical distribution of the process. Thus, for assignable causes, a change in process performance is not driven simply by common-cause variation.

attribute-based control charts   A special form of control chart that only distinguishes between defective and nondefective items. Such control charts should be used if it is not possible to capture the quality conformance of a process outcome in one variable.

authorization level   For a fare class, the percentage of capacity that is available to that fare class or lower. An authorization level is equivalent to a booking limit expressed as a percentage of capacity.

availability   The proportion of a time a process (single resource or buffer) is able to either process (in the case of a resource) or admit (in the case of a buffer) incoming flow units.

average labor utilization   Measures the percentage of paid labor time that is spent on actual production as opposed to idle time; measures the efficiency of the process as well as the balance of work across workers.

B

back order   If demand occurs and inventory is not available, then the demand can be back-ordered until inventory becomes available.

back-order penalty cost   The cost incurred by a firm per back order. This cost can be explicit or implicit (e.g., lost goodwill and future business).

balancing resources   Attempting to achieve an even utilization across the resources in a process. This is equivalent to minimizing idle time by reallocating work from one resource to another.

base stock level   Also known as the order-up-to level. In the implementation of an order-up-to policy, inventory is ordered so that inventory position equals the base stock level.

batch   A collection of flow units.

batch flow operation   Those processes where flow units are batched to benefit from scale economies of production and/or transportation. Batch flow operations are known to have long flow times.

batch ordering   A firm batch orders when it orders in integer multiples of a fixed batch size. For example, if a firm's batch size is 20 cases, then the firm orders either 0, 20, 40, 60, . . . cases.

bid price   With bid price control, a bid price is assigned to each segment of capacity and a reservation is accepted only if its fare exceeds the bid prices of the segments of capacity that it uses.

bid price control   A method for controlling whether or not to accept a reservation. This method explicitly recognizes that not all customers paying the same fare for a segment of capacity are equally valuable to the firm.

blocking   The situation in which a resource has completed its work on a flow unit, yet cannot move the flow unit to the next step (resource or inventory) downstream as there is not space available.

booking limit   The maximum number of reservations that are allowed for a fare class or lower.

bottleneck   The resource with the lowest capacity in the process.

buckets   A booking limit is defined for a bucket that contains multiple fare class–itinerary combinations.

buffer   Another word for inventory, which is used especially if the role of the buffer is to maintain a certain throughput level despite the presence of variability.

buffer inventory   Allows resources to operate independent from each other, thereby avoiding blocking and starving (in which case we speak of a decoupling buffer).

buffer-or-suffer principle The inherent tension between inventory and flow rate. In a process that suffers from setup times or variability, adding inventory can increase the flow rate.

bullwhip effect The propagation of demand variability up the supply chain.

business model Articulates how a firm aims to create a positive net utility to the customer while making a profit. Typically involves choices with respect to the process timing, the process location, and the process standardization.

business model innovation A substantial shift in a firm's business model either relative to others in the industry or to its previous practice.

buy-back contract A contract in which a supplier agrees to purchase leftover inventory from a retailer at the end of the selling season.

C

capability index The ratio between the tolerance level and the actual variation of the process.

capacity Measures the maximum flow rate that can be supported by a resource.

capacity-constrained A process for which demand exceeds the process capacity.

capacity pooling The practice of combining multiple capacities to deliver one or more products or services.

capital turns The ratio between revenues and invested capital; measures how much capital is needed to support a certain size of a company.

carbon dioxide equivalent (CO_2e) For a given gas, the weight of CO_2 that has the equivalent warming potential as 1 kilogram of that gas.

carbon footprint The total creation of carbon dioxide equivalents an organization is responsible for. Can be analyzed in the form of scope 1, 2, or 3.

channel assembly The practice in the PC industry of having final assembly completed by a distributor (e.g., Ingram Micron) rather than the manufacturer (e.g., IBM).

channel stuffing The practice of inducing retailers to carry more inventory than needed to cover short-term needs.

coefficient of variation A measure of variability. Coefficient of variation = Standard deviation divided by the mean; that is, the ratio of the standard deviation of a random variable to the mean of the random variable. This is a relative measure of the uncertainty in a random variable.

collaborative planning, forecasting, and replenishment A set of practices designed to improve the exchange of information within a supply chain.

common causes of variation Constant variation reflecting pure randomness in the process. Such causes are hence a result of pure randomness as opposed to being the result of an assignable cause.

conservation-of-matter law A law that states that, on average, the flow into a system must equal the flow out of the system, otherwise the quantity within the system will not be stable.

consignment inventory Inventory that is kept at a customer's location but is owned by the supplier.

consolidated distribution The practice of delivering from a supplier to multiple locations (e.g., retail stores) via a distribution center.

continuous process A process in which the flow unit continuously flows from one resource to the next; different from discrete process, in which the flow units are separate entities.

contract manufacturer A firm that manufactures or assembles a product for another firm. Contract manufacturers typically manufacture products from multiple competitors, they are generally responsible for procurement, but they do not design or distribute the products they assemble.

control charts Graphical tools to statistically distinguish between assignable and common causes of variation. Control charts visualize variation, thereby enabling the user to judge whether the observed variation is due to common causes or assignable causes.

control limits Part of control charts that indicate to what extent a process outcome falls in line with the common cause variation of the process versus being a result of an assignable cause. Outcomes above the upper control limit (UCL) or below the lower control limit (LCL) indicate the presence of an assignable cause.

cost of direct labor Measures the per-unit cost of labor, which includes both the labor content (the actual labor going into completing a flow unit) and the idle time that occurs across all workers per completed flow unit.

critical path A project management term that refers to all those activities that—if delayed—would delay the overall completion of the project.

critical ratio The ratio of the underage cost to the sum of the overage and underage costs. It is used in the newsvendor model to choose the expected profit-maximizing order quantity.

cross docking The practice of moving inventory in a distribution facility from the inbound dock directly to the outbound loading dock without placing the inventory in storage within the distribution facility.

cycle inventory The inventory that results from receiving (producing) several flow units in one order (batch) that are then used over a time period of no further inflow of flow units.

cycle time The time that passes between two consecutive flow units leaving the process. Cycle time = 1/Flow rate.

D

decision tree A scenario-based approach to map out the discrete outcomes of a particular uncertainty.

decoupling inventory See buffer inventory.

demand pooling   combining demands from multiple sources to reduce overall variability.

discovery-driven planning   A process that emphasizes learning about unknown variables related to a project with the goal of deciding whether or not to invest further resources in the project.

demand aggregation   The idea to supply multiple demand streams with the same resource and thereby generate economies of scale.

demand-constrained   A process for which the flow rate is limited by demand.

demand-pull   An inventory policy in which demand triggers the ordering of replenishments.

density function   The function that returns the probability the outcome of a random variable will exactly equal the inputted value.

dependency matrix   Describes the dependencies among the activities in a project.

design specifications   Establish how much a process outcome is allowed to vary before it is labeled a defect. Design specifications are driven by customer requirements, not by control limits.

distribution function   The function that returns the probability the outcome of a random variable will equal the inputted value or lower.

diversion   The practice by retailers of purchasing product from a supplier only to resell the product to another retailer.

diverters   Firms that practice diversion.

double marginalization   The phenomenon in a supply chain in which one firm takes an action that does not optimize supply chain performance because the firm's margin is less than the supply chain's total margin.

DuPont model   A financial framework built around the idea that the overall ROIC of a business can be decomposed into two financial ratios, the margins and the asset turns.

E

earliest completion time (ECT)   The earliest time a project activity can be completed, which can be computed as the sum of the earliest start time and the duration of the activity.

earliest start time (EST)   The earliest time a project activity can start, which requires that all information providing activities are completed.

economies of scale   Obtaining lower cost per unit based on a higher flow rate. Can happen, among other reasons, because of a spread of fixed cost, learning, statistical reasons (pooling), or the usage of dedicated resources.

Efficient Consumer Response   The collective name given to several initiatives in the grocery industry to improve the efficiency of the grocery supply chain.

efficient frontier   All locations in a space of performance measures (e.g., time and cost) that are efficient, that is,

improvement along one dimension can occur only if the level of another dimension is reduced.

electronic data interchange (EDI)   A technology standard for the communication between firms in the supply chain.

elimination of flow units   Discarding defective flow units instead of reworking them.

e-lot system   A decoupling buffer that is tracked to detect any systemic variation that could suggest a defect in the process; it is thereby a way to direct managerial attention toward defects in the process that would otherwise be hidden by inventory without immediately losing flow rate.

empirical distribution function   A distribution function constructed with historical data.

EOQ (economic order quantity)   The quantity that minimizes the sum of inventory costs and fixed ordering cost.

erlang loss formula   Computes the proportion of time a resource has to deny access to incoming flow units in a system of multiple parallel servers and no space for inventory.

expected leftover inventory   The expected amount of inventory left over at the end of the season when a fixed quantity is chosen at the start of a single selling season with random demand.

expected lost sales   The expected amount of demand that is not satisfied when a fixed quantity is chosen at the start of a single selling season and demand is random.

Expected Marginal Seat Analysis   A technique developed by Peter Belobaba of MIT to assign booking limits to multiple fare classes.

expected sales   The expected amount of demand that is satisfied when a fixed quantity is chosen at the start of a single selling season and demand is random.

exponential distribution   Captures a random variable with distribution $\text{Prob}\{x < t\} = 1 - \exp(-t/a)$, where a is the mean as well as the standard deviation of the distribution. If interarrival times are exponentially distributed, we speak of a Poisson arrival process. The exponential distribution is known for the memoryless property; that is, if an exponentially distributed service time with mean five minutes has been going on for five minutes, the expected remaining duration is still five minutes.

external setups   Those elements of setup times that can be conducted while the machine is processing; an important element of setup time reduction/SMED.

F

FCFS (first-come, first-served)   Rule that states that flow units are processed in the order of their arrivals.

fences   Restrictions imposed on a low-fare class to prevent high-fare customers from purchasing the low fare. Examples include advanced purchase requirements and Saturday night stay over.

FIFO (first-in, first out)   See FCFS.

fill rate   The fraction of demand that is satisfied; that is, that is able to purchase a unit of inventory.

flexibility   The ability of a process to meet changes in demand and/or a high amount of product variety.

flow rate (R)   Also referred to as throughput. Flow rate measures the number of flow units that move through the process in a given unit of time. *Example:* The plant produces at a flow rate of 20 scooters per hour. Flow rate = Min{Demand, Capacity}.

flow time (T)   Measures the time a flow unit spends in the process, which includes the time it is worked on at various resources as well as any time it spends in inventory. *Example:* A customer spends a flow time of 30 minutes on the phone in a call center.

flow unit   The unit of analysis that we consider in process analysis; for example, patients in a hospital, scooters in a kick-scooter plant, and callers in a call center.

forecast   The estimate of demand and potentially also of the demand distribution.

forward buying   If a retailer purchases a large quantity during a trade promotion, then the retailer is said to forward buy.

G

gamma distribution   A continuous distribution. The sum of exponential distributions is a gamma distribution. This is a useful distribution to model demands with high coefficients of variation (say about 0.5).

Gantt chart   A graphical way to illustrate the durations of activities as well as potential dependencies between the activities.

H

heijunka   A principle of the Toyota Production System, proposing that models are mixed in the production process according to their mix in customer demand.

hockey stick phenomenon   A description of the demand pattern that a supplier can receive when there is a substantial amount of order synchronization among its customers.

holding cost rate   The cost incurred to hold one unit of inventory for one period of time.

horizontal pooling   Combining a sequence of resources in a queuing system that the flow unit would otherwise visit sequentially; increases the span of control; also related to the concept of a work cell.

I

idle time   The time a resource is not processing a flow unit. Idle time should be reduced as it is a non-value-adding element of labor cost.

ikko-nagashi   An element of the Toyota Production System. It advocates the piece-by-piece transfer of flow units (transfer batches of one).

implied utilization   The workload imposed by demand of a resource relative to its available capacity. Implied utilization = Demand rate/Capacity.

incentive conflicts   In a supply chain, firms may have conflicting incentives with respect to which actions should be taken.

independent arrivals   A requirement for both the waiting time and the loss formulas. Independent arrivals mean that the probability of having an arrival occur in the next x minutes is independent of how many arrivals have occurred in the last y minutes.

information turnaround time (ITAT)   The delay between the occurrence of a defect and its detection.

innovation   A novel match between a solution and a need that creates value.

in-stock probability   The probability all demand is satisfied over an interval of time.

integrated supply chain   The supply chain considered as a single integrated unit, that is, as if the individual firms were owned by a single entity.

interarrival time   The time that passes between two consecutive arrivals.

internal setups   Those elements of setup times that can only be conducted while the machine is not producing. Internal setups should be reduced as much as possible and/or converted to external setups wherever possible (SMED).

inventory (I)   The number of flow units that are in the process (or in a particular resource). Inventory can be expressed in (a) flow units (e.g., scooters), (b) days of supply (e.g., three days of inventory), or (c) monetary units ($1 million of inventory).

inventory cost   The cost a process incurs as a result of inventory. Inventory costs can be computed on a per-unit basis (see Exhibit 2.1) or on a per-unit-of-time basis.

inventory level   The on-hand inventory minus the number of units back-ordered.

inventory policy   The rule or method by which the timing and quantity of inventory replenishment are decided.

inventory position   The inventory level plus the number of units on order.

inventory turns   How often a company is able to turn over its inventory. Inventory turns = 1/Flow time, which—based on Little's Law—is COGS/Inventory.

Ishikawa diagram   Also known as fishbone diagram or cause–effect diagram; graphically represents variables that are causally related to a specific outcome.

J

jidoka   In the narrow sense, a specific type of machine that can automatically detect defects and automatically shut down itself. The basic idea is that shutting down the machine forces human intervention in the process, which in turn triggers process improvement.

just-in-time   The idea of producing units as close as possible to demand, as opposed to producing the units earlier and then leaving them in inventory or producing them later and thereby leaving the unit of demand waiting. Just-in-time is a fundamental part of the Toyota Production System as well as of the matching supply with demand framework postulated by this book.

K

kaizen   The continuous improvement of processes, typically driven by the persons directly involved with the process on a daily basis.

kanban   A production and inventory control system in which the production and delivery of parts are triggered by the consumption of parts downstream (pull system).

key performance indicator   An operational variable with a strong marginal impact on ROIC (value driver) that is used as an indicator of current operational performance.

L

labor content   The amount of labor that is spent on a flow unit from the beginning to the end of the process. In a purely manual process, we find labor content as the sum of all the activity times.

labor productivity   The ratio between revenue and labor cost.

labor utilization   How well a process uses the labor involved in the process. Labor utilization can be found based on activity times and idle times.

latest completion time (LCT)   The latest time a project activity has to be completed by to avoid delaying the overall completion time of the project.

latest start time (LST)   The latest time a project activity can start without delaying the overall completion time of the project.

lead time   The time between when an order is placed and when it is received. Process lead time is frequently used as an alternative word for flow time.

lean operations   An operations paradigm built around the idea of waste reduction; inspired by the Toyota Production System.

line balancing   The process of evenly distributing work across the resources of a process. Line balancing reduces idle time and can (a) reduce cycle time or (b) reduce the number of workers that are needed to support a given flow rate.

Little's Law   The average inventory is equal to the average flow rate times the average flow time ($I = R \times T$).

location pooling   The combination of inventory from multiple locations into a single location.

loss function   A function that returns the expected number of units by which a random variable exceeds the inputted value.

M

machine-paced line   A process design in which flow units are moved from one resource to another by a constant speed dictated by the conveyor belt. There is typically no inventory between the resources connected by a conveyor belt.

make-to-order   A production system, also known as assemble-to-order, in which flow units are produced only once the customer order for that flow unit has been received. Make-to-order production typically requires wait times for the customer, which is why it shares many similarities with service operations. Dell Inc. uses make-to-order with personal computers.

make-to-stock   A production system in which flow units are produced in anticipation of demand (forecast) and then held in finished goods inventory.

margin arithmetic   Equations that evaluate the percentage increase in profit as a function of the gross margin and the percentage increase in revenue.

marginal cost pricing   The practice of setting the wholesale price to the marginal cost of production.

materials requirement planning   A system to control the timing and quantity of component inventory replenishment based on forecasts of future demand and production schedules.

maximum profit   In the context of the newsvendor model, the expected profit earned if quantity can be chosen after observing demand. As a result, there are no lost sales and no leftover inventory.

mean   The expected value of a random variable.

mismatch cost   The sum of the underage cost and the overage cost. In the context of the newsvendor model, the mismatch cost is the sum of the lost profit due to lost sales and the total loss on leftover inventory.

mixed model production   See heijunka.

MRP jitters   The phenomenon in which multiple firms operate their MRP systems on the same cycle, thereby creating order synchronization.

muda   One specific form of waste, namely waste in the form of non-value-adding activities. Muda also refers to unnecessary inventory (which is considered the worst form of muda), as unnecessary inventory costs money without adding value and can cover up defects and other problems in the process.

multiple flow units   Used in a process that has a mix of products or customers flowing through it. Most computations, including the location of the bottleneck, depend on the mix of products.

N

negative binomial distribution   A discrete distribution function with two parameters that can independently change the mean of the distribution as well as the standard deviation. In contrast, the Poisson distribution has only one parameter and can only regulate its mean.

nested booking limits   Booking limits for multiple fare classes are nested if each booking limit is defined for a fare class or lower. With nested booking limits, it is always the case that an open fare class implies all higher fare classes are open and a closed fare class implies all lower fare classes are closed.

newsvendor model   A model used to choose a single order quantity before a single selling season with stochastic demand.

nonlinear   The relationship between variables if the graph of the two variables is not a straight line.

normal distribution   A continuous distribution function with the well-known bell-shaped density function.

no-show   A customer that makes a reservation but cancels or fails to arrive for service.

O

on allocation   A product whose total amount demanded exceeds available capacity.

on-hand inventory   The number of units currently in inventory.

on-order inventory   Also known as pipeline inventory. The number of units of inventory that have been ordered but have not been received.

one-for-one ordering policy   Another name for an order-up-to policy. (With this policy, one unit is ordered for every unit of demand.)

options contract   With this contract, a buyer pays a price per option purchased from a supplier and then pays an additional price later on to exercise options. The supplier is responsible for building enough capacity to satisfy all of the options purchased in case they are all exercised.

order batching   A cause of the bullwhip effect. A firm order batches when it orders only in integer multiples of some batch quantity.

order inflation   The practice of ordering more than desired in anticipation of receiving only a fraction of the order due to capacity constraints upstream.

order synchronization   A cause of the bullwhip effect. This describes the situation in which two or more firms submit orders at the same moments in time.

order-up-to level   Also known as the base stock level. In the implementation of an order-up-to policy, inventory is ordered so that inventory position equals the order-up-to level.

order-up-to model   A model used to manage inventory with stochastic demand, positive lead times, and multiple replenishments.

origin-destination control   A revenue management system in the airline industry that recognizes passengers that request the same fare on a particular segment may not be equally valuable to the firm because they differ in their itinerary and hence total revenue.

out-of-stock   When a firm has no inventory.

overage cost   In the newsvendor model, the cost of purchasing one too many units. In other words, it is the increase in profit if the firm had purchased one fewer unit without causing a lost sale (i.e., thereby preventing one additional unit of leftover inventory).

overbooking   The practice of accepting more reservations than can be accommodated with available capacity.

P

pallet   Literally the platform used (often wood) by a forklift to move large quantities of material.

par level   Another name for the order-up-to level in the order-up-to model.

Pareto principle   Principle that postulates that 20 percent of the causes account for 80 percent of all problems (also known as the 80-20 rule).

period   In the order-up-to model, time is divided into periods of time of equal length. Typical period lengths include one day, one week, and one month.

phantom orders   An order that is canceled before delivery is taken.

pipeline inventory   The minimum amount of inventory that is required to operate the process. Since there is a minimum flow time that can be achieved (i.e., sum of the activity times), because of Little's Law, there is also a minimum required inventory in the process. Also known as on-order inventory, it is the number of units of inventory that have been ordered but have not been received.

point-of-sale (POS)   Data on consumer transactions.

Poisson distribution   A discrete distribution function that often provides an accurate representation of the number of events in an interval of time when the occurrences of the events are independent of each other. In other words, it is a good distribution to model demand for slow-moving items.

Poisson process   An arrival process with exponentially distributed interarrival times.

poka-yoke   A Toyota technique of "fool-proofing" many assembly operations, that is, by making mistakes in assembly operations physically impossible.

pooling   The concept of combining several resources (including their buffers and their arrival processes) into one joint resource. In the context of waiting time problems, pooling reduces the expected wait time.

preference fit   The firm's ability to provide consumers with the product or service they want or need.

price protection   The practice in the PC industry of compensating distributors due to reductions in a supplier's wholesale price. As a result of price protection, the price a distributor pays to purchase inventory is effectively always the current price; that is, the supplier rebates the distributor whenever a price reduction occurs for each unit the distributor is holding in inventory.

precedence relationship The connection between two activities in a project in which one activity must be completed before the other can begin.

priority rules Used to determine the sequence with which flow units waiting in front of the same resource are served. There are two types of priority rules: service time independent (e.g., FCFS rule) and service time dependent (e.g., SPT rule).

process Resources, inventory locations, and a flow that describe the path of a flow unit from its transformation as input to output.

process analysis Concerned with understanding and improving business processes. This includes determining the location of the bottleneck and computing the basic performance measures inventory, flow rate, and flow time.

process capability The tolerance level of the process relative to its current variation in outcomes. This is frequently measured in the form of the capability index.

process capacity Capacity of an entire process, which is the maximum flow rate that can be achieved in the process. It is based on the capacity of the bottleneck.

process flow diagram Maps resources and inventory and shows graphically how the flow unit travels through the process in its transformation from input to output.

process utilization To what extent an entire process uses its capacity when supporting a given flow rate. Process utilization = Flow rate/Process capacity.

processing time The duration that a flow unit has to spend at a resource, not including any waiting time; also referred to as activity time or service time.

product pooling The practice of using a single product to serve two demand segments that were previously served by their own product version.

production batch The collection of flow units that are produced within a production cycle.

production cycle The processing and setups of all flow units before the resource starts to repeat itself.

production smoothing The practice of smoothing production relative to demand. Used to manage seasonality. In anticipation of a peak demand period production is maintained above the current flow rate, building up inventory. During the peak demand, production is not increased substantially, but rather, the firm satisfies the gap by drawing down previously accumulated inventory.

productivity ratio The ratio between revenue as a measure of output and some cost (for example labor cost) as a measure of input.

project A temporary (and thus nonrepetitive) operation consisting of a set of activities; different from a process, which is a repetitive operation.

protection level The number of reservations that must always be available for a fare class or higher. For example, if a flight has 120 seats and the protection level is 40 for the high-fare class, then it must always be possible to have 40 high-fare reservations.

pull system A manufacturing system in which production is initiated by the occurrence of demand.

push system A manufacturing system in which production is initiated in anticipation of demand.

Q

quality at the source The idea of fixing defects right when and where they occur. This is a fundamental idea of the Toyota Production System. Fixing defects later on in the process is difficult and costly.

quantity discount Reduced procurement costs as a result of large order quantities. Quantity discounts have to be traded off against the increased inventory costs.

quantity flexibility contracts With this contract, a buyer provides an initial forecast to a supplier. Later on the buyer is required to purchase at least a certain percentage of the initial forecast (e.g., 75 percent), but the buyer also is allowed to purchase a certain percentage above the forecast (e.g., 125 percent of the forecast). The supplier must build enough capacity to be able to cover the upper bound.

quartile analysis A technique to empirically analyze worker productivity (e.g., in the form of their processing times) by comparing the performance of the top quartile with the performance of the bottom quartile.

queue The accumulation of flow units waiting to be processed or served.

queuing system A sequence of individual queues in which the outflow of one buffer/server is the inflow to the next buffer/server.

Quick Response A series of practices in the apparel industry used to improve the efficiency of the apparel supply chain.

R

random variable A variable that represents a random event. For example, the random variable X could represent the number of times the value 7 is thrown on two dice over 100 tosses.

range of a sample The difference between the highest and the lowest value in the sample.

R-bar charts Track the variation in the outcome of a process. R-bar charts require that the outcome of a process be evaluated based on a single variable.

reactive capacity Capacity that can be used after useful information regarding demand is learned; that is, the capacity can be used to react to the learned demand information.

resource The entity of a process that the flow unit has to visit as part of its transformation from input to output.

returns policy See buy-back contract.

revenue management Also known as yield management. The set of tools used to maximize revenue given a fixed supply.

revenue-sharing contracts With this contract, a retailer pays a supplier a wholesale price per unit purchased plus a fraction of the revenue the retailer realizes from the unit.

rework An approach of handling defective flow units that attempts to invest further resource time into the flow unit in the attempt to transform it into a conforming (nondefective) flow unit.

rework loops An iteration/repetition of project or process activities done typically because of quality problems.

ROIC Return on invested capital, defined as the ratio between financial returns (profits) and the invested capital.

round-up rule When looking for a value inside a table, it often occurs that the desired value falls between two entries in the table. The round-up rule chooses the entry that leads to the larger quantity.

S

safety inventory The inventory that a firm holds to protect itself from random fluctuations in demand.

salvage value The value of leftover inventory at the end of the selling season in the newsvendor model.

scale economies Cost savings that can be achieved in large operations. Examples are pooling benefits in waiting time problems and lower per-unit setup costs in batch flow operations.

scope 1 emissions All direct emissions of an organization, such as fuel burned in its own trucks, or oil burned in its own machines.

scope 2 emissions All emissions of an organization associated with purchased electricity, heat, steam, or other forms of energy.

scope 3 emissions All emissions of an organization, including emissions created upstream in the value chain (suppliers) as well as downstream in the value chain (customers using the product or service).

seasonal arrivals Systemic changes in the interarrival times (e.g., peak times during the day, the week, or the year).

seasonal inventory Arises if the flow rate exceeds the demand rate in anticipation of a time period when the demand rate exceeds the flow rate.

second buy An opportunity to request a second replenishment, presumably after some demand information is learned.

service level The probability with which a unit of incoming demand will receive service as planned. In the context of waiting time problems, this means having a waiting time less than a specified target wait time; in other contexts, this also can refer to the availability of a product.

service time The duration that a flow unit has to spend at a resource, not including any waiting time; also referred to as activity time or processing time.

setup cost Costs that are incurred in production whenever a resource conducts a setup and in transportation whenever a shipment is done. Setup costs drive batching. It is important to include only out-of-pocket costs in the setup costs, not opportunity costs.

setup time The duration of time a resource cannot produce as it is either switched from one setting to the other (e.g., from producing part A to producing part B, in which case we speak of a changeover time) or not available for production for other reasons (e.g., maintenance step). Setup times reduce capacity and therefore create an incentive to produce in batches.

setup time reduction See SMED.

shortage gaming A cause of the bullwhip effect. In situations with a capacity constraint, retailers may inflate their orders in anticipation of receiving only a portion of their order.

single segment control A revenue management system in the airline industry in which all passengers on the same segment paying the same fare class are treated equally.

six sigma In its narrow sense, refers to a process capability of two. This means that a process outcome can fall six standard deviations above or below the mean and still be within tolerance (i.e., still not be a defect). In its broader meaning, refers to quality improvement projects that are using statistical process control.

slack time The difference between the earliest completion time and the latest completion time; measures by how much an activity can be delayed without delaying the overall project.

SMED (single minute exchange of dies) The philosophy of reducing setup times instead of just finding optimal batch sizes for given setup times.

span of control The scope of activities a worker or a resource performs. If the resource is labor, having a high span of control requires extensive training. Span of control is largest in a work cell.

specification levels The cut-off points above (in the case of upper specification level) and below (in the case of lower specification level) which a process outcome is labeled a defect.

SPT (shortest processing time) rule A priority rule that serves flow units with the shortest processing time first. The SPT rule is known to minimize the overall waiting time.

standard deviation A measure of the absolute variability around a mean. The square of the standard deviation equals the variance.

standard normal A normal distribution with mean 0 and standard deviation 1.

starving   The situation in which a resource has to be idle as there is no flow unit completed in the step (inventory, resource) upstream from it.

stationary arrivals   When the arrival process does not vary systemically over time; opposite of seasonal arrivals.

statistical process control (SPC)   A set of statistical tools that is used to measure the capability of a process and to help monitor the process, revealing potential assignable causes of variation.

stochastic   An event that is random, that is, its outcome cannot be predicted with certainty.

stockout   Occurs if a customer demands a unit but a unit of inventory is not available. This is different from "being out of stock," which merely requires that there is no inventory available.

stockout probability   The probability a stockout occurs over a predefined interval of time.

supply chain   The series of firms that deliver a good or service from raw materials to customer fulfillment.

supply chain efficiency   The ratio of the supply chain's actual profit to the supply chain's optimal profit.

supply-constrained   A process for which the flow rate is limited by either capacity or the availability of input.

sustainable operations   An operations paradigm built around the idea of not depleting or destroying scarce resources, including the atmosphere, water, materials, land, and people.

T

takotei-mochi   A Toyota technique to reduce worker idle time. The basic idea is that a worker can load one machine and while this machine operates, the worker—instead of being idle—operates another machine along the process flow.

tandem queue   A set of queues aligned in a series so that the output of one server flows to only one other server.

target wait time (TWT)   The wait time that is used to define a service level concerning the responsiveness of a process.

tasks   The atomic pieces of work that together constitute activities. Tasks can be moved from one activity/resource to another in the attempt to improve line balance.

throughput   See flow rate.

tolerance levels   The range of acceptable outcomes of a process. See also design specifications.

Toyota Production System   A collection of practices related to production, product development, and supply chain management as developed by the Toyota Motor Corporation. Important elements discussed in this book are the idea of permanent improvement (kaizen), the reduction of waste (muda), inventory reduction (just-in-time, kanban), mixed model production (heijunka), and reduction of setup times (SMED).

trade promotion   A temporary price discount off the wholesale price that a supplier offers to its retailer customers.

transactional efficiency   Measures how easy it is to do business with a firm. Consists of the subdimension customer effort and the elapsed time between need articulation and need fulfillment.

transfer batch   A collection of flow units that are transferred as a group from one resource to the next.

trunk inventory   The inventory kept by sales representatives in the trunk of their vehicles.

tsukurikomi   The Toyota idea of integrating quality inspection throughout the process. This is therefore an important enabler of the quality-at-the-source idea.

turn-and-earn   An allocation scheme in which scarce capacity is allocated to downstream customers proportional to their past sales.

U

underage cost   In the newsvendor model, the profit loss associated with ordering one unit too few. In other words, it is the increase in profit if one additional unit had been ordered and that unit is sold.

universal design/product   A product that is designed to serve multiple functions and/or multiple customer segments.

unknown unknowns (unk-unks)   Project management parlance to refer to uncertainties in a project that are not known at the outset of the project.

utilization   The extent to which a resource uses its capacity when supporting a given flow rate. Utilization = Flow rate/Capacity.

V

value chain   See supply chain.

value curve   A graphical depiction of the key attributes of a product or service. Can be used to compare a new business model with an incumbent solution. Common attributes are the transactional efficiency, the preference fit, as well as price and quality.

value driver   An operational variable that has a strong marginal effect on the ROIC.

variance   A measure of the absolute variability around a mean. The square root of the variance equals the standard deviation.

vendor-managed inventory   The practice of switching control of inventory management from a retailer to a supplier.

virtual nesting   A revenue management system in the airline industry in which passengers on different itineraries and paying different fare classes may nevertheless be included in the same bucket for the purchase of capacity controls.

virtual pooling   The practice of holding inventory in multiple physical locations that share inventory information data so that inventory can be moved from one location to another when needed.

W

waiting time   The part of flow time in which the flow unit is not processed by a resource.

waiting time formula   The average wait time, T_q, that a flow unit spends in a queue before receiving service.

waste   An abstract word that refers to any inefficiencies that exist in the process; for example, line imbalances, inadequate batch sizes, variability in service times, and so forth. Waste can be seen as the distance between the current performance of a process and the efficient frontier. Waste is called "muda" in the Toyota Production System.

win–win   A situation in which both parties in a negotiation are better off.

work cell   A resource where several activities that were previously done by separate resources (workers, machines) are combined into a single resource (team of workers). Work cells have several quality advantages, as they have a short ITAT; they are also—by definition—more balanced.

work in process (WIP)   The inventory that is currently in the process (as opposed to inventory that is finished goods or raw material).

worker-paced line   A process layout in which a worker moves the flow unit to the next resource or buffer when he or she has completed processing it; in contrast to a machine-paced line, where the flow unit moves based on a conveyor belt.

workload   The request for capacity created by demand. Workload drives the implied utilization.

X

X-bar charts   Track the mean of an outcome of a process. X-bar charts require that the outcome of a process be evaluated based on a single variable.

Y

yield management   Also known as revenue management. The set of tools used to maximize revenue given a fixed supply.

yield of a resource   The percentage of flow units processed correctly at the resource. More generally, we also can speak of the yield of an entire process.

Z

zero-sum game   A game in which the total payoff to all players equals a constant no matter what outcome occurs.

z-statistic   Given quantity and any normal distribution, that quantity has a unique z-statistic such that the probability the outcome of the normal distribution is less than or equal to the quantity equals the probability the outcome of a standard normal distribution equals the z-statistic.

References

Abernathy, F. H., J.T. Dunlop, J. Hammond, and D.Weil. *A Stitch in Time: Lean Retailing and the Transformation of Manufacturing—Lessons from the Apparel and Textile Industries.* New York: Oxford University Press, 1999.

Antonio Moreno, Christian Terwiesch, "Pricing and Production Flexibility: An Empirical Analysis of the U.S. Automotive Industry," Working Paper.

Anupindi, R., S. Chopra, S. D. Deshmukh, J. A. Van Mieghem, and E. Zemel. *Managing Business Process Flows.* Upper Saddle River, NJ: Prentice Hall, 1999.

Bartholdi, J. J., and D. D. Eisenstein. "A Production Line That Balances Itself." *Operations Research* 44, no. 1 (1996), pp. 21–34.

Beatty, S. "Advertising: Infinity and Beyond? No Supply of Toys at Some Burger Kings." *The Wall Street Journal,* November 25, 1996, p. B-10.

Belobaba, P. "Application of a Probabilistic Decision Model to Airline Seat Inventory Control." *Operations Research* 37, no. 2 (1989), pp. 183–97.

Bohn, R. E., and R. Jaikumar. "A Dynamic Approach to Operations Management: An Alternative to Static Optimization." *International Journal of Production Economics* 27, no. 3 (1992), pp. 265–82.

Bohn, R. E., and C.Terwiesch. "The Economics of Yield-Driven Processes." *Journal of Operations Management* 18 (December 1999), pp. 41–59.

Breyfogle, F. W. *Implementing Six Sigma.* New York: John Wiley & Sons, 1999.

Brown, A., H. Lee, and R. Petrakian. "Xilinx Improves Its Semiconductor Supply Chain Using Product and Process Postponement." *Interfaces* 30, no. 4 (2000), p. 65.

Brynjolfsson, E., Y. Hu, and M. D. Smith. "Consumer Surplus in the Digital Economy: Estimating the Value of Increased Product Variety." *Management Science* 49, no. 11 (2003), pp. 1580–96.

Buzzell, R., J. Quelch, and W. Salmon. "The Costly Bargain of Trade Promotion." *Harvard Business Review* 68, no. 2 (1990), pp. 141–49.

Cachon, G. "Supply Chain Coordination with Contracts." In *Handbooks in Operations Research and Management Science: Vol. 11. Supply Chain Management, I: Design, Coordination, and Operation,* ed. T. Kok and S. Graves. Amsterdam: North-Holland, 2004.

Cannon, J., T. Randall, and C. Terwiesch. "Improving Earnings Prediction Based on Operational Variables: A Study of the U.S. Airline Industry." Working paper, The Wharton School and The Eccles School of Business, 2007.

Chan Kim, W., R. Mauborgne. *Blue Ocean Strategy.* Harvard Business School Press. 2005.

Chase, R. B., and N. J. Aquilano. *Production and Operations Management: Manufacturing and Services.* 7th ed. New York: Irwin, 1995.

Chopra, S., and P. Meindl. *Supply Chain Management: Strategy, Planning and Operation.* 2nd ed. Upper Saddle River, NJ: Pearson Prentice Hall, 2004.

Cross, R. "An Introduction to Revenue Management." In *Handbook of Airline Economics,* ed. D. Jenkins, pp. 453–58. New York: McGraw-Hill, 1995.

Cross, R. *Revenue Management: Hard-Core Tactics for Market Domination.* New York: Broadway Books, 1997.

De Groote, X. Inventory Theory: A Road Map. Unpublished teaching note. INSEAD. March 1994.

Diwas Singh KC and Christian Terwiesch, An Econometric Analysis of Patient Flows in the Cardiac Intensive Care Unit, Manufacturing and Service Operations Management, msom.1110.0341; published online before print September 2, 2011.

Drew, J., B. McCallum, and S. Roggenhofer. *Journey to Lean: Making Operational Change Stick.* New York: Palgrave Macmillan, 2004.

Feitzinger, E., and H. Lee. "Mass Customization at Hewlett-Packard: The Power of Postponement." *Harvard Business Review* 75 (January–February 1997), pp. 116–21.

Fisher, M. "What Is the Right Supply Chain for Your Product." *Harvard Business Review* 75 (March–April) 1997, pp. 105–16.

Fisher, M., K. Rajaram, and A. Raman. 2001. "Optimizing Inventory Replenishment of Retail Fashion Products." *Manufacturing and Service Operations Management* 3, no. 3 (2001), pp. 230–41.

Fisher, M., and A. Raman. "Reducing the Cost of Demand Uncertainty through Accurate Response to Early Sales." *Operations Research* 44 (1996), pp. 87–99.

Fujimoto, T. *The Evolution of a Manufacturing System at Toyota.* New York: Oxford University Press, 1999.

Gans, N., G. Koole, and A. Mandelbaum. "Telephone Call Centers:Tutorial, Review, and Research Prospects." *Manufacturing & Service Operations Management* 5 (2003), pp. 79–141.

Gaur, V., M. Fisher, A. Raman. "An Econometric Analysis of Inventory Turnover Performance in Retail Services." *Management Science* 51. (2005). pp. 181–194.

Geraghty, M., and E. Johnson. "Revenue Management Saves National Rental Car." *Interfaces* 27, no. 1 (1997), pp. 107–27.

Hall, R. W. *Queuing Methods for Services and Manufacturing.* Upper Saddle River, NJ: Prentice Hall, 1997.

Hansell, S. "Is This the Factory of the Future." *New York Times,* July 26, 1998.

Harrison, M. J., and C. H. Loch. "Operations Management and Reengineering." Working paper, Stanford University, 1995.

Hayes, R. H., and S. C. Wheelwright. "Link Manufacturing Process and Product Life Cycles." *Harvard Business Review,* January–February 1979, pp. 133–40.

Hayes, R. H., S. C. Wheelwright, and K. B. Clark. *Dynamic Manufacturing: Creating the Learning Organization.* New York: Free Press, 1988.

Hillier, F. S., and G. J. Lieberman. *Introduction to Operations Research.* 7th ed. New York: McGraw-Hill, 2002.

Holweg, M., and F. K. Pil. *The Second Century: Reconnecting Customer and Value Chain through Build-to-Order, Moving beyond Mass and Lean Production in the Auto Industry.* New ed. Cambridge, MA: MIT Press, 2005.

Hopp, W. J., and M. L. Spearman. *Factory Physics I: Foundations of Manufacturing Management.* New York: Irwin/McGraw-Hill, 1996.

Jordon, W., and S. Graves. "Principles on the Benefits of Manufacturing Process Flexibility." *Management Science* 41 (1995), pp. 577–94.

Juran, J. *The Quality Control Handbook.* 4th ed. New York: McGraw-Hill, 1951.

Juran, J. *Juran on Planning for Quality.* New York: Free Press, 1989.

Karmarkar, U. "Getting Control of Just-in-Time." *Harvard Business Review* 67 (September–October 1989), pp. 122–31.

Kaufman, L. "Restoration Hardware in Search of a Revival." *New York Times,* March 21, 2000.

Kavadias S., C. H. Loch, and A. DeMeyer, "DragonFly: Developing a Proposal for an Uninhabited Aerial Vehicle (UAV)," Insead case 600-003-1.

Kimes, S. "Revenue Management on the Links I: Applying Yield Management to the Golf-Course Industry." *Cornell Hotel and Restaurant Administration Quarterly* 41, no. 1 (February 2000), pp. 120–27.

Kimes, S., R. Chase, S. Choi, P. Lee, and E. Ngonzi. "Restaurant Revenue Management: Applying Yield Management to the Restaurant Industry." *Cornell Hotel and Restaurant Administration Quarterly* 39, no. 3 (1998), pp. 32–39.

Koller, T., M. Goedhart, and D. Wessels. *Valuation.* 4th ed. New York: John Wiley & Sons, 2005.

Lee, H. "Effective Inventory and Service Management through Product and Process Redesign." *Operations Research* 44, no. 1 (1996), pp. 151–59.

Lee, H., V. Padmanabhan, and S. Whang. "The Bullwhip Effect in Supply Chains." *MIT Sloan Management Review* 38, no. 3 (1997), pp. 93–102.

Loch C. H., A. DeMeyer, and M. T. Pich, *Managing the Unknown: A New Approach to Managing High Uncertainty and Risk in Projects,* John Wiley & Sons, 2006.

Magretta, J. 1998. "The Power of Virtual Integration: An Interview with Dell Computer's Michael Dell." *Harvard Business Review* 76 (March–April 1998), pp. 72–84.

McGill, J., and G. van Ryzin. "Revenue Management: Research Overview and Prospects." *Transportation Science* 33, no. 2 (1999), pp. 233–56.

McWilliams, G., and J. White. "Others Want to Figure out How to Adopt Dell Model." *The Wall Street Journal,* December 1, 1999.

Moreno, Antonio, Christian Terwiesch, Pricing and Production Flexibility: An Empirical Analysis of the US Automotive Industry, Working paper at the Kellogg School of Management and at the Wharton School Cannon et al is still a working paper.

Motorola. "What Is Six Sigma?" Summary of Bill Weisz's videotape message, 1987.

Nahmias, S. *Production and Operations Analysis.* 5th ed. New York: McGraw-Hill, 2005.

Ohno, T. *Toyota Production System: Beyond Large-Scale Production.* Productivity Press, March 1, 1998.

Olivares, Marcelo, Christian Terwiesch, and Lydia Cassorla, "Structural Estimation of the Newsvendor Model: An Application to Reserving Operating Room Time," *Management Science,* Vol. 54, No. 1, 2008 (pp. 45–55).

Padmanabhan, V., and I. P. L. Png. "Returns Policies: Make Money by Making Good." *Sloan Management Review,* Fall 1995, pp. 65–72.

Papadakis, Y. "Operations Risk and Supply Chain Design." Working paper. The Wharton Risk Center, 2002.

Pasternack, B. "Optimal Pricing and Returns Policies for Perishable Commodities." *Marketing Science* 4, no. 2 (1985), pp. 166–76.

Petruzzi, N., and M. Dada. "Pricing and the Newsvendor Problem: A Review with Extensions." *Operations Research* 47 (1999), pp. 183–94.

Porter, M., M. Kramer. Creating Shared Value: How to Reinvent Capitalism and Unleash a Wave of Innovation and Growth. *Harvard Business Review.* Jan-Feb, 2011.

Porteus, E. *Stochastic Inventory Theory.* Palo Alto, CA: Stanford University Press, 2002.

Ramstad, E. "Koss CEO Gambles on Inventory Buildup: Just-in-Time Production Doesn't Always Work." *The Wall Street Journal,* March 15, 1999.

Sakasegawa, H. "An Approximation Formula $L_q = \alpha\beta^p (1 - \rho)$." *Annals of the Institute of Statistical Mathematics* 29, no. 1 (1977), pp. 67–75.

Sechler, B. "Special Report: E-commerce, behind the Curtain." *The Wall Street Journal,* July 15, 2002.

Silver, E., D. Pyke, and R. Peterson. *Inventory Management and Production Planning and Scheduling.* New York: John Wiley & Sons, 1998.

Simchi-Levi, D., P. Kaminsky, and E. Simchi-Levi. *Designing and Managing the Supply Chain: Concepts, Strategies, and Case Studies.* 2nd ed. New York: McGraw-Hill, 2003.

Simison, R. "Toyota Unveils System to Custom-Build Cars in Five Days." *The Wall Street Journal,* August 6, 1999.

Smith, B., J. Leimkuhler, and R. Darrow. "Yield Management at American Airlines." *Interfaces* 22, no. 1 (1992), pp. 8–31.

Stevenson, W. *Operations Management.* 8th ed. McGraw-Hill/Irwin, 2006.

Stringer, K. "As Planes Become More Crowded, Travelers Perfect Getting 'Bumped.' " *The Wall Street Journal,* March 21, 2002.

Talluri, K., and G. van Ryzin. *The Theory and Practice of Revenue Management.* Boston: Kluwer Academic Publishers, 2004.

Terwiesch, Christian, and Karl T. Ulrich, *Innovation Tournaments: Creating and Selecting Exceptional Opportunities,* Harvard Business School Press, 2009.

Terwiesch, C. "Paul Downs Cabinet Maker." Teaching case at The Wharton School, 2004.

Terwiesch, C., and C. H. Loch. "Pumping Iron at Cliffs and Associates I: The Cicored Iron Ore Reduction Plant in Trinidad." Wharton-INSEAD Alliance case, 2002.

Tucker, A. L. "The Impact of Operational Failures on Hospital Nurses and Their Patients." *Journal of Operations Management* 22, no. 2 (April 2004), pp. 151–69.

Ulrich, K. T., and S. Eppinger, *Product Design and Development,* 5th ed., McGraw Hill Irwin, 2011.

Upton, D. "The Management of Manufacturing Flexibility." *California Management Review* 36 (Winter 1994), pp. 72–89.

Upton, D. "What Really Makes Factories Flexible." *Harvard Business Review* 73 (July–August 1995), pp. 74–84.

Vitzthum, C. "Spain's Zara Cuts a Dash with 'Fashion on Demand.' " *The Wall Street Journal,* May 29, 1998.

Wadsworth, H. M., K. S. Stephens, and A. B. Godfrey. *Modern Methods for Quality Control and Improvement.* New York: John Wiley & Sons, 1986.

Weatherford, L. R., and S. E. Bodily. "A Taxonomy and Research Overview of Perishable-Asset Revenue Management: Yield Management, Overbooking and Pricing." *Operations Research* 40, no. 5 (1992), pp. 831–43.

Whitney, D. *Mechanical Assemblies: Their Design, Manufacture, and Role in Product Development.* New York: Oxford University Press, 2004.

Whitt, W. "The Queuing Network Analyzer." *Bell System Technology Journal* 62, no. 9 (1983).

Womack, J. P., D. T. Jones, and D. Roos. *The Machine That Changed the World: The Story of Lean Production.* Reprint edition. New York: Harper Perennial, 1991.

Zipkin, P. *Foundations of Inventory Management.* New York: McGraw-Hill, 2000.

Zipkin, P. "The Limits of Mass Customization." *Sloan Management Review,* Spring 2001, pp. 81–87.

Index of Key "How to" Exhibits

Summary of Key Notation and Equations

Chapter 2: Process Flow

$$\text{Little's Law: Average inventory} = \text{Average flow rate} \times \text{Average time}$$

Chapter 3: Capacity/Bottleneck Analysis

$$\text{Implied utilization} = \frac{\text{Capacity requested by demand}}{\text{Available capacity}}$$

Chapter 4: Labor Content

$$\text{Flow rate} = \text{Min}\{\text{Available input, Demand, Process capacity}\}$$

$$\text{Cycle time} = \frac{1}{\text{Flow rate}}$$

$$\text{Cost of direct labor} = \frac{\text{Total wages}}{\text{Flow rate}}$$

$$\text{Idle time across all workers at resource } i = \text{Cycle time} \times (\text{Number of workers at resource } i) - \text{Processing time at resource } i$$

$$\text{Average labor utilization} = \frac{\text{Labor content}}{\text{Labor content} + \text{Total idle time}}$$

Chapter 7: Batching

$$\text{Capacity given batch size} = \frac{\text{Batch size}}{\text{Setup time} + \text{Batch size} \times \text{Time per unit}}$$

$$\text{Recommended batch size} = \frac{\text{Flow rate} \times \text{Setup time}}{1 - \text{Flow rate} \times \text{Time per unit}}$$

$$\text{Economic order quantity} = \sqrt{\frac{2 \times \text{Setup cost} \times \text{Flow rate}}{\text{Holding cost}}}$$

Chapter 8: Waiting Time Systems

$m = $ number of servers

$p = $ processing time

$a = $ interarrival time

CV_a = coefficient of variation for interarrivals

CV_p = coefficient of variation of processing time

$$\text{Utilization } u = \frac{p}{a \times m}$$

$$T_q = \left(\frac{\text{Processing time}}{m} \right) \times \left(\frac{\text{Utilization}^{\sqrt{2(m+1)}-1}}{1 - \text{Utilization}} \right) \times \left(\frac{CV_a^2 + CV_p^2}{2} \right)$$

$$\text{Flow time } T = T_q + p$$

$$\text{Inventory in service } I_p = m \times u$$

$$\text{Inventory in the queue } I_q = T_q / a$$

$$\text{Inventory in the system } I = I_p + I_q$$

Chapter 10: Quality

$$\text{Yield of resource} = \frac{\text{Flow rate of units processed correctly at the resource}}{\text{Flow rate}}$$

Chapter 12: Newsvendor

Q = order quantity

C_u = Underage cost

C_o = Overage cost

μ = Expected demand

σ = Standard deviation of demand

$F(Q)$ = Distribution function

$\Phi(Q)$ = Distribution function of the standard normal

$L(Q)$ = Loss function

$L(z)$ = Loss function of the standard normal distribution

$$\text{Critical ratio} = \frac{C_u}{C_o + C_u}$$

$$\text{A/F ratio} = \frac{\text{Actual demand}}{\text{Forecast}}$$

$$\text{Expected profit-maximizing order quantity: } F(Q) = \frac{C_u}{C_o + C_u}$$

$$\text{z-statistic or normalized order quantity: } z = \frac{Q - \mu}{\sigma}$$

$$Q = \mu + z \times \sigma$$

$$\text{Expected lost sales with a standard normal distribution} = L(z)$$

$$\text{Expected lost sales with a normal distribution} = \sigma \times L(z)$$

$$\text{In Excel: } L(z) = \sigma*\text{Normdist}(z, 0, 1, 0) - z*(1 - \text{Normdist}(z))$$

$$\text{Expected lost sales for nonnormal distributions} = L(Q) \text{ (from loss function table)}$$

$$\text{Expected sales} = \mu - \text{Expected lost sales}$$

$$\text{Expected leftover inventory} = Q - \text{Expected sales}$$

$$\text{Expected profit} = [(\text{Price} - \text{Cost}) \times \text{Expected sales}]$$
$$- [(\text{Cost} - \text{Salvage value}) \times \text{Expected leftover inventory}]$$

$$\text{In-stock probability} = F(Q)$$

$$\text{Stockout probability} = 1 - \text{In-stock probability}$$

$$\text{In Excel: In-stock probability} = \text{Normdist}(z)$$

$$\text{In Excel: } z = \text{Normsinv}(\text{Target in-stock probability})$$

Chapter 13: Reactive Capacity

$$\text{Mismatch cost} = (C_o \times \text{Expected leftover inventory}) + (C_u \times \text{Expected lost sales})$$
$$= \text{Maximum profit} - \text{Expected profit}$$

$$\text{Maximum profit} = (\text{Price} - \text{Cost}) \times \mu$$

$$\text{Coefficient of variation} = \text{Standard deviation/Expected demand}$$

Chapter 14: Order-up-to Model

$$l = \text{Lead time}$$

$$S = \text{Order-up-to level}$$

$$\text{Inventory level} = \text{On-hand inventory} - \text{Back order}$$
$$\text{Inventory position} = \text{On-order inventory} + \text{Inventory level}$$
$$\text{In-stock probability} = 1 - \text{Stockout probability}$$
$$= \text{Prob}\{\text{Demand over } (l + 1) \text{ periods} \leq S\}$$

$$z\text{-statistic for normalized order quantity: } z = \frac{S - \mu}{\sigma}$$

$$\text{Expected back order with a normal distribution} = \sigma \times L(z)$$

$$\text{In Excel: Expected back order} = \sigma*(\text{Normdist}(z, 0, 1, 0) - z*(1 - \text{Normdist}(z)))$$

$$\text{Expected back order for nonnormal distributions} = L(S) \text{ (from loss function table)}$$

$$\text{Expected inventory} = S - \text{Expected demand over } l + 1 \text{ periods}$$
$$+ \text{ Expected back order}$$

$$\text{Expected on-order inventory} = \text{Expected demand in one period} \times \text{Lead time}$$

Chapter 15: Pooling

$$\text{Expected pooled demand} = 2 \times \mu$$

$$\text{Standard deviation of pooled demand} = \sqrt{2 \times (1 + \text{Correlation})} \times \sigma$$

$$\text{Coefficient of variation of pooled demand} = \sqrt{\frac{1}{2}(1 + \text{Correlation})} \times \left(\frac{\sigma}{\mu}\right)$$

Chapter 16: Revenue Management

$$\text{Protection level: Critical ratio} = \frac{C_u}{C_o + C_u} = \frac{r_h - r_l}{r_h}$$

$$\text{Low-fare booking limit} = \text{Capacity} - Q$$

$$\text{Overbooking: Critical ratio} = \frac{C_u}{C_o + C_u} = \frac{r_l}{\text{Cost per bumped customer} + r_l}$$

Index

500

THE
PHILOSOPHICAL
JOURNEY

THE
PHILOSOPHICAL
JOURNEY
An Interactive Approach

William F. Lawhead
University of Mississippi

MAYFIELD PUBLISHING COMPANY
Mountain View, California
London • Ontario

To my grandchildren,
Lauren and Will.
May your lives be filled with the two dimensions
of philosophy: love and wisdom.

Library of Congress Cataloging-in-Publication Data

Lawhead, William F.
   The philosophical journey : an interactive approach / William Lawhead.
      p.   cm.
   Includes bibliographical references and index.
   ISBN 0-7674-0218-9
   1. Philosophy—History.   I. Title.
B72.L373   1999
100—dc21   99-37468
                                                               CIP

Manufactured in the United States of America
10   9   8   7   6   5   4   3   2

Mayfield Publishing Company
1280 Villa Street
Mountain View, California 94041

Sponsoring editor, Kenneth King; *developmental editors,* Kathleen Engelberg and Barbara Armentrout; *production editor,* Carla White Kirschenbaum; *manuscript editor,* Karen Dorman; *text designer,* Ellen Pettengell; *cover designer,* Linda Robertson; *design manager,* Susan Breitbard; *art editor,* Robin Mouat; *manufacturing manager,* Randy Hurst. The text was set in 11/13 Garamond (PMS 660) by Thompson Type and printed on 45# Consolidated Orion by R. R. Donnelley & Sons Company.

Cover image: Mike McQueen/Tony Stone Images

This book is printed on acid-free paper.

Preface

Socrates once complained in the *Protagoras* that eloquent orators and books are alike in that they provide massive amounts of information, "but if one asks any of them an additional question . . . they cannot either answer or ask a question on their own account." As I wrote this book, my challenge was to see to what degree I could provide a counterexample to Socrates's claim. Of course, Socrates is correct: there is no substitute for live philosophical conversations and debates. However, as you get acquainted with this book, you will find that it does ask you questions and provokes you to ask questions in turn. Instead of simply presenting information for you to passively absorb, its many exercises require your active involvement and some will even provide the opportunity for you to dialogue with your friends about the philosophical issues discussed. For this reason, I chose the title *The Philosophical Journey: An Interactive Approach.*

Rather than being like a slide show of landscapes you have never visited, this book is a guided, exploratory journey in which you will have to scout the terrain yourself. I hope that the journey will be fun, but there is also much to be done en route. This philosophy text is as interactive as is possible within the medium of paper and ink. Students taking courses in philosophy are often asked "What can you do with philosophy?" After taking this philosophical journey I have planned for you, I hope that you will realize that the really important question is "What can philosophy do with you?" You will certainly not agree with everything you will read in these pages, but do anticipate the fact that engaging with these ideas will not leave you unchanged.

Organization

This book presents philosophy by introducing the major philosophical topics, questions, positions, and philosophers. The different chapters are independent enough that they could be read in a different order if one so desired. However, everyone should start with the overview (section 1.0) in Chapter 1, which will prepare you for the journey. The remaining five chapters then lead into each of the major areas of philosophy. The first section of each chapter, as well as each subtopic, has the following features:

- *Scouting the Territory*—a scenario that raises engaging, philosophical questions.
- *Charting the Terrain*—a more precise presentation of the topic and its significance.

- *Choosing a Path*—a presentation of the opposing alternatives to help you clarify your own thinking on the issue.
- *What Do I Think?*—a questionnaire that will help you identify your current stand on the issue. An answer key will show you how philosophers label your own position and which answers are incompatible.

The opening section of each topic will be followed by sections that present and analyze the different alternatives that can be taken on the issue. Each of these sections has the following format:

- *Leading Questions*—a series of questions, asked from the standpoint of the position in question that will get you thinking about the philosophy and its merits.
- *Surveying the Case for...*—a presentation of the position under consideration and the arguments supporting it.
- *A Reading from...*—several brief readings will provide you with practice in analyzing philosophical passages and arguments. As always, you will be provided with guidelines for getting the most out of the passage.
- *Looking through X's Lens*—an exercise in which you will be asked to draw out the implications of the philosopher's position and apply the theory to novel situations.
- *Examining the Strengths and Weaknesses of X*—a series of considerations and questions that will guide you in forming your own response to the position.

Throughout the book, there will be a number of exercises that will require you to interact philosophically with the issues. These include:

- *Philosophy in the Marketplace*—a question, survey, or scenario that will allow you to apply the Socratic method of doing philosophy through structured conversations with friends outside of class.
- *Thought Experiments*—exercises that will give you the opportunity to make your own philosophical discoveries and to compare your conclusions with those of the great philosophers as well as classmates.
- *Stop and Think Boxes*—a brief pause in your reading to form some tentative conclusions about an issue.
- *Spotlight on...*—additional information that helps illuminate the topic.

(For a more detailed explanation of these unique features of *The Philosophical Journey*, turn to pages 10–13.) Both students and teachers will find that these features provide a great deal to think about and talk about. In my attempts to make philosophy an activity and not just a course, I began developing this approach to introducing philosophy more than twelve years ago. The activities I have experimented with that have made it into the book have been the ones that my students most enjoyed and that have made my task as a teacher easier. I hope that both the students and teachers using this book will find this to be true for them as well.

Teaching and Learning Package

Instructor's Manual Written by myself, this manual begins with an overall introduction to *The Philosophical Journey* and a general discussion of how to use the sundry pedagogical features to advantage in the classroom. This discussion is followed by a chapter-by-chapter, section-by-section series of lecture and discussion tips, including how to use some of the specific Thought Experiments and other interactive activities in the text. Finally, the manual contains a series of objective and essay test questions tailored to each chapter and section. Carefully crafted as a true teaching tool, the various elements of this instructor's manual provide an excellent resource for both first time and experienced philosophy teachers.

Presentation software with PowerPoint Lecture Outlines Prepared by Julius J. Jackson, Jr., San Bernardino Valley College, these slides outline important concepts, ask questions, and provide discussion topics. The presentational software can be used with either PC or Macintosh-based computers.

Talking Tutorial CD-ROM Developed by Julius J. Jackson, Jr., of San Bernardino Valley College, this unique CD-ROM Study Guide offers audio guided tours that highlight important chapter concepts, audio mini-lectures that provide in-depth study for selected concepts and philosophers, audio pronunciation guides for key terms, as well as flash cards, true-false, multiple choice, and fill-in-the-blank questions. This study guide can be used with either PC or Macintosh-based computers, and it is included **free** with each copy of *The Philosophical Journey.*

The Philosophical Journey Web Site Your students can continue their journey into philosophy online at *www.mayfieldpub.com/lawhead,* perhaps the first Web site designed specifically to accompany and supplement an introduction to philosophy text. The Web site, developed by Eric J. Salahub of Front Range Community College, has the following features:

- A *Hyperlinked Glossary* contains links to outside Web resources for further information on the philosophers and concepts described in the book.
- A *Contemporary Connections* section attempts to relate philosophical concepts from each chapter to modern dilemmas and current events. An *Extended Discussion* section contains chat room discussion links at outside institutions. An *Explorations* section invites students to investigate philosophical questions on their own on the Web.
- *Interactive Polls and Questionnaires* allow students to answer various philosophical questions of opinion and see the results contributed by their peers.
- *Multiple Choice and True/False Questions* are self-assessment quizzes for students distinct from those in the *"Talking Tutorial"* CD-ROM.

- *Instructors' Resources* include a syllabus builder and PowerPoint Lecture Outlines in Adobe Acrobat® format.

Acknowledgments

From the first rough outline to the final chapter revisions I have had the help of numerous reviewers who read it with an eye to its suitability for the classroom as well as its philosophical clarity and accuracy. I appreciate the comments of the following reviewers: Anne DeWindt, Wayne County Community College; Eric Gampel, California State University at Chico; Garth Gillan, Southern Illinois University; Achim Kodderman, State University of New York College; Mark A. Michael, Austin Peay State University; Benjamin A. Petty, Southern Methodist University; John F. Sallstrem, Georgia College; and Nancy Shaffer, University of Nebraska-Omaha.

I am particularly grateful to my colleagues for sharing their expertise with me. Laurie Cozad answered numerous questions on Asian religions, Michael Lynch on epistemology, and Robert Westmoreland on ethics and political philosophy. In addition to stimulating conversations about metaphysics, Michael Harrington, my chair, assisted me by ignoring the impact on our budget of copier, phone, and overnight mailing costs, as well as vigorously supporting my application for a sabbatical. In granting me a sabbatical, the University of Mississippi turned the impossible time demands I faced into only moderately impossible demands. Finally, I have to thank all of my Mississippi Governor's School students who interacted with me during the summers of 1987 to 1999 and who were the first to test out many of the exercises in this book.

I also owe a debt of gratitude to the many people associated with the Mayfield Publishing Company who worked so hard on the book. Ken King, my editor, was the driving force (and I do mean driving). He persuaded me that the time to write the book was now and helped me take it from a bright idea to a finished work. My development editors, first Barbara Armentrout and then Kate Engelberg, quickly caught my vision of what the book was all about and helped me realize its potential. Carla Kirschenbaum was understanding, efficient, and everything a production editor should be. While the copyediting stage can be one of the less pleasant aspects of writing, Karen Dorman's insightful suggestions were instructive and I enjoyed working with her.

Whether you are a student or a teacher, I hope that you will enjoy interacting with my book as much as I enjoyed writing it. I would be glad to hear about your experiences with the book and its exercises as well as any suggestions you have for future improvements. You may write to me at Department of Philosophy and Religion, University of Mississippi, University, MS, 38677 or e-mail me at wlawhead@olemiss.edu.

William Lawhead

Contents

CHAPTER 3   The Search for Ultimate Reality   250

INTRODUCTION TO THE PHILOSOPHICAL JOURNEY

Where Are We Going and How Will We Get There?

In a nineteenth-century work, the Danish philosopher and literary genius Søren Kierkegaard depicted one of his fictional characters sitting in a café worrying about the fact that he has no mission or purpose in life.* He despairs over the fact that many in his age have served humanity and have achieved fame and admiration by making life easier and easier for people. He mentions the convenience and ease that have been brought by the invention of railways, buses, steamboats, the telegraph, and easily accessible encyclopedias. With a sense of failure he asks himself, "And what are you doing?" It seems clear to him that he could not compete with other people in making life easier. Searching for his mission in life, he finally comes up with this idea:

> Suddenly this thought flashed through my mind: "You must do something, but inasmuch as with your limited capacities it will be impossible to make anything easier than it has become, you must, with the same humanitarian enthusiasm as the others, undertake to make something harder." This notion pleased me immensely, and at the same time it flattered me to think that I, like the rest of them, would be loved and esteemed by the whole community. For when all combine in every way to make everything easier, there remains only one possible danger, namely, that the ease becomes so great that it becomes altogether too great; then there is only one want left, though it is not yet a felt want, when people will want difficulty. Out of love for mankind, and out of despair at my embarrassing situation, seeing that I had accomplished nothing and was unable to make anything easier than it had already been made, and moved by a genuine interest in those who make everything easy, I conceived it as my task to create difficulties everywhere.[1]

STOP AND THINK

Why would someone want to make life more difficult? In what ways could a philosopher such as Kierkegaard make life more difficult for his readers? Even more important, why would we want to read an author who took this as his mission in life?

PHILOSOPHY AND AEROBICS

You might get some perspective on the questions in the box if you notice that those things that are cheap and come easiest in life are usually those things that are worth little in the long run. A quarter will get you a gum ball from a machine. A gum ball is cheap and easy to obtain, but its only value is a few minutes of pleasure. On the

---

*Although it is not always safe to assume that the words of Kierkegaard's fictional characters reflect his own sentiments, in this case they repeat what Kierkegaard says many times over about himself.

other hand, the mother's labor pains bring forth new life, the musician's long hours of practice produce musical perfection, the athlete's pain and determination are rewarded with self-mastery and athletic records, and the writer's creative struggles in the face of dozens of rejection slips may produce a great novel. In each case, something of value was gained, but only as the result of great difficulty and persistent effort.

Perhaps Kierkegaard's point is that only by facing the really difficult issues in life will we gain something that is truly valuable. His mission was to coax us, to irritate us, and to provoke us into making the effort necessary to overcome our reticence to face one of life's most difficult but rewarding tasks: honest, personal reflection. For Kierkegaard, this activity was the heart and soul of philosophy. Like many other strenuous but valuable activities, becoming a philosopher can involve intellectual labor pains, practice, determination, and creative struggling. But philosophy obviously does not produce the tangible rewards of the sort enjoyed by the mother, musician, athlete, or novelist. What, then, is the reward of doing philosophy? According to Kierkegaard, what philosophy can give us is *self-understanding*. Self-understanding involves knowing who I really am apart from the masks I present to others, the social roles I fulfill, or the labels and descriptions imposed on me by my society and my peers. It also involves understanding my beliefs and values and being aware of why I act the way I do, including knowing whether my actions result from my own authentic choices or from taken-for-granted, unexamined assumptions or the influences of my culture.

At first glance, it would seem that self-understanding is something that everyone would desire. But Kierkegaard thought that it was not only the most important goal in life, but the most difficult one. Furthermore, he claimed that it is something that we are often tempted to avoid. It is much easier to be complacent, to be self-satisfied, and to stick with beliefs that are comfortable and familiar than to be painfully and fully honest with ourselves and to subject our deepest convictions to examination. Fitness centers promote the saying, "No pain, no gain." The same is true with our struggles to become fully realized and actualized persons. In fact, philosophy could be viewed as "aerobics for the human mind." In Kierkegaard's day, everyone was claiming to provide the answers to everyone else's problems. Kierkegaard, however, thought that his greatest contribution to society would be to provide the problems to everyone's answers. Only in this way, he thought, would we be goaded into searching for those answers that are worthy of our belief. Kierkegaard has provided us with our first definition of philosophy: *Philosophy is the search for self-understanding.*

PHILOSOPHY AND LOVE

The term *philosophy* literally means "the love of wisdom." It is said that the first one to call himself a philosopher was Pythagoras, a Greek who lived somewhere between 570 and 495 B.C. and spent most of his life in southern Italy. He is, of course, best known for his famous mathematical theorem. When once asked if he was wise, he replied that no one could be wise but a god, but that he was a lover of wisdom. To love something does not mean to possess it but to focus our life on it. Whereas Pythagoras introduced the term *philosopher,* it was Socrates who made it famous. He said that the philosopher was one who had a passion for wisdom and who was intoxicated by this love. This description makes quite a contrast with the image of the philosopher as being cold and analytical—sort of a walking and talking computer. On the contrary, the cognitive and the emotional are combined in philosophy, for we do not rationally deliberate about those issues in life that are deeply trivial. When I pick up my copy of the daily campus newspaper, for example, I don't stand there and reason about which copy to grab. On the other hand, those issues that are most important to us are such things as our religious commitments (or lack of them), our moral values, our political commitments, our career, or (perhaps) who we will share our lives with. Unlike the trivial task of choosing a newspaper, such issues as our deepest loves, convictions, and commitments demand our deepest thought and most thorough rational reflection. Philosophy, in part, is the search for that kind of wisdom that will inform the beliefs and values that enter into these crucial decisions. Thanks to Pythagoras and Socrates, we now have a second definition: *Philosophy is the love and pursuit of wisdom.*

PHILOSOPHY AND PEANUT BUTTER

Everyone knows that philosophy deals with questions, with very basic questions such as, "Is there a God?" "Does life have meaning?" "Do I have freedom or am I determined by forces beyond my control?" "How do I decide what is morally right?" What makes these questions *philosophical* questions? One answer is that philosophical questions deal with our most basic concepts such as God, meaning, freedom, moral rightness. To get a better grasp on the nature of philosophical questions, try the following thought experiment.[2]

 THOUGHT EXPERIMENT: *Questions*

1. Consider the following two questions.
   Where can I find the peanut butter?
   Where can I find happiness?

In what ways are these two questions similar? In what ways are they different? Which question is the easiest to answer? Which question is the most important one?

2. Look at what is represented on the cover of this book and answer this question: Is this a flimdoggal?

Are you having difficulty answering the question? Why?

3. Suppose that someone slipped you a drug that made it impossible for you to answer the following questions: Is this a hat or an ice cream sundae? Is this belief true or false? Is this real or an illusion? Is this action morally good or evil? Now ask yourself: What would be some practical problems created by these confusions?

The questions about where to find the peanut butter or happiness seem very similar, yet there is a world of difference between them. We have a tendency to suppose that the "real" issues are ones that are concrete and have verifiable and certain answers. If we believe that tendency, then we never ask any questions more profound than, "Where is the peanut butter?" The answer is concrete ("On the top shelf behind the mustard"), and we can be sure when we have found the answer ("Yep, this tastes like peanut butter"). On the other hand, we have many conflicting opinions about where to find happiness (religion, sensual pleasure, wealth, fame, a meaningful career, service to others, and on and on). We may think we have found happiness, but we can spend the rest of our lives trying to make sure that what we found is really it. Clearly, happiness is much more abstract and elusive than peanut butter. But maybe the goals in life that are the most abstract and elusive are the ones that are the most important to pursue.

Obviously, you could not decide if the cover of this book represented a flimdoggal because you did not know what such a thing is. What you would need in order to answer the question are the criteria for determining whether something is a flimdoggal, or a precise definition of the word *flimdoggal*. We have the same problem with words such as *God, meaning, freedom,* or *moral goodness.* However, because these words are so familiar (unlike *flimdoggal*), we often assume that we understand the corresponding concepts. Yet the concepts that philosophy analyzes are those that we dare not leave unclarified. If you could not distinguish a hat from an ice cream sundae, it could lead to some embarrassing moments as you tried to put a sundae on your head. But most of your life would be unaffected. On the other hand, if you were confused about the concepts of "true," "false," "real," "illusion," "good," or "evil," your life would be deeply impaired.

George Orwell, in his novel *1984,* depicts a totalitarian society that controls its citizens' minds by controlling their language. The society's official language of "Newspeak" does not have a word for freedom. Without the word *freedom,* people do not have the concept of freedom, without the concept they cannot think about freedom, and if they cannot think about freedom they cannot aspire toward it. The citizens feel a vague sense of discomfort with their society, but the government has robbed them of the ability to speak and think about the causes of this dissatisfaction. This novel illustrates why the meanings of words are so very important to philosophy. Sometimes philosophy is accused of simply being "arguments about words." It is true that some verbal disputes are fruitless, but not all. Words give us a grasp of our fundamental concepts, which govern our thinking, and our thinking in turn guides the way we deal with reality, the actions we perform, and the decisions we make. This discussion gives us our third definition of philosophy: *Philosophy is the asking of questions about the meaning of our most basic concepts.*

PHILOSOPHY AND COLDS

The topic of examining our lives and examining our beliefs introduces an important point about philosophy. In one sense, everyone is a philosopher. Everyone has some beliefs (no matter how tentative) about the existence of God, about how to determine if a statement is true or false, and about what is morally right and wrong (among other things). Whether you realize it or not, philosophical conclusions are woven into the conduct of your daily life. As you go through this book, you will find that many of your beliefs have been shared by some of the great philosophers in history. You will also find philosophical labels for many of your beliefs as well as arguments supporting them or arguments opposing them. With respect to philosophy, you are not like a spectator sitting in the stands, watching the professionals engage in a game of tennis. Instead, you are down on the court, already a participant in the activity of philosophy.

Whereas in a certain sense everyone is a philosopher, in another sense philosophy as a way of looking at things has to be learned and practiced. The problem is that too often we acquire our ideas, beliefs, and values the way we catch a cold. Like the cold virus, these ideas, beliefs, and values are floating around in our environment and we breath them in without realizing it. The cold belonged to someone else, and now it is our cold. The beliefs and values were those of our culture, but now they are our own. It could be that they are true beliefs and excellent values, but how are we to know if we have internalized them unthinkingly? In examining our own and other peoples' fundamental beliefs, we must ask: Are these beliefs justified? What reasons do we have to suppose that they are true? What evidence counts against them? Thus, while everyone has philosophical beliefs, the philosophical journey takes us one step further. This acknowledgment gives us the fourth aspect of philosophy: *Philosophy is the search for fundamental beliefs that are rationally justified.*

If we summarize the discussion thus far, we have a multidimensional, working definition of philosophy. As you read through this book, note how each philosopher or philosophy addresses these four points. Philosophy is the

1. search for self-understanding
2. love and pursuit of wisdom
3. asking of questions about the meaning of our basic concepts
4. search for fundamental beliefs that are rationally justified

WHAT DO PHILOSOPHERS STUDY?

Many people have no idea what philosophy is all about. The term *philosophy* often conjures up the image of a vague, fuzzy realm of irreducibly subjective opinions. A common question is, "What do philosophers study?" No one seems to have this problem with other disciplines. For example, (to put it glibly) biologists study frogs, geologists study rocks, historians study wars, and astronomers study stars. But what part of the universe or human experience do philosophers examine? The short answer, as one philosopher put it, is that "philosophy's center is everywhere and its circumference nowhere."[3] But someone could raise the objection that this definition makes it seem as though philosophy covers the same territory that the other disciplines do. The answer to this objection is that philosophy is unique in comparison to other areas of study *not* because it thinks about different things, but because it thinks about things differently. This feature of philosophy can be made clear by comparing the sorts of questions asked by different disciplines with the sorts of questions asked by the philosopher in six different areas: logic, epistemology, metaphysics, philosophy of religion, ethics, and political philosophy.

Logic

The psychologist studies *how* people think and the *causes* of people's beliefs, whether their thinking is rational or irrational. But the philosopher studies how we *ought* to think if we are to be rational and seeks to clarify the good *reasons* for holding a belief. The study of the principles for distinguishing correct from incorrect reasoning is the area of philosophy known as logic, which is discussed at the end of this chapter under the heading "1.2: Argument and Evidence: How Do I Decide What to Believe?"

Epistemology

The historian seeks to increase our knowledge of the Civil War by gathering facts and determining which accounts of the events are the most true. The philosopher asks, What is knowledge? What is a fact? What is truth? How could we know that something is true or not? Is there objective truth, or are all opinions relative? Fundamental questions about the nature and source of knowledge, the concept of truth, and the objectivity or relativity of our beliefs are the concern of the theory of knowledge, or epistemology, which you encounter in chapter 2, "The Search for Knowledge."

Metaphysics

The physicist studies the ultimate constituents of physical reality such as atoms, quarks, or neutrinos. On the other hand, the philosopher asks, Is physical reality all that there is? The neurobiologist studies the activity of the brain, but the philosopher asks, Are all mental events really brain events, or is the mind something separate from the brain? The psychologist attempts to find causal correlations between criminal behavior and the individual's genetic inheritance or social influences. The philosopher, on the other hand, asks, Is all behavior (good or bad) causally determined, or do we have some degree of genuine freedom that cannot be scientifically explained? Is there necessarily a conflict between the scientific attempt to explain and predict behavior and our belief in human freedom? Metaphysics is the area of philosophy concerned with fundamental questions about the nature of reality. In chapter 3, "The Search for Ultimate Reality," you encounter different models of what reality is like as well as questions concerning *human* reality such as, What is the relationship between the mind and the body? and Are we free or determined?

Philosophy of Religion

The astronomer studies the laws that govern the heavenly bodies such as the stars. However, the philosopher asks these questions: Is the existence and nature of the universe self-explanatory, or does it need an explanation or a divine creator that lies outside it? How do we account for the order in the world that makes science possible? Is the evidence of design sufficient to prove a designer?

The meteorologist asks, What causes hurricanes? and the medical researcher asks, What causes childhood leukemia? On the other hand, the philosopher asks, Is there any rational way to believe in a good, all-powerful God who permits the undeserved destruction of hurricanes or the suffering of innocent children? Or is the evidence of undeserved suffering an argument against such a God?

The sociologist studies the religious beliefs of various groups and the social needs that these beliefs fulfill without making any judgments about the truth or rationality of these beliefs. However, the philosopher asks, Is faith opposed to reason, compatible with reason, or supported by reason, or is faith something that necessarily goes beyond reason? These sorts of questions about the existence of God, the problem of evil, and the relationship of faith and reason constitute the area of philosophy known as philosophy of religion and is discussed in chapter 4, "The Search for God."

Ethics

The anthropologist studies the moral codes of various societies and describes both their similarities and differences, but does not decide which ones are best. On the other hand, the philosopher asks, Are there any objectively correct ethical values, or are they all relative? Which ethical principles (if any) are the correct ones? How do we decide what is right or wrong? These questions are the concern of ethics, which is the topic of chapter 5, "The Search for Ethical Values."

Political Philosophy

The political scientist studies various forms of government, but the philosopher asks, What makes a government legitimate? What is justice? What is the proper extent of individual freedom? What are the limits of governmental authority? Is disobeying the law ever morally justified? These questions fall under the heading of political philosophy and are discussed in chapter 6, "The Search for the Just Society."

Survey ten friends who have not taken a philosophy class and ask them, What is philosophy? After you have collected all the responses, evaluate them on your own by considering the following questions:

- Are there any common themes throughout the ten answers?
- How do the answers compare to the description of philosophy in this chapter?
- Are there any features about philosophy that are missing in the responses?
- Which answers do you think are best? Why?
- Which answers do you think are least satisfactory? Why?

PHILOSOPHY AS A JOURNEY

Just so you will be forewarned, what you are holding in your hands is not merely a book *about* philosophy but a guidebook to a philosophical journey in which you will be *participating*. In each chapter you will have not only things to read but also things to do. I have chosen this approach because philosophy is not just a set of ideas, it is an activity. For this reason, the title of the book is *The Philosophical Journey*. I hope that you will find the philosophical journey to be fun, but it will also be a working expedition in which many tasks are to be accomplished. This book is for explorers who will be actively involved in making discoveries, not just passive viewers of a travelogue. Hence, each chapter provides sections that will engage you in intellectual versions of scouting the territory, charting terrain, choosing paths, surveying arguments, viewing perspectives, and critically examining what you have found. But you will not have to make these explorations unassisted, for this book is a field manual. It will point out significant landmarks, provide maps to the territory, caution you about crucial crossroads and pitfalls, and introduce you to some experienced trailblazers: the philosophers who have preceded you on this journey.

When I set out on my first canoe trip, I was not very good at it. Initially, my paddle thrashed around in the water and my efforts were rewarded more by sore muscles than by progress down the river. But in a short time I got the hang of canoeing and my paddle strokes became more productive. Soon my boat was gliding smoothly through the water, and I learned to anticipate obstacles or difficult stretches of water and to maneuver successfully around them. Learning to read, write, and think about philosophy is no different than learning any other skill. By the time you reach the end of this book, you should be better at it than when you began. The "philosophy as a journey" metaphor does have one limitation. Usually we take a journey to get to a specific destination (the campsite downriver, Grandma's house, back to school). The philosophical journey is different because it is never finished. There are always new ideas to explore, new problems to solve, and old territory to explore in fresh ways. In this way philosophy is more like the journey we take in a lifelong friendship than a short canoe trip.

GUIDEPOSTS FOR YOUR JOURNEY

To help you on your journey, here are some of the guideposts and activities to look for in each chapter. Do not skip over them, because the discussion following them will not be as meaningful. Each chapter is titled "The Search for . . ." and covers one of five main topics in philosophy. Specifically, these topics are the theory of knowledge, or epistemology (chapter 2), theories about reality, or metaphysics (chapter 3), philosophy of religion (chapter 4), ethics (chapter 5), and political philosophy (chapter 6). Some chapters contain subtopics that focus on a specific issue under the main heading. Each discussion on a main topic or subtopic is titled "Overview" and begins with an event that scouts the territory.

SCOUTING THE TERRITORY

The event in this section may be a story, a scenario, or a newspaper account that challenges you with philosophical puzzles concerning the topic. It usually does not consist of an explicit philosophical discussion but shows how philosophical issues make themselves felt in every area of life.

CHARTING THE TERRAIN—WHAT ARE THE ISSUES?

The next section consists of a more precise presentation of the philosophical problem and its significance. It makes you aware of the philosophical questions you need to answer as you make your way through the material.

CHOOSING A PATH—WHAT ARE MY OPTIONS?

This section contains a brief description of the opposing alternatives on the issue. Typically, the section contains a chart that shows how the various positions line up on different aspects of the main issue. Besides giving you an initial comparison of the available viewpoints, the section helps you to clarify your own thinking on the issue.

WHAT DO I THINK?

Finally, the initial section on a philosophical topic or subtopic includes a brief questionnaire to enable you to see where you currently stand on the issue. (I say "currently" because it is perfectly permissible to change your mind as you study the different options in more detail.) The questions you are asked do not presuppose any prior knowledge of philosophy and are not factual in nature, so your honest opinion is all that is expected.

KEY TO THE QUESTIONNAIRE

After the questionnaire, the answers are analyzed in this key section. This key does not tell you which answers are right or wrong. Instead, it provides you with the philosophical labels for your own opinions. Do not worry if these labels are unfamiliar; they will be explained in time. Just keep your own position in mind, because in the remaining sections of the chapter, you will find that your own views have been defended or criticized by some of the great philosophers. As you read the remainder of each chapter, keep the following thoughts in mind: The issues being discussed are issues on which you have opinions. Some of the philosophers will agree with you and will be providing resources for your own thought. Do you find these resources helpful? Why? Other philosophers will be stepping on your toes. They will be issuing challenges to your thinking. How will you respond? They are trying to get you to buy their ideas. Are you buying? They will be trying to lock you into their position with their arguments. Can you evade the force of their arguments? If not, does your position need to be refined, modified, better supported, or abandoned?

LEADING QUESTIONS

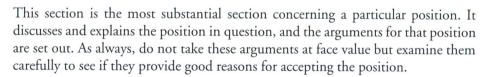

Following the overview of each particular philosophical issue is a section on each position. Each philosophical alternative is introduced with the leading questions exercise. This exercise consists of brief questions that are leading questions in two senses: they lead into the discussion of a particular philosophical position, and they are biased in favor of the position to be examined. The purpose of the questions is to make you initially sympathetic to the position that is being explained as well as to motivate you to be critical of how the questions are formulated. Hence, in answering the questions, look for the hidden assumptions they contain.

SURVEYING THE CASE FOR . . .

This section is the most substantial section concerning a particular position. It discusses and explains the position in question, and the arguments for that position are set out. As always, do not take these arguments at face value but examine them carefully to see if they provide good reasons for accepting the position.

A READING FROM . . .

Most of the sections on a particular point of view include brief readings from a philosopher that give you some practice in analyzing philosophical arguments. Questions are provided to suggest what to look for in the passage and to assist you in analyzing it. These passages have been selected because they are important to your understanding of the philosophical ideas. Do not skip over them, because you will miss some important material. Just as you cannot learn how to ski by reading about skiing but never getting out on the slopes, so you cannot develop philosophically without engaging with philosophical writings.

LOOKING THROUGH X'S LENS

Each philosophy is like a lens through which we can view human experience and the world at large. Each philosopher is claiming that his or her philosophy gives you the best picture of life. Accordingly, in this section you are asked: "If you were a follower of philosopher X, how would you view the following issues?" This exercise enables you to "try on" the philosopher's point of view in order to understand the position, see its implications, and discover its practical impact.

EXAMINING THE STRENGTHS AND WEAKNESSES OF X

This section concludes the discussion of each philosophy. Philosophy is more than just a parade of opinions. Your philosophical journey will just be aimless meandering unless you absorb all the information and arguments available to you and make up your mind as to which viewpoints make the most sense. Probably no philosophy is 100 percent right or 100 percent wrong. So, you are asked to assess both the strengths and weaknesses of the position under discussion. Instead of telling you what to think about the position, the book provides questions that suggest both positive and negative points; it will be up to you to draw your own conclusions as to whether the strengths of the position outweigh its weaknesses.

BOXED EXERCISES

Scattered throughout each chapter are a number of other, boxed exercises that ask you to pause and think about a particular issue. Here are some examples of what you will be asked to do.

PHILOSOPHY *in the* **MARKETPLACE**

From time to time, you are asked to survey your friends who are not taking this course concerning their opinions on a particular issue. The survey questions do not assume that your friends know anything about the technical details of philosophy. Socrates thought that the best way to search for the truth was in dialogue with others. Accordingly, he spent his time in the marketplace, questioning his fellow Athenians about their views. These surveys give you the opportunity to try out the Socratic method of doing philosophy outside of class. My own students have reported that this exercise often provoked an evening-long discussion of the issue with their friends. Perhaps the answers you get on these surveys will raise issues that you will want to share with your professor and your classmates.

Finally, at the end of each of the six chapters is a checklist to help you review the material in that chapter. It lists the names of the major philosophers covered in the chapter, mentions the key concepts, and includes suggestions for further reading.

As you can see, the philosophical journey is something more than simply learning facts, names, and dates. It is also more than simply clinging to personal opinions or passing them back and forth the way kids trade baseball cards. The philosophical journey involves the challenging work of reflecting on, evaluating, and seeking the justification for your own and other peoples' fundamental beliefs. But making this journey and sticking to it will bring you one of life's richest rewards, which is nothing less than *self-understanding*. To help you on your journey, this book attempts to achieve what Immanuel Kant, the eighteenth-century German philosopher, took as his goal as a teacher: "You will not learn from me philosophy, but how to philosophize, not thoughts to repeat, but how to think."[4]

SOCRATES
(470–399 B.C.)

The prisoner was housed in the state prison, only a stone's throw to the southwest of the agora, the bustling marketplace in Athens.* It seemed like just yesterday he had been walking in that very marketplace, discussing philosophy and questioning people on their views about all possible topics of human concern: knowledge, moral goodness, psychology, politics, art, and religion. But a month ago a jury made up of 500 citizens of Athens had voted to condemn him to death on the two charges of corrupting the minds of the youth and teaching about gods other than the official gods of Athens. Under normal circumstances the prisoner would have been executed soon after the trial, but an annual religious festival delayed his death by a month.

On the morning of his death, a group of friends arrived at his jail cell just as his wife and small baby were leaving to get some rest after spending the night with him. The group consisted of more than ten of his local friends as well as five others who came from out of town. The prisoner was massaging his leg, which had just been released from its chains. He looked as he always had, as though this day was just another day in his life. The morning light streaming through the window reflected off his bald head and highlighted his curly, gray beard. His mantle, as always, hung awkwardly on his seventy-year-old, short and stocky frame. People were always amused that one whose mind was so precise and orderly had such a humorous and unimposing physical appearance. But the solemnity of the occasion prevented any amusement on this day. The room was charged with emotion, and some friends were even weeping shamelessly. However, the condemned prisoner was extraordinarily calm and even cheerful as he waited for his death.

The year was 399 B.C., and the man facing execution for his ideas was Socrates, who had taught the wisdom of philosophy to many Athenians, including his best-known student, Plato. In the hours remaining in his life, Socrates revealed to his followers the secret of his calm composure. The philosopher is a person, he said, whose soul has been liberated by wisdom. Such a person has learned to know and therefore participate in ultimate Truth, Beauty, and Goodness. Since these concepts are eternal and are unchanged by the changes of the physical aspects that illustrate them, our ability to know these eternal truths indicates something eternal within us. Since the soul within us is eternal and immaterial, Socrates argued, and since it alone is the real person, then no harm that occurs to the body can ever affect it. Socrates argued long and patiently throughout the day about his and everyone's immortality. While his followers dreaded the impending loss of their friend, Socrates looked forward to being freed from the injustice of the state and reveled in the hope of entering into a realm of perfect justice where his teachings would be vindicated.

---

*This account is loosely based on the *Phaedo,* Plato's dialogue about Socrates' last hours.

Jacques Louis David's 1787 painting *The Death of Socrates*

As sunset approached, Socrates' children were brought to see him one final time. The oldest was a young man, the middle one was a boy, and the youngest was still a baby. After they left, the prison warden, who had grown quite fond of Socrates and had visited him every day, came into the cell to say good-bye. He thanked Socrates for the conversations they had enjoyed together; then he burst into tears. By now Socrates was ready to leave, and he asked to receive the drink of poison hemlock that was to be the means of execution. He drank the cup in one breath; soon his legs began to feel heavy, and he lay down on his back. The prison guard monitored Socrates' body as the coldness and numbness started moving up from his limbs to his heart. Socrates' last words to his friends were instructions to make a sacrifice to Asclepius, the god of healing. At first the friends thought that strange, for one gave thanks to Asclepius after recovering from an illness and being returned to health. But then they remembered what Socrates had taught them and they knew that he believed he was soon to find wholeness and to be healed of the spiritual infirmities and limitations of this earthly life. About Socrates' death, his disciple Phaedo is reported to have said, "Such was the end . . . of our friend, whom I may truly call the most wise and just and best of all men I have ever known."[5]

Most accounts of a great figure's life begin with his or her birth. But in Socrates' case, his death tells us the most about his character and his life. Several questions arise out of this account of Socrates' death.

- Why was a philosopher considered so dangerous that he had to be put to death?
- Why was Socrates so committed to his philosophical ideas that he was willing to die for them?

The answers to these questions should become more evident the more you learn about this great philosopher. For now, it may be helpful to consider what you can learn about yourself from Socrates' example.

STOP AND THINK

Socrates lived and died in another land and in another time, but his life and death can provoke us to ask a number of questions about our own lives. To get an appreciation of Socrates' situation, ask yourself the following questions:

- What would make an idea dangerous?
- What ideas (if any) do I find to be uncomfortable, troubling, or even dangerous? Why?
- Can I think of any ideas in the past that society thought were dangerous but that turned out to be true?
- Can I think of any ideas that I once thought were dangerous but that I now accept?
- What ideas are worth living for?
- What ideas would I be willing to die for?

SOCRATES' LIFE AND MISSION

Now that we have learned about Socrates' death, what do we know about his life? Socrates was born in 470 B.C. in Athens. Unlike most of Socrates' students, who came from some of Athens' finest families, Socrates came from humble economic circumstances. His father was a sculptor and his mother a midwife. There are interesting similarities between Socrates' method of doing philosophy and the occupations of his parents, which he observed as a young boy. A sculptor takes a raw hunk of marble and chisels away at it, removing all the extraneous material until a finished, polished statue emerges. Similarly, in his conversations with the citizens of Athens, Socrates would take the raw, unrefined ideas of his contemporaries and hammer away at their opinions, removing what was unclear or erroneous, until he gradually achieved a closer approximation to the truth. Thinking, no doubt, of his mother, Socrates referred to himself as the "midwife of ideas." He claimed not to be able to teach anybody anything, but instead he asked artful questions that sought to bring to birth the truth that lay hidden within every human soul.

The most definitive information about Socrates' life comes from the account of his trial recorded by Plato in the *Apology*. (The term *apology* here does not mean weakly expressing regret but refers to a formal defense such as one might introduce into a court of law.) In the following passage, Socrates tells the court how he got into so much trouble in the first place. The account begins with an event that was the turning point in Socrates' life.

Apology[6]

O men of Athens, I must beg you not to interrupt me, even if I seem to say something extravagant. For the word which I will speak is not mine. I will refer you to a witness who is worthy of credit, and will tell you about my wisdom—whether I have any, and of what sort—and that witness shall be the god of Delphi. You must have known Chaerephon; he was early a friend of mine, and also a friend of yours, for he shared in the exile of the people, and returned with you. Well, Chaerephon, as you know, was very impetuous in all his doings, and he went to Delphi and boldly asked the oracle to tell him whether—as I was saying, I must beg you not to interrupt—he asked the oracle to tell him whether there was anyone wiser than I was, and the Pythian prophetess answered that there was no man wiser. Chaerephon is dead himself, but his brother, who is in court, will confirm the truth of this story. Why do I mention this? Because I am going to explain to you why I have such an evil name. When I heard the answer, I said to myself, "What can the god mean and what is the interpretation of this riddle? I know that I have no wisdom, great or small. What can he mean when he says that I am the wisest of men? And yet he is a god and cannot lie; that would be against his nature." After a long consideration, I at last thought of a method of trying the question. I reflected that if I could only find a man wiser than myself, then I might go to the god with a refutation in my hand. I should say to him, "Here is a man who is wiser than I am; but you said that I was the wisest."

- In the passage you just read, what did the god say about Socrates through the voice of the prophetess?
- How does Socrates propose to disprove the god's statement?
- In the next passage, what advantage does Socrates say he has over the politicians of his day?

Accordingly I went to one who had the reputation of wisdom, and observed to him—his name I need not mention; he was a politician whom I selected for examination—and the result was as follows: When I began to talk with him, I could not help thinking that he was not really wise, although he was thought wise by many, and wiser still by himself; and I went and tried to explain to him that he thought himself wise, but was not really wise; and the consequence was that he hated me, and his hatred was shared by several who were present and heard me. So I left him, saying to myself, as I went away: "Well, although I do not suppose that either of us knows anything really beautiful and good, I am better off than he is—for he knows nothing, and thinks that he knows. I neither know nor think that I know. In this latter particular, then, I seem to have an advantage over him." Then I went to another, who had still higher philosophical pretensions, and my conclusion was exactly the same. I made another enemy of him, and of many others besides him.

After this I went to one man after another, being aware of the hatred which I provoked, and I lamented and feared this: but necessity was laid upon me. The word of the god, I thought, ought to be considered first. And I said to myself, "I must go to all who appear to know, and find out the meaning of the oracle." And I swear to you, Athenians, by the dog I swear!—for I must tell you the truth—the result of my mission was just this: I found that the men most in repute were all but the most foolish; and that some inferior men were really wiser and better.

I will tell you the tale of my wanderings and of the "Herculean" labors, as I may call them, which I endured only to find at last the oracle irrefutable. When I left the politicians, I went to the poets; tragic, dithyrambic, and all sorts. And there, I said to myself, you will be detected; now you will find out that you are more ignorant than they are. Accordingly, I took them some of the most elaborate passages in their own writings, and asked what was the meaning of them—thinking that they would teach me something. Will you believe me? I am almost ashamed to speak of this, but still I must say that there is hardly a person present who would not have talked better about their poetry than they did themselves. That showed me in an instant that not by wisdom do poets write poetry, but by a sort of genius and inspiration; they are like diviners or soothsayers who also say many fine things, but do not understand the meaning of them. And the poets appeared to me to be much in the same case; and I further observed that upon the strength of their poetry they believed themselves to be the wisest of men in other things in which they were not wise. So I departed, conceiving myself to be superior to them for the same reason that I was superior to the politicians.

At last I went to the artisans, for I was conscious that I knew nothing at all, as I may say, and I was sure that they knew many fine things; and in this I was not mistaken, for they did know many things of which I was ignorant, and in this they certainly were wiser than I was. But I observed that even the good artisans fell into the same error as the poets; because they were good workmen they thought that they also knew all sorts of high matters, and this defect in them overshadowed their wisdom. Therefore I asked myself on behalf of the oracle, whether I would like to be as I was, neither having their knowledge nor their ignorance, or like them in both. I answered to myself and the oracle that I was better off as I was. This investigation has led to my having many enemies of the worst and most dangerous kind, and has given occasion also to many falsehoods. I am called wise, for my hearers always imagine that I myself possess the wisdom which I find wanting in others.

Socrates is still convinced that he is ignorant and has nothing to teach, but now he knows why the god said he was wiser than anyone else in Athens.

- In what way is he wise?

In the next passage, Socrates anticipates that the court may let him go free on the condition that he cease to do philosophy and stop asking his annoying questions.

- What is his response to this potential offer of a plea bargain?
- What does he say is the mistake that the citizens of Athens are making?
- What does Socrates see as his mission?

Men of Athens, I honor and love you; but I shall obey the god rather than you, and while I have life and strength I shall never cease from the practice and teaching of philosophy, exhorting anyone whom I meet after my manner, and convincing him, saying: O my friend, why do you who are a citizen of the great and mighty and wise city of Athens, care so much about laying up the greatest amount of money and honor and reputation, and so little about wisdom and truth and the greatest improvement of the soul, which you never regard or heed at all? Are you not ashamed of this? And if the person with whom I am arguing says: Yes, but I do care; I do not depart or let him go at once; I interrogate and examine and cross-examine him, and if I think that he has no virtue, but only says that he has, I reproach him with undervaluing the greater, and overvaluing the less. And this I should say to everyone whom I meet, young and old, citizen and alien, but especially to the citizens, inasmuch as they are my brethren. For this is the command of the god, as I would have you know; and I believe that to this day no greater good has ever happened in the state than my service to the god.

I do nothing but go about persuading you all, old and young alike, not to take thought for your persons and your properties, but first and chiefly to care about the greatest improvement of the soul. I tell you that virtue is not given by money, but that from virtue come money and every other good of man, public as well as private. This is my teaching, and if this is the doctrine which corrupts the youth, my influence is ruinous indeed. But if anyone says that this is not my teaching, he is speaking an untruth. Wherefore, O men of Athens, I say to you, do as Anytus bids or not as Anytus bids, and either acquit me or not; but whatever you do, know that I shall never alter my ways, not even if I have to die many times.

STOP AND THINK

- Socrates has accused his fellow citizens of not keeping their priorities straight. If Socrates were to cross-examine you, what examples might he find in your life of placing great value on that which is trivial and undervaluing that which is of utmost importance?
- Socrates was a man who had a sense of mission in life—a mission that he would not forsake even to save his life. You, no doubt, are planning to get an education

(. . . continued)

> and to pursue a career that will give you an income. Apart from simply earning income, do you have a sense of mission in life?
> - If so, how would you describe your mission?
> - Is it important to have a sense of mission about your life? Why?

- In the next passage, why do you think that Socrates says that a bad person cannot harm a good person? Do you agree with this statement? Why?
- Why does Socrates think that his accusers (Meletus and Anytus) are harming themselves by prosecuting him?

Men of Athens, do not interrupt, but hear me; there was an agreement between us that you should hear me out. And I think that what I am going to say will do you good: for I have something more to say, at which you may be inclined to cry out; but I beg that you will not do this. I would have you know that, if you kill such a one as I am, you will injure yourselves more than you will injure me. Meletus and Anytus will not injure me: they cannot; for it is not in the nature of things that a bad man should injure one better than himself. I do not deny that he may, perhaps, kill him, or drive him into exile, or deprive him of civil rights; and he may imagine, and others may imagine, that he is doing him a great injury: but in that I do not agree with him; for the evil of doing as Anytus is doing—of unjustly taking away another man's life—is far greater.

- In the next passage, Socrates says to the jury that he is arguing not for his sake but for theirs. Why does he think that it is the citizens of Athens who are really being judged by the outcome of this trial and not him?
- Socrates goes on to compare himself to a gadfly (a large horsefly). Why does he describe himself in this way?
- What evidence does he give that his intentions were to unselfishly serve the people of Athens?

And now, Athenians, I am not going to argue for my own sake, as you may think, but for yours, that you may not sin against the god, or lightly reject his favor by condemning me. For if you kill me you will not easily find another like me, who, if I may use such a ludicrous figure of speech, am a sort of gadfly, given to the state by the god; and the state is like a great and noble steed who is tardy in his motions owing to his very size, and requires to be stirred into life. I am that gadfly which the god has given the state and all day long and in all places am always fastening upon you, arousing and persuading and reproaching you. And as you will not easily find another like me, I would advise you to spare me. I dare say that you may feel irritated at being suddenly awakened when you are caught napping; and you may think that if you were to strike me dead, as Anytus advises, which you easily might, then you would sleep on for the remainder of your lives, unless the god in his care of you gives you another gadfly. And that I am given to you by

God is proved by this: If I had been like other men, I should not have neglected all my own concerns, or patiently seen the neglect of them during all these years, and have been doing yours, coming to you individually, like a father or elder brother, exhorting you to regard virtue; this I say, would not be like human nature. And had I gained anything, or if my exhortations had been paid, there would have been some sense in that; but now, as you will perceive, not even the impudence of my accusers dares to say that I have ever exacted or sought pay of anyone. They have no witness of that. And I have a witness of the truth of what I say; my poverty is a sufficient witness.

 STOP AND THINK

Ask yourself the following questions:

- Who have been the gadflies in my life?
- Who were the people who challenged me and made me uncomfortable, but in doing so, made me a better person?
- In what way did they perform this role for me?

The list may include persons that you know, such as family, friends, or teachers, persons you have read about, and books, movies, or songs that have changed you.

In a trial such as Socrates', the defendant was expected to weep and beg for mercy from the court. He was also expected to bring his children, relatives, and friends into the courtroom to plead on his behalf. However, Socrates refused to resort to these emotional strategies, for he wanted to do as he always had done, to argue forcefully for the truth. If he was to be judged, he wanted to be judged on the basis of his life and ideas.

When the verdict was announced, 280 of the jury had declared him guilty and 220 voted for acquittal; the prosecutor recommended the death penalty. The custom in the Athenian court was for the defendant to now propose his own penalty and try to convince the jury to accept a lesser punishment. If Socrates had proposed that he be sent into exile, never to return to Athens, he might have satisfied his accusers. But Socrates would not play their game. He argued that he had been sent by his personal god to serve the citizens of Athens with his probing questions and he had done nothing but provide a great benefit to the city. Therefore, he proposed that he should receive what he really deserved and that was the honor reserved for the winners in the Olympics and the military heroes—a lifetime of free meals at the banquet table of the state's heroes. What was perceived as extraordinary arrogance turned the crowd against him, and the vote for the death penalty won by an even larger majority than before: 360 to 140.

After this crushing verdict, Socrates continued to philosophize in his final speech to the jury. The real danger in life is not death, he said, but living an evil life. We should not be willing to do or say anything to avoid death, thinking that by corrupting our souls we have gained any advantage.

The difficulty, my friends, is not in avoiding death, but in avoiding unrighteousness; for that runs faster than death. I am old and move slowly, and the slower runner has overtaken me, and my accusers are keen and quick, and the faster runner, who is unrighteousness, has overtaken them. And now I depart hence condemned by you to suffer the penalty of death, and they, too, go their ways condemned by the truth to suffer the penalty of wickedness and wrong. I must abide by my award—let them abide by theirs. I suppose that these things may be regarded as fated—and I think that they are as they should be. . . .

Wherefore, O judges, be of good cheer about death, and know this truth—that no evil can happen to a good man, either in life or after death. He and his are not neglected by the gods; nor has my own approaching end happened by mere chance. But I see clearly that to die and be released was better for me; and therefore my inner spiritual voice gave no sign. For which reason also, I am not angry with my accusers, or my condemners. They have done me no harm, although neither of them meant to do me any good; and for this I may gently blame them. . . .

The hour of departure has arrived, and we go our different ways—I to die, and you to live. Which is better only the god knows.

Socrates lived and died a philosopher—a lover of wisdom. Wisdom was, he thought, the most important goal we could pursue. Without it, we would be cursed with the most dire poverty a person could endure. The survey in "Philosophy in the Marketplace" asks you to think about and have others think about what it means to be wise.

SOCRATES' METHOD

If wisdom is the most important goal in life to Socrates, how did he go about pursuing it? Socrates' method of doing philosophy was to ask questions. That method was so effective that it has become one of the classic techniques of education; it is known as the Socratic method, or Socratic questioning. Plato referred to the method as *dialectic*, which comes from a Greek word for conversation. Typically, Socrates' philosophical conversations go through seven stages as he and his partner continually move toward a greater understanding of the truth:

1. Socrates unpacks the philosophical issues in an everyday conversation. (The genius of Socrates was his ability to find the philosophical issues lurking in even the most mundane of topics.)
2. Socrates isolates a key philosophical term that needs analysis.
3. Socrates professes ignorance and requests the help of his companion.
4. Socrates' companion proposes a definition of the key term.

Ask at least five people from different backgrounds the following questions:

1. Name at least three commonly known persons (living or dead) whom you consider to be wise.
2. Why do you consider these persons to be wise?

Note: The stipulation to choose commonly known people is meant to rule out relatives and others whom most people would not know. A subject who answers with only religious leaders (e.g., Buddha, Solomon, or Jesus) should be asked also for some other examples in order to guarantee variety.

Review the answers: Are any categories of people notable by their absence? (e.g., were any women mentioned? artists? scientists?) Are any categories of people notable by their frequency? (e.g., are most of the people mentioned political figures? religious figures?) Were any philosophers mentioned? Do you find any other patterns in the answers? What can we learn about people's notions of wisdom from this survey? Do you agree with these conceptions of wisdom? Why?

PHILOSOPHY
in the
MARKETPLACE

5. Socrates analyzes the definition by asking questions that expose its weaknesses.
6. The subject produces another definition, one that improves on the earlier one. (This new definition leads back to step 5, and on close examination the new definition is once again found to fail. Steps 5 and 6 are repeated several times.)
7. The subject is made to face his own ignorance. (Finally, the subject realizes he is ignorant and is now ready to begin the search for true wisdom. Often, however, the subject finds some excuse to end the conversation or someone else makes an attempt at a new definition.)

Socrates' hope in utilizing this method was that in weeding out incorrect understandings, he and his conversational partner would be moving toward a clearer picture of the true answer. Since Socrates believed that the truth about the ultimate issues in life lay deeply hidden within us, this process of unpacking the truth within was like that of a midwife helping a mother in labor bring forth her child.

One of Socrates' most skillful techniques for showing the weakness of someone's position was his use of the *reductio ad absurdum* form of argument. This term means "reducing to an absurdity." Socrates would begin by assuming that his opponent's position is true and then show that it logically implies either an absurdity or a conclusion that contradicts other conclusions held by the opponent. Deducing a false statement from a proposition proves that the original assumption was false.

You can view the Socratic method in action by working through a passage from Plato's dialogue the *Republic*. (Because Socrates did philosophy by engaging in conversations and not by writing, everything we know about him comes from the writings of Plato and other contemporaries. Plato's earlier dialogues, such as the

Apology, are thought to represent the historical Socrates. The *Republic* was written in Plato's middle period. The ideas, while expressed through the voice of Socrates, are thought to be Plato's own elaboration on and expansion of his teacher's thought.) The story begins with Socrates and his friends meeting in town on the occasion of a religious festival. They end up at the home of Polemarchus and meet his father, Cephalus, a retired and wealthy businessman. Cephalus talks about the joys of growing old and the virtue of having lived a fulfilled life. Socrates is keenly interested in what he has to say and begins to ask him about what has filled his life with peace and happiness. At this point in the story, we begin at the first step of Socrates' philosophical dialectic.

Unpacking the Philosophical Issues

Cephalus replies that the secret of his peace and happiness is a life lived on the basis of justice and piety. Socrates then begins to ask Cephalus about his concept of justice, which takes the two men to the next step of the dialectic.

Isolating a Key Philosophical Term

The result is that Socrates examines Cephalus's and the others' notions of justice and finds that none of their definitions is satisfactory. At that point, Thrasymachus, a rather smug and outspoken teacher, cannot contain himself any more and jumps into the conversation. He insists that Socrates stop playing games with them and offer his own definition of justice. As usual, Socrates claims that he is not knowledgeable on this issue and begs Thrasymachus to enlighten him with his wisdom. Thus, Socrates begins his conversation with Thrasymachus at the third step of his dialectic.

Professing Ignorance and Requesting Help

The following passage begins with Thrasymachus's cynical reply.

 FROM PLATO
Republic[7]

Behold, he said, the wisdom of Socrates; he refuses to teach himself, and goes about learning of others, to whom he never even says thank you.

That I learn of others, I replied, is quite true; but that I am ungrateful I wholly deny. Money I have none, and therefore I pay in praise, which is all I have: and how ready I am to praise any one who appears to me to speak well you will very soon find out when you answer; for I expect that you will answer well.

Having flattered Thrasymachus's rather enormous ego, Socrates moves the conversation to the fourth step of his dialectic.

Proposing a Definition

- In the next passage, identify Thrasymachus's definition of justice.
- What arguments could be made in favor of this definition of justice?
- What are some of the implications of this definition?
- Does Thrasymachus offer a satisfactory notion of justice? Why?

Listen, then, he said; I proclaim that justice is nothing else than the interest of the stronger. And now why do you not applaud me? But of course you won't.

Let me first understand you, I replied. Justice, as you say, is the interest of the stronger. What, Thrasymachus, is the meaning of this? . . .

Well, he said, have you never heard that forms of government differ; there are tyrannies, and there are democracies, and there are aristocracies?

Yes, I know.

And the government is the ruling power in each state?

Certainly.

And the different forms of government make laws democratic, aristocratic, tyrannical, with a view to their several interests; and these laws, which are made by them for their own interests, are the justice which they deliver to their subjects, and him who transgresses them they punish as a breaker of the law, and unjust. And that is what I mean when I say that in all states there is the same principle of justice, which is the interest of the government; and as the government must be supposed to have power, the only reasonable conclusion is, that everywhere there is one principle of justice, which is the interest of the stronger.

With Thrasymachus's definition on the table, Socrates now moves to the next step of his philosophical method.

Analyzing the Definition by Asking Questions

In the following passage, notice how Socrates uses a reductio ad absurdum argument to show that Thrasymachus's position leads to a contradictory conclusion. Socrates' love of irony is evident at the end of this passage as he refers to Thrasymachus as the "wisest of men" just as he demolishes Thrasymachus's position.

- What is the contradictory conclusion that Socrates infers from the definition?
- How do you think Thrasymachus could modify his definition to avoid this absurd conclusion?
- Set out the steps of Socrates' argument in this passage.

Now I understand you, I said; and whether you are right or not I will try to discover. . . . Now we are both agreed that justice is interest of some sort, but you go on to say "of the stronger"; about this addition I am not so sure, and must therefore consider further.

Proceed.

I will; and first tell me, Do you admit that it is just for subjects to obey their rulers?

I do.

But are the rulers of states absolutely infallible, or are they sometimes liable to err?

To be sure, he replied, they are liable to err.

Then in making their laws they may sometimes make them rightly, and sometimes not?

True.

When they make them rightly, they make them agreeably to their interest; when they are mistaken, contrary to their interest; you admit that?

Yes.

And the laws which they make must be obeyed by their subjects,—and that is what you call justice?

Doubtless.

Then justice, according to your argument, is not only obedience to the interest of the stronger but the reverse?

What is that you are saying? he asked.

I am only repeating what you are saying, I believe. But let us consider: Have we not admitted that the rulers may be mistaken about their own interest in what they command, and also that to obey them is justice? Has not that been admitted?

Yes.

Then you must also have acknowledged justice not to be for the interest of the stronger, when the rulers unintentionally command things to be done which are to their own injury. For if, as you say, justice is the obedience which the subject renders to their commands, in that case, O wisest of men, is there any escape from the conclusion that the weaker are commanded to do, not what is for the interest of the stronger, but what is for the injury of the stronger? . . .

At this point, two members of the group, Polemarchus and Cleitophon, argue over whether Socrates has trapped Thrasymachus. To resolve their debate, Socrates asks Thrasymachus to clarify his position. This response gives Thrasymachus the chance to add an important qualification to his definition to avoid the contradiction Socrates has exposed. We are now at the sixth step of Socrates' dialectical method.

Producing an Improved Definition

- How does Thrasymachus modify the notion of ruler from that of his original definition?

Tell me, Thrasymachus, I said, did you mean by justice what the stronger thought to be his interest, whether it really is so or not?

Certainly not, he said. Do you suppose that I call him who is mistaken the stronger at the time when he is mistaken?

Yes, I said, my impression was that you did so, when you admitted that the ruler was not infallible but might be sometimes mistaken.

You argue like a quibbler, Socrates. Do you mean, for example, that he who is mistaken about the sick is a physician in that he is mistaken? or that he who errs in arithmetic or grammar is an arithmetician or grammarian at the time when he is making the mistake, in respect of the mistake? True, we say that the physician or arithmetician or grammarian has made a mistake, but this is only a way of speaking; for the fact is that neither the grammarian nor any other person of skill ever makes a mistake in so far as he is what his name implies; they none of them err unless their skill fails them, and then they cease to be skilled artists. No artist or sage or ruler errs at the time when he is what his name implies; though he is commonly said to err, and I adopted the common mode of speaking. But to be perfectly accurate, since you are such a lover of accuracy, we should say that the ruler, in so far as he is the ruler, is unerring, and, being unerring, always commands that which is for his own interest; and the subject is required to execute his commands; and therefore, as I said at first and now repeat, justice is the interest of the stronger.

In the previous passage, Socrates goaded Thrasymachus into thinking about the ideals that are embodied in any profession. Thus Socrates gets him to admit that a physician who harms a patient is not really fulfilling the ideals of medicine, but is only acting as a would-be physician. In this way Socrates tricks Thrasymachus into saying that someone is a true ruler, strictly speaking, only when he or she is faithfully practicing the skill of ruling. By using analogies from the arts of medicine, horsemanship, and piloting, Socrates gets his companion to admit that true rulers are those who look after the interests of their subjects and do not merely serve their own, selfish interests. The next passage begins with the voice of Socrates as he repeats the cycle of his dialectic on the new, revised definition of justice.

Reanalyzing the Definition by Asking More Questions

- Follow the steps of Socrates' argument by analogy as he gets Thrasymachus to reverse his original position.

Is the physician, taken in that strict sense of which you are speaking, a healer of the sick or a maker of money? And remember that I am now speaking of the true physician.

A healer of the sick, he replied. . . .

Now, I said, doesn't every art have some interest which it serves?

Certainly.

And does not every art exist to consider and provide for these interests?

Yes, that is the aim of art.

And the interest of any art is to be as perfect as possible—this and nothing else?

What do you mean?

I mean what I may illustrate negatively by the example of the body. Suppose you were to ask me whether the body is self-sufficing or has wants, I should reply: Certainly the body has wants; for the body may be ill and require to be cured, and has therefore interests to which the art of medicine ministers; and this is the origin and intention of medicine, as you will acknowledge. Am I not right?

Quite right, he replied. . . .

Then medicine does not consider the interest of medicine, but the interest of the body?

True, he said.

Nor does the art of horsemanship consider the interests of the art of horsemanship, but the interests of the horse; neither do any other arts care for themselves, for they have no needs; they care only for that which is the subject of their art?

True, he said.

But surely, Thrasymachus, the arts are the superiors and rulers of their own subjects?

To this he assented with a good deal of reluctance.

Then, I said, no science or art considers or commands the interest of the stronger or superior, but only the interest of the subject and weaker?

He made an attempt to contest this proposition also, but finally acquiesced.

Then, I continued, no physician, in so far as he is a physician, considers his own good in what he prescribes, but the good of his patient; for the true physician is also a ruler having the human body as a subject, and is not a mere money-maker; that has been admitted?

Yes.

And the pilot likewise, in the strict sense of the term, is a ruler of sailors and not a mere sailor?

That has been admitted.

And such a pilot and ruler will provide and prescribe for the interest of the sailor who is under him, and not for his own or the ruler's interest?

He gave a reluctant "Yes."

Then, I said, Thrasymachus, there is no one in any rule who, in so far as he is a ruler, considers or enjoins what is for his own interest, but always what is for the interest of his subject or suitable to his art; to that he looks, and that alone he considers in everything which he says and does.

When we had got to this point in the argument . . . every one saw that the definition of justice had been completely upset.

At this point, the first round of Socrates' intellectual bout with Thrasymachus comes to an end. With Thrasymachus's initial definition of justice defeated, we reach the seventh step of Socrates' dialectic.

Facing Ignorance

Thrasymachus is bloodied, but not defeated. He tacitly admits Socrates' point that justice is serving the interests of one's subjects. But now he takes a totally new approach and says that *injustice* is the only lifestyle that is profitable and is the one that the smart person would choose. So, instead of continuing to tout his perverse definition of justice (which Socrates has unraveled), Thrasymachus now makes injustice the ideal. Socrates' refutation of this thesis takes up most of the remainder of the *Republic,* and it leads him into a large-scale discussion of human nature, knowledge, reality, morality, and politics.

WHAT IS THE PRACTICAL VALUE OF PHILOSOPHY?

Although Socrates was obviously very clever in debates, he was not clever enough to argue himself out of the death penalty. Why, then, did he value philosophy so highly when his contemporaries seemed to value it so little? One of Socrates' contemporaries, the satirical playwright Aristophanes, wrote a play titled the *Clouds* in which the actor representing Socrates delivered his speeches while suspended from the clouds in a basket. For many people, this image typifies the philosopher—someone who does not have his or her feet on the ground. Philosophy is often thought to be an optional enterprise, a detached, erudite hobby for the intellectually elite or the socially disabled. Someone once defined the philosopher as "a person who describes the impossible and proves the obvious."

In order to answer the question, What is the practical value of philosophy? we need to follow the example of Socrates and first clarify the concepts and question the assumptions contained in the question. What does it mean for something to be "practical"? A good answer might be that something is practical if it is an efficient and effective means for achieving a goal. If your goal is to learn your French vocabulary words for a test, a practical (efficient and effective) way to achieve this goal is to write the words on note cards that you can review throughout the day. But when we ask, Is philosophy practical? what goal do we have in mind? To answer this question we need to know what goals, ends, or values are really important in life in order to measure whether philosophy is or is not a practical means for achieving them. By now you may realize that to think about these issues is to think philosophically. Ironically, to ask whether philosophy is a useful activity you must have made some previous philosophical assumptions about what is important in life. In other words, unlike any other discipline, a person cannot criticize philosophy without having first engaged in philosophy!

SOCRATES' TEACHINGS

As you may suspect, Socrates had some opinions about the practical value of philosophy. His trial illustrated the fact that his main philosophical concern was with ethics. While he also philosophized about such topics as the nature of knowledge, the nature of reality, human nature, religion, and political philosophy, Socrates was interested in those topics primarily for the light they could shed on the question, How should we live if we are to be successful and fulfilled human beings? Socrates' teachings on this issue can be summarized in three theses. After listing them, I discuss each one in turn.

1. The unexamined life is not worth living.
2. The most important task in life is caring for the soul (the real person).
3. A good person cannot be harmed by others.

The Unexamined Life is Not Worth Living

As was evident from his remarks at his trial, Socrates was concerned that his contemporaries were like dozing cattle who, at the end of their life, would sleepily look around, not knowing who they were, why they were that way, or what their life had been all about. In contrast, Socrates chose as his motto the inscription on the temple at Delphi: "Know thyself." The examined life and examined beliefs lead to lives that are responsible and fully awake. To use a metaphorical cliché, everyone in Socrates' society was so busy "keeping the ball rolling," they had never asked what the ball was, or why it was so important to keep it rolling, or where it was going. For Socrates, what is important was not so much what we do, for our activities and careers can change. What is important is who we are and who we are trying to become. Socrates' thesis is that making oneself as good as possible is the true goal in life and the key to genuine success.

The Most Important Task in Life is Caring for the Soul

According to Socrates, the soul is not some ghostly shadow accompanying us, as Homer and the Greek poets assumed. Instead, the soul is the real person. It is our core personality or character and is the source of all our thoughts, values, and decisions. The state of a person's soul makes him or her either foolish or wise. Like the body, the soul (or the inner person) can be healthy or diseased, and for Socrates, ignorance is the most deadly disease of the soul. Of course, this ignorance is not the kind of ignorance that could be cured by memorizing an encyclopedia. Instead, the unhealthy soul is one that is ignorant of the true priorities in life. Although Socrates seemed to have believed in life after death, this belief was not his motive for being concerned about the moral health of his soul. As Gregory Vlastos says,

> The soul is as worth caring for if it were to last just twenty-four more hours, as if it were to outlast eternity. If you have just one more day to live, and can expect nothing but a blank after that, Socrates feels that you would still have all the reason you need for improving your soul; you have yourself to live with that one day, so why live with a worse self, if you could live with a better one instead?[8]

In Socrates' day there was an influential group of philosophers known as the **Sophists.** The Sophists were traveling educators who would offer practical courses for the payment of a fee. One of their main teachings was **skepticism,** the belief that we cannot have knowledge, because there is no such thing as objective truth. Hence, to the Sophists, "moral goodness" and "truth" are just sounds that we make with our mouths; they do not refer to anything. One opinion is just as good as another, they taught. If we cannot know what is true or right, then the only goal in life is to achieve success by whatever means possible. Accordingly, the Sophists taught their students how to argue and how to influence people with their opinions. (Thrasymachus in the previous reading was a leading Sophist.)

Socrates was upset that although the Sophists were offering people a map of how to get through life, it was the wrong map. The Sophists claimed to teach people how to achieve success; however, they and their students assumed that success meant achieving wealth, fame, or power. To creatively superimpose the status symbols of our day onto theirs, Socrates' contemporaries thought that success meant driving a BMW chariot, wearing a Calvin Klein tunic, being a high-priced lawyer charging 100 drachmas an hour, or getting your picture on the front page of the *Athens Times.* But Socrates claimed that his contemporaries had not really examined what it meant to be a success in life. They were busy trying to be successful businesspersons, politicians, lawyers, physicians, athletes, or artists, but they never considered that realizing their potential as persons was the most important occupation they had in life.

A Good Person Cannot Be Harmed by Others

This statement follows from the rest of Socrates' teachings. If the real me, the most important part of who I am, is not my possessions nor the outward, physical part of me, then no one can corrupt me or damage me from outside. An evil person can cause great pain or even kill me, but what makes me the person I am cannot be affected or harmed by any outward force. More precisely, I cannot be harmed by others unless, of course, I allow my values, my beliefs, my emotions, and my direction in life to be influenced unthinkingly by those around me. To paraphrase Socrates' view, we can choose to be like driftwood, floating on the surface of life, passively turning this way or that as each wave or gust of wind influences our motion. In this case, we are allowing ourselves to be vulnerable to the effects and harm produced by others. On the other hand, we can choose to be like the captain of a sailboat who sets his or her own direction with the rudder and the sails. If we set our sights on wisdom, then our values, like the keel of the boat, will keep us on the course we set. We have to respond to the winds in society that are blowing about us, but we are in control and we make the winds serve our purpose rather than being at their mercy. Hence, the Socratic vision of the life of philosophical wisdom is one in which self-examination leading to self-knowledge gives us the wisdom to care for the best part of ourselves and liberates us from the control and harm of everything outside, making us inner-directed and fulfilled persons.

Sophists traveling educators during Socrates' day who would offer practical courses for a fee and who taught the doctrine of skepticism

skepticism the belief that we cannot have knowledge because there is no such thing as objective truth

Socrates is probably one of the best known philosophers in history. See how much people know about him by asking five to ten people who have not had a philosophy class the following questions.

- Who was Socrates?
- What is the Socratic method of teaching?
- What were some of Socrates' teachings?
- Why was he put to death by the people of Athens?

It might be uncharitable to criticize your friends' answers unless they ask you what you think. Nevertheless, after you have collected various answers, rank them according to which ones you think are the most accurate and the least accurate. Based on your survey, how much does the general public know about Socrates?

1.2 ARGUMENT AND EVIDENCE: HOW DO I DECIDE WHAT TO BELIEVE?

To begin thinking about the nature of arguments, try to evaluate the following arguments. Do this by asking yourself, Does the conclusion (the statement following "therefore") logically follow from the other statements (the premises)? Or in other words, ask yourself, *If* the premises were true, would the conclusion have to be true? Notice that it is not necessary to agree that the premises are true to decide that the conclusion logically follows from them. If the conclusion does not follow (it is a bad argument), imagine how you would explain to someone else why it is a bad argument.

1. If the universe shows evidence of design, then there is a God. The universe shows evidence of design. Therefore, there is a God.
2. If Jones is a mother, then Jones is a parent. But Jones is not a mother. Therefore, Jones is not a parent.
3. If Thomas Aquinas's arguments for God are good ones, then there is a God. But Thomas Aquinas's arguments for God are not good ones. Therefore, there is not a God.
4. After a lifetime of proclaiming the death of God, Friedrich Nietzsche died completely insane. Therefore, his arguments for atheism must be worthless.
5. No one has proven that there is not a God. Therefore, God must exist.
6. If there was not a God, I could not bear to live my life. Therefore, there is a God.

Do not feel stressed if you had problems figuring these arguments out, because such analysis is what this section is all about. These same examples will be repeated again in our discussion of arguments, so the answers to these exercises will appear later on.

In section 1.0 I said that philosophy is the search for fundamental beliefs that are justified. When you read what a philosopher has written, avoid the bottom-line syndrome. This problem involves simply agreeing or disagreeing with the author's conclusion without paying attention to whether the philosopher has provided good reasons for believing the conclusion. Responding in this way defeats a major goal of philosophy—the goal of seeing whether our beliefs or those of others are justified. For example, someone who believes in God (a theist) would agree with the conclusion of Thomas Aquinas's arguments (i.e., "There is a God"). But some theists do not think that Aquinas's arguments are strong. It is important to realize that in demonstrating that an argument is weak, we have not shown that its conclusion is false. We have merely shown that the reasons the author has given for the conclusion do not guarantee its truth. Nevertheless, if the only arguments that can be found to support a conclusion are weak, we really have no reason to suppose that the conclusion is true. Remember, evaluating philosophies is not like tasting foods ("I like this. I don't like that."). Instead, it is an attempt to find objective reasons why we should or should not believe that a claim is true. In this section, I briefly cover some techniques for evaluating philosophical claims and arguments.

EVALUATING PHILOSOPHICAL CLAIMS AND THEORIES

In order to evaluate and choose between competing philosophical claims and theories, philosophers have agreed on a number of criteria, or tests. We will consider the six most common ones. I have formulated each criterion so that it contains a keyword that begins with the letter *c* in order to make the points easy to remember. The criteria are (1) conceptual *clarity*, (2) *consistency*, (3) rational *coherence*, (4) *comprehensiveness*, (5) *compatibility* with well-established facts and theories, and (6) having the support of *compelling* arguments. We will briefly look at each one in turn.

Clarity

Conceptual clarity is the first test that a philosophy must pass. If the terms or concepts in which the philosophy is expressed are not clear, then we don't know precisely what claim is being put forth. Suppose someone says, "The only thing in life that has value is pleasure." We need to ask, What does the author mean by "pleasure"? Is the term referring only to physical sensations, or do intellectual pleasures count? If it makes me feel good to sacrifice my own needs for those of others, am I really pursuing pleasure?

Consistency

Consistency is the second test that a philosophy must pass. A philosophy cannot contain any contradictions. One way a philosophy flunks this test is through

logical inconsistency
two assertions that
could not both be
true under any pos-
sible circumstances

self-referential incon-
sistency an assump-
tion that implies that
it itself cannot be
true, cannot be
known to be true,
or should not be
believed

logical inconsistency, which consists in making two assertions that could not both be true under any possible circumstances. The most obvious case of this inconsistency would be any claim of the form, "A is true and not-A is true." For example, if I claim that God determines everything that happens in the world at the same time that I claim that humans have free will, I appear to have an inconsistency. The first claim implies that God determines what choices we make, but this claim seems to conflict with the claim that we freely make our own choices. The terms *determines* and *free will* would have to be defined differently than they normally are to avoid the inconsistency. A second kind of inconsistency is more subtle. It is called **self-referential inconsistency,** and it occurs if an assertion implies that it itself cannot be true, or cannot be known to be true, or should not be believed. My statement that "All opinions are false" implies that the opinion I just expressed is false. Similarly, my claim that "Only statements that can be scientifically proven should be believed" is a statement that cannot be scientifically proven.

Coherence

Rational coherence is a criterion that considers how well the various parts of a philosophy "hang together." The elements of a philosophy may not be explicitly contradictory, but they can still fail to fit together very well. A philosopher who believes that God acts in the world but who fails to explain how that belief fits together with the belief that nature runs according to universal physical laws has articulated a philosophy that lacks coherence. Similarly, philosopher René Descartes argued that humans are made up of a physical body and a nonextended, nonphysical mind. Although he believed that the two interacted, he failed to make clear how such different types of substances could causally influence one another. This gap in his theory earned him low points on the coherence criteria in the minds of many critics.

Comprehensiveness

We evaluate a philosophy positively if it makes sense out of a wide range of phenomena; we evaluate it negatively if it ignores significant areas of human experience or raises more questions than it answers. A philosophy that illuminates humanity's scientific, moral, aesthetic, and religious experience is better than one that explains only science but ignores the rest of human experience. To take a more specific example, a philosopher who claims that all knowledge is based on sensory data but who fails to explain how we can have mathematical knowledge or moral knowledge falls short on this criterion. Similarly, a philosopher who claims that all morality is derived from the Ten Commandments but who fails to explain how some cultures have developed similar moral principles even if they never heard of these commandments fails in terms of comprehensiveness.

Compatibility

Compatibility with well-established facts and theories is important because a good theory (in philosophy or science) is one that increases our understanding by unifying our knowledge. Hence, a theory that flies in the face of the rest of our understanding of the world may require us to lose more than we gain. For example, a philosophical theory about the mind should fit with the well-established findings of biology and psychology. There are, however, exceptions to this rule. Throughout history, well-argued theories in philosophy and science have sometimes required us to violate common sense and abandon centuries-old beliefs, resulting in new knowledge. Nevertheless, we should do so only when the new theory is better than its competitors and promises to replace our current beliefs with an increase in understanding.

Compelling Arguments

Before I discuss the sixth criterion, I think it will be worthwhile to discuss a special type of reasoning that is commonly used in philosophy (as well as science). This form of reasoning is known as an **inference to the best explanation.** (This sort of reasoning is sometimes called abduction.) Unlike the sorts of arguments we will be discussing shortly, an inference to the best explanation does not try to directly prove the truth of a theory; it tries to show that the theory is superior to all its competitors and that it is therefore the one most likely to be true. This way of showing that a particular theory is the best one makes use of the five criteria discussed thus far. An inference to the best explanation has the following form:

inference to the best explanation a form of reasoning that tries to show that a particular theory is superior to all its competitors and that it is therefore the one most likely to be true; sometimes called abduction

1. There is a collection of data that needs an explanation.
2. A theory is proposed that offers an explanation of the data.
3. This theory offers the best explanation of all known alternatives.
4. Therefore, until a better explanation is proposed, it is rational to believe this theory.

This method of reasoning can best be illustrated by an example from science. In the 1930s, scientists were puzzled by a type of event, known as beta decay, in which an atom disintegrates into its parts. The problem was that a measurable sum of energy seemed to disappear into thin air in the process, thus violating the conservation of energy, a sacred principle in physics. Wolfgang Pauli, a twenty-year-old physicist, proposed that the missing energy could be accounted for by supposing that an unobserved particle was included with the other particles that were flung off from the atom. The problem was that to balance the numbers in the equations, this unknown particle had to have no electric charge, its mass had to be nearly zero or equal to zero, and besides being extremely small, it had to travel near the speed of light. In short, the mystery particle (which came to be called the neutrino) had to be completely incapable of being observed.

Physicists were reluctant to accept the existence of the neutrino because of the criterion of compatibility. It was incompatible with the long and firmly held belief that all entities accepted by science had to be observed. On the other hand, this theory was not only compatible with the conservation of energy, but it saved this more fundamental principle from being abandoned. Furthermore, in terms of the other criteria, the neutrino theory was clear and consistent, it brought coherence by preserving the closely-knit fabric of physics, and it scored high on comprehensiveness because it eventually explained other events besides beta decay. Almost thirty years later, physicists designed a very elaborate and expensive experiment whose results suggested that they could detect the effects of a neutrino interacting with another particle. However, no matter how useful the neutrino postulate is and how many events it explains, we will never directly observe one. The only reason scientists believe in it is because it makes sense out of so many other events we believe and can observe.

The evidence and explanations that are offered in science (as in the case of the neutrino) can provide very helpful models for understanding the explanations that are provided by philosophical theories. First, scientists cannot always directly observe the entities or events postulated by their theories (neutrinos, quarks, black holes, the big bang). Similarly, in philosophy we cannot directly observe with our senses the presence or absence of God, free will, moral values, or justice. Second, inferences to the best explanation in science and philosophy are evaluated using the five criteria that we have discussed thus far and can be used to justify belief in either neutrinos or in the claims made by philosophers. For example, various philosophers attempt to justify claims such as the following: there is a God, mental events are really brain events, humans have free will, the morality of an action is determined by the consequences. Even though the defense of such claims cannot take the form of a confirming observation, philosophers can try to show that these theories make the best sense of what we do know and observe.

In addition to arguing that a philosophical theory provides the best explanation of what we are trying to understand, philosophers also try to justify their theories more directly. They do this through the support of compelling arguments. This method of justifying a claim attempts to show that from certain true (or plausible) statements, the claim either necessarily follows or is highly probable. The rest of this chapter is a discussion of the nature of arguments and how to decide whether they are compelling.

THE NATURE OF ARGUMENTS

Philosophers attempt to establish the truth of their claims by means of arguments. But the word *argument* has two different meanings in everyday discourse. Suppose that two students were discussing whether there is a God, and they began shouting at each other, saying, "Yes there is," "No there isn't," "Yes there is," "No there isn't." If the exchange began to be quite heated, we might say that they were having an argument. In this context, *argument* would mean "a contentious dispute." However, this definition is not what philosophers mean by argument. In philosophy, an **argument** is a set of statements in which one or more of the statements attempt to provide reasons or evidence for the truth of another statement. A **premise** is a statement in an argument that serves to provide evidence for the truth of a claim. A **conclusion** is the statement in an argument that the premises are claimed to support or imply.

An important step in analyzing an argument is deciding which statements are the premises and which is the conclusion. Often the conclusion is the last statement in a passage. However, an author may place the conclusion first or even in the middle. Using common sense and grasping the author's intentions are the best ways to figure out the elements of a particular argument. Key terms are often used to indicate which statements are premises and which are conclusions. **Premise indicators** are terms that usually indicate that a premise will follow. Typical examples of premise indicators are *since, because, for, given that*. **Conclusion indicators** are terms that usually indicate that a conclusion will follow. Typical examples of conclusion indicators are *therefore, so, hence, thus, consequently*.

When it comes to determining whether an argument is acceptable, we can get some tips from the field of architecture. In the late Middle Ages, cathedral architects were obsessed with the goal of designing each successive cathedral to reach higher into the skies than the previous ones. The crowning glory of the architects' craft was thought to be the Beauvais Cathedral in France, whose ceiling rose to a height of 157 feet. This competition to break architectural records came to a sudden halt in 1284, however, when the main structural arches of Beauvais collapsed, unable to bear the weight that had been imposed on them.

Recently, I visited a college campus in which the focal point was a six-story administrative building. The outside walls were made from a newly invented composite material containing concrete and stone that had been formed into huge panels. Unfortunately, the new material did not hold up and large chunks of the stone slabs began falling off the building. After pouring hundreds of thousands of dollars into vain attempts to fix the problem, the building finally had to be torn down.

argument a set of statements in which one or more of the statements attempt to provide reasons or evidence for the truth of another statement

premise a statement in an argument that serves to provide evidence for the truth of a claim

conclusion the statement in an argument that the premises are claimed to support or imply

premise indicators terms that usually indicate that a premise will follow

conclusion indicators terms that usually indicate that a conclusion will follow

 STOP AND THINK

So what does architecture and building construction have to do with philosophy? Think of the ways in which constructing a building and constructing a philosophical position or argument are similar. Consider what is necessary for a building to be solid and well designed. Compare that with what is necessary for an argument to be solid and well designed. Think about the ways that the buildings mentioned in the text failed and the ways in which a philosophical argument can fail. Can you think of any further analogies or connections between buildings and philosophy?

The two examples of the failed buildings are not alike. In the case of the Beauvais Cathedral there was nothing wrong with the materials used; they were the solid blocks of stone used in all cathedrals. The problem was a structural one. The arches of the building were not designed to support the weight of the ceiling. Similarly, a philosophical argument can fail because of structural defects. These defects occur when the form of the argument is such that the premises do not provide adequate support for the conclusion. In the case of the contemporary college building, the architect's design of the skeletal structure of the building was okay but the materials that were attached to it were faulty. The concrete slabs cracked, fell apart, and disintegrated. Similarly, an argument can be defective if the premises are known to be false or are, at least, implausible.

Here is an example of an argument in which the form is structurally flawed even though the premises are true (nothing is wrong with the materials composing the argument):

1. If Ronald Reagan was a U.S. president, then he was famous.
2. Ronald Reagan was famous.
3. Therefore, Ronald Reagan was a U.S. president.

I think that your logical intuitions will tell you that even though both premises are true and the conclusion is true, the conclusion does not logically follow from the premises. This lack of logic can be shown by the fact that in 1960 both premises were true but the conclusion was false, because Ronald Reagan was famous for being a movie star and not a president. Hence, even though the conclusion happens to be true, it does not logically follow from the premises.

In the next example, the form of the argument is a good one, but the premises are false (the materials that fill out the form are faulty):

1. If President George Washington was a horse, then he had five legs.
2. President George Washington was a horse.
3. Therefore, President George Washington had five legs.

In this case, *if* the premises were true, the conclusion would have to be true. In other words, the conclusion logically follows from the premises. The problem, of course, is that this argument starts from false premises.

These examples provide us with two basic questions to ask about an argument: (1) If the premises were true, would they provide adequate logical support for the conclusion? and (2) Are the premises true (or at least plausible)? The answer to the first question concerns **logic,** the study of methods for evaluating arguments and reasoning. Any standard textbook in logic will provide many techniques for determining how strongly the premises support the conclusion, but in this chapter I can only provide a few guidelines. A rather simple way to approach the question is to ask yourself, How easy would it be to imagine that all the premises were true at the same time the conclusion was false? If there are many ways to imagine that the premises were true and the conclusion false, this finding may indicate that the truth of

logic the study of methods for evaluating arguments and reasoning

the premises do not provide strong support for the truth of the conclusion. No standard technique exists for answering the second question. Basically, you have to decide what sort of claim is being made in each premise and then decide what sort of evidence or sources of information would help in checking the truth of each premise.

A good argument establishes a "price" for rejecting the conclusion. In other words a good argument shows that if you believe the premises, then you must believe the conclusion because it either logically follows from the premises or the premises show that it is most probably true. Hence, if you reject the conclusion of a logical argument, you can do so only by rejecting one or more of the premises. But in a very good argument, it would be implausible to reject the premises.

In evaluating the form of the reasoning, two kinds of arguments are acceptable. First, if it is impossible for the premises to be true and the conclusion false, then we say that the argument is **valid.** Another way of putting this is to say that in a valid argument, *if* the premises are true, the conclusion *must* be true. Notice that the definition does not say that a valid argument will always have true premises. Furthermore, a true conclusion does not indicate that the argument is valid. The truth of the conclusion must logically follow from the premises. An argument whose author claims that it provides this sort of support for its conclusion but fails to do so is **invalid.** An argument that is valid or that the author claims is valid is called a **deductive argument.** A valid argument with true premises is a **sound argument.** In this case, the truth of the conclusion would be absolutely certain.

Second, if the argument is such that true premises would make the conclusion highly probable, then we say that the argument is a **strong argument.** A strong argument that actually does have true premises is a **cogent argument.** A cogent argument does not absolutely guarantee the conclusion (as does a sound argument), but it does give us good reasons for believing the conclusion. If the author does not claim that the conclusion necessarily follows from the premises but claims merely that the premises make the conclusion highly probable, we say that the argument is an **inductive argument.** Most of science is based on inductive arguments. For example, before a pharmaceutical drug is released on the market, it is tested extensively. Researchers may conclude from these tests on a sample group of patients that the drug is safe for anyone to use. Of course, there is no guarantee that some dangerous side effects have not been discovered yet. However, adequate testing makes a strong inductive argument that the drug is safe.

DEDUCTIVE ARGUMENTS

In this section, I will examine a number of valid argument forms that are very common (and a few that are invalid). As we go through these examples, keep the following complementary definitions of validity in mind: In a valid argument, it is impossible for the premises to be true and the conclusion false; and in a valid argument, *if* the premises are true then the conclusion *must* be true. The argument forms that I discuss are so frequently employed that they have been given names,

valid argument an argument in which it is impossible for the premises to be true and the conclusion false

invalid argument an argument in which the truth of the conclusion fails to logically follow from the premises

deductive argument an argument that is valid or that the author claims is valid

sound argument a valid argument with true premises

strong argument an inductive argument in which true premises would make the conclusion highly probable

cogent argument a strong argument that actually does have true premises

inductive argument an argument in which it is claimed that the premises make the conclusion highly probable.

sometimes in Latin. In each case, I represent the skeletal structure of the argument in terms of various letters, such as P and Q. The letters are variables that stand for propositions. To the right of each argument form, I add flesh to the skeleton by replacing the letter variables with actual propositions. To make this discussion of logic relevant to our philosophical journey, I then provide a simple philosophical argument that makes use of the form in question. While examining these examples of valid or invalid arguments for a philosophical conclusion, do not suppose that the example is the last word on the particular issue or that the arguments are the best ones available for the conclusion. In each case, if the argument is valid and you disagree with the conclusion (e.g., "there is a God" or "there is not a God"), then try to figure out a basis for questioning one or more of the premises.

Before discussing the first set of argument forms, we need to examine the nature of conditional statements (also known as hypothetical statements). A **conditional statement** contains two simpler statements that are connected with the words *if-then*. For example:

> If it is raining, then the ground is wet.
> If you study, then you will get good grades.
> If Jones is pregnant, then Jones is a female.

The first part of a conditional statement (which follows the "if") is called the **antecedent.** The second part (which follows the "then") is called the **consequent.** In the examples the antecedents are "it is raining," "you study," and "Jones is pregnant." The consequents are "the ground is wet," "you will get good grade," and "Jones is a female."

A conditional statement claims that the truth of the antecedent is a **sufficient condition** for the truth of the consequent. To say that A is a sufficient condition for B means that if A is true, then B is true. Sometimes the conditions that would make the antecedent true would *cause* conditions that would make the consequent true (as in the first two of the previous examples). However, Jones being pregnant does not *cause* Jones to be a female. So the notion of a sufficient condition has to do with the relationship between the truth of each statement and does not always express a causal relationship. A conditional statement also claims that the consequent is a **necessary condition** for the antecedent to be true. To say that A is a necessary condition for B means that for B to be true, A must be true. For example, being a female is a necessary condition for being pregnant. However, being a female is not a sufficient condition for being pregnant. These remarks about conditional statements are illustrated by the first five argument forms, which all contain conditional statements.

conditional statement two simpler statements that are connected with the words *if* and *then*

antecedent the first part of a conditional statement (the *if* clause)

consequent the second part of a conditional statement (the *then* clause)

sufficient condition statement A is a sufficient condition for statement B if the truth of A guarantees the truth of B

necessary condition statement A is a necessary condition for statement B if the truth of B requires the truth of A

Modus Ponens

1. If P, then Q.   1. If Spot is a dog, then Spot is a mammal.
2. P.   2. Spot is a dog.
3. Therefore, Q.   3. Therefore, Spot is a mammal.

Philosophical Example of Modus Ponens

1. If the universe shows evidence of design, then there is a God.
2. The universe shows evidence of design.
3. Therefore, there is a God.

Modus ponens is also known as *affirming the antecedent.*

Modus Tollens

1. If P, then Q.
2. Not-Q.
3. Therefore, not-P.

1. If John is eligible for the award, then he is a junior.
2. John is not a junior.
3. Therefore, John is not eligible for the award.

Philosophical Examples of Modus Tollens

1. If we are morally responsible for our actions, then we have freedom of the will.
2. We do not have freedom of the will.
3. Therefore, we are not morally responsible for our actions.

1. If God exists, there would be no unnecessary evil in the world.
2. There is unnecessary evil in the world.
3. Therefore, God does not exist.

Since modus tollens (also known as *denying the consequent*) is a valid argument form, it is clear that this argument about God's existence is valid. That is, if the premises are true, then the conclusion logically follows. Consequently, a theist who rejects the conclusion would have to find reasons for rejecting at least one of the premises. The first premise seems consistent with the traditional concept of God. So a theist would probably want to question the truth of the second premise by asking, Do we really know that there is unnecessary evil in the world? and Isn't it possible that all apparent evil is justified in terms of some greater good that the evil achieves? I explore these issues further in the section on the problem of evil in chapter 4 (section 4.5).

Fallacy of Denying the Antecedent

A **fallacy** is an argument form that is logically defective because the premises provide little or no support for the conclusion. Two invalid arguments (deductive fallacies) can be confused with either modus ponens or modus tollens. The first is the fallacy of denying the antecedent, which has this form:

1. If P, then Q.
2. Not-P.
3. Therefore, not-Q.

1. If Jones is a mother, then Jones is a parent.
2. Jones is not a mother.
3. Therefore, Jones is not a parent.

As the example illustrates, this argument form is invalid because we can imagine a situation in which the premises are true and the conclusion false. If Jones is a father, then it is true that Jones is not a mother but false that Jones is not a parent.

Philosophical Example of the Fallacy of Denying the Antecedent

1. If Thomas Aquinas's arguments for God are valid, then there is a God.
2. Thomas Aquinas's arguments for God are not valid.
3. Therefore, there is not a God.

This example is an argument about arguments, and it illustrates an important point. If you refute a philosopher's argument, you have not shown that his or her conclusion is false, you have merely shown that this particular proof for the conclusion fails. A theist could agree with both premises of the previous argument but still not accept the conclusion, for other arguments besides those of Aquinas could prove God's existence. Furthermore, some theists, such as Blaise Pascal and Søren Kierkegaard (see section 4.4), would claim that from a lack of rational arguments for God's existence it does not follow that God does not exist, but merely that reason is not the correct means to find God.

Fallacy of Affirming the Consequent

The fallacy of affirming the consequent is another invalid argument form that is also a counterfeit version of the valid forms of modus ponens and modus tollens.

1. If P, then Q.	1. If George Washington was assassinated, then he is dead.
2. Q.	2. George Washington is dead.
3. Therefore, P.	3. Therefore, George Washington was assassinated.

Philosophical Example of the Fallacy of Affirming the Consequent

1. If morality is completely subjective, then people will differ in their moral beliefs.
2. People do differ in their moral beliefs.
3. Therefore, morality is completely subjective. (There are no objective truths about what is morally right or wrong.)

One way to show that an argument is invalid is to construct another argument that has the same form as the original but goes from true premises to a false conclusion. This argument would be an invalid argument because a valid argument will always carry us from true information to a true conclusion. However, if the form of reasoning is the same as the original argument, the counterexample will show that the original argument is invalid also. Because the following argument is the same as the argument about morality except for the subject matter, it shows that the previous argument is invalid.

1. If medical science is completely subjective, then people will differ in their medical beliefs.
2. People do differ in their medical beliefs. (Some people believe that sacrificing twin babies will cure the community of a plague; on the other hand, our society doesn't believe this.)
3. Therefore, medical science is completely subjective. (There are no objective truths about what will or won't cure disease—a false conclusion.)

Hypothetical Syllogism

A **syllogism** is a deductive argument with two premises and a conclusion. Some logic books call the following type of syllogism a *pure* hypothetical syllogism to distinguish it from arguments such as modus ponens and modus tollens, which are partially hypothetical in that they contain one hypothetical (or conditional) premise.

syllogism a deductive argument with two premises and a conclusion

1. If P, then Q.
2. If Q, then R.
3. Therefore, if P, then R.

1. If I learn logic, then I will write better essays.
2. If I write better essays, then I will get better grades.
3. Therefore, if I learn logic, then I will get better grades.

Philosophical Example of a Valid Hypothetical Syllogism

1. If the methods of science give us only information about physical reality, then science cannot tell us whether a nonphysical reality exists.
2. If science cannot tell us whether a nonphysical reality exists, then science cannot tell us whether we have a soul.
3. Therefore, if the methods of science give us only information about physical reality, then science cannot tell us whether we have a soul.

Notice that the key to a hypothetical syllogism is that the consequent (Q) of one premise is the antecedent (Q) of the other premise such that the premises could be linked up like a chain if they were laid end to end. This connection would be true even if the order of the premises were reversed. Furthermore, the antecedent of the conclusion (P) is the beginning of the chain formed by the premises, and the consequent of the conclusion (R) is the end of the chain. Any other arrangement will be invalid, as in the following examples.

Counterfeit (Invalid) Hypothetical Syllogisms

1. If P, then Q.
2. If R, then Q.
3. Therefore, if P, then R.

1. If P, then Q.
2. If Q, then R.
3. Therefore, if R, then P.

See if you can substitute statements for the letter variables in the previous invalid hypo-thetical syllogisms. Try to construct arguments that follow the given forms but in which true premises lead to a false conclusion in order to show that something is wrong with these types of arguments.

Disjunctive Syllogism

disjunctive state-ment a statement that asserts that at least one of two alter-natives is true

A disjunctive argument contains a disjunctive statement in a premise. A **disjunctive statement** asserts that at least one of two alternatives is true. It typically is expressed as an *either-or* statement. Normally a disjunctive statement asserts that at least one alternative is true and possibly both. For example, if Sherlock Holmes determines that the murder was an inside job, he might state, "Either the butler is guilty or the maid is guilty." Obviously, the fact that one of them must be guilty also includes the possibility that both of them are guilty. Here is what a disjunctive syllogism looks like:

1. Either P or Q.   1. Either the bulb is burnt out or it is not receiving electricity.
2. Not-P.   2. The bulb is not burnt out.
3. Therefore, Q.   3. Therefore, the bulb is not receiving electricity.

Philosophical Example of a Disjunctive Syllogism

1. Either the universe contains in itself a sufficient reason for its existence or it was caused to exist.
2. The universe does not contain in itself a sufficient reason for its existence.
3. Therefore, the universe was caused to exist.

Fallacy of Affirming the Disjunct

1. Either P or Q.   1. Either the bulb is burnt out or it is not receiving electricity.
2. P.   2. The bulb is burnt out.
3. Therefore, not-Q.   3. Therefore, it is not receiving electricity.

The fallacy of affirming the disjunct is an invalid argument form that is a counterfeit of the disjunctive syllogism. In the example just given, the fact that the bulb is burnt out does not exclude the possibility that there are problems with the electricity as well. Since both alternatives could be true in a normal disjunction, simply affirming one alternative does not prove that the other is false. However, if the disjunction contained two contradictories (two statements that could not both be true), then this type of argument would be valid. For example, if the first premise was "Either Howard is married or he is single," then the truth of one statement would imply the falsity of the other.

Philosophical Example of the Fallacy of Affirming the Disjunct

1. Either reason is the source of moral principles or divine revelation is.
2. Reason is the source of moral principles.
3. Therefore, divine revelation is not the source of moral principles.

In this case, the conclusion does not follow because the two statements in the disjunction could both be true. (Some philosophers, such as Thomas Aquinas, believed that both reason and revelation could provide us with moral principles.)

Reductio ad Absurdum Arguments

The label of the **reductio ad absurdum argument,** a valid argument form, means "reducing to an absurdity." To use this technique, you begin by assuming that your opponent's position is true and then you show that it logically implies either an absurd conclusion or one that contradicts itself or that it contradicts other conclusions held by your opponent. Deducing a clearly false statement from a proposition is definitive proof that the original assumption was false and is a way of exposing an inconsistency that is lurking in an opponent's position. When the reductio ad absurdum argument is done well, it is an effective way to refute a position. Typically, the argument follows this form:

1. Suppose the truth of A (the position that you wish to refute).
2. If A, then B.
3. If B, then C.
4. If C, then not-A.
5. Therefore, both A and not-A.
6. But 5 is a contradiction, so the original assumption must be false and not-A must be true.

reductio ad absurdum argument argument form that begins with an assumption that the opponent's position is true and then proceeds to show that that position logically implies an absurd conclusion, a conclusion that contradicts itself, or a conclusion that contradicts other conclusions held by the opponent

Philosophical Example of a Reductio Ad Absurdum. As I mentioned in the previous section, Socrates' philosophical opponents, the Sophists, believed that all truth was subjective and relative. Protagoras, one of the most famous Sophists, argued that one opinion is just as true as another opinion. The following is a summary of the argument that Socrates used to refute this position.[9]

1. One opinion is just as true as another opinion. (Socrates assumes the truth of Protagoras's position.)
2. Protagoras's critics have the following opinion: "Protagoras's opinion is false and that of his critics is true."
3. Since Protagoras believes premise 1, he believes that the opinion of his critics in premise 2 is true.

4. Hence, Protagoras also believes it is true that: "Protagoras's opinion is false and that of his critics is true."
5. Since individual opinion determines what is true and *everyone* (both Protagoras and his critics) believe the statement "Protagoras's opinion is false," it follows that
6. Protagoras's opinion is false.

INDUCTIVE ARGUMENTS

Unlike deductive arguments, inductive arguments do not show that the conclusion necessarily follows from the premises. Instead, these arguments try to demonstrate that if the premises are true, then it is highly probable that the conclusion is true. One common form of inductive argument starts from the observation that a number of similar cases have a certain property in common and concludes that all other cases of this type will also have that property. For example, a medical researcher finds that everyone who has a rare form of cancer was exposed to a certain toxic chemical; when she encounters a new patient with this disease, she will suspect that this person has been exposed to the same chemical. Here are two examples of philosophical arguments based on inductive reasoning. Since different philosophers will evaluate these arguments differently, I leave it up to you to decide how strong you think these arguments are.

1. Every event that we have observed has had a cause.
2. Therefore, it is rational to presume that all events have a cause.

1. In the past, when something seemed mysterious and unexplainable (such as solar eclipses), eventually it was found that it could be scientifically explained as the result of physical causes.
2. Consciousness seems mysterious and unexplainable.
3. Therefore it is probable that someday consciousness will be scientifically explained as the result of physical causes.

Although a large part of our everyday lives and the scientific method is based on inductive reasoning, inductive arguments do not have the simple techniques that deductive arguments do for deciding whether the arguments are strong or weak. There are, however, a few rules to keep in mind when watching out for fallacious inductive arguments. I discuss three such fallacious inductive arguments here.

hasty generalization fallacy in which a general conclusion is drawn from premises that are not based on a sufficient number of observations or from premises in which the sample is not representative

Hasty Generalization Fallacy

When generalizing from facts about some cases of a certain type to a conclusion about all cases of that type, you must be sure that the premises are based on a sufficient number of observations and that the sample is representative. Failure to do so is to commit the fallacy of **hasty generalization.**

Philosophical Examples of the Hasty Generalization Fallacy. The physician and psychologist Sigmund Freud was the founder of the twentieth-century theory of psychoanalysis. In developing his theory he formed conclusions about the nature of religious belief. He speculated that religion was embraced by people who were emotionally weak and who projected the image of their own father onto the cosmos to create a heavenly father who would always be there for them. The problem was that as a therapist, Freud was exposed to multitudes of patients who were emotionally disturbed. Given the times and the culture, most of them were also religious. So, Freud studied numerous cases of emotionally disturbed religious people and concluded that religion was psychologically dysfunctional. Given the biased sample of religious people he studied, it is likely that he committed the fallacy of hasty generalization. Since then, psychologists of religion have also studied emotionally mature religious people and developed a more balanced view of religious belief.

The citizens of a small, rural town were shocked when a local teenager took a gun to school and massacred many of his classmates. It was discovered that he belonged to a cult of like-minded youths who engaged in satanic practices and read the philosopher Nietzsche. Some ministers used this incident as evidence that people who read "weird stuff" like philosophy are dangerous to society. But this hasty generalization ignores the millions of people who have read and enjoyed Nietzsche but who did not kill their colleagues. It also assumes that reading Nietzsche was the cause of the student's violence. The student may have been psychologically compelled to violence even if he had not read Nietzsche (see the false cause fallacy discussed next).

"There have been a number of financial and sexual scandals involving television evangelists in recent years. Therefore, it is likely that all religious people are frauds." This argument is a hasty generalization because the conclusion is about all religious people but it is based on a small and unrepresentative sample of this group.

False Cause Fallacy

Another form of induction reasons to the causes of a given event. The **false cause fallacy** is committed when we assume that simply because event X occurred before event Y, we may conclude that X caused Y. Causal connections are very difficult to establish; simple priority in time all by itself is usually insufficient to draw these connections.

false cause fallacy
the assumption that because event X occurred before event Y, X caused Y

Philosophical Examples of the False Cause Fallacy. "Nietzsche spent a lifetime publishing his atheistic philosophy. He died totally insane. Therefore, his own, dismal philosophy drove him mad." This causal reasoning overlooks the fact that some religiously pious people have gone insane and ignores the evidence that Nietzsche had a neurological disease.

"As sexually explicit movies have increased in number over the years, so have the number of sex crimes. Therefore, the movies have caused the crimes." These data are insufficient to establish a causal connection. It is also a fact that church attendance has increased over the years. Could we then conclude that the movies have caused church attendance to rise or that the increase in church attendance has caused the increase in crime?

False Analogy Fallacy

Some inductive arguments are based on an analogy. An argument from analogy is one in which the premises state that two cases share one or more properties in common. It is then concluded that a further property of the first case will also be a property of the second case. Some analogies can be useful, as when we learn about human physiology by studying that of primates. However, the **false analogy fallacy** is committed when there are more differences between the two situations than there are similarities. For example, if I have a 1980 gas-guzzling car that is blue and my friend has a brand new compact car that is blue, the similarity in color is not sufficient to conclude that my car will get the same gas mileage as hers.

Philosophical Examples of the False Analogy Fallacy. "No body can be healthful without exercise, neither natural body or politic; and certainly to a kingdom or estate, a just and honourable war is the true exercise. A civil war indeed is like the heat of a fever; but a foreign war is like the heat of exercise, and serveth to keep the body in health."[10] This defense of war by Francis Bacon fails to note that there are significant differences between individuals and nations and that individual exercise, unlike war, does not kill people.

It was common in the eighteenth century to argue for God's existence from the evidence of design in the world. It was said, for example, that the regular movements of the planets were like those of a clock. Since a clock had a designer, so the universe must have had a divine designer. The skeptic David Hume countered by saying, in effect, that this argument committed the fallacy of false analogy. It picked out one analogy in preference to many other possible ones. By way of counterexample, he suggested that the universe could more likely be compared to a vegetable than a clock. The particles given off by comets, for example, might function like the seeds given off by trees. After the comet passes through our galaxy, it sprouts new planetary systems in the outer darkness. Hume's point was that the clock analogy of the theists is no more likely than this analogy.[11]

INFORMAL FALLACIES

In this section, I survey several types of defective arguments known as informal fallacies. **Informal fallacies** are types of bad reasoning that can only be detected by examining the content of the argument. In most cases, if you set out the formal structure of the arguments using the letters P and Q as we did previously, the problem with the reasoning would not be evident. On the surface, the following invalid argument has the valid form of a modus ponens argument: "If something is a ruler, then it is twelve inches long, and the Queen is a ruler, so the Queen is twelve inches long." Actually, it only superficially has the form of a modus ponens argument because the term *ruler* shifts its meaning from one premise to the next. The following selection of informal fallacies is not an exhaustive list, but it contains many of the typical kinds of bad reasoning that you are likely to encounter in philosophical discussions.

Ad Hominem (Abusive)

Ad hominem means "against the person." The abusive ad hominem fallacy consists of an attempt to reject someone's conclusion by attacking the person making the claim. The problem is that simply providing negative information about a person does not prove that his or her claims are false.

Philosophical Examples of the Abusive Ad Hominem Fallacy. "After a lifetime of proclaiming the death of God, Friedrich Nietzsche died completely insane. Therefore, his arguments for atheism must be worthless."

"Immanuel Kant was a rigid neurotic who never traveled more than sixty miles from the place of his birth. How could anyone who was so limited and inexperienced have anything worthwhile to say about morality? Therefore, we do not need to bother looking at Kant's arguments for an objective morality."

Ad Hominem (Circumstantial)

Someone using the circumstantial ad hominem argument does not verbally abuse the opponent but dismisses his or her arguments by suggesting that the opponent's circumstances are the sole reason why he or she embraces the conclusion. In other words, this argument is a way of ignoring the opponent's arguments and of refusing to evaluate them on their own terms.

Philosophical Examples of the Circumstantial Ad Hominem Fallacy. "We do not need to consider Thomas Aquinas's arguments for the existence of God, because he was a Christian monk. Of course he thought belief in God was reasonable. In putting forth his proofs he was simply trying to rationalize a faith he already held."

"We do not need to consider philosopher Bertrand Russell's arguments against the existence of God. He was raised in a very strict religious home, which turned him against religion. That upbringing is the real reason he was an atheist."

Appeal to Ignorance

The appeal to ignorance fallacy occurs when lack of evidence against a conclusion is used to prove the conclusion true or when lack of evidence for a conclusion is used to prove a conclusion false. For example, "The president of this university is a spy for a foreign power, because you cannot prove that he isn't." Generally, the person making an extraordinary claim has the burden of proof to provide positive arguments for the conclusion. Lack of evidence against the conclusion is not sufficient. When a person's character is being maligned (as in the previous example), the principle of law that states "innocent until proven guilty" should prevail.

Philosophical Examples of the Appeal to Ignorance. "There must be a God, because no one has ever proven there isn't."

"Atheism is true, because no one has ever proven there is a God."

With respect to philosophical issues such as the existence of God, if we really believe there is a lack of compelling evidence either way, then we should suspend judgment.

Begging the Question

Begging the question also goes by the name of *circular reasoning* for reasons that will soon be evident. This fallacy is committed when the premises assume the truth of the conclusion instead of providing independent evidence for it. In the simplest version begging the question has the form, "P is true, therefore P is true." For example, "The dean is a liar because he never tells the truth." If you did not believe the conclusion, you would not believe the premise either, for they make identical claims.

Philosophical Examples of Begging the Question. "God exists because the Bible says he does, and we can trust the Bible because the Bible is the inspired word of God, and we know the Bible is the word of God because God has told us in II Timothy 3:16 that 'All scripture is inspired by God.'" This argument contains two pieces of circular reasoning. It assumes the words in the Bible are the words of God and uses this assumption as evidence for the claim that the words in the Bible are the words of God. Furthermore, it assumes that there is a God who inspired the words in the Bible and uses the claims in the Bible as evidence that there is a God.

In one of his arguments against belief in divine miracles, the eighteenth-century philosopher David Hume said that the laws of nature have been established not simply by the majority of human experiences but by their unanimous testimony that collectively forms "a firm and unalterable experience." Furthermore, he claimed that there is "a uniform experience against every miraculous event."[12] But Hume could know this statement is true only if he knew that all the reports of miracles were false. And he could know this claim only if he knew that miracles never happened. At this point in his essay, it appears he is arguing in this fashion:

1. No miracle has ever happened.
2. So, all reports of miracles are false.
3. Human experience universally counts against miracles.
4. Therefore, no miracle has ever happened.

Composition

In the fallacy of composition a person argues from a property of each part of a whole (or member of a group) taken individually and concludes that this property also may be attributed to the whole (or group). A silly example: "Every member of this 100-student class weighs less than 500 pounds. Therefore, the class as a whole weighs less than 500 pounds." A more subtle but equally fallacious example: "This essay is well written because every sentence in it is well written." Taken individually, each sentence may be well written, but the essay as a whole may be poorly written because it rambles, is disorganized, and lacks a central theme. Another example: "Because every member of this organization is a veteran, this organization must be a veteran's organization."

Philosophical Examples of the Fallacy of Composition. In a famous debate with Father Frederick Copleston on the existence of God, Bertrand Russell accused Copleston of committing the fallacy of composition. Copleston had argued that because everything in the universe has a cause, the universe as a whole must have had a cause. Russell responded with this counterexample: "Every man who exists has a mother, and it seems to me that your argument is that therefore the human race must have a mother, but obviously the human race hasn't a mother—that's a different logical sphere."[13] (Copleston responded by arguing that the notion of *cause* in his argument differed from that in Russell's counterexample.)

Early in the twentieth century, physicists discovered that the behavior of sub-atomic particles was random and not perfectly predictable. This discovery is called Heisenberg's principle of indeterminacy and is part of quantum mechanics. Some philosophers have used this principle as a premise in the following argument: "Because the behavior of subatomic particles is not determined but is unpredictable, and because we are made up of such particles, it follows that our behavior is unpredictable, not determined, and that we have freedom." But, critics respond, this argument is the fallacy of composition. For example, the particles making up my desk may be moving in random ways, but the statistical average of their behavior as exhibited in the desk as a whole is very predictable and determined. The same could be true of our behavior.

Division

The fallacy of division is the exact reverse of composition. Here the premise asserts that a whole or a group has some property and the argument concludes that this property applies to each one of the parts or members of the group as well. Example: "Since every third child born in New York is Roman Catholic, Protestant families there should not have more than two children." Even though the population as a whole may be one-third Catholic, it does not follow that a particular, individual family will be one-third Catholic.

Philosophical Example of the Fallacy of Division. "If there is no God, then the universe has no purpose. It follows that our individual lives have no purpose." But if the universe as a whole has no purpose, that does not mean that some parts of the universe (such as you and I) cannot find purpose in our own lives.

Equivocation

The fallacy of equivocation occurs when a word or phrase changes its meaning in the course of the argument. Consider this obvious example of equivocation: "My client, your honor, should not be sent to jail, for by your own admission he is a good burglar. Surely someone who is good does not belong in jail." (In the first statement *good* means "competent" or "skilled." A "good burglar" is a competent burglar. In the second statement *good* means morally good.)

Philosophical Examples of Equivocation. "I had a legal *right* to foreclose on this widow's property without giving her a chance to negotiate, so how can you say that what I did is not *right*?" Here the speaker confuses a *legal* right with doing what is *morally* right. Obviously, the two are different.

The famous nineteenth-century British philosopher John Stuart Mill (see chapter 5, section 5.3) seems to be guilty of equivocation in one of his arguments for hedonistic utilitarian ethics. He claims that happiness (which he defines as the experience of pleasure and the absence of pain) is the only thing desirable in itself. His argument is that

> the only proof capable of being given that an object is visible is that people actually see it. The only proof that a sound is audible is that people hear it: and so of the other sources of our experience. In like manner, I apprehend, the sole evidence it is possible to produce that anything is desirable is that people actually desire it.[14]

Now it is true that *visible* means "capable of being seen." But does the same sort of definition apply to *desirable*? Two meanings of the word *desirable* seem to be lurking in this passage: (1) It is trivially true that if someone desires something, we can say that for that person the thing is desirable; (2) But in ethics, *desirable* does not mean simply "desired," it means "worthy of being desired" or "something that *ought* to be desired." The two meanings of the word that Mill confuses is illustrated by this sentence: "Trixie finds drugs desirable (meaning 1), but compulsive drug addiction is not a very desirable (meaning 2) lifestyle for anyone to pursue."

"Doctors are saying the new pill that cures baldness is nothing short of miraculous. Therefore, religious people are correct in saying that miracle healings can occur." In the premise, saying the new pill is "miraculous" is a metaphorical exaggeration, but in the conclusion, the word is being used literally.

False Dichotomy

The false dichotomy fallacy is also known as *false dilemma,* the *either-or fallacy,* *bifurcation,* or the *black or white fallacy.* It is called the black or white fallacy because one of the premises assumes that the only alternatives are the extremes of black or white (figuratively speaking), and it ignores the fine shades of gray in between. A false dichotomy argument begins with a disjunction (P or Q). However, the fallacy is committed when one or more other alternatives, such as R, are not being acknowledged. If there are other possibilities, then both P and Q could be false. Thus, by eliminating P, you have not proven that Q is true. A simple example: "Son, you will either graduate from college and make something of yourself or you will be a bum all your life." Are there other possibilities? Bill Gates, the chairman and CEO of the Microsoft Corporation and one of the richest persons in the world, dropped out of Harvard University.

On the surface, an argument based on a false dichotomy has the valid form of a disjunctive syllogism, which is the argument on the left in the following example, whereas the real situation, represented in the argument on the right, makes clear the fallacious reasoning.

(apparent form)   *(real situation)*
1. P or Q.   1. P or Q or R
2. Not-P.   2. Not-P.
3. Therefore, Q. 3. Therefore, Q.

Philosophical Example of a False Dichotomy. The seventeenth-century mathematician, scientist, theologian, and philosopher Blaise Pascal proposed his famous wager in which he suggested that considering religious belief is like making a bet as to which option had the best possible payoff and the least risk (see section 4.4). Pascal's argument went like this:

1. We are faced with two choices in life: either to believe in atheism or to believe in the biblical God.
2. It is not prudent to believe in atheism. (For if we are wrong, then we will lose eternal life.)
3. Therefore, it is prudent to believe in the biblical God.

As with all cases of a false dichotomy, the problem is with the disjunction. The only alternatives are not limited to atheism or belief in the biblical God. There are many other religions, some of which have quite different ideas about the afterlife and some in which there is no notion of the afterlife. There is also **agnosticism,** the decision to believe in neither atheism nor religion until more convincing evidence is found for one view or the other. So, even a rejection of atheism does not automatically prove the wisdom of belief in Pascal's version of the biblical God.

agnosticism the decision to believe in neither atheism nor religion until more convincing evidence is found for one view or the other

Strawman

The strawman fallacy occurs when someone attacks a weak version of an opponent's position or attacks a conclusion that the opponent does not support. This fallacy is like knocking over a strawman and claiming that in doing so you have defeated the world heavyweight boxing champion.

Philosophical Examples of the Strawman Fallacy. "Thomas Aquinas argues that we should believe in God, but having religious faith requires that we throw our reason out the window. So, Aquinas thinks we should commit intellectual suicide." Because Aquinas thought that reason can show that belief in God is rational, he did not hold that we should "commit intellectual suicide" (see section 4.1).

"My opponent claims that we evolved from the lower animals. Therefore, because he believes we are just animals, he must believe that we should live without any civil laws, without any moral rules, and that we should mate in the streets just like dogs." But supporting the theory of evolution obviously does not entail any of the conclusions the speaker attributes to his opponent.

Wishful Thinking

Sometimes we may be tempted to believe a claim because we find the opposite conclusion to be so unpleasant. But whether we find a claim to be subjectively pleasant or not tells us nothing about its truth or falsity. Sometimes the truth about reality may be unpleasant and we simply have to face it. The problem with wishful thinking is illustrated by this example: "If I thought there was no money in my checking account, I could not sleep at night. Therefore, there must be money in my account." Here is another example of the wishful thinking fallacy: "If there was no God, I could not bear to live my life. Therefore, there is a God." A similar example: "If there is a God, then we could not live our lives any way we please. Since human beings must have moral freedom to have dignity, there cannot be a God."

LEARNING MORE ABOUT ARGUMENTS AND EVIDENCE

Much more could be said about evaluating arguments and claims. If you want to learn more about this skill, pick up a book on logic or critical reasoning in the library or bookstore. Better yet, take a course in the subject.

REVIEW FOR CHAPTER 1

Philosophers

1.0 Overview of the Journey
   Søren Kierkegaard
   Pythagoras
   Socrates
1.1 Socrates and the Search for Wisdom
   Thrasymachus
   Sophists

Concepts

1.0 Overview of the Journey
  philosophy
  wisdom
  self-understanding
  understanding the meaning of our basic concepts
  rational justification of belief
  logic
  philosophy of religion
  epistemology
  metaphysics
  ethics
  political philosophy

1.1 Socrates and the Search for Wisdom
  Socrates as the midwife of ideas
  Socrates' wisdom
  Socrates as a gadfly
  the Socratic method
  reductio ad absurdum argument
  "the unexamined life is not worth living"
  "know thyself"
  Socrates' view of the soul
  skepticism
  "a good person cannot be harmed by others"

1.2 Argument and Evidence: How Do I Decide What to Believe?
  six criteria for evaluating claims and theories
    conceptual clarity
    consistency
    rational coherence
    comprehensiveness
    compatibility with well-established facts and theories
    support of compelling arguments
  logical inconsistency
  self-referential inconsistency
  inference to the best explanation
  argument (in philosophy)
  premises
  conclusion
  premise indicators
  conclusion indicators
  valid and invalid
  deductive argument
  sound argument

strong argument
cogent argument
inductive argument
conditional statement
antecedent and consequent
sufficient condition and necessary condition
modus ponens
modus tollens
fallacy
denying the antecedent fallacy
affirming the consequent fallacy
syllogism
hypothetical syllogism
disjunctive syllogism
disjunctive statement
affirming the disjunct fallacy
reductio ad absurdum argument
hasty generalization fallacy
false cause fallacy
false analogy fallacy
informal fallacies
ad hominem (abusive) fallacy
ad hominem (circumstantial) fallacy
appeal to ignorance
begging the question
composition fallacy
division fallacy
equivocation
false dichotomy
agnosticism
strawman fallacy
wishful thinking fallacy

SUGGESTIONS FOR FURTHER READING

General Works on Philosophy

Audi, Robert. *The Cambridge Dictionary of Philosophy.* Cambridge: Cambridge University Press, 1995. A very helpful summary of the central topics in philosophy.

Blackburn, Simon. *The Oxford Dictionary of Philosophy.* Oxford: Oxford University Press, 1996. A concise and readable reference work.

Copleston, F. C. *History of Philosophy.* 9 vols. New York: Doubleday, Image, 1946–1974. A comprehensive coverage of the history of philosophy. This series is a classic.

Craig, Edward, ed. *Routledge Encyclopedia of Philosophy.* 10 vols. London and New York: Routledge, 1998. This reference work is the latest and most complete on all philosophical topics.

Edwards, Paul, ed. *Encyclopedia of Philosophy.* 8 vols. New York: Macmillan, 1967. A good place to start to research a philosopher or topic. For current information, see Donald M. Borcher, ed., *The Encyclopedia of Philosophy Supplement* (New York: Simon & Schuster Macmillan, 1996).

Gaarder, Jostein. *Sophie's World: A Novel about the History of Philosophy.* Translated by Paulette Møller. New York: Berkley Books, 1994. This popular novel is the story of a young girl who finds a piece of paper on which two questions are written: Who are you? and Where did the world come from? Her search for the answers takes her on a journey through the world of philosophy.

Kolak, Daniel. *The Mayfield Anthology of Western Philosophy.* Mountain View, Calif.: Mayfield, 1998. One hundred thirteen of the most important selections by fifty-two of the major philosophers of all time.

Lawhead, William F. *The Voyage of Discovery: A History of Western Philosophy.* Belmont, Calif.: Wadsworth, 1996. A chronological survey of philosophy by the author of this text.

Nagel, Thomas. *What Does It All Mean? A Very Short Introduction to Philosophy.* Oxford: Oxford University Press, 1987. A very readable, short introduction to philosophy.

Palmer, Donald. *Does the Center Hold? An Introduction to Western Philosophy.* 2d ed. Mountain View, Calif.: Mayfield, 1996. An amusing but informative coverage of the major philosophical topics, complete with the author's own philosophical cartoons.

―――. *Looking at Philosophy: The Unbearable Heaviness of Philosophy Made Lighter.* 2d ed. Mountain View, Calif.: Mayfield, 1994. A breezy, historical survey of the major philosophers with more than 350 of the author's cartoons.

Pojman, Louis. *Classics of Philosophy.* Oxford: Oxford University Press, 1998. More than seventy-five works (many of them complete) by the major philosophers.

Waithe, Mary Ellen, ed. *A History of Women Philosophers.* 4 vols. Dordrecht: Martinus Nijhoff/Kluwer Press, 1987, 1989, 1991, 1995. Covers women philosophers from ancient times to the twentieth century.

Woodhouse, Mark. *A Preface to Philosophy.* 5th ed. Belmont, Calif.: Wadsworth, 1994. A practical handbook on reading, writing, and thinking about philosophy.

Socrates

Guthrie, W. K. C. *Socrates.* Cambridge: Cambridge University Press, 1971. A very clear introduction to the life and teachings of Socrates.

Lawhead, William. "The Sophists and Socrates." Chap. 3 in *The Voyage of Discovery: A History of Western Philosophy.* Belmont, Calif.: Wadsworth, 1996. An overview of Socrates and the Sophists.

Plato. *Apology, Euthyphro, Crito, Protagoras, Gorgias, Republic,* and *Phaedo.* These dialogues provide Plato's depiction of the style and teachings of Socrates. They are available in numerous inexpensive paperback translations.

Stone, I. F. *The Trial of Socrates*. New York: Doubleday, Anchor Books, 1988. A national bestseller, this book provides useful information about Socrates and the Athenian culture. Stone tends to be more critical than most concerning Socrates' defense.

Vlastos, Gregory. *Socrates: Ironist and Moral Philosopher*. Ithaca, N.Y.: Cornell University Press, 1991. A readable book by a leading Socrates scholar.

Arguments and Critical Reasoning

Engle, S. Morris. *With Good Reason: An Introduction to Informal Fallacies*. 5th ed. New York: St Martin's Press, 1994. A very good coverage of the informal fallacies, including many not covered in this chapter.

Hurley, Patrick. *A Concise Introduction to Logic*. 6th ed. Belmont, Calif.: Wadsworth, 1997. One of the best traditional introductions to logic.

Moore, Brooke, and Richard Parker. *Critical Thinking*. 5th ed. Mountain View, Calif.: Mayfield, 1997. A very readable and entertaining introduction to logic and critical thinking.

Teays, Wanda. *Second Thoughts: Critical Thinking from a Multicultural Perspective*. Mountain View, Calif.: Mayfield, 1996. An introduction to critical thinking with an emphasis on current social issues and the media.

Tidman, Paul, and Howard Kahane. *Logic and Philosophy: A Modern Introduction*. 8th ed. Belmont, Calif.: Wadsworth, 1999. A readable but slightly more advanced coverage of basic logic.

NOTES

1. Søren Kierkegaard, *Concluding Unscientific Postscript,* trans. David F. Swenson and Walter Lowrie (Princeton: Princeton University Press, 1941), pp. 165–66.
2. I am grateful to David Schlafer, my former colleague, for some of the examples used in this thought experiment.
3. Maurice Merleau-Ponty, "Everywhere and Nowhere," in *Signs,* trans. Richard C. McCleary (Evanston, Ill.: Northwestern University Press, 1964), p. 128.
4. Quoted by T. K. Abbott in "Memoir of Kant," in *Kant's Critique of Practical Reason and Other Works on the Theory of Ethics,* trans. T. K. Abbott (London: Longmans, 1st ed. 1879; 6th ed., 1909; photo reprint, 1954), p. xxxiii (page citation is to the 1954 reprint).
5. Plato, *Phaedo* 118, in *The Dialogues of Plato,* 3d ed., rev., 5 vols., trans. Benjamin Jowett (New York: Oxford University Press, 1892).
6. Plato, *Apology* 20e–23a, 29d–31c, 39a–b, 41c–d, 42, in *The Dialogues of Plato.* Minor changes have been made to the punctuation and a few words have been changed for greater readability in this classic nineteenth-century translation.
7. Plato, *Republic* 338b–343a, in *The Dialogues of Plato.* Minor changes have been made in the translation.
8. Gregory Vlastos, "Introduction: The Paradox of Socrates," in *The Philosophy of Socrates,* ed. Gregory Vlastos (Garden City, N.Y.: Anchor Books, Doubleday, 1971), pp. 5–6.
9. Plato, *Theaetetus* 171a,b.
10. Francis Bacon, "Of the True Greatness of Kingdoms and Estates," in *The Complete Essays of Francis Bacon* (New York: Washington Square Press, 1963), p. 83.

11. David Hume, *Dialogues Concerning Natural Religion,* pt. 7.
12. David Hume, "Of Miracles," in *An Enquiry Concerning Human Understanding,* sec. 10, pt. 1.
13. Bertrand Russell and F. C. Copleston, "A Debate on the Existence of God," in *Bertrand Russell on God and Religion,* ed. Al Seckel (Buffalo: Prometheus Books, 1986), p. 131.
14. John Stuart Mill, *Utilitarianism,* chap. 4.

CHAPTER 2

THE SEARCH FOR KNOWLEDGE

SCOUTING THE TERRITORY: *What Can I Know?*

In a science fiction story, philosopher Jonathan Harrison tells of a famous neurologist, Dr. Smythson, who was pushing forward the frontiers of science in the year A.D. 2167[1] Smythson was presented with the case of a newly born infant whose brain was normal but whose body was afflicted with so many problems that it was on the verge of ceasing to function. In a desperate attempt to preserve the child before his body shut down completely, the scientist separated the brain and its accompanying sensory nerves from the rest of the body. He then kept the brain alive by attaching it to a machine that replaced the abandoned body's support system.

So that his patient (now a conscious brain attached to a machine) could continue his cognitive development, Dr. Smythson used an electrical hallucination machine to stimulate the sensory nerves, which caused the brain to experience sights, sounds, smells, tastes, and tactile sensations. Hence, through this computer-controlled, electrical stimulation of the brain, Smythson created a virtual reality for the patient (now named Ludwig) that was indistinguishable from the experiences of reality you and I enjoy. By means of another electrical contraption, the doctor was able to read Ludwig's brain waves and monitor the patient's cognitive and emotional life. Eventually, by learning from his simulated world produced by the simulated bodily sensations (which Ludwig assumed was the real world and a real, physical body), Ludwig's intellectual development was equivalent to that of a well-educated and experienced adult.

To further enrich Ludwig's intellect, Dr. Smythson stimulated Ludwig's optic nerve with the contents of great works in philosophy. Ludwig studied the works of the skeptics who argued that, because we can only know the immediate contents of our own, internal, conscious experience, we cannot know whether there is a world external to our experience. Ludwig was shaken by this argument and worried about the possibility that his life was a dream from which he might someday awake and discover that all the objects and people he had previously experienced had been illusions. Upon thinking the argument through, however, he found it impossible to doubt that this solid, hard chair he now sat on was not real. (At this point the doctor was giving Ludwig's brain the same sorts of sensations you and I have when sitting on a chair.) Furthermore, Ludwig concluded that his two hands were certainly real, material objects (as the machine fed him simulated experiences comparable to that of holding up one's hands).

During this time period, Ludwig also read about researchers who discovered that the brain could be electrically stimulated such that the patient experienced artificial sensations that appeared to be coming from the body's contact with the external world. However, Ludwig rejected the skeptical possibility that one's entire experience of the world could be of this sort. At this point, although Ludwig considered these skeptical possibilities to be only fictional or hypothetical scenarios (not realizing that they described his actual lot in life), Dr. Smythson ceased allowing

Ludwig to experience books that left him preoccupied with worries about illusion and reality.

The important point about this rather bizarre story is that it is logically possible that an incident like this could happen, even though at this point in our scientific research it is not yet medically possible to give someone the experience of an illusory world (although we do have the ability to stimulate the brain and produce a limited set of artificially created sensations). The theoretical possibility of someone being a brain in a vat and experiencing a virtual reality serves to raise the question of how we know that our experiences give us knowledge about the external world. However, we do not have to rely on the unusual scenario of this story to consider the possibility that all our knowledge could be mistaken. Stop and reflect on the difficulties you have had in determining what is true or false, reality or illusion within your experience.

STOP AND THINK

Think about a time when you were absolutely convinced that something was true, only to find out later that you were wrong. If this situation has happened to you, how do you know that *anytime* you are certain of something, you are not similarly mistaken in thinking it is true when it is not?

Poor Ludwig was convinced that he was directly experiencing the external world when, in fact, he was simply a brain who was having illusory but seemingly real experiences of books, chairs, hands, sunsets, and so on. The problem is that, like Ludwig, you cannot jump outside your experience to compare its contents with the world outside. Everything you know about what exists outside your experience is mediated by means of your experiences. Because you have frequently found that your experiences can be wrong, how can you be sure they are ever right? The following thought experiment will explore the notions of knowledge, certainty, and justification.

THOUGHT EXPERIMENT

Knowledge, Certainty, Justification

1. Place a quarter on the table. Look at it from above. It will look like a circular patch of silver. Now look at it from an angle. You will see an elliptical silver image in your visual field. If you look at its edge straight on, it will appear to be a silver line. Now look at it from across the room. The item in your visual field will be a very small silver speck. Presumably, the quarter is not constantly changing its shape and size. But the image present to your eyes *is* changing its shape and size. It follows that

(Continued . . .)

(. . . continued)

what you see cannot be the quarter itself but merely a changing image of the quarter. Can we say therefore that the real quarter has a constant shape and size that is causing the changing images in your experience? But how can we make such a statement, because we can never jump outside our experience to see the real quarter? How do we know that there is any relationship between what appears within experience and what lies outside of it?

2. Write down five statements that you believe are true. (Try to vary the subject matter of these items.) In terms of the relative degree of certainty you have about these statements compared to one another, rank these statements from the most certain to the least certain. Which three of these statements have the highest degree of certainty for you? Why these three? For the remaining two statements, try to imagine conditions or new information that would raise doubts about their truth. How plausible are these possible doubts? Among the three statements that have the highest degree of certainty, which one would you be least likely to doubt? Why? Try to formulate some general principles or criteria that you use in deciding whether the truth of a statement is more or less certain.

3. Is it important that we be able to justify our beliefs? What would be the problem with having beliefs that we believe are true but that we could not justify? Is it important to provide evidence for our beliefs to ourselves or only to others? Are there any problems with attempting to justify all our beliefs?

CHARTING THE TERRAIN OF KNOWLEDGE:
What Are the Issues?

The questions raised in this thought experiment concern the nature and possibility of knowledge and truth as well as the justification of our beliefs. The area of philosophy that deals with questions concerning knowledge and that considers various theories of knowledge is called **epistemology.** The Greek word *episteme* means "knowledge" and *logos* means "rational discourse." Hence, epistemology is the philosophy of knowledge. To get clear on the different dimensions of knowledge, try the following thought experiment.

epistemology the area of philosophy that deals with questions concerning knowledge and that considers various theories of knowledge

THOUGHT EXPERIMENT

Dimensions of Knowledge

The following list contains three categories of statements (1, 2, 3). In each category, what do the three knowledge claims (a, b, c) have in common? On the other hand, how do the kinds of knowledge in the three major groups (1, 2, 3) differ from one another?

1. (a) I know the president of our university on a personal basis.
   (b) I know the streets of London intimately.
   (c) I know what it is like to face death.

(Continued . . .)

(. . . continued)

2. (a) I know how to speak German.
   (b) I know how to play the piano.
   (c) I know how to write a computer program.
3. (a) I know that Chicago is in Illinois.
   (b) I know that George Washington was the first president of the United States.
   (c) I know that all the points on a circle are equidistant from its center.

Types of Knowledge

The first three statements in the thought experiment (1a, 1b, 1c) are examples of *knowledge by acquaintance.* This knowledge is not the sort that can be communicated in a book, because it requires some sort of direct experience with the person, thing, or event that is the object of knowledge. The second three statements represent *competence knowledge,* or "knowing how." This kind of knowledge is involved in learning a skill. This knowledge is more than a matter of knowing certain propositions to be true; it entails being able to do something. The last three statements are examples of *propositional knowledge,* or "knowing that." Here, the object of knowledge is the truth of some proposition or statement of fact. This sort of knowledge does not require direct acquaintance with what is being discussed, nor does it directly involve acquiring a skill. You can know truths about someone without ever meeting him or her. You can know that Chicago is in Illinois without knowing how to get there. Although some epistemologists have concerned themselves with the first two kinds of knowledge, most theories of knowledge focus on propositional knowledge. Hence, our primary interest here concerns knowledge that can be stated in propositions.

Having limited our discussion to a particular kind of knowledge—propositional knowledge—we may now ask, What are the *necessary* and *sufficient* conditions for having this sort of knowledge? Perhaps the following thought experiment will help guide your intuitions on this matter.

 THOUGHT EXPERIMENT

Necessary and Sufficient Conditions for Knowledge

Consider the following scenarios. In each case decide why it would or would not be correct to say that "Ernest *knows* that Brenda's birthday is today."

1. (a) Ernest believes that his friend Brenda's birthday is today.
   (b) Brenda's birthday really is next week.
2. (a) Ernest has no opinion about the date of Brenda's birthday.
   (b) Brenda's birthday is today.

(Continued . . .)

3. (a) Ernest randomly throws a dart at the calendar while shouting "Brenda," and the dart lands on today's date.

   (b) Based on this chance result, Ernest decides that today is Brenda's birthday.

   (c) As a matter of fact, today is Brenda's birthday.

4. (a) Ernest glances at Brenda's driver's license and notices that today is her birthday.

   (b) Ernest has no reason to believe that the date on Brenda's license is inaccurate.

   (c) Based on these considerations, Ernest believes that today is Brenda's birthday.

   (d) It is true that today is Brenda's birthday.

The Definition of Knowledge

What did you decide about the four scenarios in the thought experiment? Going as far back as Plato, philosophers have traditionally defined knowledge as *true justified belief.* If we accept this analysis, here is what we would have to say about the four scenarios. In case 1, Ernest could not be said to have knowledge because his belief is false. There is no such thing as false knowledge. However, we can have a false belief and mistakenly think we have knowledge. That is why, when we find out our mistake, we say, "I thought I knew the answer to the question, but I guess I didn't." In case 2, Ernest obviously does not have knowledge concerning Brenda's birthday because he has no beliefs about it whatsoever.

Case 3 is different from the first two because Ernest believes today is Brenda's birthday and his belief happens to be true. Nevertheless, it would be reasonable to

Ask five or more people the following question: Why do people believe what they do?[2] They can answer both in terms of their own, personal belief system or, more generally, what they think are the causes or reasons for most people's beliefs.

Write down their answers and later organize them under the following headings:

- Sociological reasons: One's beliefs are based on the influence of one's family, friends, or society.
- Psychological reasons: One's beliefs satisfy internal needs (for hope, meaning, purpose, identity, pleasure, and so on).
- Religious reasons: One's beliefs are based on a religious tradition, authority, revelation, or experience.
- Philosophical reasons: One's beliefs are based on logic, evidence, scientific facts, reasoning, sense experience, and so on.
- Other

Now evaluate each specific reason by asking, If this basis for belief is the only reason I could give myself for believing what I believe, would I be justified in continuing to hold this belief? Compare and discuss with several friends the answers you have gathered and your evaluations of them.

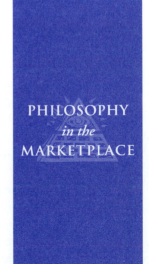

PHILOSOPHY
in the
MARKETPLACE

say that he doesn't really *know* this fact because his belief, though true, is not justified. Beliefs that are based on a lucky guess or a happenstance throw of a dart seem to fall short of what is required to have knowledge. This conclusion lacks some sort of reasons or justification that would support his belief. The method Ernest used to form his belief in case 3 could just as easily have led him to a false belief. Case 4 has all the necessary and sufficient conditions for knowledge. Ernest has a true, justified belief concerning Brenda's birth date. As we will see in later sections, philosophers disagree about what counts as justification. Is absolute certainty required for justification? Is the impossibility of error? Or is a justified belief merely a highly probable belief that is beyond any reasonable doubts? In recent years, some philosophers have questioned this definition of knowledge. Nevertheless, while quibbling over the details, most philosophers throughout history have agreed that knowledge is true justified belief. Because the notion of *certainty* has played such a large role in epistemology, the following "Stop and Think" box will ask you to assess its importance.

 STOP AND THINK

How important is it to be absolutely certain of your fundamental beliefs? Is there a difference between having a psychological feeling of confidence in your beliefs and having objective certainty? Is it even possible to achieve absolute certainty about any of your beliefs? If you think certainty is possible, what sorts of beliefs can provide you with such certainty? Is the basis of this certainty something that could be convincing to someone other than you? Is a high degree of probability an adequate substitute for absolute certainty? Why?

The Issue of Reason and Experience

One of the most important issues in a theory of knowledge is the relationship between reason and experience. Philosophers use a number of specialized terms to talk about this issue. This terminology was introduced by Immanuel Kant in the eighteenth century. Nevertheless, it can be applied to most of the theories of knowledge of previous centuries. The following terms will be useful in our discussions of some of the philosophical positions in this chapter.

analytic statement a statement possessing the following properties: (1) its truth or falsity is determined solely by the meaning of its terms, and (2) even if it is true, it does not give us any real, factual information about the world

An **analytic statement** is one that has the following properties: (1) its truth or falsity is determined solely by the meaning of its terms, and (2) even if it is true, it does not give us any real, factual information about the world. For example, if we analyze the meaning of the term *bachelor,* we find that the notion of unmarried is contained within it. We do not have to interview thousands of bachelors to determine that the statement "all bachelors are unmarried" is analytically true. Similarly, the following statement is a sure bet: "Either my university's football team will win their next game or they won't." Even if the team ties or the game is canceled, these circumstances would fulfill the "they won't win" part of the prediction. Hence, though this statement is analytically true, it does not give us real, factual information about what will happen in the world.

A **synthetic statement** has the following properties: (1) its truth or falsity is *not* determined solely by the meaning of its terms, and (2) it does make a factual claim about the way the world is. For example, the statement "rabbits are animals found in America" is true, but this fact could not be known by analyzing the meaning of the term *rabbit*. Similarly, the previous statement about rabbits and the claim that "unicorns are animals found in America" both make factual claims about the way the world is. However, the statement about unicorns happens to be false. Synthetic statements synthesize, or bring together, two concepts that are not logically connected. The concepts of "rabbit" and "animals found in America" are linked together in the previous claim even though there is not a necessary relationship between them.

The box on this page stands for the concept of a square. Contained within the box are some of the properties that are necessarily contained within the concept of a square. Hence, the statement "A square has four equal sides" is an analytic statement because the property of having four equal sides is already contained within the concept of a square.

Square
• closed, plane figure
• four equal sides
• four right angles

 However, the statement "There is a black square on this page" is a synthetic statement because, even though it is true, it combines three concepts that are not necessarily related. These concepts are:

Black	+	Square	+	On this page

Several other terms are traditionally used to discuss knowledge. **A priori knowledge** is knowledge that is gained independently of (or prior to) experience. What kinds of knowledge could be gained without any appeal to experience? Certainly, we can know the truth of an analytic statement apart from experience. Hence, definitions and logically necessary truths are examples of **analytic a priori knowledge.** "All mothers are parents" is true by definition and "Green apples are green" is a logically necessary truth, and both are examples of analytic a priori knowledge. The second kind of knowledge is **a posteriori knowledge,** or knowledge that is based on (or posterior to) experience. Similarly, the adjective **empirical** refers to anything that is based on experience. Any claims based on experience would be cases of **synthetic a posteriori knowledge,** for they add new information to the subject. Hence, "Water freezes at 32 degrees Fahrenheit" and "Tadpoles become frogs" would be examples of synthetic a posteriori knowledge. Thus far, most philosophers would agree on these points.

The difficult question now arises: Is there any **synthetic a priori knowledge?** What would that knowledge be like? It would be knowledge expressible in a synthetic statement, which means that (1) its truth is not determined solely by the

synthetic statement a statement possessing the following properties: (1) its truth or falsity is *not* determined solely by the meaning of its terms, and (2) it does make a factual claim about the way the world is

a priori knowledge knowledge gained independently of or prior to experience

analytic a priori knowledge analytic knowledge gained independently of or prior to experience, for example, definitions and logically necessary truths

a posteriori knowledge knowledge based on or posterior to experience

empirical based on experience

synthetic a posteriori knowledge knowledge that is based on experience and that adds new information to the subject

synthetic a priori knowledge knowledge that is acquired through reason, independently of experience, and that provides information about the way the world is

meaning of its terms, and (2) it does provide information about the way the world is. Furthermore, since it is a priori, it would be knowledge that we could acquire through reason, independently of experience. The question, then, is whether reason alone can tell us about the ultimate nature of reality. The philosophers discussed in this chapter take different positions on this question.

Three Epistemological Questions

The previous "Philosophy in the Marketplace" survey probably demonstrated that even among nonphilosophers there is a wide range of opinions concerning how to justify our beliefs. As you read the rest of this chapter, try to see if some of your friends' answers match up with the views of any of the philosophers discussed. These different philosophies are attempts to answer basic questions about knowledge. Although an enormous number of philosophical problems concern knowledge, I am going to focus on three of the major problems. The philosophies I discuss in the remaining sections of this chapter are various attempts to answer the following three epistemological questions. (As you read these questions, you might consider whether you would answer each one with a yes or a no at this point in your understanding.)

1. Is it possible to have knowledge at all?
2. Does reason provide us with knowledge of the world independently of experience?
3. Does our knowledge represent reality as it really is?

CHOOSING A PATH: *What Are My Options Concerning Knowledge?*

skepticism the claim that we do not have knowledge

Skepticism is the claim that we do *not* have knowledge. Most skeptics accept the traditional view that knowledge is true, justified belief, but go on from there to argue that it is impossible to have justified beliefs or that no one has provided any reasons to think that our beliefs are capable of being justified. Hence, the skeptics give a negative answer to the first epistemological question. Because skeptics think that knowledge is unattainable, they consider the remaining two questions to be irrelevant. The philosophers represented by the remaining positions think we *can* obtain knowledge, and hence, in contrast to the skeptic, they answer the first question in the affirmative. The disagreements among the nonskeptics concern the source and nature of knowledge.

rationalism the claim that reason or the intellect is the sole source of our fundamental knowledge about reality

Rationalism claims that reason or the intellect is the sole source of our fundamental knowledge about reality. Nonrationalists agree that we can use reason to draw conclusions from the information provided by sense experience. However, what distinguishes the rationalists is that they claim that reason can give us knowledge *apart* from experience. For example, the rationalists point out that we can arrive at mathematical truths about circles or triangles without having to measure, experiment with, or experience circular or triangular objects. We do so by constructing rational, deductive proofs that lead to absolutely indubitable conclusions that are always universally true of the world outside our minds (synthetic a priori knowledge). Obviously, the rationalists think the second question should be answered affirmatively.

Empiricism is the claim that sense experience is the sole source of our knowledge about the world. Empiricists insist that when we start life, the original equipment of our intellect is a tabula rasa, or blank tablet. Only through experience does that empty mind become filled with content. Various empiricists give different explanations of the nature of logical and mathematical truths. They are all agreed, however, that these truths are not already latent in the mind before we discover them and that there is no genuine synthetic a priori knowledge about the nature of reality. The empiricists would respond "No!" to the second epistemological question. With respect to question 3, both the rationalists and the empiricists think that our knowledge does represent reality as it really is.

Constructivism is used in this discussion to refer to the claim that knowledge is *neither* already in the mind *nor* passively received from experience, but that the mind *constructs* knowledge out of the materials of experience. Immanuel Kant, an eighteenth-century German philosopher, introduced this view. He was influenced by both the rationalists and the empiricists and attempted to reach a compromise between them. While Kant did not agree with the rationalists on everything, he did believe we can have synthetic a priori knowledge of the world as we experience it. Although Kant did not use this label, I call his position *constructivism* to capture his distinctive account of knowledge. One troubling consequence of his view was that because the mind imposes its own order on experience, we can never know reality as it is in itself. We can only know reality as it appears to us after it has been filtered and processed by our minds. Hence, Kant answers question 3 negatively. Nevertheless, because Kant thought our minds all have the same cognitive structure, he thought we are able to arrive at universal and objective knowledge *within* the boundaries of the human situation.

Epistemological relativism is the claim that there is no universal, objective knowledge of reality because all knowledge is relative to either the individual or his

empiricism the claim that sense experience is the sole source of our knowledge about the world

constructivism the claim that knowledge is neither already in the mind nor passively received from experience but that the mind constructs knowledge out of the materials of experience

epistemological relativism the claim that there is no universal, objective knowledge of reality because all knowledge is relative to either the individual or his or her culture

TABLE 2.1 *Three Epistemological Questions and Five Positions on Them*			
	Is knowledge possible?	Does reason provide us with knowledge of the world independently of experience?	Does our knowledge represent reality as it really is?
Skepticism	No	—	—
Rationalism	Yes	Yes	Yes
Empiricism	Yes	No	Yes
Constructivism (Kant)	Yes	Yes	No
Relativism	Yes	No	No

or her culture. In other words, the relativist believes that there is no one, true story about reality, but that there are many stories. Since we can no more jump outside our respective ways of viewing the world than we can our own skins, there is no way to say that a particular claim about reality is the only true one. It may seem that the relativist is denying knowledge the way the skeptic does. However, the relativists would insist that we *do* have knowledge but would deny that this knowledge is universal and objective. Knowledge is always knowledge *for* someone and is shaped by each knower's psychological, philosophical, historical, or cultural circumstances. Hence, while answering question 1 affirmatively, the relativist would respond with a no to the remaining two questions. There are many varieties of relativism as it has been defined here: existentialism, pragmatism, and some forms of feminism are discussed in later sections to illustrate this epistemological outlook.

Table 2.1 presents the three epistemological questions just discussed and lists the answers provided by the five different positions.

The next exercise asks you to register your agreement or disagreement with ten statements. In some cases, you may not be sure what you think; nevertheless, choose the response that you think seems to be the most correct.

 WHAT DO I THINK? *Questionnaire on Knowledge, Doubt, Reason, and Experience*

	Agree	Disagree
1. It is impossible to ever truly know anything, for all we can ever have are merely opinions and beliefs.		✓
2. It is possible to have objective knowledge of what reality is like in itself.	✗	✓
3. When my reason convinces me that something must be true, but my experience tells me the opposite, I trust my experience.	✓	
4. When we come into the world at birth, the mind is like a blank tablet. In other words, all the contents of the mind, anything that we can think about or know to be true, must have come to us originally through experience.		✓
5. Our knowledge about reality can never be absolutely certain. However, if a belief is true and we have sufficient evidence of its probability, we have knowledge.	✓	
6. When my experience convinces me that something is the case, but my reason tells me it is illogical, I trust my reason.		✓

7. At least *some* of the following ideas are directly known by the mind and are not learned from experience: (a) the laws of logic (b) the basic principles of mathematics (c) "every event has a cause" (d) the concept of perfection (e) the idea of God (f) moral concepts and principles (such as "it is wrong to torture an innocent person.")		✓
8. Through reason, it is possible to have knowledge about reality that is absolutely certain.		✓
9. We can have universal and objective knowledge of how reality consistently *appears* to the human mind, but we cannot know what reality is like *in itself.*	✓	
10. There is no absolute truth, for when I say that something is "true," I am saying nothing more than "it is true for me" or that "the majority of the people in my society agree that it is true."		✓

KEY TO THE QUESTIONNAIRE ON KNOWLEDGE

Statement 1 is an expression of skepticism. Strictly speaking, the skeptic would disagree with all the other statements, and all the other positions would disagree with this statement.

Statement 2 expresses epistemological objectivism. Some empiricists and all traditional rationalists would agree with this statement.

Statement 3 represents empiricism. It conflicts with statement 6.

Statement 4 represents empiricism. It conflicts with statement 7.

Statement 5 represents empiricism. It conflicts with statement 8.

Statement 6 represents rationalism. It conflicts with statement 3.

Statement 7 represents rationalism. It conflicts with statement 4.

Statement 8 represents rationalism. It conflicts with statement 5.

Statement 9 represents Kantian constructivism. This position would disagree with statements 1, 2, and 10. With qualifications, the Kantian constructivist could agree with some of the statements of empiricism and rationalism.

Statement 10 represents epistemological relativism. The subjectivist (or subjective relativist) says "true" equals "true for me," because according to this position, the individual is the measure of truth. The cultural relativist (or 'conventionalist) believes that "*x* is true" equals "the majority of one's culture or society agrees that *x* is true." Generally, the relativist disagrees with skepticism, rationalism, and Kantian constructivism. However, some forms of empiricism would be consistent with relativism.

Which position seems closest to your own? How consistent were your answers? In other words, did you agree with two statements that conflict with each other?

 LEADING QUESTIONS: *Skepticism*

1. How do we know that our sense experience ever reveals reality to us? We think that the water in our drinking glass is real because we can touch it (unlike the illusory water we see on the road). But maybe what we think we experience in the drinking glass is simply a deeper and more persistent illusion. After all, the illusory water on the road *looks* like real water even though it isn't. Similarly, maybe the water in the glass *feels* and *tastes* likes real water even though it isn't. Perhaps everything we think is water is really like the illusory water on the road. While the latter fools only our eyes, maybe all the other kinds of illusory water are capable of fooling all five senses.

2. Take some ordinary, simple belief that you have. It might be something like "There is a book in front of me right now." Consider what reasons you have for thinking this belief to be true. Now, consider why you think each of those reasons is true. Continue this process as far as you can until you arrive at your most fundamental beliefs. Now, what reasons do you have for these fundamental beliefs? Does the process of finding reasons for our beliefs ever come to an end? Does it end with some beliefs we simply hold onto tenaciously without any reason? Or is there another alternative?

3. Right now, as you read this sentence, you believe that you are awake and not dreaming. But isn't it usually the case that when we are dreaming, we also think that we are awake and actually experiencing the events in the dream? In our waking experience we believe that we are awake. But when we dream, we also believe we are awake. So how do we tell the difference? How do you know that right now you are not dreaming that you are reading about dreaming while you are really sleeping soundly in your own bed?

 ## SURVEYING THE CASE FOR SKEPTICISM

Skepticism is the claim that we do not have knowledge. It makes sense to begin our discussion of epistemology with skepticism, for if the skeptic is right, there is no point in examining all the other approaches to knowledge. *Universal* skeptics claim that we have no knowledge whatsoever. They think that every knowledge claim is unjustified and subject to doubt. On the other hand, *limited* skeptics allow that we may have some knowledge, but they focus their skeptical doubts on particular types of knowledge claims. For example, one type of limited skeptic might agree that we can have mathematical or scientific knowledge, but might doubt that we know the truth or falsity concerning other types of claims such as moral judgments or religious claims. On the other hand, another limited skeptic might claim that mystical experience provides us with the truth about reality, but that science does not give us anything more than conjectures, guesses, and likely stories. The following thought experiment explores the degree to which you and your friends are or are not skeptical about three major domains of knowledge.

 THOUGHT EXPERIMENT

Skepticism and Knowledge

For each of the following statements, check the box corresponding to one of the following three responses:

- I tend to either agree or disagree with this statement. (I do have knowledge.)
- At this point, I am not sure if this statement is true or false, but I think it is possible to find the answer. (Knowledge is possible, but I do not know the answer.)
- I do not believe it is ever possible to find the answer. (Knowledge is impossible.)

	I do have knowledge	Knowledge is possible, but I do not know the answer	Knowledge is impossible
1. There is a God.	1	2	3
2. There are no such events as supernatural miracles.	1	2	3
3. There is life after death.	1	2	3
4. One particular religion is the true one.	1	2	3
5. Science gives us our best information about reality.	1	2	3
6. Science can tell us about the origins of the universe.	1	2	3
7. Science can tell us about the origins of human life.	1	2	3
8. Scientists will one day be able to explain all human behavior.	1	2	3
9. Some actions are objectively right or wrong.	1	2	3

(Continued . . .)

(. . . continued)

10. The conventions of one's society determine what is right or wrong.	1	2	3
11. Pleasure is the only thing in life that has value.	1	2	3
12. Sometimes it could be one's moral duty to lie.	1	2	3

The responses to each statement have the point value that is indicated. In other words, every answer in the first column is worth one point. Each answer in the second column is worth two points, and each answer in the third column is three points.

Add up your scores for statements 1 through 4. This total is your religion score. If your religion score is 4–6, you are very confident that knowledge is possible concerning religious questions and are not a skeptic. If your score is 7–9, you tend to believe that there are answers to religious questions, but you are uncertain about the answers or have a moderate degree of skepticism. If your score is 10–12, you are very skeptical about the possibility of having knowledge concerning religious issues. Notice that *both* the religious believer and the atheist would be nonskeptics. The atheist would say that the statement "There is a God" is false. Hence, contrary to the skeptic, the atheist believes we can know the truth about this issue.

Add up your scores for statements 5 through 8. This total is your science score. If your science score is 4–6, you are nonskeptical about scientific knowledge. If your score is 7–9, you have some confidence in scientific knowledge along with a degree of skepticism on some issues. If your score is 10–12, you are very skeptical of the possibility of scientific knowledge.

Add up your scores for statements 9 through 12. This total is your score on moral knowledge. If your moral knowledge score is 4–6, you believe moral knowledge is possible and are not a skeptic. If your score is 7–9, you believe moral knowledge is possible, but have reservations about some issues. If your score is 10–12, you think we can have little or no knowledge about the truth or falsity of moral claims.

Those people who embrace skepticism must be able to give reasons for that skepticism. On the other hand, those people who reject skepticism must wrestle with the skeptic's arguments and show where those arguments go wrong. Remember that the traditional view of knowledge involves three conditions: truth, justifi-

PHILOSOPHY
in the
MARKETPLACE

Try the previous thought experiment on five friends whose answers are likely to differ from yours. In each case, note any differences of the degree of skepticism between the various respondents. Discuss the reasons for your differences.

cation, and belief. If these conditions are essential for having knowledge, the skeptic, in order to show that we do not have knowledge, has to show that one of these conditions is missing. The most obvious target of the skeptic's attacks on knowledge claims is condition 2, which states that our beliefs must be justified in order for them to count as knowledge.

Before reading further, look at the highway picture for an example of a classic experiment in perception. Did you get the right answer, or were your eyes fooled? One way that skeptics attack knowledge claims is to point to all the ways in which we have been deceived by illusions. Our experience with perceptual illusions shows that in the past we have been mistaken about what we thought we knew. These mistakes lead, the skeptic claims, to the conclusion that we can never be certain about our beliefs, from which it follows that our beliefs are not justified.

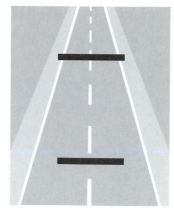

In this picture of a highway, which one of the two horizontal bars is the longest? Use a ruler to check your judgment.

Another, similar strategy of the skeptic is to point to the possibility that our apprehension of reality could be systematically flawed in some way. The story of Ludwig, the brain in the vat who experienced a false virtual reality, would be an example of this strategy. Another strategy is to suppose that there is an inherent flaw in human psychology such that our beliefs never correspond to reality. I call these possible scenarios **universal belief falsifiers.** The characteristics of a universal belief falsifier are (1) it is a theoretically possible state of affairs, (2) we have no way of knowing if this state of affairs is actual or not, and (3) if this state of affairs is actual, we would never be able to distinguish beliefs that are true from beliefs that seem to be true but are actually false. Note that the skeptic does not need to prove that these possibilities are actual. For example, the skeptic does not have to establish that we really are brains in a vat, but merely that this condition is possible. Furthermore, the skeptic need not claim that all our beliefs are false. The skeptic's point is simply that we have no fail-safe method for determining when our beliefs are true or false. Given this circumstance, the skeptic will argue that we cannot distinguish the situation of having evidence that leads to true beliefs from the situation of having the same sort of evidence plus a universal belief falsifier, which leads to false beliefs.

universal belief falsifiers strategies used by skeptics to attack knowledge claims by showing that there are possible states of affairs that would prevent us from ever distinguishing true beliefs from fake ones

Obviously, the skeptic believes that nothing is beyond doubt. For any one of our beliefs, we can imagine a set of circumstances in which it would be false. For example, I believe I was born in Rahway, New Jersey. However, my birth certificate could be inaccurate. Furthermore, for whatever reasons, my parents may have wished to keep the truth from me. I will never know for sure. I also believe that there is overwhelming evidence that Adolf Hitler committed suicide at the close of World War II. However, it could be true (as conspiracy theorists maintain) that his death was faked and that he lived a long life in South America after the war. The theme of the skeptic is that certainty is necessary for there to be knowledge, and if doubt is possible, then we do not have certainty.

We now have the considerations in place that the skeptic uses to make his or her case. There are many varieties of skeptical arguments, each one exploiting some possible flaw in either human cognition or the alleged evidence we use to justify our beliefs. Instead of presenting various specific arguments, we can consider a "generic skeptical argument."

Generic Skeptical Argument

1. We can find reasons for doubting any one of our beliefs.
2. It follows that we can doubt all our beliefs.
3. If we can doubt all our beliefs, then we cannot be certain of any of them.
4. If we do not have certainty about any of our beliefs, then we do not have knowledge.
5. Therefore, we do not have knowledge.

STOP AND THINK

- What do you think of the generic skeptical argument? Is there any premise or inference you would question?
- Do you agree with the claim that if we do not have absolute certainty, we do not have knowledge?

EARLY GREEK SKEPTICS

Skepticism arose in ancient Greek philosophy after several centuries of philosophical speculation that yielded little agreement about what reality was like. Some philosophers concluded that this massive amount of disagreement meant that no one had knowledge and that we possessed only a diversity of unfounded opinions. One of the earliest and most cantankerous of the skeptics was Cratylus, who was a fifth-century Athenian and a younger contemporary of Socrates. Cratylus believed that little could be known because everything was changing, including oneself. This belief led him to become skeptical about even the possibility of communication. Since the world, the speaker, the listener, and the words were in a constant state of flux, there was no possibility of stable meanings. Cratylus is said to have been true to his own skepticism by refusing to discuss anything. When someone attempted to assert an opinion, Cratylus merely wagged his finger, indicating that nothing could be known nor communicated.

Pyrrho of Elis (360–270 B.C.), a philosopher in ancient Greece, inspired a skeptical movement that bore his name (Pyrrhonian skepticism). Pyrrho was skeptical concerning sense experience. He argued that for experience to be a source of knowledge, our sense data must agree with reality. But it is impossible to jump outside our experience to see how it compares with the external world. So, we can never know whether our experience is giving us accurate information about reality.

Furthermore, rational argument cannot give us knowledge either, Pyrrho said, because for every argument supporting one side of an issue, another argument can be constructed to prove the opposing case. Hence, the two arguments cancel each other out and they are equally ineffective in leading us to the truth. The followers of Pyrrho stressed that we can make claims only about how things appear to us. You can say, "The honey *appears* to me to be sweet" but not "The honey *is* sweet." The best approach, according to these skeptics, was to suspend judgment whenever possible and make no assumptions at all. They believed that skeptical detachment would lead to serenity. "Don't worry about what you cannot know," they advised.

Although Plato spent his life attempting to refute skepticism, an influential group of skeptics arose within the Academy, the school that Plato originally founded. The most clever of these was Carneades (who lived about 214–129 B.C.). Carneades represented Athens as an ambassador to Rome along with two other philosophers. The Romans were most interested in his public lectures because those lectures were their first exposure to philosophy. On the first day Carneades argued in favor of justice and eloquently commended its practice to the Romans. The next day, he argued the opposite position, using equally brilliant rhetoric to downgrade justice. This two-faced arguing was a favorite method of the Greek skeptics for undermining the belief that we can know anything to be true. Later skeptics, following Pyrrho, formalized lists of arguments supporting Pyrrho's philosophy. Some skeptics distilled these arguments down into two simple theses. First, nothing is self-evident, for any axiom we start with can be doubted. Second, nothing can be proven, for either we will have an infinite regress of reasons that support our previous reasons or we will end up assuming what we are trying to prove.

RENÉ DESCARTES (1596–1650)

Descartes's Life

Some of the best known arguments for skepticism were produced by the French philosopher René Descartes. Descartes lived in exciting times. He was born almost one hundred years after Columbus sailed to the Americas and half a century after Copernicus published the controversial thesis that the earth revolves around the sun. About the time that Descartes was born, Shakespeare was writing *Hamlet*. Descartes came from a wealthy, respected family in France. His inherited family fortune gave him the freedom to travel and write without having to provide for his own support. It also enabled him to receive one of the best educations available to a young man in France at that time.

In spite of the reputation of his college, Descartes felt a sense of disappointment and even bitterness about his education. He said about the philosophy he was taught that "it has been cultivated for many centuries by the most excellent minds and yet there is still no point in it which is not disputed and hence doubtful."[3]

RENÉ DESCARTES
(1596–1650)

Feeling unsettled and restless, he decided to remedy the limitations of his formal education by traveling and studying "the great book of the world." On November 10, 1619, the harsh German winter confined him to a lonely stove-heated room where he spent the day in intense philosophical thought. There, Descartes says, he "discovered the foundations of a wonderful new science." The following night, his excitement over this discovery culminated in three vivid dreams during which he felt "the Spirit of Truth descending to take possession" of him. This experience convinced him that his mission in life was to develop a new philosophy, based on mathematical reasoning, that would provide absolute certainty and serve as the foundation of all the other sciences.

Descartes spent most of his life in Holland, whose liberal atmosphere provided a safe refuge for intellectuals working on controversial ideas. In 1633 he finished *The World,* a book on physics that contained the controversial thesis that the sun, not the earth, was the center of our universe. He was set to publish it when he learned that Galileo had been formally condemned by the Inquisition in Rome for promoting the same idea. Descartes prudently hid his manuscript with a friend, and it was only published after his death. However, he did go on to publish numerous other works on philosophy, mathematics, and science, and he became world famous. In spite of his tensions with the theologians of his day, Descartes remained a sincere Catholic and always hoped that his works would be of service to theology.

Among Descartes's many correspondents was Queen Christina of Sweden, who was not only a monarch but a person with keen philosophical abilities. She read some of Descartes's manuscripts and sent him critiques of his arguments. In 1649, she invited him to come to Sweden to be her tutor. He wrote to a friend that he was reluctant to go to the land of "bears, rocks and ice." Nevertheless, he did not feel that he could turn down her request, and so he accepted the position. The new position turned out to be disastrous. Descartes had suffered from frail health all his life, and the frigid weather and the five o'clock in the morning tutoring sessions wore him down until he contracted pneumonia and died on February 11, 1650.

The Quest for Certainty

Descartes's lifelong passion was to find certainty. He felt as though his education had given him a collection of ideas based on little else but tradition; many of these ideas had been proven false by his own research. In despair he wrote, "I found myself beset by so many doubts and errors that I came to think I had gained nothing from my attempts to become educated but increasing recognition of my ignorance."[4] While his quest for certainty was a matter of great personal concern, Descartes also thought the quest was essential before science could make any real progress. Looking at the philosophical presuppositions of the sciences of his day, Descartes concluded that "nothing solid could have been built upon such shaky foundations."[5]

Although Descartes did not end up a skeptic, he initially used skeptical doubt as a test to decide which beliefs were absolutely certain. Hence, his strategy for finding certainty could be called *methodological skepticism.* Descartes's method was to bathe every one of his beliefs in an acid bath of doubt to see if any survived. Descartes employed a very rigorous standard here. If he could think of any possibility that a belief of his could be mistaken, no matter how improbable this basis of doubt was, then he would suspend judgment concerning that belief. He realized that most of his beliefs would dissolve when subjected to such intense scrutiny, but if even one belief survived the skeptical attack, then he could be absolutely certain about that belief. Before we trace Descartes's journey through skeptical doubt, see if you can anticipate the path he will take by working through the next thought experiment.

THOUGHT EXPERIMENT

Skeptical Doubt

Use your imagination to see if you can find a way to doubt the truth of each of the following statements. In other words, try to conceive of a set of circumstances (no matter how improbable) that would cause your belief in the truth of each statement to be mistaken.

1. Lemons are yellow.
2. The moon is much farther away from me than the tops of the trees are.
3. I am (fill in your age) years old.
4. American astronauts have walked on the moon.
5. I am now reading a book.
6. This room is filled with light.
7. $2 + 3 = 5$
8. This page has four edges.
9. I am now doubting.
10. I exist.

Were you able to find possible grounds for doubting any of these statements? Were you able to doubt all of them? Compare your answers with Descartes's in the following readings.

Descartes carried out his project of philosophical demolition and reconstruction in a work called *Meditations on First Philosophy*. This work consisted of six meditations that traced his journey from skeptical doubt to absolute certainty. He opens his book with the resolution to critically examine all his opinions.

FROM RENÉ DESCARTES

Meditations on First Philosophy[6]

Some years ago I was struck by the large number of falsehoods that I had accepted as true in my childhood, and by the highly doubtful nature of the whole edifice that I had subsequently based on them. I realized that it was necessary, once in the course of my life, to demolish everything completely and start again right from the foundations if I wanted to establish anything at all in the sciences that was stable and likely to last. But the task looked an enormous one, and I began to wait until I should reach a mature enough age to ensure that no subsequent time of life would be more suitable for tackling such inquiries. This led me to put the project off for so long that I would now be to blame if by pondering over it any further I wasted the time still left for carrying it out. So today I have expressly rid my mind of all worries and arranged for myself a clear stretch of free time. I am here quite alone, and at last I will devote myself sincerely and without reservation to the general demolition of my opinions.

STOP AND THINK

What do you think of Descartes's radical program for revising his belief system? The following questions will help you formulate your response.

- What are some beliefs that you once held that you abandoned in recent years?
- What factors caused you to reject those beliefs?
- What are the psychological (and other) advantages of simply hanging on tenaciously to your beliefs and not raising any questions about them?
- Do you agree or disagree with Descartes that it is better to examine and question your beliefs? Why?

When Descartes finds that he can doubt a belief, he does not mean that he has reasons to believe it is false, merely that it is *possible* for it to be false. If he discovers the possibility of falsity, he will neither continue to embrace the belief nor disbelieve it; instead, he will suspend judgment concerning it.

- In the next passage, Descartes realizes that it would be impossible to examine all his beliefs one by one. What alternative strategy does he employ?

But to accomplish this, it will not be necessary for me to show that all my opinions are false, which is something I could perhaps never manage. Reason now leads me to think that I should hold back my assent from opinions which are not completely certain and indubitable just as carefully as I do from those which are patently false. So, for the purpose of rejecting all my opinions, it will be enough if I find in each of them at least some reason for doubt. And to do this I will not need to run through them all individually, which would be an endless task. Once the foundations of a building are undermined, anything built on them collapses of its own accord; so I will go straight for the basic principles on which all my former beliefs rested.

As the first step of his methodological skepticism, Descartes examines his *general sense experiences* (such as statements 1 and 2 in the previous thought experiment). Our senses are imperfect instruments and can be led astray by optical illusions or other causes of mistaken judgments. Hence, they cannot provide a indubitable base on which to build our knowledge. However, having said this, are there any sense experiences that are so vivid that they can provide us with certainty?

Whatever I have up till now accepted as most true I have acquired either from the senses or through the senses. But from time to time I have found that the senses deceive, and it is prudent never to trust completely those who have deceived us even once.

Yet although the senses occasionally deceive us with respect to objects which are very small or in the distance, there are many other beliefs about which doubt is quite impossible, even though they are derived from the senses—for example, that I am here, sitting by the fire, wearing a winter dressing-gown, holding this piece of paper in my hands, and so on. Again, how could it be denied that these hands or this whole body are mine? Unless perhaps I were to liken myself to madmen, whose brains are so damaged by the persistent vapours of melancholia that they firmly maintain they are kings when they are paupers, or say they are dressed in purple when they are naked, or that their heads are made of earthenware, or that they are pumpkins, or made of glass. But such people are insane, and I would be thought equally mad if I took anything from them as a model for myself.

 STOP AND THINK

Think of some times when your senses deceived you. What was it like to find out you were led into error? Do you agree with Descartes that a past deception makes it prudent never to completely trust your senses again?

You may find yourself agreeing with Descartes that while you have been deceived by your senses on some occasions, other sense experiences seem so real that one would think only a lunatic would doubt them. For example, it would be hard to doubt your belief that you are now surrounded by various real, physical objects (such as books, chairs, a floor). However, in the next passage, Descartes finds it possible to doubt even these sorts of beliefs.

- Can you guess Descartes's reason for doubting these sorts of *vivid sense experiences?*

A brilliant piece of reasoning! As if I were not a man who sleeps at night, and regularly has all the same experiences while asleep as madmen do when awake—indeed sometimes even more improbable ones. How often, asleep at night, am I convinced of just such familiar events—that I am here in my dressing-gown, sitting by the fire—when in fact I am lying undressed in bed! Yet at the moment my eyes are certainly wide awake when I look at this piece of paper; I shake my head and it is not asleep; as I stretch out and feel my hand I do so deliberately, and I know what I am doing. All this would not happen with such distinctness to someone asleep. Indeed! As if I did not remember other occasions when I have been tricked by exactly similar thoughts while asleep! As I think about this more carefully, I see plainly that there are never any sure signs by means of which being awake can be distinguished from being asleep. The result is that I begin to feel dazed, and this very feeling only reinforces the notion that I may be asleep.

At this point, Descartes's doubts become deeper and more severe. By thinking of his experiences in dreams he came up with a way to doubt the contents of his current experience. When Descartes wrote the previous passage, he was not claiming that he actually was dreaming, but merely that dreams can be so real that he had no way of knowing if he was dreaming or awake.

Even though dreams can confuse us about where we are and what we are doing, the *simple truths of arithmetic and geometry* seem to elude these doubts (statements 7 and 8 in the previous thought experiment).

Arithmetic, geometry and other subjects of this kind, which deal only with the simplest and most general things, regardless of whether they really exist in nature or not, contain something certain and indubitable. For whether I am awake or asleep, two and three added together are five, and a square has no more than four sides. It seems impossible that such transparent truths should incur any suspicion of being false.

So, has Descartes finally found his bedrock of certainty? Unfortunately, he has not, for he finds a reason to doubt even mathematical truths. At the end of *Meditation I,* Descartes stretches his imagination to come up with a universal belief falsifier that would make it possible to be mistaken even about seemingly obvious truths.

> I will suppose therefore that . . . some malicious demon of the utmost power and cunning has employed all his energies in order to deceive me. I shall think that the sky, the air, the earth, colours, shapes, sounds and all external things are merely the delusions of dreams which he has devised to ensnare my judgement. I shall consider myself as not having hands or eyes, or flesh, or blood or senses, but as falsely believing that I have all these things.

Once again, Descartes did not necessarily believe that such an evil demon exists but merely that its existence is logically possible. If the demon is possible, then it is possible that $2 + 3 = 17\frac{1}{2}$ (contrary to what we and Descartes believe), and it is possible that we and Descartes do not have bodies but that our minds are deluded into thinking we do. For example, a recent series of popular horror films were based on the idea of an evil being who manipulates the dreams and minds of his victims. We could construct a nonsupernatural version of the demon hypothesis by considering the story of Ludwig discussed at the beginning of the previous section. We could also imagine we are being victimized by a malicious psychologist who has injected us with a hallucinatory drug or that we are under the spell of a very skillful hypnotist. Hence, the deceiver hypothesis seems to be conceivable.

The End of Doubt

Descartes had hoped to use this method of doubt to distinguish beliefs that were certain from those that could be doubted. But now he seems to be overwhelmed by a flood of skeptical doubt from which he cannot recover. Ironically, at this point Descartes finds a lifeboat of certainty within his sea of doubt.

- Can you anticipate how Descartes will find certainty at this point?

 FROM RENÉ DESCARTES
Meditations on First Philosophy[7]

So serious are the doubts into which I have been thrown as a result of yesterday's meditation that I can neither put them out of my mind nor see any way of resolving them. It feels as if I have fallen unexpectedly into a deep whirlpool which tumbles me around so that I can neither stand on the bottom nor swim up to the top. Nevertheless I will make an effort and once more attempt the same path which I started on yesterday. Anything which admits of the slightest doubt I will set aside just as if I had found it to be wholly false; and I will proceed in this way until I recognize something certain, or, if nothing else, until I at least recognize for certain that there is no certainty. Archimedes used to demand just one firm and immovable point in order to shift the entire earth; so I too can hope for great things if I manage to find just one thing, however slight, that is certain and unshakeable.

I will suppose then, that everything I see is spurious. I will believe that my memory tells me lies, and that none of the things that it reports ever happened. I have no senses. Body, shape, extension, movement and place are chimeras. So what remains true? Perhaps just the one fact that nothing is certain. . . .

I have convinced myself that there is absolutely nothing in the world, no sky, no earth, no minds, no bodies. Does it now follow that I too do not exist? No: if I convinced myself of something then I certainly existed. But there is a deceiver of supreme power and cunning who is deliberately and constantly deceiving me. In that case I too undoubtedly exist, if he is deceiving me; and let him deceive me as much as he can, he will never bring it about that I am nothing so long as I think that I am something. So after considering everything very thoroughly, I must finally conclude that this proposition, *I am, I exist,* is necessarily true whenever it is put forward by me or conceived in my mind.

Descartes's great discovery is that if he tries to doubt that he is doubting, then he is necessarily confirming the fact that he is doubting. Even the evil deceiver could not make him mistaken about this. Furthermore, if doubting or deception is occurring, *someone* has to do the doubting and be the victim of deception. None of this doubting could take place unless Descartes existed. Hence, Descartes's method of doubt led him to the bedrock certainty of the belief that "*I am, I exist.*" In other writings, Descartes expressed this certitude as *cogito ergo sum,* or "I think, therefore I am."

 STOP AND THINK

Review your responses to statements 9 and 10 of the previous thought experiment. Did you, like Descartes, have trouble doubting the fact that you were doubting or that you existed?

Obviously, if the only thing he was certain about was his own existence, Descartes had not gotten very far beyond total skepticism. In a later section on rationalism, however, we will see how Descartes attempts to build on this foundation to recover many of his former beliefs, but this time to acquire them in the form of genuine knowledge (true justified beliefs). My purpose for discussing Descartes here was to focus on the skeptical arguments that served as the first step in his project of reconstructing his belief system. Our next historical trail blazer is David Hume, one of the most radical skeptics of all time. Among other things, Hume will raise doubts as to whether it is possible for Descartes or anyone to escape the skeptical doubts Descartes raised.

DAVID HUME (1711–1776)

Hume's Life

David Hume is considered to be one of the greatest skeptics of all time. Even those philosophers who do not accept his conclusions admire him for the rigorous consistency of his reasoning.

David Hume was born in Edinburgh, Scotland, into a Calvinist family of modest means. He attended Edinburgh University where he studied the standard subjects of classics, mathematics, science, and philosophy. He went on to publish a number of important works on human nature, the theory of knowledge, religion, and morality. However, his skeptical and religious opinions were too controversial for the people of that time and he was never able to obtain an academic position. He was first rejected for a position in ethics at Edinburgh University in 1745. (To rectify their oversight, the philosophy department there is now housed in a building named after him.) Twelve years later, he was also rejected for an academic position at the University of Glasgow.

DAVID HUME
(1711–1776)

His scandalous reputation was further enhanced by his *Natural History of Religion* released in 1757. It was a less than sympathetic account of the origins of the religious impulse in human experience. Learning from his previous experiences and having a desire "to live quietly and keep remote from all clamour," when Hume finished his *Dialogues Concerning Natural Religion,* he requested that it not be published until after his death. It has since become a classic in the philosophy of religion.

Although his philosophy was filled with the hard edges of skepticism, Hume was actually a kind and gentle soul in his personal relationships. His friends loved to call him "St. David," and as a result, the street on which he lived is still called St. David Street today.

Hume's Skeptical Arguments

Throughout his writings, Hume forcefully argued for skepticism by using his wrecking-ball logic against all our most fundamental and taken-for-granted beliefs. Descartes began his quest for knowledge with the assumption that if he had rational certainty concerning his beliefs, he necessarily had knowledge, and if he did not have certainty, he did not have knowledge. Hume began with the same assumption. Where they differ is that Descartes finally believed that there were a number of things of which he could be certain. However, Hume doubted whether Descartes or anyone could be certain about these things. Hence, lacking certainty, Hume believed we lacked knowledge.

Hume was an empiricist, for he believed that all knowledge about the world comes through experience. The contents of consciousness are what he calls *perceptions.* Perceptions include our original experiences, which he labels *impressions.* There are two kinds of impressions. First, there are sense data (such as visual data, sounds, odors, tastes, and tactile data). Second, we also have impressions of the "internal" world composed of the contents of our psychological experiences. Hence, Hume defines impressions as "all our more lively perceptions, when we hear, or see, or feel, or love, or hate, or desire, or will."[8] Perceptions also include what he calls *ideas,* or the contents of our memories and imagination. Obviously, our impressions are more vivid and trustworthy than the copies of them we find in our ideas. For an idea to have any meaning or legitimacy, it must be traced back to our original impressions. From this starting point, Hume drives empiricism to a radical extreme. His basic skeptical argument is: If all we know are the contents of experience, how can we know anything about what lies outside our experience?

 STOP AND THINK

Think about the similarities and differences between (1) this book and (2) all your sense experiences of this book. Can you do it? Apparently not, because you can never leap outside your experience of the book to compare it with the book itself. How, then, do you know that your experiences of the book really do correspond to the object outside your experience?

In a series of devastating arguments, Hume examines what we can know about the world. However, from the limited fund of our sense experience, Hume contends, we can learn nothing about what lies outside the subjective contents found within our experiences. According to Hume, most of our knowledge about the world is based on our understanding of causes and effects. But our ability to infer causal connections between events assumes the principle of induction. The **principle of induction** could be summarized as the assumption that "the future will be like the past." This principle requires belief in the **uniformity of nature,** or the thesis that the laws of nature that have been true thus far will continue to be true tomorrow. But how do we know that the uniformity of nature is true? As you will see, Hume argues that just because we have discovered certain things to hold true in the past does not make it logically necessary that they will be true in the future.

principle of induction the assumption that the future will be like the past

uniformity of nature the thesis that the laws of nature that have been true thus far will continue to be true tomorrow

 FROM DAVID HUME

An Enquiry Concerning Human Understanding (1)[9]

All reasonings concerning matter of fact seem to be founded on the relation of *Cause and Effect.* . . . A man finding a watch or any other machine in a desert island, would conclude that there had once been men in that island. All our reasonings concerning fact are of the same nature. And here it is constantly supposed that there is a connexion between the present fact and that which is inferred from it. Were there nothing to bind them together, the inference would be entirely precarious. The hearing of an articulate voice and rational discourse in the dark assures us of the presence of some person: Why? because these are the effects of the human make and fabric, and closely connected with it. If we anatomize all the other reasonings of this nature, we shall find that they are founded on the relation of cause and effect, and that this relation is either near or remote, direct or collateral. Heat and light are collateral effects of fire, and the one effect may justly be inferred from the other.

The assumption that some events cause other events is central to our daily life as well as to modern science. If you suddenly feel a piercing pain in your foot, you will look around to find its cause. If you find that you stepped on a tack, you will understand why you felt the pain. The question now is, "How do we arrive at our knowledge of the relation between particular causes and effects?" In the next passage, find the answers to the following questions.

- What judgment do we make when we find that particular objects are "constantly conjoined" in experience?
- What would someone like the biblical Adam originally know about the world?
- If you had no experience with the physical world, what are some possible guesses you might make concerning the effect of two billiard balls colliding?
- Why does Hume say "every effect is a distinct event from its cause"? What are the implications of this statement?

Note: throughout this and subsequent passages, the word *a priori* means "prior to experience."

If we would satisfy ourselves, therefore, concerning the nature of that evidence, which assures us of matters of fact, we must enquire how we arrive at the knowledge of cause and effect.

I shall venture to affirm, as a general proposition, which admits of no exception, that the knowledge of this relation . . . arises entirely from experience, when we find that any particular objects are constantly conjoined with each other. Let an object be presented to a man of ever so strong natural reason and abilities; if that object be entirely new to him, he will not be able, by the most accurate examination of its sensible qualities, to discover any of its causes or effects. Adam, though his rational faculties be supposed, at the very first, entirely perfect, could not have inferred from the fluidity and transparency of water that it would suffocate him, or from the light and warmth of fire that it would consume him. No object ever discovers, by the qualities which appear to the senses, either the causes which produced it, or the effects which will arise from it; nor can our reason, unassisted by experience, ever draw any inference concerning real existence and matter of fact. . . .

We fancy, that were we brought on a sudden into this world, we could at first have inferred that one Billiard-ball would communicate motion to another upon impulse; and that we needed not to have waited for the event, in order to pronounce with certainty concerning it. Such is the influence of custom, that, where it is strongest, it not only covers our natural ignorance, but even conceals itself, and seems not to take place, merely because it is found in the highest degree.

But to convince us that all the laws of nature, and all the operations of bodies without exception, are known only by experience, the following reflections may, perhaps, suffice. Were any object presented to us, and were we required to pronounce concerning the effect, which will result from it, without consulting past observation; after what manner, I beseech you, must the mind proceed in this operation? It must invent or imagine some event, which it ascribes to the object as its effect; and it is plain that this invention must be entirely arbitrary. The mind can never possibly find the effect in the supposed cause, by the most accurate scrutiny and examination. For the effect is totally different from the cause, and consequently can never be discovered in it. Motion in the second Billiard-ball is a quite distinct event from motion in the first; nor is there anything in the one to suggest the smallest hint of the other. A stone or piece of metal raised into the air, and left without any support, immediately falls: but to consider the matter *a priori,* is there anything we discover in this situation which can beget the idea of a downward, rather than an upward, or any other motion, in the stone or metal?

And as the first imagination or invention of a particular effect, in all natural operations, is arbitrary, where we consult not experience; so must we also esteem the supposed tie or connexion between the cause and effect, which binds them together, and renders it impossible that any other effect could result from the operation of that cause. When I see, for instance, a Billiard-ball moving in a straight line towards another; even suppose motion in the second ball should by accident be suggested to me, as the result of their contact or impulse; may I not conceive, that a hundred different events might as well follow from that cause? May not both these balls remain at absolute rest? May not the first ball return in a straight line, or leap off from the second in any line or direction? All these suppositions are consistent and conceivable. Why then should we give the preference to one, which is no more consistent or conceivable than the rest? All our reasonings a priori will never be able to show us any foundation for this preference.

In a word, then, every effect is a distinct event from its cause. It could not, therefore, be discovered in the cause, and the first invention or conception of it, a priori, must be entirely arbitrary. And even after it is suggested, the conjunction of it with the cause must appear equally arbitrary; since there are always many other effects, which, to reason, must seem fully as consistent and natural. In vain, therefore, should we pretend to determine any single event, or infer any cause or effect, without the assistance of observation and experience.

Hume has argued that causes and effects are distinct events and the only reason we connect a particular cause with a particular effect is because the two have been "constantly conjoined" in our experience. In our past experience, for example, whenever a flame touched gunpowder, an explosion resulted. We expect that this result will be true in the future because we trust the principle of induction and believe that "the future will be like the past." But what grounds do we have for supposing this belief to be true? As you read the next passage, keep the following questions in mind.

- According to Hume, what do we always presume? Note: "sensible qualities" refers to the properties of an object that we experience (such as the red color of an apple) and "secret powers" refers to the capacity within an object to have causal effects.
- Why does Hume think that past experience cannot give us knowledge of the future?
- What two propositions are completely different, according to Hume? Do you agree?

FROM DAVID HUME
An Enquiry Concerning Human Understanding (2)[10]

We always presume, when we see like sensible qualities, that they have like secret powers, and expect that effects, similar to those which we have experienced, will follow from them. . . . It is allowed on all hands that there is no known connexion between the sensible qualities and the secret powers; and consequently, that the mind is not led to form such a conclusion concerning their constant and regular conjunction, by anything which it knows of their nature. As to past *experience,* it can be allowed to give *direct* and *certain* information of those precise objects only, and that precise period of time, which fell under its cognizance: but why this experience should be extended to future times, and to other objects, which for aught we know, may be only in appearance similar; this is the main question on which I would insist. The bread, which I formerly ate, nourished me; that is, a body of such sensible qualities was, at that time, endued with such secret powers: but does it follow, that other bread must also nourish me at another time, and that like sensible qualities must always be attended with like secret powers? The consequence seems nowise necessary. At least, it must be acknowledged that there is here a consequence drawn by the mind; that there is a certain step taken; a process of thought, and an inference, which wants to be explained. These two propositions are far from being the same: *I have found that such an object has always been attended with such an effect, and I foresee, that other objects, which are, in appearance, similar, will be attended with similar effects.* I shall allow, if you please, that the one proposition may justly be inferred from the other: I know, in fact, that it always is inferred. But if you insist that the inference is made by a chain of reasoning, I desire you to produce that reasoning. The connexion between these propositions is not intuitive.

How do you know that if you touch a flame right now, you will experience pain? How do you know that if you taste sugar, it will be sweet? The answer is probably found in the two propositions Hume mentions in the previous passage. You probably are reasoning in this way: (1) *In the past, I have found that fire causes pain and sugar is sweet;* therefore, (2) *when I encounter similar examples of fire or sugar, their effects will be similar to the past cases.* Statement 1 is certainly true, but does it provide irrefutable evidence for statement 2? To get from statement 1 to statement 2 you need the following intermediate step: (1a) *The future always will be like the past.* But how do you know statement 1a is true? Is it possible to prove the truth of this statement?

- Why can't we simply argue in the following way: "We know that the future will be like the past because our past experience shows that events always follow this rule"?
- In what way is appealing to past experience to justify the principle of induction really arguing in a circle?

For all inferences from experience suppose, as their foundation, that the future will resemble the past, and that similar powers will be conjoined with similar sensible qualities. If there be any suspicion that the course of nature may change, and that the past may be no rule for the future, all experience becomes useless, and can give rise to no inference or conclusion. It is impossible, therefore, that any arguments from experience can prove this resemblance of the past to the future; since all these arguments are founded on the supposition of that resemblance. Let the course of things be allowed hitherto ever so regular; that alone, without some new argument or inference, proves not that, for the future, it will continue so. In vain do you pretend to have learned the nature of bodies from your past experience. Their secret nature, and consequently all their effects and influence, may change, without any change in their sensible qualities. This happens sometimes, and with regard to some objects: Why may it not happen always, and with regard to all objects? What logic, what process or argument secures you against this supposition?

Hume's skepticism even extends to doubts about the existence of the external world. Since Hume's empiricism dictates that all judgments about the world must be grounded in sense impressions, it follows that our belief in the external world must be based on experience. Certainly, we *seem* to have experiences of such objects as chairs, books, and trees that have a continuous and independent existence outside of us. But can we really know that such experiences are connected to an external world?

- In the following passage, why does Hume say we cannot know that there is an external world?

FROM DAVID HUME

An Enquiry Concerning Human Understanding (3)[11]

By what argument can it be proved, that the perceptions of the mind must be caused by external objects, . . . and could not arise either from the energy of the mind itself, . . . or from some other cause still more unknown to us? . . .

It is a question of fact, whether the perceptions of the senses be produced by external objects, resembling them. How shall this question be determined? By experience, surely, as all other questions of a like nature. But here experience is and must be entirely silent. The mind has never anything present to it but the perceptions, and cannot possibly reach any experience of their connexion with objects. The supposition of such a connexion is, therefore, without any foundation in reasoning.

The problem that Hume raises is that impressions are always data that are *internal* to our subjective experience, and hence, we have no data about what is *external* to our experience. We tend to believe in a world that continues to exist apart from our experience because of the repeated experiences of similar impressions throughout time. For example, you believe that this book is the same one that you held yesterday because it looks the same as the previous one and you found it exactly where you left it. But all we can say, based strictly on experience, is that the impressions you are having now are similar to the impressions you had yesterday. To this data, the mind adds the ungrounded hypothesis that even when you were not having impressions of this book, the same entity existed continuously between yesterday and today.

We might be tempted to argue that only by postulating an external world can we explain how our impressions are caused. But as we discussed previously, Hume says that causality is only a relation that *we* impute to two kinds of events that have repeatedly occurred together *within* experience. Hence, we cannot make causal judgments about what lies *outside* of experience. It is important to note that Hume does not actually deny that the external world exists. He agrees that it is a natural and almost unavoidable belief that we have. His point is that our fundamental beliefs are based on psychological habits that carry us far beyond what logic and experience could ever prove to us.

 THOUGHT EXPERIMENT

Humean Doubt

Descartes thought that his mind, or his essential self, could not be doubted because he was directly acquainted with it. Do you think this belief is true? Let's try a Humean experiment. Introspect on your own, conscious experience right now. What do you find? You will probably find visual images, sensations, ideas, moods, and feelings. For example,

(Continued . . .)

Skepticism   **91**

(. . . continued)

you may find you are experiencing the whiteness of this page, the texture and weight of your clothes, the temperature of your room, and the thoughts that are going through your head as well as tiredness, curiosity, perplexity, and other psychological phenomena. Now, describe what is left when you subtract this passing flow of sensations and psychological states. When you ignore the momentary contents of your experience and mental life, do you find a continuous self or mind underlying them? Apart from these temporary psychological states, can the permanent self be an item within experience, or do you just assume that there is a self behind it all?

At this point, Hume has ended up where Descartes initially did in doubting everything external to his mind and its experiences. Does Hume then conclude, with Descartes, that at least he can be certain that he is a continuously existing self? No he doesn't, for even here he finds that our beliefs and assumptions have no foundation, but that they flow through the sieve of his skeptical arguments, leaving nothing behind but doubts. We often hear the popular phrase "I am trying to find myself." But can the self ever be found? What would the self look like if we found it? Answer the following questions as you read Hume's analysis of the self.

- Why can't there be any impression (experience) of the self?
- What does Hume find when he introspects on what he calls "myself"?
- What metaphor does he use to describe the mind?
- How can this metaphor mislead us?

FROM DAVID HUME

A Treatise of Human Nature[12]

There are some philosophers who imagine we are every moment intimately conscious of what we call our SELF; that we feel its existence and its continuance in existence; and are certain, beyond the evidence of a demonstration, both of its perfect identity and simplicity. . . .

Unluckily all these positive assertions are contrary to that very experience which is pleaded for them, nor have we any idea of *self*. . . . For from what impression could this idea be derived? . . . If any impression gives rise to the idea of self, that impression must continue invariably the same, through the whole course of our lives; since self is supposed to exist after that manner. But there is no impression constant and invariable. Pain and pleasure, grief and joy, passions and sensations succeed each other, and never all exist at the same time. It cannot, therefore, be from any of these impressions, or from any other, that the idea of self is derived; and consequently there is no such idea. . . .

For my part, when I enter most intimately into what I call myself, I always stumble on some particular perception or other, of heat or cold, light or shade, love or hatred, pain or pleasure. I never can catch myself at any time without a perception, and never can observe anything but the perception. . . .

The mind is a kind of theater, where several perceptions successively make their appearance, pass, re-pass, glide away, and mingle in an infinite variety of postures and situations. . . . The comparison of the theater must not mislead us. They are the successive perceptions only, that constitute the mind.

In other words, in our experience we only find a flow of psychological contents, but we do not find any mental container (the mind) that persists apart from them. In summary, Hume's skeptical conclusion concerning the self is based on the following argument. If all we can know are sensory impressions or our internal psychological states, then we can never experience the self. First, we cannot experience a self, because it is not something that has a color, shape, sound, odor, taste, or texture. Second, we cannot experience a continuously existing, substantial self, because our psychological states are only momentary phenomena.

Although Hume originally thought that philosophy could provide us with the foundations of all knowledge, his empiricism ended him up in skepticism concerning, among other things, the uniformity of nature, causality, the external world, the self, and God. Given the extent and severity of his skepticism, how did Hume go on living? Hume's answer was simple and can be distilled into two propositions: (1) Reason cannot demonstrate even our most fundamental beliefs; (2) But there is no need to rationally demonstrate our fundamental beliefs for them to be practically useful. For Hume, skepticism is a theoretical position that reminds us to be less dogmatic and more modest and reserved about our beliefs, realizing that they are never completely justified. What saves us from the harsh implications of skepticism and returns us to life is the combination of nature, our gut-level instincts, the powerful demands of practical necessity, and even the distractions of our non-philosophical life.

> Most fortunately it happens, that since reason is incapable of dispelling these clouds, nature herself suffices to that purpose, and cures me of the philosophical melancholy and delirium. . . . I dine, I play a game of backgammon, I converse, and am merry with my friends; and when after three or four hours' amusement, I wou'd return to these speculations, they appear so cold, and strain'd, and ridiculous, that I cannot find in my heart to enter into them any farther.[13]

LOOKING THROUGH THE SKEPTIC'S LENS

1. Human history is replete with wars being waged and people being killed in the name of dogmatic convictions that were allegedly "known" to be true. According to the skeptics, how would their view lead to a more tolerant society?

2. Is it possible to live our lives without knowledge? If knowledge is unattainable, should we just do nothing but curl up and die? Hume would reply that skepticism is simply a reminder of the limitations of reason; it leaves us with a more

modest view of ourselves and our powers. When Hume takes a break from his philosophical speculations and goes about his practical life, he doesn't let his doubts bother him. Is Hume's theory and his practice objectionably inconsistent, or has he shown that a person can be a thoroughgoing skeptic and still be practical and enjoy life?

3. Even though the skeptics claim we cannot have genuine knowledge, could they still claim that some beliefs are more worthy of being embraced than others?

EXAMINING THE STRENGTHS AND WEAKNESSES OF SKEPTICISM

Positive Evaluation

1. Weeding a garden is not sufficient to make flowers grow, but it does do something valuable. In what way could the skeptics be viewed as providing a "philosophical weeding service" by undercutting beliefs that are naively taken for granted?

2. The skeptics are unsettling because they force us to reexamine our most fundamental beliefs. Is it better to live in naive innocence, never questioning anything, or is it sometimes worthwhile to have your beliefs challenged?

Negative Evaluation

1. The skeptics make the following claim: "knowledge is impossible." But isn't this claim itself a knowledge claim that they declare is true? Is the skeptic being inconsistent?

2. The skeptics use the argument from illusion to show that we cannot trust our senses. But could we ever know that there are illusions or that sometimes our senses are deceived unless there were occasions when our senses weren't deceived?

3. Some skeptics would have us believe that it is possible that all our beliefs are false. But would the human race have survived if there was never a correspondence between some of our beliefs and the way reality is constituted? We believe that fire burns, water quenches thirst, vegetables nourish us, and eating sand doesn't. If we didn't have some sort of built-in mechanism orienting us toward true beliefs, how could we be as successful as we are in dealing with reality?

4. Is skepticism liveable? Try yelling to someone who claims to be a skeptic, "Watch out for that falling tree limb!" Why is it that a skeptic will always look up? Think of other ways in which skeptics might demonstrate that they *do* believe they can find out what is true or false about the world.

5. Hume's rigorous empiricism led to skepticism concerning a continuously existing self. He bases this argument on the fact that we do not find anything

enduring within experience, only fleeting, fragmentary sensations. But could we even know this fact if there was no such thing as a continuous self? If we know we are experiencing a succession of loose and separate impressions, as Hume claims, don't we as experiencers have to be something more than a series of loose and separate states ourselves? According to Hume's theory, the self is nothing more than "a bundle or collection of different perceptions, which . . . are in a perpetual flux and movement." But if this theory were true, wouldn't each moment of time be our first conscious experience, and wouldn't we lack awareness of what proceeded it?

6. Is either Descartes's or Hume's demand for absolute certainty unreasonable? Can't we have justified beliefs based on inferences to the best explanation, probability, or practical certainty? Does certainty have to be either 100 percent or 0 percent?

LEADING QUESTIONS: *Rationalism*

1. Why don't mathematicians need laboratories to discover mathematical truths about numbers the way chemists need laboratories to discover chemical truths? How do mathematicians make their discoveries?

2. You know that the following statement is true: "All triangles have angles that add up to 180 degrees." What sort of method do we use to prove that this statement is true? Do we cut out hundreds of paper triangles and measure their angles? Why is it that we do not have to take a survey of numerous triangles to know the truth of this statement? Why do we believe that this property will necessarily be true of every possible triangle even though we can never examine every triangle?

3. Touch your nose. Now touch your ear. Now touch your rights. Why can't you touch or see your rights? Is it because your eyes aren't good enough? Is it because rights do not really exist? Most people believe that every person has basic rights and that entire cultures can be mistaken about what these rights are (think about Nazi Germany). If the judgments we make about human rights are not, in some sense, objective, then your rights are simply what your society decides they are. But if this conclusion is true, how could we ever accuse a society of violating human rights? On the other hand, if we do have basic, intrinsic rights, then they cannot be discovered in sensory experience. Rights have no shape, taste, sound, odor, or color. Is there any other alternative but to say that the truths about human rights are discovered through some sort of rational intuition?

4. You can think about dogs because you have the idea or concept of a dog. But where did your idea of a dog come from? Obviously, you can think about dogs

because you have seen dogs. On the other hand, you can think about unicorns even though (presumably) they do not exist. The reason is that your idea of a unicorn is composed out of the parts of things you *have* experienced, such as horses and horned creatures. Now, what about your idea of perfection? Have you ever found anything in your experience that was absolutely perfect? If everything we experience falls short of perfection in some way, then it seems we could not have derived the idea of perfection from the data of our five senses. How, then, did we ever arrive at the idea of perfection?

SURVEYING THE CASE FOR RATIONALISM

"Seeing is believing"—or so we say. After all, what else but experience could be the basis of our knowledge about reality? Not only is observation the key ingredient in science, but eyewitness testimony is one of the most powerful kinds of evidence in a court of law. It seems that sense experience is the final court of appeal when it comes to deciding what is true and what reality is like. But let's take a second look at this assumption. Do we always base our beliefs on sense experience? I once went to a theater to see the famous illusionist David Copperfield. Throughout the show, objects appeared from nowhere or disappeared before our eyes, people magically changed places, and an assistant was sawed in half and restored. For two full hours the laws of physics took a holiday within the theater.

Those of us in the audience were amazed at what we experienced and had no explanations for it. Nevertheless, we still rejected the testimony of our eyes by thinking, "These things could not have happened. Our senses have been tricked by the magician's skill." Why were we so skeptical when we had witnessed such extraordinary phenomena with our own eyes? The answer is that our reason tells us that "something cannot come from nothing" and "material objects do not vanish into thin air." We will distrust our senses before we will abandon these beliefs. Hence, our reason seems to have veto power over our sense experience. We often trust our reason even in the face of apparently solid, experiential evidence. The rationalists raise this trust in reason into a full-fledged theory of knowledge.

Rationalism is a very influential theory about the source and nature of knowledge. This position may be summarized in terms of the three anchor points of rationalism. As you read through the three points, complete the following tasks. (1) In each case, make sure you understand the point being made and think about how you would explain it in your own words to a friend. (2) Decide whether you agree or disagree with the position. (3) Make sure you can explain the basis for your opinions. (4) Compare your degree of agreement with rationalism with the answers you originally gave on the "What Do I Think?" questionnaire on the problem of knowledge in section 2.0.

THE THREE ANCHOR POINTS OF RATIONALISM

Reason Is the Primary or Most Superior Source of Knowledge about Reality

According to the rationalist, it is through reason that we truly understand the fundamental truths about reality. For example, most rationalists would say the truths in the following lists are some very basic truths about the world that will never change. Although our experience certainly does illustrate most of these beliefs, our experiences always consist of particular, concrete events. Hence, no experiences of seeing, feeling, hearing, tasting, or touching specific objects can tell us that these statements will always be true for every future event we encounter. The rationalist claims that the following statements represent synthetic a priori truths. The truths are synthetic because they do give us genuine knowledge about the world. They are a priori because they can be known apart from experience.

Logical Truths

A and not-A cannot both be true at the same time (where A represents some proposition or claim). This truth is called the law of noncontradiction. (For example, the statement "John is married and John is not married" is necessarily false.)

If the statement X is true and the statement "If X, then Y" is true, then it necessarily follows that the statement "Y" is true.

Mathematical Truths

The area of a triangle will always be one-half the length of the base times its height.

If X is larger than Y and Y is larger than Z, then X is larger than Z.

Metaphysical Truths

Every event has a cause.

An object with contradictory properties cannot exist. (No matter how long we search, we will never find a round square.)

Ethical Principles

Some basic moral obligations are not optional.

It is morally wrong to maliciously torture someone for the fun of it.

Sense Experience Is an Unreliable and Inadequate Route to Knowledge

Rationalists typically emphasize the fact that sense experience is relative, changing, and often illusory. An object will look one way in artificial light and will look different in sunlight. Our eyes seem to see water on the road on a hot day, but the image is merely an optical illusion. The rationalist claims that we need our reason to sort out what is appearance from what is reality. While it is obvious that a rationalist could not get through life without some reliance on sense experience, the rationalist denies that sense experience is the only source of knowledge about reality. Furthermore, experience can only tell us about particular things in the world, it cannot give us universal, foundational truths about reality. Sensory experience can tell me about the properties of *this* ball, but it cannot tell me about the properties of spheres in general. Experience can tell me that when I combine *these* two oranges with *those* two oranges, they add up to four oranges. However, only reason can tell me that two plus two will always equal four, and that this result will be true not only for these oranges, or all oranges, but for *anything* whatsoever.

The Fundamental Truths about the World Can Be Known a Priori: They Are Either Innate or Self-Evident to Our Minds

innate ideas ideas that are inborn; ideas or principles that the mind already contains prior to experience

Innate ideas are ideas that are inborn. They are ideas or principles that the mind already contains prior to experience. The notion of innate ideas is commonly found in rationalistic philosophies, but it is rejected by the empiricists. The theory of innate ideas views the mind like a computer that comes from the factory with numerous programs already loaded on its disk, waiting to be activated. Hence, rationalists say that such ideas as the laws of logic, the concept of justice, or the idea of God are already contained deep within the mind and only need to be brought to the level of conscious awareness. Innate ideas should not be confused with instinct. Instinct is a noncognitive set of mechanical behaviors, such as blinking the eyes when an object approaches them.

The theory of innate ideas is one account of how we can have a priori knowledge. Other rationalists believe that if the mind does not already contain these ideas, they are, at least, either self-evident or natural to the mind and the mind has a natural predisposition to recognize them. For example, Gottfried Leibniz (1646–1716), a German rationalist, compared the mind to a block of marble that contains veins or natural splitting points that allow only one sort of shape to be formed within it. Thus, the mind, like the marble, has an innate structure that results in "inclinations, dispositions, habits, or natural capacities" to think in certain ways. In contrast to this view, John Locke (a British empiricist) said: "There is nothing in the intellect that was not first in the senses." In response, Leibniz tagged the following rationalistic qualification at the end of Locke's formula, "except for the intellect itself."

Obviously, in saying that the mind contains rational ideas or dispositions, the rationalists do not believe a baby is thinking about the theorems of geometry. Instead, they claim that when a person achieves a certain level of cognitive development, he or she will be capable of realizing the self-evident truth of certain ideas. Leibniz pointed out that there is a difference between the mind *containing* rational principles and *being aware* of them. Rationalists give different accounts of how the mind acquired innate ideas in the first place. Socrates and Plato believed that our souls preexisted our current life and received knowledge from a previous form of existence. Theistic rationalists, such as Descartes, tend to believe that God implanted these ideas within us. Others simply claim that these principles or ideas naturally accompany rational minds such as ours.

THE RATIONALISTS' ANSWERS TO THE THREE EPISTEMOLOGICAL QUESTIONS

Section 2.0 contained three questions concerning knowledge: (1) Is knowledge possible? (2) Does reason provide us with knowledge of the world independently of experience? and (3) Does our knowledge represent reality as it really is? While differing on the details, all the rationalists give the same answers to these three questions. First, they all believe that knowledge is possible. Generally, we are able to discern that some opinions are better than others. For example, in the discipline of mathematics some answers are true and some are false. We could not know this fact if obtaining knowledge was impossible. Second, the rationalists agree that only through reason can we find an adequate basis for knowledge. For example, in mathematics and logic we are able through reason alone to arrive at truths that are absolutely certain and necessarily true. Third, rationalists agree that beliefs that are based on reason do represent reality as it truly is. In the following sections, I examine three classical rationalists to see how they illustrate the three anchor points of rationalism and answer the three epistemological questions.

SOCRATES (C. 470–399 B.C.)

In chapter 1, I introduced Socrates, one of the most interesting philosophical characters in history. He walked the streets of Athens in a disheveled toga, questioning everyone he met on topics ranging from philosophy to poetry. Although Socrates' conversations were typically full of banter and wit, underlying them was a serious commitment to some of the most fundamental axioms of rationalism. Specifically, Socrates believed in innate ideas, for he claimed that true knowledge and wisdom lay buried within the soul. Accordingly, he took it as his mission in life to serve as the midwife of ideas, helping others bring those insights into the light of day. For this reason, he denied that he could teach people anything, for a midwife does not give anyone a baby but merely assists in its birth.

In his dialogue the *Meno,* Plato portrays Socrates and his friend Meno examining a dilemma involved in the search for truth. Meno expresses the difficulty this way:

> But how will you look for something when you don't in the least know what it is? How on earth are you going to set up something you don't know as the object of your search? To put it another way, even if you come right up against it, how will you know that what you have found is the thing you didn't know?[14]

Socrates' answer is that we can have knowledge deep within us (innate ideas) but not be aware of it. Hence, gaining knowledge is more like remembering something we had forgotten than it is acquiring new and unfamiliar information. To illustrate this point, Socrates helps a nearby uneducated boy discover the geometrical relationship between the sides of a square and its area. Without ever giving the boy any answers, Socrates asks him a series of insight-provoking questions until the young boy eventually arrives at the answer himself. According to Socrates' version of rationalism, the knowledge was written on the boy's soul in a previous life and lay there sleeping until Socrates awakened it. The following thought experiment provides some insights on why Socrates believes we have innate knowledge.

 THOUGHT EXPERIMENT

Innate Knowledge

Try to give precise and adequate definitions of the terms *justice, love,* and *truth.* Ask some of your friends for their definitions. Compare and critique each other's definitions. It is hard to define such terms, isn't it? We use such terms in our daily discourse, but when put on the spot to define them, we feel as though our formulations fall short of what we are trying to describe. You might say, "I can't define *love,* but I know what it is." If I said that *love* is "using another person for your own advantage," you would reject that definition. Similarly, if I said *justice* is "treating those who have power better than those who are weak," you would not consider my definition an adequate statement of what justice is. So, the question is, How can we (1) use these terms in our conversations, (2) recognize justice, love, and truth when we encounter them, and (3) reject some definitions of these terms as being inadequate if we can't state clearly what the words mean?

Socrates' answer would be that terms such as *justice, love,* and *truth* are different from terms such as *chiliarch,* which only a specialist in Greek military history might know. Socrates would say that the concept of love is written on the soul, but apart from philosophical inquiry we cannot know it explicitly. However, we must have some tacit understanding of love to recognize what is and what is not an example of love and to know which definitions of the term approximate the truth and which are inadequate. Hence, knowledge of these fundamental ideas must be innate and already contained within the human soul.

Socrates' answers to the three epistemological questions should be clear. (1) We are able to distinguish true opinions from false ones, so we must know the standards for making this distinction. (2) These standards could not be derived from experience so they must be unpacked through a rational investigation of the reservoir of all truth—the soul. (3) Since our rational knowledge provides us with information that enables us to deal successfully with the world and our own lives, it must be giving us an accurate picture of reality.

PLATO (c. 428–348 B.C.)

Plato's Life

Plato came from an aristocratic Athenian family who groomed him to become a leading statesman in his society. To this end, he received the best education available in Athens. However, while still a young man, Plato's life took a completely different course as the result of meeting Socrates and becoming his student. When Socrates ran into trouble with the authorities and was put to death in 399, Plato and several other disciples of Socrates fled Athens to escape persecution. Plato roamed the world for several years, seeking wisdom. As his own philosophical thought developed, he began to write his famous series of dialogues as a tribute to Socrates and as an attempt to work out the implications of Socrates' teachings. Eventually, he returned to Athens and started a school of philosophical studies, which could be considered the first university in the Western world. His school was called the Academy because it was located in a grove outside the city wall that was dedicated to the hero Academus. The school was still operating nine hundred years later, but was closed in A.D. 529 by Christian rulers who had no tolerance for this stronghold of pagan thought. Nevertheless, the spirit of inquiry that Plato initiated lives on in education today in our contemporary use of the terms *the Academy* and *academics*.

PLATO
(c. 428–348 B.C.)

It is difficult to neatly separate Socrates' and Plato's thought. Socrates never wrote anything and most of what we know of Socrates comes from Plato's dialogues in which he uses the character of his teacher to present his ideas. A common interpretation is that Plato's earlier writings give us a more or less faithful representation of the historical Socrates. However, as Plato matured philosophically, the philosophical theories in his dialogues begin to expand and blossom. Hence, it is thought that in the later writings, Plato used the voice of Socrates to present distinctively Platonic doctrines. Nevertheless, while Plato gave us one of the most engaging, original, and influential versions of rationalism, his philosophy was always permeated by the spirit of his beloved teacher.

Plato on the Possibility of Knowledge

Plato began his theory of knowledge with an examination of the popular theory that sense experience is the basis of our knowledge (the position we now call empiricism). Because the Sophists of Plato's day based their opinions on sense experience, they were led into relativism and even skepticism. For example, the room can feel too hot to you and too cold to your friend. From examples like this, the Sophists argued that there is no objective truth, for everything is a matter of subjective opinion. However, according to Plato, since the physical world is constantly changing, sense perception gives us only relative and temporary information about changing, particular things. Being a typical rationalist, Plato thought that ultimate knowledge must be objective, unchanging, and universal. Furthermore, he argued that there is a difference between true opinions and knowledge, for our beliefs must be rationally justified to qualify as knowledge. Finally, Plato believed that the object of knowledge must be something that really exists. If sense experience was our only source of information, then Plato would agree with the Sophists that genuine knowledge is not possible. However, he agreed with Socrates that because we can recognize that some opinions are false, we must be capable of having knowledge. Therefore, reason must be able to provide us the knowledge we seek. Before we discuss Plato's version of rationalism, try the following thought experiment, which touches on some Platonic themes.

THOUGHT EXPERIMENT

Reason and Knowledge

1. Where are the multiplication tables? You may be tempted to say that they are in your head and written in books. In one sense, you would be right. But if there were no persons to think about multiplying numbers and all books containing these tables were destroyed, would the laws of mathematics still be true? Would they still, in some sense, exist? We can write down $2 \times 2 = 4$. However, the truths of mathematics are not literally identical to the ink on the page. Instead, the marks we make are simply ways we represent these truths. In what sense do mathematical truths come to us through reason and not through the eyes?

2. Compare the quantity and quality of justice in America's institutions, laws, and practices today with the degree of justice in the era of slavery. List several contemporary nations that exhibit a high degree of justice. List examples of nations that offer very little justice. If we are comparing two people in terms of how closely they resemble Elvis Presley, we know what sort of procedure to use. We hold up a photograph of Elvis and see who matches it the best. But how do you compare two nations in terms of their degree of justice? We can't see justice with our eyes, nor can we measure it with our scientific instruments. There are no "justice scopes" or "justice meters." What is *justice* that we can use it as a standard of comparison? How is it possible for us to know about it?

Plato and the Role of Reason

Do mathematical truths, such as those in the multiplication tables, exist within the mind or do they exist outside the mind? Plato would say both. If mathematical truths exist only in the mind, then why does physical reality conform to these truths? If mathematical truths are only mind-dependent ideas, then why can't we make the truths about triangles be anything we decide them to be? The world of *Alice's Adventures in Wonderland* was created in the mind of Lewis Carroll. He could have made the world's properties be anything he decided. But obviously, we can't make up such rules for the properties of numbers. We don't create these truths, we *discover* them. Thus, Plato would argue, these truths are objective and independent of our minds. But if they are independent of our minds, then they must refer to something that exists in reality. Although the number seven, for example, has objective properties that we discover, these properties are not physical. We do not learn the truths about numbers by seeing, tasting, hearing, smelling, or touching them. From this concept, Plato concludes that the world of mathematics consists of a set of objective, mind-independent truths and a domain of nonphysical reality that we only know through reason.

What about justice? What color is it? How tall is it? How much does it weigh? Clearly, these questions can apply to physical things, but it is meaningless to describe justice in terms of observable properties. Furthermore, no society is perfectly just. Hence, we have never seen an example of perfect justice in human history, only frail, human attempts to approximate it. Because reason can contemplate Justice Itself,* we can evaluate the deficient, limited, degrees of justice found in particular societies. Particular nations come and go and the degree of justice they manifest can rise or fall. But the objects of genuine knowledge such as true Justice or true Circularity are eternal and unchanging standards and objects of knowledge.

In the following passage, Plato uses the character of Socrates to talk about perfect Justice, Beauty, Goodness, and Equality. He points out that we have never seen these standards in our experience of the physical world. For example, no matter how carefully we draw a circle on paper, the points on the drawn circle are not perfectly equal in distance from the center, but in true circles they are. Find out in this reading how Plato answers these questions through the voice of Socrates:

- Are the "equal" things we find in our experience (e.g., two sticks) the same as absolute equality?
- How is it that we can think about the perfect standards of Justice, Beauty, Goodness, and Equality if they are never found in our experience?
- Find the words that complete this sentence: "What we call learning will be _____, and surely we should be right in calling this _____." What does Socrates mean by this statement?
- According to Socrates, are absolute Equality, Goodness, and the rest simply ideas in our minds, or are they realities that exist independently of us?
- How does Socrates use his discussion of what we can know as an argument for the soul's existence in a previous form of life?

FROM PLATO

Phaedo (1)[15]

Well, but there is another thing, Simmias: Is there or is there not an absolute justice?

Assuredly there is.

---

*Following common practice, I capitalize terms such as *Justice Itself* and *Universals* to indicate that Plato gives a special meaning to these terms.

And an absolute beauty and absolute good?

Of course.

But did you ever behold any of them with your eyes?

Certainly not. . . .

And shall we proceed a step further, and affirm that there is such a thing as equality, not of wood with wood, or of stone with stone, but that, over and above this, there is equality in the abstract? Shall we affirm this?

Affirm, yes, and swear to it, replied Simmias, with all the confidence in life.

And do we know the nature of this abstract essence?

To be sure, he said. . . .

And must we not allow that when I or anyone look at any object, and perceive that the object aims at being some other thing, but falls short of, and cannot attain to it—he who makes this observation must have had previous knowledge of that to which, as he says, the other, although similar, was inferior?

Certainly.

And has not this been our case in the matter of equals and of absolute equality?

Precisely.

Then we must have known absolute equality previously to the time when we first saw the material equals, and reflected that all these apparent equals aim at this absolute equality, but fall short of it?

That is true. . . .

Then before we began to see or hear or perceive in any way, we must have had a knowledge of absolute equality, or we could not have referred to that the equals which are derived from the senses—for to that they all aspire, and of that they fall short?

That, Socrates, is certainly to be inferred from the previous statements.

And did we not see and hear and acquire our other senses as soon as we were born?

Certainly.

Then we must have acquired the knowledge of the ideal equal at some time previous to this?

Yes.

That is to say, before we were born, I suppose?

True.

And if we acquired this knowledge before we were born, and were born having it, then we also knew before we were born and at the instant of birth not only equal or the greater or the less, but all other ideas; for we are not speaking only of equality absolute, but of beauty, goodness, justice, holiness, and all which we stamp with the name of essence in the dialectical process, when we ask and answer questions. Of all this we may certainly affirm that we acquired the knowledge before birth?

That is true. . . .

But if the knowledge which we acquired before birth was lost by us at birth, and afterwards by the use of the senses we recovered that which we previously knew, will not that which we call learning be a process of recovering our knowledge, and may not this be rightly termed recollection by us?

Very true. . . .

Then may we not say, Simmias, that if, as we are always repeating, there is an absolute beauty, and goodness, and essence in general, and to this, which is now discovered to be a previous condition of our being, we refer all our sensations, and with this compare them—assuming this to have a prior existence, then our souls must have had a prior existence, but if not, there would be no force in the argument? There can be no doubt that if these absolute ideas existed before we were born, then our souls must have existed before we were born, and if not the ideas, then not the souls.

Yes, Socrates; I am convinced that there is precisely the same necessity for the existence of the soul before birth, and of the essence of which you are speaking: and the argument arrives at a result which happily agrees with my own notion. For there is nothing which to my mind is so evident as that beauty, goodness, and other notions of which you were just now speaking have a most real and absolute existence; and I am satisfied with the proof.

In the passage you just read, Plato builds on the views of his teacher, Socrates, and argues that knowledge of perfect things, such as perfect Justice or absolute Equality, must be innate, for what we find in experience are only imperfect copies of these ideals. How can we know that something approximates, but falls short of, perfect Justice or Equality unless we are already familiar with true Justice or Equality? To use an analogy, you can recognize that someone is imitating Elvis only if you had some previous exposure to the real thing. Plato believed that the knowledge of these perfect ideals was written on the soul in a previous form of existence. Though it is there within us, we do not apprehend this knowledge clearly, because it is as though we have forgotten it. Hence, coming to know, for Plato, is a process of recollection in which we realize at the level of full, conscious awareness what we already possessed in a hazy, tacit manner. Have you ever had the experience of coming to know something for the first time although you felt as though you were unpacking and making explicit something you already understood albeit in a vague and implicit way? Think of some examples in your own experience that are similar to those in the next thought experiment.

 THOUGHT EXPERIMENT

Knowledge and Awareness

Is it possible to know something and not know it? Certainly, we have all had the experience of trying to remember something, and after a great deal of effort, we recover the

(Continued . . .)

(. . . continued)

memory. For this reason, Plato uses the term *recollection* to speak of the process of discovery, which is really a process of *recovery*. Sometimes, this "bringing to birth" of understanding is facilitated by someone who serves as the midwife of our own ideas. How many of the following scenarios have been true in your experience?

- You are struggling to find the solution to a mathematical problem. Suddenly, you have a flash of insight and the solution emerges. The answer was not the result of new information you acquired. Instead, what you already knew came together in a new way.
- You are reading a novel in which a character describes the human situation in a particularly insightful way. You find that these words describe what you have always felt, but until now, you did not have the words to appropriate your own understanding.
- You feel vaguely uneasy about a course of action you are considering. You discuss it with a friend. She does not give advice but merely serves as a sounding board to your own reflections. In the course of this dialogue, your own thinking becomes clarified and your uneasiness is explained. You realize that you had known all along that the action would be wrong, but now you understand why it would be wrong.

Not all rationalists would agree that everything that was discovered in these examples would be cases of innate knowledge, although Socrates, for one, would say that problem solving, discovering the meaning of life, and ethical insights all arise out of innate understanding. Nevertheless, these cases illustrate how you might understand something but not be fully aware of what you know until it comes to the level of explicit awareness.

Plato on Universals and the Knowledge of Reality

Thus far, Plato has argued that there are some things that we could not know about (Justice, Goodness, Equality) if experience was our only source of knowledge. The soul must have somehow acquired knowledge independently of the senses. But what, exactly, are the objects of this special sort of knowledge? In answering this question, Plato builds on the distinction he has made between the here-and-now realm of sense experience and the unchanging realm of rational knowledge. He says that in the world of sense experience we find that particulars fall into a number of stable, universal categories. Without these categories, we could not identify anything nor talk about particulars at all. For example, Tom, André, Maria, and Lakatria are all distinct individuals, yet we can use the universal term *human being* to refer to each of them. In spite of their differences, something about them is the same. Corresponding to each common name (such as "human," "dog," "justice") is a Universal that consists of the essential, common properties of anything within that category. Circular objects (coins, rings, wreathes, planetary orbits) all have the Universal of Circularity in common. Particular objects that are beautiful (roses, seashells, persons, sunsets, paintings) all share the Universal of Beauty. Particulars come into being, change, and pass away but Universals reside in an eternal, unchanging world. The rose grows from a bud, becomes a beautiful flower, and then turns brown and ugly and fades away. Yet the Universal of Beauty (or Beauty Itself) remains eternally the same. As we will see in our discussion of Plato's view of reality (section 3.0), Plato believes that Universals are more than concepts, they are actually the constituents of reality. Hence, in answer to the third epistemological question, Plato believes that knowledge of Universals provides us with knowledge of the fundamental features of reality, which are nonphysical, eternal, and unchanging. The following thought experiment will help you appreciate Plato's emphasis on Universals and universal truth.

 THOUGHT EXPERIMENT

Universals and Universal Truth

Are Universals the basis for all knowledge?

- Have a friend write down a description of you. Have this person make it complete enough that someone who knew you would be likely to recognize that it was a description of you.
- Now, you do the same for your friend.
- Pick out several words in each description and think of someone else they would describe.

Did you find that in trying to describe someone, you had to resort to using universal concepts? Did you also find that every word that was used in the descriptions is a term that also describes other people? How does this exercise illustrate Plato's point that we always think and speak in terms of universals? Do you agree with Plato that universal concepts are the necessary means to make intelligible what we encounter in experience? *Is knowing universal truth more important than being individualistic?*

- What is the answer to 3 + 5 = ?
- Is it wrong to torture people for the fun of it?

Why is it that any rational person would answer these questions by saying "8" and "Yes, torture is wrong"? If someone insisted that the answer to the first question was "11," would we give him or her high marks for uniqueness, individuality, and originality? If someone said "torturing people is fun," would we admire this person's independent thinking? Or, would we consider him or her irrational? If someone sincerely proclaimed that "squares are round" and that "triangles have both three and ten sides," wouldn't we consider this person out of touch with reality? Persons who are insane typically think, speak, and act in ways that are unique, individual, idiosyncratic, and hence, irrational. On the other hand, it seems that the more you and I are rational, the more our thinking will be alike. How do these questions illustrate Plato's point that our ability to understand

(Continued . . .)

(. . . continued)

reality correctly depends on our ability to rise above our individuality and think in ways that are objective and universal?

In the next reading, Plato contrasts the unchanging reality of the Universals known through reason with the world known by the senses.

- What implications does Plato's comparison have for the following topics: the nature of reality; the nature of the soul; the sort of knowledge we should be pursuing; and the meaning of life?

FROM PLATO

Phaedo (2)[16]

Well, but is Cebes equally satisfied? for I must convince him too.

I think, said Simmias, that Cebes is satisfied: although he is the most incredulous of mortals, yet I believe that he is convinced of the existence of the soul before birth. . . .

Very true, Simmias, said Cebes . . .

Socrates said: Then now let us return to the previous discussion. Is that idea or essence, which in the dialectical process we define as essence of true existence—whether essence of equality, beauty, or anything else: are these essences, I say, liable at times to some degree of change? or are they each of them always what they are, having the same simple, self-existent and unchanging forms, and not admitting of variation at all, or in any way, or at any time?

They must be always the same, Socrates, replied Cebes.

And what would you say of the many beautiful [things]—whether men or horses or garments or any other things which may be called equal or beautiful—are they all unchanging and the same always, or quite the reverse? May they not rather be described as almost always changing and hardly ever the same either with themselves or with one another?

The latter, replied Cebes; they are always in a state of change. And these you can touch and see and perceive with the senses, but the unchanging things you can only perceive with the mind—they are invisible and are not seen?

That is very true, he said.

Well, then, he added, let us suppose that there are two sorts of existences, one seen, the other unseen.

Let us suppose them.

And to which class may we say that the body is more alike and akin?

Clearly to the seen: no one can doubt that. . . .

And what do we say of the soul? is that seen or not seen?

Not seen.

Unseen then?

Yes.

Then the soul is more like to the unseen, and the body to the seen?

That is most certain, Socrates.

And were we not saying long ago that the soul when using the body as an instrument of perception, that is to say, when using the sense of sight or hearing or some other sense (for the meaning of perceiving through the body is perceiving through the senses)—were we not saying that the soul too is then dragged by the body into the region of the changeable, and wanders and is confused; the world spins round her, and she is like a drunkard when under their influence?

Very true.

But when returning into herself she reflects; then she passes into the realm of purity, and eternity, and immortality, and unchangeableness, which are kindred, and with them she ever lives, when she is by herself and is not let or hindered; then she ceases from her erring ways, and being in communion with the unchanging is unchanging. And this state of the soul is called wisdom?

That is well and truly said, Socrates, he replied.

STOP AND THINK

Go back over the three anchor points of rationalism. Explain how Plato's thought illustrates each of these points.

Plato's philosophy had an extraordinary influence on Western thought. With some degree of exaggeration, perhaps, the philosopher-historian Alfred North Whitehead has said, "the safest general characterization of the European philosophical tradition is that it consists of a series of footnotes to Plato."[17] The rationalism Plato developed was given a new twist when René Descartes gave birth to modern philosophy in the seventeenth century.

RENÉ DESCARTES

Recall from the section on skepticism that Descartes was a seventeenth-century mathematician, scientist, and philosopher. He is considered the founder of modern rationalism because of his arguments that reason could unlock all the secrets of reality. Descartes began his philosophical journey with the attempt to doubt every one of his beliefs to see if he could find any that were certain beyond any possible doubt. Consequently, he discovered that the one thing he could not doubt was his own existence.

But this bedrock of certainty did not carry him very far. As Descartes said, "I am, then, in the strict sense only a thing that thinks; that is, I am a mind, or intelligence, or intellect, or reason."[18] In other words, the only thing he was certain about was the existence of his mind or consciousness. But wasn't he directly acquainted with the existence of his own body? Descartes did not think so. In our dreams we have the experience of running, eating, swimming, and engaging in all sorts of bodily activities. But the experiences we have of our bodies in dreams are illusory. Hence, at this point, Descartes could not be sure that the "body-like" experiences he was currently having really did correspond to a physical body.

Descartes on the Possibility of Knowledge

Although Descartes was certain he could not be deceived about his own existence, the possibility of a Great Deceiver cast a shadow over all his other beliefs. Unless he could find something external to his mind that would guarantee that the contents of his mind represented reality, there was little hope for having any knowledge other than that of his own existence. Descartes sought this guarantee in an all-powerful, good God. Hence, Descartes says, "As soon as the opportunity arises I must examine whether there is a God, and, if there is, whether he can be a deceiver. For if I do not know this, it seems that I can never be quite certain about anything else."[19] If Descartes could prove that such a God exists, then he could know that knowledge is possible. But notice how limited are the materials Descartes has at his disposal for proving God's existence. He cannot employ an empirical argument based on the nature of the external world, for that is an issue that is still in doubt. So, he must construct a rationalistic argument that reasons only from the contents of his own mind.

Descartes on the Role of Reason

In the following passage from *Meditation III,* Descartes says the "natural light of reason" shows him that (1) something cannot arise from nothing and (2) there must be at least as much reality in the cause as there is in the effect.

- What examples does he use to illustrate each of these principles?
- How does he apply these two principles to the existence of his own ideas?

FROM RENÉ DESCARTES

Meditations on First Philosophy[20]

Now it is manifest by the natural light that there must be at least as much <reality> in the efficient and total cause as in the effect of that cause. For where, I ask, could the effect get its reality from, if not from the cause? And how could the

Spotlight on the Phantom Limb

Is it crazy for Descartes to worry about whether he has a body? Descartes was familiar with a phenomenon known as the "phantom limb." Someone who has had a leg amputated often feels itching in the missing foot. By habit, the person will reach down to scratch it, only to be reminded that the foot is no longer there! Apparently, the severed nerves in the stump send pain messages to the brain, which the brain mistakenly interprets as coming from the missing foot. If a person can experience a foot that no longer exists, it seemed logical to Descartes that he could not rule out the possibility that his mind was experiencing a "phantom body."

cause give it to the effect unless it possessed it? It follows from this both that something cannot arise from nothing, and also that what is more perfect—that is, contains in itself more reality—cannot arise from what is less perfect. . . . A stone, for example, which previously did not exist, cannot begin to exist unless it is produced by something which contains . . . everything to be found in the stone; similarly, heat cannot be produced in an object which was not previously hot, except by something of at least the same order <degree or kind> of perfection as heat, and so on. But it is also true that the *idea* of heat, or of a stone, cannot exist in me unless it is put there by some cause which contains at least as much reality as I conceive to be in the heat or in the stone. . . . For if we suppose that an idea contains something which was not in its cause, it must have got this from nothing; yet the mode of being by which a thing exists objectively <or representatively> in the intellect by way of an idea, imperfect though it may be, is certainly not nothing, and so it cannot come from nothing. . . .

. . . So it is clear to me, by the natural light, that the ideas in me are like <pictures, or> images which can easily fall short of the perfection of the things from which they are taken, but which cannot contain anything greater or more perfect.

The longer and more carefully I examine all these points, the more clearly and distinctly I recognize their truth. But what is my conclusion to be? If the objective reality of any of my ideas turns out to be so great that I am sure the same reality does not reside in me . . . and hence that I myself cannot be its cause, it will necessarily follow that I am not alone in the world, but that some other thing which is the cause of this idea also exists.

In examining the origins of his own ideas, Descartes concludes that his ideas of physical objects, animals, and other persons could be constructed from the ideas he has of himself, by creatively modifying the materials of his own experience. However, he does not think that he could have invented the idea of an infinite and perfect God. Why not? His reason for this conclusion goes back to the principle that "there must be at least as much <reality> in the . . . cause as in the effect." Pay attention to his discussion of whether the ideas of "infinite" and "perfect" could be derived from his ideas of "finite" and "imperfect" or whether the opposite must necessarily be the case.

So there remains only the idea of God; and I must consider whether there is anything in the idea which could not have originated in myself. By the word 'God' I understand a substance that is infinite, <eternal, immutable,> independent, supremely intelligent, supremely powerful, and which created both myself and everything else (if anything else there be) that exists. All these attributes are such that, the more carefully I concentrate on them, the less possible it seems that they could have originated from me alone. So from what has been said it must be concluded that God necessarily exists.

It is true that I have the idea of substance in me in virtue of the fact that I am a substance; but this would not account for my having the idea of an infinite substance, when I am finite, unless this idea proceeded from some substance which really was infinite.

And I must not think that, just as my conceptions of rest and darkness are arrived at by negating movement and light, so my perception of the infinite is arrived at not by means of a true idea but merely by negating the finite. On the contrary, I clearly understand that there is more reality in an infinite substance than in a finite one, and hence that my perception of the infinite, that is God, is in some way prior to my perception of the finite, that is myself. For how could I understand that I doubted or desired—that is, lacked something—and that I was not wholly perfect, unless there were in me some idea of a more perfect being which enabled me to recognize my own defects by comparison?

Nor can it be said that this idea of God is perhaps materially false and so could have come from nothing . . . On the contrary, it is utterly clear and distinct, and contains in itself more objective reality than any other idea; hence there is no idea which is in itself truer or less liable to be suspected of falsehood. This idea of a supremely perfect and infinite being is, I say, true in the highest degree; for although perhaps one may imagine that such a being does not exist, it cannot be supposed that the idea of such a being represents something unreal . . . The idea is, moreover, utterly clear and distinct; for whatever I clearly and distinctly perceive as being real and true, and implying any perfection, is wholly contained in it. It does not matter that I do not grasp the infinite, or that there are countless additional attributes of God which I cannot in any way grasp, and perhaps cannot even reach in my thought; for it is in the nature of the infinite not to be grasped by a finite being like myself. It is enough that I understand the infinite, and that I judge that all the attributes which I clearly perceive and know to imply some perfection—and perhaps countless others of which I am ignorant—are present in God either formally or eminently. This is enough to make the idea that I have of God the truest and most clear and distinct of all my ideas.

Descartes's argument here is that the ideas of "infinite" and "perfect" could not have come from himself or his experience, because neither he nor anything in his experience are infinite and perfect. Hence, they must have come from a being who has these qualities, namely, God. Ordinarily, the fact that I have certain ideas in my mind does not tell me there is an external reality that corresponds to them. However, Descartes argues that the idea of perfection is unique. If I could not have produced it myself, Descartes says, then "it will necessarily follow that I am not alone in the world, but that some other thing which is the cause of this idea also exists." In a passage in the beginning of *Meditation III* (that was not quoted), Descartes had concluded that the reason that he could be certain about his own existence was that this idea was absolutely clear and distinct. From then on, as illustrated in his discussion of God, if any idea is clear and distinct, he is confident that it also is true.

Descartes has argued that only if there is an infinite and perfect being (God) could Descartes have acquired the ideas of "infinite" and "perfect." The remaining question is how God gave him the idea of God. Here, Descartes illustrates the basic principle of rationalism, which is that an idea must be innate or already in the mind if it cannot be based on anything we have experienced.

Altogether then, it must be concluded that the mere fact that I exist and have within me an idea of a most perfect being, that is, God, provides a very clear proof that God indeed exists.

It only remains for me to examine how I received this idea from God. For I did not acquire it from the senses; it has never come to me unexpectedly, as usually happens with the ideas of things perceivable by the senses, when these things present themselves to the external sense organs—or seem to do so. And it was not invented by me either; for I am plainly unable either to take away anything from it or to add anything to it. The only remaining alternative is that it is innate in me, just as the idea of myself is innate in me.

And indeed it is no surprise that God, in creating me, should have placed this idea in me to be, as it were, the mark of the craftsman stamped on his work.

The argument that Descartes has given us in the previous passages can be summarized in this way:

1. Something cannot be derived from nothing. (In other words, all effects, including ideas, are caused by something.)
2. There must be at least as much reality in the cause as there is in the effect.
3. I have an idea of God (as an infinite and perfect being).
4. The idea of God in my mind is an effect that was caused by something.
5. I am finite and imperfect, and thus I could not be the cause of the idea of an infinite and perfect God.
6. Only an infinite and perfect being could be the cause of such an idea.
7. Therefore, God (an infinite and perfect being) exists.

Originally, Descartes found it possible to doubt something as obvious as $2 + 3 = 5$. But now he embraces the more complex and controversial metaphysical principle that "there must be at least as much <reality> in the efficient and total cause as in the effect," claiming that the "light of nature" makes this principle evident to us. How certain are you of this principle? Why do you have this degree of certainty about it? Do you agree or disagree with Descartes that it is impossible to doubt this principle? Why?

Does Descartes have a problem here? Has he relaxed his standards and failed to carry through his rigorous method of doubt by assuming his principles concerning causality? Is he slipping assumptions into his argument without warrant? What do you think?

Descartes on the Representation of Reality

Having satisfied himself that a perfect God exists, Descartes also knows that this God would not deceive him, for such an action would make God morally imperfect. In *Meditation IV* Descartes considers what progress this knowledge offers him in the area of epistemology. Since God is not malicious or deceptive and has created our cognitive faculties, Descartes is confident that when he uses his reason properly, it cannot fail to lead him to the truth about reality. Any error he falls into is a result of carelessness in reasoning or in allowing his beliefs to go beyond what he can clearly and distinctly know. Having found a rational ground for trusting his sense experience, Descartes is now confident that he can have knowledge of the existence and nature of his body and the external world.

 STOP AND THINK

Go back over the three anchor points of rationalism. Explain how Descartes's thought illustrates each of these points.

 ## LOOKING THROUGH THE RATIONALIST'S LENS

1. In spite of the differences between cultures, many moral principles seem almost universal. For example, the Golden Rule in Christianity states, "Do unto others as you would have them do unto you." In ancient Hebrew thought we find, "Love thy neighbor as thyself." Similarly, in the ancient Chinese writings, Confucius says, "Never do to others what you would not like them to do to you." How would the rationalist explain the fact that many moral principles are universal throughout all cultures?

2. In the American Declaration of Independence, Thomas Jefferson wrote, "We hold these truths to be self-evident, that all men are created equal, that they are

endowed by their Creator with certain unalienable rights, that among these are life, liberty, and the pursuit of happiness." Since "rights" are not something that we can observe with the five senses, how would the rationalist explain our common conviction that people have rights?

3. Most of us are convinced of the truth of this statement: "Every event must have a cause." Even if we are unable to determine the cause of some event, we are convinced that one exists. What is the basis of our certainty about this statement? Just because our experience tells us that *most* events we have examined have had causes, is this observation a sufficient basis for concluding that *all* events will have causes? Since our experience of the world is limited, why are we convinced of the necessity of universal causality? What would a rationalist say about our certainty concerning this metaphysical principle?

4. In our world, grass is green. But we can imagine that the world had turned out differently so that grass was red. Typically, science fiction writers conceive of worlds very different from our own. However, are there any statements that are true about the world that would necessarily have to be true in any conceivable world? Are there any truths about the world that we cannot imagine could have been false? What would a rationalist say?

EXAMINING THE STRENGTHS AND WEAKNESSES OF RATIONALISM

Positive Evaluation

1. Do the rationalists have a trump card in their observation that from a very few intuitively known mathematical axioms, reason can derive a body of theorems that (amazingly) hold true in our exploration of the physical world? How do we account for this correlation between what the mind rationally proves and what we observe in experience?

2. Are the rationalists correct in claiming that without reason, experience would be a kaleidoscope of sights, sounds, tastes, odors, and textures without any intelligibility?

3. How do we know the laws of logic are correct? How could we ever prove the laws of logic, since all proofs assume them? Does the impossibility of proving the laws of logic indicate that we must know certain truths innately before we can gain any knowledge at all?

Negative Evaluation

1. The rationalists claim that the fundamental truths about reality are innate or self-evident to reason. Yet, the rationalists disagree among themselves and give contradictory accounts of the nature of reality, God, the self, and the principles of ethics. For example, Descartes thought that reason points to the existence of the traditional, biblical God. On the other hand, Spinoza, another rationalist, thinks

that pantheism is the only rational view. Pantheism is the position that everything, including physical nature and ourselves, is part of God's being. Does this disagreement undermine the rationalists' claim that reason can give us universal and necessary truths on these issues? How might a rationalist attempt to explain this disagreement?

2. Some ancient and medieval rationalists claimed that the notion of a vacuum was rationally absurd and, hence, that it was impossible for one to exist. As the result of experiments, scientists eventually discovered that vacuums are possible, and we can create nearly perfect vacuums with our technology. Does this discovery cast doubt on the rationalists' claims that reason alone can tell us about reality?

3. Descartes and other rationalists argued that the idea of perfection must be innate because we never discover perfection in our experience. Can you use your imagination to think about the qualities of the perfect baseball player, chess player, lover, rose, and other such ideals? Obviously, we have never experienced a perfect baseball player or any representatives of the other ideals listed. Yet, it seems absurd to suppose that the idea of the perfect baseball player is innate within our minds. Does this exercise suggest (contrary to the rationalists) that we can construct the notion of perfection from the elements of our finite and imperfect experiences?

2.3 EMPIRICISM

 LEADING QUESTIONS: *Empiricism*

1. What does rattlesnake meat taste like? What is the taste of squid, turtle, or ostrich meat? How do seaweed cakes or a chrysanthemum salad taste? Is there any way to answer these questions if you have never had the experience of tasting the food in question? To what degree do these examples suggest that experience is the source of all our knowledge about the world?

2. Suppose you were created just a minute ago. (You can imagine that either God or Dr. Frankenstein brought you into existence.) Imagine that you have all the mental capacity of a normal adult, but since you are newly created, you have not yet had much experience with the world. In looking at a bright dazzling fire, would you have any way of knowing that it produces excruciating pain when you touch it? Without any previous experience, could you look at an ice cube and know that it would be cold?

3. Think about different things that exist in our world, such as a particular object, a group of things, or a person. For example, you could think about the Eiffel Tower, apples, or Abraham Lincoln. In each case, can you imagine the world without this entity? Since the nonexistence of these items is logically possible, how do you know that they exist? Could we know that something either did or did not exist apart from experience? By merely sitting at our desk and reasoning about the

world, would we ever know what it contains? Isn't it experience and not reason that tells us about reality?

SURVEYING THE CASE FOR EMPIRICISM

The empiricists' theory of knowledge, like the rationalist's theory of knowledge, can be formulated in terms of three anchor points. Think about the reasons for your agreement or disagreement with each point. Contrast these three points with the corresponding ones for rationalism to see how the positions differ. After reading this section, consider your responses to the "What Do I Think?" questionnaire on the problem of knowledge in section 2.0. Are there any answers you would now change?

THE THREE ANCHOR POINTS OF EMPIRICISM

The Only Source of Genuine Knowledge Is Sense Experience

The empiricists compare the mind to a blank tablet upon which experience makes its marks. Without experience, they claim, we would lack not only knowledge of the specific features of the world, but also the ability even to conceive of qualities such as colors, odors, textures, sounds, and tastes. For example, if you had no taste buds you could not even conceive what "bitter" might mean. If you had no eyes, the notion of "color" would be without content.

In saying that experience is our source of knowledge, the empiricist believes we have to be content with conclusions that are probable rather than absolutely certain, because most reasoning that is based on sense experience takes the form of inductive arguments.* Sense experience may be incapable of providing the absolute certainty that rationalists demand, but it is all we have to go on, the empiricists say. Why not, therefore, be content with knowledge that is probable and that leads us to successful engagements with the external world? John Locke, the seventeenth-century British empiricist, compared the scope of human knowledge to a light. We may wish the full light of the sun (absolute certainty) by which to see, but we must be content with what light we have. Hence, "the candle that is set up in us shines bright enough for all our purposes. The discoveries we can make with this ought to satisfy us."[21]

Reason Is an Unreliable and Inadequate Route to Knowledge Unless It Is Grounded in the Solid Bedrock of Sense Experience

The empiricists accuse the rationalists of taking fanciful flights of speculation without any empirical data to anchor them to reality. According to the empiricists,

---

*See section 1.2 for a discussion of inductive arguments.

every idea, concept, or term must be tested by tracing it back to an original experience from which it was derived. For example, Hume says that "impressions" (sensory data) are what give our terms (or words) meaning:

> When we entertain, therefore, any suspicion that a philosophical term is employed without any meaning or idea (as is but too frequent), we need but enquire, from what impression is that supposed idea derived? And if it be impossible to assign any, this will serve to confirm our suspicion. By bringing ideas into so clear a light we may reasonably hope to remove all dispute, which may arise, concerning their nature and reality.[22]

So the empiricists insist that both the meaning of our terms as well as the credibility of our beliefs must be subjected to a reality-based empirical test. Apart from experience, all we can do is compare one idea to another. However, it is possible to have a completely coherent, but false, system of ideas. For example, the universe described in George Lucas's "Star Wars" films is a coherent story woven around a series of allegedly historical events. But as coherent as the story may be, it does not describe anything real.

Because reason is not a sufficient guide to truth, the empiricists claim, it is not surprising that the various rationalists offer different and conflicting accounts of the nature of reality, God, and ethics. For example, within the rationalist tradition, Descartes thought that we had free will, but Spinoza said it is rationally necessary that everything is determined. Both Descartes and Leibniz provided rational arguments for the benevolence of God, but Spinoza argued that God was wholly without passions and could not have emotional feelings concerning us.

In spite of their critique of the rationalists' emphasis on reason, even the empiricists recognize the importance of reason in making our experience intelligible. They believe that the primary role that reason plays in the acquisition of knowledge is to organize the data of experience and draw conclusions from it. Nevertheless, contrary to the rationalists, empiricists claim that reason without experience is like a potter without clay or a computer without data. The mind needs something to reason *about* and where would it get this but from experience?

There Is No Evidence of Innate Ideas Within the Mind That Are Known Apart from Experience

The empiricists offer a number of arguments to undermine the hypothesis that there are innate ideas latent within the mind. First, they point out that not everyone possesses these so-called self-evident truths. When we come into the world as infants, the mind is a blank tablet, and experience must teach us what we need to know. For example, Jean Piaget, a developmental psychologist, showed that babies and young children do not know about causality, quantitative relationships, or object permanence. If a quantity of water in a short, wide beaker is poured into a tall, narrow beaker, young children believe that the water has increased in size because it is now "taller." Hence, some of the most basic facts about reality have to be learned through experience. Second, as was mentioned previously, the empiricists point out that the rationalists disagree among themselves concerning what ideas are rational and "innate."

Finally, even if we discover truths that seem to be universally known and that always hold true, these truths can be explained without positing innate ideas. Empiricists would say that such universal truths are either (1) expressions of the relations of our ideas (analytic a priori truths) or (2) generalizations from experience (synthetic a posteriori truths). In no case are there synthetic a priori truths that both tell us about the world and are known apart from experience.

The empiricists who stress alternative 1 claim that the rationalists' certitudes *do* consist of truths that can be known apart from experience, but for that reason, those truths do not tell us about the world. According to this view, the mathematical, logical, or metaphysical statements that the rationalist appeals to are based on definitions or linguistic conventions. For example, you can know a priori that "everything that has a shape has a size," because both properties are included in our definition of a spatial object. Hence, the rationalists' absolutely certain, necessary, and "innate" truths are no more mysterious and no more innate than the analytic statement "all bachelors are single."

The empiricists who emphasize alternative 2 claim that the rationalists' universal truths are really highly probable generalizations from experience. For example, consider the claim "every event has a cause." Rather than being a synthetic a priori truth, the statement really expresses the empirical claim that, in general, whenever something happened, experience has shown us that it had a cause. We then use that experience as a basis for concluding that this statement is likely to be true in every case. Some empiricists would deny that we can ever know that statement to be true. Instead, they interpret "every event has a cause" as a methodological principle such as "It is useful always to look for causes of events."

THE EMPIRICISTS' ANSWERS TO THE THREE EPISTEMOLOGICAL QUESTIONS

Remember once again that our three questions concerning knowledge were (1) Is knowledge possible? (2) Does reason provide us with knowledge of the world independently of experience? and (3) Does our knowledge represent reality as it really is? As we will see, while all the empiricists start from the same three anchor points of empiricism just discussed, they come to different answers to these three questions about knowledge. This discrepancy illustrates the point that philosophy involves not just taking positions on fundamental questions, but also working out the implications of that position. The three classical empiricists we examine—John Locke, George Berkeley, and David Hume—provide us with three different accounts of the implications of empiricism. We examine each philosopher's answers to the three epistemological questions under the headings of (1) the possibility of knowledge, (2) the role of reason, and (3) the representation of reality.

JOHN LOCKE (1632–1704)

Locke's Life

JOHN LOCKE
(1632–1704)

Although the roots of empiricism go back to ancient Greece, it was the English philosopher John Locke who laid the foundations of modern empiricism. A man of many talents and diverse interests, Locke studied theology, natural science, philosophy, and medicine at Oxford University. For about seventeen years, he served as the personal physician and advisor to Lord Ashley (later to become the Earl of Shaftesbury). Locke was active in political affairs, and in addition to holding a number of public offices, he helped draft a constitution for the American Carolinas in 1669.

It is commonly held that the Age of Enlightenment was ushered in with the publication of Locke's seminal work *An Essay Concerning Human Understanding* in 1690. With the possible exception of the Bible, no book was more influential in the eighteenth century than Locke's *Essay*. According to his own account, the idea for the work began when Locke and five or six friends were engaged in a vigorous debate over matters concerning morality and religion. Locke soon realized that these very difficult matters could never be resolved until Locke and his friends first made an assessment of the capabilities and limits of our human understanding. As Locke put it, "If we can find out how far the understanding can extend its view; how far it has faculties to attain certainty; and in what cases it can only judge and guess, we may learn to content ourselves with what is attainable by us in this state."[23]

Locke on the Possibility of Knowledge

Locke thought that it was obvious that experience gives us knowledge that enables us to deal successfully with the world external to our minds. Therefore, Locke gives an affirmative answer to question 1: Is knowledge possible? Knowledge, however, is not something lying out there in the grass; it is located in our minds. So to understand knowledge we have to analyze the contents of our minds and see what they tell us about the world.

According to Locke, the building blocks of all knowledge are what he calls *ideas*. It is important to understand the unique meaning Locke gives to this term because it differs from the meaning it has for us today. He says that an idea is anything that is "the immediate object of perception, thought, or understanding."[24] He offers us a random collection of examples to illustrate what he means by ideas. Ideas are the sorts of things that are expressed by the words "whiteness, hardness, sweetness, thinking, motion, man, elephant, army, drunkenness and others."[25]

Like a chemist analyzing a compound down into its simplest elements, Locke tries to find the basic units composing our knowledge. The most fundamental and original atoms of thought are *simple ideas*. The mind cannot invent a brand-new simple idea or know an idea that it has not experienced. For example, a dictionary will define *yellow* as the color of a ripe lemon. The dictionary can refer you only to the elements of your experience to make the idea clear.

Simple ideas come in two varieties. The first kind consists of *ideas of sensation,* which are the ideas we have of such qualities as yellow, white, heat, cold, soft, hard, bitter, and sweet. The second category of simple ideas are *ideas of reflection,* which are gained from our experience of our own mental operations. This concept is what we today would refer to as knowledge from introspection. Hence, we have ideas of perception, thinking, doubting, believing, reasoning, knowing, and willing as well as of the emotions and other psychological states. Because we can observe the mind at work, we can think about thinking (or any other psychological activity or state).

Like the camera film that receives and records the light that enters through its lens, so the human mind passively receives simple ideas through experience. However, these ideas are single sounds, colors, and other isolated bits of sensation. Where do we get the ideas of unified objects such as books and elephants? Locke believed that although the mind cannot originate simple ideas, it can process them into more *complex ideas.* Complex ideas are combinations of simple ideas that can be treated as unified objects and given their own names. Locke classifies complex ideas according to the three activities of the mind that produce them: compounding, relating, and abstracting. The first sort of complex ideas are formed by *compounding,* or uniting together two or more simple ideas. We can combine several ideas of the same type. For example, we can compound our limited experiences of space to form the idea of immense space spoken of by astronomers. We can also combine several different ideas. The idea we have of an apple is the combination of the simpler ideas of red, round, sweet, and so on.

By *relating* one idea with another, we can come up with complex ideas concerning relationships. For example, the idea of taller could only come about by relating and comparing our ideas of two things. Husband and wife, father and son, bigger and smaller, cause and effect are examples of ideas that are not experienced alone but are derived from observing relations.

Finally, *abstracting* from a series of particular experiences provides us with general ideas. Locke says that we can form the general idea of book by abstracting all the qualities particular books have in common and ignoring their individual distinctions. For example, individual books come in specific colors and sizes, but all books-in-general are rectangular objects containing pages with writing or pictures on them. When we refer to dogs, humans, buildings, or any other groups of things, we are abstracting the common properties found in our experiences of particular individuals.

Locke and the Role of Reason

Concerning the second question, Does reason alone provide us with knowledge of the world? Locke says "no." Locke attacked the notion of innate ideas with the arguments discussed under the third anchor point of empiricism earlier in this section. To Locke, the notion that we could have innate knowledge that we were not aware of was "rubbish" because "no proposition can be said to be in the mind which it never yet knew, which it was never yet conscious of."[26] In contrast to the rationalists' theory that the mind naturally contains certain ideas, Locke proposes this model:

> Let us then suppose the mind to be, as we say, white paper, void of all characters, without any ideas; how comes it to be furnished? Whence comes it by that vast store, which the busy and boundless fancy of man has painted on it with an almost endless variety? Whence has it all the materials of reason and knowledge? To this I answer, in one word, from experience. In that all our knowledge is founded, and from that it ultimately derives itself.[27]

In other words, without experience the mind would have no content. However, once we have some experiences, then reason can process these materials by compounding, relating, and abstracting our ideas to produce more complex ideas. So reason alone cannot give us knowledge apart from experience.

A major dispute between the rationalists and empiricists concerns the origin of our ideas. They would both agree that our idea of "banana" had to come from experiencing bananas. However, what about our idea of perfection? This issue is comparable to the question, Which came first, the chicken or the egg? The rationalists think the idea of perfection is innate within the mind and from this fundamental idea we derive the idea of imperfection. You will recall that one of Descartes's arguments for God was based on the notion that the idea of perfection had to be planted in the mind by a perfect being, since it could not have come from experience. However, Locke says that we first arrive at the concept of imperfection from the things we experience and then imaginatively remove these imperfections until we form the concept of perfection. For example, I am aware that my knowledge of computers is limited. But my understanding is continually growing as my ignorance is replaced with knowledge. Accordingly, I can imagine a being whose knowledge does not have any of the gaps that mine has, and this image would be the concept of perfect knowledge. Hence, from within our experience we can reason about things that we don't experience. Try this Lockean way of arriving at concepts yourself in the following thought experiment.

 THOUGHT EXPERIMENT

The Origin of Ideas

How would Locke give an empirical account of the origin of the following ideas by compounding, relating, and abstracting from the ideas formed through experience?

1. infinity
2. God*
3. moral goodness or evil

*Note that the issue here is not how could we know that God *exists*, but the prior question of how can we entertain the idea of "God" at all and give it *meaning*?

The empiricists think that our idea of infinity, similar to our idea of perfection, can begin with our idea of the finite (drawn from our own, limited experience), from which we derive the idea of infinity. We achieve this concept, Locke says, by imaginatively repeating and compounding our experiences of limited space, duration, and number, continuing this thought process without end. However, he cautions that we can have the idea of the infinity of space (imagining a body moving through space without end), but we cannot actually contain an infinite quantity in our finite minds. Our idea of infinity is more like a pointer to an unlimited quantity rather than the infinite quantity itself. To know the latter in all its fullness would require an infinite mind.

Similarly, we can derive the idea of God by imagining ourselves repeating and endlessly compounding our finite experiences of existence, duration, knowledge, power, wisdom, and all other positive qualities until we arrive at our complex idea of God. When it actually comes to demonstrating that such a being exists, Locke resorts to the traditional empirical evidence presented in the cosmological argument and the argument from design (see chapter 4 on the philosophy of religion).

Finally, Locke thinks that ethics can be put on an empirical foundation. Because we have no direct sensations that correspond to the concepts of good and evil, we must find some other sensations from which these notions may be derived. As is typical of empiricist moral theories, Locke's theory begins with our experiences of pain and pleasure. He says we call "good" whatever tends to cause us pleasure and "evil" anything that tends to produce pain. In this way, experience can teach us that certain types of behavior are morally good (such as keeping promises and preventing harm), because they lead to the most satisfying results. Locke contends that, in spite of all the cultural differences, the moral codes of most cultures have a great number of similarities. This commonality is because morality consists of the wisdom derived from the collective experience of the human race. Experience teaches us that a society based on treachery and deceit will not be a very pleasant place to live, nor is it likely to survive very long. Even though he thought experience can teach us what we need to know about morality, Locke tried to make this view consistent with his Christian beliefs. He believed that God made human experience such that living in conformity with divine law will produce the most satisfying experiences in the long run, both for the individual and for society.

Locke was so convinced of the truth of empiricism that he boldly issued a challenge to his readers to try to prove him wrong. Stated in his own words, the challenge is:

Let any one examine his own thoughts, and thoroughly search into his understanding; and then let him tell me, whether all the original ideas he has there, are any other than of the objects of his senses, or of the operations of his mind. . . . And how great a mass of knowledge soever he imagines to be lodged there, he will, upon taking a strict view, see that he has not any idea in his mind but what one of these two have imprinted.[28]

Locke on the Representation of Reality

The third epistemological question was, Does our knowledge represent reality as it really is? Locke believes it does, but he says we must get clear on what parts of our experience objectively represent reality and what parts only reflect our own subjectivity. His view of objective properties and subjective properties can be made clear by the following thought experiment.

THOUGHT EXPERIMENT

Objective and Subjective Properties

1. Have you found that the perceived color of a piece of clothing changes when you view it by the light of a lightbulb, a neon light, semidarkness, or sunlight? For example, have you ever thought that you were putting on matching socks only to find when you stepped outside that one was black and one was blue?
2. Why doesn't the shape, size, or motion of an object appear to change in different lights?
3. Have you ever disagreed with a friend as to whether the room is too hot or the iced tea too sweet? Why doesn't it make any sense to say one of you is right and the other is mistaken?
4. Hold a cut, raw onion under your nose as you bite into an apple. Does the normal taste of the apple appear to be different under these circumstances?

primary qualities the properties of an object that can be mathematically expressed and scientifically studied, that is, the properties of solidity, extension, shape, motion or rest, and number

secondary qualities the properties of an object that are subjectively perceived, that are the effects the object has on our sense organs, and whose appearances are different from the object that produces them, that is, the properties of color, sound, taste, smell, and texture

These thought experiments illustrate the fact that some properties, such as size, shape, or motion, are constant, whereas other properties, such as color, temperature, or taste, can change from one circumstance to another and are perceived differently by different people. Locke explains this difference by distinguishing between the two kinds of properties that an object may have. Properties that are objective, that are independent of us, and that are part of the makeup of the object itself are called **primary qualities.** The primary qualities of an object are its properties of solidity, extension, shape, motion or rest, and number. In other words, they are the properties that can be mathematically expressed and scientifically studied. Properties that are subjectively perceived, that are the effects the object has on our sense organs, and whose appearances are different from the object that produces them are **secondary qualities.** Secondary qualities are properties of color, sound, taste, smell, and texture. Locke sets out this theory in the following passage.

- In paragraph 12, how does Locke say that external bodies produce ideas of their primary qualities in us?
- In paragraphs 13 through 15, how does he distinguish primary qualities from secondary ones?

 FROM JOHN LOCKE

An Essay Concerning Human Understanding[29]

How Bodies produce Ideas in us. . . .

12. *By motions, external and in our organism.*—If then external objects be not united to our minds when they produce ideas therein; and yet we perceive these *original* qualities in such of them as singly fall under our senses, it is evident that some motion must be thence continued by our nerves, or animal spirits, by some parts of our bodies, to the brains or the seat of sensation, there to produce in our minds the particular ideas we have of them. And since the extension, figure, number, and motion of bodies of an observable bigness, may be perceived at a distance by the sight, it is evident some singly imperceptible bodies must come from them to the eyes, and thereby convey to the brain some motion; which produces these ideas which we have of them in us.

13. *How secondary qualities produce their ideas.*—After the same manner, that the ideas of these original qualities are produced in us, we may conceive that the ideas of *secondary* qualities are also produced, viz. by the operation of insensible particles on our senses. . . . Let us suppose at present that the different motions and figures, bulk and number, of such particles, affecting the several organs of our senses, produce in us those different sensations which we have from the colours and smells of bodies; v.g. that a violet, by the impulse of such insensible particles of matter, of peculiar figures and bulks, and in different degrees and modifications of their motions, causes the ideas of the blue colour, and sweet scent of that flower to be produced in our minds. It being no more impossible to conceive that God should annex such ideas to such motions, with which they have no similitude, than that he should annex the idea of pain to the motion of a piece of steel dividing our flesh, with which that idea hath no resemblance.

14. *They depend on the primary qualities.*—What I have said concerning colours and smells may be understood also of tastes and sounds, and other . . . sensible qualities; which, whatever reality we by mistake attribute to them, are in truth nothing in the objects themselves, but powers to produce various sensations in us; and depend on those primary qualities, viz. bulk, figure, texture, and motion of parts as I have said.

15. *Ideas of primary qualities are resemblances; of secondary, not.* From whence I think it easy to draw this observation,—that the ideas of primary qualities of bodies are resemblances of them, and their patterns do really exist in the bodies themselves, but the ideas produced in us by these secondary qualities have no

resemblance of them at all. There is nothing like our ideas, existing in the bodies themselves. They are, in the bodies we denominate from them, only a power to produce those sensations in us: and what is sweet, blue, or warm in idea, is but the certain bulk, figure, and motion of the insensible parts, in the bodies themselves, which we call so.

- In paragraphs 16 and 17, how does Locke use fire and snow to illustrate the distinction between the two kinds of qualities?

16. *Examples.*—Flame is denominated hot and light; snow, white and cold; and manna, white and sweet, from the ideas they produce in us. Which qualities are commonly thought to be the same in those bodies that those ideas are in us, the one the perfect resemblance of the other, as they are in a mirror, and it would by most men be judged very extravagant if one should say otherwise. And yet he that will consider that the same fire that, at one distance produces in us the sensation of warmth, does, at a nearer approach, produce in us the far different sensation of pain, ought to bethink himself what reason he has to say—that this idea of warmth, which was produced in him by the fire, *is actually in the fire;* and his idea of pain, which the same fire produced in him the same way, is not in the fire. Why are whiteness and coldness in snow, and pain not, when it produces the one and the other idea in us; and can do neither, but by the bulk, figure, number, and motion of its solid parts?

17. *The ideas of the primary alone really exist.*—The particular bulk, number, figure, and motion of the parts of fire or snow are really in them,—whether any one's senses perceive them or no: and therefore they may be called *real* qualities, because they really exist in those bodies. But light, heat, whiteness, or coldness, are no more really in them than sickness or pain is in manna. Take away the sensation of them; let not the eyes see light or colours, nor the ears hear sounds; let the palate not taste, nor the nose smell, and all colours, tastes, odours, and sounds, *as they are such particular ideas,* vanish and cease, and are reduced to their causes, i.e. bulk, figure, and motion of parts.

To return to the third epistemological question, our experience of primary qualities gives us knowledge of reality as it really is, but our experience of secondary qualities registers how the objective world affects our particular sense organs. Hence, we find it easy to agree on the size, number, position, and shape of a glass of ice tea because these are its objective, or primary, qualities. However, we might disagree on whether the tea is too sweet. This disagreement is because sweetness is a secondary quality that is not really in the tea but reflects the subjective ways that the tea affects different taste buds. One result of Locke's view of secondary qualities is that it strips the external world of all those features that artists represent and poets describe. What we have left is the world that science studies, a world of quantifiable, material properties. As we will see, George Berkeley criticizes Locke's distinction and argues that Locke's view leads to some surprising results.

STOP AND THINK

Go back over the three anchor points of empiricism. Explain how Locke's thought illustrates each of these points.

GEORGE BERKELEY (1685–1753)

Berkeley's Life

George Berkeley, Ireland's most famous philosopher, received his education at Trinity College in Dublin. There he was exposed to the philosophies of Descartes and Locke as well as the work of Newton and other leading scientists. In 1710 he was ordained as a priest in the Anglican Church and later became one of its bishops. He traveled to America in an attempt to set up a college for the sons of English planters and the native American Indians. Though his project failed for lack of funding, he had a decisive effect on American education. He provided Yale University with the finest library in America at that time and also donated books to Harvard University. Kings College (later to become Columbia University) was founded with his advice. In a poem, he praised the fresh, new spirit of America and predicted that American civilization would expand all the way to the western coast. As a result, the state of California established a university in a city named after Berkeley.

GEORGE BERKELEY
(1685–1753)

Berkeley on the Possibility of Knowledge and the Role of Reason

With Locke, Berkeley gave affirmative answers to the first two basic questions of epistemology. First, he believed that we do have knowledge. Second, he believed that it was only through experience and not reason that we have any knowledge of reality. However, it will soon be clear that Berkeley differed radically with Locke concerning what sort of reality is revealed to us within experience.

Berkeley began his philosophy where Locke began—with an analysis of experience. Following Locke, he refers to the concrete contents of our experience as ideas. Ideas are such things as the redness of a rose, the coldness of ice, the smell of freshly mown grass, the taste of honey, and the sound of a flute. We also have ideas of our own psychological states and operations because we experience our own willing, doubting, and loving. Thus, ideas are images, feelings, or sense data that are directly present to the mind either in vivid sensory or psychological experiences or in the less vivid presentations of either memory or imagination. Hence, when Berkeley says we have the idea of an apple, he is not referring to an abstract concept but to the experience or memory of the combined ideas (experiences) of roundness, redness, hardness, and sweetness.

Berkeley's Theory of Experience

While agreeing with Locke on these points, Berkeley believed Locke had not been a consistent enough empiricist, and so Berkeley resolved to carry the theory of empiricism to its logical conclusions. In doing so, Berkeley ended up with the rather astonishing position that since (1) all we know is what we find in experience, it follows that (2) we can never know nor even make sense of a material world that allegedly lies outside of our own, private experiences. Read those last two claims over again to get clear on how Berkeley argues from (1) Locke's empiricism to (2) the denial of a world of independently existing matter. Berkeley's philosophy is commonly referred to as *subjective idealism,* although he himself called it *immaterialism.* **Idealism** is a position that maintains that ultimate reality is mental or spiritual in nature. Berkeley's position is known as subjective idealism because he believes reality is made up of many individual minds rather than one cosmic mind. According to Berkeley, reality is nonphysical and everything that exists falls into one of two categories: (1) minds (or spirits) and (2) the ideas they perceive. Hence, Berkeley claims that all the objects we encounter in experience (books, apples, rocks) fall into category (2) and are nothing more than mind-dependent collections of ideas. Berkeley expressed this belief by saying *Esse est percipi,* or "To be is to be perceived." For Berkeley, the only reasonable position possible is that

> all the choir of heaven and furniture of the earth, in a word, all those bodies which compose the mighty frame of the world, have not any subsistence without a mind— that their *being* is to be perceived or known.[30]

Berkeley's goal was made clear in the complete title of his 1710 work: *A Treatise concerning the Principles of Human Knowledge wherein the chief causes of error and difficulty in the Sciences, with the grounds of Scepticism, Atheism and Irreligion, are inquired into.* Even though Berkeley knew that Newton and Locke were Christians, he complained that their science and philosophy paved the way for atheism and skepticism. If nature is made up of particles of matter in motion, following deterministic laws, as Newton claimed, then there is no need to appeal to God to explain events. Similarly, if we can only know our own ideas (experiences), but reality exists apart from them, as Locke claimed, then we can never be sure that our ideas accurately represent reality, leaving us hopelessly mired in skepticism. In contrast, Berkeley argued that our experiences of objects in our environment necessarily come from God and not from matter, thus eliminating atheism. Furthermore, by arguing that there is no external, material reality beyond our ideas, then we are always in direct contact with reality (the contents of our experience) and skepticism has been refuted.

In the opening paragraphs of his *Principles,* Berkeley introduces his claim that empiricism entails that all the objects of experience are mind-dependent.

idealism the position that maintains that ultimate reality is mental or spiritual in nature

- According to Berkeley, what do we mean when we say something "exists"?
- Why is it a contradiction to suppose that houses, mountains, and rivers exist apart from our perception of them?

FROM GEORGE BERKELEY
A Treatise Concerning the Principles of Human Knowledge[31]

1. It is evident to any one who takes a survey of the *objects* of human knowledge, that they are either ideas actually imprinted on the senses, or else such as are perceived by attending to the passions and operations of the mind, or lastly, ideas formed by help of memory and imagination—either compounding, dividing, or barely representing those originally perceived in the aforesaid ways. By sight I have the ideas of light and colors, with their several degrees and variations. By touch I perceive hard and soft, heat and cold, motion and resistance, and of all these more and less either as to quantity or degree. Smelling furnishes me with odors, the palate with tastes, and hearing conveys sounds to the mind in all their variety of tone and composition. And as several of these are observed to accompany each other, they come to be marked by one name, and so to be reputed as one thing. Thus, for example a certain color, taste, smell, figure and consistence having been observed to go together, are accounted one distinct thing signified by the name *"apple"*; other collections of ideas constitute a stone, a tree, a book, and the like sensible things—which as they are pleasing or disagreeable excite the passions of love, hatred, joy, grief, and so forth.

2. But, besides all that endless variety of ideas or objects of knowledge, there is likewise something which knows or perceives them and exercises divers operations, as willing, imagining, remembering, about them. This perceiving, active being is what I call *mind, spirit, soul,* or *myself.* By which words I do not denote any one of my ideas, but a thing entirely distinct from them, wherein they exist or, which is the same thing, whereby they are perceived—for the existence of an idea consists in being perceived.

3. That neither our thoughts, nor passions, nor ideas formed by the imagination, exist without the mind is what everybody will allow. And it seems no less evident that the various sensations or ideas imprinted on the sense, however blended or combined together (that is, whatever objects they compose), cannot exist otherwise than in a mind perceiving them.—I think an intuitive knowledge may be obtained of this by any one that shall attend to what is meant by the term *exists,* when applied to sensible things. The table I write on I say exists, that is, I see and feel it; and if I were out of my study I should say it existed—meaning thereby that if I was in my study I might perceive it, or that some other spirit actually does perceive it. There was an odor, that is, it was smelled, there was a sound, that is, it was heard; a color or figure, and it was perceived by sight or touch. This is all that I can understand by these and the like expressions. For as to what is said of the absolute existence of unthinking things without any relation to

their being perceived, that seems perfectly unintelligible. Their *esse* is *percipi*,* nor is it possible they should have any existence out of the minds or thinking things which perceive them.

4. It is indeed an opinion strangely prevailing amongst men, that houses, mountains, rivers, and in a word, all sensible objects have an existence, natural or real, distinct from their being perceived by the understanding. But, with how great an assurance and acquiescence soever this principle may be entertained in the world, yet whoever shall find in his heart to call it in question may, if I mistake not, perceive it to involve a manifest contradiction. For, what are the forementioned objects but the things we perceive by sense? and what do we perceive besides our own ideas or sensations? And is it not plainly repugnant that any one of these, or any combination of them, should exist unperceived?

Berkeley's argument in the preceding paragraph could be formulated in the following manner:

The Argument from the Mental Dependency of Ideas

1. Sensory objects (houses, mountains, rivers, and so on) are things present to us in sense experience.
2. What is presented to us in sense experience consists solely of our ideas (or sensations).
3. Ideas exist solely in our minds.
4. Therefore, sensible objects exist solely in our minds.

 THOUGHT EXPERIMENT

Mind-Dependent Ideas

Does the Argument from the Mental Dependency of Ideas seem plausible to you? If not, why not? Let's explore Berkeley's line of reasoning further. Pick up a pencil. What are you experiencing? You are probably having visual sensations of a particular color, visual and tactile sensations of an extended length with round or hexagonal sides, and tactile sensations of hardness. Press the point of the pencil into your palm and now you will have the experience of pain associated with the pencil. But where is your pain? Obviously, it is not located out in the external world. Pain is an idea (in Berkeley's sense of the word) or an item within your experience. Yet, this mind-dependent idea is part of your experience of the pencil. But Berkeley would say that all the other properties of the pencil have the same status. The sensations of color, shape, and extension in your experience are just that—items within your experience. In describing the properties of the pencil, you did not refer to anything external to your experience. How could you? If you met Bishop Berkeley, how would you respond to this argument?

---

*Their being is to be perceived.

Berkeley on the Ideas of Matter

By means of multiple, ingenious arguments, Berkeley hammered away at the notion of matter, arguing that it is unintelligible and empty of content. According to him, *matter* is either (1) a misleading term for the collection of sensory experiences we have, such as texture and hardness (in which case it is internal to the mind) or (2) something external to the mind that is without shape, color, odor, taste, or texture. A mind-independent object could not have these qualities since these kinds of sensations are experienced within the mind. But if the objects did not have any such qualities, then it would be a kind of nothingness that we can never experience, know, or imagine.

Berkeley on the Representation of Reality

The third epistemological question was, Does our knowledge represent reality as it really is? On this issue Berkeley and Locke part company. According to Locke, we do not directly experience external objects, but their primary qualities (such as shape and size) produce ideas in us that accurately represent these real properties of the objects. This view is known as **representative realism.** Thus, what appears to us within experience is a trustworthy copy of the objective features of reality. However, Berkeley thought that this view was a dangerous one because it raised the question of how we can know that experience really is telling us what the world outside of our experience is like. Berkeley's position is that we can only know what reality is like if our ideas (the contents of our experience) is the only reality there is to be known. Because our experience presents us with both primary and secondary qualities and because there is no world external to our experience, then primary and secondary qualities must be equally objective and must both be the real properties of things.

In the next set of passages, Berkeley attacks Locke's representative realism (paragraph 8), the distinction between primary and secondary qualities (paragraphs 9 and 10), and argues that it is impossible to know an external world of matter (paragraph 18).

representative realism the view that we do not directly experience external objects, but their primary qualities (such as shape and size) produce ideas in us that accurately represent these real properties of the objects

---

Spotlight on an Attempt to Refute Berkeley

Samuel Johnson, the famous English writer and contemporary of Berkeley's, tried to demonstrate the foolishness of Berkeley's denial of matter by kicking a stone into the air and saying, "I refute him thus!" But what did Johnson show? He showed that he was feeling the experience of hardness and experiencing a round, gray image flying through his visual field. However, as the pain in his toe might have suggested to him, these sensations were internal to his experience and did not provide evidence of a material stone external to his perceptions, a stone to which his perceptions supposedly corresponded.

SPOTLIGHT
on

- What two sorts of reasons does Berkeley give to show that it is impossible for the ideas in our mind to resemble external objects? (paragraph 8)
- Why can we not make a distinction between mind-dependent secondary qualities and external primary qualities? (paragraphs 9 and 10)
- Why can neither sense experience nor reason tell us about matter? (paragraph 18)

8. But, say you, though the ideas themselves do not exist without the mind, yet there may be things like them, whereof they are copies or resemblances, which things exist without the mind in an unthinking substance. I answer, an idea can be like nothing but an idea; a color or figure can be like nothing but another color or figure. If we look but ever so little into our thoughts, we shall find it impossible for us to conceive a likeness except only between our ideas. Again, I ask whether those supposed originals or external things, of which our ideas are the pictures or representations, be themselves perceivable or no? If they are, then they are ideas and we have gained our point; but if you say they are not, I appeal to any one whether it be sense to assert a color is like something which is invisible; hard or soft, like something which is intangible; and so of the rest.

9. Some there are who make a distinction betwixt *primary* and *secondary* qualities. By the former they mean extension, figure, motion, rest, solidity or impenetrability, and number; by the latter they denote all other sensible qualities, as colors, sounds, tastes, and so forth. The ideas we have of these they acknowledge not to be the resemblances of anything existing without the mind, or unperceived, but they will have our ideas of the primary qualities to be patterns or images of things which exist without the mind, in an unthinking substance which they call "matter." By "matter," therefore, we are to understand an inert, senseless substance, in which extension, figure, and motion do actually subsist. But it is evident from what we have already shown that extension, figure, and motion are only ideas existing in the mind, and that an idea can be like nothing but another idea, and that consequently neither they nor their archetypes can exist in an unperceiving substance. Hence, it is plain that the very notion of what is called *matter* or *corporeal substance* involves a contradiction in it.

10. They who assert that figure, motion, and the rest of the primary or original qualities do exist without the mind in unthinking substances, do at the same time acknowledge that colors, sounds, heat, cold, and suchlike secondary qualities, do not—which they tell us are sensations existing in the mind alone, that depend on and are occasioned by the different size, texture, and motion of the minute particles of matter. This they take for an undoubted truth which they can demonstrate beyond all exception. Now, if it be certain that those original qualities are inseparably united with the other sensible qualities, and not, even in thought, capable of being abstracted from them, it plainly follows that they exist only in the mind. But I desire any one to reflect and try whether he can, by any abstraction of thought, conceive the extension and motion of a body without all other sensible qualities. For my own part, I see evidently that it is not in my power to frame an

idea of a body extended and moved, but I must withal give it some color or other sensible quality which is acknowledged to exist only in the mind. In short, extension, figure, and motion, abstracted from all other qualities, are inconceivable. Where therefore the other sensible qualities are, there must these be also, to wit, in the mind and nowhere else. . . .

18. But, though it were possible that solid, figured, movable substances may exist without the mind, corresponding to the ideas we have of bodies, yet how is it possible for us to know this? Either we must know it by sense or by reason. As for our senses, by them we have the knowledge only of our sensations, ideas, or those things that are immediately perceived by sense, call them what you will; but they do not inform us that things exist without the mind, or unperceived, like to those which are perceived. This the materialists themselves acknowledge. It remains therefore that if we have any knowledge at all of external things, it must be by reason, inferring their existence from what is immediately perceived by sense. But what reason can induce us to believe the existence of bodies without the mind, from what we perceive, since the very patrons of matter themselves do not pretend there is any necessary connection betwixt them and our ideas? I say it is granted on all hands (and what happens in dreams, frenzies, and the like, puts it beyond dispute) that it is possible we might be affected with all the ideas we have now, though there were no bodies existing without resembling them. Hence, it is evident the supposition of external bodies is not necessary for producing our ideas; since it is granted they are produced sometimes, and might possibly be produced always in the same order, we see them in at present, without their concurrence.

According to Locke, primary qualities such as shape and extension are objective qualities existing in external objects, whereas secondary qualities such as color are subjective qualities. The difficulty is that because we can't get outside our minds to compare our ideas or experiences with the external world, how can we make this distinction between ideas that do and do not correspond to what is out there? For example, how do you know an apple is round? You know this because the experience of an apple is always the experience of a round, red patch in your visual field. Its roundness and its redness always go together in our experience. Hence, Berkeley argues, our experience of the primary qualities is always inseparable from our experience of the secondary qualities. Since the latter are subjective and mind-dependent (as Locke admits), it follows that the primary qualities are also.

Notice that in paragraph 18 Berkeley attempts to undermine skepticism. He agrees with the skeptic that we can never know if our experiences and ideas correspond with a reality outside our minds. But for that very reason Berkeley questions whether the notion of an externally existing matter is even intelligible, since the notion could never have any content. Instead, he postulates that reality is nothing more than our experiences (ideas) and everything that exists is exactly as it appears to us. If so, then skepticism is defeated, because we are always directly acquainted with the only reality there is.

The Cause of Our Ideas

There remains one, last question: What is the cause of our ideas if it is not an externally existing material world? Obviously, you produce some of your own ideas (your daydreams, for example), but you are not the cause of the sensations of the color, weight, and texture of the book that you are currently experiencing. So, what causes your ideas of the book? In the following passage, find Berkeley's answer to this question and the following ones.

- What is the cause of our sensations, if not matter? When Berkeley refers to "some other will or spirit," who is the "Author" of our ideas; who is he referring to?
- How do we distinguish between the ideas we produce in our imagination and the ideas that are "real things"?
- Without a world of matter, what are scientists discovering when they observe the "laws of nature"?

29. But, whatever power I may have over my own thoughts, I find the ideas actually perceived by Sense have not a like dependence on my will. When in broad daylight I open my eyes, it is not in my power to choose whether I shall see or no, or to determine what particular objects shall present themselves to my view; and so likewise as to the hearing and other senses; the ideas imprinted on them are not creatures of my will. There is therefore some *other* will or spirit that produces them.

30. The ideas of sense are more strong, lively, and distinct than those of the imagination; they have likewise a steadiness, order, and coherence, and are not excited at random, as those which are the effects of human wills often are, but in a regular train or series, the admirable connection whereof sufficiently testifies the wisdom and benevolence of its Author. Now the set rules or established methods wherein the mind we depend on excites in us the ideas of sense, are called the *laws of nature;* and these we learn by experience, which teaches us that such and such ideas are attended with such and such other ideas in the ordinary course of things.

31. This gives us a sort of foresight which enables us to regulate our actions for the benefit of life. And without this we should be eternally at a loss; we could not know how to act anything that might procure us the least pleasure or remove the least pain of sense. That food nourishes, sleep refreshes, and fire warms us; that to sow in the seed-time is the way to reap in the harvest; and in general that to obtain such or such ends, such or such means are conducive—all this we know, not by discovering any necessary connection between our ideas, but only by the observation of the settled laws of nature, without which we should be all in uncertainty and confusion, and a grown man no more know how to manage himself in the affairs of life than an infant just born. . . .

33. The ideas imprinted on the senses by the Author of Nature are called *real things;* and those excited in the imagination being less regular, vivid, and constant,

are more properly termed *ideas,* or *images of things,* which they copy and represent. But then our sensations, be they never so vivid and distinct, are nevertheless ideas, that is, they exist in the mind, or are perceived by it, as truly as the ideas of its own framing. The ideas of sense are allowed to have more reality in them, that is, to be more strong, orderly, and coherent than the creatures of the mind; but this is no argument that they exist without the mind. They are also less dependent on the spirit, or thinking substance which perceives them, in that they are excited by the will of another and more powerful spirit; yet still they are *ideas*; and certainly no idea, whether faint or strong, can exist otherwise than in a mind perceiving it.

According to Berkeley, only a mind can produce ideas. If our minds did not produce the ideas or experiences we encounter, then God's mind must have created them within us. God directly gives us the world of our experience without the intermediate step of external physical matter. Furthermore, God continuously maintains the world in existence, for even if we are not experiencing a particular object, it still exists within God's mind. Descartes worried that a malicious demon might be inserting experiences within his mind that were radically different from the reality that existed outside his mind. Berkeley, however, believed that a benevolent God was producing experiences within our minds and that these experiences are the only reality. Notice that Berkeley is not claiming that, say, the book you are reading does not exist or that it is not real. He is merely analyzing what he thinks it means to say something "exists." Since all our knowledge is derived from experience, then the contents of our experiences are all that can be meaningfully said to exist. This concept is what Berkeley means when he says, "To be is to be perceived."

Berkeley's immaterialism has also eliminated the problem of how the mind relates to the body (a problem I discuss in chapter 3). According to Berkeley, what we call our body is simply a collection of sensations experienced by the mind. Likewise, space is simply a series of visual and tactile sensations. When our visual image of a car looks unusually small, we say "it is far away." When our visual image begins to grow larger, we say "it is coming closer." Berkeley's notion that space (and time) are relative was a precursor to the views of modern physicists such as Albert Einstein.[32]

Knowing that we might consider his position wild and fantastic, Berkeley reassures us that in arguing for immaterialism,

> I do not argue against the existence of any one thing that we can apprehend either by sense or reflection. That the things I see with my eyes and touch with my hands do exist, really exist, I make not the least question. The only thing whose existence we deny is that which philosophers call matter or corporeal substance.[33]

We can still enjoy the coolness of water and the warmth of a fire. The only difference is that we will realize that these experiences are in the form of mental events provided us by God. According to Berkeley, you can reject the theory of an external, mind-independent, physical world and still have a world of real objects within your experience. Furthermore, science is still possible as long as we view it as the recording of regularities within our experiences and the predicting of future experiences based on this view.

STOP AND THINK

Go back over the three anchor points of empiricism. Explain how Berkeley's thought illustrates each of these points.

DAVID HUME

Hume on the Possibility of Knowledge

We encountered David Hume in the section on skepticism. Hume arrived at his skepticism by developing the radical implications of empiricism in directions that even Berkeley was not willing to go. The problem raised by Berkeley's empiricism is that if all we can know are the sensory contents of experience, how can we know spiritual substances such as our own minds, other minds, or even God? Minds as enduring nonphysical substances are not contents within experience as is the sweetness of sugar or the redness of an apple. Certainly, I can experience my own mental operations, such as doubting, believing, or willing. But these operations are temporary items within my stream of consciousness and are not identical with a substantial mind that supposedly underlies them. If we cannot experience our own minds, even less can we experience other minds or God. Hume is more consistent than Berkeley, for he stays within the bounds of experience and says we can neither know minds nor God. All we are left with, according to Hume, is the flow of sensory data. It is ironic that Locke, Berkeley, and Hume started out trying to avoid the ethereal speculation of the rationalists by grounding knowledge in the rock-solid foundation of experience. Instead Hume showed that a rigorous empiricism merely leaves us with the subjective contents of our own experience and does not allow us to draw any inferences about what lies beyond that limited domain. Hence, in response to our first question about the possibility of knowledge, Hume says that all we can know are the subjective contents of our individual minds. But this belief means that it is impossible to distinguish between the way things appear to us and the way things really are. (Thus we lack a necessary condition for having knowledge, according to Hume.) So, Hume says, we cannot have knowledge.

Hume on the Role of Reason

Our second question was, Does reason alone tell us about reality? Hume's answer is that not only can experience not tell us about reality, but reason can't either. Reason can only tell us about the relationship between our own ideas. In other words, reason can map the connections between the ideas in our minds, but it cannot establish connections between those ideas and the external world.

- In the following passage, what does Hume say are the two kinds of objects of reasoning?
- Which kind of reasoning is the most certain?
- Why can this certainty not tell us anything about the external world?

FROM DAVID HUME

An Enquiry Concerning Human Understanding[34]

ALL the objects of human reason or enquiry may naturally be divided into two kinds, to wit, Relations of Ideas, and Matters of Fact. Of the first kind are the sciences of Geometry, Algebra, and Arithmetic; and in short, every affirmation which is either intuitively or demonstratively certain. That the square of the hypothenuse is equal to the square of the two sides, is a proposition which expresses a relation between these figures. That three times five is equal to the half of thirty, expresses a relation between these numbers. Propositions of this kind are discoverable by the mere operation of thought, without dependence on what is anywhere existent in the universe. Though there never were a circle or triangle in nature, the truths demonstrated by Euclid would for ever retain their certainty and evidence.

Matters of fact, which are the second objects of human reason, are not ascertained in the same manner; nor is our evidence of their truth, however great, of a like nature with the foregoing. The contrary of every matter of fact is still possible; because it can never imply a contradiction, and is conceived by the mind with the same facility and distinctness, as if ever so conformable to reality. That the sun will not rise tomorrow is no less intelligible a proposition, and implies no more contradiction than the affirmation, that it will rise. We should in vain, therefore, attempt to demonstrate its falsehood. Were it demonstratively false, it would imply a contradiction, and could never be distinctly conceived by the mind.

In this passage, Hume points to a huge gulf between reason and the world. He agrees with the rationalists that the logical relations between our ideas are absolutely certain and necessary. If we start with Euclid's definitions and axioms, for example, then the Pythagorean theorem absolutely follows. But this conclusion only establishes a certain relationship between two sets of ideas. It does not demonstrate that the Pythagorean theorem will be true in the physical world. We can only know this truth from observation. The fact that this theorem has always worked every time we have built a house does not guarantee that it will work tomorrow. We can deny any matter of fact (such as "the sun will always rise in the morning") without falling into a logical contradiction. The fact that we feel confident about certain facts about the world is merely the result of our expectations, which are based on past experience. But why should we suppose that reality will conform to our expectations or that what has been true in the past will always be true?*

Hume and the Representation of Reality

The third question about knowledge was, Does our knowledge represent reality as it really is? By now, Hume's answer should be clear. According to Hume's analysis, the only certainty we can have concerns what we have called analytic a priori judgments. But these judgments concern only the realm of ideas and do not tell us about the external world. If so, then the attempt of the rationalists to *reason* about the ultimate nature of reality is doomed to failure. It also follows that any knowledge about reality must be based on synthetic a posteriori judgments. But Hume maintains that these judgments are never certain and merely give us information about what has been true in past experience. As the result of Hume's analysis, many empiricists concluded that insofar as metaphysics is understood to be the attempt to know what reality is really like, then it is an impossible goal. Accordingly, the empiricists who followed Hume concluded that the task of philosophy was much more limited than had been previously supposed. Philosophers, they said, could either analyze the logical relations between our concepts or draw generalizations from everyday experience and the findings of scientists. Beyond those analyses, however, little else could be known.

Hume drew some very brutal conclusions from his epistemology, as illustrated in one of his most famous passages.

> When we run over libraries, persuaded of these principles, what havoc must we make? If we take in our hand any volume; of divinity or school metaphysics, for instance; let us ask, Does it contain any abstract reasoning concerning quantity or number? No. Does it contain any experimental reasoning concerning matter of fact and existence? No. Commit it then to the flames: for it can contain nothing but sophistry and illusion.[35]

 THOUGHT EXPERIMENT

Hume's Two Tests for the Worth of Ideas

Hume has given us two questions for evaluating the worth of any book that makes assertions or puts forth truth claims. These questions may be paraphrased as (1) Does it contain mathematical reasoning? and (2) Does it contain reasoning about what can be experienced through the senses?

- Based on these criteria, find concrete examples of books that Hume would want to burn.

(Continued . . .)

---

*See Hume's skeptical arguments concerning the principle of induction in section 2.1.

(. . . continued)

- Do you agree with Hume that they "contain nothing but sophistry and illusion"?
- If you think that Hume's criteria are inadequate, what other criteria would you propose for evaluating books and the truth claims they contain?

STOP AND THINK

Go back over the three anchor points of empiricism. Explain how Hume's thought illustrates each of these points.

THOUGHT EXPERIMENT

Metaphors for the Mind

The mind is notoriously difficult to conceptualize and discuss. Typically, therefore, much of our mental terminology is replete with concrete metaphors drawn from the physical world. Locke's metaphor of the mind as a "blank white paper" that is written on by experience is an example. The following list consists of metaphors related to the education of young minds. In each case, try to decide if the metaphor best fits with a rationalist's or an empiricist's view of knowledge. First decide on the correct answer yourself, and then check your answers with those in the endnote.[36]

1. The teacher is a midwife of ideas who helps the students bring to birth the ideas latent within their minds.
2. The mind is like a rubber band that encompasses the information that it acquires from the world. Hence, the job of the teacher is to stretch the students' minds so that they can accommodate ever larger amounts of data.
3. The students' minds contain the seeds of understanding. The teacher is merely a gardener who prepares the soil and provides it with nourishment, so that the seeds can grow and produce fruit.
4. The teacher is a lamplighter who illuminates the students' minds so that the truth within will shine forth.
5. The mind is like a copy machine that reproduces images of the data it has scanned from the external world.
6. The teacher is a tour guide who leads the students into new and unfamiliar terrain.
7. The teacher is an archeologist who helps the students discover the treasures buried in the depths of their own minds.
8. The mind is like a window that provides access to the outside world. Ignorance, prejudice, and dogmatism are like a haze or obstacles that the teacher must remove in order for the light of truth to shine through the window of the intellect.
9. The mind is like a computer. Its capabilities are only as good as the data it receives.
10. The mind is like a computer. Without some built-in internal content such as logic circuits and an operating system, it is incapable of processing external data.

SUMMARY OF RATIONALISM AND EMPIRICISM

The rationalists claimed that we can have knowledge independent of experience. While rejecting this thesis the empiricists countered with the alternative thesis that all genuine knowledge is based on experience. However, from this basic premise Locke developed a (more or less) commonsense philosophy, while Berkeley argued for the radical conclusion that it is meaningless to posit a material world that exists external to our minds. Finally, Hume argued that empiricism implies that we can know virtually nothing at all except for the logical relationships between our own ideas and the flow of sensations within experience. Immanuel Kant, an eighteenth-century German philosopher, faced this great divide between the rationalists and the empiricists and concluded that each position had insights to offer but that each was plagued with difficulties. As we see in the next section, Kant attempted to construct an alternative view that incorporated elements of both rationalism and empiricism while leaving their problems behind.

LOOKING THROUGH THE EMPIRICIST'S LENS

1. Many cultures that are otherwise diverse have similar moral codes that command honoring parents, caring for children, speaking the truth, and administering impartial justice in the courts. The rationalist might say that the universality of these moral principles is evidence that they are innate within every human mind. However, how might an empiricist argue that these moral principles and others like them are really based on our common, human experience?

2. Since an empiricist believes that all our knowledge is derived from experience, how would an empiricist's approach to the education of young children differ from that of a rationalist?

3. Review what John Locke said about complex ideas. Randomly choose one page each out of several books (e.g., a novel, a science text, a political work, a religious work). Examine every idea or concept discussed in these pages. How might an empiricist attempt to explain these ideas as complexes built up from the simple ideas that originate in our experience?

EXAMINING THE STRENGTHS AND WEAKNESSES OF EMPIRICISM

Positive Evaluation

1. In ancient Greece and throughout the Middle Ages, the views of most philosophers and scientists were influenced by rationalistic assumptions. They reasoned that it was logically necessary for an object that was in motion to be continuously acted on by some force that kept it in motion. They also reasoned that the heavenly bodies must move in perfectly circular orbits, since the circle is the most perfect of all the geometrical figures. Scientists eventually discovered that

these conclusions were false. Empiricism stresses that we can only know about the world through observation and not by reasoning about the way the world must be. In what way do you think empiricism might have been conducive to the rise of modern science and a more adequate understanding of the world?

2. One virtue of basing our beliefs on experience, empiricists claim, is that experience is a self-correcting process. If our conclusions are mistaken, further experience can reveal our mistakes to us. For example, since the swans in Britain and Europe were at one time exclusively white, people in these countries concluded that whiteness was an essential property of swans. Later, as world travel increased, they discovered black and brown swans in New Zealand and had to revise their conception of swans. Do you think that the self-correcting nature of experience is a distinct advantage of empiricism?

Negative Evaluation

1. Empiricists such as Hume assert the following claim: "There are no logically necessary truths about the world." Because of this assertion, empiricists think that only experience and not reason can tell us what reality is like. But is this assertion based on logic? If so, isn't this assertion itself a claim to have logically necessary knowledge about the nature of the world? If this claim is not a logically necessary truth, then how could experience ever reveal its truth to us? If Hume's knowledge claim cannot be explained in terms of his own theory of knowledge, is something wrong with his claim? If so, are the rationalists then right that reason can give us knowledge about the world?

2. John Locke believed that our experiences tell us about the nature of reality. But how could we ever know if Locke's belief is true, since we cannot jump outside our experience to compare it with reality?

3. In his attempt to make Locke's empiricism more rigorous, Berkeley was led to deny the existence of an external material world. Similarly, Hume's thoroughgoing empiricism led to skepticism about almost everything we believe. Are these conclusions the inevitable result of empiricism? By confining our knowledge to what may be obtained within our experience, do we end up with a great deal of knowledge about ourselves but very little about the reality outside our experience? How can an empiricist avoid these extreme results?

4. Because we do not experience such things as human rights, moral duties, moral good and evil, and justice with the five senses, is it possible to have a viable empirical theory of ethics? Locke says that experience can provide us with the data for inferring what is morally right or wrong. But does it? Or does experience simply tell us the effects of behavior without providing a basis for determining whether these results are morally good or evil? Hume says morality is based on our emotions. Hence, does the empiricist leave us with nothing more than facts about human psychology, but nothing that would make possible a genuine ethical theory concerning right and wrong, good and evil?

LEADING QUESTIONS: *Constructivism*

1. The rationalists argue that experience alone cannot give us knowledge, for our knowledge requires the rational principles found in the mind. The empiricists argue that reason cannot give us knowledge, for we require the contributions of experience. Is it possible that each philosophy is partially correct and partially wrong? Is it possible that some sort of combined position will be more adequate? Why not opt for a rational-empiricism or an empirical-rationalism that views knowledge as the combined product of both reason and experience?

2. How do you know that every event must have a cause? You have experienced particular events and their causes in the past, but what grounds do you have for saying *every* event in the future will have a cause? This universal claim does not seem to be based on a posteriori knowledge of individual events. On the other hand the statement does not seem to be an analytic statement, for there is no *logical* contradiction in saying that something happened without a cause. Why then, are we so certain that the statement "every event must have a cause" is true?

3. Look at some object from different angles (a coin, coffee cup, a book). Look at its top, bottom, edge, front, and back. What you literally see are a series of different visual impressions, each with a different shape and perhaps other aspects that change as the object is rotated. Now, suppose that you were unable to relate these different impressions together to see them as multiple aspects of the *same* object. What would your world be like if you simply experienced a succession of phenomena without being able to synthesize them into the experience of meaningful objects? The fact that you *do* see these multiple experiences as representing aspects of one object means that you interpret these experiences by means of the categories of unity, plurality, identity, object, properties, and so on. These categories cannot be derived from experience, because it is in terms of these categories that your successive experiences are made to be coherent and meaningful. Where, then, do these categories come from?

4. Try to imagine an apple that grew to be blue instead of red. Try to imagine a tree that is like every other living tree except that it is as transparent as glass. Try to imagine that diamonds were soft and rubbery instead of hard. Such natural anomalies are unlikely, but it is possible to imagine dramatic changes in nature that would produce such objects. Now try to imagine an apple or a tree or a diamond that does not exist in space or time. It is fairly clear that you could not experience such objects apart from experiencing them as having spatial and temporal qualities. Why can we imagine objects lacking their normal color and solidity, but we cannot imagine them lacking spatial and temporal dimensions? Most properties of objects (such as their color or density), we learn from experience and we can imagine them

being different than they are. On the other hand, space and time seem to be necessary preconditions for any experience at all. Spatiality and temporality do not seem to be optional qualities of the objects that appear within experience. Why?

SURVEYING THE CASE FOR KANTIAN CONSTRUCTIVISM

IMMANUEL KANT (1724–1804)

Kant's Life

Immanuel Kant was born in Königsberg in what was then known as East Prussia (now Kaliningrad, Russia), and he lived there all his life. He was raised in Pietism, a Protestant sect that emphasized faith and religious feelings over reason and theological doctrines. Although Kant later took the position that knowledge is necessarily confined within the bounds of reason, he was always sensitive to the longings of the heart that aspire to transcend these limits. Being one of the most brilliant intellectuals of his day, he spent his life as a professor at the local university where he lectured on everything from philosophy to geography.

IMMANUEL KANT
(1724–1804)

By most standards Kant's life was rather rigid and orderly, as is described for us in the charming portrait of the poet Heinrich Heine:

> I do not believe that the great clock of the cathedral there did its daily work more dispassionately and regularly than its compatriot Immanuel Kant. Rising, coffee drinking, writing, reading college lectures, eating, walking, all had their fixed time, and the neighbors knew that it was exactly half past three when Immanuel Kant in his grey coat, with his bamboo cane in his hand, left his house door and went to the Lime tree avenue, which is still called, in memory of him, the Philosopher's Walk.[37]

However, while Kant's daily life was routine and mundane, the same could not be said of his ideas. Although his political ideas were relatively conservative, his theory of knowledge (epistemology) was revolutionary. It began with a devastating critique of the dominant philosophical traditions (rationalism and empiricism) and ended by radically revising how we think about knowledge. As a result, we now categorize all philosophy as either pre-Kantian or post-Kantian.

Kant's Agenda

Kant began his epistemology with the conviction that we *do* have knowledge. He thought it was undeniable that the disciplines of arithmetic, Euclidian geometry, and Newtonian physics provide us with information about our world. He also believed that these disciplines involve universal and necessary principles such that no future discoveries will ever shake our conviction of their truth. For example, it seems to be the case that necessarily anything we experience will conform to the following rules:

- The shortest distance between two points will always be a straight line.
- All events will have a cause.

The problem is that principles such as these give us universal and certain knowledge about the world and yet, as Hume pointed out, no collection of particular experiences could ever provide an absolutely necessary basis for such universal claims about all possible experience. For example, you may have observed a cause for every time your car does not start (no gas, a loose wire, a dead battery). But the most that these experiences can tell you is that on these particular occasions, these particular events had a cause. Though you may have observed that every event you have experienced has had a cause, this observation doesn't provide a basis for knowing with certainty that every future event you will experience will have a cause. In other words, a finite collection of examples cannot prove a necessary truth. Nevertheless, as Kant observed, we do think that it is necessarily true that "all events will have a cause."

The question then for Kant was, How is such universal and necessary knowledge possible? He thought that the rationalists and the empiricists each provided us with one-half of the answer and that a compromise between them was required. In other words, Kant concluded that both reason and experience play a role in constructing our knowledge. Accordingly, Kant's epistemology could justifiably be called "rational-empiricism" or "empirical-rationalism." He himself called it "critical philosophy" because he wanted to critique reason, which means that he wanted to sort out the legitimate claims of reason from groundless ones.

Hume maintained that the only way we could have knowledge that was universal, necessary, and certain is if it was analytic a priori knowledge. Hence, we can know that it is necessarily true that "All gray elephants are elephants." The problem is that such knowledge doesn't tell us about the world because from the truth of that statement alone we could not know that there are any elephants or, if there are any, that they are gray. Knowledge that does give us information, Hume said, had to be synthetic a posteriori knowledge. An example of such knowledge would be "Lemon juice is acidic." This knowledge is synthetic because it synthesizes, or brings together, the concepts of "lemon juice" and "acidic." The two concepts are not logically related the way that "bachelor" and "unmarried" are, because we can imagine lemon juice being nonacidic. Hence only through experience (a posteriori knowledge) could we know that statement to be true. Unlike Hume and the empiricists, the rationalists thought that we also could have synthetic a priori knowledge. This knowledge would not be derived from experience, would be universal and necessary, but would also give us information about the world. With the rationalists, Kant thought that statements such as "All events have a cause" provided us with synthetic a priori knowledge. However, Kant also believed with the empiricists that all knowledge began with experience. Hence, he accused the rationalists of attempting to fly above experience to know what reality is like beyond our experience. But he agreed with Hume that this stepping out of experience cannot be done. So the problem Kant faced was, How, within the bounds of experience, is synthetic a priori knowledge possible?

Kant once said that he did not fear being refuted but he did fear not being understood. His fears were well-founded, for both his ideas and his writing style are difficult. But if you can grasp the gist of what he was saying, you will be rewarded by having understood one of the most influential and revolutionary theses in the history of thought. As the first step in his reconstruction of epistemology, Kant begins his major work, the *Critique of Pure Reason,* with a discussion of the sources of our knowledge.

- The first sentence of each of the first two paragraphs begins with a statement of the relationship between knowledge and experience. What are the two points that Kant makes?
- Which of these two points sounds like empiricism? Which one sounds like rationalism?

 FROM IMMANUEL KANT

Critique of Pure Reason (1)[38]

There can be no doubt that all our knowledge begins with experience. For how should our faculty of knowledge be awakened into action did not objects affecting our senses partly of themselves produce representations, partly arouse the activity of our understanding to compare these representations, and, by combining or separating them, work up the raw material of the sensible impressions into that knowledge of objects which is entitled experience? In the order of time, therefore, we have no knowledge antecedent to experience, and with experience all our knowledge begins.

But though all our knowledge begins with experience, it does not follow that it all arises out of experience. For it may well be that even our empirical knowledge is made up of what we receive through impressions and of what our own faculty of knowledge (sensible impressions serving merely as the occasion) supplies from itself. If our faculty of knowledge makes any such addition, it may be that we are not in a position to distinguish it from the raw material, until with long practice of attention we have become skilled in separating it.

This, then, is a question which at least calls for closer examination, and does not allow of any off-hand answer:—whether there is any knowledge that is thus independent of experience and even of all impressions of the senses. Such knowledge is entitled *a priori,* and distinguished from the *empirical,* which has its sources *a posteriori,* that is, in experience.

- Read the second paragraph again. Kant says that our empirical knowledge (our knowledge about the world) is made up of elements from two sources. What are they? Note: "faculty of knowledge" refers to the mind.
- Note that in the third paragraph he suggests (in effect) that there can be genuine knowledge (synthetic knowledge) that is a priori.

A few pages later, Kant criticizes the rationalists (such as Plato) for supposing that reason can operate without the materials of experience. What metaphor does he use to make this point?

The light dove, cleaving the air in her free flight, and feeling its resistance, might imagine that its flight would be still easier in empty space. It was thus that Plato left the world of the senses, as setting too narrow limits to the understanding, and ventured out beyond it on the wings of the ideas, in the empty space of the pure understanding. He did not observe that with all his efforts he made no advance—meeting no resistance that might, as it were, serve as a support upon which he could take a stand, to which he could apply his powers, and so set his understanding in motion.

In what you just read, Kant says, "all our knowledge begins with experience." On this issue there is no question that Kant cast his lot with the empiricists. But he was well aware that if the only source of knowledge was experience, then Humean skepticism is the logical outcome. To avoid this outcome Kant adds: "But though all our knowledge begins with experience, it does not follow that it all arises out of experience," thus indicating that some of the rationalists' assumptions were still needed. However, he cautions that reason operating apart from experience is like the dove flapping its wings in empty space. In both cases, reason and the dove's wings need something (experience or air) to work with or against to be effective.

In this brief passage, we can see Kant attempting to negotiate a tricky tightrope between the positions of rationalism and empiricism by standing firm on their insights without falling into the problems that each position had produced. He agreed with the empiricists that our knowledge could not soar beyond the limits of experience, that the contents of experience provided the materials for all knowledge. Hence, any metaphysical conclusions about what reality is like *beyond the limits of experience* had to be ruled out as ungrounded. This conclusion meant that a nonphysical self, the infinity of the universe, or God could not be objects of human knowledge. Notice that he did not say that such things could not exist but merely that we could not have knowledge of them. While he agreed with Hume that knowledge claims about such metaphysical topics were illusions, Kant still was convinced that these concepts played an important role in human life. The problem was how to understand their appropriate role. Furthermore, while confining knowledge to the bounds of experience, Kant resisted Hume's conclusion that all we have left is a series of fragmented, discrete sensations. If this conclusion were true, then the sort of absolutely certain and universal laws that are essential to science could never be found. The problem Kant faced was how to have the rationalists' certain and necessary knowledge (a priori knowledge) without doing the impossible—leaping outside human experience to a Godlike view of reality. On the other hand, Kant wanted to start where Hume started (in experience), without ending up where Hume ended up (in skepticism).

Kant's Revolution

Kant received an insight concerning the nature of knowledge from the example of Copernicus's great innovation. Copernicus rejected the theory that the sun revolves around the earth because he thought it did not give us a well-ordered picture of the data. Accordingly, he proposed that we switch the center of focus and see if it would make more sense to suppose that the earth revolves around the sun. Similarly, Kant proposed a "Copernican revolution" in epistemology. The empiricists thought that the mind is passive when confronting the world and that the mind simply records the impressions provided by the senses. In this picture, *knowledge conforms to its objects.* But can we know that it does? To know this, you would have to leap outside your mind and compare the contents of your experience with the contents of reality. In order to stay within experience while avoiding Hume's skepticism, Kant (like Copernicus) reversed this commonsense picture. He asks us to consider the possibility that *objects conform to our knowledge.*[39] In other words, Kant suggests that the only way the fluctuating, fragmented assortment of sense data can provide us with the experience of *objects* is if the mind imposes a certain rational structure on it.

The rationalists argued that science is possible because there is a correspondence between the mind and the world. Kant agreed, but he changed the character of this correspondence. He says the "world" that science studies is not something beyond experience but is a world of experience that the mind has actively filtered, digested, shaped, and organized according to the mind's own structure. Hence, Hume was correct in saying that a series of particular observations cannot give us certainty and universal laws. What Hume did not realize, according to Kant, was that we can find certainty and universal knowledge within experience if the mind organizes experience in a necessary and universal way. In this sense, the mind does not conform to an external world, but the contents found in experience do conform to the structure of the mind. The mind *constructs* its objects out of the raw materials provided by the senses. For this reason, I have labeled Kant's position on knowledge *constructivism.*

It is important to get clear on what Kant is and is not saying here. He is not saying that the mind brings reality into existence out of nothing. But he is saying that the way in which reality *appears* to us (the only reality that we can know) depends on the contribution of both the senses and the intellect. The mind imposes its own form on the sense data, and through this activity we have objects to be known. The only world we can know is the world of our experience which is (partially) constructed by the mind. This world consists of things-as-they-appear-to-us, which Kant refers to as the **phenomena** (or the phenomenal realm). Outside our experience are the things-in-themselves known as the **noumena** (or the noumenal realm). Since we can't jump outside our experience to see reality as it actually is, we cannot assign any positive content to the notion of the noumena. The concept is merely a limiting concept or a way of pointing to what lies beyond any possible experience.

phenomena in Kant's theory, the things-as-they-appear-to-us that exist in the world of our experience, which is partially constructed by the mind

noumena in Kant's theory, the things-in-themselves that exist outside our experience

Obviously, in our discussion of Kant, it will be impossible for us to leap outside experience to compare our view of the world as structured by the mind with the way reality is in itself. However, throughout this chapter I use analogies from within experience to illustrate the way that our experience is both a product of what is out there and a product of the distinctive way in which we organize, process, and shape what appears. Keep in mind that in these examples we will be comparing one kind of datum *within* experience (appearance 1) with another kind of datum (appearance 2) as a rough analogy of the relationship between the objects of human experience (phenomena) and the reality that lies *outside* experience (noumena).

 THOUGHT EXPERIMENT

The Objects of Experience

1. If you require glasses to read, take them off and look at the words on this page. If you don't need glasses, you can still achieve the same effect by moving the page close to your nose until the words are hopelessly blurred. Do the same with a small, colored picture that has many complex details. The effect is that no longer are you presented with meaningful objects, whether these objects are the words on this page or the details in the picture. Instead, your visual field consists of indistinguishable shapes and splotches of gray or patches of color. However, under optimal conditions (you are wearing your glasses or the book is a normal distance from your eyes) you will see words or pictures of objects. In much the same way, Kant says, we do not simply see the world as a swirl of shapes and colors, for the mind functions like the lenses to provide us with an array of representations that present themselves as objects within experience.

2. Suppose I made the prediction that when I turn on the television to watch the evening news tonight that the male anchor (say, Dan Rather) will be wearing a tie colored in various shades of gray.[40] Furthermore, suppose that I claim this knowledge about the real world is known a priori, independently of my past experience of seeing what sorts of ties he wears. Whether the tie is striped, polka dot, paisley, or whatever, I know ahead of time it will be shades of gray. How can I make this prediction? The answer will be provided in the discussion to follow.

Kant's project involved the search for the universal and necessary conditions of any possible experience. If we find that certain conditions are necessary for us to have any experience at all, then these conditions would provide us with synthetic a priori knowledge of what must be true of the world-as-we-experience-it. In the eyeglasses example, the objects that appear within the person's visual experience are a product of both the sensory data and the way in which the lenses process this input. The eyeglasses do not create reality, but they do influence how that reality will appear.

We could extend the analogy and suppose that the glasses are red-tinted and that they cause everything to appear triangular in shape. Imagine further that there is no way to remove the lenses and see the world without them. Under these conditions, you still could not know the contents of a room apart from experiencing it. However, if you understood the nature of the glasses, you would understand the universal conditions of any possible experience you could have. While the specific contents of your experiences would vary, you would know prior to experience that whatever appeared, it would be a red-tinted and triangular object. Furthermore, if everyone viewed the world through the same kind of lenses, we could have objective and universal knowledge (prior to specific experiences) of the general character of any possible human experience. However, since the glasses cannot be removed, what we could not know is what the world was like outside our ways of experiencing it. This analogy illustrates the point Kant was making when he said that the objects within experience conform to the order that the mind imposes on sensation.

In the case of the news anchor, I could know a priori that his tie would be gray if I knew that I would be watching him on a black and white television set. Imagine that we all had the same kind of television set and that our only knowledge of the world was what we saw on it. Our television sets then would have two effects: (1) they would make it possible for us to have experiences of such things as the news anchor's tie, and (2) they would only allow us to see the world in a certain way. In an analogous way, Kant says that the mind makes it possible for us to have meaningful experiences, but it also causes us to experience the world in certain ways. The tie as it really is in the studio corresponds to the noumenal realm, and the tie as it appears on our television sets corresponds to the phenomenal realm. Only a being (perhaps God) who did not have the limitations of our cognitive apparatus could know what reality is like in itself. But once we know the way that our minds necessarily condition experience, we can have universal and necessary knowledge of what reality-as-experienced will be like.

Our Experience of Space and Time

Exactly how does Kant think the mind structures our experience of reality? Kant says that the mind imposes a spatial and temporal form on experience. Space and time are not mysterious "things" that appear within experience; instead they are fundamental frames of reference within which objects appear to us. As an example of spatial perception, look at the objects about you in your room. Perhaps you are seeing books, a coffee cup, and a CD player. However, the books are not literally in your mind. Instead, you have certain images that are appearing in your experience. But no matter what the specific contents of your experience may be, these images are always located within a spatial framework. The fact that objects have a spatial appearance is one way in which the mind structures experience, according to Kant. But aren't objects in the external world literally in space? The only way you could know that they are would be to jump outside your experience to experience reality-in-itself. Hence, it is meaningless to talk about space apart from the spatial perspective found within experience.

The same sort of mental activity provides a temporal dimension to your experience. Time is not an entity existing in itself out there in the world. Instead it is a framework within which objects are presented to us. Imagine someone striking a bell three times. If you had instant amnesia after hearing each note, you would not experience *three* strikes of the bell. Hence, in addition to receiving each bit of sense data, the mind must remember each one, relate them together within a temporal sequence, and synthesize them as three successive experiences of the same thing.

 THOUGHT EXPERIMENT

Space and Time

Kant offers us two thought experiments to show that space and time are necessary features of our experience.[41]

1. One by one, imaginatively subtract all the objects from the world until nothing is left but empty space without objects. This image seems to be conceivable. Now try to imagine a world in which there are objects but no space. For example, think what it would be like to experience a box that didn't have three dimensions. It can't be done. Why not? The reason is that spatial qualities are different from the qualities and objects of sensation. The mind arranges sensations through the form of space, but space is not itself a sensation. We don't experience space but we experience objects that are spatially structured in a particular way.

2. Try to imagine time without any objects enduring through it. In other words, imagine yourself viewing an empty universe in which there are no objects, but as you are viewing this void, time is still ticking on. If Kant is correct, you could imagine one temporal moment after another that is empty of events. Now try to imagine yourself experiencing objects (trees, a sunset, moving clouds) but without any temporal succession. If Kant is correct, this image is impossible. The reason, he says, is that time is a universal condition for the very possibility of there being objects of experience at all. The form of temporality structures every possible experience of objects. Yet time is not itself a "thing" because it is not something with sensory properties.

Kant's theory of space and time seems rather fantastic. The spatial and temporal nature of our experience is so familiar we have a hard time imagining that these qualities could be only forms of our human experience. To make Kant's view even more plausible, imagine how the world appears to a fly, with its multifaceted eyes. Its experience of space is one in which every object appears hundreds of times. The fly's world is spatially structured in a very different way from ours. So *our* experience of space is not the only possible one. Similarly, to make it plausible that both our spatial and temporal experiences are uniquely human, Kant suggests that some other sort of being (perhaps God) might experience reality without our spatial limitations and might be able to know the past, present, and future in one, simultaneous experience.[42] So once again, maybe *our* spatially and temporally formed experience is not the only way that reality could be known. Even though we can suppose that reality could be experienced in radically different ways by God, our experience will always have a particular kind of spatial and temporal dimension.

THOUGHT EXPERIMENT

Spatial Interpretation

Look at the drawing of the two tables.[43] Which table is longer?

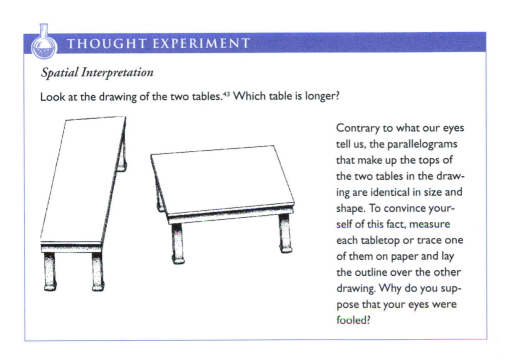

Contrary to what our eyes tell us, the parallelograms that make up the tops of the two tables in the drawing are identical in size and shape. To convince yourself of this fact, measure each tabletop or trace one of them on paper and lay the outline over the other drawing. Why do you suppose that your eyes were fooled?

When you looked at the drawings of the tables in the thought experiment, you perceived them as three-dimensional objects. Accordingly, your mind imposed a spatial perspective on the picture that gave the appearance that the left table is receding away from you, while the long axis of the right table appears to be closer to your position in space. Once you imposed a depth interpretation on the collection of lines, your mind formed the judgment that the left table must be longer. In much the same way, when we look about our room, our visual field consists of rectangular, circular, or triangular shapes (among others). These shapes appear to us within a spatially structured field of vision. Of course, unlike the drawing, we can move about the room. But the movement only gives us a series of tactile sensations that we have learned to correlate with our visual images. In the final analysis, Kant says, the experience of space and time is something that universally and necessarily characterizes our experienced world. But always remember that we are talking about *our experience of the world* and not what it is like outside our experience.

The Categories of the Understanding

To understand what comes next, it is important to know that Kant refers to the raw data of sense perception as *intuitions*. This term should not be confused with our use of the word to refer to a special gift of insight or a gut feeling. Instead, *intuition* in Kant's sense means "the object of the mind's direct awareness." For example, to experience the redness of a rose is to have a sensory intuition. Kant believes that two powers of the mind are at work in experience; he calls these powers *sensibility* and *understanding*. Sensibility is a passive power; it is the ability of the mind to receive sensory intuitions. The understanding is an active power that enables us to organize the intuitions we receive into meaningful objects by applying concepts to our experience.

Thus far Kant has been talking about our passive reception (sensibility) of perceptual data (intuitions) and the way in which the mind gives a spatial and temporal form to this data. However, if our experience consisted only of spatially and temporally organized intuitions, we would not have knowledge. Instead, we would experience a confusing barrage of unrelated colors and sounds within space and time (perhaps not unlike a newborn baby's experience). Hence, a further set of organizing principles is needed. These principles are provided by the understanding and are called the *categories of the understanding*. The understanding provides us with concepts (categories) that enable us to form intuitions into meaningful objects that can be the basis of thought. To use an analogy, imagine a cylindrical cookie press into which you place dough and squeeze it out the other end through a star-shaped hole. Just as the cookie is the product of a certain content (the dough) being processed by a shape (the cookie press), so knowledge is the product of our sensibility providing us with spatial and temporal intuitions and the understanding using its conceptual categories to organize these intuitions. For Kant, a concept is not a kind of image, for it has no content in itself (any more than the star-shaped hole in the cookie press has content). Instead, a concept is a rule for organizing our intuitions into objects of experience. In the next passage, think of intuitions as the dough and sensibility as that part of our cognitive apparatus that allows us to receive intuitions (the cookie press that holds the dough). Furthermore, think of the understanding as the source of our concepts and think of our concepts as the star-shaped hole (or round hole, or tree-shaped hole) in the cookie press that organizes and shapes the raw materials.

FROM IMMANUEL KANT
Critique of Pure Reason (2)[44]

There are two stems of human knowledge, namely, *sensibility* and *understanding*, which perhaps spring from a common, but to us unknown root. Through the former, objects are given to us; through the latter, they are thought. . . .

To neither of these powers may a preference be given over the other. Without sensibility no object would be given to us, without understanding no object would be thought. Thoughts without content are empty, intuitions without concepts are blind. It is, therefore, just as necessary to make our concepts sensible, that is, to add the object to them in intuition, as to make our intuitions intelligible, that is, to bring them under concepts. These two powers or capacities cannot exchange their functions. The understanding can intuit nothing, the senses can think nothing. Only through their union can knowledge arise.

- What does Kant mean when he says "thoughts without content are empty, intuitions without concepts are blind"? Rephrase this quote in your own words and try to explain it to a friend.

THOUGHT EXPERIMENT

Perceptual Objects

1. Consider the following collection of multishaded squares. Can you cause your eyes to form them into a pattern representing a well-known face? (Hint: hold the image at some distance from your eyes and squint your eyes, causing the individual squares to blur and merge.)

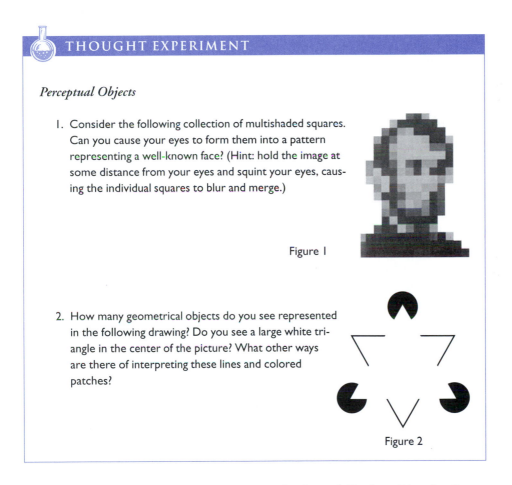

Figure 1

2. How many geometrical objects do you see represented in the following drawing? Do you see a large white triangle in the center of the picture? What other ways are there of interpreting these lines and colored patches?

Figure 2

Most people see Figure 1 as representing the face of Abraham Lincoln. But at first glance, the figure appears to be a chaotic collection of shaded patches. To see them as representing an object, the mind must form them into a single, unified pattern. Obviously, to recognize the figure as a picture of Lincoln you would have had to have seen a picture of Lincoln previously. Seeing the picture *as* Lincoln is a matter of past experience, but seeing the patches *as* an object is a matter of the mind's innate capacity for organizing your sensations. In other words, more is going on in perception than just light hitting the retina. The mind must take that data and impose a unity on it.

It is normal to view Figure 2 as containing three circles that are overlaid with two triangles. However, notice that what is actually presented to the eyes are three partial circles with a missing pie-shaped slice, and three open-ended angles (a total of six figures). Your mind takes this data and interprets the three curved shapes as complete circles that are partially obscured by a white borderless triangle laid over them. Similarly, your mind takes the three open angles and views them as the corners of a large triangle with a black border that is also partially obscured by the large white triangle. Notice that the white borderless triangle *literally is not in the picture*. The mind takes the empty, white space between the other shapes and creates the image of a triangle. This figure is a striking example of the mind creating its own objects out of the data presented to it.

These optical experiments do not exactly represent Kant's Copernican revolution, but they do show how what we experience is a composite of both sense data and the work of the mind. In these examples, the mind did not produce the data; it was imposed on you from without in the form of light rays from the picture hitting your retina. But this data appeared to you as a collection of shapes because your mind formed the data into meaningful objects. This aspect of our experience leads to an important feature of Kant's account of knowledge. Some concepts, such as "Lincoln," "dog," or "apple," obviously do not reside in the mind but are based on what we learn from experience. Kant calls these concepts *empirical concepts*. But before you could recognize that something is an apple, you first would have to recognize it as a unified object containing certain properties. Hence your distinct sensations of redness, roundness, sweetness, and crunchiness are collected together and viewed as composing a single substance. Without the category of substance you would just have a chaos of sensations (intuitions). But substance is not something we experience as we do the sensations making up our experience of the apple. For this reason, Kant says that *substance* is a *pure concept*. It is one of the categories of the understanding that we do not derive from our sensations but that we bring to experience to organize it in terms of unified objects. Other categories include causality, unity, plurality, possibility, necessity. Kant identifies twelve categories in all that serve as the framework within which all our judgments about the world are made.

It will be helpful to contrast Kant's account of experience with that of Hume. According to Hume, we are passive spectators of a world of continuously changing sensations (colors, shapes, sounds, smells, and textures). Within experience, Hume said, we find

> perceptions which succeed each other with an inconceivable rapidity and are in a perpetual flux and movement. . . . The mind is a kind of theatre, where several perceptions successively make their appearance; pass, re-pass, glide away, and mingle in an infinite variety of postures and situations.[45]

However, these sensations are not exactly what we experience, according to Kant. We do not experience mere patches of colors nor unrelated sounds and other bits of sensation. Instead, we experience a world of meaningful objects. Things in experience could only appear that way if the mind was taking the fragmented "pings" of sensation and arranging them together into distinct objects that appear in space and have identity through time.

Since we can never turn off the mind's structuring of the sense data, we can never have a pure, unmediated experience of the world. However, we may come close through experiences such as the alarm clock going off in the morning. For a moment, we are bombarded with sensations (the raucous sound of the alarm and daylight streaming through the window). These nearly raw, unconceptualized experiences intrude on us as a "buzzing, blooming confusion" (as psychologist-philosopher William James once described the experience of a baby). Eventually, we begin to make sense of the experience when the following stream of thoughts occur: "This uncomfortable sensation is a sound—this sound is a buzzer—caused by the alarm—which means morning—which means I have to get going." Even before this level of mental processing begins, however, the mind has already structured the experience in terms of the *forms* of (a) time and (b) space and the *categories* of (c) substance and (d) causality. For example, your first awareness of the alarm clock takes this form: "(a) There is an enduring stimulus (time), (b) external to me (space), (c) it is some object (substance), (d) but what is causing it? (causality)" Hence, even the most raw level of experience will be structured by the mind, and only because the mind brings order to experience are sensations able to become knowledge.

What Is Reality Like?

The good news of Kant's epistemology is that we can have objective, universal, and necessary knowledge of the world. The reason we can have this knowledge is that the world we know is always the world of experience, and the world of experience, no matter how much its content may vary, will always have a certain structure. Because of this structure, synthetic a priori judgments are possible. Just as I can know that the newscaster's tie will be gray, so I can know that "every event has a cause." In the first case, the judgment about the tie is an empirical one based on my knowledge of my receiving instrument. (Of course, this example is merely an analogy of what goes on in all experience.) In the second case (the one Kant is concerned with), the judgment about causality is a necessary one based on the nature of the human mind. What is crucial for Kant is that every human mind will structure experience in the same universal and necessary way. The bad news of Kant's position is that we can never know reality in itself because we can never jump outside our minds and see what reality is like before our minds have done their job of processing and filtering it. Think again about the representation of the news anchor on the black and white television. If our eyes were like that television set and unable to represent colors to us, then our entire world of experience would be in shades of black, white, and gray. We could never know about the colors in the real world. For Kant, that analogy is very similar to our actual lot in life. The only world we know is the world that appears to us in experience (phenomena). But because experience is structured by the mind, we can never know reality in itself (noumena).

Self, Cosmos, and God

If we accept Kant's account of how the mind and experience work together, then it is clear that the categories of the mind cannot give us knowledge of anything that transcends experience, any more than the cookie press by itself can give us cookies. The categories are merely empty forms of thought that must be filled with sensory content to produce knowledge. As twentieth-century philosopher Norman Melchert says about the categories,

> Compare them to mathematical functions, such as x^2. Until some number is given as x, we have no object. If a content for x is supplied, say 2 or 3, then an object is specified, in these cases the numbers 4 or 9. The categories of substance, cause, and the rest are similar. They are merely operators, the function of which is to unite "in one consciousness the manifold given in intuition."[46]

The implications of Kant's epistemology are enormous. It means that we cannot know such things as the self, the world-as-a-whole, or God, for these things are outside the bounds of any possible experience. Kant refers to the attempt to reason about these topics "transcendent illusions." First, with respect to the self, we can, of course, know our own moods, feelings, thoughts, and the other contents of our internal experience. But as Hume pointed out, these items are simply fleeting experiences and do not give us the experience of a substantial, enduring self. The problem is that we want to use the concept of substance to think of that real self that underlies all these experiences. But since "substance" can only apply to our sensations, we can't use it to refer to a mysterious reality that underlies these experiences.

The second metaphysical illusion is the assumption that we can reason about the cosmos (or the world-as-a-totality). The problem is that all we can know are bits and pieces of world experience, but the totality is never experienced. Thus, to think of the world as a whole, we would have to take a Godlike perspective outside of space and time. To make clear what happens when reason tries to fly beyond experience (remember the example of the dove), Kant gives a series of arguments that lead to conflicting conclusions (called "antinomies"). For example, he first argues that the world is finite in space and time and then turns around and argues that it is infinite. He argues that some events are free and then that all events are determined. Kant says that because rational arguments can establish contradictory conclusions on these topics, reason has gone beyond its proper bounds.

Finally, if our knowledge is limited to only what we can experience, then we are prevented from reasoning about God. He says that attempts to demonstrate God's existence are "altogether fruitless and by their nature null and void."[47] For example, we cannot reason about the cause of the world, for causality is only a way of relating the items within our experience. But if the limits of reason prevent us from proving God's existence, they also prevent us from disproving it as well. So in Kant's epistemology the theist and the atheist are in the same boat. In the final analysis, the notions of self, cosmos, and God are illusory if we think we can have knowledge of their objects, but Kant considers them important and irresistible notions. Though the ideas lack empirical content, they do serve the useful function of regulating our thought. They provide us with an ideal toward which we will always strive: knowledge that is a complete, unified, and systematic whole. Perhaps we can think of these notions like the converging lines in a painting that lead to an infinite point beyond the horizon. Like the perspective indicators in the painting, the concepts of self, cosmos, and God provide a meaningful framework for that which we actually do experience. With respect to God, Kant suggested that though we cannot have rational knowledge of this topic, we might still find the idea indispensable to make sense of morality. Hence, in the preface to his *Critique,* Kant says, "I have therefore found it necessary to deny *knowledge,* in order to make room for *faith.*"[48]

To summarize, Kant believed that (1) we can *never know* reality as it is in itself, because (2) our minds *structure* our experience of reality. Furthermore, (3) there is a *single* set of forms and categories by which this structuring is done, which are *universal* to every human knower, and (4) this process is fundamentally *rational.* In the remaining sections of this chapter, we see that many of the philosophers after Kant accepted (1) and (2), but they discarded (3) and sometimes (4), leading to a wide range of post-Kantian philosophies that took a radically different direction from the one that he had charted.

LOOKING THROUGH KANT'S LENS

1. Look about you and briefly take note of the objects in your current experience (books, tables, chairs, a coffee cup). As you are viewing your surroundings, try to imagine that you had lost the ability to organize your sensations into a collection of objects and could only experience a fragmented, unrelated, and unintelligible flow of sensations (patches of colors and shapes). What would this experience be like? Does this exercise suggest that the mind plays a very important role in the construction of our experience of the world?

2. Try an experiment to imagine what your experienced world would be like without the form of spatiality imposed on it. Watch a car (or a person) as it comes from the distance toward you. Focus on what is actually appearing within your experience while trying to suspend any spatial interpretations you make about it. Think of the experience as a very small, carlike image that is growing in size within your visual field. If we did not organize our sensations spatially, this growing image

is all we would see. We would have small images growing into large images instead of the experience of a car of constant size that appears in the distance and then moves closer to us.

4. Kant says that because all we can know is the world of experience (phenomena), science cannot tell us about any reality in the noumenal realm outside our physical sensations. Science tells us about the world only as it is perceived, measured, manipulated, experimented upon, and so on. Even though the world apart from our scientific interpretations is (strictly speaking) unknowable, we can formulate laws, explanations, and predictions within the realm of human experience. Given the fact that science cannot tell us about reality itself, why does Kant think that scientific knowledge is adequate? Given these limitations of science, why does Kant think that science could never be a threat to religious faith?

 ## EXAMINING THE STRENGTHS AND WEAKNESSES OF KANTIAN CONSTRUCTIVISM

Positive Evaluation

1. Does Kant's recognition of the contributions of both reason and sensation in forming our knowledge make his epistemology more adequate than that of either the rationalists or the empiricists?

2. Try to imagine that you had a cognitive defect such that you could not think of the world in terms of causes and effects, yet your experience remained the same as it is now. Under these circumstances, flipping a switch followed by the light going on would be no different than coughing while at an intersection followed by the traffic light turning green. However, the fact is that we do connect flipping the switch and the light because the sequence is a regular and ordered one, but we do not connect coughing and the green light, because this sequence is not regular and does not follow any particular order. This scenario illustrates Kant's point that causality is not an item of experience (like the sensation of light), but is a way in which we inevitably organize our experiences into those sequences that are regular and those that are not. Could you imagine what life would be like if the mind did not have this feature?

Negative Evaluation

1. Kant says that the mind shapes and forms the reality we experience. But in order for this shaping and forming to take place, must there not be some measure of affinity between the categories of the mind and the nature of reality in itself? If the mind can interact with reality at all, isn't it unlikely that their respective structures are totally different? If there is this inevitable correspondence between the way in which the mind works and the way in which reality works, then is Kant wrong in claiming that we can never know what reality is like outside the mind?

2. Biology tells us that species that adapt to external conditions survive and those that do not adapt do not survive. Has the human species done so well in surviving because our cognitive abilities have developed in response to the external environment? If so, then isn't it true that our minds must conform to reality rather than our experience of reality conforming to the structure of the mind? Does this conclusion mean that Kant's Copernican revolution is mistaken?

3. Anthropologists have discovered that people in different cultures perceive spatial and temporal relationships differently. Does this discovery undermine Kant's theory that space and time are a priori and universal ways of shaping experience that are built into every human mind?

4. According to Kant, because our knowledge is confined within the boundaries of human experience, we can know nothing about reality as it is in itself (the noumenal realm). How, then, does he even know that the noumenal realm exists? To be consistent, shouldn't he suspend judgment and remain silent about a reality external to our experience?

2.5 EPISTEMOLOGICAL RELATIVISM

LEADING QUESTIONS: *Epistemological Relativism*

1. What are facts? We speak of facts as being hard, cold, objective, and stubborn. We are asked for the plain, observable, unvarnished facts. We are told to face the facts, to collect them, or to check them out. These comments might lead us to think that facts are physical things out there in the world, independent of us. But are facts items in the world alongside trees, rocks, and grass? We can trip over a rock, but can we trip over a fact? The moon looks round but what does a fact look like? We can photograph a sunset but can we photograph facts? We can weigh apples but can we weigh facts? You can say how many objects are in your room but how many facts are in your room? Is there space enough for all of them? If these questions have convinced you that facts are not out in the world, then where are they? Could we say that facts are somehow embedded in our language or belief systems? If so, then is a fact a function of who we are, how we see the world, and how we think or speak about it? What would be the implications of this "fact"?

2. We believe that the material objects of our everyday lives are incapable of vanishing into thin air by magic. If we can't find our keys, we believe that they are *somewhere*; they did not just cease to exist. But imagine a culture in which the people do believe that material objects sometimes disappear into nothingness (without being crushed, melted, burned up, or destroyed in other ways according to *our* laws of physics).[49] So, when you lose your keys in this culture and never find them again, these people would assume that the keys had just dematerialized without a trace. According to *their* laws of physics, nature sometimes behaves this way. We

have all had the experience of pulling a load of laundry out of the dryer and finding that one sock is missing. Sometimes, no matter how hard we search (in the laundry bag, in the washer, inside other clothing), we never find the missing sock. "So there you have it," the people from this culture say, "irrefutable evidence that occasionally things can simply vanish." How would you convince these people that they are wrong and that our laws of physics are right?

3. What do you see when you look at this diagram? You probably said that the picture was that of a cube or a box. In some cultures that do not have our conventions for drawing perspective, the people can only see the figure as a two-dimensional pattern, much like a plaid pattern. Their cultural conventions prevent their eyes from interpreting the drawing as representing a three-dimensional object. (Now see if *you* can visualize the figure as a flat pattern and not as a box.) Is it possible that our entire perspective on the world is like this exercise? Is it possible that your perceptual, conceptual, moral, aesthetic, and scientific ways of interpreting the world are merely how *you* see it and are no more objectively true or correct than other ways of interpreting it?

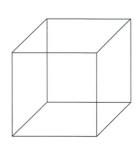

SURVEYING THE CASE FOR RELATIVISM

From Kant to Relativism

The philosophers whose views of knowledge and truth we have studied, such as Socrates, Plato, Descartes, Locke, and Berkeley, disagreed over the nature of knowledge and the best method for obtaining it. But they were all in agreement that if we obtain knowledge, we will have arrived at objective, universal truths about the world. In other words, they all agreed that there is one true story about the world.

The positions of all the philosophers just mentioned are various versions of objectivism. **Objectivism** (in epistemology) is the claim that there is one set of universal truths or facts about the world and that these truths are independent of us. Sometimes objectivism is called *absolutism*. However, because some people associate absolutism with a kind of nasty, dogmatic, authoritarian, and intolerant attitude, I have chosen to use *objectivism* instead. I would maintain that you can hold to objectivism (the belief that there are universal, mind-independent truths) without claiming that you necessarily have all the truth; thus you can still be open-minded, willing to modify your beliefs, and tolerant and respectful of the views of others. We talk about "searching for the truth," but that search only makes sense if there is something to be found (unlike the search for the mythical pot of gold at the end of the rainbow).

Immanuel Kant was an objectivist, although he added a new twist to the position. His Copernican revolution in knowledge advanced the thesis that our knowl-

objectivism the claim that there is one set of universal truths or facts about the world and that these truths are independent of us

edge of reality is not direct and unmediated, for our experience is always structured by the categories of the mind. From this thesis it follows that we can never know reality-in-itself. Still, Kant believed that the way in which our minds structure experience is the same for everyone. So Kant concluded that within the realm of human experience (what other realm could we know?), universal and objective knowledge was not only a possibility but an accomplished fact.

Now suppose Kant's revolution was correct (the mind structures our experience of reality). But suppose that he was wrong in maintaining there is one universal way in which all human minds are structured or only one way in which it is possible to make sense out of the world. It would then follow that different people would experience the world in different ways. There would be no one set of truths about the world, and no particular set of opinions would be more true than another. I may think that my position is more "true" and a more "accurate" account of reality than yours, but I am always viewing your position and reality itself through my particular mental lens. We cannot jump outside our minds to compare our mental concepts with reality itself.

If you have followed this journey from Kant's objectivism (with its singular set of rational, mental categories) to the proposal that there are multiple ways of structuring experience, then you are beginning to understand what relativism is all about. *Epistemological relativism* is the claim that there can be no universal, objective knowledge of reality because all knowledge is relative to the conceptual system of either the individual or one's culture. In other words, epistemological relativism is the belief that the world has not one true story, but many stories.

This position is variously called conceptual, cognitive, or epistemological relativism, since it asserts the relativity of all concepts, beliefs, and knowledge claims. In chapter 5 we examine ethical relativism, which holds to the same sort of claim about ethical principles, judgments, and statements. The epistemological relativist says that *all* claims are relative, so this statement would necessarily include ethical claims. Hence, if you accept the first position, you would have to adopt the second as well. However, the reverse is not true, for you could believe that ethical beliefs are relative while holding that other sorts of beliefs (scientific beliefs, for example) are objective.

 STOP AND THINK

Many popular phrases express the sentiments of relativism: "That may be true for you, but it's not true for me." "Beauty is in the eye of the beholder." "When in Rome, do as the Romans do." "We all have our own opinion about the matter, and who's to say whose belief is right?" "Different strokes for different folks." "It all depends on your point of view." "I believe this because that's just where I'm coming from."

- Can you think of other common ways of expressing relativism?
- Find examples in everyday conversations of expressions that suggest relativism.

Degrees of Relativism

To further focus the issue it is worth noting that there are several trivial forms of relativism that even an objectivist could accept. "For you, oysters taste delicious, but for me, they taste awful." Hardly anyone would deny that taste in foods is a relative matter that depends on individual preferences. One person's claim that oysters are delicious and my claim that they taste awful could be equally true because we are really not making a claim about the objective properties of oysters at all, but about our personal tastes. Hence, claims about the tastes of foods always imply that the phrase "to me" is implicitly tagged on to the end of the claim. Similarly, if I am standing on the front steps of the library, then for me, the library is "here." If you are across the street, then for you, the library is "there." Obviously, the terms *here* and *there,* as well as *left* and *right,* are always relative to the location of the speaker. But these "relative" statements really contain objective claims because the relative terms could be replaced by more objective spatial locators (such as the coordinates on a map).

Finally, a third kind of statement could be consistent with either objectivism or relativism, depending on how it is interpreted: "That's true for you but it is not true for me." This statement is ambiguous because it could have two different meanings. On the following interpretation the statement is trivially true: "If someone believes X, *then for that person* X is *thought* to be true." Of course! From the standpoint of medieval science it was "true" that the earth was flat. Similarly, according to some cultures it is "true" that the birth of twins will bring an evil curse to the society, so they must be destroyed. But this way of interpreting the original statement assumes that the statement is merely making a claim about the speaker's belief state, which still allows us to go on to ask if the belief in question really is true. (For the medievals it was true that the earth is flat, but is it *really*? Is there *really* a causal relationship between the birth of twins and bad fortune as these people think there is?) However, under another interpretation the original statement could be a full-fledged statement of relativism. Hence, the claim that "That's true for you but it is not true for me" could mean: "There is no objective truth about the matter, there are only different opinions, and one opinion is just as true as another."

 THOUGHT EXPERIMENT

Objective and Relative Truth

The following is a list of different issues. You might have a certain opinion on the issue, but your opinion is not relevant for the purposes of this exercise. What is relevant is whether you think the issue is one for which there is an objectively true answer and objectively false answers. To say that a claim is "objective" means that the truth or falsity of the claim is independent of whether any individual or culture believes it to be true or false. In this sense, you can judge that a claim or an issue is objective even though you are not sure what

(Continued . . .)

(. . . continued)

the true answer might be. If you think a particular issue is an objective one, put a mark in the "objective" column by that claim. However, if you do not think that the issue has either an objectively true or false answer, that it is solely a matter of opinion, then decide whether the truth or falsity of the answer is a matter of individual opinion (check "individually relative") or is a matter that is relative to one's culture (check "culturally relative").

Issue: Whether or not . . .	Objective	Individually Relative	Culturally Relative
1. Asparagus is delicious.			
2. Picasso's paintings have artistic merit.			
3. Johann Sebastian Bach is the greatest composer who ever lived.			
4. The Bible gives us the truest account of the purpose of life.			
5. Abortion is morally wrong, no matter what the circumstances.			
6. The institution of slavery in the United States was morally bad.			
7. Democracy is the best form of government.			
8. The earth is more than a billion years old.			
9. The color of your eyes is determined by your genes.			
10. The earth has been visited by space aliens.			

How you answered the questions indicates the degree to which you are a relativist. Statement 1 has to do with tastes in foods. Most people would say that this issue is relative to individual opinion. Statements 2 and 3 have to do with aesthetic judgments. You could be a relativist on these sorts of issues but an objectivist on others. If you think statement 4 is either true or false, you are an objectivist on religious issues. On the other hand, a religious relativist would say that this claim, like all religious claims, is purely a matter of personal choice, for there is no one, correct answer. Statements 5 and 6 deal with ethical claims. You could be a relativist on some ethical issues while believing that other ethical claims are objectively true no matter what an individual or culture believes. Statement 7 is a normative political judgment. Some objectivists would say it is true and others that it is false. A relativist would say that it depends solely on the preferences of the individual or a society. Statements 8, 9, and 10 are *claims* about empirical facts. To say that these statements are claims does not mean that they are true. You may think that the evidence shows that the earth is either older or younger than is claimed here. Furthermore, most (but not all) people think that the claim about aliens in statement 10 is false. The issue here is whether a fact about the matter makes the claim true or false independent of our beliefs about it. Someone who thinks these last three issues are simply a matter of personal or cultural opinion is probably as thoroughgoing a relativist as one can be. How many issues did you label as either individually or culturally relative? Were there any issues that you said were objective ones? How do you distinguish between issues that are objective and those in which there is no higher truth other than personal or cultural opinion?

Skepticism versus Relativism

Is there a difference between truth and falsehood? Or does it just depend on how you look at it?

On these and similar issues, it is important to distinguish between the positions of skepticism and relativism. Although the skeptic and relativist both reject the possibility of arriving at objectively true answers to philosophical questions, they do so for different reasons. The skeptic may accept the possibility that a philosophical question has one true answer, but simply claim that it is impossible for us to know the truth about the matter. In section 4.2, for example, we will see that David Hume took the objectivist stance that either there is an all-powerful, personal God who created the universe or there is not. He simply insisted that we had no way of knowing which alternative is true. On the other hand, the relativist says that there is no one true answer to any philosophical question. Truth claims are always relative to the beliefs of the individual or society. Hence, the relativist insists that any time you make a truth claim about God, the nature of reality, ethics, politics, and so on, your claim could only be true with respect to your point of view or that of your society. To put it simply, the relativist claims that all truth is relative in the same way that tastes in food are relative. For the relativists, we are always immersed within our particular historical age, particular culture, or personal perspective and can no more rise above these circumstances than we could jump out of our skins or lift ourselves up by our own bootstraps.

But does the relativist believe that there is no reality outside our belief systems? Well, yes and no. *Reality,* like *fact, rationality,* and *truth,* is a word and a concept. As such, it is always rooted in a particular conceptual and linguistic scheme. To ask if our belief system conforms to reality is like trying to use a pair of pliers to grab itself. We use our particular notion of reality to get a grip on our experience, but we can't use it to get a grip on our conceptual scheme because it is a part of what constitutes that scheme. To switch metaphors, I view the world through my eyeglasses, but I cannot take my glasses off and examine them without using some other glasses through which to see them. But how can I tell if this second pair of glasses is adequate unless I examine them through some other lenses? According to the relativists, we always and necessarily view the world through some sort of conceptual lenses, but there is no neutral instrument by means of which we can examine and evaluate our own or anyone else's conceptual lenses.

STOP AND THINK

Imagine that you were to make a list of all your beliefs. Now imagine that you made a second list of everything that was true. Would the lists be any different? Surely not. If you believe something, you do so because you think it is true, and if you consider something to be true, then you believe it. Is the relativist therefore correct in claiming that truth is always a function of our web of beliefs? Can we ever break out of our belief system to compare it with what lies outside of it?

So here we are—stuck within the human situation and unable to lift ourselves up by our own bootstraps to see the world from a Godlike perspective. So what do we do? According to contemporary philosopher Richard Rorty, we keep talking. He says that the point of philosophy is "to keep the conversation going rather than to find objective truth."[50] Different personal, historical, and cultural viewpoints about philosophical, religious, and ethical issues (to name just a few) are like the images created by the turns of a kaleidoscope. Thousands of patterns are possible, each view is different and is fascinating in itself, some may work better for *us* than others, but no particular image is the "right" one or the most "accurate" one or the only one that everyone is compelled to view. To say that a belief is "true" is simply to claim that we find it good for *us* to believe it, according to Rorty.

THOUGHT EXPERIMENT

Changing Perspectives

Here are a few examples of how the same situation can be viewed differently, described differently, and evaluated differently, depending on your particular perspective.

- In American history books, the American Revolution is presented as one of the great turning points in world history. However, one of my professors once said that when he was a schoolboy in England, his history book covered the American Revolution in only a footnote, referring to it simply as "the revolt of the colonies."
- History books refer to 1492 as the year that "Columbus discovered America." However, that expression irritates Native Americans. How could Columbus "discover" America if it had never been hidden because their ancestors were already here? Instead, Native Americans view Columbus's "discovery" as "the invasion of our homelands by the Europeans."

(Continued . . .)

(. . . continued)

- Sydney J. Harris, a newspaper columnist, loved to point out how the same facts could be described by different people in different ways. Some of my favorites are:
  - My children are permitted to engage in "self-expression," but your children are "spoiled."
  - I turn down invitations because I "enjoy privacy," but you turn down invitations because you are "antisocial."
  - I won't change my mind because I have "firm principles," but you won't change your mind because you are "fanatical."

Can you think of other examples in which the same facts are described in different ways?

Varieties of Relativism

You may have noticed that implicit in our discussion thus far has been the distinction between different kinds of relativism. When someone claims that all knowledge or truth is relative, the question that arises is, "Relative to what?" One answer is that beliefs are relative to each person's individual perspective. This assertion of individual relativism is commonly called **subjectivism.** The Greek Sophist Protagoras is said to have claimed:

subjectivism the claim that beliefs are relative to each person's individual perspective

> Each one of us is a measure of what is and of what is not; but there is all the difference in the world between one man and another just in the very fact that what is and appears to one is different from what is and appears to the other.[51]

Similarly, the nineteenth-century existentialist Friedrich Nietzsche repeatedly preached subjectivism in passages such as this one:

> Gradually it has become clear to me what every great philosophy so far has been: namely, the personal confession of its author and a kind of involuntary and unconscious memoir.[52]

When a young man came to the contemporary French philosopher Jean-Paul Sartre seeking ethical advice, the only advice Sartre would give him was "You are free, therefore choose—that is to say, invent."[53] If all truth claims are subjective and relative to an individual's perspective, then what could any assertion be except a "personal confession"? Hence, the subjectivist thinks that the qualifier "true for me" is implicit in all assertions.

On the other hand, we could claim that all beliefs are relative to a particular culture. For obvious reasons, this claim is called **cultural relativism.** For example, the anthropologist Ruth Benedict claimed that rather than viewing Western culture as superior to those of "primitive" cultures, we should see it as merely one way people in society adjust to one another. As she puts it, "Modern civilization, from this point of view, becomes not a necessary pinnacle of human achievement but one entry in a long series of possible adjustments."[54] Is it wrong for women to wear blue jeans? It all depends. In American culture it is an everyday occurrence, while

cultural relativism the claim that all beliefs are relative to a particular culture

in other parts of the world it is deeply offensive and immoral. Can science tell us all that there is to know about reality? Many people in our society believe it can. But for Plato and for some people in our own time, science can provide us with only a partial view of reality at best, or at worst, it can give us knowledge of appearances only. It all depends on your particular conception of reality. But how can we compare or evaluate different conceptions of reality, the cultural relativist says, when any evidence or data or standards of rationality that could be used to evaluate our own or another's position will always be defined, accepted, rejected, or applied in terms of our particular conception of reality? Such an action is like filling out a job application and listing yourself as a reference.

Contemporary philosopher Willard V. O. Quine (born 1908) has given us an interesting presentation of this perspective. (W. V. O. Quine spent most of his professional career at Harvard University. His writings on epistemology and meta-physics have been very influential within contemporary philosophy.) Quine de-scribes each person's view of the world as a partially stable and partially fluctuating "web of belief." The "facts" cannot prove or disprove a conceptual scheme, because what we accept or reject as a fact and how we interpret it will always be decided in terms of the whole fabric of our web of belief. However, in the face of a particularly "recalcitrant experience," we may decide to modify or even jettison deep features of our belief system, for no foundational beliefs are incapable of being revised. Nevertheless, it is always *we* who are deciding what to do with the evidence rather than the evidence dictating our response. At the most fundamental level, Quine seems to be saying that large-scale, conflicting belief systems present alternatives that we embrace or reject based on our preferences, cultural traditions, and practical needs. Quine says, for example, that twentieth-century people's belief in physical objects and the accompanying natural laws we associate with them are used to explain physical events. In contrast, Homer told stories of the gods and their activities to explain what happened in the world. Quine prefers his web of belief over Homer's, but he recognizes that in the final analysis both sets of beliefs are merely different cultural and conceptual frameworks.

> For my part I do, qua lay physicist, believe in physical objects and not in Homer's gods; and I consider it a scientific error to believe otherwise. But in point of epistemological footing the physical objects and the gods differ only in degree and not in kind. Both sorts of entities enter our conception only as cultural posits.[55]

Is there no way to argue the superiority of contemporary physics over Greek myth-ology? The problem is that, from the standpoint of cultural relativism, what we define as "mythology" are merely those belief systems that differ significantly from our own. Quine says that he prefers his "myth" (the conceptual scheme of science) because it is the one that is most effective in making predictions and organizing our experiences.

> The myth of physical objects is epistemologically superior to most in that it has proved more efficacious than other myths as a device for working a manageable structure into the flux of experience.[56]

However, once Quine has headed down the road of cultural relativism, the fact that science is a tool that can accomplish this end does not prove that it is more rational a scheme than Homer's. It merely reflects Quine's choice as to what he will count as "rational."

historical relativism the claim that each historical age had different conceptual frameworks such that there are no universal truths but only truths that are correct for a particular age

Another form of relativism is **historical relativism.** There are significant differences between the way that we look at the world and the way that the ancient Greeks, the medievals, and people in the Renaissance viewed the world in their respective eras. The German philosopher Georg W. F. Hegel (1770–1831) was most influential in promoting the view that each historical age had different conceptual frameworks. He believed that each phase of history contained a "spirit of the age" that produced the cultural and intellectual life of the people. Hence, he claimed that ideas are not eternal truths but are reflections of their time and that the truth of any idea has to be evaluated in terms of its own historical setting.

> As far as the individual is concerned, each individual is in any case a *child of his time;* thus philosophy, too, is *its own time comprehended in thoughts.* It is just as foolish to imagine that any philosophy can transcend its contemporary world as that an individual can overleap his own time.[57]

Ironically, however, Hegel did not believe that relativism was the last word. He believed that there was a rational pattern to the evolution of ideas, such that each historical era provided a partial and incomplete perspective on the one, absolute truth. Furthermore, according to the Hegelian story, each new moment in history was bringing us closer to this universal truth. Hence, Hegel's picture was that of objectivism on the installment plan. Although he was an objectivist, Hegel (like Kant) provided fuel for relativism, for many thinkers adopted his historical relativism but discarded his view that objective truth would ultimately emerge from this changing kaleidoscope of historical perspectives.

One of the most well-known contemporary defenders of epistemological relativism was Nelson Goodman (1906–1998), who was a professor of philosophy at Harvard University. The title of one of his best-known books, from which the next reading is taken, is *Ways of Worldmaking.* Notice that the title implies that the world as we know it is "made" by our linguistic and conceptual schemes and not "discovered." He talks about the vast variety of versions of the world, referring to the various representations of the world given in the sciences and various philosophies and in the works of artists and writers. While most people would acknowledge that there are various stories about the world, they would insist that only one version can be right. Goodman, however, says that there can be countless "right versions" of the world even though they are incompatible. For this reason, he describes his position as radical relativism.

- What does Goodman say about frames of reference? Can we describe the world apart from a frame of reference?
- Some philosophers think that all "right versions" of the world can be reduced to the story that physics tells. Does Goodman agree with this view?

FROM NELSON GOODMAN

Ways of Worldmaking[58]

Questions

. . . My aim in what follows is less to defend certain theses . . . than to take a hard look at some crucial questions they raise. In just what sense are there many worlds? What distinguishes genuine from spurious worlds? What are worlds made of? How are they made? What role do symbols play in the making? And how is worldmaking related to knowing? These questions must be faced even if full and final answers are far off.

Versions and Visions

. . . Consider, to begin with, the statements "The sun always moves" and "The sun never moves" which, though equally true, are at odds with each other. Shall we say, then, that they describe different worlds, and indeed that there are as many different worlds as there are such mutually exclusive truths? Rather, we are inclined to regard the two strings of words not as complete statements with truth-values of their own but as elliptical for some such statements as "Under frame of reference A, the sun always moves" and "Under frame of reference B, the sun never moves"—statements that may both be true of the same world.

Frames of reference, though, seem to belong less to what is described than to systems of description: and each of the two statements relates what is described to such a system. If I ask about the world, you can offer to tell me how it is under one or more frames of reference; but if I insist that you tell me how it is apart from all frames, what can you say? We are confined to ways of describing whatever is described. Our universe, so to speak, consists of these ways rather than of a world or of worlds. . . .

Yet doesn't a right version differ from a wrong one just in applying to the world, so that rightness itself depends upon and implies a world? We might better say that "the world" depends upon rightness. We cannot test a version by comparing it with a world undescribed, undepicted, unperceived, but only by other means that I shall discuss later. While we may speak of determining what versions are right as "learning about the world", "the world" supposedly being that which all right versions describe, all we learn about the world is contained in right versions of it; and while the underlying world, bereft of these, need not be denied to those who love it, it is perhaps on the whole a world well lost. For some purposes, we may want to define a relation that will so sort versions into clusters that each cluster constitutes a world, and the members of the cluster are versions of that world; but for many purposes, right world-descriptions and world-depictions and world-perceptions, the ways-the-world-is or just versions, can be treated as our worlds.

Since the fact that there are many different world-versions is hardly debatable, and the question how many if any worlds-in-themselves there are is virtually empty, in what non-trivial sense are there . . . many worlds? Just this, I think: that many different world-versions are of independent interest and importance, without any requirement or presumption of reducibility to a single base. The pluralist, far from being anti-scientific, accepts the sciences at full value. His typical adversary is the monopolistic materialist or physicalist who maintains that one system, physics, is preeminent and all-inclusive, such that every other version must eventually be reduced to it or rejected as false or meaningless. If all right versions could somehow be reduced to one and only one, that one might with some semblance of plausibility be regarded as the only truth about the only world. But the evidence for such reducibility is negligible, and even the claim is nebulous since physics itself is fragmentary and unstable and the kind and consequences of reduction envisaged are vague. . . . I am the last person likely to underrate construction and reduction. A reduction from one system to another can make a genuine contribution to understanding the interrelationships among world-versions; but reduction in any reasonably strict sense is rare, almost always partial, and seldom if ever unique. To demand full and sole reducibility to physics or any other one version is to forego nearly all other versions. The pluralists' acceptance of versions other than physics implies no relaxation of rigor but a recognition that standards different from yet no less exacting than those applied in science are appropriate for appraising what is conveyed in perceptual or pictorial or literary versions.

So long as contrasting right versions not all reducible to one are countenanced, unity is to be sought not in an ambivalent or neutral *something* beneath these versions but in an overall organization embracing them. . . . My approach is . . . through an analytic study of types and functions of symbols and symbol systems. In neither case should a unique result be anticipated; universes of worlds as well as worlds themselves may be built in many ways.

Goodman goes on to list several processes that we employ in constructing our view of the world. (1) *Composition and Decomposition.* On the one hand, we collect together different components of our experience and lump them under one label. Let me give some examples to illustrate Goodman's point. The ancients grouped separate stars together as constellations and gave them the names of people and objects. We talk about our "college experience" even though it consists of thousands of experiences. On the other hand, we divide a whole into parts, as when we label the parts of the body. (2) *Weighting.* Different people give different emphasis to the same features of the world. We call some facts "relevant" and others "irrelevant." The pessimist says the glass is half empty and the optimist says it is half full. (3) *Ordering.* For various purposes, we take some things as fundamental and others as derivative. To tell if your car is rolling, you assume that the earth is stationary and compare your position to it. But in astronomy, we assume the sun is stationary and measure the motion of the earth with respect to it. (4) *Deletion and Supplementation.* We are more attentive to some portions of our experience and ignore other portions. In the midst of a noisy crowd, you are more likely to hear your name being called than a stranger's name. Goodman cites research that shows if a subject is shown two flashes of light in succession and a short distance apart, the viewer will tend to see one spot of light moving continuously from one position to the next. (5) *Deformation.* We stretch and mold reality to fit our expectations. A scientist's data never conforms to a perfect pattern. Nevertheless, the scientist will assume that the data is approaching an ideal formula or approximates a pattern that the scientist is imposing on the world.

In the next passage, Goodman speaks about "true" or "right" versions of the world.

- Why can't truth be defined in terms of "agreement with 'the world'"?
- Why does Goodman say truth is a "docile and obedient servant"?

Trouble with Truth

With all this freedom to divide and combine, emphasize, order, delete, fill in and fill out, and even distort, what are the objectives and the constraints? What are the criteria for success in making a world?

Insofar as a version is verbal and consists of statements, truth may be relevant. But truth cannot be defined or tested by agreement with "the world"; for not only do truths differ for different worlds but the nature of agreement between a version and a world apart from it is notoriously nebulous. Rather—speaking loosely . . . a version is taken to be true when it offends no unyielding beliefs and none of its own precepts. Among beliefs unyielding at a given time may be long-lived reflections of laws of logic, short-lived reflections of recent observations, and other convictions and prejudices ingrained with varying degrees of firmness. Among precepts, for example, may be choices among alternative frames of reference, weightings, and derivational bases. But the line between beliefs and precepts is neither sharp nor stable. Beliefs are framed in concepts informed by precepts; and if a Boyle ditches his data for a smooth curve just missing them all, we may say either that observational volume and pressure are different properties from theoretical volume and pressure or that the truths about volume and pressure differ in the two worlds of observation and theory. Even the staunchest belief may in time admit alternatives; "The earth is at rest" passed from dogma to dependence upon precept.

Truth, far from being a solemn and severe master, is a docile and obedient servant. The scientist who supposes that he is single-mindedly dedicated to the search for truth deceives himself. He is unconcerned with the trivial truths he could grind out endlessly; and he looks to the multifaceted and irregular results of observations for little more than suggestions of overall structures and significant generalizations. He seeks system, simplicity, scope; and when satisfied on these scores he tailors truth to fit. . . . He as much decrees as discovers the laws he sets forth, as much designs as discerns the patterns he delineates.

According to Goodman, what makes a version true is not that it corresponds to the way the world really is, for we cannot jump outside our ways of representing the world to see the world independent of them. Instead, we have to see how well a version of the world coheres with beliefs we already embrace ("offends no unyielding beliefs") and if it is internally consistent ("offends . . . none of its own precepts"). Using these criteria, we can reject some versions as inadequate, but there will remain countless different versions of the world that satisfy these internal criteria.

Relative Reality

Shouldn't we now return to sanity from all this mad proliferation of worlds? Shouldn't we stop speaking of right versions as if each were, or had, its own world, and recognize all as versions of one and the same neutral and underlying world? The world thus regained, as remarked earlier, is a world without kinds or order or motion or rest or pattern—a world not worth fighting for or against.

We might, though, take the real world to be that of some one of the alternative right versions (or groups of them bound together by some principle of reducibility or translatability) and regard all others as versions of that same world differing from the standard version in accountable ways. The physicist takes his world as the real one, attributing the deletions, additions, irregularities, emphases of other versions to the imperfections of perception, to the urgencies of practice, or to poetic license. The phenomenalist regards the perceptual world as fundamental, and the excisions, abstractions, simplifications, and distortions of other versions as resulting from scientific or practical or artistic concerns. For the man-in-the-street, most versions from science, art, and perception depart in some ways from the familiar serviceable world he has jerry-built from fragments of scientific and artistic tradition and from his own struggle for survival. This world, indeed, is the one most often taken as real; for reality in a world, like realism in a picture, is largely a matter of habit.

Ironically, then, our passion for *one* world is satisfied, at different times and for different purposes, in *many* different ways. Not only motion, derivation, weighting, order, but even reality is relative. That right versions and actual worlds are many does not obliterate the distinction between right and wrong versions, does not recognize merely possible worlds answering to wrong versions, and does not imply that all right alternatives are equally good for every or indeed for any purpose. Not even a fly is likely to take one of its wing-tips as a fixed point; we do not welcome molecules or concreta as elements of our everyday world, or combine tomatoes and triangles and typewriters and tyrants and tornadoes into a single kind; the physicist will count none of these among his fundamental particles; the painter who sees the way the man-in-the-street does will have more popular than artistic success. And the same philosopher who here metaphilosophically contemplates a vast variety of worlds finds that only versions meeting the demands of a dogged and deflationary nominalism suit his purposes in constructing philosophical systems.

Moreover, while readiness to recognize alternative worlds may be liberating, and suggestive of new avenues of exploration, a willingness to welcome all worlds builds none. Mere acknowledgment of the many available frames of reference provides us with no map of the motions of heavenly bodies; acceptance of the eligibility of alternative bases produces no scientific theory or philosophical system; awareness of varied ways of seeing paints no pictures. A broad mind is no substitute for hard work.

In the next and final passage, Goodman denies that his radical relativism implies that "everything goes." Just because there are many acceptable versions of the world doesn't mean that there are not others that are unacceptable. He says we have a yearning for something *stolid* underneath our world-stories, meaning something fixed and impassive.

- What does Goodman say about the relationship between facts and theories? Do you find what he says plausible?

Means and Matter

What I have said so far plainly points to a radical relativism; but severe restraints are imposed. Willingness to accept countless alternative true or right world-versions does not mean that everything goes, that tall stories are as good as short ones, that truths are no longer distinguished from falsehoods, but only that truth must be otherwise conceived than as correspondence with a ready-made world. Though we make worlds by making versions, we no more make a world by putting symbols together at random than a carpenter makes a chair by putting pieces of wood together at random. The multiple worlds I countenance are just the actual worlds made by and answering to true or right versions. Worlds possible or impossible supposedly answering to false versions have no place in my philosophy.

Just what worlds are to be recognized as actual is quite another question. Although some aspects of a philosophical position have a bearing, even what seem severely restrictive views may recognize countless versions as equally right. . . .

To speak of worlds as made by versions often offends both by its implicit pluralism and by its sabotage of what I have called "something stolid underneath."

Let me offer what comfort I can. While I stress the multiplicity of right world-versions, I by no means insist that there are many worlds—or indeed any; for as I have already suggested, the question whether two versions are of the same world has as many good answers as there are good interpretations of the words "versions of the same world" . . .

. . . Of course, we want to distinguish between versions that do and those that do not refer, and to talk about the things and worlds, if any, referred to; but these things and worlds and even the stuff they are made of—matter, anti-matter, mind, energy, or whatnot—are themselves fashioned by and along with the versions. Facts, as Norwood Hanson says are theory-laden; they are as theory-laden as we hope our theories are fact-laden. Or in other words, facts are small theories, and true theories are big facts. This does not mean, I must repeat, that right versions can be arrived at casually, or that worlds are built from scratch. We start, on any occasion, with some old version or world that we have on hand and that we are stuck with until we have the determination and skill to remake it into a new one. Some of the felt stubbornness of fact is the grip of habit: our firm foundation is indeed stolid. Worldmaking begins with one version and ends with another.

 THOUGHT EXPERIMENT

Culture and Perception

Before reading further, look at the figure here and answer the following questions:

1. Is this picture of a family or a group of strangers?
2. How many adults are in the picture?
3. Is this picture an indoor scene or an outdoor scene?
4. Are the people happy or sad?

After you have answered the questions yourself, present the picture and the questions to a number of friends. If you have friends who are international students, it would be particularly interesting to see how their answers compare with yours. Actually, the only important question is the third one. The rest were rather obvious and served merely to take the spotlight off the third question.

From *Simple Reading for Adults: Its Preparation and Use.* Copyright © 1963 UNESCO. Reproduced by permission of UNESCO.

(Continued . . .)

(. . . continued)

Did you say this picture was an indoor scene? If so, what were the clues that led you to this answer? If you are like me, you assumed that the rectangular figure "behind" the woman to the left of center is a window revealing some foliage outside. Furthermore, the Y-shaped figure rising up to the top of the picture looks like the corner of a room bathed in shadows. However, subjects from East Africa, when asked what they saw, described a family group in which a young woman is carrying a four-gallon tin on her head (a common sight in that region). Since North Americans do not have the convention (nor the skill) of balancing and transporting large objects on their head, they assume that the rectangular drawing is not a solid object but a window in the wall behind the woman. This simple example shows how our culture influences what we see and the judgments that we make.

An interesting example of cultural relativism at work is found in the writings of Carlos Castaneda. In 1960 he abandoned his earlier studies in art and psychology and began graduate work in anthropology at U.C.L.A. As part of his field research he began interviewing don Juan, a Yaqui Indian sorcerer who lived in the Southwest and who originally came from Sonora, Mexico. This research became Castaneda's master's thesis, which was published by a university press as *The Teachings of Don Juan: A Yaqui Way of Knowledge.**

In his initial interviews Castaneda viewed the claims of don Juan through the eyes of a Western behavioral scientist. As such, his conceptual framework had typically Western epistemological conceptions concerning rationality, plausibility, evidence, and experience. Likewise, his thought functioned within a particular metaphysical framework that dictated the nature of reality, possibility, impossibility, causality, and natural order. On the other hand, don Juan, a self-proclaimed sorcerer, lived in a world of magic and mind-boggling supernatural events. His world was populated by friendly and evil spirits who could take the form of various animals and who could either enlighten you or destroy you. In the interaction between Castaneda's and don Juan's conceptual frameworks, we have a "war of the worlds." Castaneda continually tried to find some sort of neutral, rational grounds in terms of which he could discuss don Juan's claims. He always failed, however, because all data, evidence, and experiences ended up being interpreted through either Western eyes or Yaqui eyes.

In one of the most popular accounts in all of Castaneda's books, he tries to enter don Juan's world by experiencing what sorcerers experience. To do so he applies a paste to his body made of Jimson weed (devil's weed or *Datura inoxia*). As a result, he experiences himself flying high above the clouds and circling the mountains while don Juan is watching far below on the earth. Shortly after experiencing

---

*By the spring of 1973 Castaneda's master's thesis had sold 300,000 copies in paper and was selling at a rate of 16,000 copies per week. For the years 1972 through 1974, one or more of his four books were on the list of top ten college best-sellers. Castaneda died in 1998.

himself landing back on the ground like a bird, Castaneda blacks out. Of course, Jimson weed contains a hallucinogenic drug, and the anthropologist's experience was the result of its chemical effects on his brain. Or was it? It all depends on your framework. In the following passage Castaneda tries to use his scientific framework to sort out the experience with don Juan.

FROM CARLOS CASTANEDA
The Teachings of Don Juan[59]

There was a question I wanted to ask him. I knew he was going to evade it, so I waited for him to mention the subject; I waited all day. Finally, before I left that evening, I had to ask him, "Did I really fly, don Juan?"

"That is what you told me. Didn't you?"

"I know, don Juan. I mean, did my body fly? Did I take off like a bird?"

"You always ask me questions I cannot answer. You flew. That is what the second portion of the devil's weed is for. As you take more of it, you will learn how to fly perfectly. It is not a simple matter. A man *flies* with the help of the second portion of the devil's weed. That is all I can tell you. What you want to know makes no sense. Birds fly like birds and a man who has taken the devil's weed flies as such [*el enyerbado vuela así*]."

"As birds do? [*¿Así como los pájaros?*]"

"No, he flies as a man who has taken the weed [*No, así como los enyerbados*]."

"Then I didn't really fly, don Juan. I flew in my imagination, in my mind alone. Where was my body?"

"In the bushes," he replied cuttingly, but immediately broke into laughter again. "The trouble with you is that you understand things in only one way. You don't think a man flies; and yet a brujo* can move a thousand miles in one second to see what is going on. He can deliver a blow to his enemies long distances away. So, does he or doesn't he fly?"

In this initial exchange, Castaneda has failed to get don Juan to make a distinction based on the categories of Western science: (1) flying "as a bird does" (really flying in the air) and (2) flying "in my imagination" (a hallucination caused by the drug). So Castaneda tries once again to get don Juan to approach the situation scientifically by asking if the alleged flying would be verified by the intersubjective agreement of objective, neutral observers. But don Juan is a conceptual relativist. He explains that what the observers would see would depend on their conceptual framework, their past experiences, or their expectations and assumptions. In other words, there are no theory-neutral observations or facts.

---

*As Castaneda has explained earlier, the Spanish word *brujo* means medicine man, healer, witch, or sorcerer.

"You see, don Juan, you and I are differently oriented. Suppose, for the sake of argument, one of my fellow students had been here with me when I took the devil's weed. Would he have been able to see me flying?"

"There you go again with your questions about what would happen if. . . . It is useless to talk that way. If your friend, or anybody else, takes the second portion of the weed all he can do is fly. Now, if he had simply watched you, he might have seen you flying, or he might not. That depends on the man."

"But what I mean, don Juan, is that if you and I look at a bird and see it fly, we agree that it is flying. But if two of my friends had seen me flying as I did last night, would they have agreed that I was flying?"

"Well, they might have. You agree that birds fly because you have seen them flying. Flying is a common thing with birds. But you will not agree on other things birds do, because you have never seen birds doing them. If your friends knew about men flying with the devil's weed, then they would agree."

Finally, Castaneda proposes a scientific experiment. Would he still fly if his body was chained to a rock? If a bird (who can really fly as verified by science) were chained, then it could not fly under those circumstances. But if Castaneda still has the experience of flying while chained to the rock, that result proves that the "flying" is not real but is a hallucination. Once again, don Juan refuses to accept the Western dichotomy that supposes that Castaneda either flew in a manner that was verifiable by scientific, objective observers or that the "flying" was merely a mental event in his imagination.

"Let's put it another way, don Juan. What I meant to say is that if I had tied myself to a rock with a heavy chain I would have flown just the same, because my body had nothing to do with my flying."

Don Juan looked at me incredulously. "If you tie yourself to a rock," he said, "I'm afraid you will have to fly holding the rock with its heavy chain."

 STOP AND THINK

How would you try to get don Juan to distinguish between really flying (in the sense of physically leaving the ground) and only having the sensation of flying?

As this dialogue suggests, no scientific experiments or data would force don Juan to abandon his views, for all such data would be understood in terms of a set of assumptions and a worldview that he rejects. Even if we pointed out that the flying experiences occur only when someone has been affected by the Jimson weed, he might argue that the plant did not *cause* the realities experienced but merely produced a spiritual *window* through which the other dimensions of reality could be revealed.

Try this exercise to get some distance from your own conceptual scheme. Those of us who are members of twentieth-century Western scientific cultures believe that electrons exist and that they explain a great deal of what happens in the world we experience. But imagine that you have not been raised to think this way. (Perhaps you are an Yaqui Indian sorcerer.) With this approach in mind, interview students majoring in the sciences (particularly chemistry or physics) about electrons. If you are bold enough, you might even interview professors in these disciplines. Ask them this simple question: Why do you believe that electrons exist?

Whatever their answer may be, follow up with other questions as to why the subject thinks the reasons and explanations he or she has provided are true. After all, we cannot literally see electrons. Their existence is either assumed or deduced from other assumptions that we make about how the whole of reality is put together as well as how to interpret our scientific instruments. Keep pressing them with the questions and see if they reach a point at which they can only say something like, "That's just the way it is!" (Try to avoid irritating them.)

I have found that many of my colleagues who have Ph.D.s in chemistry are taken aback by this line of questioning. The existence of electrons is such an unquestioned and significant part of the framework in which we think, that people see little need to examine the grounds for this belief. Sometimes scientists respond that by postulating the existence of electrons they are able to make predictions and carry on successful experiments. In other words, the belief in electrons "works" as a guide to action. (You may want to keep their reasons in mind when you read section 2.7 on pragmatism and see the degree to which their responses are similar to William James's pragmatic theory of truth.) Finally, after interviewing the experts, ask the same question of several nonscience majors to see what sorts of justifications they provide. To complete this exercise, answer the following questions yourself.

- Do you agree or disagree with the following statement: "In the final analysis, belief in electrons depends on accepting the large-scale conceptual framework of the modern scientific worldview." Why did you answer as you did?
- Could you ever convince someone that electrons existed if that person did not accept this conceptual framework?
- Do these considerations lend support to the conceptual relativist, or is it possible to justify the view that there is one true story about the world and electrons are a significant part of it?

The Standard Criticism of Relativism

Throughout his writings, Plato attacked the relativists of his day, a group of philosophers known as the Sophists. As I mentioned previously, the Sophist Protagoras said that "man is the measure of all things." By this statement, Protagoras was claiming that individual or social opinion is the only standard we have and all opinions are equally true. In response, Plato gives this exchange between Socrates and the mathematician Theodorus:

SOCRATES: Protagoras, for his part, admitting as he does that everybody's opinion is true, must acknowledge the truth of his opponents' belief about his own belief, where they think he is wrong.

THEODORUS: Certainly.

SOCRATES: That is to say, he would acknowledge his own belief to be false, if he admits that the belief of those who think him wrong is true?

THEODORUS: Necessarily.[60]

Through the voice of Socrates, Plato is arguing that relativists do not really believe that all opinions are equally true. Relativists believe they are *correct* and their opponents are *wrong* in their opinions about knowledge. The relativist seems to be making two claims: (1) "There is no objective truth," and (2) "Statement 1 is objectively true." With these statements, Plato claims, relativists have contradicted themselves.*

Plato's argument against the relativism of Protagoras is one version of what I will call the "Standard Criticism" of relativism, which could be formulated in this way:

1. The relativist makes the following claim R: "There are no universal, objective truths about the world."
2. But statement R is a claim about the world.
3. If statement R is considered to be an objective truth, then it contradicts itself.
4. If statement R is considered to be a relative truth, then the relativist is simply reporting on how he or she personally views the world and is really not making a claim about how things really are.
5. Since points 3 and 4 are the only alternatives, then either way the relativist's claim undermines itself.

Because this sort of criticism is at least as old as Plato, relativists are well aware that this argument is a major challenge that they must face. Different relativists respond to the criticism in different ways.

PREVIEW OF COMING ATTRACTIONS

After concluding our discussion of relativism, I devote the remaining sections of this chapter to examining three philosophical positions on knowledge that all fall under the heading of "Rethinking the Western Tradition." These three philosophies are existentialism, pragmatism, and feminism. Unlike the Asian philosophies

---

*In our discussion of logic (section 1.2), I set out a reconstructed version of this argument and labeled it a reductio ad absurdum argument. That is, this argument is a technique of refuting an opponent by first assuming his or her position and showing that it leads to an absurdity or a contradiction.

of religion that will be discussed in section 4.6, which challenged the assumptions of Western thought from outside its boundaries, the next three positions all arose as movements within the Western philosophical tradition. Nevertheless, the three movements all engage in a radical critique of their own family tree. Western philosophy has always been characterized by disagreements, controversies, and divisions, such as theism versus atheism or rationalism versus empiricism. But existentialism, pragmatism, and feminism contend that the majority of the debates throughout this tradition have always been staged on the platform of objectivism. Hence, these three views of knowledge, two of which arose in the late nineteenth century (existentialism and pragmatism) and the other in the twentieth century (feminism), take as their initial defining point their rejection of the majority's commitment to unqualified objectivism throughout Western philosophy. The various proponents of these three philosophies have views ranging over (1) full-fledged subjectivism, (2) moderate, qualified relativism, or (3) a mixture of attitudes toward relativism, but they all agree that there are no context-free truths, that experience of the world is, at best, always mediated through our personal lenses, and that our theories of knowledge and reality must focus on the knower as well as on that which is allegedly known. The degree to which these theses commit these philosophers to a full-blown relativism will have to be judged in each individual case.

 ## LOOKING THROUGH THE RELATIVIST'S LENS

1. If we all became convinced that relativism is true, what would be lost by giving up the belief in objective truth? After all, most objectivists agree that human knowledge is fallible and that our best knowledge is always imperfect. Even the Bible's Apostle Paul, a paragon of objectivism, said that "it is as though we see through a dark glass" and "the knowledge I now have is imperfect."[61] Even though most people would agree that we have not finally resolved the question of "what are the absolutely correct set of objective truths?" we seem to have beliefs that work for us (and our culture) and that enable us to get through life satisfactorily. Why do we need to suppose there is only one way to live or to view the world? On the other hand, if we all suddenly became convinced that there is one set of objective truths, accepting that fact alone would not cause us to change most of the beliefs that we currently have. Each of us would be convinced that the beliefs we held were the best account of the one true story of the world. So, in practical terms, what difference does objectivism make?

2. Some relativists, such as Protagoras, claim that both (1) all beliefs are relative and (2) all beliefs are of equal value. Could a relativist hold to statement 1 but reject statement 2? Couldn't a relativist reject some beliefs or entire systems of beliefs because they are contradictory or because they fail according to their own criteria or even because they bear very little correspondence to the world? Couldn't a relativist reject some beliefs as absurd while still claiming that there remain many incompatible beliefs that are equal in the degree to which they correspond to the

world? Isn't this distinction between plausible and implausible relative beliefs consistent with relativism?

EXAMINING THE STRENGTHS AND WEAKNESSES OF RELATIVISM

Positive Evaluation

1. Since the beginning of civilization to our own day, human history has been one long string of differing opinions and debates over fundamental issues in philosophy, morals, religion, politics, and so forth, with each participant in the debate claiming that his or her position is the true one and the others are wrong. Even in science, physicists and astronomers have differing opinions over which physical theory is the correct one on many issues. Just when scientists would reach a consensus, a new generation of scientists would come along and overthrow it. If there is one true story about the world, why is it so hard to figure out what it is? Doesn't the relativist have a simple and logical answer to that question?

2. Wouldn't a healthy dose of relativism be an antidote to all the dogmatism and intolerance in the world? Wouldn't it make people more humble and willing to consider alternative points of view? Would we have had all the wars, persecutions, and tyrannies in human history if people did not believe that they held the absolute truth?

Negative Evaluation

1. Does the fact that people disagree over fundamental issues necessarily prove that there is no objective truth? If you asked five people to give their opinion of the length of this line down to the nearest sixteenth of an inch, isn't it likely that you would get five different opinions? Do these differing opinions mean that there is no truth about the matter?

When opinions differ (as in the case of the line), there are several possibilities: (1) one opinion is correct and the others are wrong; (2) all the opinions are wrong but some are closer to the truth than others. But the relativist supposes that the only possibilities are (3) all opinions are of equal value, or at least, (4) there is no objective truth about which these opinions differ. Why should we suppose that (3) and (4) are the only alternatives? As in the case of the line, the fact that people's opinions differ does not mean that there is not one, correct truth about the matter.

2. Consider the following statements. Don't these sorts of statements make up a great deal of our everyday conversation as well as underlie some of the most important themes in human life?

(1) I was mistaken in underestimating Susan's character.
(2) Our culture is wrong in neglecting the rights of this particular group.

(3) Nazi Germany was mistaken in supposing the Aryan race is superior to all others.

(4) The medievals were mistaken in believing that the moon has a perfectly smooth surface.

The problem is that every one of these meaningful statements seems meaningless from the perspective of relativism. Statement 1: If subjectivism is correct, can I ever say that my previous beliefs were incorrect? Mustn't I simply say that I have now chosen to change my beliefs? What would ever make me think my belief was mistaken if I am unable to apprehend a reality that is independent of my opinions about it? Statement 2: If cultural relativism is correct, can we ever say that our culture is morally wrong or factually mistaken if our standard of truth is relative to our particular culture? Statement 3: If we were all relativists, then prior to World War II, shouldn't America simply have said that we and the Nazis should "agree to disagree" and leave it at that? If relativism is correct, then how can we ever assert that the Nazis were wrong? Aren't we condemned to the rather bland statement that "The Aryan race is superior within the Nazi's conceptual framework, while all races are equal within the equalitarian framework"? Statement 4: In what sense were the medievals wrong if their belief fit comfortably with their entire conceptual framework?

2.6 RETHINKING THE WESTERN TRADITION: EXISTENTIALISM

 LEADING QUESTIONS: *Existentialism*

1. Imagine yourself making the following statements to a friend. Assume that all the statements are true.

(1) 236 + 513 = 749.
(2) The distance between the earth and the moon is 238,857 miles.
(3) I love you.

How is statement 3 different from the first two? Describe all the ways that the truth being asserted in this case is different from the sort of truth asserted in the other two statements. Do these differences suggest that there are different kinds of truths based on the speaker's relationship to and involvement in the truth that is being asserted?

2. A witness in a courtroom trial may be urged to "tell the truth." What notion of truth do we have in mind here when we say that the witness's statements are "true"? On the other hand, what notion of truth does a speaker employ when she urges you to "be true to yourself"? Likewise, what does it mean to be "true" to another person with whom you are romantically involved? In these cases, are we

simply talking about uttering true statements about yourself or your love? What would we mean if we said someone "knows the truth but is not living the truth"? Obviously, the kind of truth that is being spoken of in these latter cases is different from the notion of propositional truth that is used in evaluating the witness's testimony. How would you characterize these different notions of truth?

SURVEYING THE CASE FOR EXISTENTIALISM

What Is Existentialism?

Existentialism is a philosophical movement that arose in the nineteenth century in the writings of two disparate philosophers: Søren Kierkegaard, a passionate Christian, and Friedrich Nietzsche, an equally intense atheist. Their writings were not appreciated in their own time, but like intellectual time bombs, their ideas exploded in the twentieth century and existentialism became one of the most popular movements in the contemporary age. Some of the leading existential philosophers in the twentieth century were Jean-Paul Sartre,* Maurice Merleau-Ponty, Gabriel Marcel, Karl Jaspers, and Martin Heidegger. From its very beginnings in the writings of Kierkegaard and Nietzsche, existentialism attracted both religious and nonreligious thinkers. Sartre was an outspoken atheist, Merleau-Ponty was nonreligious, Marcel was a Catholic, and Jaspers and Heidegger, while not explicitly religious, incorporated a number of religious themes in their writings that influenced theologians. The influence of existentialism spread far beyond the confines of philosophy and had an impact on literature, art, drama, psychology, and theology.

Because individualism is one of the major themes of existentialism, there is no common list of doctrines to which all the existentialists subscribe. They are a diverse group of thinkers whose personalities differ as much as their writings. However, a number of themes persist throughout all existentialist thought. Some of the hallmarks of existentialism are the priority of subjective choosing over objective reasoning, concrete experience over intellectual abstractions, individuality over mass culture, human freedom over determinism, and authentic living over inauthenticity. Because my concern is with the existentialists' view of epistemology, I touch only on the first two points in this section.

existentialism a philosophical movement that believes in subjective choosing over objective reasoning, concrete experience over intellectual abstractions, individuality over mass culture, human freedom over determinism, and authentic living over inauthenticity

From Kant to Existentialism

To understand the existentialist outlook as it applies to the theory of knowledge, it is important to see existentialism as one of the many shoots that grew from the intellectual soil of Immanuel Kant's constructivism. Recall that Kant did not

---

*See the discussion of Sartre's view of freedom in section 3.7.

believe that the mind was a passive instrument that simply received data from the world. Instead, he said, the mind imparts its own structures on experience so that the resulting knowledge is both the product of the external data and the constructive activity of reason. What was crucial for Kant was the assumption that everyone's mind works in the same way. In other words, Kant believed there was a *single* way of structuring experience that was carried out by the categories of the human mind that were *universal to everyone* and that were fundamentally *rational.* For Kierkegaard and Nietzsche, however, there are *multiple* ways of structuring experience that are *relative to each individual* and that are driven by our fundamentally *nonrational* nature including our passions and our subjective interests, needs, and motives. Although all existentialists agree that we cannot have objective knowledge of ultimate things, religious existentialists such as Kierkegaard do believe we can have subjective knowledge of an absolute God, whereas atheistic existentialists such as Nietzsche and Sartre believe that there are no absolutes and that we can never escape the limits of our own subjectivity.

SØREN KIERKEGAARD (1813–1855)

SØREN KIERKEGAARD
(1813–1855)

I discussed Søren Kierkegaard in the opening pages of chapter 1, where I presented his idea of philosophy as the search for self-understanding. I also discuss his fideism and subjective approach to religious knowledge in section 4.4. While Kierkegaard's thought was permeated by his Christian perspective and his view that faith takes priority over reason, much of what he says can be expanded beyond the topic of religious knowledge per se to cover the whole of our human engagement with the world. For this reason, Kierkegaard's existentialist outlook has influenced not only religious philosophers and theologians, but nonreligious writers as well.

Kierkegaard's Life

Born in Copenhagen, Denmark, Søren Kierkegaard was the youngest of seven children. The first great influence in his life was that of his father, who was not only a highly successful merchant, but also a devout and pious Lutheran. However, the father was tormented throughout his whole life by a morbid sense of guilt for all his moral failures, which included the seduction of the young housemaid soon after his first wife died. Consequently, he gave his son a very oppressive religious upbringing in a vain attempt to spare the boy from similar miseries.

When Kierkegaard was seventeen, he enrolled in the University of Copenhagen and began studying theology to please his father. However, he soon found that he had little interest in theology and began studying philosophy and literature instead. Rebelling against what he considered a crazy religious upbringing, he spent most of his time drinking, partying, and making grand appearances at the theater to enhance his public image as a carefree, cultured, sophisticate. While outwardly he was known as the life of the party, inwardly he was in despair and suicidal. Just before his father's death in 1838, Kierkegaard reconciled with his father. The son realized that his father's harsh religious training was actually a loving attempt to spare him from the melancholy and guilt his father experienced. With this new understanding of his father's love, Kierkegaard returned back to Christianity, returned to the study of theology, and became one of Christendom's most passionate writers.

The second major influence on Kierkegaard's philosophy was his engagement to Regina Olsen. It was a tortuous experience for Kierkegaard. He was passionately in love with her and yet felt that his melancholy personality would be like a dead weight that would drag her down. As he wrestled with the question of what to do, he realized that logic and abstract theories could not make the decision for him, because it was an intensely individual, subjective choice as to what he would do and who he would choose to be. Eventually, for Regina's sake and his own, he distanced himself from her, causing her to break the engagement. His love for her had inspired the writer within him to emerge. He found it easier, however, to revel in the abstract inspiration of this love than to be in her concrete, personal presence. The tension between the abstract and the concrete that he experienced in this love relationship became an important theme throughout all his writings.

The rest of Kierkegaard's life was singularly devoted to writing literary, philosophical, and theological works. Though they represented a wide variety of styles and specific topics, his writings were all directed to calling individuals to live authentic, passionate, and honest lives, repudiating the temptation to find our meaning and identity in institutions or abstractions. In the course of preaching this message, he found himself in a lifelong, vicious battle with both the popular press and his own Danish State Church. He accused the press of undermining individuality and promoting mediocrity and inauthenticity by creating the abstraction of the faceless, anonymous "public." He accused the church of the same thing, saying that it had turned authentic Christianity into a comfortable, taken-for-granted, cultural institution. Nearly broke and in poor health, Kierkegaard died at the age of forty-two on November 11, 1855.

Truth Is Subjectivity

Throughout history, most philosophers have thought that the main problem of epistemology was how to rise above our subjectivity to obtain objective truth. For Kierkegaard, however, objectivity is the easiest stance to take. Objectivity is comfortable because I can hide behind the masks of logic and empirical evidence and do not have to reveal myself. In doing so I can even fool myself into thinking that my beliefs are based on objective, impersonal reason rather than bearing the burden of recognizing them as my own choice of a personal stance for which I and I alone am responsible. Kierkegaard found that it is not objectivity but authentic subjectivity that requires the greatest effort.

The reason why so many traditional philosophers have been suspicious of subjectivity is that they assumed that it is necessarily bad. But there is both a good and a bad sort of subjectivity. The bad kind of subjectivity occurs when someone's personal interests and prejudices interfere with his or her ability to judge a situation correctly. Subjectivity in this pejorative sense is associated with the terms *arbitrary,* *idiosyncratic,* and *biased,* as when a referee unfairly favors one team over another because he has placed a bet on the game. However, *subjective* can also mean "necessarily related to the subject." In this sense (the type of subjectivity that concerns the existentialists), to say that an outlook or decision is "subjective" means that it is inescapably related to the agent's needs, interests, or values. In this sense, your choices concerning a career, relationships, ethical commitments, and religion are subjective choices.

Kierkegaard has never been accused of writing in a mild, carefully qualified style. He preferred to state things in a way to get our attention. Consequently, in contrast to philosophers' emphasis on objectivity, he boldly states that "truth is subjectivity." What does he mean by that statement? He certainly does not mean that the truth is whatever you want it to be. Instead, he is stressing that to know the truth in the fullest sense, it must be personally appropriated, it must make a difference to your life, and you as a person must be intimately involved in it. In the "Leading Questions" exercise at the beginning of this section, the truths of mathematics and astronomy were objective truths. It does not make any difference who states those truths, and believing them does not involve who you are as a person. But the truth of the statement "I love you" is a truth that involves the person who says it. Kierkegaard does believe that it is possible for truth to be impersonal and objective when it comes to mathematics and the sciences. He once said, "all honor to the pursuits of science."[62] For example, the Pythagorean theorem and the distance between the earth and the moon clearly are not just "true for me." But when the issue is religious or moral truth or the meaning of life (what Kierkegaard called "essential truth"), then there is no neutral, objective, impersonal standpoint from which these issues can be approached through the avenue of cool, detached reason.

Similarly, in the second set of leading questions, a difference is expressed between speaking true propositions and "being true." The difference is between knowing the truth as something out there external to me and living the truth as something that affects every aspect of my life. For example, a person could intellectually embrace a very elevated moral theory but be a scoundrel in actual practice. Such a person would objectively know the truth but would not be subjectively living in that truth. In contrast, a person could live a morally exemplary life but be incapable of articulating those moral principles in a propositional form. These points are brought out in our first selection from Kierkegaard's writings.

- In the following reading, note the kinds of contrasts Kierkegaard makes between objectivity and subjectivity.
- What is his complaint with modern philosophy?

Concluding Unscientific Postscript[63]

For an objective reflection the truth becomes an object, something objective, and thought must be pointed away from the subject. For a subjective reflection the truth becomes a matter of appropriation, of inwardness, of subjectivity, and thought must probe more and more deeply into the subject and his subjectivity. . . .

Modern philosophy has tried anything and everything in the effort to help the individual to transcend himself objectively, which is a wholly impossible feat; existence exercises its restraining influence, and if philosophers nowadays had not become mere scribblers in the service of a fantastic thinking and its preoccupation, they would long ago have perceived that suicide was the only tolerable practical interpretation of its striving. But the scribbling modern philosophy holds passion in contempt; and yet passion is the culmination of existence for an existing individual—and we are all of us existing individuals. . . .

When the question of truth is raised in an objective manner, reflection is directed objectively to the truth, as an object to which the knower is related. Reflection is not focussed upon the relationship, however, but upon the question of whether it is the truth to which the knower is related. If only the object to which he is related is the truth, the subject is accounted to be in the truth. When the question of the truth is raised subjectively, reflection is directed subjectively to the nature of the individual's relationship; if only the mode of this relationship is in the truth, the individual is in the truth even if he should happen to be thus related to what is not true. Let us take as an example the knowledge of God. Objectively, reflection is directed to the problem of whether the object is the true God; subjectively, reflection is directed to the question whether the individual is related to a something *in such a manner* that his relationship is in truth a God-relationship. On which side is the truth now to be found?

Kierkegaard presents the previous points in a concrete way in one of his most famous parables. He depicts someone who has theologically correct ideas, but no passion. He contrasts this person with a man who has theologically incorrect ideas but is passionate about his relationship to God.

• In the following parable, who does Kierkegaard favor? Why?

If one who lives in the midst of Christendom goes up to the house of God, the house of the true God, with the true conception of God in his knowledge, and prays, but prays in a false spirit; and one who lives in an idolatrous community prays with the entire passion of the infinite, although his eyes rest upon the image of an idol: where is there most truth? The one prays in truth to God though he worships an idol; the other prays falsely to the true God, and hence worships in fact an idol.

Knowing the Truth versus Being in the Truth

While Kierkegaard's examples were primarily concerned with a person's relationship to God, later existentialists broadened his view of truth to include all stances toward life, religious or not. Kierkegaard's dichotomy between *knowing the truth* and *being in the truth* is a good example of a general principle that can be appropriated both within and without a religious context. He once said that there were two kinds of people, those who suffer and those who become professors of suffering. His comment explains the difference between knowledge that can only be gained by participating in life and knowledge that is approached in a detached, academic sort of way. For Kierkegaard "the professor" is not just an occupation, it is an attitude toward life. His point was reflected in the words of a little-known author, Friedrich Hebbel, who once said:

> The hell-fire of life consumes only the select among men.
> The rest stand in front of it, warming their hands.[64]

This Kierkegaardian theme can be illustrated with several analogies. For example, here is how to ride a bike: Adjust the curvature of your bicycle's path in proportion to the ratio of your unbalance over the square of your speed.[65] Obviously, knowing that physics formula will not enable you to ride a bicycle (even though it is objectively true). You learn to ride a bicycle through participating in that reality and having the subjective experience of feeling the point of balance and not through an intellectual understanding of a physics formula.

The distinction between objectively knowing the truth and subjectively being in the truth is related to another distinction Kierkegaard makes between the result and the process. In some cases the result and the process can be separated. For example, you can look up the distance from the earth to the moon in a book. You can get the results without having to go through the process of calculating it yourself. On the other hand, you cannot become physically fit in a secondhand way. The only way to get the result is to go through a certain process yourself. For Kierkegaard, the kinds of truths that really matter (self-knowledge, the way one should live, or religious understanding) are more similar to physical fitness than to

SPOTLIGHT
on

The Intellectual versus the Existential Meaning of Death

Leo Tolstoy's story "The Death of Ivan Illych" concretely illustrates the difference between knowing the truth intellectually and knowing it subjectively and existentially. Ivan Illych had always known the truth of the statement "all men are mortal." But "men" in that statement was abstract. Ivan could not envision it as including him. One day at his doctor's office, however, Ivan discovered that *he* was dying. Suddenly, the objective truth he had always known took on a new meaning. The inevitability of death was easy to contemplate when it referred to humanity in general. But when Ivan realized that "I, Ivan Illych, am dying," the concept of mortality suddenly changed for him.

mathematical information. *What* you know is bound up with *how* you know it. The journey to self-understanding is a tortuous one that only you can take.

One last example will help make Kierkegaard's point clear. During a graduate philosophy seminar I was in, a philosopher who was famous for his defense of the ontological argument for God had reduced the argument to logical symbols that were spread all over the blackboard.* At the end of this clutter of mathematical symbols was the conclusion: "God, the greatest possible being, necessarily exists." One of my friends exclaimed to me, "Damn! The argument is sound. I can find no logical errors in it." Then a look of horror came over his face because he was a Ph.D. student in philosophy who was committed to living his life on the basis of reason and who had just been presented with an argument for God's existence that he thought was sound. Yet he realized that he would leave the room and his life would be no different. Kierkegaard would have understood what this young man was feeling, because he believed that objective truth was sterile, dry, cold, and useless if it did not make a subjective impact on a person's life. He makes these points eloquently in the following selection.

FROM SØREN KIERKEGAARD

The Journals[66]

What would be the use of discovering so-called objective truth, of working through all the systems of philosophy and of being able, if required, to review them all and show up the inconsistencies within each system; what good would it do me to be able to develop a theory of the state and combine all the details into a single whole, and so construct a world in which I did not live, but only held up to the view of others; what good would it do me to be able to explain the meaning of Christianity if it had *no* deeper significance *for me and for my life;* what good would it do me if truth stood before me, cold and naked, not caring whether I recognized her or not, and producing in me a shudder of fear rather than a trusting devotion? I certainly do not deny that I still recognize an *imperative of understanding* and that through it one can work upon men, *but it must be taken up into my life,* and *that* is what I now recognize as the most important thing. That is what my soul longs after, as the African desert thirsts for water.

STOP AND THINK

Was there a time when you knew something was true with your intellect, but it made no impact on your life (as in the case of the philosophy student contemplating a proof of

(Continued . . .)

---

*See the discussion of the ontological argument in section 4.3.

(. . . continued)

God's existence)? Did you ever have the sort of experience that occurred to Ivan Illych, that something you had known abstractly became concretely and personally real? Is it possible to know something intellectually, but not know it subjectively?

Kierkegaard and Relativism

Kierkegaard proclaimed that "truth is subjectivity," but doesn't that statement clearly identify him as a relativist? Kierkegaard as a relativist would be problematic because he was a sincere, orthodox Christian. As such, he did not believe that just any story about the world and human existence will do. From his Christian perspective, only if we view the world and our lives through the lens of faith will we ever achieve self-fulfillment. Hence, contrary to what some people suppose, Kierkegaard clearly was not a relativist. How then did he reconcile the subjectivity of his existentialism with the objectivity claimed by his faith? Perhaps the best way to understand this discrepancy is to note that Kierkegaard believed that God is an objective reality at the same time that he believed God must be subjectively appropriated. While Kierkegaard believed that there is no objective truth about issues that really matter, he did believe that there is an objective reality (God) whose existence and nature is independent of human conceptual frameworks. Accordingly, he thought that everyone is either moving subjectively toward this objective reality or subjectively away from it. When he says "truth is subjectivity," he does not mean that the truth as such will be different for every person. Something can be *known* subjectively without it *being* subjective. Because Kierkegaard is not a relativist, the usual objections to relativism do not apply to him. Nevertheless, as we will see in the evaluation at the end of this section, a number of questions still remain.

In the next section, I discuss Friedrich Nietzsche to see what an existentialist epistemology looks like when it is developed within an atheistic framework. It was unfortunate that Nietzsche never got around to reading Kierkegaard, his religious counterpart. It would have been interesting to have Nietzsche's own account of where he agreed and disagreed with Kierkegaard. Lacking that, you will have to compare and contrast the two thinkers yourself.

FRIEDRICH NIETZSCHE (1844–1900)

Nietzsche's Life

The atheistic wing of existentialism was founded by the German philosopher Nietzsche. He was religiously devout in his younger years (we even have examples of his religious poetry), but he gradually drifted away from his earlier piety, and by the time he was in his twenties he was a spirited spokesman for antireligious thought. Nietzsche was a brilliant student and distinguished himself at the universities of Bonn and Leipzig where he studied classics and philology (the analysis of

FRIEDRICH NIETZSCHE
(1844–1900)

ancient texts). Plagued throughout his life by illness, he abandoned an academic career and devoted himself to his writings. Despite his problems, he wrote eighteen books and a lengthy unfinished manuscript during the years 1872 to 1888. The ideas he left behind are disturbing and difficult, as was his life. In his final years, his physical and mental health collapsed from what appears to be a neurological disorder. Now considered a visionary who predicted some of the cultural crises that would plague the twentieth century, he handed the torch over to the new century when he died on August 25, 1900.

Radical Perspectivism

Nietzsche's theory of knowledge can be stated quite simply: *we don't have any objective knowledge at all.* He is a paradigm case of a subjective relativist. The only reality we can know, he says, is the reality that is subjectively constructed by each individual. Ironically, Nietzsche seemed to have arrived at this position because he held to the correspondence theory of truth, one of the most common starting points for an objectivist epistemology. The **correspondence theory of truth** states that (1) reality has a determinant, objective character and (2) a belief or statement is true or false to the degree to which it corresponds to or represents the objective features of reality. The cruel catch, according to Nietzsche, is that we can never have that sort of relationship to reality. By setting a high standard for truth and noting that we can never reach this ideal, Nietzsche concluded that we can never have objective truth. Like a goldfish who is confined to its bowl, looking out at the world from within it, each of us thinks, speaks, and lives within our own, subjective perspective. But what about facts? Aren't they out there, independent of us, and don't they function as an objective standard for the truth of falsity of our beliefs? "Not at all!" says Nietzsche:

> No, facts is precisely what there is not, only interpretations. We cannot establish any fact "in itself": perhaps it is folly to want to do such a thing.[67]

There cannot be any uninterpreted "facts" or "truths," for everything we encounter is seen from one perspective or another. Nietzsche calls this approach his theory of **perspectivism.** If Nietzsche is correct, then to suppose that there is an impersonal, objective, and perspective-free outlook on reality is like supposing that we could take a picture of the Lincoln Monument in which the perspective was neither from the north, east, south, west, or any direction whatsoever. Although there is obviously no *visual* perspective-free perception, most objectivists claim that a *conceptual* perspective-free standpoint is possible. Some have called this standpoint the "view-from-nowhere" assumption. But Nietzsche believes there is no such standpoint, for every judgment is made from someone's concrete, personal perspective.*

correspondence theory of truth a theory that states that (1) reality has a determinant, objective character, and (2) a belief or statement is true or false to the degree to which it corresponds to or represents the objective features of reality

perspectivism the theory that there cannot be any uninterpreted "facts" or "truths," because everything we encounter is seen from one perspective or another

---

*Feminist epistemologists agree with Nietzsche on this point. See section 2.8.

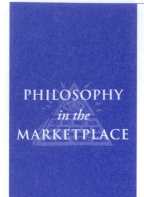

PHILOSOPHY
in the
MARKETPLACE

Read the following message inside the triangle, then look up from your book and repeat what you saw.

People typically fail to read this message accurately because they bring to the text their expectations, their assumptions, their past experience, and their background knowledge. That misinterpretation is Nietzsche's point. We "see" what our conceptual frameworks or perspectives allow us to see or what they direct us to see. Did you say that the message was "Paris in the spring"? If so, your reading of the message was incorrect. Put your finger on each word of the message as you read it. If you are like me, the first time you repeated the message you got it wrong. If something as simple as this message can be reconstructed and interpreted according to our own framework of assumptions, what makes us think we operate any differently with the whole of reality?

Try this same experiment with five friends and see how they do.

To understand Nietzsche's approach to truth, it is helpful to remember that he was a philologist.[68] In studying ancient texts, such as a Greek play, we never have the original manuscripts. What we have are copies of copies of copies that were passed down through the centuries and were put together from multiple, partial, and sometimes inconsistent versions of the original. During this process it was inevitable that errors and mistakes crept into the copies that were then passed on as part of the manuscript. Because of these errors, it was necessary for each ancient scribe copying the text or a present-day scholar reading the text to interpret and reconstruct it to make the best possible sense out of it. But in reconstructing the text, the copyist's or the scholar's outlook, their personal judgment, and the biases in their interpretations became part of the text itself.

Much in the same way, Nietzsche thought, each of us interprets the "text" of the world. In perceiving and thinking about the world, we are not like mirrors that passively record what is out there. Instead, we are reconstructing and interpreting the data to create a vision of the world that not only makes sense to us but that conforms to our subjective needs. The notion that we play an active role in constructing our knowledge is taken from Kant's insight. But the thesis that this role is based on our subjectivity and not on impersonal reason is a radical, existentialist modification of Kant's thesis.

Romantic Primitivism

According to Nietzsche, if most people suddenly realized that what they considered to be most real and true was just a subjective perspective, they could not bear this shattering of their illusions. For this reason, Nietzsche thought that our perspectives arose from a very deep stratum within human consciousness that we are inclined to suppress and deny. (Nietzsche's analysis of the unconscious drives within us both foreshadowed and influenced the thought of Sigmund Freud, the founder of psychoanalysis.) I have called this aspect of Nietzsche's thought "romantic primitivism," for like the artists and poets within the romantic movement, Nietzsche believed that our primary interaction with the world is in terms of feelings rather than ideas. It is a "primitivism" because he believed that these emotional responses operated at the level of primitive, animal instincts. Nietzsche said that all judgments arise out of our "instincts, likes, dislikes, experiences, and lack of experiences"[69] and knowledge is "actually nothing but a *certain behavior of the instincts toward one another.*"[70] Think about how radically this epistemology differs from those of both the rationalists and empiricists, who believed that knowledge was produced by an intellectual consideration of rational and empirical truths.

Rather than reason being the primary instrument of knowledge, Nietzsche believed it is just a mask we use to disguise a primitive drive that controls our cognitive life. This drive is what he calls the *will to power.* It manifests itself as the desire to overcome, to dominate my environment, to make my personal mark on the world, to create, or to express myself.

> "Truth" is therefore not something there, that might be found or discovered—but something that must be created and that gives a name to a process, or rather to a will to overcome that has in itself no end—introducing truth, as a *processus in infinitum,* an active determining—not a becoming-conscious of something that is in itself firm and determined. It is a word for the "will to power."[71]

STOP AND THINK

Can you think of a time when you tried to rationalize a belief, decision, or action of yours? That is, you tried to find rational reasons for what you did when you really knew that it was based on emotional or other nonrational factors. To what degree is Nietzsche's analysis of human psychology illustrated by your own, personal experience?

Nietzsche's view on knowledge is expressed in the following sections of one of his best-known books.

- In section 3, what does Nietzsche say secretly guides the thinking of the philosopher?
- What stands behind all logic?
- In section 4, what is said to be more important than the truth or falsity of a judgment?

FROM FRIEDRICH NIETZSCHE
Beyond Good and Evil[72]

3

After having looked long enough between the philosopher's lines and fingers, I say to myself: by far the greater part of conscious thinking must still be included among instinctive activities, and that goes even for philosophical thinking. We have to relearn here, as one has had to relearn about heredity and what is "innate." As the act of birth deserves no consideration in the whole process and procedure of heredity, so "being conscious" is not in any decisive sense the *opposite* of what is instinctive: most of the conscious thinking of a philosopher is secretly guided and forced into certain channels by his instincts.

Behind all logic and its seeming sovereignty of movement, too, there stand valuations or, more clearly, physiological demands for the preservation of a certain type of life. For example, that the definite should be worth more than the indefinite, and mere appearance worth less than "truth"—such estimates might be, in spite of their regulative importance for us, nevertheless mere foreground estimates, a certain kind of *niaiserie** which may be necessary for the preservation of just such beings as we are. Supposing, that is, that not just man is the "measure of things"—

4

The falseness of a judgment is for us not necessarily an objection to a judgment; in this respect our new language may sound strangest. The question is to what extent it is life-promoting, life-preserving, species-preserving, perhaps even species-cultivating. And we are fundamentally inclined to claim that the falsest judgments (which include the synthetic judgments *a priori*) are the most indispensable for us; that without accepting the fictions of logic, without measuring reality against the purely invented world of the unconditional and self-identical, without a constant falsification of the world by means of numbers, man could not live—that renouncing false judgments would mean renouncing life and a denial of life. To recognize untruth as a condition of life—that certainly means resisting accustomed value feelings in a dangerous way; and a philosophy that risks this would by that token alone place itself beyond good and evil.

- In the next paragraph (section 5), why does Nietzsche accuse philosophers of being dishonest?
- Nietzsche refers to philosophers as "advocates" (i.e., lawyers). What is the significance of comparing them to lawyers? Is he praising them or criticizing them?
- As you read sections 5 and 6, make a list of all the ways Nietzsche characterizes the real source of philosophers' ideas.

5

What provokes one to look at all philosophers half suspiciously, half mockingly, is not that one discovers again and again how innocent they are—how often and

---

*Folly, stupidity, silliness: one of Nietzsche's favorite French words. [Translator's note.]

how easily they make mistakes and go astray; in short, their childishness and childlikeness—but that they are not honest enough in their work, although they all make a lot of virtuous noise when the problem of truthfulness is touched even remotely. They all pose as if they had discovered and reached their real opinions through the self-development of a cold, pure, divinely unconcerned dialectic (as opposed to the mystics of every rank, who are more honest and doltish—and talk of "inspiration"); while at bottom it is an assumption, indeed a kind of "inspiration"—most often a desire of the heart that has been filtered and made abstract—that they defend with reasons they have sought after the fact. They are all advocates who resent that name, and for the most part even wily spokesmen for their prejudices which they baptize "truths"—and *very* far from having the courage of the conscience that admits this, precisely this, to itself; very far from having the good taste of the courage which also lets this be known, whether to warn an enemy or friend, or, from exuberance, to mock itself. . . .

6

Gradually it has become clear to me what every great philosophy so far has been: namely, the personal confession of its author and a kind of involuntary and unconscious memoir; also that the moral (or immoral) intentions in every philosophy constituted the real germ of life from which the whole plant had grown.

Indeed, if one would explain how the abstrusest metaphysical claims of a philosopher really came about, it is always well (and wise) to ask first: at what morality does all this (does *he*) aim? Accordingly, I do not believe that a "drive to knowledge" is the father of philosophy; but rather that another drive has, here as elsewhere, employed understanding (and misunderstanding) as a mere instrument. But anyone who considers the basic drives of man to see to what extent they may have been at play just here as *inspiring* spirits (or demons and kobolds) will find that all of them have done philosophy at some time—and that every single one of them would like only too well to represent just *itself* as the ultimate purpose of existence and the legitimate *master* of all the other drives. For every drive wants to be master—and it attempts to philosophize in *that spirit.*

To be sure: among scholars who are really scientific men, things may be different—"better," if you like—there you may really find something like a drive for knowledge, some small, independent clockwork that, once well wound, works on vigorously *without* any essential participation from all the other drives of scholar. The real "interests" of the scholar therefore lie usually somewhere else—say, in his family, or in making money, or in politics. Indeed, it is almost a matter of total indifference whether his little machine is placed at this or that spot in science, whether the "promising" young worker turns himself into a philologist or an expert on fungi or a chemist: it does not *characterize* him that he becomes this or that. In the philosopher, conversely, there is nothing whatever that is impersonal; and above all, his morality bears decided and decisive witness to *who he* is—that is, in what order of rank the innermost drives of his nature stand in relation to each other.

Nietzsche believed that a new kind of philosopher would arise. These new thinkers would transcend the dogmas of the past and would have the courage to realize that their thought did not arise out of impersonal reason, but that it was an expression of their own subjectivity.

- In the remaining sections, how does Nietzsche describe these new philosophers?
- In section 43, why does he say that there cannot be a "common good"?

42

A new species of philosophers is coming up: I venture to baptize them with a name that is not free of danger. As I unriddle them, insofar as they allow themselves to be unriddled—for it belongs to their nature to *want* to remain riddles at some point—these philosophers of the future may have a right—it might also be a wrong—to be called *attempters*.* This name itself is in the end a mere attempt and, if you will, a temptation.

43

Are these coming philosophers new friends of "truth"? That is probable enough, for all philosophers so far have loved their truths. But they will certainly not be dogmatists. It must offend their pride, also their taste, if their truth is supposed to be a truth for everyman—which has so far been the secret wish and hidden meaning of all dogmatic aspirations. "My judgment is my judgment": no one else is easily entitled to it—that is what such a philosopher of the future may perhaps say of himself.

One must shed the bad taste of wanting to agree with many. "Good" is no longer good when one's neighbor mouths it. And how should there be a "common good"! The term contradicts itself: whatever can be common always has little value. In the end it must be as it is and always has been: great things remain for the great, abysses for the profound, nuances and shudders for the refined, and, in brief, all that is rare for the rare.

44

Need I still say expressly after all this that they, too, will be free, *very* free spirits, these philosophers of the future—though just as certainly they will not be merely free spirits but something more, higher, greater, and thoroughly different that does not want to be misunderstood and mistaken for something else.

---

*[The translator, Walter Kaufmann, points out that the German word *Versucher* can mean attempters, tempters, or experimenters. Nietzsche is making a triple play on words here.]

Nietzsche and the Death of Absolutes

If there is no objective truth, no standard apart from us by which our ideas may be measured, then it logically follows that there is no God. For if God existed, he would be an absolute standard of truth and value. But if Nietzsche is right, if our minds swim in a sea of personal interpretations, then belief in God is simply a symptom of the human craving for absolutes. God provides a safe harbor for those who are afraid to venture out into the open seas of thought with no craft other than their own judgments and opinions. Nietzsche believed that there was a growing realization that "God is dead," meaning that this ideology was no longer a live, cultural force in Western culture.

> The greatest recent event—that "God is dead," that the belief in the Christian god has become unbelievable—is already beginning to cast its first shadows over Europe.[73]

However, in spite of this cultural revolution, Nietzsche recognized that there would still be those who felt the need for God along with the need for absolute truth and for a rational, metaphysical knowledge of the "true world." Nietzsche thought that humanity falls into two categories. The first category consists of those who need absolutes and security, who have no confidence in their own abilities, and who wear the masks of objectivity to hide the awesome responsibilities of their own subjectivity. He calls these people "sheep," "little gray people," "shallow ponds," "the herd," "the psychologically weak," "the vulgar," "the lower types," and "slaves." The second category consists of the new philosophers, people who are self-affirming, who need no philosophical or spiritual crutches, and who celebrate both the limits and the glories of their humanity. Nietzsche calls them "the psychologically strong," "the noble," "the higher types," the "masters."

This dualistic personality theory amplifies Nietzsche's theme that philosophy is a personal confession and that all thought is a reflection of the type of person we are (psychologically weak or strong). Although you think that you have been judging Nietzsche's ideas, he wants you to know that his ideas have been judging you all along. Like Kierkegaard, Nietzsche meant his writings to force you to face yourself, along with your fears, convictions, and sacred idols. If you find his ideas challenging, intoxicating, and life-enhancing or if you find them terrifying, offensive, and abhorrent, he will have been successful in evoking this form of self-revelation and he would have cared little about what you thought of him.

Nietzsche and Relativism

Because Nietzsche is clearly a relativist, how does he handle the Standard Criticism against relativists?* The critic would ask Nietzsche, "Why should I accept your

---

*See section 2.5 for the Standard Criticism of relativism.

theory of knowledge if, by your own account, all beliefs are nothing more than personal perspectives or interpretations?" Nietzsche loved to turn the tables on those who opposed him, so instead of evading the criticism, he enthusiastically embraced it. His reply to the people who criticized his relativism was, "Supposing that this also is only interpretation—and you will be eager to make this objection?—well, so much the better."[74] In other words, Nietzsche is willing to admit that his view is only one perspective among many in the hopes that you will recognize that your view is merely a subjective perspective as well. As his fictional character Zarathustra says, "This is my way; where is yours?"[75] We cannot compare our conflicting perspectives to reality in order to decide which is correct because all we have is reality-as-interpreted from some personal standpoint: Nietzsche's perspective, yours, mine, or someone else's. For this reason the world of thought is like the world of nature, where the survival of the fittest is the reigning principle. Philosophy is a struggle of egos as each person exercises his or her will to power.

If there is no objective truth, if all human judgments are nothing more than interpretations, then Nietzsche concludes that we should live our lives with a spirit of "experimentalism." An interesting theory should not be thought of as a photograph of reality, but should be treated as an invitation to view life in a new way. Thus, the proper response to an idea is not to ask, "Is it true?" but to exclaim, "Let us try it!"[76] A great thinker is one who "sees his own actions as experiments and questions."[77] By "experiment" Nietzsche means testing an outlook by dwelling within it and seeing whether it enhances or diminishes your life. In the final analysis, the superior ideas for Nietzsche are those that are the most life-enhancing, the most useful, or even the most interesting. Accordingly, he considered the search for variety more important than the quest for certainty.

> Deeply mistrustful of the dogmas of epistemology, I loved to look now out of this window, now out of that; I guarded against settling down with any of these dogmas, considered them harmful.[78]
>
> That the value of the world lies in our interpretation . . . that every elevation of man brings with it the overcoming of narrower interpretations; that every strengthening and increase of power opens up new perspectives and means believing in new horizons—this idea permeates my writings.[79]

LOOKING THROUGH THE EXISTENTIALIST'S LENS

1. If you were to agree with Kierkegaard that there is a personal God, then wouldn't it be likely that knowledge of him would require some sort of freely chosen, personal involvement in the knowing process? How might Kierkegaard argue that arriving at our ultimate commitments is *unlike* the process of knowing rationally compelling mathematical or scientific truths? Is personal choice absent in our mathematical or scientific beliefs? Is it inescapable in our beliefs about ultimate things?

2. Nietzsche said that if you want to understand someone's beliefs about reality (metaphysics), then consider what sort of morality he or she is promoting. Think of some examples of how one's beliefs about the nature of reality could be driven by underlying personal concerns. Is this association inevitable, as Nietzsche seems to think? If so, would it make rational discussion of our differences impossible? What would be the implications of this impossibility?

3. Concerning Kierkegaard's claim that there is a dichotomy between the objective and the subjective, contemporary philosopher Louis Pojman says, "It presumes an impossibility of being impartial and passionate at the same time, and it assumes that objectivity and neutrality are somehow closely related or even near-synonyms." Instead, Pojman argues, "Reason can be very passionate" and "one can seek the best objective evidence by passionate inquiry."[80] Because Socrates claimed that philosophy is the "love of wisdom," would he agree with Pojman? How would you argue for either Kierkegaard's, Nietzsche's, Pojman's, or Socrates' position on this issue?

EXAMINING THE STRENGTHS AND WEAKNESSES OF EXISTENTIALISM

Positive Evaluation

1. Isn't there a difference between abstractly knowing the truth (whatever it may be) and incorporating that truth within your individual life? What positive changes would be made to your life if you passionately lived on the basis of what you claimed to believe? Are the existentialists on to something here?

2. There is no way to rationally justify the value of rationality without arguing in a circle. Doesn't it follow that to strive to be rational involves a subjective commitment to that goal? Are Kierkegaard and Nietzsche right, then, that subjectivity is the foundation of all our engagements?

3. Both Kierkegaard and Nietzsche claimed that we use objective reason as an impersonal mask to hide behind. In fact, we sometimes hide our own underlying subjective motives from ourselves. If we adopted their approach, would there be much more honesty between persons? Would we be much more honest with ourselves? Wouldn't this be a positive outcome?

Negative Evaluation

1. The existentialists face a dilemma. Either they are making truth-claims or they are not. If not, then aren't they merely sharing their own personal feelings, inclinations, or subjective attitudes? If so, what relevance does their subjectivity have for our own situations? Furthermore, why do the existentialists make the effort to convince us of the truth of their position if everything is simply a matter of subjective commitment or preference? On the other hand, if existentialists are making truth-claims about the nature of human knowledge or if they are claiming

that there is a God (Kierkegaard) or that belief in God is simply an outmoded cultural phase (Nietzsche), then they are making claims about the objective nature of reality. In this case, isn't it important to be concerned with the objective truth of our own claims and not just with their subjective meaning for us?

2. Science purports to be an objective, rational search for the principles that govern physical reality. The successes of science indicate that it is doing something right. If science is on the right track, then shouldn't a philosophy try to incorporate some of these discoveries about the world and about human nature in its scope? Wouldn't a philosophy that incorporates scientific discoveries force us out of the realm of the purely subjective back into the domain of the rational search for objective truth?

3. Kierkegaard puts the emphasis on passionate commitment rather than the objective content of a belief. Granted that the former is important, but can passionate commitment have any value if our beliefs are radically out of touch with reality? Likewise, Nietzsche loves the joy of experimenting with new interpretations. But can't such experimentation be dangerous? Doesn't reality sometimes cruelly tell us our interpretations are wrong?

4. Could there be a society of Kierkegaards or a community of Nietzsches, each one pursuing his or her individual notion of the truth? Wouldn't such as organization lead to chaos? Doesn't living together require us to strive for universal truths and common values to make our society work? Could a common society be achieved within the individualistic, subjective philosophy of existentialism?

2.7 RETHINKING THE WESTERN TRADITION: PRAGMATISM

 LEADING QUESTIONS: *Pragmatism*

1. Suppose you have a friend who claims she has a certain belief. (It could be a belief concerning religion, ethics, politics, science, or any other topic.) But suppose that all her actions seem contrary to that belief. Would her actions be evidence that she did not really hold the belief she thought she did? Could we say that genuinely held beliefs will always make some sort of actual or potential difference in our actions?

2. We can say of a tool that it works, is efficient, gets the job done, is useful, lives up to our expectations, is better than the competition's, and serves our needs. To what extent could the same descriptions apply to an idea or a belief? Are some beliefs better than others because they are more useful when applied within our everyday lives? If this way of evaluating beliefs makes sense, what does this approach tell us about the nature of ideas and their role in our lives?

3. Have you ever rejected a belief for the sole reason that it didn't work when you used it to guide your actions?

SURVEYING THE CASE FOR PRAGMATISM

If philosophies came in colors, pragmatism would be painted red, white, and blue. It is the only major philosophical movement that was American-grown. The foremost pioneers of pragmatic thought were the Americans Charles Sanders Peirce, William James, and John Dewey, all of whom lived in the latter part of the nineteenth century and the early twentieth century. The key terms in pragmatism radiate the spirit of American culture. For example, pragmatism is concerned with action and practical consequences, it judges ideas by how successful they are in getting their job done, and it urges us to calculate the "cash-value" of our ideas (to use William James's phrase). Unlike some philosophies that never escaped the confines of the academic ivory tower, pragmatism achieved an admirable degree of popular fame. For example, politicians and businesspersons love to speak of themselves as pragmatists. However, like so many philosophies that have become popularized, the philosophy in its original form is much more sophisticated than its popular adaptations are.

Pragmatism is a philosophy that stresses the intimate relation between thought and action by defining the meaning of our conceptions in terms of the practical effects we associate with them and the truth of our beliefs in terms of how successfully they guide our actions. For the pragmatist every belief is like a scientific hypothesis and every action based on that belief is like an experiment that either confirms or refutes the viability of that belief. It is no accident that two of the original pragmatists were scientists before they moved into the field of philosophy (Peirce and James). However, their concern with science was not with this or that particular result but with science as a method of inquiry. The pragmatists believed that this method of finding knowledge applied not simply to performing experiments in the laboratory, but also to making a moral decision, working out the meaning of life, educating our children, and setting public policy.

The popular notion is that pragmatic is opposed to theoretical, but the pragmatists oppose this false dichotomy. They stress that the best theories will make a practical difference in concrete life and that nothing can be practical if it is not undergirded by sound theory. Rather than viewing philosophy as an obscure, elitist enterprise that searches for eternal truths that lay far beyond the horizon of human experience, the pragmatists seek to bring philosophy out of the clouds and down to earth. Pragmatic philosophy, they believe, could be a creative instrument of change, addressing the problems of the contemporary culture in which we all live and bringing clarity and coherence to the science, art, religion, politics, and morality of a particular time. Before discussing the main themes of pragmatism, it will be helpful to learn a little bit about its founders and the key differences in their versions of pragmatism.

pragmatism a philosophy that stresses the intimate relation between thought and action by defining the meaning of our conceptions in terms of the practical effects we associate with them and the truth of our beliefs in terms of how successfully they guide our actions

Charles Sanders Peirce (1839–1914)

CHARLES SANDERS
PEIRCE
(1839–1914)

C. S. Peirce was trained as a scientist, having received a master's degree in chemistry from Harvard. After working at the Harvard astronomical observatory for three years, he spent the next thirty years of his career doing scientific work for the U.S. Coast and Geodetic Survey. During this time he also lectured intermittently at Harvard and at Johns Hopkins University, although his nonconformist personality prevented him from ever securing a permanent academic position. Peirce wrote volumes of essays during his life, but his works, with the exception of a few articles, never saw the light of day until they were published long after his death. Although he was relatively unknown during his lifetime, he is now recognized as one of the most significant philosophers in the early twentieth century.

William James (1842–1910)

WILLIAM JAMES
(1842–1910)

James was born in New York into a well-to-do family for whom intellectual and cultural debates were part of the dinner table conversation. His brother Henry James was the well-known novelist. After spending years traveling the world and studying science, medicine, and painting abroad and in the United States, William James earned his medical degree from Harvard in 1869. He pioneered the then infant discipline of scientific psychology and in 1890 published *Principles of Psychology,* one of the first textbooks in the field. Eventually he made philosophy his full-time occupation and taught in Harvard's philosophy department. James not only achieved fame in the academic community but was in demand as a popular lecturer. He took Peirce's somewhat technical and obscure philosophy and made *pragmatism* a household word. Although the two men were friends and James continually helped Peirce with his financial problems, the original founder of pragmatism was never happy with James's popular version of the philosophy. Finally, Peirce gave up on the term and let James use it as he wished, announcing that his own philosophy should henceforth be known as "pragmaticism," saying that this label "is ugly enough to be safe from kidnappers."[81]

John Dewey (1859–1952)

JOHN DEWEY
(1859–1952)

Dewey earned his doctorate at Johns Hopkins University (where Peirce was one of his professors). After teaching at the University of Michigan for a decade, he went to the University of Chicago as the head of the department of philosophy, psychology, and education. At Chicago he developed his ideas into a theory of progressive education and created an experimental elementary school to serve as a laboratory for testing his educational theories. Then, from 1904 to his retirement in 1929, he taught at Columbia University. Because of the broad scope of his philosophy and his educational ideas, Dewey was perhaps the most widely influential of the pragmatists. His theory of education became quite famous and transformed American school systems. Furthermore, he lectured in Japan, China,

Turkey, Mexico, and the Soviet Union, and his works have been translated into every major language.

The Varieties of Pragmatism

Although Peirce, James, and Dewey agreed on the basic principles of pragmatism, they differed in their application of this philosophy. Peirce was primarily interested in developing a theory of inquiry and meaning that would apply to our scientific conceptions. Although James shared with Peirce a background in the sciences, James was primarily concerned with the issues of psychology, morality, religion, and practical living. When Peirce spoke of the "practical consequences" and "usefulness" of our beliefs, he was speaking primarily of the sort of public, empirical observations that would lend themselves to scientific analysis. Unlike Peirce, James believed the consequences of a belief included the personal and practical impact it has in the life of an individual.

Dewey made pragmatism a comprehensive philosophy with implications for our understanding of nature, knowledge, education, values, art, social issues, religion, and just about every area of human concern. Of all the pragmatists, he was most concerned with the social applications of knowledge. Dewey believed that the scientific method, broadly conceived, could lead our society to creative solutions to our educational and social problems. In his mind, there was no dichotomy between science and human values. Science can only succeed, he said, in the context of free communication, free action, and mutual dialogue that includes as many points of view as possible. Hence, his pragmatism and his faith in science led him to vigorously defend the American ideal of democracy.

 STOP AND THINK

Before examining the pragmatists' way of thinking about knowledge, take a minute to consider how you would answer the following two questions:

- What does it mean for a belief to be true?
- Why is it important to have true beliefs?

When you are finished reading the material by and about the pragmatists, I will ask you to answer these two questions again as a pragmatist might answer them.

The Role of Belief and the Nature of Ideas

The pragmatists criticized what they called "the spectator theory of knowledge." According to this outlook, the mind is like a passive mirror that reflects an external reality. Or to use another metaphor, the traditional view held that the mind was a container that holds ideas. But according to the pragmatists, this divorces meaning, truth, and knowledge from our practical engagement with the world. Dewey once said that the model of knowledge should not be that of a spectator viewing a painting but that of the artist producing the painting. Accordingly, epistemology should focus less on "knowledge" (a noun) and more on "knowing" (a verb). Since the world is changing, our society is changing, and our experience is continually changing, knowing the world is an ongoing, active process rather than the accumulation of static, finished results. For the pragmatists, cognition is a way of dealing with the dilemmas, perplexities, and problems that arise in experience and finding creative solutions that will enable us to act in effective ways. The word *pragmatism* can be traced back to a Greek word that means "action," "deed," or "practice." Accordingly, the pragmatists viewed ideas and beliefs as guides to action. As contemporary philosopher Abraham Kaplan says,

> Every actual case of knowing is one in which we are involved with what we know. We must do something with the object of knowledge for it to become known: manipulate it, take it apart, experiment on it.[82]

Besides rejecting the spectator view of knowledge, the pragmatists similarly criticized the *correspondence theory of truth.* This theory was the view that a statement or belief is true to the degree that it corresponds to reality. The problem is that a statement or belief is not a photograph of the external world, so in what sense does that statement or belief "correspond" to it? A statement has no magical powers to relate itself to reality. Similarly, if a belief is thought of as simply a piece of mental furniture it doesn't really relate to the world either. For the pragmatists the issue is not so much how a statement or belief relates to the world but how *we* can use that statement or belief in *our* relationship to our world. As Peirce says, "our beliefs guide our desires and shape our actions."[83] Similarly, James said that "the true is the name of whatever proves itself to be good in the way of belief."[84] For example, if I believe that "the dog is dangerous," "the glass is fragile," or "sugar is soluble," these beliefs will lead to certain expectations of future experience that will guide me in the fulfillment of my aims, and if they are satisfactory beliefs, they will enable me to act in effective ways. Dewey called his version of pragmatism "instrumentalism," because he viewed ideas and beliefs as instruments for dealing with the situations we face in life. A saw is an effective instrument for cutting wood, but it is not much use for driving nails. Likewise, in evaluating our beliefs we have to ask, "how will this belief put me in a more successful relationship with my experience than its alternatives?" Aristotle's physics answered many questions the ancient Greeks asked about nature, but it was abandoned in favor of Galileo's physics, since the latter could answer more questions more satisfactorily. In other words, Galileo's physics proved to be a more effective conceptual instrument in its own time.

If my actions always met with successful results, if my experience never raised any questions or posed any problems, I could rest comfortably in the beliefs I have, for they are doing their job. Peirce believed that inquiry and reasoning begin when my ideas prove inadequate to experience or when doubts are raised, which leads me to realize that I need to rethink my relationship to the environment. Similarly, Dewey said that inquiry is a transitional process between two stages: "a perplexed, troubled, or confused situation at the beginning and a cleared-up, unified, resolved situation at the close."[85] For example, every morning I turn the key in my ignition, believing that my car will start. But if the car does not start, then I must reassess the data, form hypotheses ("Perhaps the battery is low"), test my idea through overt action ("Do my lights still go on?"), and keep working at it until I find a set of ideas that unifies my experience, resolves the perplexity, and enables me to continue on with my tasks. Although this example is obvious and simplistic, the pragmatists claimed that *all* human inquiry proceeds in just this way. Hence, all thinking is problem solving, and there is no absolute division between the pattern of inquiry in the sciences, common sense, politics, morality, and religion. In every case, thinking involves a problem, hypotheses, plans of action, observations, facts, testing, and confirmation.

The intimate relationship between belief and action in the world is the basis of the pragmatists' rejection of skepticism. When Descartes went through his skeptical phase, he wondered whether the beliefs in his mind really corresponded with the external world.* What gave him away, the pragmatists would say, is that as he was pondering skepticism, he still got up to stoke the stove when he was cold. Obviously, in spite of his theoretical skepticism (Peirce called it "paper doubt"), Descartes's actions showed that he had beliefs about the world that were successful in guiding his actions. There is no dichotomy between the knower and the world, the pragmatists say, because our ideas are always formed in interaction with the world, and if any of our ideas are mistaken, our experience will reveal those mistakes to us. Thought is not the process of moving from one idea to another and then wondering if any of those ideas have anything to do with reality. Instead, thought begins by being immersed in the world, and it is a process of moving from the present set of world experiences to future experiences.

A corollary of the pragmatists' view of inquiry as problem solving is the view that we have no guarantee that any particular belief will ever be immune from the need to be revised. An idea that leads us to successful action today may fail us when we face tomorrow's challenges. The position that all our knowledge is tentative and subject to revision is known as *fallibilism.* Peirce once made the paradoxical claim that the only infallible statement is that all statements are fallible.[86] For the pragmatists, the quest for knowledge is not the search for eternal, necessary, foundational beliefs that are absolutely certain. Instead, they said, what we have are (1) provisional beliefs that work in practice thus far, joined with (2) a method of arriving at better beliefs.

---

*See the discussion of Descartes's struggle with skepticism in section 2.1.

The Pragmatic Theory of Meaning

The pragmatists emphasized that their philosophy did not aim to produce a set of dogmas, doctrines, or particular results. Instead, what they claimed to offer was a method for clarifying our conceptions. One of Peirce's best-known contributions to philosophy was his pragmatic theory of meaning published in a popular article called, "How to Make Our Ideas Clear." Contrary to some traditional theories, he did not think that the act of grasping the meaning of a concept was simply some interior mental state, nor did he consider meaning to be some sort of ghostly "halo" that attaches to a word or idea. Instead, Peirce described the meaning of a concept in terms of our interactions with the world and the publicly observable ways that the world responds. Accordingly, he summarized the pragmatic method in this way:

> Consider what effects, that might conceivably have practical bearings we conceive the object of our conception to have. Then, our conception of these effects is the whole of our conception of the object.[87]

When I say "the water is boiling," what do I mean? I mean that I can expect to see the water bubbling, that it will hurt if I touch it, that it will melt sugar, that it will register 212 degrees on a thermometer, and so on. Meaning is spelled out in terms of expected experiences and the results of my actions.

 THOUGHT EXPERIMENT

Applying Peirce's Method

Using Peirce's method, consider what practical effects you would expect in each of the following cases if the belief presented is correct.

- This diamond is genuine.
- Maria is trustworthy.
- This dog is friendly.
- If you study, tomorrow's exam will be easy.

James modified Peirce's conception of the pragmatic method by expanding it beyond the realm of scientific, physical concerns and applying it to our large-scale worldviews. Here is James's description of the pragmatic method:

> The pragmatic method is primarily a method of settling metaphysical disputes that otherwise might be interminable. Is the world one or many?—fated or free?—material or spiritual?—here are notions either of which may or may not hold good of the world; and disputes over such notions are unending. The pragmatic method in such cases is to try to interpret each notion by tracing its respective practical consequences. What difference would it practically make to any one if this notion rather than that notion were true? If no practical difference whatever can be traced, then the alternatives mean prac-

tically the same thing, and all dispute is idle. Whenever a dispute is serious, we ought to be able to show some practical difference that must follow from one side or the other's being right.[88]

The key difference between Peirce and James concerned how they understood the "practical consequences" of a conception. Peirce was concerned with the question, What differences would it make to our observations if this proposition were true? James was concerned with that question also, but he would go on to ask a further question as well: What practical differences would it make to *my* life if I *believed* this proposition were true? To use one of James's questions, what difference would it make as to whether we believe the world to be material or spiritual? In terms of visual data, when the atheist and the theist look at the night sky, they have the same expectations and see the same things. For Peirce this observation was sufficient to declare that their conception of the night sky was the same. However, James would not agree. The atheist thinks of the night sky as part of an impersonal universe that is governed by blind physical laws. In contrast, the Psalmist looks at the night sky and says, "the heavens declare the glory of God." James would count these approaches as two different effects based on two different conceptions of the world. Unlike Peirce, James included the emotional impact of a belief as part of its experiential consequences. James's emphasis on the *personal* consequences of belief is what made his pragmatism so extraordinarily popular.

 THOUGHT EXPERIMENT

Clarifying Meaning

William James tells the story of coming across a group of people in a heated debate. One of their members was chasing a squirrel around a tree. However, no matter how quickly he moved, the squirrel would move around to the other side of the tree, always keeping the tree between himself and the man. Some of the members argued that the man had gone round the squirrel because he had completely circled the tree and the squirrel was on the tree. The other group argued that the man had not gone round the squirrel because he had never faced the squirrel's backside.

- Is there any practical difference between the two sides of the dispute?
- How might the pragmatic theory of meaning clear up the debate?
- Have you ever been in an argument that could have been resolved if the members of the opposing sides had bothered to clarify the meaning of their terms?

The Pragmatic Theory of Truth

Another way in which James modified Peirce's pragmatic method of clarifying meaning was by expanding it into a pragmatic theory of truth. James said that true beliefs have the characteristic that they pay or have practical cash value. He defined truth in terms of what works or what gives satisfaction, or in terms of the practical consequences of our beliefs. It is important to notice that an advocate of the correspondence theory of truth could agree that the workability of a belief, or its tendency to lead to successful action, is an *indicator* that the belief provides an accurate picture of reality without agreeing that this factor *defines* what we mean by "truth."

However, James was not content to argue for this pragmatic test of truth. Instead, he put forth a radically new, pragmatic definition of what it means for a belief to be true. According to his definition, truth means *"that ideas (which themselves are but parts of our experience) become true just in so far as they help us to get into satisfactory relation with other parts of our experience."*[89] In section 4.4 on pragmatic justifications for religious belief, we will read James's argument that faith could be pragmatically justified even if it could not be rationally demonstrated to be true. The religious application of his pragmatic theory of truth is captured in the following passage:

> [Pragmatism's] only test of probable truth is what works best and combines with the collectivity of experience's demands, nothing being omitted. If theological ideas should do this, if the notion of God, in particular, should prove to do it, how could pragmatism possibly deny God's existence? [Pragmatism] could see no meaning in treating as "not true" a notion that was pragmatically so successful.[90]

However, James thought that this pragmatic approach to truth applied to every issue in life and not just the religious sphere.

We can gain a window onto James's approach to philosophy by examining an experience he had at the beginning of his career that changed the course of his life. As a result of years of studying science and medicine, James became morbidly depressed by the thought that human beings might be nothing more than determined mechanisms doomed to live in a closed universe where nothing escapes the domination of physical laws. If determinism is true, James believed, then his life had no meaning, for all his choices would then be as inevitable and purposeless as the blind motion of atoms. On the other hand, if he was genuinely free, then the future was open and his choices made a difference both to the course of his life and to the world on which he acted. The problem was that he did not think that there could be any definitive scientific or philosophical proof of either belief. If reason could not tell him what to believe on a certain issue, James thought, it made sense to choose the belief that would maximize his life and produce the most value when put into action. For this reason, James resolved that if he was to go on living and find any sort of meaning in life at all, he would have to commit himself to the thesis that free will is not an illusion and base his actions on that conviction. Accordingly, in an 1870 diary entry, written when he was twenty-eight and one year out of medical school, James resolved:

> My first act of free will shall be to believe in free will. . . . I will go a step further with my will, not only act with it, but believe as well; believe in my individual reality and creative power. . . . Life shall be built in doing and suffering and creating.[91]

This personal example illustrates James's version of the pragmatic method for forming our beliefs. As he has said, truth is a function of "what works best and combines with the collectivity of experience's demands." In some cases this definition will mean that an idea can be directly verified in terms of experimental, scientific data. For example, if I believe that an object is made out of iron, then it should be attracted to a magnet. However, the thesis of free will or the thesis of determinism do not produce any sorts of simple predictions concerning future experiences. Nevertheless, according to James, it is better to believe in free will because it will allow us to believe that our choices make a difference to the world and it will make our moral struggles meaningful, whereas determinism will not. Hence, in this very personal sense, the consequences of believing in free will lead to better results. James articulates this very broad pragmatic criteria for resolving philosophical issues in the following way:

> Of two competing views of the universe which in all other respects are equal, but of which the first denies some vital human need while the second satisfies it, the second will be favored by sane men for the simple reason that it makes the world seem more rational.[92]

Many critics accused James of saying that we should believe whatever it is comfortable to believe. James, however, always insisted that a belief would have pragmatic value only if it could be integrated with the rest of our beliefs or experiences and if it would successfully guide us in the long run. Hence, based on these considerations there are many *comfortable* beliefs that we should not entertain (e.g., "I don't need to study") because they would lead to conflicts with experience, would not be good guides to action, and would thereby be impractical. Similarly, there are many *uncomfortable* beliefs that I may have to embrace (e.g., "I have diabetes"), simply because they will provide the best guide to action over time.

When Dewey spoke about truth, he often fell back on Peirce's and James's notions of truth as "successfully guiding action," "satisfying the needs and conditions evoked by a problem," "working in action," and so on.[93] However, Dewey avoided using the word *truth* as much as possible, for it carried with it too much traditional, philosophical baggage. Typically, truth has been viewed as a static property of a proposition and has been viewed in terms of the correspondence theory. Because these views are ones that Dewey wanted to discard, he rarely used the word *truth* in his own philosophical writings.*

Instead of using the tainted word *truth,* Dewey typically explained the idea of knowledge in terms of the notion of "warranted assertibility."[94] This phrase means that those propositions that it is best for us to believe (or assert) are those that have arisen out of a process of inquiry, that have most successfully fit with our experience, and that seem best suited to guide us in our future engagements with the

---

*In an entire book devoted to the nature of inquiry (*Logic: The Theory of Inquiry*), Dewey mentions the word *truth* only once, in a footnote.

world. Of course, since the world and our experience are constantly changing, what we are warranted in asserting at this point may change as our growing experiences create new conditions that our beliefs must fulfill. This notion captures Dewey's conviction that there is no final end of inquiry at which our ideas will be perfectly adequate and beyond the need of further revision.

Pragmatism and Relativism

The different pragmatists take various positions on the issue of relativism. Peirce was clearly an antirelativist. According to his epistemology, two completely different beliefs could not be equally true, for in the long run experience would always favor one over the other. As Peirce put it:

> There are real things, whose characters are entirely independent of our opinions about them; those realities affect our senses according to regular laws, and . . . by taking advantage of the laws of perception, we can ascertain by reasoning how things really and truly are.[95]

While Peirce emphasized the fact that our beliefs were always tentative and continually needed to be revised, he was confident that the self-correcting nature of the scientific method would guarantee that human inquiry was continually converging on truth and reality.

> The opinion which is fated to be ultimately agreed to by all who investigate is what we mean by the truth, and the object represented in this opinion is the real. That is the way I would explain reality.[96]

By defining truth with reference to community opinion, Peirce is not saying that truth is all a matter of convention. Instead, he is expressing his conviction that if the process of inquiry is carried on long enough, the difference between truth and error eventually will manifest itself in the court of human experience and we will discover how things really and truly are.

James was unclear on the issue of relativism. He was frequently criticized for preaching a thoroughgoing relativistic philosophy, but in response to these criticisms he reaffirmed his belief in a reality that existed independently of us. Nevertheless, the relativist within James comes out in passages such as this one:

> There is nothing improbable in the supposition that an analysis of the world may yield a number of formulae, all consistent with the facts. . . . Why may there not be different points of view for surveying it, within each of which all data harmonize, and which the observer may therefore either choose between, or simply cumulate upon another?[97]

Perhaps the most generous interpretation of James's views is that he was a pluralist about truth. This interpretation means that James believed that there were different kinds of truths, and consequently, the practical consequences of belief or disbelief would differ depending on the subject matter. That is, on some issues he was an objectivist while on other issues he was a relativist. For example, James says that "the future movements of the stars or the facts of past history are determined now once for all, whether I like them or not."[98] Here he is speaking like an objectivist by claiming that some facts are independent of our beliefs about them. On other issues, however, where science and logic alone do not resolve the issue for us, James was a relativist. Is there a purpose to the universe or is it purposeless? Since science cannot give us a definitive answer, James thought that each person should answer the question based on his or her own experience with life. On these sorts of issues, he says, "it is almost certain that personal temperament will here make itself felt, and that although all men will insist on being spoken to by the universe in some way, few will insist on being spoken to in just the same way."[99] Suppose we believe, he says, that a particular theory solves the problem we face more satisfactorily than another. "But that means more satisfactorily to ourselves, and individuals will emphasize their points of satisfaction differently. To a certain degree, therefore, everything here is plastic."[100]

Dewey believed, with the relativists, that there were no free-floating absolute truths that were completely independent of us and our concrete situation. However, he did not think that what we should believe was completely a matter of individual, subjective choice. All experience begins within a biological and cultural matrix and what we should believe will depend on our concrete situation and our goals. There are no truths or values that are valid for all time, but only beliefs or values that are optimal for a particular society in a particular context. For this reason, his position could be called contextualism. For example, Newton's physics worked for solving the scientific problems people faced in previous centuries, but in the twentieth century, it proved inadequate to address the problems that arose at the level of subatomic events and in new discoveries in astronomy. Hence, some of the fundamental ideas of physics had to be revised. According to Dewey, inquiry is a continual process of adjusting means to ends. But as new ends arise within a changing world, we need new means, new ideas, and new theories. According to Dewey's instrumentalism, theories are instruments just like the slide rule. Just as slide rules are no longer used, so theories are not so much refuted as they are abandoned when we require new and more adequate instruments to meet our needs.

Are the pragmatists inconsistent in claiming that truth is not objective or fixed while apparently claiming that pragmatism is true? Perhaps to avoid this criticism, Dewey said that his or any philosophy had to be evaluated pragmatically:

> There is . . . . a first rate test of the value of any philosophy which is offered to us: Does it end in conclusions which, when they are referred back to ordinary life-experiences and their predicaments, render them more significant, more luminous to us, and make our dealings with them more fruitful?[101]

Obviously, Dewey thinks that pragmatism meets this test. Therefore, Dewey is saying, even though truth is not absolute, objective, and fixed, pragmatism should be adopted because it is a pragmatically useful way to approach experience.

The core of pragmatism's conception of truth was eloquently expressed in the following famous passage by James.

- As you read through this passage, write down all the ways in which James uses the words *practical, instruments,* and *useful,* and refers to the way that ideas have *cash-value, lead us, work,* and *pay.* What do these words tell you about his view of ideas and truth?
- In the first section, how does James describe the intellectualist position?
- What questions does the pragmatist ask of an idea?
- How does James define *true ideas?*

 FROM WILLIAM JAMES

Pragmatism's Conception of Truth[102]

I fully expect to see the pragmatist view of truth run through the classic stages of a theory's career. First, you know, a new theory is attacked as absurd; then it is admitted to be true, but obvious and insignificant; finally it is seen to be so important that its adversaries claim that they themselves discovered it. Our doctrine of truth is at present in the first of these three stages, with symptoms of the second stage having begun in certain quarters. . . .

Truth, as any dictionary will tell you, is a property of certain of our ideas. It means their "agreement," as falsity means their disagreement, with "reality." Pragmatists and intellectualists* both accept this definition as a matter of course. They begin to quarrel only after the question is raised as to what may precisely be meant by the term "agreement," and what by the term "reality," when reality is taken as something for our ideas to agree with.

. . . The great assumption of the intellectualists is that truth means essentially an inert static relation. When you've got your true idea of anything, there's an end of the matter. You're in possession; you *know;* you have fulfilled your thinking destiny. You are where you ought to be mentally; you have obeyed your categorical imperative; and nothing more need follow on that climax of your rational destiny. Epistemologically you are in stable equilibrium.

Pragmatism, on the other hand, asks its usual question. "Grant an idea or belief to be true," it says, "what concrete difference will its being true make in any one's actual life? How will the truth be realized? What experiences will be different from those which would be obtained if the belief were false? What, in short, is the truth's cash-value in experiential terms?"

The moment pragmatism asks this question, it sees the answer: *True ideas are those that we can assimilate, validate, corroborate and verify. False ideas are those that*

---

*When James speaks of "intellectualists," he is referring to rationalists.

we cannot. That is the practical difference it makes to us to have true ideas; that, therefore, is the meaning of truth, for it is all that truth is known-as.

This thesis is what I have to defend. The truth of an idea is not a stagnant property inherent in it. Truth *happens to* an idea. It *becomes* true, is *made* true by events. Its verity *is* in fact an event, a process: the process namely of its verifying itself, its verification. Its validity is the process of its *validation.*

But what do the words verification and validation themselves pragmatically mean? They again signify certain practical consequences of the verified and validated idea. It is hard to find any one phrase that characterizes these consequences better than the ordinary agreement-formula—just such consequences being what we have in mind whenever we say that our ideas "agree" with reality. They lead us, namely, through the acts and other ideas which they instigate, into or up to, or towards, other parts of experience with which we feel all the while—such feeling being among our potentialities—that the original ideas remain in agreement. The connexions and transitions come to us from point to point as being progressive, harmonious, satisfactory. This function of agreeable leading is what we mean by an idea's verification. Such an account is vague and it sounds at first quite trivial, but it has results which it will take the rest of my hour to explain.

- In the next section, what does James say is the value of "extra" ideas (ideas that have no immediate use)?

Let me begin by reminding you of the fact that the possession of true thoughts means everywhere the possession of invaluable instruments of action; and that our duty to gain truth, so far from being a blank command from out of the blue, or a "stunt" self-imposed by our intellect, can account for itself by excellent practical reasons.

The importance to human life of having true beliefs about matters of fact is a thing too notorious. We live in a world of realities that can be infinitely useful or infinitely harmful. Ideas that tell us which of them to expect count as the true ideas in all this primary sphere of verification, and the pursuit of such ideas is a primary human duty. The possession of truth, so far from being here an end in itself, is only a preliminary means towards other vital satisfactions. If I am lost in the woods and starved, and find what looks like a cow-path, it is of the utmost importance that I should think of a human habitation at the end of it, for if I do so and follow it, I save myself. The true thought is useful here because the house which is its object is useful. The practical value of true ideas is thus primarily derived from the practical importance of their objects to us. Their objects are, indeed, not important at all times. I may on another occasion have no use for the house; and then my idea of it, however verifiable, will be practically irrelevant, and had better remain latent. Yet since almost any object may some day become temporarily important, the advantage of having a general stock of *extra* truths, of ideas that shall be true of merely possible situations, is obvious. We store such extra truths away in our memories, and with the overflow we fill our books of reference. Whenever such an extra truth becomes practically relevant to one of our emergencies, it passes from cold-storage to do work in the world and our belief in it grows active. You can say of it then either that "it is useful because it is true" or that "it is true because it is useful." Both these phrases mean exactly the same thing, namely that here is an idea that gets fulfilled and can be verified. True is the name for whatever idea starts the verification-process, useful is the name for its completed function in experience. True ideas would never have been singled out as such, would never have acquired a class-name, least of all a name suggesting value, unless they had been useful from the outset in this way.

From this simple cue pragmatism gets her general notion of truth as something essentially bound up with the way in which one moment in our experience may lead us towards other moments which it will be worth while to have been led to. Primarily, and on the common-sense level, the truth of a state of mind means this function of *a leading that is worth while.* When a moment in our experience, of any kind whatever, inspires us with a thought that is true, that means that sooner or later we dip by that thought's guidance into the particulars of experience again and make advantageous connexion with them.

 STOP AND THINK

Notice in the passage you just read that when a belief grows active for us, according to James, you can say of it that (1) "it is useful because it is true" or that (2) "it is true because it is useful" and that "both these phrases mean exactly the same thing." But are they the same? Why?

Plato, Locke, Descartes, or any other traditional philosopher would agree that true ideas are useful, but they would vehemently deny that being useful is what makes an idea true. For example, the medievals held beliefs about the motions of the planets that were false. Yet, these false ideas endured for centuries because they still led astronomers to make successful predictions. (They were useful but false ideas.) However, James would reply that within the context of their times, for the tasks that they faced, these ideas had cash-value, they worked, they functioned as instruments of action. Hence, he might say that these ideas were true for the medievals, whereas they are false for us since they no longer function to fulfill our current needs or fit within the bounds of our greatly expanded experience.

- In the next passage, what does James mean by saying an idea "agrees" with reality?

To "agree" in the widest sense with a reality *can only mean to be guided either straight up to it or into its surroundings, or to be put into such working touch with it as to handle either it or something connected with it better than if we disagreed.* Better either intellectually or practically! And often agreement will only mean the negative fact that nothing contradictory from the quarter of that reality comes to interfere with the way in which our ideas guide us elsewhere. To copy a reality is, indeed, one very important way of agreeing with it, but it is far from being essential. The essential thing is the process of being guided. Any idea that helps us to *deal,* whether practically or intellectually, with either the reality or its belongings, that doesn't entangle our progress in frustrations, that *fits,* in fact, and adapts our life to the reality's whole setting, will agree sufficiently to meet the requirement. It will hold true of that reality.

Notice that in the next paragraph, James introduces what is now called the pragmatic or instrumentalist view of science. Because we cannot see subatomic particles (such as atoms or electrons) nor can we fully imagine them, and because the descriptions of them frequently fly in the face of common sense and our ordinary experience, James denies that scientists are giving us a literal description of what is present in experience. Instead, scientists are viewing reality *as if* it behaved this way and are constructing theoretical entities and formulas that work in making predictions. To use a rough analogy, statistics tell us that the average American family has 2.4 children. Obviously, no real family has this many children. However, the theoretical construct of the average family is a useful one and enables policy makers to predict the housing needs in the nation.

- In the next passage, what do our theories mediate between, according to James?
- If two theories are equally compatible with all our other truths, how do we decide between them?
- Does making this choice necessarily mean that the chosen theory is a "copy" of reality?
- If not, then what is its value?
- In what ways is the pursuit of truth similar to the pursuit of health and other goals in life?

Such is the large loose way in which the pragmatist interprets the word agreement. He treats it altogether practically. He lets it cover any process of conduction from a present idea to a future terminus, provided only it run prosperously. It is only thus that "scientific" ideas, flying as they do beyond common sense, can be said to agree with their realities. It is, as I have already said, *as if* reality were made of ether, atoms or electrons, but we mustn't think so literally. The term "energy" doesn't even pretend to stand for anything "objective." It is only a way of measuring the surface of phenomena so as to string their changes on a simple formula.

Yet in the choice of these man-made formulas we cannot be capricious with impunity any more than we can be capricious on the common-sense practical level. We must find a theory that will *work;* and that means something extremely difficult; for our theory must mediate between all previous truths and certain new experiences. It must derange common sense and previous belief as little as possible, and it must lead to some sensible terminus or other that can be verified exactly. To "work" means both these things; and the squeeze is so tight that there is little loose play for any hypothesis. Our theories are wedged and controlled as nothing else is. Yet sometimes alternative theoretic formulas are equally compatible with all the truths we know, and then we choose between them for subjective reasons. We choose the kind of theory to which we are already partial; we follow "elegance" or "economy." Clerk-Maxwell somewhere says it would be "poor scientific taste" to choose the more complicated of two equally well-evidenced conceptions; and you will all agree with him. Truth in science is what gives us the maximum possible sum of satisfactions, taste included; but consistency both with previous truth and with novel fact is always the most imperious claimant.

Our account of truth is an account of truths in the plural, of processes of leading, . . . and having only this quality in common, that they *pay*. They pay by guiding us into or towards some part of a system that dips at numerous points into sense-percepts, which we may copy mentally or not, but with which at any rate we are now in the kind of commerce vaguely designated as verification. Truth for us is simply a collective name for verification-processes, just as health, wealth, strength, etc., are names for other processes connected with life, and also pursued because it pays to pursue them. Truth is *made*, just as health, wealth and strength are made, in the course of experience.

- In the next paragraph, what does James mean when he says that what is true is "the expedient"? How does this theory differ from the correspondence theory of truth?

"The true," to put it very briefly, is only the expedient in the way of our thinking, just as "the right" is only the expedient in the way of our behaving. Expedient in almost any fashion; and expedient in the long run and on the whole of course; for what meets expediently all the experience in sight won't necessarily meet all further experiences equally satisfactorily. Experience, as we know, has ways of *boiling over,* and making us correct our present formulas. . . .

. . . In the realm of truth-processes facts come independently and determine our beliefs provisionally. But these beliefs make us act, and as fast as they do so, they bring into sight or into existence new facts which redetermine the beliefs accordingly. So the whole coil and ball of truth, as it rolls up, is the product of a double influence. Truths emerge from facts; but they dip forward into facts again and add to them; which facts again create or reveal new truth (the word is indifferent) and so on indefinitely. The "facts" themselves meanwhile are not *true.* They simply are. Truth is the function of the beliefs that start and terminate among them.

STOP AND THINK

In the final paragraph of the previous reading, James says it makes no difference whether we say the facts "create" or "reveal" new truths. What is the significance of blurring this distinction? (Think about the difference between creating a message in the sand and revealing one that is already there but that we didn't notice previously.) Why would Descartes and Locke (unlike James) insist that the methods of science and philosophy reveal truths but do not create them?

If to reveal truths is the same as creating them, as James says, then they must not already be there until we make them. To illustrate James's point, the sculptor Michelangelo could "see" a statue in the block of marble. Of course, it wasn't *really* there until he carved and formed the marble. Still, he had to decide which forms would fit with the veins of the marble and which forms the marble would not support. In the same way, James is suggesting that our theories and beliefs must fit the facts, but that they are not already latent in the facts or dictated by them. We create those truths for our present situation that are "expedient" and that we can weave into our past and future experiences most effectively.

LOOKING THROUGH THE PRAGMATIST'S LENS

1. The pragmatists claim that ideas are instruments for engaging with the world of our experience and that a true belief is one that will lead to successful actions in the long run. How would they use these notions to respond to the skeptic's claim that we can never know if our beliefs are true or false?

2. The pragmatists test the adequacy of a claim in terms of its practical consequences. How would they use the pragmatic method to show why we should believe the following ideas?

- The Pythagorean theorem
- Unjustified killing is wrong
- Democracy is a better political system than is a monarchy
- There is no social problem so severe that solutions to it cannot be found.

3. At the beginning of this section on the pragmatists, you were asked two questions about truth. Now imagine that you are a pragmatist and answer these same questions from that point of view.

- What does it mean for a belief to be true?
- Why is it important to have true beliefs?

In what ways (if any) do the pragmatist's answers differ from your original ones? Do you feel inclined to change your original answers? Why?

EXAMINING THE STRENGTHS AND WEAKNESSES OF PRAGMATISM

Positive Evaluation

1. The pragmatists remind us of the tentative and probable nature of all human knowledge. Individually and as a culture, our ideas are continually undergoing revision as experiences and new problems arise for which our current ideas are inadequate. Pragmatists have pointed out that the certitudes and dogmas of previous ages frequently turn out to be myths and superstitions in the light of new experiences and knowledge. In what ways is this observation a valuable insight?

2. The pragmatists have pointed to the intimate relationship between belief and action. Our actions demonstrate what we truly believe as opposed to what we think we believe or say we believe. Furthermore, all actions that are not simply blind physiological reactions are based on our beliefs about the world and our expectations about future experiences. Aren't the pragmatists on to something here in tying together belief and action?

3. The pragmatists emphasize the practical consequences of ideas, they view each belief as a tentative hypothesis to be embraced if it works or abandoned if it doesn't, and they stress that our beliefs enable us to move from one set of experiences to future experiences. In what ways is the pragmatic approach to truth similar to the scientific method? To what degree do these similarities help support pragmatism as a viable theory of truth?

Negative Evaluation

1. The pragmatists have said that an idea or belief is true or not depending on whether it works or leads to satisfactory results. But doesn't this definition of truth suggest the following problems?

- We can never say that an idea is true or false because we can never know all its long-range consequences.
- The same idea can be both true and false, since its consequences may be satisfactory for some people and unsatisfactory for others.

2. Isn't the pragmatic notion of truth paradoxical? For an idea to have pragmatic value for me, for it to work, isn't it necessary that I think in terms of the correspondence theory of truth? For example, suppose that my belief in life after death has value for me in James's sense. It fills my life with hope, it gives me confidence in the face of death, and it keeps me from despairing over the thought that after seventy years or so I will cease to exist. But is it possible for this belief to have this pragmatic value for me unless I suppose that this belief corresponds to what will happen after my death? Could it have pragmatic truth for me or could I even believe it if I thought its *only* value was the benefits I received from believing it?

3. Based on pragmatic considerations, James chose to believe in free will. This belief brought meaning to his life and gave him confidence that his actions mat-

tered and could change the course of the future. But is this result enough to warrant a belief? Couldn't it be the case that his belief led to success but that his desire to believe in free will was inevitably determined by his personality and upbringing, and that everything he did and thought was actually determined?* Doesn't it seem that it is possible for this belief to be pragmatically successful and to have cash-value and yet for it to be a false picture of reality? Do these conclusions throw us back to correspondence with reality as the defining feature of truth?

4. Critics claim that James failed to distinguish between the psychological factors that lead a person to hold to a particular belief and the rational factors that would make that belief justified. Do you think this criticism is a strong one?

2.8 RETHINKING THE WESTERN TRADITION: FEMINIST EPISTEMOLOGY

LEADING QUESTIONS: *Feminist Epistemology*

1. A man is walking past a large hospital when he sees a physician in a white coat and a little girl coming toward him. As they come closer, he realizes the physician is an old friend whom he has not seen since their college days. They greet each other warmly and the friend says, "Since we last saw each other in college, I went on to medical school and I am now a surgeon at this hospital. I also married someone whom you don't know and have never met, and this is our daughter, Nancy." The man says to the little girl, "Nancy, you not only have your mother's name, but you also have her brown eyes." How did he know?

2. The words *man, he,* and *his* can obviously be used to refer to males. However, the English language has had the tradition of also using these words in a gender-neutral way to refer to the human race as a whole or to any human being. But can *man* ever have a completely gender-neutral use? For example, in the sentence, "If an individual wishes to protect his family, then he should have adequate insurance," the words "he" and "his" are presumed to refer to *any* individual, whether male or female. If so, then we should see nothing strange about this sentence: "If an individual wishes to protect his husband, wife, or children, then he should carry adequate insurance." But we find the phrase "his husband" peculiar because "his" is not really gender-neutral. On the other hand, the sentence, "If one wishes to have an abortion, then one should be free to do so" does not sound strange because "one" is genuinely free of any gender bias. But to say, "If a person wishes to have an abortion, then he should be free to do so" sounds odd because "he," unlike "one," is not gender-neutral.[103] In these examples, are the uses of the terms *man* or *he* really as generic and gender-neutral as has been claimed?

---

*See the discussion on freedom and determinism in the next chapter, sections 3.5 to 3.8.

Answer the following questions yourself and then pose them to at least five females and five males.

- Do men and women think in different ways? How so? Give some examples.
- Do you believe that it is possible to get a man to think like a woman or, at least, to appreciate the female perspective on a given issue, and vice versa? Why?

3. If you are a female, what things do you think males just don't understand? Why do you suppose this is? If you are a male, what things do you think females just don't understand? Why do you suppose this is? Are there situations that evoke distinctively male and female ways of looking at things? If so, how should this fact be taken into account when constructing a theory of knowledge?

SURVEYING THE CASE FOR FEMINIST EPISTEMOLOGY

The Background of Feminist Theory

Feminism is another contemporary movement that questions some of the underlying assumptions of the Western tradition in philosophy and seeks to develop a new model for doing philosophy. Like any living movement that is breaking new ground, feminists have many different and conflicting visions of what the character and agenda of their movement should be. However, although there is not an official creed or set of doctrines that all feminists agree upon, their thinking revolves around some common themes. **Feminism** is a movement within philosophy and other disciplines that (1) emphasizes the role of gender in shaping how we think and how society is structured, (2) focuses on the historical and social forces that have excluded women from full participation in the intellectual and political realms, and (3) strives to produce a society that recognizes women and men as both different and equal.[104] These three themes illustrate that feminism includes both a theoretical understanding of the way things are and an attempt to use this knowledge to transform the status quo.

A quick glance at standard works on the history of philosophy will reveal the notable absence of women prior to the twentieth century, which is one example of the way in which women's voices have been excluded from our intellectual traditions. Actually, there were a number of women philosophers in every historical period starting with ancient Greece.[105] The reason that women intellectuals have had a hard time getting their voices heard is illustrated by the views about women held by notable philosophers. While the history of disparaging remarks that male philosophers have made about women is a long story, one of the earliest and most influential accounts was given by the Greek philosopher Aristotle. He believed that the normal outcome of mating was that of a male fetus, but if there was some

feminism a movement within philosophy and other disciplines that (1) emphasizes the role of gender in shaping how we think and how society is structured, (2) focuses on the historical and social forces that have excluded women from full participation in the intellectual and political realms, and (3) strives to produce a society that recognizes women and men as both different and equal

deficiency in the process, a female would be formed. For this reason, he referred to females as "mutilated males" and said that the female character is "a sort of natural deficiency." Furthermore, he believed that the female contributed the material portion of the embryo while the male contributed the "principle of soul" or the capacity for reason.[106] Aristotle's biology of the sexes was repeated throughout the Middle Ages and beyond.[107]

There have been some notable exceptions to this disparagement and exclusion of women. For example, Plato in his *Republic* argued that it is inevitable that any given society would produce some women whose intellect and abilities would be superior to those of the average person. In his ideal society, these gifted women would take their place with men of like abilities to receive specialized training to make them the intellectual and political leaders of the nation. Similarly, John Stuart Mill, the nineteenth-century English philosopher, wrote a work on *The Subjection of Women* in which he argued that his society was cutting itself off from the benefits of utilizing the contributions of gifted women. Mill himself was married to a brilliant woman, Harriet Taylor, who collaborated with him on many of his philosophical writings. For the most part, however, Aristotle's attitude prevailed in the philosophical tradition. He claimed that only the free adult male is qualified to rule society, because only he is invested by nature with full rational capacity. Hence, Aristotle says, "the courage of a man is shown in commanding, of a woman in obeying" and "silence is a woman's glory."[108]

The "Leading Questions" that opened this section indicate how deeply gender biases are rooted in our thinking. Were you able to figure out the answer to question 1? In responding to this story, many people (both male and female) are puzzled as to how the man could know the name and appearance of the girl's mother if he had never met her. Some suppose that the man knew the birth mother of the girl even though he did not know her adoptive mother (the current wife of the surgeon). Like so many issues in philosophy, the solution is found by questioning your underlying assumptions. Nothing in the story indicates that the surgeon is a man. However, when people think of a surgeon, they tend to imagine a man. Obviously, the simplest way to account for the facts of the story is to suppose that the college friend and surgeon is Nancy's mother.

Question 2 shows some problems with using male terms (such as *man*) to refer generically to both men and women. Yet in spite of these problems, this use is a traditional and common practice. For example, the glossary of one author's book has this entry: "Man (*as used throughout this book*) A human being, or the human

---

Try out the story of the surgeon and the little girl on a diverse collection of friends and acquaintances. Make sure half the respondents are females and half are males. How did they do? On the whole, were the females better than the males in finding the solution?

PHILOSOPHY
in the
MARKETPLACE

creature regarded abstractly and without regard to gender; hence, the human race, or humanity."[109] But if it is possible to use *man* in this way, then there should not be anything odd about this sentence: "Man, like all mammals, is an animal that breast-feeds his young."[110] The pragmatist John Dewey published *Problems of Men* in 1946.[111] We might suppose from the title that the book discusses typical male problems such as baldness and diseases of the prostate. However, the book is really a discussion of the philosophical problems that *humanity* has faced through the ages. Feminists point out that these examples show the tendency to treat men and men's psychology and experiences as the standard while viewing women's experiences as unimportant, exceptional, subsidiary, or deviant.

Varieties of Feminism

Historically, the feminist movement can be divided into two eras. The period prior to about 1945 sometimes is known as first-wave feminism. The resurgence of the movement in the latter half of the twentieth century often is referred to as second-wave feminism. Apart from these historical divisions, however, there are two varieties of feminists. The first group consists of (what are variously called) equity or liberal feminists. The equity feminists believe that basic social structures and intellectual traditions of Western culture should be retained. Their cause is that of allowing women to have full intellectual and political participation in society. The terms *freedom* and *opportunity* describe the focus of their concern. The second group of feminists are called gender or radical feminists. Gender feminists do not simply want to be included within the status quo because they are challenging and attempting to change the fundamental structures, assumptions, methods, and discourse of society, claiming that those aspects of society reflect male-dominated distortions. To put it glibly, equity feminists want their piece of the pie, while gender feminists radically critique the pie itself.

Whereas all enlightened persons, whether male or female, are in favor of the full intellectual and political equality of women, the second form of feminism (gender feminism) provokes a swirl of controversy in philosophy. (For the record, it would be a mistake to suppose that all female philosophers are feminists in this second sense and that all male philosophers are nonfeminists.)[112] A distinction is frequently made between the terms *sex* and *gender*. *Sex* is a biological category that refers to the obvious physical differences between males and females. *Gender* is a concept that is much more subtle and difficult to define because it includes social and psychological factors. *Gender* includes (but is not limited to) the notions of masculine-feminine, social roles, sexuality, and the apparent psychological differences between men and women.

Within gender feminism, some feminists are *essentialists,* claiming that there is a distinct and essential female nature. Essentialists differ as to whether this essential female nature is the product of women's biology or of relatively stable cultural factors that create the unique and common features of women's experiences. Feminists who are *nonessentialists* or *nominalists* deny that gender characteristics are fixed in any way at all. Furthermore, they tend to view descriptions of "women's nature" as social constructs that prevent women from changing and redefining themselves. Simone de Beauvoir was one of France's most celebrated twentieth-century writers and an influential voice in the feminist movement. De Beauvoir expressed the nonessentialist position in her famous quote "One is not born, but rather becomes, a woman."[113] Her point was that gender characteristics are not biologically determined, but they can be either socially imposed or subjectively chosen.

Ann Garry and Marilyn Pearsall provide a good introduction to feminist philosophy in the following passage. (Ann Garry is professor of philosophy at California State University, Los Angeles. Her publications are in feminist philosophy, philosophy of mind, and applied ethics. Marilyn Pearsall has taught philosophy and women's studies at a number of universities. She has edited several works on feminist studies.) In reading this selection, answer the following questions:

ANN GARRY
(1943–   )

- What disagreements do feminists have with traditional philosophy?
- What do feminists hope to accomplish with respect to the discipline of philosophy?
- What do the authors say is "one of the hardest questions" that feminist philosophers face?

FROM ANN GARRY AND MARILYN PEARSALL
Women, Knowledge, and Reality[114]

Feminist philosophy has two sources—the feminist movement and traditional academic philosophy. The feminist movement has opened our eyes to the deep and varied ways in which the ideals and institutions of our culture oppress women. In addition to providing a devastating critique of male-dominated society, feminists have affirmed the positive value of women's experience. Academic feminist philosophers build upon and contribute to the insights and work of the women's movement. Feminist philosophers examine and criticize the assumptions and presuppositions of the ideals and institutions of our culture. We write about a wide range of topics, from the most overtly political issues such as job discrimination, rape, and the use of sexist language, to the subtle underlying metaphysical and epistemological assumptions of our culture and our philosophical traditions.

Feminist philosophy, especially in its academic forms, also has its roots in traditional philosophy. Although traditional philosophy has been shaped by men who have taken their experiences, their values, and their views of the world as the standard for all human beings, it is in the philosophical traditions of these men that academic feminist philosophers were educated. Even today the philosophical methods we are taught to practice and the subject matter we are taught to consider appropriate for philosophy are by and large not feminist; they are the traditional male methods, fields, and topics of philosophy.

As feminist philosophers incorporated insights from our political practice into our academic work, we became aware that the androcentric* character of traditional philosophy made it limited, biased, and liable to oppressive use. This is true of theories not only in social and political philosophy and ethics, but also in metaphysics and theory of knowledge, the fields some consider the core of the western philosophical tradition. Although there is too much diversity in philosophy to permit easy generalization, we can say that feminist philosophers call attention to the themes pervading the various strands of western male thought that have led to distortion and bias in philosophy itself and have lent themselves readily to the oppression of women and other subordinate groups. . . .

There is more to feminist philosophy than the continuing critique and analysis of what has gone wrong. Feminist philosophers are trying in many diverse ways to reconstruct philosophy. We want to redefine the methods and subject matter of philosophy in ways that value women's experiences and enable women to move from the position of object to positions of subject, of knower, and of agent. We want to redeem philosophy, to "get philosophy right," recognizing the difficulty in even thinking about what standards, if any, there are for doing it "right."

In trying to reconstruct philosophy, one of the hardest questions is what can be salvaged from traditional philosophy and what should be rejected. While it would be foolish to disregard valuable insights of male philosophers, one cannot determine quickly what, if anything, is free from androcentric assumptions. This is an ongoing process that requires feminist philosophers to build upon each other's contributions, for what appears to be gender neutral one year may look obviously androcentric the next. Feminist philosophers realize that reconstructing or "revisioning" philosophy is a very large, open-ended project.

In the remaining portion of the passage, Garry and Pearsall give a brief answer to the question, "What can one expect to find when reading feminist philosophy?" Without attempting to set out rigid boundaries, they present some of the central themes found throughout feminist philosophical writings.

To start with, feminist philosophers are saying in a multiplicity of ways that gender matters—even in very abstract theories in which one might not suspect that it would. Because gender matters, we are prone to resist easy moves to speak in a "neutral," nongendered voice. We are also likely to focus on the ways in which values underlie and permeate theories; again, this is not just in fields one might expect, such as political philosophy, but also in the most fundamental questions of metaphysics and theory of knowledge.

Feminist philosophers also strive to connect theories to everyday experience. We ask fundamental philosophical questions about life, meaning, value, and be-

---

*male-centered

ing. Yet we try to ensure that our answers are not merely about some abstract "meaning of life," but are informed by the meaning of real lives and experiences. We place high value on differing experiences of diverse women, whether diverse in class, race, ethnicity, sexual orientation, age, or able-bodiedness. We try to be especially attentive to the ways in which the oppressions associated with these categories, e.g., racism or class oppression, intersect with sexism. The diversity among women has led to interesting controversies about the possibility of speaking in a "woman's voice" or a "feminist voice."

In addition, feminist philosophers often seek to integrate what is valuable to their work from different disciplines, from several traditions within a discipline, or from different fields of study within a discipline. For example, a feminist philosopher writing about the self might draw on anthropologists and poets as well as philosophers from more than one tradition; she might also call attention to the ways in which questions of value cannot be separated from metaphysical theories of the self. She might find that traditional styles of writing philosophy are too limiting; her style might be more personal or otherwise different from those of traditional philosophers.

 STOP AND THINK

From what you have just read, what do you think feminists will say about the role of gender and values in philosophizing about knowledge? What will be their notion of experience and the role it plays in epistemology?

ISSUES AND THEMES IN FEMINIST EPISTEMOLOGY

While there are many divisions and disagreements within feminism, some similar threads of thought run throughout all feminist theory. A common theme throughout feminist epistemology is the critique of four, traditional, interrelated assumptions:

1. *The Generic Humanity Assumption:* There is one universal human nature. Epistemology, therefore, is the attempt to describe the cognitive structures common to all individuals.
2. *The View from Nowhere Assumption:* The particular identity of a knower (including gender, race, class, and historical circumstances) is irrelevant to the production and assessment of that person's knowledge claims.
3. *The Pure, Impersonal Reason Assumption:* (This view of rationality results from the view from nowhere assumption.) The ideal of rationality is that of pure objectivity, untainted by subjectivity or the emotions and interests of the knower.

4. *The Robinson Crusoe Assumption:** The acquisition of knowledge is primarily a project of isolated individuals, and this knowledge is independent of any social context and free of political implications.

The Generic Humanity Assumption

Feminists claim that the picture of one, universal, human nature has been created by taking men's experiences and psychology as the paradigm. Other points of view and models of humanity, particularly those that incorporate women's experiences, have been excluded from consideration or marginalized for being too subjective or unconventional. This exclusion is comparable to ducks claiming that there is only one standard for all well-formed water birds and describing this universal standard in such a way that it just happens to fit the description of a typical duck. To carry this analogy further, imagine that in applying this standard of excellence, the ducks proclaim that swans are imperfect, deformed ducks because of their very unduck-like curved neck. Obviously, the problem is not that swans are deficient ducks but that the ducks have taken one particular standard for water birds and made this the norm while excluding all others from the realm of acceptability.

CAROL GILLIGAN
(1936–   )

A study that questions the assumption that male psychology defines human nature is *In a Different Voice: Psychological Theory and Women's Development,* published in 1982 by Harvard psychologist Carol Gilligan.[115] It has subsequently become one of the most influential books in feminist theory. After reviewing the leading research on the development of moral reasoning, Gilligan discovered that the studies were done on mostly male subjects. Consequently, while these studies claimed to provide data on *human* moral development, they ended up taking *male* reasoning as the norm.†

As a result of her own research, Gilligan found that males and females solve ethical dilemmas with different sets of criteria. Males tend to employ a "judicial" model, which emphasizes equality, justice, rights, impartiality, objectivity, universal principles, and logic. On the other hand, females tend to approach ethics in a more person-centered way, stressing care, compassion, trust, mercy, forgiveness, preventing harm, and feelings. Gilligan theorized that these two alternative approaches were the result of the different ways that males and females are socialized. The problem is that the traditional, male-oriented, psychological theories characterized the judicial (male) approach as the highest stage of moral development and the more relational (female) approaches as less mature stages. However, Gilligan argued

---

*Robinson Crusoe was the lead character in Daniel Defoe's eighteenth-century novel by that name. Crusoe was a sailor who was shipwrecked on an isolated tropical island. This metaphor is my own and is not common in the literature, but it summarizes a common theme in feminist theory.
†The primary focus of Gilligan's research was the work of Lawrence Kohlberg, one of the leading researchers in the area of moral development.

that these two different approaches cannot be ranked on a single, hierarchical scale and that each perspective complements the other.

Feminists claim that this tendency to make male perspectives the norm infects most traditional theories of knowledge. Feminist philosopher Lorraine Code makes this charge, for example, against a contemporary work on rationality by a male philosopher.[116] She notes that "Richard Foley appeals repeatedly to the epistemic judgments of people who are 'like the rest of us.'" The problem is, Code says, "nowhere does he address the question of who 'we' are." She suggests that the standard knowers referred to by "we" in the coded language of epistemology are tacitly assumed to be people just like the author: "an adult (but not *old*), white, reasonably affluent (latterly middle-class) educated man of status, property, and publicly acceptable accomplishments."[117] By contrast, knowers who do not fit this description (women) and whose perspectives, experiences, approaches to knowledge, and standards of rationality do not fit the preferred model are considered to be outsiders and their viewpoints are dismissed as irredeemably subjective, irregular, or irrational.

LORRAINE CODE
(1937–)

The View from Nowhere Assumption

Traditional epistemology has supposed that the ideal knower will look at reality free of any particular perspective or historical background and will carry out the project of knowing without any individual interests, engagements, or concerns. But such a knower would be a disembodied computer with no personal history or would have attained a disinterested, godlike perspective. For human knowers, however, such stances are both undesirable and impossible. Our personal history and concrete standpoint influences what we can know. For example, if I look out at the world from the top story of a building (or from the top level of the social hierarchy), while you view it from the basement (or at the lowest social, political, or economic level), what we see and how we see it will differ. Although she does not support this approach, philosopher Harriet Baber summarizes the feminist complaint against this perspective-free, view from nowhere epistemology in the following way:

> Advocates of feminist epistemology . . . reject [this approach] specifically on the grounds that the norms it embodies are male norms and hence that their acceptance sets standards which women find it difficult, or impossible, to meet. In particular they hold that the traditional epistemic ideal of an objective, detached observer, conducting his investigations in isolation from any historical or social context, is alien to women's engaged, concrete, contextual way of knowing.[118]

As Baber suggests, some feminists believe that the view from nowhere assumption is alien to women's ways of knowing the world and so excludes them from the category of being fully adequate knowers. However, most feminists think that the assumption is incoherent and that all knowers (feminist or nonfeminist, female or male) always approach the world from within some particular context, whether this context is defined by conceptual scheme, language, culture, gender, or whatever. According to this more expanded critique, the view-from-nowhere assumption is not just alien to women's approaches, but is an incorrect description of human knowledge in general.

The notion that the "typical knower" is a standardized, impersonal, faceless, nameless, featureless abstraction has been institutionalized in the practice of science. Science students are taught to depersonalize their reports with such statements as "the test tube was heated and a white precipitate was formed," as though no human agents or observers in the laboratory were conducting the experiment. We are familiar with locutions such as "the facts show that" or "science says" or "the data indicate that," as though the facts, science, and data have a voice of their own and speak their own interpretations to us. However, knowledge does not drop down from the heavens but is humanly created. Hence, when feminists talk about "knowledge," they also focus on "knowledge production" and ask, Who is making the knowledge claim? or What is his or her standpoint? For example, feminist philosopher Sandra Harding titled her book *Whose Science? Whose Knowledge?* to remind us that there is always a subjective person and point of view behind every knowledge claim.[119]

The claim that there is a point of view behind every knowledge claim is not unique to feminists. Particularly in the twentieth century, this claim is made by a number of philosophers who otherwise would not be labeled as feminists. However, feminists are noted for stressing the role that gender plays in the point of view that a person brings to the knowing situation. Is gender important in the process of knowledge production? It would seem that gender is as incidental to what we can know as are physical attributes such as height, weight, or hair color. But according to feminists, gender plays too important a role in society not to take it into account in examining how knowledge arises. As Code says, "in cultures in which sex differences figure prominently in virtually every mode of human interaction, being female or male is far more fundamental to the construction of subjectivity than are such attributes as size or hair color."[120] Accordingly, Code argues for an epistemology that takes subjectivity into account (including gender) without sliding into an "anything goes" subjectivism:

> Knowledge is at once subjective and objective: subjective because it is marked, as product, by the processes of its construction by specifically located subjects; objective in that the constructive process is constrained by a reality that is recalcitrant to inattentive or whimsical structurings.[121]

The Pure, Impersonal Reason Assumption

The view-from-nowhere assumption leads to a certain kind of value-laden dichotomy when it comes to discussing rationality. The rational thinker is presumed to be one who has attained the objective, impersonal perspective idealized in the view-from-nowhere assumption. On the other hand, those for whom personal, subjective perspectives are considered important (feminists) are thereby considered to be less than adequately rational. I have called this description of rationality the "pure, impersonal reason" assumption.

Feminist epistemologists frequently refer to bipolar thinking by means of which traditional epistemologists posit strict dichotomies such as reason vs. emotion, objective vs. subjective, mind vs. body, logic vs. intuition, or intellect vs. imagination. They have two criticisms of this approach. First, the paired concepts in each case are not mutually exclusive dichotomies as has been supposed.[122] For example, feminists claim that knowledge has both subjective and objective components and that we don't have to choose between one or the other.* Second, when epistemologists assert or assume these dichotomies, they place high priority on the first member of the pair, assuming that it describes the ideal knower, while they devalue the second member of the pair. Furthermore, the preferred alternative (such as objectivity) is taken to describe the male approach and the second (subjectivity) is assumed to be a stereotypically female trait. Feminists claim, however, that the psychological assumptions and value choices inherent in this approach are rarely questioned. Feminist writer Adrienne Rich summarized the problem, for example, by claiming that "objectivity" is nothing other than male "subjectivity."[123]

A practical consequence of this false ideal of rationality can be seen in the history of artificial intelligence research. Back in the 1950s when the attempt was first made to simulate human intelligence in computers, the research was carried out by male mathematicians and engineers, most of whom had served in the military. When they considered the range of skills that defined the core of intelligence, they decided that an intelligent computer would be one that thought just like them! (Remember the duck example.) Accordingly, they focused on the skills of chess playing, theorem proving, and problem solving.[124] Although the researchers made some progress on this limited range of topics, they were disappointed to find that their "intelligent" computers were still many decades away from acquiring the cognitive abilities of a four-year-old child. Feminist critics point out that these researchers ignored the fact that other people, particularly women, might define intelligence in terms of other competencies such as social skills and the ability to concretely interact with the world as opposed to the model of disembodied, abstract symbol processing.[125]

In an essay titled "The Man of Reason," Genevieve Lloyd, an influential feminist philosopher, discusses this traditional, one-sided ideal of rationality.[126] She demonstrates from the history of philosophy that reason has been so narrowly defined and women have been stereotyped in such a way that the ideal of "the man of reason" necessarily excludes women. Hence, men's areas of responsibility were intellect, reason, logic, and the life of the mind. Women were said to complement

---

*This point is the fallacy of the false dichotomy that is discussed in the section on logic in chapter 1 (section 1.2).

men with their gifts of a rich emotional life, imagination, intuition, and sensuousness. But the whole picture could be distilled down to the following two equations: male equals rational and female equals nonrational. According to Lloyd, "If women's minds are less rational than men's, it is because the limits of reason have been set in a way that excludes qualities that are then assigned to women."[127] However, Lloyd's solution is not to accept the traditional dichotomies and then embrace the "softer" half of each pair (such as intellect vs. emotion), elevating it to the position of prominence. She says that this approach was the mistake of the nineteenth-century romantics who rejected analytical reason in favor of the emotions. Instead, she rejects the classical dichotomies altogether and calls for a broader notion of reason that will include both men and women in its scope. Speaking about the "Man of Reason" ideal, she says, "What is needed for the Man of Reason is realization of his limitations as a *human* ideal, in the hope that men and women alike might come to enjoy a more human life, free of the sexual stereotypes that have evolved in his shadow."[128]

Not all feminists question these traditional dichotomies, however. Some have accepted the stereotypical distinctions between men and women, but have called for a reversal of priorities and valuations, claiming that women's ways of knowing are superior to those of men. Although she does not necessarily agree with this approach, Code lists the "feminine" traits that are said to give women an epistemological advantage:

> Features of women's experiences commonly cited are a concern with the concrete, everyday world; a connection with objects of experience rather than an objective distance from them; a marked affective tone; a respect for the environment; and a readiness to listen perceptively and responsibly to a variety of "voices" in the environment, both animate and inanimate, manifested in a tolerance of diversity.[129]

These traits seem to overlap the attributes commonly thought to characterize a good mother. Accordingly, in her book *Maternal Thinking*, Sara Ruddick, a well-known feminist ethical theorist, celebrates the values traditionally associated with mothering and femininity and generates a model of knowledge from such maternal traits as caring, intimacy, responsibility, and trust. She builds her case on the premise that "distinctive ways of knowing and criteria of truth arise out of practices."[130] For example, scientific thinking as a method of knowing reality developed within the laboratory but can be practiced in other areas of life as well, even by those who are not professional scientists. Similarly, Ruddick claims, maternal thinking can characterize a person's approach to every dimension of life (not just child care) and can be practiced by males and childless women as well.

To cite one final example, feminist philosopher Alison Jaggar believes both that women have a richer emotional life than men and that this fact makes them better knowers.[131] Taking her cue from recent work in the philosophy of science, Jaggar argues that all observation is selective and involves our values, motivations, interests, and emotions. These "subjective" factors direct our cognitive pursuits, shape what we know, and help determine its significance.* Furthermore, she argues that the emotions of marginalized people (such as women) make them epistemologically privileged with respect to some issues. Because they are "outsiders" to the mainstream of intellectual life and political power, women can have a much more discerning perspective on the prevailing cognitive and social structures while such structures remain invisible to men.

Although some feminists applaud this attempt to highlight the positive features of women's distinctive ways of knowing, others are concerned that this form of essentialism will reinforce the stereotypes that have been used in the past to marginalize women. These concerns are expressed by Code:

> There is a persistent tension in feminist thought between a laudable wish to celebrate "feminine" values as tools for the creation of a better social order and a fear of endorsing those same values as instruments of women's continued oppression.[132]

Similar tensions have arisen as feminists have come to terms with scientific modes of knowing. A group of researchers have pointed out that a central issue among feminists is "the equation of the masculine with objectivity, science, and the scientific method in its emphasis on manipulation, control, and distance from the objects of study."[133] In reaction against this scientific mode of knowing, some feminists have opted for extreme subjectivism and an antiscience stance. However, Evelyn Fox Keller, who has published numerous articles in biology and the history and philosophy of science, has cautioned feminists to avoid the temptation "to abandon their claim for representation in scientific culture and, in its place, to invite a return to a purely 'female' subjectivity, leaving rationality and objectivity in the male domain, dismissed as a product of a purely male consciousness."[134]

The Robinson Crusoe Assumption

Like the fictional Robinson Crusoe who was isolated on his little island, some philosophers have supposed that the search for knowledge is an individual project that is free from social or political entanglements. The best example of this assumption is Descartes, who thought he could suspend all his former beliefs as he searched for the grounds of certainty within the confines of his own mind. Descartes was able to maintain his self-image of being a completely independent and autonomous thinker because the seventeenth-century philosophical and cultural assumptions that permeated every step of his thinking remained completely invisible to him. In contrast, Code stresses that "knowledge production is a social practice of embodied,

---

*Jaggar suggests, for example, that anthropologist Jane Goodall's important scientific contributions to our understanding of chimpanzee behavior was made possible only by her love and empathy for these animals.

gendered, historically, racially, and culturally located knowers whose products bear the marks of their makers and whose stories need, therefore, to be told."[135]

For philosopher Helen Longino, knowledge always arises within a social context: "The development of knowledge is a necessarily social rather than individual activity, and it is the social character of scientific knowledge that both protects it from and renders it vulnerable to social and political interests and values."[136] To paraphrase poet John Donne, "No knower is an island." Our knowledge is initially transmitted to us by our culture, and our further search for knowledge is carried out within a community that informs our endeavors and to which we are responsible. In contrast, Descartes thought he could divorce himself from his community and begin the search for knowledge anew as an isolated individual. For Descartes, knowledge is purely an individual possession, and any facts about communal knowledge are reducible to the knowledge held by individuals. Longino, however, claims that knowledge is first and foremost the product of communities, and individual knowers acquire that knowledge insofar as they are members of a community and accept its norms and background beliefs.

If it is the community of knowers that not only transmits knowledge but brings it to birth, then the more diverse that group of knowers is, the more likely it is that their multiple perspectives will prevent the quest for knowledge from following well-established ruts in the road while ignoring other possible alternatives. Since women have traditionally been "outsiders" with respect to the mainstream intellectual traditions, they tend to be more open to diverse and nontraditional points of view. Furthermore, feminists claim, women are in a better position to understand and critique the prevailing, taken-for-granted assumptions of these traditions.

If the good news in Longino's account is that the social nature of knowledge allows it to be refined by ongoing social criticism, the bad news is that the social character of knowledge production makes it possible for the process to be skewed by the values, ideology, and background assumptions of the dominant powers within society. For example, feminists observe that the appeal to "impersonal, objective thought" often disguises underlying personal interests and power structures. In criticizing the traditional ideal of reason, Lloyd says that besides making women second-class citizens in intellectual matters, the traditional, narrow definition of rationality has had negative political consequences for women. "Exclusion from reason has meant exclusion from power."[137] Similarly, in criticizing a recent work on rationality, Code asserts, "Critics must ask for whom this epistemology exists; whose interests it serves; and whose it neglects or suppresses in the process."[138]

Knowledge production cannot be divorced from power structures, for ideas will get a hearing, will be encouraged, will flourish, and will receive funding, institutional support, and legitimacy when they correspond to the prevailing social structure. On the other hand, those ideas that do not comply with the dominant discourse will be marginalized or dismissed. Hence, to the second-wave feminist movement, women's struggles for equality cannot be confined to just courts of law or legislatures. To change society, second-wave feminists say, we must change the ideas on which society is built.

FEMINIST EPISTEMOLOGY AND THE PROBLEM OF RELATIVISM

Does the feminist perspective in the theory of knowledge imply a problematic form of relativism? This issue has divided feminist thinkers. The tensions this topic provokes is suggested by Code: "Feminist epistemologists often find themselves working within an uneasy relationship to vexed questions about relativism: within an uneasiness generated out of the very act of identifying oneself as a *feminist* epistemologist."[139] While all feminists emphasize the point that there is no view from nowhere and that knowledge is always to some degree relative to the particular circumstances and needs of a particular knower or community of knowers, many feminists are nevertheless decidedly opposed to any form of strong relativism. Their motivation is very clear. If they were to claim that "one opinion is as true as another opinion," they would be vulnerable to the Standard Criticism of relativism.* That is, they would be committed to saying that their observations, claims, and theories are *just* their opinion, merely a personal confession or a subjective preference (like tastes in foods) that have no more validity than opposing opinions. But there is a more specific reason why some feminist epistemologists wish to avoid slipping into relativism. If all opinions are of equal value, if reality does not dictate the superiority of some opinions over others, then the opinions of the Nazis, racists, and sexists have just as much value as those of the feminists.

Because of these unacceptable consequences of relativism, some feminists disassociate themselves from the position altogether. For example, Harding says, "One might be tempted to relativist defenses of feminist claims. . . . However, this temptation should be resisted. . . . Feminist inquirers are never saying that sexist and anti-sexist claims are equally plausible."[140] Similarly, feminist philosopher Jane Duran insists that "one can be contextually sensitive (aware of and responsive to relativistic concerns) without being a relativist."[141]

Philosopher Lorraine Code, however, argues that feminism and relativism are compatible. Code is distinguished research professor in the Department of Philosophy at York University in Toronto, Canada. In addition to authoring several books, she has published numerous articles in epistemology and feminist theory and her work frequently appears in anthologies on these topics. In opposition to the feminist antirelativists, Code tries to defend a version of relativism while avoiding the slippery slope that leads to an "anything goes" total relativism. Accordingly, she argues for a *mitigated relativism* (preferring this term to *mitigated objectivism*,

---

*See the discussion of the Standard Criticism of relativism in section 2.5.

which some philosophers have suggested she should use). In the following passage, she defends a feminist relativism against its critics and argues that it is consistent with the highest ideals of feminism.

- In what ways does Code say that relativism is an "enabling" position?
- Code claims that there may be many valid perspectives; what criteria does she use to evaluate the adequacy of a conceptual scheme?

FROM LORRAINE CODE
What Can She Know?[142]

It is true that, on its starkest construal, relativism may threaten to slide into subjectivism, into a position for which knowledge claims are indistinguishable from expressions of personal opinion, taste, or bias. But relativism need not be construed so starkly, nor do its *limitations* warrant exclusive emphasis. There are advantages to endorsing a measure of epistemological relativism that make of it an enabling rather than a constraining position. By no means the least of these advantages is the fact that relativism is one of the more obvious means of avoiding reductive explanations, in terms of drastically simplified paradigms of knowledge, monolithic explanatory modes, or privileged, decontextualized positions. For a relativist, who contends that there can be many valid ways of knowing any phenomenon, there is the possibility of taking several constructions, many perspectives into account. Hence relativism keeps open a range of interpretive possibilities. At the same time, because of the epistemic choices it affirms, it creates stringent accountability requirements of which knowers have to be cognizant. Thus it introduces a moral-political component into the heart of epistemological enquiry.

There probably is no absolute authority, no practice of all practices or scheme of all schemes. Yet it does not follow that conceptual schemes, practices, and paradigms are radically idiosyncratic or purely subjective. Schemes, practices, and paradigms evolve out of communal projects of inquiry. To sustain viability and authority, they must demonstrate their adequacy in enabling people to negotiate the everyday world and to cope with the decisions, problems, and puzzles they encounter daily. From the claim that no single scheme has absolute explanatory power, it does not follow that all schemes are equally valid. Knowledge is qualitatively variable: some knowledge is *better* than other knowledge. Relativists are in a good position to take such qualitative variations into account and to analyze their implications.

Traditional theories of knowledge have attempted to analyze the phrase "S knows that p" where "p" is a proposition and "S" is the subject or knower. However, it has been supposed by this analysis that the specific circumstances of the knower make no difference to the evaluation of his or her knowledge. In referring to the

"Who is S?" question in the next passage, Code shows her disagreement with this approach.

- In discussing knowledge evaluation in the next passage, does Code say that the sex of the knower is all that matters, does she say that the sex is of no consequence, or does she take a third position?
- In taking subjectivity into account, is Code asserting the truth of outright subjectivism?

Even if these points are granted, though, it would be a mistake to believe that posing the "Who is S?" question indicates that the circumstances of the knower are *all* that counts in knowledge evaluation. The point is, rather, that understanding the circumstances of the knower makes possible a more *discerning* evaluation. The claim that certain of those circumstances are epistemologically significant— the sex of the knower, in this instance—by no means implies that they are definitive, capable of bearing the entire burden of justification and evaluation. This point requires special emphasis. Claiming epistemological significance for the sex of the knower might seem tantamount to a dismissal, to a contention that S made such a claim only because of his or her sex. Dismissals of this sort, both of women's knowledge *and* of their claims to be knowers in any sense of the word, are only too common throughout the history of western thought. But claiming that the circumstances of the knower are not epistemologically definitive is quite different from claiming that they are of no epistemological consequence. The position I take in this book is that the sex of the knower is one of a cluster of *subjective* factors (i.e., factors that pertain to the circumstances of cognitive agents) constitutive of received conceptions of knowledge and of what it means to be a knower. I maintain that subjectivity and the specificities of cognitive agency can and must be accorded central epistemological significance, yet that so doing does not commit an inquirer to outright subjectivism. Specificities count, and they require a place in epistemological evaluation, but they cannot tell the whole story.

LOOKING THROUGH THE LENS OF FEMINIST EPISTEMOLOGY

1. From what you have just read, how would the adoption of a feminist perspective transform your understanding of the history of philosophy, theory of knowledge, metaphysics, ethics, political theory and practice, religion, and business? If women had not been excluded from social and intellectual life throughout history, how would our culture be different today?

2. Imagine that you had been born a member of the opposite sex. What are some possible advantages this act might give you as a knower, as a member of society, or in other ways? What disadvantages would you face that you currently do not have? To what degree are these advantages or disadvantages the result of how society has been structured in the past? To what degree are they the result of natural

differences between males and females? Still imagining that you are a member of the opposite sex, what changes would you want to make in society?

3. A number of issues that divide feminists have been mentioned in this section. The following pairs of opposing claims have *all* been defended by feminists: (1a) There is an essential female nature; (1b) Other than strictly biological facts, any content associated with *woman* or *female* is a social construct and has no fixed meaning; (2a) Traits typically associated with females (caring, emotional, intuitive) are male stereotypes and tools of oppression; (2b) Such female characteristics are real and enable women to have insights not available to men; (3a) Objectivity is a myth, and feminists should embrace relativism and subjective ways of approaching the world; (3b) Without a strong commitment to the possibility of objective knowledge, feminist's knowledge claims would be inconsequential. Imagine that you are attempting to develop your own, coherent version of feminism. Consistent with this project, argue for one or the other position on each of these controversial issues.

4. Most feminists have developed their philosophy out of the experience of being oppressed or excluded and marginalized from the mainstream of intellectual and social life. What if feminists achieved their political goals? What if women and women's perspectives achieved full intellectual, social, and political equality (or even dominance) in our society? Under these conditions, would there be any continuing need for a distinctively *feminist* philosophy? If so, would these changed conditions require a change in the direction and agenda of feminist thought? Or is feminist philosophy merely a stopgap measure necessitated by the current biases in society? Taking a position sympathetic to feminism, argue for one or the other of these conclusions.

5. What are some similarities between feminist epistemology and existentialism? What are the similarities between feminist epistemology and pragmatism?

EXAMINING THE STRENGTHS AND WEAKNESSES OF FEMINIST EPISTEMOLOGY

Positive Evaluation

1. Traditional empiricists saw experience primarily in terms of isolated units of sensation (colors, sounds, tastes, odors, textures). However, feminists have a broader conception of experience that enables them to analyze experiences such as love, harassment, empowerment, self-awareness, or the subjective experience of being a woman or a man. Which approach to experience do you think provides the best basis for doing philosophy?

2. Because feminists emphasize the role of subjectivity, values, and vested interests in the production of knowledge, their complaint is not so much that male philosophers' approaches to knowledge have been developed out of their own

experiences, values, and interests but that the presence of these biases has been denied. Instead of denying our subjectivity, isn't it better to honestly come to terms with our own subjectivity as knowers so that it can be examined, critiqued, evaluated, and possibly modified?

3. Feminist philosophers have spotlighted the social influences on knowledge, even with respect to science. They have also pointed out that theories and knowledge claims have political implications. In what ways are these concerns important to address?

4. It is obvious that women have been excluded from or marginalized within the domain of intellectual discourse. Now that women are making their voices heard within all the disciplines, what do you think are the sorts of insights they have to offer or changes they will make to the ways in which we think?

Negative Evaluation

1. Feminist thought emphasizes the concrete social-political-historical standpoint of a knower. But how many perspectives need to be taken into account? Recently, feminists have noted that their writings primarily represent the perspectives of white, middle-class, American, British, or European academic theorists and have ignored the different perspectives of women of color, working-class women, and African, Asian, Middle Eastern, and Latin American women. Because the experiences and perspective of a knower in relationship to a particular concrete community are central in feminist thought, doesn't this point imply that there will be as many perspectives as there are communities of knowers? Is there any common ground between the experiences of a white, single, agnostic, American woman academic living in a secular, liberal-democratic society and those of a black, married, Catholic, third-world, working woman living in a rigidly traditional and oppressive society? In the final analysis, are we left with a spectrum of irresolvable, multiple perspectives? If so, by what right do feminists suppose that they have the authority to speak for *all* women, much less to propose theories that apply to all knowers? In other words, does feminist theory reduce to the sociology of a series of unique, specific communities?[143]

2. Many feminists claim that there are multiple and equally plausible interpretations of reality and that whether a theory or point of view is accepted as rational is a function of the prevailing social-political power structures. If so, does this claim diminish the importance of the pursuit of truth and, instead, place the priority on achieving social dominance and political power? In rejecting the self-interested perspective of male-dominated epistemology that is said to be driven by a social agenda, are feminists merely proposing an alternative, equally self-interested perspective that is a product of their own social agenda?[144]

3. Is there a problem with the term *feminist epistemology*? Feminists want to develop an epistemology that includes women's experiences and perspectives. But

does the qualifier "feminist" imply that this theory is not a theory of knowledge per se but an account of knowledge as viewed specifically from a female standpoint or from the standpoint of those who embrace a certain ideology? Does this implication tend to segregate women philosophers' contributions to epistemology and give their insights the same limited status as women's sports, women's rest rooms, and women's health care issues?[145] How can feminist philosophy serve to "remap the epistemological terrain," as feminists claim, if it is merely a circumscribed region within that geography? Or should feminists follow the lead of Harding and strive for "hypotheses that are free of gender loyalties"?[146] If this goal was accomplished, would feminists then have to drop the qualifier *feminist* from their theories?

REVIEW FOR CHAPTER 2

Philosophers

2.1 Skepticism
   Cratylus
   Pyrrho of Elis
   Carneades
   René Descartes
   David Hume
2.2 Rationalism
   Gottfried Leibniz
   Socrates
   Plato
   René Descartes
2.3 Empiricism
   John Locke
   George Berkeley
   David Hume
2.4 Kantian Constructivism
   Immanuel Kant
   David Hume
2.5 Epistemological Relativism
   Immanuel Kant
   Willard V. O. Quine
   Georg W. F. Hegel
   Nelson Goodman
   Carlos Castaneda
   Plato
   Protagoras
2.6 Existentialism
   Søren Kierkegaard
   Friedrich Nietzsche

Concepts

Descartes's evil demon
Descartes's bedrock certainty
perceptions (Hume)
impressions (Hume)
ideas (Hume)
principle of induction
uniformity of nature
a priori
Hume's skeptical arguments concerning causality, the external world, the self

2.2 Rationalism
three anchor points of rationalism
innate ideas
Plato's reasons for rejecting sense experience
Universals
Plato's argument for Universals
phantom limb
Descartes's argument for God

2.3 Empiricism
three anchor points of empiricism
empiricists' arguments against innate ideas
ideas (Locke and Berkeley)
ideas of sensation
ideas of reflection
simple and complex ideas
compounding, relating, abstracting ideas (Locke)
Locke on primary and secondary qualities
Berkeley's immaterialism
argument from the mental dependency of ideas
representative realism
Berkeley on primary and secondary qualities
Berkeley on the cause of our ideas
Hume's view of the possibility of knowledge
Hume's view of reason
Hume's view of the representation of knowledge
Hume's two tests for the worth of ideas

2.4 Kantian Constructivism
critical philosophy
Kant's revolution
constructivism
phenomena
noumena
intuitions
sensibility
understanding

categories of the understanding
empirical concepts
pure concepts
Kant's view of our concepts of self, cosmos, and God

2.5 Epistemological Relativism
objectivism
epistemological relativism
subjectivism
cultural relativism
historical relativism
standard criticism of relativism

2.6 Existentialism
truth is subjectivity
knowing the truth versus being in the truth
correspondence theory of truth
perspectivism
romantic primitivism

2.7 Pragmatism
pragmatism
spectator theory of knowledge
correspondence theory of truth
pragmatic theory of meaning
pragmatic theory of truth

2.8 Feminism
feminism
first-wave feminism
second-wave feminism
equity feminists
gender feminists
sex vs. gender
essentialists vs. nonessentialists
generic humanity assumption
view from nowhere assumption
pure, impersonal reason assumption
Robinson Crusoe assumption

SUGGESTIONS FOR FURTHER READING

General Epistemology

Baergen, Ralph. *Contemporary Epistemology.* Fort Worth, Texas: Harcourt Brace College
    Publishers, 1995. A readable book that covers both the basic and advanced issues in
    epistemology.
Pojman, Louis. *What Can We Know? An Introduction to the Theory of Knowledge.* Belmont,
    Calif.: Wadsworth, 1994. A good overview of the topic.

Skepticism

Klein, Peter. *Certainty: A Refutation of Skepticism.* Minneapolis: University of Minnesota Press, 1981. A critical examination of skepticism.

Stroud, Barry. *The Significance of Philosophical Skepticism.* Oxford: Oxford University Press, 1984. A sympathetic analysis of skepticism.

Unger, Peter. *Ignorance: A Case for Skepticism.* Oxford: Clarendon Press, 1975. A challenging defense of radical skepticism.

Rationalism

Cottingham, John. *The Rationalists.* Vol. 4 of *A History of Western Philosophy.* Oxford: Oxford University Press, 1989. A readable and helpful discussion of Descartes and the early modern rationalists.

Descartes, René. *The Philosophical Writings of Descartes.* 2 vols. Translated by John Cottingham, Robert Stoothoff, and Dugald Murdoch. Cambridge: Cambridge University Press, 1985. One of the best translations of Descartes's works, including his *Meditations.*

Empiricism

Berkeley, George, David Hume, and John Locke. *The Empiricists.* New York: Anchor-Doubleday, 1961. An inexpensive collection of the major works of these three philosophers.

Woolhouse, R. S. *The Empiricists.* Vol. 5 of *A History of Western Philosophy.* Oxford: Oxford University Press, 1988. A good survey of the thought of Locke, Berkeley, Hume, and other early empiricists.

Kantian Constructivism

Jones, W. T. *Kant and the Nineteenth Century.* 2d. ed., rev. Vol. 4 of *History of Western Philosophy.* New York: Harcourt Brace Jovanovich, 1975. A good overview of Kant's philosophy, situating it in his century and developing his influences on later philosophy. It also includes short selections from Kant's writings.

Kant, Immanuel. *Prolegomena to Any Future Metaphysics.* Translated by James W. Ellington. Indianapolis, Ind.: Hackett Publishing, 1977. Kant is notoriously difficult to read, but this short introduction to his epistemology is a good place to begin.

Scruton, Roger. *Kant.* Oxford: Oxford University Press, 1983. A short introduction to Kant for beginners.

Epistemological Relativism

Gifford, N. L. *When in Rome: An Introduction to Relativism and Knowledge.* Albany: State University of New York Press, 1983. A helpful overview of relativism and the problem of knowledge.

Existentialism

Barrett, William. *Irrational Man.* New York: Doubleday, 1958. One of the classic introductions to existentialism; covers both the philosophical and literary impact of the movement.

Bretall, Robert, ed. *A Kierkegaard Anthology.* Princeton, N.J.: Princeton University Press, 1974. A good sampling drawn from Kierkegaard's books and journals.

Kaufmann, Walter, ed. *Existentialism from Dostoevsky to Sartre.* New York: Meridian, 1989. A helpful anthology containing selections from the leading existentialists.

Kaufmann, Walter, ed. *The Portable Nietzsche.* New York: Viking Press, 1968. A good collection of readings drawn from Nietzsche's major works.

Sartre, Jean-Paul. *No Exit and Three Other Plays.* New York: Vintage, 1989. Complete texts of Sartre's best-known existentialist plays.

Solomon, Robert. *From Rationalism to Existentialism: The Existentialists and Their Nineteenth-Century Backgrounds.* Atlantic Highlands, N.J.: Humanities Press, 1972. A good discussion for both beginners and advanced students of each of the main existentialists as well as their predecessors.

Pragmatism

Thayer, H. S. *Meaning and Action: A Critical History of Pragmatism.* 2d ed. Indianapolis, Ind.: Hackett, 1981. One of the most comprehensive surveys of pragmatism.

Thayer, H. S. *Pragmatism: The Classic Writings.* Indianapolis, Ind.: Hackett, 1982. A good group of selections drawn from the writings of the leading figures in the movement.

Feminist Epistemology

Garry, Ann, and Marilyn Pearsall, eds. *Women, Knowledge, and Reality: Explorations in Feminist Philosophy.* Boston: Unwin Hyman, 1989. Contains some of the classic articles in feminist philosophy.

Tanesini, Alessandra. *An Introduction to Feminist Epistemologies.* Oxford: Blackwell, 1999. A very readable, well-organized introduction to the topic.

Tong, Rosemarie. *Feminist Thought: A More Comprehensive Introduction.* 2d ed. Boulder, Colo.: Westview, 1998. A helpful overview of the origins and development of feminist philosophy.

NOTES

1. Jonathan Harrison, "A Philosopher's Nightmare or the Ghost Not Laid," *Proceedings of the Aristotelian Society* 67 (1966–1967): 179–88.

2. This exercise was taken from James W. Sire, *Why Should Anyone Believe Anything at All?* (Downers Grove, Ill.: InterVarsity Press, 1994).

3. René Descartes, *Discourse on the Method,* in *the Philosophical Writings of Descartes,* vol. 1, trans. John Cottingham, Robert Stoothoff, and Dugald Murdoch (Cambridge: Cambridge University Press, 1985), 1.8, pp. 114–15. The page references are to the part number and page number in the classic French edition, followed by the page number in this edition.

4. Ibid., 1.4, p. 113.

5. Ibid., 1.4, p. 115.

6. René Descartes, *Meditations on First Philosophy,* revised ed., trans. John Cottingham (Cambridge: Cambridge University Press, 1996), 1.17–23, pp. 12–15. The page references are to the meditation number and page number in the classic French edition, followed by the page number in this edition.

7. Ibid., 2.24–25, pp. 16–17.

8. David Hume, *An Enquiry Concerning Human Understanding,* ed. L. A. Selby-Bigge (Oxford: Clarendon Press, 1894), sec. 2.

9. Ibid., sec. 4, pt. 1.

10. Ibid., sec. 4, pt. 2.

11. Ibid., sec. 12, pt. 1.

12. David Hume, *A Treatise of Human Nature,* ed. L. A. Selby-Bigge (Oxford: Clarendon Press, 1896), bk. 1, pt. 4, sec. 6.

13. Ibid., bk. 1, pt. 4, sec. 7.

14. Plato, *Meno* 80d, trans. W. K. C. Guthrie, in *Collected Dialogues of Plato,* ed. Edith Hamilton and Huntington Cairns (New York: Bollingen Foundation, Pantheon Books, 1961). To allow the reader to find the selections from Plato in other editions, the references are made to the standard section numbers of Plato's manuscripts.

15. Plato, *Phaedo* 65d, 74–75, 76e–77a, trans. Benjamin Jowett (1892).

16. Plato, *Phaedo* 77a–c, 78d–79d, ibid.

17. Alfred North Whitehead, *Process and Reality: An Essay in Cosmology* (New York: Harper Torchbooks, Harper & Brothers, 1957), p. 63.

18. René Descartes, *Meditations on First Philosophy,* revised ed., trans. John Cottingham (Cambridge: Cambridge University Press, 1996), 2.27, p. 18. The page references are to the meditation number and page number in the classic French edition, followed by the page number in this edition.

19. Ibid., 3.36, p. 25.

20. Ibid., 3.40–51, pp. 28–35. The terms in angle brackets are clarifications that Descartes added to the French version of his Latin text.

21. John Locke, "Introduction," sec. 5 in *Essay Concerning Human Understanding,* vol. 1. Because there are so many editions of the empiricists' works, all references to them here are made in terms of the authors' original division numbers. A number of versions are available on the Internet and may be found by submitting the philosopher's name to any of the standard search engines. Some of these sites provide their own search tool, which enables you to find all the passages in which the philosopher uses a particular word.

22. Hume, *An Enquiry Concerning Human Understanding,* sec. 2.

23. Locke, "Introduction," sec. 4.

24. John Locke, *Essay,* bk. 2, chap. 8, sec. 8.

25. Ibid., bk. 2, chap. 1, sec. 1.

26. Ibid., bk. 1, chap. 1, sec. 5.

27. Ibid., bk. 2, chap. 1, sec. 2.

28. Ibid., bk. 2, chap. 1, sec. 5.

29. Ibid., bk. 2, chap. 8, sec. 12–17.

30. George Berkeley, *Treatise Concerning the Principles of Human Knowledge,* pt. 1, sec. 6.

31. Ibid., pt. 1, sec. 1–4, 8–10, 18, 29–31, 33.

32. See Karl Popper, "A Note on Berkeley as Precursor of Mach and Einstein," in *Conjectures and Refutations* (N.Y.: Harper and Row, 1965), pp. 166–74.

33. Berkeley, *Treatise,* pt. 1, sec. 35.

34. Hume, *An Enquiry Concerning Human Understanding,* sec. 4, pt. 1.

35. Ibid., sec. 12, pt. 3.

36. R=Rationalism and E=Empiricism; 1-R, 2-E, 3-R, 4-R, 5-E, 6-E, 7-R, 8-E, 9-E, 10-R.

37. Heinrich Heine, *Germany, Works,* vol. 5, pp. 136–37, quoted in *The Age of Ideology: The Nineteenth Century Philosophers,* ed. Henry D. Aiken (New York: New American Library, 1956), pp. 27–28.

38. Immanuel Kant, *Critique of Pure Reason,* trans. Norman Kemp Smith (New York: St. Martin's Press, 1965), B1–B2, pp. 42–43, 47. Kant published two editions of this work, the first in 1781 (referred to as A) and the second in 1787 (referred to as B). The references to this work are given in terms of the pagination of the original editions, which are indicated in the margins of most English translations, and then in the page numbers of the Kemp Smith edition.

39. Kant, *Critique of Pure Reason,* Bxvi, p. 22.

40. This example was taken from Merold Westphal, " A User-Friendly Copernican Revolution," in *In the Socratic Tradition: Essays on Teaching Philosophy,* ed. Tziporah Kasachkoff (Lanham, Md.: Rowman & Littlefield, 1998), p. 188.

41. Kant, *Critique of Pure Reason,* A24/B39, p. 68; A31/B46, p. 74–75.

42. Ibid., B71–72, pp. 89–90.

43. From Roger N. Shepard, *Mind Sights* (New York: W. H. Freeman, 1990), p. 48.

44. Kant, *Critique of Pure Reason,* A15/B29, pp. 61–62; A51/B75, p. 93.

45. David Hume, *A Treatise of Human Nature,* 2d ed., ed. P. H. Nidditch (Oxford: Clarendon Press, 1978), pp. 252–53.

46. Norman Melchert, *The Great Conversation,* 3d ed. (Mountain View, Calif.: Mayfield, 1999), p. 447.

47. Kant, *Critique of Pure Reason,* A636/B664, p. 528.

48. Ibid., Bxxx, p. 29.

49. This example was inspired by Norman Malcolm's article, "The Groundlessness of Belief," in *Reason and Religion,* ed. Stuart C. Brown (Ithaca, N.Y.: Cornell University Press, 1977), pp. 143–44.

50. Richard Rorty, *Philosophy and the Mirror of Nature* (Princeton: Princeton University Press, 1979), p. 377.

51. Plato, *Theaetetus* 166d, trans. F. M. Cornford, in *Collected Dialogues of Plato,* p. 872.

52. Friedrich Nietzsche, *Beyond Good and Evil* sec. 6, trans. Walter Kaufmann (New York: Random House, Vintage Books, 1966), p. 13.

53. Jean-Paul Sartre, "Existentialism Is a Humanism," trans. Philip Pairet, in *Existentialism from Dostoevsky to Sartre,* rev. and exp., ed. Walter Kaufmann (New York: Meridian, 1975), p. 356.

54. Ruth Benedict, "Anthropology and the Abnormal," in *The Journal of General Psychology* 10 (1934): 59.

55. Willard Van Orman Quine, "Two Dogmas of Empiricism," in *From a Logical Point of View,* 2d ed., rev. (New York: Harper & Row, 1961), p. 44.

56. Ibid.

57. G. W. F. Hegel, *Elements of the Philosophy of Right,* ed. Allen W. Wood, trans. H. B. Nisbet (Cambridge: Cambridge University Press, 1991), preface, pp. 21–22.

58. Nelson Goodman, *Ways of Worldmaking* (Indianapolis, Ind.: Hackett Publishing, 1978), pp. 1–5, 17–18, 20–21, 94, 96–97.

59. Carlos Castaneda, *The Teachings of Don Juan: A Yaqui Way of Knowledge* (Berkeley: University of California Press,1968), pp. 93–94.

60. Plato, *Theaetetus* 171a,b, trans. F. M. Cornford, in *Collected Dialogues of Plato,* pp. 876–77.
61. 1 Corinthians 13:12.
62. Søren Kierkegaard, *Concluding Unscientific Postscript,* trans. David F. Swenson and Walter Lowrie (Princeton, N.J.: Princeton University Press, 1941), p. 135.
63. Ibid., pp. 171, 176, 178, 179–80.
64. Quoted in Dallas M. High, *Language, Persons, and Belief* (New York: Oxford University Press, 1967), p. 11.
65. This example was taken from Michael Polanyi, *Personal Knowledge* (Chicago: The University of Chicago Press, 1962), p. 50.
66. Søren Kierkegaard, *The Journals of Søren Kierkegaard,* August 1, 1835, trans. Alexander Dru, in *A Kierkegaard Anthology,* ed. Robert Bretall (New York: Modern Library, 1946), p. 5.
67. Friedrich Nietzsche, *The Will to Power,* trans. Walter Kaufmann and R. J. Hollingdale (New York: Vintage Books, 1967), sec. 481, p. 267.
68. For this insight on Nietzsche, I am indebted to W. T. Jones's book, *A History of Western Philosophy,* 2d ed., rev., vol. 4, *Kant and the Nineteenth Century* (New York: Harcourt Brace Jovanovich, 1975), pp. 236–37.
69. Friedrich Nietzsche, *The Gay Science,* trans. Walter Kaufmann (New York: Vintage Books, 1974), sec. 335, pp. 263–64.
70. Ibid., sec. 333, p. 261.
71. Nietzsche, *The Will to Power,* sec. 552, p. 298.
72. Friedrich Nietzsche, *Beyond Good and Evil: Prelude to a Philosophy of the Future,* trans. Walter Kaufmann (New York: Vintage Books, 1966), pp. 11–14, 52–53.
73. Nietzsche, *The Gay Science,* sec. 343, p. 279.
74. Nietzsche, *Beyond Good and Evil,* sec. 22, pp. 30–31.
75. Friedrich Nietzsche, *Thus Spoke Zarathustra,* pt. 3, "On the Spirit of Gravity," sec. 2, in *The Portable Nietzsche,* trans. and ed. Walter Kaufmann (New York: Viking Press, 1968), p. 307.
76. Nietzsche, *The Gay Science,* sec. 51, p. 115.
77. Ibid., sec. 41, p. 108.
78. Nietzsche, *The Will to Power,* sec. 410, p. 221.
79. Ibid., sec. 616, p. 330.
80. Louis Pojman, *The Logic of Subjectivity: Kierkegaard's Philosophy of Religion* (University: University of Alabama Press, 1984), p. 143.
81. C. S. Peirce, *The Collected Papers of Charles Sanders Peirce,* vols. 1–6, ed. Charles Hartshorne and Paul Weiss (Cambridge, Mass.: Harvard University Press, 1931–1935), 5.276–77. References to Peirce's works are in terms of the volume number of this collection followed by the section number.
82. Abraham Kaplan, *The New World of Philosophy* (New York: Vintage Books, 1961), p. 28.
83. Peirce, "The Fixation of Belief," in *Collected Papers,* 5.371.
84. William James, "What Pragmatism Means," Lecture II in *Pragmatism: A New Name for Some Old Ways of Thinking* (New York: Longmans, Green, 1907), reprinted in William James, *Essays in Pragmatism,* ed. Albury Castell (New York: Collier Macmillan, Hafner Press, 1948), p. 155.

85. John Dewey, *How We Think* (Boston: Heath, 1933), p. 106.

86. Peirce, *Collected Papers,* 2.75.

87. Peirce, "How to Make Our Ideas Clear," in *Collected Papers,* 5.402.

88. James, "What Pragmatism Means," in *Essays in Pragmatism,* p. 142.

89. Ibid., p. 147.

90. Ibid., pp. 157–58.

91. *The Letters of William James,* vol. 1, ed. Henry James (Boston: Atlantic Monthly Press, 1920), pp. 147–48.

92. William James, *Meaning and Truth: A Sequel to "Pragmatism"* (New York: McKay, 1909; reprint, Westport, Conn.: Greenwood Press, 1968), preface.

93. John Dewey, *Reconstruction in Philosophy,* enl. ed. (Boston: Beacon Press, 1948), pp. 156–57.

94. John Dewey, *Logic: the Theory of Inquiry* (New York: Holt, Rinehart, & Winston, 1938), p. 9.

95. Peirce, "The Fixation of Belief," in *Collected Papers,* 5.384.

96. Peirce, "How to Make Our Ideas Clear," in *Collected Papers,* 5.407.

97. James, "The Sentiment of Rationality," in *Essays in Pragmatism,* p. 12.

98. Ibid., p. 27.

99. Ibid., p. 21.

100. James, "What Pragmatism Means," in *Essays in Pragmatism,* p. 149.

101. John Dewey, *Experience and Nature,* 2d ed. (La Salle, Ill.: Open Court, 1929), pp. 9–10.

102. William James, "Pragmatism's Conception of Truth," Lecture IV in *Pragmatism: A New Name for Some Old Ways of Thinking,* reprinted in James, *Essays in Pragmatism,* pp. 159–62, 166–68, 170–71.

103. These examples were taken from Brooke Noel Moore and Richard Parker, *Critical Thinking,* 4th ed. (Mountain View, Calif.: Mayfield, 1995), p. 59.

104. In addition to the many books and anthologies that are now available on feminist philosophy, *Hypatia: A Journal of Feminist Philosophy* provides many examples of the current discussions in this field. (Hypatia was a fifth-century female leader of the Neoplatonist philosophical movement who was condemned to death as a heretic and died a brutal death at the hands of Christian fanatics.)

105. For a comprehensive survey of women in the history of philosophy, see *A History of Women Philosophers,* ed. Mary Ellen Waithe, 4 vols. (Dordrecht, Netherlands: Kluwer Academic, 1987–1994). This series covers women philosophers from ancient Greece through the twentieth century.

106. Aristotle, *Generation of Animals,* 767b, 20–24; 737a, 27–8; 775a, 15; 730b, 1–30; 737a, 29.

107. For further examples of some male philosophers' conceptions of women, see Mary Briody Mahowald, ed., *Philosophy of Woman: Classical to Current Concepts* (Indianapolis, Ind.: Hackett, 1978).

108. Aristotle, *Politics,* 1260a, 23–30.

109. Samuel Enoch Stumpf, *Philosophy: History and Problems,* 5th ed. (New York: McGraw-Hill, 1994), p. 937.

110. See Casey Miller and Kate Swift, *Words and Women* (Garden City, N.Y.: Anchor Press/Doubleday, 1976), pp. 25–26.

111. John Dewey, *Problems of Men* (New York: Philosophical Library, 1946).

112. To get a glimpse of this disparity, see *The Monist* 77, no. 4 (October 1994), which is devoted to the topic "Feminist Epistemology: For and Against." Some of the articles and references include female philosophers who are critical of feminist thought as well as male philosophers who are sympathetic to it.

113. Simone de Beauvoir, *The Second Sex,* trans. H. M. Parshley (New York: Knopf, 1975), p. 267.

114. Ann Garry and Marilyn Pearsall, eds., introduction to *Women, Knowledge, and Reality: Explorations in Feminist Philosophy* (Boston: Unwin Hyman, 1989), pp. xi–xiv.

115. Carol Gilligan, *In a Different Voice: Psychological Theory and Women's Development* (Cambridge, Mass.: Harvard University Press, 1982).

116. Richard Foley, *The Theory of Epistemic Rationality* (Cambridge, Mass.: Harvard University Press, 1987).

117. Lorraine Code, *What Can She Know? Feminist Theory and the Construction of Knowledge* (Ithaca, N.Y.: Cornell University Press, 1991), p. 8, fn. 7.

118. Harriet Baber, "The Market for Feminist Epistemology," in *The Monist* 77, no. 4 (October 1994): p. 403.

119. Sandra Harding, *Whose Science? Whose Knowledge?: Thinking from Women's Lives* (Ithaca, N.Y.: Cornell University Press, 1991).

120. Code, *What Can She Know?* p. 11–12.

121. Ibid., p. 255.

122. This objection is also a key theme in the writings of postmodernist philosophers. See, for example, Jacques Derrida, *Margins of Philosophy,* trans. Alan Bass (Chicago: University of Chicago Press, 1982).

123. Adrienne Rich, *On Lies, Secrets, and Silence: Selected Prose: 1966–78* (New York: Norton, 1979), p. 207.

124. I would like to thank Anne Foerst for this example.

125. T. Athanasiou, "Artificial Intelligence: Cleverly Disguised Politics," in T. Solomonides and L. Levidow, eds., *Compulsive Technology: Computer as Culture* (London: Free Association books, 1985), pp. 13–35.

126. Genevieve Lloyd, "The Man of Reason," in *Women, Knowledge, and Reality: Explorations in Feminist Philosophy,* ed. Ann Garry and Marilyn Pearsall (Boston: Unwin Hyman, 1989), pp. 111–28. See also Lloyd's book *The Man of Reason: "Male" and "Female" in Western Philosophy* (Minneapolis: University of Minnesota Press, 1984).

127. Lloyd, "The Man of Reason," p. 124.

128. Ibid., p. 127.

129. Code, *What Can She Know?* p. 13.

130. Sara Ruddick, *Maternal Thinking: Toward a Politics of Peace* (Boston: Beacon, 1989), p. 13.

131. Alison M. Jaggar, "Love and Knowledge: Emotion in Feminist Epistemology," in Garry and Pearsall, *Women, Knowledge, and Reality,* pp. 129–55.

132. Lorraine Code, *What Can She Know?* p. 17.

133. Mary Field Belenky, Blythe McVicker Clinchy, Nancy Rule Goldberger, and Jill Mattuck Tarule, eds., *Ways of Knowing: the Development of Self, Voice, and Mind* (New York: Basic Books, 1986), p. 72.

134. Evelyn Fox Keller, "Feminism and Science," in *Signs: Journal of Women in Culture and Society* 7, no. 3 (1982): p. 593.

135. Lorraine Code, "Voice and Voicelessness: A Modest Proposal?" in *Philosophy in a Feminist Voice: Critiques and Reconstructions,* ed. Janet A. Kourany (Princeton, N.J.: Princeton University Press, 1998), p. 223.

136. Helen Longino, *Science as Social Knowledge: Values and Objectivity in Scientific Inquiry* (Princeton, N.J.: Princeton University Press, 1990), p. 12.

137. Lloyd, "The Man of Reason," p. 127.

138. Lorraine Code, "Taking Subjectivity into Account," in *Feminist Epistemologies* ed. Linda Alcoff and Elizabeth Potter, (New York: Routledge, 1993), p. 23.

139. Lorraine Code, *Rhetorical Spaces: Essays on Gendered Locations* (New York: Routledge, 1995), p. 185.

140. Sandra Harding, "Feminist Justificatory Strategies," in Garry and Pearsall, *Women, Knowledge, and Reality,* p. 196.

141. Jane Duran, *Toward a Feminist Epistemology* (Savage, Md.: Rowan & Littlefield, 1991), p. 197.

142. Code, *What Can She Know?* pp. 3–4.

143. These worries are expressed in several feminist writings, such as the following: "How can feminist theory base itself upon the uniqueness of the female experience without reifying thereby one single definition of femaleness as the paradigmatic one—without succumbing, that is, to an essentialist discourse on gender?" (Seyla Benhabib and Drucill Cornell, "Introduction: Beyond the Politics of Gender," in *Feminism as Critique: Essays on the Politics of Gender in Late-Capitalist Societies,* ed. Seyla Benhabib and Drucill Cornell [Minneapolis: University of Minnesota Press, 1987], p. 13.)

144. One feminist writer complains about feminist theories that imply that "there is no truth, and that knowledge based on the female subject is as valid as knowledge based on an androcentric [male-centered] subject. . . . Only power can determine which epistemology will prevail." (Marnia Lazreg, "Women's Experience and Feminist Epistemology: A Critical Neo-Rationalist Approach," in *Knowing the Difference: Feminist Perspectives in Epistemology,* ed. Kathleen Lennon and Margaret Whitford [London: Routledge, 1994], p. 56.)

145. Lazreg cautions against the "intellectual ghettoization" of feminist epistemology (Lazreg, "Women's Experience and Feminist Epistemology"). Similarly, Baber worries that the growing industry of feminist scholarship will lead to "academic pink-collar ghettos" (Harriet Baber, "The Market for Feminist Epistemology," *The Monist* 77, no. 4 [October 1994]: 419).

146. Sandra Harding, *The Science Question in Feminism* (Ithaca, N.Y.: Cornell University Press, 1986), p. 138.

CHAPTER 3

THE SEARCH FOR ULTIMATE REALITY

SCOUTING THE TERRITORY: *What Is Reality?*

Go outside and look at the night sky this evening. You will see an overwhelming number of stars. It would seem to be completely obvious that these stars exist at the same time that you are viewing them. To confirm the testimony of your eyes, you could take a picture of these stars and they will leave their image on the film. However, astronomers tell us that many of these stars no longer exist! The reason is that light takes an enormous amount of time to travel from the distant stars to the earth. (For example, the center of the band of stars that make up the Milky Way is 25,000 light-years away from the earth. A light-year is the distance that light can travel in a year, which is about 5.88 trillion miles.) During this time, as the light from these stars is traveling through space, some of the stars may burn out or be destroyed by a meteoroid. Hence, a star can exist in our current experience because we are experiencing its light, while it does not currently exist at the point from which its light originated. Think about that statement for a minute. On the one hand, such a star obviously does not exist, because its material substance has been destroyed. On the other hand, the star obviously does exist because it affects our experience and has causal effects on our instruments and photographic equipment. In our part of the universe, the star is as real and capable of scientific observation and measurement as the chair on which you are sitting. So, are these stars real or not? Can we experience the reality of something in our spatial-temporal corner of the universe at the same time that it does not exist in other locations? Of course, to decide if some specific thing is real or not requires us to examine a more fundamental question: What is reality?

Exploring questions about the nature of reality is our next stop on the philosophical journey. The awe-inspiring experience of contemplating the night sky can give us a sense of continuity with the ages. As you gaze up at the moon or the Big Dipper constellation, consider the fact that thousands of years before you were born, the ancients were looking at the same breath-taking display. Furthermore, we not only see the same heavens that the ancients saw, but we also ask some of the same questions about the universe such as, What is the cosmos like and what is my place in it? As you take your own philosophical journey, keep in mind that many explorers before you have traveled the same terrain and in their writings have left you "maps" of what they found. Their findings can guide you in your journey, but you must not follow them uncritically. These guides can make you notice features of the territory that you might have missed, but their maps also may contain errors and lead you into dead ends and even dangerous territory. You must decide when the accounts of other explorers are helpful and when they need to be revised.

Philosophical questions about the nature of reality fall under the heading of **metaphysics.** The term *metaphysics* was originally coined by a scholar in the first century B.C. who was editing the manuscripts of the Greek philosopher Aristotle (384–322 B.C.). One of Aristotle's studies of nature was titled *Physics,* and it was

metaphysics the area of philosophy concerned with fundamental questions about the nature of reality

followed by an unnamed work about the more general principles of reality. The editor assigned the title of *Metaphysics* to this later work. (The term literally means "that which comes after physics.") Even though *metaphysics* originally referred to the order of Aristotle's manuscripts, it has come to designate that area of philosophy that deals with the nature of reality. The original meaning is still appropriate, however, because the philosophical domain of metaphysics is "after" physics in the sense that it concerns those questions that remain after we have dealt with the factual questions that can be answered by the natural sciences.

CHARTING THE TERRAIN OF METAPHYSICS:
What Are the Issues?

The philosophical area of metaphysics contains some of the most difficult, profound, and abstract theories produced by the human mind. But in spite of their complexity, metaphysical questions actually arise out of some very basic human concerns. From day one, as tiny infants, we are faced with the task of coming to terms with reality and drawing conclusions about it without any previous knowledge to guide us. Similarly, at the dawn of Western philosophy in ancient Greece (around 600 B.C.), the early philosophers began to examine the nature of reality for themselves and began to think critically about the traditional stories and folk tales that had served to explain the universe prior to the development of philosophy and science. I would like to suggest a similarity between the cognitive development of a little child and the intellectual development of humanity. There used to be a theory in biology concerning the physical development of a human fetus. That theory was expressed in the slogan, "ontogeny recapitulates phylogeny," which means that the stages of development of the individual organism within the womb repeat the stages of development of the human species as a whole. Whether or not this concept is useful in biology, I think that something like this idea has a measure of truth when applied to the history of thought.

What Is the Nature of Ultimate Reality?

The cognitive development of the baby illustrates in many ways the intellectual growth of the human race throughout history. For example, within the changing kaleidoscope of his experience, the baby must sort out what sensations represent objects that persist independently of him (such as a rattle) and what are simply transitory sensations (such as an itch). Some researchers believe that around age five or six months, a baby begins to develop a firm sense of object permanence.

Just as the baby must learn to sort out what is permanent in the world from what is changing, so the early Greeks were concerned with the *problem of permanence and change.* On the one hand, everything seems to be changing. The tides come and go, the seasons rotate, the planets shift their positions, there are floods and there are droughts. Yet, some constants seem to remain throughout these changes. What is permanent throughout the changes in the world? What can we count on? Where can we find a source of stability in the cosmos? Does some fundamental, physical element persist throughout all the changes? Or does some nonmaterial eternal principle control the form that physical transformations take?

For our next example, think about a toddler noticing her image in a mirror for the first time. She is intrigued by the little child she sees. She waves to her and the other child waves back. She jumps and the other girl jumps. Once again, the child eventually makes a breakthrough discovery. The thought occurs to her that "The other child is me!" "But how can that be?" she thinks. "I am here and she is there!" This child is encountering another metaphysical problem: how to distinguish between appearance and reality.

The *problem of appearance and reality* is encountered in the toddler's experience with the world, and it was also one of the first problems that arose in humanity's intellectual infancy. A stick looks straight when we hold it, yet it seems bent when stuck in water. Fire appears to be more powerful than water when it causes water to evaporate, but water appears to be more powerful than fire when it extinguishes the flame. The moon looks small when it is high in the sky, but large when it is on the horizon. These experiences led the ancient Greeks to ask: In all our experiences, what things are just appearances and what things are real?

Why is understanding reality important? From the very beginnings of critical, systematic inquiry in ancient times, philosophers and scientists thought that taking the time and effort to understand the nature of reality was vitally important even if there was never a practical payoff for having this knowledge. Plato, however, thought that an understanding of reality also had momentous practical consequences. He believed reality is that which we dare not misunderstand if we are to be truly fulfilled persons. To use a modern analogy of his view, if we live our lives on the basis of a false view of reality, we would be like travelers trying to find their way around New York City by following a map of Chicago. A wise person, Plato said, would always choose truth (no matter how uncomfortable it may be) over the short-term happiness of illusions. Do you think Plato is right? Isn't it often the case that our illusions and false beliefs can bring comfort while reality can be cruel and distressing? Give the following test to yourself and a few friends to see to what degree a correct understanding of reality is important to you and your friends.

What Is the Nature of Human Reality?

While many metaphysical issues concern the nature of reality "out there," a major part of metaphysics focuses on that part of reality that we know from both the inside and the outside—ourselves. Some philosophers have supposed that by examining our own nature we may get a clue as to the nature of the larger cosmos in which we live. Accordingly, in addition to questions about the nature of reality in general, I explore several related problems concerning the type of reality that characterizes persons.

Let's return to the case of the toddler studying her own reflection. Her fascinating encounter with the mirror teaches her that she can experience herself both as a

Present several friends with the following survey and answer the questions yourself.

- Think of four or five beliefs you have that are very important to you and your conception of the world. (You do not need to share these beliefs if you don't want to.) Possible examples are:
  1. There is a God.
  2. There is life after death.
  3. The scientific account of the world is essentially correct.
  4. The universe conforms to the laws of logic.
  5. I am a reasonably smart person.
  6. There is some ultimate meaning or purpose to human life.
  7. The significant other in my life is faithful to me.

- Now, suppose you begin to worry about the possibility that one or more of your beliefs are false. Yet you also realize that it is possible you might continue on in blissful ignorance all your life without ever finding out the truth. To solve this problem, scientists have developed a "reality meter" for testing beliefs. By pushing its button, you will be told which of your beliefs conform to reality and which are nothing but illusions. Think of your list again. Let's assume you are comfortable believing these things to be true and if you found out otherwise, you would be deeply troubled. Would you decide to continue holding these beliefs because they give you a sense of peace, or would you activate the reality meter in spite of the chance that your new and more accurate knowledge of reality would be disillusioning? What would you do and why?

subject and as an object. As a subject, she is immersed within the world as a subjective center of consciousness. But she can also stand back and view herself as an object to study and understand. One of the mysteries little children eventually begin to wrestle with is the relationship between me and my experiences on the one hand, and that which is not me on the other.

Similarly, in the beginnings of philosophy in the Western world, the ancient Greek philosophers at first asked questions only about the cosmos out there. Gradually, like the infant, they became more self-aware. As they contemplated the stars, it occurred to them that if they take one step back (conceptually), another question arises: Who or what is the self that is contemplating the stars? Eventually, metaphysical questions about reality in general were supplemented with metaphysical questions about human nature. The two major metaphysical questions about the nature of persons concern (1) the mind-body problem and (2) freedom and determinism.

The Mind-Body Problem

Think about your experience of viewing the stars once again. Physical events are going on as light impinges on your retina, which sends signals through your optical nerve to the brain. But mental events are also going on, such as the thought, "The night sky is so beautiful!" How are we to understand these two dimensions? You are a part of the world as one object among many. You have spatial location, you can move, fall down, and be hit by a falling apple just like anything else. But you also have a sense of being separate from the world. You experience yourself as an island of consciousness that is not out there among the other objects. Within the world of your conscious, subjective experiences, for example, you encounter inner realities such as pain or joy, which seem to be different from the objects in the outer world such as rocks and flowers. You may have the sense that you know the contents of your experience by somehow "looking" inside, but how is the inside related to the outside? What sort of reality (if any) do the words *consciousness* or *mind* refer to, and how is it related to the reality of bodies, brains, and chemical elements? Is it possible that everything that happens to you and within you (including your thoughts) can be explained by physical laws? Perhaps there is no inner nonphysical world at all. Maybe what *appears* to be the inner world of your mind and your thoughts is *really* a series of events that happen in nature just like the beating of your heart. On the other hand, would such a physical explanation leave out something that needs to be explained? Such questions are metaphysical questions and fall under the heading of the *mind-body problem;* they are addressed in greater detail in section 3.1, and positions on the problem are discussed in sections 3.2, 3.3, and 3.4.

Freedom and Determinism

As you look at the stars, you have no control over how the light affects your retina. That effect is simply something that happens to you. But what about your other responses? Are they also simply something that happens to you? You may think any number of things as you view the stars: "Isn't that romantic," or "I wish I knew more about astronomy." Are these thoughts and responses freely chosen or are they the inevitable outcome of your personality or your culture? Are you just as determined as the stars or the planets you are studying? Perhaps your response to the stars depends on whether you tend to be primarily a romantic person or an intellectual person. Either way, did you choose your personality, or was it determined by your genes or your environmental influences? If all your behavior and choices are determined either by your genes, social conditioning, or (perhaps) by God's will, then can you ever be held morally responsible for what you do? These metaphysical questions fall under the heading of *freedom and determinism;* they are discussed in further detail in section 3.5, and positions on the problem are discussed in sections 3.6, 3.7, and 3.8.

This introduction has been a brief overview of three metaphysical problems: (1) the nature of ultimate reality, (2) the mind-body problem, (3) freedom and determinism. These three problems concerning the nature of reality do not cover all the issues in metaphysics, but if you work your way through these three crucial issues, you will have gone a large way toward deciding what sort of universe you live in and your place within it. In the remaining sections of this chapter, I focus on the last two problems (mind-body, freedom-determinism). Issues concerning the nature of reality will not receive separate treatment, because they reveal themselves in the debates over the other two problems.

In chapter 4, I treat the existence of God under the topic of philosophy of religion. But obviously this topic could just as easily fall under metaphysics, because the question about the existence of God is a question about the ultimate nature of reality. The stance you take on any one of these four issues (God, reality, mind, and freedom) does not necessarily lock you into a specific answer on the other three questions. Nevertheless, some combinations of positions from each of these issues fit together better than others. For example, some people believe that reality is permeated by intelligence and purpose. Others believe that reality is basically made up of matter and that everything that happens is the result of either mechanistic causes or chance. Obviously, a person who believes in God would tend to favor the first view over the second. Some philosophers, however, have said that the world is like God's body, so that he is at least partly material in nature just as we are. Furthermore, some philosophers have suggested that God could have made the world to function like a machine while allowing some events to be random rather than preplanned. So don't think that there is necessarily only one way to work out the connections between the various aspects of metaphysics. Try your hand at figuring out some of the possible connections.

 THOUGHT EXPERIMENT

The Implications of Theism and Atheism

- If you believed in God, which of the following positions on the nature of reality, mind, and freedom would fit best with this belief? Are several alternatives equally compatible with theism? Which positions would be the hardest to reconcile with the claim that there is a God? Are any alternatives absolutely contradictory to the notion that there is a God?
- If you did not believe in God, which positions on the nature of reality, mind, and freedom would fit best with this belief? Are several alternatives equally compatible with atheism? Which positions would be the hardest to reconcile with the claim that there is no God? Are any alternatives absolutely contradictory to the notion that there is no God?

1. Everything that happens in the world happens to fulfill some purpose.
2. Many events simply happen and do not have a purpose.
3. Humans are completely physical beings.
4. Humans have a nonphysical mind.
5. Everything that happens in the world (including human actions) is determined and inevitable.
6. Some events are not determined.

CHOOSING A PATH—WHAT ARE MY OPTIONS CONCERNING METAPHYSICS?

As I mentioned previously, this chapter consists of two subtopics (mind-body, freedom-determinism). Hence, I save the discussion of the options on these questions for the appropriate sections. For now, I briefly set out some of the options concerning the nature of ultimate reality that show up in all discussions of specific topics in metaphysics. To paint the picture of metaphysics in broad brush strokes, I divide philosophers into two main groups: (1) those who claim there is only one kind of reality and (2) those who claim there are two kinds of realities. The first position is **metaphysical monism** and the second is **metaphysical dualism.**

There are basically two kinds of monism. The first kind is **metaphysical materialism,** which claims that reality is totally physical in nature. Obviously, the materialist would say that if the word *mind* has any meaning at all, it has to be explained in terms of the body (for example, the brain and its states). The materialist does not accept the existence of a nonphysical mind. When I discuss the mind-body problem, I use a special term (*physicalism*) to refer to materialism as applied to the mind-body problem. (The reasons for using this term will be explained later.)

The second type of monism is **idealism.** The idealist believes that reality is entirely mental or spiritual in nature. An idealist using everyday conversation is optimistic, is a visionary, and has a pie-in-the-sky outlook. In this sense, even a materialist could have a very idealistic personality. In metaphysics, however, *idealism* does not refer to a personal stance toward life but to a claim about the ultimate nature of reality.

In our discussion of Asian religions in section 4.6, we will encounter metaphysical idealism in the ancient Hindu tradition. A dominant theme in many versions of Hinduism is that our individual minds are really partial manifestations of God's mind and that all of reality is an expression of the divine mind, much as the world of Hamlet poured forth from Shakespeare's mind. In our discussion of empiricism in section 2.3, we looked at how George Berkeley derived his subjective idealism from empiricism. He argued that since we can never experience an external, material reality that is independent of our minds, the very idea of matter is meaningless. Immanuel Kant (see section 2.4) sought to distinguish his view from Berkeley's. However, Kant ended up with his own version of idealism (called *transcendental idealism*), because he believed that space and time were forms that the mind imposed on experience and that all the objects of experience were constructed by the mind. So idealism has been a persistent position throughout the span of human history. Because idealism is discussed in other chapters (especially the reading from Berkeley), I do not address it in a separate section in this chapter.

Both forms of monism have the advantage of simplicity. That is, both forms claim that reality can be explained in terms of a single principle or category (whether it is physical or mental). Accordingly, they both argue that a dualism that posits both minds and matter as equally real will never be able to explain how these

metaphysical monism a metaphysical position that claims that there is only one kind of reality

metaphysical dualism a metaphysical position that claims that there are two kinds of realities

metaphysical materialism a type of monism that claims that reality is totally physical in nature

idealism a type of monism that claims that reality is entirely mental or spiritual in nature

TABLE 3.1	Three Metaphysical Positions and Their Responses to Central Metaphysical Questions		
	Can there be more than one type of reality?	Is matter a fundamental type of reality?	Is mind a fundamental type of reality?
Materialism	No	Yes	No
Idealism	No	No	Yes
Dualism	Yes	Yes	Yes

two very different types of reality could ever fit together into one unified universe. Both forms agree that trying to relate an independent physical reality and the mental are like trying to plug an American-made hair dryer into an European electrical system. The two just can't work together. This criticism of dualism, which both materialists and idealists share, will be discussed in section 3.2.

The major alternative to monism is dualism. The dualist maintains that one part of reality is physical and another part is nonphysical. Typically, minds and/or God are the leading candidates for this other half of reality. Dualism is obviously a compromise position, because the dualist (along with the materialist) can accept physical reality and the physicists' explanation of it while insisting that there is more to the big picture than the physical dimension alone. On the other hand, the dualist (with the idealist) claims that the mind is fully real and cannot be explained in terms of the physical. While dualism has a more complicated, bi-level view of reality than does either of the monisms, dualists would maintain that they better capture the complexity of reality as we experience it. In section 3.2 we examine René Descartes's arguments for dualism.

The three positions discussed so far are summarized in Table 3.1.

CONCEPTUAL TOOLS: *The Basics of Metaphysics*

Simplifying Complexity

One of Lewis Carroll's short stories tells of a country in which its geographers prided themselves on how far they had advanced the science of mapmaking. Their ultimate project was to create a map that was so accurate that one inch on the map would represent one inch of their country. The humor of the story is that instead of being the perfect map that the geographers envisioned, it would be totally useless, for it would be as complex and large as the territory it was representing. Similarly, a theory of reality that consisted simply of a list of all the objects and events encountered in the world would not be very useful. The goal of understanding the world is achieved by following three principles: (1) simplify, (2) simplify, and (3) simplify. In the face of the overwhelming multiplicity of things, qualities, and events in our experience, we continually seek to understand them in terms of as few categories and principles as possible.

Let's return to our child metaphor again. Before long, a young child comes to understand that in spite of the differences between knives, pencils, needles, and thornbushes, they all have the property of being pointed and sharp and that sharp, pointed things have the property of causing pain. Consequently, when she encounters an unfamiliar sharp, pointed object in the future, she will be able to relate it to what she already understands. Having developed this elementary classification of reality, she has simplified her world in a way that will enable her to deal with it more effectively. Furthermore, once she begins to acquire language, she will have the powerful tools of linguistic and conceptual categories to divide up reality. Hence, while metaphysics carried out at a sophisticated philosophical level can be abstract, intimidating, abstruse, and seemingly disengaged from practical life, it is actually the unavoidable outgrowth of our lifelong project of coming to terms with reality.

The principle motivating this quest to simplify our understanding of reality has come to be called **Ockham's razor** (named after William of Ockham, the fourteenth-century thinker who formulated it). This principle states that we should "shave" off all unnecessary entities and explanatory principles in our theories. The great physicist Isaac Newton, for example, showed that events as diverse as the falling of an apple, the motion of the tides, and the orbits of the planets could be explained with a few basic physical laws instead of a complicated series of numerous principles that explained each type of phenomenon. With these mathematically formulated laws he brought an elegant simplicity to our understanding of nature.

Ockham's razor the principle that we should eliminate (shave off) all unnecessary entities and explanatory principles in our theories

Science and Metaphysics

Speaking of Newton, the thought may have occurred to you, "Isn't it the job of scientists to tell us about reality? What contribution can metaphysics possibly make?" Two quick answers will have to suffice. First, the question, Is there more to reality than that portion that science can discover? is not a scientific question. To ask it we must stand outside of science and philosophically discern its limits and range of competence. If it is possible that reality consists of more than the physical world (e.g., nonphysical minds, God, values), then through philosophical reasoning and not through science alone can we learn whether this dimension exists and what it is like. Second, metaphysics integrates our scientific understanding of the world with our nonscientific concerns. For example, how does our scientific view of the world cohere with the belief that persons have freedom and moral responsibility? The problem is that if we don't understand the distinction between scientific questions and metaphysical questions, we find it too easy to slide from rather well-established scientific theories to controversial philosophical conclusions, not realizing that we have sneaked philosophical assumptions into our science.

In spite of these differences, there are some broad methodological similarities between science and metaphysics. As I pointed out in section 1.2, both science and philosophy evaluate theories on the basis of the six criteria: conceptual clarity, consistency, rational coherence, comprehensiveness, compatibility with well-established facts and theories, and having the support of compelling arguments. Furthermore, both science and metaphysics go beyond what is observed and try to construct large-scale theories that will explain and make sense out of what is observed. Consequently, both science and metaphysics cannot directly verify their theories but must make use of the method of *inference to the best explanation* (see section 1.2).

The Bottom-Line Issue in Metaphysics

ontology the area of metaphysics that asks what is most fundamentally real

Ontology is that area of metaphysics that asks the question, What is most fundamentally real? We briefly examine this question here. Although you will face many other sorts of metaphysical issues, such as the mind-body problem or freedom and determinism, the stance you take on ontology will set the tone for all your other metaphysical inquiries. How do we define *fundamental reality*? If you read between the lines of most metaphysicians' writings, you will find that they use at least two principles for characterizing what is fundamentally real.[1] (1) *Fundamental reality is that upon which everything else depends.* For some people, this reality may be a spiritual reality, such as God. While all theists say that God is the one ultimate reality on which everything depends, some theists say that God has created other, semi-independent realities such as minds, souls, or the physical world. Once God has created these other realities, they say, these things have their own form of existence and cannot be reduced to anything more basic. For other thinkers, fundamental reality may be physical particles, forces, or energy. (2) *Fundamental reality is that which cannot be created or destroyed.* If we found out that what we accept to be fundamentally real could be brought into being or destroyed by something else, then it would be dependent, which would violate the first criterion because there would be something even more fundamental than it. For the theist, God cannot be created or destroyed. On the other hand, if the physical world is ultimate, then it had no beginning. Someone who took this position might say that a table can be created or destroyed but the particles or energy composing it were never created nor can they be destroyed. Given these two principles, and ignoring all the myriads of fascinating details for the moment, every metaphysical theory attempts to lump things into the following three broad categories: things that are not real; realities that can be reduced to more fundamental realities; and things that are fundamentally real.

Things That Are Not Real. Most adults would say, for example, that even though Santa Claus is a pleasant story, he is not real. On the other hand, children for whom Christmas is a part of their family tradition think that Santa Claus is the explanation for the presents under the Christmas tree. As an adult, your metaphysical picture is much simpler. Instead of believing in a world that contains the *three* entities of parents, presents, and Santa, you now believe that the situation only requires the *two* entities of parents and presents and that the former is the cause of the latter. Similarly, for example, some philosophers believe that there are two kinds of events: those that result from deterministic causes and those that result from human free will. Others (analogous to the case of Santa) claim that free will does not exist and that everything, including human actions, can be understood in terms of deterministic causes. This approach could be called the *eliminativist strategy* for simplifying and ordering reality.

Realities That Can Be Reduced to More Fundamental Realities. We frequently talk about "the weather." Do these conversations mean that "weather" is something that exists? Obviously, weather is not a fiction the way the tooth fairy is. "The weather" is just a term that we use to refer to more basic realities such as temperature, high and low pressure fronts, humidity, precipitation, and so on. Every time we refer to the weather, we are referring to these more basic entities and processes. This is where the issue of appearance and reality comes in. Suppose you are driving along the road on a hot day. You see a puddle of water on the road up ahead, but when you drive closer, it disappears. What you saw appeared to be water, but it really wasn't water. It wasn't nonexistent, for you really did see something. The water vision can be explained in terms of heat waves that duplicate some of the visual appearances of water. Similarly, metaphysicians continually apply the "this-is-really-that" approach. Some say that "minds are really brain-events," others claim that "what appears to be a physical object is really a collection of mental events." This approach could be called the *reductionist strategy* in metaphysics.

Things That Are Fundamentally Real. This category is the bottom-line aspect of metaphysics. The question posed here is, What is ultimately real in terms of which everything else can be explained? As you read about each philosopher in this chapter, ask yourself, What does this philosopher believe is the most ultimate reality?

PLATO'S METAPHYSICS

It may be useful to begin our tour of metaphysics by looking at one of its earliest expressions. The ancient Greek philosopher Plato (c. 428–348 B.C.) is noted for being one of the first systematic metaphysicians. (A brief account of Plato's life was given in section 2.2 in the discussion of his rationalism.) Everybody makes some assumptions about what is real. However, Plato made his theory of reality the foundation of all his philosophical endeavors. Although Plato is dead, his ideas are alive, for he left behind one of the most intriguing and influential philosophies in the history of Western thought. However, before we discuss Plato's view of reality, try the following thought experiments, which touch on some Platonic themes.

What Is Real?

1. What would you call this object? Most likely, you said that it is a circle. But notice several things about this object.
   - A magnifying glass would reveal that the points are not equidistant from the center, for the particles of ink are somewhat jagged.
   - The line has a width that could be measured in minute fractions of an inch.
   - The line has depth, for it is made up of a layer of ink imposed on the paper.
   - This object can fade or be destroyed by fire.

   Go back over each item and ask if it is the property of a circle. If not, then how can this object be a circle? If it is not a true circle, how should we describe it? If this object is not really a circle, then what is a true circle and how can we know it?

2. Consider the following pieces of four conversations.
   - "Henry may be the biological father of his children, but his abuse and neglect of them shows that he is not a *real* father."
   - "Dr. Higgins may be listed as a professor of philosophy in the college catalog, but he doesn't care about his students. He's not a *real* teacher."
   - "I have stood in this registration line for one hour and still do not have a class schedule. This college is *unreal!*"
   - "Hitler was one of the most evil villains in history. He was *inhuman.*"

   What do we mean when we say a biological father is not a real father? How can someone teach but not be a real teacher? How can a college be unreal? How can someone be a biological human and yet be inhuman?

In addressing the first question in the thought experiment, Plato would remind us that the points forming a true circle are perfectly equidistant from the center, have neither width nor depth, and cannot change or be destroyed. Hence, the figure in the thought experiment cannot be a genuine circle but is merely a *representation* of a circle. Circles are real entities because we can discover their properties through mathematical proofs. As the following passage illustrates, Plato would say that we cannot see true circularity but can only know it with our intellect.

> You also know how [students of geometry] make use of visible figures and discourse about them, though what they really have in mind is the originals of which these figures are images: they are not reasoning, for instance, about this particular square and diagonal which they have drawn, but about *the* Square and *the* Diagonal; and so in all cases. The diagrams they draw and the models they make are actual things, which may have their shadows or images in water; but now they serve in their turn as images, while the student is seeking to behold those realities which only thought can apprehend.[2]

When we say that the father in the thought experiment is not a real father, the teacher is not a real teacher, the college registration procedures are unreal, and a human dictator is inhuman, Plato would say we are comparing particular, deficient, physical realities with universal, perfect, nonphysical realities. In each case, a *real* father, teacher, college, or human being is one that is moral, caring, and rational.

Nonphysical Realities

In discussing the rationalists' theory of knowledge in section 2.2, I said that Plato considered Universals to be the objects of genuine knowledge. (Following convention, I will capitalize terms such as *Universals, Ideas, Forms, Circularity,* and *Justice* to indicate that Plato uses these terms in a special way.) It is because we can rise above the realm of particulars and understand the Universals they exemplify that we can understand anything at all. Are Universals, then, simply ideas or concepts in our head? According to Plato, there are at least two reasons why Universals are more than that. (1) For something to be an object of knowledge it must be something real. Since Circularity is an object of knowledge, it must be something real. (2) Even if we did not exist, Circularity along with its mathematical properties would still exist. Thus, besides being rational concepts, Universals are also *nonphysical realities* that exist independently of our thoughts about them. Plato frequently uses the term *Ideas* (as in the *Idea of Justice*) to talk about Universals or the objects of knowledge. But for Plato, if there were no minds to know them, the Idea of Justice and the Ideas expressed in mathematical laws would still exist as nonphysical realities. Fortunately, to avoid the notion that Ideas depend on our minds, Plato uses another term for the Ideas, which can be translated as *Forms*. Notice that *Form* does not necessarily refer to shape. Certainly, an essential feature of triangles is their three-sided shape. However, the Form of Justice has nothing to do with shape. The essential qualities that make an action an example of Justice are its moral qualities and not its physical qualities. These Universals or Forms are the true objects of knowledge that can be known only through reason. They are real things that constitute the essence of the many particular things that exemplify them. Particular things (like the drawing of a circle or a particular father, teacher, or human) *represent* their appropriate Form to various degrees of approximation.

To use one of Plato's favorite examples, What is Justice if it is not a physical entity but can be a standard for evaluating concrete practices? There may be a number of ways to approach this question, but the two answers Plato considered are: (a) what we call *justice* is merely what different individuals think it is according to their subjective opinion, or (b) the word *justice* refers to something objective and real but something that we can only know with our minds, not with our physical senses.

 STOP AND THINK

Which of the two answers about Justice seems most correct to you? Can you think of any other answers concerning the nature of justice? From these considerations, what can you conclude about the nature of moral properties such as justice?

Plato's answer is that alternative b is the only reasonable answer. If Justice is not a nonphysical reality, then *justice* is merely a mark on this paper or a sound we make with our mouths that expresses our respective, subjective opinions. If there is no objective standard against which to measure our opinions, then one opinion can be no more true than another opinion. To shine a Platonic light on our own time, how can we say that sexual discrimination is wrong or the policies of Nazi Germany were unjust if *justice* refers to nothing more than what different individuals think it is? If it is all a matter of subjective opinion, then why are our opinions any better than those of the sexists or the Nazis? Plato would reply that if the nature of Justice is more than subjective opinion, then it must be something that we can know. For anything to be the object of knowledge, it must be something real. Therefore, Justice must be something real.

We have difficulty understanding Plato's thesis that the Forms are both nonphysical and actual realities that exist independently on their own apart from any mind. Perhaps this difficulty is because we have been culturally conditioned to think that anything real is something that can be detected directly or indirectly through the senses. But Plato would say that numbers are real things beyond the marks we make on paper. For example, the number seven, its properties, and its relations to other numbers existed before any humans did.

If the nonphysical Forms are what are ultimately real, what is their relationship to the world of individual, physical things? Plato says that particular things *participate* in their Form. A photograph of someone you love has a certain sort of reality. It is a piece of glossy paper that sits in your wallet and evokes warm feelings. When someone asks of the photograph, "Who is that?" you might say, "That is the love of my life." But your statement is not meant literally; the photograph is not the real person, it is but an image of another reality. As an image it lacks some of the essential features and reality of the real person. But what makes the picture so special to you is that it *participates* in the reality of the person you love and reminds you of his or her essence. Similarly, we speak of Henry in the thought experiment as the father of his children because he has some of the features of a father. That is, he biologically contributed to their existence and provided one-half of their genes. But when we say he is not a real father, we are saying that Henry (like a painting of money) lacks some of the essential features of the real thing. He fails to participate fully in the reality of Fatherhood.

Degrees of Reality

In describing the relationship between particular physical things and their nonphysical Forms, Plato suggests the amazing thesis that the two categories of *real* and *unreal* are insufficient to describe the world. Instead, he says, there are degrees of reality, and every thing in the world is located somewhere on the continuum of reality. According to Plato, therefore, any particular thing in the physical world will always have some degree of reality. But we can only know what that degree of reality is by recognizing the thing's relationship to a higher reality that it represents.

Speaking Platonically, I am not a real teacher. Every time I step into the classroom I am trying to be a teacher. Some days I come closer to that goal than others, but I always fall short to some degree. Furthermore, every particular thing participates in more than one Form. For example, I am (to some degree of reality) a husband, father, teacher, human being, animal, and organic life. As this list suggests, some Forms are more general than others, and the lower level Forms participate in the more general, higher level Forms.

To make clear the notion of a hierarchy of degrees of reality, Plato asks us to consider the physical world at the level of shadows, images, reflections, or copies. These items are lower level realities, because they represent, participate in, and depend on the higher stage of reality of the physical objects that they copy. The relationship between shadows and the physical objects they represent is analogous to the relationship between the entire physical domain and the world of Forms. Everything in the physical world (such as an individual father or teacher) is an imperfect representation (like a shadow) of a higher reality (the Form of Fatherhood or the Form of the Ideal Teacher).

If degrees of reality are arranged in a hierarchy, what stands at the very top? What is it that is most fully real and imparts its reality to the whole show? Plato says that it is the Form of Forms, which he calls the Good. While later Platonic Christian philosophers would identify this top level with God, Plato considered the Good to be an impersonal source of order, intelligibility, reality, and value. To get a sense of what he has in mind here, we could compare the Good to the laws of mathematics (which Plato says are lower Forms). The mathematical order pervades everything (even art and music reflect mathematical principles). Yet although the laws of mathematics govern the world and make it intelligible, they do not represent a personal, purposive force in reality. Similarly, at a much higher level, the Good is the highest Form, which provides the basis for all reality, order, intelligibility, goodness, and beauty in the world.

Plato's Allegory of the Cave

Plato's view of reality as well as his view of knowledge and personal enlightenment are represented in his famous Allegory of the Cave, which has become a classic story in Western literature. As you read the story, answer the following questions.

- What do the shadows stand for?
- What are the shadows in our society? In your life?
- According to this story, what is enlightenment?
- In what sense does the freed prisoner *not* understand the shadows as well as his friends do when he returns back to the cave? In what sense does he understand the shadows *better* than his friends do?
- How might this story be used as an analogy to illustrate Plato's view of the levels of reality and the relationship between the physical world and the intelligible world?

- In terms of Plato's metaphysics, what does the sun represent?
- Summarize what philosophical points you think Plato is making in this allegory.

 FROM PLATO

Republic[3]

SOCRATES: And now, let me show in a parable how far our nature is enlightened or unenlightened. Imagine human beings living in an underground den, which has a mouth open towards the light. Here they have been from their childhood, and have their legs and necks chained so that they can not move, and can only see before them, being prevented by the chains from turning their heads around. Above and behind them a fire is blazing at a distance, and between the fire and the prisoners there is a raised walk; and you will see, if you look, a low wall built along the walkway, like the screen which marionette players have in front of them, over which they show the puppets.

GLAUCON: I see.

SOCRATES: And do you see men passing along the wall carrying all sorts of vessels, and statues and figures of animals made of wood and stone and various materials, which appear over the wall? Some of them are talking, others silent.

GLAUCON: You have shown me a strange image, and they are strange prisoners.

SOCRATES: Like ourselves; and they see only their own shadows, or the shadows of one another, which the fire throws on the opposite wall of the cave.

GLAUCON: True; how could they see anything but the shadows if they were never allowed to move their heads?

SOCRATES: And of the objects which are being carried in like manner they would only see the shadows?

GLAUCON: Yes.

SOCRATES: And if they were able to converse with one another, would they not suppose that they were naming what was actually before them?

GLAUCON: Very true.

SOCRATES: And suppose further that the prison had an echo which came from the cave wall, would they not be sure to believe when one of the passers-by spoke that the voice which they heard came from the passing shadow?

GLAUCON: No question.

SOCRATES: To them, the truth would be literally nothing but the shadows of the images.

GLAUCON: That is certain.

SOCRATES: And now look again, and see what will naturally follow if the prisoners are released and disabused of their error. At first, when any of them is liberated and compelled suddenly to stand up and turn his neck round and walk and look towards the light, he will suffer sharp pains. The glare will distress him, and he will be unable to see the realities of which in his former state he had seen the shadows; and then conceive some one saying to him, that what he saw before was an illusion, but that now, when he is approaching nearer to reality and his eye is turned towards more real existence, he has a clearer vision. What will be his reply? And you may further imagine that his instructor is pointing to the objects as they pass and requiring him to name them—will he not be perplexed? Will he not believe that the shadows which he formerly saw are truer than the objects which are now shown to him?

GLAUCON: Far truer.

SOCRATES: And if he is compelled to look straight at the light, will he not have a pain in his eyes which will make him turn away to take refuge in the shadows which he can see, and which he will conceive to be clearer than the things which are now being shown to him?

GLAUCON: True.

SOCRATES: And suppose once more, that he is reluctantly dragged up a steep and rugged ascent, and held fast until he is forced into the presence of the sun itself, is he not likely to be pained and irritated? When he approaches the light his eyes will be dazzled, and he will not be able to see anything at all of what are now called realities.

GLAUCON: Not all in a moment.

SOCRATES: He will need to grow accustomed to the sight of the upper world. And first he will see the shadows best, next the reflections of men and other objects in the water, and then the objects themselves; then he will gaze upon the light of the moon and the stars and the spangled heaven; and he will see the sky and the stars by night better than the sun or the light of the sun by day?

GLAUCON: Certainly.

SOCRATES: Last of all he will be able to see the sun, and not mere reflections of it in the water, but he will see the sun in its own proper place, and not in another; and he will contemplate the sun as it is.

GLAUCON: Certainly.

SOCRATES: He will then proceed to argue that this is what gives the season and the years, and is the guardian of all that is in the visible world, and in a certain way the cause of all things which he and his fellows have been accustomed to behold?

GLAUCON: Clearly, he would first see the sun and then reason about it.

SOCRATES: And when he remembered his old habitation, and the wisdom of the den and his fellow-prisoners, do you not suppose that he would felicitate himself on the change, and pity them?

GLAUCON: Certainly, he would.

SOCRATES: And if they were in the habit of conferring honors among themselves on those who were quickest to observe the passing shadows and to remark which of them went before, and which followed after, and which were together; and who were therefore best able to draw conclusions as to the future, do you think that he would care for such honors and glories, or envy the possessors of them? Would he not say with Homer, "Better to be the poor servant of a poor master" and to endure anything, rather than think as they do and live after their manner?

GLAUCON: Yes, I think that he would rather suffer anything than entertain these false notions and live in this miserable manner.

SOCRATES: Imagine once more, such a one coming suddenly out of the sun to be replaced in his old situation; would he not be certain to have his eyes full of darkness?

GLAUCON: To be sure.

SOCRATES: And if there were a contest, and he had to compete in measuring the shadows with the prisoners who had never moved out of the den, while his sight was still weak, and before his eyes had become steady (and the time which would be needed to acquire this new habit of sight might be very considerable), would he not be ridiculous? Men would say of him that up he went and down he came without his eyes; and that it was better not even to think of ascending; and if any one tried to loose another and lead him up to the light, let them only catch the offender, and they would put him to death.

GLAUCON: No question.

SOCRATES: This allegory is connected to the previous argument about the ascent of knowledge. The prison-house-cave is the world of sight; the light of the fire is the sun; and the journey upwards is the ascent of the soul into the intellectual world. My view is that in the world of knowledge the idea of the Good appears last of all, and is seen only with great effort; and when seen, is also inferred to be the universal author of all things beautiful and right, parent of light and of the lord of light in this visible world [the sun], and the immediate source of reason and truth in the higher world [the world of Forms]; and that this is the power upon which he who would act rationally either in public or private life must have his eye fixed.

GLAUCON: I agree, as far as I am able to understand you.

SOCRATES: Moreover, you must not wonder that those who attain to this wonderful vision are unwilling to descend to human affairs; for their souls are ever hastening into the upper world where they desire to dwell; which desire of theirs is very natural, if our allegory is to be trusted.

GLAUCON: Yes, very natural.

To conclude this overview of metaphysics, I will ask you to develop a sense of your own metaphysical views by ordering a rather common list of items with respect to their reality.

WHAT DO I THINK? *Questionnaire on What Is Most Real*

Rank each of the following items on a scale of zero to ten according to its degree of reality. Items that you think don't exist should be given a zero, and items that are most real should be given a ten. Anything in between is a lesser or derivative kind of reality.

Rank		Rank	
	1. your body		9. a rose
	2. your mind		10. beauty
	3. Einstein's brain		11. a friend
	4. Einstein's ideas		12. love
	5. electrons		13. the U.S. Supreme Court building
	6. God		14. justice
	7. your car		15. a tooth
	8. your car appearing in a dream		16. the tooth fairy

What sorts of items received a zero? Do they have anything in common? What sorts of items received a ten? Do they have anything in common? What principle(s) did you use to decide if an item was more than zero but less than ten? Do you think there can be degrees of reality, or is everything either a zero or ten?

There is no key for your answers because there are too many ways to approach these issues. Instead, keep in mind your rankings as well as your answers to the follow-up questions so that you can compare your position with those we discuss next. We turn now to one of the most difficult issues in philosophy, the mind-body problem.

3.1 OVERVIEW: THE MIND-BODY PROBLEM

SCOUTING THE TERRITORY: *What Is the Mind? What Is the Body?*

What is your mind, and what is its relationship to your body? The ancient Greeks wrestled with this mystery and could not resolve it to everyone's satisfaction. The difficulty of the problem is indicated by the fact that it is still with us today, with many competing, alternative solutions being offered and the proponents of each position claiming that theirs is the absolutely correct one. The following story gives one perspective on the controversy.

FROM HUGH ELLIOT

Tantalus[4]

Suppose there existed a Tantalus* who was condemned for evermore to strike with a hammer upon an anvil. Suppose that Tantalus, his hammer, and his anvil were concealed from the observer's view by a screen or otherwise, and that a light, carefully arranged, threw the shadow of the hammer and anvil upon a wall where it could easily be seen. Suppose an observer, whose mind was *tabula rasa* [a blank tablet] were set to watch the shadow. Every time the shadow of the hammer descended upon the shadow of the anvil, the sound of the percussion is heard. The sound is only heard when the two shadows meet. The hammer's shadow occasionally beats fast, occasionally slow: the succession of sounds exactly corresponds. Perhaps the hammer raps out a tune on the anvil; every note heard follows upon a blow visible in the shadows. The two series correspond invariably and absolutely; what is the inevitable effect upon the observer's mind? He knows nothing of the true cause of sound behind the screen: his whole experience is an experience of shadows and sounds. He cannot escape the conclusion that the cause of each sound is the blow which the shadow of the hammer strikes upon the shadow of the anvil.

The observer is in the position of an introspective philosopher. Introspection teaches us nothing about nerve currents or cerebral activity: it speaks in terms of mind and sensation alone. To the introspective philosopher, it is plain that some mental or psychical process is the condition of action. He thinks, he feels, he wills, and then he acts. Therefore the thinking and feeling and willing are the cause of the acting. Introspection *can* get no farther. But now the physiologist intervenes. He skillfully dissects away the screen and behold! there is a real hammer and a real anvil, of which nothing but the shadow was formerly believed to exist. He proves that states of consciousness are shadows accompanying cerebral functioning; he shows that the cause of action lies in the cerebral functioning and not in the shadows which accompany it.

Elliot's point in telling this story is to suggest that we naively think that the cause of all our thoughts, feelings, and activities is a nonphysical mind. However, the mind and its activities are compared to the shadow images that are really the products of the physical hammer and anvil that lie behind the screen. Eliot believes that the real you is your brain, which is the seat and cause of all your cognitive functioning. What you find in introspection is merely an appearance or an illusion.

---

*Tantalus was a figure in Greek mythology who was punished by having to carry out an eternal task.

However, the metaphor of shadows reminds us of Plato's Allegory of the Cave ...ussed in section 3.0. So we could take our cue from Plato and interpret Elliot's ... differently than he did. Plato would say that the shadows, or the appearances, ...lliot's story refer to the physical world known by the senses. The real world, ...ding to Plato, represented by the hammer and the anvil behind the screen, is ... nonphysical world in which the soul or the mind resides. In introspection, we ...cover the real world of our minds and their ideas. Because science can only ...amine physical data, it cannot penetrate the screen of physical events to discover ...e mental reality behind it.

So we now have two major perspectives. Each one gives a different account of the true cause of our thinking, feeling, and willing. Is the brain the source of all our activities, and what we call *the mind* merely a faulty interpretation of the neurochemical events taking place behind the scenes, as Elliot suggests? Or is it that "behind the screen" of our physical embodiment is a nonphysical mind that is the seat of consciousness through which we control all that we think and do? The nature of the mind and its relationship to the body is one of the most perplexing problems in philosophy. Some philosophers think that recent research on the brain has solved the problem, while others think that it has only made the problem more complex. In the next few sections, I examine the different dimensions of the mind-body problem and the alternative solutions that have been proposed.

 THOUGHT EXPERIMENT

Physical and Mental Properties

Complete the following six tasks (A1 to B3):

A1. Add to this list five more specific kinds of physical objects: quarters, oxygen atoms, tomatoes, dictionaries, ball bearings, . . .

A2. Add to this list five more specific items that describe properties of various physical objects: green, weighs ten lbs., wet, thirty ft. tall, square, . . .

A3. Add to this list five more types of physical locations, positions, or motions that could describe a friend: across the room, sitting, running, jumping, shouting, waving, . . .

B1. Add to this list five more kinds of mental contents: hopes, ideas, dreams, pains, doubts, . . .

B2. Add to this list five more items that could be used to describe different people's minds: intelligent, imaginative, pessimistic, clever, devious, . . .

B3. Add to this list five more items that describe a mental activity: thinking, guessing, hoping, wondering, doubting, . . .

- Compare the list of properties in A2 with those in B2. Write down some of the general ways in which they differ.
- Compare the list of activities in A3 with those in B3. Write down some of the general ways in which they differ.

(Continued . . .)

(. . . continued)

- Apply some of the adjectives in A2 to the items in B1 and add a location or some of the activities in A3 to this description, for example, "a green hope that is sitting in the car."
- Apply some of the adjectives in B2 and B3 to the items in A1, for example, "intelligent, thinking quarters."

Why is it that we end up with nonsense when we combine items from lists A and B? Of course these descriptions *could* make sense if we were speaking metaphorically (we could take "sharp" as it applies to knives and speak of a "sharp" mind). However, our concern here is only with literal descriptions. Thus, it seems to make no sense to say that your idea of God is two inches long, weighs one-eighth of a gram, is located precisely three inches away from your idea of justice, and is the color red. Neither could we say that your mind was triangular in shape. Similarly, it makes no sense to say that a beaker of chemicals is doubting or believing. Why?

This exercise illustrates the fact that we have two ways of speaking: words that describe *physical* bodies, properties, and events, and words that describe *mental* contents, properties, and events. Do these two completely different ways of *speaking* suggest that there are two completely different kinds of *reality* (bodies and minds)? If so, what are some other reasons to think that bodies and minds are different sorts of things? On the other hand, if you think the body and the mind are not separate realities, then why is the language of physical events so different from that of mental events?

In addition to the different properties of minds and bodies, there is another issue. This issue has to do with the relation between the mind and the body and arises from the fact that the mind and the body seem to causally affect one another. To explore this issue, follow the instructions in A4 and B4 of the next thought experiment.

 THOUGHT EXPERIMENT

Mental and Physical Causation

A4. Complete sentences 3 and 4, and in sentence 5, add one or more specific examples of your own about how your mind affects your body:

1. I worry (mental event) and lose my appetite (physical event).
2. I think I am driving too fast, so I press the brake.
3. I desire to have another piece of pizza, and my hand . . .
4. I decide to vote for a particular candidate, and I . . .
5.

B4. Complete sentences 3 and 4, and in sentence 5, add one or more specific examples of your own about how your body affects your mind:

(Continued . . .)

(... continued)

1. I drink too much coffee (physical event), causing me to become irritable (mental event).
2. I stub my toe, and I experience pain.
3. I didn't get any sleep last night, and in class, my mind...
4. Someone special hugs me, and I feel...
5.

This exercise suggests that not only do we commonly think of the mind and body as two different things, but we think of them as interacting. Some mental events seem to cause physical events, and some physical events seem to cause mental events. Even though we ordinarily speak this way, philosophers make it their task to examine our taken-for-granted assumptions. In the final analysis, we might conclude that there are good philosophical reasons for our ordinary ways of speaking. On the other hand, we may find that these common assumptions need to be clarified, revised, or even abandoned.

CHARTING THE TERRAIN OF THE MIND-BODY PROBLEM: *What Are the Issues?*

The previous exercises support three commonsense beliefs that characterize our traditional concept of the mind and the body:

1. The body is a physical thing.
2. The mind is a nonphysical thing.
3. The mind and body interact and causally affect one another.

Having listed these beliefs, we still face one nagging problem: Exactly how does a nonphysical thing (the mind) interact with a physical thing (the body)? Physical things interact by pushing, pulling, merging, energizing, attracting, magnetizing, and so forth. However, all these sorts of interactions involve physical forces that can be explained by the laws of physics. Most people, if asked, would tend to agree with the statement, "The motion of a physical body is completely subject to physical laws." However, if the mind is not a physical thing, then it cannot affect a body through gravitational, electrical, magnetic, or mechanical force. How, then, can there be any causal relationship between the mind and body? To explain this interaction by referring to the brain is of very little help, because the brain is simply another sort of physical body. The difficulty in understanding how a nonphysical thing such as the mind can have any causal interaction with a physical body suggests a fourth proposition:

4. Nonphysical things cannot causally interact with physical things.

We now seem to have four, equally plausible propositions, but they cannot all be true. You can believe any combination of three of them, but when you add the

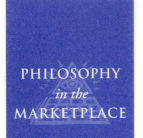

Answer the following questions yourself, and ask them of five of your friends.

- At this point in your thinking, which three of the following statements do you believe the most strongly? Or in other words, which one of the four statements do you think is the least plausible?
- What are your reasons for your three affirmative choices and your one negative choice?

1. The body is a physical thing.
2. The mind is a nonphysical thing.
3. The mind and body interact and causally affect one another.
4. Nonphysical things cannot causally interact with physical things.

mind-body dualism the claim that the mind and the body (which includes the brain) are separate entities.

remaining proposition, you end up in a contradiction. It seems that we are forced to decide which one of the four preceding propositions we are going to reject. Unfortunately, there is a price to pay for rejecting any of them, and that price is the necessity of rejecting the commonsense reasons that led us to think that particular belief was plausible in the first place. As we will see, each of the positions on the mind-body problem avoids the difficulty by rejecting one of the four propositions. In the "Philosophy in the Marketplace" survey, you and your friends will be asked how you avoid the difficulty by indicating which of the four statements you reject.

CHOOSING A PATH: *What Are My Options concerning the Mind and the Body?*

physicalism the theory that human beings can be explained completely and adequately in terms of their physical or material components

interactionism a type of dualism that claims that the mind and body, though different, causally interact with one another

A number of positions have been taken on the mind-body problem, but two of them stand out as being the most significant alternatives. These positions are mind-body dualism and physicalism. **Mind-body dualism** is the claim that the mind and the body (which includes the brain) are separate entities. The body is a physical thing, whereas the mind is a nonphysical (immaterial or spiritual) thing. (For the sake of brevity, whenever I discuss dualism with respect to the mind and body in the remainder of this chapter, I will refer to mind-body dualism as simply *dualism*.) **Physicalism** is the claim that the self is identical to or the product of the activities of the body or the brain and that there is no nonphysical aspect of a person.

The most common version of dualism is called **interactionism.** Interactionism adds to the dualistic thesis the claim that the mind and body, though different, causally interact with one another. This version of dualism was defended by the seventeenth-century French philosopher Descartes and represents the common-sense view of the issue that we explored earlier. Note that many religious views commonly identify the real person with his or her soul, which is said to be a nonphysical or spiritual entity. In discussing dualism, we will assume that the terms *soul* or *mind* may be used interchangeably, because they both refer to the nonphysical component within us that constitutes the real person.

To get a clearer picture of these two philosophies, let's see how each position would explain an everyday event like answering the phone. Dualistic interactionism can be represented by the following diagram. The symbol BS stands for a brain state or event, and the symbol MS stands for a mental state or event.

Dualistic Interactionism. The phone rings, causing electrical signals to be sent to the brain (BS_1). These electrical signals cause other brain states (BS_2), which produce the sensation of sound in the mind (MS_a). This mental event causes more brain activity (BS_3, BS_4), which causes the mental event of recognizing that the phone is ringing (MS_b). This mental event, or thought, causes the desire to pick up the phone (MS_c). This mental desire leads to the mental act of willing to pick up the phone (MS_d). This mental act sets in motion further brain activity (BS_5), which causes your hand to pick up the phone.

Keeping the original labels of the brain states the same, let's transform the mental states into brain states. We now have the physicalist's diagram of the same event.

Physicalism. The phone rings, causing electrical signals to be sent to the brain (BS_1). These electrical signals cause other brain states (BS_2), which produce the sensation of sound (BS_a). This sensation causes more brain activity (BS_3, BS_4), which produces the recognition that the phone is ringing (BS_b). This recognition causes you to want to pick up phone (BS_c), which causes you to decide to pick up the phone (BS_d), which causes more brain activity (BS_5), which causes your hand to pick up the phone. Some brain states are unconscious (BS_1 to BS_5), while some brain states operate at a very high level that we call consciousness (BS_a to BS_d). Nevertheless, whether conscious or not, the physicalist claims that all events are neurochemical events in the brain.

Even though interactionism and physicalism are the most common positions throughout the history of philosophy, several other options are worth mentioning. The overview of metaphysics at the beginning of this chapter discussed idealism. Idealism is like the photographic negative of physicalism. Whereas the physicalist says that human beings are nothing but matter, the idealist says that human beings (and all of reality) are nothing but mental substances. The idealist solves the mind-body problem by believing that the mind and the body are not really two different, irreducible kinds of reality. Instead, the idealist claims, the physical world and the body are just a collection of mental experiences or are aspects of a larger mental reality. The idealist's view of the mind has been presented previously in discussing the views of George Berkeley in section 2.3.

During the time of Descartes, two other forms of dualism were developed as alternatives to interactionism. Each of them claimed that the mind and body were separate realities while denying that the two causally affected one another. In this way these forms of dualism avoided the problem that interactionism faced of explaining how our nonphysical mind can interact with our physical body. The first alternative form of dualism is known as **parallelism.** This position claims that mental events cause only other mental events and that physical events cause only other physical events. These two separate series of events only seem to interact because they always operate parallel to one another. Arnold Geulincx (1624–1669), for example, said God arranges the two parallel series of mental and physical events to work together like two clocks that are set to strike the hour at the same time. Because God has foreseen that I am now willing my pen to write on this paper, he has arranged the physical world so that my hand and the pen move simultaneously with my mental willing. The second position is that of **occasionalism.** It is very similar to parallelism except that there is no preestablished harmony created by God. Instead, on the occasion of a physical event, God causes a mental event and vice versa. Hence, when the telephone produces physical sound waves, God causes you to experience the sound of ringing. When you think relaxing thoughts, God causes your blood pressure to go down. Nicholas Malebranche (1638–1715) was a leading defender of occasionalism.

There are also different varieties of physicalism. The two most common versions are **identity theory** (or **reductionism**) and **eliminativism.** Even though identity theorists deny that there is a separate, nonphysical mind, they think it is meaningful to talk about the mind because they claim that all talk about the mind can be translated into talk about brain states. On the other hand, the eliminativist thinks that our mental vocabulary should be eliminated altogether in favor of a physiological vocabulary. Hence, for the eliminativists, to talk about whether the mind is or is not physical or whether it does or does not interact with the body is like asking, "Are leprechauns in favor of nuclear disarmament?" or "Do ghosts enjoy modern art?" Once you have decided that leprechauns and ghosts do not exist, these questions are meaningless. Similarly, the eliminativists want to discard all language that refers to mental events because they believe there are no such things.

The various positions that we have discussed are summarized in table 3.2 in terms of their answers to five questions.

Notice that table 3.2 contains five questions and five positions. Each one of the positions avoids the mind-body problem by answering *No* to one of the questions. Both varieties of physicalists refrain from answering the fifth question because they do not think there is any nonphysical mental reality at all. The eliminativists also refrain from answering questions 3 and 4 because they deny that the term *mind* refers to anything.

TABLE 3.2 *Positions on the Mind-Body Problem*					
	Is the body a physical thing?	Do we have a mind?	Is the mind a nonphysical thing?	Do the mind and body interact?	Is it impossible for a nonphysical thing to interact with a physical thing?
Dualism: Interactionism	Yes	Yes	Yes	Yes	No
Dualism: Occasionalism, Parallelism	Yes	Yes	Yes	No	Yes
Idealism	No	Yes	Yes	Yes	Yes
Physicalism: Identity Theory (Reductionism)	Yes	Yes	No	Yes	—
Physicalism: Eliminativism	Yes	No	—	—	—

One more position, called **functionalism,** is discussed in a later section. Functionalism could not be placed on the chart because its advocates question the way that the mind-body issue has been divided up in the chart. They reject the dualist's claim that the mind is a separate substance. Yet they reject the identity theorist's claim that mental events are identical to brain events. They also reject the eliminativist's claim that there are no mental events. Instead, functionalists argue that the realm of the mental is characterized by particular patterns of input-processing-output. Hence, functionalists claim that the brain is like the physical hardware of the computer and the mind is like the computer program that is run on the hardware but is logically distinct from it. In sections 3.2, 3.3, and 3.4, we take a closer look at dualism, physicalism, and functionalism, respectively.

functionalism a philosophy that claims that the mind is characterized by particular patterns of input-processing-output

WHAT DO I THINK? *Questionnaire on Mind and Body*

Before reading any further, complete this survey. Express your opinion by putting an X in the appropriate box to the right of each statement. If you agree with the statement, mark "Agree" and if you disagree, mark "Disagree." Do not write anything in the boxes that are shaded. You may not feel strongly one way or another and wish to say "undecided." However, you must mark whichever answer seems *most* likely to you at this point. This questionnaire is only a survey of your opinions, so there are no right or wrong answers for the purposes of this exercise.

	A1	B	A2
1. The physical world is the only kind of reality there is.	Agree	Disagree	
2. The mind is something nonphysical yet real.		Agree	Disagree

(continued)

	A1	B	A2
3. The *mind* is nothing more than a word that refers to the sum of those cognitive activities produced by the brain.	Agree	Disagree	
4. The mind and the brain interact even though they are different entities.		Agree	Disagree
5. When I make a decision, the immediate cause of this event is the physical events occurring in my brain.	Agree	Disagree	
6. The act of making a mental decision is *not* a physical event, *nor* does it have a physical cause.		Agree	Disagree
7. A physical event can only be caused by another physical event.	Agree	Disagree	
8. An act of my will is *not* a physical event, but it can cause my body to perform some physical action.		Agree	Disagree
9. Even if we cannot accomplish this as yet, everything that a person does or thinks or feels is capable of a scientific explanation.	Agree	Disagree	
10. The mind and its activities will never be completely explained by the science of the brain.		Agree	Disagree
	A1	**B**	**A2**

KEY TO THE MIND-BODY QUESTIONNAIRE

Add up all the answers you checked in column A1. (This column has only "Agree" answers.) Place this total in the box marked A1 at the bottom of the column. Next, add up all the answers you checked in column A2. (This column has only "Disagree" answers.) Place this total in the box marked A2 at the bottom of the column. Add together the scores in boxes A1 and A2 and place the total in the shaded box here. Finally, add together all the answers (both "Agree" and "Disagree") that you checked in column B. Transfer this total to the unshaded box here.

A1 + A2 = [shaded box]   B = [box]

The shaded box (A1 + A2) represents the position of physicalism. The unshaded box (B) represents the position of dualism. Whichever box contains the larger number is the position closest to your own. As I have mentioned, other positions can be taken on the mind-body problem (such as functionalism) that disagree with the dichotomies assumed by this questionnaire. Nevertheless, if you had to choose between dualism and physicalism, this questionnaire does indicate which position you would favor.

3.2 DUALISM

LEADING QUESTIONS: *Dualism*

1. In the movie *All of Me,* the mind of the character played by Lily Tomlin took over the body of the character played by Steve Martin. Of course, the premise of one person inhabiting another's body provided a great deal of slapstick comedy material. In spite of the physical impossibility of such an event, is it still conceivable? Can you imagine remaining the person you are while inhabiting a different body?

2. Can you imagine yourself witnessing your own funeral? Is it conceivable that you could see your body in the casket, with your grieving friends silently viewing it, while you were a bodiless spirit or a center of consciousness watching this event from a remote position? Whether or not you believe in personal immortality, is it possible to at least imagine this scenario?

3. Most of us spend a great deal of time communicating with computers. Our computers send us messages such as, "You used an invalid filename." Through artificial intelligence research, computers have developed extraordinary abilities. They now can play very challenging games with chess masters. No matter how technologically advanced computers become, however, will they ever have minds? When you play chess, you are conscious and aware of what is going on. However, can we imagine that the collection of circuits and software in a computer will someday produce consciousness? In the final analysis, isn't the computer a calculating machine that lacks anything approaching the internal subjective experience you have?

4. You can frequently know what is going on in someone's mind. For example, a person's facial expression can reveal that he or she is experiencing puzzlement, joy, anger, fear, or boredom. But in spite of these ways in which our bodies and behavior give clues of our mental life, isn't a large portion of what is going on in your mind private and known by you alone? Isn't there a rather clear boundary between your private mental contents and that part of you that is public?

The assumptions underlying these questions represent some very traditional and common intuitions about the mind and the body. Even though our mind and our body seem to be joined together throughout our lives, most people can imagine the possibility of the two existing separately. But even though we think we can imagine this possibility, is it really coherent? Furthermore, even if it is coherent, are there any reasons to suppose that the mind actually is separate from the body? The dualist wants to convince you that the answer to both of these questions is yes.

SURVEYING THE CASE FOR DUALISM

The seventeenth-century philosopher René Descartes is not merely a representative of mind-body dualism, he is its most famous advocate. Hence, we can get a very good look at dualism by surveying Descartes's views.

In the section on skepticism (section 2.1), we examined Descartes's attempts to find certainty by doubting every one of his beliefs to see if any withstood critical examination. The one belief he could not doubt was "I exist." However, the certainty of his own existence applied only to his existence as a mind, a mental substance distinct from his body. Descartes believed he was directly and immediately acquainted with his mind or his consciousness, but his belief that he had a physical body that existed in the external world was simply something he inferred from his physical sensations. The problem is that in dreams and hallucinations we can experience bodily sensations that are illusions and that do not reflect what is really in the external world. As I pointed out in the discussion of rationalism, however, when Descartes developed his rationalistic proof for the existence of God, this problem was solved. Because he found the existence of a perfect God rationally irrefutable, he was confident that this God would not allow him to be massively deceived about the existence of his own body and the external world.

Based on these considerations, Descartes concluded not only that he was not just a mind but also that his mind was associated with a body. The picture that emerges is that human beings are made up of two different kinds of reality that are somehow linked together. On the one hand, we have bodies and are a part of the physical world. According to Descartes, the body is a machine made out of flesh and bone. Your joints and tendons act like pivots, pulleys, and ropes. Your heart is a pump and your lungs are bellows. Because the body is a physical thing, it is subject to the laws of physics and is located in space and time. According to Descartes, animals are also machines, and their behavior is sheerly a product of mechanical laws. Humans, however, are unique in that in addition to their bodies, they also possess minds. According to Descartes, your mind (which is identical to your soul and your consciousness) is the "real" you. If you lose an arm or a leg, your bodily mechanism is impaired but you are still as complete a person as before. Descartes's position can be called mind-body dualism, or *psychophysical dualism*. Since Descartes has given the classic statement of this position, it is also commonly referred to as *Cartesian dualism* in his honor.

DESCARTES'S ARGUMENTS FOR MIND-BODY DUALISM

Descartes's Basic Premise

Descartes offers several arguments to convince us that the mind and body are two separate realities. Although he argues for his dualism in a number of different ways, implicit within all his arguments is the same basic premise, often labeled the *Prin-*

ciple of the Nonidentity of Discernibles: If two things do not have exactly identical properties, then they are not identical.

On the face of it, this principle seems to be fairly clear and obvious. For two things to really be the same thing, they must have the same properties. If there are discernible differences between them, then they must be different things. For example, the nineteenth-century figure Samuel Clemens and the popular American writer Mark Twain are the same individual. Hence, anything that is true of the person designated by "Samuel Clemens" will be true of the person referred to by "Mark Twain" and vice versa. On the other hand, according to this strict definition of identity, so-called identical twins are different persons who have some very basic similarities. If nothing else, they differ (or are discernible) because they occupy different portions of space.

Let's examine a practical application of this principle. Suppose Ziggy is accused of breaking down the locked cafeteria door with an axe and stealing a banana cream pie. The crime lab analyzes the blows to the door and determines that the thief had to be left-handed and more than six feet tall. Furthermore, the police discover blond hairs on the discarded axe that obviously belong to the trespasser. However, Ziggy is right-handed, five feet tall, and has black hair. Because the properties of Ziggy differ from the properties of the thief, the two cannot be the same person. Therefore, Ziggy is innocent.

 THOUGHT EXPERIMENT

Applying Descartes's Principle

Apply the method of reasoning we just learned to the mind-body problem.

- List typical properties of minds that differ from the properties of bodies.
- Does it seem as though these differences are sufficient to establish that the mind and the body are different things?
- In the discussion that follows, see how your list compares with Descartes's.

Descartes has a standard form of argument that he frequently uses to show that the mind and body are different. This form of argument makes use of the Principle of the Nonidentity of Discernibles, because he examines the properties of both minds and bodies to show that minds and bodies are different sorts of realities. These arguments for dualism have this generic form:

1. The body has property A.
2. The mind has property non-A.
3. If two things do not have exactly identical properties, then they cannot be identical.
4. Therefore, the mind and the body are not identical. They are two completely different entities.

The Argument from Doubt

One of Descartes's central arguments is based on what can and cannot be doubted. In his *Discourse on the Method* he recounts his journey out of skepticism when he realized he could not doubt his own existence, even though he could doubt the existence of the external world, including his own body.

FROM RENÉ DESCARTES
Discourse on the Method[5]

Next I examined attentively what I was. I saw that while I could pretend that I had no body and that there was no world and no place for me to be in, I could not for all that pretend that I did not exist. I saw on the contrary that from the mere fact that I thought of doubting the truth of other things, it followed quite evidently and certainly that I existed. . . . From this I knew I was a substance whose whole essence or nature is simply to think, and which does not require any place, or depend on any material thing, in order to exist. Accordingly this "I"—that is, the soul by which I am what I am—is entirely distinct from the body, and indeed is easier to know than the body, and would not fail to be whatever it is, even if the body did not exist.

Descartes's argument could be expressed like this:

The Argument from Doubt

1. I can doubt my body exists.
2. I cannot doubt my mind exists.
3. If two things do not have exactly identical properties, then they cannot be identical.
4. Therefore, the mind and the body are not identical.

Premises 1 and 2 identify two different properties of the body and the mind that Descartes discovered when he employed his method of doubt. He found he could be absolutely certain of his mind, but because of the possibility of illusion (dreams and hallucinations), he could be mistaken and hence uncertain about the existence of his body. Descartes offered this argument as a logical proof that the mind and the body could not be the same thing.

This argument has problems, however. The property of being subject to doubt is not the same sort of property as being six feet tall or being bald. The fact that I can doubt something is as much a psychological property of me as it is of the object of my doubt. To see the difficulties with this argument, consider the following argument that has essentially the same form:

1. I am in doubt as to whether the sixteenth president of the United States ever had a beard.
2. I am not in doubt that Abraham Lincoln had a beard.

3. If two things do not have exactly identical properties, then they cannot be identical.
4. Therefore, the sixteenth president of the United States and Abraham Lincoln are not identical.

Everyone knows that Lincoln had a beard, but some people are not sure about whether the sixteenth president did. The problem is that some people do not realize that Abraham Lincoln was the sixteenth president of the United States. Hence, it is possible that Descartes is more certain about his mind than he is of his body simply because he does not understand the nature of each fully enough to see that they are identical.

The Argument from Divisibility

The following argument makes use of the same argument form as before but avoids the difficulty of dealing with our psychological attitudes. See if you can extract the outline of the argument from this passage.

FROM RENÉ DESCARTES
Meditations on First Philosophy (1)[6]

The first observation I make at this point is that there is a great difference between the mind and the body, inasmuch as the body is by its very nature always divisible, while the mind is utterly indivisible. For when I consider the mind, or myself in so far as I am merely a thinking thing, I am unable to distinguish any parts within myself; I understand myself to be something quite single and complete. Although the whole mind seems to be united to the whole body, I recognize that if a foot or arm or any other part of the body is cut off, nothing has thereby been taken away from the mind. As for the faculties of willing, of understanding, of sensory perception and so on, these cannot be termed parts of the mind, since it is one and the same mind that wills, and understands and has sensory perceptions. By contrast, there is no corporeal or extended thing that I can think of which in my thought I cannot easily divide into parts; and this very fact makes me understand that it is divisible. This one argument would be enough to show me that the mind is completely different from the body, even if I did not already know as much from other considerations.

Using the same generic argument form as before, we could summarize the previous passage in this way:

The Argument from Divisibility

1. The body is divisible.
2. The mind is indivisible.

3. If two things do not have exactly identical properties, then they cannot be identical.
4. Therefore, the mind and the body are not identical.

In this argument, Descartes's first premise is based on the notion that all material objects are spatially extended and anything spatially extended is divisible. Hence, because the body is a material object, it can always be divided in two and divided and divided again (as in an autopsy).

It seems easy enough to grant Descartes the truth of the first premise, but what about the second premise? Certainly if we assume that the mind is a spiritual substance, then because a spiritual thing lacks extension, it cannot be divided (or at least divided in the way a body is). But the notion that the mind is a spiritual entity is what Descartes is trying to prove, so simply assuming this point seems to beg the question. Without making this assumption, can we simply look at our mental experience and discover that, whatever the mind might be, it is not the sort of thing that has parts or can be divided? Or is Descartes's second premise questionable? Is it possible for the mind to have divisions or distinguishable parts in some sense?

 STOP AND THINK

Have you ever felt as though you were of "two minds" about something? Have you ever felt conflicts or tensions within your mind? Have you ever experienced conflicts between memories, beliefs, or feelings? Do these sorts of divisions within the mind count against Descartes's premise 2? What would he say?

Some would argue, contrary to Descartes, that our mental life seems to be divided. For example, we can feel both love and anger at the same time toward someone. Or we frequently find that our moral principles pull us in one direction and our feelings in another. The annals of psychiatry are full of cases of multiple personalities, or cases in which someone knows some discomforting fact in one part of the psyche while another part of the person's mind works overtime to deny it. One type of brain surgery, known as cerebral commissurotomy, is commonly used to treat epilepsy. The surgeon severs the bundle of nerves (the corpus callosum) that connects the two hemispheres of the brain. Patients with these split brains experience a fragmentation within their experience. The part of the brain that processes visual data cannot communicate with the part that processes things linguistically. These considerations seem to indicate that whatever it is that makes up the mind, it is something that has components. This conclusion at least makes plausible the suggestion that different parts of our brain produce different facets of our mental life and, hence, results in diluting the sharp distinction Descartes is trying to draw here between the mind and the body.

The Argument from Consciousness

Yet another argument can be found in Descartes's writings, one that is based on the fact that his mind is a thinking thing while his body is not. By *thinking* Descartes does not simply mean *reasoning*. Descartes uses the word *thinking* to refer to the entire range of conscious states such as knowing, doubting, wishing, willing, imagining, sensing, and so on. Hence, his point is that his mind is unlike anything in the natural world, because he is conscious. By way of contrast, Descartes says "when I examine the nature of the body, I find nothing at all in it which savours of thought."[7] The argument from consciousness (or thinking) is found in passages such as the following one.

FROM RENÉ DESCARTES
Meditations on First Philosophy (2)[8]

Thus, simply by knowing that I exist and seeing at the same time that absolutely nothing else belongs to my nature or essence except that I am a thinking thing, I can infer correctly that my essence consists solely in the fact that I am a thinking thing. It is true that I may have (or to anticipate, that I certainly have) a body that is very closely joined to me. But nevertheless, on the one hand I have a clear and distinct idea of myself, in so far as I am simply a thinking, non-extended thing; and on the other hand I have a distinct idea of body, in so far as this is simply an extended, non-thinking thing. And accordingly, it is certain that I [that is, my soul, by which I am what I am], am really distinct from my body, and can exist without it.

The outline of the argument from consciousness follows the outlines of previous arguments, except that Descartes includes the premise that "material objects cannot have the property of consciousness." Because the body is a material object, it cannot be conscious, but we know from our own immediate experience that our mind is conscious. From these premises, Descartes arrives again at his dualist conclusion.

STOP AND THINK

Do you think the argument from consciousness supports the theory that the mind is different from the body? Why? How might a physicalist respond to this alleged difference between the mind and the body?

Descartes's Compromise

Descartes's theory of dualism has sometimes been called the Cartesian compromise. Descartes was an enthusiastic champion of the new, mechanistic science. He was

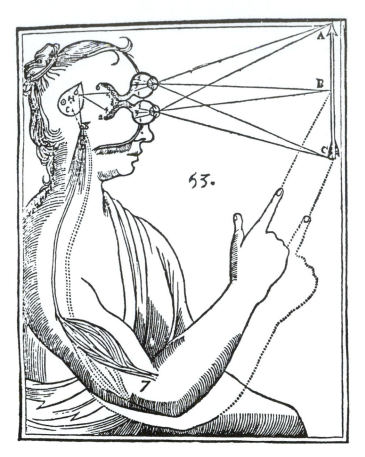

Diagrams from a work on physiology by Descartes showing the brain and the pineal gland. Descartes believed this gland to be the locus of the soul (mind) and its point of contact, or interaction, with the body.

also a sincere Catholic. One of his concerns, therefore, was to reconcile the scientific and religious views of the world. By dividing reality up into completely separate territories, he was able to accomplish this goal. One part of reality is made up of physical substances that can be studied by science and explained by mechanistic principles. This part of the universe is a giant, clocklike mechanism. All events in this realm are determined by the laws that physicists discover. Hence, we make observations, formulate physical laws, and make accurate predictions about physical events. In so far as we are bodies, science can explain our physical motions. The other part of reality consists of mental or spiritual substances. Our minds are free to think and will as we wish because mental substances are not governed by mechanical laws. In this way, persons (unlike their bodies) have genuine free will. If you jump into a swimming pool, for example, the falling of your body is governed by the laws of nature. Your decision to make that jump, however, is freely chosen and cannot be explained by physics.

In the physical realm, science is the dominant authority and gives us the truth. We do not consult the Church or the Bible to see how fast the heart pumps its blood; science informs us about such facts. But according to the Cartesian compromise, science cannot tell us about the eternal destiny of our souls, it can tell us only about our bodies. Hence, in the spiritual realm, says Descartes, religion still retains its authority and truth.

Descartes had one remaining problem. Although the mind and body are separate, he was convinced that they interact. Accordingly, Descartes's specific version of dualism is called *interactionism*. It seems easy to understand how mental entities interact (one idea leads to the thought of another idea), and it seems easy to understand how physical entities interact (a billiard ball collides with another one, setting it in motion). The problem is, however, how can a spiritual substance (the mind) causally interact with a physical substance (the body)?

Descartes was well aware of this problem; nevertheless, his attempts to answer this question were the least satisfactory part of his philosophy. In his day, scientists were aware of the existence of the pineal gland at the base of the brain, but they did not know what the gland did. So, Descartes had an organ (the pineal gland) whose function was unknown. He had a function (mind-body interaction) whose location was unknown. He concluded that he could solve both these problems with one hypothesis: the pineal gland is where the mind and body interact. Descartes thought that the pineal gland was affected by "vital spirits," and through this intermediary, the soul could alter the motions in the brain, which then could affect the body and vice versa.[9] Obviously, explaining mind-body interaction by referring to the pineal gland does not solve the problem, because this gland is merely another material object that is part of the body. If the "vital spirits" that mediate the causal interaction are some sort of physical force like magnetism, then we still do not know how the physical can affect the mental and vice versa. The same problem exists if "vital spirits" are mental in nature.

LOOKING THROUGH THE DUALIST'S LENS

1. How does the dualist's view of the mind and body imply that scientific, physical explanations of persons are incomplete?

2. How does dualism allow for deterministic explanations of nature while preserving human freedom?

3. How does dualism allow for a compromise between science and religion?

4. How does dualism serve to explain immortality?

5. If you were a disciple of Descartes, how would you improve on his explanation of the interaction of the mind and body?

6. Artificial intelligence programs are now able to play superior chess and do many other tasks that duplicate what human intelligence can accomplish. What

would be Descartes's view of artificial intelligence programs? Would he agree that computers can think? Why?

EXAMINING THE STRENGTHS AND WEAKNESSES OF DUALISM

Positive Evaluation

1. Descartes's view allows him to accept the scientific account of the physical world while retaining traditional notions of the mind and human freedom. How important is this advantage?

2. Descartes's view claims that the properties of matter could never produce something as mysterious and marvelous as consciousness or self-awareness, because these qualities could only come from a type of reality that is nonmaterial. Do you think Descartes's theory explains consciousness better than any physicalist theory ever could?

Negative Evaluation

1. Descartes had a major problem explaining how a nonspatial mind can influence a spatially located brain. Do you think Descartes's account of where and how mind-body interaction takes place is satisfactory? If not, can you even conceive of another explanation that does not fall into the same problems?

2. If the mind is the seat of our mental life and consciousness while the body is simply a machine made out of flesh, as Descartes thought, why does physical damage to the brain have such a dramatic effect on a person's mental life?

3. What happens to your mind when you are knocked unconscious or are given anesthesia? Both situations cause a disruption to the brain's normal functioning. But if the mind is separate from the body, we would expect that in these situations we would continue to experience mental awareness even though the connections between the mind, the brain, and the body were temporarily impaired. If the real you is your mind, and your mind is identical to your conscious mental life, as Descartes maintains, then where does your mind (and you) go when you are unconscious?

3.3 PHYSICALISM

LEADING QUESTIONS: *Physicalism*

1. Why is it not a good idea to have an all-night party before a big test? Why do the labels on cough and allergy medicines caution against driving or operating machinery while taking the medicine? Why do most people have trouble concentrating in class after they have had a big meal? What effects do multiple cups of

coffee tend to have on a person's mental state or temperament? Why do these sorts of changes in our bodies affect not only our physical performance but our mental performance as well?

2. Why do animals such as frogs or rabbits have relatively small brains, while high level mammals such as dogs, apes, and humans have larger and more complex brains? Why is there a correlation between the size and complexity of the brain and the level of intelligent behavior exhibited by a species?

3. You think to yourself, "I am thirsty." You then decide to get a drink. Obediently, your hand reaches out to grab a glass of ice water. How did your thoughts produce this motion in the physical world? What sort of links in the causal chain run from your thoughts to your body's muscles?

4. We know that our nervous system automatically governs such functions as our digestion and heartbeat apart from our conscious control of them. However, we like to think that our mental life is under our conscious control. But how do we explain the fact that images, thoughts, or unpleasant memories spontaneously intrude into our consciousness? Why is it that thinking about one idea often will cause another idea to spring up unexpectedly within our mind? How can the contents of our minds be affected by causes that we do not voluntarily control?

SURVEYING THE CASE FOR PHYSICALISM

Both the problems with dualism and our increasing knowledge of how the brain functions have led some philosophers to the proposal that the mind is not a special kind of nonphysical entity that somehow interacts with the body. One of the leading alternatives to mind-body dualism is physicalism, the theory that human beings can be explained completely and adequately in terms of their physical or material components. Accordingly, the physicalist claims that when we talk about the mind or mental processes, we are really talking about something physical (such as brain activity) or else we are talking about something that doesn't exist at all. There are many varieties of physicalistic theories of the person. The psychological theory of behaviorism, for example, is a form of physicalism (behaviorism is discussed under the topic of freedom and determinism). Some versions of functionalism are also examples of physicalism (see section 3.4). The two versions of physicalism I discuss in this section are identity theory (or reductionism) and eliminative materialism.

Most physicalists claim that *all* elements of reality (not just human beings) are 100 percent physical and capable of being explained by science. This claim implies that there are no spiritual or supernatural realities (such as God), and such physicalists would embrace metaphysical materialism. However, because a few theists are physicalists *only* with regard to the mind-body problem, I will use the term *physicalism* in a narrow sense to refer only to a certain position within the philosophy of mind. Basically, the physicalist's case rests on two pillars. The first pillar is the problems with dualism, which the physicalist believes are unsolvable. The second pillar is based on all the progress that has been made in brain science. After the "Philosophy in the Marketplace" exercise, I present each of these pillars in turn.

The Problems with Dualism

Many arguments have been raised against Cartesian dualism. However, the following four considerations are among those arguments that are raised most frequently.

Where Does Interaction Take Place? The most common form of dualism is dualistic interactionism, which is the two-fold claim that (1) the mind and body are separate entities and (2) they are capable of causal interaction. This position was defended by Descartes and is a position that retains a great deal of common-sense appeal to the average person. Because dualistic interactionism is the most popular version of dualism, it's the version I discuss here. Although dualistic interactionism is a very common position, it has a number of problems. Its critics have raised the question of where this interaction takes place. Every brain event has a physical location, but a nonphysical mental event could not. Yet, if the mind is to interact with the body (presumably through the brain), it would seem that this interaction would have to take place in some spatial location. Descartes suggested that the pineal gland is this location. However, we now have no reason to believe that the pineal gland plays any role with respect to consciousness, and there are no other plausible candidates to take its place. So the dualist has a major gap in his or her story of the person.

How Does Interaction Occur? Every physical event involves the employment of force. Physicists understand force as the product of mass and acceleration. But if nonphysical mental events have neither mass nor motion, how can they exert the force necessary to cause changes in the physical world? Mental events cannot push or pull physical objects. Neither can they electrically stimulate them nor exert gravitational or magnetic force on them. In other words, mental events cannot employ the sort of causality that produces changes in the physical world. Furthermore, since mental events are nonphysical, it would seem that they cannot be affected by the sorts of causal forces that operate within the body. Therefore, it seems impossible for minds to affect bodies and vice versa.

What about the Conservation of Energy? A fundamental principle that is essential to science is the principle that the amount of energy in a closed physical system remains constant. To set a billiard ball in motion requires us to expend some energy. This energy is transformed into the ball's motion as well as the heat that is produced by friction. Because energy is a physical property, it cannot be found in a nonmaterial mind. But if your body is set in motion by a mental event, then new energy has entered the world and the principle of the conservation of energy is violated. Similarly, if motion in your body is translated into a nonmaterial mental event, then energy has been lost from the physical world.

What about the Success of Brain Science? A standard principle in forming scientific theories is the principle of simplicity (see the discussion of Ockham's razor in section 3.0). The physicalist claims that if we can account for all "mental" phenomena in terms of brain events, then the notion of a nonmaterial mind becomes extraneous. Once research on the brain is complete, we will not be plagued by the mysteries of the mind-body problem because this problematic dualism will no longer exist. The physicalist claims that we already know enough about the brain and how it affects cognition to be confident that brain events tell the whole story about us.

THOUGHT EXPERIMENT

The Case of the Missing Socks

While doing our laundry, we all have had the experience of pulling our clothes out of the dryer, only to discover that one sock is missing. Often, we will search everywhere and not be able to find the missing sock. After a time we may even build up a whole collection of single socks that lack a partner. Imagine that someone proposed the theory that a species of invisible, alien beings called "sockgrabbers" are inhabiting laundry rooms. The sockgrabbers steal our socks, eat them, and through some mysterious process convert them into energy that sustains their form of life.

- Would you find this theory plausible? Why?
- The sockgrabber believer can argue that we have irrefutable evidence that *something* is taking the socks, because they frequently disappear without a trace. How might you argue, against the believer, that it is irrational to believe in sockgrabbers?
- How might Ockham's razor be used to question the plausibility of the sockgrabber theory?

A Brain Injury

On the morning of September 13, 1848, Phineas P. Gage, a twenty-five-year-old railroad man, survived one of the most bizarre and brutal accidents ever recorded in medical history. Before the accident, this construction foreman for the Rutland and Burlington Railroad was known to his friends and coworkers as an easygoing, friendly, and intelligent person. However, the event that forever changed his life occurred when he was packing a load of explosives down a narrow hole that had been drilled into a huge rock. As he was tamping the gunpowder with an iron rod, the friction created a spark, which caused the charge to explode with a tremendous force. The 3½-foot-long iron rod, weighing thirteen pounds, was propelled like a rocket, hitting Gage in the head. It entered his cheek just below his left eye, tore through a portion of his brain, and ripped through his skull, eventually landing fifty feet away.

His coworkers loaded him into an oxcart and took him to a hotel, where two doctors did their best to clean the massive wound. From the time he was injured and throughout the doctors' attempts to stop the bleeding, Gage never lost consciousness. Over the next couple of weeks he bled severely, became quite confused, and lost the sight in his left eye. However, Phineas Gage lived for thirteen more years, which most physicians consider to be a medical marvel. The skull of Phineas Gage and the metal rod that injured him are currently on display at the Warren Anatomical Museum in Boston, Mass.

While Gage survived physically, his former personality did not. The Phineas Gage who was a likeable, gentle, intelligent man became someone who was a mean, undependable, slow-witted dolt. Although most of his brain continued to function more or less normally, the portion of the brain that controls the personality had been irreparably changed. The affable person his friends once knew was gone, and an ill-tempered and stupid brute remained. Given these changes, was Gage still Gage? To what extent do you think *your* personality is a product of the state of your brain?

Obviously most of us would reject the sockgrabber theory. It just does not fit with everything we know about the world. This theory answers one question (Where did the socks go?) but leaves too many other, unanswerable questions in its wake. Besides, there is a much simpler account. We frequently lose things (e.g., keys, reading glasses, library cards), and sometimes we find them again and sometimes we do not. However, even when we cannot find an item, we have no reason to suppose that it just vanished or was eaten by some sort of invisible creature. Even if we think we put only complete pairs of socks in the wash, we could be mistaken. Hence, this commonsense theory allows us to account for the data in question in a way that is consistent with the rest of our knowledge about the world. The chief virtue of this approach is that we do not need to postulate additional, unobservable entities such as sockgrabbers who have mysterious properties unlike anything else in reality. The point of the story is obvious. The physicalist believes that explaining the activities of the person by referring to an immaterial mind is analogous to explaining the missing socks by referring to invisible, alien sockgrabbers. In both cases, there is a simpler, scientific, and physicalistic explanation.

The Positive Case for Physicalism

The second pillar of physicalism is the positive case based on brain research. For example, scientists have studied people who have suffered damage to various portions of the brain and have found that different kinds of brain damage produce regular and specific breakdowns in a person's psychological functioning. Also, studying the activities of normal brains with our sophisticated medical instruments show that when a person is performing a certain task (imagining a scene, speaking, calculating a sum), characteristic changes take place in the brain.

There seems to be a very clear correlation between what we normally think of as mental events and changes in brain states. The constant correlation between mental events and brain events plus the principle of Ockham's razor makes physicalism seem very attractive. Physicalism, it is claimed, is simply the result of an inference to the best explanation.

What about the dualist's argument that the properties of the mind and body are irreducibly different? The physicalist would say that their respective properties *appear* to be different but that nevertheless the properties and activities of the mind can be explained by the properties and activities of the body (the brain). Consider a compact disc (CD) recording. If we examine the surface of the CD, we will observe nothing that has the characteristics of sound. The sounds produced by a CD player have such properties as being melodious, dissonant, lively, haunting, and so forth. Obviously, these properties are not part of the physical description of the disc's surface. However, we realize that every sound produced by the CD is caused by the physical makeup of the disc as it is acted upon by the CD player. Hence, even though our mental activities seem to be different from physical processes, maybe they are nothing more than the events happening in our brains, just as the sounds we hear are nothing more than physical events produced by the CD player.

This concept is not so mysterious, for we commonly find that the same entity can take on different forms and have different properties. For example, H_2O can take on the form of a gas (steam), a solid (ice), or a liquid (water). Yet, for all the differences in their physical properties, these forms are all essentially the same substance. Furthermore, a complex combination of entities can produce properties that are not found in the parts. Hence, emergent properties can be produced that originally were not there. Hydrogen and oxygen by themselves will fuel a fire, but when chemically combined to form water, the product will quench a fire. Similarly, the tail of the firefly contains two chemicals that produce light when they interact even though light is not a property of either chemical by itself. Hence, the properties of the whole are not always the properties of the parts. Each individual neuron of the brain, by itself, is neither conscious nor intelligent. Perhaps the cumulative effect of neuronal interaction, however, is the sort of phenomena we know as consciousness and intelligence. Consciousness may be nothing more than a by-product of low-level physical processes, much as a rainbow is the result of the interaction of light and raindrops.

The Physicalist's View of the Person

R. Buckminster Fuller (1895–1983) was an engineer, architect, essayist, poet, inventor, and all-around visionary. Educated at Harvard and the United States Naval Academy, Fuller had a long career in industry and lectured at Yale, Harvard, and a host of other universities. He designed the geodesic dome and invented the Dymaxion three-wheeled automobile in the 1930s. His books include *No More Secondhand God, Education Automation, Ideas and Integrities, The Unfinished Epic Poem of Industrialization,* and *An Operating Manual for Spaceship Earth.* The excerpt that follows is from *Nine Chains to the Moon* (1938).

In reading this tongue-in-cheek description of a human, try to figure out what part of you is being described in each phrase. (Please ignore the outdated convention of referring collectively to human beings as "man.") Do you think this sort of description is adequate? Does it leave anything out?

What's a Man?—R. Buckminster Fuller[10]

"What is that, mother?"

"It's a man, darling."

"What's a man?"

Man?

A self-balancing, 28-jointed adapter-base biped; an electrochemical reduction-plant, integral with segregated stowages of special energy extracts in storage batteries, for subsequent actuation of thousands of hydraulic and pneumatic pumps, with motors attached; 62,000 miles of capillaries; millions of warning signal, railroad and conveyor systems; crushers and cranes (of which the arms are magnificent 23-jointed affairs with self-surfacing and lubricating systems, and a universally distributed telephone system needing no service for 70 years if well managed); the whole, extraordinarily complex mechanism guided with exquisite precision from a turret in which are located telescopic and microscopic self-registering and recording range finders, a spectroscope, *et cetera,* the turret control being closely allied with an air conditioning intake-and-exhaust, and a main fuel intake.

Within the few cubic inches housing the turret mechanisms, there is room, also, for two sound-wave and sound-direction-finder recording diaphragms, a filing and instant reference system, and an expertly devised analytical laboratory large enough not only to contain minute records of every last and continual event of up to 70 years' experience, or more, but to extend, by computation and abstract fabrication, this experience with relative accuracy into all corners of the observed universe. There is, also, a forecasting and tactical plotting department for the reduction of future possibilities and probabilities to generally successful specific choice.

Identity Theory

Physicalists disagree over the details of their theory. The *identity theory* (or *reductionism*) treats mental events as real but claims that they are *identical* to brain events. Hence, when we talk about beliefs, pains, desires, we can *reduce* these terms to talk about brain states. For example, a brain scientist could translate the statement,

"Phoebe is feeling pain in her hand" to "A particular C-fiber is signaling neurons in the S1 region of the cortex, approximately 30 millimeters up from the lateral fissure." Or if I say, "Raul believes that Scott is up to no good," I am really saying that "There is a certain configuration in Raul's cortex that causes various verbalizations such as 'Scott is slime' in certain situations and that causes certain other kinds of negative behavioral or physiological responses in Raul." Hence, the identity theory claims a one-to-one identity between a particular mental state and a particular brain state.

We can continue to use our mentalistic language as long as we keep in mind the real object of our talk. To use an analogy, we still talk of the sun "rising" and "setting." We now realize, however, that we are really talking about the rotation of the earth. The identity theorist cautions that nouns such as *mind, belief, desire, motive,* or *pain* tempt us to suppose that these terms refer to certain kinds of nonphysical entities. However, when we speak of *the dance,* we are not referring to some entity apart from the motions of various people's bodies. It would be silly for someone to say, "I hear the music and see the couples moving about, but where is *the dance? The dance* simply is the music and the motions of the couples. Hence, when we speak of *beliefs, desires,* and *thoughts,* we are not referring to anything apart from different states or activities in the brain.

According to the identity theory, the relationship between the mind and the body is analogous to the relationship between Superman and Clark Kent, or between Lewis Carroll (the author of *Alice's Adventures in Wonderland*) and the Reverend Charles Dodgson, or between Samuel Clemens and the writer Mark Twain. In each case, the two entities are identical. Hence, every mental state you have, such as the sensation of red, a pleasant memory, a stabbing pain, your belief that "Mars is a planet," your desire for a good job, a feeling of guilt, your decision to rent the movie *Gone with the Wind,* and so on, is numerically identical to some physical state, event, or process in your brain.

There are a number of advantages to the identity theory. As with all versions of physicalism, with identity theory the mind is no longer viewed as a mysterious, immaterial substance. Everything that we need to know about the mind can be discovered through empirical brain research. Furthermore, the causal interaction between the mind and the body is no longer a problem. Mental events simply are physical events and have physical causes and consequences. Your decision to rent a movie is a brain event that is caused by your previous brain states and, perhaps, by some outside stimuli. What you experience as a decision is a brain event that sets into motion other brain events and a complex set of physiological reactions that result in you hopping in the car to drive to the video store.

The chief advantage of the identity theory over the other forms of physicalism is that we can retain our ordinary ways of speaking while still claiming that neurological research will ultimately give us the final story on all mental events. In other words, we can still talk about beliefs, desires, hopes, and fears as causing other mental states as well as causing behavior as long as we keep in mind that these terms are just traditional, layperson's ways of talking about brain processes.

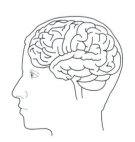

Are your mental states of believing, loving, and choosing identical to brain states?

Eliminativism

The other form of physicalism is *eliminativism.* The eliminativist believes that our mentalistic talk is so deeply flawed that it must be abandoned, because there is no hope of correlating our talk about beliefs and desires with our talk about brain states, as the identity theorist does. The eliminativist labels traditional psychological theories as **folk psychology.** Before the rise of modern science, people relied on folk science or bizarre theories about what causes events in the world. For example, the ancient Greeks explained the falling of a stone by saying the stone *desired* to return to its mother, the earth. Similarly, fate was thought to be a real force in the world that caused events to happen. References to desires in stones or to the activity of fate cannot be translated into the terminology of modern physics. Since rocks do not have desires and fate is not a causal force, the Greeks were not talking about anything at all. Hence, we abandoned these folk theories and now talk in terms of an entirely different characterization of physical and historical events. Similarly, the eliminativist believes that as our brain research advances, we will abandon our traditional mentalistic terminology and explanations just as we have abandoned the mythological folk science of the Greeks. The eliminativist claims we literally do not have beliefs or desires, nor are there really such states or activities as believing or desiring going on within us. Instead, we merely have certain kinds of brain states and processes. Because the theories of dualism, identity theory, and functionalism all talk about mental states and activities, they would all be considered examples of folk psychology, according to the eliminativist.

folk psychology perjorative term used by eliminativists to characterize traditional psychological theories

THOUGHT EXPERIMENT

Are There Mental Events?

Are there such things as mental events? For example, are there such things as beliefs? In what sorts of situations is it correct to explain behavior by referring to what the subject *believed*? In the following cases, check *yes* or *no* to indicate whether you think it is meaningful to literally attribute a belief to the subject in question.

1. Harry smelled smoke and called the fire department because he *believed* his house was on fire.	Yes	No
2. When Pavlov's dogs heard the bell ring, they began to salivate because they *believed* food was coming.	Yes	No
3. The robin poked at the ground because it *believed* a worm was beneath the surface.	Yes	No
4. The amoeba oozed around the particle because it *believed* it was food.	Yes	No
5. Someone held a flame under the thermostat and, even though the room was 50 degrees, the mechanism turned the air conditioner on because it *believed* the room was too warm.	Yes	No

(Continued . . .)

(. . . continued)

Were there any situations in which you thought it did make sense to speak of the behavior as caused by a belief? Were there any situations in which you thought it did not make sense to speak of a belief as playing a causal role in the action? What was the basis of your yes and no answers?

Most dualists would say that beliefs can only be present to conscious, intelligent minds such as Harry's. Identity theorists claim that beliefs are really particular kinds of brain states, so only creatures with a brain, such as Harry (and perhaps the dog), can have beliefs. Some artificial intelligence researchers and functionalists would say that everything from Harry down to the thermostat has beliefs. These theorists view mental activities as patterned processes by means of which inputs are transformed into outputs. Hence, both brains and intelligent machines are capable of exhibiting the same sorts of patterns. The eliminativist, on the other hand, would agree with the dualist that it makes no sense to attribute mental qualities like "believing" to a thermostat, for it is simply a mechanism that is following the laws of physics. However, for the same reason, the eliminativist says that we do not need the category of "belief" to explain Harry's actions. His behavior is the product of the neurochemical events taking place in his brain.

The following reading is by Paul Churchland, a professor of philosophy at the University of California at San Diego. As a thoroughgoing eliminativist, he argues that talk about the mind and mental events follows from a mistaken theory about human behavior and should be replaced with a scientific theory that is based on an understanding of how the brain works. In the reading, the term *intertheoretic reduction* refers to a situation in which the terms and principles of an older theory are translated into the terms and principles of a new and more powerful theory. When we talk about rainbows, for example, we now know we are really talking about the refraction, reflection, and dispersion of the sun's rays in water droplets. Similarly, the identity theorist believes that talk about the mind (folk psychology) can be reduced to talk about brain states. However, Churchland believes that folk psychology is so deeply flawed that it must be eliminated entirely.

FROM PAUL CHURCHLAND
Matter and Consciousness[11]

The identity theory was called into doubt not because the prospects for a materialist account of our mental capacities were thought to be poor, but because it seemed unlikely that the arrival of an adequate materialist theory would bring with it the nice one-to-one match-ups, between the concepts of folk psychology and the concepts of theoretical neuroscience, that intertheoretic reduction requires. . . .

As the eliminative materialists see it, the one-to-one match-ups will not be found, and our common-sense psychological framework will not enjoy an intertheoretic reduction, *because our common-sense psychological framework is a false and radically misleading conception of the causes of human behavior and the nature of cognitive activity.* On this view, folk psychology is not just an incomplete representation of our inner natures; it is an outright misrepresentation of our internal states and activities. Consequently, we cannot expect a truly adequate neuroscientific account of our inner lives to provide theoretical categories that match up nicely with the categories of our common-sense framework. Accordingly, we must expect that the older framework will simply be eliminated, rather than be reduced, by a matured neuroscience.

In the next passage, Churchland draws some parallels between folk psychology's postulation of mythical entities (the mind, beliefs, desires, and fears) and previous cases in history in which people embraced a type of explanation that we have now discarded. For example, the ancients believed that the planets and stars were literally attached to a series of crystalline spheres that rotated around the earth.

Before Copernicus' views became available, almost any human who ventured out at night could look up at *the starry sphere of the heavens,* and if he stayed for more than a few minutes he could also see that it *turned,* around an axis through Polaris. What the sphere was made of (crystal?) and what made it turn (the gods?) were theoretical questions that exercised us for over two millennia. But hardly anyone doubted the existence of what everyone could observe with their own eyes. In the end, however, we learned to reinterpret our visual experience of the night sky within a very different conceptual framework, and the turning sphere evaporated.

Witches provide another example. Psychosis is a fairly common affliction among humans, and in earlier centuries its victims were standardly seen as cases of demonic possession, as instances of Satan's spirit itself, glaring malevolently out at us from behind the victims' eyes. That witches exist was not a matter of any controversy. One would occasionally see them, in any city or hamlet, engaged in incoherent, paranoid, or even murderous behavior. But observable or not, we eventually decided that witches simply do not exist. We concluded that the concept of a witch is an element in a conceptual framework that misrepresents so badly the phenomena to which it was standardly applied that literal application of the notion should be permanently withdrawn. Modern theories of mental dysfunction led to the elimination of witches from our serious ontology.

The concepts of folk psychology—belief, desire, fear, sensation, pain, joy, and so on—await a similar fate, according to the view at issue. And when neuroscience has matured to the point where the poverty of our current conceptions is apparent to everyone, and the superiority of the new framework is established, we shall then be able to set about *re*conceiving our internal states and activities, within a truly adequate conceptual framework at last. Our explanations of one another's behavior will appeal to such things as our neuropharmacological states, the neural activity in specialized anatomical areas, and whatever other states are deemed relevant by the new theory. Our private introspection will also be transformed, and may be profoundly enhanced by reason of the more accurate and penetrating framework it will have to work with—just as the astronomer's perception of the night sky is much enhanced by the detailed knowledge of modern astronomical theory that he or she possesses.

The magnitude of the conceptual revolution here suggested should not be minimized: it would be enormous. And the benefits to humanity might be equally great. If each of us possessed an accurate neuroscientific understanding of (what we now conceive dimly as) the varieties and causes of mental illness, the factors involved in learning, the neural basis of emotions, intelligence, and socialization, then the sum total of human misery might be much reduced. The simple increase in mutual understanding that the new framework made possible could contribute substantially toward a more peaceful and humane society. Of course, there would be dangers as well: increased knowledge means increased power, and power can always be misused.

Churchland now gives several reasons why eliminative materialism is a superior form of explanation compared to folk psychology.

First, the eliminative materialist will point to the widespread explanatory, predictive, and manipulative failures of folk psychology. So much of what is central and familiar to us remains a complete mystery from within folk psychology. We do not know what sleep is, or why we have to have it, despite spending a full third of our lives in that condition. (The answer, "For rest," is mistaken. Even if people are allowed to rest continuously, their need for sleep is undiminished. Apparently, sleep serves some deeper functions, but we do not yet know what they are.) We do not understand how *learning* transforms each of us from a gaping infant to a cunning adult, or how differences in *intelligence* are grounded. We have not the slightest idea how *memory* works, or how we manage to retrieve relevant bits of information instantly from the awesome mass we have stored. We do not know what *mental illness* is, nor how to cure it.

In sum, the most central things about us remain almost entirely mysterious from within folk psychology. . . .

The second argument tries to draw an inductive lesson from our conceptual history. Our early folk theories of motion were profoundly confused, and were eventually displaced entirely by more sophisticated theories. Our early folk theories of the structure and activity of the heavens were wildly off the mark, and survive only as historical lessons in how wrong we can be. Our folk theories of the nature of fire, and the nature of life, were similarly cockeyed. And one could go on, since the vast majority of our past folk conceptions have been similarly exploded. All except folk psychology, which survives to this day and has only recently begun to feel pressure. But the phenomena of conscious intelligence is surely a more complex and difficult phenomenon than any of those just listed. So far as accurate understanding is concerned, it would be a *miracle* if we had got that one right the very first time, when we fell down so badly on the others.

THE FAR SIDE By GARY LARSON

What do the words *jitters, heebie jeebies, creeps,* and *willies* refer to? If you say "He gives me the creeps," why is it absurd for me to ask, "How many creeps did he give you?" What is the source of humor in this Far Side cartoon? Why would the eliminativist claim that the dualist is making the same sort of mistake? (Used by permission.)

Folk psychology has survived for so very long, presumably, not because it is basically correct in its representations, but because the phenomena addressed are so surpassingly difficult that any useful handle on them, no matter how feeble, is unlikely to be displaced in a hurry.

Finally, Churchland addresses and dismisses the argument that our own introspective experience demonstrates that folk psychology is true.

Eliminative materialism is false, runs the argument, because one's introspection reveals directly the existence of pains, beliefs, desires, fears, and so forth. Their existence is as obvious as anything could be.

The eliminative materialist will reply that this argument makes the same mistake that an ancient or medieval person would be making if he insisted that he could just see with his own eyes that the heavens form a turning sphere, or that witches exist. The fact is, all observation occurs within some system of concepts, and our observation judgments are only as good as the conceptual framework in which they are expressed. In all three cases—the starry sphere, witches, and the familiar mental states—precisely what is challenged is the integrity of the background conceptual frameworks in which the observation judgments are expressed. To insist on the validity of one's experiences, *traditionally interpreted,* is therefore to beg the very question at issue. For in all three cases, the question is whether we should *re*conceive the nature of some familiar observational domain.

THOUGHT EXPERIMENT

Dualism, Identity Theory, and Physicalism

To review, the Cartesian dualist believes that the mind and body are *separate* entities, although mental events can *cause* physical events and vice versa. The identity theorist believes that mental events and brain events are really *identical* even though they may be described differently. The eliminativist believes that all talk about mental events assumes a prescientific folk psychology that should be *eliminated* in favor of the latest scientific theories about the brain.

To test your understanding of the three theories discussed thus far, consider the relationship between each of the following pairs of events. In each row, decide whether the relationship between the two events (A and B) is *analogous* to the relationship between the mind and body as described by dualism (D), identity theory (IT), or eliminativism (E). After making your choices, check them with the answers in the footnote.*

Event A	Event B	Positions		
1. The sun came up in the morning.	1. The rooster crowed.	D	IT	E
2. A haunting melody is emanating from the violin.	2. The friction of the bow on the strings is producing sound waves.	D	IT	E
3. The presents were left under the tree by Santa Claus.	3. The presents were left under the tree by your parents.	D	IT	E
4. The people in the town were stricken with boils caused by a witch's curse.	4. The drinking water was contaminated by a virus, which caused a plague to spread throughout the town.	D	IT	E
5. Lightning bolts flashed across the sky.	5. There was a sudden discharge of electrons between the clouds.	D	IT	E
6. Someone flipped the light switch.	6. The ceiling light went on.	D	IT	E

*1 = D, 2 = IT, 3 = E, 4 = E, 5 = IT, 6 = D

LOOKING THROUGH THE PHYSICALIST'S LENS

1. Refer back to Fuller's description of a human being. If the physicalist is correct, this sort of description of persons is more accurate than our traditional ways of talking. For example, if we say that "Jeff is attracted to Anya," we are really saying that "Jeff's neurological response to the visual, auditory, olfactory, and tactile data he receives from Anya produces brain states that cause verbalizations such as "Let's go out Friday night.' Furthermore, when he is in spatio-temporal proximity to Anya, his heart rate will increase and there will be an increase in hormonal activity." Using similar techniques, could we form adequate translations of each one of the following sentences about the mind into a purely physicalistic language?

    a. Shakespeare had a very creative mind.
    b. Mother Teresa was very compassionate.
    c. Nikki believes that gambling is immoral.

2. Injuries to the brain of Phineas Cage caused his personality to change for the worse. Does it not, then, seem plausible that we could use chemicals and other means to change a person's personality for the better? What if we could create saintly persons by adjusting the chemicals in their brains? Is this action plausible? How would such an ability change our concept of persons? How would it change our concept of moral responsibility?

3. Refer back to the Far Side cartoon. This cartoon is based on comments such as "He gives me the heebie jeebies" or "She makes me have the willies" or "I get the jitters whenever I speak in public." From these phrases, the cartoon foolishly and humorously implies that the heebie jeebies, willies, or jitters are literally *things* that we can give, have, or get. What would be a more logical way of describing what we mean when we make these assertions? That you do not think the heebie jeebies are things indicates that you are a reductionist or eliminativist with respect to these entities. How is this example relevant to the physicalist's stance toward mentalistic language?

EXAMINING THE STRENGTHS AND WEAKNESSES OF PHYSICALISM

Positive Evaluation

1. For some time now, brain researchers have been able to attach wires to a person's head and study the brain's electrical impulses by projecting their images onto the screen of a monitor. For example, when a person is asked to mentally choose a playing card, researchers can determine precisely when the choice has been made by watching the patterns of the brain waves on the screen. To what degree does this research support the physicalist's claims over those of the dualist?

2. From all that we know today, doesn't it seem undeniable that the brain is an essential part of all our mental activities? To what degree does this connection

support the physicalist's claim that all the advances in the brain sciences indicate that nothing is left for a nonphysical mind to explain?

3. The thesis of physicalism provides a unified account of all human phenomena by integrating our explanations of mental processes with our explanation of physical processes. Hence, while dualism fragments the person into two separate parts and has to explain how the parts interact, the physicalist does not have this problem. How important is this more unified account in evaluating the plausibility of physicalism?

4. Can you think of any feature or activity of the mind that could not, in principle, be given a physicalistic explanation?

Negative Evaluation

1. The biologist J. B. S. Haldane said, "It seems to me immensely unlikely that mind is a mere by-product of matter. For if my mental processes are determined wholly by the motions of atoms in my brain, I have no reason to suppose that my beliefs are true. . . . And hence I have no reason for supposing my brain to be composed of atoms."[12] In your own words, restate the argument against physicalism that Haldane is making here. Do you agree or disagree with his point?

2. Let us suppose that there is a brain scientist who is completely color-blind.[13] She only experiences black, white, and gray. Theoretically, she could have *complete* scientific knowledge of your brain states while you were experiencing a sunset. However, she still would not know what it was like to experience color. In this case, would it be legitimate to say that a scientific knowledge of the brain only gives us a partial account of the sorts of things that the mind experiences? Are there aspects of our mental life that can only be known by a conscious subject through his or her subjective experiences and that cannot be known through third-person, scientific, objective descriptions of the brain? Does this example show that your mental experiences cannot be completely reduced or understood in terms of brain states? How would a physicalist respond?

3. The philosopher, mathematician, and scientist Gottfried Wilhelm Leibniz (1643–1716) used this thought experiment to show that even if a machine's output produced what seemed like thoughts or perception, we would never find *conscious* perception within this physical system.

> Supposing that there were a machine whose structure produced thought, sensation, and perception, we could conceive of it as increased in size with the same proportions until one was able to enter into its interior, as he would into a mill. Now, on going into it he would find only pieces working upon one another, but never would he find anything to explain Perception.[14]

If he were writing today, Leibniz might say that even if a computer can defeat a human chess master, we will only find electronic chips and wires within this mechanism; we will not find conscious awareness within it. In what way is Leibniz's argument a criticism of physicalism? How strong is this criticism?

4. One of the physicalist's arguments is that mental events (making a decision, feeling a pain, recognizing a symbol) always seem to be correlated with measurable brain events. However, does the fact that two things always occur together necessarily imply that they are identical? For example, every mammal with a heart is also a creature with kidneys. The two conditions always occur together in nature. Obviously, however, having a heart is not identical to having a kidney. How might a dualist use this fact as an analogy to explain the relation between mental events and changes in the brain?

3.4 FUNCTIONALISM AND ARTIFICIAL INTELLIGENCE

 LEADING QUESTIONS: *Functionalism and Artificial Intelligence*

1. Artificial light really *is* light. It exposes camera film in the same way that natural light does. Hence, the fact that it is "artificial" does not mean that it is fake or simulated light. It simply means that it was created by human technology and not nature. So, if scientists create artificial intelligence in computers that can duplicate the cognitive activities of humans, wouldn't it make sense to consider their artificial intelligence to be real intelligence?

2. How do we know that a person is intelligent? Don't we know by the way the person behaves and responds to situations and, in particular, by how well he or she does on intelligence tests? Since some computers in research laboratories today can successfully perform many of the tasks on intelligence tests, shouldn't we say that such computers are intelligent and can think? If not, are we being inconsistent in not judging a computer's intelligence by the standards we use to judge human beings?

3. Suppose that even the most advanced computers will never have emotions. Does that deficiency mean that they could not have minds? Some science fiction films depict alien beings who clearly have minds but not the sort of emotional life that we have. Is it necessary to have emotions to have a mind?

4. Computers today do not have consciousness nor self-awareness. How important is consciousness to cognition? How many of our cognitive activities are carried out in full consciousness? We tie our shoes, drive a car, or find our way to class without consciously thinking about what we are doing. Nevertheless, we take in data, process it, make judgments, make adjustments in our bodily motions, and perform tasks without conscious attention to these activities. Could someone (or something) have a mind and not have self-awareness? When we are asleep, do we still have minds?

5. Suppose we encounter extraterrestrial beings who have brains very different from our own. Suppose their brains consisted of some strange, organic compound made up of a substance called PQR instead of proteins. But suppose that these beings experienced pain similar to the way that we do and that they clearly had beliefs, desires, and attitudes. In other words, suppose that their psychological life was the same as ours. Would it make sense to say they had minds even though their brain matter was different? Now suppose that their brains were not made out of organic stuff but were complex metallic mechanisms. If their psychological makeup was still the same, would we say they had minds?

6. Descartes and the dualists believe that minds must be nonphysical things. But suppose our bodies contained an immaterial substance that had the cognitive capabilities of an oyster. Would we want to call this substance a mind? In the final analysis, isn't a mind identified not by what it is made out of (physical or spiritual substance), but by how it functions?

While some contemporary thinkers look to brain science to answer our questions about the mind, others look to computer science or artificial intelligence. Whatever you conclude about artificial intelligence, looking more closely at it will help you clarify what constitutes a mind. I continue our exploration of philosophy of mind by examining the answers provided by two related movements that have arisen in the latter half of the twentieth century. These two movements are a philosophy of mind known as *functionalism* and a theory about cognition known as *strong artificial intelligence*. To provide some historical background, it will be useful to look at a controversy that occurred in the nineteenth century.

THE AMAZING CHESS-PLAYING MACHINE

In 1836, the poet Edgar Allan Poe wrote an essay entitled "Maelzel's Chess-Player" in *The Southern Literary Messenger*. The subject of the essay was an alleged chess-playing machine invented by a Wolfgang von Kempelen that was being exhibited by J. N. Maelzel (the inventor of the musician's metronome). The chess-playing device consisted of a cabinet that contained a system of densely packed machinery: metal wheels, rods, levers, and so on. The top of the cabinet contained a chessboard presided over by a mechanical human figure whose left arm was moved by the machinery within the cabinet. During exhibitions, the arm would move the chess pieces and the machine would play a respectable game of chess with a human opponent. In his essay, Poe argued that the machine was a fraud and suggested that a small man concealed within the cabinet was making the moves. (In fact, Poe's suspicions were correct.) His most interesting point, however, was the thesis that *in principle* no machine could play the game of chess. Poe argued that machines can make mathematical calculations but cannot play chess because there is an unbridgeable gulf between these two activities. In Poe's own words:

> Arithmetical or algebraical calculations are, from their very nature, fixed and determinate. Certain *data* being given, certain results necessarily and inevitably follow. These

Kasparov (left) in the first game. Deep Blue (center) is telling the moves to its assistant.

results have dependence upon nothing, and are influenced by nothing but the *data* originally given. And the question to be solved proceeds, or should proceed, to its final determination, by a succession of unerring steps liable to no change, and subject to no modification. . . . But the case is widely different with the Chess-Player. With him there is no determinate progression. No one move in chess necessarily follows upon any one other. From no particular disposition of the men at one period of a game can we predicate their disposition at a different period.[15]

The gist of his argument is quite simple. Almost at every point in a chess game, a number of moves are possible (usually about thirty). The moves made by an expert do not follow by logical necessity as in a mathematical series. Hence, since the sequence of moves is not determined, a *choice* must be made. This choice (Poe assumed) made it impossible for a machine to play chess. His conclusion concerning Maelzel's chess-playing "machine" was that "it is quite certain that the operations of the Automaton are regulated by *mind* and by nothing else."[16] Hence, Poe thought that there were some absolute limits on the possibilities of artificial intelligence (hereafter referred to as AI).

Poe would have been surprised and deeply troubled if he knew that on May 11, 1997, an IBM computer named Deep Blue defeated Garry Kasparov, the world chess champion, in a six-game chess match. A year earlier, Deep Blue had defeated Kasparov in their very first encounter, even though the human player went on to either win or tie the remaining games. Speaking about one of Deep Blue's moves, Kasparov said "it was a wonderful and extremely human move. . . . I had played a lot of computers but I had never experienced anything like this. I could feel—I could *smell*—a new kind of intelligence across the table."[17]

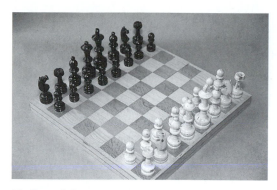

Traditional chess pieces

STOP AND THINK

In the light of recent developments in AI, we could take one of three possible positions concerning Poe's argument:

1. Poe was right. You need a mind to play chess and, therefore, many of today's computers have minds.
2. Poe was wrong. You don't need a mind to play chess.
3. Computers don't *really* play chess, but only simulate it.[18]

Which of these three positions do you favor at this point? Why?

SURVEYING THE CASE FOR FUNCTIONALISM

Before we get into the controversies surrounding computer intelligence, it will be helpful to look at a recent theory within the philosophy of mind known as functionalism. Consider the following questions. What is a belief? What distinguishes the mental state of "believing that X is true" from that of "doubting that X is true"? Compare these questions with another one. What distinguishes a chess pawn from a queen? In answering this question, you might be tempted to refer to the characteristic shape of each piece. But on further reflection it is clear that this answer is not correct. You can buy chess sets in which the pieces have many different, unconventional shapes. Some chess sets are made up of American civil war figures. Other chess sets use very modernistic, abstract shapes. In fact, you do not even need a board or chess pieces to play chess; many people play the game by mail. The squares on the board and the individual pieces are represented by numbers and letters. What makes it a movement of a *pawn* in chess is not the chemical composition of the piece nor its shape, but the distinctive pattern of its movement as well as its powers and relations to the other pieces. Chess moves have to be made with *something,* but this something can be many types of things (pieces of wood, symbols on paper, or even human beings). This sort of property is what philosophers call

A chess game played with live, human figures

multiple realizability
the property by
which something can
be realized, embod-
ied, instantiated in
multiple ways and in
different media

multiple realizability. The same chess move can be realized (embodied, instantiated) in multiple ways and in different media. This concept is important in
understanding the philosophy of functionalism.

Functionalism consists of both a negative critique and a positive theory. The
negative part describes what mental states are not. They are *not* what the identity
theory and behaviorism say they are. The identity theory says that mental events
or states (believing, doubting, willing, feeling pain, and so on) are identical to
a particular brain state. However, the functionalist argues that what is essential
to a mind is not a certain sort of material (the wet, gray, fleshy-stuff of the
brain). Instead, the functionalist claims, minds are constituted by a certain pattern or relation between the parts of a system, independent of the material that
embodies the system. In other words, mental events have the property of multiple
realizability. Even if it turns out that our brains are what produce *our* psychological properties, there could be other ways that psychological states could occur.
Hence, minds have the property of multiple realizability. (Think of the analogy
with chess.)

We could formulate a similar functionalist critique of dualism. Let's agree with
the dualist that reality is made up of physical substances and immaterial substances. However, we could imagine that the latter was simply a hunk of dumb,
inert, immaterial stuff. Certainly, this stuff would not constitute a mind. To be
a mind, this immaterial substance would have to embody a series of functional
states that bore the sorts of causal relations to each other and to inputs and outputs that we would identify as psychological states (beliefs, hopes, fears, desires,
and so on).

Strictly speaking, functionalism is neutral on the issue of dualism versus physicalism. There is no official position on what a system must be made out of to have
mental states. However, the fact is that most functionalists are physicalists. They
would say that it happens to be the case that our functional mental states are

identified with brain states. However, Jerry Fodor, a leading functionalist, suggests that functional mental states could be embodied in all kinds of media.

> Could calculating machines have pains, Martians have expectations and disembodied spirits have thoughts? The modern functionalist approach to psychology raises the logical possibility that they could.[19]

Hence, the functionalist would say that we could imagine alien beings (Martians) that have a completely different biochemistry from ours but the same sort of psychological makeup. This belief is why we find plausibility in science fiction stories that contain aliens like ET or loveable robots like R2D2 and C3PO. Fodor also suggests (perhaps tongue in cheek) that if it is possible to imagine intelligent, immaterial spirits (such as angels), then functionalism would apply to their psychological constitution as well.

Functionalism also differs from behaviorism. The behaviorist claims we can do psychology simply by studying the way certain external stimuli are correlated with external behavior. Nay, nay, says the functionalist. We must also understand the internal, psychological processing that is going on. Functionalists claim that mentalistic terms (*belief, desire, love*) do not refer to behavior or dispositions to behavior alone. Unlike the behaviorist, the functionalist says that mental states can function as the inner causes of behavior. Furthermore, the functionalist claims that behavior cannot be explained without understanding the internal processes that produce it. Hence, contrary to behaviorism, functionalism believes that internal states such as beliefs, desires, and wishes play a causal role within the organism. These states may be realized in brain states, but they also could be realized in other ways.

The positive side of functionalism is the theory that mental states are defined in terms of their causal role (how they function). What does it mean to desire something? According to the functionalist, desiring (as with any type of mental state) has certain causal relations to (1) sensory inputs, (2) other mental states, and (3) actions or responses. For example, if I desire a drink of water and if I see (1) a glass of liquid that causes me to have the belief that "this liquid is water," then this desire plus this belief will produce (2) a volitional state that results in (3) the action of my picking up the glass and drinking the water. Note that the functionalist differs from the behaviorist in claiming that relations between mental states have to be taken into account to explain the behavior.

Let's use another analogy: an antique, mechanical adding machine and an electronic calculator are very different in terms of their physical operations, but functionally they are equivalent. Each machine takes (1) inputs representing numbers and arithmetic operations, which activate (2) internal procedures for processing the inputs according to the laws of mathematics, and each machine has (3) a number-display system to represent the results. Similarly, by defining mental states in terms of their functional roles and not in terms of the substance in which they are found, the functionalist can claim that creatures that lack our biochemistry can still have the same cognitive life that we have, whether these creatures be extraterrestrial aliens or computers.

In the following reading, Jerry Fodor sets out some of the advantages of functionalism.

FROM JERRY FODOR
The Mind-Body Problem[20]

In the past 15 years a philosophy of mind called functionalism that is neither dualist nor materialist has emerged from philosophical reflection on developments in artificial intelligence, computational theory, linguistics, cybernetics and psychology. All these fields, which are collectively known as the cognitive sciences, have in common a certain level of abstraction and a concern with systems that process information. Functionalism, which seeks to provide a philosophical account of this level of abstractions, recognizes the possibility that systems as diverse as human beings, calculating machines and disembodied spirits could all have mental states. In the functionalist view the psychology of a system depends not on the stuff it is made of (living cells, metal or spiritual energy) but on how the stuff is put together.

Fodor goes on to discuss two alternative theories. The first is identity theory, which identifies mental states with brain states. The second theory is logical behaviorism, which attempts to translate all mental terms into talk about behavior or behavioral dispositions. He states that in the 1970s, these theories were the only viable alternatives to dualism, yet each theory had its problems.

- According to Fodor, how does functionalism combine the best points of both theories?
- What is the comparison the functionalist makes with computer science?

All of this emerged 10 or 15 years ago as a nasty dilemma for the materialist program in the philosophy of mind. On the one hand the identity theorist (and not the logical behaviorist) had got right the causal character of the interactions of mind and body. On the other the logical behaviorist (and not the identity theorist) had got right the relational character of mental properties. Functionalism has apparently been able to resolve the dilemma. By stressing the distinction computer science draws between hardware and software the functionalist can make sense of both the causal and the relational character of the mental.

According to the functionalist, the hardware of the computer (the wires, chips, and so on) are like the brain or whatever substance underlies the mental states. The software is a set of logical relationships that direct the processing of inputs, the changing states of the system, and the outputs. Software is analogous to the mind. Hence, differently designed computer systems can run functionally similar software (e.g., a chess game). In both systems, the logical relationships will be the same (the software will allow the pawns to move only one square at a time), even though what is happening at the hardware level may be completely different. Similarly, the mind is a pattern of relationships that could be embodied in different kinds of substances.

- In the final passage, find where Fodor describes a headache in terms of its causal relations to (1) inputs, (2) other mental states, and (3) responses.
- How does Fodor distinguish functionalism from both logical behaviorism and eliminativism?

The intuition underlying functionalism is that what determines the psychological type to which a mental particular belongs is the causal role of the particular in the mental life of the organism. . . . A headache, for example is identified with the type of mental state that among other things causes a disposition for taking aspirin in people who believe aspirin relieves a headache, causes a desire to rid oneself of the pain one is feeling, often causes someone who speaks English to say such things as "I have a headache" and is brought on by overwork, eyestrain and tension. . . .

Functionalism construes the concept of causal role in such a way that a mental state can be defined by its causal relations to other mental states. In this respect functionalism is completely different from logical behaviorism. Another major difference is that functionalism is not a reductionist thesis. It does not foresee, even in principle, the elimination of mentalistic concepts from the explanatory apparatus of psychological theories.

SURVEYING THE CASE FOR ARTIFICIAL INTELLIGENCE

Functionalists tend to find important analogies between human psychology and computers. In computer jargon we make a distinction between hardware and software. Hardware is the actual physical computer, including its chips and circuits. The software is the program giving the computer its instructions. Hence, the same hardware could run a word processor, an action game, a music synthesizer, or an artificial intelligence program that plays world-class chess. Similarly, two computers with different hardware designs (a Macintosh and an IBM) could run exactly the same program. Using the computer analogy, the identity theorist would explain our mental states by examining the hardware of the brain. On the other hand, the functionalist would say the makeup of the brain is irrelevant. What constitutes a mind is the software, or the patterns of activity that characterize different mental states, including the causal role of these states in the life of the organism. Hence, the transition from functionalism to artificial intelligence is easy. If computers could be programmed to have cognitive states functionally equivalent to those states in human psychology that we identify as thinking, believing, wanting, remembering, willing, and so on and if their ability to process information is comparable to ours, it would seem to follow that such computers would be intelligent and would have minds.

Minds versus Computers

Look through this list of activities and put a check in column A if the activity requires a mind. Put a check in column B if the activity can be performed by today's computers. Put a check in column C if you think it is at least possible that computers will be able to do this activity someday. Obviously, if you already put a check in column B for a particular activity, you should not also put a check in C.

Activity	(A) Requires a mind	(B) Today's computers can do it	(C) It is possible that future computers will be able to do it
1. Add up a sum of numbers			
2. Play chess			
3. Learn from experience			
4. Understand language			
5. Read a story and paraphrase it			
6. Read a story and draw inferences from it			
7. Make decisions			
8. Write poetry			
9. Have emotions			
10. Have consciousness			
Totals:	**(A)**	**(B)**	**(C)**
		(B) + (C)	

First, add together the number of checks you placed in column A and enter the total at the bottom of that column. *For the remaining two columns, consider only those rows in which you placed a check in column A.* Now, for all those rows (*and only those rows*), add together the number of the checks you placed in column B and enter that total at the bottom. Do the same for column C. Finally, add together the totals for columns B and C.

In tabulating your responses to the thought experiment, the degree to which the combined totals of columns B and C are equal to or almost equal to the total for column A is the degree to which you agree with a position known as strong artificial intelligence. The strong AI thesis states that it is possible for computers to literally have the same sorts of mental states and powers that humans have. The degree to which the combined totals of columns B and C are closer to zero indicates your disagreement with the position of strong AI. I now discuss the position of strong AI.

Does the Turing Test Measure Intelligence?

To answer the question, "Can computers think?" we need a criterion of what constitutes thinking. How do we measure human intelligence? We do so through IQ tests, which consist of a series of cognitive problems. Let us suppose that a computer could do about as well on a standard IQ test as an average person. This result would be a score of 100. If this score is a measure of human intelligence, why shouldn't we acknowledge that computers are intelligent if they perform just as well?

In our everyday life, of course, we do not give intelligence tests to one another. Nevertheless, we can recognize that other people have normal intelligence. How? One way is to talk to them. If they give reasonable answers in the context of a conversation, we are inclined to say that they have normal intelligence. In 1637, Descartes claimed that being able to use language flexibly was a skill that definitively separated humans from machines. He imagined that a very sophisticated robot could be designed to utter words and even say "ouch" if you touched it in a particular place. However, in the following passage, Descartes insisted that a machine would never have the versatility of human rationality.

> But it is not conceivable that such a machine should produce different arrangements of words so as to give an appropriately meaningful answer to whatever is said in its presence, as the dullest of men can do.[21]

ALAN TURING
(1912–1954)

In 1950 the British mathematician Alan Turing proposed a test to determine whether a computer can think or not.[22] Turing is considered to be the founding father of modern computer science. Although he never built a computer himself, he laid the theoretical and mathematical foundations that were essential for designing our modern computers. Here is a contemporary version of his proposal, which has since become immortalized as the **Turing Test** (Turing himself called it "the imitation game"). Let us suppose that you and several other judges are seated in a room in front of a computer terminal. Your terminal is communicating with a terminal in another room. You communicate interactively with the unseen person in the other room by typing in questions on your keyboard and reading the other person's responses on your monitor. The key feature of the test is that in some of the sessions you are not communicating with a flesh-and-blood person but with an artificial intelligence program running on a computer. Turing's claim was that if the computer program could fool a panel of judges into thinking they were communicating with a human being a significant percentage of the time, this deception would be proof that the computer program was capable of thought. Hence, Turing replaced the abstract and rather vague question, "Can computers think?" with an

Turing Test test produced by Alan Turing to determine whether a computer can think or not

operational test of intelligence—"Can computers pass the Turing Test?" The theory behind this test can be summed up by the cliché, "If it looks like a duck, walks like a duck, and quacks like a duck—it is a duck!" In other words, if a computer's responses fulfill the criteria we use to judge that a human is intelligent, then we are committed to saying that the computer is intelligent.

 STOP AND THINK

- What questions would you ask to determine whether you were communicating with a computer?
- Why do you think a computer could not (could never) give humanlike answers to these questions?

Descartes was convinced that machines could never be intelligent because they do not have immaterial minds and because he thought having such a mind is necessary to be a thinking being. Based on the technology of his day, he assumed that machines were mechanically rigid and inflexible in the sorts of operations they could perform. He also believed that understanding language requires a mind that possesses the ability to process an infinite variety of sentences. Hence, Descartes argued that understanding language was a criterion that could be used to distinguish machine responses from genuine intelligence. Descartes's argument could be summarized in this fashion:

1. Machines have the sort of intelligence we have if and only if they can understand language.
2. Machines cannot understand language.
3. Therefore, machines cannot have the sort of intelligence we have.

Alan Turing agreed with Descartes's first premise but was optimistic about the abilities of future machines. Consequently, his argument was:

1. Machines have the sort of intelligence we have if and only if they can understand language.
2. Machines can understand language.
3. Therefore, machines can have the sort of intelligence we have.

Although Turing realized that the machines of his day could not pass the Turing Test, he believed that someday machines would be technologically capable. In fact, he claimed that by the year 2000 (fifty years from the time he was writing), machines would be fooling human interrogators a significant percentage of the time.

> I believe that at the end of the century the use of words and general educated opinion will have altered so much that one will be able to speak of machines thinking without expecting to be contradicted.[23]

Some philosophers have expanded Turing's thesis into the claim that the ability to pass the Turing Test is a logically sufficient condition for having a mind. In other words, an appropriately programmed computer really *is* a mind and can be said to *literally* understand, believe, and have other cognitive states. This thesis is known as the **strong AI thesis.** The **weak AI thesis** is the relatively innocuous claim that artificial intelligence research may help us explore various theoretical models of human mental processes, while acknowledging that computers only simulate mental activities. There is a clear connection between functionalism and strong AI. Functionalism claims that a mind is anything that has the functional capabilities to behave in ways characteristic of human minds. The materials composing the system (wet gray matter or electrical circuits) are irrelevant to its status as a mind. Hence, if a computer running an artificial intelligence program has the same psychological constitution as human beings, then it has a mind.

strong AI thesis the claim that an appropriately programmed computer really is a mind and can be said to literally understand, believe, and have other cognitive states

weak AI thesis the claim that artificial intelligence research may help us explore various theoretical models of human mental processes, while acknowledging that computers only simulate mental activities

Is the Turing Test an effective way to test for intelligence? If a computer passes the Turing Test, can we be sure that this computer thinks or has a mind? Why?

Marvin Minsky and Strong AI

MARVIN MINSKY
(1927–   )

One of the leading defenders of strong AI is Marvin Minsky. For most of his professional career, Minsky has been involved in groundbreaking artificial intelligence research at the Massachusetts Institute of Technology. In the following passage, he predicts that someday computers will not only equal human intelligence, but will surpass it and that machines will achieve self-consciousness.

FROM MARVIN MINSKY

Why People Think Computers Can't[24]

When people ask if a machine can be self-conscious, they always seem to expect the answer to be no. I propose to shock the reader by explaining why machines may be capable, in principle, of possessing even more and better consciousness than people have. . . .

When and if we choose to build more artfully conceived intelligent machines, we should have many new options that were not available during the brain's evolution, for the biological constraints of vertebrate evolution must have dictated many details of the interconnections of our brains. In the new machines, we will be able to provide whatever paths we wish. Though the new machines still cannot possibly keep track in real time of everything they do, we surely should be able (at least in principle) to make those new, synthetic minds vastly more self-conscious than we are, in the sense of being more profound and having insightful knowledge about their own nature and function. Thus, in the end, those new creatures should have more interesting and richer inner lives than do people. . . .

There is absolutely no known technical reason to doubt that we could build truly intelligent machines. It may take a very long time, though, to learn enough about commonsense reasoning to make machines with manlike versatility. We already know some ways of making useful, specialized, expert systems. We don't yet know that many ways of making these systems learn enough to improve themselves in interesting ways. However, there are already some ideas about this topic on the scientific horizon. . . .

In years to come, we will learn more ways of making machines behave sensibly. . . . We will learn more about new kinds of knowledge and processes and how to use them to make still more new knowledge. We will come to think of learning and thinking and understanding not as mysterious, single, special processes, but as entire worlds of ways to represent and transform ideas. In turn, those new ideas will suggest new machine architectures, and they in turn will further change our ideas about ideas. No one can now tell where all these new ideas will lead. One thing is certain, though: there must be something wrong with any reasoned claim today to know any fundamental differences between men and possible machines. And there is a simple reason why such arguments must be erroneous: we simply do not know enough yet about the real workings of either men or possible machines.

STOP AND THINK

In the passage just quoted, Marvin Minsky suggests the following claims. For each one, set down the reasons why you either agree with the claim or disagree with it.

1. Someday, computers will be able to have greater self-understanding than we do.
2. Learning, thinking, and understanding are not "mysterious" but are basically complex "ways to represent and transform ideas."
3. It is possible that in the future there will be no basic differences between human minds and those of machines.

John Searle's Chinese Room

Whether artificial intelligence programs will ever be able to pass the Turing Test is primarily a technological question. The really interesting philosophical question is, Assuming that a computer could pass the Turing Test, would this result be a sufficient condition for saying that the computer has a mind? The contemporary philosopher John Searle attempted to refute the strong AI thesis held by Marvin Minsky and others by offering his famous 1980 Chinese room thought experiment.[25]

JOHN SEARLE
(1932–)

Try this simplified version of the Chinese room thought experiment yourself. We shall begin by assuming you have no knowledge of the Chinese language. Now, imagine that you are in a room with a rather large rulebook giving directions (in English) on how to respond to Chinese sentences with appropriate Chinese replies. The instruction manual does not contain stock sentences, for there is no way to predict what sentences it will need to process. Furthermore, it does not explain the meaning of the symbols to you. Instead, the manual contains formal rules for syntactically analyzing one set of Chinese symbols and constructing another set of Chinese symbols that a native speaker would recognize as an appropriate response. Chinese speakers slip messages under the door written in Chinese. These papers contain various marks made up of straight and curved lines, none of which you understand. You look these figures up in the book. Next, following the instructions, you write out another set of symbols and pass this message back to the Chinese speakers outside. Unknown to you, their messages are questions and, thanks to the rulebook, your responses are articulate answers to these questions written in Chinese.

THOUGHT EXPERIMENT

Searle's Chinese Room

To imagine what this process would be like, we can use typographical symbols to mimic the Chinese rulebook. Let us suppose that you are given the following set of symbols:

   & ! ¶ @ %

You look up the symbols in the book and find that the following rules are relevant:

   #357 When you encounter the symbols **& !**, replace them with the symbols **£ ¥**.

   #938 When you encounter the symbol **@**, replace it with ℞ and leave everything following it the same.

Following these rules, figure out what your response should be. This task should be easy enough, but the answer is in the footnote.*

   response:

   Unknown to you, the message means "Are you enjoying my questions?" and your response means "I am enjoying your questions."

Let us suppose that you are so successful at conversing in written Chinese by means of the rulebook that those on the outside agree that they have been communicating with a competent speaker of the Chinese language.

- What would be the implications of this result?
- Would this experiment support or count against the strong AI thesis?

*According to the rules, your response should be: **£ ¥ ¶ ℞ %**.

You can see that Searle is trying to construct something like a Turing Test for understanding Chinese. At this point, Searle appeals to our intuitions. You have passed the Turing Test by fooling the people on the outside that you are fluent in Chinese. However, in spite of this success, you still do not understand a single word of Chinese. Clearly, something different is going on when you are manipulating Chinese symbols than when you are receiving and responding to messages in English, which you do understand.

STOP AND THINK

How would you describe the difference between manipulating Chinese symbols according to formal rules and responding to English messages?

Searle claims that this formal manipulation of symbols is comparable to what goes on in a computer's AI program. His point is that no matter how effective a computer program may be in simulating conversation, it will never produce real understanding. Hence, a computer program can simulate intelligence, but it cannot duplicate it. Contrary to the strong AI thesis, Searle claims a computer program is nothing like a mind because *its* states are different from *our* cognitive states. To put it more technically, the computer lacks intentionality. **Intentionality** is a feature of certain mental states (such as beliefs) by which they are directed at or are about objects or states of affairs in the world. Intentionality is defined in terms of content and not formal relationships. For example, if you believe that a particular object is an apple, not only are you in a certain psychological state, but your state is one that is directed at a particular object in the world.

Let's apply Searle's concern about intentionality to the case of the Chinese rulebook. Suppose the rulebook tells you that the response to symbol #### is the symbol &&&&. But for you, these symbols lack any meaning. In other words, they do not refer to anything external to themselves (intentionality is lacking). On the other hand, the symbol "dog" is more than a set of marks for you. It produces a mental state that refers to a certain type of furry creature. If you ask a computer running an AI program, "Can dogs fly?" it may not have the answer programmed into it. But from the information in its database that "dogs do not have wings" and "most things that fly have wings," it might be able to infer the answer and generate the sentence, "Dogs do not fly." The point is that in producing this answer, the computer is manipulating and generating symbols just as you were in the Chinese room. Therefore, the computer's states do not have intentionality. The symbol "dog" in its memory is related to other symbols but it does not refer to the real world. Only a mind with intentionality, such as yours, is capable of using that symbol to refer to something else. It follows from Searle's position that, at best, passing the Turing Test may be *evidence* that the producer of the apparently intelligible responses has a mind, but this feat alone does not *constitute* having a mind.

Searle used this thought experiment to argue against behaviorism and functionalism. It is interesting to note that Searle himself is a physicalist. He believes that our mental states are caused by the unique causal powers of our brain. His point is that a computer program that merely manipulates symbols could never have the causal powers to produce understanding. Hence, Searle claims the behaviorist and the functionalist are wrong because they ignore the unique causal powers of the physical brain in their philosophy of mind. However, dualists have used his example to argue not only against behaviorism and functionalism but also against physicalism. We will see later in this section why dualists think Searle's conclusions point in this direction.

Some people think that Searle misses the point. He contends that computers can simulate cognitive processes but they cannot duplicate them. In another article, Searle points out that

> We can do a computer simulation of the flow of money in the British economy, or the pattern of power distribution in the Labour party. We can do computer simulation of rain storms in the home counties, or warehouse fires in East London. Now, in each of

intentionality a feature of certain mental states (such as beliefs) by which they are directed at or are about objects or states of affairs in the world

these cases, nobody supposes that the computer simulation is actually the real thing; no one supposes that a computer simulation of a storm will leave us all wet, or a computer simulation of a fire is likely to burn the house down. Why on earth would anyone in his right mind suppose a computer simulation of mental processes actually had mental processes?[26]

Searle's argument is a pretty good one, isn't it? Well, not everyone thinks it is. Daniel Dennett, a philosopher of mind at Tufts University replies to Searle's argument in this way:

> But now suppose we made a computer simulation of a mathematician, and suppose it worked well. Would we complain that what we had hoped for was *proofs,* but alas, all we got instead was mere *representations* of proofs? But representations of proofs *are* proofs, aren't they?[27]

In other words, in some cases (a rainstorm) the simulation or representation of something is quite different from the real thing. In other cases, the representation of something (a mathematical proof) is equivalent to the real thing. The word *artificial* is ambiguous because it can serve two purposes. We might use it to make this contrast: artificial versus genuine. In this sense, artificial flowers or artificial diamonds are not real flowers or diamonds, but only simulate the genuine articles. On the other hand, we can use *artificial* to make a different sort of contrast: artificial versus natural. Artificial light is not natural because it is produced by human technology. But in contrast to artificial flowers, artificial light is *real* light. So maybe intelligence can be artificial in that it is created by computer programs rather than nature at the same time that it can be real intelligence.

The Chess-Playing Machine Revisited

At this point, it will be useful to examine the three responses to Edgar Allan Poe's critique of the chess-playing machine mentioned in the "Stop and Think" box at the beginning of this section. As we go through these points, consider whether you have changed your mind about the original issue. The first response was:

1. Poe was right. You need a mind to play chess and, therefore, many of today's computers have minds.

This response correlates to the theory of strong AI. If computers can perform those tasks that we associate with human intelligence, then computers have minds.

The second response was:

2. Poe was wrong. You don't need a mind to play chess.

This response is one way that a critic of strong AI would deal with the fact that computers now play chess. This response points to an interesting tendency. Critics of strong AI use arguments of this form:

1. If something has a mind, it can do X.

2. Computers cannot do X.
3. Therefore, computers do not have minds.

In Poe's case, X was the ability to play chess. Other examples of X might be the ability to understand language, the ability to learn, the ability to write original poetry, the ability to make intelligent decisions, or the ability to solve problems. There are two difficulties here. The first is that many people cannot learn to play chess or write poetry. Nevertheless, we still consider them to have minds. We should not necessarily expect computers to do things that many humans cannot do. Another difficulty is that every time a computer program is developed that does X, then the ante is raised, so to speak. Poe assumed that computers could never play chess. We now know that computers can play chess. So, critics of strong AI now reject the chess-playing version of premise 1. But if we keep changing our criteria for what constitutes having mental abilities merely to avoid attributing these abilities to computers, then we really are not playing fair.

The third response was:

3. Computers don't *really* play chess, but only simulate it.

This response is similar to Searle's response concerning the ability of computers to understand language. We have already discussed Searle's and Dennett's disagreement over what constitutes a simulated performance and a genuine performance. Other versions of this response insist that conscious awareness is necessary for actions to be genuinely intelligent or for something to have a mind. These sorts of arguments run like this:

1. If something has a mind, it has subjective, conscious experiences.
2. Even computers that pass the Turing Test do not have subjective, conscious experiences.
3. Therefore, even computers that pass the Turing Test do not have minds.

Many theorists would say that this point is the one that Searle should have made from his thought experiment. Although the person manipulating Chinese symbols according to rules has consciousness, he or she does not have an understanding of what those symbols mean. Even less does a computer have understanding, for it lacks both intentionality and consciousness. The missing ingredient seems to be some sort of subject-related understanding and awareness. This subjective awareness does not fit well with identity theory nor with the computational model of the mind.

Here is where the dualist rejoins the battle. The dualist would agree with the functionalist that the unique nature of mental events are not explained by the specific physical makeup of our brains. The dualist would agree with Searle and the antifunctionalists that abstract, formal relationships cannot constitute minds. The existence of consciousness and subjective points of view are brute facts about our world, and it could be argued that, as yet, there are no plausible explanations of how they arise out of physical systems. The problem with this argument is that

it is hard to put your finger on consciousness and describe it. One philosopher has said: if you have it you know what it is, and if you don't have it there is no use trying to explain it to you. But how large a role does conscious awareness play in our activities? Is consciousness simply a surface-level phenomenon that floats on all the cognitive processing that occurs below it? If it is, then is it less important than the dualist thinks it is?

 STOP AND THINK

Think about all the ways in which cognitive processing (e.g., problem solving, decision making, driving a car) occurs at the subconscious level. To what degree is conscious awareness present or absent in activities that are considered to be intelligent?

LOOKING THROUGH THE LENS OF FUNCTIONALISM AND STRONG AI

1. To treat severe cases of epilepsy, physicians will remove half the patient's brain. They have found that, in time, the person can resume a normal life because the remaining half of the brain takes over most of the cognitive and motor skills once performed by the missing half. How does this research support the functionalist's claim that our mental states are not identical with any particular physical embodiment, but that they are a collection of psychological patterns and causal relations that could be realized in different sorts of physical media?

2. In the movies *ET* and *Star Wars* (numerous other science fiction films would also be relevant), we have creatures, such as aliens (ET) or robots (R2D2, C3PO), whose physical makeup is quite different from ours. Yet these creatures have beliefs, desires, and feelings just like ours, and they embody a psychology similar to ours. In the context of the story, if the robots R2D2 or C3PO were opened up, we would find nothing but wires. Still, we can imagine ourselves relating to them just as we would any other companion. We would feel sorry for them if they became damaged. Do our emotional reactions to these characters indicate that we would have a disposition to treat such advanced but different beings as psychologically like us? Does this indication lend some plausibility to functionalism?

3. Most functionalists do not address the question of life after death, but could a functionalist still believe in immortality? Hint: my ideas are embodied in the physical ink and paper of this book. If the only copy of this book were destroyed, could the ideas in this book be "resurrected" in some other medium for future generations of students to ponder? Benjamin Franklin's tombstone expresses a somewhat functionalist notion of life after death:

This body of B. Franklin in Christ Church cemetery,
Printer, Like the Cover of an old Book,
Its Contents torn out,
And stript of its Lettering and Gilding,
Lies here, Food for Worms.
But the work shall not be lost;
For it will, as he believed,
Appear once more in a new and more elegant Edition,
Corrected and Improved by its Author.

4. People frequently object to the strong AI thesis by claiming that computers are not really intelligent, but are merely doing what they have been programmed to do. But in what sense is this statement true of you? If you play chess, you follow the rules that you have been taught just as a computer does. When a computer learns to play chess, it is not only programmed with the rules, but it receives feedback and correction when it makes a strategic mistake. Subsequently, it makes decisions based on probable outcomes learned from experience. Is education, then, simply a sophisticated form of programming? If so, do computers learn and make decisions differently than humans do? What would an advocate of strong AI say?

5. Skeptics concerning artificial intelligence frequently say that computers will never reach the level of having minds because they will never be able to have emotions. Are emotions necessary in order to have a mind? Don't our emotions sometimes interfere with our ability to think? Without emotions, can computers, therefore, be better thinkers than we are? But maybe computers or robots will be able to have emotions some day. When a bully harasses us, we may feel the emotion of fear or anger. But what is fear? Fear is based on the judgment that something is dangerous to our well-being. It is also the disposition to respond by running or taking other actions. Isn't it possible to create a computer to have causal responses functionally identical to fear? In the movie *Star Wars,* the robots C3PO and R2D2 exhibited emotions. Hence, could the advocate of strong AI reasonably say that either emotions are not necessary to have a mind or that emotional response patterns could be part of a computer's program?

6. Because the advocate of strong AI believes that computers will eventually have all the capabilities that will enable them to have minds like ours and because a computer behaves in the way it has been programmed to behave, does it

necessarily follow that an advocate of strong AI is committed to the position that we, like computers, are "programmed" or determined in our behavior?

EXAMINING THE STRENGTHS AND WEAKNESSES OF FUNCTIONALISM AND STRONG AI

Positive Evaluation

1. Throughout the history of AI research, critics have continually said that computers will never really be intelligent, because they cannot do X (play chess, understand language, make decisions). However, every time a computer accomplishes one of these cognitive tasks, the critics still are not convinced. Are the critics raising the standard every time computers achieve it? What criteria would you use to decide whether computers really were intelligent? Are there any reasons to suppose that future computers will not be able to fulfill these criteria?

2. You can do many things without consciously attending to exactly how you do them. For example, you can judge if a tree is close or far away, decide if a poem is good or is drivel, determine if a person is angry or happy, decide if it is likely that the football team will win its next game. Because you can do these things, doesn't it make sense that you are unconsciously following some procedure to do them? Why can't the procedures we use to carry out our cognitive tasks be formulated and taught to computers?

Negative Evaluation

1. One of the most important features that we normally associate with minds is consciousness. Both the functionalists and strong AI advocates talk about the relations between inputs, the various states of cognitive processing, and outputs, but consciousness is never discussed. Can the functionalist's theory account for the fact that our minds exhibit conscious awareness? If functionalists cannot account for this awareness, can their theory of the mind and its cognitive activities still be complete? Is it possible that something we would recognize as consciousness could emerge from a very sophisticated computer? If a computer does not have consciousness, can it meaningfully be said to think? Do negative answers to all these questions refute functionalism and strong AI?

2. Give a functionalist's account of the mental state of pain in terms of the inputs that cause it, the relations it has to other mental states, and the behavior it produces. Furthermore, imagine a computer realizing all these functional states. Does this account contain anywhere the subjective feeling of being in pain that we associate with the mental state of pain? If not, does this absence count against the functionalist's theory that a particular mental state is simply a pattern of causal relations between inputs, other mental states, and actions? Does this absence count against the strong AI claim that computers can have minds?

SCOUTING THE TERRITORY: *Freedom and Determinism*

On February 9, 1979, identical twins Jim Lewis and Jim Springer met for the first time. Separated at birth, the twins had lived completely apart for thirty-nine years. During this time, there had been no contact between the two brothers nor between the two sets of adoptive parents. In the midst of their euphoria over their rediscovery of each other, the twin brothers became aware of a series of eerie similarities in their lives and behavior:

Both had been named James by their adoptive parents.
Both had been married twice.
Both of their first wives were named Linda.
Both of them married women named Betty the second time.
Both of them gave nearly the same name to the oldest son:
    James Alan and James Allan.
Both of them chain-smoked the same brand of cigarettes.
Both of them drank the same brand of beer.
Both had served as sheriff's deputies.

As they shared further details of their separate lives, they discovered further facets of their lifestyles that had developed along parallel tracks. Both of them had owned dogs named Toy, pursued a hobby of making miniature furniture in garage workshops, drove Chevys, vacationed on the same beach in the Florida Gulf Coast, and lived in the only house on their block.

Identical twins that have been reared apart are an ideal living laboratory for behavioral scientists. This case and thousands like it are helping scientists get a handle on one of humanity's oldest mysteries: To what degree is human behavior influenced by heredity or environment, genes or life experiences, nature or nurture? If identical twins are raised in separate and different environments, any similarities in their behavior provide support for the thesis that much of our behavior is a product of our genes. On the other hand, the differences between such twins would have to be a result of differences in their environment or life's experiences.

A month after the twin Jims met, Dr. Thomas Bouchard of the University of Minnesota paid them to spend a week at his research center. When he gave them a test that measured personality variables, the twins' scores were so close that they appeared to be the test scores of the same person taking the test twice. Brain-wave tests produced graphs that looked like the skyline of the same city. Measurements of their intelligence, mental abilities, gestures, voice tones, likes and dislikes were remarkably similar as well. Similar studies of identical twins raised in different environments have shown a high correlation between twins' beliefs and attitudes, including their social, political, moral, and religious views.[28]

What are we to make of these studies? Obviously you did not choose many of the features that make you the person you are: the color of your eyes, hair, and skin; your sex; or your height. It would seem to be equally obvious that many facts about you are the result of decisions that you freely made: your favorite music, your spouse, your job, the name of your dog, and your ethical beliefs. Throughout your life you feel as though it is up to you to examine the alternatives, to deliberate, and to make a choice. Surely the twins in these studies felt as though they were freely making these sorts of decisions. Yet it appears as though they were being forced down parallel tracks by causes of which they were not aware. In the context of this chapter, we say that a person's action or choice is *determined* when it is the inevitable result of prior causes operating on the person. These causes could be the result of psychological or physiological forces.

The studies just described focus on the possible influence of people's genes on their behavior. However, it must not be overlooked that there are always many differences between identical twins. In one study, identical twins who had been separated seemed to have developed different interests because of differences in their upbringing. One twin became a concert pianist; the other had no interest in playing the piano. However, even if our genes do not account for the whole story of our lives, we still have to contend with the claim that who we are is determined by our upbringing and life experiences.

Although the verdict on these issues is not yet in and behavioral scientists are still debating the data, many theorists claim that we are a lot more determined in the decisions we make than we would like to think. In other words, these theorists claim that our decisions are not the spontaneous result of free will, but are the necessary outcome of psychological or physiological causes operating on us, just as our blood pressure is determined by biological causes. But then what happens to our sense of self? Are we completely determined? What reasons do we have for thinking we are not determined? If we are determined, what are the implications for moral responsibility? These questions are some of the most puzzling but unavoidable ones in philosophy today. The following thought experiment explores the notions of choices and their causes as well as the concepts of action and responsibility.

THOUGHT EXPERIMENT

Actions and Responsibility

1. List three different things you did simply because they were what you wanted to do (e.g., going to a particular movie, reading a novel, taking a nonrequired course).

   a. _____

   b. _____

   c. _____

   Why do you like the activities on your list?

   Did you choose to like the things that you like to do?   YES   NO   (Circle one)

   a. If your answer is YES: What caused you to like the things that you like to do?

   b. If your answer is NO: How did you come to like the things that you like to do?

   (Continued . . .)

(. . . continued)

2. Suppose a friend of yours swings his or her arm and knocks over an object that has a great deal of sentimental value to you, shattering it into a million pieces.
   a. Under what circumstances would you say this person clearly was morally responsible for the action?
   b. List as many circumstances as you can in which the person definitely caused the item to be broken but in which you would *not* consider him or her to be morally responsible for this event in the fullest sense of the word.
   c. List circumstances (if any) in which you would not be sure whether the person was morally responsible for breaking the item. (Your uncertainty should not be based on any lack of knowledge concerning the relevant facts.)

CHARTING THE TERRAIN OF FREEDOM AND DETERMINISM: *What Are the Issues?*

The previous thought experiment touched on the first issue that concerns us here; that issue is the question of how to account for the origin of our actions. Think about the last movie you watched or novel you read. Why did you watch *that* movie or read *that* novel? Presumably, your action was the result of an act of your will, based on a choice, that reflected what you wanted to do at that moment. But this presumption raises the question, How do your acts of will, choices, and wants come about? Are they psychological events that simply pop into being without any cause? Is this sudden appearance what you mean when you say that you freely made a decision? If so, why does one mental choice rather than another happen to pop into your head? Another possibility is that your choices and wants are themselves brought about by other events, such as your previous psychological states and other causes operating on you. But this possibility only pushes the question back further, and we must again figure out whether our choices are uncaused events or the result of a series of linked causes extending back into the past. As we shall see, each of these alternatives has its problems.

The other issue raised in the thought experiment concerns moral responsibility. When are we morally responsible for our behavior, and what sorts of circumstances would diminish our responsibility? If our actions are ultimately the result of causes over which we have no control, can we ever be morally responsible?

W. Somerset Maugham's novel *Of Human Bondage* contains a conversation in which the character Philip says,

> "Before I do anything I feel that I have a choice, and that influences what I do; but afterward, when the thing is done, I believe that it was inevitable from all eternity."— "What do you deduce from that?" asked Hayward.—"Why merely the futility of regret. It's no good crying over spilt milk, because all the forces of the universe were bent on spilling it."[29]

Philip's comments represent one perspective on the issues I have just introduced. The first issue concerns freedom. We feel free, but are we genuinely free? If I *feel* nauseated, then it follows that I *am* genuinely nauseated. But does freedom work this way? If we *feel* as though we *are* free, does it necessarily follow that we *are* free? Isn't it possible to be mistaken about whether we are free? Philip says that when we do something, such as spilling milk, "all the forces of the universe were bent on spilling it." Is his conclusion true? Are our actions simply the product of the forces of nature acting on or within us? Is it possible that there is a scientific explanation (genetic, physiological, psychological) for everything we do? Why? How do actions that are the outcome of natural causes affect our sense of autonomy, dignity, and freedom? Another issue arises in Philip's comments. If we are determined to act the way we do, is it meaningless to feel regret over our actions? Can we judge another person to be morally responsible or capable of either blame or praise if his or her actions were inevitable? After you complete the next "Stop and Think" exercise, the "Philosophy in the Marketplace" survey will allow you to discuss these issues with your friends.

STOP AND THINK

Imagine yourself talking to Philip on the phone. Explain to him why you agree or disagree with the following two claims he made:

1. All our actions are "inevitable from all eternity."
2. If all our actions are determined, it is foolish to feel regret for our actions.

CONCEPTUAL TOOLS: *Thinking about Freedom*

Before I set out the alternatives, I need to clarify the word *freedom* because everyone has a different notion of what it means to be free. Basically, two kinds of freedom are relevant to our discussion of philosophy. Different authors have given these two freedoms different labels, but what is important is the distinction being made and not the terminology.

circumstantial freedom the ability and the opportunity to perform whatever action we choose; that is, freedom *from* external forces, obstacles, and natural limitations that restrict or compel our actions

We have **circumstantial freedom** when we have the ability and the opportunity to perform whatever action we choose. Circumstantial freedom is a negative condition, because it means we are free *from* external forces, obstacles, and natural limitations that restrict or compel our actions. In this sense, you would not be free to go to the movies if you were tied up or if someone was holding a gun to your head (external forces). Similarly, you are not free to jump fifty feet in the air (a natural limitation). Loosely speaking, we could say that even inanimate objects can have circumstantial freedom. For example, a bicycle wheel is "free" to turn when we remove the lock from it.

Notice that the fact that you have circumstantial freedom says nothing about how your choices originate. Bees constructing a honeycomb have circumstantial freedom even though their activity is driven by blind instinct. Similarly, all philosophers would agree that your choice of a particular career is circumstantially free

Do the following exercise yourself, and present it to at least five friends. Consider each one of the following scenarios as separate cases, that is, the facts in one case do not carry over to the other cases. In each situation, decide whether Dave was morally responsible or worthy of blame for killing Todd. In other words, answer the following two questions:

a. In which of these cases should Dave be sentenced as a criminal who committed murder?

b. In which of these cases should we say that even though Dave tragically caused the death of Todd, Dave was not fully morally responsible for this event?

1. Dave had an undiagnosed brain tumor that one day suddenly caused muscle spasms in his arm and hand. This unexpected spasm caused Dave to involuntarily pull the trigger of his gun and fatally wound Todd while the two were in the woods hunting.

2. Dave was suffering from shell shock and mental instability after serving in a brutal war overseas. Waking up from a blackout, he hallucinated that he was still in the war and that his good friend Todd was the enemy. Thinking that he was acting in self-defense, Dave shot and killed Todd.

3. Dave is normally a quiet, gentle person, but was he hypnotized by an evil psychiatrist and ordered to kill Todd. While in a deep, hypnotic trance, Dave carried out the order.

4. Dave was showing off his handgun to his neighbor Todd. Because Dave did not realize that the gun was loaded, he was handling it carelessly. It accidentally went off and killed Todd.

5. One night in a bar, Dave had way too much to drink. He got into a vicious argument with Todd, who was also drunk and verbally abusive. In a state of alcoholic rage, Dave went to his car and came back with a gun and shot Todd. Dave woke up the next morning in jail with no memory of what happened the night before.

6. Dave's father was a violent and brutal drug dealer who finally took off forever when Dave was eight years old. Thereafter, Dave's mother had an unending succession of abusive, live-in boyfriends. Dave never experienced love but only physical and psychological abuse. He carried the emotional pain and anger deep within his twisted personality like a ticking time bomb. Finally, at age twenty-two, Dave's bomb exploded. Dave was provoked into a meaningless, heated argument with Todd (a total stranger who reminded him of his abusive father). In a fit of uncontrollable rage, Dave pulled out a gun and shot Todd.

7. Dave was having an affair with Todd's wife and wanted her husband out of the way. After weeks of planning and stalking Todd, Dave shot and killed him as Todd left his gym.

(assuming no one is holding a gun to your head). However, your freedom in this sense does not rule out the possibility that your career choice is the inevitable outcome of your genetic inheritance, personality, biochemistry, social conditioning, or other determining causes. All philosophers would agree that it is possible for us to have the circumstantial freedom to choose and to act as we desire. The controversy is whether we have the second kind of freedom.

**metaphysical free-
dom** the power of
the self to choose
among genuine alter-
natives; free will

I have called the second freedom **metaphysical freedom** because whether we have this kind of freedom depends on what sort of universe we live in and on what is fundamentally true about human nature. As we will see, some philosophers deny that we have this freedom. Metaphysical freedom is identical to what we ordinarily mean when we talk about free will, a concept that refers to the power of the self to choose among genuine alternatives. Metaphysical freedom does not relate to external circumstances but to our internal condition. Here, the self is the creative, originating cause of a decision or action. If we have metaphysical freedom, then our ability to initiate a particular action is *not* simply the result of external, determining causes acting on us. If we have this freedom, then we could have made different choices in the past than the ones we did.

It follows that if we have metaphysical freedom (free will), then the given circumstances and our psychological makeup prior to a decision are *not* sufficient to make a particular choice necessary or inevitable. External circumstance and our personality may exert some influence over our decisions, but in the final analysis, which of several alternatives we act on is decided by our free, spontaneous choice. Naturally, our ability to exercise our metaphysical freedom on a particular occasion could be limited by our lack of circumstantial freedom. Nevertheless, metaphysical freedom allows the self the capacity to make free and undetermined choices within the bounds of its external limitations. Because all philosophers agree that normally we have a certain amount of circumstantial freedom, the main controversy is whether we have metaphysical freedom.

CHOOSING A PATH: *What Are My Options concerning Human Freedom?*

We can formulate the issue of freedom and determinism in terms of three statements and different combinations of responses to these statements. The three statements are:

1. We are determined.
2. If we are determined, then we lack the freedom necessary to be morally responsible.
3. We do have the freedom necessary to be morally responsible.

These statements create an inconsistent triad, which means it is impossible for all three statements to be true. You can accept any two of these statements, but to do so requires that you reject the third statement.

 STOP AND THINK

Try picking different pairs of the three statements and convince yourself that each pair implies the falsehood of the remaining statement.

You can take one of three positions on the issue of freedom and determinism: libertarianism, hard determinism, and compatibilism. Each position is defined by which two statements are accepted and which one is rejected. Let's briefly examine each of these statements while I introduce the three philosophical alternatives.

Statement 1: We Are Determined

Those philosophers who agree with this statement do so because they believe in universal causation. **Universal causation** is the thesis that all events are the necessary result of previous causes. **Determinism** is the claim that universal causation is true. If universal causation were true and if it were possible to have complete knowledge of the universe at the present moment, then we could predict not only the state of the universe in the next minute but also everything that will happen in the future. The French astronomer Pierre-Simone Laplace (1749–1827) expressed this idea by imagining the perspective of a superintelligent being:

> We ought then to consider the present state of the universe as the effect of its previous state and as the cause of that which is to follow. An intelligence that, at a given instant, could comprehend all the forces by which nature is animated and the respective situation of the beings that make it up, if moreover it were vast enough to submit these data to analysis, would encompass in the same formula the movements of the greatest bodies of the universe and those of the lightest atoms. For such an intelligence nothing would be uncertain, and the future, like the past, would be open to its eyes.[30]

Because our choices, beliefs, desires, and actions are themselves events, the determinist claims that they, too, are the necessary result of previous causes. Determinists disagree as to which type of cause is most important in producing our behavior, whether it be our genetic inheritance, biochemistry, behavioral conditioning, or God's will. Nevertheless, they all agree that everything that happens in nature and in human behavior is the inevitable outcome of the causal order. Determinists acknowledge that we can have circumstantial freedom but deny that we have metaphysical freedom. As the discussion of these statements continues, you will see that there are two forms of determinism (hard determinism and compatibilism), but both of them begin by affirming statement 1.

Libertarianism is the position that rejects determinism. Hence, the libertarian rejects statement 1. (Libertarianism here is a metaphysical position and is entirely different from the political philosophy of the same name.) In contrast to the determinist, the libertarian claims that we *do* have metaphysical freedom. If so, then at least some human actions are free and exempt from causal necessity. Free actions are originated by the self; that is, they are grounded in the free will of the person and, hence, are not the inevitable result of previous causes. Accordingly, the libertarian claims that it is often impossible (even in principle) to predict every detail of a person's behavior.

It is important that you understand the significance of these opposing viewpoints. If you are a determinist, you would have to agree that the following statement by John Stuart Mill, a nineteenth-century British philosopher, applies to you.

universal causation the thesis that all events are the necessary result of previous causes

determinism the thesis that universal causation is true

libertarianism the thesis that we *do* have metaphysical freedom; a rejection of determinism

Correctly conceived, the doctrine called Philosophical Necessity is simply this: that, given the motives which are present to an individual's mind, and given likewise the character and disposition of the individual, the manner in which he will act might be unerringly inferred: that if we knew the person thoroughly, and knew all the inducements which are acting upon him, we could foretell his conduct with as much certainty as we can predict any physical event.[31]

On the other hand, in his short novel, *Notes from Underground,* Fyodor Dostoyevsky has his character express the libertarian conviction that determinism would strip us of our humanity and that we would end up being no more than parts in the machine of nature, much like an organ stop (part of the mechanism of a pipe organ).

Indeed, if there really is some day discovered a formula for all our desires and caprices—that is, an explanation of what they depend upon, by what laws they arise, how they develop, what they are aiming at in one case and in another and so on, that is a real mathematical formula—then, most likely, man will at once cease to feel desire, indeed, he will be certain to. For who would want to choose by rule? Besides, he will at once be transformed from a human being into an organ-stop or something of the sort; for what is a man without desire, without freewill and without choice, if not a stop in an organ?[32]

Statement 2: If We Are Determined, Then We Lack the Freedom Necessary to Be Morally Responsible

incompatibilism the claim that determinism is incompatible with the sort of freedom required to be morally responsible for our behavior

This statement expresses the thesis of **incompatibilism,** for it claims that determinism is incompatible with the sort of freedom required to be morally responsible for our behavior. What does it mean to be morally responsible for an action? It means that we deserve praise or rebuke, credit or blame, reward or punishment for that action. The issue is not whether rewards or punishments are effective in causally determining a person's behavior. Instead, for the incompatibilists, moral responsibility is a question of whether we *deserve* reward or punishment. We can only deserve these consequences, they say, if we had genuine alternatives such that we could have chosen to act otherwise than we did. In other words, the incompatibilist claim is that having moral responsibility requires that we have metaphysical freedom.

hard determinism the dual claims that (1) having metaphysical freedom is a necessary condition for people to be morally responsible for their choices in any meaningful sense of the word and (2) we do not have the metaphysical freedom required for moral responsibility

Libertarians accept statement 2, because they believe that metaphysical freedom and not the more minimal circumstantial freedom is necessary for persons to be considered free and responsible for their choices and behavior. Remember, however, that the libertarian maintains that we do have metaphysical freedom. Hard determinists also accept statement 2. The position of **hard determinism** consists of two claims: (1) having metaphysical freedom is a necessary condition for people to be morally responsible for their choices in any meaningful sense of the word and (2) we do not have the metaphysical freedom required for moral responsibility. Hence, libertarians and hard determinists agree that being determined is incompatible with moral responsibility (incompatibilism), but libertarians say we have moral responsibility because we are not determined, whereas hard determinists say we lack moral responsibility because we are determined.

The position that rejects statement 2 represents another variety of determinism, known as compatibilism. **Compatibilism** is the claim that we are both determined *and* have the sort of freedom necessary to be morally responsible for our actions. Since compatibilists are determinists, what sort of freedom do they think we have? According to the compatibilist, an action is free to the degree that it is not the product of external compulsion. If the immediate cause of your action is your own will, choices, values, or desires, then it is a free or voluntary action for which you can be held responsible. At the same time, the compatibilist insists that your personality, motives, and values are completely determined by previous causes. In other words, the compatibilist denies that we have metaphysical freedom. However, contrary to the hard determinist and the libertarian, the compatibilist believes that circumstantial freedom is the only kind of freedom necessary for us to be responsible for our choices and actions.

compatibilism the thesis that we are both determined *and* have the sort of freedom necessary to be morally responsible for our actions; sometimes called soft determinism

Statement 3: We Do Have the Freedom Necessary to Be Morally Responsible

All three positions agree that some sort of freedom is a necessary condition for moral responsibility. Kant expressed this belief by saying "ought implies can." Accordingly, all three positions would agree that if you lack circumstantial freedom in a situation (a gun is held to your head, you are drugged or tied up), then you cannot be responsible for what you do or don't do when suffering from these constraints. However, as we already discussed, both the hard determinist and the libertarian agree that a necessary condition for being capable of moral responsibility is metaphysical freedom, or free will. Without metaphysical freedom, both philosophers claim, the whole category of moral responsibility must be eliminated, since our character and actions are the inevitable product of forces beyond our control. Hard determinists deny that we have metaphysical freedom, so they also deny that we have the capacity to be morally responsible. Libertarians believe we do have metaphysical freedom, so they believe we have the capacity to be morally responsible. In a speech to prisoners in jail, Clarence Darrow, the famous defense attorney, forthrightly expressed the hard determinist's denial of moral responsibility.

> I do not believe there is any sort of distinction between the real moral conditions of the people in and out of jail. One is just as good as the other. The people here can no more help being here than the people outside can avoid being outside. I do not believe that people are in jail because they deserve to be. They are in jail simply because they cannot avoid it on account of circumstances which are entirely beyond their control and for which they are in no way responsible.[33]

Darrow's position was that if we want to prevent people from becoming criminals, we must eliminate the social conditions that make people criminals. In response,

TABLE 3.3 *Three Positions on Freedom and Determinism*			
Philosophical Positions	1 We are determined.	2 If we are determined, then we lack the freedom necessary to be morally responsible.	3 We are morally responsible.
Hard Determinist	Agrees	Agrees	Disagrees
Libertarian	Disagrees	Agrees	Agrees
Compatibilist	Agrees	Disagrees	Agrees

the libertarian would assert that people have moral responsibility because they are free and are not completely determined by their circumstances.

On the other hand, the compatibilist says that whenever you have circumstantial freedom and your action is the outcome of who you are and what you believe, value, or desire, then you are morally responsible for that action, even though your wants, desires, and motives are causally determined.

Our discussion of the three positions on freedom and determinism is summarized in Table 4.3.

 STOP AND THINK

Go back over the seven scenarios concerning Dave's shooting of Todd. In each case, decide what the hard determinist, libertarian, and compatibilist would say about Dave's responsibility for his actions. Note: in a few of the scenarios, it might be debatable which answer would be consistent with the position in question.

 WHAT DO I THINK? *Questionnaire on Freedom and Determinism*

For each statement, mark whether you agree or disagree. Note that each numbered statement has two answers that are the same. If the response you choose for a particular statement has two identical answers, be sure to check them both. In other words, if you agree with statement 1, you should check agree twice.

1. Everything that happens in the world is a necessary result of previous causes.	Agree	Disagree	Agree
2. If it would be possible for scientists to know my past, my biochemical makeup, and all the causes acting on and within me, then my behavior would be perfectly predictable.	Agree	Disagree	Agree

	H	L	C
3. When I feel that a decision is completely spontaneous and uncaused, that simply means that I am ignorant of all the causes that necessarily generated that decision.	Agree	Disagree	Agree
4. Some choices I make are not the necessary result of previous causes.	Disagree	Agree	Disagree
5. Sometimes I regret a decision I made. In these cases I believe that at the time I made the particular decision I genuinely could have made a different choice.	Disagree	Agree	Disagree
6. While physiological, sociological, and psychological conditions *influence* my choices, they do not totally *determine* them.	Disagree	Agree	Disagree
7. For an action to be free, it cannot be completely determined by previous causes.	Agree	Agree	Disagree
8. Even if I am 100 percent determined to behave the way I do, my actions are free if they result from my own choices, values, and desires.	Disagree	Disagree	Agree
9. If everything I think, decide, or do is completely determined by physiological or psychological causes that control me, then it is impossible for me to be morally responsible for any of my actions.	Agree	Agree	Disagree
10. Even if my choices are completely determined by previous causes, I am morally responsible for a particular action as long as the immediate cause of that action was my own choice and not some form of external coercion.	Disagree	Disagree	Agree
Add up the number of checks in each column (H, L, C) and put the total in the box for that column.			
	H	**L**	**C**

KEY TO THE QUESTIONNAIRE ON FREEDOM AND DETERMINISM

The H column contains the answers for *hard determinism.* The L column represents *libertarianism.* The C column represents *compatibilism.* Whichever column had the most checks is the position closest to your own.

Statements 1 through 6 deal with the issue of determinism

Statements 1, 2, 3: If you answered "Agree" to any of these statements, you should have answered the same for all three. If you answered "Agree" to these statements, you are a determinist.

Statements 4, 5, 6: If you answered "Agree" to any of these statements, you should have answered the same for all three. If you answered "Agree" to these statements, you are a libertarian. Your answer to statements 1, 2, and 3 should be the opposite of the answers for 4, 5, and 6.

Statements 7 and 8 deal with the issue of freedom

Statement 7: If you answered "Agree," you are an incompatibilist, which means you are either a hard determinist or a libertarian. If you answered "Disagree," you are a compatibilist.

Statement 8: If you answered "Agree," you are a compatibilist. If you answered "Disagree," you are an incompatibilist and either a hard determinist or a libertarian. Your answer here should be the opposite of that for statement 7.

Statements 9 and 10 deal with the issue of moral responsibility

Statement 9: If you answered "Agree," you are an incompatibilist and either a hard determinist or a libertarian. If you answered "Disagree," you are a compatibilist.

Statement 10: If you answered "Agree," you are a compatibilist. If you answered "Disagree," you are an incompatibilist and either a hard determinist or a libertarian. Your answer here should be the opposite of that for statement 9.

- Which position did your answers favor?
- How consistent were your answers?

3.6 HARD DETERMINISM

 LEADING QUESTIONS: *Hard Determinism*

1. Suppose you have laid down your hard-earned cash to purchase the car of your dreams. As you take it out for a drive, however, you find that the windshield wipers spontaneously go on and off for no apparent reason, as does the radio and the horn. Frustrated and irate, you drive the car back to the dealer. After the car has been in the shop for an hour, the dealer comes out and says to you, "It's really strange. There is no cause for the behavior of your car. These events are just happening on their own." Would you accept this explanation? Why?

2. Think about your unique personality traits. Are you an extrovert or an introvert? Are you an assertive or passive person? Are you very emotional, or are you naturally calm, stable, and unmoveable? Are you decisive or indecisive? Did you choose these personality traits? Could you decide to be an emotional person on Mondays, Wednesdays, and Fridays and an even-tempered, rocklike person on Tuesdays, Thursdays, Saturdays? Why? If you did not choose your personality, then where did it come from or what caused it?

3. How does your personality affect your behavior and choices? If you did not choose your personality, then are you morally responsible for actions that result from it?

THE DEBATE OVER DETERMINISM

The twentieth-century psychologist B. F. Skinner wrote the novel *Walden Two* to present his ideas about human behavior. It contains the following dialogue between a behavioral scientist (Frazier) and a philosopher (Castle). Frazier (who represents Skinner) maintains that everything we do is determined by prior conditioning. Castle opposes him by maintaining that we have free will. As you read the dialogue, decide which character comes closest to representing your viewpoint.

FROM B. F. SKINNER
Walden Two[34]

"My answer [to the question of freedom] is simple enough," said Frazier. "I deny that freedom exists at all. I must deny it—or my program [of developing a science of behavior] would be absurd. You can't have a science about a subject matter which hops capriciously about. Perhaps we can never *prove* that man isn't free; it's an assumption. But the increasing success of a science of behavior makes it more and more plausible."

"On the contrary, a simple personal experience makes it untenable," said Castle. "The experience of freedom. I *know* that I'm free. . . ."

"The 'feeling of freedom' should deceive no one," said Frazier. "Give me a concrete case."

"Well right now," Castle said. He picked up a book of matches. "I'm free to hold or drop these matches."

"You will, of course, do one or the other," said Frazier. "Linguistically or logically there seem to be two possibilities, but I submit that there's only one in fact. The determining forces may be subtle but they are inexorable. I suggest that as an orderly person you will probably hold—ah! you drop them! Well, you see, that's all part of your behavior with respect to me. You couldn't resist the temptation to prove me wrong. It was all lawful. You had no choice. The deciding factor entered rather late, and naturally you couldn't foresee the result when you first held them up. There was no strong likelihood that you would act in either direction, and so you said you were free."

"That's entirely too glib," said Castle. "Its easy to argue lawfulness after the fact. But let's see you predict what I will do in advance. Then I'll agree there's law."

"I didn't say that behavior is always predictable, any more than the weather is always predictable. There are often too many factors to be taken into account. We can't measure them all accurately, and we couldn't perform the mathematical operations needed to make a prediction if we had the measurements."

- Do you think Frazier is correct in claiming that science requires us to deny human freedom?
- Why does Castle believe he is free?
- Do you think Castle has a good reason for believing in freedom?
- How does Frazier reconcile the fact that our behavior is not always predictable with his belief in determinism?
- Do you tend to agree with Frazier or Castle? Why?

SURVEYING THE CASE FOR HARD DETERMINISM

One afternoon, I walked into the student union at my university and found that a large crowd had gathered to watch a professional hypnotist demonstrating his skills. The main attraction was three male students with glazed-over eyes seated on chairs. They had obviously been placed in a hypnotic trance and were responding to everything the hypnotist said. He told them that they were on a spaceship hurtling through space, which caused them to press back against their chairs and grimace as he described the effects of acceleration on them. Next, he told them that they were making a rather rough landing on a planet, and the three students rocked and jerked as the hypnotist's fictional scenario became reality within their minds. Finally, he told them the planet was very cold and they needed to fight the onset of hypothermia. To the delight of the spectators, these three strangers began to huddle together and embrace each other while shivering from the "frigid" air. It is certain that they would not have behaved this way if they had not been in a hypnotic trance and under the control of the hypnotist.

We have all read similar accounts of how a person's ability to make free decisions has been diminished by hypnosis or brainwashing or by the effects of drugs, disease, or some form of mental incapacity. When someone's behavior is being caused by factors over which he or she has no control, it seems fairly clear that such an individual would lack the capacity to exercise free will. But are these cases exceptions to the general rule? Do we normally have free will except under these extreme conditions? The determinist would say that hypnotism, brainwashing, or abnormal medical conditions are simply unusual ways by which our behavior or mental states may be caused. According to the determinist, our behavior, even under conditions that we may consider "normal," is still the inevitable result of causes that are acting on and within us.

The philosophy of hard determinism is one variety of determinism. It is based on three main pillars. The first pillar consists of the problems the determinist finds with libertarianism (the belief in free will). The second pillar is the collection of positive arguments for determinism. Both versions of determinism (hard determinism and compatibilism) share these initial points. Third, hard determinism denies the possibility of moral responsibility. This third pillar distinguishes the hard determinist from the compatibilist, for the compatibilist believes we are capable of moral responsibility. Let's examine each of these three components in turn.

THE PROBLEMS WITH LIBERTARIANISM

Libertarianism Is in Conflict with the Scientific View of the World

Throughout history, science has progressed by replacing explanations of events based on voluntary, spontaneous acts of free will with explanations in terms of deterministic laws. For example, the ancient Greeks believed that a stone fell to the ground because it *desired* to be reunited with its mother the earth. Other natural events such as solar eclipses, plagues, bountiful crops, or thunderstorms were thought to be caused by the arbitrary will of the gods. Our ability to understand the world took a great leap forward when people came to realize that the causes of these events have nothing to do with stones or gods desiring or willing anything. Instead, we came to view such events as rooted in a deterministic system of natural laws. Applying this system to our own day, the determinist would point out that we are gaining a better understanding of human behavior by looking for the causal laws that explain it. As the psychologist B. F. Skinner said, "A scientific analysis of behavior must, I believe, assume that a person's behavior is controlled by his genetic and environmental histories rather than by the person himself as an initiating, creative agent."[35]

Libertarianism Requires the Problematic Notion of Uncaused Events

According to the determinist, the belief that human actions are a product of free will implies that some events (acts of the will) simply happen without any cause to produce them or explain them. For example, if you decide to join a political party, what caused your decision? Why did you decide to join *that* party while your neighbor decided to join an opposing party? You might explain your choice in terms of your values, beliefs, or ideals, but where did these values, beliefs, and ideals come from? At some point, the determinist claims, the belief in free will requires us to suppose that some psychological events simply happen and happen in a certain way, but without any cause that can explain them. While some determinists still find it appropriate to explain human actions in terms of wants, desires, or motives that activate the will, they still would insist that these psychological states must have a causal history that explains them.

Libertarianism Fails to Explain the Fact That We Can Influence Other People's Behavior

A common presupposition of all human interaction, says the determinist, is that it is possible to causally affect one another's behavior. If human actions and volitions were not the result of causes acting on them, it would be useless to reward or punish people. In a world that has no deterministic causes, the way people behaved would be completely unpredictable and capricious. However, it is obvious that we can, to a large degree, predict and influence how people will behave. This ability implies causal connections between the causes that precede an act of the will and the behavior that results. The degree to which we can understand a person's psychological state and the causes operating on it is the degree to which we can predict what that person will do. The degree to which we can control the causes acting on a person is the degree to which we can influence what that person will do. The activities of parenting, educating, rewarding, and punishing all assume determinism.

THOUGHT EXPERIMENT

Behavior Modification and Prediction

- List several occasions in the recent past when you successfully influenced or modified the behavior of another person. (It can be a trivial example.) What means did you use? How is it possible to affect another person's behavior?
- List several occasions when you predicted a friend's behavior or anticipated his or her response to a situation. How is it possible to know ahead of time what another person will do?

THE POSITIVE CASE FOR DETERMINISM

The determinist claims that human actions are just as much the product of causal necessity as is any other event in nature. The basic argument of the determinist could be formulated in the following way:

1. Every event, without exception, is causally determined by prior events.
2. Human thoughts and actions are events.
3. Therefore, human thoughts and actions are, without exception, causally determined by prior events.

Premise 1 is a statement of the thesis of universal causation. The only way to avoid determinism is to reject the thesis of universal causation. But is it plausible to reject this thesis? We all believe that changes in the weather, the behavior of our car, the interaction of chemicals, and every other kind of event in the physical world is the necessary result of previous causes. However, libertarians like to think that human behavior is an exception to the rest of nature, because they believe that our choices (including those of the determinists) are freely arrived at and not determined by prior events. The determinist would reply that the defenders of free will are being inconsistent. Why should we think that what we do is somehow immune from the sort of causal necessity that operates in the rest of the world?

It is important to be clear about the fact that the determinist is claiming that every event is 100 percent determined by prior causes. Most defenders of free will would acknowledge that we have certain psychological tendencies (one person tends to like crowds and another prefers solitude) and would agree that we are influenced by the way we were raised. However, the recognition that we all have certain behavioral tendencies and we all have influences on our behavior falls short of the thesis that everything you think, feel, choose, and do is 100 percent determined by the causes acting on you. The issue of universal causation offers only two extremes and no middle ground. Either *all* human behavior is determined by previous causes (determinism), or *some* human behavior is not determined by previous causes (libertarianism).

It is also important to realize that this issue is not one of personal preference. You miss the point if you say, "It's fine for the determinists if they like to think that their actions are controlled by previous causes, but as for me, I prefer to think my behavior is free." We are not talking about attitudes toward life here but about the nature of reality. Either the determinist is right about the way reality works and the libertarian is wrong, or vice versa. The truth about this issue has nothing to do with what view of human nature you find subjectively pleasing to believe.

Typically, determinists believe that all of reality is physical in nature and that all events are controlled by natural laws. However, some thinkers are **theological determinists** who believe that God is the ultimate cause of everything that happens in the world, including human actions. According to this form of determinism, you make the choices that you do because God made you the sort of person that you are. Hence, all your actions were predetermined by God before the creation of the world.

theological determinist one who believes that God is the ultimate cause of everything that happens in the world, including human actions

THOUGHT EXPERIMENT

Does Theism Imply Determinism?

How would you respond to the following argument?

Theism (belief in God) logically implies determinism, for the following reasons. Assuming that there is a God, when he created the world he knew ahead of time that you would be born and that you would make all the choices you did in the past and will make in the future. If he did not want you to do the things you have done, then he would have created a world

(Continued . . .)

(. . . continued)

in which you were never born or he would have created a world in which you turned out to be a different sort of person than the one he actually created. Furthermore, he could have made you a person that made other choices. Hence, you and your choices are a product of God's creation in the same way that Hamlet and his choices are a product of Shakespeare's creation.

One of the advantages of determinism is that if it is true, a science of human behavior is possible. Such behavioral sciences as psychology, sociology, and economics attempt to formulate laws that allow us to predict and explain human behavior. Although these sciences are still incomplete, it would be hard to argue that we have learned nothing about human behavior from the research done in these disciplines. The question is, will it ever be possible to have a complete science of human behavior or at least one that is complete enough to explain the causes of human thoughts, emotions, and actions the way the biologist, chemist, physicist, and astronomer explain the causes of events in nature?

Typically, we think of human behavior as the result of psychological factors such as our beliefs, desires, attitudes, emotions, motives, intentions, values, and personality. Because these factors are considered to be "internal," we feel as though we are not causally determined by external forces (unlike the motion of a billiard ball). But where did your personality come from? Did you decide what it would be? How did you come to have the moral values that you have? If you say that you simply chose them, what caused you to choose one set of values over another set? You have not finished explaining your action by saying, "I *wanted* to do it." The question still remains, "What caused you to want the things that you do?" It seems likely that our psychological makeup did not spring up spontaneously from nowhere. The determinist would insist that your choice of a particular course of action and your possession of certain values and desires are facts about the world that need explaining just as much as the fact that you were born with a certain hair color or that you have the flu.

That much of your behavior originates from within (unlike the billiard ball) is consistent with the determinist's claims. Everything we choose to do is a result of our psychological state and the surrounding circumstances or external stimuli at a

PHILOSOPHY
in the
MARKETPLACE

Pose the following questions to five acquaintances, and record their answers *and* the reasons for their answers. When you are finished gathering responses, decide which person gave you the strongest reasons for his or her position.

• Will science ultimately be able to explain you completely and adequately? The "you" that is to be explained includes your personality, values, choices, and actions. Why?

particular time. Consequently, the picture the determinist paints concerning the cause of an action looks like this:

$$\boxed{\textbf{Psychological State}} \ + \ \boxed{\textbf{External Circumstances}} \ \rightarrow \ \textbf{Behavior}$$

Your psychological state is the immediate, determining cause of your behavior in a given situation, but your psychological state was itself the product of a multitude of previous causes.

Response to Objections

A number of objections are typically raised against determinism. I will examine four of them and present the determinist's response. In each case, consider whether you think the determinist gives an adequate reply.

1. *When I make a choice, I have the undeniable feeling that the choice is free.* Many of us resist the notion that there are causes of our behavior. We like to think of ourselves as free. Indeed, we typically have the feeling that we are acting freely. But feeling we are free and actually being free are two different matters. The determinist would say that we feel we are free because we are ignorant of all the external and internal forces (physical and psychological) acting on us.

2. *When I make a choice, I could always have chosen differently.* We have the sense that there is nothing inevitable about the choices we make because we can imagine ourselves acting differently than we did in the past. Let us suppose, for example, that a young woman has to decide between a scholarship offering her a free education at Middleline University (an adequate but quite ordinary state school) and an opportunity to go, without a scholarship and at great expense, to Highstatus University, a very prestigious school. Suppose she chooses Highstatus U. but insists she could have gone to the other school if she had chosen to do so. Doesn't it seem as though she made a free choice and was not compelled to decide as she did?

How does the determinist respond to the "I could have done otherwise" argument? The determinist would claim that whenever you say "I could have done otherwise," you simply mean, "I would have done otherwise if I had wanted to, which is to say, if those psychological states that determined my action had been different." In our example, the woman's desire to go to the prestigious school was stronger than her desire to save money. She could have chosen otherwise only if her psychological makeup at the time had been different. Given her psychological state and the external circumstances, her choice was inevitable. Notice that we often think about "what could have been" even when we know an event was determined by previous causes. Suppose you are driving along a mountain road and a huge boulder comes crashing down, hitting the highway behind you where you were a half second ago. You say, "I could have been killed." But what you mean is that if the causes acting on the boulder had been different, the results would have been tragically different. You do not mean that the boulder could have freely behaved differently from the way it did, given all the causes acting upon it. So when you say, "I could have done otherwise," you're saying that if your psychological state had been different or if the external circumstances had been different, you would have acted differently. But given your psychological state and the external conditions, your behavior was just as inevitable as that of the boulder.

 THOUGHT EXPERIMENT

Decisions

Think about some decision you made that had a lot of significance for you (call it decision A). Now, relive your making of that decision in your imagination, but imagine yourself making a different decision (call it decision B). Do you find that you also need to imagine yourself having different beliefs, attitudes, motives, or desires in order to produce a different decision? If so, is the determinist correct in saying that our decisions are a product of our psychological states? If you can imagine yourself making a different decision without a change in your psychological state, then why did your original psychological state produce decision A when it could have equally produced decision B? Is there some component of your decision making that is random and uncaused? Does it make sense to say that purely random behavior is any more free than determined behavior?

3. *The fact that sometimes I have to deliberate to make a decision proves that I am not determined.* Another reason we feel free is that we frequently have to deliberate at length when we have trouble making up our minds. In such situations, we feel as though the decision is not already "programmed" within us, but that the outcome is entirely up to what we freely decide. If our behavior is determined, why is it sometimes so hard to make a decision?

In this situation, according to the determinist, we are caught between two conflicting causes, each one pulling us in a different direction. For example, we want to earn money for the summer, but we also want to travel with friends. Each choice has positive and negative aspects (more money means less fun, more fun in traveling means less money). Our difficulty in deciding is a sign that the causal determinants acting on us are almost equal. If we do make a decision, it is because the marginally stronger desire won out over the weaker one. The fact that we have these conflicting desires is, itself, the result of our causal history.

4. *It is impossible to predict another person's behavior.* While agreeing that a person's behavior may not be perfectly *predictable in practice,* the determinist would say that all human behavior is *predictable in principle.* We may never be 100 percent

accurate in predicting an individual's behavior because a human's psychological makeup is so complex that we cannot know someone's total psychological state in detail. To use an analogy, we cannot predict the weather perfectly. However, we do know enough about its causes to make some fairly good probability judgments. The reason that our predictions are not perfect is that the variables that affect the weather's behavior are too complex and numerous to make an accurate prediction possible.

Even though the behavior of the weather is not predictable in detail, we do not suppose that this unpredictability is because the forces of nature have free will to do as they please. We recognize that the weather's behavior conforms perfectly to the forces of causal necessity such that if we had perfect knowledge of all the variables, we would be able to predict every detail of this weekend's weather. Similarly, the determinist claims, *if* we knew *all* the causes operating on you at a particular time, then your behavior would be as predictable as the rolling of a billiard ball. However, we do know enough about human psychology to know in general how people will behave. In fact, isn't it true that the more you get to know a person, the more you can anticipate how he or she will react to a particular situation?

THE DENIAL OF MORAL RESPONSIBILITY

Thus far, we have discussed the first two pillars of hard determinism: the problems with libertarianism and the positive case for determinism. These pillars are shared with compatibilism, the other form of determinism. It is the third pillar, the denial of moral responsibility, that sets the hard determinist apart from the compatibilist. We are morally responsible for an action when we can be justly praised or blamed for it and are capable of deserving either reward or punishment. The muscle spasm that causes your arm to jerk could not be helped; you could not be blamed for this behavior because it was just something that happened to you. The question is, If we are completely determined, can we be responsible for any of our behavior? Under these circumstances, is it meaningful to say that some actions are voluntary? The hard determinist claims that determinism is incompatible with moral responsibility, whereas the compatibilist believes the two can be reconciled.

To begin thinking about this issue, consider the following passage from Samuel Butler's utopian satire *Erewhon* in which a judge is passing sentence on a prisoner. The judge considers the possible defense that the prisoner was not responsible for his crime because he was a victim of an unfortunate childhood and past events that caused him to be the sort of person who violated the laws of the state.

- Do you agree that it is possible that this criminal's upbringing could prevent him from being morally responsible for his crimes?
- On the contrary, do you agree with the judge that a criminal's causal history is irrelevant and that it is just to punish him for any crimes he committed?

Erewhon[36]

"Prisoner at the bar, you have been accused of [a] great crime . . . and after an impartial trial before a jury of your countrymen, you have been found guilty. Against the justice of the verdict I can say nothing: the evidence against you was conclusive, and it only remains for me to pass such a sentence upon you as will satisfy the ends of the law. That sentence must be a very severe one. It pains me much to see one who is yet so young, and whose prospects in life were otherwise so excellent brought to this distressing condition by a constitution which I can only regard as radically vicious; but yours is no case for compassion: this is not your first offense: you have led a career of crime and have only profited by the leniency shown you upon past occasions to offend yet more seriously against the laws and institutions of your country. . . .

"It is all very well for you to say that you came of unhealthy parents, and had a severe accident in your childhood which permanently undermined your constitution; excuses such as these are the ordinary refuge of the criminal; but they cannot for one moment be listened to by the ear of justice. I am not here to enter upon curious metaphysical questions as to the origin of this or that—questions to which there would be no end were their introduction once tolerated. . . . There is no question of how you came to be wicked, but only this—namely, are you wicked or not? This has been decided in the affirmative, neither can I hesitate for a single moment to say that it has been decided justly. You are a bad and dangerous person, and stand branded in the eyes of your fellow countrymen with one of the most heinous known offences."

No doubt, many citizens would agree with these sentiments. On the evening news, we hear of crafty defense attorneys arguing that their client was not responsible for committing a crime because he or she was under psychological distress or had a deprived childhood or was temporarily insane. Are these defenses nothing more than feeble attempts to excuse criminals for making immoral and illegal choices? In response to these courtroom tactics, we might be provoked to say, "Who cares about the defendant's upbringing, past experiences, or psychological problems? Did he commit the crime or didn't he? If he did, then to jail with him!" However, Butler has played a joke on us. The "crime" in the previous passage is pulmonary consumption. The judge points out that the defendant had been arrested for previous offenses such as aggravated bronchitis and did not learn a lesson. The point of the satire, however, is that it is foolish to hold a sick person responsible for conditions over which he or she had no control. Butler believed that our criminal system is just as unreasonable as the one in Erewhon. If every event in the universe has a cause, then both the criminal's and the saint's behavior is the outcome of causal processes that they were powerless to prevent. If Butler is correct, then the criminal, like the person with a lung disease, should not be punished but should be treated and his condition modified so that he will no longer be harmful to society.

Remember that both the hard determinist and the defender of free will (the libertarian) are incompatibilists because they agree with the statement that if we are determined, then we lack the freedom necessary to be morally responsible. They would also both agree with the statement that if we are not determined, then we do have the freedom necessary to be morally responsible. For both the hard determinist and the libertarian, metaphysical freedom is a necessary condition for moral responsibility. Even if we have circumstantial freedom when we act (e.g., no one is holding a gun to our head), if our will is not free of determining causes, then we can no more be held responsible for our actions than we can for the genes we have inherited. Of course, the hard determinist and the libertarian differ over the first clause of each statement, so they differ in their conclusions concerning our capacity to be morally responsible. While the hard determinists recognize that we do make choices, they believe these choices result from our personality, values, interests, desires, or motives, which are ultimately the products of deterministic causes. For this reason, moral responsibility, according to the hard determinist, is not a human possibility.

A good example of the hard determinists' denial of moral responsibility can be found in the courtroom strategies of Clarence Darrow (1867–1938), one of America's most famous criminal attorneys. In a celebrated case, Darrow defended two teenagers for murdering a fourteen-year-old boy. The confessed killers were Nathan Leopold Jr. (age nineteen) and Richard Loeb (age eighteen). Both came from wealthy Chicago families and were brilliant students; Leopold had already graduated from the University of Chicago and Loeb from the University of Michigan. The murder was the result of an intellectual "experiment" in which they attempted to commit the perfect crime. When they were captured, an outraged public demanded the death penalty. However, Clarence Darrow argued that the two boys were the helpless victims of their heredity and environment. Hence, they were no more responsible for their crime, he said, than they were for the color of their eyes. After Darrow had spoken for twelve hours presenting his final arguments, the silence of the courtroom was broken only by the judge's weeping. The jury was moved by his arguments and chose life sentences for the boys over the death penalty. The following passage is an excerpt from Darrow's summation. Find the phrases that indicate that Darrow was not only a determinist, but a hard determinist as well.

FROM CLARENCE DARROW
The Leopold and Loeb Trial [37]

This weary old world goes on, begetting, with birth and with living and with death; and all of it is blind from the beginning to the end. I do not know what it was that made these boys do this mad act, but I do know there is a reason for it. I know that they did not beget themselves. I know that any one of an infinite number of causes reaching back to the beginning might be working out in these boy's minds, whom you are asked to hang in malice and in hatred and injustice. . . .

Nature is strong and she is pitiless. She works in her own mysterious way, and we are her victims. We have not much to do with it ourselves. Nature takes this job in hand, and we play our parts. In the words of Omar Khayyam, we are only:

But helpless pieces in the game He plays
Upon this checkerboard of nights and days;
Hither and thither moves and checks, and slays,
And one by one back in the closet lays.

What had this boy to do with it? He was not his own father; he was not his own mother; he was not his own grandparents. All of this was handed to him. He did not surround himself with governesses and wealth. He did not make himself. And yet he is to be compelled to pay. . . .

I know that one of two things happened to Richard Loeb: that this terrible crime was inherent in his organism, and came from some ancestor; or that it came through his education and his training after he was born. . . .

To believe that any boy is responsible for himself or his early training is an absurdity that no lawyer or judge should be guilty of today. Somewhere this came to the boy. If his failing came from his heredity, I do not know where or how. None of us are bred perfect and pure; and the color of our hair, the color of our eyes, our stature, the weight and fineness of our brain, and everything about us could, with full knowledge, be traced with absolute certainty to somewhere. . . .

If it did not come that way, then I know that if he was normal, if he had been understood, if he had been trained as he should have been it would not have happened. . . .

Every effort to protect society is an effort toward training the youth to keep the path. Every bit of training in the world proves it, and it likewise proves that it sometimes fails. I know that if this boy had been understood and properly trained—properly for him—and the training that he got might have been the very best for someone; but if it had been the proper training for him he would not be in this courtroom today with the noose above his head. If there is responsibility any-where, it is back of him; somewhere in the infinite number of his ancestors, or in his surroundings, or in both. And I submit, Your Honor, that under every princi-ple of natural justice, under every principle of conscience, of right, and of law, he should not be made responsible for the acts of someone else.

What are the practical consequences of such a view? Should we release all the criminals from jail, since they were not morally responsible for their crimes any more than they were for their eye color? Darrow's position was that we should cure the ills in society that cause criminal behavior. Most hard determinists claim that the criminal is someone with a psychological problem who should be treated the way we treat someone who has a physical disease. We confine someone with an infectious disease to prevent harm to others even though the patient may not have done anything to contract the disease. Furthermore, we would try to cure the patient so that he or she no longer carries the infection.

As Butler's satirical piece suggests, the fact that you are a law-abiding citizen and others are criminals is the result of differences between your background and those of criminals, just as there are differences between a person who came from a healthy home and one who came from a disease-ridden home. How many social psycho-paths came from normal, loving homes? Hence, the hard determinist would say that to protect society, it is reasonable to confine criminals if they cannot help but commit crimes. The unpleasant consequences of crime will be determining causes that will help prevent future crimes. While removed from society, the criminal can receive therapy or behavior modification that will change the psychological state that resulted in the criminal act in the first place. What the hard determinist would not agree to is punishment for punishment's sake or punishment that assumes the criminal had the freedom to do otherwise than he or she did.

THOUGHT EXPERIMENT

Determinism and Differences in Behavior

Critics of determinism frequently point to cases in which two people, even two siblings, grew up under the same adverse circumstances, but one became a criminal and the other a respectable citizen. How would the determinist respond to the fact that the (appar-ently) same social conditions produce radically different behaviors?

We can use the following illustration to see how the determinist would tackle this objection. Take two identical pieces of paper and hold them in front of you side by side. Now release them at the same time. The papers will twist and turn in different ways as they drift to the ground and will land in different positions.

- Since the initial conditions seemed the same but the results were different, does it follow that the papers must have freely chosen how they would fall?

(Continued . . .)

(. . . continued)
- Isn't it reasonable to assume that a difference in two effects must be traced to a difference in their causes?
- According to the determinist, what would be the application of this analogy to human behavior?

BENEDICT (BARUCH) SPINOZA (1632–1677)

Spinoza's Life

Spinoza was a seventeenth-century philosopher who is noted for his vigorous denial of human freedom. Spinoza's parents were Portuguese Jews who fled to Holland to escape religious persecution. As a young man, Spinoza showed great promise and was raised to be a rabbi. However, at age twenty, he began to study philosophy and encountered what was then considered to be the "radical" ideas of the French philosopher Descartes. As Spinoza's own philosophy began to develop, it expanded beyond the boundaries of orthodox Jewish teachings. Finally, when he was nearly twenty-four years old, the Ecclesiastical Council condemned him as a heretic and forbade any member of the Jewish community from even speaking with him. Spinoza spent the rest of his life writing philosophy while supporting himself by grinding lenses for scientific instruments.

Spinoza's Determinism

pantheism the belief that God constitutes the whole of reality and that everything in nature, including individual persons, are modes or aspects of God's being

Spinoza's position on the nature of reality is called **pantheism,** for he believed that God constituted the whole of reality. It follows from this belief that everything in nature, including individual persons, are modes or aspects of God's being. Spinoza was also a thoroughgoing determinist, for he believed that all things existed and happened by necessity. Even God does not act from freedom of the will, because his actions flow from the necessities built into his own nature. Furthermore, God's nature could not be other than it is, for either this would mean that God was caused by something outside himself and, thereby, he would not be supreme, or it would mean that God's nature was the cause of his own nature, which would be absurd since the effect would be identical to the cause. Hence, for Spinoza, "all things follow from the eternal decree of God, according to that same necessity by which it follows from the essence of a triangle that its three angles are equal to two right angles."[38] Spinoza thought that we could find peace of mind if we realized that all things are as they necessarily must be. He claimed this philosophical viewpoint would free us from the tyranny of our emotions, because it is useless to be agitated by the emotions of fear, anger, regret, hope, or joy when the details of our lives are as necessary as the properties of a triangle.

The implications of Spinoza's position for freedom of the will are clear. Free will is an illusion based on inadequate knowledge of the divine nature and of how the whole scheme of things logically proceeds from that nature. Spinoza suggested that if a stone traveling through the air were conscious, it would feel as though it were free and were choosing to move and land where it does.[39] To see the force of Spinoza's point, I have constructed the following imaginary dialogue between Spinoza and the stone.

A Dialogue with a Virtuous Stone

SPINOZA: Mr. Stone, I am going to let go of you and we will see what happens. (Spinoza lets go of the stone, and naturally, it falls to the ground.)

SPINOZA: Mr. Stone, when I let go of you just then, you fell downward. Why is that?

STONE: I fell downward because I chose to. I could have flown upward if I had wanted to do so.

SPINOZA: In that case, show me how you can fly upward when I release you this time.
(Spinoza lets go of the stone, and once again, it falls downward.)

SPINOZA: What's wrong? Why didn't you fly upward?

STONE: I could have chosen to fly upward, but I didn't. Flying up is an immoral, disgusting thing to do. It would be obscene. No self-respecting stone would do anything other than go down. I've been taught to know the difference between right and wrong, you see.

SPINOZA: In other words, you were completely free to fall down and completely free to choose to fly upward. However, you will always choose the former alternative because of your personal values and morals.

STONE: That is exactly right. Everything I do is based on my own, free choices. Other things such as planets and cannonballs may be determined to behave a certain way, but stones have free will.

SPINOZA: I see.

 STOP AND THINK

Think about a decision you made recently in which you had to choose between what was morally right and wrong. On what did you base your decision? Did you have the freedom to make a choice different from the one you actually made? What inclined your will one way rather than another? Is it possible that you are like Spinoza's stone, thinking that your decision was completely free when it was actually determined by psychological forces acting on you? Why?

According to Spinoza, we are like that stone in all relevant respects. First, we think that we are an exception to the rest of nature. "Whereas causal laws control what happens in the world outside of me," we say, "my uncaused free will allows me to choose what I will do." But are we as foolish as the stone in thinking we are the grand exception to all of nature? Second, Spinoza says people are like the stone in that they

> are deceived because they think themselves free, and the sole reason for thinking so is that they are conscious of their own actions, and ignorant of the causes by which those actions are determined.[40]

In other words, if we correctly understood reality, we would realize that events (including human choices) do not spring into being out of a vacuum. Everything that happens is a product of preceding causes. Put the same stone in the same set of circumstances and its behavior would be the same in each case. According to the determinist, if we could keep constant the exact psychological state you were in when you made a particular choice (who to date, what school to attend, what subject to major in) and if we could put you back into the exact same set of circumstances, your behavior would always be the same. Obviously, you sometimes change your mind or choose differently from the way you did in the past. However, the hard determinist would say that it takes a difference to make a difference. If your choices change from what they were in the past, it is because of something different about your psychological state or something different about the circumstances.

B. F. SKINNER (1904–1990)

Skinner's Life

B. F. SKINNER
(1904–1990)

behaviorism a psychological theory that limits the scope of psychology to the scientific study of publicly observable behaviors and their causes while rejecting any explanations that refer to interior mental states or processes

The beginning of this section featured a passage from B. F. Skinner's novel, *Walden Two*. However, Skinner is best known not as a fiction writer but as the researcher who made behaviorism one of the most influential theories in the twentieth century. From his childhood years to the end of his life, Skinner had a fondness for gadgets, music, and literature. After graduating from college he had a brief and unsuccessful career as a literary writer. Upon reflection, Skinner realized that his interest as a writer had been in investigating human behavior and decided that psychology might be another way to achieve this goal. Consequently, he went on to earn a Ph.D. in psychology at Harvard University. After that, Skinner spent most of his career at Harvard, teaching and conducting his classic experiments on conditioning until his retirement in 1974. Throughout his long and illustrious career, he was one of the most influential advocates for behaviorism, presenting his theories in technical research articles as well as popular books.

The Theory of Behaviorism

Behaviorism is a psychological theory that limits the scope of psychology to the scientific study of publicly observable behaviors and their causes while rejecting any explanations that refer to interior mental states or processes. There are several varieties of behaviorism, but B. F. Skinner's **radical behaviorism** is the most interesting and controversial version of this theory. Skinner claims that all mental terms (*belief, desire, thinking,* and so on) can be reduced to scientific statements about behavioral probabilities. Just as the medical researcher seeks to study and control the causes of various diseases, so the behavioral scientist studies the causes of behavior. According to radical behaviorism, everything you do is the result of prior causes or conditioning, which is why psychology is a science.

radical behaviorism
B. F. Skinner's version of behaviorism that claims that all mental terms can be reduced to scientific statements about behavioral probabilities

THOUGHT EXPERIMENT

Influences on Behavior

Why do you do the things you do? What are the causes of your working hard in school (or not working hard)? Why did students in the 1970s wear Brady Bunch haircuts, gigantic collars, paisley shirts, and bell-bottoms, whereas you think those styles look goofy? What makes you prefer to dress the way you do? Why are you attracted to some persons and not to others? Do you choose what sorts of persons will attract you? What causes you to support a particular political candidate? What makes you obey the law (or not obey it)? How would your having been born in a completely different culture have affected your religious views, your taste in fashion, your food preferences, or your political views? Perhaps we can get a better focus on questions like these by considering the following scenario.

Suppose you tell a female friend something in confidence that is causing you anxiety. Consider the effect on your future behavior of each of the following consequences.

1. She gives you good advice that helps you with your problem.
2. She tells you she is deeply moved by the fact that you shared your innermost secrets with her.
3. Her response is neither negative nor positive, but you are less preoccupied with the problem by having talked about it.
4. She laughs at you and says this is the stupidest thing she has ever heard.
5. She tells everyone she meets about your secret.

Ask yourself in each case:

- What is the likelihood that you will tell her something in confidence again?
- What is the likelihood that you will continue to be her friend?

The questions in the thought experiment may help confirm Skinner's claim that his theory of human behavior is illustrated throughout our everyday life. Basically, his theory states that the behaviors we learn and repeat, as well as the behaviors we avoid or cease performing, are directly a function of the past consequences of those types of behaviors. A large number of those consequences are provided by society.

Controlling Behavior

Skinner first worked out his psychological theories by experimenting on rats and pigeons. He found that with the right sort of conditioning, he could teach pigeons to dance, to play Ping Pong, and to respond appropriately to linguistic symbols. While admitting that people are more complex than pigeons, Skinner insisted that the basic principles that govern our behavior are the same. Many psychologists agreed with him. His ideas were put to practical use in schools, mental hospitals, prisons, and business firms. Doctors using his techniques in mental hospitals found that they could make apathetic or rebellious patients behave more like healthy human beings. Similarly, psychologists tested these techniques with hardcore juvenile criminals in a youth center and found that reinforcing healthy behavior increased its frequency and extinguished unproductive patterns of behavior.

Skinner's behaviorism is clearly a form of *determinism*. Skinner readily concludes that "man is a machine in the sense that he is a complex system behaving in lawful ways."[41] What you do and what choices you make today are the inevitable result of the way you have been conditioned by past experiences and their consequences. Of course, as Frazier pointed out in his dialogue with Castle, we cannot always perfectly predict a person's behavior any more than we can perfectly predict the weather. However, in the case of the weather, we do not suppose that its unpredictability is due to the fact that it has a free will. Why not suppose that the situation is the same with respect to human actions? In both cases, the complexity of the variables make precise calculations impossible. In both cases, however, we can make fairly good probability judgments.

Not content to limit his theories to the discipline of psychology, Skinner developed his research into a large-scale philosophy of human nature and society. He believed that the science of behavior could solve all the problems related to human behavior. This solution would require, however, that we give up our belief in the "illusions" of human freedom, responsibility, and dignity. As Skinner expresses it,

> The free inner man who is held responsible for the behavior of the external biological organism is only a prescientific substitute for the kinds of causes which are discovered in the course of a scientific analysis. All these alternatives lie *outside* the individual.[42]

In denying that we are free and responsible for our behavior, Skinner is clearly a *hard determinist*. As a determinist and a scientist, Skinner believed that every event (including human behavior) has a cause. The astronomer studies the behavior of bodies in outer space, and the chemist studies the behavior of chemical elements under different conditions. Based on their observations and experiments, they formulate scientific laws that enable them to predict and control events in the world. Similarly, Skinner thought that once we improve our scientific knowledge of human behavior, we will be able to predict and control human behavior more effectively than we do now.

If the idea of controlling human behavior sounds chilling, Skinner would point out that control is the goal of many of our social interactions. Parents use various methods (such as persuasion, role modeling, punishment or reward, and verbal rebuke or praise) to make their children behave appropriately and develop into well-mannered, considerate, moral persons. Society uses various means to make its citizens' behavior consistent with the good of society. Education, religion, peer pressure, advertising, and the law are just a few of the ways in which society tries to influence and control our behavior. If we did not have the ability to predict and influence human behavior, civilization would be impossible. (Or so Skinner claims.)

In the following reading selection, Skinner analyzes the notion of creativity. Human creativity in art, poetry, and every other area of life is commonly thought to be based on free choices and free actions. In other words, we resist the notion that creativity is simply a product of environmental causes that act on the artist and for which he or she is not responsible. Skinner attempts to argue that even creativity can be explained on the basis of behaviorism. After reading all the sections, decide if you think he makes his case.

- Skinner compares having a baby to both producing a poem and giving his lecture. What would you guess will be the point of his comparison?
- In what ways does Skinner suggest the poet is like the hen?

FROM B. F. SKINNER

A Lecture on "Having" a Poem[43]

What I am going to say has the curious property of illustrating itself. The quotation marks in my title are intended to suggest that there is a sense in which having a poem is like having a baby, and in that sense I am in labor; I am having a lecture. In it I intend to raise the questions of whether I am actually originating anything and to what extent I deserve credit or blame. . . .

I am to compare having a poem with having a baby, and it will do no harm to start with a lower class of living things. Samuel Butler suggested the comparison years ago, when he said that a poet writes a poem as a hen lays an egg, and both feel better afterward.

But there are other points of similarity, and on one of them Butler built a whole philosophy of purposive evolution. The statement was current in early post-Darwinism days that "a hen is only an egg's way of making another egg." It is not, of course, a question of which comes first, though that is not entirely irrelevant. The issue is who *does* what, who *acts* to produce something and therefore deserves credit. Must we give the hen credit for the egg or the egg for the hen? Possibly it does not matter, since no one is seriously interested in defending the rights of hen or egg, but something of the same sort can be said about a poet, and then it does matter. Does the poet create, originate, initiate the thing called a poem, or is his behavior merely the product of his genetic and environmental histories?

- In what sense is the mother responsible or not responsible for the positive characteristics of her baby?
- What is the comparison Skinner makes between the mother and the poet?
- According to Skinner, what is the ultimate origin of the elements of a poem?

The issue will be clearer if we turn to a biological parallel—moving from the oviparous hen to the viviparous human mother. We say that a woman "has" a baby, where "has" means little more than possess. To have a baby is to come into possession of it. The woman who does so is then a mother, and the child is her child. But what is the nature of her contribution? She is not responsible for the skin color, eye color, strength, size, intelligence, talents, or any other feature of her baby. She gave it half its genes, but she got those from *her* parents. She could, of course, have damaged the baby. She could have aborted it. She could have caught rubella at the wrong time or taken drugs, and as a result the baby would have been defective. *But she made no positive contribution.*

A biologist has no difficulty in describing the role of the mother. She is a place, a locus in which a very important biological process takes place. She supplies protection, warmth, and nourishment, but she does not design the baby who profits from them. The poet is also a locus, a place in which certain genetic and environmental causes come together to have a common effect. Unlike a mother, the poet has access to his poem during gestation. He may tinker with it. A poem seldom makes its appearance in completed form. Bits and pieces *occur* to the poet, who rejects or allows them to stand, and who puts them together to *compose* a poem. But they come from his past history, verbal and otherwise, and he has had to learn how to put them together.

- In what ways is nature creative and a producer of novelty?
- According to Skinner, how do novelties emerge in nature?
- What results from the fact that the poet "is not aware of the origins of his behavior"?

But can this interpretation be correct if a poem is unquestionably new? Certainly the plays of Shakespeare did not exist until he wrote them. Possibly all their parts could be traced by an omniscient scholar to Shakespeare's verbal and nonverbal histories, but Shakespeare must have served some additional function. How otherwise are we to explain the creation of something new?

The answer is again to be found in biology. A little more than a hundred years ago the act of creation was debated in a very different field. The living things on the surface of the earth show a fantastic variety—far beyond the variety in the works of Shakespeare—and they had long been attributed to a creative Mind. . . .

The key term in Darwin's title is "Origin." Novelty could be explained without appeal to prior design if random changes in structure were selected by their consequences. It was the contingencies of survival that created new forms. Selection is a special kind of causality, much less conspicuous than the push-pull causality of nineteenth-century physics, and Darwin's discovery may have appeared so late in the history of human thought for that reason. The selective action of the consequences of behavior was also overlooked for a long time.

The poet often knows that some part of his history is contributing to the poem he is writing. He may, for example, reject a phrase because he sees that he has borrowed it from something he has read. But it is quite impossible for him to be aware of all his history, and it is in this sense that he does not know where his behavior comes from. Having a poem, like having a baby, is in large part a matter of exploration and discovery, and both poet and mother are often surprised by what they produce. And because the poet is not aware of the origins of his behavior, he is likely to attribute it to a creative mind, an "unconscious" mind, perhaps, or a mind belonging to someone else—to a muse, for example, whom he has invoked to come and write his poem for him.

 STOP AND THINK

Do ideas sometimes just pop into your head? How can you have ideas that you do not consciously create and thoughts that you cannot control? Where do they come from? What would Skinner say?

- In the following passage, what does Skinner mean by "the autonomy of the poet"? Why does he reject it?
- What does Skinner say are the benefits of learning about the causes that produce creative ideas?

Writing a poem is the sort of thing men and women do as men and women, having a baby is the sort of thing a woman does as a woman, and laying an egg is the sort of thing a hen does as a hen. To deny a creative contribution does not destroy man qua man or woman qua woman any more than Butler's phrase destroys hen qua hen. . . .

What is threatened, of course, is the autonomy of the poet. The autonomous is the uncaused, and the uncaused is miraculous, and the miraculous is God. For the second time in little more than a century a theory of selections by consequences is threatening a traditional belief in a creative mind. And is it not rather strange that although we have abandoned that belief with respect to the creation of the world, we fight so desperately to preserve it with respect to the creation of a poem?

But is there anything wrong with a supportive myth? Why not continue to believe in our creative powers if the belief gives us satisfaction? The answer lies in the future of poetry. To accept a wrong explanation because it flatters us is to run the risk of missing a right one—one that in the long run may offer more by way of "satisfaction." Poets know all too well how long a sheet of paper remains a *carte blanche*. To wait for genius or a genie is to make a virtue of ignorance. If poetry is

Hard Determinism   357

a good thing, if we want more of it and better, and if writing poems is a rewarding experience, then we should look afresh at its sources.

Perhaps the future of poetry is not that important, but I have been using a poem simply as an example. I could have developed the same theme in art, music, fiction, scholarship, science, invention—in short, wherever we speak of *original* behavior. We say that we "have" ideas, again in the simple sense of coming into possession of them. An idea "occurs to us" or "comes to mind." And if for "idea" we read "the behavior said to express an idea," we come no closer to an act of creation. By analyzing the genetic and individual histories responsible for our behavior, we may learn how to be more original. The task is not to think of new forms of behavior but to create an environment in which they are likely to occur.

- What does Skinner think will be the outcome of having a "deliberate design" or "scientific analysis" of human behavior?
- Do you agree with his optimism? Why?
- At the end of the selection, how does Skinner characterize his own lecture and its origins?
- What sorts of conditions does he say would have made him write a different lecture?

Something of the sort has happened in the evolution of cultures. Over the centuries men and women have built a world in which they behave much more effectively than they could in a natural environment, but they have not done much of this by deliberate design. A culture evolves when new practices arise that make it more likely to survive. We have reached a stage in which our culture induces some of its members to be concerned for its survival. A kind of deliberate design is thus possible, and a scientific analysis is obviously helpful. We can build a world in which men and women will be better poets, better artists, better composers, better novelists, better scholars, scientists—in a word, better people. We can, in short, "have" a better world. . . .

And now my labor is over. I have had my lecture. I have no sense of fatherhood. If my genetic and personal histories had been different, I should have come into possession of a different lecture. If I deserve any credit at all, it is simply for having served as a place in which certain processes could take place. I shall interpret your polite applause in that light.

 STOP AND THINK

- What is your assessment of Skinner's account of creativity?
- Defend one of the following two positions: Skinner does (does not) deserve credit for his lecture.
- How does his lecture demonstrate the fact that he is a hard determinist?

LOOKING THROUGH THE HARD DETERMINIST'S LENS

1. Every society is based on the assumption that what we do can affect people's behavior. Parents raise their children a certain way, the schools try to produce informed, responsible citizens, and the laws try to prevent people from committing crimes. Granted, we sometimes fail in these tasks. But when our methods of changing behavior fail, we seek causal explanations for these failures. We say that our children were influenced too much by television, our educational methods need changing, or a particular criminal was too warped by an antisocial background for the laws to have any deterrent effect. If behavior is not caused, then why do we even try to produce certain behaviors in people? How do our parenting practices and our educational and criminal systems support the determinist's claim that there are causal factors behind every behavior?

2. How would a determinist explain each of the following items?
   a. your choice of friends
   b. the career choices you have made or are considering
   c. your moral values
   d. why some people, such as Mother Teresa, turn out to be humanitarians and others, such as Adolf Hitler, become tyrants

3. If hard determinism is true, people are not morally responsible for their actions. If our society accepted this claim, what changes would be made to our public policy? How would these changes affect our treatment of criminals?

EXAMINING THE STRENGTHS AND WEAKNESSES OF HARD DETERMINISM

Positive Evaluation

1. Does it seem that determinism captures some of the basic intuitions we assume in our daily life? For example, we do assume that the more we understand a person's personality, the better we are able to anticipate or predict his or her behavior. We assume that we are able to causally influence other people's behavior. We assume that a person who does something (risks her life, commits a heinous crime, shows mercy to his enemy, turns down a job offer) can offer an explanation for what he or she did. Don't these facts lend support to determinism?

2. Since science has opened up our understanding of nature by formulating the laws that explain events, isn't it likely that a science of behavior will likewise enable us to understand the causes that determine human actions?

3. Isn't it a strength of determinism that it eliminates the need to postulate the existence of events such as acts of the will for which there is no cause or explanation?

4. Doesn't it make sense to say with the hard determinist that we cannot blame or praise people for events they could not control? If our actions and choices are the result of a long series of causes, just as our eye color, our physical condition, and our personalities are, can we really be held responsible for them?

Negative Evaluation

1. Have Skinner and the other determinists made an illegitimate jump from the observation that "*some* behavior is conditioned and predictable" to the much stronger claim that "*all* behavior is conditioned and predictable"? Do Skinner's experimental results, at best, support the claim that "it is useful to look for the causes of behavior" (methodological behaviorism), instead of the stronger claim that "all behavior is caused" (radical behaviorism)?

2. Does it make sense to develop and defend a theory that says that all human activities, including that of developing theories and defending them, are ultimately the product of external causes over which we have no control and for which we are not responsible? Does determinism imply that our philosophical beliefs are as much the outcome of a series of causes as is the production of an egg within a chicken? Does it follow from this implication that you are conditioned to be either a determinist or a libertarian and there is nothing you can do about it? If so, is this conclusion a problem? Is there any room in such a theory for notions such as rational or logical or even true? If not, is the lack of such notions a problem for this theory?

3. If hard determinism is true, there is no such thing as moral responsibility. According to this position, some people have been conditioned to behave in socially acceptable ways and others have been determined to act antisocially. What do you think are the implications of doing away with the notion of moral responsibility? Do you think this is even possible?

3.7 LIBERTARIANISM

 LEADING QUESTIONS: *Libertarianism*

1. Think about a time when you had difficulty making up your mind. Perhaps you did not feel strongly drawn to either of two alternatives, but you finally just decided on one of them. Or maybe you were strongly inclined toward two completely opposite alternatives and, after a great deal of struggle and deliberation, you resolutely made your choice. Doesn't the fact that your choice required deliberation indicate that it was not already "programmed" in you but that the decision was, at that moment, entirely up to you?

2. Think of something you did that was entirely spontaneous and out of character. Perhaps your friends were surprised to see you behave in such an unpredictable way. Doesn't this action indicate that sometimes we simply initiate our behavior on the spot without it being the inevitable and predictable outcome of antecedent causes?

3. As you matured and became your own person, didn't you find that you had to choose which of your parents' values and beliefs you would continue to embrace and which ones you wanted to modify or reject? Because we can sometimes choose which influences we will allow to guide our lives and which ones we won't, doesn't this choice indicate that we have some measure of freedom over our lives and are not just conditioned to behave in a certain fashion?

SURVEYING THE CASE FOR LIBERTARIANISM

Recall that the libertarian claims that (1) we are not determined, and because of that fact, (2) we do have freedom of the will (metaphysical freedom) and (3) we have the capacity to be morally responsible for our actions. In setting out the case for libertarianism, first, I examine some of the mistakes that determinists allegedly make (according to libertarians); next, I examine three views of freedom corresponding to three types of antideterminism; finally, I examine some of the positive arguments for libertarianism.

THE PROBLEMS WITH DETERMINISM

The Determinist Makes an Unwarranted Generalization from a Limited Amount of Evidence

The determinist may be able to show that our genetic makeup, our biochemical condition, or our past experiences have an influence on our behavior and choices. But there is a difference between being *influenced* by previous causes and being totally *determined* by them. Influences may create certain tendencies, but their outcome is neither inevitable nor perfectly predictable. The presence of a determining cause, however, necessarily produces the effect and makes it perfectly predictable. For example, if you had a religious upbringing as a child, it would not be surprising if this religious background had an influence on your present values and beliefs. However, since many people break with their parents' belief system, it seems clear that our upbringing can influence us but not determine us. Furthermore, the most that the determinist can claim, based on experiments and case studies, is that "*some* behavior is determined." But it is a big leap from that statement to the conclusion that "*all* behavior is determined." Determinism, therefore, can never be decisively proven. Before considering the next criticism, think through the following thought experiment.

Reasons and Causes

In which of the following cases would you say that Maria is rational in believing that "Candidate Dale Miller is the best choice for mayor"?

1. Maria has analyzed Miller's platform and believes that his ideas are better than those of any other candidate.
2. Maria has a strange brain tumor that causes her to like Miller, but without that tumor, she would support Miller's opponent.
3. A Freudian psychiatrist analyzes Maria and finds that Miller's physical appearance subconsciously reminds her of her father, whom she adored. So she supports Miller, thinking she likes him because of his policies when she is really working out her childhood relationship with her father.

- Is there a difference between behavior that is caused and behavior that is based on reasons? How could this difference be characterized?
- When we find that someone's thoughts or choices are based on causes over which the person has no control, doesn't this discovery diminish the degree to which we take this person seriously?
- What is our reaction when we find that our *own* thoughts or choices are based on causes that control us and not our own reasons ("I was tired," "I felt pressured," "I was irritable from too much coffee")? Doesn't this discovery diminish the degree to which we feel that those thoughts and choices are our own?

Determinism Undermines the Notion of Rationality

The previous thought experiment suggested two ways that you may arrive at a belief. It can be the result of *causes* within or without you over which you have no control, or it can be the product of *reasons* that you have freely chosen to guide your behavior. We tend not to take seriously beliefs that are the result of impersonal, irrational causes. However, the determinist would have to say that the brain tumor or the Freudian dynamics that caused Susan's behavior are not exceptions to the normal course of events, because all behavior is deterministically caused. According to this viewpoint, the psychological factors that produce your deliberations, thoughts, and behavior are ultimately the result of external causes over which you have no control. But if your thoughts are the result of impersonal, irrational causes, can they really be considered rational?

The British astronomer Arthur Eddington expressed this argument in the following way:

If the mathematical argument in my mind is compelled to reach the conclusion which a deterministic system of physical law has preordained that my hands shall write down, then reasoning must be explained away as a process quite other than that which I feel it to be. But my whole respect for reasoning is based on the hypothesis that it *is* what I feel it to be.[44]

Determinism Confuses the Methodological Assumptions of Science with Metaphysical Conclusions

According to the deterministic psychologist B. F. Skinner, "A scientific analysis of behavior must, I believe, assume that a person's behavior is controlled by his genetic and environmental histories rather than by the person himself as an initiating, creative agent."[45] But two objections may be raised against Skinner's account of behavioral science. First, this methodological assumption is not necessary. Can't a behavioral scientist study the tendencies or probabilistic regularities within human behavior without assuming that behavior is 100 percent determined or inevitable down to the last detail? Second, this methodological assumption may be useful without being a true description of reality. The methodological principle "it is helpful to think of humans *as though* they are mechanisms ruled by causes" may be helpful in guiding us to seek out the regularities in human behavior. However, that assumption in no way guarantees that such causal regularities are present in all behavior. To borrow an analogy from the twentieth-century British philosopher Bertrand Russell (one that was used for other purposes), the prospector bases his activity on the principle "always look for gold," but that principle does not imply that there will always be gold to be found. Likewise, it is fruitful for the behavioral scientist to follow the rule "always look for causes," but that rule doesn't mean that all human behavior is caused. Before looking at the libertarian's positive arguments, we need to examine the different views of freedom held in the antideterminist camp.

THREE VIEWS OF FREEDOM

There are three varieties of antideterminism. All three of these views argue that we have free will. In other words, they all agree that at least some of our behavior is free from determining causes. These three views are indeterminism, agency theory, and radical existentialist freedom. I discuss each one in turn.

Indeterminism

The **indeterminist** contends that, contrary to determinism, some events are uncaused. This view has become popular as a result of startling discoveries in twentieth-century physics. Previously, Newtonian physics had assumed that every event in the universe had a cause. This assumption was illustrated by the French astronomer Pierre-Simone Laplace (1749–1827), who claimed that if someone knew the position and motion of every particle in the universe, he or she could predict the state of every particle at any future time. However, with the rise of quantum mechanics in the twentieth century, physicists now say that Laplace was wrong. According to the Heisenberg Uncertainty Principle (named after the scientist Werner Heisenberg, who discovered it), there is a significant amount of unpredictability at the subatomic level. Heisenberg and other physicists claimed that this

indeterminist one who contends that some events are uncaused

unpredictability was not due to the limitations of human knowledge, but rather resulted from the fact that there is genuine randomness and indeterminacy in nature. For example, if we precisely determine the position of a particle, we cannot predict its motion in the next moment. It seems that there is a causal gap between the particle's behavior up to this point and its behavior in the immediate future. This fact led to the conclusion that some events in nature are uncaused.

Many philosophers and physicists alike were quick to argue that this newly found indeterminacy in nature opened the door to human freedom. As the scientist Arthur Eddington proclaimed, "The revolution of theory which has expelled determinism from present-day physics has therefore the important consequence that it is no longer necessary to suppose that human actions are completely predetermined."[46] According to the indeterminist, human actions are included among the events in nature that are uncaused. However, does the indeterminist's notion of uncaused events provide us with the sort of freedom we refer to when we speak of free will? To answer this question, consider the following thought experiment.

 THOUGHT EXPERIMENT

Indeterminism

In his discussion of indeterminism, philosopher Richard Taylor asks us to consider the following scenario. While reading this passage, imagine *yourself* in the role of the speaker.

> Suppose that my right arm is free, according to this conception; that is, that its motions are uncaused. It moves this way and that from time to time, but nothing causes these motions. Sometimes it moves forth vigorously, sometimes up, sometimes down, sometimes it just drifts vaguely about—these motions all being wholly free and uncaused. Manifestly I have nothing to do with them at all; they just happen, and neither I nor anyone can ever tell what this arm will be doing next. It might seize a club and lay it on the head of the nearest bystander, no less to my astonishment than his. There will never be any point in asking why these motions occur, or in seeking any explanation of them, for under the conditions assumed there is no explanation. They just happen, from no causes at all.[47]

- If this scenario really happened, in what way would it be a refutation of determinism?
- Under these circumstances, would you consider your behavior to be free? Why?
- Can there be any other notion of free will besides that of uncaused behavior?

Taylor's point is that an uncaused motion of my body could hardly be considered a free action. By freedom of the will we ordinarily mean that our actions are not the inevitable outcome of previous causes, and neither are they random, uncaused events. If the determinist views us as puppets, manipulated by the strings of our causal history, the indeterminist implies that our thoughts and actions are random, spontaneous events that are equally beyond our control. However, to be free means that *we* are the cause of our actions. We produce them and initiate them; they do not simply happen. Because the indeterminist rejects determinism, *indeterminism* is sometimes considered to be a synonym for *libertarianism*. However, most libertarians argue for a richer view of freedom than simply the uncaused events of the indeterminist. Therefore, we consider the two positions of indeterminism and libertarianism to be distinct.

Agency Theory

As an alternative to simple indeterminism, some philosophers, such as Roderick Chisholm and Richard Taylor, have argued for libertarianism by developing a position known as **agency theory.** They reject the following dichotomy: "An event is either (1) the necessary outcome of previous causes or (2) an uncaused, random event that simply happens." This version of libertarianism rejects both determinism and indeterminism. While agency theorists may agree that both kinds of events occur in the world (e.g., the motion of billiard balls and subatomic events), these philosophers insist on a third category of events as well, events that are brought about by agents. Another way of explaining this theory is to say that there are two kinds of causes operating in the world. On the one hand, there is **event-causation,** which occurs when a prior event necessarily causes a subsequent event. Examples of event-causation would be a solar eclipse, an earthquake, the rise in my blood pressure after drinking coffee, the boiling of water, or an acorn falling to the earth. On the other hand is **agent-causation.** Any event that is brought about through the free action of an agent (person, self) is the result of agent-causation. Examples of agent-causation would be voting, choosing to see a particular movie, making a promise, phoning a friend.

The notion of agent-causation seems to capture what we ordinarily mean when we say that our actions are free. We have a sense that *we* make choices and initiate actions, that *we* have the power to act or not act in certain ways, and that *we* decide which action to take. This view implies that the universe is such that not all events are caused by the sort of causes studied by the physicists. It also implies that agents or persons are unique entities who do not follow the laws that govern electrons, rocks, sunflowers, or frogs. I do not freely choose to will my heart to beat because this automatic event is caused by the sorts of causes that scientists study. However, according to the agency theory, I do freely choose to support a political candidate, to stick to my diet, or to read a novel.

It is important to note that the libertarian does not need to make the claim that *all* human actions are free and undetermined. A libertarian merely asserts that *some* human actions are free and undetermined. In other words, the libertarian could recognize that under unusual circumstances (brainwashing, hypnotism, states of psychological or physical stress) a person's behavior might not be free. If such circumstances were not under the agent's control, the libertarian would say that person was not morally responsible for what he or she did. However, the libertarian claims that for the most part, while our decisions may be *influenced* by a number

agency theory a version of libertarianism that rejects both determinism and indeterminism; this theory claims that events are brought about by agents

event-causation when a prior event necessarily causes a subsequent event

agent-causation when an event is brought about through the free action of an agent (person, self)

of factors, they are not causally *determined* by previous conditions (prior psychological states or external factors).

Radical Existential Freedom

The most extreme version of libertarianism has been proposed by the famous French existentialist philosopher and novelist Jean-Paul Sartre (1905–1980). Sartre claims that we are always free, even in situations in which most other libertarians would acknowledge that we are not. As Sartre expresses it, "Man can not be sometimes slave and sometimes free; he is wholly and forever free or he is not free at all."[48] Sartre was an atheist, and he based his radical view of freedom on the claim that each of us is thrust into existence without anyone or anything determining what we are or what our purpose shall be. This view means that for humans, "their existence comes before their essence." Sartre explains this phrase in one of his most famous essays.

> What is meant here by saying that existence precedes essence? It means that, first of all, man exists, turns up, appears on the scene and, only afterwards, defines himself. If man, as the existentialist conceives him, is indefinable, it is because at first he is nothing. Only afterward will he be something, and he himself will have made what he will be. Thus, there is no human nature, because there is no God to conceive it. Not only is man what he conceives himself to be, but he is also only what he wills himself to be after this thrust toward existence.[49]

Sartre expresses his radical view of freedom by saying that freedom is not something that we *have* but something which we *are*. In his memorable phrase, he says we are "condemned to be free." But can this radical view of freedom be reconciled with the facts of our experience? I did not choose many of the features of my past or my present. I was born an American, I am a male, I grew up near Chicago. These facts are some of the givens of my situation that I was not free to choose and yet they seem to set limits on the course of my life. Sartre calls these features a person's **facticity.** Yet for Sartre, facts by themselves do not have any meaning, for it is only by our choices that we invest facts with meaning. I was born an American. My birth is part of my facticity because it cannot be changed. But what significance do I attach to that fact? Do I swell up with nationalistic pride and wave the flag, or do I burn it in shame for America's past and present sins? I am a male. But what does that fact mean? Does it mean that I am a tough, macho man who expresses his manhood by dominating women, hunting, spitting, and drinking beer while watching football? Or do I choose to be a sensitive male, one who is not afraid to eat quiche, cry, and be moved by great art? Of course these images are stereotypes, but they illustrate the point that in spite of our facticity, freedom prevails in the end, for we continually decide how the facts of our situation fit into our present self-conception and projects. Likewise, the women's movement in the latter part of the twentieth century was (and still is) an attempt to define and give meaning to the facticity of being a female. Simone de Beauvoir, a famous French

facticity Sartre's term for those features of our past or present that we were not free to choose and yet they seem to set limits on the course of our lives

writer and Sartre's lifelong companion, expressed this struggle by saying, "One is not born, but rather becomes, a woman."[50] Briefly, her view was that what it means to be a woman is not biologically determined; a female either allows socially defined roles to be imposed on her or she freely chooses what her identity as a woman shall be.

In addition to our facticity, there is what Sartre calls our **transcendence.** Transcendence is the root of our freedom, for it refers to the fact that we define ourselves by our possibilities and by all the ways in which each of us is continually creating our own future in terms of our choices, our plans, our dreams, and our ambitions. Because of our transcendence, what we have been or done in the past does not dictate our future. Sartre acknowledges that it seems as though my past actions weigh on me and determine who I am, but only because of the way they enter into my present engagements. For example, he says that my marriage vows limit my possibilities and dictate my conduct, but only because each day I continue to embrace them and define myself as a committed husband. I could view my vows as a stupid mistake, as something that is now void and inoperative, as having no more hold over me, and as something to be set aside as part of the dead past.[51] Hence, each moment of our existence we are creating our present selves out of the possibilities that define our transcendence. If there is continuity in our lives (such as a long-lasting relationship), it is only because we have continually reaffirmed past choices. Even to refuse to choose and to stoically let things happen is itself a choice.

Sartre goes so far as to say that even our emotions or passions are not forces that control us; instead they are ways that we apprehend the world and act in it. For example, a man may be unable to solve a problem and responds in anger by tearing up the paper it is written on. In doing so, he relieves himself of the burdens of his failure by eliminating the situation that caused them.[52] In another example, Sartre cites the case of a patient who is on the verge of revealing her deepest secrets to a psychiatrist, but her sobbing prevents her from continuing. Described in this way, her emotions appear to be a mechanistic cause that inhibits her freedom. However, Sartre argues that she sobs in order to be free of the obligation of continuing her confession.[53] Again, he points out that if I am threatened (say, in war), I may flee my responsibilities and run because of my fear of dying. But the emotion of fear enters into my behavior only because I have chosen living as the supreme value. Another person may stand by his or her post in the face of danger because of a commitment to duty and honor. We do not have passion on the one hand and moral fortitude on the other as causes of the two reactions. Instead, both are manifestations of fundamental, free choices.

When we deny our freedom and our responsibility for who we are, Sartre says we are in **bad faith.** Recognizing the radical nature of our freedom leads to anguish because we are burdened with the responsibility of having to make choices and being unable to fall back on any excuses. Hence, we are continually tempted to think we can escape our freedom, and by doing so, we fall into bad faith. Bad faith can be an attempt to deny my facticity. For example, I can refuse to acknowledge

transcendence
Sartre's term for the root of our freedom, for our ability to define ourselves by our possibilities and all the ways in which each of us is continually creating our own future in terms of our choices, our plans, our dreams, and our ambitions

bad faith Sartre's term for when we deny our freedom and our responsibility for who we are

Garfield ® by Jim Davis

In what sense is Garfield guilty of bad faith? (© 1983 Paws, Inc. Reprinted with permission of Universal Press Syndicate.)

that I have repeatedly committed cowardly actions and, instead, think of myself as having the heart and soul of a hero in spite of the fact that I have never acted heroically.[54] On the other hand, bad faith can result when I deny my transcendence and refuse to acknowledge that I am continually faced with possibilities and choices. For example, I can say "I am a coward" and view this fact as an unalterable feature of my identity. In this way I can seek to escape the burden of being responsible for my actions and suppose that they are determined by my nature just as iron filings are necessarily drawn to a magnet.

STOP AND THINK

Have there been times in your life when you have been guilty of bad faith and have tried to escape the burden of being responsible for your life? Were these incidents cases of denying your facticity? (You rationalized your behavior or wouldn't face what you had done.) Or were some of these cases a matter of denying your transcendence? (You made yourself think you didn't have any other possibilities, or you said "I am a [coward, loser, lazy person, fool in love, emotional person, shy person, victim of my circumstances, or whatever]" and used that definition of yourself as an excuse for what you did, as though it determined your actions for all time.)

Before we conclude our discussion of Sartre's radical view of freedom, two points are worth noting. First, I said earlier that Sartre tied human freedom to his claim that there is no God who defines human nature. However, a number of religious existentialists reject his atheism while agreeing with most of his analysis of the dynamics of freedom, responsibility, and bad faith.* Second, Sartre embodies a very

_____

*Although he lived before Sartre, Søren Kierkegaard would be an example of a religious existentialist who had a lot in common with Sartre. See discussions of Kierkegaard's thought in sections 1.0, 2.6, and 4.4.

radical kind of libertarianism. He believed that we are either 100 percent determined or 100 percent free. However, most libertarians have no problems acknowledging that there are some extreme situations in which our freedom is diminished or even negated. They simply insist that the majority of our everyday actions are not determined.

THOUGHT EXPERIMENT

Facts and Meaning

List four or five facts about you that you cannot change (your facticity). These facts could include where you grew up, your race, your physical characteristics, traumatic events in your past, and so on. Now try to apply Sartre's theory. For each fact, describe alternative ways you could view, interpret, or assign significance to it. Think of different ways these facts could have either negative or positive value for you. Think of alternative ways in which you could view each fact as being insignificant from your present perspective, and then think of ways in which each fact could play a role in how you view yourself today. Think of events in your past (the same ones you've already listed or different ones) whose meaning, value, or significance has changed over the years. Why did your assessment of these events change?

- In comparing your own experience with Sartre's analysis, do you agree with his claim that facts have no meaning until we give them meaning?
- Contrary to the determinist, who claims that events causally determine what we are and do, Sartre insists that we have total freedom over events from our past because we decide their meaning, significance, and role in our lives. To what degree do you agree with Sartre on this point?

THE POSITIVE ARGUMENTS FOR LIBERTARIANISM

Now that I have presented the various views of freedom among the antideterminists, we now look at the arguments that libertarians provide for their position. Although there are several arguments for libertarianism, the following three are the most common.

The Argument from Introspection

What is your right hand doing at this present moment? Holding this book? Taking notes with a pen? Scratching your head? Before you read further, I want you to do something different with your hand. Did you do it? Did you feel as though that action was the inevitable result of previous causes acting on you? Of course, you were responding to my directive, but you really didn't have to do anything. You could have chosen to ignore my little object lesson. Hence, what you did (or didn't do) was a matter of your own decision. Now do something different (e.g., stand up, stick your foot out). Once again, did you feel as though that action was caused or inevitable? Didn't you have the sense that you could have acted differently than you did?

According to the libertarian, this ordinary sort of experience that our actions are freely chosen and that we could have acted otherwise than we did provides forceful counterexamples to the determinist's claim that our actions are determined and inevitable. The determinist claims, however, that in those situations in which we face multiple alternatives and feel as though we are freely choosing among them, there is always one motivating cause within our current psychological state that compels us because it is the strongest one. For example, you may be torn between wanting to see a movie or going to a concert. If you decide to see the movie, the determinist would say, it is because your psychological state was such that the desire to see the movie was the stronger determining cause acting on you at that time. Therefore the determinist claims that "persons always act upon their strongest desire." But in a specific case, how can we identify our "strongest desire" except by identifying it (after the fact) with the desire upon which we acted? Now it looks as though the determinist's claim is "persons always act upon the desire upon which they act." This claim, of course, is an empty truth and does nothing to advance the determinist's case.

Contrary to what the determinist claims, the libertarian would argue that some-times we can choose or overrule our desires. The alcoholic would certainly say that the desire to drink is a compelling one. But through treatment and sheer will power, the alcoholic can learn to control that desire and even extinguish it. Part of the process of moral development is learning to control some desires and encourage others. The fact that this process takes time and effort suggests that we are not "programmed" to behave in one specific way.

By way of rebuttal, the determinist would be quick to point out that our feeling of freedom could be an illusion and that our introspective accounts are sometimes mistaken. However, our own actions are the only type of event in the world that we know both from the inside and the outside. Hence, the libertarian argues, we should give a high priority to the prima facie evidence of our own experience on this issue. According to his biographer, the famous eighteenth-century English writer Samuel Johnson once said, "All theory is against freedom of the will; all experience for it."

The Argument from Deliberation

Frequently our choices and actions are preceded by a period of deliberation during which we weigh the evidence, consider the pros and cons of our alternatives, calculate the probable consequences of an action, and evaluate all these data in terms of our values and desires. In this situation, the libertarian claims, we experi-ence the fact that the decision is not already latent in the causes acting on us; instead, we have a distinct sense that we are actively deciding what the decision will be. Contrary to the determinist's account, when we deliberate we are not simply like a metal ball suspended between two opposing magnetic fields. Rather than passively awaiting the outcome of the war between our conflicting motives, goals, or desires, we often find ourselves actively choosing which one will prevail.

The Argument from Moral Responsibility

If someone devotes his or her spare time to building houses for the poor, we might say that person's actions are morally good, commendable, admirable, laudable, and praiseworthy. On the other hand, if someone emotionally hurts people by pretending to love them only to get something from them, we might say that person's behavior was morally bad, shabby, despicable, contemptible, and blameworthy. But could we make these judgments about a person if his or her actions were the inevitable outcome of deterministic causes? It seems that making moral judgments about persons and praising or blaming them requires that their actions be freely chosen. If the determinist is correct in saying that all our behavior is the result of causes over which we have no control, then a tyrant such as Hitler and a great humanitarian such as Mother Teresa are morally equal, since both of them simply behaved as they were caused to behave. Looked at in this way, Mother Teresa should no more be praised for her actions nor Hitler condemned for his than Mother Teresa should be applauded for having low blood pressure and Hitler denounced for having high blood pressure. In the final analysis, determinism implies that our eye color, blood pressure, and moral character are all products of causes that operate upon us and whose outcomes we did not choose. But doesn't this philosophy wreak havoc with morality, one of the most significant features of our humanity?

 STOP AND THINK

What do you think would happen if you cheated, defamed, lied, or broke an important promise to a hard determinist? Do you think he or she would dismiss your behavior as unfortunate but excusable (since everyone's behavior is allegedly determined), or would you imagine that the determinist would think ill of you, responding no differently than a libertarian would? To what degree is this scenario relevant or irrelevant to the assessment of determinism?

The libertarian claims that if determinism is true, then our moral judgments and ethical struggles are absurd. As the scientist Arthur Eddington aptly expressed it:

What significance is there in my mental struggle to-night whether I shall or shall not give up smoking, if the laws which govern the matter of the physical universe already pre-ordain for the morrow a configuration of matter consisting of pipe, tobacco, and smoke connected with my lips?[55]

The hard determinist would respond that just because a theory conflicts with our sensibilities does not mean that it is false. Maybe we have to "bite the bullet" and abandon our notion of moral responsibility. However, the libertarian would respond that there are more reasons to believe in moral responsibility than there are for believing in universal, deterministic causality. To quote Arthur Eddington once again:

> To me it seems that responsibility is one of the fundamental facts of our nature. If I can be deluded over such a matter of immediate knowledge—the very nature of the being that I myself am—it is hard to see where any trustworthy beginning of knowledge is to be found.[56]

If the libertarian is correct about these issues, then at least *some* behavior is the result of agent-causation and is freely chosen, initiated, and performed by persons based on their rational deliberations and value choices. In the final analysis, the libertarian does not need to claim that the issue is one of a simple dichotomy between being totally free or totally unfree (as Sartre claims). Maybe realizing our potential to be free is like realizing our potential to be a good tennis player. It is all a matter of degree. On the one hand, we can allow ourselves to be like objects, buffeted about by the forces acting on us (personality dispositions, peer pressure, cultural influences), or on the other hand, we can strive to rise above those influences and take charge of who we are and what we do.

In the following passage, the contemporary sociologist Peter Berger tries to account for the fact that we are often causally conditioned (like puppets). But he also contends that through greater self-knowledge, we can become liberated from the causal influences acting on us and experience true, libertarian freedom.

> We see the puppets dancing on their miniature stage, moving up and down as the strings pull them around, following the prescribed course of their various little parts. We learn to understand the logic of this theater and we find ourselves in its motions. We locate ourselves in society and thus recognize our own position as we hang from its subtle strings. For a moment we see ourselves as puppets indeed. But then we grasp a decisive difference between the puppet theater and our own drama. Unlike the puppets, we have the possibility of stopping in our movements, looking up and perceiving the machinery by which we have been moved. In this act lies the first step towards freedom.[57]

In the following reading contemporary American philosopher Richard Taylor argues for free will on the basis of agency theory. He admits that this theory may seem strange initially, for it posits a kind of causality seen nowhere else in nature. Nevertheless, he thinks it does the best job of accounting for human experience.

- According to Taylor, what two conditions are necessary for an action to be free?
- Why do you think Taylor distinguishes between the "reason for an action" and the "cause of an action"?
- Why does Taylor not consider his pulse to be *his* action?

The only conception of action that accords with our data is one according to which people—and perhaps some other things too—are sometimes, but of course not always, self-determining beings; that is, beings that are sometimes the causes of their own behavior. In the case of an action that is free, it must be such that it is caused by the agent who performs it, but such that no antecedent conditions were sufficient for his performing just that action. In the case of an action that is both free and rational, it must be such that the agent who performed it did so for some reason, but this reason cannot have been the cause of it.

Now, this conception fits what people take themselves to be; namely, beings who act, or who are agents, rather than things that are merely acted upon, and whose behavior is simply the causal consequence of conditions that they have not wrought. When I believe that I have done something, I do believe that it was I who caused it to be done, I who made something happen, and not merely something within me, such as one of my own subjective states, which is not identical with myself. If I believe that something not identical with myself was the cause of my behavior—some event wholly external to myself, for instance, or even one internal to myself, such as a nerve impulse, volition, or whatnot—then I cannot regard that behavior as being an act of mine, unless I further believe that I was the cause of that external or internal event. My pulse, for example, is caused and regulated by certain conditions existing within me, and not by myself. I do not, accordingly, regard this activity of my body as my action, and would be no more tempted to do so if I became suddenly conscious within myself of those conditions or impulses that produce it. This is behavior with which I have nothing to do, behavior that is not within my immediate control, behavior that is not only not free activity, but not even the activity of an agent to begin with; it is nothing but a mechanical reflex. Had I never learned that my very life depends on this pulse beat, I would regard it with complete indifference, as something foreign to me, like the oscillations of a clock pendulum that I idly contemplate.

- In the next passage, what two notions are said to be completely different from the ones we apply to the rest of nature?
- Why does Taylor hesitate to use the word *cause* when referring to the origin of human actions?

Now this conception of activity, and of an agent who is the cause of it, involves two rather strange metaphysical notions that are never applied elsewhere in nature. The first is that of a *self* or *person*—for example, a man—who is not merely a collection of things or events, but a self-moving being. For on this view it is a person, and not merely some part of him or something within him, that is the cause of his own activity. . . .

Second, this conception of activity involves an extraordinary conception of causation according to which an agent, which is a substance and not an event, can nevertheless be the cause of an event. Indeed, if he is a free agent then he can, on this conception, cause an event to occur—namely, some act of his own—without anything else causing him to do so. . . .

This conception of the causation of events by things that are not events is, in fact, so different from the usual philosophical conception of a cause that it should not even bear the same name, for "being a cause" ordinarily just means "being an antecedent sufficient condition or set of conditions." Instead, then, of speaking of agents as *causing* their own acts, it would perhaps be better to use another word entirely and say, for instance, that they *originate* them, *initiate* them, or simply that they *perform* them.

- Taylor says that, at first, his notion of the nature of persons may seem "dubious." Why then does he think it is superior to the accounts of indeterminism and determinism? Do you agree or disagree?

Now this is, on the face of it, a dubious conception of what a person is. Yet it is consistent with our data, reflecting the presuppositions of deliberation, and appears to be the only conception that is consistent with them, as determinism and simple indeterminism are not. The theory of agency avoids the absurdities of simple indeterminism by conceding that behavior is caused, while at the same time avoiding the difficulties of determinism by denying that every chain of causes and effects is infinite. Some such causal chains, on this view, have beginnings, and they begin with agents themselves. Moreover, if we are to suppose that it is sometimes up to me what I do, and understand this in a sense which is not consistent with determinism, we must suppose that I am an agent or a being who initiates his own actions, sometimes under conditions which do not determine what action I shall perform. Deliberation becomes, on this view, something that is not only possible but quite rational, for it does make sense to deliberate about activity that is truly my own and depends in its outcome upon me as its author, and not merely upon something more or less esoteric that is supposed to be intimately associated with me, such as my thoughts, volitions, choices, or whatnot.

 THOUGHT EXPERIMENT

Behavior and Choices

Consider the following list of four kinds of actions or behaviors. For each category, list several actions you have performed that would fit in that category. You may find that you will have no items to list under one or more of the categories.

1. Behaviors that clearly were not a matter of choice in that they did not result from an act of your will. In other words, what you did was the inevitable outcome of

(Continued . . .)

(. . . continued)

causes over which you had no control. (An example might be blinking your eyes when a bright light flashed.)

2. Actions that did result from an act of your will but that you felt you were forced to do because your options were limited or because you were operating under some sort of coercion.

3. Actions in which causal factors had an influence on what you did but did not determine your action completely and inevitably, because you felt as though you did choose among genuine alternatives.

4. Actions that were truly your own and that you freely chose to perform without any causal influences affecting the outcome of your own act of willing.

- Did you leave any categories empty? If so, why?
- What criteria did you use to decide if an action was or was not free of causal influences?
- For which of the actions you listed would you accept moral responsibility for what you did? In other words, which actions would justly merit you praise or blame? What criteria do you use to decide the degree to which you are morally responsible for what you do? Or do you agree with the hard determinist that there is no such thing as moral responsibility?
- If you listed examples under category 3 or 4, what made you choose to do what you did and not something else? In what sense was this factor *not* a determining cause that made your action inevitable?

JEAN-PAUL SARTRE (1905–1980)

Sartre's Life

Sartre was born in Paris and lived most of his life there. After receiving an education at one of France's most prestigious universities, he began his career by teaching philosophy. However, his rise to fame as a writer began in 1938 when he published *Nausea,* his first novel and a best-seller. Four years later Sartre resigned his professorship and for the rest of his life was able to live on his literary income alone. When World War II broke out, Sartre was called into military service but was captured and confined to a Nazi prison camp for approximately a year. While there, he wrote and produced plays for his fellow prisoners. He was allowed to return to Paris because of poor health, but he immediately became active in the underground movement of the French Resistance, writing for a number of anti-Nazi newspapers. In 1943, he published his philosophical masterpiece, *Being and Nothingness: A Phenomenological Essay on Ontology.* It has been called "the principle text of modern existentialism." In recognition of his many novels and plays, Sartre was awarded the Nobel prize for literature in 1964, but he refused to accept the honor and the substantial cash prize because he did not want to become a tool of the establishment. On April 15, 1980, Sartre died of heart failure. As the hearse bearing his

JEAN-PAUL SARTRE
(1905–1980)

body drove to the cemetery, a crowd of about 50,000 people, most of them students, accompanied it through the streets of Paris.

Being and Nothingness

In the following passage from his major work, Sartre expresses his view of radical freedom. He claims that even if I am thrown into a situation I did not create, a war for example, I am always free in terms of how I choose to respond to it. To be free, for Sartre, is not to float high above all concrete situations. To be free is to choose and to act, which cannot be done unless there is a set of circumstances in which to choose and act. So the facts of my life are not limits or obstacles to my freedom, they are the arena within which my freedom may be exercised. I may have not chosen a war in which I find myself, but it is still *my* war for I must now define myself in terms of it. I can accept it wholeheartedly, or I can escape it through suicide or desertion. If these latter alternatives seem too drastic, it is because *I perceive them* as drastic and choose to prefer the war over them. (Sartre's service in the French underground during World War II had a definite impact on his philosophical writings about freedom, choices, responsibility, and anguish.)

FROM JEAN-PAUL SARTRE
Being and Nothingness[59]

Thus there are no *accidents* in life; a community event which suddenly bursts forth and involves me in it does not come from the outside. If I am mobilized in a war, this war is *my* war; it is in my image and I deserve it. I deserve it first because I could always get out of it by suicide or by desertion; these ultimate possibles are those which must always be present for us when there is a question of envisaging a situation. For lack of getting out of it, I have *chosen* it. This can be due to inertia, to cowardice in the face of public opinion, or because I prefer certain other values to the value of the refusal to join in the war (the good opinion of my relatives, the honor of my family, *etc.*). Any way you look at it, it is a matter of a choice. This choice will be repeated later on again and again without a break until the end of the war. Therefore we must agree with the statement by J. Romains, "In war there are no innocent victims." If therefore I have preferred war to death or to dishonor, everything takes place as if I bore the entire responsibility for war. Of course others have declared it, and one might tempted perhaps to consider me as a simple accomplice. But this notion of complicity has only a juridical sense, and it does not hold here. For it depended on me that for me and by me this war should not exist, and I have decided that it does exist. There was no compulsion here, for the compulsion could have got no hold on a freedom. I did not have any excuse; for as we have said repeatedly in this book, the peculiar character of human-reality is that it is without excuse. Therefore it remains for me only to lay claim to this war.

Sartre goes on to point out that it is useless to imagine what my life would have been like if I had lived in another time in which there was no war, for that would not have been me. Who I am is this present person facing this present war. I must integrate it into the self that I am in the process of creating and take responsibility for what I make of myself and what I make of this war. As Sartre says, "I must be without remorse or regrets as I am without excuse; for from the instant of my upsurge into being, I carry the weight of the world by myself alone without anything or any person being able to lighten it."[60] As he says in the next passage, this weight of responsibility includes my own existence.

Yet this responsibility is of a very particular type. Someone will say, "I did not ask to be born." This is a naive way of throwing greater emphasis on our facticity. I am responsible for everything, in fact, except for my very responsibility, for I am not the foundation of my being. Therefore everything takes place as if I were compelled to be responsible. I am *abandoned* in the world, not in the sense that I might remain abandoned and passive in a hostile universe like a board floating on the water, but rather in the sense that I find myself suddenly alone and without help, engaged in a world for which I bear the whole responsibility without being able, whatever I do, to tear myself away from this responsibility for an instant. For I am responsible for my very desire of fleeing responsibilities. To make myself passive in the world, to refuse to act upon things and upon Others is still to choose myself, and suicide is one mode among others of being-in-the-world.

Sartre points out that my being born is not simply a brute fact (nothing is); it is part of my facticity that I invest with meaning as I choose who I am and the stance I take toward my life. In the next section he goes on to list possible ways of viewing my birth, all of which are ways in which I embrace the fact of my existence and "choose" my birth.

I am ashamed of being born or I am astonished at it or I rejoice over it, or in attempting to get rid of my life I affirm that I live and I assume this life as bad. Thus in a certain sense I *choose* being born. This choice itself is integrally affected with facticity since I am not able not to choose, but this facticity in turn will appear only in so far as I surpass it toward my ends. Thus facticity is everywhere but inapprehensible; I never encounter anything except my responsibility. That is why I can not ask, "*Why* was I born?" or curse the day of my birth or declare that I did not ask to be born, for these various attitudes toward my birth—*i.e.,* toward the *fact* that I realize a presence in the world—are absolutely nothing else but ways of assuming this birth in full responsibility and of making it *mine.* Here again I encounter only myself and my projects so that finally my abandonment—*i.e.,* my facticity— consists simply in the fact that I am condemned to be wholly responsible for myself.

In this way, Sartre says that every event presents itself as an opportunity, but an opportunity that we can make use of or neglect. Although we are initially thrown into a world not of our own making, we are, nevertheless, faced with the responsibility (and anguish) of making choices and bearing our absolute freedom without making excuses. However, he points out that "most of the time we flee anguish in bad faith."

Dirty Hands

The next reading selection includes the climactic lines from Sartre's play *Dirty Hands*. (The title refers to the theme that the road to an authentic life involves getting our hands dirty in the mire of human events and not being a detached intellectual.) It was first performed in 1948 in Paris.

The events in the play take place during World War II in Eastern Europe. Hugo (the main character) has just been released from prison and calls on Olga, a former comrade in one of the factions of the local communist party. Hugo had been in prison for killing Hoederer, the leader of the party. Most of the play is a flashback as Hugo tells Olga about the events leading up to the killing. The party had assigned Hugo the task of assassinating the party's leader because they thought Hoederer's political strategies amounted to betrayal and compromise with the enemy. Hugo landed a job as Hoederer's personal secretary in order to accomplish his mission. However, Hugo had trouble carrying out the murder, both because he was a timid intellectual and because he fell under the sway of Hoederer's charisma. While trying to work up the courage for the assassination, Hugo catches his wife in Hoederer's arms and quickly pulls out his gun and shoots the man. The question is, Was the murder a crime of passion or a political assassination?

The answer to the question is important, because Olga reveals to Hugo that the party has changed its mind about Hoederer's political policies. They now realize Hoederer's ideas were correct and if Hugo killed him because of his ideas, then Hugo is dangerously out of line with the party's current ideology. Hence, Olga's job is to find out if Hugo is "salvageable," while the party's assassins wait outside for the verdict. Hugo will no longer be a threat to the party if he was a victim of his passions.

FROM JEAN-PAUL SARTRE
Dirty Hands[61]

OLGA: Look at me and answer me frankly, for what I am going to ask now is very important. Are you proud of your deed? Do you claim it as your own? Would you do it again if necessary?

HUGO: Did I even do it? It wasn't I who killed—it was chance. If I had opened the door two minutes sooner or two minutes later, I wouldn't have surprised them in each other's arms, and I wouldn't have fired. [*A pause.*] I was coming to tell him that I would let him help me.

OLGA: Yes.

HUGO: Chance fired three shots, just as in cheap detective stories. Chance lets you do a lot of "iffing": "*If* I had stayed a bit longer by the chestnut trees, *if* I had walked to the end of the garden, *if* I had gone back into the summerhouse. . . ."

But me? *Me?* Where does that put me in the thing? It was an assassination without an assassin.

Hugo is complaining that if a chance collection of events had completely determined his actions, then his status as an agent would have disappeared. The action would not have been his but would have been the end product of the circumstances and the causes acting on him. Hence, it would be "an assassination without an assassin." Hugo realizes that if determinism is true, then there is no self but only a series of caused events in which he is just a passive pawn in nature's game.

At this point, Hugo complains that his crime has no "weight" because he has not yet claimed it as his own nor decided its meaning. It was a series of events that happened, and he was just the "location" where they converged (as B. F. Skinner would say). He is still viewing his actions from the outside as events that occurred in the world, but he has not yet decided what their meaning was nor what his role as a free agent may have been. Hence, it is as though these actions do not belong to him.

HUGO: I thought I was too young. I wanted to hang a crime round my neck, like a stone. And I feared it would be too heavy for me to carry. How wrong I was! It's light, horribly light. It has no weight at all. . . . I don't feel that it's there. It's not around my neck, nor on my shoulders, nor in my heart. It has become my destiny, do you understand? It controls my life from outside, but I can't see it or touch it, it's not mine, it's a fatal disease that kills painlessly. Where is my crime? Does it exist? And yet I fired. . . .

But as he searches for the meaning of his actions, he realizes that the party's need to treat Hoederer's death as an accident, a crime of passion over a woman, would demean the man as well as Hugo himself. Refusing to view himself as a passive object buffeted about by uncontrollable emotions, circumstances, and deterministic causes, Hugo declares his freedom by deciding in the present what the meaning of his past actions shall be. He declares that he is Raskolnikov (the code name he was given as an assassin) and labels himself "unsalvageable."

HUGO: A man like Hoederer doesn't die by accident. He dies for his ideas, for his political program; he is responsible for his death. If I openly claim my crime and declare myself Raskolnikov and am willing to pay the necessary price, then he will have the death he deserves. [A rap on the door.]

OLGA: Hugo, I—

HUGO: [going to the door]: I have not yet killed Hoederer, Olga. Not yet. But I am going to kill him now, along with myself. [*More knocking.*]

OLGA: [*shouting*]: Go on! Get out!
[*Hugo kicks open the door.*]

HUGO: [shouting]: Unsalvageable!

Hugo says "I have not yet killed Hoederer" because, according to the perspective of chance/determinism he has been employing up until now, the events are just something that happened. Only if he decides that the actions were the result of his own agent-causation and not event-causation will the event be a murder for which he is responsible and not just an accident that occurred because of his uncontrollable passions.

Hugo comes to understand that it is impossible to know what his past motives and intentions were. The events of the past are gone, so they cannot dictate to us today what their meaning is to be. However, Hugo can, in the present, decide how his past actions are to be viewed. Accordingly, in the last minute of his life, he decides that he was and is a freely acting assassin and not the product of circumstances and deterministic psychological causes. In doing so, he declares the meaning of his actions and of Hoederer's death.

LOOKING THROUGH THE LIBERTARIAN'S LENS

1. If you were a libertarian judge or social planner, how would your view of the treatment of criminals differ from that of a determinist?

2. If you were a libertarian educator, how might your method of teaching differ from that of a determinist such as B. F. Skinner?

3. How might a libertarian psychologist's methods of dealing with a client's emotional problems differ from those of a determinist?

4. What religious conceptions of God, human nature, and moral evil would be consistent with the libertarian's view of human freedom? What religious conceptions would be incompatible with libertarianism? For example, some theologians say that God controls *everything* that happens in the world, which implies that God controls every human action. What would a libertarian say?

5. If you were a libertarian, what criteria would you use to decide if a person was morally responsible for his or her actions? In answering this question, you might reconsider the cases concerning Dave and Todd in section 3.6.

6. All day tomorrow, imagine that you are a libertarian. How does being a libertarian affect your view of your own and others' actions? The next day, imagine that you are a hard determinist. What difference does being a hard determinist make to your attitudes and reactions? Thinking over the events of these two days, consider the different accounts the libertarian and the hard determinist would give of the same event.

7. Consider an action you performed or a choice you made in which you felt as though you had no alternatives and the choice was one you were forced to make. How would Sartre explain that you were really free?

EXAMINING THE STRENGTHS AND WEAKNESSES OF LIBERTARIANISM

Positive Evaluation

1. Doesn't libertarianism do the best job of explaining what we experience internally when we deliberate, choose, and act? You can observe another person from the outside and entertain the following theory: "She is like a machine, because her internal psychological states, including her present thoughts, are the result of causes that she did not control." But can you meaningfully make the same claim about yourself and think that it is true?

2. Apart from the libertarian notion of agent-causation, can we ever say that anyone's beliefs have been arrived at rationally? If determinism is true, then the determinist's conclusions are ultimately the product of impersonal causes acting on him or her. Likewise, the libertarian's conclusions are ultimately the product of impersonal causes acting on him or her. We simply believe what we have been determined to believe and have no power to change that. Doesn't libertarianism offer a better perspective than this one on human cognition?

3. The philosopher William James (1842–1910) said that

> I cannot understand the willingness to act, no matter how we feel, without the belief that acts are really good and bad. I cannot understand the belief that an act is bad, without regret at its happening. I cannot understand regret without the admission of real, genuine possibilities in the world.[62]

In what way are James's comments an argument for free will and against determinism?

Negative Evaluation

1. According to the libertarian, we experience our own freedom when we make choices. But in our dreams, we have the feeling that we are making choices even though we know that dreams are the product of the physiological and psychological causes that produce them. Hence we can feel as though we are free even though causes are producing our behavior.

2. According to some thinkers, the scientific view of the world is based on the conviction that events follow fixed laws and that there is a cause for everything being the way that it is. If this statement is a correct account of science, does libertarianism then fly in the face of modern science? If so, because nothing can compete with modern science in unveiling the nature of reality, don't these facts negate libertarianism?

3. According to libertarianism, every free act is based on a volition or an act of the will. But in a given case, why did a particular volition come about at the precise time that it did and why was it directed toward this or that outcome? (Why did you decide to listen to music at this precise time and not three minutes earlier or

later? Why did you decide to listen to this particular CD and not the others that were available?) Isn't the libertarian forced to admit that either our volitions pop into our heads uncaused (in which case, they are unexplained, indeterministic events that *happen* to us) or they are the result of previous acts of the will? In the latter case, we are caught in an infinite regress. For example, your decision to listen to music was based on your decision to relax, which was based on your decision to take a break from studying, which was based on your decision to, and so on. Doesn't it seem that libertarianism leads to the notion that our free actions are based on an absurd and impossible infinite series of willings?

4. Isn't it the case that the better you get to know a person, the more his or her actions are predictable? Doesn't this finding indicate that the more knowledge we have of people's past, their personality, and the present circumstances that are affecting them, the more we understand the causes that are operating on them to produce their behavior? Aren't we convinced that a person's past experiences are a key to understanding why he or she became a saint or a serial killer? If so, doesn't this argument undermine libertarianism?

3.8 COMPATIBILISM

 LEADING QUESTIONS: *Compatibilism*

1. The hard determinist claims that all human actions are caused or determined by previous events and concludes from this claim both that we never act freely and that we are never morally responsible for our actions. But if you shoved a hard determinist, wouldn't it make a difference to him or her whether you did it voluntarily (because you meant to do it) or involuntarily (because you were shoved by someone yourself)? Isn't it impossible to deal with human interactions without the category of moral responsibility? No matter what our theory about human behavior, don't we all make a distinction between voluntary and involuntary behavior?

2. Even though the libertarians believe that we can act freely, don't they try to cause others to behave in a certain ways? Like anyone else, libertarians use praise and blame, reward and punishment to affect other people's behavior. How can we change someone else's behavior if there are no causal forces affecting what people do?

3. In each of the following scenarios, what is the difference between the *a* version and the *b* version? (1a) John broke the vase because he was shoved into it. (1b) John broke the vase because he was angry at its owner. (2a) Nikki cried out because she stepped on a tack. (2b) Nikki cried out because she wanted to get people's attention. In each set of cases, the external behavior is the same (breaking the vase, crying out). In each set of cases, there is a cause for the behavior (a shove, anger, pain, or need for attention). Is it important to distinguish whether the cause was external or whether it came from the agent's own, psychological state? If so, why is this distinction important?

Both the hard determinist and the libertarian claim that the concepts of determinism and freedom are inconsistent notions. In their view, the terms *free* and *determined* are like the terms *round* and *square*. In neither case can both pairs of terms be true of something at the same time. In other words, both the hard determinist and the libertarian agree that (1) if we are determined, then we are not free, and (2) if we are free, then we are not determined. They also agree that mere circumstantial freedom is not a sufficient condition for moral responsibility. To be responsible for your actions, you must also have metaphysical freedom (free will). Hence, they both accept the doctrine of *incompatibilism:* If we are determined, we lack the freedom necessary to be morally responsible.

But are these two positions the only options? If we were to reject their common assumption of incompatibilism, then we would be able to reconcile determinism and moral responsibility. Those philosophers who do just that embrace the position known as compatibilism. As we stated in section 3.5, *compatibilism* is the claim that we are determined *and* have the sort of freedom necessary to be morally responsible for our actions. Whereas hard determinism and libertarianism take an "either-or" stance on the issue of freedom and determinism, the compatibilist takes a "both-and" position. By doing so, the compatibilist claims to avoid the severe implications of hard determinism, such as the elimination of our traditional notions of moral responsibility and human freedom. In the same stroke, the compatibilist hopes to sweep away the alleged difficulties associated with libertarianism.

Sometimes compatibilism is called **soft determinism.** However, do not interpret this label to mean that the compatibilist is "soft" on determinism. The compatibilist agrees with the hard determinist that the thesis of universal causation applies to all human actions. In other words, the compatibilist believes human actions are 100 percent determined just as much as the hard determinist does. The difference between the two positions is that the compatibilist believes that the implications of determinism are not as hard and severe as the hard determinist believes. (hence the label *soft* determinism). Because the two types of determinism share many areas of agreement, I do not have to spend as much time presenting the arguments for compatibilism. All the arguments presented for the determinism half of hard determinism would apply to compatibilism as well. What we do need to explore is why compatibilists reject the thesis of incompatibilism and how they hope to reconcile determinism and freedom. To put the issue in the form of a question, Can the compatibilists reconcile what seems irreconcilable? In other words, can they "eat their cake and have it too"? Only a careful examination of the case for compatibilism will tell.

soft determinism see compatibilism

SURVEYING THE CASE FOR COMPATIBILISM (SOFT DETERMINISM)

Question: How will the compatibilists try to convince us that being determined is consistent with being free? Answer: They argue for their position by arguing for a particular conception of freedom. They claim that free actions are those that are done voluntarily. To say that an action is voluntary, according to the compatibilist, does not mean that the action lacks determining causes. Instead, a voluntary action is said to be one in which the determining causes reside within the agent as opposed to being external to him or her. *External* causes are such things as physical forces or physical conditions. On the other hand, *internal* causes are the agent's own personality, values, motives, beliefs, desires, and other psychological states. Of course, the compatibilist would say that these internal factors do not appear out of nowhere, for they have their origin in the agent's causal history. The major difference between compatibilism and the other two positions is that the compatibilist does not believe that a lack of causal determination is necessary to have moral responsibility. Basically, the compatibilist says that you are acting freely if you have circumstantial freedom. You are free and responsible as long as your choices and actions are not forced by external conditions but are controlled mainly by your own psychological states.

In question 3 of the "Leading Questions," John and Nikki were not acting freely when he was shoved into the vase and she involuntarily cried out in pain. But they were acting freely or voluntarily when he broke the vase to get even and she cried out to get attention. In the latter two cases, they were both acting on the basis of their own, internal desires and motives. The person you have come to be is a product of many kinds of causes (genetic, cultural, past experience, and so on). Hence, you did not make yourself, but were made by these causes. But when I want to know if you should be blamed or praised for your actions, I only need to know if these actions came from your own beliefs, values, desires, motives, or choices. I do not need to know the rather complicated story of how you came to be the sort of person you are.

Are you starting to think of questions you would like to ask the compatibilist? One question that may come to mind is, "How could I have been free in performing an action unless I had genuine alternatives? In other words, if I performed action X freely, then it must have been the case that I could have done otherwise." In response the compatibilist would say you were caused to choose action X by your own psychological states, but you *could have* chosen to do action Y *if* your psychological state had been significantly different at the time. This point is illustrated by the following thought experiment.

 THOUGHT EXPERIMENT

The Context of Choices

To understand the compatibilist's combination of determinism and freedom, let's consider the case of Vernon. His physician has warned him that he is overweight and needs to reduce his calorie intake. On his way home from work, Vernon passes a bakery and purchases a pound of fudge candy, which he immediately consumes. What caused him to take this action? We can imagine that the following circumstances and psychological factors played major roles in Vernon's decision.

(Continued . . .)

(. . . continued)

1. Vernon tends to lack self-discipline.
2. He tends to choose immediate gratification over long-term goals.
3. He is not concerned about his weight or how he looks.
4. Because he feels good, he is not too concerned about his physician's warning.
5. He craves fudge candy.
6. He has just received three rejections of the novel he is seeking to publish.
7. The disappointment causes him to feel sorry for himself.
8. When he eats fudge he feels happy.
9. He was too busy to stop for lunch and is very hungry.
10. The fudge candy is prominently displayed in the store window.

- Given all these conditions, was it inevitable that Vernon would eat the fudge?
- Was Vernon acting freely when he ate the fudge?
- Can Vernon be held responsible for making a bad choice? That is, can he be blamed, criticized, and scolded for not taking care of himself?

The compatibilist, being a determinist, would say that given the psychological and physical conditions preceding this action, it was inevitable that Vernon acted as he did. If we could roll back time a dozen times to the exact instant Vernon made his choice with all the same conditions, he would always choose to eat the fudge. It would be inconceivable, the compatibilist would say, that under those same exact conditions the decision could have been different. What could have caused the outcome to be different except some difference in the conditions preceding it? To think otherwise is to suppose that Vernon's action was uncaused, inexplicable, and mysterious. If his action was not caused, then it was the result of some psychological coin flip in his head. But even coin flips and their outcome have causes, even though the results may be unpredictable. Vernon's action was obviously caused, for it had to be the result of the strongest desire that he had at the time.

Vernon could have chosen to do otherwise than he did only if a difference in the external or internal conditions had caused his strongest desire to be different. Suppose, for example, he only received two rejection slips and was still waiting to hear from the third editor or he was feeling in poor health that day or he had eaten lunch previously or the fudge was not displayed in the window. Any one of these factors may have swung the decision the other way. The same is true if his psychological state had been different at the time. For example, suppose he had an ounce more of self-discipline or he was worried about his weight or he tended to react stoically to rejection instead of getting depressed.

At the same time, the compatibilist would say (unlike the hard determinist) that Vernon was acting freely and was responsible for his behavior, even though it was inevitable. Vernon did what he wanted to do and his action was based on his own personality, desires, wants, motives, and volition. His action was voluntary, because he was not forced to behave the way he did by any external compulsion. The external factors played a role, but only because he responded to them on the basis of his own psychological needs and desires. What more could we want in the way of freedom?

You now reply, "But don't we sometimes behave one way in a certain set of circumstances and then later behave another way in exactly the same set of circumstances? Doesn't this behavior show that we are not determined?" The answer is that the two sets of circumstances are never exactly the same. Furthermore, *you* are never exactly the same from one minute to the next. Perhaps you find it boring to always make the same choices or perhaps the outcome of the first choice was not completely satisfactory so you decided to choose differently the second time. Choosing to act a certain way not only has effects on your external environment, it has internal effects as well. For this reason, your preferences and desires and, consequently, your choices can vary from moment to moment.

Again you ask, "Granted that my actions are the product of my desires, values, and motives, don't I sometimes choose to change my desires, values, and motives?" Yes, but what caused this change in your psychological state? Why did you decide to change at this point in time and not earlier or later? Furthermore, what caused you to change in exactly this particular way? The motive to change some features of your personality had to grow from a seed that already existed in your personality. This seed produced the desire to change your psychological makeup only when it was activated by some cause (e.g., an experience, something you read, or your own reflections on your life). For example, some people's personalities are such that they are very set in their ways and choose not to change, whereas other people are more flexible. So it would seem that any desire to change your personality is actually rooted in an even deeper desire in your personality (such as the desire to always be growing and improving). Such a change is your free choice, but it is a choice that comes from the person you are and how your personality is put together. In the final analysis, of course, you did not originally create or choose your personality. So determinism reigns supreme. Yet, the compatibilist insists, no matter how your personality was formed and by what causal mechanisms, your personality is *you,* and as long as your decisions are made by you, freedom also reigns supreme.

Traditional Compatibilism: W. T. Stace

A very forceful defense of compatibilism was given by W. T. Stace (1886–1967). (Walter T. Stace was born in Britain and received his education at Trinity College in Dublin. In 1932 he came to the United States to teach at Princeton University.) Stace agrees with the hard determinist that every human action is as much determined by previous causes as is any other event in the world. However, he agrees with the libertarian that without free will there can be no morality. To be morally responsible for an action requires that you freely chose to perform the action on the basis of your own motives, desires, and values. You cannot be either blamed or praised for an action if you were compelled to do it. But how can we consistently combine determinism with free will? Don't they exclude one another? Stace claims that the problem is merely a verbal one, that it is based on an incorrect definition of free will.

To provide a clear-cut case of how a wrong definition can lead to a false conclusion about reality, Stace imagines that someone defines "man" as a type of five-legged animal and, on the basis of this definition, denies the existence of men. The true story, of course, is not that men do not exist, but that "man" has been incorrectly defined. Similarly, Stace thinks that "free will" has been incorrectly defined, which is why it seems incompatible with determinism and why both hard determinists and libertarians think determinism is inconsistent with moral responsibility. In the following reading, Stace explains why a better understanding of the notion of freedom will resolve all the difficulties and controversies.

- What is the incorrect definition of free will, according to Stace?
- What has this incorrect definition led to?

FROM WALTER T. STACE

Religion and the Modern Mind[63]

Throughout the modern period, until quite recently, it was assumed, both by the philosophers who denied free will and by those who defended it, that *determinism is inconsistent with free will.* If a man's actions were wholly determined by chains of causes stretching back into the remote past, so that they could be predicted beforehand by a mind which knew all the causes, it was assumed that they could not in that case be free. This implies that a certain definition of actions done from free will was assumed, namely that they are actions not wholly determined by causes or predictable beforehand. Let us shorten this by saying that free will was defined as meaning indeterminism. This is the incorrect definition which has led to the denial of free will. As soon as we see what the true definition is we shall find that the question whether the world is deterministic, as Newtonian science implied, or in a measure indeterministic, as current physics teaches, is wholly irrelevant to the problem.

To clarify the correct understanding of *free will,* Stace provides several imaginary dialogues that illustrate how the phrase is used in ordinary conversation. In each of these cases, ask yourself whether the action was voluntary or involuntary.

JONES: I once went without food for a week.

SMITH: Did you do that of your own free will?

JONES: No. I did it because I was lost in a desert and could find no food.

But suppose that the man who had fasted was Mahatma Gandhi. The conversation might then have gone:

GANDHI: I once fasted for a week.

SMITH: Did you do that of your own free will?

GANDHI: Yes. I did it because I wanted to compel the British Government to give India its independence.

Take another case. Suppose that I had stolen some bread, but that I was as truthful as George Washington. Then, if I were charged with the crime in court, some exchange of the following sort might take place:

JUDGE: Did you steal the bread of your own free will?

STACE: Yes. I stole it because I was hungry.

Or in different circumstances the conversation might run:

JUDGE: Did you steal of your own free will?

STACE: No. I stole because my employer threatened to beat me if I did not.

At a recent murder trial in Trenton some of the accused had signed confessions, but afterwards asserted that they had done so under police duress. The following exchange might have occurred:

JUDGE: Did you sign the confession of your own free will?

PRISONER: No. I signed it because the police beat me up.

- In the next conversation, what does the philosopher (a hard determinist) say is irrelevant to the case?
- Why are the philosopher's comments absurd?

Now suppose that a philosopher had been a member of the jury. We could imagine this conversation taking place in the jury room.

FOREMAN OF THE JURY: The prisoner says he signed the confession because he was beaten, and not of his own free will.

PHILOSOPHER: This is quite irrelevant to the case. There is no such thing as free will.

FOREMAN: Do you mean to say that it makes no difference whether he signed because his conscience made him want to tell the truth or because he was beaten?

PHILOSOPHER: None at all. Whether he was caused to sign by a beating or by some desire of his own—the desire to tell the truth, for example—in either case his signing was causally determined, and therefore in neither case did he act of his own free will. Since there is no such thing as free will, the question whether he signed of his own free will ought not to be discussed by us.

The foreman and the rest of the jury would rightly conclude that the philosopher must be making some mistake. What sort of a mistake could it be? There is only one possible answer. The philosopher must be using the phrase "free will" in some peculiar way of his own which is not the way in which men usually use it when they wish to determine a question of moral responsibility. That is, he must be using an incorrect definition of it as implying action not determined by causes.

Suppose a man left his office at noon, and were questioned about it. Then we might hear this:

JONES: Did you go out of your own free will?

SMITH: Yes. I went out to get my lunch.
But we might hear:

JONES: Did you leave your office of your own free will?

SMITH: No. I was forcibly removed by the police.

We have now collected a number of cases of actions which, in the ordinary usage of the English language, would be called cases in which people have acted of their own free will. We should also say in all these cases that they *chose* to act as they did. We should also say that they could have acted otherwise, if they had chosen. For instance, Mahatma Gandhi was not compelled to fast; he chose to do so. He could have eaten if he had wanted to. When Smith went out to get his lunch, he chose to do so. He could have stayed and done some work, if he had wanted to. We have also collected a number of cases of the opposite kind. They are cases in which men were not able to exercise their free will. They had no choice. They were compelled to do as they did. The man in the desert did not fast of his own free will. He had no choice in the matter. He was compelled to fast because there was nothing for him to eat. And so with the other cases. It ought to be quite easy, by an inspection of these cases, to tell what we ordinarily mean when we say that a man did or did not exercise free will. We ought therefore to be able to extract from them the proper definition of the term. Let us put the cases in a table:

Free Acts	Unfree Acts
Gandhi fasting because he wanted to free India.	The man fasting in the desert because there was no food.
Stealing bread because one is hungry.	Stealing because one's employer threatened to beat one.
Signing a confession because one wanted to tell the truth.	Signing because the police beat one.

Leaving the office because one wanted one's lunch.	Leaving because forcibly removed.

It is obvious that to find the correct definition of free acts we must discover what characteristic is common to all the acts in the left-hand column, and is, at the same time, absent from all the acts in the right-hand column. This characteristic which all free acts have, and which no unfree acts have, will be the defining characteristic of free will.

Is being uncaused, or not being determined by causes, the characteristic of which we are in search? It cannot be, because although it is true that all the acts in the right-hand column have causes, such as the beating by the police or the absence of food in the desert, so also do the acts in the left-hand column. Mr. Gandhi's fasting was caused by his desire to free India, the man leaving the office by his hunger, and so on. Moreover there is no reason to doubt that these causes of the free acts were in turn caused by prior conditions, and that these were again the results of causes, and so on back indefinitely into the past. Any physiologist can tell us the causes of hunger. What caused Mr. Gandhi's tremendously powerful desire to free India is no doubt more difficult to discover. But it must have had causes. Some of them may have lain in peculiarities of his glands or brain, others in his past experiences, others in his heredity, others in his education. Defenders of free will have usually tended to deny such facts. But to do so is plainly a case of special pleading, which is unsupported by any scrap of evidence. The only reasonable view is that all human actions, both those which are freely done and those which are not, are either wholly determined by causes, or at least as much determined as other events in nature. It may be true, as the physicists tell us, that nature is not as deterministic as was once thought. But whatever degree of determinism prevails in the world, human actions appear to be as much determined as anything else. And if this is so, it cannot be the case that what distinguishes actions freely chosen from those which are not free is that the latter are determined by causes while the former are not. Therefore, being uncaused or being undetermined by causes, must be an incorrect definition of free will.

- If the presence or absence of determining causes is not what distinguishes voluntary from involuntary actions, what does make them different?

What, then, is the difference between acts which are freely done and those which are not? What is the characteristic which is present to all the acts in the left-hand column and absent from all those in the right-hand column? Is it not obvious that, although both sets of actions have causes, the causes of those in the left-hand column are *of a different kind* from the causes of those in the right-hand column? The free acts are all caused by desires, or motives, or by some sort of internal psychological states of the agent's mind. The unfree acts, on the other hand, are all caused by physical forces or physical conditions, outside the agent. Police arrest means physical force exerted from the outside; the absence of food in the desert is a physical condition of the outside world. We may therefore frame the following rough definitions. *Acts freely done are those whose immediate causes are psychological states in the agent. Acts not freely done are those whose immediate causes are states of affairs external to the agent.*

It is plain that if we define free will in this way, then free will certainly exists, and the philosopher's denial of its existence is seen to be what it is—nonsense. For it is obvious that all those actions of men which we should ordinarily attribute to the exercise of their free will, or of which we should say that they freely chose to do them, are in fact actions which have been caused by their own desire, wishes, thoughts, emotions, impulses, or other psychological states.

- In the next passage, why does Stace assert that determinism is consistent with the notions of moral responsibility, blame, and punishment?

But that determinism is incompatible with moral responsibility is as much a delusion as that it is incompatible with free will. You do not excuse a man for doing a wrong act because, knowing his character, you felt certain beforehand that he would do it. Nor do you deprive a man of a reward or prize because, knowing his goodness or his capabilities, you felt certain beforehand that he would win it. . . .

Suppose that your child develops a habit of telling lies. You give him a mild beating. Why? Because you believe that his personality is such that the usual motives for telling the truth do not cause him to do so. You therefore supply the missing cause, or motive, in the shape of pain and the fear of future pain if he repeats his untrustful behavior. And you hope that a few treatments of this kind will condition him to the habit of truth-telling, so that he will come to tell the truth without the infliction of pain. You assume that his actions are determined by causes, but that the usual causes of truth-telling do not in him produce their usual effects. You therefore supply him with an artificially injected motive, pain and fear, which you think will in the future cause him to speak truthfully.

The principle is exactly the same where you hope, by punishing one man, to deter others from wrong actions. You believe that the fear of punishment will cause those who might otherwise do evil to do well.

We act on the same principle with non-human, and even with inanimate, things, if they do not behave in the way we think they ought to behave. The rose bushes in the garden produce only small and poor blooms, whereas we want large and rich ones. We supply a cause which will produce large blooms, namely fertilizer. Our automobile does not go properly. We supply a cause which will make it go better, namely oil in the works. The punishment for the man, the fertilizer for the plant, and the oil for the car, are all justified by the same principle and in the same way. The only difference is that different kinds of things require different kinds of causes to make them do what they should. Pain may be the appropriate remedy to apply, in certain cases, to human beings, and oil to the machine. It is, of course, of no use to inject motor oil into the boy or to beat the machine.

- In his final argument, why does Stace claim that moral responsibility, praise or blame, reward or punishment are not only consistent with determinism, but require it?

Thus we see that moral responsibility is not only consistent with determinism, but requires it. The assumption on which punishment is based is that human behavior is causally determined. If pain could not be a cause of truth-telling there would be no justification at all for punishing lies. If human actions and volitions were uncaused, it would be useless either to punish or reward, or indeed to do anything else to correct people's bad behavior. For nothing that you could do would in any way influence them. Thus moral responsibility would entirely disappear. If there were no determinism of human beings at all, their actions would be completely unpredictable and capricious, and therefore irresponsible. And this is in itself a strong argument against the common view of philosophers that free will means being undetermined by causes.

Hierarchical Compatibilism: Harry Frankfurt

HARRY FRANKFURT
(1929–   )

The traditional form of compatibilism we have been discussing (such as that of W. T. Stace) states that even though your actions are determined they still can be free if they (1) result from an act of your will and (2) are not externally constrained or compelled. But this statement assumes that the only kind of force preventing voluntary action is an external one. Isn't it possible that a person's ability to voluntarily perform or not perform an action can be impeded by psychological compulsions? In such a case the person is being forced to act a certain way against his or her desires because of a compelling internal force. Consider the following two cases. (1) Sally chooses to wash her hands because she is about to eat dinner. (2) Chang has a psychological neurosis that compels him to wash his hands hundreds of times a day. He has the desire to wash his hands again and again even though he knows this desire is abnormal. Clearly Sally is acting freely, because she is acting on her desire to be clean and because she wants to have this desire. On the other hand, it is just as clear that Chang is not acting freely even though his actions result from his own choice and he was not compelled by any *external* causes. It seems then that freedom from external compulsions is not a sufficient basis for defining a compatibilist notion of voluntary action.

Contemporary philosopher Harry Frankfurt (born 1929) has developed a solution to this problem with a position that some have called *hierarchical compatibilism.* (Harry Frankfurt is a professor of philosophy at Yale University who has made important contributions to the study of free will.) Frankfurt offers the insight that people often have within them a hierarchy of different desires. *First-order desires* are directed toward objects or states of affairs. For example, we desire such things as food, shelter, knowledge, friends, pleasure, money, health, and comfort. However, we not only desire certain things or conditions, but we also desire to have or not have our first-order desires. A person who is trying to diet, for example, may have a strong desire for a piece of pie (a first-order desire). At the same time, however, he may wish that he didn't have this desire for dessert. Desires that are concerned with our first-order desires are called *second-order desires.* The desire not to be the sort of person who craves fattening foods, for example, would be a second-order desire.

According to Frankfurt, the capacity to form second-order desires is what makes it possible to have genuine freedom of the will. An animal such as a lion has desires, makes choices, and does what he wants to do. He desires fresh meat and chooses to prey on an antelope, for example. Even though he is free to do what he wants, however, he always acts on the basis of his instincts and his strongest desire; he never evaluates the desirability of his first-order desires and does not concern himself with whether he wants to have these desires. Hence, animals and small children may act freely on their desires, but they do not have freedom of the will because they are not able to choose among their desires.

Merely having second-order desires is not sufficient to explain free actions. We can have several second-order desires that are in conflict. For example, one part of me can desire to be a person who is moved by pity at the same time that I can desire to be a hardheaded businessperson who is not ruled by my emotions. Or we can have second-order desires that we do not wish to be effective. For example, the fourth-century philosopher St. Augustine struggled to change from being a promiscuous playboy to being a pious Christian. During his time of transition he prayed, "Lord, make me sexually pure, but not just yet." He had a second-order desire to be free of his first-order lusts, but was not yet willing for that desire to control his will. For this reason, Frankfurt says that what really counts is our *second-order volitions.* When we identify ourselves with a second-order desire and want it to constitute our will, it becomes a second-order volition.

On this analysis, having free will is not identical to the condition of having circumstantial freedom, and it is more than the liberty to act on one's first-order desires. Frankfurt defines free will in the following way:

> A person's will is free only if he is free to have the will he wants. This means that, with regard to any of his first-order desires, he is free either to make that desire his will or to make some other first-order desire his will instead.[64]

To put it another way, we act freely when we act on a second-order volition. If we do not have second-order desires (such as the lion) or if we are unable to act on the ones we have (such as Augustine), then we will be unable to act freely, because we will be ruled by our first-order desires. On the other hand, the dieter who wants to overcome her cravings and who can effectively carry out this second-order volition is acting freely, because she is choosing to have the will she wants. This theory can best be made clear by considering some of Frankfurt's own examples. He considers two kinds of drug addicts who have the same first-order desire for drugs. However, they differ in terms of their second-order volitions concerning whether they wish to have their desire for drugs.

> One of the addicts hates his addiction and always struggles desperately, although to no avail, against its thrust. He tries everything that he thinks might enable him to overcome

his desires for the drug. But these desires are too powerful for him to withstand, and invariably, in the end, they conquer him. He is an unwilling addict, helplessly violated by his own desires.

The unwilling addict has conflicting first-order desires: he wants to take the drug, and he wants to refrain from it. In addition to these first-order desires, however, he has a volition of the second order. He is not neutral with regard to the conflict between his desire to take the drug and his desire to refrain from taking it. It is the latter desire, and not the former, that he wants to constitute his will; it is the latter desire rather than the former, that he wants to be effective and to provide the purpose that he will seek to realize in what he actually does.

The deepest part of the unwilling addict, the desire he identifies with, is the second-order volition that one of his desires (to not want the drug) be the strongest one. However, he is not free because he is unable to act on this second-order volition and is incapable of directing his will toward the healthy desire. In the end, his own desire for the drug is like an alien force within him that his will is unable to control. Frankfurt contrasts this case with that of the willing addict.

Suppose that his addiction has the same physiological basis and the same irresistible thrust as [the addiction of the unwilling addict], but that he is altogether delighted with his condition. He is a willing addict, who would not have things any other way. If the grip of his addiction should somehow weaken, he would do whatever he could to reinstate it; if his desire for the drug should begin to fade, he would take steps to renew its intensity.

In one sense, the willing addict is determined, because no matter what he might wish to be the case, his physiological addiction will make his desire for the drug the one that constitutes his will. In the compatibilist's sense, however, he also has free will, for he *wants* to be a person who desires drugs. Hence, unlike the unwilling addict, this second addict is deeply and willingly identified with his addiction. There is a consistency between his second-order volition and his strongest desire. Hence, according to the hierarchical compatibilist, such a person has both freedom of the will and moral responsibility. As Frankfurt says about such a person:

Since the will that moved him when he acted was his will because he wanted it to be, he cannot claim that his will was forced upon him or that he was a passive bystander to its constitution. Under these conditions, it is quite irrelevant to the evaluation of his moral responsibility to inquire whether the alternatives that he opted against were actually available to him.

Because both the hard determinist and the libertarian are incompatibilists, they would not be satisfied with such an attempt to make freedom and determinism compatible. According to the hierarchical compatibilist, the issue is not so much whether your behavior is determined, but whether it is consistent with your second-order volitions or what you deeply wish your will to be. But the incompatibilist would want to know what, if anything, causes your second-order volitions to be what they are. If they are determined by forces not under your control, then even though you are doing what you want to do, your wants are not something over which you have any power. The following thought experiment illustrates the incompatibilist's concern.

THOUGHT EXPERIMENT

Determinisn and Responsibility

Let's suppose that Lisa enters a room in which she is shown a mediocre science fiction movie. She becomes fascinated by the movie and without any struggle with her conscience or second thoughts, she happily decides to stay and watch the movie to the end even though she will be missing her philosophy class. Unknown to her, the door to the room has been locked so that she could not leave to attend class even if she had wanted to.

- Under these circumstances, is Lisa morally responsible for missing her class?

Frankfurt would conclude that she *is* responsible for missing her class. True, she did not have the physical freedom to attend class because of the locked door. However, she freely willed to miss class, even though (unknown to Lisa) her willing to act otherwise would have been ineffective. Her missing class was consistent with what she wanted to do and what she chose to do.

Now let's suppose that we discover that Lisa's wanting to be the sort of person who desires to watch cheap movies instead of improving herself is a second-order volition caused by a drug that a malicious scientist secretly gave her. The drug causes her to want to be a couch potato and to ignore all desires to be otherwise.

- Under these circumstances, would it make sense to say that Lisa is responsible for her choices?

Referring back to Frankfurt's willing addict, the locked door represents his physical addiction to the drug. It is inevitable that he will take the drug, whether he wants to or not. Likewise, it is inevitable that Lisa will stay in the room whether she wants to or not. Yet in both cases, Frankfurt would say these persons are acting freely because they did what they wanted to do. However, is there any significant difference between a person's actions being directly caused by external forces not under his or her control and a person's second-order desires and volitions being caused by external forces not under his or her control? In deciding whether a person is free and morally responsible, is there any significant difference between a person's desires being programmed by a malicious scientist and a person's desires being "programmed" by nature (such as genetics or environment)?

LOOKING THROUGH THE COMPATIBILIST'S LENS

1. Think about a choice that you believe you made freely, and then answer the following questions. What indicates to you that this decision genuinely was your own choice (a free choice) and not one that you were coerced into making? Can you ever know completely all the causal factors that made you the person that you are? Can you ever know completely all the causal factors that made you choose as

you did? Is it necessary to know the answers to the last two questions in order to answer the first question?

2. To what degree do you think your actions are predictable by your friends or family? To what degree are your friends' actions predictable? How can an action be predictable with a certain degree of probability unless it is determined to that degree? Can an action be predictable, yet still be said to be free? What would a compatibilist say? What do you say?

EXAMINING THE STRENGTHS AND WEAKNESSES OF COMPATIBILISM

Positive Evaluation

1. By rejecting the claim that some events (or actions) are uncaused, is the compatibilist's position more consistent with the most well-founded principles of physics and the behavioral sciences than that of the libertarian?

2. In building a theory around the notions that some actions are voluntary and some are involuntary, that some are free and some are not, is the compatibilist more consistent with the way we ordinarily speak than is the hard determinist?

3. Does compatibilism provide an effective way of preserving moral responsibility while also explaining why praise, blame, reward, punishment, laws, education, and experience in general can shape, modify, and change people's behavior?

Negative Evaluation

1. Suppose you found out that since the age of eight, you have been the subject of a scientific experiment. Scientists found that from a distance, they could bombard your brain with ultrasonic rays that would cause you to have the particular values, likes, dislikes, and beliefs that you now have. Your tastes in foods, your choice of a career, your musical preferences, your personality traits, your moral and political beliefs, and your attitude toward religion were all part of a master plan that was programmed into you. Furthermore, not only your desires but your positive or negative evaluations of those desires have been inserted into you. Would this discovery change how you viewed your life? Why? Even though your choices have been based on your own psychological dispositions, is it meaningful to say they were free, since your psychological states were programmed by scientists? Do these considerations pose a problem for the compatibilist claim that we have free will even if we are determined?

2. What do you think of the following critique of compatibilism?

> If determinism is true, then our acts are the consequences of the laws of nature and events in the remote past. But it is not up to us what went on before we were born, and neither is it up to us what the laws of nature are. Therefore, the consequences of these things (including our present acts) are not up to us.[65]

REVIEW FOR CHAPTER 3

Philosophers

3.0 Overview of Metaphysics
  Aristotle
  Plato
3.1 Overview: The Mind-Body Problem
  Hugh Elliot
  René Descartes
  Arnold Geulincx
  Nicholas Malebranche
3.2 Dualism
  René Descartes
3.3 Physicalism
  Paul Churchland
3.4 Functionalism and Artificial Intelligence
  Jerry Fodor
  René Descartes
  Alan Turing
  Marvin Minsky
  John Searle
  Daniel Dennett
3.5 Overview: Freedom and Determinism
  John Stuart Mill
  Fyodor Dostoyevsky
  Clarence Darrow
3.6 Hard Determinism
  B. F. Skinner
  Samuel Butler
  Clarence Darrow
  Benedict Spinoza
3.7 Libertarianism
  Jean-Paul Sartre
  Arthur Eddington
  Peter Berger
  Richard Taylor
3.8 Compatibilism
  W. T. Stace
  Harry Frankfurt

Concepts

3.0 Overview of Metaphysics
  metaphysics
  the problem of permanence and change

the problem of appearance and reality
the mind-body problem
the problem of freedom and determinism
Ockham's razor
ontology
two characteristics of fundamental reality
three categories for classifying things
the eliminativist strategy
the reductionist strategy
dualism
Platonic Forms
Plato on the relationship between particulars and their Forms
Plato's concept of the Good
Plato's Allegory of the Cave

3.1 Overview: The Mind-Body Problem
four commonsense propositions about the mind and body
dualism
physicalism
interactionism
Cartesian dualism
idealism
parallelism
occasionalism
identity theory (reductionism)
eliminativism
functionalism

3.2 Dualism
mind-body dualism (psychophysical dualism)
Cartesian dualism
Principle of the Nonidentity of Discernibles
Descartes's argument from doubt
Descartes's argument from divisibility
Descartes's argument from consciousness
Descartes's compromise
interactionism

3.3 Physicalism
physicalism
four problems of dualism
identity theory (reductionism)
eliminativism
folk psychology

3.4 Functionalism and Artificial Intelligence
functionalism
multiple realizability

SUGGESTIONS FOR FURTHER READING

General Metaphysics

Taylor, Richard. *Metaphysics,* 4th ed. Englewood Cliffs, N.J.: Prentice Hall, 1992. An easy introduction to the topic, including chapters on the mind-body problem and freedom-determinism.

van Inwagen, Peter. *Metaphysics.* Boulder, Colo.: Westview Press, 1993. An engaging, contemporary introduction to metaphysics.

The Mind-Body Problem

Beakley, Brian, and Peter Ludlow, eds. *The Philosophy of Mind: Classical Problems and Contemporary Issues.* Cambridge, Mass.: MIT Press, 1992. A good anthology, covering a range of positions.

Carruthers, Peter. *Introducing Persons: Theories and Arguments in the Philosophy of Mind.* Albany: State University of New York Press, 1986. A fairly accessible discussion of the various theories and issues.

Churchland, Paul. *Matter and Consciousness.* Cambridge, Mass.: MIT Press, 1990. An accessible and important introduction to the issues from a physicalist perspective.

Dennett, Daniel. *The Intentional Stance.* Cambridge, Mass.: MIT Press, 1989. An entertaining but somewhat advanced discussion of the contemporary debate.

Flanagan, Owen. *The Science of the Mind.* 2d ed. Cambridge, Mass.: MIT Press, 1991. A discussion of the leading positions.

Gregory, R. L. *The Oxford Companion to the Mind.* Oxford: Oxford University Press, 1987. An important resource.

Guttenplan, Samuel. *A Companion to the Philosophy of Mind.* Oxford: Blackwell, 1994. A useful reference guide to the subject.

Kim, Jaegwon. *Philosophy of Mind.* Boulder, Colo.: Westview Press, 1996. A somewhat advanced overview of the various topics and theories.

Lycan, William, ed. *Mind and Cognition.* Oxford: Blackwell, 1991. Another good anthology.

Rosenthal, David, ed. *The Nature of Mind.* Oxford: Oxford University Press, 1991. A well-known anthology.

Dualism

Descartes, René. *Meditations on First Philosophy,* Meditations II and VI. Many translations are available. The classic statement of dualism.

Nagel, Thomas. *The View from Nowhere.* Oxford: Oxford University Press, 1986. While Nagel is not a radical dualist like Descartes, he does maintain that the mental cannot be reduced to the physical.

Robinson, Howard, ed. *Objections to Physicalism.* Oxford: Oxford University Press, 1997. A collection of articles criticizing the physicalist solution to the mind-body problem.

Swinburne, Richard. *The Evolution of the Soul.* Rev. ed. Oxford: Oxford University Press, 1997. Swinburne is a contemporary dualist who attempts to reconcile this position with the findings of recent science.

Physicalism

Levin, Michael E. *Metaphysics and the Mind-Body Problem.* Oxford: Clarendon Press, 1979. A vigorous defense of physicalism.

Functionalism and Artificial Intelligence

Fodor, Jerry. "The Mind-Body Problem." *Scientific American,* January 1981, pp. 114–23. A popular presentation of the functionalist's solution to the mind-body problem.

Lieber, Justin. *Can Animals and Machines Be Persons?* Indianapolis: Hackett, 1985. An entertaining fictional dialogue dealing with the nature of the mind in the light of animal and machine intelligence.

Moody, Todd. *Philosophy and Artificial Intelligence.* Englewood Cliffs, N.J.: Prentice Hall, 1993. An introduction to the implications of artificial intelligence for philosophy of mind.

Searle, John. *Mind, Brains, and Science.* Cambridge, Mass.: Harvard University Press, 1984. An engaging analysis of the issues; includes a version of Searle's classic Chinese room refutation of functionalism.

Freedom and Determinism

Trustead, Jennifer. *Free Will and Responsibility.* Oxford: Oxford University Press, 1984. A readable introduction to the topic.

Watson, Gary, ed. *Free Will.* Oxford: Clarendon Press, 1982. A collection of important articles on the topic.

Hard Determinism

Honderich, Ted. *How Free Are You? The Determinism Problem.* Oxford: Oxford University Press, 1993. A readable argument against the belief in free will.

Skinner, B. F. *Walden Two.* New York: Macmillan, 1948. A highly entertaining novel depicting a utopian community based on the philosophy of hard determinism.

Libertarianism

Kane, Robert. *The Significance of Free Will.* Oxford: Oxford University Press, 1996. Considered to be one of the best recent defenses of libertarianism.

Compatibilism

Dennett, Daniel. *Elbow Room: The Varieties of Free Will Worth Wanting.* Cambridge, Mass.: MIT Press, 1984. An entertaining and well-argued defense of compatibilism.

van Inwagen, Peter. *An Essay on Free Will.* Oxford: Clarendon Press, 1982. A highly original study that is strongly critical of compatibilism.

NOTES

1. Robert Solomon makes these points in *The Big Questions.* 4th ed. (Fort Worth, Texas: Harcourt Brace Jovanovich, 1994), p. 108.

2. Plato, *The Republic of Plato,* trans. Francis M. Cornford (London: Oxford University Press, 1941), bk. 6, 510d.

3. Plato, *The Republic,* Bk. 7, Sec. 514–18, in *The Dialogues of Plato,* vol. 1, trans. Benjamin Jowett (Oxford: Oxford University Press, 1920; reprinted, New York: Random House, 1937), pp. 773–77. Some changes have been made to the punctuation and wording to make the text more readable to a modern reader.

4. Hugh Elliot, "Tantalus," in *Modern Science and the Illusions of Professor Bergson* (1912), quoted in Daniel Kolak and Raymond Martin, *The Experience of Philosophy,* 3d ed. (Belmont, Calif.: Wadsworth, 1996), p. 411.

5. René Descartes, *Discourse on the Method,* in *the Philosophical Writings of Descartes,* vol. 1, trans. John Cottingham, Robert Stoothoff, and Dugald Murdoch (Cambridge: Cambridge University Press, 1985), 4.32–33, p. 127. The references are to the part number and page number in the classic French edition, followed by the page number in this edition.

6. René Descartes, *Meditations on First Philosophy,* revised ed., trans. John Cottingham (Cambridge: Cambridge University Press, 1996), 6.85–86, p. 59. The references are to the meditation number and page number in the classic French edition, followed by the page number in this edition.

7. René Descartes, *Author's Replies to the Fourth Set of Objections,* in *The Philosophical Writings of Descartes,* vol. 2, trans. John Cottingham, Robert Stoothoff, and Dugald Murdoch (Cambridge: Cambridge University Press, 1984), p. 160.

8. Descartes, *Meditations on First Philosophy,* 6.78, p. 54.

9. René Descartes, *Passions of the Soul,* in *The Philosophical Writings of Descartes,* vol. 1, 1.31, p. 340.

10. R. Buckminster Fuller, "The Phantom Captain," in *Nine Chains to the Moon* (Carbondale: Southern Illinois University Press, 1938), pp. 18–19.

11. Paul M. Churchland, *Matter and Consciousness: A Contemporary Introduction to the Philosophy of Mind,* rev. ed. (Cambridge, Mass.: MIT Press, Bradford, 1988), pp. 43–48.

12. J. B. S. Haldane, *Possible Worlds and Other Papers* (New York: Harper & Brothers, 1928), p. 220.

13. For an extended discussion of this argument, see Frank Jackson, "Epiphenomenal Qualia," *Philosophical Quarterly* 32 (1982): 127–36 and "What Mary Didn't Know," *Journal of Philosophy* 83 (1986): 291–95.

14. Gottfried Leibniz, *The Monadology,* sec. 17, in *Discourse on Metaphysics/Correspondence with Arnauld/Monadology,* trans. George Montgomery (La Salle, Ill.: Open Court Publishing Co., 1902; reprint ed., 1968), p. 254.

15. Edgar Allan Poe, "Maelzel's Chess-Playing Machine," *Southern Literary Messenger* (April, 1836); reprinted in *The Portable Poe,* ed. Philip Van Doren Stern (New York: Penguin Books, 1977), pp. 511–12.

16. Poe, "Maelzel's Chess-Playing Machine," p. 513.

17. Garry Kasparov, "The Day That I Sensed a New Kind of Intelligence," *Time Magazine,* 25 March 1996, p. 55.

18. These three responses to Poe's articles were suggested by Todd C. Moody, *Philosophy and Artificial Intelligence* (Englewood Cliffs, N.J.: Prentice Hall, 1993), p. 9.

19. Jerry Fodor, "The Mind-Body Problem," *Scientific American,* January 1981, p. 114.

20. The three passages are from Fodor, "The Mind-Body Problem," pp. 114, 118, and 118, respectively.

21. Descartes, *Discourse on the Method,* 5.56–57, p. 140.

22. Alan Turing, "Computing Machinery and Intelligence," *Mind* 59, no. 236 (1950); reprinted in *The Mind's I,* ed. Douglas Hofstadter and Daniel Dennett (New York: Bantam Books, 1981), pp. 57–67.

23. Turing, "Computing Machinery and Intelligence," p. 57.

24. Marvin Minsky, "Why People Think Computers Can't," in *The Computer Culture,* ed. Denis P. Donnelly (Cranbury, N.J.: Associated University Presses, 1985), pp. 40–43.

25. John R. Searle, "Minds, Brains, and Programs" in *The Behavioral and Brain Sciences,* vol. 3, reprinted in Hofstadter and Dennett, *The Mind's I,* pp. 353–73.

26. John Searle, *Minds, Brains, and Science* (Cambridge, Mass.: Harvard University Press, 1984), p. 37–38.

27. Hofstadter and Dennett, *The Mind's I,* p. 94.

28. For more information on the case of the two Jims, see Donald Dale Jackson, "Reunion of Identical Twins, Raised Apart, Reveals Some Astonishing Similarities," *Smithsonian* 11 (October 1980): 48–56. For further studies of twins separated at birth, see Lawrence Wright, "Double Mystery," *The New Yorker,* August 7, 1995, pp. 44–62, and Lawrence Wright, *Twins: And What They Tell Us about Who We Are* (New York: John Wiley & Sons, 1997).

29. W. Somerset Maugham, *Of Human Bondage* (New York: Penguin Books, Signet Classic, 1991), pp. 357–58.

30. Pierre-Simone Laplace, *Philosophical Essay on Probabilities,* trans. Andrew I. Dale (New York: Springer-Verlag, 1995), p. 2.

31. John Stuart Mill, *A System of Logic,* bk. 6, chap. 2, sec. 2 in *Collected Works of John Stuart Mill,* vol. 8, ed. J. M. Robson (Toronto: University of Toronto Press, 1974), pp. 836–37.

32. Fyodor Dostoyevsky, *Notes from Underground,* trans. Constance Garnett, in Walter Kaufmann, *Existentialism from Dostoyevsky to Sartre,* rev. and exp. ed. (New York: Meridian, 1975), p. 72.

33. Clarence Darrow, "Address to the Prisoners in the Cook County Jail," in *Attorney for the Damned,* ed. Arthur Weinberg (New York: Simon and Schuster, 1957), pp. 3–4.

34. B. F. Skinner, *Walden Two* (New York: Macmillan, 1948), pp. 257–58.

35. B. F. Skinner, *About Behaviorism* (New York: Alfred Knopf, 1974), p. 189.

36. Samuel Butler, *Erewhon and Erewhon Revisited* (New York: Random House, The Modern Library, 1927), pp. 106–7.

37. State of Illinois *versus* Leopold and Loeb.

38. Benedict de Spinoza, *Ethics,* ed. James Gutmann, trans. William Hale White and Amelia Hutchinson Stirling (New York: Hafner, 1966), 2.49, Note. The first number in the reference refers to the book number of Spinoza's manuscript and the number following the decimal point indicates the proposition number.

39. Letter 58 (to G. H. Schuller) in Baruch Spinoza, *The Ethics and Selected Letters,* ed. Seymour Feldman, trans. Samuel Shirley (Indianapolis: Hackett, 1982), p. 250.

40. Spinoza, *Ethics,* 2.35, Note.

41. B. F. Skinner, *Beyond Freedom and Dignity* (New York: Alfred Knopf, 1972), p. 202.

42. B. F. Skinner, *Science and Human Behavior* (New York: Macmillan, 1953), pp. 447–48.

43. B. F. Skinner, "A Lecture on 'Having' a Poem," in *Cumulative Record: A Selection of Papers,* 3d ed. (New York: Appleton-Century-Crofts, 1972), pp. 345–55.

44. Arthur Eddington, *New Pathways in Science* (New York: Macmillan, 1935), pp. 90–91.

45. Skinner, *About Behaviorism,* p. 189.

46. Eddington, *New Pathways in Science,* p. 87.

47. Richard Taylor, *Metaphysics,* 4th ed. (Englewood Cliffs, N.J.: Prentice-Hall, 1992), p. 48.

48. Jean-Paul Sartre, *Being and Nothingness,* trans. Hazel E. Barnes (New York: Simon & Schuster, Washington Square Press, 1956), p. 569.

49. Jean-Paul Sartre, "Existentialism," trans. Bernard Frechtman, in *Existentialism and Human Emotions* (New York: Philosophical Library, 1957), p. 15.

50. Simone de Beauvoir, *The Second Sex,* trans. H. M. Parshley (New York: Knopf, 1975), p. 267.

51. Sartre, *Being and Nothingness,* p. 640.

52. Jean-Paul Sartre, *The Emotions: Outline of a Theory,* trans. Bernard Frechtman (New York: Philosophical Library, 1948), p. 37.

53. Ibid., pp. 26–32.

54. Sartre, *Being and Nothingness,* p. 111.

55. Arthur Eddington, quoted in L. Susan Stebbing, *Philosophy and the Physicists* (New York: Dover Publications, 1958), p. 242.

56. Eddington, *New Pathways in Science,* p. 90.

57. Peter L. Berger, *Invitation to Sociology: A Humanistic Perspective* (Garden City, N.Y.: Doubleday, Anchor Books, 1963), p. 176.

58. Taylor, *Metaphysics,* pp. 51–53.

59. Sartre, *Being and Nothingness,* pp. 708–11.

60. Ibid., p. 710.

61. Jean-Paul Sartre, *Dirty Hands,* in *No Exit and Three Other Plays,* trans. I. Abel (New York: Random House, Vintage International, 1989), pp. 234–36, 241.

62. William James, "The Dilemma of Determinism," in *Essays in Pragmatism* (New York: Macmillan, Hafner Press, 1948), p. 59.

63. W. T. Stace, *Religion and the Modern Mind* (New York: Lippincott, 1952), pp. 249–258.

64. All the quotations by Harry Frankfurt are taken from his article "Freedom of the Will and the Concept of a Person," *Journal of Philosophy* 68, no. 1 (January 1971): 5–20.

65. Peter van Inwagen, *An Essay on Free Will* (Oxford: Clarendon Press, 1983), p. 16.

CHAPTER 4

THE SEARCH FOR GOD

SCOUTING THE TERRITORY: *The Impact of Religion*

Love and anger, guilt and ecstasy, humor and solemnity, optimism and cynicism, peace and doubt, hope and despair—religion seems capable of evoking a response corresponding to every peak and valley on the spectrum of human emotional life. Why is this? Philosopher and theologian Peter Kreeft attempts to assess the impact of the idea of God in the following passage.

FROM PETER KREEFT

Does God Exist?[1]

The idea of God is either a fact, like sand, or a fantasy, like Santa.

If it is a fantasy, a human invention, it is the greatest invention in all of human history. Measure it against all the other inventions, mental or physical. Put on one side of the scale the control of fire, the domestication of animals, and the cultivation of wheat; the wheel, the ship, and the rocket ship; baseball, the symphony orchestra, and anesthetics—and a million other similarly great and wonderful things. Then put on the other side of the scale a single idea: the idea of a being that is actual, absolute, perfect, eternal, one, and personal; all-knowing, all-loving, all-just, all-merciful, and all-powerful; undying, impervious, unbribeable, uncompromising, and unchangeable; a cosmic creator, designer, redeemer, and provider; cosmic artist, musician, scientist, and sage; the infinite abyss of pure Being who is yet a person, a self, an "I." It is disputable whether such a being is a fact or a fantasy, but it is indisputable that if it is a fantasy, it is by far the greatest fantasy in history. If it is humanity's invention, it is humanity's masterpiece.

The idea of God has guided or deluded more lives, changed more history, inspired more music and poetry and philosophy than anything else, real or imagined. It has made more of a difference to human life on this planet, both individually and collectively, than anything else ever has. To see this clearly for yourself, just try this thought experiment: suppose no one in history had ever conceived the idea of God. Now, rewrite history following that premise. The task daunts and staggers the imagination. From the earliest human remains—religious funeral artifacts—to the most recent wars in the Mideast, religion—belief in a God or gods—has been the mainspring of the whole watch that is human history.

STOP AND THINK

Try Kreeft's thought experiment by answering the following questions.

- How would human history be different if no one had ever conceived of God?

(Continued . . .)

(. . . continued)

- How would the absence of religion have affected the following areas of human experience: art, literature, music, science, morality, politics, law, philosophy?
- What would have been better in human experience if there had been no religion?
- What would have been worse in human experience if there had been no religion?
- To what degree, if any, do such considerations count for or against the truth of religious claims?

CHARTING THE TERRAIN OF RELIGION: *What Are the Issues?*

Many people have found the idea of God to be comforting, inspiring, and the source of hope. But the philosophy of religion is concerned not with the psychological benefits of believing in the idea of God, but rather with the question of whether the word *God* refers to anything in reality. As Kreeft put it, "God is either a fact, like sand, or a fantasy, like Santa." But once we start raising questions about the existence of God, a number of other questions arise. How can we decide whether God exists? Are there rational arguments that demonstrate that God exists or, at least, that his existence is probable? Is there evidence that counts against God's existence? Is it impossible or inappropriate to approach this question in an objective way? Should we fall back on faith or subjective considerations in making up our minds? What about the existence of suffering in the world? Isn't it pretty hard to square this fact with the belief in an all-powerful, loving God?

Most of our discussion surrounding these questions deals with the monotheistic conception of God found in such religions as Judaism, Islam, and Christianity. **Monotheism** claims that one God created the world and sustains it while transcending it. (Hereafter, I refer to this position as simply "theism.") But to limit philosophy of religion to these particular traditions assumes that a prior question has been raised and answered in favor of monotheism. This question is, If God exists, what is the nature of this being? To increase our range of options, we examine Hinduism, an Indian religion that has a completely different conception of God from that which predominates in Western thought. Finally, in asking whether the notion of God is essential to religion at all, we examine Buddhism, one of the world's great religions, yet one in which the notions of God and the supernatural are noticeably absent.

monotheism the claim that one God created the world and sustains it while transcending it

CHOOSING A PATH: *What Are My Options concerning Religious Belief?*

The claim that belief in God must be supported by objective evidence is known as **evidentialism.** Both religious believers and atheists can be evidentialists. The theistic evidentialist thinks that there is objective evidence for God. The atheistic evidentialist believes that we must have evidence in order for our belief in God to be rational, but goes on to argue that such evidence is lacking. Generally, all

evidentialism the claim that belief in God must be supported by objective evidence

agnostics, that is, people who do not think there is sufficient evidence either for theism or atheism, are evidentialists.

The theists who are evidentialists would, of course, agree that it is possible to demonstrate the existence of God through rational, objective arguments. They believe in the possibility and success of natural theology. **Natural theology** is the project of attempting to provide proofs for the existence of God based on reason and experience alone. In other words, the natural theologian does not appeal to supernatural revelation or faith of any sort to support his or her claims about God. The natural theologian does not necessarily reject revelation or faith, but he or she believes that it is possible to demonstrate God's existence, and perhaps the truth of other religious claims, solely through philosophical reasoning. The objective evidence that is used to support this belief is the subject of the sections that follow. The three main forms of objective arguments for God are the cosmological argument, the teleological, or design, argument, and the ontological argument.

Atheism is the claim that God does not exist. Typically, atheists are evidentialists. However, while all atheists deny that God's existence may be proven, many atheists also would say that you cannot absolutely prove that God *doesn't* exist. They make this claim because in most cases it is impossible to prove, beyond any possible doubt, a negative claim concerning the existence of something.

STOP AND THINK

- Can you absolutely prove that Santa Claus does not exist? How would you go about proving that there is no possibility that he exists?
- If you cannot prove his *non*existence, then you have the following two responses to choose from:
  1. I do not know whether Santa Claus does or does not exist.
  2. Because no plausible evidence suggests that Santa Claus exists, the rational person will believe that he does not exist.
- Which of these options do you think is more reasonable? Why?

Most rational adults believe that there is no Santa Claus even though they cannot provide *direct* evidence for this claim. It is very difficult to prove the *non*existence of something (such as leprechauns, unicorns, life in outer space, and so on). The fact that no credible person has ever seen a leprechaun does not rule out the possibility that they might be lurking out there in the woods somewhere. After all, we were once unaware of the existence of viruses because we did not have the instruments to detect them. Nevertheless, unless some hard, positive evidence turns up for the existence of leprechauns or Santa Claus, a rational person is justified in doubting their existence. The reason for this doubt is twofold: (1) The burden of proof is on those who make claims concerning the existence of extraordinary beings such as Santa Claus (as well as elves, space aliens, vampires, or unicorns) and (2) all

---

natural theology the project of attempting to provide proofs for the existence of God based on reason and experience alone

atheism the claim that God does not exist

the phenomena that we once needed the Santa hypothesis to explain (toys under the Christmas tree) can now be explained through other, more naturalistic hypotheses (indulgent parents). While we cannot prove the nonexistence of such beings with the certainty of a mathematical proof, the lack of evidence of their existence and the reasonableness of alternative hypotheses makes disbelief rational.

Similarly, the atheist argues that most of us (even the religious believer) live on the assumption that the events that happen around us are the result of natural causes. Those people who assert the existence of an extraordinary being such as God, a being who defies scientific explanation and who transcends the world of nature, have the burden of providing the evidence for their thesis. Furthermore, the atheist would say that, analogous to the Santa hypothesis, people once appealed to God or supernatural causes to explain things for which they had no other explanation (solar eclipses, disease, the origin of biological species, and so on). Hence, many atheists believe that they do not need to absolutely prove the truth of atheism. Instead they claim it is sufficient merely to show that the religious believer has failed to provide valid arguments establishing the existence of God. The task for the atheist, then, is to show that all the rational arguments of the natural theologian are invalid or inconclusive.

On the other hand, most atheists do think that there is positive evidence for the thesis that God does not exist. Although a number of different arguments are used,[2] the most common argument that atheists appeal to is based on the problem of evil. They claim that the existence of evil (such as the suffering of innocent people due to natural disasters) is evidence that casts doubt on the God hypothesis. This problem is discussed in section 4.5.

Agnosticism is the position that not enough evidence exists for us to know whether there is or is not a God. This position is sometimes called *religious skepticism*. Agnostics are evidentialists, for they agree that objective evidence is necessary to believe in God's existence, but they believe that such evidence is unavailable. However, they also say that objective evidence is necessary to claim that God does *not* exist. Hence, unlike both the theist and the atheist, the agnostic does not think we can know anything concerning God's existence. Accordingly, the agnostic thinks we must suspend judgment on this issue. I do not devote a separate section to agnosticism, because the agnostic could be viewed as a person who agrees with the negative case of both the theist and the atheist. In other words, the agnostic agrees with the atheist that the believer's arguments are fallacious or inconclusive. In fact, many of the refutations of the arguments for God have actually been made by agnostics. However, the agnostic also agrees with the believer that the atheist's arguments against God's existence are also fallacious or inconclusive.

Those people who embrace **nonevidentialism** hold that it is not necessary to have objective, rational evidence for our basic beliefs and stance toward life. The nonevidentialist claims that there is a basis for religious belief other than reason. Accordingly, the nonevidentialist says that we must and, in fact, do form our ultimate commitments on the basis of subjective, personal factors and not on rational arguments. Although there are people on both sides of the God issue who

agnosticism the claim that there is not enough evidence for us to know whether God does or does not exist; sometimes called religious skepticism

nonevidentialism the claim that it is not necessary to have objective, rational evidence for our basic beliefs and stance toward life

reject evidentialism, it is a position that appeals more to theists than atheists. There are several varieties of theistic nonevidentialists. The first category consists of people who maintain that the rational, objective arguments for God are either ineffective or unnecessary, while at the same time offer subjective or pragmatic considerations to move an individual in the direction of faith. These thinkers believe that objective evidence cannot decide the God issue, but that there are practical or subjective reasons for believing in God. The considerations referred to here differ from the typical forms of objective evidence and argument used in natural theology, because they make a direct appeal to the subjective concerns of the individual and his or her stance toward life. To illustrate this appeal, I provide readings from Blaise Pascal, the seventeenth-century mathematician and philosopher, and William James, the twentieth-century pragmatist.

fideism the claim that religious belief must be based on faith alone and cannot be justified by appeal to either objective or subjective reasons

A second, more radical form of nonevidentialism is **fideism,** which claims that religious belief must be based on faith alone and cannot be justified by appeal to either objective or subjective reasons. The fideist believes that there is a tension between faith and reason such that we must choose between the two. If we know something on the basis of objective evidence, the fideist claims, then it makes no sense to say we believe it on faith. For example, if a woman hired a detective to maintain a twenty-four-hour surveillance of her husband to see if he was cheating on her, it would be obvious that she did not have faith in him. Hence, for the fideist, faith is a kind of leap or a subjective commitment that goes far beyond what we can know on the basis of objective evidence. According to the fideist, God must be approached through faith, by following your heart, and not by searching for evidence in the sterile, dry valley of objective reason. If subjective and pragmatic considerations are seen as arguments or justifications for religious belief, then the extreme fideist would reject these considerations as well. Later in this chapter, I use passages from Søren Kierkegaard, the nineteenth-century founder of religious existentialism, to illustrate fideism.[3]

Just for the record, a few atheists have been nonevidentialists. The most striking example is Friedrich Nietzsche, the nineteenth-century founder of the movement of atheistic existentialism, who was discussed in section 2.6. Nietzsche believed that there are no rational, objective grounds for choosing a worldview. All of a person's beliefs are based on his or her personal stance toward life. Timid people will subjectively choose the comfort of religion, he said, while emotionally strong, self-reliant people will subjectively choose atheism. He was fond of expressing his nonevidentialism in statements such as: "Gradually it has become clear to me what every great philosophy so far has been: namely, the personal confession of its author and a kind of involuntary and unconscious memoir."[4]

The spectrum of viewpoints we have discussed are summarized in Table 4.1.

CONCEPTUAL TOOLS: *Arguments for the Existence of God*

All arguments fall into two main groups, and the arguments for the existence of God are no exception. First, there are a posteriori arguments. (*A posteriori* in Latin means "from what comes later"; in other words, it refers to what comes after

TABLE 4.1 *Spectrum of Viewpoints on the Existence of God*

	Theistic Evidentialism (Natural Theology)	Atheistic Evidentialism	Agnosticism	Nonevidential Theism (Pragmatism, Subjectivism)	Fideism
1. Objective evidence is required for religious belief.	Agree	Agree	Agree	Disagree	Disagree
2. Objective evidence is available.	Agree	Disagree	Disagree	Disagree	Disagree
3. Persuasive practical or subjective reasons for belief are available.	(May agree or disagree)	Disagree	Disagree	Agree	Disagree
4. Belief in God must be based on faith alone and not on reasons.	Disagree	Disagree	Disagree	Disagree	Agree
5. God exists.	Agree	Disagree	Undecided	Agree	Agree
6. God does not exist.	Disagree	Agree	Undecided	Disagree	Disagree
7. We cannot know if God does or does not exist.	Disgree	Disagree	Agree	Disagree	Depends on what you mean by "know"

experience.) These arguments depend on premises that can only be known on the basis of experience. For example, we may *observe* the order in the world and from that conclude that it exhibits a design that is the product of an intelligent, cosmic designer. Knowledge that is based on experience is sometimes called empirical knowledge. Second, there are a priori arguments. (*A priori* in Latin means "from what is prior," referring to what is prior to experience.) An a priori argument is based on reason and does not require empirical premises. Let's take an example from the realm of mathematics. In Euclidean geometry we begin with axioms that are considered to be self-evident; from these, we deduce a number of theorems. We learn the essential truths about triangles by reasoning about them a priori and not by observing or measuring dozens of triangles. In the sections to come, we look at two a posteriori arguments for the existence of God: the cosmological argument and the argument from design. We also look at one of the most famous a priori arguments in philosophy: the ontological argument for God. But first, take the following questionnaire to see where you stand on these issues.

WHAT DO I THINK? *Questionnaire on the Existence of God*

	Agree	Disagree
1. For someone's belief in God to be rational, he or she must have objective evidence supporting this belief.		
2. It is possible to demonstrate the existence of God through rational, objective arguments.		
3. Objective evidence cannot decide the God issue, but there are practical or subjective reasons for believing in God.		
4. Belief in God must be based on faith alone and cannot be justified either by objective or subjective reasons.		
5. God exists.		
6. God does not exist.		
7. God might exist, but there is no basis for knowing whether God does or does not exist.		

KEY TO THE QUESTIONNAIRE ON THE EXISTENCE OF GOD

Statement 1: If you agree with this statement, you are an evidentialist, either of the theistic, atheistic, or agnostic variety. If you disagree, you are a nonevidentialist.

Statement 2: If you agree, you are a theistic evidentialist or, in other words, a supporter of natural theology. If you disagree, you are an opponent of natural theology and are either a nonevidentialist theist or an atheist or agnostic.

Statement 3: If you agree, you are a nonevidentialist theist and are either a religious pragmatist or subjectivist.

Statement 4: If you agree, you are a fideist, a form of nonevidential theism.

Statement 5: If you agree, you are a theist.

Statement 6: If you agree, you are an atheist.

Statement 7: If you agree, you are an agnostic.

Notice that statements 5, 6, and 7 represent three conclusions concerning the existence of God. However, as I pointed out in chapter 1, an important issue in philosophy is not just *what* you believe, but the reasons *why* you and others have these beliefs. Hence, statements 1 through 4 concern what reasons are available or necessary to justify beliefs about God.

4.1 THE COSMOLOGICAL ARGUMENT FOR GOD

LEADING QUESTIONS: *The Cosmological Argument*

1. A magician walks into the spotlight on stage and rolls up his sleeves. He convincingly shows you and the rest of the audience that both hands are empty. He then cups his hands together and out pops a live, fluttering, white dove. You are astonished and bewildered. Would this experience convince you that things like doves can simply pop into existence without a cause? Or would you insist that the magician is a masterful sleight-of-hand artist rather than accept what your eyes apparently saw? Why?

2. Walking downtown, you notice a light being reflected off the side mirror of a pickup truck. Curious about the source of this light, you notice that it is coming from the surface of a store window. The question now is, What is the source of the light beam bouncing off the window? You now notice that it is coming from light being reflected by the store window across the street. You still want to know: What is the ultimate source of the mysterious light? The following scenarios are three proposed answers to this question. Which one do you think is most plausible? Why?

- The light has no ultimate source; it is an infinite number of light beams and reflective surfaces. For every surface that is reflecting the light, there is another reflective surface that is bouncing light to it. Thus, every manifestation of the light has a source, and each one of these sources has another source that is sending it light. This series of causes and effects goes on infinitely.
- The light has no ultimate source; it does not have a cause. Light simply arose spontaneously within the system of reflective surfaces.
- The ultimate source of the light is the sun, which generates its own light and is the first cause of the light being progressively reflected from one surface to the next.

SURVEYING THE CASE FOR THE COSMOLOGICAL ARGUMENT

These simple examples from show business and optics present some of the basic principles of the cosmological argument for God. Both cases dealt with the issues of causality and dependency and the notion that something cannot come from nothing. Doves and beams of light just do not pop into existence out of thin air. They both have a cause for appearing when and where they do. To put it another way, doves and beams of light depend on something outside themselves for their existence. While there are many versions of the cosmological argument, they all begin with the fact that the universe is not self-explanatory and argue from there that the cosmos depends on a self-sufficient cause outside itself. Hence, the cosmological argument seeks to provide an answer to the question, Why is there something rather than nothing?

ST. THOMAS AQUINAS (1225–1274)

ST. THOMAS AQUINAS
(1225–1274)

One of the foremost defenders of the cosmological argument was Thomas Aquinas. He was born into a noble family who resided in southern Italy about halfway between Rome and Naples. Aquinas was groomed by his family for a career of service in the Church. His parents' motives, however, were not as pious as they may seem; their dream was that Aquinas would rise to a position of ecclesiastical authority where he would be politically influential and even wealthy.

Around age fourteen Aquinas was sent to the University of Naples. It was an exciting place to be, for it abounded with new ideas; the recently discovered Aristotelian texts were beginning to have an impact on Christian thought. Aquinas came under the influence of the newly formed Dominican Order, which he joined sometime around 1244. His parents' plans seemed to be proceeding nicely, but they were not pleased, because the Dominicans did not aspire to be influential administrators but were humble and impoverished preachers and scholars. Nevertheless, Aquinas persuaded his family that the Dominicans were his calling and went on to earn the highest degree in theology.

Aquinas spent the remainder of his life lecturing and writing while residing alternately in Paris and Italy; he also made frequent journeys to conduct the business of his order and the Church. Aquinas died at age forty-nine, on his way to attend the Council of Lyons to carry out a diplomatic mission.

He was an astoundingly prolific writer; his works fill some twenty-five volumes. He is said to have kept four secretaries busy at once, dictating different manuscripts in progress to them, which they would then transcribe. Although his philosophy is considered the official model for Catholic thought, Aquinas has influenced Protestant philosophers and other religious thinkers as well.

The First Cause Argument

One version of the cosmological argument is sometimes called the "first cause argument." It argues that since the world contains things whose existence was caused, there necessarily had to be a First Cause of the entire series. Aquinas produced a famous version of this argument. Actually, he offered five arguments for the existence of God (or "the five ways," as he called them). The argument that is based on the notion of causation is his "second way."

FROM THOMAS AQUINAS
Summa Theologica[5]

The second way is from the nature of efficient cause.* In the world of sensible things we find there is an order of efficient causes. There is no case known (neither is it, indeed, possible) in which a thing is found to be the efficient cause of itself; for so it would be prior to itself, which is impossible. Now in efficient causes it is not possible to go on to infinity, because in all efficient causes following in order, the first is the cause of the intermediate cause, and the intermediate is the cause of the ultimate cause, whether the intermediate cause be several, or one only. Now to take away the cause is to take away the effect. Therefore, if there be no first cause among efficient causes, there will be no ultimate, nor any intermediate, cause. But if in efficient causes it is possible to go to infinity, there will be no first efficient cause, neither will there be an ultimate effect, nor any intermediate efficient causes; all of which is plainly false. Therefore it is necessary to admit a first efficient cause, to which everyone gives the name of God.

The first cause argument that Aquinas uses could be formulated in this way:

1. The world contains things that were brought into existence by some cause.
2. Everything that exists is either uncaused or caused to exist by another.
3. There cannot be an infinite regress of causes.
4. So there must be an uncaused first cause.
5. An uncaused first cause is (in part) what we mean by God.
6. Therefore, God exists.

Almost no one would object to the first premise. Every moment of our lives we are confronted with examples of things that came into existence as a result of previous causes. The second premise is a crucial one. It claims that something is either the sort of thing that requires no cause or its cause lies outside itself. Two options are ruled out by this premise. First, this premise implies that it is impossible for something to cause itself to come into existence. The reason is (as Aquinas points out) that for something to cause its own existence, it would have to exist prior to its own existence in order to bring itself into being, and this situation is absurd. Second, this premise denies that things that begin to exist can simply pop into existence. If something did not always exist, its status had to be changed

---

*When Aquinas uses the term *efficient cause,* he is speaking about one of the four kinds of causes described by Aristotle. Basically, "efficient cause" refers to the same thing that we in the twentieth century refer to as simply a cause. The "first cause" is a cause beyond which there is no further cause. It is the original cause that brought about all the subsequent causes and effects. When he refers to the "ultimate cause" he is referring to the very last cause in a series that actually brings about a certain effect. By "sensible things" he simply means physical things, or those things that can be perceived by the senses.

somehow from that of a nonexisting thing to that of an existing thing. Hence, the only two options for something that is real is that its existence does not depend on anything outside itself or its existence is dependent. Notice that the argument never says that "*everything* has a cause for its existence," for this premise would imply that God's existence had a cause.

What is the basis for the claim that "Everything that exists is either uncaused or caused to exist by another"? Many of the philosophers in the seventeenth and eighteenth centuries believed that this premise followed from the **principle of sufficient reason.** This principle (which I abbreviate as PSR) states that everything that exists must have a reason that explains why it exists and why it has the properties it does. This reason could be that the being in question is uncaused, that is, it is self-sufficient and does not depend on anything outside itself. Or the being in question could be caused by something else that provides a sufficient explanation why it exists and exists just the way it does and not otherwise. In the next reading, Richard Taylor makes explicit use of this principle.

principle of sufficient reason the principle that everything that exists must have a reason that explains why it exists and why it has the properties that it does

---

STOP AND THINK

What is the basis for the truth of the principle of sufficient reason? The following four options are the most common ones. Which one do you think best explains PSR?

- It is a generalization from human experience. We have always found that everything has a cause or an explanation.
- It is a necessary truth, like the laws of logic. It is impossible to conceive of it being false, for it is intuitively obvious.
- It is a presupposition of all inquiry. Without it, we could not make anything intelligible. It is involved in all our reasoning about the world.
- It is a questionable principle, and we have no reason to suppose that it is true.

Critics have had the most problems with the third premise of Aquinas's argument. Why can't there be an infinite series of causes? Isn't the series of whole numbers an infinite series? One possible reply to this objection is that numbers are abstractions and not concretely existing things like mountains or galaxies. It makes sense for scientists to inquire into the origins of mountains or galaxies, but it does not make sense to ask how and when did the number seven begin to exist.

Nevertheless, some critics of the cosmological argument claim it is possible to conceive of an infinite series of physical causes going back into an infinite past. In other words, they think it is reasonable to suppose that the past is without a beginning. They argue in fact, that since Aquinas believed that it makes sense to say there must be an uncaused first cause (God), why couldn't this uncaused cause of the universe simply be matter or energy instead?

- Does it make sense to suppose that the series of causes producing a present event could go on infinitely, never ending in a first cause?
- Does it make sense to speak of an uncaused being, such as God?
- Which of these two ideas is the most implausible?

The Argument from Contingency

A second version of the cosmological argument is the argument from contingency. Aquinas uses this method of reasoning in his third way. This argument begins with the fact that the world is a collection of things that are **contingent.** For something to be contingent means that its existence depends on something outside itself. In other words, neither its existence nor its nonexistence is logically necessary. If we accept PSR, then we believe that there has to be a sufficient reason for the existence of anything. However, because a contingent being does not contain the reason for its existence within itself, then whether it exists or not is dependent on some outside cause. For example, flowers exist, but only because the temperature, soil, moisture, sunshine, and other causes make their existence possible. Since the world consists of contingent things, the argument goes, so the world itself is contingent. Ultimately, everything could not be contingent, so there has to be a reason for the world's existence that is noncontingent, nondependent, self-sufficient, and uncaused. Sometimes the opposite of a contingent being is said to be a **necessary being.** A necessary being is one who contains the reason for its existence within its own nature. In other words, it does not depend on anything for its existence and nothing can prevent it from existing. Obviously, God would be such a being.

> **contingent being** a being whose existence depends on something outside itself, such that neither its existence nor nonexistence is logically necessary

> **necessary being** a being who contains the reason for its existence within its own nature

At this point it is worth noting that Aquinas believed, with the Greek philosopher Aristotle, that it is logically possible that the world always existed. Aquinas believed that even if the world was eternal, it would be eternally dependent on something outside itself to sustain it in existence. Thus, in the argument from contingency, when Aquinas talks about the cause of the world, he does not necessarily mean a first cause in time but instead a cause that is responsible for all other causes that are currently operating. Think about it this way. Right now your existence as a living, breathing human is dependent on there being oxygen in the atmosphere. But the existence of oxygen in your environment is dependent on there being plants and the earth's gravity. Likewise, these causes are at this present moment dependent on other conditions for their existence. These conditions are dependent on other conditions and so forth. So right here and now, there is a hierarchical series of causes on which your existence depends. Aquinas's point is that this whole series that is operating here and now must be dependent on something that is not itself dependent on something else. For Aquinas, this situation would be true even if the world had always existed. As a matter of fact, Aquinas did believe that the universe had a beginning, but he based this belief on the Bible and not on philosophical arguments. There is, however, a version of the argument known as the *kalām* cosmological argument, defended by some medieval Islamic, Jewish, and Christian philosophers, that begins with the premise that the universe had a beginning in time.[6]

In the following passage, the contemporary American philosopher Richard Taylor (born 1919) develops the argument from contingency. (Richard Taylor was a professor of philosophy at the University of Rochester and is now retired.) Taylor argues that even if the world had no beginning, it would still need a cause.

- After reading this passage, try to figure out what Taylor's point will be concerning the mysterious, translucent ball.
- How does Taylor define and defend the PSR?

FROM RICHARD TAYLOR

Metaphysics[7]

The Principle of Sufficient Reason

Suppose you were strolling in the woods and, in addition to the sticks, stones, and other accustomed litter of the forest floor, you one day came upon some quite unaccustomed object, something not quite like what you had ever seen before and would never expect to find in such a place. Suppose, for example, that it is a large ball, about your own height, perfectly smooth and translucent. . . .

. . . Now whatever else you might wonder about it, there is one thing you would hardly question; namely, that it did not appear there all by itself, that it owes its existence to something. You might not have the remotest idea whence and how it came to be there, but you would hardly doubt that there was an explanation. The idea that it might have come from nothing at all, that it might exist without there being any explanation of its existence, is one that few people would consider worthy of entertaining. . . .

The principle involved here has been called the principle of sufficient reason. Actually, it is a very general principle, and is best expressed by saying that, in the case of any positive truth, there is some sufficient reason for it, something which, in this sense, makes it true—in short, that there is some sort of explanation, known or unknown, for everything. . . .

The principle of sufficient reason can be illustrated in various ways, . . . and if one thinks about it, he is apt to find that he presupposes it in his thinking about reality, but it cannot be proved. It does not appear to be itself a necessary truth, and at the same time it would be most odd to say it is contingent. If one were to try proving it, he would sooner or later have to appeal to considerations that are less plausible than the principle itself. Indeed, it is hard to see how one could even make an argument for it, without already assuming it. For this reason, it might properly be called a presupposition of reason itself. . . . We shall, then, treat it here as a datum—not something that is provably true, but as something that people, whether they ever reflect upon it or not, seem more or less to presuppose. . . .

- In the next passage, how does Taylor apply PSR to the world?
- Why does he claim that if we apply PSR to individual things in the world (such as the ball), we must apply it to the world itself?

The Existence of a World

From the principle of sufficient reason it follows, of course, that there must be a reason, not only for the existence of everything in the world but for the world itself, meaning by "the world" simply everything that ever does exist, except God, in case there is a god. This principle does not imply that there must be some purpose or goal for everything, or for the totality of all things; for explanations need not, and in fact seldom are, teleological or purposeful. All the principle requires is that there be some sort of reason for everything. And it would certainly be odd to maintain that everything in the world owes its existence to something, that nothing in the world is either purely accidental, or such that it just bestows its own being upon itself, and then to deny this of the world itself. . . .

Consider again the strange ball that we imagine has been found in the forest. Now we can hardly doubt that there must be an explanation for the existence of such a thing, though we may have no notion what that explanation is. It is not, moreover, the fact of its having been found in the forest rather than elsewhere that renders an explanation necessary. It matters not in the least where it happens to be, for our question is not how it happens to be *there* but how it happens to exist at all. If we in our imagination annihilate the forest, leaving only this ball in an open field, our conviction that it is a contingent thing and owes its existence to something other than itself is not reduced in the least. If we now imagine the field to be annihilated, and in fact everything else as well to vanish into nothingness, leaving only this ball to constitute the entire physical universe, then we cannot for a moment suppose that its existence has thereby been explained, or the need of any explanation eliminated, or that its existence is suddenly rendered self-explanatory. If we now carry this thought one step further and suppose that no other reality ever has existed or ever will exist, that this ball forever constitutes the entire physical universe, then we must still insist on there being some reason independent of itself why it should exist rather than not. If there must be a reason for the existence of any particular thing, then the necessity of such a reason is not eliminated by the mere supposition that certain other things do *not* exist. And again, it matters not at all what the thing in question is, whether it be large and complex, such as the world we actually find ourselves in, or whether it be something small, simple and insignificant, such as a ball, a bacterium, or the merest grain of sand. We do not avoid the necessity of a reason for the existence of something merely by describing it in this way or that. And it would, in any event, seem plainly absurd to say that if the world were comprised entirely of a single ball about six feet in diameter, or of a single grain of sand, then it would be contingent and there would have to be some explanation other than itself why such a thing exists, but that, since the actual world is vastly more complex than this, there is no need for an explanation of its existence, independent of itself.

Beginningless Existence

It should now be noted that it is no answer to the question, why a thing exists, to state *how long* it has existed. A geologist does not suppose that he has explained why there should be rivers and mountains merely by pointing out that they are old. Similarly, if one were to ask, concerning the ball of which we have spoken, for some sufficient reason for its being, he would not receive any answer upon being told that it had been there since yesterday. Nor would it be any better answer to say that it had existed since before anyone could remember, or even that it had always existed; for the question was not one concerning its age but its existence. If, to be sure, one were to ask where a given thing came from, or how it came into being, then upon learning that it had always existed he would learn that it never really *came* into being at all; but he could still reasonably wonder why it should exist at all. If, accordingly, the world—that is, the totality of all things excepting God, in case there is a god—had really no beginning at all, but has always existed in some form or other, then there is clearly no answer to the question, where it came from and when; it did not, on this supposition, *come* from anything at all, at any time. But still, it can be asked why there is a world, why indeed there is a beginningless world, why there should have perhaps always been something rather than nothing. And, if the principle of sufficient reason is a good principle, there must be an answer to that question, an answer that is by no means supplied by giving the world an age, or even an infinite age.

- In the next passage, what is the analogy Taylor makes concerning the flame and the beams of light?
- Even if the world had *always* existed, why does this fact not eliminate the need for a God?

Creation

This brings out an important point with respect to the concept of creation that is often misunderstood, particularly by those whose thinking has been influenced by Christian ideas. People tend to think that creation—for example, the creation of the world by God—*means* creation *in time*, from which it of course logically follows that if the world had no beginning in time, then it cannot be the creation of God. This, however, is erroneous, for creation means essentially *dependence*, even in Christian theology. If one thing is the creation of another, then it depends for its existence on that other, and this is perfectly consistent with saying that both are eternal, that neither ever came into being, and hence, that neither was ever created at any point of time. Perhaps an analogy will help convey this point. Consider, then, a flame that is casting beams of light. Now there seems to be a clear sense in which the beams of light are dependent for their existence upon the flame, which is their source, while the flame, on the other hand, is not similarly dependent for its existence upon them. The beams of light arise from the flame, but the flame does not arise from them. In this sense, they are the creation of the flame; they derive their existence from it. And none of this has any reference to time; the relationship of dependence in such a case would not be altered in the slightest if we supposed that the flame, and with it the beams of light, had always existed, that neither had ever *come* into being.

Now if the world is the creation of God, its relationship to God should be thought of in this fashion; namely, that the world depends for its existence upon God, and could not exist independently of God. If God is eternal, as those who believe in God generally assume, then the world may (though it need not) be eternal too, without that altering in the least its dependence upon God for its existence, and hence without altering its being the creation of God. The supposition of God's eternality, on the other hand, does not by itself imply that the world is eternal too; for there is not the least reason why something of finite duration might not depend for its existence upon something of infinite duration—though the reverse is, of course, impossible.

- How do the previous considerations provide reasons for the existence of God?
- Is it implausible to suppose that the world depends on nothing but itself?

God

If we think of God as "the creator of heaven and earth," and if we consider heaven and earth to include everything that exists except God, then we appear to have, in the foregoing considerations, fairly strong reasons for asserting that God, as so conceived, exists. Now of course most people have much more in mind than this when they think of God, for religions have ascribed to God ever so many attributes that are not at all implied by describing him merely as the creator of the world; but that is not relevant here. Most religious persons do, in any case, think of God as being at least the creator, as that being upon which everything ultimately depends, no matter what else they may say about him in addition. It is, in fact, the first item in the creeds of Christianity that God is the "creator of heaven and earth." And, it seems, there are good metaphysical reasons, as distinguished from the persuasions of faith, for thinking that such a creative being exists.

If, as seems clearly implied by the principle of sufficient reason, there must be a reason for the existence of heaven and earth—i.e., for the world—then that reason must be found either in the world itself, or outside it, in something that is literally supranatural, or outside heaven and earth. Now if we suppose that the world—i.e., the totality of all things except God—contains within itself the reason for its existence, we are supposing that it exists by its very nature, that is, that it is a necessary being. In that case there would, of course, be no reason for saying that it must depend upon God or anything else for its existence; for if it exists by its very nature, then it depends upon nothing but itself, much as the sun depends upon nothing but itself for its heat. This, however, is implausible, for we find nothing about the world or anything in it to suggest that it exists by its own nature, and we do find, on the contrary, ever so many things to suggest that it does not. For in the first place, anything which exists by its very nature must necessarily be eternal and indestructible. It would be a self-contradiction to say of anything that it exists by its own nature, or is a necessarily existing thing, and at the same time to say that it comes into being or passes away, or that it ever could come into being or pass away. Nothing about the world seems at all like this, for concerning anything in the world, we can perfectly easily think of it as being annihilated, or as never having existed in the first place, without there being the slightest hint of any absurdity in such a supposition. . . .

. . . Ultimately, then, it would seem that the world, or the totality of contingent or perishable things, in case it exists at all, must depend upon something that is necessary and imperishable, and which accordingly exists, not in dependence upon something else, but by its own nature.

A common criticism of the argument from contingency is that the notion of a necessary being is unclear. Necessity, critics claim, is a property that applies only to propositions. For example, "all bachelors are unmarried" is a necessary proposition in the sense that it is impossible for it to be false. But what would it mean for the *existence* of something to be "necessary"? Anything that we can imagine existing, they say, we can also imagine not existing. It certainly seems logically possible to imagine God as not existing, so what sense can we make of the notion that God's existence is necessary? In a later part of his essay, Taylor responds to this objection by saying that the existence of a square circle is impossible (its nonexistence is necessary). Hence, if there are things whose nonexistence is necessary, why can't there be something whose existence is necessary? If there are things whose existence is dependent, why can't there be something whose existence is nondependent?

 STOP AND THINK

Do you think Taylor's response is plausible? Or is the notion of a necessarily existing being an odd concept that has been manufactured simply to make the argument from contingency work? Can we imagine the possibility that God does not exist? If so, then does it make sense to say that his existence is necessary? Which view of necessary existence makes the most sense?

Another criticism of the argument from contingency makes the accusation that it commits the fallacy of composition (discussed in section 1.2). Critics claim that the argument reasons in this way:

1. Every contingent being requires a sufficient reason for its existence.
2. Therefore, the collection of contingent beings known as the universe requires a sufficient reason for its existence.

However, the existence of any member of the collection could be explained by some other member of the collection without the whole collection itself requiring an explanation. Once you have explained the existence of every house on your street by referring to some builder or another who constructed each one, you don't need an additional explanation for the collection of houses. The agnostic Bertrand Russell attempted to show the fallacy in the previous argument by constructing an obviously fallacious argument that uses the same reasoning.

1. Every human being has a mother.
2. Therefore, the entire collection of human beings has a mother.

Of course, as I mentioned previously, when the critics of the cosmological argument maintain that there is not an uncaused first cause of the universe, they must either assume that it is meaningful to conceive of an infinite series of contingent causes going back into an infinite past or that the universe popped into being out of nothing. Although it is difficult to imagine an infinite series of past events, the critics point out that the limits of our imagination may not be the final word. Many of the scientific discoveries of the twentieth century would have defied the imagination of previous generations. In making up your own mind as to whether the cosmological argument is plausible, consider the pros and cons that have been discussed.

LOOKING THROUGH THE LENS OF THE COSMOLOGICAL ARGUMENT

1. Why is there something rather than nothing? The answer provided by the cosmological argument is clear. However, think about all the other possible answers. Three possibilities are: (1) The universe is just there and that is all we can say. We can't ask about its cause. (2) The universe came into being out of nothing. (3) Every event had a cause that preceded it in the past, and this series goes back in time forever. Can you think of any other alternatives? How would a defender of the cosmological argument respond to each of these alternative answers?

2. Since the universe appears to be expanding, scientists have now concluded that the existence of the universe is the result of a singular event, called the Big Bang, that happened 10 to 20 billion years ago. They believe that from an infinitesimal point, a cataclysmic explosion occurred that produced all the energy, matter, space, and time in the universe as we know it. Hence, this well-accepted scientific theory suggests that the universe has not always existed, but that it had its origins in a singular event. In what ways does the big bang theory lend support to the cosmological argument?

EXAMINING THE STRENGTHS AND WEAKNESSES OF THE COSMOLOGICAL ARGUMENT

Positive Evaluation

1. Science is the search for the causes of all the events in our world. But while each particular event can be explained by referring to some particular set of causes that preceded it, what is the cause of this whole series of causes and effects itself? Doesn't the cosmological argument attempt to carry forward and complete the scientific activity of seeking for causes by asking about the ultimate cause of everything?

2. It seems possible to imagine an infinite and unending future by imagining that each event will be followed by yet one more event. But can we conceive of an infinite past? If the universe had no beginning and always existed, then an infinite series of events would have occurred in the past. But that infinite series of events would have taken an infinite amount of time to complete, and we would never have reached our present point in time. Doesn't the cosmological argument avoid the paradox of an infinite past by arguing that the past is finite and that there was a point at which it all began?

Negative Evaluation

1. Critics have argued that the cosmological argument begins with the claim that the universe could not exist without a cause and then concludes that an uncaused being (God) is the explanation. But as the nineteenth-century philosopher Arthur Schopenhauer said, the law of universal causation "is not so accommodating as to let itself be used like a hired cab, which we dismiss when we have reached our destination." Is the proponent of the cosmological argument being inconsistent here? Why is the notion of God as an uncaused cause accepted when the notion of an uncaused universe is rejected?

2. Does the cosmological argument commit the *fallacy of composition* (see section 1.2)? The argument claims that in addition to each event having an immediate cause, the entire series of cause and effects (the universe) must itself have a cause. But consider this analogous argument: "Each person in this class has a mother, therefore, the entire class itself must have had a mother." Obviously, what is true of each member of the class (each had a mother) is not true of the class as a whole. Similarly, just because every individual event in the universe has a cause, does it follow that the universe as a whole must have had a cause?

3. The cosmological argument for God concludes that there is a first cause that brought the universe into being. But even if we accept this argument, does it prove the existence of the God of religion, a being who is infinite, intelligent, benevolent, and purposeful? Couldn't the cause of the universe be a finite, random, and impersonal cause? Does the cosmological argument give us any grounds for supposing that the first cause is singular? Couldn't a number of causes have worked together to form the universe? Isn't it too great a leap from the need for the universe to have a cause to the conclusion that this cause is a monotheistic God?

LEADING QUESTIONS: *The Argument from Design*

1. Suppose that scientists received an unusual sequence of radio signals that originated somewhere in outer space. Furthermore, suppose that the signals could be interpreted as representing numbers and that the numbers were an ordered sequence of prime numbers (1, 3, 5, 7, 11, 13, 17, . . .). Would these signals be evidence that there is intelligent life in outer space?

2. Suppose you were walking along a beach and came across numerous sticks that had apparently been washed up by the tide. However, suppose that amidst the random clutter of sticks, some of them were arranged in this way: I LOVE PAM. How probable is it that this arrangement came about by chance? How probable is it that the arrangement was the result of intelligent planning?

3. Suppose you are playing poker with a character known as Slick. He gives the deck a thorough shuffle and deals the cards. He wins the first round because he has four aces in his hand. You know that the odds of drawing four aces from a shuffled deck is 1 in 54,145. You play again and again and again. No matter how many hands are dealt and who the dealer is, Slick always wins by having the four aces. It is logically possible that Slick is very, very lucky and that he was randomly dealt the aces each time. Nevertheless, how likely is it that you would suspect that Slick's winning hands were the result of planning and trickery and not chance?

SURVEYING THE CASE FOR THE DESIGN ARGUMENT

All the leading questions are examples of apparent design. I call it "apparent" design because it is not impossible that the results came about through blind chance. However, in each case, we would find it highly unlikely that sheer randomness is the explanation. The most likely explanation is that the results were the product of intelligent, purposeful design. It is probable that the series of prime numbers were generated by a being who knows mathematics, the message in the sand was written by a lover, and the winning poker hands were the result of Slick's deceptive card manipulation. The issue of chance versus design is the central theme in this section's argument for God.

One of the most popular arguments for God's existence is based on the evidence of design in the world. For obvious reasons, this argument is called "the argument from design," but philosophers usually call it the **teleological argument** for the existence of God. The name comes from the Greek word *telos,* which means "end" or "goal." The argument is called the teleological argument because it points to the fact that many things and processes in the universe seem as though they were designed to fulfill purposeful ends or goals. Like the cosmological argument, the

teleological argument
the argument for God's existence based on the evidence of design in the world

teleological argument is an a posteriori argument, because it reasons from certain observed features of the world. The data that it uses constitute evidence of apparent design in the world. Its main thesis is "evidence of design implies a designer." Any argument for God based on the evidence of design must address two issues. First, how do we distinguish the mere appearance of design from genuine design? Second, can the order in nature be explained by any hypothesis other than that of an intelligent, purposeful cause that is above nature but operates on it?

 THOUGHT EXPERIMENT

Chance versus Design

Sometimes we find objects in nature that were obviously created by impersonal, natural causes (rock formations, dandelions, moss growing on trees). Other times, we find objects lying about that were obviously created by intelligent, purposeful causes (arrowheads, a coin, initials scratched onto a rock). At times, archeologists and explorers may not be sure whether the objects they found are products of nature or human craftsmanship. For example, archeologists might find a collection of rocks that appear to be placed in the pattern of an arrow, but that pattern could conceivably have appeared by coincidence. Similarly, explorers might dig up a metallic deposit that is normally found in the earth but that appears to be shaped in the form of some symbol. In both cases the question "design or chance?" is the issue.

- In ambiguous cases like these, what sorts of criteria would you use to decide whether something is the result of random, natural causes or purposeful design?
- Have you ever made the mistake of thinking something was humanly designed when it was really the product of chance, natural causes? How did you find out you were mistaken?
- To what degree does the problem of deciding whether something exhibits design or not affect the teleological argument?

WILLIAM PALEY (1743–1805)

One of the most famous and clearest versions of the teleological argument was given by William Paley, a British clergyman and philosopher. The following excerpt is from his book *Natural Theology, or Evidences of the Existence and Attributes of the Deity Collected from the Appearances of Nature* (1802).

WILLIAM PALEY
(1743–1805)

 FROM WILLIAM PALEY
Natural Theology[8]

In crossing a heath, suppose I pitched my foot against a *stone,* and were asked how the stone came to be there, I might possibly answer that for anything I knew to the contrary it had lain there for ever; nor would it, perhaps, be very easy to shew the absurdity of this answer. But suppose I had found a *watch* upon the ground, and it should be inquired how the watch happened to be in that place. I should hardly think of the answer which I had before given, that for any thing I knew the watch might have always been there. Yet why should not this answer serve for the watch as well as for the stone; why is it not as admissible in the second case as in the first? For this reason, and for no other, namely, that when we come to inspect the watch, we perceive—what we could not discover in the stone—that its several parts are framed and put together for a purpose, e.g., that they are so formed and adjusted as to produce motion, and that motion so regulated as to point out the hour of the day; that, if the different parts had been differently shaped from what they are, or placed after any other manner or in any other order than that in which they are placed, either no motion at all would have been carried on in the machine, or none that would have answered the use that is now served by it. . . . This mechanism being observed . . . the inference we think is inevitable, that the watch must have had a maker—that there must have existed, at some time and at some place or other, an artificer or artificers who formed it for the purpose which we find it actually to answer, who comprehended its construction and designed its use. . . .

. . . For every indication of contrivance, every manifestation of design, which existed in the watch, exists in the works of nature, with the difference on the side of nature of being greater and more, and that in a degree which exceeds all computation.

The teleological argument (or the design argument) has this general form:

1. The universe exhibits apparent design, that is, the ordering of complex means to the fulfillment of intelligible goals, ends, or purposes.
2. We have usually found a purposive, intelligent will to be the cause of such design or order.
3. Therefore, it is reasonable to conclude that the universe was caused by a purposive, intelligent will.

There are several things to notice about the teleological argument. First, it is based on an analogy. It attempts to draw our attention to the alleged similarities between human creations (clocks, statues, computer programs, and so on) and the universe as a whole. Hence, the strength of the argument depends on how confident we are that meaningful similarities exist. The teleological argument's claim that the universe exhibits evidence of design is much less obvious than the cosmological argument's claim that contingent beings exist and depend on prior causes. Second, most versions of the argument take the form of probabilistic arguments or arguments to the best explanation. In other words, they do not show that it is absolutely necessary that the universe had a designer but that a designer is the most probable explanation. Finally, of all the theistic arguments, the teleological argument probably is the least abstract, the easiest to understand, and has the most popular appeal.

SCIENCE AND COSMIC DESIGN

In contrast to the common notion that science has replaced religion, some scientists claim that the more we learn about the complexity and intricate balance of the universe, the stronger the case becomes for an intelligent designer.[9] For example, although Charles Darwin's theory of evolution is often thought to be in conflict with religion, Darwin himself was a theist when he first published *Origin of Species* in 1859. (His only earned academic degree was in theology.) Even though he became an agnostic later in life, Darwin originally saw his scientific findings as confirming divine design. He said that the strongest argument for the existence of God was

> the extreme difficulty or rather impossibility of conceiving this immense and wonderful universe, including man with his capacity of looking far backward and far into futurity, as the result of blind chance or necessity. When thus reflecting I feel compelled to look to a First Cause having an intelligent mind in some degree analogous to that of man; and I deserve to be called a Theist.[10]

The famous astronomer Fred Hoyle is reported to have had his atheism shaken when he discovered the remarkable nuclear resonance structure of carbon and oxygen that is critical to the existence of life.[11] Hoyle compared the formation of life by the random shuffling of molecules to "a whirlwind passing through an aircraft factory and blowing scattered components into a functioning Boeing 747." This discovery led him to conclude that the order of the universe is not an accident but that "the universe is a put-up job."[12]

The renowned British mathematical physicist Paul Davies says that it is hard to imagine that the thousands of carefully arranged atoms in the DNA molecule could have come about randomly. "It is easy to estimate the odds against random permutations of molecules assembling DNA. It is about $10^{40,000}$ to one against! That is the same as tossing a coin and achieving heads roughly 130,000 times in a row."[13] Although Davies recognizes that the significance of these discoveries is subject to interpretation, the structure of DNA and dozens of other examples of the intricate framework of the universe led him to conclude that

> It is hard to resist the impression that the present structure of the universe, apparently so sensitive to minor alterations in the numbers, has been rather carefully thought

out . . . the seemingly miraculous concurrence of these numerical values remain the most compelling evidence for cosmic design.[14]

DAVID HUME

Not everyone has been persuaded by argument. David Hume, the Scottish skeptic, provided a formidable series of objections to the argument from design. Hume was introduced in the discussion of skepticism (section 2.1), and details of his life may be found there. Hume's critique of the design argument was presented in his *Dialogues Concerning Natural Religion,* published in 1779, three years after his death. Ironically, although these criticisms came out twenty-three years before William Paley wrote his book and even though Paley criticized Hume on other issues, he never directly responded to Hume's objections to the arguments for God. As the title of his book suggests, Hume's arguments are presented in the course of a conversation between three fictional characters. Cleanthes is a natural theologian who presents some of the standard arguments for God. Demea is an orthodox believer who alternates between faith and rational arguments to justify his beliefs. Finally, Philo the skeptic provides the refutations of the traditional religious arguments.

In the course of the dialogue, Cleanthes presents the following version of the argument from design:

1. In human creations (watches, houses, ships) we find the adaptation of means to ends that are the result of design, thought, wisdom, and intelligence.
2. In nature we find a similar adapting of means to ends, but on a much grander scale.
3. From similar effects we may infer similar causes.
4. So, it must be the case that the magnificent mechanism of the universe is the result of a very great, wise, intelligent designer.

In responding to this argument, Philo employs a twofold strategy. The arguments that compose the first strategy deny that there are relevant similarities between human machines and nature. The second strategy concedes this point but claims that the design argument does not give us anything like the Judeo-Christian God.

Philo's First Strategy

Philo claims that the analogy between human creations (such as machines or houses) and the universe is weak, for there are too many differences between them to know anything about the cause of the universe. Under this strategy (which I call A), Hume has at least three arguments (A1, A2, and A3). The following passage presents strategy A1 through the voice of Philo.

- See if you can formulate Philo's argument in your own words.
- Why can we infer that a house had a creator, but cannot infer that the universe did?

FROM DAVID HUME
Dialogues Concerning Natural Religion[15]

That a stone will fall, that fire will burn, that the earth has solidity, we have observed a thousand and a thousand times; and when any new instance of this nature is presented, we draw without hesitation the accustomed inference. The exact similarity of the cases gives us a perfect assurance of a similar event; and a stronger evidence is never desired nor sought after. But wherever you depart, in the least, from the similarity of the cases, you diminish proportionably the evidence; and may at last bring it to a very weak *analogy,* which is confessedly liable to error and uncertainty. . . .

If we see a house, CLEANTHES, we conclude, with the greatest certainty, that it had an architect or builder; because this is precisely that species of effect which we have experienced to proceed from that species of cause. But surely you will not affirm, that the universe bears such a resemblance to a house, that we can with the same certainty infer a similar cause, or that the analogy is here entire and perfect. The dissimilitude is so striking, that the utmost you can here pretend to is a guess, a conjecture, a presumption concerning a similar cause; and how that pretension will be received in the world, I leave you to consider.

In the preceding argument (A1), Philo insists that in order to infer the nature of something, it must be similar to other things with which we are familiar. In an example not included in the previous quotation, he says that if we have observed the circulatory system in many humans, we may conclude that it will be the same in other humans that we have not examined. But if you only knew about the circulatory system in frogs or fishes or the movement of fluids within plant life, your ability to conclude anything about humans would become successively weaker in each case. Similarly, in the preceding passage, Philo argues that the differences between a house and the universe are so great, the fact that the first had an intelligent designer does not allow us to infer that the universe did also.

- In the following passage, what is Philo's point concerning the hair and the leaf?

But can you think, CLEANTHES, that your usual phlegm and philosophy have been preserved in so wide a step as you have taken, when you compared to the universe houses, ships, furniture, machines, and, from their similarity in some circumstances, inferred a similarity in their causes? Thought, design, intelligence, such as we discover in men and other animals, is no more than one of the springs and principles of the universe, as well as heat or cold, attraction or repulsion, and a hundred others, which fall under daily observation. It is an active cause, by which some particular parts of nature, we find, produce alterations on other parts. But can a conclusion, with any propriety, be transferred from parts to the whole? Does not the great disproportion bar all comparison and inference? From observing the growth of a hair, can we learn any thing concerning the generation of a man? Would the manner of a leaf's blowing, even though perfectly known, afford us any instruction concerning the vegetation of a tree?

In the preceding argument (A2), Philo asks that because (human) intelligence and design is only a fraction of the many kinds of causality that we observe operating in the world, why do we pick out intelligence as the factor that caused the whole system? He then argues that we cannot reason from the part to the whole. By observing a hair or a leaf, we could not learn how a human or a tree originates. Since we only know about limited portions of the universe, how can we conclude anything about how the whole universe was produced?

 STOP AND THINK

On this last point, the theist might reply that scientists today frequently argue from the part to the whole. From a single hair, scientists can infer what species it came from. Furthermore, if it is a human hair, they can determine the owner's gender, race, and what diseases he or she had.

- Can you think of any other ways in which we reason from the part to the whole?
- In the light of these examples, what do you think of Philo's second argument (A2)?

- In the next passage, what does Philo say is a major difference between our knowledge of the causes of ships or cities and our attempts to reason about the origin of the world?

When two *species* of objects have always been observed to be conjoined together, I can *infer*, by custom, the existence of one wherever I *see* the existence of the other: And this I call an argument from experience. But how this argument can have place, where the objects, as in the present case, are single, individual, without parallel, or specific resemblance, may be difficult to explain. And will any man tell me with a serious countenance, that an orderly universe must arise from some thought and art like the human; because we have experience of it? To ascertain this reasoning, it were requisite that we had experience of the origin of worlds; and it is not sufficient, surely, that we have seen ships and cities arise from human art and contrivance.

In the passage you just read (argument A3), Philo claims that we have an insufficient database for causal reasoning about the cosmos. We can infer that x causes y when we have observed many repeated cases of events of type x followed by events of type y. For example, research on the causes of Alzheimer's disease would get nowhere if scientists only had one patient to examine. Similarly, we have only one example of a universe to study. So we have no information about what sorts of causes produce a universe.

Philo's Second Strategy

In Philo's second strategy (B), he concedes the premises of his opponent and assumes that we can reason from like effects to like causes in the case of machines and the universe. But then he turns Cleanthes' own argument against him. Philo argues that the teleological argument leaves us with an all-too-human deity.

- According to Philo, what are several consequences of comparing a machine and its human creator to the universe and its creator?

Now, CLEANTHES, said PHILO, with an air of alacrity and triumph, mark the consequences. *First,* by this method of reasoning, you renounce all claim to infinity in any of the attributes of the Deity. For, as the cause ought only to be proportioned to the effect, and the effect, so far as it falls under our cognisance, is not infinite; what pretensions have we, upon your suppositions, to ascribe that attribute to the Divine Being? You will still insist, that, by removing him so much from all similarity to human creatures, we give in to the most arbitrary hypothesis, and at the same time weaken all proofs of his existence.

Secondly, You have no reason, on your theory, for ascribing perfection to the Deity, even in his finite capacity, or for supposing him free from every error, mistake, or incoherence, in his undertakings. There are many inexplicable difficulties in the works of Nature, which, if we allow a perfect author to be proved *a priori,* are easily solved, and become only seeming difficulties, from the narrow capacity of man, who cannot trace infinite relations. But according to your method of reasoning, these difficulties become all real; and perhaps will be insisted on, as new instances of likeness to human art and contrivance. At least, you must acknowledge, that it is impossible for us to tell, from our limited views, whether this system contains any great faults, or deserves any considerable praise, if compared to other possible, and even real systems. Could a peasant, if the *Aeneid* were read to him, pronounce that poem to be absolutely faultless, or even assign to it its proper rank among the productions of human wit, he, who had never seen any other production?

But were this world ever so perfect a production, it must still remain uncertain, whether all the excellences of the work can justly be ascribed to the workman. If we survey a ship, what an exalted idea must we form of the ingenuity of the carpenter who framed so complicated, useful, and beautiful a machine? And what surprise must we feel, when we find him a stupid mechanic, who imitated others, and copied an art, which, through a long succession of ages, after multiplied trials, mistakes, corrections, deliberations, and controversies, had been gradually improving? Many worlds might have been botched and bungled, throughout an eternity, ere this system was struck out; much labour lost, many fruitless trials made; and a slow, but continued improvement carried on during infinite ages in the art of world-making. In such subjects, who can determine, where the truth; nay, who can conjecture where the probability lies, amidst a great number of hypotheses which may be proposed, and a still greater which may be imagined?

Here Philo takes Cleanthes' own point that like effects prove like causes and argues that if the universe is to be compared to the creation of a human machine, then the following conclusions are more probable than that of the biblical God: (1) God is not infinite, for a finite effect (the universe) only requires a finite cause; (2) God is not perfect, for, from our limited perspective, we cannot tell if his creation is as good as possible (In fact, the presence of natural evil and suffering suggest that the world is very defective.); (3) God is not perfectly intelligent, for human inventions came about through trial and error.

In the remainder of this part of the discussion, Philo suggests other ways in which the analogy between the creators of machines and the creator of the universe would imply that the cause of the universe has all the limitations we find in human inventors. He says, for example, that we may as well conclude that God did not work alone, for the most complex of human machines are produced by a crew of designers and workers. Furthermore, if the cause of the universe is similar to human creators, then it is mortal, comes in two genders, and is physical. Finally, Hume has Philo suggest that instead of comparing the universe to a machine, we could just as easily think of it like an animal or a vegetable that evolves through blind, organic, natural processes.

It is important to note that in putting forth these counterarguments to the teleological argument, Hume is not claiming that there is no God or that he is finite and stupid or that there are a plurality of gods. Hume is simply saying that the evidence does not give us any more reason for believing in the biblical God than it does for these other alternatives. The most we can conclude from nature, he says, is that "the cause or causes of order in the universe probably bear some remote analogy to human intelligence."[16] However, this conclusion is too ambiguous or obscure to give much comfort to the theist. In the final analysis, Hume is an agnostic or a religious skeptic. He believes that we have no evidence for thinking that God does or does not exist.

EVOLUTION VERSUS DESIGN

In the nineteenth century, the design argument ran against one of its most difficult problems in the scientific work of Charles Darwin (1809–1882). Until then the hypothesis of intelligent design seemed to be the best explanation available for the order manifested within biological systems. For example, though there are countless varieties of teeth in nature, each creature has the type of teeth necessary to chew the sort of food its stomach requires. Canines have sharp teeth for ripping meat, and meat is the type of food that their stomachs can process. On the other hand, a canine's teeth would not work for horses, who must eat grass to sustain themselves. Many theistic scientists prior to Darwin argued that this harmony between each animal's teeth and its dietary needs could not be the product of chance, but had to be the result of an intelligent, benevolent, and purposeful design.[17]

With the 1859 publication of Darwin's theory of evolution in *Origin of Species,* however, the teleological argument seemed to lose some of its persuasive force. Darwin's findings can be briefly summarized as follows: (1) *random variations* occur in animals and plants that are inherited by their offspring. (2) Since more offspring are produced than the environment can sustain, there is a *struggle for survival.* (3) Those individuals in which the variations are advantageous will be more likely to survive than the others, resulting in the *survival of the fittest.* Consequently, those individuals will tend to live longer, produce more offspring, and pass on their advantageous biological traits. (4) Over a long period of time the process of *natural selection* produces populations of organisms that are highly developed and well-suited for survival. In short, the defenders of the teleological argument assumed that divine design preceded the creation of each species and that it explained why there is so much harmony, efficiency, and order in the biological realm. Darwin's theory of natural selection, however, presented the reverse picture. In this alternative view, nature produces random changes with no purpose in mind and the appearance of design is the end result of blind, natural selection. A forceful presentation of the Darwinian objection to divine purpose is made in biologist Richard Dawkins's best-selling book *The Blind Watchmaker,* which has the subtitle *Why the Evidence of Evolution Reveals a Universe without Design.* His reply to Paley's argument is, "All appearance to the contrary, the only watchmaker in nature is the blind forces of physics."[18]

As I mentioned at the beginning of this section, Darwin initially thought that his own theory of evolution was consistent with the notion of divine purpose and design. He theorized that God supervised the overall scheme of nature while allowing chance to play a role in the details.[19] Although Darwin later had doubts about even this very general notion of design, other scientists, theologians, and philosophers took up his thesis that evolution posed no threat to the teleological argument. F. R. Tennant (1866–1957), who represented all three of those professions, developed a "wider teleological argument" that allowed particular instances of design, such as the development of the human eye, to be explained by natural causes but argued that natural processes and laws were merely instruments used by God. Thus, the evidence of design was found in the universe as a whole and the system of laws that made evolution possible.[20] More recently, contemporary philosopher Richard Swinburne has provided a probabilistic argument from design that attempts to evade the force of the Darwinian objection.[21] Hence, modern versions of the argument reject Paley's analogy in which God, like a watchmaker, designs every detail of the system of nature at a single point in time. Instead, we have purposeful design on the "installment plan," which takes place over the long process of evolution, allows for some randomness in nature, and looks for design in the total system rather than in every detail.[22] On the other hand, in contrast to those who propose a happy marriage between evolution and divine purpose, both atheists who embrace evolutionary biology and conservative religious critics of evolution maintain that we must choose between blind evolution and divine design, for the two theses present radically different pictures of nature. Most contemporary philosophers believe that Paley's version of the argument from design, at least as it applies to biological nature, is no longer plausible in the light of the Darwinian objection.

LOOKING THROUGH THE LENS OF THE ARGUMENT FROM DESIGN

1. Although science has sometimes been considered the enemy of religion, the fact remains that many of the great scientists since the beginnings of modern science to our day (e.g., Copernicus, Galileo, Kepler, Newton, Einstein) have also been persons of great religious faith. What connections might there be between the belief in a God of reason and order who created the universe and the belief that studying the world scientifically will be fruitful?

2. According to atheism, we are just complex collections of particles of matter who seek to create our little islands of meaning within an otherwise meaningless universe. According to theism, however, our search for meaning, purpose, and values fits into the grand scheme of things. The argument from design says that both the universe as a whole and the human beings in it are the products of an intelligent, purposeful, and benevolent divine architect. What implications does the argument from design have for how we should treat nature and one another? Does theism provide a better basis for explaining why we think of ourselves and our neighbors as having a special dignity and worth?

EXAMINING THE STRENGTHS AND WEAKNESSES OF THE ARGUMENT FROM DESIGN

Positive Evaluation

1. Theism provides an explanation for the delicate balance of complex variables that maintains the universe and makes the existence of life on our planet possible. On the other hand, the atheist must chalk this balance up to an enormous series of fortunate but random events that had no prevision of the ends they were achieving. But modern science was first developed by theists who believed that the world has a rational order, and science continues to require this belief. For this reason, the scientist and religious mystic Albert Einstein referred to the belief that the world is mathematically ordered as a "miracle creed." Although the argument from design

is not absolutely conclusive, could it be argued that theism provides the best explanation for the order in the universe?

2. Many scientists today are searching for signs of intelligent life in outer space. For example, they are analyzing radio signals from space to see if the signals contain anything other than random noise. If, for example, scientists received a packet of signals that represented a significant portion of the prime number series, they would conclude that this signal could not have happened by chance but that it was the product of intelligence. How is this scientific search for intelligence, using design and purposive patterns as criteria, supportive of the approach taken by the argument from design for the existence of a divine intelligence?

Negative Evaluation

1. Progress in science has continually replaced explanations of events in terms of God's purposes with impersonal, natural explanations. For example, disease was once thought to be the result of God's punishment. But we now know that disease is the result of viruses and other natural causes and that both believers and atheists alike are subject to the same diseases. Similarly, the harmonious functioning among the biological systems of our bodies was once thought to be the result of divine planning. But we now know that only those species whose systems function well will survive. Don't these examples suggest that all the so-called evidence of design in the world will eventually be seen as the result of random, impersonal processes?

2. If we add up all the evidence of design, purpose, and benevolence in the world and compare that with all the evidence of randomness, chance, and evil, don't they balance each other out? Don't we have a tendency to impose patterns of design on the phenomena, much as we do when we "see" meaningful faces or shapes in the clouds? When we roll two dice one hundred times, it is likely that combinations adding up to seven will occur more often than the combinations adding up to two or twelve. However, this "pattern" is not the result of any design but is based on the law of probabilities. Is all the evidence of design in the world the result of our tendency to impose meaningful patterns on random processes? Do we have any reason to believe that the patterns in nature are purposeful and not the result of probability and chance? Isn't the claim that the world exhibits design really rather doubtful?

4.3 THE ONTOLOGICAL ARGUMENT FOR GOD

 LEADING QUESTIONS: *The Ontological Argument*

1. Suppose I told you that in my pocket was a round square. Would you believe me? Why not? How could you know that a round square does not exist even though you have had no experience of the contents of my pocket? Do these questions suggest that reason can give us some information about existence?

2. The most common conception of God in Western thought is that he is a perfect being. It would be absurd to suppose that God had all the properties commonly attributed to him, except that he was absent-minded and forgetful. Forgetfulness is a deficiency that could not be part of the nature of a perfect God. Similarly, could we imagine that there is a God, but that he just happens to be hanging around the universe? Could God's existence be a fluke or something that was dependent on other conditions? Don't these questions suggest that the concept of God is the concept of a being whose existence is necessary and who does not depend on anything else for existence?

SURVEYING THE CASE FOR THE ONTOLOGICAL ARGUMENT

The preceding questions raise the following issues: Can reason alone tell us about what does or does not exist in reality? Is it possible to say that the concept of God is that of a perfect being at the same time we say that such a perfect being lacks existence? Does God necessarily exist? Is it meaningful to attribute necessary existence to anything? These issues are central to an argument for God's existence known as the ontological argument. The adjective *ontological* is derived from the Greek and literally means "having to do with the science of being." Thus this argument attempts to derive God's existence from the very concept of God's being. Before looking at the argument itself, consider the following thought experiment borrowed from contemporary philosopher William Rowe.[23]

THOUGHT EXPERIMENT

Existence and Nonexistence

The following table consists of two lists. On the left are things that exist and on the right are things that do not exist.

Things That Exist	Things That Do Not Exist
1. The Empire State Building	1. The Fountain of Youth
2. Dogs	2. Unicorns
3. The Planet Mars	3. The Abominable Snowman
4. ?	4. Round Squares

Notice that the first three items on each list has this feature in common: it is logically possible that the world could have been such that they were on the other list. For example, dogs exist, but we can imagine that this world could have been one in which there were no dogs. Real, live unicorns do not exist, but there is no logical absurdity in imagining that they could have been on the left list if the world had turned out differently. These sorts of things, whose existence and nonexistence is possible, are known as *contingent beings*. When we discussed the cosmological argument I pointed out that contingent beings are sometimes identified as dependent beings. They can either exist or not exist;

(Continued . . .)

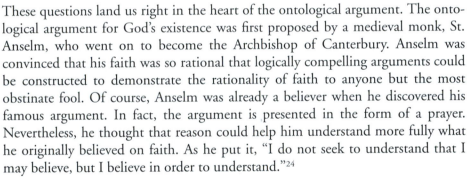

(. . . continued)

consequently, if they do exist it is because their existence is dependent on causes outside themselves.

The last item on the right list is unique. Round squares do not exist, but unlike the other items on this list, it is logically impossible for them to have been on the left list. It is logically impossible for round squares to exist. Think of some other things that belong on the right list but that are *logically* impossible to put on the left list.

The question is whether there could there be an item on the left list that *logically could not* be on the right list. Such an item would be something that necessarily exists; it would be logically impossible for this item not to exist. We can summarize our results in this way. There are things that (1) exist, but whose nonexistence is logically possible (dogs), (2) do not exist, but whose existence is logically possible (unicorns), and (3) do not exist and whose existence is logically impossible (round squares). Now, why shouldn't there be a final category, (4) something that exists and whose *nonexistence* is *logically impossible*? What would be in this category? Some philosophers say that this category is precisely what we mean by God. Before going on, answer these remaining questions: Could there be something in category 4? Is the notion of a necessary being meaningful? Why or why not?

ST. ANSELM (1033–1109)

ST. ANSELM
(1033–1109)

These questions land us right in the heart of the ontological argument. The ontological argument for God's existence was first proposed by a medieval monk, St. Anselm, who went on to become the Archbishop of Canterbury. Anselm was convinced that his faith was so rational that logically compelling arguments could be constructed to demonstrate the rationality of faith to anyone but the most obstinate fool. Of course, Anselm was already a believer when he discovered his famous argument. In fact, the argument is presented in the form of a prayer. Nevertheless, he thought that reason could help him understand more fully what he originally believed on faith. As he put it, "I do not seek to understand that I may believe, but I believe in order to understand."[24]

- In the following passage, what does Anselm mean when he defines God as "a being than which nothing greater can be conceived"?
- What is the distinction Anselm makes between something "existing in the understanding alone" and "existing in reality"?
- Why can the greatest conceivable being not exist in the understanding alone?

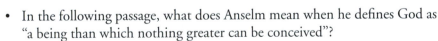

FROM ST. ANSELM

Proslogium[25]

And so, Lord, do thou, who dost give understanding to faith, give me, so far as thou knowest it to be profitable, to understand that thou art as we believe; and that thou art that which we believe. And indeed, we believe that thou art a being than which nothing greater can be conceived. Or is there no such nature, since the fool hath said in his heart, there is no God? (Psalms 14:1). But at any rate, this very fool, when he hears of this being of which I speak—a being than which nothing greater can be conceived—understands what he hears, and what he understands is in his understanding; although he does not understand it to exist.

For, it is one thing for an object to be in the understanding, and another to understand that the object exists. When a painter first conceives of what he will afterwards paint, he has it in his understanding, but he does not yet understand it to be, because he has not yet painted it. But after he has made the painting, he both has it in his understanding and he understands that it exists, because he has made it.

Hence, even the fool is convinced that something exists in the understanding, at least, than which nothing greater can be conceived. For, when he hears of this, he understands it. And whatever is understood, exists in the understanding. And assuredly that, than which nothing greater can be conceived, cannot exist in the understanding alone. For, suppose it exists in the understanding alone: then it can be conceived to exist in reality; which is greater.

Therefore, if that, than which nothing greater can be conceived, exists in the understanding alone, the very being, than which nothing greater can be conceived, is one, than which a greater can be conceived. But obviously this is impossible. Hence, there is no doubt that there exists a being, than which nothing greater can be conceived, and it exists both in the understanding and in reality.

Anselm's version of the ontological argument could be formulated as follows:

1. I have, within my understanding, an idea of God.
2. This idea of God is the idea of a being that is the greatest that can be conceived.
3. A being is greater if it exists in reality than if it exists only in the understanding.
4. If God exists in the understanding alone, then a greater being can be conceived, namely one that also exists in reality.
5. But premise 4 is a contradiction, for it says I can conceive of a greater being than the greatest conceivable being.
6. So if I have an idea of the greatest conceivable being, such a being must exist both in my understanding and in reality.
7. Therefore, God exists in reality.

According to Anselm, to deny that God exists, it is necessary to have the idea of God in mind. Hence, God exists in the understanding (even for the atheist). Furthermore, Anselm claims that whatever we mean by "God," we must mean the most perfect, greatest possible being imaginable or "a being than which none greater can be conceived." But if I think of God (the greatest conceivable being) as existing only in my imagination, I have encountered a contradiction (premise 4). This form of argument, known as a *reductio ad absurdum,* assumes the opposite of what a person is trying to prove and goes on to show that it leads to an absurdity or contradiction. Anselm considers the atheistic possibility that God exists in the understanding alone, but argues that this possibility leads to a contradiction (the greatest conceivable being is not the greatest conceivable being). However, these premises all depend on the controversial premise 3. Does existing in reality make something better? Wouldn't it be better if cancer cells, the national debt, and automobile crashes existed in the imagination alone and not in reality? In what follows we see how premise 3 of Anselm's argument was turned against him by his critics.

Some of Anselm's critics claim that his argument proves too much. For example, Gaunilo, a monk who was a contemporary of Anselm, wrote a sarcastic reply titled "On Behalf of the Fool." Gaunilo was a fellow Christian, so he believed that God existed, but he did not think that Anselm's argument was a good one. To prove his claim, Gaunilo argued that the same form of argument could be used to demonstrate the necessary existence of a perfect island. To see Gaunilo's point, work through the following thought experiment.

 THOUGHT EXPERIMENT

The Perfect Island

Go over the argument again and whenever it mentions God (or "a being than which nothing greater can be perceived"), plug in one of the following entities instead: a perfect island, the perfect boyfriend (or girlfriend), the perfect baseball player. This argument counters Anselm's reductio ad absurdum with another reductio ad absurdum. Surely there is something wrong, the critic charges, if an argument for God also allows us to prove the existence of a perfect island.

- Do you think Gaunilo's point is a fatal objection to Anselm's argument?
- Is there a significant difference between using the argument to prove God's existence and using it to prove the existence of a perfect island?
- How might Anselm reply to this objection?

Another objection made against the ontological argument states that *existence* is not a property that can be listed among the other properties that define God's perfection, such as wisdom, benevolence, power, and so on. This criticism was put forth by Immanuel Kant (1724–1804) among others. To see the force of this objection, try the two thought experiments in the next box.

 THOUGHT EXPERIMENT

The Property of Existence

1. Imagine a gold ring circling one of your fingers. Now add to your image of the ring the year of your graduation etched into the metal. Think of the ring as also bearing the name of your school. Now add to this image a large, perfect diamond set into the ring. Now add to your image of the ring the property of existence. Has this last step

(Continued . . .)

(. . . continued)

changed your concept of the ring at all? While I was describing the ring, you could add the various properties to your image or concept of the ring. In thinking about the ring, however, you were already thinking of it as though it existed. Hence, existence does not seem to be another property that could enhance the concept of the ring.

2. Suppose that the following two lists represent Julie's and Christin's conception of the "perfect" partner.

Julie's perfect partner	Christin's perfect partner
1. Intelligent	1. Intelligent
2. Sensitive	2. Sensitive
3. Sense of humor	3. Sense of humor
4. Good cook	4. Good cook
	5. Existence

Notice that the two lists are identical, with one exception. Unlike Julie, Christin has added the property of existence to the list. Are their lists really different? Has Christin really added anything in addition to Julie's concept of the perfect partner? Wouldn't it be true that anyone whose properties matched up with Christin's list would also match up with Julie's list? Does this experiment show that existence really isn't a property that can make the concept of something better?

LOOKING THROUGH THE LENS OF THE ONTOLOGICAL ARGUMENT

1. With respect to most things in the world, the *idea* of something tells us nothing about its *existence*. For example, to have the idea of a kangaroo does not tell you whether kangaroos exist in the world. But isn't the idea of God absolutely unique? Shouldn't we expect that the idea of God would have logically unique properties? This world just happens to be one in which strange creatures like kangaroos do exist and Santa Claus does not exist. But could this world be one in which God just happens to exist or not exist?

2. Some philosophers (such as David Hume) maintain that logic does not tell us about the world but only about the relations between our ideas. But what would be the point of having logically well-ordered ideas if our ideas told us nothing whatsoever about reality? According to the proponents of the ontological argument, does logic tell us anything about reality?

EXAMINING THE STRENGTHS AND WEAKNESSES OF THE ONTOLOGICAL ARGUMENT

Positive Evaluation

1. With respect to most things we can think about (e.g., giraffes and unicorns), it is possible that they exist and also possible that they do not exist; experience is the only way we have of telling us which is which. But there are some things whose

nonexistence is logically necessary (round squares). Logic (and not experience) tells us that they cannot exist. Accordingly, couldn't there be something (God) whose existence is logically necessary and whose nonexistence is logically impossible? If logic can tell us about reality in the case of round squares, why can't it tell us about the existence of God?

2. If we can imagine that something does not exist, it is because we can imagine conditions that prevented its existence. For example, unicorns do not exist because the biological conditions that would cause them to evolve never occurred. Snowflakes do not exist in the desert, because the high temperatures prevent them from forming. Can you imagine any conditions that would prevent a nondependent being such as God from existing? If the concept of God is the concept of a being who could not be caused to exist nor prevented from existing, then isn't the concept of God necessarily that of an existing being? If so, then doesn't God necessarily exist?

Negative Evaluation

1. Isn't atheism a logically possible position? Can't we conceive of a logically possible universe in which there is no God? If so, doesn't our ability to imagine such a universe imply that God's existence is not logically necessary? Doesn't the fact that we can conceive of an atheistic universe undermine the ontological argument?

2. The concept of a unicorn contains the idea of a creature with one horn. Hence, if a unicorn exists, then it follows that a one-horned creature exists. But the "if" in the last sentence indicates that it is not necessary that a one-horned creature exists. Similarly, couldn't we agree with the ontological argument that the idea of God contains the idea of a necessarily existing being? Hence, *if* God exists, then it follows that a necessarily existing being exists. But, like the "if" in the sentence describing the unicorn and its properties, doesn't the "if" in the previous sentence indicate that we cannot assume that a necessarily existing being is real? In other words, doesn't the ontological argument simply show the properties that are contained within the *idea* of God? But is this argument enough to show that God and his properties do exist?

4.4 PRAGMATIC AND SUBJECTIVE JUSTIFICATIONS

 LEADING QUESTIONS: *The Pragmatic and Subjective Justifications for Belief*

1. Have you ever faced an unavoidable decision when you did not know which choice was the correct one? Lacking knowledge concerning the correct choice, what considerations entered into your making the decision?

2. Can you think of situations in which refusing to make a choice actually commits you to a choice by default? (For example, deciding whether to marry a

person you have been dating for a long time, or deciding whether to accept a particular job.)

3. Is it possible to prove everything we believe? If so, how would we prove the premises of every single proof for all our beliefs? Are there other grounds for belief besides logically airtight proofs?

SURVEYING THE CASE FOR PRAGMATIC AND SUBJECTIVE JUSTIFICATIONS

Not all theists believe that is necessary or even possible to prove the existence of God before a person chooses to believe in him. Theists who take this position could be broadly categorized as *nonevidentialist* theists. Ironically, these religious philosophers agree with Hume and other critics that the philosophical arguments for God fail. Nevertheless, nonevidential theists think that other considerations besides rational proofs could lead an individual on a personal journey to a belief in and relationship with God. I have characterized these considerations as pragmatic and subjective justifications for religious belief. In this section, we examine Blaise Pascal, William James, and Søren Kierkegaard as representatives of this approach. While these different writers each have their unique approach to the issue of faith, reason, and belief in God, they tend to agree on the following three essential points.[26]

1. *The insufficiency of reason with regard to God's existence.* These writers all believe that theoretical, philosophical, or rational arguments can neither prove nor disprove the existence of God. God is infinite, but human reason, knowledge, and experience are finite. Thus, it is a mathematical impossibility to start from within the human situation and reason ourselves to God. If we stopped here, the nonevidentialists would be no different from an agnostic such as Hume, and they would have to conclude with him that we must suspend judgment with regard to God. However, it is with the next point that nonevidentialists break with agnosticism.

2. *The impossibility of the neutral standpoint.* We cannot be neutral when it comes to the question of God, say these authors. We will either live our lives as though there is a God, or by default, we will live our lives as though there is not a God. I can suspend judgment on whether there is life in outer space. If the evidence is not compelling one way or another, I can refuse to believe either option, for it will not make any difference to my daily life. However, I don't have the leisure to suspend judgment with respect to the religious option. To borrow an example from William James, it is as though we are lost in a snowstorm on a mountain. We can choose to stay put and hope that a rescue party will find us, but we risk being frozen to death while we wait. Or we can try to make our way down the mountain ourselves, risking the possibility that we will take the wrong path and fall down an icy precipice. The point is that we have to choose. To do nothing is to choose the first option. Either way, however, we must act without knowledge. These three authors claim this situation is what we face with religious belief.

3. *The reasonableness of subjective justifications.* Even though we lack knowledge and evidence, these philosophers believe they can offer some personal and practical considerations that will make the religious option the most appealing. However, they do not believe that we should use subjective considerations for every decision (Pascal was a mathematician and scientist, and James was trained as a medical doctor). When objective evidence and reasons are available, we should use them. These philosophers claim, however, that it is legitimate to listen to the heart when we are forced to choose and when the intellect cannot give us guidance in making this choice. For Pascal and James, the subjective grounds for religious belief took the form of practical arguments that would enable faith to go beyond the limits of reason and objective evidence. In Kierkegaard's case, however, his fideism presented the subjectivity of religious belief as a "leap of faith." It was a leap that not only transcended reason's limits (Pascal's and James's position) but also allowed the believer to embrace what seemed absurd or irrational from the standpoint of objective reason.

BLAISE PASCAL (1623–1662)

BLAISE PASCAL
(1623–1662)

The French thinker Blaise Pascal was a brilliant mathematician, physicist, inventor, and philosopher. As a child growing up in Paris, he demonstrated his remarkable intellectual gifts. He published his first mathematical discovery at the age of sixteen and later provided the basis for the modern theory of probability. He later invented a calculating machine that was more powerful than any of that time. For this reason, the computer programming language PASCAL was named after him. Furthermore, his experiments with the barometer made important contributions to seventeenth-century science. A profound religious experience in 1654, however, changed his life and turned his interests to philosophy and theology.

Although Pascal knew well the power of reason and science, he was also convinced of their limits when it comes to the ultimate issues in human life, such as religion. Concerning these issues, he thought that only personal, subjective considerations could give us any guidance. Accordingly, he once said, "the heart has its reasons which reason does not know." In the following passage, Pascal appeals to the reasons of the heart by means of his famous "wager."

- Find Pascal's statements that illustrate the three themes of the subjective justification of faith discussed in the beginning of this section.
- According to Pascal, what considerations should lead a person to believe in God?

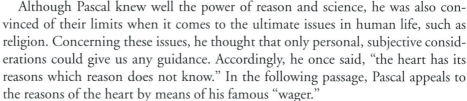

FROM BLAISE PASCAL

Thoughts[27]

"God is, or He is not." But to which side shall we incline? Reason can decide nothing here. There is an infinite chaos which separated us. A game is being played at the extremity of this infinite distance where heads or tails will turn up. What will you wager? According to reason, you can do neither the one thing nor the other; according to reason, you can defend neither of the propositions.

Do not, then, reprove for error those who have made a choice; for you know nothing about it. "No, but I blame them for having made, not this choice, but a choice; for again both he who chooses heads and he who chooses tails are equally at fault, they are both in the wrong. The true course is not to wager at all."

Yes; but you must wager. It is not optional. You are embarked. Which will you choose then? Let us see. Since you must choose, let us see which interests you least. You have two things to lose, the true and the good; and two things to stake, your reason and your will, your knowledge and your happiness; and your nature has two things to shun, error and misery. Your reason is no more shocked in choosing one rather than the other, since you must of necessity choose. This is one point settled. But your happiness? Let us weigh the gain and the loss in wagering that God is. Let us estimate these two chances. If you gain, you gain all; if you lose, you lose nothing. Wager, then, without hesitation that He is. "That is very fine. Yes, I must wager; but I may perhaps wager too much." Let us see. Since there is an equal risk of gain and of loss, if you had only to gain two lives, instead of one, you might still wager. But if there were three lives to gain, you would have to play (since you are under the necessity of playing), and you would be imprudent, when you are forced to play, not to chance your life to gain three at a game where there is an equal risk of loss and gain. But there is an eternity of life and happiness.

- In the final passage, Pascal addresses those readers who want to believe in God but find themselves in the grips of unbelief. What is his advice?

"Yes, but I have my hands tied and my mouth closed; I am forced to wager, and am not free. I am not released, and am so made that I cannot believe. What, then, would you have me do?"

True. But at least learn your inability to believe, since reason brings you to this, and yet you cannot believe. Endeavour, then, to convince yourself, not by increase of proofs of God, but by the abatement of your passions. You would like to attain faith and do not know the way; you would like to cure yourself of unbelief and ask the remedy for it. Learn of those who have been bound like you, and who now stake all their possessions. These are people who know the way which you would follow, and who are cured of an ill of which you would be cured. Follow the way by which they began; by acting as if they believed, taking the holy water, having masses said, etc. Even this will naturally make you believe, and deaden your acuteness. "But this is what I am afraid of." And why? What have you to lose?

With respect to the way reality is, Pascal seems to think that there are only two alternatives: either God does or does not exist. Similarly, with respect to my belief about the subject, I can either believe that God does or does not exist. This means

TABLE 4.2 *Pascal's Belief Alternatives*

My Belief		The Way Reality Is	
		God Exists	**God Does Not Exist**
	I Believe in God	Gain (*infinite*): an eternity of life and happiness	Gain (finite): I have lived a good life with a sense of purpose
		Loss (finite): sacrifice of autonomy and temporal pleasures	Loss (finite): sacrifice of autonomy and temporal pleasures
	I Do Not Believe in God	Gain (finite): achieve autonomy and temporal pleasures	Gain (finite): achieve autonomy and temporal pleasures
		Loss (*infinite*): no eternal life or happiness	Loss (finite): no sense of purpose or meaning

there are four possibilities, as indicated in Table 4.2. Each alternative results in a certain amount of gain or loss. However, the outcomes are not balanced, for one alternative results in infinite gain and another in infinite loss.

What If I Believe in God? First, if I should choose to believe in God, there will be a cost, for I will have to sacrifice my own autonomy. In other words, I cannot live my life any way I want to but must fulfill those moral obligations that I believe God demands of me. Accordingly, belief in God also means I cannot live life in the fast lane. I must forego many earthly pleasures that are inappropriate for a believer. If I believe in God but he does not exist, my belief and personal sacrifices are in vain. But in the long run, perhaps the loss of temporal pleasures are a relatively minor inconvenience. Furthermore, even if my belief in God is mistaken, I have led a decent life with a sense of purpose. The major point that Pascal makes here is that if I believe in God and he really does exist, I will have gained eternal life and happiness—an infinite gain beyond all price. On the other hand, if God does not exist, my loss is minimal.

What If I Do Not Believe in God? Whether God exists or not, if I am not a believer I will obtain the finite gain of being able to live my life the way I want to (autonomy) and can pursue whatever earthly pleasures I choose without fear of eternal consequences. However, if God does exist and I have failed to believe in him, then I will suffer an infinite loss. I will be deprived of the eternal life and happiness that awaits me in God's heaven.

STOP AND THINK

Have you ever made a decision when you did not know which choice was the correct one, but you decided on the basis of what the consequences of each choice would be if you were either right or wrong? Make a chart similar to table 4.2 that lists the alternatives you faced and the consequences of each outcome. Given the fact that you were acting without knowledge, was this basis a good way to make a decision? How did the decision turn out?

THOUGHT EXPERIMENT

Pascal's Wager

The following questions are based on some standard criticisms of Pascal's wager. In each case, consider the strength of the criticism that is implied and think how Pascal might reply to it.

1. Isn't it inappropriate to decide to believe in God using the same strategy we would use at the roulette wheel in a casino? Can we suppose that such a calculating, self-serving concern for the "payoff" of faith can really constitute genuine, religious faith? Aren't we expected to love God for himself and not for what we can get out of the deal? If you were Pascal, how would you reply?
2. Doesn't Pascal assume that you can simply force yourself to believe something? Suppose I told you that I would give you a million dollars if you believe the moon is made out of green cheese (and hooked you up to a lie detector to tell if you really believed my statement). Could you will yourself to believe this statement in the face of all the evidence? Can we *choose* our beliefs the way we choose our clothes, or is belief something that *happens* to us? Can we simply will ourselves to believe in God for no other reason than that this belief seems to be the best bet?
3. Pascal assumes that God will punish those people who do not believe in him. But what if someone finds it difficult or even immoral to believe in something without any evidence? Is it possible that God might reward her for being intellectually honest, even if her faithfulness to the truth as she understands it prevents her from having religious belief? How does this possibility affect Pascal's argument?
4. Pascal seems to assume that the only options are to believe in the Christian God or to not believe in the Christian God. But don't we have more options than these? Look through an encyclopedia of religion that lists all the religions from animism to Zoroastrianism to see how many there are. Because Pascal does not think that there are any objective reasons for religious belief, don't we also have to consider all these other religious options? What would Pascal's wager look like if we included all these other religious options?

- Which of these four considerations do you think is the easiest for Pascal to respond to?
- Which one is the most threatening to his pragmatic justification of religious belief?

One of the leading critics of the attempt to base belief on anything other than rigorous evidence was British philosopher W. K. Clifford (1845–1879). Clifford argued that believing has ethical implications. We have no right to believe anything unless we have earned that right through a rational, critical investigation of the belief in question. In a famous essay called "The Ethics of Belief," Clifford illustrates his point by telling the story of a shipowner who sent a ship full of families off to sea. He knew that the ship was old and probably should be inspected. However, he put aside all his doubts and convinced himself that it was seaworthy, trusting in the providence of God to see the passengers safely to their destination. In spite of his sincere convictions, the ship went down in the middle of the ocean, killing all the passengers, while the shipowner collected his insurance money.

Clifford complains that in spite of the fact that the shipowner really did end up believing the ship was sound, he had no evidence for that belief and even some evidence against it. It would have made no difference if the ship, by good fortune, had completed the trip, for the man still had no right to hold a belief without evidence. Thus, when Pascal urges us to choose to believe in God without rational evidence, Clifford would say we are being asked to disregard our ethical duty to find a foundation for our beliefs. He summarizes his position by saying, "It is wrong always, everywhere, and for any one, to believe anything on insufficient evidence."

WILLIAM JAMES

In his classic essay "The Will to Believe" (1896), William James responded to Clifford's ethics of belief (we previously encountered James in the discussion of pragmatism in section 2.7). In this essay James defines an "option" as any choice we face between two contrasting beliefs. Options may be (1) living or dead, (2) forced or avoidable, and (3) momentous or trivial. Asking you to believe in either the Greek god Zeus or the Norse god Thor would be a dead option if neither choice is a live one for you. On the other hand, facing a choice between being a Christian or an atheist might be a living option for you, depending on your circumstances and inclinations.

Next, if you faced a choice between believing that there is life in outer space or believing there is no life in outer space, you could avoid this option by suspending judgment about the issue and having no opinion. It is an avoidable option. James, however, believes that in morality and religion, we are faced with forced options. What you believe about God will affect your actions and your stance toward life. If you try to avoid thinking about the religious option, you will, by default, end up living your life as though there is no God. On this issue, you are forced to choose.

Finally, your option is either momentous or trivial. James says a trivial option is one in which the opportunity is not unique, the stake is insignificant, or the decision is reversible if it later turns out to be unwise. Following these criteria, which video you rent this weekend is a trivial matter. James agrees that when an option is avoidable, then it may be appropriate to follow Clifford's advice and withhold our belief until we get more evidence. When an option is trivial, we do not need to spend much time thinking about it at all. However, James argues that if we seriously consider the question of religious belief (it is a live option for us), then we will find that it is a forced, momentous decision. The problem is, however, James does not think reason can give us sufficient evidence to make a decision one way or another on this issue. When we face a decision that meets these three criteria (a live, forced, momentous option) and when we cannot have objective, rational certainty, then we have the right to believe what is subjectively and pragmatically appealing.

FROM WILLIAM JAMES
The Will to Believe[28]

The thesis I defend is, briefly stated, this: *Our passional nature not only lawfully may, but must, decide an option between propositions, whenever it is a genuine option that cannot by its nature be decided on intellectual grounds; for to say, under such circumstances, "Do not decide, but leave the question open," is itself a passional decision,—just like deciding yes or no,—and is attended with the same risk of losing the truth.*

James goes on to point out that every knower is faced with two duties: "We must know the truth; and we must avoid error." But these duties are not two versions of the same commandment, for a person can follow one and not the other with different results. If a scientist is willing to risk error in seeking the truth, she may spend years attempting to prove a hypothesis she only hopes and suspects is true. The great scientific discoveries have been made by researchers who have been willing to boldly seek the truth, even though they were not absolutely sure that they were on the right track. However, if a scientist's main rule is to avoid error, she will only stick with research that is absolutely certain to bring results and will avoid investing her time in any hypothesis that has the least chance of being wrong. Clifford, James says, thinks that avoiding error is the supreme principle in life and advises us to suspend judgment on matters about which we cannot be certain. But James replies that when our choices are forced and momentous, the risks of error may be inconsequential when the possibility of having really important knowledge with enormous benefits lies before us.

We see, first, that religion offers itself as a *momentous* option. We are supposed to gain, even now, by our belief, and to lose by our nonbelief, a certain vital good. Secondly, religion is a *forced* option, so far as that good goes. We cannot escape the issue by remaining sceptical and waiting for more light, because, although we do avoid error in that way *if religion be untrue,* we lose the good, *if it be true,* just as certainly as if we positively chose to disbelieve. . . . Scepticism, then, is not avoidance of option; it is option of a certain particular kind of risk. *Better risk loss* of truth than chance of error,—that is your faith-vetoer's exact position. He is actively playing his stake as much as the believer is; he is backing the field against the religious hypothesis, just as the believer is backing the religious hypothesis against the field. To preach scepticism to us as a duty until "sufficient evidence" for religion be found, is tantamount therefore to telling us, when in presence of the religious hypothesis, that to yield to our fear of its being error is wiser and better than to yield to our hope that it may be true. It is not intellect against all passions, then; it is only intellect with one passion laying down its law. And by what, forsooth, is the supreme wisdom of this passion warranted? . . .

. . . I, therefore, for one, cannot see my way to accepting the agnostic rules for truth-seeking, or willfully agree to keep my willing nature out of the game. I cannot do so for this plain reason, that *a rule of thinking which would absolutely prevent me from acknowledging certain kinds of truth if those kinds of truth were really there, would be an irrational rule.* That for me is the long and short of the formal logic of the situation, no matter what the kinds of truth might materially be.

 STOP AND THINK

Which rule do you think would provide the best guide for life?

- Clifford's rule: Better risk the loss of truth than the chance of error by believing only what we know is true.
- James's rule: Better risk the chance of error than the loss of truth by believing what might maximize our good.

SØREN KIERKEGAARD

Is truth objective, or is it personal? Is it possible to have true ideas that make no difference to your life? Which is more difficult: to acquire correct knowledge or to make correct decisions? Here are Kierkegaard's answers (see section 2.6 for details about Kierkegaard's life):

> What I really lack is to be clear in my mind *what I am to do, not* what I am to know, except in so far as a certain understanding must precede every action. The thing is to understand myself, to see what God really wishes *me* to do; the thing is to find a truth which is *true for me,* to find *the idea for which I can live and die.*[29]

With these words (written in a journal when he was a university student), Kierkegaard declared his life's mission. These brief words contain two of the major themes in his philosophy: (1) acting decisively and finding self-understanding, rather than acquiring theoretical knowledge, are the crucial tasks each of us faces in life and (2) all the objective truth in the world will be useless if I do not subjectively appropriate it, if I do not make it something that is "true for me."

With Pascal and James, Kierkegaard believed that the philosophical arguments for God's existence were logically fallacious because they attempt to compile the *finite* materials of experience and reason to arrive at a God who is *infinite*. In other words, the numbers just don't add up. Theoretical arguments, he claimed, also distract us from our real need. The word *theory* comes from a Greek word whose root is related to the word *theater*. When we are in a theater, we are spectators viewing the action on stage from a distance. Similarly, Kierkegaard complained, many people go through life as detached spectators, theorizing about it but never really becoming engaged with it. To switch metaphors, a fideist such as Kierkegaard believes that the person who presents rational arguments for God is like someone who comes upon a man dying of thirst and gives him a lecture on the chemical properties of water.

Kierkegaard also agreed with Pascal and James that it was impossible to maintain a neutral stance on the issue of religious belief. But Kierkegaard was much more of a fideist than the other two in that he believed that faith was a powerful source of belief rather than something that would tip a close balance between belief and unbelief. Indeed, he believed that faith not only could go beyond reason, but was often contrary to reason. When faith and reason are in conflict, he claimed, faith must always be given the priority. Hence, basing our beliefs on faith enables us to overcome any obstacles or objections that reason may put in our way.

Kierkegaard is often difficult to read, because he believed that the truth could only be communicated indirectly. Accordingly, he rarely presents his ideas in a straightforward fashion but instead presents them in such a way that they sneak up on you. He continually uses a number of literary devices such as pseudonyms, irony, humor, satire, parables, and thought experiments to make his points. Perhaps the best way to present his ideas on religious belief is to present a number of short selections from his writings on this topic. In the first set of quotations, Kierkegaard expresses his conviction that religious belief cannot be based on objective arguments. If we have rational arguments for a conclusion (the Pythagorean theorem, for example), then we *know* it, but we do not have *faith* in it. But belief in God must be freely chosen, not compelled by logic; it is a matter of subjective commitment, not objective truth. Accordingly, Kierkegaard sometimes refers to religious belief as a "leap of faith" to a higher plane of existence. Notice in the following passages the tension he posits between the approach of faith and that of theoretical reason.

FROM SØREN KIERKEGAARD

Selections

For if the God does not exist it would of course be impossible to prove it; and if he does exist it would be folly to attempt it.

There is no other road to faith; if one wished to escape risk, it is as if one wanted to know with certainty that he can swim before going into the water.

Belief is not a form of knowledge but a free act, an expression of the will. . . . The conclusion of belief is not so much a conclusion as a resolution, and it is for this reason that belief excludes doubt.[30]

An objective uncertainty held fast in an appropriation-process of the most passionate inwardness is the truth, the highest truth attainable for an *existing* individual. . . .

But the above definition of truth is an equivalent expression for faith. Without risk there is no faith. Faith is precisely the contradiction between the infinite passion of the individual's inwardness and the objective uncertainty. If I am capable of grasping God objectively, I do not believe, but precisely because I cannot do this I must believe. If I wish to preserve myself in faith I must constantly be intent upon holding fast the objective uncertainty, so as to remain out upon the deep, over seventy thousand fathoms of water, still preserving my faith.

Anything that is almost probable, or probable, or extremely and emphatically probable, is something he can almost know, or as good as know, or extremely and emphatically almost *know*—but it is impossible to believe.[31]

In the next passage, Kierkegaard continues the theme that Christianity is not something that can be approached objectively through the speculative, detached reason of the philosopher. Instead it must be embraced subjectively, for only if we have passion will we know the truth. At the end of the first paragraph he suggests that the truth can be found only if you are "in a specific condition." This condition is one of raw honesty and genuine spiritual thirst. The person who is complacent and self-satisfied will be closed to the truth and unable to find it. Kierkegaard liked to point out that you can sometimes achieve a result (for example, the solution to a puzzle) without having to struggle for it yourself (you look up the answer in the back of the book). For some goals in life, however, you can only achieve the result (physical fitness, for example) if you go through a certain process yourself (exercise). Kierkegaard believed that self-understanding (or, as he puts it, "becoming a self") is a result that *cannot* be obtained without going through a very difficult process of subjective inwardness ourselves. In the final paragraph of this section he expresses his belief that we can gain a true sense of our authentic self only when we stand before an infinite God who knows us as we are.

The speculative philosopher . . . proposes to contemplate Christianity from the philosophical standpoint. . . . The philosopher contemplates Christianity for the sake of interpenetrating it with his speculative thought; aye, with his genuinely speculative thought. But suppose this whole proceeding were a chimera, a sheer impossibility; suppose that Christianity is subjectivity, an inner transformation, an actualization of inwardness, and that only two kinds of people can know anything about it: those who with an infinite passionate interest in an eternal happiness base this their happiness upon their believing relationship to Christianity, and those who with an opposite passion, but in passion, reject it—the happy and the unhappy lovers. Suppose that an objective indifference can therefore learn nothing at all. Only the like is understood by the like, and the old principle: [Whatever is known is known in the mode of the knower], must be so expanded as to make room for a mode of knowing in which the knower fails to know anything at all, or has all his knowledge reduced to an illusion. In the case of a kind of observation where it is requisite that the observer should be in a specific condition, it naturally follows that if he is not in this condition, he will observe nothing.[32]

But this self acquires a new quality or qualification in the fact that it is the self directly in the sight of God. . . . And what an infinite reality this self acquires by being before God![33]

In a controversial and extreme statement of his fideism, Kierkegaard expresses the tension between reason and faith by saying that Christianity is *absurd* when viewed through the eyes of our rational understanding. Because reason has its limits, it cannot make sense of Christianity with its inadequate categories, so it must be transcended in a leap of faith. Does Kierkegaard really believe that Christianity is absurd? Perhaps not, for in the final quotation he suggests that from within the standpoint of faith, we gain a new sort of understanding that puts things into perspective.

For the absurd is the object of faith and the only object that can be believed. . . . Christianity has declared itself to be the eternal essential truth which has come into being in time. It has proclaimed itself as the *Paradox*, and it has required of the individual the inwardness of faith in relation to that which stamps itself as . . . an absurdity to the understanding.[34]

When the believer has faith, the absurd is not the absurd—faith transforms it.[35]

 THOUGHT EXPERIMENT

Objectivity and Subjectivity

1. In other areas of life, we seem to place a high value on reason and objective evidence. For example, the scientific theory that has the best arguments and the most evidence is accepted over one that has little rational support. The politician who has the best arguments for her economic proposals is favored over the opponent who has no reasons for his position. Should things be any different with religious belief? Why?
2. Why would a God give us reason if, as Kierkegaard claims, it plays little to no role in forming our religious beliefs?
3. Kierkegaard believed that Christianity was a paradox and seemed absurd to our understanding. For example, he believed that God and Jesus were one and yet that Jesus died and God the father did not. But how are we to distinguish a religious teaching like this that goes beyond our understanding from the sort of rational contradiction that even Kierkegaard would reject, such as "God is good and God is not good"? Once we go beyond or abandon reason, haven't we given up our ability to distinguish truth from nonsense?

LOOKING THROUGH THE LENS OF THE PRAGMATIC AND SUBJECTIVE JUSTIFICATIONS OF RELIGIOUS BELIEF

1. Isn't it possible for the decision to marry someone to be a reasonable decision? But isn't the decision to marry the love of your life a decision that is based on personal, subjective considerations and not universal, impersonal, logical arguments? Aren't many of the decisions that you make in life justified decisions at the same time that they are personal and subjective decisions? How does your conclusion about these questions apply to Pascal's and James's justifications of religious belief?

2. If the evidentialist is correct, then wouldn't it be true that the only persons who could be religious believers are those who are capable of providing philosophical proofs for the existence of God? Isn't there something strange about limiting religious belief only to intellectuals? If there was a personal God, isn't it reasonable to suppose that the way to discover him would be through a personal, individual journey and not through an impersonal, rational argument? What would Kierkegaard say?

EXAMINING THE STRENGTHS AND WEAKNESSES OF THE PRAGMATIC AND SUBJECTIVE JUSTIFICATIONS OF RELIGIOUS BELIEF

Positive Evaluation

1. Can every decision in life be based on rational arguments? What about the decision to be rational? Can that decision be based on rational arguments without assuming what we are trying to prove? Can the decision to believe in the scientific method be justified by the scientific method without arguing in a circle? In both of these cases, aren't we making a subjective decision about what sorts of persons we will be and how we will live our lives? According to Pascal, James, and Kierkegaard, isn't the same process involved in deciding to be religious believers?

2. What if we conclude that the philosophical arguments for and against the existence of God are equally persuasive and cancel each other out? What do we do when reason leaves us indecisive? Don't Pascal, James, and Kierkegaard have a point when they say that the neutral standpoint is impossible? Don't we have to decide to live on the basis of belief in God or else live as practical atheists? If so, aren't we justified in choosing the religious option if that option seems to make the most sense out of life?

Negative Evaluation

1. Take Kierkegaard's arguments for the priority of faith over reason, but imagine that the same arguments are being used by the following true believers:

PHILOSOPHY
in the
MARKETPLACE

- Someone who asks you to have faith in the Nazi ideology.
- Someone who asks you to have faith in communism.
- A follower of a religious cult whose faith teaches that if you sell all your
  possessions and join their community, space aliens will take you on a ship to
  a world beyond the stars where you will live for all eternity in perfect bliss.

If Kierkegaard's fideism is a sufficient basis for believing in his Christianity,
why shouldn't it provide legitimacy to these faiths as well?

2. Do Pascal, James, and Kierkegaard face a dilemma? Either they are claiming
that theism is true based on the fact that it is the most rationally justified belief, or
they are not. If they are not attempting to argue for the truth of theism, then they
are simply offering us their own autobiographical journeys. If the latter is the case,
then they are simply saying to us: "As for my own life, I have decided to be
religious." But why should their choices make any claims on us? This problem
particularly applies to Pascal and Kierkegaard because they were Christians (James's
religious beliefs were more nonspecific). As such, they presumably believed that
Christianity was true. But since not all beliefs are true, they must have some way
of deciding that Christianity is true and other options are not. However, once they
begin justifying the truth of their religious beliefs, they will be appealing to reason
and abandoning their nonevidentialism and fideism. So, could it be argued that the
claims of Pascal, James, and Kierkegaard in favor of religious belief are arbitrary
and merely autobiographical? If not, then don't they have to attempt to provide a
rational justification of their religious truth claims?

STOP AND THINK

Go back over the reasons for believing in God that have been presented in this and previous sections (the cosmological, teleological, and ontological arguments, and the pragmatic-subjective reasons). Which seems to be the strongest? What do you think is the major weakness (if any) of each argument?

4.5 THE PROBLEM OF EVIL: ATHEISTIC AND THEISTIC RESPONSES

LEADING QUESTIONS: *The Problem of Evil*

1. If you were a parent, wouldn't you do everything in your power to prevent your child from needless suffering? Since so many innocent children in the world suffer from painful diseases, how can there be a loving, powerful God?

2. If you had to make a choice between a world in which there is human freedom but also suffering, innocent children and a world in which there is no human freedom but also no children who are suffering, which one would you choose? Why?

3. Was there ever a time when you experienced suffering (emotional or physical) that seemed meaningless, but you found out later that the suffering ultimately served some good purpose?

problem of evil the difficulty of reconciling the existence of suffering and other evils in the world with the existence of God

SURVEYING THE CASE FOR ATHEISM: *The Argument from Evil*

Most atheists or agnostics base their case on the lack of evidence for God's existence. However, atheists have at least one, very powerful positive argument for their position: that there cannot be a loving, all-knowing, all-powerful God, because there is so much evil and suffering in the world. The difficulty of reconciling the existence of suffering and other evils in the world with the existence of God is called **the problem of evil.** Traditionally, philosophers have distinguished between two kinds of evil. **Moral evil** consists of the bad actions and their unfortunate results for which humans (or other moral agents) are morally responsible. Lying, theft, murder, and rape, for example, are moral evils committed by people that cause the evil results of distrust, loss of property, and physical or emotional harm. **Natural evil** consists of the suffering to humans and animals that results from natural causes such as genetic defects, diseases, earthquakes, and tornadoes. To avoid the atheist's charge of incoherence, the theist has the burden of explaining why God would allow either moral or natural evils to occur.

The problem of evil was given literary expression by the twentieth-century French novelist Albert Camus. In his novel *The Plague,* Camus tells the story of the town of Oran, which slowly becomes ravaged by an epidemic of the bubonic

moral evil bad actions and their unfortunate results for which humans (or other moral agents) are morally responsible

natural evil the suffering to humans and animals resulting from natural causes such as genetic defects, diseases, earthquakes, and tornadoes

plague. Quarantined from the outside world, the people of Oran find themselves trapped in a prison of death and agony as they and their loved ones die slow, painful deaths. Among other themes presented in the novel, the town becomes a symbol of the human situation, and the various responses of its citizens represent different attitudes toward life. The religious response is represented by the town's priest, Father Paneloux. The atheist or agnostic response is represented by Dr. Bernard Rieux, a physician who works tirelessly to alleviate the victims' suffering. The reading selection begins with the narrator's account of the death throes of a small child who has been infected by the plague.

 FROM ALBERT CAMUS
The Plague [36]

And just then the boy had a sudden spasm, as if something had bitten him in the stomach, and uttered a long, shrill wail. For moments that seemed endless he stayed in a queer, contorted position, his body racked by convulsive tremors; it was as if his frail frame were bending before the fierce breath of the plague, breaking under the reiterated gusts of fever. . . . When for the third time the fiery wave broke on him, lifting him a little, the child curled himself up and shrank away to the edge of the bed, as if in terror of the flames advancing on him, licking his limbs. . . . From between the inflamed eyelids big tears welled up and trickled down the sunken leaden-hued cheeks. When the spasm had passed, utterly exhausted, tensing his thin legs and arms, on which, within forty-eight hours, the flesh had wasted to the bone, the child lay flat, racked on the tumbled bed, in a grotesque parody of crucifixion. . . .

Paneloux gazed down at the small mouth, fouled with the sores of the plague and pouring out the angry death-cry that has sounded through the ages of mankind. He sank on his knees, and all present found it natural to hear him say in a voice hoarse but clearly audible across the nameless, never ending wail:

"My God, spare this child!"

But in spite of the priest's prayer, the child's wailing continues without ceasing. After awhile, however, the poor boy's tragic suffering comes to an end. Dr. Rieux is with him as he dies.

And now the doctor grew aware that the child's wail, after weakening more and more, had fluttered out into silence. . . . For it was over. . . . His mouth still gaping, but silent now, the child was lying among the tumbled blankets, a small, shrunken form, with the tears still wet on his cheeks.

When the plague first broke out, Father Paneloux gave a confident, moralistic sermon in which he claimed that the sickness was God's judgment on the townspeople for their sins. After viewing the suffering of this innocent child, however, his attitude changes. No longer confident, he preaches a sermon in which he says we cannot understand the reason for this suffering but still must cling to our faith in God. The following passage contains his closing remarks.

> We should go forward, groping our way through the darkness, stumbling perhaps at times, and try to do what good lay in our power. As for the rest, we must hold fast, trusting in the divine goodness, even as to the deaths of little children, and not seeking personal respite. . . .
> "My brothers"—the preacher's tone showed he was nearing the conclusion of his sermon—"the love of God is a hard love. It demands total self-surrender, disdain of our human personality. And yet it alone can reconcile us to suffering and the deaths of children, it alone can justify them, since we cannot understand them, and we can only make God's will ours."

A different response toward the suffering in the world is represented by Dr. Rieux. Throughout the novel, this physician risks his life nursing the victims of the plague. However, unlike Paneloux, Dr. Rieux thinks that there is no way to reconcile the agony of innocent people with the existence of a good God. When a friend asks the doctor why he gives of himself so selflessly when he doesn't believe in God, the physician replies as follows:

> His face still in shadow, Rieux said that he's already answered: that if he believed in an all-powerful God he would cease curing the sick and leave that to Him. But no one in the world believed in a God of that sort; no, not even Paneloux, who believed that he believed in such a God. And this was proved by the fact that no one ever threw himself on Providence completely. Anyhow, in this respect Rieux believed himself to be on the right road—in fighting against creation as he found it.

After the boy dies, Paneloux tries to comfort the doctor, but Rieux shouts at him for trying to justify the suffering of innocent children such as this one. However, Rieux then apologizes, saying, "I'm sorry. But weariness is a kind of madness. And there are times when the only feeling I have is one of mad revolt." Paneloux goes on to explain how he copes with the suffering.

> "I understand," Paneloux said in a low voice. "That sort of thing is revolting because it passes our human understanding. But perhaps we should love what we cannot understand."
> Rieux straightened up slowly. He gazed at Paneloux, summoning to his gaze all the strength and fervor he could muster against his weariness. Then he shook his head.
> "No, Father. I've a very different idea of love. And until my dying day I shall refuse to love a scheme of things in which children are put to torture."

SPOTLIGHT
on

STOP AND THINK

How would you respond to the child's death? Would you agree with Father Paneloux or with Dr. Rieux? Or is there a third approach you would take?

A Formulation of the Argument from Evil

Why do innocent people such as the boy in Camus's story suffer from apparently meaningless pain? Why didn't God spare the child from a tortuous death as the priest prayed for him to do? Why are there so many evils in nature, as Darwin suggests? Camus's story and Darwin's observations illustrate the mystery, the paradox, and the problem of evil. The problem of evil can be formulated in terms of four propositions, all of which are propositions that the traditional theist wants to affirm. However, it seems difficult to reconcile the following four statements:

1. God is perfectly good.
2. God is all-knowing (omniscient).
3. God is all-powerful (omnipotent).
4. Evil exists.

By themselves, these four propositions do not constitute a contradiction the way that the statements "Bob is a bachelor" and "Bob is a husband" contradict one another. Hence, to establish the conclusion that God does not exist, the atheist must add one more premise to complete the argument.

5. If God exists and is a being who is good, all-knowing, and all-powerful, then there would be no evil in the world.
6. Therefore, God does not exist.

This argument is valid and, hence, if you accept the premises, you must accept the conclusion. However, if you think the conclusion is false, then you must reject at least one of the five premises. Let's consider the premises of the argument to see what the theist's options are.

STOP AND THINK

If you were a theist (it doesn't matter if you really are or not), which of the five premises would you reject in order to reject the conclusion that "God does not exist"? Why do you think that premise is the best one to reject? What are the implications of rejecting that premise? What else would you have to prove in order to show that this premise is false?

RELIGIOUS RESPONSES TO THE ARGUMENT FROM EVIL

General Theistic Strategies

Most theists would not want to reject premises 1, 2, or 3. Those premises all seem central to traditional, religious conceptions of God. If God was deficient in either goodness, knowledge, or power, it is claimed, he would be not a God but a "godling," a wimpy being unworthy of worship. However, if you reject any one of these premises, the problem is solved. For example, the ancient Greeks were polytheists, and many of their gods were not good ones but were vicious, vindictive, petty beings. Hence, because the Greeks rejected premise 1 (God's goodness), they did not have any problem understanding evil. The bad things that happen in our world result from blind fate or the actions of one or more mean-spirited gods, according to the typical Greek view.

Some philosophers reject or weaken premise 2 (God is all-knowing) by arguing that God's knowledge is limited.[38] It is limited, they say, because he cannot know the future in perfect detail, since the future has not yet happened and is, in part, the product of the choices of free agents such as ourselves. But this philosophy, by itself, does not solve the problem, for even if God could not anticipate every evil that would occur, it would seem that he could intervene and eliminate the evils once they make their presence known. For example, once the Nazis made clear their plans for world domination, why didn't God cause massive mechanical failures in their tanks and gas ovens, thus preventing the Holocaust?

Another nontraditional view rejects premise 3 (God is all-powerful). John Stuart Mill, William James, personal idealists such as Edgar S. Brightman, and process philosophers such as Alfred North Whitehead, Charles Hartshorne, John Cobb, and David Ray Griffin have explored this alternative. Similarly, the best-selling book *When Bad Things Happen to Good People* by Rabbi Harold Kushner argues that God has not yet completed creation and is continually working with us to make the world better.[39] If nature and human agents have any degree of autonomy and power at all, then God is limited in what he could do to eliminate evil.

In discussing God's power, it is important to note that even traditional Christian thinkers throughout the centuries have seldom maintained that the statement "God is all-powerful" is equivalent to "God can do anything." Certainly, the whole problem of evil is based on the notion that God cannot bring about totally unjustified, irredeemable evil, for this action would be contrary to his nature. Hence, God cannot do anything, for he cannot act contrary to his nature. However, this one qualification is hardly a limit on God's power. Furthermore, most traditional philosophers and theologians have said that God cannot do what is *logically impossible*. He cannot do the following sorts of things: create a round square, make one plus one equal three, make a stone heavier than he can lift, or cause himself not to exist. Since all these notions are nonsense, God's inability to bring them about is not a limit on his rational powers. If God could do what is logically impossible, then he could be both good and evil at the same time, and it would be impossible to think about God at all. The claim that God cannot do what is logically impossible is an important one because it plays a major role in some theistic responses to the problem of evil.

What about premise 4, the claim that "evil exists"? Some Asian religions claim that evil is an illusion. That conclusion would solve the problem, but many people believe that the real-life suffering of innocent children that Camus depicted in his novel just seems too real to consider it an illusion. While he did not say that evil is an illusion, the early Christian writer St. Augustine (354–430) nevertheless claimed that evil lacks independent, substantial reality. Everything that God creates is good, he said, but what is good can become corrupted. Thus evil is something negative, for it is the absence of good. Hence, just as a shadow is not an independent reality in itself but is the absence of light, so what we perceive as evil are the ways in which the world falls short of God's goodness. Even if we view evil in this way, however, we can still ask why God allows these absences of his goodness to occur. For most theists, denying the reality of evil does not seem to be a good strategy for coping with the problem. Disease, the devastation of tornadoes and earthquakes, and other features of this world that produce pain and suffering seem to be gratuitous, brute evils that need some sort of explanation if theism is to be plausible.

Premise 5, the claim that a good and powerful God would prevent or eliminate evil, seems to be the point at which the traditional theist might want to launch his or her response. Perhaps God allows certain evils because in some way or other, these evils are necessary or are morally justified. Indeed, most theists who propose solutions to the problem of evil recognize that evils such as pain exist (they accept premise 4) but try to suggest ways in which these evils are justified or unavoidable, even for a good and powerful God (they reject premise 5). The attempt to do so is known as a **theodicy,** or a justification of God's permitting evil to occur in the world. Hence, many theodicists modify premise 5 to state "If God exists and is a being who is good, all-knowing, and all-powerful, then there would be no *unjustified* evil in the world." They then go on to defend the claim that "There are no unjustified evils in the world." In this way theodicists attempt to show that the existence of evil or suffering does not count against the existence of God. The two most common responses of theists to the problem of evil are known as the "greater

theodicy the attempt to justify God's permitting evil to occur in the world

goods defense" and the "free will defense." I discuss each strategy in turn. But first, work through the following thought experiment.

 THOUGHT EXPERIMENT

Reasons for Evil

To anticipate what is to come, consider the following situations:

1. Think of a time when you knowingly did something or entered into a situation that caused you (or someone you loved) to suffer. The suffering could be physical pain or emotional pain or some other kind of unpleasant experience. Your own or the other person's suffering was not something you desired in itself. Nevertheless, you allowed this suffering to happen because you knew that in the end, something good would come from it. In what way do you think that making this suffering or allowing it to occur was justified and unpreventable?

2. Suppose you are a parent who has a great deal of control over your children. Using the threat of punishment, you might be able to force them to behave in moral and responsible ways. For example, you could force them to clean their rooms, do their homework, and abstain from using profanity in their speech. But could you force them to *want* to do these things as a matter of their own free choice? Could you not only force them to *do* what is good, but also force them to *desire* to do what is morally good, even when you are not around and no reward or punishment is involved? If you could not force them to desire what is good, how might you, nevertheless, influence them in this direction?

- How might these two thought experiments be relevant to the problem of evil?

The Greater Goods Defense

greater goods defense the claim that God allows some evil to exist because it is necessary to the achievement of a greater good

The claim that God allows some evil to exist because it is necessary to the achievement of a greater good is known as the **greater goods defense.** This argument assumes that (1) some evils are necessary to achieving certain good ends, (2) the good that is achieved outweighs the evil, and (3) the same or a greater amount of good could not have been attained by any means that did not involve the presence of these evils. A simple example illustrates this point. When my wife and I first took our new baby to the doctor for a checkup, the pediatrician gave our child a shot that immunized him against all sorts of dread childhood diseases. Our baby, of course, did not understand what was going on. He screamed in pain and looked up at his mother with eyes that said, "I trusted you and put my faith in you. But you betrayed that trust by carrying me into this torture chamber where an evil man stuck needles into my bottom!" Why did we allow our son to suffer this pain? We did not delight in his pain and it distressed us to hear his cries, but we knew the pain was the only way to achieve the greater good of health. Hence, the evil of the pain was justified according to the threefold criteria listed previously.

Spotlight on an Ancient Chinese Parable—What Is the Meaning of It All?

There was an old man whose only wealth was the one horse he owned. One day his horse escaped and took off into the mountains. His friends and neighbors came to comfort him saying, "Old man, what bad luck you have had." The man replied, "Bad luck? Good luck? Who can say?" A week later, the horse returned and brought with him a whole herd of wild, mountain horses. The man's wealth was suddenly increased beyond measure. His friends and neighbors came to rejoice with him saying, "Old man, what good luck you have had." The man replied, "Good luck? Bad luck? Who can say?" The next day, when the man's son was trying to break in the wild horses, one of the horses threw him, causing him to break his leg. His friends and neighbors came to bring comfort saying, "Old man, what bad luck you have had." The man replied, "Bad luck? Good luck? Who can say?" The next day, the army came to town to forcibly draft all the young men to go fight in a bloody war from which few of them would return. However, the army did not take the old man's son; he was allowed to stay home because he was crippled. The man's friends and neighbors came to rejoice with him saying, "Old man, what good luck you have had." The man replied, "Good luck? Bad luck? Who can say?"

- Just for fun, can you make up some more lines to the story?
- Can we ever know what the ultimate outcome of the events in our lives will be?
- How might this story relate to the problem of evil?
- Which one of the following two meanings do you derive from this story? Why?

    1. The suffering we experience always has a purpose, even if we cannot know what it is at the time.
    2. Life is ambiguous and purposeless. Good things happen and bad things happen because of chance events, but there is no meaning to those occurrences. We can never count on how things will turn out.

In this example, the trade-off between the pain and the good it achieved was very clear to the parents but not to the child. Similarly, if there is a God, it is conceivable that we are often like the baby who does not see the big picture and, therefore, does not understand that his pain is a necessary means to avoid an even greater evil (a deadly disease) and to achieve an ultimate good (health). Some theists use such considerations to respond to the problem of evil. They claim that there is an infinite gap between God's perspective and our own. While we have sufficient reasons for believing in God, they say, we cannot explain or understand why evil exists. It will always be a mystery to be coped with on the basis of trust. Other theists while acknowledging that we can never explain the reason for each and every particular suffering that God allows, have tried to set out some ways in which we can understand how God's permitting evil to occur may be morally justified, just as my wife and I were justified in allowing our baby to experience temporary pain.

In developing the greater goods defense, theists formulate the argument that certain moral goods such as courage, compassion, fortitude, forgiveness, and forbearance are human traits and are responses that enrich us as human beings, which would not be possible if there were no evil in the world. In alleviating, resisting, and overcoming evil, not only do we help those around us and make the world a better place, but we also make ourselves better persons in the process. But couldn't God simply give us fully developed moral characters without making us struggle against evil to achieve this goal? The answer to this question is effectively presented in Aldous Huxley's futuristic novel *Brave New World*. He depicts a society in which all crime, all suffering, and every negative feature of our society has been eliminated and in which its people are model citizens and supremely happy. But rather than being a utopian paradise, the world is dehumanizing because these results have been achieved through behavioral conditioning and a happiness drug called *soma*. The director of this "brave new world" explains the benefits of his society in this way:

> There's always *soma* to calm your anger, to reconcile you to your enemies, to make you patient and long-suffering. In the past you could only accomplish these things by making a great effort and after years of hard moral training. Now, you swallow two or three half-gramme tablets and there you are. Anybody can be virtuous now. You can carry at least half your morality about in a bottle. Christianity without tears—that's what *soma* is.[40]

THOUGHT EXPERIMENT

Means versus Ends

Suppose that you could take different drugs that would instantly transform you into a moral saint, an accomplished piano player, a successful athlete in a sport of your choice, a straight A student, or a great artist. Undoubtedly, such results would gain you public admiration, fame, wealth, and other goods. But would you feel as though you were worthy of this admiration? Would you feel good about how you obtained your achievements? Is it only the results that count in life, or are the processes and the means for achieving those results important too? If you swallow a pill that makes you virtuous, are you really virtuous? Or do moral achievements necessarily involve effort and struggle?

John Hick's Greater Goods Defense. If the notion of a "brave new world" pill that makes people instantly virtuous does not seem quite right, then you can appreciate the solution to the problem of evil proposed by the Christian theologian and philosopher John Hick (born 1922). John Hick was educated at Edinburgh, Oxford, and Cambridge universities and was Danforth Professor of Religion at Claremont Graduate School until his retirement in 1994. He has published a number of highly regarded works in the philosophy of religion. Hick develops what he calls the "minority report" in the history of theology. This view is that when God initially created humanity, there was still some work to be done in making us a completed product. However, this remaining work could not be accomplished by God alone; we have to contribute to the process. Using the greater goods defense,

Hick argues that even God himself could not achieve certain results without allowing us to struggle against evil and to endure suffering.

- In the following passage, what does Hick say was "easy for divine omnipotence"?
- What cannot be performed by omnipotent power as such?

 FROM JOHN HICK

Evil and the God of Love[41]

Instead of regarding man as having been created by God in a finished state, as a finitely perfect being fulfilling the divine intention for our human level of existence, and then falling disastrously away from this, the minority report sees man as still in process of creation. . . .

And so man, created as a personal being in the image of God, is only the raw material for a further and more difficult stage of God's creative work. This is the leading of men as relatively free and autonomous persons, through their own dealings with life in the world in which He has placed them, towards that quality of personal existence that is the finite likeness of God. . . .

In the light of modern anthropological knowledge some form of two-stage conception of the creation of man has become an almost unavoidable Christian tenet. At the very least we must acknowledge as two distinguishable stages the fashioning of *homo sapiens* as a product of the long evolutionary process, and his sudden or gradual spiritualization as a child of God. But we may well extend the first stage to include the development of man as a rational and responsible person capable of personal relationship with the personal Infinite who has created him. This first stage of the creative process was, to our anthropomorphic imaginations, easy for divine omnipotence. By an exercise of creative power God caused the physical universe to exist, and in the course of countless ages to bring forth within it organic life, and finally to produce out of organic life personal life; and when man had thus emerged out of the evolution of the forms of organic life, a creature had been made who has the possibility of existing in conscious fellowship with God. But the second stage of the creative process is of a different kind altogether. It cannot be performed by omnipotent power as such. For personal life is essentially free and self-directing. It cannot be perfected by divine fiat, but only through the uncompelled responses and willing co-operation of human individuals in their actions and reactions in the world in which God has placed them. Men may eventually become the perfected persons whom the New Testament calls "children of God," but they cannot be created ready-made as this.

The value-judgement that is implicitly being invoked here is that one who has attained to goodness by meeting and eventually mastering temptations, and thus by rightly making responsible choices in concrete situations, is good in a richer and more valuable sense than would be one created *ab initio* [from the beginning] in a state either of innocence or of virtue. In the former case, which is that of the actual moral achievements of mankind, the individual's goodness has within it the strength of temptations overcome, a stability based upon an accumulation of right choices, and a positive and responsible character that comes from the investment of costly personal effort. I suggest, then, that it is an ethically reasonable judgement, even though in the nature of the case not one that is capable of demonstrative proof, that human goodness slowly built up through personal histories of moral effort has a value in the eyes of the Creator which justifies even the long travail of the soul-making process.

- In the following passage, what conception contrary to Christian thought does Hick say anti-theistic writers assume?
- Why is pleasure not the supreme value a parent tries to achieve for his or her children?
- In your own words, state what does Hick means by "soul-making"?
- According to Hick, what greater goods are achieved by God's allowing us to suffer?

If, then, God's aim in making the world is "the bringing of many sons to glory," that aim will naturally determine the kind of world that He has created. Antitheistic writers almost invariably assume a conception of the divine purpose which is contrary to the Christian conception. They assume that the purpose of a loving God must be to create a hedonistic paradise; and therefore to the extent that the world is other than this, it proves to them that God is either not loving enough or not powerful enough to create such a world. They think of God's relation to the earth on the model of a human being building a cage for a pet animal to dwell in. If he is humane he will naturally make his pet's quarters as pleasant and healthful as he can. Any respect in which the cage falls short of the veterinarian's ideal, and contains possibilities of accident or disease, is evidence of either limited benevolence or limited means, or both. Those who use the problem of evil as an argument against belief in God almost invariably think of the world in this kind of way. . . .

But if we are right in supposing that God's purpose for man is to lead him from human *Bios,* or the biological life of man, to that quality of *Zoe,* or the personal life of eternal worth, which we see in Christ, then the question that we have to ask is not, Is this the kind of world that an all-powerful and infinitely loving being would create as an environment for his human pets? or, Is the architecture of the world the most pleasant and convenient possible? The question that we have to ask is rather, Is this the kind of world that God might make as an environment in which moral beings may be fashioned, through their own free insights and responses, into "children of God"?

Such critics as Hume are confusing what heaven ought to be, as an environment for perfected finite beings, with what this world ought to be, as an environment for beings who are in process of becoming perfected. For if our general conception of

God's purpose is correct the world is not intended to be a paradise, but rather the scene of a history in which human personality may be formed towards the pattern of Christ. Men are not to be thought of on the analogy of animal pets, whose life is to be made as agreeable as possible, but rather on the analogy of human children, who are to grow to adulthood in an environment whose primary and overriding purpose is not immediate pleasure but the realizing of the most valuable potentialities of human personality.

. . . How does the best parental love express itself in its influence upon the environment in which children are to grow up? I think it is clear that a parent who loves his children, and wants them to become the best human beings that they are capable of becoming, does not treat pleasure as the sole and supreme value. Certainly we seek pleasure for our children, and take great delight in obtaining it for them; but we do not desire for them unalloyed pleasure at the expense of their growth in such even greater values as moral integrity, unselfishness, compassion, courage, humour, reverence for the truth, and perhaps above all the capacity for love. We do not act on the premise that pleasure is the supreme end of life; and if the development of these other values sometimes clashes with the provision of pleasure, then we are willing to have our children miss a certain amount of this, rather than fail to come to possess and to be possessed by the finer and more precious qualities that are possible to the human personality. A child brought up on the principle that the only or the supreme value is pleasure would not be likely to become an ethically mature adult or an attractive or happy personality. And to most parents it seems more important to try to foster quality and strength of character in their children than to fill their lives at all times with the utmost possible degree of pleasure. If, then, there is any true analogy between God's purpose for his human creatures, and the purpose of loving and wise parents for their children, we have to recognize that the presence of pleasure and the absence of pain cannot be the supreme and overriding end for which the world exists. Rather, this world must be a place of soul-making. And its value is to be judged, not primarily by the quantity of pleasure and pain occurring in it at any particular moment, but by its fitness for its primary purpose, the purpose of soul-making.

 THOUGHT EXPERIMENT

Soul Making

Suppose you had to choose between two people to be your roommate. The first person grew up in a wealthy home. As a child, she (or he) always had everything she could possibly desire. Her parents gave her expensive toys, clothes, ponies, horses, and cars. They never said "no" to her. She never faced any disappointments, sorrows, or challenges. Life had always been easy for her. Because of her childhood, she grew up to be blasé, cocky, and carefree. The second person came from very difficult circumstances. As a child, she had to earn money to help her family get by. She suffered from poverty, illness,

(Continued . . .)

Criticisms of John Hick's Argument. John Hick's theodicy has been very influential, but it has also been subjected to a great deal of criticism. Edward H. Madden and Peter H. Hare, for example, accuse Hick of committing the "all or nothing" fallacy.[42] They concede that we may become better persons if we have to face obstacles and some suffering. But Hick assumes that God's choice is between all of the tortuous amount of suffering we have in the actual world and no suffering at all.

Everyone suffers on some occasions, but some people turn out to be decent, compassionate, morally sensitive individuals without enduring the gross amount of suffering that is inflicted upon others. Hence, do we really need the amount of suffering that currently exists? As Madden and Hare state it, "Even if some undeserved and unnecessary suffering is necessary to make possible compassion, it is obvious that a minute percentage of the present unnecessary suffering would do the job adequately."

Furthermore, suffering, rather than contributing to the process of "soul-making," often brings about "soul-breaking," as people are crushed, defeated, demoralized, and dehumanized by great suffering. Accordingly, Madden and Hare argue: "One must remember that while unjust suffering may increase compassion, it also creates massive resentment. This resentment often causes individuals indiscriminately to lash out at the world. The benefits of compassion are probably more than offset by the damage done by resentment."

The Free Will Defense

free will defense the claim that God could not create creatures (such as us) who have freedom of the will but who are incapable of doing evil

Another way of dealing with the problem of evil is the **free will defense.** Its strategy is to claim that God could not create creatures (such as us) who have freedom of the will but who are incapable of doing evil. Remember that when religious philosophers say God is omnipotent, they usually mean that he has the power to do anything that is logically possible. Hence, it is not a limit on God's power to say that he cannot create free creatures who are programmed to do only what is good. Such creatures would be like well-behaved robots, and hence, it would be a contradiction to suppose that they were free. Thus God had a choice. He could create a world (A) in which there is no freedom of the will and, consequently, no moral evil, or create a world (B) with free agents and, consequently, allow for the possibility that people will use their freedom to do moral evil. Which world would be the best choice? We can imagine world A as one populated only with well-behaved robots. They would pick one another up when one fell, would never damage one another's logic circuits, and maybe would even sing praises to God with their voice synthesizers. However, these morally behaving beings would no more be able to choose to do good than a calculator can choose to give the correct sum. Hence, this world, though free of evil, would lack something that is of ultimate value both to God and ourselves, namely, human freedom.

Accordingly, the argument goes, God chose to create world B, a world in which creatures can make free choices. However, to possess freedom means that we have the ability to make good choices as well as bad choices. In creating free agents, according to this account, God took a risk. He necessarily could not guarantee that we would choose good over evil. Like a parent, he can try to influence and persuade us in the right direction, but he cannot force us to act one way as opposed to another. The result is that we live in a world in which people choose to act in ways that are courageous, compassionate, forgiving, merciful, and loving. But it is also a world in which people freely choose to act in ways that are immoral, malicious, despicable, hateful, and destructive. Hence, God does not will or cause evil to occur, but in order to allow free agents such as us to exist, he has to allow us the freedom to commit evil acts. God could prevent the inhumane evils and horrors of human history such as Hitler and Auschwitz only by excluding the great moments in humanity represented by Jesus, the Buddha, Socrates, Confucius, Michelangelo, Leonardo da Vinci, Johann Sebastian Bach, Abraham Lincoln, Mahatma Gandhi, Sojourner Truth, Helen Keller, Albert Einstein, Martin Luther King Jr., and Mother Teresa.[43]

At first glance, the free will defense might sound like a version of the greater goods defense, because it claims that the existence of freedom of the will is such a great good that the world would be impoverished without it. However, the two strategies differ, even though they are compatible. The greater goods defense claims that enduring evil is necessary for achieving certain goods of supreme value. On the other hand, the free will defense claims that the world is a better one if there is free will, but that the existence of free will necessarily makes possible the existence of evil. Hence, in this argument, evil is an unfortunate and unavoidable possibility created by something that is good rather than being an instrument for achieving a greater good. Another difference is that the greater goods defense can explain both natural evils and moral evils, because it claims that suffering can cause good results that could not be obtained without it whether this suffering has natural or human causes. The free will defense, however, is primarily an explanation of why God allows human moral evil to exist.

Critics have raised several problems with the free will defense. First, the defense assumes that it is impossible for creatures to be free at the same time that they are incapable of doing evil. This particular view of freedom is known as *libertarianism*, which claims that human freedom is incompatible with a guaranteed, predictable outcome. In chapter 3 we discussed this position as well as *compatibilism*, an opposing view that claims that if our actions are determined by our own nature and not by external constraints, then we are free. Hence, by applying the compatibilist's view of freedom to the free will defense, we are compelled to ask, Why couldn't God make us such that we would always freely choose the good? After all, God is said to be free, but his nature is such that he cannot do evil. Why couldn't these features exist in beings God has created? In many accounts of the afterlife, it is said that people will live an eternally blissful existence in heaven, will be free, and will no longer commit sins. Why couldn't God make this kind of life occur in the present world?

A second response to the free will defense admits that a certain measure of freedom of the will would make this world better than if free will was totally lacking. But couldn't we get along with a little bit less free will if it meant less suffering in the world? For example, our society seeks to preserve human freedom at the expense of allowing certain sorts of evils to occur. Under ordinary circumstances, it is not a crime to ridicule someone's looks, which causes that person emotional pain. You have the moral freedom to choose whether you will say things to others that are hurtful or that are uplifting. However, should you choose to engage in serious harm such as assaulting a person and causing him or her physical injury, society does step in to prevent such an evil. Why couldn't God do the same with the human race as a whole? For example, he could stand back and give us the freedom to make good or bad moral choices with respect to lying, malicious gossip, slandering, theft, or other forms of wickedness. At the same time, he could intervene or make us such that we would be incapable of severe evils such as murder, rape, or child abuse. Thus, the criticism is that the value of having free agents in the world does not justify the amount of moral evil that results. A moderate amount of human freedom and a moderate amount of moral evil might make a better world.

The Natural Order Defense

The greater goods defense can handle both forms of evil (natural and moral), because it claims that suffering can produce a greater good whether the suffering is caused by humans or nature. However, the free will defense views evil as a result of the immoral choices that result from human freedom. This defense addresses such evils as slavery, murder, and war, but how can it explain the suffering caused by natural events such as disease, the destructive power of a hurricane, or an earthquake that destroys homes and lives? (Think of Albert Camus's depiction of the suffering caused by a precipitous plague.)

One way in which a free will defense can account for natural evils is to say that in order for there to be free choices, whether these choices are good or evil ones, there has to be a fixed, reliable order of natural causes and effects. For example, C. S. Lewis argues that for persons (he calls them "souls") to interact in a meaningful way and for humans to be free, the physical world must have a regular order that we all can recognize and share. C. S. Lewis (1898–1963) was a Fellow of Magdalen College at Oxford University when he wrote *The Problem of Pain.* Al-

though he published many literary studies and works of fiction, he is best known for his popular defenses of Christianity.

FROM C. S. LEWIS
The Problem of Pain[44]

Society, then, implies a common field or "world" in which its members meet. . . . But if matter is to serve as a neutral field it must have a fixed nature of its own. . . .

Again, if matter has a fixed nature and obeys constant laws, not all states of matter will be equally agreeable to the wishes of a given soul, nor all equally beneficial for that particular aggregate of matter which he calls his body. If fire comforts that body at a certain distance, it will destroy it when the distance is reduced. . . .

Yet again, if the fixed nature of matter prevents it from being always, and in all its dispositions, equally agreeable even to a single soul, much less is it possible for the matter of the universe at any moment to be distributed so that it is equally convenient and pleasurable to each member of a society. If a man traveling in one direction is having a journey down hill, a man going in the opposite direction must be going up hill. If even a pebble lies where I want it to lie, it cannot, except by a coincidence, be where you want it to lie. And this is very far from being an evil: on the contrary, it furnishes occasion for all those acts of courtesy, respect, and unselfishness by which love and good humour and modesty express themselves. But it certainly leaves the way open to a great evil, that of competition and hostility. And if souls are free, they cannot be prevented from dealing with the problem by competition instead of by courtesy. And once they have advanced to actual hostility, they can then exploit the fixed nature of matter to hurt one another. The permanent nature of wood which enables us to use it as a beam also enables us to use it for hitting our neighbour on the head. The permanent nature of matter in general means that when human beings fight, the victory ordinarily goes to those who have superior weapons, skill, and numbers, even if their cause is unjust.

We can, perhaps, conceive of a world in which God corrected the results of this abuse of free will by His creatures at every moment: so that a wooden beam became soft as grass when it was used as a weapon, and the air refused to obey me if I attempted to set up in it the sound waves that carry lies or insults. But such a world would be one in which wrong actions were impossible, and in which, therefore, freedom of the will would be void; nay, if the principle were carried out to its logical conclusion, evil thoughts would be impossible, for the cerebral matter which we use in thinking would refuse its task when we attempted to frame them. All matter in the neighbourhood of a wicked man would be liable to undergo unpredictable alterations. . . . Fixed laws, consequences unfolding by causal necessity, the whole natural order, are at once the limits within which [our] common life is confined and also the sole condition under which any such life is possible. Try to exclude the possibility of suffering which the order of nature and the existence of free wills involve, and you find that you have excluded life itself.

LOOKING THROUGH THE ATHEIST'S LENS

1. Many religious people cannot understand how an atheist can live his or her life if there is no ultimate meaning or purpose to it. However, atheists reply that just because there is no ultimate *meaning* to human existence on a cosmic scale does not mean that we cannot find meaning in our daily lives, our friendships, our families, and our careers. Think about the things that happened to you this week or things that you did that were not religious in nature but that brought you happiness, were meaningful, or gave you a sense of accomplishment. Isn't it possible to live a happy, rewarding, and meaningful life on the basis of these experiences alone?

2. Many atheists throughout history have been compassionate, morally sensitive individuals, much like Dr. Bernard Rieux in Albert Camus's novel *The Plague.* Yet such people live morally exemplary lives without the guidance of sacred texts and divine commands. Does it follow from this observation that religion is not necessary for morality?

3. When we were children, we looked to our parents to take care of us, to tell us what to do, and to help us make decisions. However, as we became more mature and approached adulthood, we had to learn how to live our own lives and make our own decisions. Is it true, as some atheists claim, that atheism calls us to live our lives as adults, whereas theism appeals to our immature tendencies to be dependent and to need guidance?

EXAMINING THE STRENGTHS AND WEAKNESSES OF ATHEISM

Positive Evaluation

1. The theist argues that the world needs a cause and finds the explanation in a God who is eternal and uncaused. Is this answer any better than the atheist's answer that the universe or matter and energy themselves are eternal and uncaused?

2. Before the rise of modern science, people thought that all natural events, such as disease and the motion of the planets, were the result of God's activity. However, science has continually shown that events in the world once thought to be mysterious can be explained as the product of natural causes. Do these findings suggest that in the scientific age God is no longer a necessary hypothesis?

3. In Camus's novel *The Plague,* Dr. Rieux said that he was "fighting against creation as he found it" and that "I shall refuse to love a scheme of things in which children are put to torture." Rieux's point is that if suffering is part of God's plan, then people are not supposed to fight against suffering. In other words, if suffering makes us better persons, then I am not doing you a favor if I try to alleviate your suffering; I should simply accept your suffering as part of God's scheme of things. However, most of us, like Dr. Rieux, feel compelled to fight against suffering. Are we then fighting against God's will? Do these considerations undermine the notion that suffering serves a divine purpose?

Negative Evaluation

1. Some atheists argue with the psychiatrist Sigmund Freud that religion is a psychological crutch that emotionally weak persons use to get through life. Certainly, religion fulfills the emotional needs of many people. But can this argument be turned against the atheist? List some reasons why someone might find the existence of God to be psychologically threatening and the belief in atheism to be an emotionally comfortable crutch.

2. Most religious and secular systems of ethics have some notion of the intrinsic worth, dignity, and equality of each person. But if we are just a random collection of atoms impersonally coughed up by nature, do we have any rational basis for believing in the intrinsic worth, dignity, and equality of all persons? How can the atheist, who does not believe that we are made by a loving God and that we bear his image but who does believe that we are the product of the random, impersonal processes of physical nature, view persons as having intrinsic worth?

3. Daniel H. Osmond, professor of physiology and medicine at the University of Toronto, argues that modern science arose from the theistic belief in the divinely ordered rationality of the universe. From this historical point he goes on to explain: "To be sure, many scientists today are able to do science without necessarily believing in a Purposeful Creator. But in order to do so, they must implicitly accept an ordered universe that can be known. . . . Purpose lies outside their domain of scientific discourse much as the roots of a tree lie outside the trunk. In each case the latter cannot stand without the former though the former is hidden from view."[45] Is it plausible, as Osmond maintains, that the "trunk" of science depends on the "hidden roots" of theistic belief? Does theism have the best explanation for the existence of this intricately ordered universe and of minds that are capable of theoretically examining this order?

4.6 RETHINKING THE WESTERN TRADITION: ASIAN RELIGIONS

 LEADING QUESTIONS: *Asian Religions*

1. The Judeo-Christian tradition claims that God created the world and that the world and God are distinctly different beings. But if this claim were true, wouldn't the world limit God since it stands outside of his being? To look at it another way, if God is everywhere, don't we have to view nature as included in the very being of God? If God is all-inclusive and nothing stands apart from God, then aren't we simply an aspect of God and isn't our distinct individuality an illusion?

2. How would you define religion? Is belief in a personal God essential for an outlook or way of life to be considered a religion at all? Or could you be religious and concerned about living a spiritual life without believing in a God that is to be worshiped?

3. What is the self? If you look inward, you will find nothing but a changing kaleidoscope of sensations, feelings, thoughts, and psychological states. Is the self something more than this changing phenomena? Does some permanent, unchanging "super-self," or soul, exist beneath this passing flow of psychological states? Or is there nothing there, nothing permanent beyond the stream of consciousness you experience?

Thus far our discussion of religion has revolved primarily around the Western concept of the Judeo-Christian God. Some philosophers have argued for the existence of such a God, while others have argued against his existence. We would be remiss, however, if we failed to examine the assumption that these arguments are the only options. Consequently, a brief look at the religious traditions of Asia provides us with some alternative views. To focus our discussion, I address only two of the many Asian traditions, namely, Hinduism and Buddhism. Although both religions arose in India and share a great deal in common, they also take differing positions on the points raised in the leading questions. I discuss each religion in turn, and to best contrast these religions with each other and with Western thought, I discuss each religion in terms of its historical origins and its views on faith and reason, God, the world, the self, the goal of life, human destiny, and the problem of evil.

 STOP AND THINK

How much do you know about Hinduism and Buddhism at this point? Go back to the three leading questions on Asian religions and write down how you think a Hindu and a Buddhist would answer them. After you have read the following sections, review your answers and see how accurate they were.

SURVEYING THE CASE FOR HINDUISM

Historical Origins

Unlike religions such as Christianity, Islam, or Buddhism, Hinduism had no single founder. Its first expression came from a collection of ancient and anonymous sacred texts that came from even older hymns of worship. The earliest writings are the Vedas ("body of knowledge"). Some scholars estimate that the oldest one, the Rig Veda, may have been written approximately 1,500 years B.C. This estimate would place it hundreds of years before Moses, allowing Hindus to claim that theirs is the oldest living religion. Devout Hindus still consider the Vedas to be divinely inspired knowledge, and the writings are still commonly believed to form the basis of all later scriptures. Another set of sacred writings make up the Upanishads, which are commentaries on the Vedas. The Upanishads are the most philosophical of ancient Hindu writings, for they present the world as a rational whole. The title *Upanishads* is composed of root words that mean *near, down,* and *to sit.* Hence, the name of this collection of writings suggests the picture of a pupil sitting down near a teacher to learn the truth that liberates. There are at least 108 of these writings, but only ten to thirteen are considered the principal ones. Some scholars believe that the earliest of the Upanishads was recorded around 1,000 B.C., while others say the manuscripts evolved from 800 B.C. on. The authors of these books are anonymous, but the books are considered to be revelation produced by sages whose spiritual experience gave them special insight into divine matters.

Just as the expressions of Christianity range from the informal, emotional services of Pentecostal fundamentalists to the high rituals of the Greek Orthodox church, so the wide range of doctrines and practices found in Hinduism prevent it from being easily summarized. It is often said that anything that can be affirmed of Hinduism can be denied of it as well. For our purposes, I focus on the tradition of Advaita Vedanta pantheism, because it is one of the most philosophical forms of Hinduism and it makes the most effective contrast with Western religions. *Pantheism* is the view that God and the world are identical or are different manifestations of the same, one reality. This view is in contrast to the theistic view in which the world is dependent upon God while it remains a separate reality from the being of God.

Although many Westerners may not be familiar with the technical details of Hinduism, they have been exposed to some of its manifestations. The method of nonviolent resistance that Mohandas K. Gandhi used to bring social reform to India, for example, was inspired by the Hinduism of his youth. The Hare Krishna movement, which has drawn many American converts into its fold over the past four decades, is a form of Hinduism. Within the world of popular culture, the Beatles were influenced by the transcendental meditation of the Maharishi Mahesh Yogi, and in George Harrison's song "My Sweet Lord" the background singers sang praises to Hindu deities.[46] Likewise, the pantheism found in some versions of Hinduism has found Western expressions. The New Age movement and such entertainers as Shirley MacLaine and Tina Turner have been influenced by pantheistic

GANDHI
(1869–1948)

thought.[47] Also, movies such as the *Star Wars* series have popularized pantheistic thought. In *the Empire Strikes Back,* for example, Yoda's teachings about the Force refer to a divinelike energy that permeates everything.

Faith and Reason in Hinduism

Like many of Hinduism's doctrines, the Hindu view of religious knowledge is complex and the position expressed depends on what passages are emphasized. Similar to the Biblical writings of Western religion, the ancient Hindu scriptures are very poetic and metaphorical. Both sets of scriptures were written to awaken people to their spiritual calling and were not intended to be philosophical treatises. Nevertheless, the Upanishads contain within them seeds of philosophical arguments that later writers were able to develop. For example, the cosmological argument is hinted at by the claim that God (Brahman) is "the Self-Existent" or the "Creator of the Universe." Similarly, the teleological, or design, argument is suggested by a number of passages. After a review of the physical and organic processes in the world, we are told that "All this is guided by intelligence, is based on intelligence. The world is guided by intelligence. The basis is intelligence. [Brahman] is intelligence."[48] Another scripture says that "if there were no elements of intelligence, there would be no elements of being."[49]

A number of other passages, however, are pessimistic about the possibility of proving a supreme, infinite God from the materials of our finite experience. Speaking of God, one scripture says, "He has no master in the world, no ruler, nor is there even a sign of Him [by which He can be inferred]."[50] Another argument against natural theology is based on the notion that the world being created at some point in time is merely a metaphorical expression, for the world has eternally existed with God. Both the cosmological and the teleological arguments assume that the world is the creation of God's will. But to will something is to desire it, and we desire things because we lack something. But how can a supreme, perfect being lack anything or desire anything? As one ancient commentary on the Upanishads puts it, "What desire is possible for Him who is the fulfilment of all desires?"[51]

Some Hindu writers such as Sarvepalli Radhakrishnan express the view, similar to the position of fideism found in Western thought, that God cannot be known by reason but only through faith or religious experience. Radhakrishnan (1888–1975) was born in south India and became one of the most frequently read Indian philosophers in the Western world. Besides holding teaching positions at various Indian universities, he served as a professor of Eastern religions and ethics at Oxford University. He was not only a great scholar but a statesman as well, for he was president of India from 1962 to 1967.

Radhakrishnan explicitly agrees with Kierkegaard that truth has to be personally appropriated. As the following passage illustrates, Radhakrishnan believed that intuition, insight, and experience allowed us to know God with a directness and immediacy unavailable to reason:

Everything is known to us only through experience. Even such an abstract science as mathematics is based on the experience of stated regularities. Philosophy of religion must base itself on religious experiences. The existence of God means the real or the possible experience of this Being. If the genuine standard of knowledge is experience, we must deny the character of knowledge to our ideas of God unless they are traced to the experience of God.[52]

The Hindu View of God

The Hindu term for the ultimate reality is *Brahman.* It is derived from a root that means "to be great" or "to expand." In other words, Brahman is that Being whose greatness or expansion is unlimited. Some of the titles used to refer to Brahman are the Absolute, Lord of All, Supreme Ruler, the Soul of the Whole Cosmos, Light, Truth, the Supreme Person, and the Adorable God. Brahman is said to be infinite, indivisible oneness, all knowing, all powerful, immortal, all pervading, and unchanging as well as being supreme love and goodness. With respect to us, Brahman is the fulfillment of all desires, the source of all blessings, the upholder of all things.

At first glance, these descriptions make Brahman sound very similar to the Judeo-Christian God depicted in the Bible. The problem is that Brahman has not only all these properties, but also none of these, because the ultimate reality is inexpressible and indefinable. To try to categorize the ultimate reality in terms of human language and concepts is like trying to capture the ocean in a bucket. Paradoxically, those believers who think they understand the divine reality do not, while those who truly understand it realize they don't. The indefinable nature of Brahman is captured in the following two passages.

 FROM THE *UPANISHADS*

Not by speech, not by mind,
Not by sight can He be apprehended.
How can He be comprehended
Otherwise than by one's saying "He is"?[53]

It is conceived of by him by whom It is not conceived of.
He by whom It is conceived of, knows It not.
It is not understood by those who [say they] understand It.
It is understood by those who [say they] understand It not.[54]

The complexity of Hindu thought is illustrated by the fact that the first passage in this reading speaks of Brahman as personal ("He") and the second one uses the impersonal pronoun "It." Western minds are very dualistic. We want to categorize everything as either falling into a certain category or falling outside it. For example, Western thinkers would say that God, women, and men are personal beings, while gravity, rocks, and daisies are impersonal beings. In which category (personal or impersonal) does Hinduism place God? The answer is "both." God is both personal and impersonal, for neither category alone adequately describes the Supreme Reality. Radhakrishnan explains the use of contradictory descriptions of God in this way: "We are like little children on the seashore trying to fill our shells with water from the sea. While we cannot exhaust the waters of the deep by means of our shells, every drop that we attempt to gather into our tiny shells is part of the authentic waters. Our intellectual representations differ simply because they bring out different facets of the one central reality."[55] Accordingly, when describing Brahman we can only say what it is not. The Sanskrit expression *neti, neti* (Not thus! Not so!) is repeatedly used to speak of this incomprehensible reality.[56] In Western theology this method of describing God is known as the "way of negation."

[Brahman] is not that which is conscious of the inner (subjective) world, nor that which is conscious of the outer (objective) world, nor that which is conscious of both, nor that which is a mass of consciousness. It is not simple consciousness nor is It unconsciousness. It is unperceived, unrelated, incomprehensible, uninferable, unthinkable, and indescribable. The essence of the Consciousness manifesting as the self. . . . It is all peace, all bliss, and non-dual.[57]

As opposed to the Western emphasis on the transcendence of God and the duality between God and creation, Vedanta Hinduism sees Brahman as not only immanent in, but identical to, the world. One scripture compares Brahman to a lump of salt dissolved in water. The salt is invisible to the eye, but to those who taste the water, the flavor of the salt is pervasive throughout it.[58] Many passages such as the following present nature as though it is God's body.

The heavens are His head; the sun and moon, His eyes; the quarters [regions of space], His ears; the revealed Vedas, His speech; the wind, is His breath; the universe, His heart. From His feet is produced the earth. He is, indeed, the Inner Self of all beings.[59]

That immortal Brahman alone is before, that Brahman is behind, that Brahman is to the right and left. Brahman alone pervades everything above and below; this universe is that Supreme Brahman alone.[60]

 THOUGHT EXPERIMENT

The World and Brahman

Consider the following Hindu argument.

1. Brahman (God) is perfect to the maximum degree.
2. If Brahman is perfect to the maximum degree, then it must be unlimited.

(Continued . . .)

(. . . continued)

3. So Brahman is unlimited.
4. If the world was its own reality that existed separately from Brahman, then Brahman would be limited by it.
5. Therefore, the world does not exist as its own reality separate from Brahman. Review the argument forms in section 1.2. Can you identify the forms of reasoning in this current argument? See the answer in the following endnote.[61] Do you agree with the conclusion that the world is *not* a separate reality from God? If you do not agree, then because the argument is valid, you must reject one or more of the premises (1–4). Which premise, if any, would you reject or modify? Or do you accept the conclusion of the argument?

Anyone who has ever seen Indian art or heard the stories of their gods is familiar with the multiplicity of gods found in their popular religion. Vishnu, Siva, Kali, and Krishna are some of the most common ones. Scholars estimate that there are around 33 million gods in popular Hindu religion. Some scholars believe that primitive Indian polytheism was replaced by monotheism in the same way that the multitude of Greek gods were replaced by the one God in Western thought. But others point out that in the *Rig Veda,* the most ancient of the Indian scriptures, the creation of the world is presented as the product of one, supreme God referred to as "That One."[62] In the various Hindu scriptures, we are given a number of different stories. We are told that (1) the gods are many and each one controls a different aspect of reality, that (2) while there are many gods, Brahman is the greatest of them all, that (3) Brahman created the other gods, and that (4) all gods are really different manifestations of Brahman. The unity of all the plural deities in the one God is a persistent theme in many of the Upanishads. A typical expression of this latter interpretation is the following passage: "When they (the priests) speak of particular gods, saying: 'Sacrifice to him,' 'Sacrifice to that one,' [they are mistaken]; for these are all His manifestations: He Himself is all the gods."[63]

The notion that all the gods are merely different expressions of the same reality allows the Hindu to be very tolerant of other religions. The different gods, including the God of the Jewish faith and the God of Christianity, are like the sunlight breaking into many colors when passing through a prism. Each religion, like each color in the sunlight, gives us a partial aspect of the one reality.

The World in Hindu Thought

If all of reality is really the one, vast unified being of Brahman, why do we experience the world as a plurality of distinct things? The answer is in the doctrine of *maya.* This word is often translated as *illusion,* but this translation can be misleading. Maya is how Brahman appears from our perspective, so the image is not completely unreal, as is, say, the illusory water in the desert seen by a thirsty, hallucinating traveler. Hindu writers tell the story of a man going through a forest at night who jumped back when he saw a snake on the ground in front of him.

When he returned to that spot in the daytime, he realized it was only a rope. Likewise the world we experience is really there, but is not seen for what it is. Hence, the world of our senses—the world of many, distinct, individual objects— is maya. To use another metaphor, the world we experience is like the reflection on the surface of a mirror. The reflection is really there, but we must not mistake it for reality itself. The person who views the world as a collection of many attributes or substances will live a life that is scattered and fragmented. "As rainwater falling on a mountain peak runs down the rocks in all directions, even so he who sees the attributes as different from Brahman verily runs after them in all directions."[64]

The Self in Hindu Thought

If Brahman is the only reality, then who or what are you? You are like a drop of water floating on the crest of a wave on the surface of the ocean. The drop may feel as though it is a distinct individual with its own identity and independent destiny. But that feeling is an illusion, because when the wave subsides, the drop will merge with that great body of water from which it came. Similarly, you are an aspect of and are enfolded within the undivided being of Brahman. But you may protest, "I experience myself as a distinct individual with my own unique feelings, bodily sensations, thoughts, and desires. How can this experience be an illusion?" Look at it in this way. Your feelings, sensations, thoughts, and desires are fleeting, ephemeral, transitory phenomena. One day you are depressed because things are not going your way and the whole world looks gloomy. The next day you get an A on your calculus test or you receive a letter from a close friend, and you are now buoyant and elated. But what is it that stays the same, what is it that is the real *you* throughout all the mood swings, changing psychological states, and passing thoughts? You not only experience tiredness, anger, doubt, joy, but you are also aware of and reflect on the feelings you are experiencing. It is almost as though what exists is the self that is having the experiences and a higher self that is observing the lower self and its experiences.

Hinduism says that the changing, temporal self, *jiva,* is the self that you experience most directly and immediately, but it is insubstantial, for it changes and dissipates with each passing moment. The real you, that which endures throughout all changes, is *atman*. Atman is that part of you that allows you to be an ongoing, continuous being through time; atman is that part of you that is eternal and indestructible.

 STOP AND THINK

Have you ever been so caught up in the whirl of your daily life, rushing from one event to another or always trying to be what others expect you to be, that you felt as though you were losing contact with the deep, inner core of who you are? Or perhaps you have

(Continued . . .)

(. . . continued)

asked, "Who am I?" That question is easy enough to answer by giving your name or by defining yourself in terms of your academic major, relationships, or affiliations. But this response is not really adequate, for these circumstances could have been different or they could change, and you would still be *you*. People sometimes say, "I am trying to *find* myself." But what is the self that it is capable of getting "lost"? Are you nothing more than your outward activities or your physical location and properties or just the changing flow of your inward psychological states, or is there something more to you—something that can't be pinned down, defined, or studied scientifically? If these questions make sense to you, then you are trying to sort out the jiva from the atman. You are trying to find that true self that stands behind all the outward appearances and activities.

Now comes the crucial turn. Hinduism teaches that the eternal soul of each individual (atman) is the same as the Soul (Atman) of the cosmos. Furthermore, this cosmic Soul—Atman (capitalized)—is one and the same as Brahman. In teaching about Brahman, the Hindu scriptures frequently add, "That art thou." The following passages stress the unity of each individual with God (Brahman) or the soul of the universe (Atman).

Then Ushasta, the son of Chakra, questioned him. "Yājnavalkya," said he, "explain to me the Brahman that is immediately and directly perceived—the self that is within all."

"This is your self that is within all."[65]

For truly, everything here is Brahma; this self (atman) is Brahma.[66]

These rivers, my dear, flow, the eastern toward the east, the western toward the west. They go just from the ocean to the ocean. They become the ocean itself. As there they know not "I am this one," "I am that one"—even so, indeed, my dear, all creatures here, though they have come forth from Being, know not "We have come forth from Being." . . . That which is the finest essence—this whole world has that as its soul. That is Reality. That is Atman (Soul). That art thou.[67]

Let's try an analogy to explain the Hindu view of the self. Imagine a street with ten houses, and each house has a completely different stained glass window on its southern side. Each resident thinks that the source of the light streaming through his or her window is unique, for its colors and patterns are different than that of the neighbors' windows. But the fact is that the same sun is illuminating the interior of each person's house. The light only appears to be different in each case because it is being filtered through different panes of glass. Now suppose that the inhabitants had been imprisoned in their own houses all their lives with no windows other than the stained glass one through which to view the outside world. If the window only transmitted light but was too dark to show much else, the residents would have a diminished view of what the world was like outside their individual house. They even might think that the window itself was the source of light rather than being simply an opening through which they experienced a partial manifestation of something greater. Now suppose that the doors to the houses were unlocked and the residents were able to step outside into the brilliance and majesty of the fully visible sun itself. Can you imagine what a change of perspective that experience would cause? The sun, of course, is Brahman, and the individual windows are jiva. The experience of seeing the sun itself and basking in its undiluted light corresponds to what the Hindu scriptures call liberation.

If this view is correct, then the Western individualistic culture is based on an ideal that is at odds with the nature of reality. We and the rest of nature are all part of the one, majestic being of Brahman. We eat the fruit grown on trees and vegetables that come from the earth, so the being of those plants and the minerals in their soil now become part of our bodies. When we die, our bodies will return to the soil. Every time you inhale, the oxygen produced by plants and the air that others have breathed becomes a part of your physical system. Every time you breathe out, some of your physical being now becomes a part of nature. As these examples illustrate, the divisions between individual things in the world are artificial, for ultimately we are all bonded together in the one being of Brahman.

The Goal of Life in Hinduism

According to Hinduism, the goal in life is to overcome the illusion of duality and separateness and to realize our oneness with the Absolute Being. We are told that "if a man knows Atman here, he then attains the true goal of life"[68] and "he who knows the Supreme Brahman verily becomes Brahman."[69] Kabīr, a religious teacher, says that God is not a far-away, absent deity that we must hunt for, but is as close to us as water is to the fish.

> I laugh when I hear that the fish in the water is thirsty. You wander restlessly from forest to forest while the Reality is within your own dwelling. . . . The truth is here!
> . . . Until you have found God in your own soul, the world will seem meaningless to you.
> Your Lord is near; yet you are climbing the palm-tree to seek him.[70]

Hinduism offers many roads to the one goal of spiritual fulfillment. Since people are not all the same and since they start their spiritual journey at different points, there must be different ways available for achieving this goal. These various paths take the form of different kinds of *yoga.* This word is related to the English word *yoke,* which means both to unite and to place under discipline. Briefly, all forms of yoga involve disciplining the body and the mind to achieve physical and spiritual integration and to unite the person with the divine dimension within. One form is the way of wisdom, an approach that appeals to intellectuals. The way of wisdom leads a person to spiritual fulfillment through correct thinking and overcoming ignorance. A second yoga is the path of devotion, which is for those who relate to life with their emotions. Here a person seeks a relationship of intense love with the divine. A third path is for those people who are oriented toward action. It focuses on moral action in the world without concern for personal consequences. The fourth path is for people who are more experimental; it involves participation in physical, psychological, and spiritual exercises that lead to a serene, detached awareness. More or less nonreligious versions of this fourth form of yoga have become popular in the West as a form of mental and physical exercise.

Hinduism and Human Destiny

Although achieving oneness with the cosmic Soul is our ultimate destiny, it doesn't happen overnight; it takes time and effort. To understand this effort, we need to look at the best known and least understood concept in Indian philosophy—the doctrine of karma. **Karma** is the moral law of cause and effect that governs our actions in the world. In the physical realm, laws govern everything that happens and dictate that every cause has a definite effect. In the same way, the Hindu scriptures teach, a law of cause and effect governs the moral and the spiritual realm. Every action you perform will have its effect not only on the world around you but also on your own soul, depending on the moral quality of the action. Every action, thought, word, and desire shapes our future experiences. The doctrine of karma is sometimes thought to be a form of fatalism, as though we are in the grip of forces we cannot control. This approach is incorrect, however, because your own actions control your destiny such that whatever you sow, that is what you shall reap.

While your karma may have immediate effects, it is impossible for all the consequences of your actions to be realized in your current life. Therefore, Indian thought affirms **reincarnation,** the doctrine that your soul came from a previous form of existence and that when you die you will be reborn into another life. Each successive rebirth reflects the moral development (or lack of it) in your previous life. Hence, karma not only affects your condition in this present life, but also in the next life, whether you find yourself to be a king, a slave, or a mosquito. "As a person puts on new garments, giving up old ones, the soul similarly accepts new material bodies, giving up the old and useless ones."[71]

karma in Hinduism, the moral law of cause and effect that governs our actions in the world

reincarnation the doctrine that your soul came from a previous form of existence and that when you die you will be reborn into another life

 STOP AND THINK

Westerners sometimes have trouble accepting the notion of reincarnation because it is largely foreign to our tradition. The question that we sometimes ask is, "How can I have been reincarnated from a previous life if I have no memory of my former mode of existence?" One answer that Hindu thinkers give is to point to your belief that you are continuous with and the same person as the little baby you once were even though you have no memories of that former state of your existence. Hence, we can accept continuity of the self even without conscious connection in our memories between our current experiences and the experiences of the baby. "As the embodied soul continuously passes, in

(Continued . . .)

(. . . continued)

his body, from boyhood to youth to old age, the soul similarly passes into another body at death. A sober person is not bewildered by such a change."[72]

- How would you reply to this argument?
- Is the analogy between the successive phases of your present life and the doctrine of reincarnation a good one?

The ultimate goal of our deepest longings (whether we realize it or not) is the final release of *moksha*. Moksha is best translated as "liberation" rather than "salvation." When we achieve moksha, we are released from all the finite and mortal conditions of life. There are many names for the goal: God-realization, oneness with the Absolute, supreme bliss, cosmic consciousness, or simply release or freedom. When we become spiritually perfected, we find release from the karma-driven cycle of birth, death, and rebirth.

Unenlightened souls who are still caught up in their own individuality return to earth to pursue their unfulfilled desires, but not so for the person who has transcended the individual self and its unquenchable desires:

But as to the man who does not desire—who is without desire, who is freed from desire, whose desire is satisfied, whose only object of desire is the Self—[his breath does not depart]. Being Brahman, he merges in Brahman.

Regarding this there is the following verse:
"When all the desires that dwell in his heart are got rid of, then does the mortal become immortal and attain Brahman in this very body."
Just as the slough of a snake lies, dead and cast away, on an ant-hill, even so lies this body. Then the self becomes disembodied and immortal Spirit, the Supreme Self . . ., Brahman, the Light.[73]

Because a person achieves this eternal state of bliss by overcoming the illusion of the individual self and by realizing that he or she is one with God, there is no sense of the individual, personal immortality found in Western thought. The liberated souls are compared to many rivers that have merged with the ocean and are no longer this or that river.[74] In a striking analogy, this unity with Brahman is compared to a romantic embrace (or sexual ecstasy) in which the lovers are absorbed in the pure pleasure of the moment and are not thinking about themselves or anything else.[75]

Hinduism and the Problem of Evil

If everything is an aspect of God, how does Hinduism account for the existence of evil in the world? One answer is that the law of karma implies that all suffering is just and is the outcome of choices that we have made in this life or a previous life. There are problems with this answer, however, just as there are with theistic solutions. This response implies that the innocent victim of suffering (say, someone who has a painful disease) is really to be blamed for his or her condition, which would suggest that we should not feel as compassionate for such a person as we normally are.

While the karmic answer to the problem of evil has a number of problems with it, the Hindu treatment of moral good and evil is equally radical. We are told that the distinction between good and evil, in the final analysis, is not fully real. As long as we have not yet achieved spiritual fulfillment, we are still required to wrestle with the issue of moral versus immoral choices. But in Brahman there is only total unity, and when we experience our identity with this oneness, all opposing dualities are dissolved. Hence, when a person achieves freedom from the dreamworld of this life, good and evil are no longer an issue. The enlightened person becomes untroubled, accepting reality as it is, and achieves detachment from everything, including all past, present, and future actions. This teaching is reiterated in many passages such as the following four scriptures.

When a seer sees the brilliant
Maker, Lord, Person, the Brahma-source,
Then, being a knower, shaking off good and evil,
Stainless, he attains supreme identity [with Him].[76]

Him [who knows this] these two do not overcome—neither the thought "Hence I did wrong," nor the thought "Hence I did right." Verily, he overcomes them both. What he has done and what he has not done do not affect him.[77]

Now, the Soul (Atman) is the bridge [or dam], the separation for keeping these worlds apart. Over that bridge [or dam] there cross neither day nor night, nor old age, nor death, nor sorrow, nor well-doing, nor evil-doing.[78]

Just as one driving a chariot looks down upon the two chariot-wheels, thus he looks down upon day and night, thus upon good deeds and evil deeds, and upon all the pairs of opposites. This one, devoid of good deeds, devoid of evil deeds, a knower of Brahma, unto very Brahma goes on.[79]

SURVEYING THE CASE FOR BUDDHISM

Historical Origins: The Buddha's Life

Contrary to popular opinion, Buddha is the title (but not a name) of Siddhartha Gautama (563–483 B.C.), the historical founder of Buddhism. The title "Buddha" means "the enlightened one." Siddhartha, the one who would become a Buddha, was born in northeastern India and was raised in the Hindu tradition. His father was a wealthy ruler who sought to provide his son with every luxury while sheltering him from the cruel world outside. When he was sixteen, while still living within the confines of his father's palace, Siddhartha married a young woman who bore

BUDDHA
(563–483 B.C.)

him a son. However, when he was in his early twenties, he escaped from his carefully supervised environment and slipped out to visit a nearby city. There, according to legend, he encountered four life-changing sights. First, he saw a gaunt, trembling old man whose body manifested the degeneration of old age. Next, he saw a man suffering from a dread disease, lying by the roadside. Third, he passed a funeral procession with the corpse surrounded by grief-stricken relatives. Still stunned by his first encounters with the sufferings produced by old age, illness, and death, Siddhartha saw a monk experiencing the peace of deep meditation.

These experiences showed him the vanity of seeking fulfillment in the physical realm and started him on his quest for the solution to the human condition. One night, at age twenty-nine, he could no longer suppress his spiritual longings, and he silently said goodbye to his wife and son while they slept and fled into the forest to seek enlightenment. There he exchanged his fine garments with a ragged beggar, shaved his head, and renounced the carefree life of luxury he had enjoyed up until then. Siddhartha began his spiritual journey by spending seven years as a beggar-monk and sought enlightenment through Hindu asceticism (the practice of self-denial and extreme fasting). His self-imposed diet of a few seeds, herbs, rice, and fruit led to a physical collapse. Later he said of this stage in his life, "if I sought to feel my belly it was my backbone which I found in my grasp." One day, overcome by malnourishment, he fell unconscious. Shortly thereafter a girl from a nearby village revived him with a bowl of warm rice. This experience made him realize that ascetic practices do not lead to enlightenment but only to self-destruction.

After traveling until nightfall, Siddhartha sat down under a fig tree, resolving that he would not move from this spot until he had found the answers he sought. He sat there all night, passing through various stages of awareness, experiencing all his previous lives, and seeing the web of all beings who are interwoven into a ceaseless drama of birth, death, and rebirth until the mystery of human life became revealed to him. At this point, when Siddhartha was thirty-five years old, he became the Buddha, an "Enlightened One" or "One who is awake." Having found enlightenment, he spent most of the next half-century going about teaching his answer to the problems of life and proposing his "Middle Way," a balance between sensual indulgence and fanatical asceticism. He founded a religious order and was eventually joined by his wife and son. At the age of eighty he passed away in the arms of one of his disciples, saying "Decay is inherent in all compound things. Work out your own salvation with diligence."

Because of the power of Siddhartha's personality and teachings, Buddhism spread very rapidly. After the Buddha's death, his followers split into several factions. Ultimately, two major traditions emerged, each with its own interpretation of the master's teachings. The Theravada school sees the Buddha as a holy man who attained enlightenment and pointed others to the way. They stick very closely to the original teachings of their master. The Mahayana Buddhists, however, see the Buddha as a savior. In addition to considering him divine and praying to him, they have expanded and added to the original doctrines. In this discussion of

Buddhism, I present the Theravada interpretation because it closely follows the most ancient Buddhist scriptures.

Faith and Reason in Buddhism

The relationship between faith and reason has been a major concern throughout Western religious philosophy. What did the Buddha have to say about these topics? The answer is that he had little use for either faith or reason. With respect to reason, the Buddha was opposed to all speculating, theorizing, and debating. In early Buddhist thought there is nothing to compare to the philosophical arguments found in Western philosophy. Instead the Buddha continually pointed people to their own experience as a means of persuading them of the value of his insights.

- In the following passage, what does the Buddha say about our ability to study his "Way"?
- What is his attitude toward analytic thinking?

 FROM THE BUDDHA

Selected Teachings

We merely talk about "studying the Way" using the phrase simply as a term to arouse people's interest. In fact, the Way cannot be studied. If concepts based on [factual] study are retained, they only result in the Way being misunderstood. . . . If you will now and at all times, whether walking, standing, sitting, or lying, only concentrate on eliminating analytic thinking, at long last you will inevitably discover the truth.[80]

In a writing called "Questions Not Tending to Edification," the story is told that a man once approached the Buddha and wanted all his philosophical questions answered before he would practice the way that Buddha taught. Here is how the Buddha responded:

It is as if a man had been wounded by a poisoned arrow and when attended to by a physician were to say, "I will not allow you to remove this arrow until I have learned the caste, the age, the occupation, the birthplace, and the motivation of the person who wounded me." That man would die before having learned all this. In exactly the same way, anyone who should say, "I will not follow the teaching of the Blessed One until the Blessed One has explained all the multiform truths of the world"—that person would die before the Buddha had explained all this.[81]

Not only is the value of analytic reason diminished in Buddhist thought, but Buddhism also offers little that corresponds to the notion of faith. Rather than presenting himself or his teachings as the object of faith, the Buddha claimed that his own teachings were merely a means to an end that may be abandoned once the teachings have carried us to our destination. In a well-known parable Buddha tells the story of a man on a journey who comes upon a great river that restricts his progress. On his side of the river are many perils that he wants to escape, while on the other bank it is calm and peaceful. So he constructs a raft that he uses to carry himself across the river. Once the man has crossed to the safety of the other side, the Buddha asks, would anyone consider this man to be wise if he continued to carry his raft with him on his shoulders when he no longer needed it? The Buddha concludes the story by saying, "In this way I have taught you Dharma [the truth], like the parable of the raft, for getting across, not for retaining."[82]

The Question of God in Buddhism

What is remarkable about early Buddhist thought is the almost complete absence of any mention of the gods or the supernatural realm. Accordingly, some people say the Buddha's teaching was basically atheistic, while others say he was a religious skeptic (an agnostic). What is clear is that the Buddha's silence concerning theology pointed to the irrelevance of any God or gods to the human condition. Even when he does mention the gods of traditional Indian religion, they are always treated as rather minor, unimportant, and unknowable beings. As I mentioned previously, the earlier followers of Buddha and those who still practice Theravada Buddhism do not consider their founder to be a god but simply a man who showed the way to liberation through his teachings and his example. Although followers later added the edifice of institutional religion onto Buddhist teaching, the Buddha himself seemed to be opposed to the religious authorities, rituals, and traditions of his day. In many Buddhist shrines, the Buddha is represented solely by a footprint, symbolizing that he is no longer here but has left his mark and has showed us the direction in which we should go. This view of the Buddha is captured by the following well-known story.

> It is said that soon after his enlightenment the Buddha passed a man on the road who was struck by the Buddha's extraordinary radiance and peaceful presence. The man stopped and asked,
> "My friend, what are you? Are you a celestial being or a god?"
> "No," said the Buddha.
> "Well, then, are you some kind of magician or wizard?"
> Again the Buddha answered, "No."
> "Are you a man?"
> "No."
> "Well, my friend, then what are you? The Buddha replied, "I am awake."[83]

The way to salvation or liberation is a journey that people must make for themselves, using their own resources and knowledge of the truth. They must not look for the external help of any god or even the Buddha himself. On his deathbed he said these last words to his followers.

Be ye lamps unto yourselves. Rely on yourselves, and do not rely on external help. Hold fast to the truth as a lamp. Seek salvation alone in the truth. Look not for assistance to any one besides yourselves. . . . Those who, either now or after I am dead, shall be a lamp unto themselves, relying upon themselves only and not relying upon any external help . . . it is they . . . who shall reach the very topmost height![84]

The Buddhist View of the World

A central concept in Buddhism is the transitory nature and perpetual perishing of every natural object. The Buddha once said,

Thus shall ye think of all this fleeting world:
A star at dawn, a bubble in a stream;
A flash of lightning in a summer cloud,
A flickering lamp, a phantom, and a dream.[85]

We view the world as made up of "things," but according to Buddhism the world is actually an interwoven series of processes. Our concepts and words are like photographs that freeze and fragment the world, whereas reality is more like an ongoing movie. The Buddha frequently used the metaphor of a wave to make this point. We watch the wave from the beach as it moves across the surface of the water. "It" starts in the distance and rapidly makes "its" way toward us. In speaking of it as "*the* wave," we delude ourselves into thinking it is one, continuous, singular object, whereas the shape and motion of the wave is actually made up of completely different particles of water from moment to moment. The point is that once we understand that everything is fleeting and perishable, we will not look to the physical world for our source of fulfillment.

The Self in Buddhist Philosophy

Everything in the world lacks permanence, and the same is true of the self. The Buddha's famous *anatta* ("no-self") doctrine states that there is no soul, self, or mind that is an enduring object that persists through time. Contemporary science tells us that your surface skin cells are discarded and replaced every thirty days. The rest of the cells in your body change every seven years. So when you see an old friend whom you haven't seen for some time, you are literally looking at completely different particles of matter. Thousands of years before this fact was known, the Buddha taught that there is nothing permanent in your physical makeup. Similarly there is nothing permanent in your psychological makeup, for you are a stream of consciousness that is constantly changing. This doctrine is remarkably similar to that of David Hume, the eighteenth-century Scottish philosopher introduced in section 2.1, who said, "What we call mind is nothing but a heap or bundle of different perceptions united together by certain relations."

If there is no permanent soul or self, then who (or what) are you? The Buddha taught that you are made up of five transient streams or aggregates. These are material shape, the feelings, the perceptions, the dispositions (or impulses), and consciousness. In the following passage, you are compared to musical sounds or moving air. We use nouns to refer to them ("the melody" or "the wind"), but there is no enduring entity within or behind these transitory events.

When body and mind dissolve, they do not exist anywhere, any more than musical notes lay heaped up anywhere. When a lute is played upon, there is no previous store of sound; and when the music ceases it does not go anywhere in space. It came into existence on account of the structure and stem of the lute and the exertions of the performer; and as it came into existence so it passes away.

In exactly the same way, all the elements of being, both corporeal and non-corporeal, come into existence after having been non-existent; and having come into existence pass away.

There is no self residing in body and mind, but the cooperation of the conformations produces what people call a person. Paradoxical though it may seem: There is a path to walk on, there is walking being done, but there is no traveler. There are deeds being done, but there is no doer. There is blowing of the air, but there is no wind that does the blowing. The thought of self is an error and all existences are as hollow as the plantain tree and as empty as twirling water bubbles.[86]

In other words, a melody is simply a collection of the notes, but it does not exist apart from them. Similarly, the blowing of the air and the wind are not two things; there is nothing more to the wind but the blowing of the air. Likewise, you are simply the collection of all the processes and activities that are happening right now, but there is no self that exists apart from these processes. There is no enduring personal identity throughout all your activities, because apart from your activities that are happening at any given time, there is nothing left over to constitute the self. The Hindu believes that the individual self is an illusion because it is really a manifestation of Atman, the Soul of the cosmos, or God (Brahman). In contrast, the Buddhist believes that the individual self is an illusion because there is really nothing there beyond the passing flow of events.

Buddhism and the Problem of Evil

It is necessary to introduce the topic of evil earlier in the discussion of Buddhism than I did for Western religion or Hinduism because the problem of evil and the existence of suffering is the main theme of the Buddha's teachings. According to Buddhism, the cause of suffering is twofold. First, much of our suffering is the result of our own desires and our preoccupation with the illusion of the self.

Second, suffering is simply a fact of life that we must face; no divine purpose is being achieved by suffering. We will look at each of these causes in turn.

The theme of suffering is addressed in the most fundamental creed of Buddhism, which is called the "Four Noble Truths." The first two diagnose the human condition and the last two point to the solution. These truths may be briefly stated in the following way: (1) We experience suffering in life. (2) Suffering is caused by selfish cravings and desires. (3) There is a way to end suffering. (4) The way to end suffering is through enlightened living. These Four Noble Truths were presented by the Buddha in his first sermon, which was delivered in a park at the edge of town soon after he received enlightenment. Here is how one translator renders the truths.

And this is the Noble Truth of Sorrow. Birth is sorrow, age is sorrow, disease is sorrow, death is sorrow; contact with the unpleasant is sorrow, separation from the pleasant is sorrow, every wish unfulfilled is sorrow—in short, all the five components of individuality are sorrow.

And this is the Noble Truth of the Arising of Sorrow. It arises from craving, which leads to rebirth, which brings delight and passion, and seeks pleasure now here, now there—the craving for sensual pleasure, the craving for continued life, the craving for power.

And this is the Noble Truth of the Stopping of Sorrow. It is the complete stopping of that craving, so that no passion remains, leaving it, being emancipated from it, being released from it, giving no place to it.

And this is the Noble Truth of the Way which leads to the Stopping of Sorrow. It is the Noble Eightfold Path—[having] Right Views, Right Resolve, Right Speech, Right Conduct, Right Livelihood, Right Effort, Right Mindfulness, and Right Concentration.[87]

Buddhism is sometimes accused of being pessimistic, for it seems to dwell on the negative features of life. On the contrary, the Buddha did not deny that life can have its moments of pleasure and happiness, but his point is that all pleasures are momentary events that come to an end and leave us with regret and a longing for more. As long as we pin our sense of well-being on that which is fated to slip through our hands, we will always be restless and empty. The word that was translated as "sorrow" in the last passage is *dukkha*, which can also mean "suffering," "pain," "evil," and "disease," as well as "impermanence," "emptiness," "imperfection," and "frustration." The word is sometimes used to refer to an axle of a wheel that is off-center. It can also refer to a bone that has slipped out of its socket.[88] Accordingly, the contemporary historian of religion Huston Smith rephrases the First Noble Truth in this way:

Life as typically lived is out of joint. Something is awry. Its pivot is not true. This restricts movement (blocks creativity), and causes undue friction (interpersonal conflict).[89]

We are like a child who has reached into a jar of candy and gotten his hand stuck. He doesn't realize that the cause of his distress is that his hand is clenched into a fist around the candy, making it too large to slip out of the opening. If he would just let go, his hand would be freed. Similarly, the cause of suffering and the obstacle to enlightenment is our tendency to cling to such notions as "I," "me," "mine," and "self." We are filled with grasping desires, but we do not control our desires—they control us. They are like raging beasts inside us that drive us on in a never-ending, frantic quest to feed them. From our desires come frustration, resentment, greed, selfishness, self-conscious anxieties, inadequacy, fear, and all the negative attitudes and emotions that cause suffering. But if we desire nothing, if we learn contentment, we will never be frustrated. To eliminate desire and, hence, to eliminate suffering, we must stop saying "I want, I want" and stop thinking in terms of "me, me, me."

 THOUGHT EXPERIMENT

Desire and Freedom

1. Think about yourself as a little child. Try to recall the things that caused this little child joy, sadness, fear, anxiety, envy, and yearning, things that you now realize were of little significance and that no longer have any emotional effect on you. What caused you to change? Is it because you are now more informed, mature, wiser, and have a broader understanding than you did as a child? Now consider the things that cause you joy, sadness, fear, anxiety, envy, and yearning *today*. Can you imagine that someday you might grow to see these things of little significance as well? Is it possible that forty years from now, you will consider all your current emotional crises to be somewhat trivial in the context of the big picture? Does this experiment suggest anything about the transitory and ephemeral nature of our desires?

2. Consider the following argument for the Buddhist perspective:
   (1) If there are things we desire, either we will get all that we want or we won't.
   (2) If we *do* get all that we want, we will suffer from both boredom, for there will be nothing more for which to strive, and anxiety, because of the fear that we will lose what we have.
   (3) If we do *not* get all that we want, we will suffer from frustration.
   (4) So, if we have desires, we will suffer.
   (5) Therefore, freedom from suffering comes only by being free from desire.
   Is this argument a good one? Why?

The other explanation for suffering (as the First Noble Truth explained) is that it is simply an inevitable fact of life. Since Buddhism does not have the Judeo-Christian notion of an all-powerful, loving God whose sovereign will controls every event in the world, it does not have to justify the presence of suffering. The Buddhist attitude toward suffering is illustrated by this ancient story.

Once a woman was stricken with grief over the death of her young boy. She came to the Buddha hoping that he could bring her son back to life. He instructed her to go to every house in the village and fetch some mustard seeds from every home in which no one had died. She came back empty-handed, for everyone she had met had been touched by the sorrow of death. Holding her son's body in her arms, she said, "Dear little son, I thought that you alone had been overtaken by this thing which men call death. But you are not the only one death has overtaken. This is a law common to all mankind." After laying her son's body to rest, she sought refuge in the way of the Buddha.[90]

The Goal of Life in Buddhism

While the Buddha did not offer a magic pill to save us from the intrusion of illness, pain, old age, and death, he did teach a way of being immune from their hold over us. It consists of being free from our narrow concern with ourselves and our interests; eliminating our grasping nature and our desires, passions, wants, and cravings; achieving a sense of distance from the transitory features of the world; mastering ourselves and all that is negative and destructive within us; cultivating a peaceful, focused, and purified outlook and lifestyle; and concentrating on that which really matters.

Buddhism and Human Destiny

The Buddha retained the Hindu doctrine of karma—the law of cause and effect. He believed that harmful actions cause harmful results, much like a stone hitting the water causes ripples that continue on long after the stone has sunk. Likewise he believed in reincarnation, which he called the "Wheel of Rebirth." But now the obvious question is, How can one be reborn if there is no permanent self to make the journey from one life to another? To answer this question, the Buddha frequently used the example of a candle flame. Suppose a candle is burning down until its wick is almost all consumed and you then light another candle with it. As this second candle starts to go out, you light yet another candle from its flame. Is the flame in the third candle the same one you had at the beginning? Is the flame some sort of permanent substance that passes from candle to candle the way a water pitcher can be passed from one person to another? Obviously there is continuity in this process, since each candle is lit from the flame of the previous candle. However, the flame is not one continuous object lighting three successive candles. It is not even a continuous object from moment to moment when it is burning in one candle. In this way, the cycle of rebirth takes place without a continuous soul or self.

Even though the Buddha believed in karma and rebirth, he did not think that being reborn in another life is punishment imposed upon us for past actions. Instead, rebirth is a sign that a person has not let go of the self sufficiently. If we have not yet attained liberation, we will get what we think we want, but what we think we want is not what we need. Clinging to our own desire for individuality, we will be trapped in its illusions and limitations.

nirvana In Buddhism, an unchanging, peaceful state of mind that allows us freedom from the illusion of individuality and the limitations of the self

To escape the prison of our desires and our illusions is to achieve **nirvana.** The word refers to the extinguishing of a flame from lack of fuel. Nirvana is not a place (like heaven) but is a state of mind. It is not to be found somewhere over the rainbow but in the here and now. A person who achieves nirvana enters an unchanging, peaceful state and achieves freedom from the illusion of individuality and the limitations of the self. Nirvana is like a deep, relaxing sleep, only better. However, in the final analysis, it cannot be described.

> Nirvana grants all one can desire, brings joy, and sheds light. As a mountain peak is lofty and exalted, so is Nirvana. As a mountain peak is unshakable, so is Nirvana. As a mountain peak is inaccessible, so in Nirvana inaccessible to all the passions. As no seeds can grow on a mountain peak, so the seeds of all the passions cannot grow in Nirvana. And finally, as a mountain peak is free from all desire to please or displease, so is Nirvana.[91]

It might seem as though a person who had been liberated from the passions and who has achieved perfect contentment would be oblivious to the needs and suffering of those about him or her. But Buddhists follow the example of their master who, after achieving nirvana, did not choose to stay alone in his state of perfect bliss but turned back to care for those who were still suffering and in need of enlightenment. The Buddha continually taught that we must live a life of compassion, but we can have compassion without being a victim of passion. You can imagine a child who is injured and whose father is emotionally distraught. Because the parent is so overwhelmed and focused on his own emotional state, he is ineffective in tending to the needs of the child. However, a physician who is emotionally uninvolved can calmly dress the wound. The physician's detachment serves to make her compassion that much more effective.[92] Likewise, a life of detachment is compatible with a life of compassion and service to others.

 THOUGHT EXPERIMENT

Experiencing Nirvana

You can use your own experience to get a glimpse of what the Buddha is saying. When have you been most miserable? It probably has been when you were totally absorbed in yourself. You were nurturing emotional hurts or feeling sorry for yourself. Perhaps you were in a situation in which you were painfully self-conscious, worrying about how you looked, how you were dressed, what people thought of you. On the other hand, you probably can remember times during which you experienced the joy of being totally absorbed with others or with some project. You "came out of yourself" because you were immersed within someone else's joy or with their suffering. You found happiness in your total in-

(Continued . . .)

---

volvement with others or with something larger than yourself because you were no longer focusing on yourself and your petty concerns. This experience of self-abandonment is but a glimpse of the experience of nirvana.

The Buddha's disciples frequently asked what happens when a person has achieved nirvana and then dies. Is this person reborn to a better life, or does he or she go to heaven? The Buddha refused to delve into speculative questions, considering them irrelevant. In the following passage the Buddha (Gotama) explains this irrelevancy to Vaccha, a wandering ascetic.

"But, Vaccha, if the fire in front of you were to become extinct, would you be aware that the fire in front of you had become extinct?"

"Gotama, if the fire in front of me were to become extinct, I should be aware that the fire in front of me had become extinct."

"But, Vaccha, if some one were to ask you, 'In which direction has that fire gone,—east, or west, or north, or south?' what would you say, O Vaccha?"

"The question would not fit the case, Gotama. For the fire which depended on fuel of grass and wood, when that fuel has all gone, and it can get no other, being thus without nutriment, is said to be extinct."

"In exactly the same way, Vaccha, all that form has been abandoned, uprooted, pulled out of the ground like a palmyra-tree, and become non-existent and not liable to spring up again in the future. The saint, O Vaccha, who has been released from what is styled form, is deep, immeasurable, unfathomable, like the mighty ocean. To say that he is reborn would not fit the case. To say that he is not reborn would not fit the case. To say that he is both reborn and not reborn would not fit the case. To say that he is neither reborn nor not reborn would not fit the case.[93]

The religious life . . . does not depend on the dogma that the world is eternal; nor does the religious life . . . depend on the dogma that the world is not eternal. Whether the dogma obtain . . . that the world is eternal, or that the world is not eternal, there still remain birth, old age, death, sorrow, lamentation, misery, grief, and despair, for the extinction of which in the present life I am prescribing.[94]

SUMMARY OF HINDU AND BUDDHIST THOUGHT

In Herman Hesse's moving novel about the life of Siddhartha Gautama and how he attained enlightenment, Hesse has captured the Asian sense of the unity of the cosmos, a unity in which all distinctions between the self and others, the self and nature, pleasure and sorrow, good and evil are dissolved. In the climactic passage of the story Siddhartha bends down and listens to the message of the river. The final message is the humming sound of "Om," a word that has no specific intellectual content, for it refers to anything and everything. Asian mystics use it both to refer to the ultimate meaning of the cosmos, its total unity, and perfection and to transport themselves to the highest level of awareness. The following passage could represent the experience sought for by both the Hindu and the Buddhist.

FROM HERMAN HESSE
Siddhartha[95]

Siddhartha tried to listen better. The picture of his father, his own picture, and the picture of his son all flowed into each other. Kamala's picture also appeared and flowed on, and the picture of Govinda and others emerged and passed on. They all became part of the river. It was the goal of all of them, yearning, desiring, suffering; and the river's voice was full of longing, full of smarting woe, full of insatiable desire. The river flowed on towards its goal. Siddhartha saw the river hasten, made up of himself and his relatives and all the people he had ever seen. All the waves and water hastened, suffering, towards goals, many goals, to the waterfall, to the sea, to the current, to the ocean and all goals were reached and each one was succeeded by another. The water changed to vapor and rose, became rain and came down again, became spring, brook and river, changed anew, flowed anew. But the yearning voice had altered. It still echoed sorrowfully, searchingly, but other voices accompanied it, voices of pleasure and sorrow, good and evil voices, laughing and lamenting voices, hundreds of voices, thousands of voices. . . .

. . . He could no longer distinguish the different voices—the merry voice from the weeping voice, the childish voice from the manly voice. They all belonged to each other: the lament of those who yearn, the laughter of the wise, the cry of indignation and the groan of the dying. They were all interwoven and interlocked, entwined in a thousand ways. And all the voices, all the goals, all the yearnings, all the sorrows, all the pleasures, all the good and evil, all of them together was the world. All of them together was the stream of events, the music of life. When Siddhartha listened attentively to this river, to this song of a thousand voices; when he did not listen to the sorrow or laughter, when he did not bind his soul to any one particular voice and absorb it in his Self, but heard them all, the whole, the unity; then the great song of a thousand voices consisted of one word: Om— perfection.

LOOKING THROUGH THE HINDU'S AND THE BUDDHIST'S LENS

1. Much of human history has been scarred by the conflict between competing religions. However, a common Hindu teaching is that the different religious traditions are like different paths up the same mountain. According to Radhakrishnan, we can overcome the conflict between religions "only if we accept something like the Hindu solution, which seeks the unity of religion not in a common creed

but in a common quest." How would world history have been different if every-body had accepted the Hindu solution?

2. Most Hindu traditions teach that Brahman (God) is immanent within nature and that the world is his body. How would embracing this view affect our society's tendency to abuse our natural environment?

3. What examples can you find in literature, magazines, television, and everyday conversation of the emphasis that our society places on the self and individuality? What would the Buddhist say about this emphasis?

4. Advertisers and others in our society try to make you believe that your worth and the measure of your success in life is determined by the amount of wealth you have accumulated, the car you drive, the clothes you wear, the status of your profession, or the organizations to which you belong. What would the Hindu or Buddhist say about these sorts of values that are prevalent in our society? How would they define success?

5. Both Hinduism and Buddhism teach that we must view the material world the way we view a child's toy—as something trivial and of no lasting importance to us. If you were to follow the advice of these Asian religious philosophies, what would be the childish "toys" in your life that are keeping you from spiritual and ethical enlightenment?

6. Suppose that a friend's home caught on fire and your friend not only lost all his or her possessions and shelter but was also severely burned and scarred for life. How would the theist seek to comprehend such suffering? How would an atheist explain it? A Hindu? A Buddhist?

EXAMINING THE STRENGTHS AND WEAKNESSES OF HINDUISM AND BUDDHISM

Positive Evaluation

1. Hinduism presents a view of the universe that can offer both intellectual and spiritual satisfaction. Everything in the world is permeated by the divine. Ulti-mately there is no fragmentation or dichotomy between God and nature or the sacred and the secular, for the world is one with God's own nature. Wouldn't this outlook bring unity and harmony to our fragmented lives?

2. If everyone believed with the Hindus that every individual soul is really a manifestation of the divine soul, wouldn't it transform human relationships? Would hatred, war, and racism be possible in the light of that belief?

3. How would your personality, times of diminished self-esteem, or self-doubt be transformed if you believed as Hindus do that below the surface of your person-ality you are really identical with the soul of God?

4. To what degree would you find release from emotional suffering if you adopted the Buddhist perspective of floating on the surface of life's waves instead of letting them engulf you? If you viewed your daily hurts, frustrations, and sorrows as though they were as temporal and ephemeral as yesterday's shadows, wouldn't this view make a significant difference to your life?

Negative Evaluation

1. Hindu thought claims that Brahman (God) transcends language, reason, and the laws of logic. For this reason, Hindus describe Brahman in contradictory terms (personal and impersonal, other than the world and identical with it). And yet in making this claim, don't they assume that our logic and conceptual categories are applicable to Brahman? For example, Hindus use the law of excluded middle in assuming that reason either is or is not applicable to Brahman.* They also use the law of contradiction in assuming that Brahman cannot be both limited and not limited.**

2. Hindu pantheism claims that the individual self is really one with the universe, while the Buddhist no-self doctrine claims that the self is an illusion. But how is it that within this unified, undifferentiated universe, aspects of this universe arose that suffer from the illusion of an individual self? To the degree that my beliefs are false, I genuinely am something apart from the rest of the fabric of reality. How can I be one with the universe, as these Asian philosophies claim, at the same time that my beliefs alienate me from the way the universe is?

3. Certainly the Buddhist is correct to point out that we would be happier and more content if we let go of some of our self-obsessive cravings and desires. But throughout history there have been creative geniuses who were driven by the thirst to achieve success or to accomplish some sort of personal goal. Many of these people have had enormous egos at the same time they made enormous contributions to humanity. From these personal desires and strivings, for example, have come great inventions or advances in medicine and science that have reduced human suffering, enriched our lives, and advanced civilization. Wouldn't the world and the quality of human life have been poorer if these history-changing people had done nothing but led contemplative lives and abandoned their strivings and thirst to achieve their individual goals? Is desire the problem in human life (as Buddhism claims) or only wrongly directed desires?

4. Buddhism teaches that we should neutralize our emotions and live a life of detachment from everything that is passing. In the 1960s, folk singer Paul Simon wrote a song in which his fictional character sang, "I am a rock, I am an island. And a rock feels no pain; and an island never cries."[96] While a rock (a person who strives for detachment) is invulnerable to pain, he or she also is closed to the

---

*The law of excluded middle: for any property *A*, something is either *A* or not-*A*.
**The law of contradiction: for any property *A*, something cannot be both *A* and not-*A*.

possibility of love and could never have a deep friendship, be an effective parent, or become emotionally involved in the fight for a just cause. Aren't there times when directed passion is appropriate and justified (for example, when a person is fighting social injustice)?

REVIEW FOR CHAPTER 4

Philosophers

4.1 The Cosmological Argument for God
St. Thomas Aquinas
Richard Taylor

4.2 The Design Argument for God
William Paley
David Hume

4.3 The Ontological Argument for God
St. Anselm
Gaunilo
Immanuel Kant

4.4 Pragmatic and Subjective Justifications of Religious Belief
Blaise Pascal
W. K. Clifford
William James
Søren Kierkegaard

4.5 The Problem of Evil: Atheistic and Theistic Responses
Albert Camus
John Hick
C. S. Lewis

4.6 Rethinking the Western Tradition: Asian Religions
Buddha

Concepts

4.0 Overview of Philosophy of Religion
monotheism
evidentialism
natural theology
atheism
agnosticism (religious skepticism)
nonevidentialism
fideism
existentialism
a posteriori arguments
empirical knowledge
a priori arguments

4.1 The Cosmological Argument for God
cosmological argument
first cause argument
principle of sufficient reason
argument from contingency
contingent
necessary being

4.2 The Design Argument for God
argument from design (teleological argument)
David Hume's critique of the design argument
Darwinian objection to the design argument

4.3 The Ontological Argument for God
ontological argument
reductio ad absurdum argument
Gaunilo's critique of the ontological argument
Immanuel Kant's objection to the ontological argument

4.4 Pragmatic and Subjective Justifications of Religious Belief
pragmatic and subjective justifications of belief
nonevidentialist theism
three essential points of the nonevidentialist theists
Pascal's wager
Clifford's ethics of belief
James's view of religious belief
Kierkegaard's view of religious belief

4.5 The Problem of Evil: Atheistic and Theistic Responses
the problem of evil
moral evil
natural evil
theodicy
greater goods defense
free will defense
libertarianism
compatibilism

4.6 Rethinking the Western Tradition: Asian Religions
Hinduism
pantheism
Brahman
jiva
atman
karma
reincarnation
God in Buddhism
self in Buddhism
nirvana

SUGGESTIONS FOR FURTHER READING

General Philosophy of Religion

Peterson, Michael, William Hasker, Bruce Reichenbach, and David Basinger. *Reason and Religious Belief.* New York: Oxford University Press, 1991. A clearly written examination of the issues from a theistic perspective.

Pojman, Louis, ed. *Philosophy of Religion: An Anthology.* 3d ed. Belmont, Calif.: Wadsworth, 1998. A balanced collection of readings on the topic. One of the best.

Rowe, William. *Philosophy of Religion: An Introduction.* 2d ed. Belmont, Calif.: Wadsworth, 1993. A clearly written but scholarly introduction to the main issues.

Wainwright, William J. *Philosophy of Religion.* 2d ed. Belmont, Calif.: Wadsworth, 1999. A readable and well-argued text from a theistic perspective.

The Classical Arguments for God, and Their Critics

Hick, John, ed. *The Existence of God.* New York: Macmillan, 1964. A good collection of articles about the standard theistic arguments.

Hume, David. *Dialogues Concerning Natural Religion,* 1779. Available in many different paperback editions. Contains not only the classical critique of the argument from design but Hume's skeptical attacks on the other theistic arguments as well.

Moreland, J. P., and Kai Nielsen. *Does God Exist? The Debate between Theists and Atheists.* Amherst, N.Y.: Prometheus Press, 1993. A lively debate on the existence of God and other religious issues by a theist and an atheist.

Swinburne, Richard. *The Existence of God.* Rev. ed. Oxford: Oxford University Press, Clarendon Press, 1991. A thoroughgoing, contemporary defense of theism.

Arguments for Atheism

Mackie, J. L. *The Miracle of Theism: Arguments For and Against the Existence of God.* Oxford: Oxford University Press, 1982. A clear and lively discussion of theism by a leading atheistic philosopher. According to Mackie, the "miracle" is that anyone is a theist.

Martin, Michael. *Atheism: A Philosophical Justification.* Philadelphia: Temple University Press, 1990. Perhaps the most complete critique of theism and justification of atheism in print.

Smith, George H. *Atheism: The Case Against God.* Amherst, N.Y.: Prometheus Press, 1980. A popular presentation of the case for atheism.

The Problem of Evil

Adams, Marilyn McCord, and Robert Merrihew Adams, eds. *The Problem of Evil.* Oxford: Oxford University Press, 1990. A collection of contemporary articles on the subject by a wide range of authors.

Howard-Snyder, Daniel, ed. *The Evidential Argument from Evil.* Bloomington, Ind.: Indiana University Press, 1996. A well-balanced collection of contemporary articles.

Lewis, C. S. *The Problem of Pain.* New York: Simon & Schuster, Touchstone Books, 1996. A popular theistic analysis of the problem of evil.

World Religions

Carmody, Denise L., and John T. Carmody. *Ways to the Center: An Introduction to World Religions.* 4th ed. Belmont, Calif.: Wadsworth, 1993. A well-received introduction to world religion with a coverage of Hinduism and Buddhism.

Molloy, Michael. *Experiencing the World's Religions: Tradition, Challenge, and Change.* Mountain View, Calif.: Mayfield, 1999. A survey of the world's religions, including Hinduism and Buddhism.

NOTES

1. Peter Kreeft, introduction to J. P. Moreland and Kai Nielsen, *Does God Exist? The Great Debate* (Nashville: Thomas Nelson, 1990), p. 11.

2. For some good summaries of atheistic arguments, see Michael Martin, *Atheism: A Philosophical Justification* (Philadelphia: Temple University Press, 1990) and George H. Smith, *Atheism: The Case against God* (Amherst, N.Y.: Prometheus Press, 1980).

3. Contrary to this view, some commentators see Kierkegaard as providing subjective justifications for why we should take the leap of faith. See Marilyn Gaye Piety, "Kierkegaard on Rationality," *Faith and Philosophy* 10, no. 3 (July 1993); C. Stephen Evans, "The Epistemological Significance of Transformative Religious Experiences: A Kierkegaardian Exploration," *Faith and Philosophy* 8, no. 2 (April 1991); and Merold Westphal, *Kierkegaard's Critique of Religion and Society* (Macon, Ga.: Mercer University Press, 1987).

4. Friedrich Nietzsche, *Beyond Good and Evil,* trans. Walter Kaufmann (New York: Random House, Vintage Books, 1966), sec. 6, p. 13.

5. Thomas Aquinas, *Summa Theologica,* in *Basic Writings of Saint Thomas Aquinas,* vol. 1, ed. Anton C. Pegis (New York: Random House, 1945), part I, question 2, article 3, p. 22.

6. For an extensive discussion of this argument, see William Lane Craig. *The Kalām Cosmological Argument* (New York: Barnes and Noble, 1979).

7. Richard Taylor, *Metaphysics,* 4th ed. (Englewood Cliffs, N.J.: Prentice-Hall, 1992), pp. 100–105, 107.

8. William Paley, *Natural Theology: Selections* (Indianapolis: Bobbs-Merrill, Library of Liberal Arts, 1963), pp. 3–4, 13.

9. Ten scientists at such universities as Harvard, Oxford, and Cambridge expressed this conclusion in *Evidence of Purpose: Scientists Discover the Creator,* ed. John Marks Templeton (New York: Continuum, 1996).

10. Charles Darwin, *The Life and Letters of Charles Darwin,* vol. 1, ed. Francis Darwin (New York: Basic Books, 1959), p. 282.

11. Reported by Hoyle's friend and Harvard astronomer Owen Gingerich in "Dare a Scientist Believe in Design?" in Templeton, *Evidence of Purpose,* p. 24.

12. Hoyle's comments are reported by Paul Davies in *Are We Alone?* (New York: HarperCollins, BasicBooks, 1995), pp. 27–28, 118.

13. Davies, *Are We Alone?,* p. 28.

14. Paul Davies, *God and the New Physics* (New York: Simon and Schuster, 1983), p. 189.

15. David Hume, *Hume's Dialogues Concerning Natural Religion,* ed. Norman Kemp Smith (London: Oxford University Press, 1935), Part II: pp. 178; 182–83, 185; Part IV: pp. 205–7.

16. Ibid., Part XII: p. 281.

17. See Richard S. Westfall, *Science and Religion in Seventeenth-Century England* (New Haven, Conn.: Yale University Press, 1958), especially chapter 3, "The Harmony of Existence."

18. Richard Dawkins, *The Blind Watchmaker: Why the Evidence of Evolution Reveals a Universe without Design* (New York: W. W. Norton, 1987), p. 5.

19. *The Life and Letters of Charles Darwin,* vol. 2, ed. Francis Darwin (New York: Basic Books, 1959), p. 105.

20. F. R. Tennant, *Philosophical Theology,* vol. 2, *The World, the Soul, and God* (Cambridge: Cambridge University Press, 1956), pp. 78–120.

21. Richard Swinburne, *The Existence of God* (Oxford: Oxford University Press, 1979).

22. For a brief overview of post-Darwinian teleological arguments, see Michael Peterson, William Hasker, Bruce Reichenbach, and David Basinger, *Reason and Religious Belief: An Introduction to the Philosophy of Religion,* 2d ed. (Oxford: Oxford University Press, 1998), pp. 102–6.

23. This example can be found in William Rowe, *Philosophy of Religion: An Introduction* (Belmont, Calif.: Wadsworth, 1978), p. 32.

24. St. Anselm, *Proslogium,* chap. 1, in *Saint Anselm: Basic Writings,* trans. S. N. Deane (La Salle, Ill.: Open Court, 1962).

25. St. Anselm, *Proslogium,* chap. 2, in *St. Anselm: Basic Writings.*

26. The discussion of these three points is based on C. Stephen Evans, *Subjectivity and Religious Belief: An Historical, Critical Study* (Grand Rapids, Mich.: William B. Eerdmans, Christian University Press, 1978), chap. 1.

27. Blaise Pascal, *Thoughts,* trans. William F. Trotter, The Harvard Classics, vol. 48 (New York: P. F. Collier, 1910), Sec. 233, pp. 84–87.

28. William James, "The Will to Believe," in *Essays in Pragmatism,* ed. Alburey Castell (New York: Macmillan, Hafner Press, 1948), pp. 95, 105–6, 107.

29. Søren Kierkegaard, *The Journals of Søren Kierkegaard,* August 1, 1835, trans. Alexander Dru, in *A Kierkegaard Anthology,* ed. Robert Bretall (New York: Random House, The Modern Library, 1946), pp. 4–5.

30. Søren Kierkegaard, *Philosophical Fragments,* trans. David Swenson and Howard V. Hong (Princeton: Princeton University Press, 1962), pp. 49, 103n, 103–4.

31. Søren Kierkegaard, *Concluding Unscientific Postscript,* trans. David Swenson and Walter Lowrie (Princeton: Princeton University Press, 1941), pp. 182, 189.

32. Ibid., p. 51.

33. Søren Kierkegaard, *The Sickness unto Death* in *Fear and Trembling and The Sickness unto Death,* trans. Walter Lowrie (Princeton: Princeton University Press, 1968), p. 210.

34. Kierkegaard, *Concluding Unscientific Postscript,* pp. 189, 191.

35. *Søren Kierkegaard's Journals and Papers,* vol. 1, trans. and ed. Howard and Edna Hong (Bloomington: Indiana University Press, 1967), no. 10, p. 7.

36. Albert Camus, *The Plague,* trans. Stuart Gilbert (New York: Random House, Vintage Books, 1972), pp. 199, 201, 211–12, 120, 202–3.

37. Charles Darwin, letter to Asa Gray (May 22, 1860), in *The Life and Letters of Charles Darwin,* vol. 2, ed. Francis Darwin (New York: Basic Books, 1959), p. 105.

38. A movement known as process philosophy limits God's knowledge of the future. See Charles Hartshorne, *Omnipotence and Other Theological Mistakes* (Albany: State University of New York Press, 1984).

39. Harold S. Kushner, *When Bad Things Happen to Good People* (New York: Schocken Books, 1981).

40. Aldous Huxley, *Brave New World* (New York: Harper & Row, 1946), p. 162.

41. John Hick, *Evil and the God of Love,* rev. ed. (New York: Harper & Row, 1966, 1977), pp. 253–59.

42. Edward H. Madden and Peter H. Hare, *Evil and the Concept of God* (Springfield, Ill.: Charles C. Thomas, 1968), pp. 83–90, 102–3. Reprinted in Louis Pojman, *Philosophy of Religion: An Anthology* (Belmont, Calif.: Wadsworth, 1994), pp. 181–85.

43. This way of expressing the point was borrowed and modified from a passage in David Ray Griffin, *God, Power, and Evil: A Process Theodicy* (Philadelphia: Westminster Press, 1976), p. 309.

44. C. S. Lewis, *The Problem of Pain* (New York: Macmillan, 1962), pp. 31–34.

45. Daniel H. Osmond, "A Physiologist Looks at Purpose and Meaning in Life," in Templeton, *Evidence of Purpose,* p. 148.

46. George Harrison, "My Sweet Lord," from the album *All Things Must Pass* (Apple Records, New York).

47. See Shirley MacLaine, *Out on a Limb* (New York: Bantam, 1983) and *Dancing in the Light* (New York: Bantam, 1985), and Nancy Griffin, "Tina," in *Life* (August 1985), pp. 23–28.

48. *Aitareya Upanishad* 5.3 in *The Thirteen Principal Upanishads,* trans. Robert Hume (London: Oxford University Press, 1931), p. 301. Because there are multiple translations of the Upanishads, references will be made in terms of the divisions of the original writings as well as the page numbers of the particular translation used.

49. *Kaushitaki Upanishad* 3.8, in Hume, *Thirteen Principal Upanishads,* p. 327.

50. *Svetasvatara Upanishad* 6.9, in *The Upanishads,* vol. 2, trans. Swami Nikhilananda (New York: Ramakrishna-Vivekananda Center, 1952), p. 135.

51. Acharya Gaudapada, *Karika* 1.9, in Nikhilananda, *The Upanishads,* vol. 2, p. 235.

52. Sarvepalli Radhakrishnan, *Recovery of Faith* (New York: Harper & Brothers, 1955), p. 104.

53. *Katha Upanishad* 6.12 in Hume, *Thirteen Principal Upanishads,* p. 360.

54. *Kena Upanishad* 11, in Hume, *Thirteen Principal Upanishads,* p. 337.

55. Sarvepalli Radhakrishnan, *The Hindu View of Life* (New York: Macmillan, 1927), p. 36.

56. See *Brihad-Aranyaka Upanishad* 2.3.6, in Hume, *Thirteen Principal Upanishads,* p. 97.

57. *Mandukya Upanishad* 7, in Nikhilananda, *The Upanishads,* vol. 2, p. 236.

58. *Brihad-Aranyaka Upanishad* 2.4.12, in Hume, *Thirteen Principal Upanishads,* p. 101.

59. *Mundaka Upanishad* 2.1.4, in *The Upanishads,* vol. 1, trans. Swami Nikhilananda (New York: Ramakrishna-Vivekananda Center, 1949), p. 282.

60. Ibid., 2.2.11, p. 294.

61. Steps 1 through 3 of this argument constitute a modus ponens argument, while steps 3 through 5 make a modus tollens argument.

62. *Rig Veda* 10.129, in *Sources of Indian Tradition,* ed. William Theodore de Bary, Stephen Hay, Royal Weiler, and Andrew Yarrow (New York: Columbia University Press, 1958), p. 18.

63. *Brihadaranyaka Upanishad* 1.4.6, in *The Upanishads,* vol. 3, trans. Swami Nikhilan-anda (New York: Ramakrishna-Vivekananda Center, 1956), p. 117.

64. *Katha Upanishad* 2.1.14, in Nikhilananda, *The Upanishads,* vol. 1, p.167.

65. *Brihadaranyaka Upanishad* 3.4.1, in Nikhilananda, *The Upanishads,* vol. 3, p. 214.

66. *Mandukya Upanishad* 2, in Hume, *Thirteen Principal Upanishads,* p. 391.

67. *Chandogya Upanishad* 6.10.1–3, in Hume, *Thirteen Principal Upanishads,* pp. 246–47.

68. *Kena Upanishad* 2.5, in Nikhilananda, *The Upanishads,* vol. 1, p. 240.

69. *Mundaka Upanishad* 3.2.9, in Nikhilananda, *The Upanishads,* vol. 1, p. 309.

70. Quoted in Radhakrishnan, *Recovery of Faith,* p. 112.

71. *Bhagavad-gita As It Is,* trans. A. C. Bhaktivedanta Swami Prabhupada (Sydney: The Bhaktivedanta Book Trust, 1986), 2:22, p. 104.

72. Ibid., 2:13, p. 91.

73. *Brihadaranyaka Upanishad* 4.4.6–7, in Nikhilananda, *The Upanishads,* vol. 3, pp. 293–95.

74. *Chandogya Upanishad* 6.10.1, in Hume, *Thirteen Principal Upanishads,* p. 246.

75. *Brihadaranyaka Upanishad* 4.3.21, in Nikhilananda, *The Upanishads,* p. 276.

76. *Mundaka Upanishad* 3.1.3, in Hume, *Thirteen Principal Upanishads,* p. 374.

77. *Brihad-Aranyaka Upanishad* 4.4.22, in Hume, *Thirteen Principal Upanishads,* p. 143.

78. *Chandogya Upanishad* 8.4.1, in Hume, *Thirteen Principal Upanishads,* p. 265.

79. *Kaushitaki Upanishad* 1.4, in Hume, *Thirteen Principal Upanishads,* p. 305).

80. E. A. Burtt, ed., *The Teachings of the Compassionate Buddha* (New York: Mentor, 1982), pp. 202–3.

81. Jack Kornfield, ed., *Teachings of the Buddha* (Boston: Shambhala, 1996), p. 26.

82. Ibid., p. 91.

83. Ibid., p. xiii.

84. Burtt, *Teachings of the Compassionate Buddha,* pp. 49–50.

85. Kornfield, *Teachings of the Buddha,* p. 141.

86. Ibid., p. 18.

87. de Bary et al., *Sources of Indian Tradition,* p. 102.

88. Huston Smith, *The Illustrated World's Religions* (New York: HarperCollins, Harper-SanFrancisco, 1994), p. 71.

89. Ibid.

90. Paraphrased from Burtt, *Teachings of the Compassionate Buddha,* pp. 43–46.

91. Kornfield, *Teachings of the Buddha,* p. 45.

92. This analogy is based on one from Abraham Kaplan, *The World of Philosophy* (New York: Random House, Vintage Books,1961), p. 262.

93. Sarvepalli Radhakrishnan and Charles A. Moore, eds., *A Source Book in Indian Philosophy* (Princeton, N.J.: Princeton University Press, 1957), p. 291.

94. Burtt, *Teachings of the Compassionate Buddha,* p. 35.

95. Herman Hesse, *Siddhartha,* trans. Hilda Rosner (New York: Bantam Books, 1951), pp. 134–36.

96. Paul Simon, "I Am a Rock," © 1965 Paul Simon (BMI).

CHAPTER 5

THE SEARCH FOR ETHICAL VALUES

SCOUTING THE TERRITORY: *Why Be Moral?*

Why should you worry about being a moral person? Is moral goodness something that you should pursue for its own sake, or is it desirable simply because of the consequences? To use an analogy, no one enjoys going to the dentist to get his or her teeth drilled and most people do not choose to go on a severely restrictive diet for its own sake. Instead, we take these actions only because of the results they bring—physical health. If going to the dentist or dieting did not pay in terms of better health, we would have little reason to do either one. Is morality like that? Is the only reason for being a morally good person the fact that the external consequences are desirable while the external consequences of being immoral are undesirable?

The question, Why be moral? was taken up in Plato's dialogue, the *Republic*. In this work, Glaucon (Plato's brother) asks Socrates whether justice (or moral goodness) is something that a person ought to pursue not only for its consequences but for its own sake. In order to goad Socrates, Glaucon defends the position that most reasonable people (if they were truly honest) would agree that being a just and moral person is *not* desirable in itself but is only desirable for the social rewards that it brings and the unpleasant consequences it avoids. For example, people are moral because being so will help them get along with others, give them a good reputation, and generally enhance their success in society. Similarly, people avoid being immoral because this behavior will lose them friends, damage their social standing, or land them in jail. In other words, being moral is purely an unpleasant but self-serving pursuit motivated by the desirability of the external results, similar to getting your teeth filled or going on a diet.

To make his point as sharply as possible, Glaucon tells the story of a shepherd named Gyges who discovers a ring that will make him invisible when it is turned a certain way. This ring enables him to do whatever he wishes without worrying about society's sanctions. Glaucon uses this story as a thought experiment to demonstrate his thesis. He thinks that it will reveal to us the true nature of morality. Think about it. If you had the power to make yourself invisible, you would no longer have to worry about being arrested, punished, or even rebuked. Under the cloak of invisibility, you could commit any kind of crime and misdeed you wished and the general public as well as your friends would be unaware of your evil behavior. According to Glaucon's assessment of human nature, there would be no reason to be moral under these circumstances. Based on your observable behavior, you would seem to be a model citizen. At the same time, you could act as you wished in terms of your private behavior. Hence, according to Glaucon, not only would there be no reason to be moral, there would be every reason to get away with all that you could. Only the fool would do otherwise, since only appearances and the social consequences of our actions matter.

What do you think? Do you agree with Glaucon that most people would act this way? As you read about the story of Gyges, ask yourself how you would behave if you had the magic ring. The reading begins when Gyges first discovers his extraordinary powers.

Republic[1]

Now the shepherds met together, according to custom, that they might send their monthly report about the flocks to the King. Having the ring on his finger, Gyges came into their assembly and as he was sitting among them he chanced to turn the setting of the ring inside his hand, when instantly he became invisible to the rest of the company and they began to speak of him as if he were no longer present. He was astonished at this, and again touching the ring he turned the setting outward and reappeared. He made several trials of the ring, and always with the same result—when he turned the setting inward he became invisible, when outward he reappeared. Whereupon he contrived to be chosen one of the messengers who were sent to the court; where as soon as he arrived he seduced the Queen, and with her help conspired against the King and slew him and took the kingdom. Suppose now that there were two such magic rings, and a just man put on one of them and an unjust man the other. No man can be imagined to be of such an iron nature that he would stand fast in justice. No man would keep his hands off what was not his own when he could safely take what he liked out of the market, or go into houses and lie with anyone at his pleasure, or kill or release from prison whom he would, and in all respects be like a god among men. Then the actions of the just would be as the actions of the unjust; they would both come at last to the same point. And this we may truly affirm to be a great proof that a man is just, not willingly or because he thinks that justice is any good to him individually, but of necessity, for wherever anyone thinks that he can safely be unjust, there he is unjust. For all men believe in their hearts that injustice is far more profitable to the individual than justice, and he who argues as I have been supposing, will say that they are right. If you could imagine anyone obtaining this power of becoming invisible, and never doing any wrong or touching what was another's, he would be thought by the lookers on to be a most wretched idiot, although they would praise him to one another's faces, and keep up appearances with one another from a fear that they too might suffer injustice.

To expand on this experiment, Glaucon then asks us to imagine two men. One is perfectly unjust, or evil, and the other has a perfectly just, or moral, character. However, the evil man (being very clever) manages to fool his society and he maintains a spotless reputation while committing the worst crimes and immoral actions imaginable. On the other hand, the society totally misunderstands the good man. Although he is perfectly just, his society wrongly inflicts him with an evil reputation and persecutes and torments him because of it. Under these circumstances, would there be any point in being moral? Glaucon entertains the cynical view that it is not really necessary to be a truly moral person. It is sufficient merely to *appear* to be moral to one's society *if one could get away with it*. When John F. Kennedy was considering entering into national politics, his family members debated among themselves whether he would be a successful congressman. His father,

Joseph Kennedy, ended the discussion by saying, "You must remember—it's not what you are that counts, but what people think you are."[2] Perhaps the elder Kennedy was right—people's opinions of you are important to being a successful candidate. However, do people's opinions make you a *qualified* candidate? Even if putting forth the appearance of success is useful in politics or business, is appearance all that matters in ethics? Glaucon thinks it is. What do you think?

Some people say that we can fool society in this way, but we can't fool God. They say the true reason for being moral (both on the inside as well as in our behavior) is to be rewarded in the afterlife and avoid unpleasant consequences. But isn't this viewpoint just a variation on Glaucon's? In both cases, the motive for being a moral person is a matter of the carrot or the stick (reward versus punishment). It's only a matter of detail as to whether you think it is society or God that wields the carrot and the stick.

Perhaps this issue can be made clearer with another analogy. We can imagine a young man who is engaged to an enormously wealthy young woman. With great eloquence he insists that he loves her for herself and not for her money. But upon finding out that she gave away all her fortune to the poor, he breaks off the engagement, admitting that he no longer has any reason to marry her. It is one thing to love a person for his or her own sake and for how your lover causes you to become enriched and fulfilled as a person. This relationship has rewards, but they are internal and intimately related to the person you love. It is quite another thing to profess love for that person for sake of the external rewards that the relationship will bring, such as money, purely physical pleasure, or status. Similarly, there is a difference between desiring to be a moral person for its own sake (including internal rewards such as self-respect) and being moral because of the external rewards it brings in society (or the afterlife).

 STOP AND THINK

If you were like Gyges and had the power to make yourself invisible so that no one would know what you did and there would be no negative consequences for immoral behavior, would this power cause any changes in how you behave? If you were convinced there was no afterlife in which your behavior would be either rewarded or punished, would this belief make any changes in your ethical decisions? Would you choose to be the immoral person who was mistakenly thought to be a saint by your society, or would you choose to be the genuinely moral person who was misunderstood and punished by your society? Under these circumstances would you agree or disagree with Glaucon that there would be no point in being just and moral? Why?

While all the philosophical questions discussed in this book have far-reaching and practical consequences for how we live, none have such a direct and immediate impact on the persons we are and how we conduct our daily lives as does our thinking about morality. Although the topic of ethics is complex and has many dimensions, the questions raised by Plato's story of the ring cut to the heart of the issue. As you go through the various theories on ethics covered in this chapter, you should consider how the different philosophers would respond to Glaucon. At the end of this introductory section on ethics, we briefly consider Glaucon's questions once again. But before we do that, we need to look more closely at the nature of morality.

CHARTING THE TERRAIN OF ETHICS: *What Are the Issues?*

What Is Ethics?

Ethics is quite a different philosophical field from those that we have studied thus far. In previous chapters we have asked questions such as: Does God exist? What is knowledge? How is the mind related to the body? Do we have free will? In our studies of all the previous philosophical fields, we have been attempting to *describe* what *is* true about the world. In ethics, however, we are concerned with what we *ought* to do, what consequences *ought* to be achieved, and what sort of persons we *ought* to become. In other words, ethics is a *normative* inquiry and not a descriptive one. It seeks to establish and prescribe norms, standards, or principles for evaluating our actual practices. Some authors distinguish morality and ethics. They speak of *descriptive morality* as referring to the actual practices of a people and a culture and its beliefs about which behaviors are good or bad. In this sense, anthropologists study and describe various cultures' moral beliefs and practices without being concerned with whether those beliefs are genuinely good. On the other hand, *normative ethics* is used to designate the philosophical task of discerning which moral principles are rationally defensible and which actions are genuinely good or bad. *Ethical theories* are the end products of this type of philosophical inquiry. Using this distinction, we could say that it was *moral* in Nazi Germany to persecute the Jews (*descriptive morality*) at the same time that we say that from the standpoint of *normative ethics* this practice was abhorrently *immoral*. However, since this chapter is not concerned simply with the practices or beliefs of this or that culture but with the normative questions of which moral beliefs are rational and which actions are genuinely good, I use *morality, ethics,* and related terms interchangeably.

CONCEPTUAL TOOLS: *Philosophical Ethics and Religion*

Because ethics seeks to establish principles that prescribe what we ought or ought not to do, it has similarities to other domains of human existence that seek to guide behavior, such as religion. In fact, many people think that religion and ethics not only overlap but that they are inseparable. It will be worthwhile, therefore, to pause on our journey to examine and distinguish philosophical ethics and religion.

It is a historical fact that religion is deeply bound up with morality. It would be hard, if not impossible, to find an established religious tradition that does not contain extensive ethical teachings. In fact, some of the great religions of the world, such as Buddhism and Confucianism, are primarily ethical outlooks on life rather than a series of doctrines about a deity. However, in spite of the historical influence of religion on our moral traditions, some authors claim that religion promotes an inferior brand of morality that inhibits mature moral development.[3] On the other hand, some would argue that religious considerations enhance morality in one or more of the following ways: religion can inspire us to be moral, reinforce our willpower to be moral, give us hope that good will ultimately prevail over evil, provide us with moral guidance, and demonstrate that morality is deeply rooted in the nature of reality itself.[4] Notice that a person could agree that religion enriches personal morality in these ways but still believe that there could be a viable morality without religion. As interesting as these claims may be, it would take us too far afield to evaluate them. Instead, we need to take a brief look at a related but much stronger claim: "Morality necessarily depends on religion." The claim that religion is necessary for morality was eloquently stated by Leo Tolstoy:

> The attempts to found a morality apart from religion are like the attempts of children, who, wishing to transplant a flower that pleases them, pluck it from the roots that seem to them unpleasing and superfluous, and stick it rootless into the ground. Without religion there can be no real, sincere morality, just as without roots there can be no real flower.[5]

The **divine command theory** is the theory that the rightness or wrongness of an action is intrinsically related to the fact that God either commands it or forbids it. There are a number of versions of this theory, and it is defended by some (but not all) theologians and religious philosophers.[6] However, many philosophers (even religious ones) think that a sound ethical theory can be developed independently of religious assumptions, and furthermore, they argue that there are problems with divine command theories. The first problem is the lack of agreement as to which religious text or authority should guide our ethical deliberations: The Bible, for example, or the Koran, the Hindu *Upanishads*, Buddha's teachings, and so on. To successfully live together in the same society, we need to arrive at some common ethical norms. But how can we do this in our pluralistic society if there is no agreement as to which religious authority (if any) should be followed? Furthermore, how can people be held ethically accountable for their behavior if many have never been exposed to whatever religious tradition is supposed to be normative? The second problem is that even if we agree to live under the guidance of a particular religious tradition, we may disagree as to how to interpret its teachings. For example, Christians both defend and attack capital punishment on the basis of the same tradition and sacred texts. Similarly, while the Bible often condemns lying, it contains passages in which God is said to reward people for lying on his behalf and even commands individuals to lie.[7] Minimally, some sort of philosophical reflection is necessary to sort out all these discrepancies. Third, some ethical questions cannot be answered by traditional religious teachings apart from philosophical considerations. Is it morally acceptable to make cloned duplicates of humans? When

divine command theory the theory that the rightness or wrongness of an action is intrinsically related to the fact that God either commands it or forbids it

numerous people need an organ transplant or a kidney dialysis machine but the medical supplies are scarce, what is the just way to allocate these resources? To what extent do journalists have an obligation to serve the public's right to know and to what extent do they have an obligation to protect an individual's privacy? Most religious traditions are clear on ethical topics such as adultery, murder, and stealing, but many ethical dilemmas in contemporary society are not addressed by these traditions.

A further problem is that the divine command theory makes it impossible or meaningless to declare that God and his will are good without some prior conception of moral goodness that is understood independently of God and his will. This point is illustrated by the following "Stop and Think" exercise.

 STOP AND THINK

Consider the following claim of the divine command theory:

- Good is defined as *that which God wills.*

Now substitute this definition of good into the following claim:

- God's will is *good.*

Why is the resulting claim an empty one?

This exercise illustrates the fact that defining "good" in terms of God's will makes it impossible to say anything meaningful about the goodness of God or his will, for we end up with the empty statement "God's will is that which God wills." Thus, it seems that we need some sort of independent concept of "good."

In Plato's dialogue *Euthyphro,* Socrates raises the question, "Do the gods approve of certain actions because these actions are good, or are certain actions good because the gods approve of them?" We can phrase this question in terms of monotheism by asking, "Does God approve of certain actions because these actions are good, or are certain actions good because God approves of them?" The first alternative is Plato's answer and the second is that of the divine command theory. Let's look at the second alternative first: if "good" and "bad" are simply arbitrary labels that God attaches to actions based on his sovereign will, then it seems that God could have declared that hatred, adultery, stealing, and murder are morally good. Some philosophers have bitten the bullet and accepted this conclusion. (William of Ockham, a fourteenth-century Christian philosopher, seems to have defended this problematic conclusion.) On the other hand, most philosophers have found this conclusion abhorrent. The philosopher Gottfried Leibniz (1646–1716) explains why:

> In saying, therefore, that things are not good according to any standard of goodness, but simply by the will of God, it seems to me that one destroys, without realizing it, all the love of God and all his glory; for why praise him for what he has done, if he would be equally praiseworthy in doing the contrary?[28]

In contrast, the first alternative's claim that "God approves of certain actions because they are good" suggests that God has a reason for approving certain actions—the reason being that they are good. But if so, then we should be able to evaluate the goodness (or badness) of the actions themselves and approve or disapprove of them for the same reason that God does, which implies that we can have a conception of ethics that is independent of God's will (although it might be consistent with it).

The final reason for questioning the necessity of religion for ethics is that many people are morally good persons but are not religious and were not raised in a religious background. Somehow these people are able to distinguish right and wrong, come to some of the same moral conclusions as religious people, and live morally commendable lives without appealing to a religious basis for their ethical stance.

These considerations suggest that whatever ethical guidance someone may find in a particular religious tradition, everyone needs to engage in philosophical reflection on ethics based on human experience and reason and not merely authority or tradition. Further considerations on this topic will be raised later in this chapter when we return to the question, Why be moral?

Dimensions of Ethical Evaluation

One problem we face in seeking to reflect on ethics is that the factors relevant to making moral decisions are so numerous that it is difficult to know what role they should play in our moral judgments. Typically, ethical theories have something to say about actions, motives, consequences, and character, and subject these factors to moral evaluation. But after all is said and done, which of these factors is most important or has priority over the others? The following thought experiment will get you thinking about these priorities and will prepare you to examine the answers offered by the various ethical theories.

 THOUGHT EXPERIMENT

Are All Cases of Truth Telling Equally Moral?

The moral evaluation of actions is certainly an important issue in ethics. We frequently judge that a person did the right thing or did what was wrong. For example, we are told that it is good to tell the truth or, even more strongly, it is our moral obligation to tell the truth and not lie. The following three scenarios depict examples of telling the truth. Consider the ways in which they differ. In each case, consider how you would evaluate the action morally and why you made the judgments you did.

I. When Andre was asked, "Did you have a good reason for missing the required morning meeting?" he is tempted to lie, saying that he had a class scheduled at that

(Continued . . .)

(. . . continued)

time. Instead, however, he tells the truth: "No, I was too lazy to get out of bed." He tells the truth because it is his moral obligation to do so.

2. When Brandee was asked, "Did you have a good reason for missing the required morning meeting?" she is tempted to lie, saying that she had a class scheduled at that time. Instead, however, she tells the truth: "No, I was too lazy to get out of bed." She tells the truth because she knows her excuse can be checked out and her lie exposed.

3. Chris says to the dean, "Do you know what? Professor Fields came to class sober today." That statement is the absolute truth because the professor never took an alcoholic drink in his life. However, Chris knows that the dean will infer that Professor Fields sometimes does not come to class sober and hopes that this inference will ruin this lousy teacher's reputation.

All things being equal, most of us would say that telling the truth is the morally right thing to do, and in these three cases, each person told the truth. However, these three cases have significant differences. Andre tells the truth because it is his moral duty to do so, even though the consequences may be bad for him. In the same situation, Brandee tells the truth not because she wants to do the right thing for its own sake but because she thinks she won't be able to get away with a lie. If Brandee believed that she could tell a lie and never be discovered, do you think she would do it? Chris tells the literal truth, but with the motive of deceiving the dean and hurting the professor. Clearly, the motive of the person who performed the action plays a role in our moral judgments. The next three cases ask you to consider the person's motives in light of other factors that are present.

 THOUGHT EXPERIMENT

How Important Are Motives?

Again, consider the ways in which each case is similar to or different from the others. Think about how you would evaluate each action morally and why you made the judgments you did.

1. Danielle's roommate Tasha asks her if she thinks the short story that Tasha has just written is any good. Danielle says that it is a wonderfully written story, which is a lie because she really thinks it is wretched. However, she doesn't want to hurt Tasha's feelings. Based on Danielle's encouragement, Tasha reads the story to a writing group and is thoroughly humiliated. She never trusts her roommate again.

2. Out of compassion, Esther gives $500 to a charity for starving children. Inspired by her example, many other students donate money to the charity that they would ordinarily spend partying. However, in order to obtain the money for the charity, Esther had to steal it from a rich stranger's purse. The stranger has so much money

(Continued . . .)

(. . . continued)

that she never realizes it is missing. As a result of Esther's generosity and example, many children are fed.

3. Fred shoves Reggie to the ground simply to be mean. Unintentionally, however, his doing so had the consequence of shoving Reggie out of the way of a falling brick that might have killed him.

In the first two cases, each person is acting from a good motive—the desire to help people. For Danielle, however, the consequences turned out badly. To what degree should this consequence affect our moral judgment of her actions? Even though Danielle thought the consequences of her lie would be for the best, could she really know what the consequences would be? Would it have been better if she had stuck with her duty of telling the truth and let the consequences take care of themselves? What if the consequences had been good? Suppose Danielle's lie had encouraged Tasha to write more and better stories? If both her motive and the consequences had been good, would her lie then be morally acceptable? Esther also had a good motive—she wanted to help children. Esther's situation had good consequences and no obviously bad consequences. Children were helped, students were inspired to be charitable, and the stranger never missed her money. Does it make a difference that Esther's generosity was the result of an act of theft? Can an action be morally wrong if the immediate consequences are good, if there are no bad consequences, and if it is done from a good motive? In Fred's case, the action (shoving someone out of harm's way) would be commendable if done by a quick-thinking, courageous person of good will. However, Fred's motive was to harm Reggie. So, do you think that motives are more important or less important than good consequences when you assess the morality of an action? The next thought experiment asks you to assess the role of consequences in making moral judgments.

 THOUGHT EXPERIMENT

How Important Are Consequences?

1. Gary has been charged with delivering a professor's painting to a museum. On his way there, he notices a small girl drowning in a river. Knowing that every second counts, he throws her the painting to use as a float until he can get to her. Unable to spare the time fooling with his clothes, he then jumps into the water wearing the good suit that he borrowed from his roommate. In spite of Gary's best efforts, the child drowns. He didn't save the child, but he ruined both the professor's painting and his friend's suit.

2. Hallie sacrifices her weekends to work on a project that builds homes for the poor. She figures that the publicity from this work will help her campaign for student body president and will look good on her resume. The families that move into the homes she has helped construct are overjoyed with the fruits of her labor.

In these last two examples, the actions considered by themselves are morally good. Gary's motive was to fulfill his duty to save lives when possible, but his consequences turned out badly. Would this fact be relevant or irrelevant in our moral assessment of Gary's actions? Hallie performed a good action and, unlike poor Gary's failed efforts, the consequences were exceedingly good both for the families and for herself. But then there is the nagging problem of her motive. She was acting only for her own selfish gain and not for the people she helped. After considering all three of these thought experiments, what role do you think the goodness or badness of actions, motives, and consequences should play in ethics? All three factors may be important, but the ethical theories we examine in this chapter give priority to one or more of these factors over the others. In terms of your current understanding, how do you think the factors should be weighted?

THE QUESTION, WHY BE MORAL? RECONSIDERED

Glaucon's Question

Before looking at various theories that concern how to decide what is right or wrong, we first need to ask why such a decision is an important issue at all. In the beginning of this chapter the question, What is the point of morality? was raised by Glaucon, one of the characters in Plato's *Republic*. This question can actually be broken down into two questions: (1) Why does society need morality? and (2) Why should I be moral?

The first question is the easier one to answer. Thomas Hobbes, a seventeenth-century British philosopher, answered that question by imagining that everybody lived in a "state of nature" in which there was no government, no society, and no commonly agreed-upon morality.[9] In such a situation, everybody would be serving his or her own individual interests without regard for anyone else. Without laws or morality you would be free to club people over the head to steal their food. The problem is that someone stronger than you could then beat you up and steal your food. Hobbes says that human existence under these conditions would be "a war of all against all" and that everybody would find life to be "solitary, poor, nasty, brutish, and short." For this reason, Hobbes says, people would come together and agree to restrict their own behavior if others restrict their behavior and would form a government to enforce these agreements. In this way, both morality and law would emerge. The end result would be, as Glaucon described, that people would behave morally to avoid social and legal sanctions.

The problem is that this account explains only why I would want there to be moral laws that people around me feel compelled to follow. This situation is clearly in my self-interest. However, it does not answer the second question: Why should *I* be moral? If everyone else was behaving morally, but I only *appeared* to be moral, I would have the best of both worlds. I could cheat, lie, and steal to my own advantage while admonishing everyone else to be honest and truthful when dealing with me. If I could successfully pull this off (and some people seem to), why

PHILOSOPHY
in the
MARKETPLACE

shouldn't I behave this way? The reply may be that it would be inconsistent or *unfair* to expect others to be honest with me when I chose to be dishonest. This answer won't do, however, for *fairness* is a moral principle and telling me I ought to be fair is telling me I ought to be moral, and that brings us back to the original question: Why should I be moral?

A Religious Answer

One way to respond to the question, "Why be moral?" is to reply, "Because God commands it." In the "Conceptual Tools" section of this chapter we discussed some problems with the attempt to base the content of ethics solely on a religious tradition. But in spite of those problems, does religion alone provide a reason to act morally? The reply "Because God commands it" could be interpreted as maintaining that you should act morally because God will reward you if you do and punish you if you don't. But as we already mentioned, this motivation is sheerly one of prudence, personal greed, and selfish, egoistic self-interest. If you are acting morally only for the sake of what you can gain by doing so, is "being moral" reduced simply to calculating what is in your best interest? So, this answer is very much like the cynical answer of Plato's Glaucon and is similar to the young man romancing the woman for the sake of her money and not for herself. A further problem is that this reason for acting morally appeals purely to God's power to reward or punish and has nothing to do with the goodness of the actions themselves. We might find it wise to be subservient to the demands of a powerful evil spirit or a human dictator, but our actions would be irrelevant to whether or not the moral legislator and his commands are good. Finally, you might protest that we should be moral not for the sake of reward or punishment but out of love for God. Certainly, this motive is better than the prudential one. However, you still must ask whether God is *worthy* of your love. Is God truly good? On what basis do we decide God is good? Once again, this answer requires some prior conception of good.

Plato's Answer

Later in the *Republic,* Plato offers his own answer to the questions about morality raised by Glaucon. In brief, Plato says it is in our self-interest to be moral. The problem with this answer is that most people find that the demands of morality are often in conflict with self-interest. It might serve my own ends to cheat on a test, lie to an acquaintance, or swindle a customer. However, if morality requires me to be honest, truthful, and fair in these situations, then it doesn't seem that being moral is in my self-interest after all. Plato would say, however, that this apparent conflict results from a misguided sense of what is in our self-interest. For Plato, morality is essential to the spiritual health of the *psyche.* This word is usually translated as "soul," but to free it of religious connotations that are much too narrow, it is best to understand the soul as the essential core of the person, or one's true self. Hence, immorality is like a disease or corruption of the inner person. To follow up on Plato's analogy, if I smoke one cigarette, eat one high-fat meal, and go one week without exercise, these actions will probably cause little noticeable harm to my body. However, a lifetime of behaving this way will begin to ruin my health. Furthermore, even if momentary lapses in a healthy lifestyle do not substantially harm me, they can make further lapses more tempting until they become self-destructive habits. Similarly, Plato thought that immoral actions would incur harm to the soul (or the real you) until you lost all control over your life and became a slave to your own impulses and desires.

Plato's view, as with most ethical theories, is based on a conception of human nature. Plato noticed that we find inner conflicts and competing forces warring within us, suggesting different faculties or psychological drives within us. The *appetites* pull us in the direction of physical gratification and material acquisition. They are the voice within us that says, "I want, I want," without regard for the consequences. The part of us that is capable of vetoing the appetites is *reason.* It also is the source of desires, but these desires are rational ones, based on truth. There is also a third element, the *spirited part* of us. This part is the willful, dynamic, executive faculty, which is associated with the passions or emotions. The spirited part is a motive force, but it receives its direction from either the appetites or reason, depending on which has the upper hand.

Plato uses several dramatic analogies to make clear how these three elements function in our moral life. For example, he imagines that inside each human is a smaller person who represents the voice of reason. There is also a lion (the spirited part) and a wild, many-headed beast (the appetites). His point is to illustrate why pursuing justice (having a moral nature) is what the wise person would choose. To say that immorality pays and that there is no point in doing right is like saying that

> it pays to feed up and strengthen the composite beast and all that belongs to the lion, and to starve the man till he is so enfeebled that the other two can drag him whither

they will. . . . On the other hand, to declare that justice pays is to assert that all our words and actions should tend towards giving the man within us complete mastery over the whole human creature, and letting him take the many-headed beast under his care and tame its wildness, like the gardener who trains his cherished plants while he checks the growth of weeds. He should enlist the lion as his ally, and, caring for all alike, should foster their growth by first reconciling them to one another and to himself.[11]

In summary, Plato argues that justice, or a moral nature, much like physical health, is a condition in which all the various elements of the person are balanced and in the right order. In contrast, immorality is like a cancer of the soul. It is an inner abnormality, deformity, or weakness, or a fatal disease that has taken over the person. A character in the dialogue sums up Plato's moral philosophy thus:

People think that all the luxury and wealth and power in the world cannot make life worth living when the bodily constitution is going to rack and ruin; and are we to believe that, when the very principle whereby we live is deranged and corrupted, life will be worth living so long as a man can do as he will, and wills to do anything rather than to free himself from vice and wrongdoing and to win justice and virtue?[12]

At the beginning of this conversation, Plato treated the question "Why be just or morally good?" as a serious question. But after he laid out the options, that question is like asking, "Why be in control of my life instead of being a slave? Why not be ravaged by the beasts and wild desires within me? Why be in the correct relationship to reality? Why be healthy instead of diseased?" When the question about the value of morality is asked in these ways, Plato thinks the only rational reply must be, "It is a ridiculous question."

"Because It's Right"

Some philosophers think that the very attempt to justify being moral is misconceived. To explain to me why I should be moral is to provide reasons for why I should act in a certain way. But either these reasons could be based on moral considerations or they would have to be based on some other interests I have or principles to which I am committed. The justification of morality cannot be based on moral considerations because the very question under consideration is why we should take moral considerations seriously. On the other hand, if we justify morality on some other basis, such as self-interest, then we are assuming that this commitment is more ultimate than morality. In this case, we could never justify sacrificing self-interest for the sake of morality. So, this position claims that the only basis for acting morally is that it is the right thing to do. Contemporary philosopher John Hospers argues this position in the following passage:

It's right to give the correct change to the blind news vendor, and *that*—not the fact (if it is a fact) that you will benefit from it—is the reason why you should do it. Perhaps you will be rewarded in heaven, perhaps not; perhaps your act will pay off for you in future benefits, and perhaps it won't; these considerations are irrelevant as reasons for why you ought to do it. The only reason that is relevant is simply the fact that it's the right thing to do. Nothing more is needed, and nothing more should be desired.[13]

Summary: Morality and the Self

Maybe the best answer to the question, "Why be moral?" is a combination of Hospers's and Plato's responses. As Hospers suggests, if morality is to be taken seriously at all, it must override all other considerations. If morality serves some other ends or interests outside the moral domain, then we might as well dispense with morality altogether and simply concern ourselves with the most efficient way to achieve those other, nonmoral goals. The moral point of view is something a person either has or does not have. People who have acquired the moral point of view by the way they were raised or through the events in their own personal development may fail in their moral endeavors and sometimes yield to temptation, but they will understand why morality should be their goal. Morality is a commitment to a certain life plan, a decision to be a certain sort of person.

On the other hand, people who reject the moral point of view will see no point in worrying about whether an action is right or wrong. They may be satisfied with their form of life, may feel themselves more or less happy and fulfilled human beings, and may manage to get along in society, but their sense of fulfillment and their development as persons are limited. Such persons are like Dickens's character Scrooge, who is blind to the value of friendship and gloats that his life is better than ours because he doesn't have to buy anyone Christmas presents.[14] Or, the person who is blind to morality is like a little child who has not yet developed the capacity to have romantic feelings. To this child, the time and effort we spend in nurturing a romantic relationship is a silly waste when we could be having the supreme pleasure of playing video games. Or, compare the morally challenged person to the totally color-blind person who sees only shades of gray and wonders why we make such a fuss over sunsets. In these analogies, the persons think they are serving their own interests and believe that they know what life is about, but only because they have not experienced an important dimension of human experience (friendship, romantic passion, or colors) that has the potential to make life richer. If Scrooge, in particular, had lived his entire life without any meaningful human relationships, he would have been left a severely limited human being. But true friendships require us to respect others and to sometimes sacrifice our own self-interests for another, and with these actions we have entered into the moral point of view.

How about Plato's answer? Can we agree with him that morality is in our best interests, that it enables us to flourish? The problem is that the just man in Glaucon's story (as well as some in our society) suffered greatly. Perhaps Plato would respond that there is a difference between short-term, superficial self-interest and long-term, deep self-interest. This difference can be explained by referring to the example of friendships once again. At the superficial level, a friendship can be costly in terms of the time, sacrifices, and emotional energy it requires. However, is there a value to close friends? Do friendships serve our self-interest? I think the answer is that friendships are for our good not because of what we *get,* but because of what we *become.* If we value friendships only for their superficial pay-offs (money, sex, social status), we are like a person who has experienced puddles, but never the ocean. A deep friendship develops capacities within us that we would have never discovered in any other way. Morality is like that.

I practice my basketball shots, play my guitar, learn to program in a new computer language, and try to solve challenging intellectual problems, but not because these pursuits will win me fame or fortune. Instead, I want to be the best person I possibly can and develop what skills and capacities I have for their own sake. Making myself the best person I can be, whether athletically, musically, intellectually, or morally, is a matter of fulfilling my long-term, deep self-interests. Particularly with respect to morality, there is a paradox here. I can best fulfill myself by making my narrow self-interests secondary to my moral commitments. Self-fulfillment and happiness are usually not found by pursuing them directly. Instead, they are a by-product of pursuits that lead us beyond ourselves. But by being less concerned with what I get out of life, I open up new dimensions of what I can become as a person. According to Socrates and Plato, our most important possession is our soul or our inner person. Our health, careers, fame, friends, and material possessions can come and go as the result of external circumstances, but nothing external can affect the persons that we are. In this area of our lives we are in control and can make ourselves as excellent or corrupt as possible. Why should we choose to live with a worse self when we can live with an excellent one instead? This focus on ethics as preserving the integrity of one's self was captured in Robert Bolton's play *A Man for All Seasons.* It tells the true story of Thomas More, a sixteenth-century government figure in England. At this time, King Henry VIII had divorced his wife to marry another woman and asserted his authority over that of the Church. He required all his officials to take an oath of allegiance to him, approving of what he had done, or be executed. However, such an oath would have violated More's ethical and religious convictions. More's wife and daughter visit him in prison, trying to convince him that an oath is just words and paying this lip service to the king would have no real ethical implications. To this, More replies:

> When a man takes an oath . . . he's holding his own self in his own hands. Like water. (*He cups his hands*) And if he opens his fingers *then*—he needn't hope to find himself again.[15]

More's words are a good description of what morality is all about. It is holding my own self in my hands and making sure that I don't lose it by grasping at other things.

CHOOSING A PATH: *What Are My Options concerning Ethics?*

Ethical relativism is the position that there are no objective or universally valid moral principles, for all moral judgments are simply a matter of human opinion. In other words, there is no right or wrong apart from what people consider to be

ethical relativism the position that there are no objective or universally valid moral principles, for all moral judgments are simply a matter of human opinion

right or wrong. This position comes in two versions, depending upon whose opinion is considered to be the standard for morality.

Subjective ethical relativism is the doctrine that what is right or wrong is solely a matter of each individual's personal opinion. Just as some people like the color purple and some detest it, and each person's judgment on this matter is simply a matter of his or her individual taste, so there is no standard other than each person's own opinion when it comes to right or wrong. This doctrine implies that it is impossible for an individual to be mistaken about what is right or wrong.

Conventional ethical relativism (conventionalism) refers to the claim that morality is relative to each particular society or culture. For example, whether it is moral for women to wear shorts is a question of whether you are talking about mainstream American society or the Iranian culture. In other words, there are no universal objective moral standards that can be used to evaluate the ethical opinions and practices of a particular culture. This doctrine implies that it is impossible for a society to be mistaken about what is right or wrong.

Ethical objectivism is the view that there are universal and objectively valid moral principles that are relative neither to the individual nor to society. Because objectivism is a very general doctrine that covers a wide range of more specific ethical theories, various objectivists will differ as to what the correct moral principles are and how we can know them. Nevertheless, they all agree that in every concrete situation there are morally correct and morally wrong ways to act. Furthermore, they would agree that if a certain action in a given situation is morally right or wrong for a particular person, then it will be the same for anyone who is relevantly similar and facing relevantly similar circumstances. Ethical objectivism implies that it is possible for an individual or an entire society to sincerely believe that their actions are morally right at the same time that they are deeply mistaken about this assumption.

The next four theories all fall under the heading of ethical objectivism. Although these theories disagree about what ethical principles should be followed, they all agree that there are one or more nonarbitrary, nonsubjective, universal moral principles that determine whether an action is right or wrong.

Ethical egoism is the theory that people always and only have a moral obligation to do what is in their own self-interest. According to this position, the locus of value is the individual and there can be no higher value for me than my own life and its well-being and no higher value for you than your own life. This theory is a version of ethical objectivism and should not be mistaken for subjective ethical relativism, for the egoist would say that my moral judgments can be wrong if I put another person's interests before my own. Of course, the egoist's principle will dictate different, and sometimes competing, courses of action. For example, it is in my best interests to promote the flourishing of the philosophy program at my university, while it is in a coach's interest to promote the flourishing of the football program. Nevertheless, the egoist would maintain that competing interests can lead to the best outcome. In business, for example, if each company tries to capture the market with the best product, society as a whole benefits. Similarly, in a court of

subjective ethical relativism the doctrine that what is right or wrong is solely a matter of each individual's personal opinion

conventional ethical relativism the claim that morality is relative to each particular society or culture; also called ethical conventionalism

ethical objectivism the view that there are universal and objectively valid moral principles that are relative neither to the individual nor to society

ethical egoism the theory that people ought always to do only what is in their own self-interest

law, each lawyer promotes the best interests of his or her client, and we presume that this procedure will help ensure that all aspects of the case will be revealed.

Utilitarianism is the theory that the right action is the one that produces the greatest amount of happiness for the greatest number of people. Accordingly, utilitarians claim that the morality of an action cannot be divorced from its consequences. The utilitarian would agree with the egoist that a person's own interests need to play a role in moral decisions. However, according to utilitarianism, a person's own interests have to balance against those of all others in calculating the morality of an action. This formula would allow the same type of action to be moral in one set of circumstances and immoral in a different situation if the consequences were different. Nevertheless, while the moral evaluation of an action may be relative to the circumstances, an unchanging, universal, ethical principle is still being followed.

Kantian ethics is a theory that states we have absolute moral duties that are determined by reason and that are not affected by the consequences. Obviously, its approach to morality is radically different from that of the utilitarians. For Kantian ethics, the rightness or wrongness of an action is intrinsic to the type of action it is. (When we examine this theory in more detail later in this chapter, we discuss how the Kantian determines what these duties are.) The Kantian, for example, would say that we have a moral obligation to tell the truth, even if it produces harm. On the other hand, lying is considered wrong, even if it produces a good outcome.

Virtue ethics refers to any theory that sees the primary focus of ethics to be the character of the person rather than that person's actions or duties. The previous theories are concerned primarily with rules or principles for deciding how to act. They do not ignore the issue of what makes a good person, but they define the goodness of persons in terms of either what actions they perform or what principles they employ. Virtue ethics, however, reverses the proper order. The good person is not one who performs good actions, but good actions are defined as those that a person with a good moral character would do. Whereas the previous theories ask, "What should I do?" virtue ethics asks, "What sort of person should I be?" Plato would fall under the heading of virtue ethics, for he gave very little specific guidance on how to make moral decisions. Instead, he talked at length on how to attain a morally sound character.

Feminist ethics is a new development in recent decades that questions some of the fundamental assumptions of traditional ethical theory. Feminist theory is still developing and full of multiple perspectives, so it is hard to summarize it in a brief statement. For example, some feminists agree with ethical relativism, while others are more aligned with some version of ethical objectivism. However, in spite of their differences, most feminists agree that there are distinctively male and female ways of viewing a situation and that these views will make a decided difference to our ethical perspective. Feminists complain that traditional ethical theories are one-sided because they typically represent the style, aims, concerns, questions, and theoretical assumptions of men. Some psychological studies, for example, seem to suggest that males tend toward a judicial model of ethical decision making where

utilitarianism the theory that the right action is the one that produces the greatest amount of happiness for the greatest number of people

Kantian ethics the theory that we have absolute moral duties that are determined by reason and that are not affected by the consequences

virtue ethics any theory that sees the primary focus of ethics to be the character of the person rather than that person's actions or duties

feminist ethics the attempt to correct male biases in traditional ethical theory by emphasizing relationships over abstract principles and compassion over analytical reason

TABLE 5.1 *Three Questions concerning Moral Relativity and the Answers of the Two Forms of Ethical Relativism*

	Are moral principles relative to human opinion?	Are moral judgments relative to each individual's opinion?	Are moral judgments relative to each society's opinion?
Subjective Ethical Relativism	Yes	Yes	No
Conventional Ethical Relativism	Yes	No	Yes

TABLE 5.2 *Five Questions concerning the Nature of Morality and the Answers of Four Kinds of Ethical Objectivism*

	Are there moral principles or truths that are objectively valid?	Is serving one's own self-interest the only moral duty?	Do the consequences of an action make it right or wrong?	Are actions right or wrong in themselves, independent of their consequences?	Is morality more concerned with the character of a virtuous person than with rules of conduct?
Ethical Egoism	Yes	Yes	Yes—but only the consequences for the individual performing the action	No	No
Utilitarianism	Yes	No	Yes	No	No
Kantian Ethics	Yes	No	No	Yes	Morality is concerned with both
Virtue Ethics	Yes	No	No	Only as they relate to certain character traits	Yes

abstract principles and reason predominate. Females, however, are more concerned with relationships and the emotional textures of a situation. These differences play out in completely different theoretical approaches to ethical issues. Whereas some feminists want to replace the male-biased approaches with new perspectives, others simply want to supplement the historically one-sided approaches with a more balanced perspective. While feminist theorists bring a fresh new perspective to ethics, they often work within and use the resources of the other theories as much as they critique the limitations of those theories.

This spectrum of ethical theories is summarized in tables 5.1 and 5.2. These tables are followed by a questionnaire for you to take. Unfortunately, it is impossible to represent feminist ethics in these simplified schemes because writers who can be characterized as representing the feminist perspective on ethics can be found within each of the traditional categories. Feminist writers are not distinguished so much by how they answer the following questions, but by the way that they bring gender issues to bear on the traditional questions and theories in moral philosophy.

Note that because both the subjective ethical relativist and the conventional ethical relativist deny that there are any moral principles that apply to all persons, they would answer "No" to the questions in table 5.2. On the other hand, because the advocates of each of the four positions in table 5.2 are all ethical objectivists, they would answer "No" to the three questions in table 5.1.

WHAT DO I THINK? *Questionnaire on Ethics, Actions, Consequences, Motives, and Character*

	Agree	Disagree
1. Moral judgments are an expression of personal opinion. Just as "Oysters are delicious" expresses the speaker's personal opinion, so *all* moral judgments, such as "Capital punishment is morally wrong" or "Physician-assisted suicide is morally permissible," are sheerly a matter of personal opinion.		
2. When we declare that an action is morally right or wrong, we simply mean that the majority of the people in our society consider it to be right or wrong.		
3. It is possible that an action (such as owning slaves) could be morally wrong even if the person who did it or all the members of that person's society sincerely believed that the action was morally permissible.		
4. The only moral duty that anyone ever has is to do those actions that will be good for him or her in some way.		

5. The only thing that counts in deciding if an action is morally good is whether it leads to the overall best possible consequences for the most number of people. Motives are irrelevant.		
6. The only thing that counts in determining whether a person acted morally or not is his or her motive. The results of the action are irrelevant.		
7. What makes an action morally right or wrong depends entirely on whether it is what a morally virtuous person would do. Any application of moral rules is secondary and after the fact.		
8. Males and females approach ethical issues with different perspectives and different concerns.		
9. It is morally wrong for anyone, in any culture, at any time, under any circumstances, to torture an innocent child for no reason at all.		
10. Even if it could be shown that cheating on a test led to the best consequences for everybody, all things considered, it would still be wrong.		
11. Even if a person acted from a morally good motive, if the action resulted in an overall sum of more unhappiness over happiness for all concerned, it would be morally wrong.		

 ### KEY TO THE QUESTIONNAIRE ON ETHICS

Statement 1 is an expression of subjective ethical relativism. It conflicts with statements 3 and 9.

Statement 2 expresses conventional ethical relativism. It also conflicts with statements 3 and 9.

Statement 3 represents ethical objectivism, because it implies that right and wrong are independent of human opinion. It conflicts with statements 1 and 2.

Statement 4 is the defining principle of ethical egoism.

Statement 5 is a statement of utilitarianism.

Statement 6 expresses Kantian ethics.

Statement 7 represents virtue ethics.

Statement 8 represents one version of feminist ethics. Since feminist theory is so diverse, different versions of feminist ethics could be compatible with any of the other statements.

Statement 9 is an expression of ethical objectivism. It conflicts with statements 1 and 2.

Statement 10 represents the denial of utilitarianism. It conflicts with statement 5.

Statement 11 expresses the denial of Kantianism. It conflicts with statements 6.

Which position seems closest to your own?

5.1 ETHICAL RELATIVISM VERSUS OBJECTIVISM

LEADING QUESTIONS:
Ethical Relativism and Ethical Objectivism

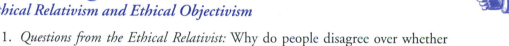

1. *Questions from the Ethical Relativist:* Why do people disagree over whether raw oysters taste good? Why do some people like tattoos and body piercing and others find these personal adornments distasteful? Why is it considered morally permissible to wear brief swimsuits in some cultures and immoral in others? Why do some people think abortion is morally permissible and others think it is absolutely wrong? Why do people disagree over the morality of capital punishment? Is there a reason why these disagreements and disputes never seem to be resolved? Could the answer be that *all* these cases are simply a matter of the preferences and viewpoints of particular individuals or society?

2. *Questions from the Ethical Relativist:* Who's to judge what is right or wrong? How can we say that the moral beliefs and practices of another individual or society are wrong simply because they differ from our own morality? Isn't it arrogant, presumptuous, and intolerant to do so? Isn't it better to live and let live, deciding for ourselves what we think is right or wrong and allowing others to do the same for themselves? Hasn't history shown that wars, persecutions, and inquisitions have resulted when people decide that they will be the moral authorities for the rest of humanity?

3. *Questions from the Ethical Objectivist:* Suppose that you have fallen into the hands of a group of scientists in another country. They want to perform medical experiments on you that will be extremely painful and will result in your death. They justify these experiments by saying that you will help them advance science and that the research leading to your death will result in life-saving drugs that will benefit thousands in their country and throughout the world. You protest that what they are about to do is morally wrong. However, they patiently explain that morality is relative and is only a matter of personal or social opinion. Since they think

that using your body for their ends is right and killing for the sake of medical research is legal in their society, they explain that your moral outrage is simply a matter of your personal opinion. They ask, "Who are you to say that we are morally wrong? Each person has to judge rightness or wrongness for himself or herself." How would you attempt to convince them that what they are about to do is morally wrong? Doesn't this scenario show that it is implausible to suppose that morality is subjective? Isn't it absurd to claim that as long as the scientists sincerely believe they are doing the right thing, no one should question their actions?

4. *Questions from the Ethical Objectivist:* Philosopher James Rachels argues that certain moral rules are essential for any society to survive and that a healthy society will condone violations of these rules only under exceptional conditions. The three rules he lists are: (1) infants should be cared for, (2) lying is wrong, and (3) murder is wrong. What would a society be like if it did not value these basic moral rules? In 1964, anthropologist Colin Turnbull discovered the Ik, an isolated tribe in northern Uganda who were facing severe conditions of starvation. Consequently, food was no longer shared, but fathers and mothers gathered it for themselves and kept it from their children. After age three, children had to fend for themselves. The desperate children learned to steal food by extracting it from the mouths of the elderly and those who were weaker. Honesty was thought foolish and clever lying was valued, while affection and trust were considered dysfunctional. According to Turnbull's account, the society was in a state of near-total cultural collapse because of the breakdown of its moral and social fabric. Isn't it implausible to suppose that moral rules such as those Rachels lists are sheerly relative and optional? Can morality be completely a matter of personal or social preference? Isn't there a universal core morality that is essential to human flourishing?

Leading questions 1 and 2 represent the viewpoint of ethical relativism. *Ethical relativism* is the theory that there are no objective or universally valid moral principles, for all moral judgments are simply a matter of human opinion. Ethical relativism is the theory in ethics that corresponds to epistemological relativism in the theory of knowledge (see section 2.5). If a person believes there is no objective truth in general (epistemological relativism), then he or she must believe that there are no ethical truths (ethical relativism). The reverse is not necessarily true, however, for a person could be a relativist in ethics but believe there are objective truths in other areas (such as science).

Ethical relativism comes in two versions depending on how the relativist answers the question, Are moral principles relative to the individual or to society? The first alternative is *subjective ethical relativism,* or *ethical subjectivism,* and the second version is *conventional ethical relativism,* or *ethical conventionalism.* Questions 3 and 4 represent the outlook of ethical objectivism. *Ethical objectivism* is the view that there are universal and objectively valid moral principles that are relative to neither the individual nor society. We first examine the two versions of ethical relativism and then survey the case for ethical objectivism.

SURVEYING THE CASE FOR ETHICAL RELATIVISM

As leading question 1 illustrates, ethical relativism seeks to account for all the disagreement in matters that touch on ethics or values. The reason for this disagreement, the relativist claims, is that there is no objective basis for deciding between conflicting moral outlooks. In contrast, other areas of human experience, such as mathematics, physics, and medicine, have clear-cut procedures for coming to agreement. Furthermore, in the sciences, at least, the objects studied (e.g., atoms or tumors) exist independently of our opinions of them, making it possible to test our theories against the brute facts. On the other hand, the subjects of ethical discourse, such as right, wrong, good, and bad, do not seem to be waiting out in the world for us to discover their properties. Hence, the ethical relativist concludes that right and wrong have no existence or properties apart from human opinions concerning them. As question 2 illustrates, relativists place a high value on tolerance because they believe there is no true story about ethics and they see ethical judgments primarily as preferences for a certain type of conduct, lifestyle, or society.

In examining ethical relativism we need to get clear on exactly what is claimed to be relative and in what ways or for what reasons it is relative. Consider the following claim:

A. What is morally right for me is not necessarily morally right for you.

The problem here is that this claim is ambiguous, and because some interpretations of it are certainly true, some people may think that ethical relativism is also true. The first interpretation is as follows:

A1. What I think is morally right is not necessarily what you think is morally right.

This statement does not establish ethical relativism, for no ethical objectivist would disagree with it. To use a nonmoral example, many of Columbus's contemporaries believed that if he sailed across the ocean, he would fall over the edge of the earth. However, Columbus did not believe this. The fact that his contemporaries had their own opinions does not imply that each opinion was equally correct. Similarly, the fact that two people have differing moral opinions does not imply that there is not a correct answer. One person could be right and the other mistaken, or they both could be incorrect and the correct moral opinion might be a third option.

The two remaining interpretations depend on the fact that either moral actions or moral principles can be relative. This distinction allows for two completely independent claims. Let's examine *action relativism* first. It is the basis of the second interpretation of our original claim:

A2. An action can be morally right for me and morally wrong for you.

Ordinarily, during the summer I water my lawn. However, for someone (call him Karim) who lives in a water-starved region where water is necessary to preserve life, watering the lawn would be immoral. Thus, the same action (watering the lawn) is morally permissible for me but morally wrong for someone else. I water my lawn because (among other reasons) I care for my neighbors (they don't want my ugly lawn lowering their property values). Similarly, Karim is showing care for his neighbors by not wasting precious water. So, even though an action is right for me and is wrong for Karim, we are adhering to the same moral standard (caring for others). So far, this interpretation is completely consistent with ethical objectivism, for a person can believe there is a single set of universal and objective moral standards at the same time he or she believes that those standards can command different actions in different concrete situations.

The third interpretation expresses *moral principles relativism*:

A3. A moral principle can be correct for me but not necessarily correct for you. Since this statement uses the normative term *correct,* it is not merely describing the fact that people have different moral beliefs, as statement A1 does. Instead, statement A3 is claiming that moral principles themselves are relative to the individual. It is this form of moral relativity that will be the focus of our discussion, because it is making a controversial and large-scale claim about the nature of morality itself. This relativity can be based on the individual's personal outlook (subjectivism) or on the fact that he or she is a member of a particular culture (conventionalism). Let's discuss each of these alternatives in turn.

Subjective Ethical Relativism (Subjectivism)

According to ethical subjectivism, when *anyone* (not just the subjectivist) makes a moral judgment such as, "It is morally right to tax the rich to support the poor" or "Nudity on late night television should be permitted," or "Abortion is wrong," he or she is simply reporting or expressing personal approval (or disapproval) of an action as well as his or her attitudes and feelings. As Ernest Hemingway wrote:

> So far, about morals, I know only that what is moral is what you feel good after and what is immoral is what you feel bad after and judged by these moral standards, which I do not defend, the bullfight is very moral to me because I feel very fine while it is going on and have a feeling of life and death and mortality and immortality, and after it is over I feel very sad but very fine.[16]

This theory reduces ethics to the same plane as individual tastes in food. Although there may be some similarities among the people of a particular culture concerning what food dishes are delicacies and what are repulsive, in the final analysis it is simply a matter of individual taste. Similarly, ethical subjectivism claims that ethics is a matter of personal opinion, even though people of like opinions will naturally tend to concentrate in a particular culture or subculture.

One of the earliest expressions of subjective ethical relativism can be found in the Sophists who taught in Greece in the fifth century B.C. (See the discussion of Socrates' arguments against the Sophists in section 1.1.) The Sophists taught that *right* and *wrong* are simply words whose meanings were arbitrary and dependent on human opinion. This belief was expressed by Protagoras's famous slogan, "Man is the measure of all things." Some of the more cynical Sophists taught that you should follow the moral conventions of society when it is prudent to do so, but do what you think is right when you can get away with it.

In the twentieth century, one of the most famous expressions of ethical subjectivism is found in the writings of the French existentialist Jean-Paul Sartre. (See the discussion of Sartre's existentialist view of human freedom in section 3.7.) Sartre quotes Dostoyevsky's statement, "If God did not exist, everything would be permitted." However, whereas Dostoyevsky was making this point to emphasize the necessity of there being a God, the atheist Sartre uses it to make clear the implications of atheism. For Sartre, because there is no God, there is no realm of values and moral rules apart from us that we can use to guide our behavior. Each of us must choose for ourselves the values that will guide our lives. Sartre stresses the enormous responsibility and even anxiety we must bear in facing this subjective choice. He tells of a young man who came to him for advice during World War II. The young man wanted to know whether the morally right action would be to stay home to care for his mother or abandon her to fight the Nazis. The advice Sartre gave to him was, "You are free, therefore choose—that is to say, invent. No rule of general morality can show you what you ought to do."[17] That comment is a classic statement of subjectivism. Morality is not discovered; it is chosen or invented by each individual, much like creating a work of art.

Subjective ethical relativism is a curious position, because it says that there are no moral principles other than those that each individual chooses for herself or himself. But if there are no moral standards other than the ones I invent for myself, then it seems impossible for me to ever do what was morally wrong. Of course, someone might be able to claim that I have failed to live according to my own moral principles. But that criticism is easy to fix, for I can simply claim that according to my beliefs, hypocrisy is morally permissible. Furthermore, it seems impossible for there ever to be a viable society of moral subjectivists, each doing his or her own thing. Minimally, a society needs some common standards of morality to which all its members are subject, to allow them to rise above the conflicts that are inevitable between individual whims, idiosyncrasies, preferences, and desires. Without a common morality, the human situation would be, in the words of the eighteenth-century philosopher Thomas Hobbes, "a war of all against all."[18] Because subjective ethical relativism is so problematic, ethical relativism would seem to rise or fall with its strongest version, which is conventionalism.

WRONG

Is there a difference between right and wrong? Or is it all relative to how you look at it?

Conventional Ethical Relativism (Conventionalism)

The theoretical problems with subjectivism as well as the practical problems of sustaining a society on that basis help make the case for the conventionalist version of ethical relativism. This theory is actually an ancient one, for morality has typically been embedded within cultural traditions throughout human history, whereas individualism of any sort was not very prevalent before the Renaissance.

Long ago the Greek historian Herodotus (485–430 B.C.) cleverly illustrated the way in which people's moral opinions are shaped by their society:

The Histories[19]

If one were to offer men to choose out of all the customs in the world such as seemed to them the best, they would examine the whole number, and end by preferring their own; so convinced are they that their own usages far surpass those of all others. . . . That people have this feeling about their laws may be seen by very many proofs: among others, by the following. Darius, after he had got the kingdom, called into his presence certain Greeks who were at hand, and asked—"What he should pay them to eat the bodies of their fathers when they died?" To which they answered, that there was no sum that would tempt them to do such a thing. He then sent for certain Indians, of the race called Callatians, men who eat the dead bodies of their fathers, and asked them, while the Greeks stood by, and knew by the help of an interpreter all that was said—"What he should give them to burn the bodies of their fathers at their decease?" [The practice of the Greeks.] The Indians exclaimed aloud, and forbade him to use such language. Such is men's customary practice; and Pindar was right, in my judgment, when he said, "Custom is the king o'er all."

To apply this story to the conventional ethical relativist's account, let's imagine that there are two Greeks, Alcinus and Xerxes, and two Callatians, Bredor and Yerbon (A, X, B, and Y for short).[20] Suppose the facts are as follows:

Greek Society (Burning the dead is moral)	Callatian Society (Burning the dead is immoral)
A believes burning the dead is moral.	B believes burning the dead is immoral.
X believes burning the dead is immoral.	Y believes burning the dead is moral.

Which one of these individuals (A, B, X, Y) has correct moral beliefs? The subjectivist would say that all are equally correct since morality is a matter of individual opinion. However, a conventionalist would say that A and B have correct moral beliefs, even though their beliefs contradict each other, because A's morality and B's morality conform to that of their society. On the other hand, the conventionalist would say X and Y have incorrect moral beliefs because they are in conflict with the morality of their respective societies. The following thought experiment asks you to consider your own moral values and the degree to which they are or are not a result of your cultural background.

 THOUGHT EXPERIMENT

How Did You Learn about Morality?

- How did you arrive at your ideas of morality? What factors played a role in your moral development (family, friends, role models, teachers, books, films)?

(Continued . . .)

(. . . continued)

- Imagine that you were born into a different family, in a different region of the world, and in a different culture. Do you think these circumstances would make a difference in your current notions of right or wrong?
- In what ways do your moral judgments and values differ from those of your parents? What factors caused your opinions to differ from theirs?
- To what degree do these reflections support or contradict the claims of conventional relativism?

RUTH BENEDICT (1887–1948)

RUTH BENEDICT
(1887–1948)

Conventionalism is typically defended by surveying the wide range of ethical beliefs and practices throughout the world. This defense is illustrated in the writings of Ruth Benedict, who used her anthropological studies to show us that much of our behavior arises from the prevailing standards of the culture in which we were raised. (Ruth Benedict was one of America's foremost anthropologists. She taught at Columbia University, and her book *Patterns of Culture* (1934) is considered a classic of comparative anthropology.) Benedict's conclusions were exceedingly controversial when she first introduced them, because they challenged the tendency of anthropologists to judge and evaluate various societies in terms of the "superior" values and "rational" outlook of Western culture. Instead, as the following selection illustrates, Benedict urged that in investigating any culture we should attempt to understand it in terms of the unique internal standards of those people without judging them to be either inferior or superior to our own.

- As you read through this selection, assess the degree to which Benedict's descriptions of other cultures either support or fail to support the thesis of ethical relativism.
- What would be some of the implications of Benedict's relativism? Are any implications good? Are any problematic?

FROM RUTH BENEDICT

Anthropology and the Abnormal[21]

The most spectacular illustrations of the extent to which normality may be culturally defined are those cultures where an abnormality of our culture is the cornerstone of their social structure. It is not possible to do justice to these possibilities in a short discussion. A recent study of an island of northwest Melanesia by Fortune describes a society built upon traits which we regard as beyond the border of paranoia. In this tribe the exogamic groups* look upon each other as prime

---

*By "exogamic groups" Benedict is referring to tribes who marry only persons from another tribe.

manipulators of black magic, so that one marries always into an enemy group which remains for life one's deadly and unappeasable foes. They look upon a good garden crop as a confession of theft, for everyone is engaged in making magic to induce into his garden the productiveness of his neighbors'; therefore no secrecy in the island is so rigidly insisted upon as the secrecy of a man's harvesting of his yams. Their polite phrase at the acceptance of a gift is, "And if you now poison me, how shall I repay you this present?" Their preoccupation with poisoning is constant; no woman ever leaves her cooking pot for a moment untended. Even the great affinal economic exchanges that are characteristic of this Melanesian culture area are quite altered in Dobu since they are incompatible with this fear and distrust that pervades the culture. They go farther and people the whole world outside their own quarters with such malignant spirits that all-night feasts and ceremonials simply do not occur here. They have even rigorous religiously enforced customs that forbid the sharing of seed even in one family group. Any-one else's food is deadly poison to you, so that commonality of stores is out of the question. For some months before harvest the whole society is on the verge of starvation, but if one falls to the temptation and eats up one's seed yams, one is an outcast and a beachcomber for life. There is no coming back. It involves, as a matter of course, divorce and the breaking of all social ties.

Now in this society where no one may work with another and no one may share with another, Fortune describes the individual who was regarded by all his fellows as crazy. He was not one of those who periodically ran amok and, beside himself and frothing at the mouth, fell with a knife upon anyone he could reach. Such behavior they did not regard as putting anyone outside the pale. They did not even put the individuals who were known to be liable to these attacks under any kind of control. They merely fled when they saw the attack coming on and kept out of the way. "He would be all right tomorrow." But there was one man of sunny, kindly disposition who liked work and liked to be helpful. The compul-sion was too strong for him to repress it in favor of the opposite tendencies of his culture. Men and women never spoke of him without laughing; he was silly and simple and definitely crazy. Nevertheless, to the ethnologist used to a culture that has, in Christianity, made his type the model of all virtue, he seemed a pleasant fellow. . . .

. . . Among the Kwakiutl it did not matter whether a relative had died in bed of disease, or by the hand of an enemy, in either case death was an affront to be wiped out by the death of another person. The fact that one had been caused to mourn was proof that one had been put upon. A chief's sister and her daughter had gone up to Victoria, and either because they drank bad whiskey or because their boat capsized they never came back. The chief called together his warriors, "Now I ask you, tribes, who shall wail? Shall I do it or shall another?" The spokesman an-swered, of course, "Not you, Chief. Let some other of the tribes." Immediately they set up the war pole to announce their intention of wiping out the injury, and gathered a war party. They set out, and found seven men and two children asleep and killed them. "Then they felt good when they arrived at Sebaa in the evening."

The point which is of interest to us is that in our society those who on that occasion would feel good when they arrived at Sebaa that evening would be the definitely abnormal. There would be some, even in our society, but it is not a recognized and approved mood under the circumstances. On the Northwest Coast those are favored and fortunate to whom that mood under those circumstances is congenial, and those to whom it is repugnant are unlucky. This latter minority can register in their own culture only by doing violence to their congenial responses and acquiring others that are difficult for them. The person, for instance, who, like a Plains Indian whose wife has been taken from him, is too proud to fight, can deal with the Northwest Coast civilization only by ignoring its strongest bents. If he cannot achieve it, he is the deviant in that culture, their instance of abnormality.

This head-hunting that takes place on the Northwest Coast after a death is no matter of blood revenge or of organized vengeance. There is no effort to tie up the subsequent killing with any responsibility on the part of the victim for the death of the person who is being mourned. A chief whose son has died goes visiting wherever his fancy dictates, and he says to his host, "My prince has died today, and you go with him." Then he kills him. In this, according to their interpretation, he acts nobly because he has not been downed. He has thrust back in return. The whole procedure is meaningless without the fundamental paranoid reading of bereavement. Death, like all the other untoward accidents of existence, confounds man's pride and can only be handled in the category of insults.

Behavior honored upon the Northwest Coast is one which is recognized as abnormal in our civilization, and yet it is sufficiently close to the attitudes of our own culture to be intelligible to us and to have a definite vocabulary with which we may discuss it. The megalomaniac paranoid trend is a definite danger in our society. It is encouraged by some of our major preoccupations, and it confronts us with a choice of two possible attitudes. One is to brand it as abnormal and reprehensible, and is the attitude we have chosen in our civilization. The other is to make it an essential attribute of ideal man, and this is the solution in the culture of the Northwest Coast.

These illustrations, which it has been possible to indicate only in the briefest manner, force upon us the fact that normality is culturally defined. An adult shaped to the drives and standards of either of these cultures, if he were transported into our civilization, would fall into our categories of abnormality. He would be faced with the psychic dilemmas of the socially unavailable. In his own culture, however, he is the pillar of society, the end result of socially inculcated mores, and the problem of personal instability in his case simply does not arise. . . .

Every society, beginning with some slight inclination in one direction or another, carries its preference farther and farther, integrating itself more and more completely upon its chosen basis, and discarding those types of behavior that are uncongenial. Most of those organizations of personality that seem to us most uncontrovertibly abnormal have been used by different civilizations in the very foundations of their institutional life. Conversely the most valued traits of our normal individuals have been looked on in differently organized cultures as aberrant.

Normality, in short, within a very wide range, is culturally defined. It is primarily a term for the socially elaborated segment of human behavior in any culture; and abnormality, a term for the segment that that particular civilization does not use. The very eyes with which we see the problem are conditioned by the long traditional habits of our own society.

It is a point that has been made more often in relation to ethics than in relation to psychiatry. We do not any longer make the mistake of deriving the morality of our locality and decade directly from the inevitable constitution of human nature. We do not elevate it to the dignity of a first principle. We recognize that morality differs in every society, and is a convenient term for socially approved habits. Mankind has always preferred to say, "It is morally good," rather than "It is habitual," and the fact of this preference is matter enough for a critical science of ethics. But historically the two phrases are synonymous.

The concept of the normal is properly a variant of the concept of the good. It is that which society has approved. A normal action is one which falls well within the limits of expected behavior for a particular society. Its variability among different peoples is essentially a function of the variability of the behavior patterns that different societies have created for themselves, and can never be wholly divorced from a consideration of culturally institutionalized types of behavior.

- State in your own words Benedict's thesis concerning normality and abnormality.
- She says that the statement "It is morally good" is synonymous with what other phrase? Do you agree that these phrases are essentially the same? Why?
- How would you summarize Benedict's view of morality?
- Do you agree with her that the differences between cultures are sufficient to prove that there are no objective rights or wrongs? Why?

Although many might agree with Benedict's descriptions of various cultures, the question remains whether such descriptions are sufficient to make the case for ethical relativism. Philosopher John Ladd defines ethical relativism (or the conventionalist version being discussed here) in the following way:

> Ethical relativism is the doctrine that the moral rightness and wrongness of actions varies from society to society and that there are no absolute universal moral standards binding on all men at all times. Accordingly, it holds that whether or not it is right for an individual to act in a certain way depends on or is relative to the society to which he belongs.[22]

As Ladd points out, two logically independent theses are embedded within this definition. The first is the *diversity thesis* (often called *cultural relativism*). This thesis states that moral beliefs, rules, and practices differ from society to society. The *dependency thesis* asserts that moral beliefs, rules, and practices are essentially dependent on the cultural patterns of the society in which they occur. Hence, if the Greeks in Herodotus's account had been raised in the Callatian society, they would have thought it right to eat the bodies of their dead fathers. Likewise, if the Callatians had been raised as Greeks, it would have been right for them to burn the bodies of their dead fathers.

Using Ladd's analysis, the argument of the ethical relativist could be formulated in the following way:

1. Whether an action is right or wrong is dependent on the moral beliefs and practices of a particular society. (Dependency thesis)
2. Moral beliefs and practices vary from society to society. (Diversity thesis)
3. Therefore, whether an action is right or wrong varies from society to society. (Conventional ethical relativism)

Conventional ethical relativism seems very appealing, for if it were widely accepted it would provide an antidote to the rabid intolerance in the world today. Intolerance leads people to set fire to a church or synagogue, or to bomb an abortion clinic or government building; intolerance motivates people of one religious or ethnic group to seek to eliminate those of another group while claiming that they are doing these acts in the name of what is "right." Ethical relativism emphasizes that just because we think a certain way doesn't give us the right to disrespect (much less destroy) others who think and act differently. Is ethical relativism, however, the only way (or even the best way) to achieve tolerance? We can answer this question only by examining the argument for relativism in more detail.

First, let's look at the dependency thesis. It is surely correct that morality is intimately intertwined with cultural traditions. But is this connection sufficient to prove that moral beliefs cannot be evaluated independently of these cultural traditions? To use a nonmoral example, it is part of our Western cultural tradition that most teenagers learn chemistry in school, but in other, nontechnological cultures teenagers might be trained in hunting and not chemistry. But should we conclude that the principles of chemistry have no validity apart from our particular culture? We recognize close to 100 chemical elements, but the ancient Greeks recognized only earth, air, fire, and water. Should we conclude that the issue of how many elements there really are is simply dependent upon culture? Similarly, the abolition of slavery in our society was motivated by a more consistent reflection on the implications of our democratic ideals and the biblical roots of our culture. But should we conclude that slavery is wrong only for people in our culture?

Furthermore, remember that in our discussion of action relativism, we noted that two cultures can share the same moral principle (caring for one's neighbors) but that the *application* of this principle may be dependent on the specific conditions of the culture (watering the lawn or not). Hence, in a weak sense it is true that morality is dependent on culture, but there are few reasons to accept the strong dependency required to establish ethical relativism.

What about the diversity thesis? Benedict has documented the wide range of moral practices and attitudes throughout the world. But in spite of this diversity, some anthropologists have argued that there is also a common core of agreement. As anthropologist Clyde Kluckhohn has noted:

Every culture has a concept of murder, distinguishing this from execution, killing in war, and other "justifiable homicides." The notions of incest and other regulations upon sexual behavior, the prohibitions upon untruth under defined circumstances, of restitution and reciprocity, of mutual obligations between parents and children—these and many other moral concepts are altogether universal.[23]

Furthermore, while it may seem at first that conflicting moral judgments are based on conflicting moral principles, the difference may actually be based on the nonmoral differences in factual beliefs. For example, in many tribal cultures it is customary to kill one's parents when they are no longer capable of providing for themselves. This practice is not only radically different from the way we are expected to treat our parents, but people in our culture would be inclined to judge it morally abhorrent. But do these tribes differ from us morally? Surprisingly, the answer is no, for the difference is to be found at the level of factual beliefs. These people kill their aged parents because they believe that the physical condition of your body at the time of death will be your condition in the afterlife throughout all eternity. Given this belief, it is important to die before you become an invalid. If your children will not perform this service for you, it is a great disgrace. Furthermore, for cultures who face a harsh environment, the struggle for existence dictates that they spend their energy and resources caring for the young and not their infirm senior members. The moral of the story is that these cultures have basically the same principles that we do: (1) honor your parents, (2) provide for the young, and (3) serve the overall good of society. However, their application of these principles differs from ours because they have different nonmoral beliefs about death and because their physical conditions are different.

Finally, the diversity thesis does not imply ethical relativism, because it merely describes what people do but does not address the issue of what they ought to do. If we found out, for example, that the majority of parents sexually abuse their children, this discovery would not mean that their actions were right. But ethical relativism makes the claim that if the majority of people in a culture believe something is right, then that belief or action is morally right for them.

LOOKING THROUGH THE LENS OF ETHICAL RELATIVISM

1. There seem to be some features of human experience that are universal, such as mating, birth, child rearing, property, some form of social organization, some system of justice, suffering, and death. How does the relativist explain the fact that every society has some form of morality based on these and other common features of human life? How can the relativist defend the view that morality is completely relative to human opinion at the same time that these common facts seem to indicate some similarities in the moral rules of different societies?

2. If everyone in history had been conventional ethical relativists, what differences would we have seen in history and in the world today? What differences would be better? What would be worse?

3. In the nineteenth century, Christian missionaries often coerced tribal people in Africa to abandon their practice of polygamy. However, since the women tended to outnumber the men (due to the death of males in war and hunting), many women were left without any means of support. Consequently, some desperate women were forced to move to the cities to become prostitutes. What would the ethical relativist say about this attempt to change a society's moral practices?

4. The ethical objectivist can explain the fact that individuals or cultures change their moral views or practices (such as abandoning slavery) by saying that they come to discover better or truer ethical standards. However, if morality is based simply on individual or social opinion and there are no objective standards against which to measure that morality, as the relativist claims, then why would people be inclined to believe that their present morality is wrong? In other words, how might the relativist explain changes in people's moral outlook?

EXAMINING THE STRENGTHS AND WEAKNESSES OF ETHICAL RELATIVISM

Positive Evaluation

1. Ethical relativism can easily explain the diversity of moral opinions and the difficulty of arriving at a consensus on controversial moral issues. How strongly does this factor count in favor of the plausibility of the relativist's position?

2. The conventionalist's moral standard is that an action is morally right or wrong if it is considered such by society. Doesn't such a standard have these advantages: it gives us a clear procedure for resolving ethical disputes, it is democratic, and it creates social harmony? Doesn't this standard reflect the approach that we often take in ethics?

3. Ethical relativism encourages people to follow the principle "live and let live." It places a high value on tolerance and is a corrective to the evils of ethnocentrism (the attitude that your society is superior to all others). It reminds us that people shouldn't be condemned just because they do things differently than we do. Aren't these attitudes laudable?

4. Ethical relativism provides for a flexible morality. People don't have to adhere to one set of moral rules etched in granite for all time; instead, ethical relativism allows morality to change as people's needs and attitudes change, as society progresses, and as circumstances change. Just as the horse and buggy gave way to the automobile, shouldn't morality be a function of society's growing needs?

Negative Evaluation

1. At the time Ruth Benedict was writing her article (1934) the Nazis were beginning to take over Europe. (Benedict was silent about this cultural "practice" in her paper.) Someone has said that no one can watch the movie *Schindler's List* (which depicts the Nazi's atrocities) and remain an ethical relativist. Wouldn't an ethical relativist have to say that the rest of the world had no right to condemn the elitist, racist, and genocidal actions of the Nazis as long as the Nazis were being consistent with their own moral ideals? Doesn't ethical relativism imply that we can never criticize the accepted practices of another society, no matter how evil those practices are? Does this approach expose a problem with ethical relativism?

2. Can morality be simply a function of what the 51 percent majority in a society says it is? Let's say the majority of people believed that physician-assisted suicide was wrong last week, but this week the polls show that the majority opinion has changed; do these polls mean that physician-assisted suicide was wrong last week but is morally right this week? Isn't this approach odd and problematic? We may be able to change people's *opinions* of the rightness or wrongness of a controversial practice through an effective advertising campaign, but do we want to say that the *morality* of a practice can be changed through a public relations campaign?

3. If conventionalism is correct, then how can we ever decide the rightness or wrongness of something that has no clear social consensus? For example, I cannot possibly decide the morality of a new medical controversy such as cloning genetically identical babies until I find out what the rest of society thinks. But likewise, no one else in society can decide the morality of this new procedure without knowing what the majority thought. In other words, when we face new moral problems that have no already-established social consensus, we could never decide for ourselves what is right, and consequently, there could never be a majority opinion about what is right.

4. If morality depends on social consensus, how large does a group have to be to constitute a valid standard for morality? Does it require 1,000 people? How about 100 people or even 10 people? While we may each be a citizen of a particular nation, we are also members of any number of subcultures within that nation that each have different cultural practices. If morality is relative to our culture, could I claim that it is right for me to murder people because I belong to the Mafia subculture in which this practice is acceptable? Furthermore, one person can belong to several different subcultures that have conflicting moral codes. Suppose, for example, that Tanya is a black, feminist, Roman Catholic living in a society that tolerates discrimination against blacks and women and that also finds abortion and pornography acceptable. Racism, sexism, abortion, and pornography each could be both morally right and wrong for Tanya depending on which of her several subcultures she uses as her standard for moral evaluation. By reducing morality to human opinion, doesn't the relativist rob it of its action-guiding function altogether?

Shouldn't human opinions be subject to moral norms and not the other way around?

SURVEYING THE CASE FOR ETHICAL OBJECTIVISM

Ethical objectivism is the position that certain moral principles are universal (they apply to all persons in all times) and objective (they are not based on the opinions of individuals or cultures). Hence, for this position, there are objectively right and wrong answers to ethical questions just as there are objectively true and false answers to questions in mathematics, medicine, or physics. Unlike ethical relativism, the ethical objectivist does not believe that morality is like tastes in food or social customs. Hence, the ethical objectivist claims that it is possible for individuals or entire cultures to be mistaken in their moral opinions and practices.

Objectivism and Absolutism

Ethical objectivism should be distinguished from ethical absolutism. **Absolutism** claims that not only are moral principles objective but also they cannot be overridden and there cannot be any exceptions to them. As we will see, Kantian ethics (section 5.4) is an example of ethical absolutism. Absolutism is a more narrow position than objectivism and could be considered a subcategory within it. Hence, all absolutists are objectivists, but the reverse is not true. The ethical absolutist, for example, would say that we have an obligation to tell the truth and not lie, and this duty cannot be violated for any reason. On the other hand, the ethical objectivist could say that a rule like "do not lie" is an objective moral principle but that this principle can be overriden when it conflicts with a more pressing obligation such as saving a life. Hence, if lying to a homicidal maniac would prevent him from killing someone, then our duty to preserve life overrides our duty to tell the truth. W. D. Ross (who is discussed in section 5.4) presents an example of the more moderate position of ethical objectivism. Although he did believe that there were universal, objective moral principles, he did not believe that any of them were absolute and without exceptions, for when two or more of these principles conflict, one would have to be subordinated to the other.

    Ethical relativism claims that "*All* moral principles are relative," whereas ethical objectivism claims that "*Some* moral principles are *not* relative." These claims are contradictory, so one is true and one is false; there could be no compromise that embraces them both. Notice, however, that the objectivist could claim that *some* moral issues are relative as long as he or she also maintains that there is a core of moral principles that are universal and objective. In other words, the objectivist does not need to say that there is only one right answer to every single ethical question, but merely has to claim that there can be wrong answers and that on *some* ethical issues there are moral principles that everyone ought to follow. For example, an objectivist might say that monogamy is best for some societies but polygamy is

absolutism the claim that not only are moral principles objective but also they cannot be overridden and there cannot be any exceptions to them

best for others, given their circumstances and conditions. At the same time, while recognizing some degree of acceptable diversity in social arrangements, the objectivist would say that treating family members with benevolence and care, doing no harm, and respecting each person's dignity and worth are universal, objective moral principles that cannot be violated. Furthermore, the specific actions that would constitute treating a family member benevolently might vary with social customs and conditions, even though the principle followed in each case would be the same. For example, the Greeks burned their dead because they thought this ritual was the proper way to honor the spirits of the dead, whereas the Callatians ate their dead for the same reason. Both were attempting to honor their family members, but did so through different specific actions.

Problems with Relativism

One of the attractions of ethical relativism is that it seems to place a high value on tolerance—something that most people think is an important principle. But just because a theory approves of something good does not imply that the theory is true. Furthermore, the objectivist would agree with the relativist that tolerance is good and intolerance is bad. However, the objectivist philosophers would say that only *they* have a right to make this claim, because tolerance is being offered as an objective moral standard that is universally binding. By claiming that all ethical opinions are of equal value, the relativist is in the uncomfortable position of having to tolerate intolerance. If tolerance is to be our sole guiding ideal, should we then consider the sincere ethical judgments of racists and Nazis to be morally acceptable?

 STOP AND THINK

I once had a student who wrote a forceful essay in defense of ethical relativism. He claimed that right and wrong are relative to individual opinion and that no one had any basis for imposing his or her conception of morality on others. The student finished the essay by writing in large letters "Everyone OUGHT to be tolerant. It is always WRONG to be intolerant."

- How might an ethical objectivist argue that this student is being inconsistent?
- What if my personal morality was one that embraced the virtue of intolerance? What could this student say about that? Wouldn't an ethical relativist have to say that for me (or for some cultures) intolerance is morally right?

Another problem with relativism (both versions) is that it makes it impossible to criticize the behavior of other persons or cultures. Our campus once had an anthropologist speak in a public forum in defense of cultural relativism. To make his point, he described many cultures whose sexual behavior and other moral practices differ radically from what is acceptable in our society. He concluded by saying, "Who can say that they are wrong, simply because their morality differs from ours?" Knowing that his wife ran the local women's and children's domestic violence shelter, I asked him if he could consistently live with his ethical relativism. After all, there are many cultures and even subcultures in our society in which violence to women is tolerated. Even many of the women victims themselves, who have been raised in the values of that culture, accept violence as the way things should be. As I suspected, however, there were limits to the anthropologist's tolerance and relativism. He replied that a minimal moral rule must be the protecting of women and children, even though he realized that this acknowledgment undermined his own thesis of ethical relativism. When ethical relativists find that their own rights or the rights of those they love are being violated, they quickly begin to see the attractiveness of ethical objectivism.

Is There a Core Morality?

Many objectivists argue that a universal core of moral principles can be found throughout every flourishing culture. Of course, we can always find cultures such as the Ik and societies such as Nazi Germany that have moral principles that seem to deviate from the norm. (The Ik culture was briefly discussed in leading question 4 at the beginning of this section.) However, the fact that the Ik culture is not flourishing and that the Nazi society was grim and paranoid and resisted by some of its own people suggests that in both cases something was wrong with these societies' moral ideals. In spite of the wide range of moral practices throughout the world and history, some anthropologists have found a number of common moral principles.

If there is a core of moral values or practices that seem to be universal among flourishing, healthy societies, this serves as counter evidence to the examples of diversity provided by Benedict and other relativists. As mentioned previously, the ethical objectivist does not need to deny that there is some measure of moral disagreement or diversity among different cultures. Such moral disagreements could be a result of the fact that people can make mistakes about what is morally correct. Just as the medievals were mistaken in believing that the earth is flat, so people in earlier centuries mistakenly believed that slavery was morally permissible. On the other hand, differences in morality also could result from the fact that some moral issues permit differences of opinion. The standards of modesty in one culture may differ from the standards of another culture. However, the objectivist might admit that moral standards with regard to clothing and behavior may be culturally based. Minimally the objectivist merely has to maintain that there are some features of morality that are not optional nor simply a matter of cultural convention.

In the following essay James Rachels proposes that the arguments for ethical relativism, which he calls "cultural relativism," fail to make their case. (James Rachels is a professor of philosophy at the University of Alabama. He is well known

A Common Core Morality

Although many examples of common moral principles could be cited, here is how different cultures have expressed two fundamental moral principles.[24]

The Law of General Beneficence

"Utter not a word by which anyone could be wounded." (Hindu)

"I have not brought misery upon my fellows." (Ancient Egyptian)

"Speak kindness . . . show good will." (Babylonian)

"Men were brought into existence for the sake of men that they might do one another good." (Roman)

"Never do to others what you would not like them to do to you." (Ancient Chinese)

"Love thy neighbour as thyself." (Ancient Jewish)

"Do unto others what you would have them do unto you." (Christian)

The Law of Good Faith and Truthfulness

"A sacrifice is obliterated by a lie and the merit of [charitable giving] by an act of fraud." (Hindu)

"With his mouth was he full of *Yea,* in his heart full of *Nay?*" (Babylonian List of Sins)

"I have not spoken falsehood." (Ancient Egyptian)

"The Master said, Be of unwavering good faith." (Ancient Chinese)

"Hateful to me as are the gates of Hades is that man who says one thing, and hides another in his heart." (Greek)

"The foundation of justice is good faith." (Roman)

"Anything is better than treachery." (Old Norse)

"Thou shalt not bear false witness against thy neighbor." (Ancient Jewish)

for his books and articles on philosophy of religion and ethics.) Furthermore, he points out that there are many reasons why we should find ethical relativism implausible and ethical objectivism correct. In the original essay, he begins by mentioning the funeral practices of the Greeks and the Callatians, which we have already discussed. The following selection begins with his discussion of traditional Eskimo customs.

- How do Eskimo practices lend support to the thesis of cultural relativism? How does Rachels later show that their treatment of babies is consistent with objectivism?
- Why does Rachels think the diversity thesis is flawed?(He calls it the "cultural differences argument.")
- What are the three consequences of cultural relativism?
- Why does Rachels believe there must be some moral rules that are common to every culture?

The Challenge of Cultural Relativism[25]

1. How Different Cultures Have Different Moral Codes

JAMES RACHELS
(1941–   )

. . . Consider the Eskimos. They are a remote and inaccessible people. Numbering only about 25,000, they live in small, isolated settlements scattered mostly along the northern fringes of North America and Greenland. Until the beginning of this century, the outside world knew little about them. Then explorers began to bring back strange tales.

Eskimo customs turned out to be very different from our own. The men often had more than one wife, and they would share their wives with guests, lending them for the night as a sign of hospitality. Moreover, within a community, a dominant male might demand—and get—regular sexual access to other men's wives. The women, however, were free to break these arrangements simply by leaving their husbands and taking up with new partners—free, that is, so long as their former husbands chose not to make trouble. All in all, the Eskimo practice was a volatile scheme that bore little resemblance to what we call marriage.

But it was not only their marriage and sexual practices that were different. The Eskimos also seemed to have less regard for human life. Infanticide, for example, was common. Knud Rasmussen, one of the most famous early explorers, reported that he met one woman who had borne twenty children but had killed ten of them at birth. Female babies, he found, were especially liable to be destroyed, and this was permitted simply at the parents' discretion, with no social stigma attached to it. Old people also, when they became too feeble to contribute to the family, were left out in the snow to die. So there seemed to be, in this society, remarkably little respect for life.

To the general public, these were disturbing revelations. Our own way of living seems so natural and right that for many of us it is hard to conceive of others living so differently. And when we do hear of such things, we tend immediately to categorize those other peoples as "backward" or "primitive." But to anthropologists and sociologists, there was nothing particularly surprising about the Eskimos. Since the time of Herodotus, enlightened observers have been accustomed to the idea that conceptions of right and wrong differ from culture to culture. If we assume that our ideas of right and wrong will be shared by all peoples at all times, we are merely naive.

2. Cultural Relativism

To many thinkers, this observation—"Different cultures have different moral codes"—has seemed to be the key to understanding morality. The idea of universal truth in ethics, they say, is a myth. The customs of different societies are all that exist. These customs cannot be said to be "correct" or "incorrect," for that implies we have an independent standard of right and wrong by which they may be judged. But there is no such independent standard; every standard is culture-bound. The great pioneering sociologist William Graham Sumner, writing in 1906, put the point like this:

> The "right" way is the way which the ancestors used and which has been handed down. The tradition is its own warrant. It is not held subject to verification by experience. The notion of right is in the folkways. It is not outside of them, of independent origin, and brought to test them. In the folkways, whatever is, is right. This is because they are traditional, and therefore contain in themselves the authority of the ancestral ghosts. When we come to the folkways we are at the end of our analysis.

This line of thought has probably persuaded more people to be skeptical about ethics than any other single thing. *Cultural Relativism*, as it has been called, challenges our ordinary belief in the objectivity and universality of moral truth. It says, in effect, that there is no such thing as universal truth in ethics; there are only the various cultural codes, and nothing more. Moreover, our own code has no special status; it is merely one among many.

As we shall see, this basic idea is really a compound of several different thoughts. It is important to separate the various elements of the theory because, on analysis, some parts of the theory turn out to be correct, whereas others seem to be mistaken. As a beginning, we may distinguish the following claims, all of which have been made by cultural relativists:

1. Different societies have different moral codes.
2. There is no objective standard that can be used to judge one societal code better than another.
3. The moral code of our own society has no special status; it is merely one among many.
4. There is no "universal truth" in ethics—that is, there are no moral truths that hold for all peoples at all times.
5. The moral code of a society determines what is right within that society; that is, if the moral code of a society says that a certain action is right, then that action *is* right, at least within that society.
6. It is mere arrogance for us to try to judge the conduct of other peoples. We should adopt an attitude of tolerance toward the practices of other cultures.

Although it may seem that these six propositions go naturally together, they are independent of one another, in the sense that some of them might be true even if others are false. In what follows, we will try to identify what is correct in Cultural Relativism, but we will also be concerned to expose what is mistaken about it.

3. The Cultural Differences Argument

Cultural Relativism is a theory about the nature of morality. At first blush it seems quite plausible. However, like all such theories, it may be evaluated by subjecting it to rational analysis; and when we analyze Cultural Relativism we find that it is not so plausible as it first appears to be.

The first thing we need to notice is that at the heart of Cultural Relativism there is a certain *form of argument*. The strategy used by cultural relativists is to argue from facts about the differences between cultural outlooks to a conclusion about the status of morality. Thus we are invited to accept this reasoning:

1. The Greeks believed it was wrong to eat the dead, whereas the Callatians believed it was right to eat the dead.
2. Therefore, eating the dead is neither objectively right nor objectively wrong. It is merely a matter of opinion, which varies from culture to culture.

Or, alternatively:

1. The Eskimos see nothing wrong with infanticide, whereas Americans believe infanticide is immoral.
2. Therefore, infanticide is neither objectively right nor objectively wrong. It is merely a matter of opinion, which varies from culture to culture.

Clearly, these arguments are variations of one fundamental idea. They are both special cases of a more general argument, which says:

1. Different cultures have different moral codes.
2. Therefore, there is no objective "truth" in morality. Right and wrong are only matters of opinion, and opinions vary from culture to culture.

We may call this the *Cultural Differences Argument*. To many people, it is very persuasive. But from a logical point of view, is it a *sound* argument?

It is not sound. The trouble is that the conclusion does not really follow from the premise—that is, even if the premise is true, the conclusion still might be false. The premise concerns what people *believe*: in some societies, people believe one thing; in other societies, people believe differently. The conclusion, however, concerns *what really is the case*. The trouble is that this sort of conclusion does not follow logically from this sort of premise.

Consider again the example of the Greeks and Callatians. The Greeks believed it was wrong to eat the dead; the Callatians believed it was right. Does it follow, *from the mere fact that they disagreed,* that there is no objective truth in the matter? No, it does not follow; for it *could* be that the practice was objectively right (or wrong) and that one or the other of them was simply mistaken.

To make the point clearer, consider a very different matter. In some societies, people believe the earth is flat. In other societies, such as our own, people believe the earth is (roughly) spherical. Does it follow, *from the mere fact that they disagree,* that there is no "objective truth" in geography? Of course not; we would never draw such a conclusion because we realize that, in their beliefs about the world, the members of some societies might simply be wrong. There is no reason to think that if the world is round everyone must know it. Similarly, there is no reason to think that if there is moral truth everyone must know it. The fundamental mistake in the Cultural Differences Argument is that it attempts to derive a substantive conclusion about a subject (morality) from the mere fact that people disagree about it.

It is important to understand the nature of the point that is being made here. We are *not* saying (not yet, anyway) that the conclusion of the argument is false. Insofar as anything being said here is concerned, it is still an open question whether the conclusion is true. We *are* making a purely logical point and saying that the conclusion does not *follow from* the premise. This is important, because in order to determine whether the conclusion is true, we need arguments in its support. Cultural Relativism proposes this argument, but unfortunately the argument turns out to be fallacious. So it proves nothing.

4. The Consequences of Taking Cultural Relativism Seriously

Even if the Cultural Differences Argument is invalid, Cultural Relativism might still be true. What would it be like if it were true?

In the passage quoted above, William Graham Sumner summarizes the essence of Cultural Relativism. He says that there is no measure of right and wrong other than the standards of one's society: "The notion of right is in the folkways. It is not outside of them, of independent origin, and brought to test them. In the folkways, whatever is, is right."

Suppose we took this seriously. What would be some of the consequences?

1. *We could no longer say that the customs of other societies are morally inferior to our own.* This, of course, is one of the main points stressed by Cultural Relativism. We would have to stop condemning other societies merely because they are "different." So long as we concentrate on certain examples, such as the funerary practices of the Greeks and Callatians, this may seem to be a sophisticated, enlightened attitude.

However, we would also be stopped from criticizing other, less benign practices. Suppose a society waged war on its neighbors for the purpose of taking slaves. Or suppose a society was violently anti-Semitic and its leaders set out to destroy the Jews. Cultural Relativism would preclude us from saying that either of these practices was wrong. We would not even be able to say that a society tolerant of Jews is *better* than the anti-Semitic society, for that would imply some sort of transcultural standard of comparison. The failure to condemn *these* practices does not seem "enlightened"; on the contrary, slavery and anti-Semitism seem wrong *wherever* they occur. Nevertheless, if we took Cultural Relativism seriously, we would have to admit that these social practices also are immune from criticism.

2. *We could decide whether actions are right or wrong just by consulting the standards of our society.* Cultural Relativism suggests a simple test for determining what is right and what is wrong: all one has to do is ask whether the action is in accordance with the code of one's society. Suppose a resident of South Africa is wondering whether his country's policy of *apartheid*—rigid racial segregation— is morally correct. All he has to do is ask whether this policy conforms to his

society's moral code. If it does, there is nothing to worry about, at least from a moral point of view.

This implication of Cultural Relativism is disturbing because few of us think that our society's code is perfect—we can think of ways it might be improved. Yet Cultural Relativism would not only forbid us from criticizing the codes of *other* societies; it would stop us from criticizing our *own*. After all, if right and wrong are relative to culture, this must be true for our own culture just as much as for others.

3. *The idea of moral progress is called into doubt.* Usually, we think that at least some changes in our society have been for the better. (Some, of course, may have been changes for the worse.) Consider this example: Throughout most of Western history the place of women in society was very narrowly circumscribed. They could not own property; they could not vote or hold political office; with a few exceptions, they were not permitted to have paying jobs; and generally they were under the almost absolute control of their husbands. Recently much of this has changed, and most people think of it as progress.

If Cultural Relativism is correct, can we legitimately think of this as progress? Progress means replacing a way of doing things with a *better* way. But by what standard do we judge the new ways as better? If the old ways were in accordance with the social standards of their time, then Cultural Relativism would say it is a mistake to judge them by the standards of a different time. Eighteenth-century society was, in effect, a different society from the one we have now. To say that we have made progress implies a judgment that present-day society is better, and that is just the sort of transcultural judgment that, according to Cultural Relativism, is impermissible.

Our idea of social *reform* will also have to be reconsidered. A reformer such as Martin Luther King, Jr., seeks to change his society for the better. Within the constraints imposed by Cultural Relativism, there is one way this might be done. If a society is not living up to its own ideals, the reformer may be regarded as acting for the best: the ideals of the society are the standard by which we judge his or her proposals as worthwhile. But the "reformer" may not challenge the ideals themselves, for those ideals are by definition correct. According to Cultural Relativism, then, the idea of social reform makes sense only in this very limited way.

These three consequences of Cultural Relativism have led many thinkers to reject it as implausible on its face. It does make sense, they say, to condemn some practices, such as slavery and anti-Semitism, wherever they occur. It makes sense to think that our own society has made some moral progress, while admitting that it is still imperfect and in need of reform. Because Cultural Relativism says that these judgments make no sense, the argument goes, it cannot be right.

5. Why There Is Less Disagreement than It Seems

The original impetus for Cultural Relativism comes from the observation that cultures differ dramatically in their views of right and wrong. But just how much do they differ? It is true that there are differences. However, it is easy to overestimate the extent of those differences. Often, when we examine what *seems* to be a dramatic difference, we find that the cultures do not differ nearly as much as it appears.

Consider a culture in which people believe it is wrong to eat cows. This may even be a poor culture, in which there is not enough food; still, the cows are not to be touched. Such a society would *appear* to have values very different from our own. But does it? We have not yet asked why these people will not eat cows. Suppose it is because they believe that after death the souls of humans inhabit the bodies of animals, especially cows, so that a cow may be someone's grandmother. Now do we want to say that their values are different from ours? No; the difference lies elsewhere. The difference is in our belief systems, not in our values. We agree that we shouldn't eat Grandma; we simply disagree about whether the cow *is* (or could be) Grandma.

The general point is this. Many factors work together to produce the customs of a society. The society's values are only one of them. Other matters, such as the religious and factual beliefs held by its members and the physical circumstances in which they must live, are also important. We cannot conclude, then, merely because customs differ, that there is a disagreement about *values.* The difference in customs may be attributable to some other aspect of social life. Thus there may be less disagreement about values than there appears to be.

Consider the Eskimos again. They often kill perfectly normal infants, especially girls. We do not approve of this at all; a parent who did this in our society would be locked up. Thus there appears to be a great difference in the values of our two cultures. But suppose we ask *why* the Eskimos do this. The explanation is not that they have less affection for their children or less respect for human life. An Eskimo family will always protect its babies if conditions permit. But they live in a harsh environment, where food is often in short supply. A fundamental postulate of Eskimo thought is: "Life is hard, and the margin of safety small." A family may want to nourish its babies but be unable to do so.

As in many "primitive" societies, Eskimo mothers will nurse their infants over a much longer period of time than mothers in our culture. The child will take nourishment from its mother's breast for four years, perhaps even longer. So even in the best of times there are limits to the number of infants that one mother can sustain. Moreover, the Eskimos are a nomadic people—unable to farm, they must move about in search of food. Infants must be carried, and a mother can carry only one baby in her parka as she travels and goes about her outdoor work. Other family members can help, but this is not always possible.

Infant girls are more readily disposed of because, first, in this society the males are the primary food providers—they are the hunters, according to the traditional division of labor—and it is obviously important to maintain a sufficient number of food gatherers. But there is an important second reason as well. Because the hunters suffer a high casualty rate, the adult men who die prematurely far outnumber the women who die early. Thus if male and female infants survived in equal numbers, the female adult population would greatly outnumber the male adult population. Examining the available statistics, one writer concluded that "were it not for female infanticide . . . there would be approximately one-and-a-half times as many females in the average Eskimo local group as there are food-producing males."

So among the Eskimos, infanticide does not signal a fundamentally different attitude toward children. Instead, it is a recognition that drastic measures are sometimes needed to ensure the family's survival. Even then, however, killing the baby is not the first option considered. Adoption is common; childless couples are especially happy to take a more fertile couple's "surplus." Killing is only the last resort. I emphasize this in order to show that the raw data of the anthropologists can be misleading; it can make the differences in values between cultures appear greater than they are. The Eskimos' values are not all that different from our values. It is only that life forces upon them choices that we do not have to make.

6. How All Cultures Have Some Values in Common

It should not be surprising that, despite appearances, the Eskimos are protective of their children. How could it be otherwise? How could a group survive that did not value its young? This suggests a certain argument, one which shows that all cultural groups must be protective of their infants:

(1) Human infants are helpless and cannot survive if they are not given extensive care for a period of years.

(2) Therefore, if a group did not care for its young, the young would not survive, and the older members of the group would not be replaced. After a while the group would die out.

(3) Therefore, any cultural group that continues to exist must care for its young. Infants that are *not* cared for must be the exception rather than the rule.

Similar reasoning shows that other values must be more or less universal. Imagine what it would be like for a society to place no value at all on truth telling. When one person spoke to another, there would be no presumption at all that he was telling the truth—for he could just as easily be speaking falsely. Within that society, there would be no reason to pay attention to what anyone says. (I ask you what time it is, and you say "Four o'clock." But there is no presumption that you are speaking truly; you could just as easily have said the first thing that came into your head. So I have no reason to pay attention to your answer—in fact, there was no point in my asking you in the first place!) Communication would then be extremely difficult, if not impossible. And because complex societies cannot exist without regular communication among their members, society would become impossible. It follows that in any complex society there *must* be a presumption in favor of truthfulness. There may of course be exceptions to this rule: there may be situations in which it is thought to be permissible to lie. Nevertheless, these will be exceptions to a rule that *is* in force in the society.

Let me give one further example of the same type. Could a society exist in which there was no prohibition on murder? What would this be like? Suppose people were free to kill other people at will, and no one thought there was anything wrong with it. In such a "society," no one could feel secure. Everyone would have to be constantly on guard. People who wanted to survive would have to avoid other people as much as possible. This would inevitably result in individuals trying to become as self-sufficient as possible—after all, associating with others would be dangerous. Society on any large scale would collapse. Of course, people might band together in smaller groups with others that they *could* trust not to harm them. But notice what this means: they would be forming smaller societies that did acknowledge a rule against murder. The prohibition of murder, then, is a necessary feature of all societies.

There is a general theoretical point here, namely, that *there are some moral rules that all societies will have in common, because those rules are necessary for society to exist.* The rules against lying and murder are two examples. And in fact, we do find these rules in force in all viable cultures. Cultures may differ in what they regard as legitimate exceptions to the rules, but this disagreement exists against a background of agreement on the larger issues. Therefore, it is a mistake to overestimate the amount of difference between cultures. Not *every* moral rule can vary from society to society.

- Having examined the pros and cons, do you think ethical relativism or ethical objectivism is the stronger position? Explain.

LOOKING THROUGH THE LENS OF ETHICAL OBJECTIVISM

1. Contemporary philosopher Louis Pojman lists four purposes of morality: (1) To keep society from falling apart, (2) to ameliorate human suffering, (3) to promote human flourishing, (4) to resolve conflicts of interest in just ways.[26] Do you agree with his list? Are there any other purposes you would add or any you would subtract? If morality in general does serve some set of goals, how strong is the implication that there is an objective set of moral principles? What are some moral principles that would be necessary to achieve one or more of these four goals?

2. Does an objectivist have to be dogmatic? Can an objectivist be humble and tentative about his or her own grasp of morality? Is it possible for an objectivist to believe that there are universal, objective moral truths without claiming that his or her moral principles are necessarily the correct ones? In other words, can a person be an ethical objectivist without claiming moral infallibility?

3. Don't individuals and societies sometimes modify and change their morality? Don't we sometimes find that we mistakenly believed something was right but now believe it is wrong, or find that in the past we thought something was wrong but now we realize it is right? In doing so, aren't we measuring our individual and social moral opinions against a moral standard that is independent of these opinions?

4. Relativists often appeal to the claim that (1) "Everyone has a right to his or her own opinion." But does this claim imply that (2) "Everyone's opinion is equally right"? What is the difference between the two claims? Could an objectivist be tolerant, respectful of the opinions of others, and believe in free speech by accepting claim 1 but still reject claim 2?

EXAMINING THE STRENGTHS AND WEAKNESSES OF ETHICAL OBJECTIVISM

Positive Evaluation

1. Is it possible to avoid having any objective moral principles at all? Is it possible to consistently live and defend relativism? Don't the relativists contradict themselves when they say, "You *should not* judge another person's or culture's morality"? Isn't this statement like saying, "You should never use the word *never*" or "You should always avoid the word *always*"? If you break a promise to a relativist or cheat him of what he is due, do you think he would accept your defense that he should not rebuke you because morality is simply a matter of opinion?

2. As long as there are at least two persons in the world, there will always be conflicts. But one of the purposes of morality is to provide an objective, rational, and impartial way to resolve conflicts. Doesn't relativism leave us without any basis for rationally resolving moral conflicts? If every person or society is allowed to embrace whatever morality pleases them or is convenient, isn't morality then useless?

Negative Evaluation

1. It is notoriously difficult to find agreement concerning what actions are right or wrong. Taking the issue one step back, it is also difficult to find agreement concerning what principles should be used to determine the rightness or wrongness of an action. There are facts about planets and stars that serve to confirm or refute our theories about them. But rightness or wrongness do not seem to be objective features of nature against which our moral theories can be tested. Unlike scientific inquiry, there are no meters, telescopes, or microscopes for observing and measuring the moral qualities of actions. Don't these considerations support the relativist's claim that morality is a function of opinions, attitudes, emotions, or social traditions rather than objective truth?

2. Even though other societies have moral codes very different from ours, many of them seem to flourish and provide a basis for human happiness. Doesn't the existence of such societies suggest that there are no moral absolutes but that morality is a matter of what works for a particular society?

5.2   ETHICAL EGOISM

 LEADING QUESTIONS: *Ethical Egoism*

1. Isn't it true that any goal that you take to be good and desirable is one that you will want to achieve? If so, then isn't any action that you count as good necessarily an action that will achieve a goal you desire? Doesn't this thinking imply that everything you consider to be morally good is that which satisfies a desire you have and serves your own ends? Are your ethics then based on selfish desires?

2. Suppose you had the choice of spending your life savings to save the life of the person you love versus spending it to save the lives of ten strangers. Which would you choose? Would it be selfish to save the life of the one person who matters to you personally instead of saving the lives of ten others? Would this choice be morally justified?

3. Is it always bad for people to be concerned only with serving their own interests? For example, you try to get the best score for yourself on a test. But if the test is graded on a curve, the better you do the worse others will do. Is there anything wrong with that? In business, each company is out to get the largest profits by capturing the market with the best product at the lowest price. But when companies seek to maximize their profits in this way, it creates the best results for the consumers. Isn't this good? Similarly, in a court of law, each lawyer promotes the best interests of his or her client, and we presume that this procedure will help ensure that all aspects of the case will be revealed. Isn't this good? If caring for others is a moral ideal, then shouldn't you *not* try to excel beyond your fellow students? Shouldn't companies seek to help their competitors? Shouldn't a lawyer help the opposition strengthen its case? Of course, all these suggestions for being a caring person are absurd. Don't these examples illustrate that, contrary to common opinion, serving your own interests can be not only morally acceptable, but even positively good?

As these questions suggest, the proper role of self-interest in life and in an ethical theory is an important topic in ethics. Philosophers debate whether selfishness is bad and even whether unselfishness is possible. These issues arise in Somerset Maugham's novel *Of Human Bondage*. In a Paris bar, Philip Carey and Cronshaw (two characters in the novel) are having a conversation. Philip expresses the belief that people sometimes act unselfishly and implies that it is a person's moral obligation to do so. This remark provides the opportunity for Cronshaw to expound his ethical philosophy.

Of Human Bondage[27]

"You will find as you grow older that the first thing needful to make the world a tolerable place to live in is to recognize the inevitable selfishness of humanity. You demand unselfishness from others, which is a preposterous claim that they should sacrifice their desires to yours. Why should they? When you are reconciled to the fact that each is for himself in the world you will ask less from your fellows. They will not disappoint you, and you will look upon them more charitably. Men seek but one thing in life—their pleasure." . . .

"Man performs actions because they are good for him, and when they are good for other people as well they are thought virtuous: if he finds pleasure in giving alms he is charitable; if he finds pleasure in helping others he is benevolent; if he finds pleasure in working for society he is public-spirited; but it is for your private pleasure that you give twopence to a beggar as much as it is for my private pleasure that I drink another whiskey and soda. I, less of a humbug than you, neither applaud myself for my pleasure nor demand your admiration."

Philip is horrified by his friend's egoistic philosophy and retorts, "But have you never known people do things they didn't want to instead of things they did?" To this Cronshaw replies:

"No. You put your question foolishly. What you mean is that people accept an immediate pain rather than an immediate pleasure. The objection is as foolish as your manner of putting it. It is clear that men accept an immediate pain rather than an immediate pleasure, but only because they expect a greater pleasure in the future. Often the pleasure is illusory, but their error in calculation is no refutation of the rule. You are puzzled because you cannot get over the idea that pleasures are only of the senses; but, child, a man who dies for his country dies because he likes it as surely as a man eats pickled cabbage because he likes it. It is a law of creation. If it were possible for men to prefer pain to pleasure the human race would have long since become extinct."

- Do you agree with Cronshaw's philosophy? Why?
- What reasons could be given to support it? On what basis could it be argued that his philosophy is false?
- Given his philosophy, how does Cronshaw explain the fact that people sometimes help one another, do what is painful, and even sacrifice their lives?

In the first two sentences of this passage, Cronshaw actually makes two claims. The first asserts the "inevitable selfishness of humanity." This comment is a psychological claim about human motivation that is known as **psychological egoism.** We examine this position shortly. What is of interest for the moment is the second

psychological egoism the theory that people always act so as to serve their own interests, or at least what they believe to be their interests

altruism the claim that we should be unselfishly concerned for the welfare of others and should act for the sake of other people's interests and needs

statement that it is "preposterous" to claim that people *should* sacrifice their desires for others. The position that Cronshaw is ridiculing here is known as **altruism,** which is the claim that we should be unselfishly concerned for the welfare of others and should act for the sake of other people's interests and needs. In contrast, Cronshaw is embracing *ethical egoism,* which is the position that people ought always to do only what is in their own self-interest. According to this position, all moral duties are ultimately duties to myself. Any supposed moral obligations I have toward others and society can only be justified if they enhance my own self-interest.

At first glance it may seem that the term *ethical egoism* is as contradictory as the term *married bachelor.* The term *egoism* is often associated with the qualities of being self-centered, selfish, egotistical, avaricious, and greedy. Egoism is condemned from the pulpit and denounced in newspaper editorials as the sanctuary of cynics, users, scoundrels, and manipulators. When baseball manager Leo Durocher said, "Nice guys finish last," there was no great rush to nominate him for the Nobel Peace Prize for humanitarian efforts. In the 1980s the media branded the youth of that time as the Me Generation because of their alleged disregard for any cause other than their own personal interests. Playing off the spirit of the times, a magazine called *Self* appeared on the scene. Best-selling books such as Robert Ringer's *Looking Out for #1* and David Seabury's *The Art of Selfishness* appealed to those seeking to rationalize the policy of "me first." The Sermon on the Mount says, "Blessed are the meek, for they will inherit the earth." However, to the egoist, the only thing the meek will inherit is the *dirt.* Given these popular conceptions of the position, isn't egoism antithetical to the very notion of ethics? Don't most ethical systems call us to rise above our own selfish interests to fulfill our duty or to serve the interests of others?

On the other hand, is self-love necessarily bad? After all, even the Bible commands that you should "love your neighbor as you love yourself." Even though it is calling for altruism, this ethical principle still makes self-love the paradigm for our attitude toward others. As I point out in the discussion to follow, ethical egoists maintain that their philosophy is maligned only because it is misunderstood. They claim either that all human behavior is motivated by self-interest or that if it is not, rationality dictates that it should be.

SURVEYING THE CASE FOR ETHICAL EGOISM

Some Common Misconceptions about Egoism

Before examining the arguments for ethical egoism, it will be worthwhile to first weed out some inaccurate conceptions of the position. First, it is sometimes thought that egoism says, "Do whatever you want to do." If so, how would it be possible for anyone ever to do what was morally wrong if doing what we want is sufficient to be ethical? This formulation of egoism must be incorrect, because the person who acts from altruistic motives is doing what he or she wants to do, but the egoist would say that acting in this way is morally mistaken. Furthermore, what you want to do at the moment may not be what is best for you. For example, your immediate desire may be to party all night instead of studying for a test. In this case, however, serving your own immediate desire is not in your best self-interest. Thus, acting on the basis of your self-interest may be different from acting on the basis of your desires.

Rather than urging us to gratify our *subjective* desires, ethical egoism says we ought to be concerned with our *objective* self-interest. But even if I always seek to serve my best interests, there is a difference between what I believe is in my self-interest and what genuinely is. I may believe that investing in a certain stock is in my self-interest, but I may be mistaken about this investment. For the egoist, therefore, miscalculation, ignorance, stupidity, and weakness of the will are obstacles to the morally fulfilled life, as they are for any ethics that is concerned with the objective consequences of our actions. Many of the immediate objections to ethical egoism can be disarmed once we realize that the most plausible versions of egoism are concerned with the long-term consequences of our actions and call for rational, enlightened self-interest, based on the best available knowledge about a person's self and circumstances.

STOP AND THINK

Can you think of a time in which you did what you wanted to do, seeking to fulfill some desire that you had, but it did not serve your best self-interest?

Another misconception of ethical egoism is to believe that we are never obligated to act in a way that will benefit other people or even to believe that it is always wrong to do so. However, seeking to serve my own interests does not necessarily lead to narrow-minded, selfish actions. To be successful in life, I probably need to have a good reputation and be liked by people so that they will be inclined to help me out and promote my interests. For example, if I am a successful businessperson, I could spend all my wealth on expensive cars, yachts, and jewelry. But if I donate a substantial amount of money to the local college, I may feel a sense of personal satisfaction, I will receive good publicity, and this public admiration will be good for my business. Egoism is primarily concerned with ends and not means. Hence, making others happy could be a means that serves the ends of my own interests. You often cannot identify an egoist by observing outward behavior alone; you must know something about the motive or moral theory that is the source of that person's behavior. Thus, a wise ethical egoist might find it rational to be pleasant toward others, help them out with their needs, give to charities, and so on. From the ethical egoist's perspective, however, the happiness we produce in others can only be incidental to what makes such actions morally right. The ethical egoist would

Egoism and Benevolence

Friedrich Nietzsche, a powerful spokesman for egoism, thought that the emotion of pity is despicable. Weak people pathetically affirm their own superiority by pitying someone more wretched than they are. In the following passage, however, he says that the noble human being (the egoist) can help the less fortunate, but only because the superior types have an abundance of psychological wealth, not because they need to feel good about themselves.

> In the foreground there is the feeling of fullness, of power that seeks to overflow, the happiness of high tension, the consciousness of wealth that would give and bestow: the noble human being, too, helps the unfortunate, but not, or almost not, from pity, but prompted more by an urge begotten by excess of power.[28]

Similarly, Ayn Rand (a contemporary advocate of egoism) said that the egoist who values his own self can value the potential and humanity in others and even help a stranger in an emergency as long as he makes no significant sacrifice of his own interests.

> The moral purpose of a man's life is the achievement of his own happiness. This does not mean that he is indifferent to all men, that human life is of no value to him and that he has no reason to help others in an emergency. But it *does* mean that he does not subordinate his life to the welfare of others, that he does not sacrifice himself to their needs, that the relief of their suffering is not his primary concern, that any help he gives is an *exception,* not a rule, an act of generosity, not of moral duty, that it is *marginal* and *incidental*—as disasters are marginal and incidental in the course of human existence—and that *values,* not disasters, are the goal, the first concern and the motive power of his life.[29]

have to say that altruistic actions are morally justified only if they ultimately serve our self-interest in the long run.

 STOP AND THINK

Can you think of a time in which you acted in a way that benefited others but you were actually benefiting yourself in doing so?

Finally, it is a mistake to suppose that an advocate of ethical egoism is necessarily an *egotist.* Egotism is a personality trait and not an ethical theory. The egotist is someone who always wants to be the center of attention and who is a pushy, narcissistic, self-promoting person with an inflated ego. Such people tend to be irritating and obnoxious and are rarely successful in winning friends and influencing people. Paradoxically, the egotist is unlikely to be successful at living out the philosophy of egoism. Hence, an enlightened egoist can be charming, amiable,

modest, and considerate of others if exhibiting these traits are to his or her advantage in the long run.

The Varieties of Ethical Egoism

Several types of ethical egoism need to be distinguished before we can analyze the philosophy in detail. First, a person who embraces *personal ethical egoism* makes the following claim: "As for me, I believe I ought to always act in ways that will maximize my self-interest, but I have no opinion about how you should act." This expression is of a personal policy, but it is not a theory about what makes an action morally right for anyone (other than the speaker). As such, it does not make an impersonal, objective claim about the nature of moral obligation that solicits our acceptance. Consequently, this claim is incapable of either defense or refutation. The only response to be made to this position is, "Thank you for sharing that with me."

On the other hand, if I were someone who advocates *individual ethical egoism* I would make the following claim: "The morally right act is the one that serves the interests of *me* (the author of this book)." According to this position, for you to be a moral person, whenever you act you should always ask, "How will this action benefit the author of my philosophy book?" Of course, this form of egoism is absurd and grotesque, and no one is likely to take it very seriously. If morality is dependent on how an action affects *me,* then before I was born there were no moral obligations and after I die morality would come to an end, because before and after I existed no action would produce any harm or benefit to me. Furthermore, this position is indefensible, for how could I make the case that I am so special that everyone ought to always serve my individual interests? Although some people may practice individual ethical egoism, it lacks the impartiality and universal appeal that is necessary to be a credible ethical theory.

The only version of ethical egoism that has any hope of persuading anyone is *universal ethical egoism.* Whereas the individual ethical egoist says, "Every person ought to do only what will further *my* interests," the universal ethical egoist says, "Every person ought to do only what will further *his or her own* interests." In other words, this position claims that when *anyone* acts (not just the speaker) the standard of right action is that person's own interests, whoever that person may be. Accordingly, this position has the impartiality and universal appeal that is necessary for a

full-fledged ethical theory. To express this position figuratively, the supreme principle of morality is that "You should cultivate your garden and I should cultivate mine." Now that we have concluded that universal ethical egoism is the only version of egoism that should be taken seriously, our next task is to examine it further by considering some important issues raised by this position.

Selfishness, Self-Interest, and Others

In ordinary usage, there is a difference between the terms *selfish* and *self-interest* when applied to motives or behavior.[30] Examples of selfish behavior would be acting to benefit myself with no regard for the harm others may suffer from my actions, or acting unfairly to gain an advantage for myself while depriving others of what they are due. However, the fact that I am acting for the sake of my own self-interest does not *necessarily* mean I am being selfish in these ways. If I exercise regularly for the sake of my health, I am acting in my own self-interest, but I am not acting selfishly.

How do ethical egoists define *self-interest*? Some egoists define self-interest in terms of pleasure. However, we should not think that they are talking only about raw, physical pleasure. There are, for example, also intellectual pleasures, the pleasures of enjoying great art, and the pleasures of friendship. The position that claims that pleasure is the only thing that has value is known as **hedonism.** (I discuss hedonism more fully in section 5.3, "Utilitarianism.") However, other egoists think

hedonism the position that pleasure is the only thing that has value that pleasure is too narrow a notion to define self-interest; they speak more broadly in terms of happiness or self-realization. Hence, for the purposes of our discussion, we will consider "acting in our self-interest" in the broadest possible way as the rational pursuit of those ends that will contribute to our personal happiness, to the achievement of the good life for ourselves, or to the maximization of our own good and well-being.

You may be inclined to think that it is impossible for an egoist to have friends or to love someone, since friendship and love often require a certain measure of self-sacrifice. In her book *The Virtue of Selfishness: A New Concept of Egoism,* Ayn Rand argues that a true sacrifice is "the surrender of a greater value for the sake of a lesser one or of a nonvalue." Obviously, this sacrifice is not something an egoist would do. However, because Rand does not think that love necessarily involves sacrifice, she finds no incompatibility between being a rational, consistent egoist and a lover. She says that, contrary to the ethics of sacrifice, the egoist is a "trader." When the egoist's actions benefit someone else at some cost to himself, he is not making a sacrifice but an exchange: he is exchanging something that has lesser value to obtain some end that has more value for him. Hence, the soldier who is willing to die fighting for the cause of freedom does so because it is in his interest to risk death rather than live in a dictatorship. Similarly, Rand says that genuine love is not self-sacrificing because it involves valuing another person who exemplifies the values and qualities we cherish in ourselves.

> Love and friendship are profoundly personal, selfish values: love is an expression and assertion of self-esteem, a response to one's own values in the person of another. One gains a profoundly personal, selfish joy from the mere existence of the person one loves. It is one's own personal, selfish happiness that one seeks, earns and derives from love.[31]

 STOP AND THINK

Do you agree with Rand's theory of love? Does it describe what most people think of as love? Does it describe what actually motivates people to fall in love? What could be said in favor of her view? How might someone criticize her account of love?

Rand goes on to give the example of a man who passionately loves his wife and spends a fortune to cure her of a serious disease. According to Rand, this example is a paradigm of egoistic (and thus moral) behavior because the wife's companionship is of greater value to the man than is his money. As she puts it, "It would be absurd to claim that he does it as a 'sacrifice' for *her* sake, not his own, and that it makes no difference to *him,* personally and selfishly, whether she lives or dies."[32] In contrast, Rand claims that if it were possible to use that money to save the lives of ten other women who meant nothing to him as opposed to saving his wife, the morality of altruism would obligate him to choose this unselfish alternative. Having clarified some of the main themes in ethical egoism, we now consider three arguments that are used to support it.

Argument 1: Psychological Egoism

Recall the opening passage from *Of Human Bondage,* where Cronshaw expressed his belief in the "inevitable selfishness of humanity" and went on to say that "Man performs actions because they are good for him." I said that this comment was an expression of psychological egoism. *Psychological egoism* is the theory that, as a matter of fact, people always act so as to serve their own interests (or at least, what they believe to be their interests). In other words, rather than claiming that altruism is simply misguided, the psychological egoist claims that human nature makes it impossible. According to this view, all apparently altruistic or self-sacrificing behavior is really a disguised egoism that serves the interests of the agent. Notice that this theory is a *psychological* theory about people's motives, inclinations, or dispositions. As such, it is not an *ethical* theory, for it does not *prescribe* how we *ought* to act but only purports to *describe* how we *do* act. In other words, psychological egoism expresses a factual statement, whereas ethical egoism establishes an ethical standard. Even though the two positions are making different claims and even though one is a psychological theory and the other an ethical theory, the fact remains that psychological egoism is frequently used to support ethical egoism. As Cronshaw argued, since the laws of nature dictate that humans inevitably serve only their own interests, it is preposterous to suppose that they have a moral obligation to do anything else but that.

 STOP AND THINK

Can you think of a time in which you (or someone else), contrary to psychological egoism, genuinely sacrificed self-interest for the sake of another person's good? Or do you agree with the psychological egoist that such a sacrifice can never happen?

The argument for ethical egoism that is currently being considered is based not only on the thesis of psychological egoism, but also on the principle that "ought" implies "can." (Immanuel Kant is the philosopher who made this principle prominent in ethical theory.) In other words, I cannot have a moral obligation to do something if it is impossible to do it. For example, I cannot have an obligation to swim to save a drowning child if I am unable to swim.

The argument can be formulated in the following way:

1. I have a moral obligation to perform an action only if I am able to do it. (Ought implies can)
2. I am able to perform an action only if I do it to maximize my own self-interest. (Psychological egoism)

Therefore

3. I have a moral obligation to perform an action only if I do it to maximize my own self-interest.

Therefore

4. Ethical egoism is true.

The part of the argument that requires the closest scrutiny is premise 2, which assumes psychological egoism. First, it seems strange to conclude that I have an obligation to always act on the basis of my self-interest if (as premise 2 states) I am incapable of doing otherwise. It is like saying "You have a moral obligation to blink when an object approaches your eye" or "You have a moral obligation to grow hair on your head." Since under normal circumstances these results are inevitable, it seems superfluous to include them within the realm of morality. Morality has to do with choices that we are free to make or not make, not with what we will do no matter what. Notice that it is precisely for this reason that the hard determinist claims that we do not have moral responsibility (see the discussion of hard determinism in 3.6 and 3.7).

A second major problem with psychological egoism is the abundant counter-examples against it. People sometimes seem to have a clear-headed understanding of what is in their best self-interest but still act contrary to it. For example, many smokers know that their habit is causing their health to deteriorate but make no effort to change their behavior. Furthermore, it seems that if psychological egoism is true, then no one would ever act unselfishly, benevolently, or altruistically, but obviously people do act this way. A sister will donate one of her kidneys to a sibling who needs it, people will give money to a charity rather than spend it on themselves, and a soldier will sacrifice his life in war for the sake of his country.

In reply to the self-destructive behavior, the psychological egoist might say that smokers have an abstract understanding of the dangers of smoking but still believe that the stimulation and psychological benefits of nicotine are of such advantage to them that it is worth the risk. To say that we always act from the motive of maximizing our self-interest does not mean that we always correctly calculate what is best for us.

In addressing the benevolent behavior, the psychological egoist recognizes that people often act in a way that serves the interests of others but denies that they do it *for the sake of others.* In other words, even when your actions benefit someone else, you are not doing it from a benevolent motive (it is claimed), but you are doing it to serve your own interests (in some way). This point is illustrated by Robert Ringer's remarks on the great social reformer Mahatma Gandhi in *Looking Out for #1.*

> Can I honestly say that I believe Gandhi was acting selfishly when he "sacrificed" himself for the freedom of the Indian people? No, I can't say that I believe it. It would be more proper to say that I know it for a fact. . . . Whatever Gandhi did, out of rational or irrational choice, he did because he chose to do it. . . . Martyrs are selfish people—the same as you and me—but with insatiable egos.[33]

It is clear that psychological egoists must claim that there is an ulterior, self-centered motive behind every allegedly benevolent action. They must even dogmatically insist that when we sincerely believe we are acting for the sake of others, we are really self-deceived about our true, egoistic motives. This position is implausible, however, because it collapses important distinctions between radically different types of behavior. According to this position, both the college student who spends his weekends partying and the one who spends them donating her labor to build homes for the poor are really acting for themselves. If psychological egoism is true, then there is no difference between the sadist and the saint, or the coward and the hero. The problem is not simply that it is objectionable to view the sadist and the saint as similiar but that it is dubious to suppose that they are operating from the same motive.

An argument to support psychological egoism could be formulated in the following manner. In examining this argument, try to decide which of the premises is the weakest.

1. Whenever we act we are always trying to achieve some goal that we desire.
2. Whenever we achieve some goal that we desire, we obtain personal satisfaction.
3. So, whenever we act we are always trying to obtain personal satisfaction.
4. Obtaining personal satisfaction serves our self-interest.
5. Therefore, whenever we act we are always trying to serve our self-interest.

Bishop Butler (1692–1752), a clergyman and famous essayist on ethics, wrote a classic refutation of this argument. He pointed out that just because a person desires something does not mean that the persons's own satisfaction is the object of that desire. For example, if I desire a cold drink, then it is true that my own physical pleasure is the ultimate object of that desire. But if I desire to delight my friend with an unexpected gift, the object of the desire is my friend's happiness. So the problem with the argument is in premise 3. It is true that we usually feel a sense of satisfaction when we get what we desire, but the personal satisfaction is often the consequence of getting what we desire, not its goal. I could not get a sense of satisfaction from making my friend happy if I did not have a prior concern for the welfare of my friend for her own sake.

These points touch on what is sometimes called the "paradox of hedonism." If we pursue pleasure (or more generally, happiness) as our all-consuming goal, we'll probably have a hard time finding it. As the following thought experiment illustrates, happiness usually comes to us as a by-product of pursuing other goals that we value.

 THOUGHT EXPERIMENT

The Pursuit of Pleasure

Have you ever been in a state of mind in which you were desperate to have fun at all costs? You had a rough week, but it is now Friday night and you are at a party. The entire

(Continued . . .)

(. . . continued)

evening you keep saying, "I hope I have a good time! Am I having a good time yet? I'll be crushed if the evening ends and I didn't have a good time. I just HAVE to have a good time!" Every time you talk to someone or dance to the music, you are constantly measuring your pleasure quotient on some sort of internal scale. Each moment you are at the party, you are worried that there is someone else you should be talking to or something else you could do to maximize the pleasure of the moment. This pathetic drive for pleasure, of course, is likely to be counterproductive. If you had relaxed and taken things as they came, you might have met some new and interesting people, participated in good conversations, and enjoyed the music, all without worrying about whether each action would adequately maximize your self-interest. When we cease to be frantically obsessed with our own pleasure, we often look back on the day's events after they are over and suddenly notice that we had a good time and really enjoyed what we had been doing. While pleasure and happiness are important ingredients in life, they often are the indirect rewards for pursuing other things that have value, such as friendships, intellectual challenges, political causes, artistic endeavors, participation in sports, nature walks, and humanitarian projects.

- Can you think of actual events in your own life when the direct pursuit of pleasure failed, but the pursuit of other goals brought personal satisfaction as a result?

Contemporary philosopher Joel Feinberg exposes a fundamental problem with psychological egoism through the following dialogue:

"All men desire only satisfaction."

"Satisfaction of what?"

"Satisfaction of their desires."

"Their desires for what?"

"Their desires for satisfaction."

"Satisfaction of what?"

"Their desires."

"For what?"

"For satisfaction"—etc., ad infinitum.[34]

In the final analysis, the relationship between psychological and ethical egoism does not seem to be tight enough to claim that one logically implies the other. On the one hand, a person could be a psychological egoist without being an ethical egoist. The Christian philosopher Augustine (354–430), for example, was a psychological egoist because he believed that our natural inclination was always to serve our own selfish ends instead of serving God. However, he was not an ethical egoist because he added that our psychological nature was corrupted by sin and only through divine grace could we rise above our egoism and be empowered to do what we ought to do. On the other hand, a person could be an ethical egoist without being a psychological egoist. The contemporary writer Ayn Rand was an ethical egoist because she believed that "the moral purpose of a man's life is the achievement of his own happiness." But Rand was not a psychological egoist, because she believed that the majority of people are muddle-headed altruists who do not behave egoistically at all. This belief is illustrated by her claim that the practice of altruism is the source of society's ills: "For a view of the nature of altruism, its consequences and the enormity of the moral corruption it perpetrates, I shall refer you to . . . any of today's newspaper headlines."[35]

Argument 2: Egoism Leads to the Best Society

Ethical egoists sometimes argue that if we were all egoists, things would be a whole lot better for everyone. The economist Adam Smith (1723–1790) argued that in a competitive, free-enterprise economic system, people try to enhance their own wealth by producing the best product at a lower price than the competitors do. Although everyone is motivated by his or her own self-interest and is not consciously trying to serve the overall good, the "invisible hand" of marketplace dynamics creates the best situation for consumers. Even if we would grant that this economic system is the best, however, some critics question whether you can apply principles that work in business transactions to the ethics of personal relations. Nevertheless, the marketplace does provide examples of how serving self-interest can also serve the greater good.

Similarly, in the following passage Ayn Rand argues that we have two choices: (1) embrace "rational selfishness," which will cause society to flourish or (2) embrace altruism, which will lead to the destruction of all that is worthwhile in society.

> It is only on the basis of rational selfishness—on the basis of justice—that men can be fit to live together in a free, peaceful, prosperous, benevolent, *rational* society. . . .
>
> It is philosophy that sets men's goals and determines their course; it is only philosophy that can save them now. Today, the world is facing a choice: if civilization is to survive, it is the altruist morality that men have to reject.[36]

To be fair to Rand, she would argue that the good of society is an *effect* of everyone adopting rational selfishness, but it is not the *reason* for adopting it. While Rand doesn't rest her case for egoism on its social benefits, she does claim there is a perfect harmony between selfishness and the social good.

The problem with the "good of society" argument is that it is paradoxical. Although the argument is used to defend ethical egoism, it actually undermines it. The argument seems to be saying that we should pursue our own self-interest, because doing so will lead to the greatest good for the greatest number. But if we are egoists, why should we be concerned with the greatest good of society? In essence, this second argument for ethical egoism actually claims that everyone pursuing his or her own interests is a *means* to the *end* of the general happiness of the many. As we see in the next section, the principle that we should maximize the greatest happiness for the greatest number of people is the fundamental ethical principle of utilitarianism. But utilitarianism is decidedly different from egoism, for it allows each individual's self-interest to count only as one vote to be tallied along with the interests of others. Furthermore, it hardly seems plausible to suppose that what is good for me or what is good for you will always neatly line up with what is good for society as a whole, as Rand and others suppose. On the contrary, it seems possible that an action that would maximize my self-interest could be harmful to the rest of humanity. For example, I could build a factory that would bring me enormous profits but would deplete the natural resources and cause pollution problems in the long run. If the cumulative, negative effects on the environment would not be felt in my lifetime, then they would not affect my self-interest.

Argument 3: Egoism Is the Ultimate Ethical Principle

The first argument for ethical egoism makes a questionable inference from an equally questionable psychological theory, and the second argument justifies egoism by appealing to nonegoistic ends. The third argument avoids these problems by claiming that if we are truly rational persons, we will realize that self-interest is a fundamental, irreducible value that is the source of all other values.

AYN RAND
(1905–1982)

This argument was forcefully articulated in the writings of Ayn Rand (1905–1982). Although Rand grew up in Russia, she rebelled against what she perceived as the excessive governmental tyranny and disintegration of free inquiry that followed the communist revolution. In 1926 she escaped to America and began her career as a Hollywood screenwriter. Throughout her life, she defended both ethical egoism and capitalism in her essays and literary works. Among her best-known novels are *We the Living* (1936), *The Fountainhead* (1943), and *Atlas Shrugged* (1959). Rand called her personal philosophy *Objectivism*. All ethical egoists are ethical objectivists, because they affirm that there are ethical principles that are universal. However, the reverse is not true, because most ethical objectivists do not embrace egoism. To avoid confusion concerning this terminology, when I use the term *objectivism* in this text, I am referring to the more general category, but when Rand uses the term, she is referring specifically to her version of ethical egoism. In the following passage, Rand argues that egoism is the ultimate ethical principle.

FROM AYN RAND
The Virtue of Selfishness [37]

An *ultimate* value is that final goal or end to which all lesser goals are the means—and it sets the standard by which all lesser goals are *evaluated.* An organism's life is its *standard of value:* that which furthers its life is the *good,* that which threatens it is the *evil.* . . .

The Objectivist ethics holds man's life as the *standard* of value—and *his own life* as the ethical *purpose* of every individual man. . . .

Value is that which one acts to gain and/or keep—*virtue* is the act by which one gains and/or keeps it. The three cardinal values of the Objectivist ethics—the three values which, together, are the means to and the realization of one's ultimate value, one's own life—are: Reason, Purpose, Self-Esteem, with their three corresponding virtues: Rationality, Productiveness, Pride. . . .

[Altruism is] the ethical theory which regards man as a sacrificial animal, which holds that man has no right to exist for his own sake, that service to others is the only justification of his existence, and that self-sacrifice is his highest moral duty, virtue and value.

Rand's argument could be formulated in the following way:

1. There can be no higher value than our own life, for without it, there could be no other values.
2. "Our own life" includes more than biological survival; it also includes our interests, projects, and the goods we earn and create for ourselves, for without these factors we would have no life worth living.
3. Rationality is the basic instrument for human survival, since we cannot live according to instinct as do animals.
4. Altruism, the opposite of egoism, is irrational, because it destroys the value of our life and thereby undermines the only basis for value in our life.
5. Ethical egoism affirms the right of each of us to make our life the ultimate value and thereby makes it possible for us to pursue any values at all.
6. Therefore, ethical egoism is the only rationally defensible ethical theory.

Notice that Rand assumes a false dichotomy between pure ethical egoism and pure ethical altruism.* Because the form of altruism she describes is so extreme, however, egoism seems like the only rational choice. For example, an empty-headed altruist might embrace the foolish principle, "Never spend money on your own health care, but always use what money you have for the health of others." But if I followed this principle, I would always have to provide money for your health care and never spend it on mine. Furthermore, if you followed this principle, you would have to take the money I gave you and spend it on someone else. Finally, if everyone followed this principle, no one would be able to get any health care. But contrary to what Rand supposes, rejecting her ethical egoism does not require us to be extreme altruists. It is morally right for me to make sure my reasonable needs and those of my family are taken care of before I tend to the needs of others (rejection of pure altruism). This moral right, however, does not mean that I have no obligation whatsoever to sacrifice some of my trivial needs or desires when possible in order to help provide for the life, health, and basic well-being of my fellow human beings (rejection of pure egoism).

> ### STOP AND THINK
>
> Can you think of a situation in which it would be morally justified to serve your own interests even if it required sacrificing someone else's interests or even if it indirectly
>
> *(Continued . . .)*

---

*See the discussion of the false dichotomy fallacy in section 1.2, "Argument and Evidence."

(. . . continued)

resulted in harm to someone else? Suppose, for example, that the only way you could save your own life would be if you allowed another innocent person to die. (Think of the Titanic, which did not have enough lifeboats for everyone.) Could a nonegoist justify this action? Why? Are there less extreme situations in which you would be morally justified to serve your own interests at the expense of someone else's interests? Could there be any situations in which serving your own interests at the expense of another's would not be justified?

Egoism and the Conflict of Interests

Some critics of ethical egoism argue that it is contradictory for me to seek to serve my own interests and not yours at the same time that I claim that others ought to seek their own interests and not mine. If I am an egoist, why would I advise you to seek any interests other than my own? However, this criticism may not be as problematic as it appears at first. For example, if I am a skilled runner who loves the excitement of competition, I will wish that I win the race at the same time that I wish for you to do your best to win the race. If I found out that my manager had bribed the other runners to allow me to win, I would be robbed of the thrill of victory. Hence, there is a difference between what I believe you ought to do and the actual outcome I desire. (I believe that if you are rational you should try to win the race, but I desire that you will be unsuccessful.)

A critic of egoism could reply to this example by saying that a race is a rather limited domain of human action and the ethical principles that work in an athletic competition may not be applicable to life in general. In the serious issues in life it seems that there can be irreconcilable conflicts of interest between people. Ethical egoism, unlike other theories, offers us no impartial way to resolve these conflicts. However, Rand argues that ethical egoism "holds that the *rational* interests of men do not clash—that there is no conflict of interests among men who do not desire the unearned, who do not make sacrifices nor accept them, who deal with one another as *traders,* giving value for value."[38] She describes a trader as "a man who earns what he gets and does not give or take the undeserved. . . . He deals with men by means of a free, voluntary, unforced, uncoerced exchange—an exchange which benefits both parties by their own independent judgment."[39] However, it is not clear that her hero, the trader, is a thoroughgoing egoist. It seems that he is a trader whose pursuit of self-interest is constrained by principles of impartiality and fairness. Rand's deviation from pure egoism becomes clear in the following example.

Suppose you and I are both pursuing the same job. If I am an ethical egoist and *if I knew I could get away with it,* don't I have the obligation to do whatever is necessary to ensure that I get the job? For example, I could spread malicious rumors about you, snatch your job application out of the mailbox, or secretly slip you a drug so that you are a babbling idiot during the interview. In other words, this ethical stance would lead to the same behavior championed by Glaucon at the beginning of this chapter. In discussing this example, however, Rand indicates that this behavior would be wrong, for it ignores the key considerations of reality, context, responsibility, and effort.[40] Here is a summary of her discussion. (1) *Reality:* The mere fact that I want the job does not mean that I am entitled to it or deserve it. (2) *Context:* For me to have a job there has to be a successful business to hire me, and a business can only be successful if it can and does choose the best candidate among a pool of competitors. (3) *Responsibility:* If I seek something I desire, I have to take responsibility for all the conditions that are required to fulfill that desire. (4) *Effort:* Rational people know that they only have a right to that which they have earned or deserve.

Rand certainly embraces a more attractive version of egoism than a vicious egoism in which people are allowed to seek their own ends while robbing others of what they deserve. However, critics claim that the degree to which her egoism is attractive is the degree to which she subordinates self-interest to the principles of rational consistency, impartiality, fairness, and justice. When she starts to work out the practical implications of her ethical egoism, it begins to sound more like Kantian ethics than egoism.* Even though getting a particular job may be in my best interests, Rand says it would be irrational for me to pursue it or even desire it if you are better qualified. Critics, however, question whether this conclusion is consistent with her egoism. Rand may be correct that the world would be better if people were *generally* rewarded according to their merit, but that could be consistent with me wanting to make myself the exception to the rule. She could object that my exception would violate the ideals of impartiality and rational consistency. But being guided by these ideals would require us to abandon the main thesis of egoism, because the principles of impartiality and rational consistency imply that we should not serve our individual interests with total disregard for the interests of others, particularly if there are no significant differences between ourselves and others or if the differences are not due to our own efforts. For example, many people have achieved much of what they have in life through their own effort and merit. But many of these same people have also had the good fortune to be born with good health, in a good family, and in a prosperous society. While it is right that they should receive the just rewards of their efforts, it is also irrational for them to suppose that they may smugly enjoy the fruits of the good fortune that they did not earn with no regard for the suffering of others, when the less fortunate may have done nothing to deserve their lot in life.

 THOUGHT EXPERIMENT

What Are the Implications of Ethical Egoism?

Some critics say that ethical egoism is unacceptable because it would justify clearly immoral actions. For example, critics charge that the ethical egoist would have to say that it

(Continued . . .)

---

*See the discussion of Kantian ethics in section 5.4 of this chapter.

(. . . continued)

would be morally wrong for the plantation owners in the 1840s to have freed their slaves or even to have treated them as fellow human beings, since it would be against the plantation owners' self-interest. On the other hand, Rand claims that, according to rational ethical egoism, slavery and racial discrimination are wrong because there could be no such thing as a "right" to enslave other people or to violate their individual rights.[41]

- Who is correct (the critics or Rand) concerning what is logically implied by egoism?

LOOKING THROUGH THE EGOIST'S LENS

1. How might an ethical egoistic justify performing the following actions? (a) Refusing to cheat on a test, even if you could get away with it; (b) helping your neighbor move some furniture; (c) diminishing your profits by giving your most productive employees a raise; (d) saving the life of the person you love at great risk to yourself.

2. The psychological egoist claims that we are all selfish. However, Rand (who is an ethical egoist but not a psychological egoist) says that while we *should* be selfish, most people are altruists. She points out, for example, that the word *selfishness* is identified with evil in popular usage. Furthermore, she complains that the well-accepted government programs of appropriating everyone's tax dollars and using them for the common good in education, health, and welfare show that our society consists primarily of brainwashed altruists. Do you agree with Rand that very few people in our society are rational egoists? Or do you think that egoism is fairly prevalent?

3. As little children we are taught to behave ethically for selfish reasons. Mother says, "If you want your friend to share her toys with you, you must share your toys with her." Furthermore, we are rewarded or praised if we are good and punished or scolded if we are bad. Popular television evangelists preach that following their precepts will bring personal success, prosperity, and health. Does selfishness play more of a role in our ethical life than most people would like to admit?

EXAMINING THE STRENGTHS AND WEAKNESSES OF EGOISM

Positive Evaluation

1. Is self-love or serving your own interests over those of others necessarily wrong? Isn't it right for you to spend the money you earned on your tuition as opposed to distributing it among others? The American Declaration of Independence says we have unalienable rights that include life, liberty, and the pursuit of happiness. Aren't these rights egoistic concerns? The document doesn't guarantee the right of everybody to be happy, nor does it say that you have an obligation to

secure other people's happiness. Instead, it says you have a right to pursue your own happiness.

2. I am the best judge of my own wants and needs and you are the best judge of yours. Each of us is also in the best position to pursue our own wants and needs effectively. On the other hand, when others try to do what they think is "best" for us, they often end up being intrusive and making a mess of things. Furthermore, when I consider other's needs more important than my own, am I not showing a lack of self-esteem? Doesn't altruism also show a lack of respect for others by treating them as helpless beggars who are dependent on me for their well-being? Isn't charity degrading to the recipients, treating them as too incompetent to look after their own interests? Isn't it a healthier ethics to place the highest value on my own self and interests and to give others the dignity and the right to pursue their interests? What do you think?

3. The Golden Rule says, "Do unto others as you would have them do unto you." Doesn't this rule imply that the reason to treat others decently is that it is to your advantage to do so, because they will be more inclined to treat you decently? Isn't the primary reason for being honest, keeping promises, and fulfilling the other demands of morality the fact that it will be in your best interests to act this way? Isn't egoism really the basis of our commonsense morality?

Negative Evaluation

1. Ethical egoists often present a choice between pure egoism (being concerned exclusively with our own interests) and pure altruism (being concerned exclusively with others' interests). Because a policy of always sacrificing our own interests is untenable, ethical egoism seems to win out by default. But isn't this argument a false dichotomy? Wouldn't a more defensible ethical theory attempt to balance our own interests with those of others?

2. Suppose you and I are only casual acquaintances who are stranded in a lifeboat in the ocean and are waiting for rescuers to find us. I have managed to bring along a quantity of food and water, but you have none. Suppose further that you are an ethical egoist. What moral advice should you give me? If you tell me that I only have an obligation to serve my own interests, then I should keep the food and water for myself and let you die. On the other hand, if you want to live, then you will tell me that I have a moral obligation to sacrifice some of my resources for your sake. But this statement would require you to renounce your ethical egoism. Does this scenario show that it is impossible to consistently live and promote ethical egoism? How might an ethical egoist respond?

3. Harvard philosopher John Rawls proposes the following thought experiment for deciding what would be the most rational and impartial principles for governing society.[42] Suppose that you had the ability to determine what sort of society you would live in and what principles will guide it. Of course, if you are a brown-eyed, female athlete named Kisha, you might like a society that gives the most benefits

to brown-eyed, female athletes named Kisha. Such a society, however, would hardly be a defensible social structure to choose, for it is not based on rational and impartial considerations. To guarantee that your choices will be rational and impartial, Rawls says you must choose behind the "veil of ignorance." You must choose your society without knowing your race, sex, natural abilities, religion, interests, social position, income, or physical and psychological makeup. Not knowing if you would be poor, disabled, or lacking in natural abilities, would you choose a society based on egoism in which all members look out for themselves? Or would you choose a society that offered some degree of altruistic concern for the least advantaged?

4. Most people consider racism and sexism to be unacceptable policies because they arbitrarily advocate treating some individuals differently without justification. In the following argument, contemporary philosopher James Rachels claims that ethical egoism is similarly an arbitrary and unacceptable doctrine:

1. Any moral doctrine that assigns greater importance to the interests of one group than to those of another is unacceptably arbitrary unless there is some difference between the members of the groups that justifies treating them differently.
2. Ethical Egoism would have each person assign greater importance to his or her own interests than to the interests of others. *But there is no general difference between oneself and others, to which each person can appeal, that justifies this difference in treatment.*
3. Therefore, Ethical Egoism is unacceptably arbitrary.[43]

Is Rachels's argument a decisive refutation? How might an ethical egoist respond?

5.3 UTILITARIANISM

LEADING QUESTIONS: UTILITARIANISM

1. Suppose I told you that it is your moral obligation to submit to a procedure that would cause you pain. Your natural reply would be, "Why do I have a moral duty to endure pain?" But suppose I then explained that your body has a one-in-a-million biochemical property such that a painful medical procedure would cause your body to produce antibodies that could be used to save the lives of hundreds of little children who are stricken with a rare and fatal disease. Does my explanation of the consequences of this action clarify why I claimed that you had a moral duty to endure the painful procedure? Similarly, aren't all our moral obligations and duties meant to lead to actions that result in the best overall consequences? Would it make any sense to say that some of our moral duties have no good effects, but only cause human misery? Aren't the consequences of an action what determines its rightness or wrongness?

2. Most people would say that it would usually be morally wrong to act in a way that violated any of the following rules: (1) tell the truth, (2) keep your promises, (3) do not kill innocent persons. Can you think of situations in which you would be morally justified to break each of those rules if doing so would create

an enormous amount of good for humanity but if adhering to the rule would create an enormous amount of human unhappiness and suffering? Are there any actions that we normally think are wrong that could not be justified in certain situations? Are moral rules anything more than "rules of thumb"?

The first leading question suggests that moral duties have a purpose. It supposes that the principle "do your duty for duty's sake" makes no sense if fulfilling an alleged moral obligation neither avoids some harm nor results in some good. The second question suggests that common moral commands are rules of thumb that produce desirable results in most cases, but they can be overridden when the circumstances and consequences require it. For example, consider the following three situations, corresponding to each of the moral rules that were listed. (1) A homicidal maniac with an axe asks you where he can find your friend. By lying to him you will save your friend and facilitate the murderer's capture. (2) You promised to help someone review for a test, but you fail to keep the promise because you suddenly have to drive an injured person to the emergency room. (3) You are fighting a just war against an evil tyrant who has murdered thousands of innocent victims in a bordering country. If a chemical warfare factory is bombed, it will save the lives of thousands of innocent civilians, but you know that three innocent people living near the factory will perish. Regardless of whether you agree with the action taken in all these cases, you are forced to think hard about the question, Does the end justify the means? The philosophers we study in this section would reply, "If the end doesn't justify the means, there is nothing else that could!" To further test your intuitions on the relationship between moral duties and consequences, consider the following thought experiment.

Compare your response in the thought experiment to the following three decisions and justifications. Which one comes closest to the answer you gave?

 THOUGHT EXPERIMENT

The Promise

You and a friend have been shipwrecked on a desert island. Only a limited amount of food remains and it is doubtful that it will keep both of you alive until you are rescued. Since your friend is injured, it is unlikely that he will survive. He tells you that you can have all the food, but makes you promise that you will see to it that his nephew gets the millions of dollars in treasure that your friend discovered. You promise him you will do exactly as he requested. A few days later your friend dies, happy in the knowledge that you will carry out his last wish. After you are rescued, you seek to fulfill your promise by looking up the man's nephew (his only living relative). However, you are dismayed to find out that the nephew is living an extravagant and wasteful life consisting of drug abuse and huge gambling losses. You realize that if you keep your promise, it would not take long for the nephew to squander the entire fortune on his self-destructive and dissipated lifestyle. You are fairly sure that your friend knew the life his nephew was leading. As you are consider-

(Continued . . .)

(. . . continued)

ing what to do, you notice an advertisement for a famous children's hospital that does research on childhood diseases such as leukemia and rare forms of cancer. If you gave the money to the hospital, it could be used to alleviate the suffering of many little children as well as fund research to prevent future suffering. Since your friend is dead, you are the only one who knows about the money and the promise. What should you do with the money? Why would your choice be the right thing to do?

Randy: I would keep the money for myself. Although my friend found the treasure, I helped him die a peaceful death, so it is morally right that I should have it. Why should I hand over any of the money to that worthless nephew? I don't even know him, and furthermore, he would only waste the money, whereas I could use it pay to for worthwhile things such as my education. Any promises I made to my friend became null and void when he died. It's unfortunate that children are dying, but I don't know them either and have no obligations toward them. I can't save the world, but I do have an obligation to do what is best for me.

Millard: I would give the money to the children's hospital or some other worthy cause. This action is morally right because it would produce the best consequences for the greatest number of people. Of course, the nephew will be deprived of the money, but he didn't know it had been promised to him anyway. Besides, he probably would have used the money in self-destructive ways, so I would actually be doing him some good by saving him from self-inflicted harm. Since my friend is dead, it would have no impact on him whether I kept my promise or how I used the money. Of course, I would love to keep the money for myself, but the happiness it would cause me would pale in comparison to the amount of good it would do for the sick children. Besides, it wouldn't be right to break the promise simply for selfish reasons, but it would be justified to help alleviate human suffering. This course of action is the morally right one for it would apparently not harm anyone, but it would produce a tremendous amount of good.

Kandice: I would keep my promise and give my friend's money to his nephew. I have no doubt that this is my moral obligation regardless of what the consequences may be. After all, can I really predict the consequences with any certainty? Maybe the nephew would be so moved by his uncle's generosity that it would turn his life around and a great deal of good would come from this transformation. If someone made a promise to me on my deathbed, I would expect that she would carry it out, no matter what she thought about my wishes. So, it would be inconsistent and unfair for me to do otherwise. I would love to give the money to the children's hospital, but it is not mine to give. At any rate, the consequences are a matter of sheer speculation, but I do know that I made a solemn promise to a friend on his deathbed and that is what defines my moral duty.

As you may have suspected, Randy is thinking like an ethical egoist. He thinks that his only moral obligation is to serve his own self-interest. Since we have already discussed this position in the previous section, it is the remaining two decisions that are our concern at present. Millard thinks that the consequences of an action determine whether it is right or wrong. Since the consequences of breaking the promise and giving the money to the hospital are far better than keeping the promise, the moral principle he follows dictates that the former action is his moral duty. Kandice thinks that the consequences should play no role in deciding what to do. She claims that the nature of the action itself (keeping a promise or breaking it) determines her moral obligations.

consequentialism
any ethical theory that judges the moral rightness or wrongness of an act according to the desirability or undesirability of the action's consequences; also called teleological ethics

deontological ethics
any ethical theory that judges the moral rightness or wrongness of an act in terms of the intrinsic moral value of the act itself

Millard's ethical reasoning identifies him as a consequentialist. **Consequentialism** refers to any ethical theory that judges the moral rightness or wrongness of an act according to the desirability or undesirability of the action's consequences. To put it glibly, the consequentialist believes that "all's well that ends well." This type of theory is also known as *teleological ethics* (from the Greek word *telos,* meaning end or purpose). Kandice, on the other hand, took a deontological approach in resolving this ethical dilemma. **Deontological ethics** (from the Greek word *deon,* meaning duty) judges the moral rightness or wrongness of an act in terms of the intrinsic moral value of the act itself. (Some philosophers call deontological theories *formalistic ethical theories* because they judge the act in terms of its form, that is, in terms of the kind of act it is.) Deontological ethics is a *nonconsequentialist* theory because it holds that our duty to perform an action (or to refrain from doing it) is based on the nature of the act itself and not on its consequences. Kandice was concerned only with the moral obligation of keeping her promise no matter what the consequences might be. In this section we examine the most common form of consequentialism, known as *utilitarianism.* In the next section, we will contrast utilitarianism with *Kantian ethics,* the most common deontological ethical theory.

Since consequentialism claims that ethics is concerned with the goodness or badness of the consequences of our actions, there are two questions that every consequentialist must answer: (1) What has intrinsic value, and (2) Who should receive this value? Something has **intrinsic value** if it is good or desirable in itself, whereas something has **instrumental value** if its desirability is in terms of other ends it achieves. For example, we might believe that health has intrinsic value, whereas getting a shot has instrumental value only because it helps us achieve health.

Technically speaking, consequentialists can disagree on what has intrinsic value. Consequentialists would agree that the good action is one that produces the best consequences, but they may disagree as to whether good consequences could be defined as those that promote God's will, or knowledge, or beauty, or so on. Most consequentialist theories, however, define intrinsic value in terms of pleasure or, more broadly, happiness. Consequentialists argue that everything else that is good (even health) has only instrumental value in helping to bring about happiness. If you ask me why I am doing something and I reply, "It makes me happy," it doesn't make any sense to go on to ask, "Why do you do things that make you happy?" Since happiness seems to have intrinsic value, the pursuit of it needs no other justification.

We have already encountered one variety of consequentialist ethics in our discussion of ethical egoism. The ethical egoist claims that acts that produce happiness or well-being have intrinsic value, but quickly adds that the proper recipient of those consequences is the person who performed the act. Utilitarianism is in agreement with the egoist on the role of consequences in ethics, but disagrees about the recipient of the value. For the utilitarian, the proper recipient of that which has value is the greatest number of people possible. If happiness has value, utilitarians argue, then that value ought to be maximized and distributed among as many people as possible.

Utilitarianism defines a morally right action as one that produces at least as much good (utility) for all people affected by the action as any alternative action that could be performed. This definition of utilitarianism is often referred to as the *principle of utility*. This definition does not specify what is good or has value, but as I just mentioned, utilitarians have typically identified value with happiness. Let's now examine utilitarianism as it has been formulated and defended by its two founders as well as several contemporary philosophers.

SURVEYING THE CASE FOR UTILITARIANISM

JEREMY BENTHAM (1748–1832)

Although the main themes of utilitarianism were developed in the eighteenth century by several Scottish philosophers (including David Hume), its first explicit and systematic formulation is credited to the British philosopher Jeremy Bentham. Bentham was the son of a London attorney who had ambitious plans for Jeremy to

JEREMY BENTHAM
(1748–1832)

become famous in a career in law. After studying law at Oxford University and graduating at age fifteen, however, Bentham discovered that although he had no interest in practicing law, he was interested in changing it. Having lived through the American Revolution, the French Revolution, the Napoleonic wars, and the rise of parliamentary government in England, Bentham was convinced that the political instability of the times was due to the irrational and chaotic foundations of the current legal systems and social structures. Accordingly, Bentham's philosophy of utilitarianism was an attempt to provide a rational and scientific foundation for law and morality. The opening lines of one of his best-known books make clear what this foundation will be.

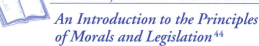

FROM JEREMY BENTHAM

An Introduction to the Principles of Morals and Legislation[44]

I. Nature has placed mankind under the governance of two sovereign masters, *pain* and *pleasure*. It is for them alone to point out what we ought to do, as well as to determine what we shall do. On the one hand the standard of right and wrong, on the other the chain of causes and effects, are fastened to their throne. They govern us in all we do, in all we say, in all we think: every effort we can make to throw off our subjection, will serve but to demonstrate and confirm it. In words a man may pretend to abjure their empire: but in reality he will remain subject to it all the while. The *principle of utility* recognises this subjection, and assumes it for the foundation of that system, the object of which is to rear the fabric of felicity by the hands of reason and of law. Systems which attempt to question it, deal in sounds instead of sense, in caprice instead of reason, in darkness instead of light.

psychological hedonism the claim that the only causes operating in human behavior are the desires to obtain pleasure and avoid pain

ethical hedonism the theory that the moral rightness or wrongness of an action is a function of the amount of pleasure or pain it produces

This passage contains the thesis of **psychological hedonism,** which is the claim that the only causes operating in human behavior are the desires to obtain pleasure and avoid pain. Basically, this thesis is a version of psychological egoism (discussed in the previous section) with the additional claim that when people pursue their self-interest they are really pursuing pleasure and avoiding pain. But Bentham says that our two "sovereign masters" of pain and pleasure not only "determine what we shall do," but they also "point out what we ought to do." Hence, from his psychological theory he attempts to derive an **ethical hedonism,** which is the theory that the moral rightness or wrongness of an action is a function of the amount of pleasure or pain it produces. Critics claim that the problems of psychological egoism discussed in the last section and the difficulties of deriving an ethical theory from it are duplicated and even magnified in Bentham's hedonistic version.

As I said before, utilitarianism is a version of consequentialism, or teleological ethics. Accordingly, in the next two paragraphs, Bentham sets out the principle of utility as the foundation of all ethics.

II. The principle of utility is the foundation of the present work: it will be proper therefore at the outset to give an explicit and determinate account of what is meant by it. By the principle of utility is meant that principle which approves or disapproves of every action whatsoever, according to the tendency which it appears to have to augment or diminish the happiness of the party whose interest is in question: or, what is the same thing in other words, to promote or to oppose that happiness. I say of every action whatsoever; and therefore not only of every action of a private individual, but of every measure of government.

III. By utility is meant that property in any object, whereby it tends to produce benefit, advantage, pleasure, good, or happiness, (all this in the present case comes to the same thing) or (what comes again to the same thing) to prevent the happening of mischief, pain, evil, or unhappiness to the party whose interest is considered: if that party be the community in general, then the happiness of the community: if a particular individual, then the happiness of that individual.

Since pleasure is the only thing that has value, an action that maximizes the greatest amount of pleasure possible is the best action. In other words, the fundamental rule of utilitarianism is, "Act always to promote the greatest happiness for the greatest number." But since there are so many different kinds of pleasures, the question now arises, Which kind of pleasure is the best one to pursue? Should we simply pursue bodily pleasures or should we, instead, pursue the "higher," more cultivated pleasures such as reading great books and enjoying significant art and music?

Bentham consistently points out that there is no sensible meaning to the notion of "higher" or "lower" pleasures. Pleasures can only differ in their quantity. Bentham expresses this point in a memorable quotation: "Prejudice apart, the game of pushpin is of equal value with the arts and sciences of music and poetry. If the game of pushpin furnish more pleasure, it is more valuable than either."[45] Pushpin was a rather trivial eighteenth-century children's game. If he were writing today, Bentham might say, "If they produce the same amount of pleasure, playing video games is as worthy a pleasure as reading poetry."

Bentham provides a method to scientifically quantify and calculate the value of different pleasures. This method is commonly referred to as Bentham's "hedonic calculus." When considering any action, we should evaluate the amount of pleasure or pain it will produce according to the following seven dimensions:

1. *Intensity:* How strong is the pleasure?
2. *Duration:* How long will the pleasure last?
3. *Certainty or Uncertainty:* How likely or unlikely is it that the pleasure will occur?
4. *Propinquity or Remoteness:* How soon will the pleasure occur?
5. *Fecundity:* How likely is it that the proposed action will produce more sensations of the same kind (either pleasure or pain)?

6. *Purity:* Will the sensations be followed by sensations of the opposite kind? (Will the pain be followed by pleasure, or the pleasure by pain?)
7. *Extent:* How many other people will be affected?

Let's look at how these criteria are applied. It is obvious that receiving $25 would not produce as much pleasure as receiving $30, so assuming that all factors are equal, you would prefer the action whose outcome was $30. However, if the $25 would be given to you now when you need it for school expenses, but the $30 would not be received for another forty years, it might be rational to choose the action that leads to the lesser but more immediate pleasure. Here's another example. Going to a party tonight would produce a high amount of immediate pleasure, but if it caused you to flunk a medical school admissions test tomorrow, the pleasure would be an impure one because the long-range pain of not pursuing your career would outweigh the immediate pleasure. Thus, all of Bentham's factors have to be taken into account in calculating which action is best.

Even when we are faced with more complicated moral dilemmas, Bentham claims that the process of calculation is simple:

1. For each person affected by a proposed action, add up the total amount of units of pleasure (or desirable consequences) produced and subtract from that figure the amount of pain (or undesirable consequences) produced.
2. Merge the calculations for each individual into the sum total of pleasure and pain produced for the community.
3. Do this calculation for alternative courses of action.
4. The morally right action is the one that produces the greatest sum total of pleasure.

Thus, on Bentham's analysis, moral dilemmas are turned into problems of addition and subtraction in which decisions are made by looking at the final balance, much as we would look at an accountant's ledger of credits and debits. While the process looks awkward and even bizarre, Bentham thinks it formalizes what we actually do in practice, for we are constantly making assessments of the pluses and minuses of the consequences of any course of action.

 STOP AND THINK

Can you think of an occasion in which you made a decision by informally following the sort of procedure and criteria Bentham recommends? How did the decision turn out? On reflection, do you think this method was the best way to decide what to do? Why?

Notice that so far we have not discussed what specifically has value. To be desired or valued by someone is all that it takes for something to have genuine value for that person. Obviously, what gives me pleasure may differ from what produces pleasure for you. Although the principle of utility provides an objective moral principle, it has no absolute standard of value, for values are claimed to be relative and subjective. Each one of us affected by an action has an equal vote in determining the worthiness of that action. Thus, ethics is not the search for some hidden, unobservable quality called "moral goodness." Ethical decisions are no more complicated or sublime than planning the menu for a dinner party in which you take into account your guests' likes and dislikes.

Bentham was basically a psychological hedonist, since he believed we are fundamentally motivated by our own pleasures and pains. Why, then, should I be interested in the seventh element of Bentham's criteria, the extent to which pleasure is distributed? The answer is found in enlightened self-interest. To be concerned about my own welfare requires that I also need to be attentive to the interests of others. For example, the aristocrats on the eve of the 1789 French Revolution were selfishly concerned only about their own interests. This self-interest was foolish, however, because the suffering of the mobs in the streets had fatal consequences for the well-being of the aristocrats. Bentham is convinced that, with the proper legislation, we can create a society in which the pursuit of personal happiness will produce those actions that lead to "the greatest good for the greatest number."

 THOUGHT EXPERIMENT

The Happiness Machine

To see whether you agree with Bentham that happiness or pleasure is the supreme goal in life, try the following thought experiment.[46]

Suppose that you had the opportunity to step into a "happiness machine" that would give you any experiences you desired. While in the machine, neurophysiologists would stimulate your brain so that, for example, you would think and feel you were winning an athletic event, writing a great novel, making a friend, or enjoying some physically and psychologically satisfying experience. To avoid boredom, the quality and types of happiness would be varied. Whatever types of experiences bring you happiness or pleasure in real life would be simulated in your brain. All the time that you are enjoying a life of uninterrupted happiness, you would be floating in a tank, with electrodes attached to your brain. Of course, while in the tank you won't have the feeling that you're there; you will feel as though the simulated experiences are actually happening. In addition to this psychological satisfaction, all the rest of your biological needs would be provided for, and your life span would not be any different than it would have been outside the happiness machine. You would be free to leave the machine at any time, although you know that everyone who ever entered the machine never chose to leave it.

- Isn't pleasure, contentment, satisfaction, and happiness what we all seek in life? If so, would there be any reason not to live your life plugged into the machine?
- Would you choose to be plugged into the machine, having a life of total contentment and pleasure from the experiences it simulates? Why?
- Would a consistent Benthamite be obligated to enter the machine?

If the unqualified pursuit of happiness or pleasure is the goal in life, then it seems that we all ought to climb into the happiness machine. However, many people think something is missing here. The artificial happiness induced by the machine is not something that we have achieved for ourselves, and it is inconsistent with our potential and dignity as human beings. In Bentham's day his philosophy was labeled the "pig philosophy," because he emphasized simply the quantity of pleasure and did not give sufficient priority to the type of pleasures that are worthy of human beings alone. For this reason, his disciple and godchild John Stuart Mill sought to develop a more refined version of utilitarianism.

JOHN STUART MILL (1806–1873)

JOHN STUART MILL
(1806–1873)

John Stuart Mill was born in London, the eldest son of nine children. His father, James Mill, was a businessman as well as a philosopher, economist, historian, and disciple of Bentham. Educated at home, Mill began studying Greek and arithmetic at age three. By the time he was thirteen years old, he was better educated than any university graduate of the time. Although he was one of history's greatest ethical and political thinkers, Mill made his living as an executive of a trading firm in London, writing philosophy on the side. His wife, Harriet Taylor, was a brilliant woman who had a deep influence on him and was his joint author in many of his most important works. While serving a term in Parliament, Mill unsuccessfully tried to amend the Reform Bill of 1867 to give women the vote. He also published *The Subjection of Women* in 1869, in which he argued for the political empowerment of women on utilitarian grounds. Mill died in Avignon, France, on May 8, 1873.

In developing his moral philosophy, Mill accepted the main outlines of Bentham's hedonism, claiming that happiness (the experience of pleasure and the absence of pain) is the only thing that is desirable in itself. This theme is introduced in the following passage.

FROM JOHN STUART MILL
Utilitarianism[47]

The creed which accepts as the foundation of morals, "Utility," or the "Greatest Happiness Principle," holds that actions are right in proportion as they tend to promote happiness, wrong as they tend to produce the reverse of happiness. By happiness is intended pleasure, and the absence of pain; by unhappiness, pain, and the privation of pleasure. To give a clear view of the moral standard set up by the theory, much more requires to be said; in particular, what things it includes in the ideas of pain and pleasure; and to what extent this is left an open question. But these supplementary explanations do not affect the theory of life on which this theory of morality is grounded—namely, that pleasure, and freedom from pain, are the only things desirable as ends; and that all desirable things (which are as numerous in the utilitarian as in any other scheme) are desirable either for the pleasure inherent in themselves, or as means to the promotion of pleasure and the prevention of pain.

Higher Quality Pleasures

Thus far, Mill's position seems indistinguishable from Bentham's. However, as Mill develops his version of utilitarianism further, he differs from Bentham on several crucial issues. The first issue is the criteria for evaluating pleasure. Bentham maintained a *quantitative* hedonism. However, Mill adds a *qualitative* hedonism, for he insists that pleasures can differ in their quality and not just in their amount. He says that those pleasures that are the product of our intellectual and more refined capacities are higher and better than physical pleasures. But how does he make the case that some pleasures are higher? Look for Mill's answer in the following passage.

If I am asked, what I mean by difference of quality in pleasures, or what makes one pleasure more valuable than another, merely as a pleasure, except its being greater in amount, there is but one possible answer. Of two pleasures, if there be one to which all or almost all who have experience of both give a decided preference, irrespective of any feeling of moral obligation to prefer it, that is the more desirable pleasure. If one of the two is, by those who are competently acquainted with both, placed so far above the other that they prefer it, even though knowing it to be attended with a greater amount of discontent, and would not resign it for any quantity of the other pleasure which their nature is capable of, we are justified in ascribing to the preferred enjoyment a superiority in quality, so far outweighing quantity as to render it, in comparison, of small account.

Now it is an unquestionable fact that those who are equally acquainted with, and equally capable of appreciating and enjoying, both, do give a most marked preference to the manner of existence which employs their higher faculties. Few human creatures would consent to be changed into any of the lower animals, for a promise of the fullest allowance of a beast's pleasures; no intelligent human being would consent to be a fool, no instructed person would be an ignoramus, no person of feeling and conscience would be selfish and base, even though they should be persuaded that the fool, the dunce, or the rascal is better satisfied with his lot than they are with theirs. They would not resign what they possess more than he for the most complete satisfaction of all the desires which they have in common with him. If they ever fancy they would, it is only in cases of unhappiness so extreme, that to escape from it they would exchange their lot for almost any other, however undesirable in their own eyes. A being of higher faculties requires more to make him happy, is capable probably of more acute suffering, and certainly accessible to it at more points, than one of an inferior type; but in spite of these liabilities, he can never really wish to sink into what he feels to be a lower grade of existence. We may give what explanation we please of this unwillingness; we may attribute it to pride, a name which is given indiscriminately to some of the most and to some of the least estimable feelings of which mankind are capable: we may refer it to the love of liberty and personal independence, an appeal to which was with the Stoics one of the most effective means for the inculcation of it; to the love of power, or to the love of excitement, both of which do really enter into and contribute to it: but its most appropriate appellation is a sense of dignity, which all human beings possess in one form or other, and in some, though by no means in exact, proportion to their higher faculties, and which is so essential a part of the happiness of those in whom it is strong, that nothing which conflicts with it could be, otherwise than momentarily, an object of desire to them.

STOP AND THINK

Is Physical Pleasure the Only Goal in Life?

Take a look at some animal that is enjoying the good life (your family pet, for example). Think about the fact that this pet has food, shelter, and medical care provided for him as well as the companionship of his human friends (and possibly other animals as well). He doesn't have to worry about classes, the complications of personal relationships, his personal values, the mind-body problem, his checking account, a career, the economy, political tensions in the world, or the environment. Instead, he naps and plays when he wishes and takes life as it comes. While in the midst of the stress and crush of your daily life, you may think it would be nice to exchange places with him. But would you really? Would you choose to permanently give up the joys and pains of learning new things and growing as a person and facing new challenges in order to have a life of pure pleasure and contentment? Does this example support Mill's point that it is not pleasure as such, but those sorts of pleasures that are appropriate to human life, that are worth pursuing?

The next passage contains one of Mill's most memorable lines. He says that it is easier for a pig or a fool to be satisfied than a Socrates is, but that the life of Socrates is far superior. Do you agree with Mill on this point?

Whoever supposes that this preference takes place at a sacrifice of happiness—that the superior being, in anything like equal circumstances, is not happier than the inferior—confounds the two very different ideas, of happiness, and content. It is indisputable that the being whose capacities of enjoyment are low, has the greatest chance of having them fully satisfied; and a highly endowed being will always feel that any happiness which he can look for, as the world is constituted, is imperfect. But he can learn to bear its imperfections, if they are at all bearable; and they will not make him envy the being who is indeed unconscious of the imperfections, but only because he feels not at all the good which those imperfections qualify. It is better to be a human being dissatisfied than a pig satisfied; better to be Socrates dissatisfied than a fool satisfied. And if the fool, or the pig, are a different opinion, it is because they only know their own side of the question. The other party to the comparison knows both sides.

Mill criticizes Bentham for having too limited a view of human nature. Human beings, Mill insists, are more than pleasure-seeking organisms. In seeking pleasure they also seek to develop their "higher faculties" and to become "well-developed human beings." Mill says that in Bentham's account,

> Man is never recognized by him as a being capable of pursuing spiritual perfection as an end; of desiring, for its own sake, the conformity of his own character to his standard of excellence, without hope of good or fear of evil from [any] other source than his own inward consciousness.[48]

However, in saying that we strive to realize our potential as human beings as an end in itself, Mill seems to have moved away from the utilitarian doctrine of psychological hedonism and has substituted for it an elevated view of human nature that emphasizes the need to fulfill our unique dignity and potential as human beings rather than to simply maximize our own or other's happiness. Otherwise, how can he say, "It is better to be a human being dissatisfied than a pig satisfied; better to be Socrates dissatisfied than a fool satisfied"?

Self-Interest or Altruism?

The second issue on which Mill disagreed with Bentham concerned the question of whether self-interest was the basis for all our actions. Bentham did recognize that we sometimes experience personal pleasure from making others happy, which he called the "pleasure of benevolence." He also noted that attending to other persons' interests is often the best way to promote our own interests. In the final analysis, however, Bentham tended toward an egoistical hedonism, for he thought that the most universal motive for action was always the individual's self-interest. On the other hand, Mill emphasized much more strongly that we naturally have social feelings for humanity and the desire for unity with our fellow-creatures. Although both Bentham and Mill believed in "the greatest happiness for the greatest number," Mill made a special effort to stress that in a utilitarian calculation,

Read the earlier thought experiment concerning the happiness machine and the first two questions accompanying it to five or more friends. What answers do they give, and what reasons do they provide? Do any of their answers sound similar to Mill's qualitative hedonism and his preference to be a dissatisfied human rather than a happy pig? Do any of your friends question the hedonistic assumption that pleasure or happiness is the only thing that has value? Or do some think the machine is a good idea? Discuss their answers with them.

PHILOSOPHY
in the
MARKETPLACE

your own happiness cannot be given any more weight than the happiness of another person.

> The happiness which forms the utilitarian standard of what is right in conduct, is not the agent's own happiness, but that of all concerned. As between his own happiness and that of others, utilitarianism requires him to be as strictly impartial as a disinterested and benevolent spectator. In the golden rule of Jesus of Nazareth, we read the complete spirit of the ethics of utility. "To do as you would be done by," and "to love your neighbour as yourself," constitute the ideal perfection of utilitarian morality.[49]

UTILITARIANISM: *Objectivism or Relativism?*

Several features of utilitarianism are important to understand. The utilitarianism theory falls under the heading of *ethical objectivism.* The utilitarian believes that there is a universal, objective moral principle that everyone ought to follow—the principle of utility. Hence, as with all varieties of ethical objectivism, the utilitarian believes that it is possible for a person to be mistaken about rightness or wrongness. The morally right action for you to perform in a particular situation (your moral duty) is not necessarily the action you think is right, nor is it necessarily identical to what you subjectively desire. The rightness or wrongness of an action is an objective matter of the goodness or badness of its consequences.

Sometimes people incorrectly think that utilitarianism is a form of relativism because the utilitarian does not hold that any given action is absolutely right or wrong in itself. However, relativity enters into morality for the utilitarian not at the level of moral principles but at the level of their application. Let's look at a nonethical example. It is a universal medical principle that "everyone ought to eat nutritious meals." Although everyone ought to follow this principle, the specific eating habits and amounts of food that this principle dictates for a 100-pound accountant will be different from those for a 250-pound football player. Similarly, the utilitar-

PEANUTS reprinted by permission of United Feature Syndicate, Inc.

ian would say that everyone ought to follow the principle of utility in making moral choices, but following this principle may dictate different actions in different, specific circumstances, depending on the persons involved, the nature of the circumstances, and the consequences of the particular action. For example, telling a lie in a court of law could have very bad consequences for all concerned, whereas telling Aunt Tillie you love her meat loaf (a lie) might be charitable. For the utilitarian, all lies are not alike, because they do not all have the same consequences; therefore, lying in general cannot be morally evaluated apart from the concrete consequences of particular lies.

If consequences determine the rightness or wrongness of an action, then the morality of a particular action can change over time if the consequences change. At one time, for example, an unwanted pregnancy and the contracting of a sexually transmitted disease were possible consequences of sexual intercourse. However, improved contraceptive technology and more effective means to prevent and cure these diseases led to more ability to control the bad consequences of sexual intercourse. From a purely utilitarian standpoint, these changes would have an effect on the morality of promiscuous sexual intercourse. With the rise of diseases, such as AIDS, that have resisted all known cures, however, the consequences of promiscuous sexual behavior changed once again, and monogamous sexual relationships gained new popularity. Of course, if you are a careful utilitarian, the previously mentioned obvious consequences of sexual behavior are not the only ones that you need to consider. Other factors might be the emotional effects of your sexual behavior on yourself and others, including how the behavior negatively or positively affects your ability to sustain long-term relationships such as marriage; the affects this behavior will have on society; and so on. Nevertheless, for the utilitarian, the three factors determining the morality of sexual behavior (or any behavior) are: consequences, consequences, and consequences.

THE CONSEQUENCES OF CONSEQUENTIALISM:
A Test Case

One of the frequent criticisms of utilitarianism is that it leads to morally problematic and even abhorrent conclusions. The questions posed in the following "Stop and Think" box will get you thinking about the plausibility, limits, and consequences of utilitarianism, or consequentialist ethics.

 STOP AND THINK

Would it be morally permissible to bring about or to allow the death of one innocent person if it spared a vast number of people from some major harm? Why? If you answered the question affirmatively, then how great would the harm being prevented have to be in order to justify one person's death? Can you think of any examples in which our

(Continued . . .)

(. . . continued)

society sacrifices the lives of some individuals for the good of the many? How about war? How about the way our society sets medical research priorities and allocates money for health care? How about the level of safety standards that are required of products and in the workplace? Are there trade-offs made here between the costs and the risks? If automobile manufacturers made all cars so safe that everyone would survive a crash, would you be able to afford a car? Are utilitarian considerations at work in these situations, even when lives are at stake?

While some people would agree that under the right circumstances it would be morally permissible to sacrifice one person to save the *lives* of many, most people would probably say that sacrificing one life for the *convenience* of the many would be morally reprehensible. This conclusion, however, has been questioned on consequentialist grounds by Alastair Norcross. (Alastair Norcross holds the William Edward Easterwood Chair of Philosophy at Southern Methodist University. He has written numerous articles in defense of consequentialist ethical theory.) Norcross argues in the spirit of utilitarianism that for a consistent consequentialist there would have to be a point at which the total sum of minor pains or inconveniences of a very large number of persons would outweigh the bad consequences of the death of one person. Furthermore, he argues for the surprising conclusion that most of us agree with practices of our society in which that exact policy is pursued. (Remember that utilitarianism is one variety of consequentialist ethics, so everything Norcross says about the latter applies to the former.)

FROM ALASTAIR NORCROSS
Comparing Harms: Headaches and Human Lives[50]

Consequentialists are sometimes unsettled by the following kind of example: a vast number of people are experiencing fairly minor headaches, which will continue unabated for another hour, unless an innocent person is killed, in which case they will cease immediately. There is no other way to avoid the headaches. Can we permissibly kill that innocent person in order to avoid the vast number of headaches? For a consequentialist, the answer to that question depends on the relative values of the world with the headaches but without the premature death, and the world without the headaches but with the premature death. If the latter world is at least as good as the former, it is permissible to kill the innocent. Furthermore, if the all-things-considered values of the worlds are comparable, and if a world with more headaches is, *ceteris paribus,** worse than a world with fewer, it is reasonable to suppose that a world with a vast (but finite) number of headaches could be worse than a world that differs from it only in lacking those headaches

---

**Ceteris paribus* means "other things being equal."

and containing one more premature death. In short, there is some finite number of headaches, such that it is permissible to kill an innocent person to avoid them. Call this claim *life for headaches*. Many people balk at *life for headaches*. In fact, many people think that there is no number of people such that it is permissible to kill one person to save that number the pain of a fairly minor headache. Deontologists might think this, because they endorse what Scheffler calls "agent-centered restrictions." Such restrictions forbid certain kinds of action, even when their results are at least as good as all alternatives. Thus, a deontologist might agree that the world without the headaches but with the premature death is better all things considered than the world with the headaches but without the premature death, and yet maintain that it is impermissible to kill the person in order to avoid the headaches. A consequentialist, however, who agrees with this ranking of the two worlds must also claim that it is permissible to kill the innocent person.

Norcross follows this introduction with a lengthy series of arguments to show that a consistent consequentialist cannot avoid the *life for headaches* conclusion. The consequentialist, of course, believes that the decision to choose one alternative over another is morally justified by calculating and comparing the total sum of good consequences and bad consequences for all affected by each proposed action, and choosing the alternative that produces the greatest amount of good (and least harm) for the greatest number of people. Therefore, Norcross argues, there is a point at which the cumulative amount of minor, individual headaches would produce a sum of pain such that the elimination of this quantity of pain would outweigh the bad consequence of sacrificing one individual.

Norcross acknowledges that his argument for *life for headaches* could appear to be a fairly weighty argument against consequentialist ethics. However, in the following passage he argues that *life for headaches* is not as unpalatable as it may seem at first. In fact, he claims, "most of us, consequentialists and nonconsequentialists alike, accept at least some other claims that do not differ significantly from *life for headaches*."

Thousands of people die in automobile accidents every year in the United States. It is highly probable that the number of deaths is positively correlated with the speed limits in force on highways, at least within a certain range. One of the effects of raising speed limits is that there are more accidents, resulting in more deaths and injuries. One of the effects of lowering speed limits is that there are fewer accidents. Higher vehicle safety standards also affect both the numbers of accidents and the severity of the injuries sustained when accidents do occur. Another effect of raising speed limits is that more gasoline is consumed, which raises the level of particulate pollution, which also leads to more deaths. Stricter standards for fuel efficiency also affect the amount of gasoline consumed. There are, then, many different measures that we, as a society, could take to lower the number of automobile-related deaths, only some of which we do take. There are also many measures we could take, that would *raise* the number of such deaths, some of which we do take. Furthermore, it is not obvious that we are wrong to fail to do all we can to reduce the number of deaths. For the purposes of this discussion, I will focus on just one aspect of this failure, the failure to impose a national speed limit of 50 miles per hour in the US.

If there were a national speed limit of 50 mph, it is overwhelmingly likely that many lives would be saved each year, as compared with the current situation. One of the costs of the failure to impose such a speed limit is a significant number of deaths. The benefits of higher speed limits are increased convenience for many. Despite this, it is far from obvious that the failure to impose a 50 mph speed limit is wrong. In fact, most people believe what I will call *lives for convenience:*

> *Lives for convenience:* We are not morally obligated to impose a national speed limit of 50 mph (or less).

If we reject *life for headaches* as obviously wrong, we must find a morally significant difference between it and *lives for convenience.*

Norcross's facts are well documented. When it was proposed that we raise the speed limits on U.S. highways, we could calculate with some degree of precision the increase in deaths this change would cause. This unfortunate result was thought to be justified because it would save the majority of people, who are not victims, the inconvenience of slower speeds and it would reduce the costs to transport goods. The actual results of raising the speed limits have supported the original predictions. Norcross says that if you think these findings show that the speed limits should be set at 50 mph, then you should support highway speed limits of 40 mph, or 30 mph, or lower, since each reduction in speed will save even more lives.

 STOP AND THINK

Do you agree with Norcross's argument that *lives for convenience* is a justified trade-off? If not, would you lobby for 20 mph highway speed limits in order to save lives? Is there a relevant moral difference between the *lives for convenience* principle that the United States and other countries have adopted and Norcross's *life for headaches* principle? What would that difference be and how would you argue for it?

In the remainder of his article, Norcross argues that there is no relevant difference between our sacrificing lives so that the majority can drive faster and his headache example. The fact that the victims of highway deaths are randomly chosen whereas the victim in the headache example is a specific, known individual does not seem to be a relevant difference. In fact, randomly bringing about the deaths of thousands of people seems to be worse than specifically targeting one person. Norcross also argues that there is no relevant difference between bringing about a death that is intended and bringing about many deaths that are merely foreseen when they could be prevented by our actions.

In the following passage, Norcross responds to yet one more attempt to argue that the highway speeds are morally justified while the *life for headaches* death is not.

> The victims of higher speed limits, even though they may have neither chosen nor benefited from those limits, have at least freely chosen to undertake the risk of being harmed. The dangers of driving, or being driven, are well known. Those who choose to travel by road, therefore, are at least partly responsible for any harm that befalls them. The same cannot be said of the prospective victim of *life for headaches*.
>
> Once again, this is clearly not applicable to the victims of higher levels of particulate pollution. Nor does it seem to be true of all the victims of road accidents. Many children are killed on the roads. Many of these may have had no say over whether they were to travel that way. Perhaps we will say that their parents voluntarily assumed the risk on their behalf. But this seems to be an inadequate reply. Would our reaction to *life for headaches* be significantly different, if the prospective victim were a child, chosen at random from among those whose parents had agreed to the selection procedure? Besides, it is not clear how *free* is the choice to travel by road, even for well-informed adults. For many of the victims of road accidents, the alternatives may have been excessively burdensome, if not nonexistent. Many people do not have access to basic services, such as groceries and health-care providers, except by road.

Norcross's arguments are troubling. They show some of the hard conclusions that may have to be accepted by a consequentialist such as the utilitarian. They also show that, whether we like it or not, we all reason like utilitarians on some issues affecting life and death.

THE PROBLEM OF JUSTICE AND RIGHTS

Many critics object to utilitarianism precisely because it leads to the sort of problematic conclusions found in the headaches case. Critics charge that there is no room in utilitarianism for justice and individual rights, which are commonly thought to be nonnegotiable concerns in moral deliberations. Since all that counts for the utilitarian is the total sum of happiness or utility, why should it matter how this happiness is distributed or whether an individual's rights are violated? Bentham, for example, had no use for the notion of natural rights, because rights are not quantifiable, they are not scientifically observable, and no one can agree on what our rights are. Although Bentham favored the American Revolution, he lamented the fact that the American political philosophy was based on a notion so vague and subject to objections as human rights. The issue of utility versus justice and rights, along with a suggestion as to how a utilitarian might deal with this problem, is the subject of the following thought experiment.

The Blacksmith and the Baker

An eighteenth-century Danish poet, Johan Herman Wessel, wrote the tale of "The Black-smith and the Baker" in verse. The story concerns a rather mean blacksmith who killed a man in a barroom brawl while in a drunken rage. The blacksmith is about to be sentenced to death by a judge when four upstanding citizens speak on his behalf. Their argument is that the man is the only blacksmith in this small town and his services are desperately needed. It would accomplish nothing to execute him, but it would be detrimental to the welfare of the community to deprive people of his skills. The judge is sympathetic to their plea but responds that the law requires a life for a life. If he let a murder go unpunished, it would undermine respect for the law and be harmful to the fabric of the society. The citizens point out that the town has an old and scrawny baker who is on the last leg of his life. He is a somewhat disreputable and unpopular fellow, although he is innocent of any crime. Since the town has two bakers, he would not be missed. So, for the greatest good of the greatest number, the judge lets the blacksmith go while framing the baker and making him pay for the murder with his life. The old baker wept pitifully when they took him away.[51]

- Does this story illustrate the problems that utilitarianism has with the principle of justice?
- Obviously, willfully condemning an innocent man to death is morally abhorrent. However, in good utilitarian fashion, keeping the blacksmith and sacrificing the baker seems to create the best consequences for the town. How would a utilitarian respond to the judge's decision? Can the utilitarian condemn the action by appealing to the *long-term* bad consequences a society would incur if it framed and executed innocent persons? Or does the problem remain that the principle of utility can always override a concern for justice?

ACT-UTILITARIANISM VERSUS RULE-UTILITARIANISM

In an attempt to avoid some of the problematic implications of utilitarianism, philosophers now distinguish two varieties of utilitarianism: act-utilitarianism and rule-utilitarianism. **Act-utilitarianism** is the doctrine that a particular action is right if it results in as much or more happiness than any other alternative available at that time in those circumstances. (Most of our discussion thus far has assumed act-utilitarianism.) Richard Brandt, a contemporary philosopher, raises the following problems with act-utilitarianism:

> It implies that if you have employed a boy to mow your lawn and he has finished the job and asks for his pay, you should pay him what you promised only if you cannot find a better use for your money. It implies that when you bring home your monthly paycheck you should use it to support your family and yourself only if it cannot be

act-utilitarianism
the doctrine that a particular action is right if it results in as much or more happiness than any other alternative available at that time in those circumstances

used more effectively to supply the needs of others. It implies that if your father is ill and has no prospect of good in his life, and maintaining him is a drain on the energy and enjoyments of others, then, if you can end his life without provoking any public scandal or setting a bad example, it is your positive duty to take matters into your own hands and bring his life to a close.[52]

However, to some utilitarians, talking about the rightness or wrongness of an action does not refer to a particular action at a particular time, but to a category of actions, such as promise keeping in general. Theorists who take this stance are rule-utilitarians, for they are concerned with the consequences of rules that permit, require, or prohibit various types of actions. We may define **rule-utilitarianism** as the doctrine that an action is right if it is required by a rule that, if generally followed, would result in the greatest amount of happiness in the long run. (While Bentham seemed to be an act-utilitarian, it is not clear whether Mill was one or not. Since there are passages in Mill that support both interpretations, the distinction between the two versions may not have concerned him.) With respect to the cases that Brandt lists, the rule-utilitarian would say that rules that command us to pay someone what we promised, support one's family, and respect our father's life are rules that will produce the best long-term consequences for society, even though there may be specific instances when the particular actions commanded by those rules do not maximize happiness.

Initially, rule-utilitarianism seems plausible, because a society in which people follow such rules as "tell the truth," "keep your promises," or "never steal" is likely to be a better society on the whole than one in which such rules are not followed. However, since the justification of the rule-utilitarian's moral commands is that they will maximize happiness, critics have complained that it is always possible to imagine situations in which breaking the general rule will maximize happiness without undermining society. Suppose that the rule "never lie" is justified on the grounds that if people follow it, the result will be the best overall consequences for society. But now suppose that I find that lying to an individual on a particular occasion will make her happier than if I told the truth and that I know my lie will never be exposed or produce any harmful effects for society as a whole. Because maximizing happiness is the goal of moral rules and because lying on *this* occasion will create a greater amount of happiness than if I strictly conform to the rule, I ought to tell the lie. But now it seems that the rule I am following is "never lie unless doing so will maximize happiness without any negative effects on society in general," and this rule returns us to the case-by-case assessment of act-utilitarianism and to some of its accompanying problems. Is there any way the rule-utilitarian can strictly adhere to general moral rules without either ceasing to be a consequentialist or collapsing back into act-utilitarianism?

Utilitarians in the twentieth century have clarified or modified some of their principles and responded to the sorts of objections discussed. Likewise, nonutilitarians have continued to provide examples and arguments to expose what they consider to be problems in the theory. Whether you think utilitarianism is for better

rule-utilitarianism the doctrine that an action is right if it is required by a rule that, if generally followed, would result in the greatest amount of happiness in the long run

or worse, a few moments' reflection will make clear how much Bentham and Mill have influenced our contemporary thinking in the moral and political spheres.

LOOKING THROUGH THE UTILITARIAN'S LENS

1. Utilitarianism is not just a historical movement in nineteenth-century British philosophy, for it is alive and well in contemporary society. Find examples of utilitarian justifications of ethical conclusions in newspaper stories, editorials, letters to the editor, political or legislative proposals, and everyday conversations. In each case, how could the author use utilitarian principles to respond to possible objections to his or her conclusions?

2. Take some current moral controversy and imagine two utilitarians arguing the opposing sides of the issue. There are, for example, utilitarian arguments both for and against abortion, based on differing assessments of the consequences for the individuals involved and for society in general of either prohibiting abortion or permitting it. Remember, many kinds of arguments can be made on both sides of an issue like abortion, but the utilitarian analysis of an issue should not appeal to any notion of intrinsic rights of the individuals involved, nor should it make use of any religious assumptions. Argue both sides of the issue as utilitarians would by assessing both the good achieved and the harms produced for all individuals affected by the action and by assessing the long-term effects on society. Now that you have considered the utilitarian pros and cons, which side of the moral controversy represents the most consistent expression of utilitarian ethical theory?

3. For each of the seven points of Bentham's hedonistic calculus, try to provide a concrete example of a pleasure that might be forbidden because it violates that principle.

4. Think of an issue on which a follower of Jeremy Bentham's ethics and a follower of John Stuart Mill's theory would differ concerning the morally correct action to take. Limiting your options to these two theories for the sake of the exercise, which position do you think provides the best ethical guidance?

5. Think of a concrete moral decision in which an ethical egoist such as Plato's Glaucon or Ayn Rand would differ with a utilitarian as to the morally right thing to do. How would the egoist and the utilitarian justify their decisions? Which position do you think provides the best ethical guidance?

6. Harriet Taylor and her husband and coauthor, John Stuart Mill, wrote a number of essays in the nineteenth century arguing that women should be accorded full social, political, and legal equality with men. However, since the notion of "natural rights" finds little room in utilitarian theory, their arguments were based on what would create the most social good. See if you can construct an argument for women's equality that is based on the utilitarian principle of maximizing the greatest good for society.

EXAMINING THE STRENGTHS AND WEAKNESSES OF UTILITARIANISM

Positive Evaluation

1. Utilitarians have an answer to the question, Why be moral? They argue both that it is in your best interests to be moral and that it fulfills the best impulses within human nature. The utilitarians link morality with our basic interests and inclinations instead of making natural enemies out of happiness and morality; does this link make their theory more convincing than other theories?

2. Utilitarianism claims to provide a clear-cut procedure for making ethical decisions instead of relying on vague intuitions or abstract principles. Furthermore, it allows us to use the findings of psychology and sociology to determine which policies will promote human happiness and the social good. To what degree do these considerations strengthen the utilitarian's case?

3. The utilitarian theory leads to impartiality, fairness, and greater social harmony because it requires us to balance our interests with those of others. In doing so, doesn't utilitarianism provide an effective antidote for the evils of discrimination based on race, gender, religion, and other unjust criteria?

4. Although people have many different and conflicting moral beliefs, everyone agrees that, all things being equal, pain is bad and pleasure is good. Given this basic fact, doesn't utilitarianism provide a common ground for a minimal, public morality? If so, isn't this finding an important consideration in its favor?

5. Because utilitarianism does not rigidly label actions as absolutely right or wrong, it allows for a great deal of flexibility and sensitivity to the particular circumstances surrounding an action. Furthermore, it allows our moral policies to be adjusted and to change with the changes in society and with the changing consequences of our actions over time. Don't these factors make utilitarianism a very practical theory?

6. Utilitarians argue that their view is commonsensical and widely practiced, for their theory underlies many of the decisions we make in everyday life and has produced many of the socially beneficial changes in the laws and policies of our society. Do you agree that these claims have merit? If so, don't they lend considerable support to utilitarianism?

Negative Evaluation

1. Most people would agree that Bentham's hedonistic utilitarianism is too vulgar. What conscientious person would affirm that living at the level of an animal and only pursuing the pleasures of the body is just as good as developing the life of the mind? On the other hand, while Mill's modified version is more appealing, how can he claim that one pleasure is "better" than another? Wouldn't we need to have some criterion other than pleasure to judge the value of competing pleasures?

Yet, if pleasure is the only criterion of value, is there any way to rank pleasures except in terms of their quantity? Doesn't this conclusion send us right back to Bentham's version?

2. The utilitarian principle can be broken down into two goals: (1) create the greatest amount of happiness, and (2) create happiness for the greatest number. In case 1, suppose you could create the greatest amount of happiness for a community of ten people by making four people supremely happy while six people were miserable. In case 2, suppose you could make all ten people moderately happy, with none experiencing any misery. However, the total amount of happiness would not be as great as in the first case. If the total amount of pleasure over pain is what counts, then case 1 is morally preferable. If creating happiness for the greatest number is what counts, then case 2 would be best. Does this example show an incoherence in the utilitarian principle? Would it be possible for the utilitarian to make adjustments to the theory to avoid this problem?

3. Wouldn't the utilitarian have to say that slavery would be morally justified if the benefits to the society outweighed the burdens of the slaves? Doesn't the greatest happiness principle imply that an unjust distribution of benefits and harms can be moral as long as the action results in a greater amount of total happiness than unhappiness when compared to any other alternative? Could the utilitarian argue that there would always be alternatives to slavery that would do a better job of maximizing utility? Do you think this reply is plausible?

4. Suppose that someone you love (a parent or a sibling) will die without a kidney transplant. You are willing to sacrifice one of your kidneys to save the life of this special person. However, you learn that a famous scientist, who is on the verge of finding a cure for cancer, also needs a donor kidney to live. Although the scientist is a stranger to you, your unique biochemistry will allow your kidney to be transplanted successfully into the body of someone who is not related to you. Your loved one holds a rather unimportant job and makes very little impact on society in general. However, no one can replace the work of the scientist and the benefits to society of her research. No kidney other than yours can be successfully transplanted in either case. Should you maximize the benefits to society by saving the scientist, or should you save the special person in your life? What would you do? Why? What would the utilitarian advise you to do? In responding to this scenario, most people would say that we have special obligations toward family members and friends that have priority over general obligations toward strangers. However, critics charge that utilitarian theory is unable to account for *special moral responsibilities,* because everyone who is affected by our choices should be counted equally in light of the total outcome for society in general. If you were a utilitarian, how would you respond? Would you defend the hard view that each of us has a moral obligation to society to give the kidney to the scientist and not to our loved one? Or would you argue that giving priority to the critical needs of those who are close to us would be best for society in the long run? Would this position permit moral obligations that conflicted with the utilitarian principle?

LEADING QUESTIONS: KANTIAN ETHICS

1. Suppose that Dr. Eunice Utilitarian is asked by a hospitalized patient how he is doing. Knowing that his health is rapidly deteriorating and fearful that the shock of hearing the truth will worsen his condition, the physician decides that she could achieve the best consequences by lying to him and waiting to tell him the truth at a better time. However, can you think of some unintended bad consequences that might result from this benevolent lie? What if the physician lied by saying, "You're doing great," and the patient died without making out a will because he thought there was no urgency? Could the physician be held morally responsible for the bad consequences of the lie? On the other hand, what if she told the truth and it so depressed the patient that he gave up his will to live? Could she then be held responsible for the bad consequences of telling the truth? Could it be that the best policy in such a situation is to avoid the known evil (lying) and let the consequences happen as they will?

2. When my children were young I had the rule, "You must always fasten your seat belt when riding in a car." One day, my son pointed out that I seldom wore my seat belt while I drove. Was I being inconsistent by giving commands that I did not follow? Was it morally wrong for me to be inconsistent? What is the problem with saying, "Do as I say, not as I do"? Why do we think that people ought to "practice what they preach"? Why is the Golden Rule, "Do unto others as you would have them do unto you," often cited as one of the supreme rules of morality? What role does consistency play in being a moral person and in deciding what rules we should follow?

3. What if we could make 100 people extremely happy by unfairly causing an undeserving innocent person cruel and humiliating embarrassment? What if the one person's emotional pain was the only bad result? Would it be morally wrong to create happiness in this way? If so, how could you convince those in favor of the action that it was wrong? If the principle "maximize happiness" could be used to justify this action, what other general moral rule could we formulate that would make it impossible to justify any actions of this sort?

4. Generally, people think that such principles as "tell the truth" and "keep your promises" are good ones to follow. However, we all have been in situations in which it seems that an exception to these rules should be made. Once we begin allowing exceptions to moral rules, isn't it pretty easy to always rationalize and justify breaking these rules when it is expedient or convenient to do so? When we don't take these moral commands as absolutes and allow exceptions to them, aren't we really watering them down into insipid rules such as, "Always keep a promise unless you think it is better not to"? Doesn't such an insipid rule allow for so many loopholes that it is ineffective in guiding our actions? If you knew that someone was following

this rule, how much confidence would you place in an important promise that she made? If *everyone* followed this rule, would there be any point in taking promises seriously?

These four leading questions draw attention to four leading themes in Immanuel Kant's deontological ethical theory: (1) the irrelevance of consequences in determining our obligations or the moral rightness and wrongness of actions, (2) the importance of consistency for living the moral life and choosing our moral rules, (3) the irreducible dignity and worth of every person, and (4) the necessity of having moral absolutes that are not qualified by any exceptions. We explore these themes in the remainder of this section.

SURVEYING THE CASE FOR KANTIAN ETHICS

IMMANUEL KANT (1724–1804)

We encountered Kant's philosophy previously in our discussion of his theory of knowledge. (See section 2.4, "Kantian Constructivism," for brief biographical information on Kant.) If he had written nothing else but his theory of knowledge, he would still be considered one of history's most important thinkers. It is a testimony to his genius, however, that he also is a landmark in the field of ethics. Writing in the late eighteenth century, Kant obviously was not attempting to refute the nineteenth-century utilitarianism of Jeremy Bentham and John Stuart Mill. Nevertheless, because Kant was responding to the British empiricists who would later influence the utilitarians, his writings read like an argument directed against Bentham and Mill. For this reason, I have presented these thinkers in reverse chronological order. Rather than being a historical museum piece, Kant's moral philosophy remains one of the most influential theories today. While many philosophers enthusiastically defend and apply his theory, and others harshly criticize it, no one who wants to think seriously about ethics can afford to ignore his ideas. Consequently, the Kantian approach to ethics still stands today as one of the leading resources of ethical insight as we face the troubling issues our contemporary culture is encountering in the areas of political, legal, medical, and business ethics.

Kant's View of Morality

We could take as the model of Kant's entire philosophy his statement that "two things fill the mind with ever new and increasing admiration and awe . . . *the starry heavens above me and the moral law within me.*"[53] The starry heavens stand for the world of sensory experience. Kant's epistemology attempted to set out the principles by which we are able to have knowledge of the world of physical nature. (This epistemology was discussed in section 2.4.) But human experience consists of more than sense data impinging upon us and the force of physical laws, for we also feel the pull of the moral law. For example, when you deeply desire to go out with friends, but this desire is vetoed by the realization that you promised a friend you would help her move, you are feeling the pull of duty.

When Kant talks about our moral experience, he looks inward to find the moral law and not outward to the consequences of our actions (such as happiness). In this one detail we get an indication that his ethical theory is going to be radically different from that of the utilitarians. Kant's moral theory emphasizes absolute duties, motives, the dignity and worth of persons, and a moral law that is absolute and unchanging. In this emphasis, he retains some of the elements of his own Christian roots. But when it comes to deciding what the moral law is, no mention is made of God and his commands. Kant says our ability to identify God with the highest good and to attribute goodness to the great religious figures in history requires that we already have a prior conception of moral perfection. Even a person who was not raised in a religious tradition possesses her innate capacities as a rational human being that both make her capable of knowing the moral law and require her to be subject to it. Thus Kant did not abandon the moral precepts of his religious tradition, but neither did he base his ethics upon them. Instead, he thought that secular, rational ethics and the best in religious morality pointed in the same direction.

Kant's uncompromising rationalism led him to insist that the principles of morality cannot be derived from any empirical facts about human practices such as we find in anthropology or psychology. Kant believed that we cannot move from a description of what *is* being done to any notion of what we *ought* to do. A statistical survey of how people actually behave would not tell us how we ought to behave. Hence, if moral principles cannot be derived from experience, then the mind must bring its own, rational principles to the realm of moral experience. (Kant's claim that in morality the principles of reason structure the content of experience is analogous to his Copernican revolution in epistemology discussed in section 2.4.) Accordingly, in Kant's analysis, acting morally can be understood in terms of acting rationally, whereas acting immorally can be considered as one species of acting irrationally.

The Good Will

Kant's moral theory begins with the claim that the only thing in the world that has absolute, unqualified moral value is a *good will.* A person who has a good will is one who acts from no motive other than the motive of doing what is right. In other words, such a person acts out of respect for the moral law and for the sake of duty, and no other considerations enter into the decision. Of course, this claim raises major questions: What is the moral law and what are our duties? Kant will get to that, but for now he is concerned with the good will as the motivating force in all morality. In the first paragraph of the following passage Kant acknowledges that there are other things that we count as good and lists twelve of them under the headings of "talents of the mind," "qualities of temperament," and "gifts of fortune." (In the second paragraph he lists three additional qualities of temperament.)

However, he argues that such things are not truly good in themselves, for without a good will, such "good" traits actually can be bad. For example, if a hardened criminal is intelligent, cool-headed, courageous, powerful, and persevering, these positive qualities would only enhance the evil he could do.

- In the following passage, why does Kant say that happiness and uninterrupted prosperity would not be good without a good will? How does this opinion differ from what the utilitarians would say?
- The utilitarians stressed that morality has to do with the consequences of our actions. What does Kant think about this approach?

FROM IMMANUEL KANT
Foundations of the Metaphysics of Morals[54]

The Good Will

Nothing in the world—indeed nothing even beyond the world—can possibly be conceived which could be called good without qualification except a *good will.* Intelligence, wit, judgment, and the other talents of the mind, however they may be named, or courage, resoluteness, and perseverance as qualities of temperament, are doubtless in many respects good and desirable. But they can become extremely bad and harmful if the will, which is to make use of these gifts of nature and which in its special constitution is called character, is not good. It is the same with the gifts of fortune. Power, riches, honor, even health, general well-being, and the contentment with one's condition which is called happiness, make for pride and even arrogance if there is not a good will to correct their influence on the mind and on its principles of action so as to make it universally conformable to its end. It need hardly be mentioned that the sight of a being adorned with no feature of a pure and good will, yet enjoying uninterrupted prosperity, can never give pleasure to a rational impartial observer. Thus the good will seems to constitute the indispensable condition even of worthiness to be happy.

Some qualities seem to be conducive to this good will and can facilitate its action, but, in spite of that, they have no intrinsic unconditional worth. They rather presuppose a good will, which limits the high esteem which one otherwise rightly has for them and prevents their being held to be absolutely good. Moderation in emotions and passions, self-control, and calm deliberation not only are good in many respects but even seem to constitute a part of the inner worth of the person. But however unconditionally they were esteemed by the ancients, they are far from being good without qualification. For without the principle of a good will they can be come extremely bad, and the coolness of a villain makes him not only far more dangerous but also more directly abominable in our eyes than he would have seemed without it.

The good will is not good because of what it effects or accomplishes or because of its adequacy to achieve some proposed end; it is good only because of its willing, i.e., it is good of itself. And, regarded for itself, it is to be esteemed incomparably higher than anything which could be brought about by it in favor of any inclination or even of the sum total of all inclinations. Even if it should happen that, by a particularly unfortunate fate or by the [stingy] provision of a stepmotherly nature, this will should be wholly lacking in power to accomplish its purpose, and if even the greatest effort should not avail it to achieve anything of its end, and if there remained only the good will (not as a mere wish but as the summoning of all the means in our power), it would sparkle like a jewel in its own right, as something that had its full worth in itself. Usefulness or fruitlessness can neither diminish nor augment this worth. Its usefulness would be only its setting, as it were, so as to enable us to handle it more conveniently in commerce or to attract the attention of those who are not yet connoisseurs, but not to recommend it to those who are experts or to determine its worth.

STOP AND THINK

Pick three of the personal qualities Kant lists in the first two paragraphs of the previous passage. Make up your own examples of how these qualities actually could be bad if the person possessing them lacked a good will.

If the notion of a good will is at the heart of morality, how do we identify such a will when we are trying to evaluate our own moral character or those of others? What is the relationship between the good will and the actual consequences of our actions as well as our intentions, motives, and feelings? Take a minute to explore these issues in the following thought experiment.

THOUGHT EXPERIMENT

The Good Will

Suppose that Gretchen sees a drowning boy, and being a good swimmer, she leaps into the water to save him. Now consider each of the following additions to this scenario, and in each case, ask if Gretchen possesses what Kant means by a good will.

1. Though the waters were dangerous, Gretchen overcame her fears because she felt a duty to attempt the rescue. Tragically, however, her efforts were in vain, for the child drowned.
2. Gretchen did her best to save the child because she knew his parents were wealthy and she figured she might be in for a substantial reward.
3. Because of the dangers, Gretchen knew no one would blame her if she decided not to risk the rescue. Nevertheless, she was moved by pity upon hearing the child's cries and she knew she would be racked with guilt feelings and could not live with herself if she didn't at least attempt a rescue.

The first two cases should have been easy. In the previous reading, Kant said that a good will would "sparkle like a jewel in its own right," and the external circumstances could neither add to or subtract from its worth. Hence, even if Gretchen's actions did not achieve the good consequence of saving the child, the goodness of her will that motivated these actions still shines brightly. In the second case, it is obvious that she was not acting out of a sense of duty (the essential feature of a good will), but only for her own selfish gain.

What about the third case, where Gretchen is driven by pity and the desire to avoid guilt? Isn't pity a morally worthy emotion and doesn't guilt often motivate us to do the right thing? In this case Gretchen is acting on the basis of her feelings, or what Kant calls *inclination*. The problem with inclination, however, is that our feelings come and go but the demands of morality are a constant. What if Gretchen happened to be emotionally numb that day and felt neither the pull of pity nor the push of guilt acting on her? Lacking these feelings, wouldn't she still have a duty to act? Kant insists that emotions cannot be the motive force in morality for sometimes the moral person must do things that he or she does not really feel like doing. For this reason, Kant insists that morality must be based on rational principles and cannot be driven by any variable conditions such as feelings or inclinations.

In the next two selections, Kant elaborates on this theme by setting out three propositions that define the essential features of duty. (Note: In this passage and later ones Kant user the term *maxim* to refer to a general rule that guides how we act.)

- In the next passage, Kant makes a distinction between (1) acting *in accordance with* duty and (2) acting *from* duty. Can you state the difference between them in your own words and by providing examples?
- Why does Kant say the merchant acted in accordance with duty but not from duty?
- Why is it normally not morally heroic to do what is necessary to sustain your own life? On the other hand, what does Kant say about the anguished man who is inclined to end his life but chooses to preserve it?

The First Proposition of Morality: To Have Moral Worth, an Action Must Be Done from a Sense of Duty

We have, then, to develop the concept of a will which is to be esteemed as good of itself without regard to anything else. It dwells already in the natural sound understanding and does not need so much to be taught as only to be brought to light. In the estimation of the total worth of our actions it always takes first place and is the condition of everything else. In order to show this, we shall take the concept of duty. It contains that of a good will, though with certain subjective restrictions and hindrances; but these are far from concealing it and making it unrecognizable, for they rather bring it out by contrast and make it shine forth all the brighter.

I here omit all actions which are recognized as opposed to duty, even though they may be useful in one respect or another, for with these the question does not arise at all as to whether they may be carried out *from* duty, since they conflict with it. I also pass over the actions which are really in accordance with duty and to which one has no direct inclination, rather executing them because impelled to do so by another inclination. For it is easily decided whether an action in accord with duty is performed from duty or for some selfish purpose. It is far more difficult to note this difference when the action is in accordance with duty and, in addition, the subject has a direct inclination to do it. For example, it is in fact in accordance with duty that a dealer should not overcharge an inexperienced customer, and wherever there is much business the prudent merchant does not do so, having a fixed price for everyone, so that a child may buy of him as cheaply as any other. Thus the customer is honestly served. But this is far from sufficient to justify the belief that the merchant has behaved in this way from duty and principles of honesty. His own advantage required this behavior; but it cannot be assumed that over and above that he had a direct inclination to the purchaser and that, out of love, as it were, he gave none an advantage in price over another. Therefore the action was done neither from duty nor from direct inclination but only for a selfish purpose.

On the other hand, it is a duty to preserve one's life, and moreover everyone has a direct inclination to do so. But for that reason the often anxious care which most men take of it has no intrinsic worth, and the maxim of doing so has no moral import. They preserve their lives according to duty, but not from duty. But if adversities and hopeless sorrow completely take away the relish for life, if an unfortunate man, strong in soul, is indignant rather than despondent or dejected over his fate and wishes for death, and yet preserves his life without loving it and from neither inclination nor fear but from duty—then his maxim has a moral import.

As Kant's examples make clear, acting *in accordance with* duty simply means that our external behavior conforms with what we ought to do. The merchant, for example, dealt honestly with his customers (which was his duty), but it served his interests to do so, because having a reputation for honesty is good for business or because he was afraid of being arrested for unfair business practices. As the case of the merchant demonstrates, we can do the right thing for prudential or selfish reasons. The problem is that doing our duty because of the desirable consequences that would result implies that if the consequences were different, we would no longer have a reason to act in accordance with duty. In this case, whether we have a reason to act in accordance with duty depends more on external circumstances over which we have no control and less on our internal moral character.

On the other hand, acting *from* duty means that the motive for acting is simply the desire to perform the action because it is right. Then and only then does the action have moral worth, for it proceeds from a good will. Kant's theory is an example of *deontological ethics,* because the nature of the action itself and the person's motive are what determines the action's moral value. His theory is in

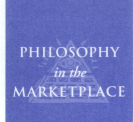

Ask several friends to decide which of the following two people best illustrates what it means to be a genuinely moral person. Ask them to explain their decision.

- Heidi frequently makes personal sacrifices to help other people who are in need. Even though emotionally she tends to be cold and indifferent to the needs of others, she knows that it is her moral duty to help others when she can.
- Kendra frequently makes personal sacrifices to help other people who are in need. She has a cheerful, compassionate disposition, and it makes her feel alive to do something good for someone else. Since helping others is second nature to her, it never occurs to her to consider it a moral obligation.

contrast with *teleological ethics,* or *consequentialism* such as the utilitarian theory, which claims that the goal or outcome of an action is what determines its moral value.

STOP AND THINK

Can you think of a time when have you done something *in accordance with* duty but not *from* duty? If duty did not motivate your behavior, what was your motive? If this motivation was not present, would you still have acted in accordance with duty?

In the next passage Kant focuses specifically on our emotions and inclinations. We have a duty to act kindly and benevolently whenever possible, and many people are moved to do so because they experience pleasure in making others happy. Surely (we might think) such people are morally praiseworthy. However, Kant argues that such responses fall short of what characterizes a good will. We do not choose our emotions and inclinations, and neither do we decide what constitutes our pleasurable experiences. That we happen to feel satisfied when we make others happy is a pleasurable experience over which we have no control. We are the passive recipients of such experiences, and for that reason, they cannot be the product of our rational choices. But ethics has to do with the choices we make and why we make them and cannot be based on our involuntary emotional reactions, our personality, or the whims of fortune.

In the following passage, which is continuous with the last one, Kant sheds further light on the first proposition of morality, that is, to have moral worth an action must be done from a sense of duty.

- Why does Kant say the actions of the naturally sympathetic person lack moral worth?
- According to Kant, do we have duties to ourselves?
- What is Kant's interpretation of the biblical command to love our neighbor?

To be kind where one can is duty, and there are, moreover, many persons so sympathetically constituted that without any motive of vanity or selfishness they find an inner satisfaction in spreading joy, and rejoice in the contentment of others which they have made possible. But I say that, however dutiful and amiable it may be, that kind of action has no true moral worth. It is on a level with [actions arising from] other inclinations, such as the inclination to honor, which, if fortunately directed to what in fact accords with duty and is generally useful and thus honorable, deserve praise and encouragement but no esteem. For the maxim lacks the moral import of an action done not from inclination but from duty. But assume that the mind of that friend to mankind was clouded by a sorrow of his own which extinguished all sympathy with the lot of others and that he still had the power to benefit others in distress, but that their need left him untouched because he was preoccupied with his own need. And now suppose him to tear himself, unsolicited by inclination, out of this dead insensibility and to perform this action only from duty and without any inclination—then for the first time his action has genuine moral worth. Furthermore, if nature has put little sympathy in the heart of a man, and if he, though an honest man, is by temperament cold and indifferent to the sufferings of others, perhaps because he is provided with special gifts of patience and fortitude and expects or even requires that others should have the same—and such a man would certainly not be the meanest product of nature—would not he find in himself a source from which to give himself a far higher worth than he could have got by having a good-natured temperament? This is unquestionably true even though nature did not make him philanthropic, for it is just here that the worth of the character is brought out, which is morally and incomparably the highest of all: he is beneficent not from inclination but from duty.

To secure one's own happiness is at least indirectly a duty, for discontent with one's condition under pressure from many cares and amid unsatisfied wants could easily become a great temptation to transgress duties. But without any view to duty all men have the strongest and deepest inclination to happiness, because in this idea all inclinations are summed up. But the precept of happiness is often so formulated that it definitely thwarts some inclinations, and men can make no definite and certain concept of the sum of satisfaction of all inclinations which goes under the name of happiness. It is not to be wondered at, therefore, that a single inclination, definite as to what it promises and as to the time at which it can be satisfied, can outweigh a fluctuating idea, and that, for example, a man with the gout can choose to enjoy what he likes and to suffer what he may, because according to his calculations at least on this occasion he has not sacrificed the enjoyment of the present moment to a perhaps groundless expectation of a happiness supposed to lie in health. But even in this case, if the universal inclination to happiness did not determine his will, and if health were not at least for him a necessary factor in these calculations, there yet would remain, as in all other cases, a law that he ought to promote his happiness, not from inclination but from duty. Only from this law would his conduct have true moral worth.

It is in this way, undoubtedly, that we should understand those passages of Scripture which command us to love our neighbor and even our enemy, for love as an inclination cannot be commanded. But beneficence from duty, when no inclination impels it and even when it is opposed by a natural and unconquerable aversion, is practical love, not pathological love; it resides in the will and not in the propensities of feeling, in principles of action and not in tender sympathy; and it alone can be commanded.

 STOP AND THINK

Do you think Kant is correct in favoring the person who is cold and indifferent but who dutifully performs an act of kindness instead of the person who is naturally sympathetic and who spontaneously and joyfully spreads happiness? Isn't it morally better for someone to be inclined to be sympathetic, benevolent, and faithful rather than grimly calculating and performing his or her moral duty? As you will see, this issue constitutes a major difference between Kant's ethics and virtue ethics (which is discussed in section 5.5).

In the next passage, Kant presents the second and third principles concerning moral duties. (Remember that a maxim is the principle that you are following when you choose to perform a concrete action.)

The Second Proposition of Morality

The second proposition is: An action performed from duty does not have its moral worth in the purpose which is to be achieved through it but in the maxim by which it is determined. Its moral value, therefore, does not depend on the realization of the object of the action but merely on the principle of volition by which the action is done, without any regard to the objects of the faculty of desire. From the preceding discussion it is clear that the purposes we may have for our actions and their effects as ends and incentives of the will cannot give the actions any unconditional and moral worth. Wherein, then, can this worth lie, if it is not in the will in relation to its hoped-for effect? It can lie nowhere else than in the principle of the will, irrespective of the ends which can be realized by such action. . . .

The Third Proposition of Morality

The third principle, as a consequence of the two preceding, I would express as follows: Duty is the necessity of an action executed from respect for law. I can certainly have an inclination to the object as an effect of the proposed action, but I can never have respect for it precisely because it is a mere effect and not an activity of a will. Similarly, I can have no respect for any inclination whatsoever, whether my own or that of another; in the former case I can at most approve of it and in the latter I can even love it, i.e., see it as favorable to my own advantage. But that which is connected with my will merely as ground and not as consequence, that which does not serve my inclination but overpowers it or at least excludes it from being considered in making a choice—in a word, law itself—can be an object of respect and thus a command. Now as an act from duty wholly excludes the influence of inclination and therewith every object of the will, nothing remains which can determine the will objectively except the law, and nothing subjectively except pure respect for this practical law. This subjective element is the maxim that I ought to follow such a law even if it thwarts all my inclinations.

Thus the moral worth of an action does not lie in the effect which is expected from it or in any principle of action which has to borrow its motive from this expected effect. For all these effects (agreeableness of my own condition, indeed even the promotion of the happiness of others) could be brought about through other causes and would not require the will of a rational being, while the highest and unconditional good can be found only in such a will. Therefore, the pre-eminent good can consist only in the conception of the law in itself (which can be present only in a rational being) so far as this conception and not the hoped-for effect is the determining ground of the will. This pre-eminent good, which we call moral, is already present in the person who acts according to this conception, and we do not have to look for it first in the result.

Thus far, Kant has been stressing that an action has moral worth if it is done for the sake of the moral law. However, he has not yet answered the question, How do we determine what is the moral law? Without an answer to this question, the good will would be well-intentioned but morally blind. A moral law is a kind of command or imperative that directs us to do something or not do something. To understand the kinds of commands that are essential to ethics, Kant says it is important to make a distinction between two kinds of imperatives. The first is a **hypothetical imperative** and says, "If you want X then do Y." This rule tells me what I ought to do, but the ought is contingent on my desiring the goal that follows the "if." For example, I may be told, "If you want a nice lawn, then you must fertilize your grass." Kant calls this type of hypothetical statement a technical imperative. It tells me what means I must use to achieve an end that I may desire. However, if I couldn't care less whether I have a nice lawn or not, then the command is of no concern to me. Hence, a genuinely moral ought cannot take the form of a hypothetical imperative, for this statement would make my moral duties dependent sheerly on what subjective goals I happen to have. A further problem with hypothetical imperatives is that they do not question whether an end is good but only provide guidance on how to attain it. For example, I may be told, "If you want to murder a rival colleague, you ought to use a strong poison." This point illustrates that some hypothetical imperatives are useful for obtaining immoral ends.

Some hypothetical imperatives fall under the heading of pragmatic imperatives, or counsels of prudence. These imperatives offer advice on how to enhance our

hypothetical imperative a rule that tells us only what means to use to achieve a desired end

own welfare and happiness. When we were children, we were given these sorts of rules by our parents, for example, "If you want people to believe you, then you ought always to tell the truth" or "If you want to be happy, you should seek other people's happiness." While the goals contained in these commands may be worthy ones, these rules are not moral commands because they depend on subjective conditions that create our own happiness.

According to Kant, a genuinely moral command is not a hypothetical imperative. Instead, the moral law is presented to us as a **categorical imperative.** It tells me what I ought, should, or must do, but it does not depend on any prior conditions or subjective wants and wishes, and it contains no qualifications. A categorical imperative takes the form, "Do X!" It is not preceded by an if-clause because it tells me what I am morally commanded to do under all conditions and at all times. However, if such a moral law does not come from some external lawgiver such as God, who issues such commands to me? The lawgiver, for Kant, is reason itself. A rational rule is one that is universal and consistent; it is universal in that it applies to all people, at all times, and in all circumstances, and it is consistent in that it does not lead to any contradictions.

Before applying the categorical imperative to morality, let's look at how rationality functions in several examples that do not directly involve ethics. In mathematics it is a rule that two plus two equals four. It does not matter who is doing the calculation or what the circumstances are, and it does not matter whether we like the consequences of applying the rule. The rule must be followed if we are to be rational. However, some rules are, by their very nature, irrational, because they could not be consistently followed by everyone or because they undermine the very activity to which the rule applies. Suppose your mother has a dinner table rule that says, "Before you serve yourself, make sure everyone else is served first." If *everyone* followed this rule, no one would ever be able to eat (thus defeating the whole purpose of the rule). Similarly, suppose a baseball player signs a contract that sets out all the conditions that bind both the employee and the employer. However, if the last line of the contract reads, "If either of the parties wishes not to abide by the above conditions, they don't have to." At that point the contract ceases to be a contract. A contractual condition that undermines the very meaning of a contract is an irrational condition. In the same way, the criterion for the rules we use in ethics is that the rules must be rationally consistent.

With these examples to build on, we can now set out the categorical imperative that Kant regards as the supreme moral principle. Actually, Kant formulates several versions of the categorical imperative. The next passage gives us the first version.

The Categorical Imperative I: Conformity to a Universal Law

There is, therefore, only one categorical imperative. It is: Act only according to that maxim by which you can at the same time will that it should become a universal law.

Now if all imperatives of duty can be derived from this one imperative as a principle, we can at least show what we understand by the concept of duty and what it means, even though it remains undecided whether that which is called duty is an empty concept or not.

The universality of law according to which effects are produced constitutes what is properly called nature in the most general sense (as to form), i.e., the existence of things so far as it is determined by universal laws. [By analogy], then, the universal imperative of duty can be expressed as follows: Act as though the maxim of your action were by your will to become a universal law of nature.

A maxim is a general rule that tells us what we should and should not do. Notice, however, that Kant has not given us any specific maxims. Instead, he has given us a principle for deciding which maxims establish our actual moral obligations and which ones do not. Actually, the first formulation of the categorical imperative has given us two principles: universalizability and reversibility. An action-guiding principle is *universalizable* if it is possible for everyone to act on it. A principle is *reversible* if we could rationally wish ("will" in Kant's terminology) that everyone would act upon it.

Let's examine one of the examples Kant uses to illustrate his categorical imperative. Suppose you need to borrow some money but to do so you must promise to repay it even though you know full well that you will not be able to keep the promise. If you apply Kant's principle, you will discover that the maxim on which you are acting is, "If I need to make a promise I may do so, even though I do not intend to keep it." But could you rationally will that this maxim would become a universal law that everyone followed? Surely not. If everyone adopted this rule, then promise making would be meaningless and there would be no point in making or accepting promises. Your deceitful promise will be accepted *only* if others have respect for promises. Hence, you can apply your rule concerning promises only if no one else follows it.

Notice that Kant's point is *not* that a society in which people did not keep their promises would be very unpleasant. With this inference, the empirical consequences of the action become the criteria of whether the action is right or wrong. Kant's point is a more subtle, logical one. What he is saying is that a moral rule governing an activity (promise making) that would eliminate the activity in question would be a self-defeating rule (and thereby an inconsistent or irrational one).

Kant's criteria of universalizing our maxims captures some of our everyday moral intuitions. When you were young your mother probably censured your behavior at some time or other by saying, "What if everyone behaved the way you do?" The Golden Rule says, "Do unto others as you would have them do unto you." We say to people, "Don't make yourself an exception. Don't be a hypocrite." Hence, the professor who flunks students for plagiarizing their papers at the same time that he steals and publishes another person's research is making himself an exception to the rule that he expects his students and colleagues to follow.

Kant's first version of the categorical imperative approached ethics at the level of formal principles. His second formulation of the categorical imperative focuses more concretely on the persons with whom we interact.

The Categorical Imperative II: Persons as Ends in Themselves

Now, I say, man and, in general, every rational being exists as an end in himself and not merely as a means to be arbitrarily used by this or that will. In all his actions, whether they are directed to himself or to other rational beings, he must always be regarded at the same time as an end. All objects of inclinations have only a conditional worth, for if the inclinations and the needs founded on them did not exist, their object would be without worth. The inclinations themselves as the sources of needs, however, are so lacking in absolute worth that the universal wish of every rational being must be indeed to free himself completely from them. Therefore, the worth of any objects to be obtained by our actions is at all times conditional. Beings whose existence does not depend on our will but on nature, if they are not rational beings, have only a relative worth as means and are therefore called "things"; on the other hand, rational beings are designated "persons" because their nature indicates that they are ends in themselves, i.e., things which may not be used merely as means. Such a being is thus an object of respect and, so far, restricts all [arbitrary] choice. Such beings are not merely subjective ends whose existence as a result of our action has a worth for us, but are objective ends, i.e., beings whose existence in itself is an end. Such an end is one for which no other end can be substituted, to which these beings should serve merely as means. For, without them, nothing of absolute worth could be found, and if all worth is conditional and thus contingent, no supreme practical principle for reason could be found anywhere.

Thus if there is to be a supreme practical principle and a categorical imperative for the human will, it must be one that forms an objective principle of the will from the conception of that which is necessarily an end for everyone because it is an end in itself. Hence this objective principle can serve as a universal practical law. The ground of this principle is: rational nature exists as an end in itself. Man necessarily thinks of his own existence in this way; thus far it is a subjective principle of human actions. Also every other rational being thinks of his existence by means of the same rational ground which holds also for myself; thus it is at the same time an objective principle from which, as a supreme practical ground, it must be possible to derive all laws of the will. The practical imperative, therefore, is the following: Act so that you treat humanity, whether in your own person or in that of another, always as an end and never as a means only.

Kant did not think that these two versions of the categorical imperative were two distinct principles; he considered them two ways of making the same point. Many commentators, however, are not sure that they are the same. Nevertheless, on Kant's behalf, it could be argued that the second version is really expressing the criteria of universalizability and reversibility of the first version by saying that we should always act toward others in ways that we would want everyone else to act toward us.

What does Kant mean when he says, "Act so that you treat humanity, whether in your own person or in that of another, always as an end and never as a means only"? This principle seems to be saying that each person has intrinsic worth and dignity and that we should not use people or treat them like things. Kant's argument for this principle could be paraphrased in the following manner. Mere things such as cars, jewels, works of art, or tools have value only if persons endow them with value. In other words, a Rembrandt painting will sell for a million dollars only because many people desire it. Accordingly, such things have only *conditional* value, because if people stop desiring them, they will be worthless. However, persons are not things. Since persons are the source of all conditional value, they cannot have conditional value themselves; they must have *absolute* or *intrinsic* value. No one can give you your worth as a person, nor can they take it away. An acquaintance may treat you like a thing whose only value is to serve his ends, but such a person is being inconsistent. He is acting as though he alone has absolute value while others are mere things to be used. Thus, he is following the maxim, "I will treat others as things," but he could not consistently want others to follow this rule in return. Consequently, he is making himself an exception.

STOP AND THINK

Have you ever experienced a situation in which someone used you merely as a means to get something that person wanted? How did that experience make you feel? Why did you feel that way? Have you ever treated someone else merely as a means? What end were you trying to achieve? If you had followed Kant's categorical imperative, how would you have behaved differently?

Sometimes it may seem as though we cannot avoid using people as things to serve our own ends. When you buy stamps from the postal clerk, for example, you are using that person as a source of stamps. However, notice that Kant said we should treat persons always as an end and never as a means *only.* Hence, even in impersonal transactions in which we are mainly interested in a person for the services that he or she can perform for us, we should never act in a rude or manipulative manner, and we should always be mindful of the fact that it is a person with whom we are dealing.

An important feature of this formulation of the moral imperative is that Kant explicitly claims that we should treat ourselves with respect and not merely as a means to some end. Many ethical theorists (the utilitarians, for example) believe that ethics governs only our relations with others. Kantian ethics implies that we have moral duties to ourselves and not just to others. For this reason, Kant condemns suicide. If I decide to terminate my life in order to escape my pains and disappointments, I am treating myself as though I were a thing that is determined by external circumstances. Instead, I should respect the dignity and worth of my own personhood and treat it as having a value that transcends every other consideration. In the act of suicide, I am destroying a person (myself) and treating that person as a means in order to achieve some other end (freedom from burdens). In another application of this principle, Kant says that even if I were stranded alone on a desert island, I would have duties to myself. For example, I should do what I could to improve myself and make use of my talents instead of lapsing into idleness and indulgence.

Absolute Duties

Kant believes that if there is to be morality at all, then moral rules must hold for all people, at all times, in all circumstances, and with no exceptions. In one respect, the notion that there are absolute moral duties is a good one. Since one rule that the categorical imperative generates is that we ought not to kill an innocent person, Kant's absolutism would forbid society from killing you even if your murder created the best consequences for society. Thus, unlike utilitarianism, Kantian ethics would not allow exceptions to the principles of justice and individual rights. However, there are problems with moral absolutism. Consider the case of the inquiring stranger in the following thought experiment.

THOUGHT EXPERIMENT

The Case of the Inquiring Stranger

Suppose that a friend is fleeing from a murderous maniac and comes to your home begging you for help. Since he is your friend and is innocent of any wrongdoing, you hide him in your attic. Moments later, the murderer comes to your door and asks if your friend is in the house. (Let's suppose that silence will tip him off that your friend is inside.)

- Should you tell the truth or lie?
- What moral principles and arguments would you use to justify this action?
- What do you think Kant would say?

Even if we agree that lying (as a general rule) is wrong, most people would say that in *this* case lying to the inquiring stranger is morally justified. Surely it is more important to save an innocent life than to tell the truth. This story is not simply a far-fetched, hypothetical case; many real-world examples of this situation exist. In World War II, for example, Europeans hid innocent people from the Nazis and lied to protect these potential victims. Kant, discussing this example in his essay "On a Supposed Right to Lie from Altruistic Motives," points out that in this case we are violating our moral duty to the truth because we think the consequences of doing so will be good. But can we ever know what the consequences will be? Suppose that you lie and say that your friend is not in your house but that you saw him running down the street. Unknown to you, your friend has slipped out the back door and *is* running down the street, where the murderer catches and kills him. Kant says that your lie would have been instrumental in causing the innocent person's death. On the other hand, Kant says that if you had told the truth, the murderer might have been apprehended by the neighbors while he searched the house. Kant's conclusion is: "Therefore, whoever tells a lie, however well intentioned he might be, must answer for the consequences, however unforeseeable they were, and pay the penalty for them. . . . To be truthful (honest) in all deliberations, therefore, is a sacred and absolutely commanding decree of reason, limited by no expediency."[55] Kant's point is that we can never be completely sure of the consequences of our actions, so they cannot play a role in determining our duty. Instead, we must stick with our known duties.

Several replies could be made to Kant's analysis. First, he is too pessimistic about our ability to always predict the consequences. Surely there are situations in which we could be reasonably sure about what will happen if we perform this or that action. Particularly when a life is at stake, we better do whatever seems to have the best chance of preserving that life. If you had acted on your duty to the truth, as Kant says you should do, and if your action had the indirect result of causing your friend's death, can you wash your hands so simply of the results of your choice?

A second problem is that Kant didn't seem to realize that qualifications and exceptions could be built into universal and absolute rules. For example, in the case of the inquiring stranger, why couldn't you follow the rule, "Always tell the truth unless doing so would cause an innocent person's death"? This rule is both universalizable and reversible, because everyone could follow it without contradiction, and we could wish that everyone did follow it. Or the rule could be, "Always tell the truth to those who have a right to know the truth." This universal rule would require us to tell the truth to a friend, an employer, or a judge, but it might allow us to be less than truthful to a murderer, a Nazi, a malicious gossip, or an acquaintance inquiring about important issues of security and confidentiality.

Finally, Kant did not address the problem of what to do when duties conflict. This situation certainly occurred in the case with the inquiring stranger, because our duties of telling the truth and preserving lives were in conflict. Some philosophers have tried to keep Kant's important insights while modifying his position to deal with the problem of conflicts between duties. W. D. Ross, for example, distinguishes between two kinds of duties.[56] A **prima facie duty** is one that is morally binding *unless* it conflicts with a more important duty. (Prima facie literally means "at first glance.") An **actual duty** is one that we are morally obligated to perform in a particular situation after we have taken all the circumstances into account. Prima facie duties are always in effect, but any particular one can be superseded by a higher duty. This rule is analogous to the law of gravity, which is always in effect but can be superseded by the more powerful force of a rocket engine. Of course, even though we may be justified in violating one prima facie duty to fulfill another one, we still have an obligation to make amends to anyone who was harmed by our doing so.

Without claiming that this list is complete, Ross sets out seven prima facie duties: (1) *fidelity*—keeping our promises, telling the truth; (2) *reparation*—compensating others for wrongs we have done; (3) *gratitude*—showing appreciation for benefits others have bestowed on us; (4) *justice*—distributing goods with impartiality and equity; (5) *beneficence*—promoting other people's good, (6) *self-improvement*—trying to become a better person; and (7) *nonmaleficence*—refraining from harming others.

Ross does not believe in any formula for ranking these duties in some sort of absolute hierarchy. To decide which of the prima facie duties is the actual duty we should act on in a given situation requires a morally sensitive and wise assessment of the circumstances. For example, my actual duty may be to stop and help a stranded motorist even though it may require me to break a promise (such as an appointment). If that promise impacts an international treaty on which world peace depends, however, then the actual duty of that promise may be more important than preventing a minor harm. Furthermore, Ross stresses the highly personal character of duty. For example, my general duty to help others is normally more pressing when it comes to my family members than it is for strangers. Although Ross does not provide us with a clear-cut procedure for determining which duty is our actual one in a given situation, he has captured Kant's concern for universally binding duties while giving us some means to resolve conflicts between them.

prima facie duty a duty that is morally binding *unless* it conflicts with a more important duty

actual duty a duty that we are morally obligated to perform in a particular situation after we have taken all the circumstances into account

LOOKING THROUGH THE LENS OF KANTIAN ETHICS

1. Kant says that we should always treat persons as ends in themselves and never merely as a means. What implications would following this principle have for your social life, including your actual or potential romantic involvements?

2. According to classical utilitarianism, ethics has to do with how our actions affect others. If I were alone on a desert island I could do whatever pleases me; I would have no moral obligations. But Kant thinks that we have moral duties to ourselves, such as the duty to preserve our own life, to develop our natural talents, to improve ourselves, and so on. What do you think? Do you have moral duties to yourself, or is it morally permissible to do anything you want as long as it doesn't affect someone else?

3. In Victor Hugo's novel *Les Miserables* (made into a musical and movie), the hero, Jean Valjean, is a former convict living under an illegal false identity. Not only is he the mayor of his town and a public benefactor, but he owns a successful business on which most of the townspeople depend for employment. He learns that some unfortunate beggar has been mistaken for him and will be sent away to prison. The real Jean Valjean decides it is his moral duty to reveal who he is, even though it may destroy all the good work he has done and cause him to be sent back to prison to serve a cruel and unjust life sentence.

- What would a Kantian say Jean Valjean should do? Why?
- What would a utilitarian say? Why?
- What do you think Jean Valjean should do? Give your reasons.

4. Peruse newspaper stories, editorials, letters to the editor, political or legislative proposals, and everyday conversations to find examples of ethical justifications that reflect the spirit of Kantian ethics.

EXAMINING THE STRENGTHS AND WEAKNESSES OF KANTIAN ETHICS

Positive Evaluation

1. Kant's ethics is admirable in emphasizing the importance of rationality, consistency, impartiality, and respect for persons in the way we live our lives. By stressing the fact that moral absolutes cannot be violated, he prevents any loopholes, self-serving exceptions, and personal biases in the determination of our duties. Consequently, he saves us from the temptation to rationalize our behavior for the sake of convenience and expediency or from doing an end run around our moral obligations.

2. Can we ever be completely sure of the consequences of our actions? Haven't there been times when you thought you were doing the best thing, based on the

anticipated consequences, but the results turned out badly? Don't such situations raise a problem with the philosophy of basing our moral decisions on the consequences? Contrary to utilitarianism and other forms of consequentialism, Kant argues that consequences should never play a role in determining our moral obligations. Based on rational, moral deliberations, we can be certain about our moral obligation to tell the truth, for example. However, we cannot know with equal certainty the good or bad consequences of either telling the truth or lying. Isn't this consideration important? Isn't it often the case that doing the right thing will sometimes make people unhappy? In such cases, don't we have to do our duty anyway?

3. Unlike utilitarianism, Kant's theory strictly prohibits some actions, such as murder, breaking promises, or violating a person's rights to serve some other end. In doing so, Kant's ethics avoids utilitarianism's problems in which (critics claim) the goodness of the overall consequences could justify some very reprehensible actions. Isn't Kant's theory a better moral theory than one in which "anything goes" as long as the overall consequences are good?

Negative Evaluation

1. Is the good will always good without qualification, as Kant supposes? Can't I be an inept, bungling do-gooder, always conscientiously trying to do my duty but creating human misery as a result? Take for example, the oppressive, controlling mother of an adult child who assumes her duty is always to be "helpful" until the child finally screams in frustration, "Please, mother, I would rather do it myself!" As the old saying goes, "the road to hell is paved with good intentions." It seems clear that many Nazis saw themselves as fulfilling a moral mandate to "save" Europe from political and cultural decay. It could be argued that my single-minded focus on my duty coupled with a self-righteous or insensitive blindness to the consequences of my actions could be a form of moral fanaticism. Is moral fanaticism a potential problem for Kantian ethics?

2. Kant tends to make a very sharp dichotomy between doing our duty for duty's sake and doing it because of our inclinations. But shouldn't you be commended if you spontaneously and joyfully do your duty because you are filled with compassion, because it is second nature to you, and because being moral has become a habitual feature of your personality? Kant seems to think that doing our duty must be a matter of rational calculation in which our inclinations and emotions play no role. Isn't there something one-sided about this approach? Shouldn't morality be related to our emotions, our habitual or spontaneous behavior, what we love, what we disdain, and what we feel good about, and not just to our actions, rational deliberations, and rules of conduct?

3. Kant's commitment to absolute duties offers us no solution when our duties conflict. In the case of the inquiring stranger, you have a duty to tell the truth, but you also have a duty to preserve life. Kant's advice is to tell the truth and let the

consequences happen as they may, since you cannot be completely certain of the consequences. Besides, he says, you will have done your duty, and it is the stranger who is responsible for the murder and not you. But aren't we responsible not only for what we do but also for what we knowingly allow to happen? If your telling the truth about the location of your friend allows the murderer to find his victim, don't you bear some responsibility for the death? Isn't the preservation of life a higher and more weighty duty than telling the truth? Shouldn't reasonable exceptions to moral rules be allowed, especially when those rules make it impossible to fulfill a higher duty?

4. Are the principles of universalizability and reversibility found in the first version of the categorical imperative subject to arbitrariness and subjectivity, contrary to what Kant thinks? For example, I find eating raw oysters disgusting, so I would make a moral rule that "No one should eat raw oysters." Or suppose I have the odd belief that "Everyone should tie his or her left shoe first." In both cases, I could universalize these principles without contradiction, willing that everyone should obey them, but then we would have arbitrary, trivial, and highly subjective moral rules. Similarly, Kant thinks that we have a moral duty to help others who are less fortunate, because if we were in their place we would want someone to help us (reversibility). But the ethical egoist Ayn Rand claims that "Everyone should tend to his or her own interests and not to the needs of others." She also claims that if she were in need she would neither expect nor want you to sacrifice your interests for hers, since she finds that being dependent on others is demeaning. So it is possible for others to universalize moral rules that are contrary to those of Kant. Does this possibility suggest that in spite of Kant's belief that his ethics is based on pure rationality, a good deal of subjectivity has crept into it?

5.5 VIRTUE ETHICS

LEADING QUESTIONS: VIRTUE ETHICS

Contemporary philosopher Michael Stocker posed the following thought experiment to test our ethical intuitions.

> Suppose you are in a hospital, recovering from a long illness. You are very bored and restless and at loose ends when Smith comes in once again. You are now convinced more than ever that he is a fine fellow and a real friend—taking so much time to cheer you up, traveling all the way across town, and so on. You are so effusive with your praise and thanks that he protests that he always tries to do what he thinks is his duty, what he thinks is best. You at first think he is engaging in a polite form of self-deprecation, relieving the moral burden. But the more you two speak, the more clear it becomes that he was telling the literal truth: that it is not essentially because of you that he came to see you, not because you are friends, but because he thought it his duty, perhaps as a fellow Christian or Communist or whatever, or simply because he knows of no one more in need of cheering up and no one easier to cheer up.[57]

1. From a utilitarian point of view, Smith was acting morally because he maximized happiness by cheering you up. From a Kantian point of view, Smith was acting morally because he was acting from a sense of duty. What, then, is the problem with his hospital visit?

2. What is the difference between someone helping you (a) for the sake of maximizing the total amount of happiness in the world, (b) for the sake of fulfilling his duties as a friend (c) to help sustain the general practice of friendship, and (d) *out of* a personal sense of friendship for the sake of you as a person whom he cherishes? Why do the first three motives seem somewhat impersonal and abstract?

3. Utilitarianism says we should act for the sake of good consequences and Kantianism says we should act for the sake of our rational moral duty, but Stocker (the author of this thought experiment) objects that in either case we are failing to value the recipient of the action as a person for his or her own sake. Such theories "treat others externally, as essentially replaceable, as mere instruments or repositories of general and non-specific value" and in doing so, these theories "preclude love, friendship, affection, fellow feeling, and community."[58] In what way does Stocker's story attempt to illustrate these points?

4. If Smith's benevolent actions, their consequences, and his sense of duty are blameless, what is it that Smith lacks?

Up until the last few decades, ethical theory has been dominated by the debate between the utilitarians and the Kantians or between those who stress the consequences of an action and those who are more concerned with whether the nature of the act itself fulfills or violates a moral duty. Nevertheless, in spite of their differences, both ethical theories are in agreement that the morality of *actions* is the primary focus of ethics. However, in ordinary life we assess the moral qualities not only of actions but of *persons* as well. We might say of a person that she is admirable, decent, good, honorable, moral, saintly, and in short, has a virtuous moral character. On the other hand, we might judge that she is bad, base, corrupt, disreputable, immoral, reprehensible, and in short, has a deplorable moral character. Some philosophers do not seem to connect morality with a person's actions. Instead, they claim, morality should be concerned with our likes and dislikes, desires, attitudes, dispositions to behave in certain ways, personal ideals and life goals, what sorts of things make us happy, and in general those personal qualities that define our stance toward life.

This position, found both in ancient and contemporary thought, is known as virtue ethics. *Virtue ethics* is an ethical theory that focuses on those character traits that make someone a good or admirable person rather than simply on the actions the person performs. According to the previously discussed theories the primary question in ethics is, What should I do? On the contrary, for virtue ethics the fundamental question in ethics is, What sort of person should I be? This point is made by Stocker's story about Smith's hospital visit, for even though Smith did the right thing and conscientiously fulfilled his moral duty according to utilitarian or

Kantian theory, he lacked the virtue of compassion. Accordingly, something is lacking in his moral development as a person. Virtue ethics says that in ethics we should first be concerned with what it means to be a virtuous person, and then the dos and don'ts of concrete action will follow from this.

STOP AND THINK

What reasons can be given in support of each of the following statements?

1. Ethics should be based on the notion of what it means to be a good person.
2. Ethics should be based on the concept of what it means for an action to be morally right or obligatory.

After weighing the reasons given in support for each one, which statement do you think best describes what should be the main concern of an ethical theory?

SURVEYING THE CASE FOR VIRTUE ETHICS

WHAT IS VIRTUE?

One difficulty in understanding the word *virtue* is the fact that it has acquired a number of diverse associations over the centuries. In our day, to say someone is "virtuous" suggests that they are very pious or, perhaps, sexually pure. Sometimes it even has a negative connotation, for example, when it is applied sarcastically to someone who is obnoxiously sanctimonious. To understand virtue ethics, we have to go back to ancient Greece where the theory began. In Greek philosophy the concept of virtue was expressed with the word *aretē*. To have *aretē* means "to have the quality of excellence" or "to be doing what you do in an excellent way." This concept of virtue is still alive today in our English word *virtuosity*. A virtuoso violinist is one who can play the violin with admirable technical skill. For the Greeks *anything* could be said to have virtue if it was an excellent example of its kind. Thus, they said that the virtue of a knife is its ability to cut things. The virtue of a race horse is to run very fast. While the shipbuilder, the wrestler, the physician, and the musician each have a particular kind of virtue related to their specific task, philosophers such as Socrates were concerned with the question, "What does it mean to be a virtuous (excellent) human being?" In other words, being fully human is a task or skill in itself, which is more fundamental than all the specific skills we may acquire. That's why we refer to a vicious tyrant as being "inhuman." He is so lacking in the virtues that constitute an excellent character that he doesn't deserve the label "human." According to Socrates and virtue ethics, being moral boils down to being successful at the art of living. People who routinely, and without any qualms, lie, cheat, exploit people, and are insensitive to the sufferings of others lack the virtues of honesty, integrity, justice, and compassion, and have the corresponding vices. According to Socrates and Plato the character of such a person is malformed, deficient, and dysfunctional and is the moral equivalent of a bodily organ that is diseased.[59] Consequently, Socrates asserted that the most important goal for humans is not just living but "living well."[60] Contrary to contemporary advertisements that equate the good life with possessing popularity, fame, fortune, and premium beverages or cars, Socrates identified "living well" with possessing a certain quality of character, for he says that "living well and honorably and justly mean the same thing."[61]

virtue a trait of character that is to be admired and desired because it is a constituent of human excellence

A **virtue** can be defined as a trait of character that is to be admired and desired because it is a constituent of human excellence. Virtues are intrinsically valuable for their own sake, but they are also valued because they promote human flourishing both for the individual who possesses them and for society in general. Typical examples of moral virtues (but not a complete list) are generosity, compassion, honesty, fidelity, integrity, justice, conscientiousness, and courage. Although the boundaries are hard to draw, moral virtues should be distinguished from personality traits such as charm or shyness. While we may find certain personality traits to be appealing or unappealing, they are not the focus of our evaluation of a person's moral character. If character traits are the subject of moral evaluation, then everyone must at least have the potential to have them. If we do not possess them, we must be able to acquire them by training, practice, and through a personal program of self-improvement. Otherwise, judging someone negatively for lacking a certain virtue would be like criticizing that person for being born with defective eyesight.

STOP AND THINK

As you look over your life, what character traits have you acquired or strengthened that made you a better human being than before? Was your acquisition of these traits facilitated by someone's influence, by your own attempts at self-improvement, or by a combination of factors? Suppose you could go to a trading post at which you could leave behind a trait, an attitude, or a desire that you think diminishes you as a human being and exchange it for one that is better. What would you leave behind, and what new characteristic would you acquire? What concrete changes would this trade make in your life? Why do you think this trade would improve you as a person?

Like most theories, virtue ethics is defended with a two-pronged approach. First, the assumptions and methods of competing theories are critiqued. Since the main alternatives to virtue ethics are utilitarianism and Kantian ethics, the virtue ethicist must demonstrate that those theories have irredeemable limitations and flaws. But simply showing that your opponents' theories have problems is not enough to show that yours should be adopted. Therefore, the second approach is to make a positive case for the theory being promoted in order to show its superiority to the alternatives. Following this two-pronged approach, I begin by discussing the virtue theorist's critique of utilitarianism and Kantian ethics.

THE PROBLEMS WITH THE UTILITARIAN VIEW

As you might suspect, the virtue ethicist charges that the utilitarian and Kantian theories are inadequate because they fail to give virtue the priority it deserves in our ethical lives. Although utilitarian and Kantian ethical theories are primarily concerned with right conduct, they do not neglect virtuous character traits entirely. In those theories, however, virtue has value mostly for its tendency to serve other ends. Thus, the two theories view virtue as having instrumental value rather than intrinsic value. First, consider the following thought experiment in the light of utilitarian theory.

THOUGHT EXPERIMENT

Are Good Actions Enough?

Suppose that someone (call her Millie) performed the following actions: (1) told the truth when pressured to do otherwise, (2) rescued a child in a dangerous situation, (3) donated time to a charity, and (4) spent her free time visiting Aunt Gertrude in the nursing home. Furthermore, let's add the stipulation that in each case Millie's actions maximized happiness more than any other alternative would.

- What judgment would the utilitarian make concerning the moral goodness of Millie's actions in each case?

Now suppose that in the previous cases Millie acted from the following motives: (1) she calculated that truth telling would earn her a reward in the afterlife, (2) she hoped that her courageous rescue would earn her fame, (3) she anticipated that her charitable work would be good for her political campaign, and (4) she hoped to inherit her aunt's fortune.

- With this additional information, what would *you say* about the moral goodness of Millie's actions?

It seems clear that the utilitarian would have to say that, in spite of her questionable motives, Millie performed the morally right action in each situation because the consequences resulted in maximizing happiness. Nothing in the utilitarian rules for right conduct talks about motives. However, if your moral intuitions are similar to mine, when we find out Millie's motives for these benevolent actions, we tend to think less of her as a person rather than admiring her. Are the utilitarians sheerly "happiness accountants" who only worry about how the figures add up? Are they totally unconcerned about people's motives and character? The answer is that utilitarian theory *does* take these factors into account. If people performed benevolent actions only to get into heaven, win fame, succeed in politics, or get an inheritance, then they would not be inclined to act morally when they believed there was no payoff. Hence, utilitarians think it is important to encourage certain character traits in people and instill them in their children, because a person who has a virtuous character is more likely to choose to do the morally right action (the action that maximizes the general good). In this theory, virtue has merely instrumental value, not intrinsic value.

THE PROBLEMS WITH THE KANTIAN VIEW

Kant seems to be more concerned with the person's character than the utilitarians are, because he says it is not enough to do the right thing (acting in accordance with duty). Instead, for an action to be genuinely moral it must be performed from the right motive (acting for the sake of duty). For Kant, the only thing that is good without qualification is the good will, or the motive to do our duty. We could characterize this motive as the virtue of *conscientiousness*. But while Kant exalts this one virtue, he dismisses the others as morally neutral or even as expressions of our inclinations and emotions. The following thought experiment illustrates the problem with Kant's narrow approach to moral virtue.

 THOUGHT EXPERIMENT

Is Acting for the Sake of Duty Enough?

Consider the following two scenarios:

1. Kantian Karl finds that someone has left a purse behind in the classroom. Seeking to find the name of its owner, he discovers that it contains a substantial amount of money. He could use the money to pay the balance on his tuition bill and has a strong inclination to keep it. Being a good Kantian, however, he realizes that his rational, moral duty is to return the purse to its owner. He seriously considers keeping the money, convincing himself that he needs it more than its owner does, but his attempts to rationalize this course of action are repeatedly interrupted by the insistent demands of the moral law within him. Breaking out in a sweat as he oscillates between temptation and duty, he finally sets his chin and decides that he will do what duty demands. He returns the purse with the money intact to its rightful owner.

2. Virtuous Virginia finds that someone has left a wallet behind in the classroom. Seeking to find the name of its owner, she discovers that it contains a substantial amount of money. Virginia believes that achieving personal excellence is the most important goal in life, so all her life she has striven to improve herself intellectually, athletically, musically, and morally. She has a mature, fully developed moral character, so honesty is part of her very being. Consequently, it does not even occur to her to keep the money for herself. Without a second thought, she immediately takes action to return the wallet with the money to its rightful owner.

Both Karl and Virginia performed the right action and did it for moral reasons. But suppose we now want to assess not just their actions, but their moral character. Which person, Karl or Virginia, has the most moral worth? How important is this consideration?

In the first scenario, Kantian Karl faithfully but grudgingly did his duty, but to do so he had to wrestle against his inclinations. In contrast, Virtuous Virginia did her duty because she had developed such moral habits that she was naturally inclined to do what is right. Kant tended to make such a rigid dichotomy between moral duty and desire that if an action (such as Virginia's) reflected our habitual way of behaving or followed from our personal nature, our emotions, desires, and inclinations, that action had no moral worth. However, Aristotle said that

> the man who does not rejoice in noble actions is not even good; since no one would call a man just who did not enjoy acting justly, nor any man liberal [generous] who did not enjoy liberal actions [generosity]; and similarly in all other cases. . . . Hence we ought to have been brought up in a particular way from our very youth, as Plato says, so as both to delight in and be pained by the things that we ought; for this is the right education.[62]

Contrary to Kant, Aristotle thought that ethics was a matter of the emotions and not simply of reason alone. Following Aristotle, contemporary virtue ethicists claim that virtuous persons not only do their duty for its own sake, but do it happily and spontaneously, and find their deepest desires and inclinations fulfilled in doing so.

In summary, utilitarianism and Kantianism, the two major ethical theories in modern philosophy, are theories based on rules or principles and focus single-mindedly on the ethics of conduct. The analogy between ethical theory and the law is obvious in these approaches. On the other hand, virtue ethics thinks this emphasis is misplaced and wants to return the focus of ethics to that of character and the emotions. If the legal metaphor underlies rule-based theories, then gardening is the metaphor of virtue ethics. The virtues are those conditions that are essential for humans to grow, blossom, and flourish. Continuing with the gardening metaphor, each one of us is both the gardener and the flower. Hence, for the virtue theorist, the question to ask about a proposed action is not "What are the consequences?" or "Could I universalize the principle on which I am acting?" Instead, the virtue theorist would ask, "What would this proposed action do to me in my project of becoming an admirable and worthy human being?"

THE POSITIVE CASE FOR VIRTUE ETHICS

The viewpoint offered by virtue ethics can be summarized by the following five themes. While different theorists will emphasize some points over others, together these themes weave a pattern depicting an alternative picture of what ethics is all about.

1. Virtues Are Necessary Conditions for Human Flourishing and Well-being

One common theme in virtue ethics is that, given our physical and psychological nature, the moral virtues are necessary for us to flourish and to fare well in life. Socrates thought that asking for a reason to be moral was like asking, "Why should

I want to flourish?" Obviously, the notion of "flourish" here does not mean that possessing the moral virtues will necessarily guarantee us friends, wealth, and a life of ease, because moral persons have often been rejected by their society, poor, and inflicted with great suffering. Whether or not we are graced with external rewards, we have a natural desire to be as excellent as possible in what we do. Few of us will win great fame or fortune for our athletic, musical, or intellectual skills. Yet we want to do as well as we can in these and other endeavors simply because striving for excellence, that is, maximizing our potential as human beings, is rewarding in itself and gives us a sense of personal accomplishment. Virtues, rather than having a causal relationship to flourishing, are said to have a constitutive relationship. A spark can *cause* an explosion, but getting the ball across your opponent's goal line does not cause your team to have a touchdown. Instead, it is what *constitutes* a touchdown. Similarly, possessing the virtues is, the argument goes, what constitutes human well-being.

Alasdair MacIntyre, one of the most influential voices in contemporary virtue ethics, describes the role that the virtues play in our individual and community endeavors:

> The virtues therefore are to be understood as those dispositions which will not only sustain practices, but which will also sustain us in the relevant kind of quest for the good, by enabling us to overcome the harms, dangers, temptations and distractions which we encounter, and which will furnish us with increasing self-knowledge and increasing knowledge of the good. The catalogue of the virtues will therefore include the virtues required to sustain the kind of households and the kind of political communities in which men and women can seek for the good together and the virtues necessary for philosophical inquiry about the character of the good.[63]

2. *Moral Rules Are Inadequate unless They Are Grounded in a Virtue-based Ethics*

While downplaying the role of moral rules in the study of ethics, the virtue ethicist does not deny their role in the moral life altogether. Nevertheless, the proponents of virtue ethics question the sufficiency of moral rules apart from a virtuous character. For example, I will not be inclined to follow moral rules nor will I be able to know how they are to be applied if I do not possess virtue. Philosopher Gregory Trianosky expresses the standpoint of virtue ethics in this way:

> It has sometimes been pointed out that rules or principles of right action must be applied, and conflicts between them adjudicated. But the rules themselves do not tell us how to apply them in specific situations, let alone how to apply them well, or indeed when to excuse people for failing to comply with them. For these tasks, it is claimed, an account of the virtues is required. . . .
>
> Next, it has been argued that much of right conduct cannot be codified in rules or principles. Moral situations are too complex; moral rules too general and simplistic. . . . Moreover, except when one can look to some morally exemplary or paradigmatic individual, the extent to which one decides well will depend largely on the extent to which one has already developed a virtuous character.[64]

3. Judgments about Character Are More Fundamental Than Judgments about the Rightness or Wrongness of Conduct

This claim goes further than the last one, for some recent utilitarians and Kantians have attempted to supplement the ethics of duty with considerations of character. However, the claim of virtue ethics is that the notion of virtue is neither a supplement to moral rules nor dependent upon them because virtue is the primary moral category. As virtue ethicist Harold Alderman says:

> Rules and other notions of the good are, at best, either analytic clarifications of what we mean by virtuous character, maps which indicate how it might be acquired, or a sign that someone actually has it.[65]

Just as the utilitarian and the Kantian will often come to the same moral judgment even though they justify it on different grounds, so the virtue ethicist will usually agree with them concerning the right thing to do in a certain situation. However, the distinctive nature of virtue ethics reveals itself in the fact that, within this position, considerations of virtue can sometimes trump considerations of utility or duty. Philosopher Justine Oakley makes this point with the following example:

> Suppose I console a close friend of mine who is grieving over the irretrievable breakdown of his marriage, and that in consoling him, I stay with him longer than would be required by my duty to him as a friend. A virtue ethicist might regard my staying longer to console him as right, even if my doing so meant cancelling an appointment with a business associate I'd promised to meet for lunch, and also meant that I thereby failed to maximise overall utility. What makes it right to console the friend here is that this is the sort of thing which someone with an appropriate conception of friendship will be disposed to do, rather than because this brings about the best overall consequences, or because this is our duty as a friend.[66]

4. Virtue Ethics Is More Comprehensive, because It Deals with the Whole Person and Not Simply the Person in So Far As He or She Performs an Action

Action and rule-based theories of ethics are too narrow, for they focus primarily on those moments in life when a person is contemplating an action and specifically only on that category of actions for which there are either good and bad consequences at stake or duties to be fulfilled or violated. Consequently, such theories promote a sort of "moral minimalism" in which the primary concern is, "How can I avoid being blameworthy for the way I acted?" Such theories divide human life into (1) moral situations and (2) nonmoral situations. Theories of conduct are concerned primarily with domain 1, in which we are faced with choices that are either obligatory or forbidden, whereas domain 2 is the realm of the permissible in which the demands of morality are indifferent to what we do. But should morality be quarantined to such a narrow slice of human life? Shouldn't morality be concerned with the whole of our lives and not just those situations in which we face possible wrongdoing? Does ethics offer any guidance to those aspects of life in which the demands of moral rules and duties are not pressing upon me? Does it have anything to say about my ideals, aspirations, desires, interests, emotional responses—all those factors that express the person I am and the person I hope to become, apart from how I behave? Does ethics concern my choices, trivial and momentous, such as what friends to cultivate, what career to pursue, what books to read, or what recreations to enjoy? For example, according to the rule-based ethics of either utilitarianism or Kantianism, the moral value of benevolence is primarily an issue in those situations in which I ought to help others and in which not doing so would be wrong. However, philosopher J. L. A. Garcia argues that this rule-based, action-oriented notion of benevolence is much too minimalistic.

> For a benevolent person will have some inclination to help others even when she is not directed (required) to do so by the moral rules, i.e. when it is supererogatory.* More important, a benevolent person will be inclined to want and hope that others prosper even when she realizes that she cannot by her actions help them and she will be in-clined to be pleased with others' good fortune and displeased with their bad fortune when their fortune is, again, unrelated to her own action. In short, the virtue of benev-olence cannot be simply a disposition to action, because it consists, not in action, but in various forms of mental response, which may or may not be expressed in action.[67]

If we go back to the story of Smith visiting you in the hospital, we can now see clearly why his benevolent actions were so disturbing. He was acting out of a sense of duty and with the intention to maximize utility, but what was lacking was a spirit of benevolence, a desire to help, a caring attitude, a disposition to feel pleasure in helping you, and happiness in seeing your spirits lifted.

In contrast to the ethics of conduct that dwells on how I perform transitory actions and the motives that direct me at those moments, virtue ethics is concerned with settled character traits that endure beyond those occasions. As the virtue ethicist David Solomon expresses it:

> The moral life is not, on this view, best regarded as a set of episodic encounters with moral dilemmas or moral uncertainty (although anyone's moral life will certainly con-tain moments of this kind); it is rather a life-long pursuit of excellence of the person. The kind of guidance appropriate to such a pursuit will be quite different from that envisioned by many modern ethical theories. . . . The task of an [ethics of virtue] is not determinately to guide action; that task is left to the virtues. Virtue theories do not propose algorithms for solving practical difficulties; they propose something more like a fitness program to get one ready to run a race.[68]

Virtue ethics has been criticized for not providing us with definitive rules for making decisions, but Solomon's point is that it does something better, it gives us

---

*Garcia is using *supererogatory* to refer to actions that are not obligatory but go beyond the demands of duty.

guidance in becoming the sorts of persons who can effectively make moral decisions.

5. The Key to Morality Is Found in the Character of Moral Role Models

While not all proponents of virtue ethics take this approach, many stress the importance of role models (also called paradigmatic individuals, ideal types, or moral exemplars) in ethical development and decision making. As little children, we acquire a good deal of our moral training by imitating people we admire, such as parents, relatives, teachers, historical figures, and even fictional characters. People such as Buddha, Confucius, Socrates, Jesus, Abraham Lincoln, Gandhi, or Mother Teresa (the list could go on) inspire us not only through their teachings but through the quality of their lives and personalities. Hence, for virtue ethics, the personalities encountered in biographies, history, literature, and even traditional children's stories such as those collected in William Bennett's *The Book of Virtues,* provide as much if not more moral insight than do all the principles of the philosophers. As Daniel Statman, a leading scholar of virtue ethics, says:

> Becoming a good person is not a matter of learning or "applying" principles, but of imitating some models. We learn to be virtuous the same way we learn to dance, to cook, and to play football—by watching people who are competent in these areas, and trying to do the same. According to [virtue ethics], education through moral exemplars is more effective than education focused on principles and obligations, because it is far more concrete.[69]

As Statman suggests, we cannot learn to dance, cook, or play football by reading a book or listening to a lecture. While there are things that accomplished persons can tell us about these activities and even principles to keep in mind that will help us catch on, in the final analysis we need to watch the actions of people who have mastered the art and practicing the activity, until we become as much like these exemplars as possible. Accordingly, Rosalind Hursthouse defines *right action* as "what a virtuous agent would do in the circumstances."[70]

STOP AND THINK

What persons have been moral role models for you? Were they all persons you knew, or were some of them people you read about? Were any of them teachers? Were some of them historical figures? Were any of them fictional characters? Did your moral paradigms change as you grew older? Why? What did you learn from them about life and about being an excellent human being? How would you have been different if you had not been influenced by them? To what degree could you put into words or express as principles what you learned from them? To what extent could the insight they gave you not be verbally expressed? Have you ever felt as though you played this role for someone else—a younger sibling or a friend perhaps?

ARISTOTLE (384–322 B.C.)

ARISTOTLE
(384–322 B.C.)

Virtue ethics in the Western world can trace its roots back to Socrates, Plato, the Stoics, and early Christianity, but Aristotle has had the most influence on the development of this perspective. Aristotle was born in Macedonia, a kingdom north of Greece. Around age eighteen, he sought out the best education offered in his day and became a student in Plato's Academy in Athens. Aristotle studied and taught there with Plato for twenty years until the latter's death. Later in life, while gratefully acknowledging Plato's influence on him, Aristotle sharply criticized his teacher's ideas, explaining that while truth and friends are both dear, we ought to honor truth above our friends. After leaving Athens, Aristotle pursued various careers, including tutoring the young Macedonian prince who would later be known as Alexander the Great.

Eventually Aristotle returned to Athens and founded his own school and research institute, called the Lyceum. There he taught a wide range of subjects that included biology, physics, medicine, psychology, chemistry, mathematics, philosophy, rhetoric, political science, and literary criticism. When Alexander the Great died in 323 B.C., a wave of anti-Macedonian rage swept through Athens, and Aristotle feared that his associations with Alexander would put him in danger. Remembering the fate of Socrates but feeling no need to be a martyr, Aristotle fled the city, "lest the Athenians should sin twice against philosophy." He died the following year.

Although his scientific ideas were overthrown long ago, Aristotle's ethical theory continues to inform contemporary philosophy. Aristotle begins his discourse on ethics by observing that all human action aims at some end. But if human life is to be something other than a fragmented and meaningless pursuit of multiple goals, all intermediate goals must ultimately aim at some final good we desire for its own sake. Aristotle says that this goal is *happiness.* Happiness must be the final, unquestioned goal in life, for it makes no sense to ask, "Why are you spending your life pursuing happiness?" The Greek term he uses is *eudaimonia.* Happiness should not be confused with pleasure; its meaning is best thought of as "well-being" or "living well" or "having a life worth living." The problem is that *happiness* is a rather vague term, and different people have different conceptions of it. But if happiness is the supreme good in life, then Aristotle says it is best understood by getting clear on the end or function of human life.

- How does Aristotle argue that humans must have a particular function or purpose?
- What function do we have that is uniquely human?

FROM ARISTOTLE

Nicomachean Ethics[71]

Book 1

The best way of arriving at such a definition [of happiness] will probably be to ascertain the function of man. For, as with a flute player, a sculptor, or any artist, or in fact anybody who has a special function or activity, his goodness and excellence seem to lie in his function, so it would seem to be with man, if indeed he has a special function. Can it be said that, while a carpenter and a cobbler have special functions and activities, man, unlike them, is naturally functionless? Or, as the eye, the hand, the foot, and similarly each part of the body has a special function, so may man be regarded as having a special function apart from all these? What, then, can this function be? It is not life; for life is apparently something that man shares with plants; and we are looking for something peculiar to him. We must exclude therefore the life of nutrition and growth. There is next what may be called the life of sensation. But this too, apparently, is shared by man with horses, cattle, and all other animals. There remains what I may call the active life of the rational part of man's being. Now this rational part is twofold; one part is rational in the sense of being obedient to reason, and the other in the sense of possessing and exercising reason and intelligence. The active life too may be conceived of in two ways, either as a state of character, or as an activity; but we mean by it the life of activity, as this seems to be the truer form of the conception.

The function of man then is an activity of the soul in accordance with reason, or not apart from reason. Now, the function of a man of a certain kind, and of a man who is good of that kind—for example, of a harpist and a good harpist—are in our view the same in kind. This is true of all people of all kinds without exception, the superior excellence being only an addition to the function; for it is the function of a harpist to play the harp, and of a good harpist to play the harp well. This being so, if we define the function of man as a kind of life, and this life as an activity of the soul or a course of action in accordance with reason, and if the function of a good man is such activity of a good and noble kind, and if everything is well done when it is done in accordance with its proper excellence, it follows that the good of man is an activity of the soul in accordance with virtue, or, if there are more virtues than one, in accordance with the best and most complete virtue. But we must add the words "in a complete life." For as one swallow or one day does not make a spring, so one day or a short time does not make a man blessed or happy. . . .

Inasmuch as happiness is an activity of the soul in accordance with perfect virtue, we must now consider virtue, as this will perhaps be the best way of studying happiness. . . . Clearly it is human virtue we have to consider; for the good of which we are in search is, as we said, human good, and the happiness, human happiness. By human virtue or excellence we mean not that of the body, but that of the soul, and by happiness we mean an activity of the soul. . . .

Aristotle thinks that happiness is to be found by living according to our nature and fulfilling what it means to be human, which entails a life lived according to a certain plan or strategy that is furnished by reason. Although Aristotle thought that philosophical contemplation was the highest and most satisfying form of happiness, he did not think that we necessarily had to be cloistered intellectuals, for he thought that involvement in politics and the life of our culture was necessary to be fully human. Instead, the rational life is one that can be lived continuously in the midst of our other engagements. When he speaks of the activity of the soul in accordance with reason or virtue, he is not talking about something specific that we do but about the manner in which we do all things in life.

Since we are rational beings as well as beings who feel, desire, and act, the road to happiness involves two dimensions. We must rationally judge what is the best way to live, and our appetites, feelings, and emotions must be disciplined to follow that judgment. As Aristotle indicates in the next passage, these two dimensions require two kinds of human excellence: *intellectual virtues* (ability at mathematics, science, and philosophy) and *moral virtues* (courage, generosity, truthfulness, justice, and so on). Although Aristotle's focus is on the moral virtues in this passage, the two kinds of virtues are mutually supportive. The good life cannot be had if either of these virtues is neglected.

- The intellectual virtues can be fostered by teaching, but how are the moral virtues acquired? In other words, how do we become just, courageous, or temperate (self-controlled)?

Book 2

Virtue then is twofold, partly intellectual and partly moral, and intellectual virtue is originated and fostered mainly by teaching; it demands therefore experience and time. Moral virtue on the other hand is the outcome of habit, and accordingly its name, *ethike,* is derived by a slight variation from *ethos,* habit. From this fact it is clear that moral virtue is not implanted in us by nature; for nothing that exists by nature can be transformed by habit.

Thus a stone, that naturally tends to fall downwards, cannot be habituated or trained to rise upwards, even if we tried to train it by throwing it up ten thousand times. Nor again can fire be trained to sink downwards, nor anything else that follows one natural law be habituated or trained to follow another. It is neither by nature then nor in defiance of nature that virtues grow in us. Nature gives us the capacity to receive them, and that capacity is perfected by habit.

Again, if we take the various natural powers which belong to us, we first possess the proper faculties and afterwards display the activities. It is obviously so with the senses. Not by seeing frequently or hearing frequently do we acquire the sense of seeing or hearing; on the contrary, because we have the senses we make use of them; we do not get them by making use of them. But the virtues we get by first practicing them, as we do in the arts. For it is by doing what we ought to do when we study the arts that we learn the arts themselves; we become builders by building and harpists by playing the harp. Similarly, it is by doing just acts that we become just, by doing temperate acts that we become temperate, by doing brave acts that we become brave. The experience of states confirms this statement, for it is by training in good habits that lawmakers make the citizens good. This is the object all lawmakers have at heart; if they do not succeed in it, they fail of their purpose; and it makes the distinction between a good constitution and a bad one.

Again, the causes and means by which any virtue is produced and destroyed are the same; and equally so in any part. For it is by playing the harp that both good and bad harpists are produced; and the case of builders and others is similar, for it is by building well that they become good builders and by building badly that they become bad builders. If it were not so, there would be no need of anybody to teach them; they would all be born good or bad in their several crafts. The case of the virtues is the same. It is by our actions in dealings between man and man that we become either just or unjust. It is by our actions in the face of danger and by our training ourselves to fear or to courage that we become either cowardly or courageous. It is much the same with our appetites and angry passions. People become temperate and gentle, others licentious and passionate, by behaving in one or the other way in particular circumstances. In a word, moral states are the results of activities like the states themselves. It is our duty therefore to keep a certain character in our activities, since our moral states depend on the differences in our activities. So the difference between one and another training in habits in our childhood is not a light matter, but important, or rather, all-important.

 STOP AND THINK

How did you learn how to be generous, self-controlled, fair, or truthful? Do you agree with what Aristotle says about how the virtues are acquired? Is it possible to practice the art of being moral, much like we practice playing a musical instrument or a sport? What practical steps could you take to develop your moral qualities?

In the next passage, Aristotle continues the theme that we acquire the moral virtues by practicing them. When a child first learns to play the piano, the teacher must show the pupil what to do. By modeling the teacher's behavior, the child begins to acquire the skill. After a while, however, the mature musician does not need the teacher to place her fingers where they go. Instead, the skilled musician looks at the music and instantly responds because of the built-in habits she has acquired. In much the same way, Aristotle thinks that the moral virtues are habits that we acquire such that moral behavior becomes an ingrained, natural response.

- In the next passage, Aristotle says that a person is not temperate or just simply because he or she does temperate or just actions. What three conditions are necessary for an action to qualify as a genuinely moral action?
- Why does Aristotle think that having the correct philosophical theory is insufficient for being a moral person? (He may have been referring to Socrates here, who thought that knowing the good would cause a person to do the good.)

Acts in accordance with virtue are not justly or temperately performed simply because they are in themselves just or temperate. The doer at the time of performing them must satisfy certain conditions; in the first place, he must know that he is doing; secondly, he must deliberately choose to do it and do it for its own sake; and thirdly, he must do it as part of his own firm and immutable character. If it be a question of art, these conditions, except only the condition of knowledge, are not raised; but if it be a question of virtue, mere knowledge is of little or no avail; it is the other conditions, which are the results of frequently performing just and temperate acts, that are not slightly but all-important. Accordingly, deeds are called just and temperate when they are such as a just and temperate person would do; and a just and temperate person is not merely one who does these deeds but one who does them in the spirit of the just and the temperate.

It may fairly be said that a just man becomes just by doing what is just, and a temperate man becomes temperate by doing what is temperate, and if a man did not so act, he would not have much chance of becoming good. But most people, instead of acting, take refuge in theorizing; they imagine that they are philosophers and that philosophy will make them virtuous; in fact, they behave like people who listen attentively to their doctors but never do anything that their doctors tell them. But a healthy state of the soul will no more be produced by this kind of philosophizing than a healthy state of the body by this kind of medical treatment.

Aristotle's description of the morally good act is consistent with Kant's analysis. Both would agree that I am not acting justly unless I am acting deliberately and on the basis of knowledge (it cannot be an accident that I did the right thing). Furthermore, they would agree that I must perform the action for its own sake (and not for some reward, for example). Nevertheless, when Aristotle emphasizes that acting morally must be an ingrained habit and when he says in the next passage that morality is concerned with both "emotions and actions," Kant would worry that such actions would be based on my inclinations, involuntary passions, and temperament instead of on a rational calculation of my duty. It is on this point that virtue ethics differs most radically from Kantian ethics.

In the next passage, Aristotle discusses his famous *doctrine of the mean.* The "mean" referred to here is the intermediate position between two extremes or vices. The virtuous person is the one who has just the right amount of a certain quality or trait.

- In the first paragraph, Aristotle lists several qualities in which there can be an excess or a deficiency as well as the correct balance. For several of them, think of concrete situations in which we would say that a person had too much, too little, or just the right amount of the quality in question.
- Having said that virtue is a balance between the extremes, Aristotle offers in the last paragraph emotions or actions for which there is no correct balance. Why does he make these exceptions to his general rule?

Every art then does its work well, if it regards the mean and judges the works it produces by the mean. For this reason we often say of successful works of art that it is impossible to take anything from them or to add anything to them, which implies that excess or deficiency is fatal to excellence but that the mean state ensures it. Good artists too, as we say, have an eye to the mean in their works. Now virtue, like Nature herself, is more accurate and better than any art; virtue, therefore, will aim at the mean. I speak of moral virtue, since it is moral virtue which is concerned with emotions and actions, and it is in these we have excess and deficiency and the mean. Thus it is possible to go too far, or not far enough in fear, pride, desire, anger, pity, and pleasure and pain generally, and the excess and the deficiency are alike wrong; but to feel these emotions at the right times, for the right objects, towards the right persons, for the right motives, and in the right manner, is the mean or the best good, which signifies virtue. Similarly, there may be excess, deficiency, or the mean, in acts. Virtue is concerned with both emotions and actions, wherein excess is an error and deficiency a fault, while the mean is successful and praised, and success and praise are both characteristics of virtue.

It appears then that virtue is a kind of mean because it aims at the mean. . . .

Virtue then is a state of deliberate moral purpose, consisting in a mean relative to ourselves, the mean being determined by reason, or as a prudent man would determine it. It is a mean, firstly, as lying between two vices, the vice of excess on the one hand, the vice of deficiency on the other, and, secondly, because, whereas the vices either fall short of or go beyond what is right in emotion and action, virtue discovers and chooses the mean. Accordingly, virtue, if regarded in its essence or theoretical definition, is a mean, though, if regarded from the point of view of what is best and most excellent, it is an extreme.

But not every action or every emotion admits of a mean. There are some whose very name implies wickedness, as, for example, malice, shamelessness, and envy among the emotions, and adultery, theft, and murder among the actions. All these and others like them are marked as intrinsically wicked, not merely the excesses or deficiencies of them. It is never possible then to be right in them; they are always sinful. Right or wrong in such acts as adultery does not depend on our committing it with the right woman, at the right time, or in the right manner; on the contrary, it is wrong to do it at all. It would be equally false to suppose that there can be a mean or an excess or deficiency in unjust, cowardly or licentious conduct; for, if that were so, it would be a mean of excess and deficiency, an excess of excess and a deficiency of deficiency. But as in temperance and courage there can be no excess or deficiency, because the mean there is in a sense an extreme, so too in these other cases there cannot be a mean or an excess or a deficiency, but however the acts are done, they are wrong. For in general an excess or deficiency does not have a mean, nor a mean an excess or deficiency. . . .

Aristotle's view that the moral virtues constitute a balance between two extremes can be illustrated with the following chart made up of his own examples.

Activity	Vice (excess)	Virtue (mean)	Vice (deficit)
Confidence in facing danger	Rashness	Courage	Cowardice
Enjoying pleasure	Self-indulgence	Temperance	Being puritanical
Giving of money	Vulgarity	Generosity	Stinginess
Truth telling about oneself	Boastfulness	Self-honesty	Self-deprecation

 STOP AND THINK

Provide your own examples of several activities in which the response of the virtuous person will be a balance between either an excess or a deficiency. In your examples, what labels would you give to the virtue and its corresponding vices?

In the previous passage Aristotle said that virtue entails finding the "mean relative to ourselves." Hence, the mean will not be the same for every individual under all circumstances. The genius of Aristotle's ethics is his recognition that universal and objective principles have relative applications for different people and within different circumstances. For example, we may praise the courage of a young child who overcomes his terror of the water and sticks his face in the water. On the other hand, it would not be an act of courage for a professional lifeguard to do the same thing. Similarly, a widow who gives a dollar to charity when this amount is a substantial portion of her income is exhibiting the virtue of generosity. If she inherits a million dollars, however, then giving only a dollar would be exhibiting the vice of stinginess. When we are deciding what to do, how are we to know where to find the right balance point? Aristotle says that it is "determined by reason, or as a prudent man would determine it." Hence, finding the right balance for ourselves is a matter of experience and learning from the examples of those virtuous persons who have practical wisdom.

THE VIRTUES IN CONFUCIAN THOUGHT

Many ethical systems in non-Western traditions also focus more on the virtuous character than on rules of conduct. The sayings of Confucius are a good example of this focus. Although there are differences between the list of Aristotelian virtues and Confucian virtues, there are also significant overlaps. Interestingly, one of the works in Confucian literature is *The Doctrine of the Mean,* which parallels Aristotle's advice to seek a balance between the extremes. The following passage contains selected proverbs from the twenty sections of the sayings of Confucius. In this passage, Confucius describes the virtues of the superior person, a word that could also be translated as "noble person," "person of honor," or "wise person."

CONFUSCIUS
(551–479 B.C.)

Confucius

An ancient version of virtue ethics is found in the thought of the great Chinese moral and spiritual leader Confucius. He was born in 551 B.C. during a time of social turmoil in China and died about 479 B.C. He was actually called K'ung Fu Tzu by his people, but he is known in the West by the Latin version of his name. During his life Confucius served his country as both a teacher and a government official, but he served people throughout the ages with the inspiration of his collected sayings. Having lived through unsettled times, he concluded that people would flourish only if there were excellent individuals who would create a harmonious society and a harmonious society that would create virtuous individuals. Although Confucianism is one of the world's great religions, Confucius did not consider himself anything more than a man, and he spoke very little about the gods but offered instead a moral system for guiding a person's life. Although Confucianism came under hard times after the Communist revolution, it has had considerable influence on Chinese culture and throughout East Asia.

FROM CONFUCIUS
The Analects[72]

1.4 I daily examine myself on three points: In planning for others, have I failed to be conscientious? In my dealing with friends, have I failed to be sincere? In teaching, have I failed to practice what I have taught?

1.8 Give a prominent place to loyalty and sincerity.

1.16 Sorrow not because men do not know you; but sorrow that you know not men.

2.14 The superior man is not one-sided.

2.24 To see what is right and not to do it, that is cowardice.

4.16 The superior man seeks what is right; the inferior one, what is profitable.

4.24 The superior man is slow to promise, prompt to fulfill.

4.25 Virtue dwells not in solitude; she must have neighbors.

5.9 Rotten wood cannot be carved.

5.15 There are the four essential qualities of the superior man; he is humble, he is deferential to superiors, he is generously kind, and he is always just.

6.18 Better than the one who knows what is right is he who loves what is right.

7.36 The superior man is always calm, the inferior (small-minded) man is constantly in a state of disturbance.

8.2 Without a sense of proportion, courtesy becomes oppressive; calmness becomes bashfulness; valor becomes disorderliness; and candor becomes rudeness.

7.36 The superior man makes the most of other people's good qualities, not the worst of their bad ones.

13.26 The superior man can be dignified without being proud; the inferior man can be proud without being dignified.

15.20　The superior man is exacting with himself; the inferior man is exacting with others.

16.10　The superior man must be mindful of nine things: to be clear in vision, quick to listen, genial in expression, respectful in manner, true in utterance, serious in duty, inquiring in doubt, self-controlled in anger, just and fair when the way to success is open before him.

A CONTEMPORARY APPLICATION OF VIRTUE ETHICS

Virtue ethics is often criticized for offering us a set of admirable ideals but failing to provide concrete guidance with respect to specific actions. What are needed, the critics say, are moral rules from which we can deduce the moral quality of an action. For many people, the moral wrongness of adultery, for example, follows from the fact that it violates a moral rule, whether that rule is from the Ten Commandments or Kant's categorical imperative or utilitarian rules about avoiding consequences that cause more harm than good. In the following passage, however, contemporary philosopher Janet Smith applies the perspective of virtue ethics to show how the moral quality of adultery can be assessed by considering whether this action is something a virtuous person would do.

FROM JANET SMITH
Moral Character and Abortion[73]

JANET SMITH

The very importance of the attempt to live an ethical life lies in the fact that in acting the individual forms herself or himself either for the better or for the worse. One of the foremost questions to be asked by the moral agent in the decision to do an action is: What kind of person will I become if I do this act?

Let us now consider how the choice to commit adultery might reveal and affect one's moral character. . . . If it is true . . . that adulterers can be said to have undesirable moral characteristics and/or that they are forming undesirable moral characters through their choice to commit adultery, this would be taken as an indication . . . that adultery is a morally bad action. . . .

For an analysis in accord with an ethics of virtue, answers to the following questions would be useful: What sort of people generally commit adultery? Are they, for instance, honest, temperate, kind, etc.? . . . Why do adulterers choose to have sex with people other than their spouses? Are their reasons selfish or unselfish ones? Do they seem to speak of their reasons for their choice honestly or do they seem to be rationalizing? What sort of lives have they been leading prior to the action that they choose; are they the sorts of lives that exhibit the characteristics we admire?

Most may agree that some true generalization could be made about adulterers that would lead us to think that in general adultery is not compatible with the moral virtues that we admire. The reaction of the American public to the extramarital affairs of [clergyman] Jim Bakker and [politician] Gary Hart reveal well the widespread view that lying predictably accompanies the act of adultery and that adulterers are not to be trusted. Certainly, if someone told us that he or she wanted to be an honest, trustworthy, stable and kind individual with good family relationships, and wanted to know if an adulterous affair would conflict with this goal, we would have little hesitation in advising against adultery.

SUMMARY OF VIRTUE ETHICS

Although it is an ancient theory, the revival of virtue ethics in our day has opened new and interesting issues in contemporary philosophy. Rather than simply repeating the ideas of the Greeks, recent proponents of this position have taken advantage of contemporary insights drawn from the fields of psychology, anthropology, history, moral education, and literature. In turn, the theory of virtue ethics has also made contributions to these and other disciplines and has brought new perspectives to the fields of business ethics and medical ethics. While virtue ethics started out as a reaction against traditional moral philosophy, its criticisms of utilitarianism and Kantianism have forced the philosophers in these traditions to take account of virtue and character more fully than Mill and Kant did. Thus attempts have been made in recent decades to modify these traditional positions and to develop utilitarian and Kantian versions of an ethics of virtue. On the other hand, some

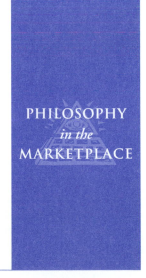

PHILOSOPHY
in the
MARKETPLACE

Read the following paragraph to five to ten people from different backgrounds and ask them the questions that follow it:

A wide range of people were asked, "What persons are good examples of moral role models—persons whose lives and personalities have guided you in your attempts to be a better person? Some of the answers given were: parents, relatives, teachers, Moses, Buddha, Confucius, Socrates, Jesus, Muhammad, St. Francis, Abraham Lincoln, Gandhi, Martin Luther King Jr., and Mother Teresa.

- Besides these common answers, what other people would you add to the list?
- What was it about these persons that made them admirable?
- Why did they have a moral influence on you or others?

After gathering the responses, study the similarities and differences between the persons listed. How many males and how many females were on the list? What were their occupations? What historical period and culture did they live in? What challenges did they face? What can your friends' responses teach you about which sorts of moral role models have the most influence?

philosophers accuse the virtue ethicists of attacking a strawman and claim that sufficient resources exist in traditional utilitarianism or Kantianism to accommodate all the legitimate concerns of virtue ethics.[74] (See the discussion of the strawman fallacy in section 1.2, "Argument and Evidence: How Do I Decide What to Believe?".) Although virtue ethics started out as a radical alternative to the traditional systems, the discussions it has produced have resulted in a movement to synthesize the ethics of duty with the ethics of virtue. As Robert Louden, a sympathetic critic of virtue ethics, concludes, "It is important now to see the ethics of virtue and the ethics of rules as adding up, rather than as cancelling each other out."[75]

 ## LOOKING THROUGH THE LENS OF VIRTUE ETHICS

1. Suppose you are a parent of a small child. It is easy to teach a list of dos and don'ts with the appropriate rewards and sanctions. But how do you instill character in your child? Can virtue be taught? How so? Besides direct teaching, what are other ways of facilitating the development of virtue in your child? What virtues would you want him or her to develop?

2. If you were a utilitarian, how would you explain to a friend that cheating on a test is wrong? How would you explain this action if you were Kant? How would you explain what is wrong with cheating if you were a virtue ethicist?

3. Have you ever made an ethical decision by imagining that you were in the shoes of a wise, virtuous person whom you admire and trying to discern how he or she would act? Whether you have or not, to what degree do you think this exercise would be a helpful way to make a decision?

4. In an influential article, philosopher Susan Wolf questions whether it is desirable to be a moral saint (a person who is as morally worthy as a human can be). She says she is glad that neither she nor any of her friends are such persons.

> For the moral virtues . . . are apt to crowd out the non-moral virtues, as well as many of the interests and personal characteristics that we generally think contribute to a healthy, well-rounded, richly developed character.
>
> In other words, if the moral saint is devoting all his time to feeding the hungry or healing the sick or raising money for Oxfam [a charity], then necessarily he is not reading Victorian novels, playing the oboe, or improving his backhand. Although no one of the interests or tastes in the category containing these latter activities could be claimed to be a necessary element in a life well lived, a life in which *none* of these possible aspects of character is developed may seem to be a life strangely barren. . . .
>
> A moral saint will have to be very, very nice. It is important that he not be offensive. The worry is that, as a result, he will have to be dull-witted or humourless or bland.[76]

Do you agree with Wolf's analysis? Is she correct in saying that the perfectly virtuous person lacks the "ability to enjoy the enjoyable in life"? What would an advocate of virtue ethics say about this analysis?

EXAMINING THE STRENGTHS AND WEAKNESSES OF VIRTUE ETHICS

Positive Evaluation

1. Virtue ethics seems to capture some important concerns in our ordinary way of thinking about ethics. As philosopher Robert Solomon says, "The very idea that the good person is one who acts according to the right principles—be they categorical imperatives or the principle of utility—has always struck me as colossally out of tune with the manner in which ordinary people (and most philosophers) think about and judge themselves and their actions. As a matter of fact it makes my blood run cold."[77] Do you agree with Solomon's account of our ordinary ethical thinking? How strongly does this approach support virtue ethics?

2. One of the standard ways of criticizing an ethical theory such as egoism, utilitarianism or Kantianism is to show that it would allow us to justify an action that is clearly morally wrong. Doesn't this argument show that moral theories are subject to our commonsense moral intuitions and not the other way around? Furthermore, it could be argued that our commonsense moral intuitions are typically tied to our conception of the sorts of actions that would be performed by the morally ideal person. Does this argument support the virtue ethicist's case that ethics starts with the notion of moral virtue and moral principles and theories follow from that?

3. The charge is sometimes made that virtue ethics is impractical because it does not provide us with rules for making moral decisions in complex situations. But in this respect is the theory any worse off than competing ethical theories? Even if we follow the rules of the utilitarian or the Kantian, are rules alone enough to guide us? Is acting in complex moral situations simply an exercise in logic in which the rules tell us what to do? Or does the application of moral rules require the sensitive judgment of a virtuous person? Daniel Statman points out that even for rule-based ethics, "the virtuous person is not the person who has excellent knowledge of some set of principles, meta-principles and meta-meta-principles, but the person who has right perception as to which rules should apply here and now. And this person must be, among other things, sensitive, compassionate and perceptive—the same features so praised in VE [virtue ethics]."[78] Does Statman's comment suggest that a virtuous character is more fundamental to ethics than rules are?

4. Defenders of virtue ethics say that it goes beyond the minimal morality of right and wrong conduct. Instead, its concern with conduct includes in its scope those traits that lead us beyond the demands of duty. Apart from actions it also emphasizes the good, the admirable, and the noble within us as well as those personal characteristics and emotional and mental responses that make us good persons. Do these considerations tip the balance in favor of virtue ethics?

Negative Evaluation

1. Virtue ethics has been criticized for assuming a classical and antiquated view of human nature. Many versions assume with Aristotle that there is an innate purpose to human life and that there is a single model of human excellence and flourishing. However, doesn't our pluralistic society exhibit a lack of agreement about the purpose of human life, the standards of excellence, and the definition of flourishing? In fact, don't many of us question whether there is one *ideal* that is applicable to all? Furthermore, isn't there a great deal of disagreement about the correct list of moral virtues? For example, Aristotle thought pride was a virtue, but for early Christianity and for Confucius, the good person is one who shuns pride and strives for humility. To what degree do these considerations undermine virtue ethics?

2. Can it be argued that the ethics of character depends on the ethics of conduct, the reverse of what the virtue ethicist claims? Could someone have the virtue of compassion if he never performed compassionate acts when appropriate? Virtue ethics defines right actions as those that a virtuous person would perform. But how can we define a virtuous person apart from saying she is a person who has a disposition to perform right actions? Hasn't this reasoning led us into a circle? For example, how can we judge that a person has the virtue of justice apart from the fact that she acts in accord with the duty of justice? Don't these considerations imply that the notions of right conduct and moral duties are more fundamental than the notion of virtuous character?

3. Virtue ethics has been accused of making moral goodness a matter of luck. For example, according to virtue ethics, it is not enough to *act* benevolently out of a sense of duty; to be a morally good person I must have benevolent *feelings* toward people. However, can I will myself to have certain feelings? If I have the virtue of benevolence it must have come in one of two ways. First, it can be a natural disposition that was given to me as a gift of nature, possibly as a result of my genetic inheritance. Or it can be inculcated within me by my social training. But these options leave out the person who lacks a benevolent nature because neither nature nor her poor home environment produced it in her. Either way, she is not at fault. Yet even if bad moral luck has cursed her with a cold and ungenerous personality, can't she (in good Kantian fashion) still dutifully act in morally good ways through a extraordinary act of will? Given these considerations, how important are moral character traits as opposed to dutiful, right actions?

4. Can virtue ethics be criticized for failing to provide us with specific action-guiding principles? Let's take as an example an ethical question that is in the news these days: is it morally permissible to clone humans? In other words, should someone be allowed to create a cloned child who is the genetic replica of the DNA donor? Although this question has no clear-cut answer, at least utilitarians and Kantians have some definite principles in terms of which the issue can be debated.

The utilitarian would assess the pluses and minuses of the likely social, psychological, and biological consequences for all who would be affected by the procedure. The Kantian would ask if the cloned child was being created merely as a means to the parent's egotistical ends and so on. But if we ask, "What would a virtuous person say about cloning?" either no answer is forthcoming or the answer would be based on utilitarian or Kantian considerations. Similarly, isn't it hard to imagine what moral exemplars such as Buddha, Jesus, or Gandhi would do with cases in medical ethics that they never encountered? Does this problem imply that virtue ethics is not as helpful as the other theories are?

5.6 RETHINKING THE WESTERN TRADITION: FEMINIST ETHICS

LEADING QUESTIONS: *Feminist Ethics*

1. The classic collection of children's stories known as Aesop's fables contains the following story of the porcupine and the moles:

> It was growing cold, and porcupine was looking for a home. He found a most desirable cave but saw it was occupied by a family of moles.
>
> "Would you mind if I shared your home for the winter?" the porcupine asked the moles.
>
> The generous moles consented and the porcupine moved in. But the cave was small and every time the moles moved around they were scratched by the porcupine's sharp quills. The moles endured this discomfort as long as they could. Then at last they gathered courage to approach their visitor. "Pray leave," they said, "and let us have our cave to ourselves once again."
>
> "Oh no!" said the porcupine. "This place suits me very well."

What is the problem here and what is the best way to solve it?

2. Think about a moral dilemma you have encountered in which you had to decide the right thing to do. Which of the following two sets of considerations (A or B) were the most important to you in solving the problem?

A. (1) using logic and reason to find a solution, (2) being aware of and concerned about the rights of those affected by my actions, (3 making sure I don't interfere with anyone's rights, (4) treating everyone equally, (5) following the principles of justice, impartiality, fairness, (6) making sure my actions can be defended in terms of rules that are universal and apply to all.

B. (1) bringing love, care, and compassion to the situation, (2) being aware of and concerned about people's needs, (3) looking for ways that I can help people, (4) trying to arrive at a solution that everyone could accept, (5) trying to connect with the people involved and working to create communication and cooperation, (6) being attentive to relationships and my responsibilities to other people.

SURVEYING THE CASE FOR FEMINIST ETHICS

In a study published in 1988, a number of adolescents were presented with the porcupine and moles dilemma you just read.[79] The majority of the males solved the problem in terms of the principles of rights and justice, saying, for example, "it is the moles' house, so the porcupine has to go." However, the majority of the females responded in terms of the principles of cooperation and care. For example, some of their solutions were "the moles and the porcupine must talk and share the house," "wrap the porcupine in a towel," or "both of them should try to get together and make the hole bigger." The researchers believe their data support the recent and much-discussed theory that there are differences in the ways that males and females typically solve moral problems.

> ## STOP AND THINK
>
> Based on your experience, do you think there are differences in the ways in which males and females approach issues in morality? If so, what are some of these differences? If you do see differences in how men and women view ethics, what implications (if any) are there for ethical theory in the fact that differences exist?

In my discussion of feminist epistemology in section 2.8, I laid out the main themes of feminist thought and their disagreements with traditional theories of knowledge. Feminists are equally dissatisfied with traditional ethical theories. According to recent feminist philosophers, traditional moral theories tend to focus on the considerations listed under (A) in the second leading question while neglecting the moral orientation represented by (B). Furthermore, they point out that, for historical reasons, the traditional moral theories have been developed by males. These facts raise a number of questions such as, Are traditional moral theories such as Kantianism and utilitarianism one-sided? Do they reflect a male bias? Theorists in the recently developed movement of feminist ethics tend to answer these questions affirmatively. In this section we address the following questions: What is feminist ethics? What is the feminist critique of traditional ethical theories? How do feminists propose to reshape the foundations of morality?

Before the 1980s, there was no field called feminist ethics. Today, however, feminist perspectives in ethics are the source of fertile discussions not only in philosophy but also in the fields of psychology, education, medicine, theology, business, and law. It is much more difficult to summarize the feminist approach to ethics than it is to give a capsule summary of the Kantian or utilitarian theories, for feminist theory is a continually developing body of thought that is the work of many different thinkers, representing a multiplicity of perspectives. While feminists see themselves as engaged in a shared project, they have many different opinions as to how that project should be realized. For example, in her book, *Feminist Thought: A More Comprehensive Introduction,* philosopher Rosemarie Tong lists nine varieties of feminist theory: liberal, radical, Marxist-socialist, psychoanalytic, gender feminism, existentialist, postmodern, multicultural-global, and ecofeminism. Under each of these categories, Tong also lists a number of subdivisions. Not only does each version of feminism have different emphases, but they often come to radically different conclusions on substantive issues. Nevertheless, for all their differences, feminists are agreed that traditional ethical theories are inadequate and one-sided, and need to be replaced or modified, because they have ignored the insights of women's moral experiences.

 THOUGHT EXPERIMENT

Different Approaches to Ethics

The following two responses were given by two different people (both adults) to the interview question, "What does morality mean to you?"[80]

Response A

I think it is recognizing the right of the individual, the rights of other individuals, not interfering with those rights. Act as fairly as you would have them treat you. I think it is basically to preserve the human being's right to existence. I think that is the most important. Secondly, the human being's right to do as he pleases, again without interfering with somebody else's rights.

Response B

We need to depend on each other, and hopefully it is not only a physical need but a need of fulfillment in ourselves, that a person's life is enriched by cooperating with other people and striving to live in harmony with everybody else, and to that end, there are right and wrong, there are things which promote that end and that move away from it, and in that way it is possible to choose in certain cases among different courses of action that obviously promote or harm that goal.

- Which response best characterizes your view of morality?
- Which response would you guess was made by a man?
- Which response would you guess was made by a woman?
- What clues in each response led you to answer the way you did?

The answers will be given later in this section when we examine Carol Gilligan's theory of moral development.

Gender Bias in Ethical Theory

Although there have been women philosophers going all the way back to ancient Greece, they were largely neglected throughout the history of philosophy. Consequently, feminists contend, the ethical theories that have shaped our understanding of morality were written by men and reflect a male point of view. For example, at the beginning of his work on ethics, Aristotle said that "the function of *man* is an activity of the soul in accordance with reason." The most charitable explanation of this wording would be that Aristotle was using *man* generically to include both males and females. If so, then any male bias in his work is limited to a rather insensitive choice of words rather than a deep-seated omission in the content of his theory. Unfortunately, when Aristotle referred to "man" in his works he really did mean *males*. According to him, males are the only creatures to have a true capacity for reasoning. Women, on the other hand, have other purposes (such as childbearing) and a different set of virtues. (See the earlier discussion of Aristotle's view of women in section 2.8.)

Other philosophers throughout history have followed Aristotle in making reason a uniquely male virtue and in focusing on the traditional male domains such as the state, law, war, and the marketplace in their ethical theories. Not only did the activities within these public spheres serve as metaphors of ethical transactions, but these arenas also were thought to be the places in which ethical dilemmas and morally significant actions were to be found. Women, on the other hand, were associated with emotions, instinct, and the biological dimension. Their natural activities were confined to what was considered to be the morally neutral private sphere in which the biological needs of food, shelter, and reproduction were met, while all that was distinctively human and of moral significance was carried out by men in the public sphere.

In the twentieth century, for example, philosopher J. O. Urmson discussed moral "saints" who make sacrifices beyond the call of duty, but he added, "Let us be clear that we are not now considering cases of natural affection, such as the sacrifice made by a mother for her child; such cases may be said with some justice not to fall under the concept of morality."[81] However, in response to this distinction, feminist philosopher Virginia Held notes that "without feminist insistence on the relevance for morality of the experience in mothering, this context is largely ignored by moral theorists. And yet from a gender-neutral point of view, how can this vast and fundamental domain of human experience possibly be imagined to lie 'outside morality'?"[82]

If women bring unique perspectives and experiences to the activity of moral inquiry, what differences do these contributions make to their ethical theories? We might suppose at first that feminist ethics will be distinguished by simply a focus on ethical issues that are of particular concern to women, issues that may not have received adequate attention from ethical theories developed by men. Indeed, many of the writings of female philosophers in ethics emphasize issues such as discrimination against women, sexual harassment, sexual assault, pornography, abortion, reproductive technologies, changing conceptions of sexuality-marriage-family, and the implications of gender differences and stereotypes. But we would be wrong to suppose that feminist ethics simply supplements traditional ethics with discussions of "women's issues." Feminist philosophers think it would be counterproductive, among other reasons, to approach issues that concern women with ethical theories that grew out of male-biased social and philosophical soil. Instead, feminists see themselves as giving ethical theory a complete overhaul by recentering it and by bringing into prominence themes, concepts, and approaches that typically have been ignored. As ethical theorists Eve Browning Cole and Susan Coultrap-McQuin say:

> [Feminists] argue that traditional moral philosophy has been a largely male-directed enterprise and has reflected interests derived predominantly from men's experience. In other words, because men's experience has often involved market transactions, their moral theories concentrate on promise-keeping, property rights, contracts, and fairness.[83]

In contrast to the paradigm of the impersonal and often anonymous contractual relationships of the public sphere, feminist writers tend to model their ethics on the person-to-person relationships and concrete contexts entailed in friendships and families. Philosophers Eva Kittay and Diana Meyers have said that

> a morality of rights and abstract reason begins with a moral agent who is separate from others, and who independently elects moral principles to obey. In contrast, a morality of responsibility and care begins with a self who is enmeshed in a network of relations to others, and whose moral deliberation aims to maintain these relations.[84]

Hence, as opposed to the abstract principles of Kantian universalizability or utilitarian maximization of the general good, feminist ethics concentrates on such concepts as care, empathy, and personal understanding. According to feminist philosopher Alison Jaggar, feminists allege that Western ethics has preferred the

> supposedly masculine or male-associated values of independence, autonomy, intellect, will, wariness, hierarchy, domination, culture, transcendence, product, asceticism, war and death over the supposedly feminine or female-associated values of interdependence, community, connection, sharing, emotion, body, trust, absence of hierarchy, nature, immanence, process, joy, peace and life.[85]

Jaggar goes on to say that feminist ethics has sometimes been construed (by both some of its proponents as well as some of its critics) as a proposal to replace a male-biased approach with a female-biased approach. In other words, it has been associated with one or more of the following goals:

> putting women's interests first; focusing exclusively on so-called women's issues; accepting women (or feminists) as moral experts or authorities; substituting "female" (or feminine) for "male" (or masculine) values; or extrapolating directly from women's moral experience.[86]

While not claiming that it would be impossible to find examples of this sort of feminist inversion of the male biases they critique, Jaggar says that most feminists would be "morally outraged" by the blatant partiality and immorality of such proposals. Similarly, while acknowledging that feminists seek to bring gender issues to the foreground in ethics, Tong denies that they are doing this in a way that replaces one wrong with another:

The fact that an approach to ethics is gendered does not necessarily mean it is sexist. An approach to ethics becomes sexist only when it systematically excludes the interests, identities, issues, and values of one or the other of the two sexes, and feminist ethicists have no plans to do unto men what nonfeminist ethicists did unto women.[87]

TWO APPROACHES TO FEMINIST ETHICS

A distinction is frequently made between what is sometimes labeled *feminine* ethics and *feminist* ethics. Philosopher Betty A. Sichel distinguishes them in the following manner:

> "Feminine" at present refers to the search for women's unique voice and, most often, the advocacy of an ethics of care that includes nurturance, care, compassion, and networks of communication. "Feminist" refers to those theorists, whether liberal or radical or other orientation, who argue against patriarchal domination, for equal rights, a just and fair distribution of scarce resources, etc.[88]

Stating the distinction in slightly different terms, philosopher Susan Sherwin asserts that a feminine approach to ethics "consists of observations of how the traditional approaches to ethics fail to fit the moral expressions and intuitions of women," whereas a feminist approach to ethics "applies a specifically political perspective and offers suggestions for how ethics must be revised if it is to get at the patterns of dominance and oppression as they affect women."[89] However, while acknowledging the accuracy of this distinction, Tong finds these labels to be misleading, because they imply that only the latter group of philosophers are genuinely feminist. Instead, she refers to the two approaches to ethics as "care-focused feminist ethics" and "power-focused feminist ethics."[90] Using Tong's labels, let's examine each approach in turn.

Care-Focused Feminist Ethics

Carol Gilligan

One of the foundational works in feminist ethics, particularly of the care-based variety, was *In a Different Voice,* published in 1982 by Harvard psychologist Carol Gilligan. (Her theories were briefly discussed in section 2.8, "Rethinking the Western Tradition: Feminist Epistemology.") Gilligan responded to the work of Lawrence Kohlberg, one of the leading researchers in the area of moral development. Kohlberg traced six stages that people go through in their moral development, starting as little children. These six stages are: (1) the "carrot and stick" orientation, in which children are motivated by reward and punishment; (2) the "you scratch my back and I'll scratch yours" orientation, in which children do what satisfies their own needs and occasionally the needs of others; (3) the "good-boy/nice-girl" orientation, in which immature adolescents conform to society's standards to receive others' approval; (4) the "law and order" orientation, in which mature adolescents do their duty to show respect for authority and to maintain the given social order; (5) the "social contract/legalistic" orientation, in which people follow insti-

tutionalized rules that are perceived as rational, and they are concerned with the general good; and (6) the "universal ethical principles" orientation, a Kantian perspective in which self-imposed, internalized, universal principles such as justice, reciprocity, and respect for persons inform people's personal conscience.

Gilligan was puzzled by the fact that in Kohlberg's studies, women and girls rarely progressed past the "good-boy/nice-girl" status of stage 3, whereas men and boys routinely were measured at stages 5 and 6. Kohlberg presumed that his six stages represented progressively higher stages of moral development which suggested that females were generally more deficient in their moral development than were males. However, Gilligan concluded that the problem was not with women's moral development but with the male bias built into Kohlberg's theory. As an alternative to this single hierarchy, Gilligan argued that there were two models in ethical reasoning. One model is an "ethics of justice" model in which rules, rights, and logic predominate, and the other is an "ethics of care" in which relationships, responsibilities, and emotions predominate. Gilligan does not think that either approach is superior; she sees them as complementary and equally important in our moral lives. In her original work and in later writings Gilligan emphasized that these two different "voices" are differentiated not by gender but by their themes. Nevertheless, most of her studies focus on the fact that males and females are socialized differently, with the result that males tend to gravitate toward the ethics of justice and females toward the ethics of care.

STOP AND THINK

How did you label the responses in the thought experiment titled "Different Approaches to Ethics"? Response A was made by a twenty-five-year-old male. He identified morality with justice (fairness, rights, the Golden Rule) and stressed the individual's right to do as he pleases as long as it doesn't intrude on another person's rights. Response B was made
(Continued . . .)

(. . . continued)

by a twenty-five-year-old female who emphasized that morality is concerned with cooperation and promoting harmonious relationships.

- How do these responses illustrate Gilligan's theory?
- How accurately do these responses represent men's and women's styles of approaching morality?
- Do you tend toward the "ethics of justice" approach or the "ethics of care" approach?

Do not be concerned with whether your approach to morality fits Gilligan's categories of "male" or "female" ethics. A number of researchers (some feminists included) question whether the evidence demonstrates that there are gender-specific modes of moral reasoning. Psychologist John Broughton, for example, cites dozens of studies that contradict Gilligan's results. Furthermore, he argues that Gilligan misinterpreted some of her own interviews, since a number of male subjects exhibited a caring, relationship-based ethics while some of the female subjects had concerns about justice and rights.[91] Some philosophers argue that the differences between males and females in ethical styles are negligible when compared to the differences between subjects ranked in terms of cognitive skills, educational level, and social class.[92] Regardless of whether either of the two moral orientations can be associated with a certain gender, feminists typically argue that the two orientations do represent two distinctly different approaches and that the care-relationships approach has been neglected in ethical theory.

In the following passage, taken from the introduction to Gilligan's book, she explains how she got started on her new approach to ethics.

FROM CAROL GILLIGAN

In a Different Voice[93]
Introduction

Over the past ten years, I have been listening to people talking about morality and about themselves. Halfway through that time, I began to hear a distinction in these voices, two ways of speaking about moral problems, two modes of describing the relationship between other and self. Differences represented in the psychological literature as steps in a developmental progression suddenly appeared instead as a contrapuntal theme, woven into the cycle of life and recurring in varying forms in people's judgments, fantasies, and thoughts. The occasion for this observation was the selection of a sample of women for a study of the relation between judgment and action in a situation of moral conflict and choice. Against the background of the psychological descriptions of identity and moral development which I had read and taught for a number of years, the women's voices sounded distinct. It was then that I began to notice the recurrent problems in interpreting women's development and to connect these problems to the repeated exclusion of women from the critical theory-building studies of psychological research.

This book records different modes of thinking—about relationships and the association of these modes with male and female voices in psychological and literary texts and in the data of my research. The disparity between women's experience and the representation of human development, noted throughout the psychological literature, has generally been seen to signify a problem in women's development. Instead, the failure of women to fit existing models of human growth may point to a problem in the representation, a limitation in the conception of human condition, an omission of certain truths about life.

The different voice I describe is characterized not by gender but theme. Its association with women is an empirical observation, and it is primarily through women's voices that I trace its development. But this association is not absolute, and the contrasts between male and female voices are presented here to highlight a distinction between two modes of thought and to focus a problem of interpretation rather than to represent a generalization about either sex. In tracing development, I point to the interplay of these voices within each sex and suggest that their convergence marks times of crisis and change.

In one of her most famous passages, Gilligan illustrates her theory by reinterpreting Kohlberg's study of children's responses to a moral dilemma.

- How would you characterize the ethical theory implicit in Jake's responses?

Images of Relationship

The dilemma that these eleven-year-olds were asked to resolve was one in the series devised by Kohlberg to measure moral development in adolescence by presenting a conflict between moral norms and exploring the logic of its resolution. In this particular dilemma, a man named Heinz considers whether or not to steal a drug which he cannot afford to buy in order to save the life of his wife. In the standard format of Kohlberg's interviewing procedure, the description of the dilemma itself—Heinz's predicament, the wife's disease, the druggist's refusal to lower his price—is followed by the question, "Should Heinz steal the drug?" The reasons for and against stealing are then explored through a series of questions that vary and extend the parameters of the dilemma in a way designed to reveal the underlying structure of moral thought.

Jake, at eleven, is clear from the outset that Heinz should steal the drug. Constructing the dilemma, as Kohlberg did, as a conflict between the values of property and life, he discerns the logical priority of life and uses that logic to justify his choice:

For one thing, a human life is worth more than money, and if the druggist only makes $1,000, he is still going to live, but if Heinz doesn't steal the drug, his wife is going to die. (*Why is life worth more than money?*) Because the druggist can get a thousand dollars later from rich people with cancer, but Heinz can't get his wife again. *(Why not?)* Because people are all different and so you couldn't get Heinz's wife again.

Asked whether Heinz should steal the drug if he does not love his wife, Jake replies that he should, saying that not only is there "a difference between hating and killing," but also, if Heinz were caught, "the judge would probably think it was the right thing to do." Asked about the fact that, in stealing, Heinz would be breaking the law, he says that "the laws have mistakes, and you can't go writing up a law for everything that you can imagine."

Thus, while taking the law into account and recognizing its function in maintaining social order (the judge, Jake says, "should give Heinz the lightest possible sentence"), he also sees the law as man-made and therefore subject to error and change. Yet his judgment that Heinz should steal the drug, like his view of the law as having mistakes, rests on the assumption of agreement, a societal consensus around moral values that allows one to know and expect others to recognize what is "the right thing to do."

Fascinated by the power of logic, this eleven-year-old boy locates truth in math, which, he says, is "the only thing that is totally logical." Considering the moral dilemma to be "sort of like a math problem with humans," he sets it up as an equation and proceeds to work out the solution. Since his solution is rationally derived, he assumes that anyone following reason would arrive at the same conclusion and thus that a judge would also consider stealing to be the right thing for Heinz to do.

Gilligan thinks that Jake's response is representative of the justice-based approach to ethics. In the next passage, she contrasts this approach with Amy's quite different form of moral justification. Amy's orientation focuses not on principles of justice but on relationships.

- Since Amy agrees with Jake that it would be right for Heinz to steal the drug, in what ways is her response different from his?
- Amy suggests another solution with respect to the druggist that Jake did not mention. What is it? How does her approach add another dimension to the solution?

In contrast, Amy's response to the dilemma conveys a very different impression, an image of development stunted by a failure of logic, an inability to think for herself. Asked if Heinz should steal the drug, she replies in a way that seems evasive and unsure:

> Well, I don't think so. I think there might be other ways besides stealing it, like if he could borrow the money or make a loan or something, but he really shouldn't steal the drug—but his wife shouldn't die either.

Asked why he should not steal the drug, she considers neither property nor law but rather the effect that theft could have on the relationship between Heinz and his wife:

If he stole the drug, he might save his wife then, but if he did, he might have to go to jail, and then his wife might get sicker again, and he couldn't get more of the drug, and it might not be good. So, they should really just talk it out and find some other way to make the money.

Seeing in the dilemma not a math problem with humans but a narrative of relationships that extends over time, Amy envisions the wife's continuing need for her husband and the husband's continuing concern for his wife and seeks to respond to the druggist's need in a way that would sustain rather than sever connection. Just as she ties the wife's survival to the preservation of relationships, so she considers the value of the wife's life in a context of relationships, saying that it would be wrong to let her die because, "if she died, it hurts a lot of people and it hurts her." Since Amy's moral judgment is grounded in the belief that, "if somebody has something that would keep somebody alive, then it's not right not to give it to them," she considers the problem in the dilemma to arise not from the druggist's assertion of rights but from his failure of response.

As the interviewer proceeds with the series of questions that follow from Kohlberg's construction of the dilemma, Amy's answers remain essentially unchanged, the various probes serving neither to elucidate nor to modify her initial response. Whether or not Heinz loves his wife, he still shouldn't steal or let her die; if it were a stranger dying instead, Amy says that "if the stranger didn't have anybody near or anyone she knew," then Heinz should try to save her life, but he should not steal the drug. But as the interviewer conveys through the repetition of questions that the answers she gave were not heard or not right, Amy's confidence begins to diminish, and her replies become more constrained and unsure. Asked again why Heinz should not steal the drug, she simply repeats, "Because it's not right." Asked again to explain why, she states again that theft would not be a good solution, adding lamely, "if he took it, he might not know how to give it to his wife, and so his wife might still die." Failing to see the dilemma as a self-contained problem in moral logic, she does not discern the internal structure of its resolution; as she constructs the problem differently herself, Kohlberg's conception completely evades her.

Instead, seeing a world comprised of relationships rather than of people standing alone, a world that coheres through human connection rather than through systems of rules, she finds the puzzle in the dilemma to lie in the failure of the druggist to respond to the wife. Saying that "it is not right for someone to die when their life could be saved," she assumes that if the druggist were to see the consequences of his refusal to lower his price, he would realize that "he should just give it to the wife and then have the husband pay back the money later." Thus she considers the solution to the dilemma to be in making the wife's condition more salient to the druggist or, that failing, in appealing to others who are in a position to help.

Just as Jake is confident the judge would agree that stealing is the right thing for Heinz to do, so Amy is confident that, "if Heinz and the druggist had talked it out long enough, they could reach something besides stealing." As he considers the law to "have mistakes," so she sees this drama as a mistake, believing that "the world should just share things more and then people wouldn't have to steal." Both children thus recognize the need for agreement but see it as mediated in different ways—he impersonally through systems of logic and law, she personally through communication in relationship. Just as he relies on the conventions of logic to deduce the solution to this dilemma, assuming these conventions to be shared, so she relies on a process of communication, assuming connection and believing that her voice will be heard. Yet while his assumptions about agreement are confirmed by the convergence in logic between his answers and the questions posed, her assumptions are belied by the failure of communication, the interviewer's inability to understand her response.

Although the frustration of the interview with Amy is apparent in the repetition of questions and its ultimate circularity, the problem of interpretation is focused by the assessment of her response. When considered in the light of Kohlberg's definition of the stages and sequence of moral development, her moral judgments appear to be a full stage lower in maturity than those of the boy. Scored as a mixture of stages two and three, her responses seem to reveal a feeling of powerlessness in the world, an inability to think systematically about the concepts of morality or law, a reluctance to challenge authority or to examine the logic of received moral truths, a failure even to conceive of acting directly to save a life or to consider that such action, if taken, could possibly have an effect. As her reliance on relationships seems to reveal a continuing dependence and vulnerability, so her belief in communication as the mode through which to resolve moral dilemmas appears naive and cognitively immature.

Yet Amy's description of herself conveys a markedly different impression. Once again, the hallmarks of the preadolescent child depict a child secure in her sense of herself, confident in the substance of her beliefs, and sure of her ability to do something of value in the world. Describing herself at eleven as "growing and changing," she says that she "sees some things differently now, just because I know myself really well now, and I know a lot more about the world." Yet the world she knows is a different world from that refracted by Kohlberg's construction of Heinz's dilemma. Her world is a world of relationships and psychological truths where an awareness of the connection between people gives rise to a recognition of responsibility for one another, a perception of the need for response. Seen in this light, her understanding of morality as arising from the recognition of relationship, her belief in communication as the mode of conflict resolution, and her conviction that the solution to the dilemma will follow from its compelling representation seem far from naive or cognitively immature. Instead, Amy's judgments contain the insights central to an ethic of care, just as Jake's judgments reflect the logic of the justice approach. Her incipient awareness of the "method of truth," the central tenet of nonviolent conflict resolution, and her belief in the restorative activity of care, lead her to see the actors in the dilemma arrayed not as opponents in a contest of rights but as members of a network of relationships on whose continuation they all depend. Consequently her solution to the dilemma lies in activating the network by communication, securing the inclusion of the wife by strengthening rather than severing connections.

But the different logic of Amy's response calls attention to the interpretation of the interview itself. Conceived as an interrogation, it appears instead as a dialogue, which takes on moral dimensions of its own, pertaining to the interviewer's uses of power and to the manifestations of respect. With this shift in the conception of the interview, it immediately becomes clear that the interviewer's problem in understanding Amy's response stems from the fact that Amy is answering a different question from the one the interviewer thought had been posed. Amy is considering not *whether* Heinz should act in this situation ("*should* Heinz steal the drug?") but rather how Heinz should act in response to his awareness of his wife's need ("Should Heinz *steal* the drug?"). The interviewer takes the mode of action for granted, presuming it to be a matter of fact; Amy assumes the necessity for action and considers what form it should take. In the interviewer's failure to imagine a response not dreamt of in Kohlberg's moral philosophy lies the failure to hear Amy's question and to see the logic in her response, to discern that what appears, from one perspective, to be an evasion of the dilemma signifies in other terms a recognition of the problem and a search for a more adequate solution.

Thus in Heinz's dilemma these two children see two very different moral problems—Jake a conflict between life and property that can be resolved by logical deduction, Amy a fracture of human relationship that must be mended with its own thread. Asking different questions that arise from different conceptions of the moral domain, the children arrive at answers that fundamentally diverge, and the arrangement of these answers as successive stages on a scale of increasing moral maturity calibrated by the logic of the boy's response misses the different truth revealed in the judgment of the girl. To the question, "What does he see that she does not?" Kohlberg's theory provides a ready response, manifest in the scoring of Jake's judgments a full stage higher than Amy's in moral maturity; to the question, "What does she see that he does not?" Kohlberg's theory has nothing to say. Since most of her responses fall through the sieve of Kohlberg's scoring system, her responses appear from his perspective to lie outside the moral domain.

In the next passage, from the last chapter of her book, Gilligan concludes with the major themes of her theory: men and women "speak different languages," women's voices and moral experiences have been undervalued and ignored, and in the final analysis, a fully mature moral perspective requires both the ethic of care and the ethic of justice.

Visions of Maturity

Given the evidence of different perspectives in the representation of adulthood by women and men, there is a need for research that elucidates the effects of these differences in marriage, family, and work relationships. My research suggests that men and women may speak different languages that they assume are the same, using similar words to encode disparate experiences of self and social relationships. Because these languages share an overlapping moral vocabulary, they contain a propensity for systematic mistranslation, creating misunderstandings which impede communication and limit the potential for cooperation and care in relationships. At the same time, however, these languages articulate with one another in critical ways. Just as the language of responsibilities provides a weblike imagery of relationships to replace a hierarchical ordering that dissolves with the coming of equality, so the language of rights underlines the importance of including in the network of care not only the other but also the self.

As we have listened for centuries to the voices of men and the theories of development that their experience informs, so we have come more recently to notice not only the silence of women but the difficulty in hearing what they say when they speak. Yet in the different voice of women lies the truth of an ethic of care, the tie between relationship and responsibility, and the origins of aggression in the failure of connection. The failure to see the different reality of women's lives and to hear the differences in their voices stems in part from the assumption that there is a single mode of social experience and interpretation. By positing instead two different modes, we arrive at a more complex rendition of human experience which sees the truth of separation and attachment in the lives of women and men and recognizes how these truths are carried by different modes of language and thought.

To understand how the tension between responsibilities and rights sustains the dialectic of human development is to see the integrity of two disparate modes of experience that are in the end connected. While an ethic of justice proceeds from the premise of equality—that everyone should be treated the same—an ethic of care rests on the premise of nonviolence—that no one should be hurt. In the representation of maturity, both perspectives converge in the realization that just as inequality adversely affects both parties in an unequal relationship, so too violence is destructive for everyone involved. This dialogue between fairness and care not only provides a better understanding of relations between the sexes but also gives rise to a more comprehensive portrayal of adult work and family relationships.

Maternal, Care-Focused Ethics

Gilligan thinks that while the ethics of justice and the ethics of care are different, they are complementary and both are needed in ethics. Contrary to Gilligan, however, some feminists argue that a care-based ethics is superior. Many of them go even further and take women's experiences of mothering to be the paradigm for understanding ethics, developing what has been called maternal ethics. However, Virginia Held does not limit the experience of mothering to women, for instead of speaking of "mother" she speaks of a "mothering person" (someone who can be either female or male) and suggests that the wording "the nurturing of children"

Male and Female Psychology

A study was done in which college students were asked to write stories about pictures they were shown. The pictures alternately depicted situations involving personal affiliation and impersonal achievement. According to Carol Gilligan, the research suggested that:

> Men and women perceive danger in different social situations and construe danger in different ways—men seeing danger more often in personal affiliation than in achievement and construing danger to arise from intimacy, women perceiving danger in impersonal achievement situations and construing danger to result from competitive success. The danger men describe in their stories of intimacy is a danger of entrapment or betrayal, being caught in a smothering relationship or humiliated by rejection and deceit. In contrast, the danger women portray in their tales of achievement is a danger of isolation, a fear that in standing out or being set apart by success, they will be left alone.[94]

For example, one of the pictures showed two trapeze artists performing high in the air—a man, hanging by his knees from the trapeze, was grasping the wrists of a woman in mid-air. Although the picture did not depict a safety net, researchers found that 22 percent of the women added nets in the stories they wrote, while only 6 percent of the men imagined the presence of a net. On the other hand, 40 percent of the men either mentioned the absence of a net in their stories or implied its absence by describing one or both of the acrobats as falling to their deaths. In analyzing the results, Gilligan says, "Thus, the women saw the scene on the trapeze as safe because, by providing nets, they had made it safe, protecting the lives of the acrobats in the event of a fall. . . . As women imagine the activities through which relationships are woven and connection sustained, the world of intimacy—which appears so mysterious and dangerous to men—comes instead to appear increasingly coherent and safe."[95]

SPOTLIGHT
on

may be preferable to "mothering."[96] Similarly, in her book *Maternal Thinking,* moral philosopher Sara Ruddick says that the maternal traits of caring, intimacy, responsibility, and trust can characterize your stance toward life and others, even if you are a childless woman or a man.[97] (Ruddick's model of maternal thinking was briefly discussed in section 2.8.)

In her often-quoted book, *Caring: A Feminine Approach to Ethics and Moral Education,* ethical theorist Nel Noddings carries out the project of "reclaiming the feminine" by arguing that those qualities such as compassion, caring, and empathetic feelings that were often ignored or given marginal status in traditional ethical theory are actually the foundation stones of moral maturity. She says that we approach human relationships not on the basis of abstract rights, but in terms of concern for a particular individual's concrete needs. As opposed to an ethical orientation based on abstract principles, a parent who is caring for a child, for example, will consult her own "feelings, needs, impressions, and . . . sense of personal ideal" and will try to identify herself with the child as closely as possible to know what is in the child's best interest.[98]

From the experience of being cared for we learn the goodness of the caring relationship, and in turn, we learn how to care for others ourselves. Once we have developed the spontaneous sentiment of *natural* caring, a more deliberative *ethical* caring becomes a moral possibility for us. However, contrary to Kant, who thought that the call of duty must give a deaf ear to our natural inclinations, Noddings believes that the "I must" of moral obligation is always related to the best of our natural inclinations. As Noddings writes, "An ethic built on caring strives to maintain the caring attitude and is thus dependent upon, and not superior to, natural caring."[99]

At this point, we might be inclined to ask, "Can the values, traits, and practices that are found in the intimate relationships of a family offer any ethical guidance as we go out into the larger world beyond the home?" Maternalistic, care-focused feminists think they can. For example, political theorist Kathy Ferguson urges women to use the "values that are structured into women's experience—caretaking, nurturance, empathy, connectedness" to create new models of society and institutions that are not based on the principle of domination.[100] In other words, although the experiences of caretaking and nurturing are more typically associated with women and especially mothers, these experiences can provide important ethical insights and serve as a paradigm for nonmothers as well. Furthermore, maternal, care-focused feminists claim that we can generalize from these concrete experiences to construct a comprehensive ethical theory that can be disseminated throughout the public sphere as a politics of compassion. Hence, to the title of her book *Maternal Thinking,* Ruddick adds the subtitle *Toward a Politics of Peace.* These feminists have no doubts that the ethics of care will be better suited than alternative theories to address the problems associated with world hunger, poverty, war, the environment, exploitation in the workplace, health care, and education. In discussing the approach taken by maternal ethics, philosopher Jean Grimshaw asks whether, "given, for instance, the experience of women in pregnancy, childbirth, and the rearing of children, might there be, for example, some difference in the way they will view the 'waste' of those lives in war."[101] In summarizing this more expanded application of care-focused ethics, political theorist Joan Tronto says, "care is not solely private or parochial; it can concern institutions, societies, even global levels of thinking."[102]

Power-Focused Feminist Ethics

The care-focused version of feminist ethics has had an enormous influence, both in terms of its critique of the limitations of traditional ethical theory as well as its positive program for recentering ethics. However, not all feminists believe that care-focused ethics is the way to go. Those who adhere to what Tong has called power-focused feminist ethics believe that ethical questions cannot be addressed in isolation from questions about the power structures in society and the patterns of dominance and oppression that exist. Tong notes that this approach emphasizes that nonfeminist philosophers subordinate women to men by "neglecting, down-

PHILOSOPHY
in the
MARKETPLACE

Read the following ethical dilemma to an equal number of males and females, and ask them the questions that follow. If their answers are too brief or vague, you might want to ask follow-up questions to make sure you understand their reasoning. After collecting their answers, analyze them by referring to the two sets of moral considerations (A and B) in leading question 2 at the beginning of this section. You may also want to compare them to Jake's and Amy's answers in the Carol Gilligan reading. Do the males and females tend to give different sorts of answers, as Gilligan suggests? Did the males tend to think more like Jake and use the factors in list A? Did the females tend to think more like Amy and use the factors in list B? What conclusions can you draw from your survey?

In Europe a woman was near death from a special kind of cancer. There was one drug that doctors thought might save her. It was a form of radium that a druggist in the same town had recently discovered. The drug was expensive to make, but the druggist was charging ten times what the drug cost to make. He paid $200 for the radium and charged $2000 for a small dose of the drug. The sick woman's husband, Heinz, went to everyone he knew to borrow the money, but he could only get together about $1000, which is half of what it cost. He told the druggist that his wife was dying, and asked him to sell it cheaper or let him pay later. But the druggist said, "No, I discovered the drug and I'm going to make money from it." So Heinz got desperate and began to think about breaking into the man's store to steal the drug for his wife.[103]

- Should Heinz steal the drug?
- Why?

playing, trivializing, or totally ignoring women's moral interests, issues, insights, and identities."[104] Jaggar says that while power-focused feminist ethicists share some of the aims of feminists in general, the former place a higher priority on the following goals: "First, to articulate moral critiques of actions and practices that perpetuate women's subordination; second, to prescribe morally justifiable ways of resisting such actions and practices; and, third, to envision morally desirable alternatives that will promote women's emancipation."[105]

Critics of Care-Focused Ethics

Ethicist Susan Mendus sums up the power-focused feminist critique of the ethics of care by citing three related problems:

The first is that its emphasis on difference implies a view of women which, historically, has been associated with policies of political exclusion. The second is that it implies an over-simple, and static, view of female identity, which misdescribes women's role in modern life, and the third is that it appeals to an inappropriate analogy between familial and political relationships.[106]

Concerning Mendus's first point on the political exclusion of women, some feminists see our current conceptions of mothering, the family, and the home as miniature versions of the more general oppression in society. Critics charge that when the care-focused feminists make these domains the paradigm for ethics, they are further solidifying women's secondary status. For example, some feminists have agreed with John Broughton, a male critic of Carol Gilligan, who states that Gilligan's theory tends to "perpetuate the status quo, to affirm the established division of labor, and to foreclose the possibility of radical transformation."[107] In other words, Broughton says, Gilligan "leaves women in almost the same position that Aristotle left them."[108] Similarly, in response to maternal ethics, political scientist Mary Dietz argues that love, intimacy, and caring cannot be the basis for political action or discourse. As she puts it, "Not the language of love and compassion, but only the language of freedom and equality, citizenship and justice, will challenge nondemocratic and oppressive political institutions."[109]

The second complaint is that care ethics provides an inappropriate description of female identity. Psychologist Zella Luria asks, "Do we truly gain by returning to a modern cult of true womanhood? Do we gain by the assertion that women think or reason in one voice and men in another?"[110] Similarly, in the title of her insightful article, philosopher Patricia Scaltsas asks the question, "Do Feminist Ethics Counter Feminist Aims?" In response to claims that empathy and care are distinctively female virtues, she says:

> Although the traditional role of women in society might have led to the development of certain virtues, the *confinement* of women to that role has had destructive results in their development as individuals in society. . . .
> . . . The danger is that these female values, ways of thinking, and experiences will degenerate into the traditional dichotomies between male and female capacities and characteristics which have been used to try to justify excluding women from educational, professional, and political opportunities and locking them into roles of irrational love-givers or love-giving simpletons.[111]

The problem, some feminists complain, is that women have been socialized to believe that their moral responsibilities require them to be sacrificially altruistic, and they think that if they fail to suppress their own identities, interests, and needs, they are being selfish. In response to this socialization, some feminists even recommend a healthy dose of egoistic self-interest as an antidote. Feminist philosopher Sara Hoagland suggests, for example, that feminists replace the questions, "Am I good?" or "Is this good?" with the question, "Does this contribute to my self-creation, freedom and liberation?"[112] Hoagland is concerned with the possibility that in following Nodding's ethics of care, "I get my ethical identity from always being other-directed," with the result that "being moral" becomes another term for "being exploited."[113]

In response to such criticisms, feminist theorist Sheila Mullett distinguishes between "distortions of caring" and "undistorted caring."[114] She says that caring cannot be authentic if a person is economically, socially, or psychologically compelled to care. She acknowledges, therefore, that an ethics of caring can only be fully realized when women achieve sexual equality and freedom from conditions that support

Two Feminist Interpretations of Relationships

Earlier we discussed Gilligan's analysis of an experiment in which men and women were told to write stories about a picture of two trapeze artists, a man holding the wrists of a woman. Gilligan found that significantly more women added safety nets in the story, which she assumed illustrated the fact that the women were more comfortable with relationships. The women saw the relationship between the man and the woman as safe, Gilligan said, because the women subjects had made it safe. Marilyn Friedman, however, says that in a male-dominated society, many women have found the current patterns of heterosexual relationships to be problematic and even oppressive. Hence, she sees a different theme in the results of the study: "Perhaps, on the contrary, women added nets as external safety devices precisely because they perceived the relationships as being, in themselves, *un*safe."[118]

male domination and female subordination. Until then, women must be cautious in caring and ask if it is serving their own, self-realization and if it is taking place within the "framework of consciousness-raising practice and conversation."[115]

Finally, many feminists agree with Mendus that the ethics of care, based as it is on the model of family relationships, is inadequate for the realm of public and political morality. For example, Dietz argues that

> maternal virtues cannot be political in the required sense because . . . they are connected to and emerge out of an activity that is special, distinctive, unlike any other. We must conclude, then, that this activity is unlike the activity of citizenship; the two cannot be viewed as somehow encompassing the same attributes, abilities, and ways of knowing.[116]

The problem is that the mother-child relationship contains an inequality of power and control, whereas the ideal political sphere allows the citizens to interact as equals. Furthermore, at the personal level it is natural for me to be partial and give priority to the needs of those with whom I am intimately involved, but such partiality is inappropriate at the political level. As John Broughton says about Gilligan's care ethics,

> Gilligan does not seem to acknowledge the importance of respect or responsibility in the relationship of a government to its nation's citizens, of nation-states to each other, or of states, governments, and citizens to past or future generations. "Caring" is limited as the basis of an ethical orientation unless it can overcome the parochiality that its association with friends and family tends to convey.[117]

Philosopher Marilyn Friedman's writings on ethics, social philosophy, and feminist theory provide a good illustration of power-focused feminist ethics. In the following selection Friedman begins with some of the standard criticisms against care-based ethics. While recognizing that the ethics of care has been neglected in traditional theories and that it is an important component in ethics, she still insists

MARILYN FRIEDMAN
(1945–)

that caring cannot be the sole or even the major moral duty that overrides all others. Instead, she says, caring must find its place in a "liberatory" feminist ethic in which "enlightened care" includes the caring of the caregiver for herself and a concern for her own "personal flourishing" as well as a willingness to abandon caring when it serves as the cause of her oppression.

• See if you can summarize and list Friedman's objections to an ethics of care.

MARILYN FRIEDMAN
Liberating Care[119]

A Critical Overview of Care Ethics

Care ethics offers at least one very alluring feature: high moral esteem for the traditional caring work done by women. Yet, because of certain problems in care ethics, feminists wonder whether, on balance, this ethic hinders more than it helps women seeking to overcome their cultural subordination. Claudia Card and Joan Tronto, for example, observe that merely presenting care ethics as a distinctively female ethic is not enough to establish its moral adequacy or its moral superiority to other ethical perspectives. Barbara Houston worries that to celebrate feminine virtues and perspectives is to risk glorifying the oppressive conditions under which they arose.

Card and Tronto point out that relationships differ in their worth, that not every relationship is valuable, and that care ethics provides no basis for critical reflection on relationships. Card suggests that, having developed under conditions of oppression, the care perspective has been needed for adaptation to those oppressive conditions and may not embody genuine virtue. In the views of both Card and Houston, care ethics ignores the possibility that a history of oppression has inflicted moral damage on women. Of special concern to feminists is the moral damage that further entrenches women's subordination, for example, the morally hazardous forms of deference that are a frequent risk when women care for men.

Card and Sarah Hoagland, in addition, both point out that care ethics lacks a political or institutional focus. It ignores the institutionally structured differentials of power and authority among different persons, especially those that constitute the gender hierarchy. It is thereby incapable of conceptualizing the oppressive, institutionally patriarchal context in which care takes place and that may compromise the otherwise high moral value of care. In Jeffner Allen's view, the nonviolence of care is a liability to women under oppressive circumstances, for it disables women from resisting whatever abuse they experience in heterosexual relationships.

Hoagland and Tronto, furthermore, recognized that care ethics ignores moral responsibilities to distant strangers and those for whom we do not feel particularly caring; care ethics thereby threatens to devolve into a mere defense of conventional relationships. Care ethics also fails to represent diversity among women.

Either it suffers from positive biases of race, class, ethnicity, and national culture, as Michele Moody-Adams charges, or, at the very least, it suffers by its simple failure to represent specific differences among women, such as the racial diversity discussed by Carol Stack. . . .

To sum up: resisting the varied forms of female subordination calls for more than simply elevating esteem for women's traditionally sanctioned forms of labor and attendant modes of consciousness. To elevate social esteem for care ethics is to combat women's subordination to the extent of resisting only one of its many manifestations. This approach, by itself, does not (yet) constitute a sufficiently rich or fully liberatory *feminist* ethic. Worse yet, care ethics appears to bolster some of the practices and conceptions that subordinate women.

To portray care ethics as a distinctively female ethic reinforces the stereotypic gender assumptions that women are especially suited for the domestic, nurturing realm, that men are unsuited for this realm, and that women are particularly unsuited for the traditionally masculine worlds of public work and activity. The apparent incapacity of care ethics to deal with the moral relationships of public life, relationships among strangers, or among persons who share no affective ties, contributes greatly to this impression. If care ethics is supposed to represent the preferred perspective of substantial numbers of women, and if its mutual integration with justice considerations is not widely convincing, then the promotion of care ethics as a female ethic cannot help but reinvigorate stereotypes of women's incapacity to handle the moral challenges of public life.

Furthermore, care ethics might also undermine women's resolve to resist, say, violence or reproductive control by others, by appearing to endorse the *overridingness* of the moral duties to care, nurture, and maintain relationship with anyone with whom one comes into intimate contact, regardless of the moral quality of the relationship. Gilligan's focus on what she sees as the inclusiveness of the caring attitude suggests this unqualified orientation simply to maintaining connections with others. A care ethic, in this respect, is vulnerable to Hoagland's objection that it morally nullifies some of the most effective strategies available to women for resistance to abuse, exploitation, and coercion, strategies such as withdrawal altogether from relationship.

In another passage (not quoted here), Friedman questioned the Gilligan thesis that caring is a distinctively female moral orientation. Nevertheless, she agrees that caring is an important dimension of the moral life, for men as well as women. In the next passage, Friedman attempts to preserve what was of value in the ethics of care by developing a notion of "enlightened care" within the context of an ethics of liberation. According to her view, the moral responsibility for caring ends when it endangers the caregiver's well-being. Furthermore, consistent with the power-focused version of feminist ethics, she suggests that caring must be viewed within the larger social context in which relationships are embedded, in which the dynamics of power, domination, and exploitation take on institutional dimensions, and in which the positive aspects of community may be developed.

Care for Women as Care Givers

A fully liberatory feminist ethic must legitimate a woman's care for herself and her pursuit of caring and nurturing from others. From the standpoint of care ethics, it is important to recognize that women, who are normally relied upon to provide the bulk of nurturant care for others, are vulnerable in various ways. The forms of care that women need are not vouchsafed in the course of our caring for others. Even though women's caring for others sustains networks of interpersonal relationships, the existence of these relationships does not guarantee women's safety or equality of social status with men. Caring remains a risky business for women.

The care that can make a moral difference to a woman's life is roughly twofold. On the one hand, there is the kind of care involved in resisting our own devaluation, denigration, harassment, marginalization, exclusion, exploitation, subordination, domination, or openly violent abuse. Systematic attempts to overcome such harms may take the form of petitioning or pressuring societal institutions either to alter their own structures toward greater gender equity or to intercede more effectively on behalf of women in so-called private affairs, as in woman-battering cases. But rescue is not always available, and some of the problems in question arise out of social institutions and practices that are culturally sanctioned and widely tolerated. To protect ourselves, we as women must often rely on our own self-assertive efforts against oppressive practices. Thus, one major form of care for oneself concentrates on the variously necessary ways of protecting oneself against harm by others.

The second major category of care for self that a fully liberatory feminist ethic should offer involves positive flourishing, self-development that goes beyond merely resisting subordination or oppression. To be fully liberatory for women, such an ethic must develop ideals for a variety of personal achievements and excellences (other than those that center around self-protection). Care ethics does, of course, glorify the virtue of caring for and nurturing others. But this is not the only sort of human excellence that women can attain. Thus, a fully liberatory feminist ethic, with an eye toward the lives of women as typical care givers, should idealize forms of personal flourishing in addition to excellent care giving.

The sort of care for oneself involved in flourishing is significantly different from the sort that concentrates on protecting oneself from harm. The familiar criticisms that the women's movement in the United States concentrates on the needs of middle-class, white women and ignores the needs of low-income women or women who are not white have much to do with this distinction. Many women in our culture lack access to the resources for forms of personal development that extend beyond self-protective and survival needs. To sue the Rotary Club for barring female applicants from membership is a different sort of feminist project from volunteering support services at a battered women's shelter. Yet each is, in its own way, a quest by women to care for themselves and for some other women, a quest to surmount some facet of subordination or oppression facing some women and to live as well as conditions permit. Both of these wide-ranging sorts of concerns, self-protection as well as personal flourishing, require moral anchorage in a notion of care for oneself.

On Nodding's formulation of care ethics, not much primary importance is attached to caring for oneself. As Hoagland observes, the responsibility to care for oneself is derivative in Noddings's system; it derives from the responsibility to maintain one's capacity to care for others, a goal that requires staying in good care-giving shape. Caring for oneself as such appears to have no intrinsic value. . . .

My emphasis on the importance of caring for oneself and of being cared for in return by those for whom one cares introduces into care ethics an emphasis on self that is lacking in Noddings's formulation and that appears only in undeveloped form in Gilligan's version. On the approach I am recommending, the self is still defined, at least in part, by her relationships. My approach, however, incorporates the recognition that the care-giving self is herself someone who needs care and that her needs as such make legitimate moral demands on those to whom she is close.

There is room in care ethics for a cautious strain of individualism, one that is consistent with a theoretical emphasis on interconnection and the social nature of persons. Responsibilities to care should not eclipse those features of the care giver that constitute her as an individual, nor should they obscure those dimensions of meaning in her life that are independent of her care-giving role. Subordination, exploitation, abuse, and oppression occur to individuals—individuals in relationships, to be sure, but individuals nevertheless. Care ethics requires a notion of individuality (together with an adequate conception of human groups) in order to illuminate who is subordinated, who is oppressed, and why and how this occurs on a daily piecemeal basis. . . .

More so than Noddings and Gilligan, then, I construe the needs, wants, hopes, fears, and so forth of the care-giving self as legitimately helping to set the moral agenda for her relationships with other adults. The caring self, in such relationships, should care for herself and should expect her loved ones to reciprocate the care that she provides for them to the extent that they are able to do so. Self-assertion is not inimical to caring but, rather, helps to ensure that caring is mutual and undefiled by subordination of the care-giver. . . .

However we respond to this assessment of caretaking practices, it seems that we can no longer take a wholly benign view of the role of caring in women's lives, especially in the context of heterosexual relationships. If my analysis is correct, then it, together with the other feminist criticisms of care ethics outlined at the beginning of this chapter, yields a complex portrait of care. On the one hand, care is essential for the survival and development of both individuals and their communities, and care giving is a noble endeavor as well as being often morally requisite. On the other hand, care is simultaneously a perilous project for women, requiring the sacrifice of other important values, its very nobility part of its sometimes dangerously seductive allure. An ethic of care, to be fully liberatory for women, must not fail to explore and reflect this deep complexity.

- How would you paraphrase and summarize Friedman's requirements for a "liberating care ethic"?

SUMMARY OF FEMINIST ETHICS

It should be clear by now that while feminists insist that women's "voices" need to be heard in the realm of ethics, they do not always speak with one voice. Some of the controversies we have examined and that are still being discussed within the feminist movement are as follows: Is there a male bias in traditional ethical theories, and is it of such proportions that a total reconstruction of moral theory is required? Is there a difference between males and females in their ethical orientations? If so, how should that difference be characterized? If there are such differences, are they rooted in our biological natures or our social conditioning? Are a justice-based ethics and a care-based ethics equally correct and complementary, or is one superior to the other? Do the insights gathered from women's experiences in nurturing provide a basis for a more satisfactory approach to ethics? Can these insights be appropriated by men? On the other hand, does a care-focused ethics reinforce sexual stereotypes and prevent women from critically examining their status in society? Should women be concerned simply with elaborating better ethical theories, or is their first priority to challenge the conditions in society that oppress them?

LOOKING THROUGH THE LENS
OF FEMINIST ETHICS

1. Annette Baier says that "the great moral theorists in our tradition not only are all men, they are mostly men who had minimal adult dealings with (and so were then minimally influenced by) women." For the most part, she says, they were "clerics, misogynists, and puritan bachelors," and thus it is not surprising that they focus their philosophical attention "so single-mindedly on cool, distanced relations between more or less free and equal adult strangers."[120] Granted that the great moral theorists were all men, but do you think that maleness affected their theories in the way that Baier claims? Think back over the readings throughout this chapter on ethics. If you had not known the gender of the different authors, would you have been able to tell if they were male or female?

2. If you were a mother (perhaps you are), do you think the experience of motherhood would affect the way you viewed ethics? How so?

3. From your own experience and from what you have read, do you think there are differences between the ways that men and women approach ethical issues? What would be the implications of differences that are rooted in our biological natures? What would be the implications of differences that are caused by our social conditioning?

4. What do you think are the contributions and limitations of an ethics of care when applied beyond personal relationships to ethical issues in society and public policy?

5. Take one of the theories within feminist ethics and imagine that this theory had been the dominant moral tradition throughout the history of our society. In this case, how would history and society be different today? What differences would this theory have made in our institutions, politics, laws, and social arrangements? Which of these changes (if any) would have been better? Which (if any) would have been worse?

EXAMINING THE STRENGTHS AND
WEAKNESSES OF FEMINIST ETHICS

Positive Evaluation

1. The feminist writers have focused attention on what they believe is a much too restrictive view of rationality. Too often, being rational is identified with being distant, cool, and abstract, while feelings are dismissed as mere sentimentality. But feminists have insisted that sympathy, compassion, and concern can provide rational grounds for moral action. Do you think this point strengthens the case for their theory?

2. Whether or not it's true that males and females have different ethical orientations, doesn't Carol Gilligan have a point when she says that the rational, justice-based approach that focuses on rules and rights and the empathetic, caring-based approach that focuses on relationships are both important and complementary? Don't we all tend to be unbalanced in one direction or the other, and wouldn't we be better persons if we learned to listen to "voices" that are different from our own?

3. It is certainly true that women's voices have been ignored or silenced in the past as well as in our contemporary world. Wouldn't our moral traditions and our political life have been better if our intellectual and political conversations had been more broadly based and more inclusive? Isn't it significant that many corporations and institutions are making voluntary efforts (and not simply for legal reasons) to step up their efforts to include women in positions of leadership? Aren't they finding that women bring insights and perspectives that would be missing without their input?

4. Whether you are a male or a female, don't you sometimes find it helpful to seek out advice or at least a sympathetic ear from a woman friend? Don't you find this conversation particularly helpful when you are dealing with a sensitive relationship problem with someone you love or a family member? Do women tend to have a better understanding of relationships or, at least, a distinctive perspective on them? If so, why? What implications does this quality have for contributions women can make and have made to ethical theory?

Negative Evaluation

1. The American Declaration of Independence talks eloquently about human equality, dignity, and innate rights at the same time that its signers owned slaves. The problem was not in the principles they embraced but in their failure to apply them consistently and impartially. Could the same be true with traditional ethical theory? Isn't it possible that all the problems feminists point to in society are the result not of the failures of our ethical traditions but of the inadequate ways they have been applied?

2. Many feminists emphasize the ethics of care, but are they the only ones who are showing concern? After all, the duty and virtue of beneficence is solidly based in Aristotelian, Kantian, utilitarian, and recent virtue ethics. For example, although some feminists complain that women have been conditioned to submerge their needs and interests to tend to the needs of the male ego, Kant reminds us that we should not treat *ourselves* merely as a means to some other end but that we should view ourselves as persons who have intrinsic worth and dignity. Furthermore, the utilitarians point out that our own desires and interests must be included in the balance when we are calculating what action will produce the most happiness. Some male philosophers in previous ages may have had demeaning attitudes toward women, but don't their ethical theories have the resources to address most of the feminists' concerns? Isn't it ironic that of all the ethical theorists presented in this

chapter, it was a woman thinker, Ayn Rand, whose ethics was most antithetical to many of the central concerns of the feminists?

3. Many feminist ethicists criticize traditional ethics for emphasizing the abstract principles of rights and justice. But shouldn't these principles be fundamental, key concepts in any viable ethical theory? In her book on human rights, Patricia Williams reflects on the bill of sale for her great-great-grandmother, which describes her ancestor as an eleven-year-old female slave. Williams says that, given the progress our society has made in overcoming racial injustice in the last century, the word "rights" is "deliciously empowering to say."[121] Similarly, hasn't all the progress that women have made in this century, and particularly in the past few decades, been the result of social and legal changes that emanate from an ethical concern for rights and justice? Haven't many of these changes been facilitated by male theorists and politicians? Does a feminist ethic undermine feminist goals?

4. Although they criticize ethical theories based on abstract, universal principles, can feminist ethicists avoid them? For example, feminist ethics seems to be based on the universal principle that *everyone* should be caring, compassionate, and attentive to others' needs. If feminist insights can be shared and can serve as guidelines in our moral lives, aren't they capable of being formulated as universal principles, the very thing feminists disdain in Kantian ethics?

REVIEW FOR CHAPTER 5

Philosophers

5.0 The Search for Ethical Values
    Plato
    John Hospers
5.1 Ethical Relativism versus Objectivism
    Protagoras
    Jean-Paul Sartre
    Herodotus
    Ruth Benedict
    John Ladd
    James Rachels
5.2 Ethical Egoism
    Friedrich Nietzsche
    Ayn Rand
    Bishop Butler
    Joel Feinberg
    Adam Smith
5.3 Utilitarianism
    Jeremy Bentham
    John Stuart Mill

Concepts

ethical egoism
egoism versus egotism
personal ethical egoism
individual ethical egoism
universal ethical egoism
selfishness versus self-interest
hedonism
5.3 Utilitarianism
consequentialism
teleological ethics
deontological ethics
intrinsic value
instrumental value
utilitarianism
psychological hedonism
ethical hedonism
Bentham's hedonic calculus
quantitative hedonism
qualitative hedonism
act-utilitarianism
rule-utilitarianism
5.4 Kantian Ethics
the good will
acting in accordance with duty versus acting from duty
deontological ethics
teleological (or consequentialist) ethics
Kant's three propositions of morality
hypothetical imperative
categorical imperative
a universalizable principle
a reversible principle
prima facie duty
actual duty
5.5 Virtue Ethics
virtue ethics
virtue
Aristotle's doctrine of the mean
the utilitarian view of virtue
the Kantian view of virtue
5.6 Rethinking the Western Tradition: Feminist Ethics
feminine ethics versus feminist ethics
care-focused feminist ethics
power-focused feminist ethics
Lawrence Kohlberg's six stages of moral development

ethics of justice versus ethics of care
maternal ethics

SUGGESTIONS FOR FURTHER READING

General Works on Ethics

Birsch, Douglas. *Ethical Insights: A Brief Introduction.* Mountain View, Calif.: Mayfield, 1999. An analysis and evaluation of the major theories along with their practical applications.

Boss, Judith. *Analyzing Moral Issues.* Mountain View, Calif.: Mayfield, 1999. An introduction to the major theories with applications to contemporary moral issues.

_____. *Perspectives on Ethics.* Mountain View, Calif.: Mayfield, 1998. A collection of readings ranging from classical to contemporary.

Newberry, Paul. *Theories of Ethics.* Mountain View, Calif.: Mayfield, 1999. A historically organized anthology ranging from Socrates to the contemporary period.

Pojman, Louis. *Ethical Theory: Classical and Contemporary Readings.* 3d ed. Belmont, Calif.: Wadsworth, 1998. An excellent anthology.

_____. *Ethics: Discovering Right and Wrong.* 3d ed. Belmont, Calif.: Wadsworth, 1999. A short and engaging introduction to the leading theories and issues.

Rosenstand, Nina. *The Moral of the Story: An Introduction to Questions of Ethics and Human Nature.* Mountain View, Calif.: Mayfield, 1994. An overview of classical and modern approaches to ethical theory that uses examples from fiction and film.

Ethical Relativism versus Objectivism

Ladd, John. *Ethical Relativism.* Belmont, Calif.: Wadsworth, 1973. A collection of basic readings on the topic.

Mackie, J. L. *Ethics: Inventing Right and Wrong.* London: Penguin Books, 1976. A defense of relativism.

Wong, David. *Moral Relativity.* Berkeley: University of California Press, 1985. Defends a sophisticated version of ethical relativism.

Egoism

Gauthier, David, ed. *Morality and Rational Self-Interest.* Engelwood Cliffs, N.J.: Prentice-Hall, 1970.

Rand, Ayn. *Atlas Shrugged.* New York: Signet, 1996. All of Rand's novels promote the virtues of egoism in fictional form. This one seemed to be her favorite and depicts her thesis of the problems of an altruistic society and the possibility and desirability of a society of pure egoists.

_____. *The Virtue of Selfishness: A New Concept of Egoism.* New York: New American Library, 1989. A collection of articles written by Rand defending her version of ethical egoism.

Utilitarianism

Bentham, Jeremy. *Introduction to the Principles of Morals and Legislation.* Edited by W. Harrison. Oxford: Oxford University Press, 1948. Bentham's classic defense of his theory.

Brandt, Richard. *A Theory of the Good and Right.* Oxford: Clarendon Press, 1979. A contemporary classic that defends a sophisticated version of utilitarianism.

Mill, John Stuart. *Utilitarianism.* Indianapolis: Bobbs-Merrill, 1957. One of the founding documents of the utilitarian movement.

Quinton, Anthony. *Utilitarian Ethics.* London: Macmillan, 1973. A clear exposition of classical utilitarianism.

Scheffler, Samuel. *Consequentialism and Its Critics.* Oxford: Oxford University Press, 1988. An advanced discussion of the strengths and limitations of consequentialist theories.

————. *The Rejection of Consequentialism.* Rev. ed. Oxford: Oxford University Press, 1994. An important discussion of the limits of consequentialism.

Smart, J. J. C., and Bernard Williams, eds. *Utilitarianism and Beyond.* Cambridge, England: Cambridge University Press, 1982. Contains a number of important readings.

Kantian Ethics

Kant, Immanuel. *The Foundations of the Metaphysics of Morals.* Translated by Lewis White Beck. Indianapolis: Bobbs-Merrill, 1959.

Wolff, Robert. *The Autonomy of Reason: A Commentary on Kant's "Groundwork of the Metaphysics of Morals."* New York: Harper & Row, 1973. A helpful commentary on Kant's work.

Virtue Ethics

Crisp, Roger, and Michael Slote, eds. *Virtue Ethics.* Oxford: Oxford University Press, 1997. A collection of important recent essays on the topic.

French, Peter, Theodore Uehling Jr., and Howard Wettstein, eds. *Ethical Theory: Character and Virtue.* Midwest Studies in Philosophy, vol. 13. Notre Dame, Ind.: University of Notre Dame Press, 1988. Contains a good collection of previously unpublished essays.

Kruschwitz, Robert, and Robert Roberts, eds. *The Virtues: Contemporary Essays on Moral Character.* Belmont, Calif.: Wadsworth, 1987. A readable collection of essays with an extensive bibliography.

Statman, Daniel, ed. *Virtue Ethics: A Critical Reader.* Washington, D.C.: Georgetown University Press, 1997. Includes contributions by both defenders and critics of virtue ethics. The editor's introduction is one of the best surveys of this topic in print.

Feminist Ethics

Cole, Eve Browning, and Susan Coultrap-McQuin, eds. *Explorations in Feminist Ethics: Theory and Practice.* Bloomington: Indiana University Press, 1992. A collection of articles representing the various viewpoints in the movement.

Frazer, Elizabeth, Jennifer Hornsby, and Sabina Lovibond, eds. *Ethics: A Feminist Reader.* Oxford: Blackwell, 1992. An anthology of both historical and contemporary articles.

Gatens, Moira, ed. *Feminist Ethics.* Aldershot, England: Dartmouth Publishing, 1998. A massive collection of articles, covering some of the main controversies in the movement.

Tong, Rosemarie. *Feminist Approaches to Bioethics.* Boulder, Colo.: Westview, 1997. Part 1 gives a helpful overview of the variety of theories in feminist ethics.

_____. *Feminist Thought: A More Comprehensive Introduction.* Boulder, Colo.: Westview, 1998. A comprehensive overview of the movement, including a discussion of the leading feminist ethical theories.

NOTES

1. Plato, *Republic,* trans. Benjamin Jowett (New York: P. F. Collier, 1901), bk 2, lines 359e–360b. I have made minor changes to the wording and punctuation for greater readability.
2. Quoted in Peter Collier and David Horowitz, *The Kennedys: An American Drama* (New York: Summit Books, 1984), p. 150.
3. See Patrick H. Nowell-Smith, "Morality: Religious and Secular," in *Philosophy of Religion: An Anthology,* 3d ed., Louis Pojman (Belmont, Calif.: Wadsworth, 1998) and James Rachels, "God and Human Attitudes," in *Religious Studies,* 7 (1971): 325–38.
4. See George Mavrodes, "Religion and the Queerness of Morality," in Pojman, *Philosophy of Religion;* Louis Pojman, "Ethics: Religious and Secular," *The Modern Schoolman* 70 (November 1992): 1–30; and Louis Pojman, "Is Contemporary Moral Theory Founded on a Misunderstanding?" *Journal of Social Philosophy* 22 (fall 1991): 49–59.
5. "Religion and Morality," in *Leo Tolstoy: Selected Essays,* trans. Aylmer Maude (New York: Random House, 1964), p. 31.
6. For discussions and defenses of the divine command theory, see Paul Helm, ed., *The Divine Command Theory of Ethics* (Oxford: Oxford University Press, 1979); Gene Outka and J. P. Reeder, eds., *Religion and Morality: A Collection of Essays* (Garden City, N.Y.: Anchor Books, 1973); and Philip Quinn, *Divine Commands and Moral Requirements* (Oxford: Oxford University Press, 1978).
7. For Biblical approval of specific acts of lying, see Exodus 1:15–20 and Joshua 2:1–6 (in conjunction with Hebrews 11:31). For divinely commanded lying, see 1 Samuel 16:1–3.
8. Gottfried Leibniz, *Discourse on Metaphysics,* sec. 2, trans. George R. Montgomery (1902).
9. Thomas Hobbes, *Leviathan* (1651). All quotes are from chapter 13.
10. This exercise was given by John Hospers in *Human Conduct* (New York: Harcourt Brace Jovanovich, 1961), p. 174.
11. Plato, *The Republic of Plato,* trans. Francis MacDonald Cornford (Oxford: Oxford University Press, 1941), bk. 9, lines 588e–589b.
12. Plato, *The Republic of Plato,* bk. 4, lines 445a–b.
13. John Hospers, *Human Conduct,* 2d ed. (New York: Harcourt Brace Jovanovich, 1982), p. 29.
14. This apt analogy was taken from Louis Pojman, *Ethics: Discovering Right and Wrong* (Belmont, Calif.: Wadsworth, 1995), p. 229.
15. Robert Bolt, *A Man for All Seasons* (New York: Random House, 1962), p. 140.
16. Ernest Hemingway, *Death in the Afternoon* (New York: Scribner, 1932), p. 4
17. Jean-Paul Sartre, "Existentialism Is a Humanism," in *Existentialism from Dostoyevsky to Sartre,* ed. Walter Kaufmann (New York: Meridian, 1989), p. 356.
18. Hobbes, *Leviathan,* chap. 13.

19. Translation adapted from George Rawlinson, trans., *The History of Herodotus* (New York: D. Appleton, 1859–1861), bk. 3, chap. 38.

20. This example was adapted from one by Emmett Barcalow, *Open Questions,* 2d ed. (Belmont, Calif.: Wadsworth, 1997), p. 289.

21. Ruth Benedict, "Anthropology and the Abnormal," *The Journal of General Psychology* 10 (1934): 59–82.

22. John Ladd, *Ethical Relativism* (Belmont, Calif.: Wadsworth, 1973), p. 1.

23. Clyde Kluckhohn, "Ethical Relativity: Sic et Non," *Journal of Philosophy* 52 (1955): 663–77.

24. These and other examples can be found in C. S. Lewis, *The Abolition of Man* (New York: Touchstone, 1975), pp. 93–95, 103–4.

25. James Rachels, "The Challenge of Cultural Relativism," in *The Elements of Moral Philosophy* (New York: Random House, 1986), pp. 13–22.

26. Pojman, *Ethics: Discovering Right and Wrong,* p. 16.

27. W. Somerset Maugham, *Of Human Bondage* (New York: Signet, 1991), pp. 229–30.

28. Friedrich Nietzsche, *Beyond Good and Evil,* trans. Walter Kaufmann (New York: Vintage Books, 1966), sec. 260.

29. Ayn Rand, "The Ethics of Emergencies," in *The Virtue of Selfishness: A New Concept of Egoism* (New York: Signet Books, 1964), p. 49.

30. For my discussion of this point I am indebted to Paul Taylor's discussion in his *Principles of Ethics: An Introduction* (Belmont, Calif.: Wadsworth, 1975), p. 42.

31. Rand, "The Ethics of Emergencies," p. 44.

32. Ibid., pp. 44–45.

33. Robert Ringer, *Looking Out for #1* (New York: Fawcett Crest, 1977), p. 50.

34. Joel Feinberg, "Psychological Egoism," in *Reason and Responsibility,* 7th ed., ed. Joel Feinberg (Belmont, Calif.: Wadsworth, 1989), p. 495.

35. Rand, *The Virtue of Selfishness,* pp. vii–viii.

36. Ibid., pp. 32, 35.

37. Rand, "The Objectivist Ethics," in *The Virtue of Selfishness,* pp. 17, 25, 34.

38. Ibid., p. 31.

39. Ibid.

40. Rand, "The 'Conflicts' of Men's Interests," in *The Virtue of Selfishness,* pp. 50–56.

41. Rand, "Racism," in *The Virtue of Selfishness,* pp. 126–34.

42. John Rawls, *A Theory of Justice* (Cambridge, Mass.: Harvard University Press, 1971), pp. 11–17.

43. James Rachels, *The Elements of Moral Philosophy* (New York: Random House, 1986), pp. 77–78.

44. Jeremy Bentham, *An Introduction to the Principles of Morals and Legislation* (1789), chap. 1.

45. Jeremy Bentham, *The Rationale of Reward,* in *The Works of Jeremy Bentham,* vol. 2, ed. John Bowring (Edinburgh: William Tait, 1843), p. 253.

46. This thought experiment is adapted from one proposed in Robert Nozick, *Anarchy, State, and Utopia* (New York: Basic Books, 1974), pp. 42–43.

47. John Stuart Mill, *Utilitarianism* (1863), chap. 2.

48. John Stuart Mill, "Bentham," in *Collected Works of John Stuart Mill,* ed. J. M. Robson, vol. 10, *Essays on Ethics, Religion, and Society* (Toronto: University of Toronto Press, 1969), p. 95.

49. John Stuart Mill, *Utilitarianism,* chap. 2.

50. Alastair Norcross, "Comparing Harms: Headaches and Human Lives," *Philosophy and Public Affairs* 26 (spring 1997): 135–36, 159–60, 163.

51. Adapted from Nina Rosenstand, *The Moral of the Story: An Introduction to Questions of Ethics and Human Nature* (Mountain View, Calif.: Mayfield, 1994), p. 148.

52. Richard Brandt, "Towards a Credible Form of Utilitarianism," in *Morality and the Language of Conduct,* ed. H. Castaneda and G. Naknikian (Detroit: Wayne State University Press, 1963), pp. 109–10.

53. Immanuel Kant, *Critique of Practical Reason,* trans. Lewis White Beck (Chicago: University of Chicago Press, 1949), pt. 2, conclusion.

54. Immanuel Kant, *Foundations of the Metaphysics of Morals,* trans. Lewis White Beck (Indianapolis: Bobbs-Merrill, Library of Liberal Arts, 1959), pp. 9–10, 13–17, 38–46. I have added my own section headings to Kant's text.

55. Immanuel Kant, "On a Supposed Right to Lie from Altruistic Motives," in *Critique of Practical Reason and Other Writings in Moral Philosophy,* trans. Lewis White Beck (Chicago: University of Chicago Press, 1949), p. 348.

56. William David Ross, *The Right and the Good* (Oxford: Oxford University Press, 1932).

57. Michael Stocker, "The Schizophrenia of Modern Moral Theories," *Journal of Philosophy* 73 (August 12, 1976): 462.

58. Ibid., pp. 460, 461.

59. Plato, *Gorgias* 479b.

60. Plato, *Crito* 48b.

61. Ibid.

62. Aristotle, *Nicomachean Ethics* 1099a, 1104b, in *The Basic Works of Aristotle,* trans. and ed. Richard McKeon (New York: Random House, 1941).

63. Alasdair MacIntyre, *After Virtue,* 2d ed. (Notre Dame, Ind.: University of Notre Dame Press, 1984), p. 219.

64. Gregory Velazco y Trianosky, "What Is Virtue Ethics All About?" in *Virtue Ethics: A Critical Reader,* ed. Daniel Statman (Washington, D.C.: Georgetown University Press, 1997), p. 52. The author's in-text citations have been omitted.

65. Harold Alderman, "By Virtue of a Virtue," in Statman, *Virtue Ethics,* p. 162.

66. Justine Oakley, "Varieties of Virtue Ethics," *Ratio* 9 (September 1996): 135.

67. J. L. A. Garcia, "The Primacy of the Virtuous," *Philosophia* 20 (July 1990): 70.

68. David Solomon, "Internal Objections to Virtue Ethics," in *Ethical Theory: Character and Virtue,* Midwest Studies in Philosophy, vol. 13 (Notre Dame, Ind.: University of Notre Dame Press, 1988), p. 437.

69. Daniel Statman, "Introduction to Virtue Ethics," in Statman, *Virtue Ethics,* p. 13.

70. Rosalind Hursthouse, "Virtue Theory and Abortion," in Statman, *Virtue Ethics,* p. 228.

71. *Aristotle's Nicomachean Ethics,* trans. James Weldon (New York: Macmillan, 1897).

72. Confucius, *The Analects,* trans. William Jennings, in *The Sacred Books of the East,* ed. Max Muller (Oxford: Clarendon Press, 1879–1910).

73. Janet Smith, "Moral Character and Abortion," in Joram Graf Haber, *Doing and Being* (New York: Macmillan, 1993), pp. 442–56.

74. See, for example, Mark Strasser, "The Virtues of Utilitarianism," *Philosophia* 20 (July 1990): 209–26; Michael Slote, "Utilitarian Virtue," in *Ethical Theory: Character and*

Virtue, Midwest Studies in Philosophy, vol. 13 (Notre Dame, Ind.: University of Notre Dame Press, 1988), pp. 384–97; and Robert Louden, "Kant's Virtue Ethics," in Statman, *Virtue Ethics,* 286–99.

75. Robert Louden, "On Some Vices of Virtue Ethics," in Statman, *Virtue Ethics,* p. 191.

76. Susan Wolf, "Moral Saints," *Journal of Philosophy* 79 (August 1982): 419–39.

77. Robert Solomon, "Beyond Reason, The Importance of Emotion in Philosophy," in *Revising Philosophy,* ed. James Ogilvy (Albany: State University of New York Press, 1992), p. 32.

78. Statman, "Introduction to Virtue Ethics," p. 23.

79. D. Kay Johnston, "Adolescents' Solutions to Dilemmas in Fables: Two Moral Orientations—Two Problem Solving Strategies," in *Mapping the Moral Domain: A Contribution of Women's Thinking to Psychological Theory and Education,* ed. Carol Gilligan, Janie Victoria Ward, and Jill McLean Taylor, with Betty Baridge (Cambridge, Mass.: Harvard University Press, 1988), pp. 49–71.

80. Lawrence Kohlberg, *Moral Education* (Cambridge, Mass.: Moral Education Research Foundation, Harvard University, 1973), quoted in Carol Gilligan, *In a Different Voice: Psychological Theory and Women's Development* (Cambridge, Mass.: Harvard University Press, 1982, 1993), pp. 19–20.

81. J. O. Urmson, "Saints and Heroes," in *Essays in Moral Philosophy,* ed. A. I. Melden (Seattle: University of Washington Press, 1958), p. 202.

82. Virginia Held, "Feminist Reconceptualizations in Ethics," in *Philosophy in a Feminist Voice: Critiques and Reconstructions,* ed. Janet Kourany (Princeton, N.J.: Princeton University Press, 1998), pp. 94–95.

83. Eve Browning Cole and Susan Coultrap-McQuin, "Toward a Feminist Conception of Moral Life," in *Explorations in Feminist Ethics: Theory and Practice,* ed. Eve Browning Cole and Susan Coultrap-McQuin (Bloomington, Ind.: Indiana University Press, 1992), p. 2.

84. Eva Feder Kittay and Diana T. Meyers, eds., *Women and Moral Theory* (Totowa, N.J.: Rowan and Littlefield, 1987), p. 10.

85. Alison Jaggar, "Feminist Ethics," in *Encyclopedia of Ethics,* ed. Lawrence Becker and Charlotte Becker (New York: Garland, 1992), p. 364.

86. Ibid.

87. Rosemarie Tong, *Feminist Approaches to Bioethics* (Boulder, Colo.: Westview Press, 1997), p. 52.

88. Betty A. Sichel, "Different Strains and Strands: Feminist Contributions to Ethical Theory," *Newsletter on Feminism* 90, no. 2 (winter 1991): 90.

89. Susan Sherwin, *No Longer Patient: Feminist Ethics and Health Care* (Philadelphia: Temple University Press, 1992), pp. 42–43.

90. Tong, *Feminist Approaches to Bioethics,* p. 38.

91. John Broughton, "Women's Rationality and Men's Virtues: A Critique of Gender Dualism in Gilligan's Theory of Moral Development," *Social Research* 50, no. 3 (autumn 1983): 597–642.

92. See some of the critical responses to Gilligan's theory reprinted in *Caring Voices and Women's Moral Frames,* ed. Bill Puka (New York: Garland Publishing, 1994).

93. Gilligan, *In a Different Voice,* pp. 1–2, 25–31, 173–74.

94. Ibid., p. 42.

95. Ibid., p. 43.
96. Virginia Held, "Non-contractual Society: A Feminist View," in *Science, Morality, and Feminist Theory,* ed. Marsha Hanen and Kai Nielsen (Calgary: The University of Calgary Press, 1987), pp. 116, 119.
97. Sara Ruddick, *Maternal Thinking: Toward a Politics of Peace* (Boston: Beacon Press, 1989).
98. Nel Noddings, *Caring: A Feminine Approach to Ethics and Moral Education* (Berkeley: University of California Press, 1984), p. 3.
99. Ibid., p. 80.
100. Kathy Ferguson, *The Feminist Case against Bureaucracy* (Philadelphia: Temple University Press, 1984), pp. 25, 119–203.
101. Jean Grimshaw, "The Idea of a Female Ethic," in *A Companion to Ethics,* ed. Peter Singer (Oxford: Blackwell, 1992).
102. Joan C. Tronto, "Care as a Basis for Radical Political Judgments," *Hypatia* 10, no. 2 (spring 1995): 145.
103. Lawrence Kohlberg, *The Psychology of Moral Development: The Nature and Validity of Moral Stages,* Essays on Moral Development, vol. 2 (San Francisco: Harper & Row, 1984), p. 640.
104. Tong, *Feminist Approaches to Bioethics,* p. 49.
105. Jaggar, "Feminist Ethics," p. 361.
106. Susan Mendus, "Different Voices, Still Lives: Problems in the Ethics of Care," *Journal of Applied Philosophy* 10, no. 1 (1993): 21.
107. Broughton, "Women's Rationality and Men's Virtues," p. 626.
108. Ibid.
109. Mary G. Dietz, "Citizenship with a Feminist Face: The Problem with Maternal Thinking," *Political Theory* 13, no. 1 (February 1985): 34.
110. Zella Luria, "A Methodological Critique," in "On *In a Different Voice:* An Interdisciplinary Forum," *Signs* 11, no. 2 (winter 1986): 320.
111. Patricia Ward Scaltsas, "Do Feminist Ethics Counter Feminist Aims?" in Cole and Coultrap-McQuin, *Explorations in Feminist Ethics,* pp. 19, 23.
112. Sara Lucia Hoagland, quoted in Tong, *Feminist Approaches to Bioethics,* p. 50.
113. Sara Lucia Hoagland, "Some Thoughts about *Caring,*" in *Feminist Ethics,* ed. Claudia Card (Lawrence: University Press of Kansas, 1991), p. 250.
114. Sheila Mullett, "Shifting Perspectives: A New Approach to Ethics," in *Feminist Perspectives,* ed. Lorraine Code, Sheila Mullett, and Christine Overall (Toronto: University of Toronto Press, 1989), p. 119.
115. Ibid.
116. Dietz, "Citizenship with a Feminist Face," pp. 30–31.
117. Broughton, "Women's Rationality and Men's Virtues," p. 614.
118. Marilyn Friedman, "Liberating Care," in *What Are Friends For? Feminist Perspectives on Personal Relationships and Moral Theory* (Ithaca: Cornell University Press, 1993), p. 150.
119. Marilyn Friedman, "Liberating Care," pp. 142–83. I have deleted Friedman's extensive footnotes.
120. Annette Baier, "Trust and Anti-Trust," *Ethics* 96 (January 1986): 247–48.
121. Patricia J. Williams, *The Alchemy of Race and Rights* (Cambridge, Mass.: Harvard University Press, 1991), p. 164.

CHAPTER 6

THE SEARCH FOR THE JUST SOCIETY

SCOUTING THE TERRITORY: *Thinking about Government*

Why is there government? What is it that makes a government legitimate? What is its purpose? What are its limits? To answer these questions, the seventeenth-century English philosopher Thomas Hobbes wrote his classic book *Leviathan* in 1651. Using a thought experiment, he imagined what human life would be like if there were no government, a condition that he called the "state of nature." Hobbes surmised that without a government to maintain order and regulate human inter-actions, this condition would be "a war of all against all" as each person did whatever he or she could get away with doing. If there were no government, then the notions of *justice* and *injustice* would be merely words. In short, Hobbes con-cluded that human life without government would be "solitary, poor, nasty, brutish, and short." From there he developed a theory about how people would go about forming a government and what powers they would assign to it.

Most of us would agree with Hobbes that a government of some sort is a practical necessity. But do we need as much government as we currently have? Does the government need to poke its nose into our personal affairs as much as it does? Every time we look at a paycheck and see how much of our original income has been eaten up by the government's voracious appetite, we are reminded of the presence of the government in our lives. Many of us despair over what we perceive as the heavy hand of the government in collecting excessive taxes, imposing unnec-essary regulations, creating huge bureaucracies, and squandering our hard-earned money on people and causes that we deem undeserving. Henry David Thoreau, the nineteenth-century American writer, expressed his antigovernment sentiments by saying, "that government governs best that governs least."

Is government as bad as Thoreau thought it was? Even though Thoreau thought his society had too much government, there was less government in his day than in our present society. However, with less government, people also had virtually no protection from harmful medicines and dangerous products sold by unscrupulous or negligent persons. The workplace had few health and safety standards. If you deposited money in a bank, you had no guarantee that you could get it back if the bank failed. In today's world, a college education would be beyond the reach of anybody but the most wealthy without government-supported financial aid and loans. Furthermore, even if a student is not receiving direct financial aid, his or her college education is made possible by tax-supported federal programs. With the high costs of technology and other resources, no major university and most colleges could not fulfill their mission if it were not for the direct or indirect support of the local, state, and federal governments.

So, we are back to Thomas Hobbes's point that government seems to be a necessary part of human life. But even if we agree on that point, we are still left with a host of questions concerning the nature of government and what exact role it should play in human affairs. These issues make up the central core of political philosophy.

The first issue we discuss in this chapter is, "What is the justification of the government's authority?" The government may have the power and the force to rule its people, but not every ruler or use of force is legitimate. So, what conditions make it legitimate for the government to be in power? Obviously, this issue is a fundamental one, for if a government is not legitimate then all other issues about the proper role of government and our relationship to it do not arise.

The second issue we discuss concerns the theory of justice. We frequently evaluate a government in terms of efficiency. During political campaigns, candidates typically promise that if they are elected to office, they will make the government do its job more effectively. But is efficiency the only criterion for judging a government? After all, it has frequently been pointed out that when the fascist dictator Benito Mussolini took charge of Italy in the 1920s, he succeeded in making the trains run on time. Similarly, the communist dictator Joseph Stalin brought mechanization to Russian agriculture during the early part of the twentieth century. Although these rules brought efficiency to their respective societies, it is clear that they did not bring justice. Obviously, we want our government to be efficient, but we also want it to be just. This point raises several questions: "What is justice?" and "How can we determine whether a government is just or not?"

The third issue we examine concerns the relationship between the individual and the state, between freedom and control. We all cherish our individual freedoms. But too much individual freedom would lead to social chaos. Hence, some degree of government control is necessary. But too much government control would lead to an unacceptable level of tyranny. So where do we draw the line between individual freedom and government control? Is the government to be thought of as our servant, doing only those things we cannot do for ourselves? Or is the government to be thought of as our parent, looking out for our best interests? In other words, is the major responsibility of government to serve us by maximizing our individual liberties but allowing us to live our individual lives as we please? Or is the major responsibility of government to produce the best results for ourselves and society in general, even if this goal requires limiting our freedom?

The final issue we examine concerns the topic of civil disobedience. If we agree that government is something necessary and even good, then it would seem that obeying the government is necessary and good. To have laws that no one obeys is no better than having no laws at all. But are there situations in which it would be bad and even immoral to obey the government? Under what conditions would it be morally permissible to break the law? These two questions are the focus of the fourth section of this chapter on political philosophy.

CHOOSING A PATH:
What Are My Options Concerning Political Philosophy?

Two positions are discussed under the topic of the justification of government. The first is an extreme position, and the second is one of the most influential theories in the history of political thought. The extreme position is *anarchism*. The anarchist replies to the question "What makes the authority of a government legitimate?" with the simple answer, "No government ever has legitimate authority." The second theory responds to the question, "What makes the authority of a government legitimate?" by saying, "A government is legitimate if it rules with the consent of its citizens." In modern history, this consent of the governed theory has been labeled the *social contract theory.*

The first position discussed in section 6.2 about the nature of justice is *justice as merit.* This position maintains that since all people do not contribute to society equally, they should not have political equality. The just society, it is argued, is one in which all people receive what they are due (especially political power) according to their merit. The next position is known as the *natural law theory.* It claims that a government is just if its laws and actions conform to a universal moral law and that this moral law exists independently of human preferences or society's decisions. The third position on justice that we examine is the *utilitarian theory.* Consistent with their ethical theory, the utilitarians claim that a just society is one that produces the greatest happiness for the greatest number of people. Finally, we survey the theory of *justice as fairness* developed by the contemporary American philosopher John Rawls. He believes that if we all were truly rational and fair, we would opt for a society in which everyone has the opportunity to succeed to the best of his or her abilities, while maintaining a minimal level of social and economic equality. This theory entails maximizing political liberty while improving the condition of the most disadvantaged.

In section 6.3 on the individual and the state, we look at two positions that are located at opposing ends of the political spectrum. One position, *individualism,* believes that the best society is the one in which individual liberty is at a maximum and the government's intrusion in our lives is kept to what is minimally necessary. We examine John Stuart Mill's *classical liberalism* as an example of this position. The opposing position states that the best results will be achieved if the government plays a large role in regulating society and providing for people's needs. This position is sometimes called *collectivism* because it claims that the collective, the common good, or the state (the government) should have the final authority over individual preferences. I use Marxism as a representative of this theory.

Finally, we examine the pros and cons of civil disobedience. The first position maintains that civil disobedience is never morally justified, and Socrates is used to represent this position. The second position maintains that there are circumstances in which obeying the law would be immoral and disobeying the law would be morally permissible, perhaps even our moral duty. We examine the arguments of Martin Luther King Jr. and Mohandas Gandhi in support of this position. Obvi-

TABLE 6.1 *Four Questions in Political Philosophy and Responses to Them*				
What is the justification of government?	Anarchism: government is not justified	Social Contract Theory: the consent of the governed		
What is justice?	Justice is Merit: giving everybody what they deserve, based on their contribution or merit	Natural Law Theory: conformity to a universal moral law	Utilitarianism: whatever produces the greatest good for the greatest number	Justice is Fairness: it includes maximizing political equality and maximizing the position of the least advantaged
Which should be given priority: individual liberty or the good of the community?	Individualism: individual liberty	Collectivism: the good of the community		
Is civil disobedience ever morally permissible?	Socrates: no	Martin Luther King Jr.: yes	Mohandas Gandhi: yes	

ously, the first position has the burden of proving why it is always wrong to disobey the government. The second position has to show why it is sometimes morally permissible to do so and to provide principles for deciding when our normal duty to obey the government may be suspended in the name of a higher moral obligation.

This chapter presents four questions in political philosophy and offers various responses to those four questions. Your answer to each question may impact your answers to the other questions, but I will let you think through their connections for yourself. Table 6.1 summarizes this overview by listing the questions and the answers that we discuss in the next four sections of this chapter.

WHAT DO I THINK? *Questionnaire on Political Philosophy*

	Agree	Disagree
1. It is never morally justified for someone to control another rational adult's life. Therefore, whatever *practical* needs the government serves, its exercise of power over us is not *morally* justified.		

2. It is morally justified for the government to exercise power over our lives if we have chosen to delegate that power to it.		
3. Those who have the most ability are the ones who should be the rulers of society and have the most political power. Hence, justice has nothing to do with democratic equality.		
4. The main criterion for determining if governments and their laws are just or not is how moral they are.		
5. The just society is simply one that maximizes the greatest happiness for the greatest number.		
6. The just society is one that maximizes political liberty while giving priority to those who are least advantaged.		
7. The best society is one that places the highest priority on maximizing individual liberty and minimizing government control.		
8. The best society is one that places the highest priority on giving government the power to make life better for everyone, even at the sacrifice of some individual freedom.		
9. Disobeying the law is never morally justified.		
10. There are circumstances in which disobeying the law might be our moral obligation, even if we go to jail for it.		

 ## KEY TO THE QUESTIONNAIRE ON POLITICAL PHILOSOPHY

Statement 1 represents anarchism. It conflicts with statement 2.

Statement 2 represents the social contract theory. It conflicts with statement 1.

Statement 3 represents the theory of justice as merit. It conflicts with statements 4, 5, and 6.

Statement 4 represents the natural law theory. It conflicts with statements 3, 5, and 6.

Statement 5 represents the utilitarian theory of justice. It conflicts with statements 3, 4, and 6.

Statement 6 represents John Rawls's theory of justice as fairness. It conflicts with statements 3, 4, and 5.

Statement 7 represents the position of individualism concerning the degree of individual liberty versus government control. It conflicts with statement 8.

Statement 8 represents the position of Marxism. It conflicts with statement 7.

Statement 9 represents the position of opponents of civil disobedience. It conflicts with statement 10.

Statement 10 represents the position of supporters of civil disobedience. It conflicts with statement 9.

6.1 THE JUSTIFICATION OF GOVERNMENT

LEADING QUESTIONS: *The Justification of Government*

1. *Leading Questions of the Anarchist:* Suppose a stranger broke into your home while you were away and, instead of robbing you, washed and folded your laundry and vacuumed your carpets. Obviously, the stranger performed a service for you, but would this action justify the stranger breaking into your home without your permission? Similarly, the government provides a number of benefits for us, but do these actions morally justify the government in exercising its power over our individual lives?

2. *Leading Questions of the Anarchist:* The government obviously has the force to impose its will on us, but having force does not equal having morally justified authority. Doesn't the power of the government violate the basic principle that each person should have autonomy and control over his or her own life? While the practical benefits of government are obvious, does it have any morally justified authority over us, or is its control simply based on its power?

3. *Leading Questions of the Social Contract Theorist:* When you accept a job, you sign a contract agreeing that you will do certain things for your employer, and your company agrees to provide you with a certain salary and benefits. If both parties are free to sign the contract or not, what could possibly be wrong with this arrangement? Isn't our relationship to the government like such a contract? We consent to allow the government to have a certain amount of authority over us for our benefit and the good of society. Isn't this arrangement an adequate justification of the government's authority?

4. *Leading Questions of the Social Contract Theorist:* As long as you live in a free society, you have the option of living in that society, obeying its laws, and receiving its services. If you don't like that arrangement, you can choose to live elsewhere. By living in your present society and accepting its benefits, haven't you consented to abide by the government's laws?

There is a distinction between having power and having the proper authority to use that power. As these leading questions suggest, this distinction is important when discussing the role of the government in our lives. The following thought experiment asks you to think about the issue of authority and the proper exercise of power.

 THOUGHT EXPERIMENT

Authority versus Power

In each pair of the following scenarios, similar actions are being performed. In each case, how does situation a differ from situation b?

1. (a) You fill out your federal income tax form and find that you owe the government $1,000. You write out a check for this amount, knowing that if you do not pay the government what it demands of you, the penalties will be severe.
   (b) While you are walking home at night, a robber with a gun steps out of the shadows and demands all the money in your wallet. You hand your money over, knowing that the consequences of not doing so will be severe.
2. (a) In a criminal trial, a judge determines that the defendant is guilty of fraud and sentences her to several years in prison.
   (b) You decide that the saleswoman who sold you a defective car is guilty of fraud and so you forcibly lock her up in your basement for several years.
3. (a) During a time of international crisis, your best friend is drafted into the army to fight for the country's interests. He doesn't particularly want to go to war but is forced to do so by the government.
   (b) You are having a dispute with your neighbor concerning the damage that the neighbor's dog did to your garden. At gunpoint, you force your unwilling friend to attack your neighbor for you.

In one sense, each of the pairs of actions in the thought experiment are similar. In the first pair of cases, you are forced to give up your money. In the second set, a wrongdoer is being punished. In the third pair, someone is being forced to fight for a cause. Obviously, all the cases labeled (a) involve what are customarily considered to be the legitimate exercise of governmental power. In all the (b) cases, however, power is being used to force someone to do something, but there is no proper authority to use that power. What does it mean to have legitimate authority to control or regulate the behavior of others? How does legitimate authority differ from simply having power? How is the government different than the robber? Or is it? Is the government's ability to restrict our freedom in various ways simply due to the fact that it has the most guns?

In the context of politics, authority means not only having power but also having the right (the legitimate authority) to use that power in certain specified ways. But what is the basis of the alleged right of the government to restrict our freedom to act as we wish? On what basis is government justified—not this or that particular government but government in general?

Throughout most of human history as we know it, there has been some form of social organization, and whenever people have come together in groups, there has been some form of leadership that implicitly or explicitly had the character of a government. But as the previous thought experiment illustrated, the claim that a person or a group of people represent the government entails the claim that their use of power is legitimate. Without this latter claim, there is no distinction between a government and a mob with weapons.

Governmental authority has been justified in several ways. The most ancient view is the *divine right theory,* which states that the king, queen, pharaoh, emperor, or whoever received his or her authority to rule from God or the gods. All the great civilizations that followed this theory of government also had moral codes and standards of justice that the ruler was expected to follow if his or her rule was to be pleasing to the divine powers. In most cases, no one in the society had the power to question whether the ruler was living up to this code (with the possible exception of a priest or priestess). Hence, the code of justice generally served little purpose in tempering the power of the ruler, who had total control over defining or interpreting what was just. In the final analysis, most governments that claimed they ruled under divine authority either actually had the consent of their subjects as well or were based on sheer power, and the religious justifications served merely as a public relations story.

Another approach to government is the *justice theory.* According to this account, the legitimacy of the government hangs directly on the issue of whether it is serving the cause of justice (however that cause is defined). The ancient Greek philosophers Plato and Aristotle, for example, seemed to justify the authority of government on this basis. In section 6.2, we examine various theories of justice. The issue of justice, however, seems to address the question of whether a government that is already in place is acting rightly or wrongly; it doesn't answer the question of why the government is legitimate in the first place.

The remainder of this section focuses on two important theories about the legitimacy of government: anarchism and the social contract theory. We discuss each of these two theories in turn.

SURVEYING THE CASE FOR ANARCHISM

As we look at various governments throughout history and in the world today, most of us naturally make the judgment that some of those governments have been bad ones (Hitler's regime, for example). One political position, however, claims that *all* governments are bad in the sense that none of them have the authority or the right to exercise their power over people. **Anarchism** is the position that there is no conceivable justification for government. At times, when we feel alienated from our own government and struggle with the laws, taxes, and the burdens it imposes on us, we are tempted to think of the government as "them" instead of as "us." At those times, anarchism has a certain emotional appeal. But the defense of anarchism must be based on arguments rather than simply negative feelings about

anarchism the position that there is no conceivable justification for government

the government. Before examining the arguments for anarchism, let's consider the various forms it can take.

Naive anarchism is characterized by the belief that in the absence of governmental control, people would exist in harmony and peace. According to this view, government is an unnecessary evil that restricts human freedom and flourishing. A critical assumption of this view is that human nature is basically good and that it is society in its current form that corrupts us and leads to bad behavior. Advocates of this position sometimes suggest that society ought to be broken down into smaller, manageable communities, such as communes, in which people would live together and relate on a personal level, much like a large, happy family. The problem is, of course, that this position is based on an implausible and far too optimistic view of human nature. Evoking the model of the family is naive, because sometimes even family relationships need to be regulated by society's authorities and laws, such as when an inheritance is contested, when domestic violence in involved, or when a divorce requires decisions about child custody and property settlements. Naive anarchism fails in the face of the obvious need for society to restrict or regulate its members' actions for the benefit of all.

Another expression of anarchism, the one that is commonly associated with the term, takes the position that if government is unjustified, then it is an evil that should be overthrown—by violent means if necessary. In the past few decades in the United States, we have seen some of its own citizens blowing up government buildings as a form of protest against the government's authority. However, this version of anarchism cannot be taken seriously, for its advocates blindly follow their principles without regard for practical consequences. Usually, greater harm results from people acting on this position than from the evils they are seeking to eradicate. Furthermore, once the government is destroyed, what then? How will we manage to coexist? Like the naive anarchists, the militant anarchists have an unrealistic view of the possibilities of human life without laws.

The only version of anarchism worth considering, therefore, is theoretical anarchism. **Theoretical anarchism** agrees with the basic premise that government has no legitimate authority, but holds that even though the exercise of governmental power is theoretically unjustified, it may be necessary, as a matter of practical necessity, to tolerate its existence.

theoretical anarchism the theory that government has no legitimate authority even though we may have to tolerate its existence as a matter of practical necessity

---

STOP AND THINK

Have you ever obeyed a law that you thought was not justified or right simply because the situation of having no laws at all would be worse than having some laws that are questionable? Have you ever followed a leader that you did not think deserved the position simply because following an undeserving leader is better than having no leader at all? If you have ever been in either of these situations, then your response is similar to that of the theoretical anarchist with respect to *all* laws, elected officials, and governments.

One of the most eloquent contemporary defenses of theoretical anarchism has been developed by Robert Paul Wolff. (Robert Paul Wolff is professor of Afro-American studies and philosophy at the University of Massachusetts, Amherst. He has written in the areas of Kantian philosophy, ethics, and social-political philosophy.) In this first passage, he sets out the difference between the power of the government (which is an obvious fact) and its alleged authority to exercise that power over its citizens (which is the point of contention).

- What does it mean for something to be a state, according to Wolff?
- How does Wolff distinguish the power of the state from its authority?

FROM ROBERT PAUL WOLFF

In Defense of Anarchism[1]

The Concept of Authority

Politics is the exercise of the power of the State, or the attempt to influence that exercise. Political philosophy is therefore, strictly speaking, the philosophy of the state. If we are to determine the content of political philosophy, and whether indeed it exists, we must begin with the concept of the state.

The state is a group of persons who have and exercise supreme authority within a given territory. Strictly, we should say that a state is a group of persons who have supreme authority within a given territory *or over a certain population.* A nomadic tribe may exhibit the authority structure of a state, so long as its subjects do not fall under the superior authority of a territorial state. The state may include all the persons who fall under its authority, as does the democratic state according to its theorists; it may also consist of a single individual to whom all the rest are subject. We may doubt whether the one-person state has ever actually existed, although Louis XIV evidently thought so when he announced, "L'etat c'est moi" [I am the State]. The distinctive characteristic of the state is supreme authority. . . .

Authority is the right to command, and correlatively, the right to be obeyed. It must be distinguished from power, which is the ability to compel compliance, either through the use or threat of force. When I turn over my wallet to a thief who is holding me at gunpoint, I do so because the fate with which he threatens me is worse than the loss of money which I am made to suffer. I grant that he has power over me, but I would hardly suppose that he has *authority,* that is, that he has a right to demand my money and that I have an obligation to give it to him. When the government presents me with a bill for taxes, on the other hand, I pay it (normally) even though I do not wish to and even if I think I can get away with not paying. It is after all, the duly constituted government, and hence it has a *right* to tax me. It has *authority* over me. Sometimes, of course, I cheat the government, but even so, I acknowledge its authority, for who would speak of "cheating" a thief?

To *claim* authority is to claim the right to be obeyed. To *have* authority is then—what? It may mean to have that right, or it may mean to have one's claim acknowledged and accepted by those at whom it is directed. The term "authority" is ambiguous, having both a descriptive and a normative sense. Even the descriptive sense refers to norms or obligations, of course, but it does so by *describing* what men believe they ought to do rather than by *asserting* that they ought to do it. . . .

What is meant by *supreme* authority? Some political philosophers have held that the true state has ultimate authority over all matters whatsoever that occur within its venue. Jean-Jacques Rousseau, for example, asserted that the social contract by which a just political community is formed "gives to the body absolute command over the members of which it is formed; and it is this power, when directed by the general will, that bears . . . the name of 'sovereignty.'" John Locke, on the other hand, held that the supreme authority of the just state extends only to those matters which it is proper for a state to control. The state is, to be sure, the highest authority, but its right to command is less than absolute. One of the questions which political philosophy must answer is whether there is any limit to the range of affairs over which a just state has authority.

In the next passage, Wolff bases his argument against government on the notion of *autonomy* (a concept he derived from Immanuel Kant). A condition for having autonomy is freedom of choice, but autonomy entails much more than that. Autonomy also involves *taking* responsibility for your actions in the sense of making your own choices, standing behind them, being accountable, and not delegating the decisions that are yours to make to anyone else. Autonomy also involves *being* responsible in making decisions, by basing them on good reasons and by reflecting on your motives and the consequences of your actions. According to Wolff, being an autonomous person is a moral obligation.

- In the following passage, how does Wolff reconcile the fact that we can learn about our moral obligations from others while still being autonomous?
- What is the difference between doing what someone tells you to do because that person tells you to do it, and doing what someone tells you to do because you can see that it is reasonable and conforms to your moral duty?

Concept of Autonomy

The fundamental assumption of moral philosophy is that men are responsible for their actions. From this assumption it follows necessarily, as Kant pointed out, that men are metaphysically free, which is to say that in some sense they are capable of choosing how they shall act. Being able to choose how he acts makes a man responsible, but merely choosing is not in itself to constitute *taking* responsibility for one's actions. Taking responsibility involves attempting to determine what one ought to do, and that, as philosophers since Aristotle have recognized, lays upon one the additional burdens of gaining knowledge, reflecting on motives, predicting outcomes, criticizing principles, and so forth.

The obligation to take responsibility for one's actions does not derive from man's freedom of will alone, for more is required in taking responsibility than freedom of choice. Only because man has the capacity to reason about his choices can he be said to stand under a continuing obligation to take responsibility for them. It is quite appropriate that moral philosophers should group together children and madmen as being not fully responsible for their actions, for as madmen are thought to lack freedom of choice, so children do not yet possess the power of reason in a developed form. It is even just that we should assign a greater degree of responsibility to children, for madmen, by virtue of their lack of free will, are completely without responsibility, while children, insofar as they possess reason in a partially developed form, can be held responsible to a corresponding degree.

Every man who possesses both free will and reason has an obligation to take responsibility for his actions, even though he may not be actively engaged in a continuing process of reflection, investigation, and deliberation about how he ought to act. A man will sometimes announce his willingness to take responsibility for the consequences of his actions, even though he has not deliberated about them, or does not intend to do so in the future. Such a declaration is, of course, an advance over the refusal to take responsibility; it at least acknowledges the existence of the obligation. But it does not relieve the man of the duty to engage in the reflective process which he has thus far shunned. . . .

The responsible man is not capricious or anarchic, for he does acknowledge himself bound by moral constraints. But he insists that he alone is the judge of those constraints. He may listen to the advice of others, but he makes it his own by determining for himself whether it is good advice. He may learn from others about his moral obligations, but only in the sense that a mathematician learns from other mathematicians—namely by hearing from them arguments whose validity he recognizes even though he did not think of them himself. He does not learn in the sense that one learns from an explorer, by accepting as true his account of things one cannot see for oneself.

Since the responsible man arrives at moral decisions which he expresses to himself in the form of imperatives, we may say that he gives laws to himself, or is self-legislating. In short, he is *autonomous*. As Kant argued, moral autonomy is a combination of freedom and responsibility; it is a submission to laws which one has made for oneself. The autonomous man, insofar as he is autonomous, is not subject to the will of another. He may do what another tells him, but not *because* he has been told to do it. He is therefore, in the political sense of the word, *free*.

In saying that we have a moral obligation to be autonomous and "self-legislating," Wolff sets up an inevitable conflict with any government that claims the authority to legislate our lives for us. Thus, he rejects the possibility of there being a de jure state, meaning a state that is legitimate and has the right to command our obedience.

- While Wolff believes the state has no legitimate authority, why does he say that an autonomous person still may believe it necessary to comply with the laws of the government?
- How does Wolff's example of obeying the laws of a foreign country illustrate his attitude toward the laws of his own country?

The Conflict Between Authority and Autonomy

The defining mark of the state is authority, the right to rule. The primary obligation of man is autonomy, the refusal to be ruled. It would seem, then, that there can be no resolution of the conflict between the autonomy of the individual and the putative authority of the state. Insofar as a man fulfills his obligation to make himself the author of his decisions, he will resist the state's claim to have authority over him. That is to say, he will deny that he has a duty to obey the laws of the state *simply because they are laws.* In that sense, it would seem that anarchism is the only political doctrine consistent with the virtue of autonomy.

Now, of course, an anarchist may grant the necessity of *complying* with the law under certain circumstances or for the time being. He may even doubt that there is any real prospect of eliminating the state as a human institution. But he will never view the commands of the state as *legitimate,* as having a binding moral force. In a sense, we might characterize the anarchist as a man without a country, for despite the ties which bind him to the land of his childhood, he stands in precisely the same moral relationship to "his" government as he does to the government of any other country in which he might happen to be staying for a time. When I take a vacation to Great Britain, I obey its laws, both because of prudential self-interest and because of the obvious moral considerations concerning the value of order, the general good consequences of preserving a system of property, and so forth. On my return to the United States, I have a sense of reentering *my* country, and if I think about the matter at all, I imagine myself to stand in a different and more intimate relation to American laws. They have been promulgated by *my* government, and I therefore have a special obligation to obey them. But the anarchist tells me that my feeling is purely sentimental and has no objective moral basis. All authority is equally illegitimate, although of course not therefore equally worthy or unworthy of support, and my obedience to American laws, if I am to be morally autonomous, must proceed from the same considerations which determine me abroad.

The dilemma which we have posed can be succinctly expressed in terms of the concept of a *de jure* state. If all men have a continuing obligation to achieve the highest degree of autonomy possible, then there would appear to be no state whose subjects have a moral obligation to obey its commands. Hence, the concept of a *de jure* legitimate state would appear to be vacuous, and philosophical anarchism would seem to be the only reasonable political belief for an enlightened man.

STOP AND THINK

What do you think of Wolff's argument? Do you think he has effectively made the case for what we have called theoretical anarchism? Why?

LOOKING THROUGH THE ANARCHIST'S LENS

1. If you broke a legal contract with an anarchist, saying that the laws governing contracts have no legitimate authority over you, how might the anarchist respond? Would it be inconsistent for the anarchist to take you to court? In other words, could the anarchist use the law to his or her benefit without violating anarchist principles?

2. History is full of shameful events in which people blindly followed the laws of a corrupt government. In these cases, if the majority of people had been anarchists, would the consequences have been different?

3. Would it be inconsistent for an anarchist to vote in either local, state, or national elections? On the one hand, the anarchist would be following his or her legitimate self-interest in supporting political leaders who will do the best job. On the other hand, by voting in elections, the anarchist is tacitly approving of the system of governmental authority. What should the anarchist do?

EXAMINING THE STRENGTHS AND WEAKNESSES OF ANARCHISM

Positive Evaluation

1. Has the anarchist made a legitimate point in stressing the importance of taking responsibility for our own lives and refusing to blindly follow an authority?

2. What would the anarchist say about the slogan of the radical patriot, "My country, right or wrong"? Do you think the anarchist's response is better than that of unquestioning patriotism?

Negative Evaluation

1. Even though Wolff is an anarchist, he says he obeys the laws on the basis of "the obvious moral considerations concerning the value of order" and "the general good consequences of preserving a system of property." In making these statements, hasn't Wolff provided reasons why government should exist and why, under the best circumstances, it can legitimately exercise authority? Hasn't he undermined his argument for anarchism?

2. Contrary to Wolff, can't we believe in the legitimacy of our government and take his argument to be merely pointing out that some extreme circumstances offer morally legitimate grounds for a revolution or civil disobedience?

3. Unless he or she lives on a desert island that is not part of any national territory, the anarchist benefits from the security and convenience of living in a state in which the government provides or supports national defense, police, legal rights, highways, educational systems, medical care, and so forth. Is it inconsistent for the anarchist to enjoy these government programs while claiming that the government has no right to collect taxes or to provide these services?

SURVEYING THE CASE FOR SOCIAL CONTRACT THEORY

social contract theory the theory that the justification of a government and its exercise of power is based on an explicit or implicit agreement made between the individuals who live under that government or between the citizens and the government

In opposition to anarchism and all other theories of government, the **social contract theory** claims that the justification of a government and its exercise of power is based on an explicit or implicit agreement made between the individuals who live under that government or between the citizens and the government. In other words, the government has the authority to make laws, enforce penalties for violating those laws, and exercise control over the lives of its citizens, only because each citizen has given the government that authority.

Thomas Hobbes's Social Contract Theory

While the basic idea of the social contract is implicit in the teachings of Socrates and other ancient thinkers, it came to the forefront in the seventeenth century. One of its earliest and most famous advocates was Thomas Hobbes (1588–1679), an English philosopher. After completing his education at Oxford University, Hobbes spent most of his life working as a tutor and companion to a prominent English family. This employment gave him the leisure to write and the opportunity to travel with them, allowing him to meet the leading thinkers of the day. Hobbes was influenced by Galileo's physics, which inspired him to take a scientific approach to the study of human nature and society. Another influence on Hobbes's thought was the Civil War in England, which began in 1642 following a long period of tension between those who supported the king and the antimonarchists. The social chaos that resulted and the persecution that Hobbes suffered from managing to alienate both sides of the conflict led him to become convinced of the need for a strong government with absolute power. The following passage is from his most famous work, in which he set out the nature of government. He begins by describing an initial condition that he called the "state of nature," in which he imagines what human life would be like prior to establishing some form of government.

- What would life be like without government, according to Hobbes?
- Does Hobbes have an optimistic or pessimistic view of human nature? What effect might this view have had on his theory of government?

THOMAS HOBBES
(1588–1679)

Leviathan[2]

The Problems and Inconvenience of a State of War

Hereby it is manifest, that during the time men live without a common power to keep them all in awe, they are in that condition which is called war; and such a war, as is of every man, against every man. For WAR consists not in battle only or the act of fighting; but in a tract of time, wherein the will to contend by battle is sufficiently known: and therefore the notion of *time,* is to be considered in the nature of war; as it is in the nature of weather. For as the nature of foul weather, lies not in the shower or two of rain; but in an inclination thereto of many days together: so the nature of war, consists not in actual fighting; but in the known disposition thereto, during all the time there is no assurance to the contrary. All other time is PEACE.

Whatsoever therefore occurs in a time of war, where every man is enemy to every man; the same occurs in the time, wherein men live without other security, than what their own strength, and their own invention shall furnish them withal. In such condition, there is no place for industry; because the fruit thereof is uncertain: and consequently no culture of the earth; no navigation, nor use of the commodities that may be imported by sea; no commodious building; no instruments of moving, and removing, such things as require much force; no knowledge of the face of the earth; no account of time; no arts; no letters; no society; and which is worst of all, continual fear, and danger of violent death; and the life of man, solitary, poor, nasty, brutish, and short.

It may seem strange to some man, that has not well weighed these things; that nature should thus dissociate, and render men apt to invade, and destroy one another: and he may therefore, not trusting to this inference, made from the passions, desire perhaps to have the same confirmed by experience. Let him therefore consider with himself, when taking a journey, he arms himself, and seeks to go well accompanied; when going to sleep, he locks his doors; when even in his house he locks his chests; and this when he knows there be laws, and public officers, armed, to revenge all injuries shall be done him; what opinion he has of his fellow-subjects, when he rides armed; of his fellow citizens, when he locks his doors; and of his children, and servants, when he locks his chests. Does he not there as much accuse mankind by his actions, as I do by my words? but neither of us accuse man's nature in it. The desires, and other passions of man, are in themselves no sin. No more are the actions, that proceed from those passions, till they know a law that forbids them: which till laws be made they cannot know: nor can any law be made, till they have agreed upon the person that shall make it.

- In the next passage, Hobbes discusses whether a state of nature could contain right and wrong, or justice and injustice, or property. Do you agree with Hobbes's position on these points?

In This State of War Nothing Is Unjust

To this war of every man, against every man, this also is a result: *that nothing can be unjust.* The notions of right and wrong, justice and injustice have there no place. Where there is no common power, there is no law: where no law no injustice. Force, and fraud, are in war the two cardinal virtues. Justice, and injustice are none of the faculties neither of the body, nor mind. If they were, they might be in a man that were alone in the world, as well as his senses, and passions. They are qualities, that relate to men in society, not in solitude. It is consequent also to the same condition, that there be no property, no ownership, no *mine* and *thine* distinct; but only that to be every man's, that he can get; and for so long, as he can keep it. And thus much for the ill condition, which man by mere nature is actually placed in; though with a possibility to come out of it, consisting partly in the passions, partly in his reason.

The Passions That Incline Men to Peace

The passions that incline men to peace, are fear of death; desire of such things as are necessary to commodious living; and a hope by their industry to obtain them. And reason suggests convenient articles of peace, upon which men may be drawn to agreement. These articles, are they, which otherwise are called the Laws of Nature.

Without any civil laws, Hobbes says that people would be governed only by the laws of nature. But he thinks that nature's laws (discovered by reason) would instruct people and make them naturally inclined to form a government.

- What are the three laws of nature that Hobbes thinks are relevant to the formation of government?
- Why does Hobbes think people would be motivated to give up some of their rights and freedoms?
- Why does Hobbes think people would form covenants?
- Why does the validity of a covenant require the existence of a government (or commonwealth)?

Of the First Three Natural Laws, and of Contracts
The Right of Nature

The right of nature . . . is the liberty each man hath, to use his own power, as he will himself, for the preservation of his own nature; that is to say, of his own life; and consequently, of doing anything, which in his own judgment, and reason, he shall conceive to be the best means thereunto.

Liberty

By LIBERTY, is understood, according to the proper signification of the word, the absence of external impediments: which impediments, may oft take away part of a man's power to do what he would; but cannot hinder him from using the power left him, according as his judgment, and reason shall dictate to him.

A Law of Nature

A LAW OF NATURE . . . is a precept or general rule, found out by reason, by which a man is forbidden to do that, which is destructive of his life, or taketh away the means of preserving the same; and to omit that, by which he thinketh it may be best preserved. For though they that speak of this subject, use to confound . . . *right* and *law*: yet they ought to be distinguished; because RIGHT, consisteth in liberty to do, or to forbear; whereas LAW, determines, and binds to one of them: so that law, and right, differ as much, as obligation and liberty; which in one and the same matter are inconsistent.

The First Law of Nature: Seek Peace

And because the condition of man, as has been shown in the precedent chapter, is a condition of war of every one against every one; in which case every one is governed by his own reason; and there is nothing he can make use of, that may not be a help unto him, in preserving his life against his enemies; it followeth, that in such a condition, every man has a right to every thing; even to one another's body. And therefore, as long as this natural right of every man to every thing endures, there can be no security to any man, how strong or wise soever he be, of living out the time, which nature ordinarily alloweth men to live. And consequently it is a precept, or general rule of reason, *that every man, ought to endeavour peace, as far as he has hope of obtaining it; and when he cannot obtain it, that he may seek, and use, all helps, and advantages, of war.* The first branch of which rule, contains the first, and fundamental law of nature; which is, *to seek peace, and follow it.* The second, the sum of the right of nature; which is, *by all means we can, to defend ourselves.*

The Second Law of Nature: Give Up What Is Necessary to Obtain Peace

From this fundamental law of nature, by which men are commanded to endeavour peace, is derived this second law; *that a man be willing, when others are so too, as far forth, as for peace, and defence of himself he shall think it necessary, to lay down this right to all things, and be contented with so much liberty against other men, as he would allow other men against himself.* For as long as every man holds this right, of doing anything he likes, so long are all men in the condition of war. But if other men will not lay down their right, as well as he; then there is no reason for any one, to divest himself of his: for that were to expose himself to prey, which no man is bound to, rather than to dispose himself to peace. This is that law of the Gospel; *whatsoever you require that others should do to you, that do ye to them.* And that law of all men, "What you do not want done to you, do not do to others."

Giving Up a Right

To *lay down* a man's *right* to anything, is to *divest* himself of the *liberty,* of hindering another of the benefit of his own right to the same. For he that renounces, or passes away his right, gives not to any other man a right which he had not before; because there is nothing to which every man had not right by nature: but only stands out of his way, that he may enjoy his own original right, without hindrance from him; not without hindrance from another. So that the effect which redounds to one man, by another man's defect of right, is but so much diminution of impediments to the use of his own right original.

Right is laid aside, either by simply renouncing it; or by transferring it to another. By *simply* RENOUNCING; when he cares not to whom the benefit thereof redounds. By TRANSFERRING; when he intends the benefit thereof to some certain person, or persons. And when a man has in either manner abandoned, or granted away his right; then is he said to be OBLIGED, or BOUND, not to hinder those, to whom such right is granted, or abandoned, from the benefit of it: and that he ought, and it is his DUTY, not to make void that involuntary act of his own: and that such hindrance is INJUSTICE, and INJURY, as being "without right," the right being before renounced, or transferred. So that *injury,* or *injustice,* in the controversies of the world, is somewhat like to that, which in the disputations of scholars is called *absurdity.* For as it is there called an absurdity, to contradict what one maintained in the beginning: so in the world, it is called injustice, and injury, voluntarily to undo that, which from the beginning he had voluntarily done. The way by which a man either simply renounces, or transfers his right, is a declaration, or signification, by some voluntary and sufficient sign, or signs, that he does so renounce, or transfer; or has so renounced, or transferred the same, to him that accepts it. And these signs are either words only, or actions only; or, as it happens most often, both words, and actions. And the same are the BONDS, by which men are bound, and obliged: bonds, that have their strength, not from their own nature, for nothing is more easily broken than a man's word, but from fear of some evil consequence upon the rupture.

Some Rights Cannot Be Surrendered

Whensoever a man transfers his right, or renounces it; it is either in consideration of some right reciprocally transferred to himself; or for some other good he hopes for thereby. For it is a voluntary act: and of the voluntary acts of every man, the object is some *good to himself.* And therefore there be some rights, which no man can be understood by any words, or other signs, to have abandoned, or transferred. At first a man cannot lay down the right of resisting them, that assault him by force, to take away his life; because he cannot be understood to aim thereby, at any good to himself. The same may be said of wounds, and chains, and imprisonment; both because no benefit proceeds from such patience; as there is to the patience of suffering another to be wounded, or imprisoned: as also because a man cannot tell, when he seeth men proceed against him by violence, whether they intend his death or not. And lastly the motive, and end for which this renouncing, and transferring of right is introduced, is nothing else but the security of man's person, in his life, and in the means of so preserving life, as not to be weary of it. And therefore if a man by words, or other signs, seem to despoil himself of the end, for which those signs were intended; he is not to be understood as if he meant it, or that it was his will; but that he was ignorant of how such words and actions were to be interpreted.

The Contract

The mutual transferring of right, is that which men call CONTRACT.

There is a difference between transferring of right to the thing; and transferring, or tradition, that is delivery of the thing itself. For the thing may be delivered together with the translation of the right; as in buying and selling with ready money; or exchange of goods, or lands: and it may be delivered some time after.

The Covenant

Again, one of the contractors, may deliver the thing contracted for on his part, and leave the other to perform his part at some determinate time after, and in the mean time be trusted; and then the contract on his part, is called PACT, or COVENANT: or both parts may contract now, to perform hereafter: in which cases, he that is to perform in time to come, being trusted, his performance is called keeping of promise, or faith; and the failing of performance, if it be voluntary, violation of faith.

When the transferring of right, is not mutual: but one of the parties transfereth, in hope to gain thereby friendship, or service from another, or from his friends; or in hope to gain the reputation of charity, or magnanimity; or to deliver his mind from the pain of compassion; or in hope of reward in heaven, this is not contract, but GIFT, FREE-GIFT, GRACE: which words signify one and the same thing.

Signs of contract, are either *express,* or by *inference.* Express, are words spoken with understanding of what they signify: and such words are either of the time *present,* or *past,* as, *I give, I grant, I have given, I have granted, I will that this be yours:* or of the future; as, *I will give, I will grant:* which words of the future are called PROMISE. . . .

When a Covenant Is or Is Not Valid

If a covenant be made, wherein neither of the parties perform presently, but trust one another; in the condition of mere nature, which is a condition of war of every man against every man, upon any reasonable suspicion, it is void: but if there be a common power set over them both, with right and force sufficient to compel performance, it is not void. For he that performs first, has no assurance the other will perform after, because the bonds of words are too weak to bridle men's ambition, avarice, anger, and other passions, without the fear of some coercive power; which in the condition of mere nature, where all men are equal, and judges of the justness of their own fears, cannot possibly be supposed. And therefore he which performs first, does but betray himself to his enemy; contrary to the right, he can never abandon, of defending his life, and means of living.

But in a civil estate, where there is a power set up to constrain those that would otherwise violate their faith, that fear is no more reasonable: and for that cause, he which by the covenant is to perform first, is obliged so to do.

The cause of fear, which maketh such a covenant invalid, must be always something arising after the covenant made; as some new fact, or other sign of the will not to perform: else it cannot make the covenant void. For that which could not hinder a man from promising, ought not to be admitted as a hindrance of performing.

The Third Law of Nature: Justice

From that law of nature, by which we are obliged to transfer to another, such rights, as being retained, hinder the peace of mankind, there followeth a third; which is this, *that men perform their covenants made:* without which, covenants are in vain, and but empty words; and the right of all men to all things remaining, we are still in the condition of war.

And in this law of nature, consists the fountain and origin of JUSTICE. For where no covenant has preceded, there has no right been transferred, and every man has right to every thing; and consequently, no action can be unjust. But when a covenant is made, then to break it is *unjust:* and the definition of INJUSTICE, is no other than *the not performance of the covenant.* And whatsoever is not unjust, is just.

But because covenants of mutual trust, where there is a fear of not performance on either part, as hath been said in the former chapter, are invalid; though the original of justice be the making of covenants; yet injustice actually there can be none, till the cause of such fear be taken away; which while men are in the natural condition of war, cannot be done. Therefore before the names of just and unjust can have place, there must be some coercive power, to compel men equally to the performance of their covenants, by the terror of some punishment greater than the benefit they expect by the breach of their covenant; and to make good that propriety which by mutual contract men acquire, in recompense of the universal right they abandon: and such power there is none before the erection of a commonwealth.

In this final passage, Hobbes sets out the solution to the state of war found in nature. He speculates that people would form a covenant to produce a peaceful society for their mutual benefit and safety, but would need a government to enforce that covenant. Hence, the government is brought into being by a social contract.

- According to Hobbes, what do people hope to gain from the social contract to form a government?

Government Created by the Social Contract

The only way to erect such a common power, as may be able to defend them from the invasion of foreigners, and the injuries of one another, and thereby to secure them in such sort, as that by their own industry, and by the fruits of the earth, they may nourish themselves and live contentedly; is, to confer all their power and strength upon one man, or upon one assembly of men, that may reduce all their wills, by plurality of voices, unto one will: which is as much as to say, to appoint one man, or assembly of men, to bear their person; and every one to own, and acknowledge himself to be author of whatsoever he that so beareth their person, shall act, or cause to be acted, in those things which concern the common peace and safety; and therein to submit their wills, every one to his will, and their judgments, to his judgment. This is more than consent, or concord; it is a real unity of them all, in one and the same person, made by covenant of every man with every man, in such manner, as if every man should say to every man, *I authorize and give up my right of governing myself, to this man, or to this assembly of men, on this condition, that thou give up thy right to him, and authorize all his actions in like manner.* This done, the multitude so united in one person, is called a COMMONWEALTH, in Latin CIVITAS. This is the generation of that great LEVIA-THAN, or rather, to speak more reverently, of that *mortal god,* to which we owe under the *immortal God,* our peace and defence. For by this authority, given him by every particular man in the commonwealth, he hath the use of so much power and strength conferred on him, that by terror thereof, he is enabled to perform the wills of them all, to peace at home, and mutual aid against their enemies abroad. And in him consisteth the essence of the commonwealth; which, to define it, is *one person, of whose acts a great multitude, by mutual covenants one with an-other, have made themselves every one the author, to the end he may use the strength and means of them all, as he shall think expedient, for their peace and common defence.*

And that he carrieth this person, is called SOVEREIGN, and said to have *sovereign* power; and every one besides, his SUBJECT.

Hobbes's vision of government was unpopular with all the political factions of his day. He saw government as a human creation, based entirely on natural, physical needs. Hence, those who believed that government was an institution created by God and that the king ruled by divine authority did not like his account. On the other hand, Hobbes believed a government could serve its purpose only if it ruled with absolute power. Hence, he did not please the more democratic anti-monarchists either. Hobbes thought that the most rational and effective government would be one ruled by one person, the monarch, who was brought into power by common consent rather than royal inheritance. But notice that the social contract theory does not specify what form the government must take. The people could choose to have a monarchy, a democracy, a socialistic government, or whatever system they wanted.

Hobbes was one of the first thinkers to develop a social contract theory of government in the modern period. This theory answers the question of why the government has the right to impose its laws upon its citizens: the citizens have formed a contract to create the government and have given it the right to exercise power over their lives for their mutual benefit. But this theory raises a problem. Since neither you nor I have had anything to do with the creation of our government, what does this theory have to say about our relationship to our government? The founders of the United States government, such as Thomas Jefferson, literally brought the government into existence, delegated powers to it in the Constitution, and signed their names to the contract. However, you and I have never entered into such an explicit agreement with the government. In response to this problem, the social contract theorist would maintain that by living in this country and being the recipients of its benefits, we have implicitly agreed to be a part of this governmental system. The government has provided us with education, with roads, with protection by the military and the police, with laws that protect our lives, property, and rights. Hence, it is claimed, by accepting the benefits of the government, we have tacitly agreed to the original contract by which it was formed. (We will see in section 6.4 that Socrates uses this point in his argument against civil disobedience.)

If you were born in the United States, you are a citizen by virtue of your birth. However, when you become an adult, you can decide for yourself whether you want to be a party to the social contract. You are, of course, always free to leave. If you emigrate to another country, however, you must go through the process of changing your citizenship. In effect, you sign a new contract with a new government.

We can imagine a government that was forced on the people by a foreign power (as the outcome of a war, for example). We can furthermore imagine that this government, nevertheless, serves its people well. But if the people did not somehow bring this government into being, then no matter how moral the government is, it has no legitimacy according to the social contract theory. Hobbes believed that if people create a government, they should give it absolute power so that it can govern effectively. Many social contract theorists, however, believe that the government must provide for regular elections to guarantee that it is ruling with the citizens' consent. The Universal Declaration of Human Rights adopted by the General

Assembly of the United Nations expresses this point when it says that "the will of the people shall be expressed in periodic and genuine elections which shall be by universal and equal suffrage and shall be held by secret vote or by equivalent free voting procedures."

John Locke's Social Contract Theory

We encountered the English philosopher John Locke in section 2.3, where we discussed his empiricist theory of knowledge. (A short account of his life can be found there.) Besides being interested in the theory of knowledge, Locke also wrote extensively on political philosophy. Locke's political philosophy consisted of many interwoven themes. First, Locke was a natural law theorist (natural law theory is discussed in section 6.2), which means, briefly, that he believed that the conduct of individuals and society was governed by a universal, objective, moral law, not a law based on human conventions. Locke believed that this moral law was instituted by God. Furthermore, he argued that this natural law guaranteed us basic, natural, inherent rights by virtue of the fact that we are human. A **right** is a justified claim to something, usually implying that others have certain duties with respect to the possessor of the right. For example, if you have the right to free speech, then others (including the government) have an obligation not to interfere with your ability to express your opinions (as long as your doing so does not violate someone else's rights).

right a justified claim to something, usually implying that others have certain duties with respect to the possessor of the right

Some rights can be granted by law. For example, a sixteen-year-old may have the right to drive a car. However, rights granted by law can be taken away (the minimum driving age can be changed to eighteen). Locke insisted, however, that some rights are natural, human rights that cannot be taken away by the government. These rights are sometimes said to be *indefeasible* (cannot be made void) or *inalienable* (cannot be taken away). According to Locke, we possess these rights in the state of nature, before government came on the scene. Among these natural, moral rights are the preservation of our life, health, liberty, and possessions. In contrast, Hobbes said that in the state of nature we have the right to anything we want, *but only as long as we have the physical power to obtain what we want.* In other words, we have no moral claims over others. For that reason, Hobbes said that without government, "nothing can be unjust." When we form a government, according to Hobbes, we renounce many of our rights and liberties. However, Locke believed that both prior to government and after we form a government, we possess God-given inherent rights.

Locke's view of rights has major implications for political theory. If we have natural, indefeasible, inalienable rights, then the government can never justifiably violate these rights. If it does so, then it is no longer a legitimate government. Locke's social contract theory has to be understood with his theory of natural rights as its background. We create the government with the social contract, but we do not surrender our rights to the government nor does it create our rights. Instead, we bring the government into being in order to protect our natural rights.

In the following reading, Locke starts out as Hobbes did by describing the hypothetical "state of nature" in which people exist prior to forming a government. Remember that Hobbes believed that, without the iron will of an absolute government, such a condition would be "a war of all against all," in which human life is "solitary, poor, nasty, brutish, and short." However, Locke gives us a somewhat different picture of this situation.

- Can you detect the differences in Locke's vision of what the state of nature would be like in contrast to Hobbes's pessimistic assessment of human nature?
- Without any civil laws, what sort of law governs rational people in nature, according to Locke?

 FROM JOHN LOCKE

An Essay Concerning the True Original, Extent and End of Civil Government [3]

The State of Nature

6. The state of Nature has a law of Nature to govern it, which obliges every one, and reason, which is that law, teaches all mankind who will but consult it, that being all equal and independent, no one ought to harm another in his life, health, liberty or possessions; for men being all the workmanship of one omnipotent and infinitely wise Maker; all the servants of one sovereign Master, sent into the world by His order and about His business; they are His property, whose workmanship they are made to last during His, not one another's pleasure. And, being furnished with like faculties, sharing all in one community of Nature, there cannot be supposed any such subordination among us that may authorize us to destroy one

another, as if we were made for one another's uses, as the inferior ranks of creatures are for ours. Everyone as he is bound to preserve himself, and not to quit his station willfully, so by the like reason, when his own preservation comes not in competition, ought he as much as he can to preserve the rest of mankind, and not unless it be to do justice on an offender, take away or impair the life, or what tends to the preservation of the life, the liberty, health, limb, or goods of another. . . .

19. And here we have the plain difference between the state of nature and the state of war, which however some men have confounded, are as far distant as a state of peace, good-will, mutual assistance and preservation, and a state of enmity, malice, violence and mutual destruction, are one from another.

Unlike Hobbes, Locke had an optimistic view of human nature and believed that most people were basically reasonable. Hence, rather than being a vicious state of war, Locke thought that life in nature would be one of peace, goodwill, and mutual assistance. There would be a few troublemakers, of course, but the rest could assist one another to address any violations of each other's natural rights. Furthermore, Hobbes and many other political thinkers thought that there could not be any property without a government to define property rights. However, Locke argued that while natural resources (air, water, soil, and plants) belong to everybody, if you mix your labor with nature (gathering fruits, tilling the soil, planting seeds), then that part of nature becomes your rightful property and no government is necessary to decide this arrangement.

- In what way does the following passage make clear that Locke believes in the social contract theory of government?

The Origins of Political Society

95. Men being, as has been said, by nature all free, equal, and independent, no one can be put out of this estate and subjected to the political power of another without his own consent, which is done by agreeing with other men, to join and unite into a community for their comfortable, safe, and peaceable living, one amongst another, in a secure enjoyment of their properties, and a greater security against any that are not of it. This any number of men may do, because it injures not the freedom of the rest; they are left, as they were, in the liberty of the state of Nature. When any number of men have so consented to make one community or government, they are thereby presently incorporated, and make one body politic, wherein the majority have a right to act and conclude the rest.

96. For, when any number of men have, by the consent of every individual, made a community, they have thereby made that community one body, with a power to act as one body, which is only by the will and determination of the majority. . . .

97. And thus every man, by consenting with others to make one body politic under one government, puts himself under an obligation to every one of that

society to submit to the determination of the majority, and to be concluded by it; or else this original compact, whereby he with others incorporates into one society, would signify nothing, and be no compact if he be left free and under no other ties than he was in before in the state of Nature. For what appearance would there be of any compact? What new engagement if he were no farther tied by any decrees of the society than he himself thought fit and did actually consent to? This would be still as great a liberty as he himself had before his compact, or any one else in the state of Nature, who may submit himself and consent to any acts of it if he thinks fit. . . .

99. Whosoever, therefore, out of a state of Nature unite into a community, must be understood to give up all the power necessary to the ends for which they unite into society to the majority of the community, unless they expressly agreed in any number greater than the majority. And this is done by barely agreeing to unite into one political society, which is all the compact that is, or needs be, between the individuals that enter into or make up a commonwealth. And thus, that which begins and actually constitutes any political society is nothing but the consent of any number of freemen capable of majority, to unite and incorporate into such a society. And this is that, and that only, which did or could give beginning to any lawful government in the world.

If, as Locke claims, the state of nature is one of complete freedom, governed by reason, goodwill, and mutual assistance, why bother with government at all? Locke provides three reasons why people would want to contract together to form a government. People need: (1) an established and unbiased interpretation of the natural moral law embedded in nature, (2) an impartial judge to apply the established law to settle disputes and conflicts of interest, and (3) a power to support the rights of those who are victims of injustice and to enforce the law.

- Whereas Hobbes thought people would set up an absolute government as an act of desperation, what does Locke say about the motivation for government in the following passage?

The Motivation for Government

127. Thus mankind, notwithstanding all the privileges of the state of Nature, being but in an ill condition while they remain in it are quickly driven into society. Hence it comes to pass, that we seldom find any number of men live any time together in this state. The inconveniences that they are therein exposed to by the irregular and uncertain exercise of the power every man has of punishing the transgressions of others, make them take sanctuary under the established laws of government, and therein seek the preservation of their property. It is this that makes them so willingly give up every one his single power of punishing to be exercised by such alone as shall be appointed to it amongst them, and by such rules as the community, or those authorised by them to that purpose, shall agree

on. And in this we have the original right and rise of both the legislative and executive power as well as of the governments and societies themselves.

For Locke, life without government is an "ill condition" and full of "inconveniences." If government is a convenience, not a necessity, then we can dictate the terms of the bargain. Instead of *surrendering* our rights and power to the government as Hobbes proposed, we *delegate* it for the mutual preservation of our lives, property, and liberties. The government is our creation; therefore, it is our servant, not an absolute power over us. As Locke puts it, the actions of the government are "to be directed to no other end but the peace, safety, and public good of the people."[4] In this theory are the foundations of what has come to be called "classical liberalism," the notion that the government should only have as much power as is necessary to do for us what we cannot (or cannot conveniently and efficiently) do for ourselves.

John Locke was one of the most influential philosophers of his time. His concepts of the state of nature, the natural moral law, natural rights, the social contract, and the right of revolution were the intellectual currency of eighteenth-century political thought. When writing the American Declaration of Independence, Thomas Jefferson said that his ideas were not new but followed the thought of writers such as Locke. When the colonists shouted, "No taxation without representation!" they were virtually quoting Locke. Through Montesquieu and others, Locke also influenced French thought. Locke might not have sanctioned the American and French revolutions (since he was too much of a moderate), but it is certain that these movements grew from seeds he had planted. Notice that for Locke, the social contract theory has implicit within it a right of revolution. If the government has been imposed on people without their consent, or if it is not fulfilling its contract (by violating people's rights, for example), then the government is no longer legitimate, citizens no longer have any obligations to the government, and a revolution is morally and politically justified.

- How many echos from John Locke's political philosophy can you find in the opening lines of the American Declaration of Independence?

The Concept of the Separation of Powers

Notice that Locke suggests that in the government there should be a separation of powers (the legislative and executive branch). Later in the essay he adds a third branch, the federative power, which is similar to our secretary of state. Taking his lesson from the problems of the king having total, absolute power, Locke came up with the brilliant idea of dividing the government into parts, each of which could limit the power of the other branches. Influenced by Locke, Montesquieu (1689–1755) suggested that the third branch should be the judicial one. When the founders of the American republic divided the government into three branches, they were drawing on the ideas of both Locke and Montesquieu.

SPOTLIGHT
on

FROM *THE DECLARATION OF INDEPENDENCE*
(JULY 4, 1776)

When in the Course of human events, it becomes necessary for one people to dissolve the political bands which have connected them with another, and to assume among the Powers of the earth, the separate and equal station to which the Laws of Nature and of Nature's God entitle them, a decent respect to the opinions of mankind requires that they should declare the causes which impel them to the separation.

We hold these truths to be self-evident, that all men are created equal, that they are endowed by their Creator with certain unalienable Rights, that among these are Life, Liberty, and the pursuit of Happiness. That to secure these rights, Governments are instituted among Men, deriving their just powers from the consent of the governed. That whenever any Form of Government becomes destructive of these ends, it is the Right of the People to alter or to abolish it, and to institute new Government, laying its foundation on such principles and organizing its powers in such form, as to them shall seem most likely to effect their Safety and Happiness.

LOOKING THROUGH THE LENS OF THE SOCIAL CONTRACT THEORY

1. Think about your own country and its constitution. If you were a social contract theorist, what events would have to occur in your nation to claim that the social contract had been broken? In other words, under what conditions would your government no longer be legitimate and would a political revolution be justified?

2. If all the governments throughout history had agreed with the principles of the social contract theory, how would history have been different?

EXAMINING THE STRENGTHS AND WEAKNESSES OF THE SOCIAL CONTRACT THEORY

Positive Evaluation

1. Doesn't this theory, by emphasizing that a government is legitimate if it rules with the consent of the governed, capture most people's intuitions about what makes a government good? Isn't it the case that the really bad governments in history and in our contemporary world are governments that have violated this principle?

2. The social contract theory says that the power of the government has been delegated to it in order to put an end to the chaos and injustice we would suffer if it was not there. Hence, isn't it a strength of this theory that it does not dictate a certain form of government but does provide a criterion for defining the scope and

limits of the government? Don't we want a government that has no more and no less power than we decide it should have?

3. The social contract theory emphasizes that the government derives its power from its citizens, that our rights cannot be violated by the government, and that the government is our servant (rather than the other way around). Hence, doesn't this theory go a long way in preserving the rights of the citizens against the coercive power of the government?

Negative Evaluation

1. The social contract theory is based on the story of a hypothetical "state of nature" in which people lived without government and then formed a "social contract" to invent a government. However, even the defenders of the theory acknowledge that they cannot point to an actual historical situation in which such a formation occurred. Instead, all we find in history are situations in which one form of government arose from a previous form of government. If the main thrust of the social contract theory is based on a hypothetical, fictional thought experiment, does this basis undermine the value of the theory as a justification of actual governments?

2. Even if all governments were actually formed in the way that this theory suggests, would this fact lend any further plausibility to the theory? Why do the origins of a government matter in deciding whether it is legitimate today? Couldn't a government have been imposed on its people hundreds of years ago in an illegitimate way, and couldn't its present-day citizens still consider it a legitimate government in its present form?

3. Historically, the United States was formed by a contract among white males. But native Americans, African slaves, and women played no role in this process. Furthermore, people in these groups were denied any participation in the political process for most of this nation's history. According to the social contract theory, wouldn't this information suggest that for the people in these groups the government is not legitimate? Even if everyone has his or her political rights protected today, can we really say that the poor and the powerless have much influence over who gets elected? Furthermore, even if the poor and the powerless are beneficiaries of the government's services, doesn't their lack of political power cast doubts on the degree to which the government rules with the "consent of the governed"? Does this theory idealize how political power really comes about?

6.2 THE QUESTION OF JUSTICE

LEADING QUESTIONS: *The Nature of Justice*

1. *Questions from Plato:* If you needed a heart operation, would you want the decisions in the operating room to be made by an accomplished heart surgeon or

by a democratic vote of your friends? Should teaching positions be open to anyone who wants them or only to those who are qualified to teach the subject matter? If you were the coach of a professional basketball team, would you attempt to choose the very best players or would you give everyone an equal chance? In all areas of society, we give people privileges, power, and opportunities based on their merit or qualifications and not on the basis of democratic equality. Likewise, when the issue is who should run our society, shouldn't the decision be based on merit and not democracy?

2. *Questions from Thomas Aquinas:* If justice is simply what the laws of a particular society declare it to be, then could we ever say that those laws were unjust? Doesn't there have to be some standard of justice that transcends human decisions and the will of the majority?

3. *Questions from John Stuart Mill:* Does it make sense to talk abstractly of the justice of a society or its laws apart from their consequences? Isn't a society just if it fulfills people's needs and produces the greatest amount of satisfaction that is possible? Do we need any concept of justice beyond that?

4. *Questions from John Rawls:* Isn't justice basically fairness? And aren't conditions fair when they are what we would choose if we were completely rational and objective and were freed from our personal biases?

These leading questions reflect the theories of justice of the four thinkers we examine in this section. When we think of justice, we typically think of the criminal justice system in which wrongdoers are tried, convicted, and punished for their crimes. Thus, when a criminal is found guilty and given an appropriate prison sentence, we say that justice has been done. Likewise, when an innocent person is declared not guilty, we consider this decision to be just. On the other hand, if a criminal is released on a technicality, we feel as though the system of justice has failed us. All these examples involve that form of justice known as *retributive justice,* or the proper allotment of punishment proportionate to the severity of a crime.

But retributive justice is only a small part of a much larger issue. Society does not merely distribute punishment. Society is organized to also distribute or regulate the attainment of positive benefits such as wealth, goods, privilege, and power. Retributive justice is concerned with giving a criminal the punishment that he or she is due. But society must also decide how people in general are to receive what they are due in terms of the burdens necessary to make society work (such as taxes) and in terms of benefits to be received (such as income, medical care, education, and political power). How should resources be distributed, given the fact that there is not enough for everyone to receive all that they would like or need? Should everyone receive an equal amount? Should those who have the most needs receive the most? Should those who make the greatest contribution to society receive the greatest share? All these issues fall under the heading of *distributive justice,* or the proper distribution of benefits and burdens among its citizens.

SURVEYING THE CASE FOR JUSTICE AS MERIT

Most accounts of justice assume that whatever it is, it involves giving everybody what they are due. But how do we determine what people are due? One answer is that the determination should be by merit. The foremost defender of this position is Plato. Plato was a thoroughly systematic philosopher, so his political theory has to be put in the context of his theory of knowledge and reality, which we encountered in sections 2.2, "Rationalism," and 3.0, "Overview of Metaphysics." Plato believed that all of life (including the life of society) had to be based on a correct assessment of what reality is like. Our understanding of reality is like a map that guides us in every decision we make. If the map is wrong, we will never be able to achieve our goals. Hence, those people who deserve the most political power are those who are best able to discern the nature of reality. But ultimate reality, according to Plato, can only be known through reason. Since people are not equal in their rational capacities, they should not be equal in their ability to exercise political power. Plato's ideal society, in which political power is proportionate to merit, is known as a **meritocracy.**

From these brief remarks, it should be clear that Plato was not a great fan of democracy. In fact, he was one of history's harshest critics of this political philosophy. By the time Plato was born, the new invention of Athenian democracy had replaced the age-old system of monarchy. The Athenians were proud of their system of government in which all laws, trials, and other public decisions were voted on by an assembly of the adult male citizens. No doubt, Plato's negative assessment of democracy was influenced by the fact that it was by a popular vote of the Athenian citizens that his teacher, Socrates, was condemned to death. This event, which Plato considered to be an outrageous miscarriage of justice, led him to spend the rest of his life searching for the blueprint of the just society. For Plato, democracy was equivalent to mob rule. He described democracy as a thousand-headed beast in which each head is pulling in its own direction, seeking to satisfy its personal desires.

Plato's alternative is based on his theory that "the state is the individual written large." To express this concept in contemporary terms, Plato believed that psychology and political science follow the same principles. Those factors that constitute either a healthy or pathological individual will be the same factors that constitute a healthy or pathological society. In Plato's psychological theory, each individual is made up of three parts: the appetites (or desires), the spirited part (which includes the emotions), and reason. The healthy individual is one in whom these three parts play their appropriate role and work together in harmony. However, this concordance occurs only when the desires and the spirited part are governed by reason.

Similarly, Plato thought that there were three kinds of people in society: (1) those who are ruled by their appetites, (2) those who are ruled by their passions and motivated by ambition, loyalty, honor, and courage, and (3) those who are fully governed by reason. The first group are called the *producers*. Since their appetitive nature inclines them toward material acquisition and physical comfort, they

meritocracy Plato's ideal society, in which political power is proportionate to merit

are best suited to care for the production of goods and services in society. This group includes not only the laborers, but also the merchants, physicians, business-people, and bankers as well. The second group are the *auxiliaries,* those whose courage and passion for ambition and honor makes them suited to be the protectors of society. This group corresponds to our police and military as well as to other federal agents and administrators who support the policies of the rulers. The final group are the *guardians,* whose intelligence qualifies them to establish the laws and policies of the state.

Plato believed that, in the same way that harmony is realized in a healthy individual, justice is realized in a society when each group plays its appropriate role and when the first two classes are ruled by the intellectual elite. Ironically, while the producers have the least political power, they are afforded the most freedom and economic gain. They can marry whom they wish, can own property, and can acquire personal wealth and luxuries as long as society does not become unbalanced with too much wealth and too much poverty. The rulers, on the other hand, cannot own property, for Plato wanted to guarantee that they would be motivated sheerly by the desire to serve society and not by the prospect of personal gain. However, they alone have political power and the ability to make political decisions and set the direction that society will take. The other two classes merely do their jobs and follow the direction of the rulers.

In the following passage, Plato presents his theory of justice through the voice of Socrates. Socrates is leading the discussion.

 FROM PLATO

Republic[5]

Well then, tell me, I said, whether I am right or not: You remember the original principle which we were always laying down at the foundation of the State, that one man should practise one thing only, the thing to which his nature was best adapted—now justice is this principle or a part of it.

Yes, we often said that one man should do one thing only.

Further, we affirmed that justice was doing one's own business, and not being a busybody; we said so again and again, and many others have said the same to us.

Yes, we said so.

Then to do one's own business in a certain way may be assumed to be justice. Can you tell me whence I derive this inference?

I cannot, but I should like to be told.

Because I think that this is the only virtue which remains in the State when the other virtues of temperance and courage and wisdom are abstracted; and, that this is the ultimate cause and condition of the existence of all of them, and while remaining in them is also their preservative; and we were saying that if the three were discovered by us, justice would be the fourth or remaining one.

That follows of necessity.

If we are asked to determine which of these four qualities by its presence contributes most to the excellence of the State, whether the agreement of rulers and subjects, or the preservation in the soldiers of the opinion which the law ordains about the true nature of dangers, or wisdom and watchfulness in the rulers, or whether this other which I am mentioning, and which is found in children and women, slave and freeman, artisan, ruler, subject,—the quality, I mean, of every one doing his own work, and not being a busybody, would claim the palm—the question is not so easily answered.

Certainly, he replied, there would be a difficulty in saying which.

Then the power of each individual in the State to do his own work appears to compete with the other political virtues, wisdom, temperance, courage.

Yes, he said.

And the virtue which enters into this competition is justice?

Exactly.

Let us look at the question from another point of view: Are not the rulers in a State those to whom you would entrust the office of determining suits at law?

Certainly.

And are suits decided on any other ground but that a man may neither take what is another's, nor be deprived of what is his own?

Yes; that is their principle.

Which is a just principle?

Yes.

Then on this view also justice will be admitted to be the having and doing what is a man's own, and belongs to him?

Very true.

Think, now, and say whether you agree with me or not. Suppose a carpenter to be doing the business of a cobbler, or a cobbler of a carpenter; and suppose them to exchange their implements or their duties, or the same person to be doing the work of both, or whatever be the change; do you think that any great harm would result to the State?

Not much.

But when the cobbler or any other man whom nature designed to be a trader, having his heart lifted up by wealth or strength or the number of his followers, or any like advantage, attempts to force his way into the class of warriors, or a warrior into that of legislators and guardians, for which he is unfitted, and either to take the implements or the duties of the other; or when one man is trader, legislator, and warrior all in one, then I think you will agree with me in saying that this interchange and this meddling of one with another is the ruin of the State.

Most true.

Seeing then, I said, that there are three distinct classes, any meddling of one with another, or the change of one into another, is the greatest harm to the State, and may be most justly termed evil-doing?

Precisely.

And the greatest degree of evil-doing to one's own city would be termed by you injustice?

Certainly.

This then is injustice; and on the other hand when the trader, the auxiliary, and the guardian each do their own business, that is justice, and will make the city just.

I agree with you.

- Do you agree with Plato that people are naturally suited to play different roles in society?
- What do you think of his argument that political power should be given to the intellectual elite and not distributed equally?

In Plato's version of a meritocracy, only those people who had wisdom and exceptional rational capacities were suited to be leaders. Accordingly, he said in the *Republic* that society would not be well-ordered and just unless "philosophers become kings or kings become philosophers." Plato thought that a child of a ruler would usually have the capacity to grow up to be a ruler, but he realized that this succession would not always be true. In some instances the child of a ruler might be best suited to be a merchant, while the child of a fisher might have the aptitude to be a ruler. To settle this problem, Plato proposed that, throughout their early life, children be tested to determine what their abilities were and how they could best serve society. As a result of this process, all children would be given the appropriate education to best develop their talents and to prepare them to best employ their abilities in serving society.

In setting out his vision of the ideal society, Plato said that the health of the state needed to be as carefully regulated as the health of the body and thus could be left neither to happenstance nor to popular opinion. Plato therefore held a very strong view of the amount of control the government should have over its citizen's lives. For example, he believed in scientific mating to ensure that the very best specimens of humanity were produced. He also believed in arranged marriages and assigned the raising of children to the community. Furthermore, just as our society controls hallucinogenic drugs, quack medicines, and other harmful substances to protect people's bodies, so Plato believed in government censorship of the arts and all forms of communication so that its citizens' minds should be kept free of harmful ideas.

LOOKING THROUGH PLATO'S LENS

1. Think about our present-day political campaigns in which candidates are packaged and marketed in the same way that a particular brand of car is promoted to the public. What would Plato have to say about our approach to the political process?

2. Plato believed that children at an early age should be tested to discover their abilities and determine what role they should play in society. How do we use

such testing in our current educational system? Are there any similarities between our system and Plato's? What are the advantages and disadvantages of Plato's proposal?

3. In Plato's society, the producers had the most freedom and personal possessions, but the least power. On the other hand, his auxiliaries and guardians had the most power, but lived disciplined, frugal lives. If you could choose (even though in Plato's society you couldn't choose for yourself), which role would you prefer to be placed into?

EXAMINING THE STRENGTHS AND WEAKNESSES OF PLATO'S THEORY OF JUSTICE

Positive Evaluation

1. While Plato's political philosophy offends our democratic sensibilities, doesn't it also have some advantages? In our society, the family you are born into, including its influence, wealth, and social standing, plays a large role in determining the opportunities you have in life. In what ways is this determination good, and in what ways is it bad? How does Plato's system avoid some of the problems of our system?

2. By structuring his society so that wealth and political power would be separated, Plato guaranteed that the rulers would be motivated solely by their desire to serve. Isn't this structure a good idea?

3. Think back to the first leading question. Don't we base a person's opportunities in medicine, education, business, sports, and other careers solely on his or her merit and not on democratic equality? Does Plato have a point in saying that the same principle should apply to our political rulers?

Negative Evaluation

1. Although Plato tried to design the perfect society based on rational principles, critics argued that it is based on a number of questionable assumptions. For example, in determining the career track that children will be channeled into, Plato assumes that he will be able to accurately discern their abilities through testing. But is this assumption always true? Aren't some people late bloomers? For example, the great physicist Albert Einstein performed terribly in mathematics as a child. In Plato's society he might have ended up a carpenter instead of a great scientist. Furthermore, Plato assumes that those people with the best intellects will also be the wisest. But is intellectual ability necessarily the same as wisdom and leadership skills?

2. Critics charge that Plato's society is a thinly veiled tyranny in which the rulers have absolute control over the society, including the censorship of the arts and the flow of information. Wouldn't this control mean that Plato's society would never

be able to change and would not accommodate new ideas that might lead it to improve?

3. Even if we accept Plato's belief that his society would be perfectly rational and efficient, are these qualities all that make up a good society? Does it make sense to say that a society is perfectly just and good if people have no autonomy and no freedom to make important decisions about their own lives? Hasn't Plato assumed that having a well-ordered society is the only element in human flourishing?

SURVEYING THE CASE FOR JUSTICE AS CONFORMITY TO THE NATURAL LAW

The advocates of the natural law theory have a number of points in common with Plato. They agree with him that justice has to do with the rational and moral ordering of society. However, they would say that the sort of ordered society he had in mind is, in many ways, not natural and would inhibit human flourishing.

The natural law theory is a conception of law and justice that has deep roots in the Western tradition and continues to inform our ways of thinking even today. It was given its initial impetus by Aristotle, found its way into the thought of the Greek Stoics around 300 B.C., helped shape the Roman conception of law, and was further developed by the medieval philosophers. The **natural law theory** claims that there is an objective moral law that transcends human conventions and decisions, governs individuals and the conduct of society, and can be known through reason and experience on the basis of the natural order of the world and the built-in tendencies of human nature.

The natural law theory applied to justice says that any civil law that human beings legislate is just (or properly called a law) only if it is in conformity to the natural law. On the other hand, if a law of a particular society violates the natural law, then it is unjust and not really a law at all. Obviously, when we are referring to the natural law in the context of ethics and political philosophy, we are not talking about scientific, physical laws (such as the law of gravity). Nevertheless, the two concepts are similar, because the natural law theorist believes that there is an objective moral order in reality that is independent of us, just as there is a physical order in nature.

Although some of the features of the natural law theory can be found in Socrates, Plato, and even some of the earlier Greeks, its explicit formulation was probably first given by Plato's student Aristotle (384–322 B.C.). (See the discussion of Aristotle's virtue ethics in section 5.5.) Aristotle did not believe that the state is a human invention; in this way his theory contrasted with the social contract theory discussed in section 6.1. Aristotle claimed that human beings are political animals whose very nature dictates that they are made to live in society. In this way, we are like other social creatures, such as ants or wolves, who live in colonies or packs and who have leaders and an implicit social structure. However, we are also different in that we have speech, reason, and the ability to discern good and evil. Hence, unlike

natural law theory the theory that there is an objective moral law that transcends human conventions and decisions, governs individuals and the conduct of society, and can be known through reason and experience on the basis of the natural order of the world and the built-in tendencies of human nature

the social structure of other animals, our social life is not governed by instinct but by our ability to make rational and moral decisions.

According to the natural law theorist, all morally aware people have the potential to recognize these laws, although as little children this potential needs to be developed through moral training. The moral principles that make up the natural law are not capable of being proven because they are so basic. As Immanuel Kant said (see section 5.4), to deny the moral law is to fall into a contradiction. Obviously, some people, through their behavior or in their theories, deny the existence of the natural law. However, the natural law theorist would say that this denial does not prove that the natural law is not real any more than the fact that color-blind people cannot distinguish blue from green or that tone-deaf people are not sensitive to music proves that colors or melodies are not real.

Because this moral law is called "natural," the point is being made that we can discover the basic principles of morality by using our natural human faculties. Although many natural law theorists were religious and believed that the natural law was ultimately rooted in God and the way we were created, it is not necessary to be a theist to be a natural law theorist. From Aristotle on, natural law theorists have believed that whether we are religious or not, we can discover the natural law by reasoning about experience and human nature.

The natural law theorist does not claim that we always have a complete and infallible knowledge of this natural law any more than we are always correct in discerning the objective physical laws. For example, the framers of the U.S. Constitution correctly realized that all persons are created equal and have basic rights at the same time that they held slaves. It took a century for our society to realize that the institution of slavery violated the natural law. It took another century to begin to change those laws in our society that discriminated against minorities and women. We are still in the process of trying to bring our society's practices and civil laws in conformity with the moral law.

Critics sometimes object that the natural law theory is an attempt to "legislate morality." But the natural law theorist would respond that legislating morality is precisely what a large portion of our current laws do. For example, stealing is wrong and so we make it illegal. But the converse is not true, that is, the reason that stealing is wrong is not that it is illegal. Furthermore, as the medieval natural law theorist Thomas Aquinas said, not every matter of morality should be legislated, because then, since none of us are perfectly moral, we would all deserve to be in jail. For example, it is immoral to ridicule someone because of his or her disability, even if we do it without that person knowing it. Under most circumstances, that sort of crude, tasteless, and moral insensitivity is not illegal, even though it is immoral. However, those issues of morality that so are so fundamental that their violation would degrade human life, impair human flourishing, and destroy society are the features of the natural law that find their way into the civil law.

Unlike the laws against actions such as murder and stealing, some laws are only indirectly derived from the natural law. Americans drive on the right side of the street, and the British drive on the left side of the street. Obviously, neither practice is more in conformity with the natural law than the other. However, our traffic laws and other such laws are derived from the natural law that human life should be preserved.

We first encountered Thomas Aquinas (1225–1274) when we discussed his proofs for God in section 4.1. Here, we examine his argument that a government and its laws are just if they conform to the natural law.

FROM THOMAS AQUINAS

Summa Theologica[6]

As Augustine says, *that which is not just seems to be no law at all.* Hence the force of a law depends on the extent of its justice. Now in human affairs a thing is said to be just from being right, according to the rule of reason. But the first rule of reason is the law of nature, as is clear from what has been stated above. Consequently, every human law has just so much of the nature of law as it is derived from the law of nature. But if in any point it departs from the law of nature, it is no longer a law but a perversion of law. . . .

Laws framed by man are either just or unjust. If they be just, they have the power of binding in conscience from the eternal law whence they are derived. . . . Now laws are said to be just, both from the end (when, namely, they are ordained to the common good), from their author (that is to say, when the law that is made does not exceed the power of the lawgiver), and from their form (when, namely, burdens are laid on the subjects according to an equality of proportion and with a view to the common good). For, since one man is a part of the community, each man, in all that he is and has, belongs to the community; just as a part, in all that it is, belongs to the whole. So, too, nature inflicts a loss on the part in order to save the whole; so that for this reason such laws as these, which impose proportionate burdens, are just and binding in conscience, and are legal laws.

On the other hand, laws may be unjust in two ways: first, by being contrary to human good, through being opposed to the things mentioned above:—either in respect of the end, as when an authority imposes on his subjects burdensome laws, conducive, not to the common good, but rather to his own cupidity or vainglory; or in respect of the author, as when a man makes a law that goes beyond the power committed to him; or in respect of the form, as when burdens are imposed unequally on the community, although with a view to the common good. Such are acts of violence rather than laws, because, as Augustine says, a law that is not just seems to be no law at all. Therefore, such laws do not bind in conscience, except perhaps in order to avoid scandal or disturbance, for which cause a man should even yield his right. . . .

Secondly, laws may be unjust through being opposed to the divine good. Such are the laws of tyrants inducing to idolatry, or to anything else contrary to the divine law. Laws of this kind must in no way be observed.

The most fundamental principles of the natural law, according to Aquinas, are the preservation of life, the propagation and education of offspring, and the pursuit of truth and a peaceful society. While the natural law is built into human nature, we can violate the natural law of morality (unlike physical laws). This feature enables us to freely make good or bad choices and, hence, to have morality at all. Nevertheless, we tend to feel that the natural order of things has been violated when someone violates the law of nature. For example, we all recognize a case of suicide as deeply tragic because, Aquinas would say, the natural tendency is for a person to want to maintain his or her life. Similarly, we are appalled when we read about a wanton murder. But why are we particularly horrified when a parent murders his or her own child? Because it is a very deep feature of the natural and right order of things for parents to love and care for their children.

LOOKING THROUGH THE LENS OF NATURAL LAW THEORY

1. If there were no natural law that stands over and above the laws made by human governments, would there be any basis for saying that a particular civil law was unjust if it had come about through a legal process?

2. The American Declaration of Independence says, "We hold these truths to be self-evident, that all men are created equal, that they are endowed by their Creator with certain unalienable Rights, that among these are Life, Liberty, and the pursuit of Happiness." What key terms in this passage indicate that the founders of the American government believed in the natural law?

3. If the natural law is available to be known by all, why is there a need to have written laws? Couldn't a society be run entirely on the basis of people's intuition of the moral law? How might a natural law theorist respond to this objection?

4. The U.S. Fugitive Slave Law of 1793 allowed slaveholders to capture and retrieve slaves who had sought freedom in other states. How would you attempt to convince the framers of this law that it was unjust? In doing so, would you have to appeal to some notion of a natural moral law that defines justice?

EXAMINING THE STRENGTHS AND WEAKNESSES OF NATURAL LAW THEORY

Positive Evaluation

1. Supporters of this theory claim that it provides a basis for critiquing the laws of a society. As a matter of fact, this theory has been explicitly or tacitly appealed to by all great social reformers throughout history, such as the antislavery movement in the nineteenth century and the civil rights movement in the 1960s led by Martin Luther King Jr. Apart from the natural law theory, would there be any theoretical basis for social reform?

2. Don't good legislators continually ask themselves, "Is this proposed legislation right? Is it just? Does it promote the common good? Does it protect the fundamental rights of our citizens?" Aren't these questions rooted in the natural law? Apart from some conception of the natural law, wouldn't legislation be based on simply the will of the 51 percent majority or on whatever the current political fashion of the day might be? Wouldn't this basis be bad?

Negative Evaluation

1. Critics maintain that even if there is a natural moral law, it is too vague and too hard to discern to be much use in political theory. The natural law is supposed to be based on human nature. But aren't we often naturally inclined to do something that is bad for us or that is immoral? Given this fact, does it make sense to define justice in terms of what is "natural"? Aren't there alternative conceptions of what is natural or good?

2. Some people object that the natural law theory is based on a particular conception of reality, one that tends to be biased toward a religious view of the world. For example, critics claim that the theory assumes that there are oughts in nature and that human nature is fixed and preordained. Given the fact that our society has so many alternate conceptions of what constitutes the best life, how can the natural law theory be the basis of law in a pluralistic society such as ours?

SURVEYING THE CASE FOR JUSTICE AS SOCIAL UTILITY

JOHN STUART MILL (1806-1873)

One of the most influential political theorists in the last two centuries was John Stuart Mill. Whether or not you have read Mill, it is likely that your ideas about society show traces of his influence. We encountered Mill previously in our discussion of utilitarian ethics (see section 5.3 for the discussion of Mill's ethics and a brief account of his life). Since Mill believed that the morally right action was one that produced the greatest happiness for the greatest number, it is natural that his ethical concerns would lead to a political theory. In the realm of politics, Mill's concern was, "What sort of society will produce the greatest happiness for the greatest number?" In previous centuries Mill's native country of England had endured a turbulent civil war that led to the rise of parliamentary government, and just a few decades before Mill was born, political unrest produced the American and French Revolutions. In Mill's own lifetime, the beginning of the industrial revolution was foreshadowing major social changes and turmoil. Consequently, Mill saw the need for a political philosophy that would ensure social stability and protect individual freedom.

Mill's solution was to argue that the just society is one that attempts to minimize social harms and maximize social benefits for the most number of people. He called this solution the "principle of utility" or "expediency." In other words, he believed that *justice* is just an empty word unless it is tied to observable consequences such as the satisfaction of the interests of the majority of people in society. The following reading by Mill illustrates the utilitarian theory of justice.

- How does Mill define the word *right*?
- What is the basis of our rights, according to Mill?
- How does Mill's notion of rights differ from Locke's notion of natural, inalienable rights? What are some implications of this difference?
- On what basis does Mill say that a society ought to defend individual rights?

FROM JOHN STUART MILL
Utilitarianism[7]

When we call anything a person's right, we mean that he has a valid claim on society to protect him in the possession of it, either by the force of law, or by that of education and opinion. If he has what we consider a sufficient claim, on whatever account, to have something guaranteed to him by society, we say that he has a right to it. . . .

To have a right, then, is, I conceive, to have something which society ought to defend me in the possession of. If the objector goes on to ask, why it ought? I can give him no other reason than general utility. If that expression does not seem to convey a sufficient feeling of the strength of the obligation, nor to account for the peculiar energy of the feeling, it is because there goes to the composition of the sentiment, not a rational only, but also an animal element, the thirst for retaliation; and this thirst derives its intensity, as well as its moral justification, from the extraordinarily important and impressive kind of utility which is concerned. The interest involved is that of security, to every one's feelings the most vital of all interests. All other earthly benefits are needed by one person, not needed by another; and many of them can, if necessary, be cheerfully foregone, or replaced by something else; but security no human being can possibly do without; on it we depend for all our immunity from evil, and for the whole value of all and every good, beyond the passing moment; since nothing but the gratification of the instant could be of any worth to us, if we could be deprived of anything the next instant by whoever was momentarily stronger than ourselves. Now this most indispensable of all necessaries, after physical nutriment, cannot be had, unless the machinery for providing it is kept unintermittedly in active play. Our notion, therefore, of the claim we have on our fellow-creatures to join in making safe for us the very groundwork of our existence, gathers feelings around it so much more intense than those concerned in any of the more common cases of utility, that the difference in degree (as is often the case in psychology) becomes a real difference in kind. The claim assumes that character of absoluteness, that apparent infinity, and incommensurability with all other considerations, which constitute the distinction between the feeling of right and wrong and that of ordinary expediency and inexpediency. The feelings concerned are so powerful, and we count so positively on finding a responsive feeling in others (all being alike interested), that *ought* and *should* grow into *must,* and recognized indispensability becomes a moral necessity, analogous to physical, and often not inferior to it in binding force.

STOP AND THINK

If, as Mill believes, our rights are granted to us by law or social opinion and are based on general utility, could society decide to change these rights when it was socially useful to do so? What would be the implications of this position? What would Locke say about Mill's notion of rights?

- In the next passage, Mill cites critics who claims that his principle of utility is too vague and should be replaced with the concept of "justice." Why does he think that justice alone cannot be the standard for evaluating a society?
- What does Mill think about the social contract theory?

We are continually informed that Utility is an uncertain standard, which every different person interprets differently, and that there is no safety but in the immutable, ineffaceable, and unmistakable dictates of justice, which carry their evidence in themselves, and are independent of the fluctuations of opinion. One would suppose from this that on questions of justice there could be no controversy; that if we take that for our rule, its application to any given case could leave us in as little doubt as a mathematical demonstration. So far is this from being the fact, that there is as much difference of opinion, and as much discussion, about what is just, as about what is useful to society. Not only have different nations and individuals different notions of justice, but in the mind of one and the same individual, justice is not some one rule, principle, or maxim, but many, which do not always coincide in their dictates, and in choosing between which, he is guided either by some extraneous standard, or by his own personal predilections.

For instance, there are some who say, that it is unjust to punish any one for the sake of example to others; that punishment is just, only when intended for the good of the sufferer himself. Others maintain the extreme reverse, contending that to punish persons who have attained years of discretion, for their own benefit, is despotism and injustice, since if the matter at issue is solely their own good, no one has a right to control their own judgment of it; but that they may justly be punished to prevent evil to others, this being the exercise of the legitimate right of self-defense. Mr. Owen, again, affirms that it is unjust to punish at all; for the criminal did not make his own character; his education, and the circumstances which surrounded him, have made him a criminal, and for these he is not responsible. All these opinions are extremely plausible; and so long as the question is argued as one of justice simply, without going down to the principles which lie under justice and are the source of its authority, I am unable to see how any of these reasoners can be refuted. For in truth every one of the three builds upon rules of justice confessedly true. The first appeals to the acknowledged injustice of singling out an individual, and making a sacrifice, without his consent, for other people's benefit. The second relies on the acknowledged justice of self-defense, and the admitted injustice of forcing one person to conform to another's notions of what constitutes his good. The Owenite invokes the admitted principle, that it is unjust to punish any one for what he cannot help. Each is triumphant so long as he is not compelled to take into consideration any other maxims of justice than the one he has selected; but as soon as their several maxims are brought face to face, each disputant seems to have exactly as much to say for himself as the others. No one of them can carry out his own notion of justice without trampling upon another equally binding. These are difficulties; they have always been felt to be such; and many devices have been invented to turn rather than to overcome them. As a refuge from the last of the three, men imagined what they called the freedom of the will; fancying that they could not justify punishing a man whose will is in a thoroughly hateful state, unless it be supposed to have come into that state through no influence of anterior circumstances. To escape from the other difficulties, a favorite contrivance has been the fiction of a contract, whereby at some unknown period all the members of society engaged to obey the laws, and consented to be punished for any disobedience to them, thereby giving to their legislators the right, which it is assumed they would not otherwise have had, of punishing them, either for their own good or for that of society. This happy thought was considered to get rid of the whole difficulty, and to legitimate the infliction of punishment, in virtue of another received maxim of justice, *Volenti non fit injuria;* that is not unjust which is done with the consent of the person who is supposed to be hurt by it. I need hardly remark, that even if the consent were not a mere fiction, this maxim is not superior in authority to the others which it is brought in to supersede. It is, on the contrary, an instructive specimen of the loose and irregular manner in which supposed principles of justice grow up. This particular one evidently came into use as a help to the coarse exigencies of courts of law, which are sometimes obliged to be content with very uncertain presumptions, on account of the greater evils which would often arise from any attempt on their part to cut finer. But even courts of law are not able to adhere consistently to the maxim, for they allow voluntary engagements to be set aside on the ground of fraud, and sometimes on that of mere mistake or misinformation. . . .

To take another example from a subject already once referred to. In a cooperative industrial association, is it just or not that talent or skill should give a title to superior remuneration? On the negative side of the question it is argued, that whoever does the best he can, deserves equally well, and ought not in justice to be put in a position of inferiority for no fault of his own; that superior abilities have already advantages more than enough, in the admiration they excite, the personal influence they command, and the internal sources of satisfaction attending them, without adding to these a superior share of the world's goods; and that society is bound in justice rather to make compensation to the less favored, for this unmerited inequality of advantages, than to aggravate it. On the contrary side it is contended, that society receives more from the more efficient laborer; that his services being more useful, society owes him a larger return for them; that a greater share of the joint result is actually his work, and not to allow his claim to it is a kind of robbery; that if he is only to receive as much as others, he can only be justly required to produce as much, and to give a smaller amount of time and exertion, proportioned to his superior efficiency. Who shall decide between these appeals to conflicting principles of justice? Justice has in this case two sides to it, which it is impossible to bring into harmony, and the two disputants have chosen opposite sides; the one looks to what it is just that the individual should receive, the other to what it is just that the community should give. Each, from his own point of view, is unanswerable; and any choice between them, on grounds of justice, must be perfectly arbitrary. Social utility alone can decide the preference.

- In the next passage, how does Mill describe the relationship between justice and expediency (utility)?

Is, then, the difference between the just and the expedient a merely imaginary distinction? Have mankind been under a delusion in thinking that justice is a more sacred thing than policy, and that the latter ought only to be listened to after the former has been satisfied? By no means. The exposition we have given of the nature and origin of the sentiment, recognizes a real distinction; and no one of those who profess the most sublime contempt for the consequences of actions as an element in their morality, attaches more importance to the distinction than I do. While I dispute the pretensions of any theory which sets up an imaginary standard of justice not grounded on utility, I account the justice which is grounded on utility to be the chief part, and incomparably the most sacred and binding part, of all morality. Justice is a name for certain classes of moral rules, which concern the essentials of human well-being more nearly, and are therefore of more absolute obligation, than any other rules for the guidance of life; and the notion which we have found to be of the essence of the idea of justice, that of a right residing in an individual implies and testifies to this more binding obligation. . . .

The considerations which have now been adduced resolve, I conceive, the only real difficulty in the utilitarian theory of morals. It has always been evident that all cases of justice are also cases of expediency: the difference is in the peculiar sentiment which attaches to the former, as contradistinguished from the latter. If this characteristic sentiment has been sufficiently accounted for; if there is no necessity to assume for it any peculiarity of origin; if it is simply the natural feeling of resentment, moralized by being made coextensive with the demands of social good; and if this feeling not only does but ought to exist in all the classes of cases to which the idea of justice corresponds; that idea no longer presents itself as a stumbling-block to the utilitarian ethics. Justice remains the appropriate name for certain social utilities which are vastly more important, and therefore more absolute and imperative, than any others are as a class (though not more so than others may be in particular cases); and which, therefore, ought to be, as well as naturally are, guarded by a sentiment not only different in degree, but also in kind; distinguished from the milder feeling which attaches to the mere idea of promoting human pleasure or convenience, at once by the more definite nature of its commands, and by the sterner character of its sanctions.

Since Mill's political philosophy is based on his ethical theory, they rise or fall together. If you think that his ethical principles are the best way of deciding what an individual ought to do, then you probably also think that his political philosophy is the best way of deciding what a society ought to do. At the same time, the objections that were made against his ethical theory are also raised against his political philosophy.

LOOKING THROUGH MILL'S LENS

1. Does Mill's theory dictate a particular form of government, or could it be applied to many different and even incompatible governmental systems? Is this quality a strength or a weakness of the theory?

2. Think about different societies in history and in the world today. In applying his political philosophy, how would Mill evaluate each one? Which ones would he say were good (or just) societies and which ones would he consider bad (or unjust) societies? Why?

3. Think about a current political controversy (e.g., abortion, legalization of marijuana, foreign policy, welfare). Try to imagine what policy Mill would recommend for that controversy in our society.

EXAMINING THE STRENGTHS AND WEAKNESSES OF MILL'S THEORY OF JUSTICE

Positive Evaluation

1. How do we decide if an educational program is a good one? How do we decide if a medicine is safe and effective? How do we decide whether a particular brand of computer is a good buy? In all areas of life, we judge the goodness or badness of a policy or practice in terms of its consequences. Shouldn't the same be true of our social and political policies?

2. What is the purpose of government if not to satisfy of the needs of its citizens? Can't we evaluate a society on this basis without worrying about the natural law or

the alleged social contract? Isn't Mill's principle of utility the most clear and efficient measure of the goodness and justice of a society?

3. Think about situations in which we decided that our society was acting unjustly and we changed the laws (e.g., slavery, discriminatory laws, the lack of women's rights). In all these situations, weren't the changes preceded by social unrest and the realization that large numbers of our citizens were not satisfied with current conditions? In other words, doesn't Mill's political theory describe how we actually go about deciding that a law is unjust?

Negative Evaluation

1. In the first paragraph of the reading, Mill suggests that individual rights are those that are recognized as such by the law or by the general opinion of the community. Is social consensus an adequate way to define an individual's rights with respect to the government? How might a natural law theorist critique this socially defined notion of "rights"?

2. Isn't it possible for the majority of society to be satisfied with the government even though the government and its policies are unjust with respect to those in the minority? Is social utility always consistent with our notion of justice? Does Mill's utilitarian theory have any way of addressing this problem?

3. Isn't it possible for a policy to result in the greatest good for society as a whole while clashing with individual interests? For example, putting a nuclear waste dump in your state (or behind your property) might serve the needs of the rest of the nation, but it might be risky or unpleasant for you. Doesn't utilitarian political philosophy give priority to the public interest over individual interests? Couldn't this priority be unjust?

SURVEYING THE CASE FOR JUSTICE AS FAIRNESS
JOHN RAWLS (BORN 1921)

John Rawls is professor of philosophy at Harvard University and has published many influential articles and books on moral and political philosophy. No book has been more in the forefront of current discussions about political philosophy than Rawls's 1971 book, *A Theory of Justice.* In this book, Rawls attempts to find a balance between individual liberty and rights on the one hand and society's duties and interest in maintaining an equitable distribution of goods on the other hand. In seeking this balance, Rawls sets out a blueprint of a society in which people are encouraged to succeed and better their position, and yet are guaranteed that no one will be hopelessly left behind.

While he doesn't discuss Plato directly, Rawls takes a dim view of a pure meritocracy such as Plato proposes. Rawls argues that people who possess merit in Plato's sense, whether measured by intelligence, personality traits, or other natural gifts, did not earn their abilities but received them as a fortunate accident of birth or circumstances. Such people are no more deserving of a larger share of society's benefits than the winner of a lottery is more deserving of the prize than are the losers. Rawls's alternative to "justice as merit" is "justice as fairness," a system in which justice is directed toward a minimal level of equality.

Rawls directly criticizes the utilitarian theory of Mill. He agrees with utilitarianism's critics that this position opens up the possibility that the general good of the majority could be pursued at the expense of the rights and well-being of some individual or group. If we were completely impartial and did not know ahead of time whether we would be included in the prospering majority, Rawls claims, we would not agree to a social system in which our rights and our goods would be sacrificed for those of the many.

According to Rawls, an adequate theory of justice must be one that will be acceptable to everyone. But how is this general acceptance possible? Each person has different needs, interests, abilities, social circumstances, and agendas. I may think, for example, that it would be just for philosophy professors to be paid the most, but English professors probably would not agree to my notion of justice. Rawls's answer is that people will accept a theory of justice only if they think it is fair. But once again, how can different people in different circumstances agree on what is fair? To solve this problem, Rawls comes up with a clever solution based on a thought experiment. He asks us to imagine that there is as yet no society, but that we are all coming together in a state of perfect equality to create a new society and to decide what principles shall govern it. Rawls calls this initial situation the "original position."

- In what ways is Rawls's notion of the original position similar to Hobbes's and Locke's notion of the state of nature?

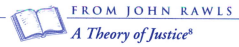

FROM JOHN RAWLS
A Theory of Justice[8]

The Main Idea of the Theory of Justice

My aim is to present a conception of justice which generalizes and carries to a higher level of abstraction the familiar theory of the social contract as found, say, in Locke, Rousseau, and Kant. In order to do this we are not to think of the original contract as one to enter a particular society or to set up a particular form of government. Rather, the guiding idea is that the principles of justice for the basic structure of society are the object of the original agreement. They are the principles that free and rational persons concerned to further their own interests would accept in an initial position of equality as defining the fundamental terms of their association. These principles are to regulate all further agreements; they specify the kinds of social cooperation that can be entered into and the forms of government that can be established. This way of regarding the principles of justice I shall call justice as fairness.

Thus we are to imagine that those who engage in social cooperation choose together, in one joint act, the principles which are to assign basic rights and duties and to determine the division of social benefits. Men are to decide in advance how they are to regulate their claims against one another and what is to be the foundation charter of their society. Just as each person must decide by rational reflection what constitutes his good, that is, the system of ends which it is rational for him to pursue, so a group of persons must decide once and for all what is to count among them as just and unjust. The choice which rational men would make in this hypothetical situation of equal liberty, assuming for the present that this choice problem has a solution, determines the principles of justice.

In justice as fairness the original position of equality corresponds to the state of nature in the traditional theory of the social contract. This original position is not, of course, thought of as an actual historical state of affairs, much less as a primitive condition of culture. It is understood as a purely hypothetical situation characterized so as to lead to a certain conception of justice.

Many philosophers would say (contrary to Rawls) that in our current society, those people who have the most gifts or the most superior character should have the greater advantage over the rest. In other words, the critics claim, if you are very intelligent, athletic, or good-looking on the one hand (natural gifts), or if you are persistent, highly motivated, or optimistic on the other hand (superior character), you have a right to reap society's richest rewards (such as wealth, fame, or opportunities) by making use of your gifts or character traits. But Rawls argues that this position is indefensible.

- In the following passage, how does Rawls respond to the suggestion that those people who are naturally superior have no obligations to others but deserve all the advantages their abilities bring them?

Perhaps some will think that the person with greater natural endowments deserves those assets and the superior character that made their development possible. Because he is more worthy in this sense, he deserves the greater advantages that he could achieve with them. This view, however, is surely incorrect. It seems to be one of the fixed points of our considered judgments that no one deserves his place in the distribution of native endowments, any more than one deserves one's initial starting place in society. The assertion that a man deserves the superior character that enables him to make the effort to cultivate his abilities is equally problematic; for his character depends in large part upon fortunate family and social circumstances for which he can claim no credit. The notion of desert seems not to apply to these cases. Thus the more advantaged representative man cannot say that he deserves and therefore has a right to a scheme of cooperation in which he is permitted to acquire benefits in ways that do not contribute to the welfare of others. There is no basis for his making this claim.

You are a person of a particular gender, race, age, physical condition, personality, education, and certain social and economic circumstances. Given these facts, what would be the ideal society for you that would enable you to flourish and achieve maximum gains?

The problem that Rawls wrestles with is that everyone has different circumstances and so would want to design a society that would enhance his or her own life. Consequently, it seems impossible to figure out how everyone could ever come to agree on the principles that will govern society in a way that will be fair to all. In the next passage, Rawls solves this problem by adding one more crucial feature to his thought experiment concerning the original position.

• State in your own words what Rawls means by the "veil of ignorance."

The Veil of Ignorance

The idea of the original position is to set up a fair procedure so that any principles agreed to will be just. The aim is to use the notion of pure procedural justice as a basis of theory. Somehow we must nullify the effects of specific contingencies which put men at odds and tempt them to exploit social and natural circumstances to their own advantage. Now in order to do this I assume that the parties are situated behind a veil of ignorance. They do not know how the various alternatives will affect their own particular case and they are obliged to evaluate principles solely on the basis of general considerations.

It is assumed, then, that the parties do not know certain kinds of particular facts. First of all, no one knows his place in society, his class position or social status; nor does he know his fortune in the distribution of natural assets and abilities, his intelligence and strength, and the like. Nor, again, does anyone know his conception of the good, the particulars of his rational plan of life, or even the special features of his psychology such as his aversion to risk or liability to optimism or pessimism. More than this, I assume that the parties do not know the particular circumstances of their own society. That is, they do not know its economic or political situation, or the level of civilization and culture it has been able to achieve. The persons in the original position have no information as to which generation they belong. These broader restrictions on knowledge are appropriate in part because questions of social justice arise between generations as well as within them, for example, the question of the appropriate rate of capital saving and of the conservation of natural resources and the environment of nature. There is also, theoretically anyway, the question of a reasonable genetic policy. In these cases too, in order to carry through the idea of the original position, the parties must not know the contingencies that set them in opposition. They must choose principles the consequences of which they are prepared to live with whatever generation they turn out to belong to. . . .

Thus there follows the very important consequence that the parties have no basis for bargaining in the usual sense. No one knows his situation in society nor his natural assets, and therefore no one is in a position to tailor principles to his advantage. We might imagine that one of the contractees threatens to hold out unless the others agree to principles favorable to him. But how does he know which principles are especially in his interests? The same holds for the formation of coalitions: if a group were to decide to band together to the disadvantage of the others, they would not know how to favor themselves in the choice of principles. Even if they could get everyone to agree to their proposal, they would have no assurance that it was to their advantage, since they cannot identify themselves either by name or description. . . .

The restrictions on particular information in the original position are, then, of fundamental importance. Without them we would not be able to work out any definite theory of justice at all. We would have to be content with a vague formula stating that justice is what would be agreed to without being able to say much, if anything, about the substance of the agreement itself. The formal constraints of the concept of right, those applying to principles directly, are not sufficient for our purpose. The veil of ignorance makes possible a unanimous choice of a particular conception of justice. Without these limitations on knowledge the bargaining problem of the original position would be hopelessly complicated. Even if theoretically a solution were to exist, we would not, at present anyway, be able to determine it.

- Imagine that while you are behind the veil of ignorance you must decide what principles should govern society. How would this cloak make it possible for you and everyone else to be impartial and fair in deciding what would be the best society?
- If you were in this situation, how would you want society to be run? What principles would you choose?

In the next passage, Rawls sets out two principles of justice that he thinks all rational persons would choose if they were ideally impartial and fair—that is, if they had to choose a political philosophy from behind the veil of ignorance.

Two Principles of Justice

I shall now state in a provisional form the two principles of justice that I believe would be chosen in the original position. . . .

The first statement of the two principles reads as follows.

First: each person is to have an equal right to the most extensive basic liberty compatible with a similar liberty for others.

Second: social and economic inequalities are to be arranged so that they are both (a) reasonably expected to be to everyone's advantage, and (b) attached to positions and offices open to all. . . .

By way of general comment, these principles primarily apply, as I have said, to the basic structure of society. They are to govern the assignment of rights and duties and to regulate the distribution of social and economic advantages. As their formulation suggests, these principles presuppose that the social structure can be divided into two more or less distinct parts, the first principle applying to the one, the second to the other. They distinguish between those aspects of the social system that define and secure the equal liberties of citizenship and those that specify and establish social and economic inequalities. The basic liberties of citizens are, roughly speaking, political liberty (the right to vote and to be eligible for public office) together with freedom of speech and assembly; liberty of conscience and freedom of thought; freedom of the person along with the right to hold (personal) property; and freedom from arbitrary arrest and seizure as defined by the concept of the rule of law. These liberties are all required to be equal by the first principle, since citizens of a just society are to have the same basic rights.

The second principle applies, in the first approximation to the distribution of income and wealth and to the design of organizations that make use of differences in authority and responsibility, or chains of command. While the distribution of wealth and income need not be equal, it must be to everyone's advantage, and at the same time, positions of authority and offices of command must be accessible to all. One applies the second principle by holding positions open, and then, subject to this constraint, arranges social and economic inequalities so that everyone benefits.

Principle 1 is the *principle of equal liberty*, which applies to our political institutions. Basically, it says that everyone should have the maximum amount of political rights and freedom as long as everyone has an equal amount of these liberties. For example, to allow everyone an equal right to have their opinion heard at a public meeting, it will be necessary to restrict one group from speaking as much as they may like. Principle 2 applies to society's social and economic institutions. Unlike in the political sphere, where absolute equality is necessary, in the social and economic spheres it is inevitable and even good that some inequalities be allowed. If a person who risked her life savings to invent a better computer received no greater reward than someone who risked nothing and produced nothing new, she would be discouraged from productivity and innovation. Rewarding people for their extraordinary achievements and hard work will motivate them to be more creative and productive, and as a result, society as a whole will benefit. If the efforts of the computer inventor are successful, more jobs will be created, the world will have better computers, and other people will strive to excel. The first half of this principle is what Rawls calls the *difference principle*. He calls it this because it focuses on the differences among people. This principle states that social and economic inequalities should be arranged so they result in everyone's advantage. What does this statement mean? Obviously, if people are unequal, then those who have more are already reaping an advantage. So, the difference principle implies that those who are on the short end of a situation of inequality also should gain some benefit from it in the long run. Indeed, in a later passage Rawls spells out this point by saying that such inequalities should be "to the greatest benefit of the least advantaged."[9] For example, if your physician earns more money than you do, isn't that still to your advantage if it means that you receive better medical care?

Rawls doesn't discuss specific policies in his book, but there are many ways to bring about this balance between the goal of allowing people to achieve all they can and the goal of providing for the least advantaged. One way is to provide food, shelter, medical care, education, and job opportunities for the least advantaged through such devices as corporate, income, and luxury taxes. Another way is for society to provide incentives for those who have achieved the most to compensate the less well-off through the creation of jobs and charitable contributions. Only in this way will society achieve stability, for revolutions are nurtured in situations in which extreme wealth and extreme poverty exist side by side. Rawls believes that rational persons in the original position would favor the difference principle because they might end up in the neediest group. Many corporate executives who used to rail against welfare came to appreciate unemployment benefits when they suddenly found themselves laid off and having difficulties securing a new job.

The latter half of the second principle is the *principle of fair equality of opportunity.* This principle says that the opportunities to achieve more than the basic minimum should be open to all. In other words, a caste system or an aristocracy in which people are locked into their social or economic niche would not be just, even if the least advantaged were being taken care of. There should be no intrinsic barriers to moving from the least advantaged to the most advantaged. This feature of society is certainly one that we all would want if we were behind the veil of ignorance and did not know where we would land in the social and economic hierarchy.

Whenever two or more principles govern our actions, the question always arises: What if the principles conflict? Which one has priority? Plato's society, for example, had a fairly even distribution of wealth. The society was not divided between the "haves" and the "have-nots." In fact, the common people were allowed to accumulate property and private possessions, while the rulers were not. However, the common people had no voice in politics and few of the political liberties we enjoy. In other words, Plato gave priority to principle 2 (economic justice) over principle 1 (political equality).

- In the following passage, how does Rawls address these issues?

These principles are to be arranged in a serial order with the first principle prior to the second. This ordering means that a departure from the institutions of equal liberty required by the first principle cannot be justified by, or compensated for, by greater social and economic advantages. The distribution of wealth and income, and the hierarchies of authority, must be consistent with both the liberties of equal citizenship and equality of opportunity.

. . . For the present, it should be observed that the two principles (and this holds for all formulations) are a special case of a more general conception of justice that can be expressed as follows.

> All social values—liberty and opportunity, income and wealth, and the bases of self-respect—are to be distributed equally unless an unequal distribution of any, or all, of these values is to everyone's advantage.

Injustice, then, is simply inequalities that are not to the benefit of all. Of course, this conception is extremely vague and requires interpretation.

As a first step, suppose that the basic structure of society distributes certain primary goods, that is, things that every rational man is presumed to want. These goods normally have a use whatever a person's rational plan of life. For simplicity, assume that the chief primary goods at the disposition of society are rights and liberties, powers and opportunities, income and wealth. . . . These are the social primary goods. Other primary goods such as health and vigor, intelligence and imagination, are natural goods; although their possession is influenced by the basic structure, they are not so directly under its control. Imagine, then, a hypothetical initial arrangement in which all the social primary goods are equally distributed: everyone has similar rights and duties, and income and wealth are evenly shared. This state of affairs provides a benchmark for judging improvements. If certain inequalities of wealth and organizational powers would make everyone better off than in this hypothetical starting situation, then they accord with the general conception.

Now it is possible, at least theoretically, that by giving up some of their fundamental liberties men are sufficiently compensated by the resulting social and economic gains. The general conception of justice imposes no restrictions on what sort of inequalities are permissible; it only requires that everyone's position be improved. We need not suppose anything so drastic as consenting to a condition of slavery. Imagine instead that men forego certain political rights when the economic returns are significant and their capacity to influence the course of policy by the exercise of these rights would be marginal in any case. It is this kind of exchange which the two principles as stated rule out; being arranged in serial order they do not permit exchanges between basic liberties and economic and social gains. The serial ordering of principles expresses an underlying preference among primary social goods. When this preference is rational so likewise is the choice of these principles in this order.

A Feminist Critique of Rawls

While John Rawls is often thought to be the spokesperson for contemporary liberalism, some feminists think that his theory of justice contains important gaps and flaws. In her book *Justice, Gender, and the Family*, Stanford University professor Susan Moller Okin critically analyzes Rawls's account. She begins with the general problem that even though American society is built on the principle of equality of opportunity, the implications of this principle have not been fully realized.

FROM SUSAN MOLLER OKIN

Justice, Gender, and the Family[10]

Yet substantial inequities between the sexes still exist in our society. In economic terms, full-time working women (after some very recent improvement) earn on average 71 percent of the earnings of full-time working men. One-half of poor and three-fifths of chronically poor households with dependent children are maintained by a single female parent. The poverty rate for elderly women is nearly twice that for elderly men.

Okin goes on to note the disproportionate burdens that women bear in child rearing and housework. Furthermore, she cites the fact that, in spite of great strides, women are still underrepresented in legislative bodies, judgeships, and other professional offices. As I pointed out earlier (section 5.6, "Rethinking the Western Tradition: Feminist Ethics"), feminists criticize ethical and political theorists who focus on public morality while ignoring what goes on in families and who ignore the role of gender in their account of human relationships. She takes this shortcoming of contemporary political theories as the focus of her book:

Yet, remarkably, major contemporary theorists of justice have almost without exception ignored the situation I have just described [the status of women]. They have displayed little interest in or knowledge of the findings of feminism. They have largely bypassed the fact that the society to which their theories are supposed to pertain is heavily and deeply affected by gender, and faces difficult issues of justice stemming from its gendered past and present assumptions. Since theories of justice are centrally concerned with whether, how, or why persons should be treated differently from one another, this neglect seems inexplicable. . . . [Justice, Gender, and the Family] is about this remarkable case of neglect. It is also an attempt to . . . point the way toward a more fully humanist theory of justice by confronting the question, "How just is gender?"

While acknowledging that Rawls's book is not blatantly sexist, Okin still finds it problematic, particularly in the male biases that creep into his choice of terms:

Men, mankind, he, and *his* are interspersed with gender-neutral terms of reference such as *individual* and *moral person.* Examples of intergenerational concern are worded in terms of "fathers" and "sons." . . .

Thus, there is a blindness to the sexism of the tradition in which Rawls is a participant, which tends to render his terms of reference more ambiguous than they might otherwise be. A feminist reader finds it difficult not to keep asking, Does this theory apply to women?

To Rawls's credit, he does say that our sex is one of the features of nature's lottery that we cannot know behind the veil of ignorance. But feminist critics such as Okin point out that Rawls appears to forget his comment when he describes the original position: "Among the essential features of this situation is that no one knows *his* place in society, *his* class position or social status, nor does any one know *his* fortune in the distribution of natural assets and abilities, *his* intelligence, strength, and the like" (emphasis added).[11] To this, Okin says, "one might think that whether or not they knew their sex might matter enough to be mentioned. Perhaps, Rawls meant to cover it by his phrase 'and the like,' but it is also possible that he did not consider it significant."[12] Okin goes on to observe that knowledge of a person's gender is more significant than Rawls seems to imply:

The significance of Rawls's central, brilliant idea, the original position, is that it forces one to question and consider traditions, customs, and institutions from all points of view, and ensures that the principles of justice will be acceptable to everyone, regardless of what position "he" ends up in. . . . The theory, in principle, avoids both the problem of domination that is inherent in theories of justice based on traditions or shared understandings and the partiality of libertarian theory to those who are talented or fortunate. For feminist readers, however, the problem of the theory as stated by Rawls himself is encapsulated in the ambiguous "he." . . . If, however, we read Rawls in such a way as to take seriously both the notion that those behind the veil of ignorance do not know what sex they are and the requirement that the family and gender system, as basic social institutions, are to be subject to scrutiny, constructive feminist criticism of these contemporary institutions follows. . . .

Finally . . . if those in the original position did not know whether they were to be men or women, they would surely be concerned to establish a thoroughgoing social and economic equality between the sexes that would protect either sex from the need to pander to or servilely provide for the pleasure of the other. They would emphasize the importance of girls and boys growing up with an equal sense of respect for themselves and equal expectations of self-definition and development. . . . In general, they would be unlikely to tolerate basic social institutions that asymmetrically either forced or gave strong incentives to members of one sex to serve as sex objects for the other.

. . . I reach the conclusions not only that our current gender structure is incompatible with the attainment of social justice, but also that the disappearance of gender is a prerequisite for the *complete* development of a nonsexist, fully human theory of justice.

 THOUGHT EXPERIMENT

The Original Position

- If you were in Rawls's original position but knew you would be a male, would you be satisfied with the way your current society treats males, or would you want to make some changes?

(Continued . . .)

(. . . continued)

- If you knew that you would be a female, would you be satisfied with your current society, or would you want to make some changes?
- If you were able to design the society in which you would live but didn't know what gender you would be in this society, are there any changes to our current society that you would make with respect to the status of either men or women?

LOOKING THROUGH RAWLS'S LENS

1. Hobbes's and Locke's social contract theory was an attempt to explain the existence of the governments that actually exist. Rawls's social contract theory, however, is not concerned with the past but is a way of thinking about what sort of government we ought to have. Do you think that his use of the social contract theory avoids some of the criticisms of Hobbes's and Locke's versions?

2. Rawls has given us principles that apply to our political, social, and economic institutions: the principle of equal liberty, the difference principle, and the principle of fair equality of opportunity. Which one of these three do you think is given priority in our society?

3. If we adopted Rawls's theory, what changes would be made in our current society? Do you think these changes would make our society better or worse?

EXAMINING THE STRENGTHS AND WEAKNESSES OF RAWLS'S THEORY OF JUSTICE

Positive Evaluation

1. Most people would agree that a just government is one that treats everyone fairly. Would you agree that Rawls's original position and veil of ignorance scenarios are an effective way of getting us to think in an objective fashion without favoritism toward anyone?

2. Most societies are faced with a dilemma. If they strive for complete economic equality by distributing wealth equally, they will stifle the incentive of the high achievers and productivity will suffer. On the other hand, since a person's abilities are mainly a gift of fortune, neglecting the disadvantaged would be unfair and the result could be vast social and economic inequalities that would make the society unstable. Rawls solves this problem by guaranteeing that any social and economic inequalities will always result in benefits to the disadvantaged. Do you think Rawls makes an effective compromise between allowing people to achieve and get all they can while not leaving the rest too far behind?

3. The French Revolution was caused (in part) by the large-scale social and economic inequalities of that society. The fall of the former U.S.S.R. was caused (in part) by the lack of political liberty and economic productivity. Hasn't Rawls

avoided these problems by insisting on both economic justice and political liberty? Doesn't his theory capture our present-day Western social, economic, and political ideals that have seemed to work reasonably well?

Negative Evaluation

1. One of Rawls's strongest critics is his Harvard colleague Robert Nozick (born 1938). Nozick charges that Rawls's theory says that society should play some role in dictating how wealth and goods should be distributed among its members. But Nozick thinks that in applying its formula, a society will have to interfere with people's political liberties. If, for example, sports fans wish to buy tickets to watch a famous basketball star and the star becomes a millionaire as a result, this economic inequality is not unjust if it is based on people's free choices. Do you think this criticism is fair?

2. Consider four poker players about to start a high-stakes game. In one sense, they are behind the veil of ignorance because none of them knows who will win. Even though some of them may lose all their money, none of them would want to change the rules of the game to redistribute the winnings after it is all over. They are each willing to risk a great loss for the chance of a big win. Does this situation suggest that people behind the veil of ignorance will not always choose to diminish inequalities as Rawls suggests?

3. Critics of Rawls, such as Nozick, who give priority to individual liberty (known as "political libertarians") say that Rawls sacrifices the individual's good for the good of society. On the other hand, critics who believe that the common good is more important than individual liberty say that society is like a biological organism whose overall well-being should receive the priority. In seeking a compromise between these two concerns, has Rawls achieved the "best of both worlds," or has he actually ended up with the "worst of both worlds"? In other words, does his political philosophy try to serve two incompatible goals?

6.3 THE INDIVIDUAL AND THE STATE

LEADING QUESTIONS: *The Individual and the State*

1. *Questions from classical liberalism:* Who potentially has the most power, the government or a single individual? Since the government obviously has the most power, shouldn't the protection of our individual liberties be the priority in any political philosophy?

2. *Questions from classical liberalism:* Who knows best what is in your own interest, you or the government? Even if you make choices that are not in your best interest, as long as those choices harm no one but yourself, does the government have the right to act as your parent by controlling your actions? Won't the best

society be achieved if people are allowed to pursue their own interests as best they can, without the government intervening?

3. *Questions from the Marxist:* Who has the most political power and influence in society, the working poor or the wealthy? Who is in the majority, the working poor or the wealthy? Isn't there something unjust about a social structure in which the workers make up the bulk of society but have the least power and the wealthy are the elite minority but have the most power?

4. *Questions from the Marxist:* Suppose you lived in a society that claimed to be perfectly just and moral. Furthermore, suppose a few people managed to accumulate all the wealth in the society and were able to pass it on to their children without sharing any of it for the common good. However, those citizens who were born disadvantaged through no fault of their own were forced by desperation to work for starvation wages and had little opportunity to break out of the chains of their poverty. Suppose further that the government and its laws served the interests of the wealthy but turned a deaf ear to the needs of the disadvantaged. Would this society be able to defend its claim of being perfectly just and moral?

As the four leading questions suggest, both the protection of individual freedoms and governmental concern for the common good are important ingredients in a good society. The problem is that there is an inevitable tension between the two. Some political thinkers try to eliminate the tension by advocating one extreme or the other. On the side of individual freedom, the most extreme position is *anarchism* (discussed in section 6.1), which claims that no government ever has a right to interfere with human autonomy. At the other extreme is *absolute totalitarianism,* which claims that individual freedom and rights always should be sacrificed for the good of the society. Under absolute totalitarianism, the government controls virtually every sphere of human life. A fictional representation of life under a totalitarian government is found in George Orwell's novel *1984.* The residence of every citizen contains a television on which the figure of Big Brother (who represents the government) shouts political propaganda and leads the citizens in state-enforced calisthenics. To make sure that each citizen's every action is in compliance with the government, television cameras monitor every movement at home and outside.

These two extreme positions are untenable to most people. There are, however, more moderate positions that place priority on either individual freedom or government control without eliminating the other concern entirely. Those positions that emphasize individual freedom could be called *individualism.* One of the most important versions of this viewpoint was classical liberalism. In this section, we look at this position as it was represented by the nineteenth-century English philosopher John Stuart Mill. Those positions that subordinate individual liberty to the needs of society could be called *collectivism* because they believe that the collective or the common good is all-important. Representing collectivism in this section is the nineteenth-century German philosopher Karl Marx. Although both these thinkers were writing more than a century ago, their ideas were so important that they still influence contemporary political philosophers.

SURVEYING THE CASE FOR CLASSICAL LIBERALISM

Today, the word *liberal* is associated with left-wing politics and the promotion of big government. However, the position we are examining here is *classical* liberalism as developed by such thinkers as the English philosophers John Locke in the seventeenth century and John Stuart Mill in the nineteenth century. (Locke's and Mill's political philosophies have been introduced in sections 6.1 and 6.2 respectively.) *Liberalism* comes from the Latin word *libertas,* which means "liberty" or "freedom." Hence, classical liberalism emphasizes the freedom of the individual. This emphasis includes individual freedom *from* inappropriate government control and the individual's freedom *to* pursue his or her legitimate individual interests. Ironically, those who are called liberals and those who are called conservatives in today's terminology, in spite of their differences, both promote this sort of freedom. One difference between them is how they work out the details. In other words, liberals and conservatives differ in their conceptions of what is "inappropriate" government control and "legitimate" individual interests. The point is that you can find the basic principles of classical liberalism woven into our whole social and political system whether you lean to the left or to the right.

JOHN STUART MILL

We first encountered John Stuart Mill in the section on utilitarian ethics (5.3), where a brief account of his life may be found. We also looked at his theory of justice in section 6.2. Previous democratic thinkers had been so concerned about defending the rights of the citizens from the tyranny of the king that they had ignored the sort of tyranny that can arise in a democracy—the tyranny of the majority. Realizing that the will of the majority, when enforced by the state, could be as oppressive as any monarch, Mill sought for principles that would limit the power of the government over individual lives. From his standpoint, censorship, intolerance, government-imposed morality, and legislated conformity are some of the greatest dangers that a society can face, for unlike a foreign invader, they arise in the midst of a society and masquerade as defenders of the social good. However, allowing total individual freedom is not feasible either, for society needs to prevent individuals from harming one another and from undermining the general welfare. With these problems in mind, Mill published *On Liberty* in 1859 to establish the proper balance between governmental control and individual freedom. Since then, it has become a classic and is one of the most influential essays ever published on this topic.

- According to Mill, what is the "one very simple principle" that determines when society is allowed to impose its will on an individual?
- Does Mill believe it is legitimate for society to force you to act in a certain way for the sake of your own self-interest?

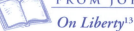

On Liberty[13]

The object of this Essay is to assert one very simple principle, as entitled to govern absolutely the dealings of society with the individual in the way of compulsion and control, whether the means used be physical force in the form of legal penalties, or the moral coercion of public opinion. That principle is, that the sole end for which mankind are warranted, individually or collectively in interfering with the liberty of action of any of their number, is self-protection. That the only purpose for which power can be rightfully exercised over any member of a civilized community, against his will, is to prevent harm to others. His own good, either physical or moral, is not a sufficient warrant. He cannot rightfully be compelled to do or forbear because it will be better for him to do so, because it will make him happier, because, in the opinions of others, to do so would be wise, or even right. These are good reasons for remonstrating with him, or reasoning with him, or persuading him, or entreating him, but not for compelling him, or visiting him with any evil, in case he do otherwise. To justify that, the conduct from which it is desired to deter him must be calculated to produce evil to some one else. The only part of the conduct of any one, for which he is amenable to society, is that which concerns others. In the part which merely concerns himself, his independence is, of right, absolute. Over himself, over his own body and mind, the individual is sovereign.

Obviously, Mill does not believe in governmental paternalism, the view that the government should play the role of our parent by forcing us to do what it thinks is best for us. Because individual autonomy is essential for people and societies to flourish, Mill says the state cannot intrude on the sphere of your personal life. He provides one exception to this rule, however. In the case of children or others who do not have the rational capacity to make their own decisions, it is legitimate for adults and even society to protect them from their own actions that may be harmful to themselves. As long as you are an adult and of a sound mind, however, and even if your actions are unwise, imprudent, or self-destructive, society has no authority to interfere with your freedom in order to protect you from yourself. In other words, it is *your* life and you have a right to live it as you please. There are only two conditions under which the government has a legitimate interest in controlling your behavior. One condition is when such interference will prevent harm to others. As the old cliché goes, your right to swing your arm ends at the tip of my nose. The second condition in which the government may compel you to act a certain way is when it is essential that you help society or another person. Examples would be serving in the army, serving on a jury, or rescuing a drowning person. In these cases, your private actions have effects on the public sphere, where the government has its proper domain of authority.

In the next passage, Mill states that his political philosophy does not rest on the notion of "individual rights." This idea is too vague and abstract for the utilitarians.

Rights are incapable of observation, which is why there is so much disagreement over what rights we have. Instead, the utilitarians want ethics and political theory to be based on empirical, scientific observations of human nature and the observable consequences of behavior. Accordingly, Mill states that his view of society is based on the principle of utility, or the principle that determines the rightness or wrongness of actions and public policies in terms of the observable good consequences they produce or the harms they prevent. While Mill sometimes talks about "rights," he believes that these rights are not intrinsic or built into human nature but are given to us by law and social consensus and are based on the principle of utility.

- In the next paragraph, Mill concerns himself with the question of when society may force you *not to do* something or punish you for what you have done. He also speaks of when society may compel you *to perform* an action or hold you responsible for failing to act. What considerations govern each of these situations?

It is proper to state that I forego any advantage which could be derived to my argument from the idea of abstract right as a thing independent of utility. I regard utility as the ultimate appeal on all ethical questions; but it must be utility in the largest sense, grounded on the permanent interests of man as a progressive being. Those interests, I contend, authorize the subjection of individual spontaneity to external control, only in respect to those actions of each, which concern the interest of other people. If any one does an act hurtful to others, there is a prima facie case for punishing him, by law, or, where legal penalties are not safely applicable, by general disapprobation. There are also many positive acts for the benefit of others, which he may rightfully be compelled to perform; such as, to give evidence in a court of justice; to bear his fair share in the common defence, or in any other joint work necessary to the interest of the society of which he enjoys the protection; and to perform certain acts of individual beneficence, such as saving a fellow-creature's life, or interposing to protect the defenceless against ill-usage, things which whenever it is obviously a man's duty to do, he may rightfully be made responsible to society for not doing. A person may cause evil to others not only by his actions but by his inaction, and in neither case he is justly accountable to them for the injury. The latter case, it is true, requires a much more cautious exercise of compulsion than the former. To make any one answerable for doing evil to others, is the rule; to make him answerable for not preventing evil, is, comparatively speaking, the exception. Yet there are many cases clear enough and grave enough to justify that exception. In all things which regard the external relations of the individual, he is de jure amenable to those whose interests are concerned, and if need be, to society as their protector. There are often good reasons for not holding him to the responsibility; but these reasons must arise from the special expediencies of the case: either because it is a kind of case in which he is on the whole likely to act better, when left to his own discretion, than when controlled in any way in which society have it in their power to control him; or because the attempt to exercise control would produce other evils, greater than those which it would prevent. When such reasons as these preclude the enforcement of responsibility, the conscience of the agent himself should step into the vacant judgment-seat, and protect those interests of others which have no external protection; judging himself all the more rigidly, because the case does not admit of his being made accountable to the judgment of his fellow-creatures.

- As you read the next passage, make a list of the various kinds of individual liberties Mill thinks the government should protect.

But there is a sphere of action in which society, as distinguished from the individual, has, if any, only an indirect interest; comprehending all that portion of a person's life and conduct which affects only himself, or, if it also affects others, only with their free, voluntary, and undeceived consent and participation. When I say only himself, I mean directly, and in the first instance: for whatever affects himself, may affect others through himself; and the objection which may be grounded on this contingency, will receive consideration in the sequel. This, then, is the appropriate region of human liberty. It comprises, first, the inward domain of consciousness; demanding liberty of conscience, in the most comprehensive sense; liberty of thought and feeling; absolute freedom of opinion and sentiment on all subjects, practical or speculative, scientific, moral, or theological. The liberty of expressing and publishing opinions may seem to fall under a different principle, since it belongs to that part of the conduct of an individual which concerns other people; but, being almost of as much importance as the liberty of thought itself, and resting in great part on the same reasons, is practically inseparable from it. Secondly, the principle requires liberty of tastes and pursuits; of framing the plan of our life to suit our own character; of doing as we like, subject to such consequences as may follow; without impediment from our fellow-creatures, so long as what we do does not harm them even though they should think our conduct foolish, perverse, or wrong. Thirdly, from this liberty of each individual, follows the liberty, within the same limits, of combination among individuals; freedom to unite, for any purpose not involving harm to others: the persons combining being supposed to be of full age, and not forced or deceived.

No society in which these liberties are not, on the whole, respected, is free, whatever may be its form of government; and none is completely free in which they do not exist absolute and unqualified. The only freedom which deserves the name, is that of pursuing our own good in our own way, so long as we do not attempt to deprive others of theirs, or impede their efforts to obtain it. Each is the proper guardian of his own health, whether bodily, or mental or spiritual. Mankind are greater gainers by suffering each other to live as seems good to themselves, than by compelling each to live as seems good to the rest.

Interpreting Mill's discussion, we could say that the sphere of individual liberty can be divided into two main sectors. The first is our inward life in which there is the absolute right to freedom of thought and expression. While Mill recognizes that speaking or publishing our opinions intrudes on the public sphere, he thinks that our personal opinions are so intimately related to the sanctity of our individual conscience that it is a natural extension of the personal sphere. The second sector of individual liberty concerns our outward life, which involves our choices and actions. Let's discuss each sphere in turn.

Mill's discussion of the first realm of freedom, the right to free expression and discussion of ideas, has been enormously influential and is the basis of much of our thinking about free speech today. Because he devotes the entire second chapter of his book to this issue, I can only summarize his main points here. Mill says that society is harmed by the suppression of free speech regardless of whether the ideas in question are true or false. First, the unpopular idea that is suppressed may, in fact, be true. In this case, it will not get a fair hearing, and society's need to correct its false beliefs will not be met. The case of Galileo showed that the majority is often wrong and the nonconformist is right. Since we are not infallible, we need to be exposed to ideas that will make us check the soundness of our beliefs. Second, even if an idea is false, we still should allow it to be heard in order to expose it to the light of free discussion so that its errors may be revealed and so that the outlines of the true opinion can be seen more clearly. Third, even when their ideas are false, dissenters from the ideological status quo make a contribution because they prevent intellectual stagnation and force us to reexamine the grounds for the prevailing convictions. Unless this scrutiny is done, a true opinion will become "a dead dogma, not a living truth." Notice that Mill defends freedom of speech not because it is an intrinsic "right" that individuals possess, but because it will produce the greatest good for society in the long run.

The only restriction on free speech Mill allowed was when it threatened to cause immediate harm. However, this situation is not really an exception to his rule, because his whole theory of personal liberty is based entirely on what will promote the social good and prevent harm. The example he provides is:

> An opinion that corn-dealers are starvers of the poor . . . ought to be unmolested when simply circulated through the press, but may justly incur punishment when delivered orally to an excited mob assembled before the house of a corn-dealer.[14]

This principle found its way into the "clear and present danger" criteria that the U.S. Supreme Court uses to determine when free speech may be limited.

With respect to the second sphere of individual liberty, that of personal choices and overt actions, Mill continues to guard the freedom of the individual from the intrusion of the government. He recognizes, however, that it is difficult to maintain the correct balance here between the individual's interests and society's interests. Let's begin with his general statement of the issue.

- Notice in the following passage that when Mill talks about "rights," he says that they are the result of "legal provision or tacit understanding." They are socially "constituted" rights, meaning they are not intrinsic to us apart from a social context. What are some implications of the view that there are no intrinsic rights apart from society?

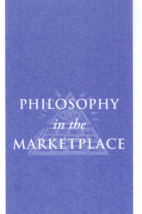

Give five people outside your class the following list. Ask them which of the following items, if any, should *not* be protected under the U.S. Constitution's guarantee of freedom of speech. Ask them to justify their answers.

1. prayer in public schools
2. expressing the opinion in public that an unpopular president should be assassinated
3. burning the country's flag as a form of political protest
4. advocating the overthrow of the government
5. expressing hate speech in public toward a particular racial group
6. distributing pornography to adults
7. shouting "fire" in a crowded theater as a joke
8. publishing sensational lies about a movie star in a Hollywood gossip magazine
9. publicly proclaiming that all religions are fraudulent

After gathering the answers, decide which views would conform most closely to Mill's principles on personal liberty and which forms of public expression Mill would not allow.

- Mill says that some actions may harm others but not to the extent that they should be punishable by law. Does he then conclude that no punishment of any sort is appropriate? Do we have to refrain from all judgments about such actions? What would be some examples of actions that are, in some sense, harmful to others but are not serious enough to be illegal? How should society respond to such actions?

What, then, is the rightful limit to the sovereignty of the individual over himself? Where does the authority of society begin? How much of human life should be assigned to individuality, and how much to society?

Each will receive its proper share, if each has that which more particularly concerns it. To individuality should belong the part of life in which it is chiefly the individual that is interested; to society, the part which chiefly interests society.

Though society is not founded on a contract, and though no good purpose is answered by inventing a contract in order to deduce social obligations from it, every one who receives the protection of society owes a return for the benefit, and the fact of living in society renders it indispensable that each should be bound to observe a certain line of conduct towards the rest. This conduct consists, first, in not injuring the interests of one another; or rather certain interests, which, either by express legal provision or by tacit understanding, ought to be considered as rights; and secondly, in each person's bearing his share (to be fixed on some equitable principle) of the labors and sacrifices incurred for defending the society or its members from injury and molestation. These conditions society is justified in enforcing, at all costs to those who endeavor to withhold fulfilment. Nor is this all that society may do. The acts of an individual may be hurtful to others, or wanting in due consideration for their welfare, without going the length of violating any of their constituted rights. The offender may then be justly punished by opinion, though not by law. As soon as any part of a person's conduct affects prejudicially the interests of others, society has jurisdiction over it, and the question whether the general welfare will or will not be promoted by interfering with it, becomes open to discussion. But there is no room for entertaining any such question when a person's conduct affects the interests of no persons besides himself, or needs not affect them unless they like (all the persons concerned being of full age, and the ordinary amount of understanding). In all such cases there should be perfect freedom, legal and social, to do the action and stand the consequences.

 THOUGHT EXPERIMENT

Private versus Public Interests

Mill has just expressed the principle that "to individuality should belong the part of life in which it is chiefly the individual that is interested; to society, the part which chiefly interests society." Consider the following list of actions (assume that they are all performed by an adult). Assign each action to one of the following three categories:

(a) This action is a matter of personal choice, and society should have nothing to say about it.

(b) This action affects the interests of society, and laws should govern it. (Ignore the question of whether the action currently is illegal or not.)

(c) This action should not be illegal, but the person should be criticized and persuaded not to do it, and should receive social rebuke.

1. In spite of numerous reports of head injuries from motorcycle accidents, Barlow refuses to wear a safety helmet when he rides his motorcycle.

2. Cassie routinely gets high on hallucinogenic drugs in the privacy of her own home, but never takes them when she is going out somewhere.

3. Williford frequently drives while intoxicated, claiming that even then he is a better driver than most drivers who are sober.

4. Lucy is in pain from a terminal disease and requests the services of a physician to help her commit suicide.

5. Dale and Britt are a same-sex couple who are sexually intimate.

6. Brenda helps people suffering from sexual disorders by having therapeutic sex with them for a fee.

7. Harriet is a single woman who spends most of her paycheck on gambling and often does not have enough money to buy food or the medicine she herself needs.

8. Brad, a single father, spends most of his paycheck on gambling and often does not have enough money to buy food or medicine for his children.

9. Chase is married to five women who all live together with him and are fully in favor of their polygamous marriage.

- For each one of your judgments, state how you would defend it to someone who disagreed with you.

- In each case, try to figure out whether Mill would agree with you.

Mill's second area of freedom, the liberty to act as we wish, was based on his undying conviction that, on the whole, individuals are the best judges of their own interest but are not always the best judges of the interests of others. In particular cases, of course, someone's personal choices concerning his or her way of life may not actually be what is best for that individual (for people do make foolish choices), but it is best to allow people to make such choices simply because it is their own choice. Hence, personal autonomy is one of the highest values in Mill's vision of society.

The implications for legal theory are enormous if we adopt Mill's principle that society has no right to infringe on an individual's freedom except when that person's actions harm others. Some of the examples he provides of *unjustifiable* interference with personal liberty are the punishment of nonviolent drunkenness; the suppression of polygamy among the Mormons; the prohibition of recreational drugs, gambling, and sexual relations between consenting adults (such as prostitution); restrictions on Sunday amusements; and restrictions on the sale of poisons. We may personally find the sorts of behavior listed here repugnant, but the persons who engage in them do not inflict harm on others. Hence, for Mill, these examples are all what are often called victimless crimes and should be tolerated.

With the right to freely engage in such behavior, however, comes the necessity of accepting that behavior's natural consequences. For example, while Mill says we are not allowed to prevent people from drinking, he points out that the offensive drunk may find that people shun his or her company. Critics of Mill have asked if we can draw the line so cleanly between actions that affect only the person engaging in them and actions that affect society. The person who gets drunk in the privacy of his own home may seem to be harming only himself, but what if this personal vice leaves his family to starve? Mill's response was that we may justly punish him for nonsupport, the only socially harmful act he has committed. We may urge the drunk, the prostitute, and the compulsive gambler to mend their ways, but society cannot otherwise interfere in their personal lifestyle choices.

In spite of the strong tone of political freedom that permeates Mill's writings, it should be remembered that personal liberty is not an intrinsic right but is always grounded in social utility. Thus, the government may always intervene in personal liberty when it serves the common good. For example, in chapter 5 of *On Liberty*, Mill says that when overpopulation threatens the economy, the state may legitimately forbid people to marry if they have insufficient means of supporting a family. Likewise, he says, justified governmental limitations on our liberty that are necessary to protect society's interests might include requiring the registration of poisons (to guard against their criminal use), enforcing sanitary conditions, or restricting the location of a casino. In his later years, Mill began to abandon the economic individualism of his earlier work and saw a greater need for state control of the distribution of wealth. It is at this point that his strong plea for individual liberty came into conflict with his concern for the public good.

Whereas classical liberals such as Mill argue for the primacy of individual liberty and minimal government interference, the advocates of collectivism claim that a concern for the big picture and more government control will guarantee the best society.

LOOKING THROUGH THE LENS OF CLASSICAL LIBERALISM

1. If John Stuart Mill were our president, what changes would he want to make in our society? In what ways would he think that our government was intruding into the sphere of individual liberty?

2. Suppose a student group wanted to bring to campus a very controversial speaker who would be offensive to many other students (e.g., a neo-Nazi, a racist, a communist, an outspoken atheist). The administration, in an attempt to avoid public controversy and to protect the sensibilities of those students who would be offended by this presentation, decides to ban this speaker. Imagine that you are Mill. What arguments would you give to the administration as to why this speaker should be allowed to publicly express his or her opinions?

3. If governments throughout history had adopted Mill's principles and had they not censored, imprisoned, or put to death people whose ideas were controversial for their time, how would history have been different? Would it be better or worse? Would the free expression of ideas have resulted in more progress, more tolerance, and a better society? Or would allowing deviant and even dangerous ideas to be freely expressed have caused more harm and social problems than Mill imagined?

EXAMINING THE STRENGTHS AND WEAKNESSES OF CLASSICAL LIBERALISM

Positive Evaluation

1. Western societies pride themselves on the amount of personal liberty they allow. They also claim that protecting freedom of speech is one of the foundation stones of a democratic, free society. Doesn't the fact that many of our current policies concerning freedom of speech were influenced by Mill's essay or are captured in it, lend credibility to his political philosophy?

2. The government can provide a number of services and benefits that will maximize the common good, but it also has a tremendous amount of power. Without strict limits on the government's power, it is hard for individuals to protect their liberties apart from radical social actions and even revolutions. Therefore, isn't Mill correct in trying to drastically limit the power of the government and giving priority to individual liberty?

3. Martin Niemoeller, a German pastor imprisoned by the Nazis, wrote this: "First the Nazis went after the Jews, but I was not a Jew, so I did not object. Then they went after the Catholics, but I was not a Catholic, so I did not object. Then they went after the Trade-Unionists, but I was not a Trade-Unionist, so I did not object. Then they came after me, and there was no one left to object." It is hard to tolerate ideas and practices that are contrary to our own. As Niemoeller suggests, it is also easy to be apathetic when groups we don't belong to are suppressed and even persecuted. But hasn't Niemoeller effectively demonstrated Mill's point that if we don't protect *everyone's* freedoms, even those freedoms that are distasteful or contrary to our values, then our freedoms as well are in jeopardy?

Negative Evaluation

1. Mill argues that the government can intervene only to prevent actions that harm others. But aren't there other types of "harms" besides physical harm? Can't hateful speech be harmful to those it targets or create a social climate that is harmful to society?

2. Mill claims that prostitution, the use of recreational drugs, and gambling may be bad for the individuals who freely engage in these activities, but that others are not harmed. Whether or not we believe in the legalization of these activities, can we really say that they have no social consequences whatsoever? In other words, isn't it hard to draw the line between activities of individuals that harm only themselves and those that negatively affect the common good? Hasn't Mill glossed over this problem?

3. Isn't there a conflict between Mill's commitment to individual liberty and his claim that the best society is one that creates the greatest amount of happiness for the greatest number? Whereas the first concern leads to a minimal government, doesn't the second concern presuppose more involvement of the government in people's lives? Isn't it dangerous for the government to assume that it is in charge of our happiness? In fact, as we read in the text, Mill later believed in a need for state control of the distribution of wealth in order to maximize the amount of satisfaction in society. Isn't this sort of "social engineering" in tension with his emphasis on individualism?

SURVEYING THE CASE FOR MARXISM

KARL MARX (1818–1883)

Marx's Life

Karl Marx was born in 1818 in the Rhineland of Germany. Although his family was Jewish, his father converted to Lutheranism (which was a political necessity at that time). As a teenager, Marx was very pious. He studied at the universities of

Bonn and Berlin, hoping to become a lawyer like his father. At the University of Berlin, however, Marx joined a group of political radicals known as the Young Hegelians, named after the German philosopher Georg W. F. Hegel. Although Hegel had been dead for five years, the German universities were charged with his influence, and philosophical debates filled the air. Marx became caught up in the excitement and abandoned law for the study of philosophy. He ended up getting a doctorate in philosophy at the University of Jena.

Although Marx was destined to be a philosophy professor, the conservative Prussian government closed this option when they prohibited political radicals such as Marx to teach in the universities. Consequently, he became a political journalist but was forced to continually move from city to city and country to country as his journals were banned by various governments. Marx finally settled in London in 1849, where he remained the rest of his life. The only stable job he ever held was as a European correspondent for the *New York Tribune* from 1851 to 1862. The rest of the time he survived on family donations, loans, and subsidies from his lifelong friend and collaborator, Friedrich Engels.

Although he is thought of as a social activist, the bulk of Marx's life was spent in the library of the British Museum, where he worked every day from nine in the morning until it closed at seven at night, researching and writing his philosophical, historical, political, and economic manuscripts. When the library closed, he would go home to his wife, Jenny, and their children, where he would work at night until he was exhausted. (Although the couple had six children, only three lived to reach adulthood. In spite of Marx's poverty and single-minded dedication to his writings, however, his children recalled that he was a wonderful, playful father.) After suffering for months from a diseased lung, Marx died on March 14, 1883, while sleeping in his favorite armchair in his study. He was buried next to his wife in a cemetery near London.

KARL MARX
(1818–1883)

Marx's Philosophy

Marx's impoverished life and his long hours of research were not fruitless. His radical, political philosophy eventually became both the rallying trumpet and the theoretical foundation of angry, impoverished, oppressed workers throughout Europe (and later the entire world). While people can debate the credibility of Marx's theories, no one can dispute their influence. No philosopher in history can claim to have had an international, organized, and activist following of such proportions. As a result of his theories, governments have been overthrown, maps have been changed, and his name became a household word. As Marx said in one of his more famous quotes, "the philosophers have only *interpreted* the world, in various ways; the point is to *change* it."

Marx's vision of history and society began as a young university student when he first encountered Georg Hegel's ideas. Hegel's philosophy taught that human history has meaning and purpose, that it is a rational, determined, evolutionary process in which each stage encounters tensions and contradictions that cause it to change and bring forth a new form of social, cultural, and political organization. Some fans of Hegel gave him a very conservative interpretation and saw his philosophy as implying that the present stage of history was thoroughly rational and inevitable. This view helped support the status quo. Marx and his friends, however, saw Hegel's philosophy as leading in a more radical direction. They believed that the historical development of society has not yet finished its journey and that the present stage will inevitably be destroyed and give way to a better, more rational social structure. It was their goal to move history along to its final, rational stage through political action.

The main themes of Marx's philosophy can be summarized in five points. Let us examine each point.

Economics Rules Everything. Marx is noted for the claim that the fundamental driving force in human behavior and history is economics. He begins with the undeniable truth that people cannot eat ideas but must live on the material products of labor. In other words, before you can philosophize, paint, write novels, do science, or practice your religion, you first have to survive. And in order to survive, you must have the means to secure food, shelter, and clothes. Economics, Marx argued, is at the root of all human existence. Hence, the changes in society and philosophy are the result of underlying changes in technology and the economic system. In the Middle Ages, with its rural economy, one set of ideas and political system prevailed; in industrial Europe, another set of ideas and political system results. This approach was quite a slap in the face to traditional philosophers, who thought that ideas brought about the changes in history. According to Marx, however, economics is the basis of all other facets of society and culture. Marx argued that whether an idea gets a hearing in society or is suppressed is the result of whether it supports the prevailing power structure. As Marx puts it: "The ideas of the ruling class are in every epoch the ruling ideas; . . . The class which has the means of production at its disposal, has control at the same time over the means of mental production."[15] Locke's theory of government, for example, stressed individualism, the fundamental right to own property, and noninterference from the government. But these ideas are supportive of the interests of those who are powerful, own property, and are well-to-do. In other words, according to Marx, Locke's philosophy supported the aristocratic establishment of which he was a part. His economic interests were the basis of his philosophical ideas.

This tendency for social institutions to protect the interests of those in power is the reason why Marx is notorious for being so opposed to religion. He said that religion is the "opium of the people" because it tells the workers to endure their earthly suffering and to focus on their eternal destiny instead of trying to change their wretched social conditions. From Marx's perspective, religion was merely one more expression of the economic status quo that said that the current social hierarchy is God-ordained.

Class Struggle Is the One Constant throughout History. According to Marx, the story of history is the story of those who have power and those who do not, a struggle between the exploiters and the exploited. With the advent of private property, human affairs became a struggle between those who have property and those who do not. In the modern era, this struggle has been carried on between two classes: the bourgeoisie and the proletariat. The *bourgeoisie* are the capitalists, or the owners of the means of industrial production (such as the factories) and the employers of wage labor. They also include the middle class, who benefit from the current economic system. The other half of society is made up of the *proletariat,* or the workers, those who own no property and who must survive by selling their labor as a commodity.

Capitalism Survives by Exploiting the Workers. In Marx's terminology, *capital* is anything that constitutes economic wealth in that it has exchange value, for example, money, property, or goods. The *capitalists* are those who control the economic resources of society, such as the factories. *Capitalism* is that political and economic system in which the means of production and economic wealth are privately controlled. In order to maintain an edge over the competition, Marx says, the capitalist must increase profits by paying workers as little as possible. In Marx's day, society did not have effective unions, minimum wage laws, grievance procedures, or government-imposed standards of health and safety. Furthermore, there was an abundance of labor, so the capitalists could treat their workers as they pleased. Marx said that the vision of hell in Dante's *Inferno* paled in comparison to the inhuman degradation of the industrial England of his time. To prove his comment, he quotes freely from the British government's own documents. One official report had this to say about the lace factories:

Children of nine or ten years are dragged from their squalid beds at two, three, or four o'clock in the morning and compelled to work for a bare subsistence until ten, eleven, or twelve at night, their limbs wearing away, their frames dwindling, their faces whitening, and their humanity absolutely sinking into a stone-like torpor, utterly horrible to contemplate.[16]

Because of these sorts of horror stories, Marx believed that the type of freedom espoused by liberal philosophers such as Mill was really a sham. For the government to allow everyone to do as he or she wished simply meant that those people who were wealthy, owned the factories, and controlled all the political power were free to exploit the rest.

History Is a Deterministic, Dialectical Process. In developing his view of history, Marx borrowed Hegel's view that history follows a dialectical pattern. The word *dialectic* derives from the Greek word for conversation and suggests a back and forth pattern (like a conversation) in which progress is made. For both Hegel and Marx, the **dialectic** is a historical process in which different, opposing forces resolve their tension by bringing into being a new stage of history. Thus, every era in history is only a temporary stopping place as history moves to its fulfillment. For Hegel, however, this dialectical development was one of *ideas,* for he believed that it was ideas that drive history. Marx turned Hegel's philosophy upside down and made it a dialectic of *material, economic forces.* Using the terminology of Hegel's predecessor, Johann Gottlieb Fichte, Marx said that each era of history goes through three stages. The initial state of affairs (called the *thesis*) develops to a point at which it produces its own contradiction (the *antithesis*). The two remain in tension until another state of affairs supersedes them (the *synthesis*). In each round of the dialectic, the deficiencies of one stage bring forth opposing forces to balance out what is lacking. Thus, conflict and struggle are an inevitable part of history.

Like Hegel, Marx had a deterministic view of history. He refers to the laws of history as "tendencies working with iron necessity towards inevitable results."[17] Thus, the various movements and stages in history are not a matter of happenstance; instead, internal laws are at work, bringing about a certain outcome. Accordingly, in Marx's theory, the oppressed class does not need to hope for social justice as merely a tentative possibility, because the laws of history are on their side and guarantee the outcome. But where is the role of human freedom in this scenario? On this topic, Marx says:

> *History* does *nothing,* it 'possesses *no* immense wealth,' it 'wages *no* battles.' It is *man,* real living man, that does all that, that possesses and fights; 'history' is not a person apart, using man as a means for *its own* particular aims; history is *nothing but* the activity of man pursuing his aims.[18]

One way of looking at Marx's theory is to compare the forces of history to a boulder that someone has sent rolling down a mountain. Once set in motion, the boulder becomes an independent force with its own momentum. Obstructions may be set in its path to slow it down, or obstacles may be minimized to speed up the boulder's

dialectic In Hegal and Marx, a historical process in which different opposing forces resolve their tension by bringing into being a new stage of history

descent. However, because of its mass and momentum, it cannot be stopped, and when it has passed through each stage of its descent, it will finally reach its destination. Thus, history is controlled by its own internal laws as well as by human actions. The goal of social activists is to help speed up the inevitable changes of social reform and revolution.

Capitalism Will Undermine Itself and Lead to Communism. According to Marx, capitalism arises as a system in which a small class of people own and control the major forces of production as their private property, and they employ workers who have no economic resources but their own labor power. Within this system a contradiction will begin to arise. The ideology of capitalism is based on individualism and private property. However, the growth of capitalism will necessarily require a highly organized, socialized base with a continually increasing size, complexity, and interdependence. As competition for profits increases, capitalists will keep wages low and replace workers with machines. These actions will result in more unemployment and will drive wages down. The stronger companies will buy up the smaller ones, monopolies will increase, and companies will expand to an international scale. In the process, the capitalists whose companies have failed will join the growing pool of the unemployed.

Using the terms of Marx's dialectic, capitalism is the *thesis* that produces its own *antithesis,* an ever-growing, international, embittered, and impoverished, but unified, class of proletarians (or workers). For this reason, Marx says of the bourgeois (or capitalist) class: "What the bourgeoisie, therefore, produces, above all, is its own grave-diggers. Its fall and the victory of the proletariat are equally inevitable." While the capitalists strive to maintain their position, the situation of the workers becomes intolerable. Society becomes like a tire continually being pumped with air until the internal pressure becomes so great that it explodes. This explosion leads to the third stage of the final cycle of history.

Once capitalism has been discarded on the junkpile of history, the final stage of the dialectic (the *synthesis*) will emerge in three phases. The first phase will be a stage of transition called "the dictatorship of the proletariat." This transition is when the proletariat use their newly gained political power to cleanse society of the last remnants of capitalism. The next phase is the first stage of communism, the stage now known as socialism. The state takes over the means of production that were formerly in the hands of private ownership. This stage, however, will eventually give way to the final stage of ultimate communism, in which the people themselves will control not only political decisions but also the economic life of the country.

The following passage is from the *Communist Manifesto* of 1848, the most popular expression of Marxist theory, written by Marx and his friend and coauthor, Friedrich Engels. In this political tract, Marx and Engels depict history as a long, sorry parade of class conflicts. Although each historical period has different social and economic structures and although the main players go by different sets of labels, in each age there are the "haves" and the "have-nots," the exploiters and the exploited, the oppressors and the oppressed. Ironically, according to Marx's theory, the so-called freedom of modern, liberal democracies is simply the freedom of those with political and economic power to exploit those who are powerless. The word *freedom* rings hollow, Marx says, when the laws, social institutions, economic systems, and even philosophies of a society are controlled by a few to maintain the status quo and promote their own interests. True freedom for the masses of society will only come about with an economic and political revolution such that society will be run by the people for the benefit of all and will guarantee them a living wage, education, health care, and cultural enrichment. According to Marx's version of collectivism, less government means less freedom and more government means more freedom. Only if the government, ruled by the workers, takes charge of things, will true freedom and well-being result.

- What does Marx believe is the dominant theme in history?
- What is the distinctive feature of our epoch?

FROM KARL MARX AND FRIEDRICH ENGELS
Communist Manifesto[19]

Bourgeois and Proletarians

The history of all hitherto existing societies is the history of class struggles.

Freeman and slave, patrician and plebeian, lord and serf, guild-master and journeyman, in a word, oppressor and oppressed, stood in constant opposition to one another, carried on an uninterrupted, now hidden, now open fight, a fight that each time ended, either in a revolutionary re-constitution of society at large, or in the common ruin of the contending classes.

In the earlier epochs of history, we find almost everywhere a complicated arrangement of society into various orders, a manifold gradation of social rank. In ancient Rome we have patricians, knights, plebeians, slaves; in the Middle Ages, feudal lords, vassals, guild-masters, journeymen, apprentices, serfs; in almost all of these classes, again, subordinate gradations.

The modern bourgeois society that has sprouted from the ruins of feudal society has not done away with class antagonisms. It has but established new classes, new conditions of oppression, new forms of struggle in place of the old ones. Our epoch, the epoch of the bourgeoisie, possesses, however, this distinctive feature: it has simplified the class antagonisms: Society as a whole is more and more splitting up into two great hostile camps, into two great classes, directly facing each other: Bourgeoisie and Proletariat.

According to Marx's dialectical view of history, each economic system based on class conflicts produces its own contradiction, which eventually becomes its undoing. In the age of capitalism, the capitalists (or bourgeoisie) require a large body of underpaid workers to make goods at low costs that the capitalists sell to make their profits. The capitalists are driven by their own nature to increase their profits by increasingly exploiting the workers. However, Marx says, the growth and centralization of modern industry has caused large bodies of workers to collect together in their common misery, allowing them to become organized into unions and social action groups. In this way, the bourgeoisie are producing their own "grave-diggers."

Hitherto, every form of society has been based, as we have already seen, on the antagonism of oppressing and oppressed classes. But in order to oppress a class, certain conditions must be assured to it under which it can, at least, continue its slavish existence. The serf, in the period of serfdom, raised himself to membership in the commune, just as the petty bourgeois, under the yoke of feudal absolutism, managed to develop into a bourgeois. The modern labourer, on the contrary, instead of rising with the progress of industry, sinks deeper and deeper below the conditions of existence of his own class. He becomes a pauper, and pauperism develops more rapidly than population and wealth. And here it becomes evident, that the bourgeoisie is unfit any longer to be the ruling class in society, and to impose its conditions of existence upon society as an over-riding law. It is unfit to rule because it is incompetent to assure an existence to its slave within his slavery, because it cannot help letting him sink into such a state, that it has to feed him, instead of being fed by him. Society can no longer live under this bourgeoisie, in other words, its existence is no longer compatible with society.

The essential condition for the existence, and for the sway of the bourgeois class, is the formation and augmentation of capital; the condition for capital is wage-labour. Wage-labour rests exclusively on competition between the labourers. The advance of industry, whose involuntary promoter is the bourgeoisie, replaces the isolation of the labourers, due to competition, by their revolutionary combination, due to association. The development of Modern Industry, therefore, cuts from under its feet the very foundation on which the bourgeoisie produces and appropriates products. What the bourgeoisie, therefore, produces, above all, is its own grave-diggers. Its fall and the victory of the proletariat are equally inevitable.

Notice in the final sentence that Marx says that the fall of capitalism and the victory of the working-class is "inevitable," which is an expression of his deterministic view of history. In the next passage, Marx proposes the abolition of private property. He does not mean that you cannot own your own toothbrush; instead, he is talking about property that produces profits for an individual capitalist, such as a factory.

Property and Freedom

All property relations in the past have continually been subject to historical change consequent upon the change in historical conditions.

The French Revolution, for example, abolished feudal property in favour of bourgeois property.

The distinguishing feature of Communism is not the abolition of property generally, but the abolition of bourgeois property. But modern bourgeois private property is the final and most complete expression of the system of producing and appropriating products, that is based on class antagonisms, on the exploitation of the many by the few.

In this sense, the theory of the Communists may be summed up in the single sentence: Abolition of private property.

We Communists have been reproached with the desire of abolishing the right of personally acquiring property as the fruit of a man's own labour, which property is alleged to be the groundwork of all personal freedom, activity and independence.

Hard-won, self-acquired, self-earned property! Do you mean the property of the petty artisan and of the small peasant, a form of property that preceded the bourgeois form? There is no need to abolish that; the development of industry has to a great extent already destroyed it, and is still destroying it daily.

Or do you mean modern bourgeois private property?

But does wage-labour create any property for the labourer? Not a bit. It creates capital, i.e., that kind of property which exploits wage-labour, and which cannot increase except upon condition of begetting a new supply of wage-labour for fresh exploitation. Property, in its present form, is based on the antagonism of capital and wage-labour. Let us examine both sides of this antagonism.

To be a capitalist, is to have not only a purely personal, but a social status in production. Capital is a collective product, and only by the united action of many members, nay, in the last resort, only by the united action of all members of society, can it be set in motion.

Capital is, therefore, not a personal, it is a social power.

When, therefore, capital is converted into common property, into the property of all members of society, personal property is not thereby transformed into social property. It is only the social character of the property that is changed. It loses its class-character.

Let us now take wage-labour.

The average price of wage-labour is the minimum wage, i.e., that quantum of the means of subsistence, which is absolutely requisite in bare existence as a labourer. What, therefore, the wage-labourer appropriates by means of his labour, merely suffices to prolong and reproduce a bare existence. We by no means intend to abolish this personal appropriation of the products of labour, an appropriation that is made for the maintenance and reproduction of human life, and that leaves no surplus wherewith to command the labour of others. All that we want to do away with, is the miserable character of this appropriation, under which the labourer lives merely to increase capital, and is allowed to live only in so far as the interest of the ruling class requires it.

In bourgeois society, living labour is but a means to increase accumulated labour. In Communist society, accumulated labour is but a means to widen, to enrich, to promote the existence of the labourer.

In bourgeois society, therefore, the past dominates the present; in Communist society, the present dominates the past. In bourgeois society capital is independent and has individuality, while the living person is dependent and has no individuality.

And the abolition of this state of things is called by the bourgeois, abolition of individuality and freedom! And rightly so. The abolition of bourgeois individuality, bourgeois independence, and bourgeois freedom is undoubtedly aimed at.

By freedom is meant, under the present bourgeois conditions of production, free trade, free selling and buying.

But if selling and buying disappears, free selling and buying disappears also. This talk about free selling and buying, and all the other "brave words" of our bourgeoisie about freedom in general, have a meaning, if any, only in contrast with restricted selling and buying, with the fettered traders of the Middle Ages, but have no meaning when opposed to the Communistic abolition of buying and selling, of the bourgeois conditions of production, and of the bourgeoisie itself.

You are horrified at our intending to do away with private property. But in your existing society, private property is already done away with for nine-tenths of the population; its existence for the few is solely due to its non-existence in the hands of those nine-tenths. You reproach us, therefore, with intending to do away with a form of property, the necessary condition for whose existence is the non-existence of any property for the immense majority of society.

In one word, you reproach us with intending to do away with your property. Precisely so; that is just what we intend.

From the moment when labour can no longer be converted into capital, money, or rent, into a social power capable of being monopolised, i.e., from the moment when individual property can no longer be transformed into bourgeois property, into capital, from that moment, you say individuality vanishes.

You must, therefore, confess that by "individual" you mean no other person than the bourgeois, than the middle-class owner of property. This person must, indeed, be swept out of the way, and made impossible.

Communism deprives no man of the power to appropriate the products of society; all that it does is to deprive him of the power to subjugate the labour of others by means of such appropriation.

- In the next passage, what does Marx say causes the changes in our views, conceptions, and consciousness?

Culture and Ideology Controlled by Those in Power

The charges against Communism made from a religious, a philosophical, and, generally, from an ideological standpoint, are not deserving of serious examination.

Does it require deep intuition to comprehend that man's ideas, views and conceptions, in one word, man's consciousness, changes with every change in the conditions of his material existence, in his social relations and in his social life?

What else does the history of ideas prove, than that intellectual production changes its character in proportion as material production is changed? The ruling ideas of each age have ever been the ideas of its ruling class.

When people speak of ideas that revolutionise society, they do but express the fact, that within the old society, the elements of a new one have been created, and that the dissolution of the old ideas keeps even pace with the dissolution of the old conditions of existence.

When the ancient world was in its last throes, the ancient religions were overcome by Christianity. When Christian ideas succumbed in the 18th century to rationalist ideas, feudal society fought its death battle with the then revolutionary bourgeoisie. The ideas of religious liberty and freedom of conscience merely gave expression to the sway of free competition within the domain of knowledge.

"Undoubtedly," it will be said, "religious, moral, philosophical and juridical ideas have been modified in the course of historical development. But religion, morality, philosophy, political science, and law, constantly survived this change."

"There are, besides, eternal truths, such as Freedom, Justice, etc. that are common to all states of society. But Communism abolishes eternal truths, it abolishes all religion, and all morality, instead of constituting them on a new basis; it therefore acts in contradiction to all past historical experience."

What does this accusation reduce itself to? The history of all past society has consisted in the development of class antagonisms, antagonisms that assumed different forms at different epochs.

But whatever form they may have taken, one fact is common to all past ages, viz., the exploitation of one part of society by the other.

No wonder, then, that the social consciousness of past ages, despite all the multiplicity and variety it displays, moves within certain common forms, or general ideas, which cannot completely vanish except with the total disappearance of class antagonisms.

The Communist revolution is the most radical rupture with traditional property relations; no wonder that its development involves the most radical rupture with traditional ideas.

But let us have done with the bourgeois objections to Communism.

- In the next passage, how does Marx say the proletariat will use its political power?
- What does Marx say about the future of class divisions?

The Future

We have seen above, that the first step in the revolution by the working class, is to raise the proletariat to the position of ruling as to win the battle of democracy.

The proletariat will use its political supremacy to wrest, by degrees, all capital from the bourgeoisie, to centralise all instruments of production in the hands of the State, i.e., of the proletariat organised as the ruling class; and to increase the total of productive forces as rapidly as possible.

Of course, in the beginning, this cannot be effected except by means of despotic inroads on the rights of property, and on the conditions of bourgeois production; by means of measures, therefore, which appear economically insufficient and untenable, but which, in the course of the movement, outstrip themselves, necessitate further inroads upon the old social order, and are unavoidable as a means of entirely revolutionising the mode of production. These measures will of course be different in different countries.

Nevertheless in the most advanced countries, the following will be pretty generally applicable.

1. Abolition of property in land and application of all rents of land to public purposes.
2. A heavy progressive or graduated income tax.
3. Abolition of all right of inheritance.
4. Confiscation of the property of all emigrants and rebels.
5. Centralisation of credit in the hands of the State, by means of a national bank with State capital and an exclusive monopoly.
6. Centralisation of the means of communication and transport in the hands of the State.
7. Extension of factories and instruments of production owned by the State; the bringing into cultivation of waste-lands, and the improvement of the soil generally in accordance with a common plan.
8. Equal liability of all to labour. Establishment of industrial armies, especially for agriculture.
9. Combination of agriculture with manufacturing industries; gradual abolition of the distinction between town and country, by a more equable distribution of the population over the country.
10. Free education for all children in public schools. Abolition of children's factory labour in its present form. Combination of education with industrial production, &c., &c.

When, in the course of development, class distinctions have disappeared, and all production has been concentrated in the hands of a vast association of the whole nation, the public power will lose its political character. Political power, properly so called, is merely the organised power of one class for oppressing another. If the proletariat during its contest with the bourgeoisie is compelled, by the force of circumstances, to organise itself as a class, if, by means of a revolution, it makes itself the ruling class, and, as such, sweeps away by force the old conditions of production, then it will, along with these conditions, have swept away the conditions for the existence of class antagonisms and of classes generally, and will thereby have abolished its own supremacy as a class.

In place of the old bourgeois society, with its classes and class antagonisms, we shall have an association, in which the free development of each is the condition for the free development of all.

The following conclusion of the *Communist Manifesto* is Marx's famous rallying cry to the workers. If you were an impoverished, exploited laborer, what effect would it have on you?

The Communists disdain to conceal their views and aims. They openly declare that their ends can be attained only by the forcible overthrow of all existing social conditions. Let the ruling classes tremble at a Communist revolution. The proletarians have nothing to lose but their chains. They have a world to win.
WORKING MEN OF ALL COUNTRIES UNITE!

LOOKING THROUGH THE LENS OF MARXISM

1. Marx believed that economics was the basis of all other cultural institutions. Based on this point, work out a Marxist analysis of the worlds of sports, music, religion, education, and politics as they exist in our society today. Do you think the Marxist analysis has captured any of the truth about these features of our contemporary culture?

2. One hundred years after the publication of *The Communist Manifesto,* philosopher Sidney Hook listed the following features of capitalism as described by Marx:

economic centralization and monopoly, the cycle of boom and depression, unemployment and the effects of technological change, political and economic class wars, excessive specialization and division of labor, the triumph of materialistic and money values on the rest of our culture.[20]

How many of these problems of capitalism described by Marx still exist in our society today?

3. Contrary to Marx's predictions, the plight of the worker has not gotten worse. Salaries, health and safety standards, the length of the working day, and benefits are all better than they were in Marx's day. However, contemporary Marxist Herbert Marcuse argues that capitalists will make working conditions better only if it serves to increase their profits. Furthermore, he says, by giving workers more materialistic benefits, capitalists have actually made them blind to their true alienation and lack of political power. In spite of the better conditions of the worker, do you think that the capitalist system is still as unjust as the Marxists claim?

4. Under capitalism, you have the opportunity to form your own corporation and, if it is successful, become a millionaire. Under communism, private, profit-making corporations did not exist and personal wealth was severely restricted. However, people received a guaranteed income, free education, and free medical care, and the costs of cultural events such as the opera were available to the common person. Very few people in our society are able to become millionaires as a result of our economic freedom. However, everyone would benefit from free education and

medical care. Do you think the individual freedom of capitalism is enough to justify the lack of these governmental benefits? Or would it be worth sacrificing some freedoms so that everyone in society would benefit from the government-provided benefits?

EXAMINING THE STRENGTHS AND WEAKNESSES OF MARXISM

Positive Evaluation

1. As Eastern Europe shifted to capitalism in the latter part of the twentieth century, there were good and bad results. People who had lived their lives under communism suddenly were confronted with unemployment, homelessness, poverty, and an increase in crime because strong governmental control and paternalistic benefits had declined in the new capitalistic economy. Do these results suggest that communism had some positive effects on society?

2. Think of the ways in which money is able to buy power and influence in our society. To what degree are wealthy individuals and large corporations able to influence political campaigns and the flow of information as well as our nation's laws and policies? Does Marx have a point in stressing the role of economics in culture and the power of the wealthy?

3. Western capitalist societies have brought about important social reforms and cured many of the evils that existed in Marx's industrial England in the nineteenth century. However, would these reforms have come about if anticapitalist critics such as Marx had not raised our social conscience by drawing attention to the plight of the workers? Would corporations have become more benevolent if they did not have to respond to the pressure of unions, social protests, and critics that were inspired by Marx's critique of capitalism?

Negative Evaluation

1. Marx seemed to assume that the only alternatives were a total laissez-faire economy in which the capitalists could do whatever they pleased and a total collectivism in which the government controlled everything. But hasn't our capitalist society actually evolved into a mixed economy that balances the power of the corporations with the common good? What would have happened if Marx had been able to view our twentieth-century society and had seen the power of the labor unions, the government's prosecution of monopolies, the extensive regulations governing the health and safety of workers, the affirmative action programs, the increased leisure of workers, and the numerous employee benefits? Wouldn't he have had to change many of his ideas and moderate his critique of capitalism?

2. Did Marx have a romantic view of human nature? He seemed to think that the motivation of self-interest and the lust for power and control were exclusively the results of the capitalist system and would not carry over to humanity under a

socialist government. But isn't it true that, for better or worse, some features of human nature will be the same in any economic system? Furthermore, haven't capitalists and corporations sometimes acted against their best interests for the common good of society (contrary to what Marx claimed)?

3. Although it is hard to deny that economic factors have played an important role in history and contemporary society, doesn't Marx overemphasize this point? Can all aspects of human life and culture be explained on the basis of economic motivations? Isn't there more to human behavior than this one, narrow dimension?

6.4 CIVIL DISOBEDIENCE

 ### LEADING QUESTIONS: *Civil Disobedience*

1. *Questions from the Opponents of Civil Disobedience:* One of the purposes of government is to maintain law and order so that its citizens can enjoy peace and security. But aren't people who break the laws (even if they believe their cause is just), undermining the stability of society? Furthermore, doesn't such behavior promote disrespect for the law?

2. *Questions from the Opponents of Civil Disobedience:* Some people claim that it is morally justified to break the law in order to draw attention to what they feel is an unjust law. But does the end justify the means? There is never going to be universal agreement about which laws are good and which ones are not. If everyone broke the laws they did not like, then lawlessness rather than order would be the norm. Even if people think that disobeying the law will cure the ills of society, isn't the cure worse than the disease?

3. *Questions from the Supporters of Civil Disobedience:* Everyone generally has an obligation to obey the law, but what about laws that are unjust and that violate people's rights? Furthermore, what if the people in power are deeply committed to the status quo and are unwilling to change? Isn't it sometimes true that the only way to draw attention to unjust laws is to disobey them?

4. *Questions from the Supporters of Civil Disobedience:* How would history have been different if everyone had believed that it was never justified to break the law? Moses and the Israelites would not have defied the Egyptian pharaoh. Socrates would have ceased to teach his philosophy in defiance of the state. Christianity might never have gotten off the ground because the early Christians were forbidden by the Jewish and Roman authorities to preach their new religion. The American revolution would never have occurred. People would not have helped slaves escape from their masters in the nineteenth century. Unsafe conditions and starvation wages for workers would have continued if workers did not go on strike at a time when striking was illegal. Who knows when or if women would have been allowed

to vote without the civil disobedience of the women protestors. The Civil Rights Act of 1964 might not have been enacted without the protests and acts of civil disobedience that led up to it. Doesn't history show that civil disobedience can be a necessary impetus for social improvement?

As leading questions 1 and 2 suggest, for there to be a government, there have to be laws. If you believe that government is generally a good thing (assuming you are not an anarchist), then you must believe that it is essential to the good of society to have laws. If people do not obey the laws, however, then there might as well not be any laws at all, and practically speaking, society would be an anarchy. So initially, it seems as though disobeying the laws of your government is never morally justified. But leading questions 3 and 4 throw a different light on the issue. What if the laws that a government passes are illegal (they violate its own constitution or the social contract)? Or what if the laws are legal but are deeply immoral? Adolph Hitler, for example, rose to power in Nazi Germany through a legal political process. Once in power, he began to change the laws (again through legal procedures) so that many of the horrors of that society, such as the confiscation of people's property and imprisonment of innocent "enemies of the state," were perfectly legal. In the eighteenth and nineteenth centuries it was legal to own slaves in portions of the United States, even though this practice is clearly immoral. Furthermore, up until the latter half of the twentieth century, racial discrimination was protected by the law in the United States. What should a citizen do in these cases? While most political philosophers agree that obedience to the law is an important foundation stone of any society, many have argued that there are limits to this obligation.

Before I go any further in examining the opposing sides of this issue, I should back up and define my terms. **Civil disobedience** is an illegal action performed for the purpose of making a moral protest. It isn't just an act of protest that frustrates or aggravates the authorities. It has to be a blatant violation of the law or a disobeying of an explicit order of some civil authority. This authority could be at the city, state, or federal level. An example of civil disobedience would be sitting in at some governmental office in order to disrupt its course of business and then refusing to leave when ordered to do so. But what is the difference between criminal disobedience and civil disobedience, since both categories involve illegal actions? The major difference is that civil disobedience (unlike criminal disobedience) is a form of moral protest. It is an attempt to protest some law, policy, or action of a governmental body in order to draw attention to the unjustness of the law, the problems with the policy, or the wrongness of a particular action on the part of the government. Ultimately, of course, the goal is to change the law or the government's behavior. In contrast, a simple criminal act does not have any sort of high-minded purpose. The criminal breaks the law for personal gain, by robbing a bank or driving with an illegal license, for example.

To be classified as an act of moral protest, the lawbreaking must be public. The authorities and the public must be aware that the government is being disobeyed.

civil disobedience an illegal action performed for the purpose of making a moral protest

Furthermore, most defenders of civil disobedience would say that protestors who cannot win their case in court must be willing to accept the penalty that follows this action, such as a jail sentence or a fine. Hence, those people who engage in civil disobedience must be willing to become martyrs for their moral cause. More important, accepting the penalty shows respect for the political system and the law in general while drawing attention to its problems. On the other hand, a criminal action is done secretly with the intent of evading the law. By this criterion, bombing an abortion clinic or a governmental office and then evading capture is a criminal act. However, placing your body in front of the door until you are arrested and dragged away by the police is an act of civil disobedience. Both types of action may be motivated by a dissatisfaction with the system, but the difference is in the means used to protest it.

Also, many social activists believe that for an action to count as a moral protest, it must be nonviolent. This approach was stressed by Mahatma Gandhi and Martin Luther King Jr., who are both known for their use of civil disobedience as a technique for social change. But where do we draw the line between violence and nonviolence? Certainly an action that caused personal injury would be an example of violence. But what about destruction of property? On one occasion, environmentalists poured sludge from a polluted river into the files of a corporation that they claimed was a major polluter. Although this action falls short of bombing the building, is it still violence? Other social activists would define violence more broadly and include the violation of an individual's legal rights. Under this definition, preventing a client from entering an abortion clinic would not be a legitimate form of protest. Now that we have our terms defined, let's go on to examine the arguments against and for civil disobedience.

SURVEYING THE CASE AGAINST CIVIL DISOBEDIENCE

If you are living in a completely totalitarian state in which the people have no freedoms and human rights are being persistently and grossly violated, you could argue that civil disobedience (even to the point of violence) is the only remedy left. To discuss whether civil disobedience is justified in this context is to make the debate too trivial. On the other hand, what if you are living in a democratic society in which the people are able to elect their leaders and have a voice in making the laws? Furthermore, what if the laws are, for the most part, just and good laws? In this society, are there any situations in which civil disobedience can be justified?

The following four arguments are the most common ones used to defend the view that civil disobedience is never morally justified. They are expressed in the voice of an opponent of civil disobedience.

A Violation of the Social Contract. By the time that you begin considering an act of civil disobedience, you have lived for a while (typically all your life) in the society whose laws you are going to violate. In doing so, you have been continuously protected by the government and have benefited from the government's services. Hence, you have tacitly entered into a agreement with the state to be one of its citizens. Since you have reaped the benefits of being a citizen of this country, you also have an obligation to the state to obey its laws. You cannot enjoy being a citizen when it is convenient, expecting the government to hold up its end of the bargain, and then turn around and disobey it when it is convenient to do so. Hence, civil disobedience is a violation of the social contract that every citizen has tacitly approved.

Majority Rule. The government is not some alien entity that has invaded our lives. The government rules according to the will of the people through our elected representatives. However, none of us is happy with the outcome of every election nor with each and every law. But whether we like the outcome or not, the government is a creation of the will of the majority. We all have an obligation to abide by the will of the majority or to seek to change it. When you dissent through civil disobedience, you are trying to accomplish through breaking the law what you were unable to accomplish through the democratic process, but in doing so, you are undermining the very principle of democracy. Therefore, civil disobedience is never justified.

Ends That Do Not Justify the Means. Let's assume, for the sake of the discussion, that you are breaking the law in the name of a good cause. But does having good motivations and trying to achieve a good end justify anything you do? The good that might be accomplished through civil disobedience has to be measured against its other results. Breaking the law, for whatever reasons, promotes a lack of respect for the law and the government. Furthermore, it leads to social chaos and other evils. The work of the government is so disrupted and officials have to spend so much time dealing with protesters that they are diverted from doing the normal and essential tasks involved in running the society. Finally, in spite of their best intentions, lawbreaking protesters often provoke violence and lawlessness. The violence may erupt from the protesters' own ranks, from members who are less disciplined and cannot channel their anger. Or perhaps the protesters ignite the strong feelings of opponents who disagree with their cause. Even if these dire outcomes never occur, the negative results of civil disobedience still outweigh its positive fruits.

Other Alternatives. The issues raised in the first three arguments culminate in this last one. A democracy always offers less drastic means than civil disobedience to make your voice heard and to affect society. Without breaking the law, you can exercise your rights to free speech, peaceful assembly, petitioning support, voting, and demonstrating. True, these methods are not as dramatic and as attention getting as civil disobedience is. Nevertheless, they can work, and they avoid the problems generated by breaking the law. Furthermore, if you really believe that your society is so evil and unjust that breaking the law is justified, then you always have the option of renouncing your citizenship and moving to a society that is more to your liking. Hence, civil disobedience is an unnecessary evil and is always wrong in a free society.

Do you find these arguments convincing? Which one do you think is the strongest? Which one is the weakest? How would a defender of civil disobedience respond to these points?

One of the classic spokespersons for opposing civil disobedience is Socrates. We have encountered the figure of Socrates throughout this book, starting with the discussion of his trial for heresy and corrupting the youth in section 1.1. In a sequel to the story of the trial, Plato tells about Socrates' discussion with one of his students while Socrates was in jail waiting for his execution. Crito, the young disciple, begs Socrates to escape from prison. In the course of the discussion, Socrates makes clear his controversial stand on civil disobedience.

- In the following reading, see how many of the four arguments against civil disobedience you can find in Socrates' discussion.

FROM PLATO

Crito[21]

SOCRATES: Why have you come at this hour, Crito? It must be quite early.

CRITO: Yes, certainly.

SOCRATES: What is the exact time?

CRITO: The dawn is breaking.

SOCRATES: I am surprised the keeper of the prison would let you in.

CRITO: He knows me because I often come, Socrates; moreover, I have done him a kindness.

SOCRATES: Did you just get here?

CRITO: No, I came some time ago.

SOCRATES: Then why did you sit and say nothing, instead of awakening me at once? . . .

CRITO: Oh, my beloved Socrates, let me entreat you once more to take my advice and escape. For if you die I shall not only lose a friend who can never be replaced, but there is another evil: people who do not know you and me will believe that I might have saved you if I had been willing to give money, but that I did not care. . . . Nor can I think that you are justified, Socrates, in betraying your own life when you might be saved; this is playing into the hands of your enemies and destroyers; and moreover I should say that you were betraying your children; for you might bring them up and educate them; instead of which you go away and leave them, and they will have to take their chance; and if they do not meet with the usual fate of orphans, there will be small thanks to you. No man should bring children into the world who is unwilling to persevere to the end in their nurture and education. . . .

SOCRATES: Dear Crito, your zeal is invaluable, if a right one; but if wrong, the greater the zeal the greater the evil; and therefore we ought to consider whether these things shall be done or not. For I am and always have been one of those natures who must be guided by reason, whatever the reason may be which upon reflection appears to me to be the best; and now that this fortune has come upon me, I cannot put away the reasons which I have before given: the principles which I have hitherto honored and revered I still honor, and unless we can find other and better principles on the instant, I am certain not to agree with you. . . .

Let us consider the matter together, and either refute me if you can, and I will be convinced; or else cease, my dear friend, from repeating to me that I ought to escape against the wishes of the Athenians: for I am extremely desirous to be persuaded by you, but not against my own better judgment. . . .

CRITO: I will do my best.

SOCRATES: Are we to say that we are never intentionally to do wrong, or that in one way we ought and in another way we ought not to do wrong, or is doing wrong always evil and dishonorable? Are all our former admissions which were made within a few days to be thrown away? And have we, at our age, been earnestly discoursing with one another all our life long only to discover that we are no better than children? Or are we to rest assured, in spite of the opinion of the many, and in spite of consequences whether better or worse, of the truth of what was then said, that injustice is always an evil and dishonor to him who acts unjustly? Shall we affirm that?

CRITO: Yes.

SOCRATES: Then we must do no wrong?

CRITO: Certainly not.

SOCRATES: When we are injured should we injure in return, as the many imagine. Or must we injure no one at all?

CRITO: Clearly not.

SOCRATES: Again, Crito, may we do evil?

CRITO: Surely not, Socrates.

SOCRATES: And what of doing evil in return for evil, which is the morality of the many—is that just or not?

CRITO: Not just.

SOCRATES: For doing evil to another is the same as injuring him?

CRITO: Very true.

SOCRATES: Then we ought not to retaliate or render evil for evil to anyone, whatever evil we may have suffered from him. But I would have you consider, Crito, whether you really mean what you are saying. For this opinion has never been held, and never will be held, by any considerable number of persons; and those who are agreed and those who are not agreed upon this point have no common ground, and can only despise one another when they see how widely they differ. Tell me, then, whether you agree with and assent to my first principle, that neither injury nor retaliation nor warding off evil by evil is ever right. And shall that be the premise of our argument? Or do you decline and dissent from this? For this has been of old and is still my opinion; but, if you are of another opinion, let me hear what you have to say. If, however, you remain of the same mind as formerly, I will proceed to the next step.

CRITO: You may proceed, for I have not changed my mind.

SOCRATES: Then I will proceed to the next step, which may be put in the form of a question: Ought a man to do what he admits to be right, or ought he to betray the right?

CRITO: He ought to do what he thinks right.

SOCRATES: But if this is true, what is the application? In leaving the prison against the will of the Athenians, do I wrong any? or rather do I not wrong those whom I ought least to wrong? Do I not desert the principles which were acknowledged by us to be just? What do you say?

CRITO: I cannot tell, Socrates, for I do not know.

SOCRATES: Then consider the matter in this way: Imagine that I am about to play truant (you may call the proceeding by any name which you like), and the laws and the government come and interrogate me: "Tell us, Socrates," they say; "what are you trying to do? Are you attempting to overturn us—the laws and the whole State, as far as you are able? Do you imagine that a State can subsist and not be overthrown, in which the decisions of law have no power, but are set aside and overthrown by individuals? " What will be our answer, Crito, to these and the like words? Anyone, and especially a clever rhetorician, will have a good deal to urge about the evil of setting aside the law which requires a sentence to be carried out; and we might reply, "Yes; but the State has injured us and given an unjust sentence." Suppose I say that?

CRITO: Very good, Socrates.

SOCRATES: "And was that our agreement with you?" the law would say; "or were you to abide by the sentence of the State?" And if I were to express astonishment at their saying this, the law would probably add: "Answer, Socrates, instead of opening your eyes: you are in the habit of asking and answering questions. Tell us what complaint you have to make against us which justifies you in attempting to destroy us and the State? In the first place did we not bring you into existence? Your father married your mother by our aid and begat you. Say whether you have any objection to urge against those of us who regulate marriage?" None, I should reply. "Or against those of us who regulate the system of nurture and education of children in which you were trained? Were not the laws, who have the charge of this, right in commanding your father to train you in music and gymnastic?" Right, I should reply. . . . What answer shall we make to this, Crito? Do the laws speak truly, or do they not?

CRITO: I think that they do.

SOCRATES: Then the laws will say: "Consider, Socrates, if this is true, that in your present attempt you are going to do us wrong. For, after having brought you into the world, and nurtured and educated you, and given you and every other citizen a share in every good that we had to give, we further proclaim and give the right to every Athenian, that if he does not like us when he has come of age and has seen the ways of the city, and made our acquaintance, he may go where he pleases and take his goods with him; and none of us laws will forbid him or interfere with him. Any of you who does not like us and the city, and who wants to go to a colony or to any other city, may go where he likes, and take his goods with him. But he who has experience of the manner in which we order justice and administer the State, and still remains, has entered into an implied contract that he will do as we command him. And he who disobeys us is, as we maintain, thrice wrong: first, because in disobeying us he is disobeying his parents; secondly, because we are the authors of his education; thirdly, because he has made an agreement with us that he will duly obey our commands; and he neither obeys them nor convinces us that our commands are wrong; and we do not rudely impose them, but give him the alternative of obeying or convincing us; that is what we offer, and he does neither.

"These are the sort of accusations to which, as we were saying, you, Socrates, will be exposed if you accomplish your intentions; you, above all other Athenians." Suppose I ask, why is this? They will justly retort upon me that I above all other men have acknowledged the agreement. "There is clear proof, Socrates," they will say, "that we and the city were not displeasing to you. Of all Athenians you have been the most constant resident in the city, which, as you never leave, you may be supposed to love. For you never went out of the city either to see the games, except once when you went to the Isthmus, or to any other place unless when you were on military service; nor did you travel as other men do. Nor had you any curiosity to know other States or their laws: your affections did not go beyond us and our State; we were your special favorites, and you acquiesced in our government of you; and this is the State in which you begat your children, which is a proof of your satisfaction.

"Moreover, you might, if you had liked, have fixed the penalty at banishment in the course of the trial—the State which refuses to let you go now would have let you go then. But you pretended that you preferred death to exile, and that you were not grieved at death. And now you have forgotten these fine sentiments, and pay no respect to us, the laws, of whom you are the destroyer; and are doing what only a miserable slave would do, running away and turning your back upon the compacts and agreements which you made as a citizen. And first of all answer this very question: Are we right in saying that you agreed to be governed according to us in deed, and not in word only? Is that true or not?"

How shall we answer that, Crito? Must we not agree?

CRITO: There is no help, Socrates.

SOCRATES: Then will they not say: "You, Socrates, are breaking the covenants and agreements which you made with us at your leisure, not in any haste or under any compulsion or deception, but having had seventy years to think of them, during which time you were at liberty to leave the city, if we were not to your mind, or if our covenants appeared to you to be unfair. You had your choice, and might have gone either to Lacedaemon or Crete, which you often praise for their good government, or to some other Hellenic or foreign State. Whereas you, above all other Athenians, seemed to be so fond of the State, or, in other words, of us her laws (for who would like a State that has no laws), that you never stirred out of her. . . . And now you run away and forsake your agreements. Not so, Socrates, if you will take our advice; do not make yourself ridiculous by escaping out of the city. . . .

"Listen, then, Socrates, to us who have brought you up. Think not of life and children first, and of justice afterwards, but of justice first, that you may be justified before the princes of the world below. For neither will you nor any that belong to you be happier or holier or more just in this life, or happier in another, if you do as Crito bids. Now you depart in innocence, a sufferer and not a doer of evil; a victim, not of the laws, but of men. . . . Listen, then, to us and not to Crito."

This is the voice which I seem to hear murmuring in my ears, like the sound of the flute in the ears of the mystic; that voice, I say, is humming in my ears, and prevents me from hearing any other. And I know that anything more which you may say will be in vain. Yet speak, if you have anything to say.

CRITO: I have nothing to say, Socrates.

SOCRATES: Then let me follow the intimations of the will of God.

 STOP AND THINK

What do you think of Socrates' arguments? Assuming that the decision of the court was wrong, did Socrates do the right thing in refusing to escape from prison? If you were Crito, how would you convince Socrates not to stay and die?

 ## LOOKING THROUGH THE LENS OF THE OPPONENTS OF CIVIL DISOBEDIENCE

1. What advice would Socrates give to a German living during the time of the Nazi regime concerning his or her response to the government?

2. At the end of their speech, the laws tell Socrates that he is "a victim, not of the laws, but of men." Is this distinction between the justice of the laws and the injustice of people's application of them a helpful one? What would be the practical application of this distinction?

3. What would be the advantages of living in a society in which everyone supported Socrates' political ideas? What would be the disadvantages?

EXAMINING THE STRENGTHS AND WEAKNESSES OF THE OPPOSITION TO CIVIL DISOBEDIENCE

Positive Evaluation

1. Doesn't the opposition to civil disobedience encourage people to find creative and legal ways to make their voices heard and to change society? On the other hand, doesn't civil disobedience run the risk of opening the floodgates of social disorder?

2. The laws said to Socrates that if he disagreed with them, he always had the option either of trying to convince them of his position or of settling in another country in which he found the laws more agreeable. Aren't these alternatives reasonable? Aren't there always ways in a democracy of dealing with a problem other than breaking the law?

3. Could we apply Kant's notion of universalizability here? (See section 5.4 on Kant's moral philosophy.) If we all followed the rule, "Always obey the law unless you think you shouldn't," wouldn't we negate the very notion of law? Because different people have different notions of what is just and unjust, wouldn't obedience to the law be a rather individualistic and subjective matter? Can we pick and choose which laws we want to obey?

Negative Evaluation

1. If we believe with Socrates that we have an agreement with our government, does it follow that we have agreed to obey any and all laws no matter what? Or is our agreement that we will obey laws that are justly written and justly applied? Doesn't this qualification allow for respect for the social contract as well as for the possibility of disobeying unjust laws and governmental actions?

2. Isn't Socrates' position rather extreme? Doesn't it support glib slogans like "My country, right or wrong!" or "Either obey your government unconditionally or leave." Isn't there some middle ground between passively accepting everything your government does and moving? Doesn't Socrates' death sentence at the hands of his government show that the government is not always justified in what it does?

3. Certainly the opponents of civil disobedience have a point in drawing attention to the dangers and possible abuses of this form of protest. But aren't they attacking a strawman in suggesting that this approach would lead to a total

disregard for the law? (See the discussion of the strawman fallacy in section 1.2.) If people who engage in civil disobedience don't resist arrest and are willing to accept punishment for their dissent, aren't they exhibiting respect for the law?

SURVEYING THE CASE FOR CIVIL DISOBEDIENCE

Although the position we just examined, represented by Socrates, maintained that it is *never* right to break the law, the opposing position does not contend that it is *always* right to break the law. Instead, the position we now discuss argues that it is *sometimes* justified to commit acts of civil disobedience. Whether breaking the law in this way is morally justified is said to depend on the circumstances. Hence, because the position contains this qualification, different people could agree on the principle of using civil disobedience as a form of moral action while disagreeing on the circumstances in which it should be used. Nevertheless, while they disagree on the details, all defenders of this position use the same basic set of arguments. In his book *Morals and Ethics,* philosopher Carl Wellman lists five arguments typically used to justify civil disobedience.[22]

Preservation of Moral Integrity. Although we normally may have a duty to obey the law, if the law is unjust, then such obedience would force a conscientious citizen to commit a moral evil. It is impossible for any one individual to eradicate all evil, but each of us does have an obligation to refuse to cooperate with evil and to preserve our moral integrity. As Wellman puts it, "Since one ought never to participate in moral wrong and since civil disobedience is sometimes the only way to refrain from being a party to moral evil, civil disobedience is sometimes right."

The Duty to Combat Immorality. Even if you refrain from participating in moral evil yourself, nonaction can facilitate the perpetuation of injustice. Hence, you have a moral duty to actively combat the evils in society by whatever means are effective. Sometimes the only effective way to fight the evils in society is through civil disobedience. Therefore, civil disobedience is sometimes a morally right action.

A Means of Social Progress. It is morally good to seek to improve your society, and you have many ways to do so. Sometimes, however, the normal methods of the political process are ineffective or thwarted; therefore, more direct action is necessary. An act of civil disobedience typically receives media coverage and draws attention to an unjust law. The challenge to the law and the courage of the dissenters can prick the conscience of a nation's citizens and lead them to reexamine society's policies. Americans in the 1960s who were isolated from the injustices of their society or who were not present at the sites of the civil rights clashes in the 1960s were forced to come to terms with their society's problems on the evening news. In this way, civil disobedience is a form of communication and an effective political technique for moving society in the right direction.

No Practical Alternative. The machinery of democracy may move too slowly to keep pace with escalation of social problems. Furthermore, even in a democratic society, the ballot box, the courts, and the press may be controlled by people who want to protect the unjust status quo. Hence, if all other alternatives are ruled out, civil disobedience may be the only means available to influence public opinion and bring about social and political change.

Government May Exceed Its Authority. Sometimes a government may violate its own constitution or may infringe on the rights of its citizens. In such cases, the laws it makes or the demands it makes on its citizens are no longer morally binding. In section 6.2, we read that Aquinas said "the force of a law depends on the extent of its justice." As Aquinas illustrates, people who justify civil disobedience frequently assume some version of the natural law theory. If the government decides what shall constitute justice, as Hobbes claimed in his version of the social contract theory (see section 6.1), then by definition, the government cannot be unjust and civil disobedience cannot be justified.

STOP AND THINK

Do you find these arguments convincing? Which one do you think is the strongest? Which one is the weakest? How would an opponent of civil disobedience respond to these points?

Although these five defenses of civil disobedience overlap somewhat, they each emphasize a slightly different point. In the remainder of this section, we examine the thoughts of two well-known political activists, Mohandas Gandhi and Martin Luther King Jr., and we look for these five defenses in their writings.

MOHANDAS K. GANDHI (1869–1948)

Gandhi's Life

Mohandas Gandhi, the great Indian political and spiritual leader, is best known by the Indian title *Mahatma,* which means "great soul." He was born in Porbandar, India, where he spent his childhood. As a young man, he studied law in London and in 1893 went to South Africa to do legal work. Although South Africa was controlled by the British at that time, and Gandhi was a British subject, he found that he and his fellow Indians were victims of discriminatory laws. He stayed there for twenty-one years, working to secure rights for the Indian people. But in 1914 he returned to India, the land he loved, and spent the rest of his life working to win India's independence from the British government by applying the method and philosophy of nonviolent civil disobedience he had developed. Gandhi was frequently jailed and beaten by the British government for his civil disobedience, and he spent a total of seven years in prison for his political activities. However, he taught that it was honorable to go to jail for a just cause.

Gandhi was so effective at organizing massive nonviolent resistance to the government that he broke Britain's will to continue its hold over India. His goal of India's independence was achieved in 1947. In January of the following year,

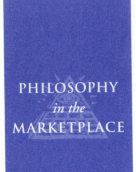

Ask five to ten people the following questions.

1. Is breaking the law ever *morally* justified? Why?
2. If so, under what conditions would breaking the law be morally justified?
3. Can you think of any examples from history in which people were justified in disobeying the law? Why do you think these cases of lawbreaking were justified?
4. Can you think of any examples from history or the news in which people sincerely believed they were justified in breaking the law, but you believe they were mistaken? Why do you think they were wrong?

After collecting the answers, compare them to Socrates' arguments for not breaking the law and to the five justifications for civil disobedience. Do you see any similarities? Did any of your friends come up with new arguments for either side? Which response do you think was the best? Why? Which response did you disagree with most? Why?

however, he was assassinated by a Hindu fanatic who opposed Gandhi's efforts to promote tolerance of all creeds and religions.

Gandhi's Philosophy

Although he is known for his opposition to violence, Gandhi acknowledged that sometimes violence is the only thing that will stop major evils; he himself took part in several wars. Nevertheless, he believed that most of the time violence only breeds worse evils. The preferred method of bringing injustice in a society to an end, Gandhi thought, is a massive movement of morally committed citizens resisting the government by refusing to cooperate with the machinery of injustice. He used such tactics as sit-ins on government property, which forced the government to haul away dozens of people who neither resisted it nor submitted to its demands. On one occasion, Gandhi led a 200-mile march to the sea to collect salt in defiance of the government monopoly on the product. He called his method *satyagraha,* a word coined from the Hindu words *satya* (truth) and *agraha* (force). His political theory grew out of his spirituality, which reflected the Hindu philosophy discussed in section 4.6. He was also influenced by the nineteenth-century American author Henry David Thoreau, who advocated resistance to unjust laws.

Gandhi's philosophy of nonviolent resistance sounds naive to some people, but he used it to win political victories in South Africa, and he and his followers showed its effectiveness by bringing the British government to its knees. His method has been a model for political action ever since. Martin Luther King Jr. and the civil rights leaders in the 1960s brought dramatic changes to American society by employing Gandhi's techniques. Furthermore, Gandhi's ideas have inspired both antiabortion and proabortion protesters, antiwar activists, environmentalists, animal rights advocates, and other groups lobbying for social change. The spirit of Gandhi's philosophy of nonviolent civil disobedience is illustrated in this passage from one of his books.

- In the following reading, see how many of the five justifications for civil disobedience you can find.

 FROM MAHATMA GANDHI

Young India[23]

The Law of Suffering

No country has ever risen without being purified through the force of suffering. The mother suffers so that her child may live. The condition of wheat growing is that the seed grain should perish. Life comes out of Death. Will India rise out of her slavery without fulfilling this eternal law of purification through suffering? . . .

. . . What then is the meaning of Non-co-operation in terms of the Law of Suffering? We must voluntarily put up with the losses and inconveniences that arise from having to withdraw our support from a Government that is ruling against our will. Possession of power and riches is a crime under an unjust government; poverty in that case is a virtue, says Thoreau. It may be that, in the transition state, we may make mistakes; there may be avoidable suffering. These things are preferable to national emasculation.

We must refuse to wait for the wrong to be righted till the wrongdoer has been roused to a sense of his iniquity. We must not, for fear of ourselves or others having to suffer, remain participators in it. But we must combat the wrong by ceasing to assist the wrongdoer directly or indirectly.

If a father does an injustice, it is the duty of his children to leave the parental roof. If the head-master of a school conducts his institution on an immoral basis, the pupils must leave the school. If the chairman of a corporation is corrupt, the members thereof must wash their hands clean of his corruption by withdrawing from it; even so, if a government does a grave injustice, the subject must withdraw co-operation wholly or partially, sufficiently to wean the ruler from his wickedness. In each of the cases conceived by me, there is an element of suffering whether mental or physical. Without such suffering, it is not possible to attain freedom. . . .

The Momentous Issue

The next few weeks should see Civil Disobedience in full working order in some part of India. With illustrations of partial and individual Civil Disobedience the country has become familiar. Complete Civil Disobedience is rebellion without the element of violence in it. An out and out civil resister simply ignores the authority of the state. He becomes an outlaw claiming to disregard every unmoral state law. Thus, for instance, he may refuse to pay taxes, he may refuse to recognise the authority of the state in his daily intercourse. He may refuse to obey the law of trespass and claim to enter military barracks in order to speak to the soldiers, he may refuse to submit to limitations upon the manner of picketing and may picket within the prescribed area. In doing all this, he never uses force and never resists force when it is used against him. In fact, he invites imprisonment and other uses of force against himself. This he does because, and when, he finds the bodily freedom he seemingly enjoys to be an intolerable burden. He argues to himself that a state allows personal freedom only in so far as the citizen submits to its regulations. Submission to the state law is the price a citizen pays for his personal liberty. Submission, therefore, to a state wholly or largely unjust is an immoral barter for liberty. A citizen who thus realises the evil nature of a state is not satisfied to live on its sufferance, and therefore appears to the others who do not share his belief to be a nuisance to society, whilst, he is endeavouring to compel the state without committing a moral breach to arrest him. Thus considered, civil resistance is a most powerful expression of a soul's anguish and an eloquent protest against the continuance of an evil state. Is not this the history of all reform? Have not reformers, much to the disgust of their fellows, discarded even innocent symbols associated with an evil practice?

Civil versus Criminal

. . . What legal remedy has the afflicted individual against the Government? There is certainly no sanction provided against the Government in law when it prostitutes the law itself to its own base ends. When therefore a Government thus becomes lawless in an organised manner, Civil Disobedience becomes a sacred duty and is the only remedy open specially to those who had no hand in the making of the Government or its laws. Another remedy there certainly is, and that is armed revolt. Civil Disobedience is a complete, effective and bloodless substitute. And it is well that by exemplary restraint and discipline in the way of submission to unjust and even illegal orders we have created the necessary atmosphere for Civil Disobedience. For thereby on the one hand the tyrannical nature of the Government has been made more manifest, and on the other by willing obedience we have fitted ourselves for Civil Disobedience.

It is equally as well that Civil Disobedience is being confined even now to the smallest area possible. It must be admitted that it is an abnormal state, even as a corrupt and unpopular Government should be in civilised society, like disease, an abnormal state. Therefore, only when a citizen has disciplined himself in the art of voluntary obedience to the state laws is he justified on rare occasions deliberately but non-violently to disobey them, and expose himself to the penalty of the breach. If then we are to achieve the maximum result in the minimum of time, whilst fiercest disobedience is going on in a limited area, perfect submission to the laws must be yielded in all the other parts so as to test the nation's capacity for voluntary obedience and for understanding the virtue of Civil Disobedience. Any unauthorised outbreak of disobedience, therefore, in any part of India will most certainly damage the cause and will betray an unpardonable ignorance of the principles of Civil Disobedience.

We must expect the Government to take the strictest measures to suppress this impending defiance of authority, for on it depends its very existence. Its instinct of self-preservation alone will actuate measures of repression adequate for suppression. And if it fails, the Government of necessity disappears. That is, it either bends to the national will or it is dissolved. The greatest danger lies in violence breaking out anywhere by reason of provocation. But it would be wrong and unmanly to invite the sternest measures and then to be incensed against them, apart from the fact that it will be a breach of our solemn pledge of non-violence. I may be arrested, thousands who take part in the peaceful revolt may also be arrested, imprisoned, even tortured. The rest of India must not lose its head. When the proper time comes, the rest of India may respond by undertaking Civil Disobedience and inviting arrests, imprisonments and tortures. It is the sacrifice of the innocent we want to make. That alone will appear pleasing to God. And therefore, on the eve of the great battle the nation is embarking upon, my earnest exhortation to every Non-co-operator is to fit himself for Civil Disobedience by fulfilling to the letter and in the spirit the conditions of Civil Disobedience laid down at Delhi, and to ensure non-violence everywhere. Let us not be satisfied that we remain non-violent individually. We boast that Non-co-operation has become universal in India. We boast that we have acquired sufficient influence even over the unruly masses to restrain them from violence. Let us prove true to our claim. . . .

The Immediate Issue

I wish I could persuade everybody that Civil Disobedience is the inherent right of a citizen. He dare not give it up without ceasing to be a man. Civil Disobedience is never followed by anarchy. Criminal Disobedience can lead to it. Every state puts down Criminal Disobedience by force. It perishes, if it does not. But to put down Civil Disobedience is to attempt to imprison conscience. Civil Disobedience can only lead to strength and purity. A civil resister never uses arms and, hence, he is harmless to a state that is at all willing to listen to the voice of public opinion. He is dangerous for an autocratic state, for he brings about its fall by engaging public opinion upon the matter for which he resists the state. Civil Disobedience, therefore, becomes a sacred duty when the state has become lawless, or which is the same thing, corrupt. And a citizen that barters with such a state shares its corruption or lawlessness.

It is, therefore, possible to question the wisdom of applying Civil Disobedience in respect of a particular act or law; it is possible to advise delay and caution. But the right itself cannot be allowed to be questioned. It is a birthright that cannot be surrendered without surrender of one's self-respect.

At the same time that the right of Civil Disobedience is insisted upon, its use must be guarded by all conceivable restrictions. Every possible provision should be made against an outbreak of violence or general lawlessness. Its area as well as its scope should also be limited to the barest necessity of the case. In the present case, therefore, aggressive Civil Disobedience should be confined to a vindication of the right of free speech and free association. In other words, Non-co-operation, so long as it remains non-violent, must be allowed to continue without let or hindrance.

MARTIN LUTHER KING JR. (1929–1968)

King's Life

**MARTIN LUTHER
KING JR.
*(1929–1968)***

Like Gandhi before him, Martin Luther King Jr. is noted not only for being an effective political leader and agent of social change but also for developing a philosophy of political action to guide his activism. King was born in Atlanta, Georgia, the son and grandson of Baptist ministers. As the result of skipping two grades, he was able to enter Morehouse College at age fifteen. While in college he felt called to follow his father's and grandfather's example and decided to become a minister. He went on to obtain a degree from Crozer Theological Seminary in Pennsylvania and then earned a doctorate in systematic theology from Boston University. While in Boston, he met and married Coretta Scott, who would become a great civil rights leader herself. Although he had offers for academic positions, Martin and Coretta returned to the South, where King became the pastor of a prominent Baptist church in Montgomery, Alabama.

In 1955, a pivotal event in American social history set the course of King's life. An African-American seamstress named Rosa Parks climbed onto a Montgomery bus after a long day of work. Because all the seats in the back of the bus were taken, she sat down on a seat in the "whites only" section. Consequently, she was forcibly removed and arrested for violating the city's segregationist laws. As a popular minister and community leader, Dr. King was elected president of an organization formed to protest the racist laws of the city. King put into effect the philosophy of nonviolent resistance that he had been developing since college. The bus boycott that he and his followers started would last a year. As a result, King's house was bombed, his life was continually threatened, and he and his associates were convicted of conspiracy. Finally, The U.S. Supreme Court ruled that Montgomery had to provide equal treatment to all people on public buses.

Building on this success, King and other African-American ministers founded the Southern Christian Leadership Conference, and King's life became a succession of protest marches, speeches, books, and other forms of political action. Seeking to refuel his spirit, he took some time off to tour India in order to deepen his understanding of Gandhi's nonviolent strategies. In August 1963, King attracted more than a quarter of a million people to Washington, D.C., for a civil rights rally. There, on the steps of the Lincoln Memorial, he delivered his famous "I Have a Dream" speech. Finally, after years of social unrest in America, Congress passed the Civil Rights Act of 1964. The following year, King became *Time* magazine's Man of the Year, and he received the Nobel Prize. In spite of these honors, King continued to be the center of controversy. In former years he had been the target of racists as well as well-meaning critics who thought he was going too far and too fast with his calls for change. Now, he was criticized by radical leaders within his own cause who argued for more aggressive techniques under the label of Black Power. King, however, continued to hold high the banner of nonviolence.

In 1967, King began to turn his struggle for political equality into one that emphasized economic rights. He had became convinced that economic poverty was just as great an evil as political discrimination. On April 4, 1968, while lending support to a garbage workers' strike in Memphis, Tennessee, King was assassinated.

The following selection is taken from Dr. King's famous "Letter from Birmingham Jail." In 1963, one year before he won the Nobel Prize, he was jailed for participating in a civil rights demonstration. Eight prominent Alabama clergy wrote an open letter critical of King's methods. In his own letter, King responded to their criticisms and provided an eloquent justification of civil disobedience.

- As you did with the Gandhi selection, try to find examples of the five justifications of civil disobedience discussed previously.
- What similarities or differences are there between King's justification of civil disobedience and Gandhi's?
- How does King respond to the criticism that he should have used negotiation instead of direct action to address the issues?

 FROM MARTIN LUTHER KING JR.

Letter from Birmingham Jail[24]

April 16, 1963

My Dear Fellow Clergymen:

While confined here in the Birmingham city jail, I came across your recent statement calling my present activities "unwise and untimely." Seldom do I pause to answer criticism of my work and ideas. If I sought to answer all the criticisms that cross my desk, my secretaries would have little time for anything other than such correspondence in the course of the day, and I would have no time for constructive work. But since I feel that you are men of genuine good will and that your criticisms are sincerely set forth, I want to try to answer your statement in what I hope will be patient and reasonable terms. . . .

You deplore the demonstrations taking place in Birmingham. But your statement, I am sorry to say, fails to express a similar concern for the conditions that brought about the demonstrations. I am sure that none of you would want to rest content with the superficial kind of social analysis that deals merely with effects and does not grapple with underlying causes. It is unfortunate that demonstrations are taking place in Birmingham, but it is even more unfortunate that the city's white power structure left the Negro community with no alternative.

In any nonviolent campaign there are four basic steps: collection of the facts to determine whether injustices exist; negotiation; self-purification; and direct action. We have gone through all these steps in Birmingham. There can be no gainsaying the fact that racial injustice engulfs this community. . . .

You may well ask: "Why direct action? Why sit-ins, marches and so forth? Isn't negotiation a better path?" You are quite right in calling for negotiation. Indeed, this is the very purpose of direct action. Nonviolent direct action seeks to create such a crisis and foster such a tension that a community which has constantly refused to negotiate is forced to confront the issue. It seeks so to dramatize the issue that it can no longer be ignored. My citing the creation of tension as part of the work of the nonviolent-resister may sound rather shocking. But I must confess that I am not afraid of the word "tension." I have earnestly opposed violent tension, but there is a type of constructive, nonviolent tension which is necessary for growth. Just as Socrates felt that it was necessary to create a tension in the mind so that individuals could rise from the bondage of myths and half-truths to the unfettered realm of creative analysis and objective appraisal, so must we see the need for nonviolent gadflies to create the kind of tension in society that will help men rise from the dark depths of prejudice and racism to the majestic heights of understanding and brotherhood.

The purpose of our direct-action program is to create a situation so crisis-packed that it will inevitably open the door to negotiation. I therefore concur with you in your call for negotiation. Too long has our beloved Southland been bogged down in a tragic effort to live in monologue rather than dialogue. . . .

- In the next passage, how does King distinguish between just laws and unjust laws? Does he present a useful distinction?
- According to King, under what conditions is it permissible to break the law?

You express a great deal of anxiety over our willingness to break laws. This is certainly a legitimate concern. Since we so diligently urge people to obey the Supreme Court's decision of 1954 outlawing segregation in the public schools, at first glance it may seem rather paradoxical for us consciously to break laws. One may well ask: "How can you advocate breaking some laws and obeying others?" The answer lies in the fact that there are two types of laws: just and unjust. I would be the first to advocate obeying just laws. One has not only a legal but a moral responsibility to obey just laws. Conversely, one has a moral responsibility to disobey unjust laws. I would agree with St. Augustine that "an unjust law is no law at all."

Now, what is the difference between the two? How does one determine whether a law is just or unjust? A just law is a man-made code that squares with the moral law or the law of God. An unjust law is a code that is out of harmony with the moral law. To put it in the terms of St. Thomas Aquinas: An unjust law is a human law that is not rooted in eternal law and natural law. Any law that uplifts human personality is just. Any law that degrades human personality is unjust. All segregation statutes are unjust because segregation distorts the soul and damages the personality. It gives the segregator a false sense of superiority and the segregated a false sense of inferiority. Segregation, to use the terminology of the Jewish philosopher Martin Buber, substitutes an "I-it" relationship for an "I-thou" relationship and ends up relegating persons to the status of things. Hence segregation is not only politically, economically and sociologically unsound, it is morally wrong and sinful. Paul Tillich has said that sin is separation. Is not segregation an existential expression of man's tragic separation, his awful estrangement, his terrible sinfulness? Thus it is that I can urge men to obey the 1954 decision of the Supreme Court, for it is morally right; and I can urge them to disobey segregation ordinances, for they are morally wrong.

Let us consider a more concrete example of just and unjust laws. An unjust law is a code that a numerical or power majority group compels a minority group to obey but does not make binding on itself. This is *difference* made legal. By the same token, a just law is a code that a majority compels a minority to follow and that it is willing to follow itself. This is *sameness* made legal.

Let me give another explanation. A law is unjust if it is inflicted on a minority that, as a result of being denied the right to vote, had no part in enacting or devising the law. Who can say that the legislature of Alabama which set up that state's segregation laws was democratically elected? Throughout Alabama all sorts of devious methods are used to prevent Negroes from becoming registered voters, and there are some counties in which, even though Negroes constitute a majority of the population, not a single Negro is registered. Can any law enacted under such circumstances be considered democratically structured?

Sometimes a law is just on its face and unjust in its application. For instance, I have been arrested on a charge of parading without a permit. Now, there is nothing wrong in having an ordinance which requires a permit for a parade. But such an ordinance becomes unjust when it is used to maintain segregation and to deny citizens the First-Amendment privilege of peaceful assembly and protest.

I hope you are able to see the distinction I am trying to point out. In no sense do I advocate evading or defying the law, as would the rabid segregationist. That would lead to anarchy. One who breaks an unjust law must do so openly, lovingly, and with a willingness to accept the penalty. I submit that an individual who breaks a law that conscience tells him is unjust, and who willingly accepts the penalty of imprisonment in order to arouse the conscience of the community over its injustice, is in reality expressing the highest respect for law.

Of course, there is nothing new about this kind of civil disobedience. It was evidenced sublimely in the refusal of Shadrach, Meshach and Abednego to obey the laws of Nebuchadnezzar, on the ground that a higher moral law was at stake. It was practiced superbly by the early Christians, who were willing to face hungry lions and the excruciating pain of chopping blocks rather than submit to certain unjust laws of the Roman Empire. To a degree, academic freedom is a reality today because Socrates practiced civil disobedience. In our own nation, the Boston Tea Party represented a massive act of civil disobedience.

We should never forget that everything Adolf Hitler did in Germany was "legal" and everything the Hungarian freedom fighters did in Hungary was "illegal." It was "illegal" to aid and comfort a Jew in Hitler's Germany. Even so, I am sure that, had I lived in Germany at the time, I would have aided and comforted my Jewish brothers. If today I lived in a Communist country where certain principles dear to the Christian faith are suppressed, I would openly advocate disobeying that country's antireligious laws. . . .

Let us all hope that the dark clouds of racial prejudice will soon pass away and the deep fog of misunderstanding will be lifted from our fear-drenched communities, and in some not too distant tomorrow the radiant stars of love and brotherhood will shine over our great nation with all their scintillating beauty.

Yours for the cause of Peace and Brotherhood,

Martin Luther King, Jr.

THOUGHT EXPERIMENT

The Pros and Cons of Civil Disobedience

Write a letter to the person with whom you *disagree* the most (Socrates, Gandhi, or King). Explain to him why he is wrong by refuting his arguments and providing a defense of the opposing point of view. Don't just disagree with him but try to be as convincing as possible, providing strong reasons for your position. How do you think he might reply?

LOOKING THROUGH THE LENS OF THE SUPPORTERS OF CIVIL DISOBEDIENCE

1. If you were a supporter of civil disobedience, how would you respond to critics who say that there are always less radical means for achieving social change?

2. Taking the point of view of the civil disobedience defender once again, how would you determine when a minor wrong should be tolerated or addressed through legal means for the sake of social stability and when the injustice is severe enough to warrant breaking the law? Think of some examples of minor injustices in which civil disobedience would not be justified and more serious infractions of justice in which civil disobedience would be justified.

3. Why do most defenders of civil disobedience believe it is important that the breaking of the law be a public event and that the protester not use further illegal means to evade the law?

EXAMINING THE STRENGTHS AND WEAKNESSES OF THE CIVIL DISOBEDIENCE POSITION

Positive Evaluation

1. You don't go in for stomach surgery whenever you have indigestion from eating too much pizza. Radical surgery is used only in severe situations in which

other remedies are not effective. Similarly, even though civil disobedience is an extreme measure that should not be used if it can be avoided, can't it be justified in extreme cases in which there are no other effective alternatives?

2. Isn't civil disobedience consistent with a love for your country, a respect for its institutions, and a general acceptance of the political system as a whole? Aren't the dangers of not doing everything possible to correct injustices just as grave and likely to lead to social unrest as are the alleged dangers of civil disobedience?

3. Hasn't history shown that significant social progress often results when people refuse to participate in an unjust system and rebuke the system by acts of civil disobedience? Wouldn't society become set in its ways and refuse to improve if there weren't dissenters, protesters, and social reformers who were willing to risk imprisonment and even death to stop the machinery of injustice?

Negative Evaluation

1. The advocate of civil disobedience claims that this method of moral protest will bring political injustice to the attention of the nation's moral conscience. But this argument implies that civil disobedience will work only if the people in a society are open and responsive to moral appeals. If so, then the citizen's moral conscience can be informed and appealed to through legal means. On the other hand, if a society has no compassion and no sense of justice or fair play, then civil disobedience will not work and will only bring more oppression. In other words, if civil disobedience will be effective, it is unnecessary, but if it is necessary, it is likely to be ineffective. Aren't the advocates of civil disobedience left in a dilemma that undermines their position?

2. Isn't civil disobedience an example of using an immoral means to achieve a supposedly moral end? Furthermore, won't the good results sought for always be an uncertain possibility? Can we ever know ahead of time if civil disobedience will be worth the price? On the other hand, aren't the social harms produced by breaking the law almost always inevitable?

3. Is it inconsistent for people engaging in civil disobedience to expect protection from the law at the same time they are breaking the law? For example, they expect the police to protect them from physical harm that their opponents might wish to inflict on them. Furthermore, isn't an individual law part of the total system of laws created and enforced by the legal institutions of the land? Is it possible to violate one law without harming the system as a whole? Doesn't every law, simply because it is part of the total system of laws, impose an obligation of obedience on us until we can get it changed?

REVIEW FOR CHAPTER 6

Philosophers

6.1 The Justification of Government

Robert Paul Wolff
Thomas Hobbes
John Locke
6.2 The Question of Justice
Plato
Thomas Aquinas
John Stuart Mill
John Rawls
Susan Moller Okin
6.3 The Individual and the State
John Stuart Mill
Karl Marx
6.4 Civil Disobedience
Socrates
Mohandas Gandhi
Martin Luther King Jr.

Concepts

6.1 The Justification of Government
authority vs. power
divine right theory
justice theory
naive anarchism
militant anarchism
theoretical anarchism
social contract theory
Thomas Hobbes's notion of the state of nature
Hobbes's three laws of nature
Hobbes's notion of the social contract
John Locke's view of rights
Locke's notion of the state of nature
Locke's notion of the social contract
6.2 The Question of Justice
meritocracy
the three kinds of people according to Plato
Plato's theory of justice
natural law theory
Thomas Aquinas's theory of justice
John Stuart Mill's theory of justice
the principle of utility
John Rawls's theory of justice
the original position
the veil of ignorance
the principle of equal liberty

SUGGESTIONS FOR FURTHER READING

General Works on Political Philosophy

Hampton, Jean. *Political Philosophy.* Boulder, Colo.: Westview, 1996. An engaging introduction to both the classical and contemporary issues.

Kymlicka, Will. *Contemporary Political Theory: An Introduction.* New York: Oxford University Press, 1990. A very good introduction to the topic.

Luper, Steven, ed. *Social Ideals and Policies: An Introduction to Social and Political Philosophy.* Mountain View, Calif.: Mayfield, 1999. A topically organized anthology containing classical and contemporary readings.

Sterba, James. *Contemporary Social and Political Philosophy.* Belmont, Calif.: Wadsworth, 1995. A discussion of current issues in social and political philosophy.

The Justification of Government

Barker, Ernest, ed. *Social Contract: Essays by Locke, Hume, and Rousseau.* Oxford: Oxford University Press, 1962. A collection of the classic essays on the topic, with an introduction by the editor.

Forman, James. *Anarchism: Political Innocence or Social Violence?* New York: Dell, 1977. A useful discussion of the topic.

Hampton, Jean. *Hobbes and the Social Contract Tradition.* Cambridge, England: Cambridge University Press, 1988. This work analyzes Hobbes's theory in the light of contemporary perspectives.

Woodcock, George. *Anarchism: A History of Libertarian Ideas and Movements.* Cleveland: Meridian Books, 1962. This author is one of the leading writers on anarchism.

The Nature of Justice

Anna, Julia. *An Introduction to Plato's "Republic"*. Oxford: Clarendon Press, 1981. A systematic introduction to Plato's most important work.

Aquinas, Thomas. *On Law, Morality, and Politics,* ed. William Baumgarth and Richard Regan, Indianapolis: Hackett, 1988. Aquinas's central writings on law, morality, and politics.

Finnis, John. *Natural Law and Natural Rights*. Oxford: Oxford University Press, 1980. A contemporary defense of natural law theory.

Kukathas, Chandran, and Philip Pettit. *Rawls: "A Theory of Justice" and Its Critics*. Stanford, Calif.: Stanford University Press, 1990. A discussion of Rawls's work, including the arguments of his critics.

Manning, Rita, and René Trujillo, eds. *Social Justice in a Diverse Society*. Mountain View, Calif.: Mayfield, 1996. A collection of essays on current issues related to justice.

Popper, Karl. *The Open Society and Its Enemies. Vol. 1, The Spell of Plato*. 5th ed., rev. Princeton, N.J.: Princeton University Press, 1966. This controversial book provides a passionate defense of democracy and an equally passionate critique of Plato's utopian vision.

Rawls, John. *Political Liberalism*. New York: Columbia University Press, 1994. In this work Rawls refines and develops his earlier theory.

Rawls, John. *A Theory of Justice*. Cambridge, Mass.: Harvard University Press, 1971. Many consider this work to be the most significant one in political philosophy in this century.

Sandel, Michael. *Liberalism and the Limits of Justice*. Cambridge: Cambridge University Press, 1982. A critique of Rawls's work.

Sterba, James, ed. *Justice: Alternative Political Perspectives*. 2d ed. Belmont, Calif.: Wadsworth, 1992. A wide range of readings on the topic.

The Individual and the State

Gray, John, and G. W. Smith, eds. *J. S. Mill's "On Liberty" in Focus*. London and New York: Routledge, 1991. A collection of important essays discussing Mill's famous work.

Marcuse, Herbert. *One-Dimensional Man*. Boston: Beacon Press, 1964. A very readable analysis of our technological society that brings Marx's critique of capitalism into the twentieth century.

Marx, Karl. *The Marx-Engels Reader*. 2d ed. Ed. Robert C. Tucker. New York: W. W. Norton, 1978. Contains selections from the full range of Marx's works.

Mill, J. S. *On Liberty*. Ed. E. Rapaport. Indianapolis: Hackett, 1978. Mill's argument for classical liberalism.

Nozick, Robert. *Anarchy, State, and Utopia*. New York: Basic Books, 1974. Nozick is famous for his political libertarianism (a position that advocates maximum individual liberty). His book is notable for its critique of Rawls's theory.

Popper, Karl. *The Open Society and Its Enemies. Vol. 2, The High Tide of Prophecy: Hegel, Marx, and the Aftermath*. 5th ed., rev. Princeton, N.J.: Princeton University Press, 1966. Contains a passionate critique of Marxist political philosophy.

Schmitt, Richard. *Introduction to Marx and Engels: A Critical Reconstruction*. 2d ed. Boulder, Colo.: Westview, 1997. One of the best introductions to Marxism.

Civil Disobedience

Bedau, Hugo Adam, ed. *Civil Disobedience in Focus.* London and New York: Routledge, 1991. A collection of the most significant essays on the topic, ranging from Socrates to contemporary thinkers.

Thoreau, Henry David. *Civil Disobedience and Other Essays.* New York: Dover, 1993. An important defense of civil disobedience by the famous nineteenth-century American writer.

NOTES

1. Robert Paul Wolff, *In Defense of Anarchism* (Berkeley: University of California Press, 1998), pp. 3–6, 12–14, 18–19.
2. Thomas Hobbes, *Leviathan* (1651). Many editions of this work are available in the public domain. The selections are taken from chapters 13, 14, 15, and 17. The section headings have been added.
3. John Locke, *An Essay Concerning the True Original, Extent and End of Civil Government,* the second essay in *Two Treatises of Government* (1680). Many versions of this essay are available in the public domain. The section headings have been added.
4. Ibid., Sec. 131.
5. Plato, *Republic,* 433a–434c, trans. Benjamin Jowett (1894).
6. Thomas Aquinas, *Summa Theologica,* I–II, ques. 95, art. 2, and ques. 96, art. 4, in *Basic Writings of Saint Thomas Aquinas,* vol. 2, ed. Anton C. Pegis (New York: Random House, 1945).
7. John Stuart Mill, *Utilitarianism,* chapter 5. Many editions of this work are available in the public domain.
8. John Rawls, *A Theory of Justice* (Cambridge, Mass.: Harvard University Press, 1971), pp. 11–12, 103–4, 136–37, 139–40, 60–63.
9. Ibid., p. 83.
10. Susan Moller Okin, *Justice, Gender, and the Family* (New York: Basic Books, 1989), pp. 3, 8, 90, 91, 101, 104–5.
11. Rawls, *A Theory of Justice,* p. 12.
12. Okin, *Justice, Gender, and the Family,* p. 91.
13. John Stuart Mill, *On Liberty.* Many editions are available in the public domain. The selections are taken from chapters 1 and 4.
14. Ibid., chap. 3.
15. Karl Marx, *The German Ideology,* in *The Marx-Engel Reader,* 2d. ed., ed., Robert C. Tucker (New York: Norton, 1978), p. 172.
16. Karl Marx, *Capital,* in *The Marx-Engel Reader,* p. 367.
17. Ibid., p. 296.
18. Karl Marx, *The Holy Family,* quoted in *Essential Writings of Karl Marx,* ed. David Caute (New York: Collier Books, 1967), 50.
19. Karl Marx and Friedrich Engels, *Communist Manifesto,* trans. Samuel Moore in 1888 from the original German text of 1848. Many versions from this edition are available in the public domain. The selections are from chapters 1 and 2. The section titles have been added.

20. Sidney Hook, "*The Communist Manifesto* 100 Years After," *New York Times Magazine,* February 1, 1948, in *Molders of Modern Thought,* ed. Ben B. Seligman (Chicago: Quadrangle Books, 1970), p. 80.
21. Plato, *Crito,* trans. Benjamin Jowett (1898). I have edited the translation.
22. Carl Wellman, *Morals and Ethics* (Glenview, Ill.: Scott, Foresman & Co., 1975), pp. 10–13.
23. Mahatma Gandhi, *Young India 1919–1922* (Madras, India: S. Ganesan, 1922), pp. 230, 233–34, 933–34, 937–39, 943–44.
24. Martin Luther King Jr., "Letter from Birmingham Jail," in *Why We Can't Wait* (New York: Harper & Row, 1964), pp. 77, 79, 81–82, 84–87, 100.

Credits

Index